SOCIETY OF BIBLICAL LITERATURE
1982 Seminar Papers

D1519485

SOCIETY OF BIBLICAL LITERATURE
SEMINAR PAPERS SERIES

Editor, Kent Harold Richards

Number 21

Society of Biblical Literature
1982 Seminar Papers

Editor, Kent Harold Richards

SOCIETY OF BIBLICAL LITERATURE
1982 SEMINAR PAPERS

Editor, Kent Harold Richards

One Hundred Eighteenth Annual Meeting
December 19–22, 1982
The New York Hilton
New York City

Scholars Press
Chico, California

SOCIETY OF BIBLICAL LITERATURE
1982 SEMINAR PAPERS

Editor, Kent Harold Richards

ISBN: 0–89130–607–2
ISSN: 0145–2711

Printed in the United States of America

INTRODUCTORY NOTE

The papers in this volume were prepared for discussion at the One Hundred Eighteenth Annual Meeting of the Society of Biblical Literature convened at the New York Hilton Hotel, 19-22 December 1982. They represent, in most cases, experimental and initial work on a subject. Therefore, they should not be considered finished works but works in progress. The Society encourages this type of publication to stimulate discussion which may lead to the refinement and precision necessary in a journal article or monograph.

The Society's publication program has generated research among its members. Younger scholars and the veteran are able to prepare papers for discussion. This dispenses with time allotments for the reading of papers and permits significant debate at the Annual Meeting.

This year an NBI 3000 Series Word Processor with a Diablo 630 Printer was used to prepare the camera-ready copy. The new format is being used experimentally and will be evaluated for use in other Society series. The Editor expresses appreciation to Drs. Maurya Horgan and Paul Kobelski for their able preparation of the text.

The Editor takes this opportunity to thank the chairs of all Annual Meeting program units for their assistance in developing a stimulating program.

Kent Harold Richards
Editor

CONTENTS

MISHNAH'S SYSTEM OF SANCTIFICATION

Alan J. Avery-Peck
Tulane University

The destruction of the Temple and the fall of Jerusalem in 70 C.E. presented a deep theological crisis for Jews living in that period. The problem was the clear dissonance between the biblical promises which until then had shaped their religious self-consciousness and the actualities of their own historical situation. The Temple, that visible sign of God's presence and dominion, was gone. With its destruction the people of Israel lost one central way in which they had acknowledged God's lordship and appealed to his mercies. The promised land itself now was under the rule of foreigners, with little hope for its return to Israelite sovereignty. All that once had represented the presence of God and holiness within Israel was destroyed. Two generations later the failed Bar Kokhba revolt greatly worsened the picture. Israelites were left with good reason to believe that God no longer cared for or ruled over them. They had lost Temple and sovereignty, the earthly signs that once had proven that God's grace and holiness filled the people of Israel.

One Israelite response to this crisis is found in the Mishnah, the earliest document of Rabbinic Judaism. Mishnah comes into being at the hands of the generation of Rabbinic authorities who lived just after the destruction of the Temple and the failed Bar Kokhba revolt. It comprises the Rabbinic statement of the character Judaism was to take in the era after the wars with Rome. Its authorities present a theology designed to overcome the dissonant situation created by the loss of the Temple and Israelite sovereignty over the land of Israel. To accomplish this, they reexamine the old biblical promises, so as to give new meaning to the biblical symbols of Temple, priesthood and land. They render applicable in the new historical circumstances the old claims that the people of Israel would rule its own land and worship in God's Temple. This means, on the one hand, that the Rabbinic response is extremely conservative. It focuses upon the Pentateuchal promises and notions of Temple, priesthood, and land. Yet with the Temple and sovereignty gone and the priesthood no more than a symbol of what once was, the Rabbinic theology contains as well a deep innovation which refocuses the age-old tradition. While on the surface speaking of priests and Temple, Mishnah's authorities concentrate at a deeper level upon the people of Israel themselves. For Mishnah, the continued existence and vitality of the people become the symbol that God's promises still have effect. By carrying out God's commandments and performing his will the people themselves prove that what has happened upon the stage of history has not altered the vision portrayed in the Hebrew Bible. God still rules over and cares for the people and land of Israel.

The nature and content of this Rabbinic response to the destruction of the Temple are clear when we examine one particular section of the Mishnah. I refer to Tractate Terumot, which outlines the early Rabbinic notion of sanctification: of what is holy, how it becomes holy, and of how that which is holy is disposed of in a Temple-less, secular world. Discussion of these issues constitutes the Rabbis' reaction to one central question which the loss of the Temple and its altar generated. The altar had been the primary locus of Israelite sanctification and holiness. If the people of Israel still are to have the role of God's holy nation now a new locus of sanctification needs to be determined. This is the problem which, in Tractate Terumot, the authorities of Mishnah address.

The specific topic through which the Mishnah outlines its system of sanctification is familiar from the Hebrew Bible's Priestly Code. Mishnah's authorities speak of an agricultural tax, derived from Num 18:8-13, called the heave-offering.[1] Like other

---

[1]Further grounds for Mishnah's identification and description of this priestly due is at Neh 10:37a. The issue of the biblical sources for Mishnah's system of tithes, and

tithes, this offering is mandated by Scripture, to be paid by Israelites from produce grown on the land of Israel. It is given in support of the Aaronide priesthood, God's cultic representatives on earth who run the Temple-cult. The theory which explains Mishnah's insistence that this agricultural offering, along with other tithes, be paid likewise is familiar from Scripture. Mishnah takes seriously the Hebrew Bible's notion that the God of Israel is proprietor of the land of Israel. He gave this land for the use of the people of Israel, so that they might grow food for their sustenance. Like all landowners, God has a right to a share of the produce. This rent represents his payment for providing the land. God mandates that his share, in the form of heave-offering and the other agricultural tithes,[2] be paid over to his representatives on earth, the priests and Levites. Certain tithes also are assigned to the poor, who have a special claim upon God for support. Viewed as a whole, the agricultural laws are not unlike modern systems of taxation. Offerings of produce are paid to God who, like a government, provides the people with specific services, in this case, use of the land, rain and sun which enable the Israelites to nurture crops.[3]

In the generation after the destruction of the Temple and the Bar Kokhba revolt the authorities of Mishnah thus reaffirm one aspect of the biblical theology which detailed the relationship between God, the priesthood, the land of Israel and the people of Israel. In speaking of heave-offering and the other agricultural tithes, the Rabbis evidence their central concern that Israelites continue to acknowledge their debt to God, who provides the land and, through it, the people's sustenance. The Rabbis' message is not deep below the surface. The loss of political control over the land of Israel does not mean to them that God's ownership of the land has ceased, or that the Lord has deserted his people. For the authors of Mishnah it is as though, on the stage of history, nothing has changed. God remains proprietor of the land, just as he was during the period of Israelite sovereignty. His designated representatives therefore retain their positions of honor and continue to receive the required shares of produce, payment for the use of the land granted the Israelite nation by God.

---

heave-offering in particular, has been discussed by Richard S. Sarason in *A History of the Mishnaic Law of Agriculture. Tractate Demai* (Leiden: Brill, 1979) pp. 6-8, and in that author's article, "Mishnah and Scripture: Preliminary Observations on the Law of Tithing in *Seder Zera^cim*," *Approaches to Ancient Judaism. Vol II*, ed. W. S. Green (Chico: Scholars Press, 1980) pp. 81-96.

[2]The other offerings set aside by the Israelite are first tithe, for the Levite, second tithe, which the householder himself eats in Jerusalem, poorman's tithe, for the poor, and first fruits, waved before the altar in Jerusalem. If the Israelite makes dough, he further must separate dough-offering which, like heave-offering goes to a priest. The Levite, for his part, takes from his first tithe an offering for the priest. This is called heave-offering of the tithe. On the structure and content of the Division of Agriculture as a whole, see Jacob Neusner, *Judaism: The Evidence of the Mishnah* (Chicago, 1981) pp. 79-86 and 126-132.

[3]The task of Mishnah Terumot, to describe what it believes all Israelites should know in order properly to pay one of the required agricultural dues, is parallel to the purpose of the other tractates in Mishnah's Division of Agriculture that deal with specific agricultural dues. I refer in particular to Tractate Peah, on the portion of the unharvested crop which must be left for the poor, Maaser Sheni, on second tithe, Hallah, on dough-offering, and Bikkurim, on first fruits. Tractate Maaserot, for its part, functions as the introduction to this whole system of tithing. It does this by indicating exactly what produce is subject to the separation of tithes, and by delimiting the point in its ripening or subsequent processing at which it becomes so subject. See Martin Jaffee, *Mishnah's Theology of Tithing. A Study of Tractate Maaserot* (Chico: Scholars Press, 1981) pp 1-6.

Yet if in its larger parameters the system of tithes claims that nothing has changed, in its deeper workings it realizes that everything now is different. For it knows that, while the priests are God's designates on earth, the priestly clan no longer has any cultic function. Moreover, the authorities behind Mishnah realize that, after the loss of the Temple and altar, the system of sanctification around which the biblical theology revolved no longer could be maintained. These facts needed to be taken into account. As we turn to the specific content of Tractate Terumot's rules, we therefore shall see the great extent to which Mishnah's authorities present a range of concepts and insights foreign to the Scriptural basis of the agricultural laws. This represents the central aspect of the Rabbinic response to the events of 70 and 135.

A single fact about heave-offering interests Mishnah's authorities and generates all of their discussion of this topic. Heave-offering is holy. It is a sanctified Holy Thing, comparable to any animal sacrifice placed on the altar in the Temple in Jerusalem. Mishnah knows this because Scripture itself states that agricultural gifts given to the priests are special. They are the property of the priests and may be eaten only by them and their families. To eat heave-offering, these individuals must be in a high state of cultic purity, just as is the case for other holy animal offerings. The central point for Mishnah Terumot, then, is that this tax, paid by Israelites to God's representatives, is consecrated.

With this much established, Mishnah Terumot takes up a very specific line of questioning. It wants to know, first, how and why these taxes, comprised of produce grown on the land of Israel, come to be holy. Most of the produce of the land may be eaten or otherwise used by anyone, without restriction. How does heave-offering come to be different? The second, closely related, issue is the effect this holy produce, heave-offering, has upon other secular food with which it is mixed. Does the heave-offering's holiness contaminate the other food, such that all now is to be deemed consecrated? This second issue is expanded to talk about other situations in which heave-offering is used as though it were secular, for instance, cases in which it is eaten by a non-priest. Finally, the authorities of Mishnah Terumot discuss the circumstances under which heave-offering ceases to be holy, the end point of the process which began with its initial sanctification.[4]

We see that the early Rabbis use the topic of an agricultural tax as a context in which to talk about their notions of sanctification. They ask how things in this world become holy, what happens to them once they are holy and, finally, how they cease to be holy. This material presents a cogent essay, a Rabbinic theology of sanctification. Through this topic the authorities of Tractate Terumot find the locus and means of sanctification which, in their day, can replace the lost Temple and altar. So as to delve deeply into this reponse to the loss of the Temple, let us examine the central details of Mishnah's system of sanctification. We must begin with a few principal laws.[5]

---

[4]It is this concern for the process of sanctification which in the first place prompted Mishnah's framers to talk about heave-offering. This is clear from the fact that the Division of Agriculture devotes tractates only to those offerings which have a consecrated status. These are heave-offering, second tithe, and first fruits. There is no tractate on first tithe, which is not holy. The inclusion of Tractate Peah, on unconsecrated offerings for the poor, is explained by the fact that the produce of which it speaks stands completely outside of the system of tithes. It is not subject to the separation of agricultural dues. This produce had to be defined if, in its other tractates, the Division of Agriculture was accurately to detail what produce is subject to and available for payment of the various dues (see, e.g., Mishnah Terumot 1:5). The whole thus forms a single, indivisible unit. It appears therefore that a theory of what Mishnah's tithing-tractates were to discuss preceded and guided all the work which actually was done on these tractates.

[5]For a complete exegesis of all of the tractate's rules, along with those of the corresponding tractate in Tosefta, see Alan J. Peck, *The Priestly Gift in Mishnah. A Study of Tractate Terumot* (Chico: Scholars Press, 1981).

The first problem Tractate Terumot addresses is how produce becomes consecrated as heave-offering. It answers that this consecration depends upon certain thoughts and deeds of Israelites. Mishnah states that it is the common Israelite—the non-priest—who, while forbidden to eat holy produce, has the power to cause produce to be deemed holy. Israelites do this by formulating the intention to consecrate produce as heave-offering. Then they pronounce a formula orally designating the intended produce to be the holy offering. Finally, they effect their intention by physically separating this designated produce from any other fruit near it. Through such thoughts and deeds, Israelites determine what produce, and how much of it, is to be deemed holy.[6]

Mishnah's point is that, in this world, common people have the power of sancti-fication.[7] The holy heave-offering comes into being only if common Israelites properly formulate the intention to sanctify a portion of their produce, and then indicate that intention through corresponding words and actions. The centrality of human will in this process is illustrated by the fact that individuals deemed to have no understanding,[8] and therefore no power of intention, may not validly designate heave-offering. It further is clear that by their actions Israelites are not simply removing from their produce food which already has a sanctified status. That no produce is intrinsically holy is easily shown. An Israelite who has two distinct batches of produce may designate and set aside from one of them the heave-offering required of both.[9] The result is that the liability of both batches to the payment of the agricultural tax is fulfilled. This could not be the case if each batch contained a quanitity of already-holy produce which had to be removed. If that were so, what the householder did with one batch could have no effect upon a different batch. According to Tractate Terumot, therefore, it is the common Israelite who imposes a status of sanctification upon produce.

This notion of the centrality of the Israelite in the process of consecration is further developed in Mishnah Terumot's second section, on cases in which heave-offering is mixed with secular food, or is used in some other way not fitting its sanctified

---

[6]These rules are at Mishnah Terumot 1:1-4:6.

[7]This must be qualified. The Israelite's power to designate food to be holy applies only to produce which, because it was grown on God's land, is susceptible to sancti-fication. Note however that even produce grown on the land of Israel is not automati-cally subject to the separation of heave-offering and tithes. It becomes subject only in response to certain desires and intentions on the part of the Israelite. Jaffee, op. cit., pp. 4-5, states: "What is striking . . . is that the entire mechanism of restrictions and privileges, from the field to home or market, is set in motion solely by the intentions of the common farmer. Priests cannot claim their dues whenever they choose, and God himself plays no active role in establishing when the produce must be tithed. Indeed, the framers of Maaserot assume a profound passivity on the part of God. For them, it is only man who is active and whose actions affect the world. God's claims against the Land's produce, that is to say, are only reflexes of those very claims on the part of Israelite farmers. God's interest in his share of the harvest . . . is first provoked by the desires of the farmer for the ripened fruit of his labor. His claim to that fruit, furthermore, becomes binding only when the farmer makes ready to claim his own rights to its use, whether in the field, or at home or market." Mishnah thus describes the intentions of the common Israelite as central in all aspects of its system of agricultural dues. This begins with the circumstances under which produce becomes subject to the separation of these dues, and includes the actual designation and, as we shall see, protection of the offerings.

[8]For example, a deaf-mute, imbecile or minor (Mishnah Terumot 1:1-3).

[9]This is with the provision that the Israelite does not violate the taxonomic categories established by God at creation, for instance, by separating the heave-offering required of a batch of olives from a batch of grapes. See Mishnah Terumot 1:4, 8, 9 and in particular, 2:4-6, as well as my discussion of these pericopae in *The Priestly Gift in Mishnah*.

status.[10] That is to say, the authorities of Mishnah realize that once heave-offering has been designated and separated by the Israelite, a new set of problems will be encountered. These problems concern the protection of heave-offering from misuse. For as long as the consecrated priestly gift remains in the Israelite's domain, it is liable to be used for some purpose other than its proper one, the benefit of the priest. For example, the heave-offering might be mixed or otherwise cooked with the Israelite's own common food. Again, it might be eaten by the non-priest, or even planted as seed. These are central points of danger in the passage of the holy produce from the domain of the Israelite to that of the priest. Tractate Terumot addresses these potential difficulties so as to deepen our appreciation of the centrality of the Israelite in the processes of sanctification. It asks of the culpability of the non-priest for the mistreatment of the holy offering. As we should expect on the basis of what we already have seen, according to Mishnah, culpability depends very much upon the intentions and perceptions of the Israelite who allows heave-offering to become mixed with his own food, or to be eaten or planted.

Two brief examples illustrate this point. The first is the case in which heave-offering is cooked with the Israelite's own common food.[11] Through the cooking, the heave-offering and profane food are turned into a single dish. We might therefore expect Mishnah's Rabbis to rule that the whole dish, including the common produce, must thereafter be treated as though it had absorbed the holiness of the heave-offering and is forbidden to the Israelite. Otherwise the non-priest would use the consecrated produce to his own benefit, which is forbidden. According to the tractate, however, this is the case only if the Israelite perceives the heave-offering to have improved his common food. If so, he must refrain from eating any of the produce, even if he succeeds in removing the heave-offering from the dish. For even if the non-priest removed the priest's share, he still would view himself as benefitting from the flavor it imparted to his food. What, on the other hand, if the householder does not desire the flavor the heave-offering imparted to his food? Now he may simply remove the heave-offering from that food, and thereafter ignore the fact that heave-offering was cooked with it. The actual flavoring power of the heave-offering is not at issue, but only the Israelite's personal likes and desires.[12] So long as he does not perceive himself as benefitting from the heave-offering, he has maintained intact the barrier between the holy and the profane.

The case in which the Israelite plants heave-offering as seed illustrates this same point.[13] We know that the Israelite should not do this, for heave-offering is set aside for the use of the priest alone. If the non-priest anyway plants the heave-offering, there are two possible outcomes. If he does so deliberately--that is, with the full intention of using the priest's share as his own--he is compelled to allow the seed to grow and to treat the crop which results as if it were holy heave-offering. This constitutes a substantial loss to the Israelite. He both loses the use of his field and may not eat the produce which grows from it. If, however, the individual unintentionally plants the heave-offering, he may plow it up, so as to prevent the growth of a consecrated crop. To be sure, he may not make personal use of what is designated for the priest. But by the same token, he is not held culpable for, or made to suffer the consequences of, what he did unintentionally.[14]

---

[10]These cases are at Mishnah Terumot 4:7-10:12.

[11]The rules for such cases are at Mishnah Terumot 10:1-12.

[12]This is implicit throughout, but is stated explicitly in the view of Judah, Mishnah Terumot 10:1, and in Simeon's view in Tosefta's corrolary material, Tosefta Terumot 8:9.

[13]These rules are at Mishnah Terumot 9:1-6.

[14]Mishnah makes the same point through cases in which a non-priest unintentionally eats heave-offering. If that happens, the non-priest simply sanctifies more produce, to replace that heave-offering which he ate. (In this case he also pays an additional fifth of the heave-offering's value, as mandated by Lev 5:16 and 22:14.) If, however, the non-

Only by his intention does an Israelite encroach upon the holy, just as it is only by his own intention that he renders produce sanctified in the first place.

The single message of Tractate Terumot thus is that holiness in this world depends upon the thoughts and deeds of common Israelites. Produce becomes holy because they wish it to be so. The holiness is maintained because these same people are intent upon protecting the sanctity. As the final passages of the tractate point out, heave-offering ceases to be holy at the point at which common Israelites no longer deem that produce worthy of a sanctified status. Then it may be used for the Israelite's own benefit, just like other common food.[15] These central notions are developed through the tractate's diverse, and sometimes arcane, rules on this topic. They shine through the haze of details which Tractate Terumot's authorities discuss and dispute.

In review, the central tenets with which we now deal are as follows: God must be paid what is owing to him for providing the land which produces the food of the people of Israel. Israelites make this payment by designating food to be holy, and by making sure that the holiness is not improperly displaced. Ultimately the food is to be given to the priests, the proper recipients of all that is holy. Yet even before this occurs, Israelites themselves might determine that the produce no longer is fit to be consecrated. People, God, priesthood and land thus form a complete system of sanctification. And as we now have seen, the people are this sytem's center and fulcrum. They cause food to become holy, assure that it properly is handled once it is holy, and through their own sensibilities determine when it will cease to be holy.

We must realize that these notions which Mishnah's Rabbis present are striking. They differ from those we should expect on the basis of the Priestly Code, the source from which Mishnah learns about heave-offering in the first place. According to that code, sanctification depends upon the priests and their service at the altar, the primary locus of the holy. The earthly representation of God's power is in the cult of the priests. This power is seen in their capacity to lay on hands and designate beasts as holy, in their service in God's Temple, and in their consumption of those parts of God's holy things which are not burned upon the altar. In concentrating upon the power of consecration of common Israelites, Mishnah's authorities thus take up and express ideas specific to themselves.

When we turn back to contemplate the facts with which this paper began, reasons for this are apparent. It becomes clear why, in the time of the Rabbis of Tractate Terumot, it is important to talk about heave-offering and the power of common Israelites to impose upon produce a status of holiness. In exactly that period in which Israelites have good reason to believe that God's lordship over and concern for the people and land of Israel have come to an end,[16] the authorities of Mishnah rehearse and make explicit the Scriptural requirement that all Israelites pay the priestly due. By doing this they put forward the powerful statement that the relationship between the people of Israel and God remains the same as it was before the wars with Rome. Events of history are to be ignored. Clearly with the Temple in ruins the priests no longer function in cultic service to God. Despite this loss of function, however, they still are to be treated as God's representatives on earth. For this reason they must receive the share which God mandated for them. This masks the deeper claim which the ideas of the tractate

---

priest intentionally eats the priestly gift, he is culpable for destroying a holy thing. He cannot replace the sanctified produce and, further, is subject to extirpation.

[15]These cases are at Mishnah Terumot 11:1-10.

[16]The tractate's only attributions to authorities who lived before 70 C.E. are in three disputes assigned to the Houses of Hillel and Shammai. As I have argued (in Neusner, op. cit., pp. 292-293), only in the case of one of these disputes are there grounds for holding that the issue actually goes back to the historical houses. It therefore is clear that the vast majority of the work on the Tractate Terumot was done after the destruction of the Temple and later, after the Bar Kokhba revolt.

express. By acknowledging the continuing status and privileges of the priests, the Rabbis of Mishnah Terumot affirm that God remains owner of the land and lord over the people of Israel. Only because God still is present and in control does his claim as a landlord remain in effect over the produce grown by his people Israel on the land he gave them.

For the authorities of Mishnah Terumot, the priesthood thus serves as a symbol evoking God's lordship and dominion. At the same time, for these Rabbis, the priestly station can be nothing more than a symbol. For as we have seen, with the Temple and cult destroyed, the priests no longer play a concrete role in the sanctification of Israelite life. There now is no Temple in which they can serve, no sacrifices which they may offer. In light of this, in focusing upon a particular locus and means of sanctification to be operative in their day, the authorities of Mishnah Terumot turn their attention away from the priests. They concentrate instead upon heave-offering, which Israelites themselves designate to be holy. In this offering, the Rabbis recognize a strong proof that the holiness they seek still abides in the world. If the people themselves may declare things to be holy, and can maintain that holy status in a secular world, it means that, even with the Temple gone, cultic sanctification still exists. The God who once moved through the priests and altar continues to rule. Now he moves in response to the intentions and perceptions of his common people, Israelites who separate and protect the offerings which God mandated. Mishnah's message is poignant. For as is clear, with the Temple destroyed and the land defiled, the intentions and perceptions of Israelites are all that remain to defy the events of history and affirm God's presence and dominion.

Bibliography

Jaffee, Martin S., *Mishnah's Theology of Tithing. A Study of Tractate Maaserot* (Chico: Scholars Press, 1981).

Neusner, Jacob, *Judaism: The Evidence of the Mishnah* (Chicago: University of Chicago Press, 1981).

Peck, Alan J., *The Priestly Gift in Mishnah. A Study of Tractate Terumot* (Chico: Scholars Press, 1981).

Sarason, Richard S., *A History of the Mishnaic Law of Agriculture. A Study of Tractate Demai* (Leiden: Brill, 1979).

Sarason, Richard S., "Mishnah and Scripture: Preliminary Observations on the Law of Tithing in *Seder Zeraᶜim*," *Approaches to Ancient Judaism. Vol II* (ed. W. S. Green; Chico: Scholars Press, 1980) pp. 81-96.

EARLY CHRISTIAN MAGICAL PRACTICES

Stephen Benko

The charges against the early Christians that are best known to us (because they were so often refuted by the Apologists) were atheism, licentiousness and infanticide. These have been analyzed often and well by experts[1] but less attention has been given to the charge that Christians were practicing harmful magic which was illegal under Roman law.[2] The recent appearance of Morton Smith's *Jesus the Magician* has finally attracted the scholarly attention the problem deserves.[3]

This paper raises the question whether the early Christians practiced magic and if so in what form. Our investigation is limited chronologically roughly to the early patristic period and to the mainstream "orthodox" church only. The reasons for this focus are obvious. In this time period the allegations are quite clear. Celsus accused the Christians of using the names of demons and incantations[4] and he even claimed to have seen magical books in the hands of Christian presbyters.[5] In *Acta Achatii V*[6] the investigating magistrate supposedly said: *Ideo magi estis, quia novum nescio quod genus religionis inducitis.* Similarly, according to the *Passion of Perpetua and Felicitas* 16 information was given to the guard that his prisoners may be secretly freed *incantationibus aliquibus magicis.* Hadrian's much debated letter to Servianus[7] counts the Christian presbyters along with Samaritans and the "chief of the Jewish synagogue" as "astrologers, soothsayers, anointers." Morton Smith has made a strong case in favor of his thesis that Pliny *Ep.* 10.96 and Tacitus, *Annales* 15.44 make sense only if one presupposes that the Romans had already formed an opinion of Christianity, namely that "it was an organization for the practice of magic."[8] In addition to these references some indirect ones could be quoted, such as Lucian's *Alexander* whose pathological fear of the presence of Christians at his ceremonies[9] may be due to the fact that he was familiar with the reputation of the Christians as effective exorcists and thus he was afraid that they may "break the spell" in his assemblies. Whether Apuleius saw the "empty rites" of the baker's wife[10] as some sort of strange magic remains unresolved. We do know for certain that Christians later were suspected of being able to confuse pagan religious rites by their presence alone[11] and this was supposedly the reason for the beginning of the Diocletian persecution.[12] These are, of course, sure signs of magicians but "Orthodox" Christians have always rejected the charge and have denied vigorously that Jesus had anything to do with magical acts as well. Any comparison between Jesus and Apollonius

---

[1]P. Labriolle, *La reaction païenne*, 1934; modern bibliography in my "Pagan Criticism of Christianity," *ANRW* 32/2, 1055-1118.

[2]*Lex Cornelia de sicariis et veneficis*; see R. MacMullen, *Enemies of the Roman Order*, 1966, pp. 95-127.

[3]For an earlier reference see A. D. Nock, "Paul and the Magus," in F. Jackson-Lake, *The Beginnings of Christianity*. I.5.

[4]Origen, *Contra Celsum* 1.6.

[5]Origen, op. cit., 6.40.

[6]Around 250; omitted as spurious by Musurillo, *The Acts of the Christian Martyrs*, Oxford, p. XII.

[7]*Historia Augusta, Saturninus* 8; D. Magie, *SHA* in the *LCL* 3, 397-401.

[8]Op. cit., p. 53. See also E. V. Dobschütz, "Charms and Amulets," *Encyclopedia of Religion and Ethics*, ed. Hastings, 3.414.

[9]Chapters 25 and 38.

[10]*Metamorphoses* 9.14.

[11]Eusebius, *HE*7.10.1-4.

[12]Lactantius, *De morte persecutorum* 10.

of Tyana or Apuleius was rejected with the very shaky argument that Jesus was "incomparably superior to magicians of every name."[13]

On the other hand, Christian "heretics," especially Gnostics were liberally accused of being magicians by their orthodox brothers. Irenaeus pointed a finger at the Carpocratians that they "practice magical acts and incantations, use philters also and love potions, and have recourse to familiar spirits, dream-sending demons and other abominations. . . ."[14] A particularly accomplished trickster must have been Markos who could turn the color of the wine in the Eucharist into purple or red.[15]

Quite often, however, in the writings of the church fathers their belief in the principles of magic surfaces. For example, they firmly believed in the existence of demons as intermediary beings and that is one of the preconditions for any system of magic. "We affirm indeed the existence of certain spiritual essences," wrote Tertullian, "nor is their name unfamiliar."[16] Indeed, Christians felt constantly surrounded by demons, they sensed them lurking under the statues and images, behind pagan oracles and divinations.[17] So firm was the belief in demonology that systematic treatises have been written about them.[18] How close this is to pagan ideas of magic becomes clear when we consider that pagan magic postulated an affinity between the spiritual and material world so that they could mutually affect each other. This cosmic "sympathy" and "antipathy"[19] means that the divine exists in the material (animals, plants, minerals, the human body and voice, etc.) and the whole secret is to find out which material contains which divine element in the purest and most abundant form. The preparation of magic potions, the use of amulets and charms, the myriads of magic prescriptions and closely defined formulas are based on these presuppositions.

Occasionally Christian authors used surprisingly candid language when they discussed magic. Such a one was Origen who argued that magic is "not an altogether uncertain thing but is, as those skilled in it prove, a consistent system."[20] Augustine similarly believed that it was possible to produce miracles by magic, because "devils are attracted . . . not by food like animals, but like spirits, by such symbols as suit their taste, various kinds of stones, woods, plants, animals, songs, rites. And that men may provide these attractions, the devils first of all cunningly seduce them . . . and thus make a few of them their disciples, who become the instructors of the multitude. For unless they first instructed men, it was impossible to know what each of them desires, what they shrink from, by what name they should be invoked or constrained to be present. Hence the origin of magic and magicians."[21] These are, of course, open admissions that magic exists but Origen went further when he asserted that Christians can heal mental disorders, exorcise, heal and even change the character of people by the use of the name of Jesus and "certain other words."[22] These, he quickly adds, cannot be considered employing spells or incantations--but he fails to tell us why not. Magical elements also appear in many early Christian practices. The following are especially blatant:

---

[13]E.g. Augustine, Ep. 138-20; Lactantius, Div. Inst. 5.3.

[14] Adv. Haer. 1.25; 2.31.2; Hippolytus, Ref. 6.7ff; 7.32; 9.14.

[15]Hippolytus, op. cit., 6.39ff. and Epiphanius, Panarion 34.

[16] Apol. 22; De test. an. 3.

[17]Minucius Felix, Octavius 27; Cyprian, Quod idola 7.

[18]Tatian, Oratio 7-18, Tertullian, Apol. 22-23; The Ps.-Clementine Homilies 9; Lactantius, Inst. Div. 2.15; 9.18; Augustine, De civ. Dei 8-10.

[19]T. Hopfner, "Mageia," Pauly's Realencyclopädie 28.310ff.; D. A. Aune, "Magic in Early Christianity," ANRW 23/2 (1980) 1507-1557, esp. p. 1513 and footnote 17 for bibliography.

[20] Contra C. 1.24, compare with Apuleius, Apol. 25.

[21] De civ. Dei 21.6.

[22]Op. cit., 1.46, 67; 7.4.

The *exorcism of demons*. Christians can do that because "the concealed power of God was in Christ the crucified before whom demons . . . tremble."[23] Indeed, exorcism was such an important part of early Christian life that it should not surprise us when outsiders often saw Christians in this light. There were so many exorcists that rules had to be established to ward off imposters who used unintelligible and terrifying words, similarly to their pagan counterparts, to impress simple people.[24] It is not difficult to imagine that the early Christian "glossolalia" may be connected with this practice, but certainly toward the outside world the use of unintelligible formulas must have appeared as something well known from magical practices.

The *name of Jesus* was instrumental in the accomplishment of miracles of exorcism. This is emphasized by all Christian authors, especially by Origen in his reply to Celsus. He has here a long discussion on the nature of names, how names were bestowed and about "powerful names" which are known to a few people only. Such names are Sabaoth and Adonai. "These names, accordingly, when pronounced with that attendant train of circumstances which is appropriate to their nature are possessed of great power."[25] The name of Jesus possesses such power over evil spirits that "there have been instances where it was effectual, when it was pronounced even by bad men. . . ."[26] It is by the use of the name of Jesus that Christians perform their miracles.

They also use the *sign and symbol of the cross*. Already Justin wrote about the power of the cross[27] and Tertullian referred to its use as an already established custom.[28] The sign of the cross was believed to have the power to expel demons and to perform miracles.[29] As a sign that is loaded with spiritual power this is hardly distinguishable from the use of pagan amulets and charms. Other objects, however, may also be charged with divine potency and their proper use could bring beneficial results. Augustine mentions a whole list of these[30] such as a bag of earth from Jerusalem, where Jesus died and rose again; this bag was hung up in the bedroom of Hesperius "to preserve him from harm." After his house was exorcised he no longer needed this protection and buried the bag of earth at a place which became a favorite meeting point of Christians. A paralytic was healed when he visited the place. Other objects with magical powers mentioned by Augustine are oil, mixed with the tears of a certain presbyter who prayed for a young woman--when the woman was anointed with this mixture she was freed from the devil; flowers that were in the procession that carried the relics of a saint restored the sight of a blind person; a dress was taken to a shrine and when it was put on the body of a dead woman she was restored to life. Of course, of all human objects most powerful magic rests in the human voice and Augustine tells us that hymns sung at evening prayer drove the demons from a young man. The list goes on and on: objects, rites, words and formulas charged with divine potency force demons to yield and force the divine power to condescend and to be of assistance in time of need to perform a desired service.

In the same category may be mentioned the use of the *sacraments,* because it is especially in here that the divine is connected with the material and that, we remember, is a basic presupposition of the function of magic. Ignatius referred to the Eucharist as

---

[23]Justin, *Dial.* 49; *Apol.* 2.6; Theophilus, *Ad. Aut.* 8; Irenaeus, *Adv. Haer.* 2.32.4-5; etc.

[24]Ps. Clementine, *De Virginitate* 1.10, 12.

[25]Op. cit., 1.24.

[26]Op. cit., 1.6; also Ps. Cyprian, *Rebaptism* 7.

[27] *Apol.* 1.55.

[28] *De corona* 3; *Ad uxorem* 2.5. See, however, Min. Felix, *Oct.* 29.

[29]Lactantius, *De morte pers.* 4.27; *Inst. div.* 4.26; *Epitome* 51; *Passio Quatuor Coronatorum.*

[30] *De civ. Dei* 22.8-10.

φάρμακον ἀθανασίας[31] and it is a well known fact that the word φάρμακον was used in the sense of magic potion, charm, poison and in a derivative sense as medicine.[32] According to Irenaeus the Logos-Christ present in the bread and wine effect immortality[33] but other authors emphasize the importance of the eucharistic prayer.[34] For Augustine the Eucharist is the "daily medicine of the Lord's body"[35] but he also stresses the importance of the attending word.[36]   No wonder that we hear about countless miracles involving the Eucharist. Typically these fall into the categories of "sympathetic" or "antipathetic" miracle, i.e. the results are sometimes beneficial at other times hostile. For the former we may mention that certain Hesperius known to Augustine, whose farm was haunted by evil spirits; they disappeared when the Eucharist was offered.[37] An example for the latter is the woman who opened the box in which the eucharistic bread was carried to her "with unworthy hands" and she saw flames coming out of it.[38]

Concerning Baptism Tertullian's treatise *De Baptismo* clearly shows how even a man like him was a child of his time. He first proceeds to explain the importance of water: it is an age old substance which is dignified by the fact that even before creation it was the seat of the Holy Spirit.[39] There was, therefore, this eternal "sympathy" (not Tertullian's word) between God and water so that water became the regulating power which resulted in creation—by "dividing the waters" the dry land was made. It was from water again that living creatures were made[40] "that it might be no wonder in Baptism if waters know how to give life." The material substance "which governs terrestrial life acts as agent likewise in the celestial."[41] It is hard to think of anything that is more in line with Greco-Roman principles of magic, but Tertullian goes on. The Spirit of God, which hovered over the waters, continues to linger over the water of Baptism. A material substance caught a spiritual quality and thus gained the power of sanctifying. "All waters, therefore, in virtue of the pristine privilege of their origin, do, after the invocation of God, attain the sacramental power of sanctification."[42]   Granted, the pagans also know the rite of sprinkling houses, temples, cities and in the Eleusian mysteries the people are even baptized and pagans attribute other miracles to waters. But if it is true that in all these instances evil angels are active in the element, a holy angel of God is effective in Christian Baptism. This holy angel prepares the way for the coming of the Holy Spirit upon the baptized, the names of Father, Son and Holy Spirit are mentioned and these divine names give the assurance of salvation. Two more acts follow: anointing with a "blessed unction," and the laying on of hands inviting the Holy Spirit. Just as it was granted possible for human ingenuity to summon a spirit into water so now through cleansed and blessed bodies willingly descends the Holy Spirit. After further meditations Tertullian gives instructions about the problems of who can baptize, who can be baptized and about the most propitious times for the administering of this

---

[31] *Eph.* 20.2.

[32] Arndt-Gingrich, *A Greek-English Lexicon, ad loc.*; Hopfner, art. cit., 320.

[33] *Adv. Haer.* 5.2.2.

[34] *Barnabas* 2.10; *Didache*; Hermas, *Mand.* 10.3.2; 1 Clem 52.2ff.; Justin, *Apol.* 1.66; *Dial.* 41.117.

[35] *Ep.* 54.3.

[36] *Sermo* 234.2., and concerning Baptism *In Jo. Ev. Tr.* 80.3: "Take away the Word and what is the water but water only? The Word is added to the element and it becomes a sacrament."

[37] *De civ. Dei* 22.8, 9, 10.

[38] Cyprian, *De lapsis* 26.

[39] Gen 1:1-2.

[40] Gen 1:20.

[41] Chap. 3.

[42] Op. cit., 4.

sacrament. Obviously, properly administered Baptism did not fail to produce miraculous results of which let us mention two from Augustine's list:[43] a gouty doctor in Carthage was to be baptized but before his Baptism in a dream he saw black wooly-haired boys who tried to prohibit him from accepting Baptism. He understood that these were devils, resisted them, although they caused him much pain, and next day in Baptism not only did his pain disappear but also his gout. Similarly an old comedian near Carthage was cured of paralysis and hernia when he received Baptism.

The preferred time for magic was *night*. So Medea went out in the middle of the night at full moon, when there was no sound, "only the stars twinkled" and prayed: "O night, faithful preserver of mysteries . . . Hecate, who knowest our undertakings and comest to the aid of the spells and arts of magicians; and thou, O Earth, who dost provide the magicians with thy potent herbs . . . be with me now."[44] Apuleius described magic with the following words: It is "as mysterious an art as it is loathly and horrible; it needs as a rule night watches and concealing darkness, solitude absolute and murmured incantations, to hear which few free men are admitted. . . ."[45] Thus, magical practices and nightly meetings were closely associated in the minds of Greeks and Romans. Tertullian was aware of the potential dangers that meant for Christians who also had nightly meetings. In his treatise to his wife he described the difficulties a Christian woman may face who had to live with a pagan husband. He may want to hinder her in the performance of her religious duties especially at night. What pagan husband "will willingly bear her being taken from his side by nocturnal convocations, if need so be? Who, finally, will without anxiety endure her absence all the night long at the paschal solemnities? Who will, without some suspicion of his own, dismiss her to attend the Lord's Supper which they defame?"[46] Then he continues, "Shall you escape notice when you sign your bed, or your body; when you blow away some impurity; when even by night you rise to pray? Will you not be thought to be engaged in some sort of magic? Will not your husband know what it is which you secretly taste before taking any food? And if he knows it to be bread, does he not believe it to be that bread which it is said to be? And will every husband, ignorant of the reason of these things, simply endure them, without murmuring, without suspicion whether it be bread or poison?"[47] Tertullian's warnings bear all the marks of a pagan's suspicion about Christians: they meet at night, perform secret rites, partake of food which may or may not be harmful. Pliny's letter to Trajan[48] from A.D. 111 contains similar elements: the Christians congregate before daylight; they sing a *carmen*, which could be heard by a pagan as "casting a spell"; they take an oath; and then later they come together to eat. The similarity with well-known magical practices is obvious and the conclusion must have been inevitable that Christians were involved in some sort of magic, as Tertullian aptly noted. And who can tell the difference?

Secrecy was another hallmark of ancient magic and this was partially the reason why it was performed under the cover of darkness. The knowledge of formulas, "true names," the elements of ingredients in potions and other parts of the rites were well kept secrets. This is true concerning the mystery religions, too, but when we come to early Christianity our sources do not provide us with a unified answer. Tertullian makes a veiled reference to the Christian wife's "secrets"[49] and in an indirect way he also refers to such a secrecy when he chides the heretics that they provide access to their services

---

[43] *De civ. Dei* 22.8-10.

[44] Ovid, *Metamorphoses* 7.180ff.; ET.: F. J. Miller, *LCL* vol. 1.

[45] *Apol.* 47; see also Theokritos II; Pidar, *Olympic Odes* 1.73ff.; Tibullus 1.8.17; 1.5.11-16; Philostratus, *Life* 8.7; Horace, *Epode* 5.5; etc.

[46] *Ad uxorem* 2.4.

[47] *Ad uxorem* 2.5.

[48] *Ep.* 10.96.

[49] 2.5.

to everybody without distinction. Their conduct thus becomes frivolous, merely human, without seriousness, without authority.[50] We know that the sacraments were available for the initiated only[51] and it was probably on this account that Celsus called Christianity a "secret system of belief."[52] Origen in his reply admits that there are certain secret doctrines of Christianity but he argues that this is not unique with Christianity and besides the basic teachings of Christianity are well known to all. Since the seventeenth century this practice of Christianity was called *disciplina arcani* and eventually it included in addition to Baptism and Eucharist the Lord's prayer and the baptismal creed. But the *disciplina arcani* was never uniformly followed: Justin Martyr did not know of it, Hippolytus tended to ignore it and even in later centuries many Christian authors treated it in a liberal way. From the fifth century on it quickly disappeared--everybody was Christian and there was nothing to be kept secret. For second or third century Greeks and Romans the most suspicious secret of the Christians was their celebration of the Eucharist and it was naturally in this connection that the worst rumors arose.[53]

---

[50] *De praescr. haer.* 41.

[51] *Didache* 9.5.

[52] Origen, op. cit., 1.7.

[53] Because of space limitations the summary has been omitted.

TRADITION AND CREATIVITY:
HERMENEUTICAL USE OF LANGUAGE IN HOSEA 1-3

George Blankenbaker
Westmont College

I. Introduction

Traditional language forms provide continuity and stability necessary for good communication. On the other hand, freshness and vitality are generated through the creative dimension which a writer or speaker brings to a new language situation. Although tradition is a guard against chaos, language is not a static but a dynamic tool for dealing with situations in life. As Wittgenstein has pointed out, there are ". . . countless different kinds of use of what we call 'symbols,' 'words,' 'sentences.' And this multiplicity is not something fixed, given once for all; but new types of language, new language-games, as we say, come into existence, and others become obsolete and get forgotten."[1] The purpose or intention of an author may be seen in the hermeneutical moves made by him as he shapes the language along certain lines.[2] It is important, then, not only to recognize traditional and new elements but also to take note of the selection and arrangement of them made by the author.

As with other language, the formation of prophetic literature has involved a dynamic tension between the traditional and the creative use of language forms. Gerhard von Rad speaks of the prophets as ". . . spokesmen of old and well-known sacral traditions which they interpreted for their own day and age."[3] This could also be said of the redactors who interpreted the words of the prophets for a new situation.

II. Hosea 1-3

Like other prophetic books, Hosea illustrates that dynamic tension of tradition and creativity both from the perspective of the prophet Hosea and from that of the redactor.

Hosea is composed of two main sections: chapters 1-3 and 4-14.[4] Since chapters 1-3 are a self-contained unit, discussion of the hermeneutical use of language in Hosea will be restricted to those chapters. Even so, not all the material in those chapters will be dealt with.[5]

It is possible in those chapters to distinguish between Hosea's use of language and the reuse of Hosea's material by a later writer. The majority of the language reflects the actual situation of Hosea; however, there is a definable non-Hoseanic element as

---

[1]L. Wittgenstein, *Philosophical Investigations*, trans. by G. E. M. Anscombe (New York: Macmillan, 1965) p. 11.

[2]Cf. G. A. Miller, *The Psychology of Communication* (London: Penguin, 1969) pp. 79-81.

[3]*Old Testament Theology*, (Vol. II; trans. by D. Stalker; New York: Harper and Row, 1965) p. 175. Of course, other than sacral traditions were used as well by the prophets.

[4]W. Rudolph, *Hosea* (KAT 13/1; Gütersloh: Mohn, 1966) p. 25; O. Eissfeldt, *The Old Testament: An Introduction* (trans. by P. Ackroyd; New York: Harper and Row, 1965) p. 385; J. Ward, *Hosea: A Theological Commentary* (New York: Harper and Row, 1966) p. vii, divides the book into three sections: chapters 1-3, 4-10, 11-14; because W. F. Stinespring, "Hosea, Prophet of Doom," *Crozer Quarterly* 27 (1950) 202, sees Hosea as a prophet of doom, he considers chapter 3 as "irrelevant to the original purpose of the book of Hosea."

[5]For a fuller discussion see G. Blankenbaker, *The Language of Hosea 1-3*, Doctoral Dissertation, Claremont Graduate School, 1975.

well. The situations which lie behind the Hoseanic material are not fully indicated in the present text. This is due to the fact that the present text was constructed with a particular intention in mind. Consequently, those elements of the previous Hoseanic material which were significant for that intention have been used, while the rest have not. The intention of the present text may be seen in the framework of chapter one and its relation to chapters two and three. Within the framework of chapter one, originally separate details have been brought together by the writer. The narrative framework utilizes the anthropological sequence of marriage, birth, and naming which is placed within the context of the commands of Yahweh. Yahweh's commands are the basis for the sequence. Chapter one emphasizes the continuing need for judgment while chapter two indicates the transition from the beginning of the word of Yahweh in judgment (chapter 1) to the final word of restoration (chapter 3).

In some cases the language of Hosea may not be the result of a conscious decision to use one or another motif or genre or phrase. The situations and intentions may quite automatically have determined the language elements which were appropriate.[6] Whether or not the author was always conscious of the selection process, the various combinations chosen convey a specific meaning, by the very fact that the language is thus and not some other way constructed. Therefore, in exploring the way in which the language of Hosea 1-3 has been structured by Hosea two main elements should be considered: the basic language forms used and the purpose served by the juxtaposition of the various formulae, motifs, or genres.

A. Hosea's Use of Language

There appear to have been three levels of expression by Hosea: sign events, justifications with secondary expansions, and abiding elements of the sign events.

The prophetic sign-event is a genre similar to that of the parable.[7] It points beyond itself. It is self-evident to the observer that more is meant than the sign-event itself. Its purpose is to stimulate the hearer to inquire about the meaning. The sign-event, then, serves a definite hermeneutical function. However, it is in the explanations that the main elements of the message of the prophet are unfolded. At the same time there is often a justification given for the nature of the sign-event. Usually the justification is stated in terms of the command of Yahweh. As Hosea evidently had pointed out, Yahweh had commanded him to perform the four sign-events, i.e., the marriage to Gomer and the naming of the three children. The choice of language is governed to a certain degree by the nature of the command. Therefore, because the commands involved marriage and naming children, Hosea's language was shaped by the institution of the family. Other motifs and genre elements have also been used by Hosea to express the message.

In justification of his marriage to Gomer, Hosea combines elements of the genres of prophetic commission and marriage. The commission lies behind the action, as the authority for it. He could have done no other; he was under orders from Yahweh. Since a prophetic commission is related to a word which must be delivered, the action commanded is to be seen as a prelude to that message.

---

[6]Cf. G. Tucker, *Form Criticism of the Old Testament*, p. 3; K. Koch, *The Growth of the Biblical Tradition*, pp. 26-28.

[7]Cf. Matt 13:3-23. At several points there are indications that parables are used, not as a full expression of a truth, but as a means of engendering inquiry. After the parable of the sower Jesus says, "He who has ears to hear, let him hear" (verse 9). In verse 18 he says, "Hear then the parable of the sower." This follows the inquiry by the disciples about the reason for his use of parables. If the parables were self-explanatory, the disciples' question would be meaningless, and the explanation (verses 19-23) would have been unnecessary.

The opening word of the Yahweh speech in 1:2b is "Go." When used in the imperative this word may convey a wide variety of meanings from simple dismissal or entreaty to depart,[8] with[9] or without blessing, to a more complex form including one or more imperatives.[10] With the addition of another imperative the emphasis most often shifts to the element of the added imperative.

An important factor connected with the use of "Go" plus a following imperative is that the activity usually is on behalf of, or could even be considered as an extension of, the person who gives the command.[11] It has been shown that when God calls a man to the office of prophet the formula of "Go" plus a following imperative is often used. Westermann speaks about what he calls "the structure of the event that we call prophecy." He continues by saying, "The three stages that constitute a message can be assumed also for the sending of a prophet: (1) the commissioning, (2) the transmission, (3) the delivery." He considers the second element the most important because, in his words,

> It is in the act of bridging the distance that it has its distinctive meaning. . . . That those who transmitted the prophetic speeches were conscious of this as the real task of the prophetic speech is seen in the formulation of the commissioning, which is almost always: 'Go and say. . . !' Each time the prophet has to bridge this distance anew with his word.[12]

The use in Hosea of לך plus the following imperative is an expression of his commission from Yahweh. However, instead of the very common formula: "Go and say . . . !" a verb of action rather than speech is used. Hosea is to "bridge the distance," but at least for the initial stage of transmission, action rather than word is commanded. The action is commanded by Yahweh, under whose authority Hosea is to act as an extension of Yahweh's authority. The action is not to be an end in itself but is to be an important step toward a specific purpose. That purpose is not stated, but since the commissioning of a prophet by Yahweh usually involves the element of speech, the ultimate purpose of the strange action was probably to create a situation in which speech could be the most meaningful. The action was meant to create a situation of inquiry so that, since they had introduced the questions, the inquirers would be more compelled to accept the responses given. This relationship of word to action is characteristic of sign events.

One of the clearest examples of this element in a context of symbolic action is found in Ezek 12:1-16. After Yahweh's command for Ezekiel to act as an exile, including digging through the wall, and after Ezekiel's performance of this symbolic action, Ezekiel records the following in verses 8-10a, "In the morning the word of the Lord came to me: 'Son of Man, has not the house of Israel, the rebellious house, said to you,"What are you doing? Say to them. . . .' " Several things are evident: the symbolic action engendered a questioning spirit on the part of those who observed it;[13] the word of explanation

---

[8]Cf. Gen 26:16; 1 Kings 1:53; 2 Kings 3:13.

[9]Cf. Exod 4:18; 1 Sam 20:42; 2 Sam 15:9.

[10]In the majority of cases there is one or more additional imperative.

[11]Cf. Gen 27:9; 2 Kings 2:29.

[12]C. Westermann, *Basic Forms of Prophetic Speech*, (trans. by H. C. White; Philadelphia: Westminster Press, 1967) pp. 102-3.

[13]That the purpose of symbolic action is to engender a situation in which people will react by asking questions is even more easily seen in Ezek 21:11. Here the fact that the question will be asked is asserted at the time the symbolic action is commanded, i.e., before the people even ask the question. Contra W. Brownlee who says, "This is no mere symbolic pantomime. . . . Ezekiel interprets his own emotion as a message from God" ("Ezekiel," *Interpreters One-Volume Commentary on the Bible* [ed. by C. Laymon; Nashville: Abingdon, 1971] p. 424).

originated with Yahweh, even as the command to perform the symbolic action had; the symbolic action is servant to the word of Yahweh.

Linking together the fact that the prophetic commission is usually cast in the formula "Go . . . say" and the fact that a symbolic action is servant to the word of Yahweh, it is evident that when the command to a prophet is "Go . . . do," he is commissioned to do more than perform a symbolic action. He is being commissioned to proclaim the word of Yahweh. Thus it must have been with Hosea when he married Gomer and named his children. Those symbolic actions would have been only a means to an end: the proclamation of the word of Yahweh.

The combination of symbolic action and word of Yahweh is a traditional form among the prophets predating the eighth century as shown by the Ahijah narrative in 1 Kings 11:29-39.[14] Thus when Hosea used this traditional method of communication, he did not have to justify the method. However, the first of these symbolic actions probably stimulated more than a simple questioning spirit. It created a condemning hostility against which Hosea had to justify himself and that particular form of symbolic action. By this symbolic action the people were forced into the role of accusers,[15] but they who had assumed the role soon found the roles reversed. The accusers became the accused when the justification, the word of Yahweh, was given. Hosea had married a harlotrous woman as an analogous representation of Israel's relation to Yahweh. That Hosea married a woman would not have been meaningful as a symbolic action adequate in itself to set the stage for that particular message of Yahweh which Hosea was to proclaim. It is the unusual, not the usual, which is basic to the prophetic use of symbolic action. The unusual creates the stimulus for questioning, which provides the situation in which the word of the prophet, the word of Yahweh, will be the most effective.

The phrase קח לך אשה originates within the context of marriage arrangements.[16] Usually such arrangements were made by the parents. A phrase similar to Hosea 1:2b occurs in Gen 28:1, 2.

. . . אשת	לך	קח	לך	הושע	אל	יהוה	ויאמר Hosea
אשה . . .	לך	וקח . . .	לך . . .		לו		ויאמר Genesis

This element of the father-son relation is usually overlooked by commentators. Instead they focus on the marriage relation and the question of Gomer's pre-marital status. Hosea is to be seen as the "son" of God who is called to minister to his own people, even entering into their situation and experiencing the consequences of their sin.

By the addition of זנונים the traditional language is given a negative meaning. Hosea must marry a woman of harlotry. Such a qualification of the traditional language is essential to Hosea's message. Within the context of what any father might say to his son, Yahweh says to Hosea what no father would ever say to his son.

Language from at least three distinct traditions is joined together to form the initial thrust of Hosea's message: (1) the prophetic call formula, which goes back to even earlier roots, (2) the marriage formula, and (3) the word for adultery. In this way the action of Hosea, his marriage to Gomer the harlot, is justified by him to those who would question the propriety of his action. He has been called by Yahweh into the prophetic

---

[14]Cf., also, Zedekiah's action and word in 1 Kings 22:11.

[15]Cf. H. W. Wolff, *Dodekapropheton 1: Hosea,* (BKAT; Neukirchener: Moers, 1965) p. 25; H. Frey, *Das Buch des Werbens Gottes um seine Kirche: der Prophet Hosea,* (Die Botschaft des Alten Testament, Bd. 23/2; Stuttgart: Calwer, 1957) pp. 12-13. W. Rudolph rejects this (*Hosea,* p. 46).

[16]Cf. R. de Vaux's chapter on marriage in *Ancient Israel* (London: Darton, Longman and Todd, 1961) pp. 24-40; also J. Pedersen, *Israel,* I-II (London: Oxford, 1953) pp. 60ff.; G. von Rad, *Genesis* (Philadelphia: Westminster Press, 1961) p. 249.

office. However, he represents Yahweh not only as prophet but also as son. As son he must obey the command of the father, even when that command involves marriage to a harlot, a woman probably associated with Baal worship. Israel, who has been the son of God,[17] is thus indicted; first by the obedient response of Hosea, the son, but even more so by the nature of the action, i.e., marriage to a harlot.

On this second level the indictment is strengthened because of another factor involved in the father-son relationship. The father is reflected in the son. Hosea's marriage to a harlot is to mirror the relation of Yahweh to his own wife, Israel. In this way Israel is indicted as a harlot, not as a reflection of what she will become but of what she already is.

According to Ezekiel, Israel's harlotry extends back to their days in Egypt.[18] The act of covenant making at Sinai, then, can be viewed as Yahweh taking a harlot as his bride. It was a gracious action. It is in this light that the imagery of Hosea must be viewed. The sign action Hosea is commanded to perform is in line with the tradition of covenant making between Yahweh and Israel. By God's grace the covenant was established. Now, in Hosea's time, the grace of God is once again exemplified, this time a gracious act on Hosea's part: his marriage to Gomer, the harlot. However, such a gracious covenant relation when broken involves judgment, for within the covenant of marriage are binding requirements.

Ezekiel appears to have utilized the tradition which developed through Hosea.[19] Thus it is interesting to follow the thought of Ezekiel 23. In verse 4 it is said of Oholah and Oholibah: ". . . they became mine, and they bore sons and daughters." This is similar to the statements in Hosea: "So he went and took Gomer the daughter of Diblaim and she conceived and bore him a son" (verse 3), ". . . a daughter" (verse 6), ". . . a son" (verse 8). Ezek 23:8 points out that the new relation of marriage did not keep Israel from again playing the harlot. In the same way, the fact that Hosea married Gomer did not keep her from again committing harlotry. In each instance the harlot who by grace had been brought into the covenant relation of marriage broke that covenant bond.

The phrase ילדי זנונים ו has created difficulties for translators and commentators. Syntactically it would usually be considered the second object of קח לך.[20] Most commentators[21] suggest that there is an elipsis requiring an additional verb such as "beget." The formula made up of the imperatives of לקח and ילד occurs only in Jeremiah 29:6. The more normative formula is probably that of blessing as found in the Isaac-Jacob narrative where Isaac says to Jacob, ". . . take a wife. . . . El Shaddai bless you and make you fruitful and multiply you. . . ."[22] The thought of having children is

---

[17]That the ideal relationship between Yahweh and Israel may be expressed as one of father-son is pointed out by Hos 2:1 where the phrase "sons of the living God" is used as a designation for Israel when once again in fellowship with Yahweh. This goes back to the exodus traditions. In the narrative of Exod 4:22, 23, Israel is spoken of as Yahweh's first-born son.

[18]Ezek 23:3, 8, 19; Josh 24:14 alludes to this also.

[19]W. Zimmerli, in *The Law and the Prophets: A Study of the Meaning of the Old Testament* (trans. by R. E. Clements; Harper Torchbooks; New York: Harper and Row, 1965) p. 71, speaks of a "unique theology of history" which became clear to Hosea when he realized Israel's loss of the true knowledge of God. He says, "Hosea xii speaks of the patriarch Jacob. The evil nature is already apparent in him. 'In the womb he took his brother by the heel . . . . The whole evil nature of Israel is already present in its ancestor, and now becomes manifest."

[20]Cf. J. Ward, *Hosea*, p. 5. Ward does not press for this, however. He says, "The obvious connotation of such a statement may be misleading . . . ."

[21]Cf. H. W. Wolff, *Dodekapropheton* 1, p. 15; J. L. Mays, *Hosea*, p. 26; W. Rudolph, *Hosea*, p. 48, et al.

[22]Gen 28:2, 3.

integral to either formulation. However, the one is in the form of imperative command while the other is in the form of blessing.

That neither of these formulae is used by Hosea is significant. The double object is to be understood in terms of the single verb, קח. The idea expressed is not that of blessing but of the solidarity between the children and the mother. When Hosea takes the woman of harlotry he also takes the children she will bear, children of harlotry. If there is an elipsis, such that a verb like ילד is omitted, it is probably a conscious one. The children are not thought of as secondary to the activity of marriage. They are one with that initial action. Chronologically, of course, they will not become a part of the actual scene until their respective births. In a real sense, however, the woman and her children represent the same entity: Israel. The mother represents the nation as a whole, while the children represent the individuals.

In the justification clause of Hos 1:2, the Sinai covenant tradition is foundational. Because of the covenant and its restriction, to turn to other gods is a sin against Yahweh, a sin described under the figure of harlotry. In Num 25:1-5[23] this simile is used to describe the Israelite defection from Yahweh. Since the use of harlotry to describe defection from Yahweh is a part of the early traditions, von Rad is probably incorrect when he says, "Hosea was the first to describe Israel's submersion in the Canaanite nature religion as 'harlotry' 'leaving Jahweh in order to play the harlot;' . . . ."[24] The close association of the term harlotry with disobedience to the initial commands of the Sinai covenant is reflected in Exod 34:15-16. An alien covenant is mentioned in verse 15, a covenant with the inhabitants of the land. This alien covenant would lead to "harlotry after their gods." The parallel of this phrase with that in Hosea 1:2c is striking.

כי זנה תזנה הארץ מאחרי יהוה   Hosea 1:2c

וזנו   אחרי אלהיהם   Exod 34:15b

The Hoseanic passage utilizes this ancient formula which is descriptive of the processes by which the covenant may be broken. This imagery is foundational to Yahweh's command that Hosea marry a harlot. Also, it is on the basis of the legal elements of the Sinai covenant that the indictment against Israel is made. She has broken covenant with Yahweh.

Since Hosea is dependent upon the tradition that covenant breaking equals harlotry, is he also dependent upon a previous tradition which uses the marriage concept as a description of the covenant relation, or is this a new development which originates with him?

In the earliest traditions[25] the terms for harlotry are used in secular settings. With the establishment of the covenant at Sinai the terms were utilized to describe unfaithfulness to the covenant relation between Yahweh and his people. Unfaithfulness to Yahweh, i.e., defection to other gods, was likened in this way to a woman being unfaithful to the marriage covenant between her husband and herself. It is probable that from very early times Israel thought of her covenant relation to Yahweh in terms of marriage, otherwise the use of negative marriage covenant terms makes little sense. If so, Hosea uses a traditional motif, rather than introducing a new one.

---

[23]O. Eissfeldt, in *The Old Testament*, pp. 195, 200, suggests that this section is a conflation of sources L and J. M. Noth, in *Numbers: A Commentary* (Philadelphia: Westminster, 1968) p. 8, says it ". . . belongs to the 'old sources' and is probably to be attributed to J . . . ."

[24]G. von Rad, *Old Testament Theology,* II, p. 142.

[25]Cf. Genesis 34 and 38.

The phrase מאחרי יהוה with the verb זנה occurs only in Hosea 1:2. Although זנה is able to stand by itself as an expression of defection, naturally מאחר cannot; some verb must accompany it. Yet, with the exception of Hos 1:2, some verb other than זנה is used. The normal formula with זנה is אחר followed by a representative form for a foreign god[26] (e.g., a name, a generic term, a pronoun, etc.). Thus, even in such contexts of defection from Yahweh (pointed out by זנה), with the use of אחר, allegiance is also stressed, allegiance to other gods.

In Hosea 1:2, two formulae are fused together: (1) verb (other than זנה) plus מאחר and (2) זנה . . . אחר. The resultant formula is זנה . . . מאחרי יהוה. The mind is forced to center on Yahweh as the one who has been wronged. It is true that the theological understanding of both formulae is embodied in the new formula. However, at this point the other gods are secondary to the magnitude of personal affront which Yahweh has suffered.

In verse 3, standard narrative formulae are used for the marriage, conception, birth sequence.[27] In this concise way the obedience of the son-prophet is expressed and the stage is set for the next Yahweh word, the command to name the child.

In narratives dealing with the sequence of events from marriage to birth, there are several basic formulae which are joined together in various ways. A nearly complete list is found in the old narrative of Gen 38:2, 3. It includes a form of לקח, indicating the element of marriage;[28] a euphemism for intercourse;[29] a statement indicating conception; a phrase about the birth of a son; and , finally, a statement about the naming of the child. There is no reason indicated for the name given, although reasons are often stated in similar narratives.[30] The fuller form, thus exhibited in Gen 38:2, 3 is not characteristic for most of these narratives. However, the narrative in Hos 1:3, 4 is quite complete. It lacks only a euphemism for intercourse. But there is a difference in the statement concerning the naming of the child. Instead of the father (or the mother) choosing a name, Hosea is told by Yahweh what to name the son. In the few other contexts where God gives the name, it is usually prior to the birth.[31] The only time it occurs after the birth is in the naming of Maher-shalal-hash-baz.[32] This is an interesting parallel. It uses, in the autobiographical form, the identical formula which Hos 1:4b uses in the biographical.

כי . . . מהר שמו קרא אלי יהוה ויאמר	Isa 8:3b
כי יזרעאל שמו קרא אליו יהוה ויאמר	Hos 1:4b

Thus, one can see what the original form of Hos 1:4b was.

---

[26]Cf. Exod 34:15, 16; Deut 31:16.

[27]For the Ugaritic parallels to these formulae, cf. M. Dahood, "Word Pairs," *Ras Shamra Parallels*, I: 173-74, 200-201.

[28]Usually "to take a woman" refers to the marriage. However, in 2 Sam 11:4 it is used of David in relation to Bathsheba, but not in the technical sense of marriage. This may indicate something of the origin of the use of this phrase for marriage. The act of possession, probably sexual possession, was the first step in a continuing relation between a man and a woman. Thus, "to take a woman" became a standard formula for marriage even when the element of physical or sexual possession was no longer primary.

[29]Usually in the narratives of conception and birth, there is simply the statement of conception. Here the euphemism is ויבא אליה. In 2 Sam 11:4 וישכב עמה is used.

[30]Cf. Gen 16:4, 15; 21:2, 3; 29:32-30:24; 1 Sam 1:20.

[31]Gen 16:11 (Ishmael); 17:19 (Isaac); Isa 7:14 (Immanuel).

[32]Isa 8:3.

The tradition that Yahweh sometimes directs the naming of a child is ancient, although not abundantly attested to. In contexts where Yahweh (or Elohim, Gen 17:19) indicates the name, an element of covenant is usually present.[33] The name of a child was probably at least a semi-public event. The naming of John the Baptist[34] is instructive since it carries forward just such an ancient tradition. On the eighth day, the day of circumcision, the people came together for the festive, if not cultic, event. The community apparently had a part in the naming of the child. It is not clear exactly what that role was. Perhaps it was nothing more than asking the question, through a spokesman, "What is his name?"[35]

What a shock it must have been when Hosea made public his son's name: Jezreel.[36] It must have aroused questions[37] which were soon vocalized. This is the most likely situation for the justification speech concerning the propriety of such a name for a person. The word of judgment which results will not only be stated by Hosea but will continually be with the people through the name of the child. He becomes a living embodiment of the word of Yahweh. Except for the son of Hosea, Jezreel, as a personal name, is found only once.[38] Otherwise it is used as a place name. By the name Jezreel, Hosea focuses upon a place, a place of frequent conflict and bloodshed.

The phrase עוד מעט is always used to signal a coming disaster. Usually the disaster was to fall as judgment on Israel's enemies.[39] In Exod 17:4, however, it is used by Moses as he is about to be stoned by the Israelites. They had risen up in judgment against him. Here, not a foreigner but an Israelite is being judged. Hosea uses this formula in a similar fashion. Israel, not a foreign nation, is about to be judged by Yahweh. That this formula is normally used as an introduction to a pronouncement of impending judgment strengthens the argument that the following statement in Hosea 1:4 is also an announcement of judgment rather than an accusation. The accusation has already been made in the justification speech of verse 2.

In the present context, then, פקד is used in the negative sense of judgment. Van Hooser points out that the form noun פקד על derives ". . . from a legal specialization . . . ."[40] Within the covenant context, Yahweh pronounces the sentence of judgment against the house of Jehu. In many instances where the agency of judgment is mentioned, it is stated in terms of the offense. It is as though the pronouncement of Yahweh activates the offense as the agent of judgment.[41]

The blood of Jezreel is a symbol of the total obliteration of Baal worship under the purge of Jehu. It is appointed by Yahweh as the emissary of judgment upon the house of Jehu. The "blood of Jezreel" is not a phrase of negation against the actions of Jehu but against the actions of the "house of Jehu."

---

[33]Cf. Genesis 16, 17; Isaiah 7.

[34]Luke 1:59-63.

[35]That the father was usually the ultimate authority in naming a child is seen in this event. After the negative reaction to the name given by Elizabeth, the people asked Zechariah what he would name him.

[36]Cf. M. J. Buss, *The Prophetic Word of Hosea*, p. 29. He considers the names of the children to be one word oracles.

[37]H. W. Wolff, *Dodekapropheton* 1, p. 18; M. J. Buss, *The Prophetic Word of Hosea*, p. 56.

[38]1 Chron 4:3.

[39]Cf. Isa 10:25; Jer 51:33; Hag 2:6; Ps 37:10.

[40]J. B. van Hooser, *The Meaning of the Hebrew Root פקד in the Old Testament*, Unpublished doctoral thesis, Harvard University, 1962, p. 108. Although van Hooser does not indicate the fact, in many cases the form is slightly different.

[41]Cf. Isa 26:21; also M. J. Buss, *The Prophetic Word of Hosea*, p. 93: "The returning of deeds expressed an intimate tie between offense and punishment."

As an indictment involving any excesses of Jehu being visited upon the nation of Israel at this time, it makes little sense in the context. The main indictment has to do with religious apostasy not excessive bloodshed. It does make sense in this context, however, to recognize the punitive element in Jehu's slaughter as a purging of apostasy from Yahweh, i.e., Baalism, and to further recognize that this concept is the basis for the new announcement of judgment upon Israel. The irony of the whole picture presented is that the line of Jehu is now to be judged rather than being the means of judgment. Though Jehu purged the apostasy from Israel, Israel has become apostate again, and the leaders of the apostasy are of the line of Jehu. Therefore, the announcement of judgment is against the house of Jehu, not against Jehu himself, and the figure of judgment, the blood of Jezreel, is used to point up more sharply the anomaly of the apostasy of the line of Jehu. The "blood of Jezreel" depicts blood of judgment not excessive bloodshed. The house of Jehu, because of Canaanite Baal worship, will be purged as the house of Ahab had been for Tyrian Baal worship.[42]

Contextually, then, the relation of verse 4 to verse 2 is much stronger than has normally been recognized. To say as Buss does that verse 4 is "directed toward the life of politics"[43] is true to a limited extent. It is directed against the political arm of the state but for religious, not political, reasons.

The formula "house of" originally referred to those under a tribal head,[44] as those of common ancestry. In Hos 1:4 it is used in a restricted sense of the dynasty of Jehu.[45] In the following sentence it is also used in the broader sense of all Israel:[46] "the house of Israel." Both the royal line and the general populace have been indicted, and now the announcment of judgment is directed against them both.

It was an accepted procedure for prophets to actively participate in the rise and fall of dynasties.[47] For Hosea to declare judgment against "the house of Jehu," or even the demise of that dynasty, would have been no rare or unheard of message. What the people were not as prepared for was the next pronouncement: Israel, the northern king-dom, would cease to have kings.

Undoubtedly Hosea had on many occasions, besides that connected with the initial naming of his son, commented on the name Jezreel. Verse 5, even though it is au-thentically Hoseanic,[48] appears to come from another situation and to be an addition to verse 4.

The introductory phrase ביום ההוא is a common formula associated with a momentous event, often warfare, either past[49] or future.[50] It is sometimes used by the prophets to speak of Yahweh's intervention in Israel's history. In such cases it often has the same sense as the phrase "Day of Yahweh."[51] In verse 5, although the statement is short, it is clear that the motif of holy war is linked to the coming Day of Yahweh. Here, as elsewhere, it is associated with the covenant traditions.

---

[42]H. W. Wolff, *Dodekapropheton* 1, p. 20; J. Bright, *History of Israel,* pp. 257-58.

[43]M. J. Buss, *The Prophetic Word of Hosea,* p. 56.

[44]Cf. Gen 24:40; 17:23.

[45]Cf. 2 Sam 3:1.

[46]Cf. 2 Sam 1:12; 6:5, 15.

[47]Cf. 1 Sam 10; 16:1, 13; 1 Kings 1:34; 11:25-35; 16:1, 11-13; 2 Kings 9:1-13.

[48]Cf. H. W. Wolff, *Dodekapropheton* 1, pp. 20-21; W. Rudolph, *Hosea,* p. 52. In discussing Isa 7:18, 20, and 23, Kaiser says, "The introduction to vv. 18, 20 and 23, the stereotyped 'in that day it will come to pass . . . .' do not argue against their authenticity . . . .": O. Kaiser, *Isaiah 1-12: A Commentary* (OTL; trans. by R. A. Wilson; Philadelphia: Westminster, 1972) p. 107.

[49]Cf. 2 Sam 18:8.

[50]Cf. Isa 7:23; 1 Kings 22:25.

[51]Cf. G. von Rad, *Old Testament Theology,* II, 119: "There are not very many passages which refer to the Day of Yahweh in so many words."

In covenant traditions, both in and outside of Israel, there were curses as well as blessings which formed a part of the procedure of covenant making and covenant renewal.[52]   The covenant curse of the "broken bow" is not elsewhere preserved in the extant literature of Israel. It may be that Hosea is drawing on the broader Near Eastern treaty curse formulae.[53]   In the "Treaty of Esarhaddon with Baal of Tyre," the following curse formula is found. "May Astarte break your bow in the thick of battle, and have you crouch at the feet of your enemy, may a foreign enemy divide your belongings."[54]

The use of the curse formula of the broken bow indicates the form the judgment will take. A battle against a foreign power will result in the military might of Israel being broken. That this will take place in the valley of Jezreel suggests an invasion by a foreign power. There is no specific mention in 2 Kings of the valley of Jezreel as a place where a decisive battle was lost to Assyria. However, because of its tradition as a place of battle and victory-defeat, Hosea uses "the valley of Jezreel" in the general sense of impending doom, not necessarily in the sense of the exact place of the decisive battle which would destroy Israel. This general understanding in connection with the valley also makes it possible to join it to the events of the Jehu-Jezreel tradition.

In this way a general tradition concerning the valley of Jezreel is united with a specific tradition of the city of Jezreel which involved judgment against Baalism. At the same time, the secular, and perhaps extra-Israelite, formula of the broken bow is united with the element of Baalism. Baalism for an Israelite is an overt expressing of broken covenent, while the broken bow is a part of treaty-curse formulae which point to the judgment to come if a covenant relation is broken. Thus, Hosea, or a redactor, has woven various traditions together to form a judgment speech which arises out of a conscious understanding that Israel is in covenant violation. She has violated the covenant which originated at Sinai and which stipulates: You shall have no other gods except me. Therefore, the negative or curse element of the covenant will be activated by Yahweh, so that instead of a day of gladness for Israel it will be "a day of darkness and gloom."[55]

Verses 6-7 form a unit, although verse 7, in a manner similar to verse 5, probably had a different origin than verse 6. The formulae used to lead up to the name of the daughter are similar to those of verses 3 and 4.

The name Lo Ruhamah is also a startling one to give a child. It indicates an alienation of family relations; but, more than that, it indicates that the parent is not going to work actively for reconciliation. From a negative stance it reflects the positive relation of parental love which expresses itself in compassion and forgiveness.[56]   The close relation of mother and child during pregnancy becomes an extended figure in the derived forms of the verb and noun. Thus they may be used to express fatherly love as well. This provides an apt figure for Yahweh's relation to Israel.[57]   But, further, this relation with Israel has been established on covenant principles. Mercy is shown to those who have offended against the covenant only if they repent.

This sign event does not speak of absolute judgment but leaves open the way of repentance. Yahweh will continue to remain faithful even in the face of Israel's unfaithfulness. He cannot, however, show mercy while the situation in Israel does not warrant it. Through the naming of this child the condition of Israel is shown to reflect not only an attitude of covenant breaking but, also, no desire on Israel's part to re-

---

[52]Cf. Josh 8:30-35; Deuteronomy 28; Leviticus 26.

[53]Cf. D. R. Hillers, *Treaty Curses and the Old Testament Prophets* (BibOr 16; Rome: Pontifical Biblical Institute, 1964) esp. pp. 13, 19, 27.

[54]J. Pritchard, ed., *Ancient Near Eastern Texts,* p. 534; cf. also pp. 354, 538.

[55]Amos 2:2.

[56]Cf. M. J. Buss, *The Prophetic Word of Hosea,* p. 111.

[57]Cf. Ps 103:13, "As a father pities his children, so Yahweh pities those who fear him."

establish the covenant relation. Therefore, they will not be forgiven but judged. This judgment is not made explicit in verse 6 but would follow the pattern of verses 4 and 5. This is spelled out by way of contrast in verse 7.

The phrase כי נשא אשא להם has caused difficulty for interpreters. Usually it has been taken as elliptical.[58] However, נשא ל means "to bear with" something or someone. It may even be extended to mean "forgive," but it basically refers to long-suffering in place of the execution of judgment.[59] On the other hand, when the idea of forgiveness is expressed, a word for sin is the direct object of נשא, not the object of the preposition ל. Therefore, the explanation for the name of the second child should read, "For I will no longer have compassion on the house of Israel, that I should bear with them any longer." The use of the infinitive absolute with the finite verb emphasizes the idea of "bearing with" so that the concept of "long suffering" is clearly meant, a long suffering which the context points out no longer will be shown.

Whether or not verse 7 is a later Judean insertion, it probably refers to a time of deliverance for Judah similar to that when Sennacharib was unable to complete the conquest of Jerusalem. However, as it now stands, it is used for more than just a promise of salvation for Judah. It is a pronouncement of judgment against Israel. It is a perfect way to needle Israel, to goad them to repent, or perhaps to make the word of judgment all the more severe.

Verse 7 parallels verse 5 as its antithesis. Instead of destruction there will be deliverance, but deliverance for Judah not Israel. In Israel's traditions, deliverance is an expression of Yahweh's mercy. Instead of military defeat, expressed under the treaty curse formula of the broken bow, Judah will not even need any weapons. The indictment here of Israel is against their trust in human ability rather than in Yahweh. The formulae of verse 7 are characteristic of the negotiations made in contexts of holy war.[60] The battle is solely Yahweh's.

Wolff acknowledges that there is a catch-word relation of verse 7 to verse 6 and that there is also a connection with 2:20. However, he considers the positive elements of verse 7 to have been written in an artificial style. According to him the use of ביהוה immediately following והושעתים is especially clumsy. As he points out, some interpreters have attempted to smooth this out by certain translational moves.[61] The range of possibilities for ביהוה is very broad: Negative stance toward Yahweh, trust in Yahweh, inquiring of Yahweh, praising or rejoicing in Yahweh, saved by Yahweh, swearing by Yahweh. Only the last two categories have any apparent relation to the main thrust of verse 7. However, Yahweh is not simply saying: I will save them by myself, instead of by men or in contrast to the power of men. Rather, by means of the swearing formula of covenant making he calls down the curse upon himself in the event he does not fulfill his promise. Thus he makes the promise all the more sure.

Three elements are expressed in verse 7b. The statement of promised salvation, the binding oath, the means of victory stated negatively. As an oath formula ביהוה need not be seen as awkward following והושעתים nor should it be too closely associated with the negated human means of battle. It has its own independent origin and meaning. Only after this is seen can its relation to the other elements of verse 7b be understood. Yahweh puts his very existence on the line in terms of the holy war in which he will participate on behalf of Israel.[62]

The main thrust of verses 6 and 7 comes from the tradition of covenant mercy which is rooted in anthropological, i.e., family traditions. Forgiveness and deliverance

---

[58]C. F. Keil, *The Twelve Minor Prophets*, I. 43-44; H. W. Wolff, *Dodekapropheton* 1, p. 7.

[59]Cf. Gen 18:24, 26; Exod 23:21; Josh 24:19.

[60]Cf. Josh 24:12; Ezek 21:5; 1 Sam 17:47; Ps 20:8; Isa 31:1.

[61]H. W. Wolff, *Dodekapropheton* 1, pp. 22-23.

[62]Cf. Isa 45:17-23; Heb 6:16-18.

are possible, but only when repentance is involved. Thus far in the judgment speeches, the matter of judgment is not yet settled in an absolute way. It is still pending. This is further stressed by the first word of verse 8. It indicates that a period of some length has gone by, during which the message of judgment is still set within the bounds of the covenant framework.

With verse 9 the covenant frame is shattered by the name Lo Ammi, the negative form of Ammi, my people. In Exod 6:7 the covenant formula is very similar to the general marriage formula. Marriage as a simile for the Sinai covenant also provides a structure for expressing the negation of the covenant. The marriage covenant was probably established by a statement such as: She is my wife and I am her husband.[63] For divorce, a similar negative statement would have been made: She is not my wife, and I am not her husband.[64] By a similar formula, the justification for the name of the third child is in essence a declaration dissolving the covenant relation. The use of the nominal sentences marks the actuality of the situation. The conditions of non-covenant already prevail because Israel has not returned to Yahweh. That the Sinai covenant is background for these transactions is again stressed by the use of אהיה. This is the name by which Moses was to identify Yahweh to the people as the God of the fathers.[65] Thus, in negating the covenant by this name, Yahweh is cutting out not only the Sinai basis but the patriarchal as well.

At this final stage, it is no longer a matter of judgment within the covenant. The final judgment speech is a pronouncement of judgment which excludes Israel from the covenant.

The prophetic word of Hosea went beyond that of judgment as his creative phrase "sons of the living God" in chapter two indicates. But for our purposes in this paper we will conclude the examination of the prophet Hosea's creative use of language at this point and turn our attention to the use of language by the redactor of the Hoseanic material.

B. The Redactor's Use of Language

Hos 1:1 introduces the whole book of Hosea,[66] whereas the statement of 1:2a has been used to introduce the specific prophetic word of Hos 1:2b-3:5. Since 1:2b-9 is not in the form of a first-person report, Hosea is probably not the author of the present structure. Perhaps a disciple of Hosea constructed this third-person report from first-person oral or written messages or reports of Hosea himself, similar in nature to chapter three which, as a first-person report, originated with the prophet himself.[67]

The word תחלת in 1:2a should be interpreted only in terms of the initial prophetic activity of 1:2b-9. Together with עוד of 3:1 the unity of thought and structure of chapters 1-3 are established. The beginning of the word of Yahweh ends in judgment. However, since it is only the beginning, the word of Yahweh must be continued if the full

---

[63]Cf. R. de Vaux, *Ancient Israel*. Buss says that 1:9 was ". . . probably influenced by a legal formula of disavowal," M. J. Buss, *The Prophetic Word of Hosea*, p. 75. He does not elaborate on this statement. However, compare his comments on 2:4; *ibid.*, pp. 87-89.

[64]This formula is found in Hos 2:4. A similar one is found in a Sumerian text which says, "If Enlil-izzu ever says to Am-sukkal, his wife, 'You are no longer my wife,' he shall return . . ."' (J. Pritchard, ed. *Ancient Near Eastern Texts*, p. 219).

[65]Exod 3:14.

[66]A. Weiser, *Das Buch der zwölf kleinen Propheten*, (I, Das Alte Testament Deutsch; Göttingen: Vandenhoeck & Ruprecht, 1959) p. 15; H. W. Wolff, *Dodekapropheton* 1, p. 2.

[67]Cf. Isa 8:16; G. von Rad, *Old Testament Theology*, I, 41; O. Eissfeldt, *The Old Testament*, p. 391.

impact of Hosea's message is to be known. Thus it is shown that the concept of salvation is not secondary to the message of Hosea. Judgment is not viewed by the writer as an end in itself but as a means to an end. The message of salvation, as well as that of judgment, originates in the initial commission and activity of the prophet Hosea. The "beginning" culminates in the ultimate judgment of being disowned as a people: You are not my עם and I am not your אהיה. But this is to be seen only as the culmination of the "beginning," not as the final word. The very structure of this narrative indicates that chapter one was constructed with the content of chapter three in mind. Since chapter three is still in the form of a first-person report, it probably influenced the development of chapter one. The catch-phrase . . . לך . . . אל יהוה ויאמר formally joins the double-commission experience of Hosea. By means of the phrase תחלת דבר יהוה, an introduction is given to the whole unit, while the form in which the author of chapter one constructs the narrative of chapter one indicates that the "beginning" does not include chapter three.

The skeletal structure is as follows.

ויאמר יהוה אל הושע	(1:2b)
ויאמר יהוה אליו	(1:4a)
ויאמר ... לו	(1:6c)
ויאמר	(1:9a)
ויאמר יהוה אלי עוד	(3:1a)

This form shows a conscious effort to indicate a point of termination not only of the people as Yahweh's people but of the "beginning" of the words of Yahweh as well. The shortening of the framework to the final ויאמר of 1:9 and the fact that 2:1ff. does not continue this framework of speeches clearly point to this conclusion. Since, however, chapter one has been built up on the basis of the catch-phrase of chapter three, what had been begun in chapter one cannot be thought of as totally finished. Thus the language frame of 3:1 indicates this and provides the conclusion to that for which Hos 1:2b-9 is only the beginning. The writer is not so much saying that judgment will ultimately result in salvation, though it will do that. What is probably more significant is his subordinating the promised blessings of chapter three to the element of judgment expressed in the narrative of chapter one which he composed out of the earlier life situations and messages of Hosea.

The first-person report is not used in chapter one because the redactor's interest is not in the prophetic word of Hosea as words which he had spoken. At no point are the actual speeches of Hosea given, unless parts of them may have survived in the explanations contained in verses 2b, 4b-5, 6, 9b. The lack of the report of the Hoseanic speeches of explanation, like those which are found in speeches of Micaiah, Amos, Isaiah, etc.,[68] leads to the conclusion that the present stress is not on the justification of the prophetic ministry of Hosea. The stress is on the compliance to the orders of Yahweh as an exact fulfillment of the Yahweh order. The emphasis is on the word of Yahweh as the ground for the names of the children. Yahweh commanded the marriage which produced the children who by the command of Yahweh are to bear specific names. In each instance the command is followed by an explanation. The explanation connected with the command to marry is an accusation. Those connected with the commands to name the children are announcements of judgment.

Although Westermann does not develop the idea, he speaks of Hosea chapters 1 and 3 as parabolic actions within his section on "Variant Formulations of the Prophetic Speech (Borrowed Speech Forms)."[69] That section deals with the place of parabolic action in judgment speeches. The term "parabolic" is not as adequate as "sign" for the

---

[68] 1 Kings 22:18-28; Amos 7:12-17; Isaiah 6.
[69] C. Westermann, *Basic Forms of Prophetic Speech*, p. 202.

context of Hosea, but the element of judgment could be carried by either. Although Westermann has not specifically discussed Hosea 1 as a judgment speech, there are some similarities in form to the judgment speeches which he has discussed earlier in the same work.[70] The judgment speech against nations is seen as a development of the judgment speech against individuals. Because there is a discernible deviation in form, especially in the writing prophets, he says, "For this reason it is impossible to rediscover the structure that was shown above in each prophetic speech. It is much more prudent to note that this framework of the prophetic judgment-speech is fundamental only to the *genre* and that the expression of an individual speech can deviate very far from it."[71]

With this in mind, Hos 1:2-6, 8, 9 may be seen as derived from a series of prophetic judgment speeches against the nation Israel. Of the four major parts, the first contains the accusation, and the last three contain the announcement(s). The structure is as follows.

Commission:	Go take . . . (action rather than speech)
Summons to hear:	Involved in the strange action of verse 3
Accusation:	For the land commits great harlotry
Announcement:	None
Continuation of Commission:	Name . . . (threefold: verses 4a, 6a, 9a)
Summons to hear:	Involved in carrying out the action of naming (which is not narrated in the present text) but more in the strange names used.
Accusation:	None
Announcement(s):	Verses 4b-5, 6b-7, 9b

This structure is dependent on the previous actions and speeches of Hosea at a specific time of challenge by those who were summoned to hear by the fulfilled commission-action of the prophet. As each commission-action was enacted before the people, they were being summoned to hear. However, only in answer to the challenge or question of "why such a strange action?" was the message given in the form of a justification for the action. The justification was at the same time either an accusation, as in the first instance, of an announcement of judgment, as in the case of the last three.

At present, the first of the four section lacks the element of announcement while the last three do not contain any explicit accusation. Together they provide the basic elements of accusation followed by announcement of judgment. The justification for the marriage sets forth the accusation, and the justifications for the names of the children provide the announcements of judgment.

The present text plays down the role of Hosea by not including the report of his naming the children or the exact speeches, speeches of judgment, which he himself made to the people. However, the residual form continues to emphasize the element of judgment.

Thus, the beginning word of Yahweh was judgment. However, this beginning did not cease with the actions and speeches of Hosea, but by the very nature of the sign actions continued to enunciate the word of judgment. The children, and more specifically the names of the children, constantly kept the word of judgment before the people.

Taking into consideration the emphasis on the names of the children and especially that these names bore the message of judgment, what might be the intention of the present report? The report lays the stress on the word of Yahweh. Often such stress in prophetic literature, when coupled with some element of a prophet's life, indicates an apologetic intention, usually in justification of the prophetic existence of the prophet.[72] Here, however, because the role of Hosea is not stressed but the names of

---

[70]Ibid., pp. 129-94.

[71]Ibid., p. 173.

[72]Cf. Amos 7; Isaiah 6; 1 Kings 22.

the children are, the apology is not directed toward the prophetic existence of Hosea but toward the names of the children. Evidently, the redactor is addressing a situation in which the names of the children had to be justified, not in the sense of why they had first been given, but in the sense of the continuing word of judgment. The challenge being met in the text is not the challenge to Hosea's right to have thus named his children; that would have come at the time he named each of them. What the text indicates is that at some time after the whole sequence of naming the children the writer is attempting to justify the continuing word of judgment expressed by the names.

Since the writer has indicated that the word of judgment was only the beginning of the word of Yahweh through Hosea, it is without doubt that the word of reconciliation or promised blessing must already have been given as well. A word of salvation is often spoken as a word of encouragement to the faithful. Such a word can easily be misunderstood by the unfaithful, especially if a previous word of judgment appears to have been fulfilled. Having come through the Assyrian encounter of 733 B.C., the unfaithful misunderstood the salvation promises which Hosea had spoken as encouragement to the faithful. The misunderstandings of the unfaithful are tied to the false understanding of the covenant. Such false notions of covenant must now be denied. The names of the children are still valid because the word of judgment is still valid. The covenant must be renewed and the people will once again become the "sons of the living God" (2:1). However, this can come only through the judgment of God upon the unfaithful who have failed to respond properly to the message of the children's names or to the hand of God in the Assyrian encounter.

The intention of chapter one, then, is to justify the continuing statement of judgment in face of (1) the further word of Hosea, a positive word, (2) the Assyrian encounter of 733 B.C., as a past event, and (3) the false understanding of the covenant relationship to Yahweh.

This apology in defense of the names of the children ties chapter one to chapters two and three. In fact chapter 2:1-2 is probably the conclusion to this apology. In other words, blessing will come but only through judgment; and blessings will derive from Yahweh's covenant, but the covenant must be a renewed covenant. Renewal of the covenant depends on genuine repentance on the part of the people. Chapter 2 indicates that, although there are two ways open for Israel's salvation, the way of disciplinary judgment is the more likely because the people have not really repented for breaking the covenant. Therefore, the author of the framework of Hos 1:2-9 joined his new construction of the material in Hos 1:2-9 (plus 2:1-2) with the already existing chapter 3 by means of the already existing chapter 2:3-25.

III. Conclusion

Hosea freely drew upon the language stock of his day to provide the vehicle for Yahweh's message to Israel. Since the traditional generic language had developed out of the experiences of the people, Hosea was able to meet them where they were by means of such language forms. At the same time, the very way he juxtaposed those language forms created the matrix for a new experience. The redactor of the Hoseanic material reused it in a creative theological way to speak the word of Yahweh to the new situation of his own day.

LINGUISTICS, SEMITICS, AND BIBLICAL HEBREW

Walter Bodine

Whatever terminology one may choose for describing the current situation in Old Testament scholarship, it must surely indicate flux. There are several reasons for this. Though this is not the place to analyze them, they would probably include the increasingly rapid appearance of new approaches to the data, such as, recently, rhetorical criticism, literary criticism, structural analysis, "canonical criticism," and the social sciences (especially sociology and anthropology); the breakup of areas of consensus (e.g., the anti-Albrightian reaction on several fronts); increasing specialization and, at the same time, concurrent awareness of greater need for cross disciplinary work; and the impact of high technology, especially the computer.

In the field of biblical Hebrew studies, there is likewise a state of change. All of the currents of influence mentioned above are having their effect. With regard to the study of the language itself, no new focus has yet become predominant after the historical-comparative linguistic emphasis which culminated in the first half of this century with the works of Brockelmann, Bergsträsser, and Bauer and Leander. It is significant that general linguistics is the most recent of the modern trends discussed in one of the most helpful published surveys of the linguistic study of biblical Hebrew from the time of Saadia Gaon to the present.[1]

The purpose of this paper and of the Consultation to be devoted to the same subject is to consider the potential for biblical Hebrew studies of a fuller interaction with modern linguistics. The following remarks will attempt, in a representative way, to survey the field of linguistics in its contact with Semitics as a whole, Semitics in its contact with linguistics, and biblical Hebrew in the same dimension and to offer some preliminary suggestions as to how a program unit in the SBL could profitably concern itself with this particular line of interdisciplinary research. No claim is made to completeness either with respect to authors or their works. In particular, no attempt will be made to even sample the philological work of the past, as distinguished from what can be called linguistic in the modern sense of the term.

Linguistics in Its Contact With Semitics

The advent of modern linguistics is generally traced to the work of F. de Saussure. In this country E. Sapir and L. Bloomfied are outstanding figures in the development of American structuralism (though the former can hardly be so simply classified). Sapir took a specific interest in Semitics and biblical Hebrew.[2] Even more concerted work in Semitic has been done by Z. Harris, who carried at least one type of structuralism to perhaps its highest power.[3]

---

[1] James Barr, "Linguistic Literature, Hebrew," Enc Jud (1971) XVI, 1397-1400. Cf. note 31 below on the place of the historical-comparative method in the study of Hebrew.

[2] Frequent reference is made to both in his Language: An Introduction to the Study of Speech (New York: Harcourt Brace Jovanovich, 1921).

[3] Barr has commented on the relatively greater impact of Harris' work of a traditional philological type, such as The Development of the Canaanite Dialects, American Oriental Series, 16 (New Haven: American Oriental Society, 1939), over against his more specifically linguistic work (James Barr, "The Ancient Semitic Languages--The Conflict Between Philology and Linguistics," Transactions of the Philological Society [Oxford: Blackwell, 1969] p. 46). Perhaps the best example of the latter type of Harris' work would be The Linguistic Structure of Hebrew (New Haven: American Oriental Society, 1941).

The generative-transformational theory of N Chomsky, which has had such a profound effect on American linguistics, began in the context of Semitics and Hebrew. His father, William Chomsky, was an accomplished scholar of biblical Hebrew;[4] Z. Harris was his teacher at the University of Pennsylvania; and his own master's thesis dealt with modern Hebrew.[5] Although Chomsky has not returned to the subject in any concerned way, to my knowledge, others within his general theoretical framework are doing so. J. L. Malone has published a number of specific studies and reports the completion in manuscript of a comprehensive generative-phonological analysis of and also a study of the morphophonology of Tiberian Hebrew.[6]

There are some pointed observations on the need for the insights and methods of structural linguistics on the part of Semitists in Harris Birkeland, "Some Reflections on Semitic and Structural Linguistics, " in *For Roman Jakobson: Essays on the Occasion of His Sixtieth Birthday,* ed. Morris Halle et al. (The Hague: Mouton, 1956), pp. 44-51. In spite of the strictures in Edward Ullendorff, "Comparative Semitics," in *Linguistica Semitica: Presente e Futuro,* ed. Giorgio Levi Della Vida (Rome: Università di Roma, Centro di Studi Semitici, 1961, p. 23, n. 16, Birkeland's comments retain their validity.

J. H. Greenberg should also be mentioned as a linguist who has done productive work in Semitic.

[4]His *Hebrew: The Eternal Language* (Philadelphia: Jewish Publication Society of America, 1957) is a popular and now dated, but helpful, survey of the entire history of Hebrew. He has a number of more technical studies in *JQR* and elsewhere. A valuable contribution to scholarship was made by his translation and edition of *David Ḳimḥi's Hebrew Grammar (Mikhlol)*(New York: Bloch Publishing Co., 1952).

[5]Now published as *The Morphophonemics of Modern Hebrew,* Outstanding Dissertations in Linguistics 12 (New York: Garland Publishing, Inc., 1979, completed in 1951).

[6]Joseph L. Malone, "Textually Deviant Forms as Evidence for Phonological Analysis: A Service of Philology to Linguistics," *JANES* 11 (1979) 71, 74. John Battle has done syntactic work in the Psalms using a transformational model, e.g., "Transformational Concepts in the Hebrew Text of the Psalms," *Papers from the Fifth Annual Kansas Linguistic Conference* (ed. Frances Ingemann; Lawrence, KA: University of Kansas Linguistics Students Association and the Department of Linguistics, 1971). A student of mine is completing a generative-phonological analysis as his master's thesis at the time of this writing in which he makes the proposal that phonemics can serve as an avenue to phonetics and seeks to demonstrate the same from his data (Ralph Gregory Enos, "The Sounds of Tiberian Hebrew: A Study in Linguistics and Philology" [Th.M. thesis, Dallas Theological Seminary, 1982]).

The rapid proliferation of offshoots of Chomsky's model and of related theoretical perspectives, such as generative semantics, relational grammar, etc., will not be discussed here. Indeed, there are those who believe that a serious weakness of generative-transformational theory, if not its ultimate undoing, lies in this--that it is too powerful.

Perhaps it would not be too bold to suggest a way in which a collaboration such as what is proposed here could benefit the field of general linguistics. The primacy of data as the basis of theory, or, at least, the necessity of theory coming to terms with data and being empirically verifiable can be underscored by ancient Near Eastern philologians, whose primary task is the elucidation of written texts. The appeal has, in fact, been expressed to linguists by one of their own company for a reduced commitment to formalism with its resulting isolation from other fields of scholarship and for a closer contact with the empirical base in language data (H. A. Gleason, Jr., "Linguistics and Philology," in *On Language, Culture, and Religion: In Honor of Eugene A. Nida,* ed. Matthew Black and William A. Smalley [The Hague: Mouton, 1974] pp. 210-12). A similar concern in the latter regard is implicit in Gene Gragg, "Linguistics, Method, and Extinct Languages: The Case of Sumerian," *Or* 42 (1973) 78-90.

Two of the presently expanding fields within general linguistics are semantics and discourse analysis. The former is receiving attention from several who are primarily Semitic philologists and whose work will be mentioned below. The latter, as practiced by R. E. Longacre, is presently being applied to the Hebrew Bible.[7]

The primary attention of linguists who have worked within Semitic has thus far been on the living dialects of Arabic, Ethiopian, Hebrew, and Aramaic.[8] This can be seen, for example, by scanning the programs of the North American Conference on Afro-Asiatic Linguistics (NACAL). Such an emphasis is not surprising, given the general assumption among linguists of the primacy of spoken over written language[9] and the obvious advantages in the use of informants over written texts.[10]

Another trend among those linguists who work in Semitic is the broader use of African languages, thus potentially enriching the whole historical and comparative Afroasiatic enterprise.[11]

Semitics in Its Contact With Linguistics

Classical Arabic has had respectable linguistic attention from such Semitists as J. Blau, F. Corriente, C. A. Ferguson, and C. Rabin. Attempts at full analyses of this phase of the language have been made by M. C. Bateson (using the categories of structural linguistics)[12] and H. Fleisch (following the process approach of Sapir and Trubetskoy).[13] The need remains, however, for an adequate analysis of the classical language, as well as for the study of many of the specific linguistic issues it raises.[14]

---

[7]See especially Robert E. Longacre, "The Discourse Structure of the Flood Narrative," *JAAR* 47 (1979), Supplement B, pp. 89-133.

[8]Many scholars are studying modern Hebrew linguistically, including S. Bolozky, M. S. Devins, A. Laufer, C. Rabin, and H. B. Rosen.

[9]On this matter, see the cautions in Gleason, pp. 207-8, and J. H. Hospers, "Applied Linguistics and the Teaching of Dead Languages," in *General Linguistics and the Teaching of Dead Hamito-Semitic Languages* (ed. J. H. Hospers; Leiden: E. J. Brill, 1978) pp. 14-15 and the bibliography cited there in n. 57. The study of graphemics is still quite young, and the relationship between language, speech, and writing is yet to be clarified with precision. Some helpful observations from an ancient Near Eastern scholar can be found in Miguel Civil, "The Sumerian Writing System: Some Problems," *Or* 42 (1973) 21-34.

[10]Gleason points out, however, that written language constitutes an important diachronic force and exhibits a whole range of synchronic patterns, both of which are usually missed because of the common attitude toward spoken and written language ("Linguistics and Philology," p. 207). Because of their obvious stake in the refinement of the discipline of graphemics, perhaps this is another area in which Semitists can contribute to general linguistics, at least in underscoring the need for a more balanced use of evidence.

[11]The term was introduced by Joseph H. Greenberg to replace Hamito-Semitic ("The Afro-Asiatic [Hamito-Semitic] Present," *JAOS* 72 [1952] 1-9). Cf., for a less positive appraisal of the widening sphere of Afroasiatic linguistics, M. H. Goshen-Gottstein, "Comparative Semitics--A Premature Obituary," in *Essays on the Occasion of the Seventieth Anniversary of the Dropsie University* (ed. Abraham Katsh and Leon Nemoy; Philadelphia: The Dropsie University, 1979) pp. 144-45 and especially n. 10.

[12]Mary Catherine Bateson, *Arabic Language Handbook* (Language Handbook Series; Washington, DC: Center for Applied Linguistics, 1967).

[13]Henri Fleisch, *L'arabe classique. Esquisse d'une structure linguistique* (MUSJ XXXIII/1; Beyrouth, 1956).

[14]The review of Fleisch by C. A. Ferguson in *Language* 34 (1958) 314-21 points out several questions in classical Arabic calling for linguistic study.

Although classical Ethiopic (Ge ez) has had competent linguistic treatment from W. Leslau, E. Ullendorff, and R. Hetzron, in all cases with benefit for Semitic studies generally, there has not appeared, to my knowledge, any full analysis of the language from the standpoint of modern linguistics.[15]

Akkadian has had the benefit of E. Reiner's analysis, focusing on the Standard Babylonian phase;[16] but there has still been no full linguistic analysis of even the phonology of the language.[17] Giorgio Buccellati has a detailed grammar in manuscript form which takes a structural approach.

With the voluminous literature that continues to appear dealing with Ugaritic, I know of no study that is formally linguistic.[18]

Aramaic, in its ancient manifestations, is in roughly the same position as the other languages already mentioned. In spite of the excellent work of Kutscher, Greenfield, Fitzmyer, and others, the field is still ripe for specifically linguistic work.[19]

Biblical Hebrew in Its Contact with Linguistics

The importance of the developing science of graphemics, mentioned briefly above, for all study of written language, especially those no longer spoken, cannot be over-estimated. A full-length analysis of the graphemic system of Tiberian Hebrew has already appeared,[20] although problems remain to be addressed.[21]

Related, but specifically addressed to the phonology of the language, is the work of S. Morag.[22] Under his editorship, the Hebrew University Language Traditions Project

---

Epigraphic South Arabic studies, already having the benefit of recent studies in spoken South Arabian, will now be helped by the publication of Joan C. Biella, *Dictionary of Old South Arabic: Sabaean Dialect* (Harvard Semitic Studies 25; Chico: Scholars Press, 1982).

[15]Thomas O. Lambdin's *Introduction to Classical Ethiopic (Geᶜez)* (Harvard Semitic Studies 24; Missoula, Montana: Scholars Press, 1978) is quite complete and helpful for an introductory grammar.

[16]Erica Reiner, *A Linguistic Analysis of Akkadian* (Janua Linguarum, Series Practica 21; The Hague: Mouton, 1966).

[17]Erica Reiner, "How We Read Cuneiform Texts," *JCS* 25 (1973) 23, n. 28. Cf. also, in this regard, Thorkild Jacobsen, "Ittallak niãti," in *Toward the Image of Tammuz and Other Essays on Mesopotamian History and Culture* (ed. William L. Moran; Cambridge: Harvard University Press, 1970) p. 467, n. 8.

[18]The dissertation of D. G. Pardee, which has been published in installments, is a rigorous philological study of the preposition (Dennis Graham Pardee,"The Preposition in Ugaritic," *UF* [1975] 329-78, 8 [1976] 215-322, 9 [1977] 205-31; cf. also D. Pardee, "More on the Preposition in Ugaritic," *UF* 11 [1975] 685-92). This may be an example in which the distinction between what is linguistic and philological is virtually meaningless.

[19]Most of the formally linguistic attention given to Aramaic thus far, as in the other cases, has been focused on spoken Neo-Aramaic (Irene Garbell, Yona Sabar, etc.). An exception is the work of J. L. Malone, especially in Mandaic.

[20]Gene M. Schramm, *The Graphemes of Tiberian Hebrew* (Berkeley: University of California Press, 1964).

[21]The linguistic study of Hebrew writing has also been undertaken in John C. L. Gibson, "Hebrew Writing as a Subject of Linguistic Investigation," *Glasgow University Oriental Society Transactions* 20 (1963-64) 49-62; "On the Linguistic Analysis of Hebrew Writing," *Archivum Linguisticum* 17 (1969) 131-60; and Harvey Minkoff, "Graphemics and Diachrony: Some Evidence from Hebrew Cursive," *Afroasiatic Linguistics* 1:7 (March, 1975) 193-208.

[22]E.g., Shelomo Morag, *The Vocalization Systems of Arabic, Hebrew, and Aramaic* (Janua Linguarum, No. XIII; The Hague: Mouton, 1962).

is publishing information on various traditions of Hebrew phonology.[23] Mention should also be made of the work of J. Barr, H. Birkeland, J. Blau, C. Rabin, and H. B. Rosen in biblical phonology.

Morphology in biblical Hebrew has received little specifically linguistic attention.[24] This is not surprising in light of the ambiguity of the discipline within general linguistics as a whole, apart from its established place within historical and comparative linguistics.[25]

Syntax is in only a relatively better condition in biblical Hebrew studies. It has been called "the stepchild of the grammarian" by Gleason, who pointed out that, whereas it is the least exhaustively and incisively treated of topics in grammars, it is more significant for exegesis than those receiving greater attention.[26] An exception to this is the recent grammar by J. F. A. Sawyer.[27] The tagmemic theory of K. L. Pike is being applied to Hebrew syntax by F. I. Anderson.[28]

With regard to semantics, the writings of J. Barr have been especially helpful in showing the need of sound methodology.[29] An effort in the direction of a theoretical context for semantic analysis is being made by J. F. A. Sawyer.[30]

---

[23]Cf. in this regard Shelomo Morag, "Oral Tradition as a Source of Linguistic Information," in *Substance and Structure of Language* (ed. Jaen Puhvel; Berkeley: University of California Press, 1969) pp. 127-46.

[24]A notable exception is M. H. Goshen-Gottstein, "Semitic Morphological Structures: The Basic Morphological Structure of Biblical Hebrew," in *Studies in Egyptology and Linguistics in Honour of H. J. Polotsky* (Jerusalem: The Israel Exploration Society, 1964) 104-16.

[25]On the uncertain status of morphology within transformational linguistics, cf. Gragg, p. 83, n. 15. An effort to define such appeared shortly before Gragg's article in P. H. Matthews, *Inflectional Morphology: A Theoretical Study Based on Aspects of Latin Verb Conjugation* (Cambridge Studies in Linguistics 6; Cambridge: At the University Press, 1972).

[26]Henry A. Gleason, Jr., "Some Contributions of Linguistics to Biblical Exegesis," *Hartford Quarterly* 4 (1963) 51. Cf. note 28 below regarding the impact of generative-transformational theory on syntactic analysis.

[27]John F. A. Sawyer, *A Modern Introduction to Biblical Hebrew* (Boston: Oriel Press, 1976).

[28]Francis I. Andersen, *The Hebrew Verbless Clause in the Pentateuch* (SBLMS 14; Nashville: Abingdon Press, 1970); *The Sentence in Biblical Hebrew* (The Hague: Mouton, 1974).

My impression is that a satisfying elucidation of syntax within a larger linguistic theory is yet to be elaborated. Whether or not Chomsky "has provided a whole generation of linguistics with a handle on syntax" (Gragg, p. 83) depends on whether one is comfortable with the assumption of the larger theory involved. Perhaps it could at least be agreed that he has dramatically called attention to the importance of syntax.

My own expectation is that the stratificational theory pioneered by S. M. Lamb and developed in various ways by D. G. Lockwood, I. Fleming, etc., will make a contribution at this point. I and Earl Bills are presently engaged in a stratificational analysis of Tiberian Hebrew in the hope of demonstrating the usefulness of the theory and, at the same time, achieving helpful results in the language.

[29]Cf. especially James Barr, *The Semantics of Biblical Language* (Oxford: Clarendon Press, 1961) and *Comparative Philology and the Text of the Old Testament* (Oxford: Clarendon Press, 1968).

[30]Cf. esp. John F. A. Sawyer, *Semantics in Biblical Research: New Methods of Defining Hebrew Words for Salvation* (SBT, 2nd ser., 24; Naperville, IL: Alec R. Allenson, Inc., 1972).

There are potential signs that historical and comparative linguistics may be emerging from a period of neglect within general linguistics as a whole. Within Semitic and biblical Hebrew studies, the eclipse of the approach has been relatively less pronounced and may, likewise, be passing.[31] While synchronic analysis has a rightly acknowledged priority over diachronic study, the latter is essential in Semitics and especially in biblical Hebrew with its peculiar problems due to the standardization tht has gone on in a literature representing virtually one thousand years of linguistic development (by almost anyone's dating) and due to the relatively limited sample of the language that is extant.[32] An example of a historical-comparative approach to a question in Semitics that is, at the same time, abreast of developments in general linguistics is the recent work of R. Steiner.[33]

Some Proposals for a Program Unit

An endeavor to integrate biblical Hebrew and linguistic studies would do well to begin with a positive attidude toward the past, extending all the way through the Medieval Jewish Grammarians. Linguistics, in its modern sense, is the newcomer. The effort is motivated by the conviction that the newcomer has something of value to offer. Yet this conviction does not require a disregard for past philological work. Rather, what is needed is a renewed impetus in that direction as well, lest we expend a great deal of energy in relearning what has already been discovered.[34] Indeed, the fresh perspective of linguistics can provide a new way of reviewing the work of past grammarians.[35]

My desire would be to see the unit, whatever its exact nature may be,[36] resolutely remain open to differing perspectives on the linguistics side, rather than become

---

[31] Whereas D. W. Thomas pronounced the publication of Bauer and Leander's *Historische Grammatik der hebräischen Sprache* in 1922, with its historical emphasis, as marking "the beginning of a revolution in Hebrew grammatical study" (David Winton Thomas, *The Recovery of the Ancient Hebrew Language* [Cambridge: University Press, 1939] pp. 34-35), Barr has more recently seen it as representing, together with Bergsträsser, a sort of culmination of the historical-comparative emphasis in Semitic ("Linguistic Literature," col. 1397). Perhaps there is something to say for both viewpoints, given the relative lack of refinement of the historical-comparative method within Semitic as contrasted with Indo-European (cf. H. Polotsky, "Semitics," in *The World History of the Jewish People* I, 1 [1964] pp. 100-103, 108).

[32] Cf. D. Winton Thomas, "The Language of the Old Testament," in *Record and Revelation* (ed. H. Wheeler Robinson; Oxford: Clarendon Press, 1938) pp. 383-88 especially and Edward Ullendorff, "The Knowledge of Languages in the Old Testament," *BJRL* 44 (1962) 455-65, the latter concluding with the observation that, in the light of the nature of the problems in biblical Hebrew, "the place of comparative Semitic linguistics can scarcely be overstated" (ibid., p. 465).

[33] Richard C. Steiner, *The Case for Fricative-Laterals in Proto-Semitic* (AOS 59; New Haven: American Oriental Society, 1977).

[34] Cf. W. Chomsky's remarks to this effect (*David Ḳimḥi's Hebrew Grammar (Mikhlol)*, p. xxxii).

[35] As, e.g., in Alan S. Kaye, "Spinoza as Linguist," *HAR* 4 (1980) 107-25 and a paper on G. Bergsträsser as a linguist read by Peter Daniels at the 1982 meeting of the North American Conference on Afroasiatic Linguistics.

[36] I am inclined to think that a Section might be most appropriate, at least in the early life of the unit, due to the differing theoretical orientations that scholars will probably bring to the task and the need to explore varied linguistic methodologies and the areas of study within biblical Hebrew.

committed to any one linguistic theory.[37] If linguists themselves have not achieved any substantial theoretical consensus, then I wonder if we would not be well advised to lay our base broadly and remain open to new developments and to participants of divergent perspectives. Since it is an effort on the part of biblical Hebrew scholars, it can, in fact, serve as a forum in which the theoretical framework of a presentation is critiqued in terms of its ability to make a tangible contribution to the understanding of the language in view.[38]

Furthermore, I would like to see various areas of linguistic study explored. Thus, there would be room for contributions in phonology, which might bring to bear the results of work in modern spoken dialects, but would not lose sight of the primary focus on biblical Hebrew. Morphology, in the sense of studies of phenomena internal to the grammatical word, could be welcomed. Syntax, semantics and lexicography, and discourse could be examined. Graphemics could be fostered; historical and comparative linguistics could be expanded; and new theoretical as well as practical proposals could be entertained.

These suggestions are admittedly quite broad, but so is my impression of what is needed. All of the above is, of course, open to discussion and modification. That is the purpose of these remarks and of the Consultation--to provoke mutual thought and effort.

In conclusion, let me say that I see this proposal not as an appeal for some new departure, but as an affirmation of what is already underway. (Indeed, much of what is now in view on the part of Semitic scholars employing general linguistics was already implicit in the older philology.[39]) Interdisciplinary work is now in progress on the part of individuals. This is a proposal that we who participate in the Society of Biblical Literature straightforwardly acknowledge the importance of the endeavor by including it in the work of our annual meeting and thereby promote a joint effort.

---

[37] This introduces a potential conflict, for, as Gleason has said, "the appraisal of a linguistic work can only be done within the framework of some general understanding of language, that is, a theory of linguistics." However, he goes on to say, "Indeed it can best be tested within the arena in which competing theories of language confront one another" ("Some Contributions," p. 50). Some may differ on this point and with to argue for a commitment within the unit to a particular linguistic theory. I expect that this question will need to be discussed.

[38] The same can also be said for the other side of the endeavor, both respect to biblical Hebrew and to Old Testament studies generally. Theories in these fields can be brought to the touchstone of a sound linguistic analysis of the literature on which they are based.

Perhaps it would be in order at this point to cite the remarks made to me in a letter from Richard Steiner in a letter of May 18, 1982 responding to my communication about this consultation: "My initial reaction is that the unit you are proposing should be more philologically oriented than NACAL, and that its main goal should be to upgrade the level of Biblical philology and exegesis by insisting on rigorous linguistic methodology, and by making explicit the assumptions about language in general and Hebrew in particular which underlie Biblical scholarship."

[39] Barr, "The Ancient Semitic Languages," pp. 53-54.

IMAGES AND CONCEPTS OF HOPE IN THE EARLY IMPERIAL CULT

Mark Edward Clark

Allegorical personifications played a major role in the Roman imperial cult. As specific virtues of the emperor, these personified forces, or *numina*, provided a means of articulating his attributes and were employed as propaganda of imperial ideology. Some virtues, such as *Libertas* and *Victoria*, have recently been subjects of individual studies, while others await detailed analysis.[1] *Spes*, the personification of Hope, is one which has not been fully examined. Standard handbooks on Roman religion offer only general information; P. G. Walsh has gone one step further in his treatment of the Roman concept in connection with early Christian views of hope, but his study has not emphasized traditional Roman beliefs.[2] In this paper we shall examine *Spes* as a Roman virtue, in particular its earliest developments in the imperial cult.

It is best to begin with a review of *Spes* in the coinage of the early empire. Coins provide extensive evidence for the concept and they show that the most popular designation of Hope was *Spes Augusta*, "the Hope of Augustus." This legend first appeared on a sestertius issued by Claudium in A.D. 41, which also depicts the deity advancing as she holds a flower (*RIC* 64). In A.D. 70 the legend reappeared with a new motif of *Spes* offering her flower to Vespasian and his sons, Domitian and Titus (*RIC* 396). Vespasian also placed *Spes* on coins bearing the legend *PRINCEPS IVVENTUT* as propaganda for Domitian and himself, although the title *Princeps iuventutis* was usually reserved for the young heir in his semi-official capacity as "Prince of youth" (*RIC* 139, 233). These coin types raise questions concerning the meaning of the Roman virtue and its incorporation into the imperial cult. For instance, some question remains whether *Spes Augusta* on Claudius' coin was intended to celebrate the birth of his son, Britannicus, who was born in A.D. 41; or whether it was meant to reflect upon hope in regards to Claudius himself, who was born on August 1, the traditional feast day of *Spes*.[3] We should, moreover, recognize that Claudius did not institute a totally new imperial virtue, for the personification had already appeared in non-western coinage of Augustus. A coin from Pella, issued in 16 B.C., bears the legend *SPES COLONIAE PELLENSIS* and implies that Augustus was "the Hope of the colony of Pella."[4] Though the coin does not represent widely disseminated propaganda, we suspect that it drew upon ideas of hope already in existence, since the colony was comprised of Roman veterans. The virtue must thus be traced to Augustus in order to appreciate the concepts which Claudius and Vespasian evoked by the legend *Spes Augusta*.

The religious cult of *Spes* also sheds light upon the Roman virtue. During the republic two major temples to *Spes* were at Rome. The first was known as "Old Hope"

[1] J. R. Fears, *Roman Liberty: An Essay in Protean Political Metaphor* (Bloomington, Ind., 1980); T. Hölscher, *Victoria Romana* (Mainz von Zabern, 1967); A. V. Stylow, *Libertas und Liberalitas. Untersuchungen zur innen politischer Propaganda* (Munich, 1972). See also L. R. Lind, "Roman Religion and Ethical Thought: Abstraction and Personification," *CJ* (1974) 108-99. The bibliography and evidence used in this paper must be selective.

[2] K. Latte, *Römische Religionsgeschichte* (Munich, 1960), 238, 322, and idem, "Spes," *RE* (2) 6. cols. 1634-36; P. G. Walsh, "*Spes Romana, Spes Christiana*," *Prudentia* 6 (1974) 33-43; G. Wissowa, "Spes," *Ausführliches Lexicon der griechischen und römischen Mythologie* (ed. W. H. Roscher; Leipzig, 1905-15) vol. 4, cols. 1295-97.

[3] See C. H. V. Sutherland, *Coinage in Roman Imperial Policy* (London, 1951) 131-32, n. 1.

[4] H. Gaebler, *Die antiken Münzen von Makedonia und Paonia* (Berlin, 1934) vol. 2, 118 and idem, "Zur Münzkunde Makedoniens," *ZN* 36 (1926) 118, 121; M. Grant, *From Imperium to Auctoritas* (Cambridge, 1946) 281.

(*Spes vetus*), while the second, and more popular, temple was maintained from 258 B.C. in the Forum Holitorium.[5] Although the second temple was destroyed in 218 and 31 B.C., it is clear that the cult enjoyed continuing, if at time interrupted, observance from the Romans.[6] The numismatic portrayal of *Spes* may have been based upon the archaic iconography of the temple in the Forum Holitorium.[7]

Spes is also mentioned in the cults of other deities. For instance, she was associated with *Fortuna* and *Fortuna primigenia*, the deity properly concerned with the firstborn of the household.[8] The Romans viewed children as the hope of the house and *Spes* had much to do with continuing the family.[9] During the imperial period she was also petitioned with *Salus* and other goddesses on behalf of the protection of the emperor and his family.[10] Her connections here suggest that *Spes* served as protectress over domestic affairs for private citizens and the imperial family.

The religious concept, however, sometimes conflicts with disparate views of hope in Latin literature. The Romans, as well as the Greeks, did not view the human quality as always consistent and dependable. Often *spes* appears as an evil force of delusion, such as "vain hope" (*spes inanis*), and even the personification is sometimes treated as a delusive deity.[11] Especially when she is connected with Fortune as a whimsical goddess, *Spes* may acquire an unstable character.[12] The pejorative aspects of the Roman conception have been previously studied and we need not dwell upon them, except to note that the view of hope as delusion sometimes prejudiced the literary portrayal of the personification.[13]

Only a limited number of literary passages thus represents the quality as a true virtue. One such passage is *De legibus* 2.27-28 in which Cicero deals with the concretization of virtues into divine abstractions. He includes *Spes* among the virtues, viewing her as a beneficent deity and not as a dubious quality or an apotropaic deity, such as *Mala Fortuna*.[14] The personification is also defined as "the expectation of good things" (*expectatio rerum bonarum*). Though Cicero's definition is general, it is appropriate for the public expectation of political benefits. The Athenians, even according to their enemies, were invariably full of good hope, confident in the future, and resilient in time of despair.[15] So too were the Romans, although we do not have such an explicit statement to that effect from a Latin source. If anything, the cult of *Spes* symbolized to the Romans their own resilience and confidence in their national destiny. This symbol, moreover, was evident as a virtue of individuals, for the personifications were actually divine qualities in great leaders, and the Romans expressed their confidence through public figures who provided them with the hope of future blessings.

A catalog of Roman leaders, both mythical and historical, whose virtue *spes* figured among their qualities, would be a lengthy study in itself. Some leaders, such as

---

[5]Livy, 2.51.2, *SHA*, *Elag.* 13.5, *CIL* 15.5929; Cicero, *Leg.* 2.28, *Nat. deor.* 2.61; R. Delbrück, *Die drei Tempel am Forum Holitorium im Rom* (Rome, 1903) 3.4.

[6]Livy, 21.62.4, 24.47.15, 25.7.6; Cassius Dio, 50.10.3.

[7]See M. Bieber, *The Sculpture of the Hellenistic Age* (2) (New York, 1961) 182.

[8]*CIL* 11.5749, 14.2853, 14.2867.

[9]For example, Cicero, *Clu.* 32.

[10]*CIL* 14.2804; *Acta Fratrum Arvalium*, (ed. G. Henzen; Berlin, 1874) 85.

[11]Cicero, *Cat.* 4.23, *Mil.* 94; Ovid, *A. A.* 1.445-46: *Spes . . . fallax . . . dea.*

[12]Horace, *Car.* 1.34.21-24. See G. Dumézil, "Les compagnes de la Fortune," *Fêtes romaines d'été et d'automne* (Paris, 1975) 238-49.

[13]A. Hackl, *Die spes als negativer Charakterisierungsbegriff in Caesars Bellum civile, Ciceros Catilinarien, Lucans Pharsalia* (Diss. Innsbruck, 1963): F. -H. Mutschler, *Erszählstil und Propaganda in Caesars Kommentarien* (Heidelberg, 1975) 64-66.

[14]See also *Nat. deor.* 2.60-61; 3.47, 61, 88.

[15]This is expressed through the adjective *euelpis*, Thucydides, 1.70, Xenophon, *An.* 2.1.18.

Scipio Africanus, stand out. According to Livy, Scipio's youth provided the Romans with a new spirit of hope during the Second Punic War; in fact, Livy cites the *spes ac magnitudo animi* of Scipio as the impetus behind his vigorous pursuit of the war.[16] Also in *De lege Manilia* Cicero implies that Pompey brought hope to the Romans. Scholars have noted that this speech, delivered in 66 B.C., portrays Pompey as a young charismatic leader and that it anticipates the subsequent crystallization of several Roman virtues in the imperial cult.[17] In Cicero's arguments *spes* figures as the hope of the people in Pompey; though the idea is not as concrete as other virtues, such as *felicitas*, it is an example of the political significance of *spes*, for Cicero even argues that it was customary for the Romans to place their hope in a single military leader.[18] Furthermore, in the *Philippics* Cicero represents Octavian and other republican leaders as the hope of liberty and peace.[19] At the end of the republic Cicero made great use of Octavian as a rallying point against the more dangerous Antony.[20] While we may question Cicero's sincerity here, his use of *spes* takes on significance for the imperial virtue.

By the time of Augustus' rise to power, then, the Roman virtue had political, as well as religious importance. In the imperial cult the political and religious aspects converged into the concept of the emperor as the hope of the Romans. This is best seen in the close identification of *Spes* with the person of the emperor. For example, the temple in the Forum Holitorium was sometimes identified as *Spes Augusta* and the Augustales, who oversaw the worship of the genius of the emperor, were referred to at times as the *Augustales Spei Augustae*.[21] Moreover, the date of Augustus' assumption of the *toga virilis*, October 18, was observed as a *supplicatio Spei et Iuventuti*.[22] The evidence thus indicates that the cult of Hope centered around the emperor and that special importance lay in *Spes* as a virtue associated with youth.

The coin issued at Pella in 16 B.C. suggests that the official process of focusing hope in the emperor began with Augustus himself and that the adjective *Augustus* was more than a generic description of the virtue. Several developments is Augustan culture substantiate this supposition. For instance, the cult of *Spes* received some attention from the emperor and was connected with the imperial family quite early. In 31 B.C. the temple in the Forum Holitorium had been destroyed, but an inscription from the time of Augustus indicates that he restored it, although it may not have been completed until 19 B.C., at which time Germanicus rededicated the shrine.[23] Germanicus was a suitable symbol of the virtue for the royal family, for as heir his youth and leadership aroused the expectations and hopes of the people.[24]

Augustan literature also contains some passages which point to a new significance of hope for the period. In Vergil's *Aeneid*, uncompleted at the poet's death in 19 B.C., the future of Rome is alluded to in symbolic language:

> hinc pater Aeneas, Romanae stirpis origo,
> sidereo flagrans clipeo et caelestibus armis

---

[16]Livy, 28.1.11, 2.14, 17.2, 35.10, 38.9-10.

[17]See J. R. Fears, *Princeps a Diis Electus: The Divine Election of the Emperor as a Political Concept at Rome* (Rome, 1977) 94-99; S. Maccormack, "Latin Prose Panegyrics," *Empire and Aftermath* (ed. T. A. Dorey; London, 1975) 148.

[18] *Manl.* 44, 52, 59, 60.

[19] *Phil.* 5.40-41, 49; 12.9.

[20]R. Syme, *The Roman Revolution* (2) (Oxford, 1951) 271-74.

[21] *CIL* 5.707-708, 8.10985, 6.760; 10.6645, 6682.

[22] *CIL* 10.8375.

[23]See A. E. Gordon, *Album of Dated Latin Inscriptions* (Berkeley, 1964) vol. 2, 15-18; Tacitus, *Ann.* 2.49; M. E. Blake, *Roman Construction in Italy from Tiberius through the Flavians* (Washington, 1959) 12.

[24]Tacitus, *Ann.* 1.33.2, 1.71.3, 2.71.4, 3.4.1.

> et iuxta Ascanius, magnae spes altera Romae,
>   procedunt castris . . . . (12.166-169)

Both father and son share in the concept of hope, here represented as an idea of the future dynasty of Rome. Aeneas, as founder and father of the Romans (*Romanae stirpis origo*), is accompanied out of the camp by his son, Ascanius, for the final battle to establish Rome. Vergil's portrayal of the young man as "the second hope of great Rome" (*magnae spes altera Romae*) enhances by implication Aeneas' own position as the first hope of Rome. The passage should be seen in light of current scholarly views of the mythical heroes in the *Aeneid* as symbols of the Augustan regime and ideology.[25]

While Vergil's focus is upon the individual heir in the mythical dynasty of Rome, Horace offers a broader glimpse of the hope of the people. In 17 B.C. Augustus celebrated the Secular Games, which looked forward to the next *saeculum* of Rome. Horace's *Carmen saeculare*, written for the occasion, was appropriately sung by a chorus of twenty-seven young boys and an equal number of girls. Together they represented the hope of continuing the family for their respective parents. The poem is a look to the future from a panoramic view of Roman history and it ends with an affirmation of good hope for the present: *spem bonam certamque domum reporto* (line 74). Though not one of Horace's best, the ode does suggest that the Romans were concerned with their future, represented by children, and that this concern took on new confidence under Augustus.

In 17 B.C. the imperial family had every reason for good hope for the dynasty. The previous year Augustus adopted as heirs Gaius and Lucius Caesar and appointed them to the semi-official status of *principes iuventutis*, which we noted was later associated with *Spes* in Vespasian's coinage.[26] The problem of establishing a dynasty was difficult for Augustus, however, and his hopes were nearly dashed. The previous heir Marcellus had died in 23 B.C., an event alluded to by Vergil who describes the hope of his ancestors (*Aeneid* 6.876: *in tantum spe tollet avos . . .*). Also, by A.D. 4 both Lucius and Gaius were dead.

In that year Augustus reluctantly adopted Tiberius. The adoption is described enthusiastically by Velleius Peterculus (2.103), whose account is designed to enhance Tiberius as a carefully selected heir.[27] Velleius is significant because we know that he wrote before A.D. 30 and this date is helpful in showing the crystallization of the virtue prior to Claudius. The passage begins with a reference to fortune--a whimsical *fortuna* which removed the "hope of a great name" (*fortuna, quae subduxerat spem magni nominis*). She returns her protection to the state through the arrival of Tiberius in Rome at the opportune moment. On the day of the adoption the city was filled with joy and the realized hope of the perpetual security and eternity of the empire; parents had hope of children, men of matrimony, masters of patrimony, and all men had the hope of salvation, quiet, peace and tranquillity, so much so that one could not hope for more, nor could it be accorded hope more fortunately:

> laetitiam illius diei concursumque civitatis et vota
> paene inserentium caelo manus spemque conceptam
> perpetuae securitatis aeternitatisque Romani imperii
> vix in illo iusto opere abunde persequi poterimus . . .
> tum refulsit certa spes liberorum parentius, viris
> matrimoniorum, dominis patrimonii, omnibus hominibus
> salutis, quietis, pacis, tranquillitatis, adeo ut nec
> plus sperari potuerit nec spei responderi felicius.

---

[25] See A. F. Stocker, "Vergil in the Service of Augustus," *Vergilius* 26 (1980) 1-9.

[26] *Res gestae* 14; see D. O. Rosenberg, "Historical Development of a Roman Coin Type," *San* 2 (1970) 34-35, 39.

[27] A. J. Woodman, *Velleius Paterculus. The Tiberian Narrative* (2.94-131) (Cambridge, 1977) 130-131. See also I. Lana, *Velleio Paterculo o della propaganda* (Turin, 1952) 221-222.

Several of the concepts here, such as *salus, quies, pax,* and *tranquillitas,* appear as later coin types of the empire. The main imperial idea, however, which links all the future blessings is *spes.* The passage is particularly appropriate as a contrast between the Roman view and the Christian concept of hope: the Roman virtue emphasized the material blessings of this life, in very concrete terms as the hope of children and domestic welfare, whereas the Christian focus was upon the afterlife and spiritual blessings.[28]

Above all, Velleius indicates that the imperial virtue was a twofold idea. On one hand it was the expectation of the people and the hope of private families. On the other hand Tiberius was the hope of the imperial family and Velleius began the description with a reference to the "hope of a great name," e.g., the name of Caesar as the hope of continuing the Augustan dynasty. The adoption was thus a public symbol to private households of continuation and perpetuity. We should imagine here the virtue as proceeding from the hope of a great name to the hope of the empire and down to the expectations of all Romans. The emanation of *spes* was a single process, for the hope of the imperial family was also the personal hope of private citizens.

These ideas clarify the subsequent propaganda of Claudius and the Flavians. Claudius' coin type was a suitable expression of hope in the emperor and in Britannicus as the hope of the Augustan dynasty. By seeking to evoke the Augustan concept, Vespasian was actually attempting to fulfill his own dynastic ambitions. The virtue had meaning for the mature emperor, as well as his designated heir, and the evidence suggests that the imperial virtue represented the hope of the people in a perpetual dynasty. The coinage as propaganda, moreover, drew upon a well established tradition of the Roman virtue.

---

[28]See Walsh (above, note 2) and St. Paul, 1 Cor 15:19. Although the term *spes immortalitatis* does appear (Cicero, *Tusc.* 1.32, 39), this cannot be applied to the Roman virtue; also, the portrayal of *Elpis* on a sarcophagus of the late first century B.C. (?) should not be taken as a representation of the concept of Hope as a public virtue of the Romans, P. Gusman, *L'Art decoratif de Rome* (Paris, 1908) vol. 2, plate 96.

YAVNEH REVISITED:
PHARISEES, RABBIS, AND THE END OF JEWISH SECTARIANISM

Shaye J. D. Cohen

Introduction

When we speak about the theological, political, economic, and social difficulties which confronted the Jews after the destruction of the Jerusalem temple in 70 C.E., we usually use the words "crisis," "trauma," and "catastrophe." We speak about the cessation of the sacrificial cult, the loss of the sacred center of the cosmos, the removal of the physical symbols of God's presence among the Jews, the public display of the power of Rome and her Gods and of the relative powerlessness of Israel and her God, the massacre of over half a million people, the failure of apocalyptic dreams and prophecies, the abolition of the sanhedrin and the cultic functions of the priesthood, and the destruction and confiscation of Judean land and property. None of us doubts that these difficulties were sufficiently numerous and severe to constitute a crisis but we must be careful lest we exaggerate. The air of crisis which pervades the apocalypses of Barukh and Ezra is conspicuously absent from tannaitic literature, even those dicta ascribed to Yavnean figures. The point of the mythic story about Rabban Yohanan ben Zakkai and Vespasian is that rabbinic life ought to continue as before, the Jews subservient to foreign rule and occupied with the study of the law. No crisis here. And even the apocalypses of Barukh and Ezra do not treat all the items on the above list. For example, neither seer is concerned about the cessation of the sacrificial cult or about the destruction of the temple *per se*.

In this essay my theme is the end of Jewish sectarianism. Although no ancient text discusses the ultimate fate of the Pharisees, Sadducees, and Essenes, I shall argue that their disappearance, as well as the disappearance of the Houses of Hillel and Shammai, is directly connected with the destruction of the temple. According to the usual view, sectarianism ceased when the Pharisees, gathered at Yavneh, ejected all those who were not members of their own party. Christians were excommunicated, the Biblical canon was purged of works written in Greek and apocalyptic in style, and the gates were closed on the outside world, both Jewish and non-Jewish. Functioning in a "crisis" atmosphere, the rabbis of Yavneh were motivated by an exclusivistic ethic; their goal was to define orthodoxy and to rid Judaism of all those who would not conform to it. In this interpretation the "synod" of Yavneh becomes a prefiguration of the council of Nicea: one party triumphs and ousts its competitors. In addition, we are told, the Sadducees, Essenes, and, presumably, all other sects, conveniently rolled over and died, thereby facilitating Pharisaic victory. The Sadducees, bereft of the temple, were bereft of a livelihood and a power base. The Essenes perished in the great war against the sons of darkness.[1]

This view is flawed on several counts. First, it is overly simplistic. Second, it presumes that we know a good deal more about Yavneh than we really do. As we shall see, there is little hard evidence to connect the Yavnean sages with the Pharisees and to ascribe to them an exclusivistic ethic. Third, it assumes an air of crisis which, as I have

---

[1]See e.g. G. F. Moore, *Judaism in the First Centuries of the Christian Era* (3 vols.; Cambridge: Harvard UP, 1927) 1.85-86; W. D. Davies, *The Setting of the Sermon on the Mount* (Cambridge: Cambridge UP, 1964) 259-86; J. Neusner, "The Formation of Rabbinic Judaism: Yavneh (Jamnia) from A.D. 70 to 100," *Aufstieg und Niedergang der römischen Welt* II, 19.2, ed. H. Temporini and W. Haase (Berlin and New York: de Gruyter) 3-42. The numerous works of Jacob Neusner have stimulated my thinking on Yavneh and, although my approach and conclusions differ from his (as many of the following notes will show), I have learned much from him.

already indicated, the rabbis may not have felt, or, at least, may not have felt in a way which would have justified the expulsion of those with whom they disagreed. Fourth, and most important, it obscures the major contribution of Yavneh to Jewish history: the creation of a society which tolerates disputes without producing sects. For the first time Jews "agreed to disagree." The major literary monument created by the Yavneans and their successors testifies to this innovation. No previous Jewish work looks like the Mishnah because no previous Jewish work, neither Biblical nor post-Biblical, neither Hebrew nor Greek, neither Palestinian nor diasporan, attributes conflicting legal and exegetical opinions to named individuals who, in spite of their differences, belong to the same fraternity. The dominant ethic here is not exclusivity but elasticity. The goal was not the triumph over other sects but the elimination of the need for sectarianism itself. As one tannaitic midrash remarks, "*lo³ titgodedu* (Deut 14:1). Do not make separate factions (*³agudot*) but make one faction all together" (Sipre, Deut 96 [p. 158 ed. Finkelstein]). I shall argue that the destruction of the temple provided the impetus for this process: it warned the Jews of the dangers of internal divisiveness and it removed one of the major focal points of Jewish sectarianism.

Sectarianism in the rabbinic period

It is generally assumed that Jewish sectarianism all but ceased after 70 C.E. This assumption seems to be correct but a brief discussion of the rabbinic and patristic evidence is in order.

Rabbinic evidence

Rabbinic literature has occasional references to various sects: Pharisees, Sadducees, Boethusians, Hemerobaptists, Samaritans, and, perhaps, others.[2] Most of these references do not locate these groups in any specific period, but those which do, invariably place these groups during the second temple period, not after 70 C.E. (The Samaritans, of course, are an exception.) Pharisees and Sadducees (or Boethusians) discuss temple rituals which disappeared after 70 C.E. Wicked Sadducean (Boethusian) high priests serve in the temple and are confronted by the Pharisees or the Sages or Rabban Yohanan ben Zakkai. No rabbi, including Yohanan ben Zakkai, is ever called a Pharisee (a point to which we shall return below), and no rabbi after Yohanan ben Zakkai is ever brought into contact with a Sadducee or a Boethusian. Only one text seems to break this pattern:

A.   Sadducean women, as long as they are accustomed to follow the ways of their ancestors, have the same status (with regard to menstrual purity) as Cuthean (i.e. Samaritan) women. When they have separated themselves (from their ancestral ways) to follow the ways of Israel, they have the same status as Israel.

B.   R. Yosi says, "they always have the same status as Israel unless they separate themselves to follow the ways of their ancestors." (m. Nid. 4:2)

In this mishnah R. Yosi argues that Sadducean women can be assumed to follow the rabbinic laws of menstruation unless we know specifically to the contrary that they

---

[2]A full collection and analysis of all such rabbinic statements (with their textual variants) is a desideratum. For the purposes of this essay a useful article is J. Lightstone, "Sadducees versus Pharisees: The Tannaitic Sources," *Christianity, Judaism, and other Greco-Roman Cults: Studies for Morton Smith*, ed. J. Neusner (SJLA 12; 4 vols.; Leiden: Brill, 1975), 3. 206-17. The best discussion of the term *minim* is R. Kimelman, "*Birkat Ha-Minim* and the Lack of Evidence an anti-Christian Jewish Prayer in Late Antiquity," *Jewish and Christian Self-Definition II: Aspects of Judaism in the Graeco-Roman Period*, ed. E. P. Sanders et al. (Philadelphia: Fortress, 1981) 226-44, esp. 228-32. Hemero-baptists are mentioned in t. Yad. end.

follow Sadducean traditions. Are the anonymous tradent of the mishnah and R. Yosi (mid-second century) referring to contemporary Sadducean women or to ancient times?[3] The former interpretation is assumed by a *beraita* quoted by the Babylonian Talmud ad loc. The text narrates a story about a Sadducee and a high priest, and concludes with the words of the wife of the Sadducee:

A.   "Although they (=we) are wives of Sadducees, they (=we) fear the Pharisees and show their (=our) (menstrual) blood to the sages."

B.   R. Yosi says, "We are more expert in them (Sadducean women) than anyone else. They show (menstrual) blood to the sages, except for one woman who was in our neighborhood, who did not show her (menstrual) blood to the sages, and she died (immediately)." (b. Nid. 33b)[4]

In this text there is chronological tension between parts A and B. A clearly refers to a woman who lived during the second temple times, while B has R. Yosi derive his expertise about Sadducean women from personal acquaintance. He recalls a Sadducean woman who lived in his neighborhood and died prematurely because (R. Yosi said) she did not accept the authority of the sages to determine her menstrual status. Compare, however, the version of the Tosefta:

A.   "Although we are Sadducean women, we all consult a sage."

B.   R. Yosi says, "We are more expert in Sadducean women than anyone else: they all consult a sage except for one who was among them, and she died." (t. Nid. 5:3)

In the Tosefta version there is no chronological tension between parts A and B since it gives no indication that R. Yosi's expertise derives from personal experience. We may assume that here, as in many other places R. Yosi is transmitting some antiquarian lore about the period of the second temple.[5] If we are correct in preferring the Tosefta to the BT version,[6] m. Nid. 4:2 does not constitute an exception to the overall pattern.

In tannaitic tradition, then, and for the most part in amoraic tradition as well, named sects disappear after 70 C.E. This is not to say that the rabbis imagined that all their Jewish contemporaries accepted their authority and followed their practices, since they frequently admit that this was not the case. But the rabbinic silence does indicate that a major change took place in Jewish sectarianism after 70.

Patristic Evidence

Numerous Christian fathers preserve in various forms a list of Jewish "heresies." Many aspects of these lists are obscure but this is not the place for a full collection and analysis of the material.[7] The crucial point for us is that most of these authors,

---

[3]The context seems to favor the former interpretation since this Mishnah is preceded by a ruling concerning the menstrual status of Samaritan women and is followed by a ruling concerning the menstrual status of gentile women. If the three mishnayot are a unit, they all refer to matters of contemporary concern. But are they a unit? They differ in style.

[4](immediately) is omitted in our vulgate edition of the Talmud but appears in codex Munich 95 and codex Vaticanus Ebr. 111.

[5]See e.g. m. R.H. 1:7; m. Yom. 6:3; t. Hag. 2:9.

[6]The phrase which makes R. Yosi a contemporary of the Sadducean woman ("who was in our neighborhood") reappears elsewhere in BT (C. and B. Kasowsky, *Thesaurus Talmudis* (Jerusalem: Ministry of Education and Jewish Theological Seminary, 1954ff), 37.436) and transfers the social reality described by m. ʿErub. 6:2 (a Sadducee and R. Gamaliel, presumably R. Gamaliel the Elder, share a courtyard) to the mishnah in Niddah.

[7]M. Simon, "Les sectes juives d'après les témoignages patristiques," *Studia Patristica I*, ed. K. Aland and F. L. Cross (TU 63; Berlin: Akademie Verlag, 1957) 526-39; M. Black, "The Patristic Accounts of Jewish Sectarianism," *BJRL* 41 (1958-59) 285-303;

beginning with Hegesippus (mid-second century), state that they are describing the sects of long ago, presumably of the period of the New Testament. Epiphanius, for example, says explicitly that these Jewish sects, including the Pharisees, no longer exist in his day (see the appendix below). The only important exception to this pattern[8] is Justin:

> For if you have fallen in with some who are called Christians, but who do not admit this (the resurrection), and venture to blaspheme the God of Abraham, and the God of Isaac, and the God of Jacob . . . do not imagine that they are Christians, even as one, if he would rightly consider it, would not admit that the Sadducees, or the similar sects of Genistai, Meristai, Galilaioi, Hellenianoi, Pharisaioi, and Baptistai, are Jews . . . but are (only) called Jews and children of Abraham, worshipping God with the lips, as God himself declared (Isa 29:13), but the heart was far from him. But I and others, who are right-minded Christians on all points, are assured that there will be a resurrection of the dead. . . . (Dialogue with Trypho 80.4-5)[9]

Eager to forestall an argument against resurrection from the opinions of various Christian sects, Justin denies that these so-called Christians really are Christians, since only those who are "orthodox" (Justin uses the term *orthognomon*) like Justin himself deserve that appellation. Similarly, Justin argues, sectarian Jews like the Genistai et al. really are not Jews although they are generally called Jews.[10] Since the first part of the passage refers to contemporary Christian sects, may we conclude that, according to Justin at least, Jewish sectarianism too was flourishing in the second century? Not necessarily. Justin is interested in ideology, not sociology. His point about the relationship of orthodoxy to heresy makes sense even if some or all of the Jewish sects listed did not exist in his own time. Furthermore, the implicit reference to Jewish "orthodoxy"--the first time such a concept is applied to Judaism--indicates that Jewish sectarianism, even if all seven groups still existed in the second century, was no longer what it had been in the first century. I shall argue below that this passage reflects the rabbinic ideology of the Yavnean period: there is one "orthodox" Judaism which, while tolerating disputes within the fold (a point not discussed by Justin here), has no room for any group--even Pharisees--which maintains a sectarian self-definition.[11]   The rabbis

---

S. J. Isser, *The Dositheans* (SJLA 17; Leiden: Brill, 1976) 11-14; S. P. Brock, "Some Syriac Accounts of the Jewish Sects," *A Tribute to Arthur Vööbus: Studies in Early Christian Literature,* ed. R. H. Fischer (Chicago: Lutheran School of Theology, 1977) 265-76. Hippolytus' account of the Essenes has been the subject of many special studies, notably C. Burchard, "Zur Nebenüberlieferung von Josephus' Bericht über die Essener Bell 2, 119-161 bei Hippolyt, Porphyrius, Josippus, Niketas Choniates und anderen," *Josephus-Studien: Untersuchungen zu Josephus . . . O. Michel . . . gewidmet,* ed. O. Betz et al. (Göttingen: Vandenhoeck & Ruprecht, 1974) 77-96 (with bibliography).

[8]Perhaps there are others too. I do not discuss here Origen, *Contra Celsum* 3.12, which bears a close resemblance to *Tri. Trac.* 112 (*The Nag Hammadi Library,* ed. J. M. Robinson [San Francisco: Harper and Row, 1977] 86). See n. 40 below.

[9]The translation is that of the *Ante-Nicene Fathers,* slightly modified.

[10]"Worshipping God with the lips" (*cheilesin homologountas*) is probably a pun on the name "Jew" which was commonly taken to mean "confessor." For this etymology in Philo, see the passages listed by J. W. Earp in vol. 10 of the LCL Philo (Cambridge: Harvard UP, 1962) 357 note *a*. For the fathers see N. De Lange, *Origen and the Jews* (Cambridge: Cambridge UP, 1976) 32 n. 29.

[11]Modern scholars have been disturbed by the presence of Pharisees in Justin's list. Harnack, emphasizing that the manuscript tradition of the Dialogue omits the *kai* between Pharisees and Baptists and that Justin identifies the Pharisees with the *didaskaloi* of his own time, argues that a copyist added Pharisees to Justin's list ("Judentum

called such groups *minim,* a term apparently reflected in Justin's Genistai and Meristai.[12] Perhaps the other five groups also existed in Justin's time, but in his view they clearly were inconsequential.

On the basis of both the rabbinic and the patristic evidence, I conclude that we may accept the usual view that 70 C.E. is a major transition point in Jewish sectarianism. Perhaps some sects, aside from the Samaritans and Christianizing Jews, lingered on for a while, but Jewish society from the end of the first century until the rise of the Karaites, was not torn by sectarian divisions. This conclusion cannot be upset by a lone beraita in the Babylonian Talmud and by an elusive passage of Justin.

Pharisees and others at Yavneh

Everyone knows that the sages of Yavneh were Pharisees or the descendants of Pharisees. Although this assumption is widely accepted, even by those who modify it,[13] the evidence on which it relies does not justify such confidence. Here is a brief assessment of evidence.[14]

1. Josephus and the NT refer to eleven named individuals who are called Pharisees or who are said to lead a Pharisaic life.[15] Two, perhaps three, of these recur in the rabbinic chain of tradition of ʾAbot 1 (where, of course, they are not called Pharisees). But if the Pharisees Gamaliel, Simon ben Gamaliel, and, perhaps, Pollio, are claimed by

---

... in Justins Dialog mit Trypho," TU 39,1 [1913] 57-58). But it is more likely that a *kai* has fallen out (or was taken out by a scribe bothered by Harnack's problem) than that "Pharisees" has fallen in. Nor does Justin identify the Pharisees with the *didaskaloi;* see n. 69 below. Black ("Patristic Accounts," 288-89) also omits *kai* and appeals to a movement of "baptizing Pharisees." Simon ("Sectes juives," 529-31) argues that Justin is writing from a Christian perspective. These suggestions result from the failure to study the connections between Pharisees and rabbis. I regret that I have not seen G. Archambault, *Justin Dialogue avec Tryphon* (2 vols; Paris: A. Picard, 1909). L. W. Barnard, *Justin Martyr His Life and Thought* (Cambridge: Cambridge UP, 1967) 50-51, does not advance the discussion.

[12] Isser, "Dositheans," 14 n. 19, quoting D. Gershenson and G. Quispel, "Meristae," *VC* 12 (1958) 19-26; Simon, "Sectes juives," 533-35.

[13] Neusner, "Formation," and "Pharisaic-Rabbinic Judaism: A Clarification," *Early Rabbinic Judaism* (SJLA 13; Leiden: Brill, 1975) 50-70 (reprinted from *HR* 12 [1973] 250-70). In *Judaism: The Evidence of the Mishnah* (Chicago: University of Chicago, 1981) 70-71, Neusner retracts the work of a lifetime and admits to uncertainty whether the Pharisees were a sect or not, and whether they are the group which stands behind the mishnah. Other scholars too have cast doubt on the Pharisaic-rabbinic connection. See e.g. J. Bowker, *Jesus and the Pharisees* (Cambridge: Cambridge UP, 1973).

[14] The following argument is not worthy of serious consideration. Since Josephus lists only four sects, and since the rabbis obviously are not Sadducees, Essenes, or the Fourth Philosophy, therefore the rabbis must be Pharisees. By the same logic sixteenth century scholars concluded that Boethusians must be the Essenes since otherwise Josephus omits the former and the rabbis omit the latter. Ignotum per ignotius.

[15] The eleven are: 1. Eleazar the Pharisee at the court of John Hyrcanus (Josephus *Ant.* 13.290 where the singular *Pharisaios* does not appear); 2. Pollion (*Ant.* 15.3 and 370; his disciple is not called a Pharisee); 3. Saddok, one of the founders of the Fourth Philosophy (*Ant.* 18.4); 4. Nicodemus (Jn 3:1); 5. Gamaliel (Acts 5:34); 6. Paul (Phil 3:5; Acts 23:6 and 26:5); 7. Simon ben Gamaliel (*Vita* 191); 8-9-10. Jonathan, Ananias, and Jozaros, three priests sent to Galilee in 66-67 (*Vita* 197); 11. Josephus (*Vita* 12). Luke mentions three individual Pharisees, all unnamed (Luke 7:36-39; 11:37-38; 18:10-11). New Testament apocrypha and Nag Hammadi texts mention additional Pharisees.

the rabbis as their own, does this prove that the rabbis generally were Pharisees or the descendants of Pharisees? Obviously not. The same list also claims Simon the righteous, a high priest of the hellenistic period, not to mention Moses himself. This list "rabbinizes" history. Perhaps some Pharisees too have been retroactively "rabbinized."[16]

2. Similarly, some of the stories which Josephus tells about the Pharisees recur in rabbinic literature as part of rabbinic history. The Josephan story about a rift between John Hyrcanus and the Pharisees recurs in almost identical form in the Talmud, but there the protagonists are Yannai the King and the sages. Josephus states that the Sadducees were unable to implement their own rulings out of fear of the populace which followed the Pharisees. The rabbinic narratives which make this same point concern Sadducees (or Boethusians) and the sages.[17] This evidence too is not irrefragable: once again, perhaps the rabbis have "rabbinized" Pharisaic history.[18]

3. Josephus and the NT ascribe certain beliefs and practices to the Pharisees which are shared by rabbinic Judaism, notably the belief in a combination of fate and free will, the belief in the immortality of the soul and resurrection, the acceptance of ancestral traditions in addition to the written law, and the meticulous observance of the laws of purity, tithing, Shabbat, and other rituals. The list is impressive, but do these practices and beliefs characterize only Pharisees to the exclusion of all other Jews? Furthermore, these parallels cannot hide the differences between Pharisaic and rabbinic piety. For example, the tannaim believe in an oral law revealed to Moses but this doctrine is never attributed to the Pharisees.[19] The Pharisees scour the entire earth to make one proselyte but the rabbis do not.[20] These and other differences might be explained by internal Pharisaic-rabbinic development or the change in the external circumstances in which the post-70 Pharisees found themselves, but the differences as well as the similarities have to be explained.

4. It has been argued that Josephus' *Jewish Antiquities,* completed in 93/4, and *Vita,* completed shortly thereafter, are more pro-Pharisaic than the *Jewish War,* completed ca. 81.[21] Similarly, it has been argued that those sections of the gospels which accord prominence to the Pharisees are post-70 additions to earlier material.[22] If these observations are correct--both have been disputed--we may assume that these literary developments mirror the rise of Pharisaic fortunes at Yavneh.[23]

---

[16]Neusner discusses the "rabbinization" of history in his mis-titled *The Rabbinic Traditions about the Pharisees before 70* (Leiden: Brill, 1971). There is no evidence that the figures discussed in this book (aside from those listed in n. 15 above) were Pharisees. The uncertainty applies to the Houses too.

[17]Rift: *Ant.* 13.288-96 and b. Qidd. 66a. Sadducees obey Pharisees: *Ant.* 18.15 and 17; t. Yoma 1:8; t. Parah 3:8; m. and t. Nid. (discussed above); t. Sukk. 3:1 and 3:16. See n. 25 below.

[18]For a clear case of the rabbinization of history, compare *Ant.* 13.372 (the people pelt Jannaeus with their citrons to protest his rule) with t. Sukk. 3:16 (the people pelt a Boethusian high priest with their citrons to protest his failure to follow a rabbinic ordinance). I am preparing a study of all the rabbinic anecdotes paralleled by Josephus.

[19]J. Neusner, *Method and Meaning in Ancient Judaism* (Missoula: Scholars Press, 1979) 69-70.

[20]The tannaim generally--not, however, the Mishnah--have a favorable attitude towards proselytes (B. J. Bamberger, *Proselytism in the Talmudic Period* [1939; repr. New York: Ktav, 1968] 149-73) but we have no indication that the rabbis ever engaged in missionary activity.

[21]S. J. D. Cohen, *Josephus in Galilee and Rome* (Leiden: Brill, 1979) 144-51. On the date of the *J.W.* see Cohen 84-90.

[22]See e.g. Morton Smith, *Jesus the Magician* (San Francisco: Harper and Row, 1978) 153-57.

[23]For a very different approach see E. Rivkin, *A Hidden Revolution* (Nashville: Abingdon, 1978). The review in *JBL* (1980) 627-29 is a bit too harsh.

Each of these four arguments depends upon Josephus and the NT to provide the Pharisaic connection for early rabbinic Judaism. Each argument is inconclusive but each aids the other. Their weight is cumulative. We may conclude that in all likelihood there was some close connection between the post-70 rabbis and the pre-70 Pharisees.

Do rabbinic texts confirm this conclusion? Do the tannaim[24] see themselves as Pharisees or as the descendants of the Pharisees? The evidence is ambiguous. On the one hand, the tannaim detail four disputes between the Pharisees and the Sadducees, one dispute between the Pharisees and the Boethusians, one dispute between the sages and the Sadducees, and two disputes between the sages and the Boethusians. In each case the victors are the Pharisees and the sages, the losers are the Boethusians and the Sadducees. Yehudah ben Tabbai, Yohanan ben Zakkai, and the anonymous "they" who figure throughout the Mishnah, perform public rituals in such a way so as to flout the rulings of the Boethusians and the Sadducees. Against Boethusian opposition the Jewish masses insist that two temple rituals be performed.[25] From all this it is clear that the tannaim saw their ancestors of the second temple period as the opponents of the Sadducees and the Boethusians. But the link between the rabbis and the Pharisees is much more tenuous, appearing only implicitly and only in the two passages which describe the five disputes between the Pharisees and the Sadducees-Boethusians. The tannaim never explicitly call themselves "Pharisees" nor is any individual rabbi ever called a Pharisee. Nor do they employ "Sadducee" as a general synonym for "reprobate" or "heretic."[26] Furthermore, in one of the disputes between the Pharisees and the Sadducees Yohanan ben Zakkai replies to the Sadducees as follows, "And is there no other argument we can advance against the Pharisees except this?", which could be interpreted to indicate that Yohanan was a Sadducee (or, at least, not a Pharisee).[27] The tannaim use *perushim* with reference not only to the Pharisees of old but also to contemporary "separatists" or "ascetics," whose conduct can be either condemned or approved. Either way, these *perushim* have no connection with the Pharisees.[28]

In contrast to the tannaim who had little interest in establishing themselves as Pharisees, the amoraim, especially the amoraim of Babylonia, began to see themselves more clearly as the descendants of the Pharisees. T. Yoma 1:8, followed by p. Yoma 1:5 (39a), speaks of the tension between the Boethusians and the sages; in b. Yoma 19b the sages are replaced by the Pharisees. In t. Nid. Sadducean women show their menstrual blood to the sages; in b. Nid. the sages are identified with the Pharisees (see above).[29]

---

[24]I exclude Babylonian beraitot from consideration here since they cannot be presumed to reflect tannaitic language.

[25]Pharisees and Sadducees: m. Yad. 4:6 and 7; t. Hag. 3:35. Pharisees and Boethusians: t. Yad. 2:20. Sages and Sadducees: m. Mak. 1:6. Sages and Boethusians: t. Yoma 1:8; t. R. H. 1:15. Yehudah: t. San. 6:6. Yohanan: t. Parah 3:8. Anonymous "they": m. Men. 10:3 and t. Men. 10:23. Jewish masses: t. Sukk. 3:1 and 16.

[26]At m. Yad. 4:8 the texts offer either *Sadducee* or *min*. Sipre, Num 112 (p. 121 ed. Horovitz) interprets the phrase "for he has abused the word of the Lord" to mean "this is a Sadducee," but many testimonia omit this from the text. I know of no other tannaitic text which employs Sadducee as a synonym for heretic.

[27]I do not think that this interpretation is correct. See D. Daube, "Three Notes Having to do with Johanan ben Zaccai," *JTS* 11 (1960) 53-56. The text is m. Yad. 4:6.

[28]Condemned: m. Sot. 3:4; t. Ber. 3:25; t. Sot. 15:11. Approved: m. Hag. 2:7; t. Shabb. 1:15. On the different meanings of the word *perushim*, see Alexander Guttmann, *Studies in Rabbinic Judaism* (New York: Ktav, 1976) 206-23 = *Rabbinic Judaism in the Making* (Detroit: Wayne State UP, 1970) 161-75, and E. Rivkin, "Defining the Pharisees," *HUCA* 40-41 (1969-70) 205-49.

[29]Lightstone, "Sadducees," 215, points out this shift. He was anticipated by Lieberman in his commentary to the Tosefta who in turn credits the observation to N. Rabbinovicz.

Similarly, in the Babylonian version of the rift between Yannai the King and the Pharisees, the latter are identified with the sages (b. Qidd. 66a). "Sadducee" is used to designate a non-rabbinic Jew, much like the term *min* (with which it is often confused in the manuscripts).[30] But even in this period the identification with the Pharisees is not so strong as to prevent the occasional use of *perushim* to indicate separatists whose conduct puts them outside the rabbinic pale (b. Pesah. 70b) or hypocrites who, like the Pharisees of the NT, feign an exaggerated piety (b. Sota 22b).[31] The overall tendency is even clearer in the post-Talmudic works Fathers according to Rabbi Nathan and Megillat Tacanit. The former describes the rebellion of Zadoq and Boethus, the putative founders of the Sadducees and the Boethusians, against the Pharisees who are led by Antigonus of Sokho, a link in the rabbinic chain of tradition; the latter (in the scholia) attributes the origin of various feast days to victories of the Pharisees or Sages over the Boethusians and Sadducees.[32]

In sum: at no point in antiquity did the rabbis clearly see themselves either as Pharisees or as the descendants of Pharisees. In tannaitic texts hostility to Sadducees and Boethusians is far more evident than is affinity with the Pharisees, i.e., the definition of the rabbis' opponents is clearer than is the self-definition of the rabbis themselves. This changes somewhat in amoraic texts, but even here identification with the Pharisees is not all that frequent and *perushim* is used as a term of abuse. The identification with the Pharisees is secure and central for the first time only in an early medieval text, the scholia to Megillat Tacanit.[33]

How can we explain the hesitation of the rabbis to identify themselves with the Pharisees? We might have argued that the rabbis were not, in fact, the descendants of the Pharisees, but this radical suggestion founders on the inconclusive yet suggestive arguments surveyed above, especially those few rabbinic texts which do allege an affinity between the rabbis and the Pharisees. Hence we must conclude that the rabbis were latter-day Pharisees who had no desire to publicize the connection. Why not? Part of the answer is the rabbinic abnegation of historical study. The rabbis had little interest in the Pharisees because they had little interest in post-Biblical history. The study of the revealed word of God was essential; the study of the works of men was, as Maimonides said centuries later, a waste of time.[34] Part of the answer is the tendency of all sects to

---

[30]See Kasowski's concordance to the Babylonian Talmud, s.v. *şeduqi;* in many of the passages there cited our vulgate texts read *min*. On the phrase "something which (even) the Sadducees acknowledge," see the *Talmudic Encyclopedia* 7 (Jerusalem, 1956) 1-4 (in Hebrew).

[31]On this list of seven types of Pharisees, see Guttmann, *Studies* 211-13 = *Rabbinic Judaism* 165-67.

[32]Abot R. Nat. A 5 = B 10 (p. 13b ed. Schechter) with "A Virgin Defiled: Some Rabbinic and Christian Views on the Origins of Heresy," *USQR* 36 (1980) 1-11; H. D. Mantel, "Megillat Tacanit and the Sects," *Studies in the History of the Jewish People and the Land of Israel in Memory of Zvi Avneri*, ed. A. Gilboa (Haifa: University of Haifa, 1970) 51-70 (in Hebrew). Not all versions of the scholia refer to the Sadducees and Boethusians; some even mention the Karaites. See Ido Hampel, *Megillat Taanit* (PhD thesis, Tel Aviv University, 1976). See note 33.

[33]Perhaps it was only in polemic with the Karaites, whom the rabbis identified with the Sadducees, that the rabbis clearly identified themselves with the Pharisees. Later medieval historians knew of the Pharisaic-rabbinic connection (e.g. Yosippon, ibn Daud's *History of the Second Temple*). For the patristic evidence bearing on this question see the appendix.

[34]Whether Maimonides meant what he said is a question; see S. Baron, "The Historical Outlook of Maimonides," *History and Jewish Historians* (Philadelphia: Jewish Publication Society, 1964) 109-63. The historical outlook of the rabbis has been a popular subject in recent years; modern discussion begins with N. Glatzer, *Untersuchungen zur Geschichtslehre der Tannaiten* (Berlin: Schocken Verlag, 1933).

refuse to see themselves as sects. They are the orthodox; the wicked multitudes are the heretics. Jewish sects (e.g. Samaritans, Christians, Qumran Essenes) call themselves "Israel"; "Pharisees," which literally means "separatists," was the opprobrious epithet hurled by opponents. Hence it is not surprising that the rabbis refer to themselves as "sages," "sages of Israel," "rabbis," etc., rather than "Pharisees" and do not acknowledge their sectarian origins.[35]

The real issue, however, is not nomenclature but ideology. Rabbinic materials preserve some relics of the ideology and organization which characterized pre-70 Pharisaism,[36] but these sectarian relics are few and far from central in rabbinic self-definition. At no point in antiquity did the rabbis develop heresiology and ecclesiology, creeds and dogmas. At no point did they expel anyone from the rabbinic order or from rabbinic synagogues because of doctrinal error or because of membership in some heretical group. Those who held incorrect beliefs were chastised or denied a share in the world to come, not denied a share in the people of Israel in this world (m. Sanh. 10 and t. Sanh. 12:9-13:12). Those who recited unacceptable liturgical formulas were silenced, not expelled (m. Ber. 5:3 and Meg. 4:8-9). Similarly, the birkat ha minim, the curse against minim ("heretics") which was inserted in the daily liturgy in the Yavnean period (b. Ber. 28b-29a), did not define which heretics were intended (all perushim, separatists, were included [t. Ber 3:25]) and, in any case, denounced but did not expel.[37] A few rabbis--not heretics!--were expelled (excommunicated or "banned"), and they were expelled because of their refusal to accept the will of the majority (see below). We never hear of the expulsion of any heretic or heretics. Nor did the rabbis of Yavneh expel heretical books from the canon. The consensus of modern scholarship is that the canonization of the Hebrew Bible was a long and complex process which neither began nor ended at Yavneh. No books, not even the books of minim, were burnt at Yavneh.[38] Rabbinic tradition is aware of opposition faced by Yohanan ben Zakkai at Yavneh but knows nothing of any expulsion of these opponents (b. R.H. 29b). Yohanan ben Zakkai was even careful to avoid a confrontation with the priests (m. ᶜEd. 8:3).

There is little evidence, then, of an exclusivistic ethic at Yavneh. Perhaps many or most of the rabbis were the descendants of the Pharisees, but their sectarian consciousness was minimal. What characterizes Yavneh (and rabbinic Judaism generally) is not uniformity but diversity. The Yavnean rabbis were rich and poor, priestly and lay, rural and urban. Some were mystics, some not. Some felt it necessary to attach their teachings to scripture, others did not. Some even had their own jargon; Akivan terminology in the Mekhilta cannot be mistaken for Ishmaelian. And everywhere are halakhic disputes on matters large and small but without the acrimony which

---

[35] Many scholars have noted that the label Pharisee ("separatist") was originally assigned by the group's opponents. See e.g. E. Schürer, The History of the Jewish People in the Age of Jesus, rev. and ed. G. Vermes et al. (Edinburgh: T. & T. Clark, 1979) 2. 396-98. The rabbis call themselves Israel to the exclusion of the Sadducees; see m. Nid. discussed above. According to one school of thought the Pharisees were not in fact a sect, but this is not the place for a discussion of the problem.

[36] I assume that the haburah described by m. and t. Dem. is a relic of the pre-70 period. The list of disputes between Pharisees and Sadducees may be a relic too, but the disputes on the whole are minor matters and betray no sectarian self-consciousness on either side. See Lightstone.

[37] See Kimelman, "Birkat Ha-Minim," and G. Stemberger, "Die sogenannte Synode von Jabne," Kairos 19 (1977) 14-21, esp. 17-18.

[38] B. Childs, Introduction to the Old Testament as Scripture (Philadelphia: Fortress, 1979) 46-68 (with bibliography). The evidence for book burning consists of the rhetorical outbursts of Tarphon and Ishmael in t. Shabb. 13:5, but there is no sign that they actually burnt any books. The context concerns the rescue of sacred books from impending destruction.

characterized the disputes between the sects and between the Houses of Hillel and Shammai before 70. This is not the work of a sect triumphant but of a grand coalition.[39]

The Temple and Sectarianism

Jewish sectarianism in antiquity, unlike Christian, defined itself in matters of law (halakha) and legal authority. What is the correct interpretation of the laws of the Torah? Who are the legitimate interpreters of the law and on what authority do they rely? All sects, including Sadducees, defended various ancestral traditions, exegetical modes, and authority figures as the only authentic representatives of Torah-true Judaism.[40] The sects debated many different laws, but the specific halakhot which always stood at the heart of Jewish sectarianism were the laws related to the temple: purity, cult, and priestly offerings. The sects advanced different theories of self-legitimation but the authority figures against whom they always defined themselves were the priests of the temple. Hence a common feature of Jewish sectarianism is the polemic against the temple of Jerusalem: its precincts impure, its cult profane, and its priests illegitimate. And just as the Jerusalem temple claimed to be the only authentic house of God ("one temple for the one God" remarks Josephus in *Against Apion* 2.193; cf. *Jewish Antiquities* 4.200-1), so too the sects, which saw themselves either explicitly or implicitly as the (temporary) replacements or equivalents of the temple,[41] advanced exclusive claims to the truth: only they understand God's will and only they perform God's law correctly. The temple priests, the other sects, and all the rest of the Jews either will convert or will be doomed to perdition in the end of days when a true temple is erected, a legitimate priestly line installed, and pure sacrifices offered.

Sectarian thought of this type began in the Persian period. For many Jews then the second temple was flawed, far inferior to the temple erected by Solomon. Constructed under the aegis of a gentile king and without the accompaniment of miracles and other explicit signs of divine favor, the second temple seemed inauthentic. Second Isaiah was aware of these objections (Isa 45:9-13). Even as it was being built, a prophetic school arose which proclaimed a vision and a program for the new temple not shared by

---

[39]Perhaps even some Sadducees sneaked in. In the nineteenth century A. Geiger tried to show traces of Sadducean halakha in rabbinic literature. See the chapter "Sadducees and Pharisees" in his *Urschrift und Uebersetzungen der Bibel* (Breslau, 1857; repr. 1928) as well as the article with the same title in his *Jüdische Zeitschrift für Wissenschaft und Leben* 2 (1863) 11-54. Cf. too J. Halévy, "Traces d'aggadot saducéennes dans le Talmud," *REJ* 8 (1884) 38-56. Were it not for the total lack of evidence, this question would be worth pursuing.

[40]M. Smith, "The Dead Sea Sect in Relation to Ancient Judaism," *NTS* 7 (1961) 347-60, anticipated to some extent by Origen, *Contra Celsum* 3.12, "There was in Judaism a factor which caused sects to begin, which was the variety of the interpretations of the writings of Moses and the sayings of the prophets" (p. 135, trans. H. Chadwick). This passage has an affinity with a Nag Hammadi text; see n. 8 above. "It was not dogma but law that was apt to produce lasting schisms in Judaism," writes L. Ginzberg, *An Unknown Jewish Sect* (New York: Jewish Theological Seminary, 1976) 105.

[41]B. Gärtner, *The Temple and the Community in Qumran and the New Testament* (Cambridge: Cambridge UP, 1965), and G. Klinzing, *Die Umdeutung des Kultus in der Qumrangemeinde und im NT* (Göttingen: Vandenhoeck & Ruprecht, 1971). The structural relationship between the sect and the temple is not uniform in ancient Judaism. Pharisees and apparently Christians tried to transfer some of the temple sanctity to themselves, but this did not prevent them from worshipping in the temple too, something which the Essenes refused to do. D. R. Schwartz, *RQ* 10 (1979-81) 83-91 and 435-46, argues that the Essenes did not see their community as a replacement for the temple; perhaps they never said so explicitly, but the implicit meaning of their texts is clear.

the temple priesthood. Increasingly disenchanted with the temple of Jerusalem, the school gradually came to regard it and its priests as wicked and corrupt. These prophets saw a glorious future for themselves which included a new temple erected and administered in consonance with their ideas.[42] A different sort of attack on the temple--not prophetic but halakhic--was mounted by Ezra and Nehemiah who did their best to weaken the power of the priesthood (on the grounds that it had intermarried and violated other norms) and to reorganize the temple cult (presumably on the grounds that the wicked priests did not know what they were doing). Nehemiah 10 may be the charter of a group of people who banded together to observe "correctly" the laws of the priestly and temple offerings. Nor would they marry outsiders--we almost have a sect.[43]

In the Maccabean period the temple's illegitimacy was revealed to all. It was profaned by a gentile monarch and by the wicked priests. True, it was regained by the Jews, but without a prophet to guide them and without miracles to authenticate their actions, who could be sure that the temple was really purified? Shortly after Jonathan illegitimately installed himself as the high priest, sectarianism emerged for the first time (Jewish Antiquities 13.171-73). What the Pharisees, Sadducees, and Essenes looked like in the second century B.C.E. we do not know, but by the first century C.E. the general outlines are clear. The Pharisees paid meticulous attention to the laws of purity and tithing, seeking to replicate the altar of the Lord at the family table. The Essenes (Qumran) rejected the Jerusalem temple and priesthood, and looked forward to the time when they would be able to observe the cult, the offerings, and the sacred calendar in the true temple erected by God (Temple Scroll). In the meanwhile the sect was the temple. The Samaritans, whatever their origin and history, also rejected the Jerusalem temple and priesthood and advocated in their stead the temple and priesthood of Gerizim. The early Christians believed that the temple was profane and that Jesus, as messiah, high priest, and/or atonement sacrifice, would replace in some way the current occupants of the temple mount. Other groups too (e.g. Zealots) presumably defined themselves vis-a-vis the temple and the priesthood. The temple--not the heavenly temple which would descend in the end of days but the earthly temple of Jerusalem--was the crucial focal point of sectarian self-definition before 70.

After 70: From Sects to Disputes

The world which produced Jewish sectarianism, nurtured it, and gave it meaning, disappeared in 70. In addition to removing the focal point of Jewish sectarianism, the destruction of the temple also facilitated the emergence of individuals as authority figures to replace the institutional authority previously exercised by the temple and the sects, and the emergence of the ideology of pluralism to replace the monism which previously characterized the temple and the sects. The net effect of these developments was the end of sectarianism and the creation of a society marked by legal disputes between individual teachers who nevertheless respected each other's right to disagree. This sketch is presented as an hypothesis, a conjectural reconstruction of an obscure period and an obscure process. A full study of each of these points is a desideratum; here is a brief discussion.

The Loss of the Focal Point
With the destruction of the temple the primary focal point of Jewish sectarianism disappeared. True, the Christians and the Samaritans continued to define themselves vis-a-vis the Jerusalem temple and the cult,[44] but this type of thinking was difficult to

---

[42]See esp. Isa 65 with P. D. Hanson, The Dawn of Apocalyptic (Philadelphia: Fortress, 1975; rev. ed. 1979).

[43]Smith, "Dead Sea Sect," who compares Neh 10 with the Manual of Discipline.

[44]Tractate Kutim (end) declares simply, "When do we take them (the Samaritans) back? When they acknowledge the temple in Jerusalem." Church fathers imagine that

maintain unless other foci were already in place; the Samaritans had Gerizim and the Christians had Christ. For most Jews, however, sectarian self-definition ceased to make sense after 70. The holiness of the Jerusalem temple, the legitimacy of its priesthood, and the propriety of its rituals were no longer relevant issues.[45] The Yavnean rabbis were much interested in the laws of the temple and the cult (Neusner even suggests that Mishnaic materials from the period of 70-132 "revolve around the altar")[46] and this is not surprising. They expected the temple to be rebuilt shortly (in "seventy years") and part of their sectarian legacy was interest in this legislation. But without a functioning temple and priesthood, whose legitimacy would be the subject of dispute, the study of temple law did not produce sects. A sect needs an evil reality against which to protest, rail, and define itself. The rabbis, however, were legislating for a messianic future. When they did define themselves they avoided putting priests in their lineage and ascribing to themselves a priestly ideology.[47] The temple was not a source of rabbinic self-definition, at least not in the Yavnean period.[48]

The Emergence of Individual Authority

Rabbinic tradition assigns few halakhot and few disputes to individual masters who lived before 70, whereas for post-70 figures the tradition is very rich. Similarly, neither the Temple Scroll nor the Manual of Discipline nor the Damascus Document nor any other Qumran scroll assigns halakhot to individuals, not even to the (unnamed!) Teacher of Righteousness. Pharisees debate Sadducees, Qumran Essenes attack the "speakers of smooth things," the House of Hillel feuds with the House of Shammai, but named individual masters are never mentioned in these discussions.[49] (The obvious exception to this pattern is Jesus who debates Pharisees, Sadducees, scribes, and elders. Is his exceptional status the point of "teaching with authority"[Mk 1:22//Mt 7:29]?)[50] Clearly

---

they have refuted Judaism when they have demonstrated the inadequacies of the sacrificial cult. See F. M. Young, "Temple Cult and Law in Early Christianity," NTS 19 (1973) 325-38 and H. W. Nibley, "Christian Envy of the Temple," JQR 50 (1959) 97-123 and 229-40 (somewhat speculative and inaccurate).

[45]The concern that without a temple atonement is impossible (ᵓAbot R. Nat. A 4 and B 8 [pp. 11a-b ed. Schechter]; Origen, Homily on Numbers 10.2) reflects the theology of the post-tannaitic period. See my "The Temple and the Synagogue," The Temple in Antiquity, ed. Truman Madsen (forthcoming).

[46] Evidence 120-21; see too Method and Meaning 133-53. Perhaps Neusner is right for the Mishnah, but this characterization is incorrect for tannaitic materials as a whole.

[47]Sects and feeling of "otherness": see the numerous works of Bryan Wilson, notably Patterns of Sectarianism. Messianic future: B. Z. Wacholder, Messianism and Mishnah (Cincinnati: Hebrew Union College, 1979). The avoidance of priests in ᵓAbot 1 has been discussed many times, most recently by M. D. Herr, Zion 44 (1979) 43-56 (Hebrew). The rabbinic use of priestly ideology needs study; cf. b. Ned. 62a.

[48]The nine taqqanot of R. Yohanan ben Zakkai (six of which are attested in the mishnah [R. H. 1:4 and 4:1], three in the talmud [b. R. H. 31b]) deal with the realities of living in a world without a temple and without a sanhedrin. They deal with very specific matters, not ideology and theology. I do not know of any evidence that the Yavneans viewed the synagogue as a temple, a view which is well attested by amoraic times. See my "The Temple and the Synagogue." The importance of the taqqanot is generally exaggerated.

[49]Not even in Acts 23:6-10; contrast Acts 5:34. Never: that is, hardly ever. Rabban Yohanan ben Zakkai appears as the spokesman of the Pharisees once (see above) although the language obscures the relationship. See n. 27 above. Several individuals are mentioned in connection with the disputes of the Houses but as far as I know never as spokesmen. The social mechanism which permitted this collective speaking is obscure.

[50]Contrast "but you (pl.) say" (Mt 15:5) with "but I say" (Mt 5:22, 28, 32, 34, 39, 44). We do not know whether Judas the Galilean and Saddoq the Pharisee, the founders of the Fourth philosophy, were considered prophets by their followers.

this phenomenon is a symptom of the crisis of religious authority which plagued second temple Judaism. The sanhedrin, priests, and scribes also spoke with collective voices. Seers of visions hid behind pseudonymity or anonymity.[51] But by defining themselves vis-a-vis the temple the sects had a special reason for their reliance on collective authority, for who but a prophet could confront the temple and the priesthood? Who but a prophet could pronounce the temple unclean and the cult unwelcome in the eyes of God? Prophecy, however, was dead. By whatever means the sects explained their origins, their fundamental claim to the antithesis/supplement/equivalent of the temple meant that the group derived its legitimacy from its status as a temple community. Hence it always spoke as a community. But after 70 there was no temple, no ultimate authority which only a community could match. The individual, although not a prophet, could now emerge, since he did not have to measure himself against the unapproachable precincts of the temple.[52]

From Monism to Pluralism

Rabbinic materials not only ascribe halakhot to named individuals, they also present individuals conflicting with each other and with "the sages." Some of these disputes, both tannaitic and amoraic, are the artificial creations of editors and redactors,[53] but most are real, the highly stylized summaries of real discussions and real arguments. But the thousands of disputes are rarely characterized by the animosity and tension which accompanied the disputes between the sects and between the Houses before 70. Rabbinic Judaism is dominated by pluralism, the ideology which allows the existence of conflicting truths. The truth is many, not one.[54]

As remarked above, the temple represents monism. "One temple for the one God." Only one holy site, one altar, one cult, and one priesthood can find favor in God's eyes. Sects defined themselves in reference to the temple and therefore arrogated the temple's exclusivistic claims. Only the sect is the true Israel and only the sect correctly fulfills God's wishes. Some of the sects admitted that the temple was still legitimate to one degree or another, but all the sects argued that every variety of Judaism other than its own is illegitimate. This is the monism of the temple transferred to the sect.[55] With the destruction of the temple in 70, the institutional basis of monism is removed.

---

[51]The anonymity of early halakhic authorities has been studied by many Jewish scholars of previous generations; see e.g. Z. Frankel, *Darkhe HaMishnah* (repr. Tel Aviv: Sinai, 1959) 5, 29, 44-45, and L. Finkelstein, "The Ethics of Anonymity among the Pharisees," *Conservative Judaism* 12,4 (1958) 1-12 (reprinted in his *Pharisaism in the Making* [New York: Ktav, 1972]). Hence the rabbinic failure to attribute many halakhot to named authorities before 70 should not be explained solely by rabbinic ignorance of the second temple period. I do not, however, endorse the view that anonymous mishnayot must be "old," i.e. of second temple origin.

[52]The dialectical tension between sectarianism as a group phenomenon and sectarianism as a vehicle for individual piety is evident at Qumran.

[53]Contrast the redactors of the Manual of Discipline and the Damascus Document who follow the biblical tradition. Without any indication of sources contradictory material is juxtaposed, thereby, presumably, homogenized.

[54]Second temple Judaism was pluralistic but had no ideology of pluralism. How the rabbis maintained their fraternal discord and to what extent halakhic dicta were merely theses for discussion and not legal decisions, are not always clear. See the statement of R. Yohanan to his daughters to follow the laws of Resh Laqish, p. Git. 7:6 (49a).

[55]The monism also derives from the prophetic critiques of society; see Hanson, *Dawn*.

Some of the rabbis were aware that their ideology of pluralism did not exist before 70. "At first there was no dispute (*mahloqet*) in Israel" (t. Hag. 2:9 and Sanh. 7:1). How did disputes begin? According to one view in the Tosefta, disputes were avoided by the adjudication of the great court which sat in the temple precincts and determined either by vote or by tradition the status of all doubtful matters. In this view, when the great court was destroyed in 70, disputes could no longer be resolved in an orderly way and *mahloqot* proliferated. According to another view, "once the disciples of Hillel and Shammai became numerous who did not serve (their masters) adequately, they multiplied disputes in Israel and became as two Torahs." In this view Jewish (i.e. rabbinic) unanimity was upset by the malfeasance of the disciples of Hillel and Shammai, a confession which would later be exploited by the Karaites. What happened to the disputes between the Houses? They ceased at Yavneh,[56] how we do not know. Amoraic tradition (p. Yeb. 1:6 [3b] and parallels) tells of a heavenly voice which declared at Yavneh, "Both these (House of Hillel) and these (House of Shammai) are the words of the living God, but the *halakha* always follows the House of Hillel." Pluralism replaces monism, individual authority replaces collective. As part of this irenic trend someone (at Yavneh?) even asserted that the disputes between the Houses did not prevent them from intermarrying or from respecting each other's purities (m. Yeb. 1:4 and ᶜEd. 4:8; t. Yeb. 1:10-12) but this wishful thinking cannot disguise the truth. The two Talmudim find it almost impossible to understand this statement and so reinterpret it as to make it almost meaningless. The Houses could not marry or sup with each other. They were virtually sects–*kitot* the Palestinian Talmud calls them (p. Hag. 2:2 [77d]).[57] At Yavneh sectarian exclusiveness was replaced by rabbinic pluralism. The creation of a Mishnah could now begin.[58]

Were there any whose words were not the words of the living God? In spite of the rabbinic hesitation, described above, to define the limits of acceptable doctrine and practice, two categories of people could not be incorporated into the Yavnean coalition: those who insisted upon a sectarian self-identification, and those who refused to heed the will of the majority. The former were not content with the name "Israel" but called themselves, or at least were distinctive enough to be called by others, "Pharisees," "Sadducees," "Christians," or whatever. All of these persistent sectarians were cursed in the *birkat ha minim*. This rabbinic ideology is reflected in Justin's discussion of the Jewish sects: there are Jews, i.e. the "orthodox," and there are sects, among them the Pharisees, who scarcely deserve the name Jew. How many such people existed before and after the institution of the *birkat ha minim* is not clear; in the light of our previous discussion, probably very few. They were denounced, not excommunicated. As a result of this effort to minimize sectarian self-identification, the rabbis themselves did not see themselves as Pharisees and showed little interest in their sectarian roots. The second category includes those sages who did not accept the will of the majority. Even an elastic society has limits. Aqavya ben Mehallalel was excommunicated because he "stood upon," i.e. insisted on the rectitude of his opinion in the face of the opposition of the majority.[59] According to amoraic narratives R. Eliezer was excommunicated because he

---

[56]Some of the House disputes are later scholarly constructs, as Neusner has shown, but these are not our concern. For an analysis of this problem from a fundamentalist perspective, see Guttmann, "The End of the Houses," *Studies* 184-200.

[57]Compare Neusner, *Traditions*, 2.192-93. Neusner assumes that the Houses are two branches of Pharisaism but I prefer to admit ignorance.

[58]On the beginnings of the mishnah at Yavneh, see t. ᶜEd. 1:1; on the citation of majority and minority views see m.ᶜEd. 1:4-5 with t. ᶜEd. 1:4. T. Sukk. 2:3 (Neusner, *Traditions*, 2. 156) gives a somewhat less glamorous view of the victory of the Hillelites. Even if the heavenly voice story is not tannaitic, the ideology is represents if inherent in the entire rabbinic enterprise.

[59]M. ᶜEd. 5:7; 5:6 is obscure. The incident probably took place at Yavneh; see E. E. Urbach, *The Sages* (Jerusalem: Magnes, 1971) 535 (Hebrew).

would not accept the legal ruling of the majority, invoking against it a heavenly voice and various miracles--a dangerous precedent (b. B. Mes. 59b; p. Moᶜed Qatan 3:1 [81c-d]). The other side of the coin is illustrated by another amoraic narrative which has R. Gamaliel deposed from the patriarchate because he sought to impose his will on the sages. Even the authority of the patriarch has limits when opposed by the majority (b. Ber. 27b-28a; p. Ber. 4:1 [7c-d]). Whatever the truth of these amoraic stories, they reflect the essential problem of the Yavnean period: the creation of a society which would tolerate, even foster, disputes and discussions but which could nonetheless maintain order. Those rabbis who could not play by the new rules were too great a danger to be punished with just a curse. They were expelled.[60]

Conclusion

"Pharisaic triumph" is not a useful description of the events at Yavneh. Perhaps many, if not most, of the sages there assembled were Pharisees or the descendants of Pharisees, but they made little of their ancestry. Their interest was the future, not the past. There is little evidence for "witch-hunting" in general and anti-Christian activity in particular.[61] Rather than view the sages as a party triumphant which closes the ranks, defines orthodoxy, and expels the unwanted, I suggest that we look at Yavneh as a grand coalition of different groups and parties,[62] held together by the belief that sectarian self-identification was a thing of the past and that individuals may disagree with each other in matters of law while remaining friends. Those who refused to join the coalition and insisted upon sectarian self-definition were branded *minim* and cursed. Those rabbis who could not learn the rules of pluralism and mutual tolerance were banned.

Josephus boasts of the unanimity of the Jewish people in its religion (*Against Apion* 2.179-81) and remarks that this unanimity provoked pagan admiration (2.283). Since this is the same author who tells us many times about the three (or four) Jewish sects, Josephus presumably means that all the Jewish "philosophies" agree on the fundamentals but dispute among themselves various details.[63] Unfortunately the sects themselves did not see things as Josephus did, and as long as the temple stood it was very hard to see things that way. Sects viewed themselves as surrogate temples and their leaders as surrogate priests. Like the archetype in Jerusalem, each sect claimed God for itself exclusively, denouncing all other temples and sects as illegitimate and profane. With the destruction of the temple these surrogate temples disappeared too. The Yavnean sages, the contemporaries of Josephus, realized that the Jewish "schools of thought" (*haireseis*) agreed with each other more than they differed. Aware of the deleterious consequences of internecine strife, the sages saw themselves as members of the same philosophical school who could debate in friendly fashion the tenets of the school.[64]

---

[60]The law of the rebellious elder, a (deliberate?) distortion of Deut 17:12, was discussed by Yavnean authorities (m. Sanh. 11:2-4 and t. Sanh. 11:7).

[61]In other words, there is little evidence for the activity most often ascribed to the Yavneans. See e.g. Davies, *Setting*, 272-86.

[62]Perhaps even some Sadducees joined; see n. 39 above. Neusner (*Early Rabbinic Judaism*, 64) once suggested that Yavneh was a coalition of five groups, but as far as I know he never developed that suggestion. Neusner has recently speculated that rabbinism is a combination of Pharisaism with scribism, a suggestion first made by the Nazarenes in the fourth century; see n. 70 below.

[63]Similarly, in the *Against Apion* 1.37-38 Josephus argues that, in contrast to the works of the Greeks, the books of the Jewish canon do not contradict each other. This statement is either an absolute endorsement of the power of midrash or an acknowledgement that the books of the Bible disagree in myriad details but agree on the fundamentals.

[64]On the rabbis as philosophers and Yavneh as a philosophical school, see S. J. D. Cohen, "Patriarchs and Scholarchs," *PAAJR* 48 (1981) 57-85 (with bibliography).

A year or two before the council of Nicea Constantine wrote to Alexander and Arius, the leaders of the contending parties, and asked them to realize that they were united by their shared beliefs more than they were separated by the *homoousion* controversy. Let them behave like members of a philosophical school who debate in civil fashion the doctrines of the school (Eusebius, *Life of Constantine* 2.71). The council of Nicea ignored the emperor's advice and expelled the Arians. The sages of Yavneh anticipated Constantine's suggestion. They created a society based on the doctrine that conflicting disputants may each be advancing the words of the living God.

Appendix:

Pharisees and Rabbis in the Church Fathers

I argued above that rabbinic self-identification with the Pharisees is only seldom attested in tannaitic literature, is somewhat more frequent in amoraic materials, but does not become secure and determinative until the early middle ages (when the rabbis were fighting the Karaites whom they regarded as latter-day Sadducees; see note 33). As far as I have been able to determine, patristic literature documents a similar development. The fathers of the second, third, and fourth centuries do not identify contemporary Judaism with Pharisaism. Tertullian, Cyprian, the Dialogue of Timothy and Aquila, and Aphrahat attempt to refute Judaism, but they either do not mention the Pharisees at all or mention them only in NT quotations. Even Origen, who lived in Palestine and knew a great deal about Judaism, does not refer to contemporary *didaskaloi* and *sophoi* as Pharisees.[65] Epiphanius, that learned purveyor of information and misinformation, explicitly declares (*Panarion* 19.5 and 20.3) that Pharisees no longer exist in his time (fourth century). He mentions that the scribes have four *deuteroseis* (traditions): those of Moses the prophet, Akibas (or Barakibas) their teacher, Andas (or Annas) who is also known as Judas, and the sons of Asamonaeus (*Panarion* 15 end). Whatever we make of this garbled passage, it is clear that Epiphanius connects rabbinic tradition not with the Pharisees but with the scribes.[66] John Chrysostom has eight orations *Against the Jews* but in none of them does he call contemporary Jews "Pharisees" or refer to their piety as "Pharisaic." All of this is somewhat surprising since the NT accords the Pharisees such a prominent role and provides so many anti-Pharisee polemics which would have been very useful to anti-Jewish writers. Obviously these fathers did not know of the connection between the Pharisees and the rabbis.[67] The only

---

[65]De Lange (*Origen* 34-35) cannot hide the fact that when Origen speaks of *didaskaloi* and *sophoi* he does not mention Pharisees, and when he speaks of Pharisees he does not mention *didaskaloi* and *sophoi*. De Lange cites three passages to prove that Origen applies Pharisees to "literalist, rabbinic Jews of his own day," but all three passages refer to NT times. The one passage in present tense (commentary on Jn 3:1, GCS 4. 510) also does not refer to contemporary times; it draws on Josephus (see de Lange 35 n. 75).

[66]The four *deuteroseis* also appear in PG 1.1456 (= J. Parkes, *The Conflict of the Church and the Synagogue* [1934; repr. New York: Atheneum, 1969] 399), a passage which almost certainly derives from Epiphanius. The study of Epiphanius' knowledge of Judaism remains a desideratum.

[67]The fathers generally do not describe contemporary Judaism since Judaism means the OT, especially the laws of the sacrificial cult (see n. 44 above) and *kashrut*. Is the identification implicit in the citation of NT passages about Pharisees? Later legends frequently refer to the Jewish leaders as Pharisees.

possible exceptions known to me are a brief passage in Irenaeus[68] and the ever elusive Justin.[69]

Sometime in the fourth century this begins to change. Jerome refers to contemporary rabbis as Pharisees and explicitly identifies the *deuteroseis* of Barachibas with the *traditiones* of the Pharisees. He quotes a Nazarene interpretation of Isa 8:14 which refers to the Houses of Hillel and Shammai "from whom the scribes and Pharisees originated, whose school was assumed by Akibas" and his successors. These Nazarenes, like Jerome himself, clearly associate the rabbis with the Pharisees (and the scribes).[70] Presumably they are deriving their information from Jewish sources. In any case, the patristic testimony concerning the Pharisees is remarkably parallel to the rabbinic: in the second century little or no connection is made between the rabbis and the Pharisees, but in the fourth the connection starts to become clear. A thorough study of the fathers is needed to confirm this observation.[71]

---

[68]Irenaeus 4.12.1, "For not only by actual transgression did they (the elders) set the law of God at nought . . . but they also set up their own law in opposition to it, which is termed, even to the present day, the pharisaical."

[69]In the *Dialogue* Justin refers dozens of times to the Jewish *didaskaloi* (Harnack, "Judentum," 55-57) and employs against them some of the NT polemic against Pharisees. For example, they wish to be called "Rabbi, Rabbi" (112.5) and they prefer human traditions to the dictates of God (38.2, 48.2, and 80.3). Contemporary *didaskaloi* fulfill the function once exercised by the Pharisees, but the two are not otherwise connected. The Jews are led by *didaskaloi,* not Pharisees. The Pharisees are a sect and do not even deserve the name Jew. The solitary reference to "Pharisaic teachers" (137.2) probably should be interpreted as follows, "Do not mock Jesus as the Pharisaic teachers once taught you and as the archisynagogues teach you now." See n. 11 above.

[70]Rabbis and Pharisees: de Lange, *Origen,* 35 (e.g. *Epistula* 127.4 [PL 22.1809 and CSEL 56.148]). *Deuteroseis: Epistula* 121.10 (PL 22.1033-34 and CSEL 56.48-49). Commentary on Isa 8:14: PL 24.119 and CChr 73.116; A. F. J. Klijn and G. J. Reinink, *Patristic Evidence for Jewish-Christian Sects* (NovTSup 36; Leiden: Brill, 1973) 220-21 and A. F. J. Klijn, "Jerome's Quotations from a Nazorean Interpretation of Isaiah," *Judéo-Christianisme: Recherches . . . offertes . . . à J. Danielou* (= *RSR* 60 [1972]) 241-55, esp. 249-51. I hope to return to this text elsewhere.

[71]Perhaps a check of patristic citations of NT passages about Pharisees might yield results. Such work is now facilitated by the *Biblia Patristica.*

KINGDOM AND CHILDREN
A STUDY IN THE APHORISTIC TRADITION

John Dominic Crossan
DePaul University, Chicago

The fairest order in the world is a heap of random sweepings.

Heraclitus (Kahn: 85)

An aphorism is a link from a chain of thoughts; it demands that the reader re-establish this chain from his own resources; this is to demand very much. An aphorism is a presumption.

Nietzsche (Mautner: 54)

To think aphoristically is the attempt to avoid the imperfection of perfection in thought.

Kasper (Margolius: 81)

Broken flesh, broken mind, broken speech. Truth, a broken body: fragments, or aphorisms; as opposed to systematic form or methods.

Brown (188)

I. APHORISM AND DIALECTIC

This first section will discuss a problem both terminological and theoretical which has been passed on from classical into contemporary analysis.

1. Classical Analysis

In Graeco-Roman education "the *Progymnasmata* were a group of elementary exercises for teaching composition, for writing and speaking. They led by a graded series of exercises from the less difficult to the more difficult, and culminated in speech-making. For this reason, the later stages were handled by the rhetor" (Spencer: 102-3). The student's first progression was, for example, through (1) Fable, (2) Story, (3) Chreia, and (4) Gnome. It is in the relationship between those last two units of speech or stages in education that a problem begins--for us.

We know about those literary genres and pedagogical steps from the written exercise books of grammarians such as Aelius Theon of Alexandria in the early second century A.D. (Spengel: 2.57-130), Hermogenes of Tarsus in the later second century (2.1-18), and Aphthonius of Antioch in the late fourth or early fifth century (2.19-56). These teachers agree very closely on the definition and division of the chreia, as may be seen in the texts given and translated by Taylor and Nicklin (Taylor: 75-90). First, "such sayings are called χρεῖαι (from ἡ χρεία --'need') probably because they were maxims which were taught to school children to impress their memories with views, ideas, and statements which would be serviceable for the various 'needs' they would experience in later walks of life" (Spencer: 90). But it is also likely that they were "useful" or "needed" in philosophical propaganda before being taken over for pedagogical instruction (Spencer: 158-60). Second, for definition, there is the third century Oxyrhynchus papyrus fragment (Anonymous: #85, pp. 157-58; Taylor: 82):

What is the Chreia? It is an Apomnemoneuma (i.e. memorandum) which is succinct, with reference to some person, told to his credit.
Why is the Chreia an Apomnemoneuma? Because it is kept in mind in order that it may be quoted.

Why is it 'succinct'? Because, in many cases, if told at length it becomes either a narrative or something else.

Why is it 'told of some person'? Because, in many cases, without a personal reference, a succinct Apomnemoneuma becomes either a Gnome or something else.

Why is it called a Chreia? Because of its serviceability.

Third, the standard division of the chreia depends on whether the response is (1) a saying, (2) an action, or (3) both saying and action (Taylor: 83; Spencer: 109-13).

The problem surfaces clearly in those distinctions and in the examples given for the first category, the purely verbal chreia (Spencer: 110): "Diogenes the philosopher, having been asked by someone how he might become of high regard, answered, 'By giving least thought to how he might become esteemed' " (Theon), or "Plato said that the Muses dwell in the souls of the fit" (Hermogenes), or "Plato's saying that seedlings of virtue burst forth through sweat and toil" (Aphthonius).

The term chreia covers aphorisms, dialogues, actions, or stories *as long as the climactic saying is attributed to some historical personage.* For example, the essential difference between chreia and gnome is that the former is so attributed but the latter is not. Put crudely but accurately: "A stitch in time saves nine" is a gnome, but "Diogenes said: 'A stitch in time saves nine' " is a chreia.

This is a very important point. It is not at all that the Graeco-Roman grammarians were confused in their categories and divisions. It is that their essential distinction was between: (1) attribution to a known and named historical person, or (2) "attribution" to an anonymous source in ancient and ancestral wisdom. "The attitude of the times was the reverse of ours. We view a maxim as if it had an existence and authority of its own, apart from its author. If we approve of it, we may be interested to find who was its author, and willing to value him for its sake. But, to them, the maxim, however impressive, had to come from an accredited person to carry the greatest weight. In short, the maxim was required to be a dictum" (Taylor: 79-80). And again, "the Chreia was, to the Hellenic mind, a fundamental form. We have to recollect, however, that it was not merely a literary form, but essentially a historical statement-- So-and-So, who was a known, historical figure, actually said or did this" (87).

This concern with historical (or, for us, possibly pseudohistorical) attribution shows up not only in the way the Graeco-Roman grammarians distinguished between chreia and gnome, but also in the first and last of the eight headings under which the poor student had to treat the given chreia. Take, for example, the text of Aphthonius (Spengel: 2.23-25) in the translation by Nadeau (266-67). The verbal chreia is: "Isocrates said that the root of learning is bitter, but sweet are its fruits." The first exercise is the "Panegyric" ('Εγκωμιαστικόν) and it begins, "It is fitting that Isocrates should be admired for his art," etc. etc. The last exercise is the "Epilogue" ('Επίλογος) and it begins, "In regard to these things, there is reason for those looking back to Isocrates to marvel at him," etc. etc. In other words, the first step was a eulogy of the historical speaker and the final step reverted to that worthy in conclusion (Spencer: 104-5).

The position of Marcus Fabius Quintilianus (ca. 35-100 A.D.), Spain's gift to Roman rhetoric, is more complicated than that of the later grammarians. It is especially important to consider together the two sections in his *Institutio Oratoria* where the subject appears, that is, in 1.9.3-5 and 8.5.1-35 (Butler: 1.156-59 & 3.280-301).

The *Institutio Oratoria* 1.9.3-5 distinguishes quite clearly between three types of pedagogical exercises "in certain rudiments of oratory for the benefit of those who are not yet ripe for the schools of rhetoric," and these are the writing of *"aphorisms* [*sententiae*] *, moral essays (chriae),* and *delineations of character (ethologiae)* . . . In all of these exercises the general idea is the same, but the form differs: *aphorisms* are general propositions, while *ethologiae* are concerned with persons [*quia sententia universalis est vox, ethologia personis continetur*]" (Butler: 1.156-59). Colson finds it curious that Quintilian should have said "concerned with persons" of the *ethologia* but not of the *chria,* and he suggests that the text be amended accordingly (151 note 2). But I think that this is a misreading of Quintilian's text. I do not think that his distinction between "*vox universalis*" and "*personis continetur*" refers to attribution and source but to application and use. Quintilian presumes that both *sententia* and *ethologia* stem from known and named persons but that they are distinguished in that the former applies to a wide variety of situations while the latter applies to some particular, individual, or personal situation. Having made that basic distinction between his first and third type (1.9.3), he proceeds immediately to focus on the second type, the *chria,* in detail (1.9.4-5). And this type is somewhat in between the "*vox universalis*" and "*personis continetur*" distinction since the chria contains examples of both those other types, but once again, the distinction is not in source but in use, not in attribution but in application. For example, it is quite clear that all the formal openings by which Quintilian distinguishes the chria, such as "he said" or "in answer to this he replied," presume in the concrete a named personage. Thus he can say that, "of *moral essays (chriarum)* there are various forms: some are akin to *aphorisms (sententiae)* and commence with a simple statement 'he said' or 'he used to say' " (1.9.4). I consider that this interpretation is confirmed by the way the phrase "*vox universalis*" is used again in the later discussion of 8.5.4 (Butler: 3.282-83).

In the *Institutio Oratoria* 8.5.1-35 the terminology, but not the theory, shifts a little. Now the overarching term is *sententia* and it is used for "striking reflexions such as are more especially introduced at the close of our periods, a practice rare in earlier days, but carried even to excess in our own" (8.5.2). Quintilian breaks the *sententia* into two main species. (1) "Although all the different forms are included under the same name, the oldest type of *sententia,* and that in which the term is most correctly applied, is the aphorism, called γνώμη by the Greeks. Both the Greek and the Latin names are derived from the fact that such utterances resemble the decrees or resolutions of public bodies. The term, however, is of wide application [*est autem haec vox universalis*] (indeed, such reflexions may be deserving of praise even when they have no reference to any special context), and is used in various ways" (8.5.3). Quintilian's "*vox universalis*" is here, once again, the universality of application and not the anonymity of attribution. this is also evident in the examples which follow. Sometimes Quintilian cites the author by name, for example, Domitius Afer, Ovid, Cicero, but even when he does not do so explicitly, the examples are not proverbs but quotations and, once again, a named author-ity is behind them (see 8.5.4-7; note footnotes in Butler: 3.282-84). Finally, it is very evident in his concluding remark: "Such reflexions are best suited to those speakers whose authority is such that their character itself will lend weight to their words. For who would tolerate a boy, or a youth, or even a man of low birth who presumed to speak with all the authority of a judge and to thrust his precepts down our throats" (8.5.8). (2) The other major type of *sententia* is declared to be "more modern," and the examples cited are instances of the chria, but there is no specific title used for them. Once again, of course, we are dealing with known and named persons.

I conclude that, for Quintilian, the *sententia,* whether distinguished from the *chria* as species from species (1.9.3) or genus from species (8.5), is always presumed to have behind it a known, named, and preferably authoritative source, just as does the *chria* itself. In this he agrees substantially with the later grammarians although they spell out more explicitly what he seems to presume implicitly, namely, historical attribution. But while they clearly distinguish the gnome, as being an anonymous saying of universal application (a proverb), Quintilian considers it an authored saying but of universal application (an aphorism).

What we are seeing here, for grammarians and rhetoricians alike, is the "renewed interest in exemplary figures in Hellenistic philosophy since the first century B.C." (Georgi: 534). Thus attribution (even if for us, pseudoattribution) or anonymity was a crucial distinction, overriding here such other distinctions as aphorism, dialogue, action, or story. But this also bequeathes us with a problem since it does not distinguish where we may want to do so, that is, its fundamental categories may not coincide with our own needed ones. And, worse still, we might not even notice that fact.

2. Contemporary Analysis

The problem has resurfaced in contemporary discussion. Since classical times the genre in question has been termed both ἀπόφθεγμα and χρεία (Latin: *chria*) and, although "apophthegms do not have the breadth of applicability which makes the chreiai useful for so many situations in life" (Spencer: 163), they may be taken for here and now as synonymous. The difficulty may be seen in Bultmann's magisterial work on the Synoptic tradition. His first two major sections were entitled "The Tradition of the Sayings of Jesus" (11-205) and "The Tradition of the Narrative Material" (209-317), that is, *sayings* and *stories*. He then commented on that division as follows (11):

> It also seems to me a secondary matter whether one begins with sayings or stories. I start with sayings. But I should reckon as part of the tradition of the sayings a species of traditional material which might well be reckoned as stories — viz. such units as consist of sayings of Jesus set in a brief context. I use a term to describe them which comes from Greek literature, and is least question-begging — 'apophthegms'. The subsequent course of this present inquiry will justify my taking the apophthegms before the sayings of Jesus that are not placed in a particular framework. The chief reason is that many apophthegms can be reduced to bare dominical sayings by determining the secondary character of their frame, and can thus be compared, in the following part of the book, with other sayings of Jesus.

There is an unfortunate ambiguity in that phrase "secondary character of their frame." A frame may be secondary in that it came later than the saying it holds. In that case the saying existed separately and independently of the frame. Or, a frame may be secondary in that it is less important than the saying it holds. But in that case the saying may never have existed separately or independently from the frame.

Bultmann then divided his "Sayings" section into "Apophthegms" (11-69) and "Dominical Sayings" (69-205). The former category includes (a) conflict, (b) scholastic, and (c) biographical apophthegms, and the initial ambiguity remains present throughout the analysis. On the one hand, he proposes a clear distinction between "unitary" and "non-unitary" apophthegms: "We must always raise the question whether we are dealing with a unitary composition, or whether the scene is a secondary construction for a saying originally in independent circulation. If the saying is comprehensible only in terms of its contextual situation, then it clearly has been conceived together with it" (47). On the other hand, he repeatedly asserts: "in general the sayings have produced a situation, not the reverse" (21), or "the sayings have commonly generated the situation, not vice-versa" (47), or "the situation has frequently been composed out of the dominical saying" (61). *But surely the unitary apophthegms would have situation and saying quite simultaneous so that dialectic rather than sequence is the heart of the composition.* And Bultmann's ambiguity has been continued and sometimes even increased in later works.

In his 1971 dissertation and 1979 book Hultgren divides the Synoptic conflict stories, like Bultmann, into unitary and non-unitary ones (1971:132-78, 179-274; 1979:67-99, 100-48). But many of his non-unitary ones involve what are actually aphoristic conclusions, that is, isolated sayings appended to a unitary story, for example, "Plucking Grain on the Sabbath" in Mark 2:23-28 (1971:271-24; 1979:111-15). Yet such aphoristic additions or conclusions are a quite separate question from the basic distinction between unitary and non-unitary apophthegms, as Bultmann already reminded us: "we must of course keep this question of the unity of the conception quite distinct from that of a secondary expansion by the addition of other sayings" (47 note 1). This simply compounds the confusion and underlines once more the inadequacy of the terminology.

The ambiguity inherited from Bultmann's inaugural analysis still haunts some very recent and very sophisticated studies rightly seeking a more adequate typology of apophthegms or pronouncements stories. There are three functional typologies to be considered: (1) by Aune (64-67) on the wisdom stories in the "Dinner of the Seven Wise Men" from *Plutarch's Moralia* (Babbitt: 2.348-449); (2) by Tannehill (1-13, 101-19) on the pronouncement stories of the Jesus tradition; and (3) by Robbins (1981b:29-52), who combines those twin typologies into a more developed third possibility, and tests it on *Plutarch's Lives* (Perrin, 1914-26). Since Robbins has thus connected Aune and Tannehill, the three analyses may be compared synoptically as in *Figure 1*. I would insist, of course, that each author's categories are to be compared and not just equated with similar ones in another.

Figure 1.

AUNE		ROBBINS			TANNEHILL
Wisdom Saying					
Wisdom Story	Gnomic	Aphoristic	Description		Description
			Inquiry		Inquiry/Test
	Agonistic	Antagonistic	Correction	Self	Correction
				Direct	
				Indirect	
			Dissent	Objection	Objection
				Rebuff	
		Affirmative	Commendation	Self	Commendation
				Direct	
				Indirect	
			Laudation		
	Paradigmatic				

My present concern is not with the basic validity of those excellent analyses but with one single problem which is not really discussed in either Tannehill or Robbins. I emphasize this point because Robbins' term "aphoristic story" is not the same as my own expression "aphoristic story." For Robbins "aphoristic stories" are one of the three sub-types of "pronouncement stories," one where the "interaction . . . is friendly or neutral, because confrontation with ideas rather than people governs the dynamics. The primary character's interaction with the idea addressed in the final utterance takes precedence over his interaction with people either within the setting or outside of it" (Robbins, 1981b:32). His term does not concern itself with the specific problem of an aphoristic saying being later developed into an aphoristic dialogue or aphoristic story. But in Robbins' analysis the problem is latent in his combination of "interaction" and "aphoristic."

Aune, however, has specifically surfaced the problem in discussing "The Dinner of the Seven Wise Men" by noting that "Plutarch has apparently elaborated the single structural element in the wisdom saying into the two-part structure characteristic of wisdom stories" (64). Among his examples (96-97) is a series of wisdom sayings (my aphoristic sayings) from Thales in Diogenes Laertius' *Lives of Eminent Philosophers* I.35 (Hicks: 1.36-37) which Plutarch converts into wisdom stories (my aphoristic dialogues). There are six sayings of which Plutarch uses five in his set of nine dialogues, as he cites Thales in "The Dinner of the Seven Wise Men," *Plutarch's Moralia* 153CD (Babbitt: 2.388-89). A single example will suffice here:

Thales, in Diogenes Laertius	Thales, in Plutarch
Of all things that are, the most ancient is God, for he is un-created	What is the oldest thing? God, said Thales, for God is something that has no beginning

In Aune's terms: wisdom sayings have become wisdom stories. In my terms: aphoristic sayings have become aphoristic dialogues.

3. Basic Distinctions

I propose, therefore, two essential distinctions. The first is by far the more important. This is between (a) the aphoristic tradition and (b) the dialectical tradition. The *aphoristic tradition* includes not only aphoristic sayings but also those cases where such units are developed into either aphoristic dialogues or aphoristic stories. These are usually "set-up" phenomena so that there will be no interaction, dynamics, or dialectics between situation and/or address and the climactic saying. It will destroy the validity of any typology based on "interaction" to include such units among the data. The *dialectical tradition* includes all those cases where a dialectic exists between, on the one hand, the *situation and/or the address,* and, on the other, the *action and/or the response.* In this tradition, even if the second part has meaning by itself, it takes on its full import only in interaction or dialectic with the first part. And in many cases the second part is vacuous or meaningless when taken by itself or as an independent aphorism. I would insist on the validity of this distinction for those working with the Jesus tradition or for any analysis which includes it. How important it is elsewhere is another question but, at least, Aune has shown it operative in one essay of Plutarch.

The second essential distinction is between (a) *dialogue* and (b) *story*. I am quite aware that either can develop into the other and that dialogue often points outside itself to story just as story often contains dialogue within it. But granted all that, I think the distinction is again important, at least for the Jesus tradition, and especially for understanding the fateful trajectories chosen differently by the gnostic and catholic destinies within it. Think, for example, of the absolutely artificial way in which the letter *Eugnostos the Blessed* (CG III, 3, & V, 1) is turned into the dialogue *The Sophia of Jesus Christ* (CG III, 4, & BG 8502, 3) by inserted questions from Matthew, Philip, Thomas, Mariamne, Bartolomew, or the disciples in general (Robinson, 1977: 206-28; Robinson-Koester: 84, 90; Koester, 1979: 536-37). Thus even when independent sayings are "set up" in artificially appended dialogues or stories *something happens.* First, one had to decide whether to choose dialogue alone or story, with or without dialogue. Second, if one chose dialogue, it was asserted thereby that questions were possible and acceptable and that answers were possible and expectable. Third, if one chose story, one tied Jesus to the earth and its pathways.

My proposed terms are, then, *aphoristic dialogues* and *aphoristic stories,* or *dialectical dialogues* and *dialectical stories.*

II. APHORISM AND KINGDOM

This second section will test the viability of those distinctions on a single but paradigmatic example, the aphorism concerning *Kingdom and Children.*

There are four independent versions to be considered: (1) Mark 10:14=Matt 19:14=Luke 18:16, and Mark 10:15=Luke 18:17; (2) Matt 18:3; (3) John 3:3, 5; *Gos. Thom.* 22.

1. Mark 10:13-16

> And they were bringing children to him, that he might touch them; and the disciples rebuked them. But when Jesus saw it he was indignant, and said to them, 'Let the children come to me, do not hinder them; for to such belongs the kingdom of God. Truly, I say to you, whoever does not receive the kingdom of God like a child shall not enter it.' And he took them in his arms and blessed them, laying his hands on them.

The text will be discussed in terms of both the general context and immediate content.

(1) Mark 8:27-10:45. Like Mark 4:1-8:26 before it (Petersen), 8:27-10:45 has a core structure which is repetitive and internally and externally triadic (Perrin, 1974: 155; Robbins, 1981a: 102-5):

(a)	Passion-Resurrection:	8:27-30	9:30-32	10:32-34
(b)	Apostolic Blindness:	8:31-33	9:33-34	10:35-41
(c)	Corrective Teaching:	8:34-9:1	9:35-50	10:42-45

(2) Mark 9:36-10:16. Within that middle section of the triad there is evidence of another large compositional unity wherein two sections concerning the child frame one concerning divorce: A (9:36-39 within 9:33-50), B (10:1-12), A' (10:13-16). The thematic importance of this juxtaposition has been explained by Kelber: "The marriage relationship is singled out as the one exception to the eschatological experience of separation and divorce. By the same token neither wife nor husband are included among the goods to be renounced (10:29) . . . While the ties to the past are severed, the link to the future is strengthened" (1974:91; note that the "children" to be abandoned in Mark 10:29 are τέκνα not παιδία). The twin framing units concerning children are carefully paralleled by a chiastic balance of positive ("whoever receives . . . child") and negative ("whoever does not receive . . . child") sayings. This is detailed in *Figure 2*, with both thematic and verbal links indicated. In that figure the balanced Greek phrases indicate the deliberate nature of the parallelism: (a) the central units in C are structured identically and the elements of reproach from Jesus to the disciples concerning their attitude to outsiders serve to continue and intensify Mark's criticism of Jesus' disciples (see Kelber, 1974:87-92); (b) the units in 9:36-37 and 10:15-16 are positioned chiastically to frame these central units, and once again, the key words are duplicated in Greek.

Figure 2.

Structural Elements		Mark 9:36-39	Mark 10:13-16
A	Action by Jesus on Child	9:36 "taking him in his arms" (ἐναγκαλισά- μενος αὐτό)	
B	Aphorism by Jesus about Child(ren)	9:37 "whoever receives ... child"(ὃς ἂν ... παιδίων δέξ- ηται)	
C	a Action by Outsiders	9:38a	10:13a
	b Reproach by Disciples	9:38b	10:13b
	b' Counter-Reproach by Jesus to Disciples	9:39a "do not forbid" (μὴ κωλύετε)	10:14a "do not hinder" (μὴ κωλύετε)
	a' Aphorism by Jesus on Action by Outsiders	9:39b	10:14b
B'	Aphorism by Jesus about Child		10:15 "whoever does not receive ... child" (ὃς ἂν μὴ δέξηται ... παιδίον)
A'	Action by Jesus on Children		10:16 "took them in his arms" (ἐναγκαλισά- μενος αὐτά)

At this point, however, it becomes quite evident whence the theme of "receiving" the Kingdom was derived in 10:15. It is not in any way pre-Markan but it represents Mark's rephrasing of his pre-Markan 10:15 *in order to underline the verbal and thematic parallel with 9:37* (B/B'). Hence any consideration of Mark 10:15 must imagine a pre-Markan version which contained nothing about "receiving" the Kingdom as a child (against Schilling).

(3) Mark 10:13-16. Bultmann had already suggested "treating v. 15 as an originally independent dominical saying, inserted into the situation of vv. 13-16" (32). But he also held that "the point of v. 14 is quite different from that of v. 15: v. 14 simply states that children have a share in the Kingdom of God" (32). I accept that former point but do not agree at all with the second one.

(a) Mark 10:15. I agree that this is an independent *aphoristic saying*. This will be confirmed by later considerations of both Matt 18:3 and John 3:3, 5. In these three independent texts there is an aphorism with similar construction: (i) solemn opening, "Truly, I say to you," with the usual doubling of the "Truly" in John; (ii) protasis formulated negatively: ἐὰν μή in Matthew and John, ὃς ἂν μή in Mark; and (iii) apodosis, also formulated negatively: οὐ μή in Mark and Matthew, οὐ δύναται in John; and (iv) the same verb, "enter," in Mark 10:15; Matt 18:3; and John 3:5.

(b) Mark 10:13, 14, 16. Bultmann said that "vv. 13-16 are a complete apophthegm without v. 15" (32) and he located Mark 10:13, 14, 16 among the biographical apophthegms (see also Spencer: 351-56). Tannehill locates 10:13-16 among those "hybrid pronouncement stories which combine . . . correction and commendation" (103). In my terminology Mark 10:13, 14, 16 is a *dialectical story*. The saying of Jesus is: "Let the children come to me, do not hinder them; for to such belongs the kingdom of God." This saying *could* make sense by itself as its frequent citation withing the Christian tradition has proved. But the emphatic and double opening with its positive ("let") and negative ("do not") imperative bespeaks at least an implicit dialectic with some previous position. It is not, therefore, an *aphoristic story* but rather a *dialectical story*.

It is possible, but not much more, to argue that there was a pre-Markan *aphoristic story* present in 10:13a+14b and that Mark, by introducing the conflict between the disciples and Jesus in 13b+14a, has himself turned this into a *dialectical story*. One might even point to the "Jesus saw" in Mark 10:14 (not accepted by either Matt 19:14 or Luke 18:16) and the "Jesus saw" in *Gos. Thom.* 22a as evidence for such a pre-Markan *aphoristic story* in 10:13a+14b.

I think, however, that a more radical solution is called for. It was Mark himself who created the entire *dialectical story* in 10:13, 14, 16 and imbedded the pre-Markan but redactionally rephrased 10:15 within it. This suggestion is supported by three considerations. (1) Structures. I have already drawn attention to how Mark built 10:13-16 in verbal parallel with the two incidents in Mark 9:36-37 and 9:38-39 (see *Figure 2*). (2) Expressions. The Markan penchant for dualism and especially for a positive followed by a negative appears in 10:14 (Neirynck: 84 and 92, see also 99, 115, 122). (3) Words. Pryke places all of 10:13 and 16 in "the redactional text of Mark" (165, see also 18, 24, 105, 107, 108, 109, and on γάρ see 128 despite 126, 133-34).

2. Matt 18:1-4

At that time the disciples came to Jesus, saying, "Who is the greatest in the kingdom of heaven?" And calling to him a child, he put him in the midst of them, and said, "Truly, I say to you, unless you turn and become like children, you will never enter the kingdom of heaven. Whoever humbles himself like this child, he is the greatest in the kingdom of heaven."

This unit will also be discussed in terms of both context and content.

(1) Matt 18:1-5. The parallels between Matt 18:1-5 and Mark are as follows:

Matt 18:1	=	Mark 9:33-34
Matt 23:11	=	Mark 9:35
Matt 18:2	=	Mark 9:36
Matt 18:3	=	Mark 10:15
Matt 18:4	=	---
Matt 18:5	=	Mark 9:37a

This means that Matthew removed Mark 10:15 from its sequence in Mark 10:13-16=Matt 19:13-15=Luke 18:15-17 and inserted it into his own smoother reformulation of Mark 9:33-37. He has thus united the two child aphorisms of Mark 9:36-37; 10:15, that is, he has noted but rewritten *Figure 2* above.

(2) Matt 18:3. That preceding description raises the question whether Matt 18:3 is just his version of Mark 10:15 or might be an independent version. On the one hand, Bultmann states emphatically that "Matt. 18:3 . . . is clearly not an independent tradition, but is the Matthean form of Mk. 10:15 in another context" (32). On the other, Lindars has argued persuasively that, "even on the assumption of Markan priority, the version of the saying in Mt. 18.3 must be regarded as equally likely to represent the original as the version in Mk. 10.15" (288). He cites four reasons for his conclusion: (a) the better balance of verb and adverbial clause in both protasis and apodosis of Matt 18:3 over Mark 10:15; (b) the verb "enter" of Matt 18:3 is less redactionally and contextually derivative than the "receive" of Mark 10:15 (ex Mark 9:37); (c) Matt 18:3 uses the plural "like children" despite the fact that Mark 10:15 has a singular and that such a singular fits far better than a plural with the other singulars in Matt 18:2, 4, 5. The plural is presumably pre-Matthean; (d) Jeremias noted that "in the Septuagint we have a whole series of double expressions which paraphrase 'again' and are analogous in structure to the στραφῆτε καὶ γήνησθε ὡς τὰ παιδία' (1971:155), that is, "turn and become" means "become again." This Semitism is a final and most important indication that Matt 18:3 is independent of and even more original than the version in Mark 10:15.

Matt 18:3 is thus another version of the *aphoristic saying* found in another context in Mark 10:15.

(3) Matt 18:4. In the table of parallels between Matt 18:1-5 and Mark which was given above, there was no Markan parallel to Matt 18:4. It is clear that 18:1 and 18:4 serve as frames for the materials in between since they both conclude with "the greatest in the kingdom of heaven." But Matt 18:4 does much more than close the complex in 18:1-4. In and by itself it almost reads like an independent aphorism. It is what I term an *aphoristic commentary*, that is, a unit which looks like an aphorism but which is appended to a preceding independent aphorism in order to comment on it. It deserves the title *aphoristic commentary* because it is formally modelled on the aphorism itself. This distinguishes it from the more obvious *commentary on an aphorism*. But it also makes it much more difficult to distinguish it from *aphoristic compounds* (two aphorisms together) or even *aphoristic clusters* (more than two aphorisms together).

By the appendage of Matt 18:4 to 18:3 Matthew tells us how he interprets the *Kingdom and Children* saying: to become like a child is to become humble like a child.

3. John 3:1-10

Now there was a man of the Pharisees, named Nicodemus, a ruler of the Jews. This man came to Jesus by night and said to him, "Rabbi, we know that you are a teacher come from God; for no one can do these signs that you do, unless God is with him." Jesus answered him, "TRULY, TRULY, I SAY TO YOU, UNLESS ONE IS BORN ANEW, HE CANNOT SEE THE KINGDOM OF GOD." Nicodemus said to him, "How can a man be born when he is old? Can he enter a second time into his mother's womb and be born?" Jesus answered, "TRULY, TRULY, I SAY TO YOU,

UNLESS ONE IS BORN OF WATER AND THE SPIRIT, HE CANNOT ENTER THE KINGDOM OF GOD. That which is born of the flesh is flesh, and that which is born of the Spirit is spirit. Do not marvel that I said to you, 'YOU MUST BE BORN ANEW.' The wind blows where it wills, and you hear the sound of it, but you do not know whence it comes or whither it goes; so it is with every one who is born of the Spirit." Nicodemus said to him, "How can this be?" Jesus answered him, "Are you a teacher of Israel, and yet you do not understand this?"

My working hypothesis concerning Johannine and Synoptic relationships involves *both* (1) the presence of Synoptically independent traditions concerning Jesus' words and deeds in John, *and also* (2) the influence of the Synoptics on the final construction of the Johannine Gospel itself (see Smith: 443).

(1) John 3:3, 5. The independence proposed for Matt 18:3 is confirmed by a consideration of John 3:3, 5 which, despite Johannine reformulation and baptismal adaptation, is another witness to the independent version underlying Matt 18:3 (Dodd: 358-59; Brown: 1.143-44).

With regard to content, Lindars has proposed that (a) John 3:5a ("of water and the Spirit") is his own reformulation of 3:3a ("anew"), and 3:3b ("See") is his own reformulation of 3:5b ("enter"): hence, "anew" (ἄνωθεν) and "enter" are prejohannine; that (b) "John's ἄνωθεν can bear the meaning 'again,' and so represents a more idiomatic translation of the Aramaic phrase which appears in Matthew's version as στραφῆτε καί" (290); that (c) John's term "born" (γεννηθῇ) is linguistically close to Matt 18:3's "become" (γένησθε), although, of course, they are not the same root; and that (d) in adapting his source and dropping any mention of children, "John intended the meaning 'from above' in verse 3, contrary to the required meaning [anew, again] of the underlying source" (292).

(2) John 3:1-10. What John has done with the aphorism is quite fascinating. (a) John 3:2b-10 is a dialogue between Nicodemus and Jesus in three exchanges: 2b/3, 4/5-8, and 9/10. (b) It is structured so that Nicodemus gets one assertion (2b) and two questions (4, 9) while Jesus gets two assertions (3, 5-8) and one question (10). And (c) the unit is framed by the ironic contrast between the "teacher" in 3:3 and 3:10.

But the most interesting feature is the way that the *aphoristic saying* has been tripled to form the armature of the dialogue in 3:3, 5, 7. In this case *aphoristic saying* has been developed into *aphoristic dialogue* with three exchanges. But each time the aphorism is cited it is varied a little. In 3:3 the apodosis has the Johannine term "see" rather than the traditional "enter" (Brown: 1.501-3). In 3:5 the protasis has the new expression which is of paramount importance for 3:5-8, "of water and the Spirit." And in 3:7 there is only an abbreviated version of the protasis as in 3:3.

After the twin citations of the aphorism in 3:5 and 7 John adds, as had Matt 18:4 after 18:3, what I term *aphoristic commentary*. Thus in 3:6 and 8 appear sentences which read like aphorisms, sentences which could be imagined as independent sayings in their own right but which are actually commentary on the preceding aphorisms. They are given, however, in a format which copies that of the basic aphorism which they interpret.

Finally, one could say that the aphorism concerning *Kingdom and Children*, having become a triple dialogue in 3:2b-10, is located as an *aphoristic story* within the overall narrative of John's gospel by 3:1-2a.

This is a small but significant confirmation of the first working hypothesis proposed by Koester concerning the development of Johannine dialogues and monologues from traditional sayings of Jesus (1979:553). And what comes next, from *Gos. Thom.* 22, seems an equal confirmation of his second proposed working hypothesis. This postulates the necessity of establishing not only material but especially formal trajectories for the transmission of canonically independent Jesus sayings from, for example, (1) Papyrus Egerton 2 (Bell & Skeat; see Mayeda), (2) through such Nag Hammadi texts as the *Gospel of Thomas*, the *Dialogue of the Savior* (see Pagels & Koester), and the *Apocryphon of*

James, on into (3) the dialogues and monologues of John's gospel (Koester, 1979: 553-54; also 1980a:119-26; 1980b:250-56).

4. *Gos. Thom.* 22.

> Jesus saw infants being suckled. He said to His disciples, "These infants being suckled are like those who enter the Kingdom." They said to Him, "Shall we then, as children, enter the Kingdom." Jesus said to them, "When you make the two one, and when you make the inside like the outside, and the outside like the inside, and the above like the below, and when you make the male and the female one and the same, so that the male not be male nor the female female; and when you fashion eyes in place of an eye, and a hand in place of a hand, and a foot in place of a foot, and a likeness in place of a likeness; then will you enter [the Kingdom] ."

(1) *Gos. Thom.* 22b. Robinson has shown most persuasively how the original *Kingdom and Children* aphorism has moved along two hermeneutical trajectories. One is the "orthodox" baptismal interpretation represented by John 3:1-10 and developed in later patristic texts (1962:106-7). The other is the "unorthodox" and gnostic interpretation represented here by *Gos. Thom.* 22b: "When one considers that repudiation of sex was a condition to admission to some Gnostic groups, somewhat as baptism was a condition of admission into the church at large, it is not too difficult to see how a logion whose original *Sitz im Leben* was baptism could be taken over and remolded in the analogous *Sitz im Leben* of admission to the sect" (1962:108). Thus Jesus' reply in *Gos. Thom.* 22b involves a fourfold "when you make," each of which contains the obliteration of bodily differences, and each of which is known by itself or in various combinations from other gnostic sources (save the fourth). Thus, "when you make the two one" reappears in *Gos. Thom.* 106, and combined as "when the two become one and the male with the female (is) neither male nor female" in the *Gospel of the Egyptians* (Hennecke-Schneemelcher: 1.168). These, and Robinson's more detailed examples (1962:108, 281-84), show that the setting and saying in *Gos. Thom.* 22a have been redactionally expanded in typically gnostic terms by the dialogue of 22b. "The result is a logion all but transformed beyond recognition, were it not that the hint provided by the basic structure is confirmed by the introduction, in which it becomes clear that the logion grew out of the saying about the children" (Robinson, 1962:109).

The only factor not adequately explained in all this is the meaning of the fourth and final "when you make" concerning eye-hand-foot. "It is tempting to propose an emendation of the text" (Kee: 312), so that it would recommend eye to replace eyes, hand hands, and foot feet. But that, as Kee admits, is but a plausible guess, and Robinson can only note Mark 9:43, 45, 47 and add a question mark. But however one explains that final "when you make (fashion)," it is clear that "a collection of various traditions" (Robinson, 1962:283 note 46) has been appended to the *Kingdom and Children* aphorism. This means that one cannot dismiss the possibility of independent tradition in *Gos. Thom.* 22a simply because of the gnostic interpretation(s) now attached to it in 22b (against Kee: 314). Any decision on 22a must be made apart from its present much longer dialogic conclusion in 22b.

(2) *Gos. Thom.* 22a. This will be considered in terms of both form and content. (a) Form. This is a classic example of an *aphoristic story,* that is, of an *aphoristic saying* developed into narrative. A setting or situation is given with "Jesus saw infants being suckled." But this situation is already verbally contained within the aphorism itself: "He said to His disciples, 'These infants being suckled are like those who enter the Kingdom.' " On the one hand, this adds little to the aphorism itself, but, on the other, it significantly chooses the narrative mode (situation) over the discourse mode (address) to develop the aphorism. Notice also that the incident begins with Jesus, with something *from Jesus* rather than something *to Jesus.* It begins when "Jesus saw." This recalls Bultmann's observation that, "It is characteristic of the primitive apophthegm that it

makes the occasion of a dominical saying something that happens to Jesus (with the exception of the stories of the call of the disciples). It is a sign of a secondary formation if Jesus himself provides the initiative" (66). (b) Content. The *aphoristic saying* in Mark 10:15; Matt 18:3; John 3:3, 5 appears as a double negative ("unless . . . not") but the *dialectical story* in Mark 10:14 and the *aphoristic story* in *Gos. Thom.* 22a is positive. The shift from saying to story has involved the shift from negative to positive as well.

(3) *Gos. Thom.* 22. The whole unit of 22 involves three steps. First, the *aphoristic saying* is developed into an *aphoristic story* in 22a. Second, this is hermeneutically expanded by means of *aphoristic dialogue.* A single exchange is created between disciples and Jesus. Their question simply picks up the language of Jesus' original saying in 22a. Three, the reply of Jesus almost overpowers the original saying in length, but it is an *aphoristic commentary* in form. If one leaves aside 22a and the opening question of 22b, the rest of 22b could be taken as an originally independent saying. It is, however, an *aphoristic commentary,* that is, a unit which looks like an independent aphorism but is appended as interpretative commentary to a preceding aphorism.

5. *Gos. Thom.* 46.

> Jesus said, "Among those born of women, from Adam until John the Baptist, there is no one superior to John the Baptist that his eyes should not be lowered (before him). Yet I have said, whichever one of you comes to be a child will be acquainted with the Kingdom and will become superior to John."

This is another version of the saying found in Q/Matt 11:11=Luke 7:28, where the "least" in the Kingdom is "greater" than John. Baker has drawn attention to other versions of this aphorism in "the homilies that pass under the name of Macarius" and which "continue to perplex scholars as to their true author, place of origin and sources" although "recent work has brought strong arguments for Asia Minor and perhaps Syria as the place and the last quarter of the fourth century as the time of composition" (215). Pseudo-Macarius' versions speak first of the "least one" (μικρότερος) as being greater than John, then equate such with the "apostles," and conclude that such a "little one" (μικρός) is greater than John (Migne: 713CD). That final text is the same as the one found in *Gos. Thom.* 46b since the Coptic word *kwi* can be translated either as "a child" or "a little one." *Gos. Thom.* 46b therefore translates either "whichever one of you comes to be a child" (Lambdin; see Guillaumont et al.) or "he who shall be among you as a little one" (Wilson: 515). This change from "least one" to "little one" is significant, "for the New Testament wishes to say that all in the Kingdom are greater than John, there-fore, even the least-- μικρότερος. Whereas the *Gospel of Thomas* and Macarius mean that only those who are small--μικρός --are greater than John" (Baker: 218). Quispel has explained the relationship between *Thomas* and Macarius by proposing "that Macarius most probably knew the *Gospel of Thomas* and alluded to it in his writings" (227) and he concludes by asserting that he is "not in the least astonished that Macarius used the *Gospel of Thomas,* because so many Syrian writers before him had done the same" (234).

I conclude, therefore, that there has been an infiltration from *Gos. Thom.* 22 into 46b which (a) mitigates the denigration of John and (b) substitutes "shall know (be acquainted with) the Kingdom" for "shall enter the Kingdom." Gärtner has summarized the situation as follows: "The categorical statement in Matt. 11.11 has been reshaped so as to state the condition for admittance into the kingdom, 'the one among you who becomes like a little one (a child) shall know the kingdom.' The resemblance to Logion 22a is striking. Indeed, behind the alteration we may discern a gnosticizing tendency which has as its object to emphasize the important term 'little,' referring to the Gnostic. This tendency is supported by another alteration, the phrase 'know the kingdom.' The New Testament uses such expressions as 'to enter the kingdom of God,' or 'to receive the kingdom of God,' but never 'to know the kingdom of God'" (224).

III. APHORISM AND HERMENEUTIC

Francis Bacon (1561-1626), Baron Verulam, Viscount St. Albans, Lord Chancellor of England, has explained and also defended his own aphoristic style by affirming that "aphorisms, representing a knowledge broken, do invite men to enquire further" (3.405), and, "aphorisms . . . did invite men, both to ponder that which was invented, and to add and supply further" (3.498), and again, "aphorisms doth leave the wit of man more free to turn and toss, and to make use of that which is so delivered to more several purposes and applications" (7.321).

In discussing the *Kingdom and Children* saying we have seen this aphoristic power at work both internally with regard to content and externally with regard to form. But it is with the *external hermeneutic,* with the ways in which such forms as aphoristic sayings, stories, dialogues, and *commentaries* are creatively interwoven in Mark, Matthew, John, and *Thomas,* that this final section is concerned. Special attention should also be drawn to Mark 10:13, 14, 16 which represents an interface between the *aphoristic* and *dialectical* traditions, since in this instance an *aphoristic saying* was expanded not just into an *aphoristic story* but into a *dialectical story.*

I propose the model given in *Figure 3* to summarize the phenomena described in section II above.

The model suggested in *Figure 3* was not just created to handle the *Kingdom and Children* aphorism. It derived from a study of about 130 aphorisms in Mark and Q which will be published as *In Fragments. The Tradition of Jesus' Aphorisms* by Harper & Row in the Fall of 1983. The model therefore requires some comments, but only in the most general terms for now.

(1) The proposal is for a dynamic and generative model rather than for a static and typological model. This suits better the tradition which very often presents the same aphorism at different locations on the model. I consider this to be a more useful sort of model than the typological one proposed for the dialectical tradition in *Semeia 20: Pronouncement Stories.*

(2) The four axes of the model are: Narrative & Discourse, Isolation & Combination. The formal trajectories of the aphoristic tradition follow along those axes.

(3) Aphoristic Compounds involve the combination of two sayings (see Gärtner: 41) and this is especially important when one then infiltrates the other.

(4) Aphoristic Clusters involve the combination of more than two sayings into verbal, formal, structural, and thematic clusters.

(5) Aphoristic Dialogues and Stories are clear enough from the example of the *Kingdom and Children* saying. So also is the possibility of interaction between these and Dialectical Dialogues and Stories. This was seen paradigmatically in Mark 10:13, 14, 16 and 10:15. Aphoristic Commentaries are also clear.

(6) Aphoristic Chronicle is cited as a possibility but is not found as such in the texts I studied.

(7) Aphoristic Core is extremely important since the aphoristic tradition begins in oral not scribal transmission. Oral memory and oral sensibility operate with *aphoristic structure* rather than with *aphoristic saying,* that is, oral memory retains a linguistic structure rather than a syntactical sequence. One could even define oral sensibility as the victory of structure over sequence. This structure/sequence interplay must allow for a certain amount of free play within the aphoristic core. This free-play is designated by the terms inside the core: contraction, expansion, conversion (from negative to positive or vice versa), substitution (of words for their equivalents), and transposition (of protasis into apodosis or vice versa, between stichs, etc.).

Figure 3: GENERATIVE MODEL FOR THE APHORISTIC TRADITION.

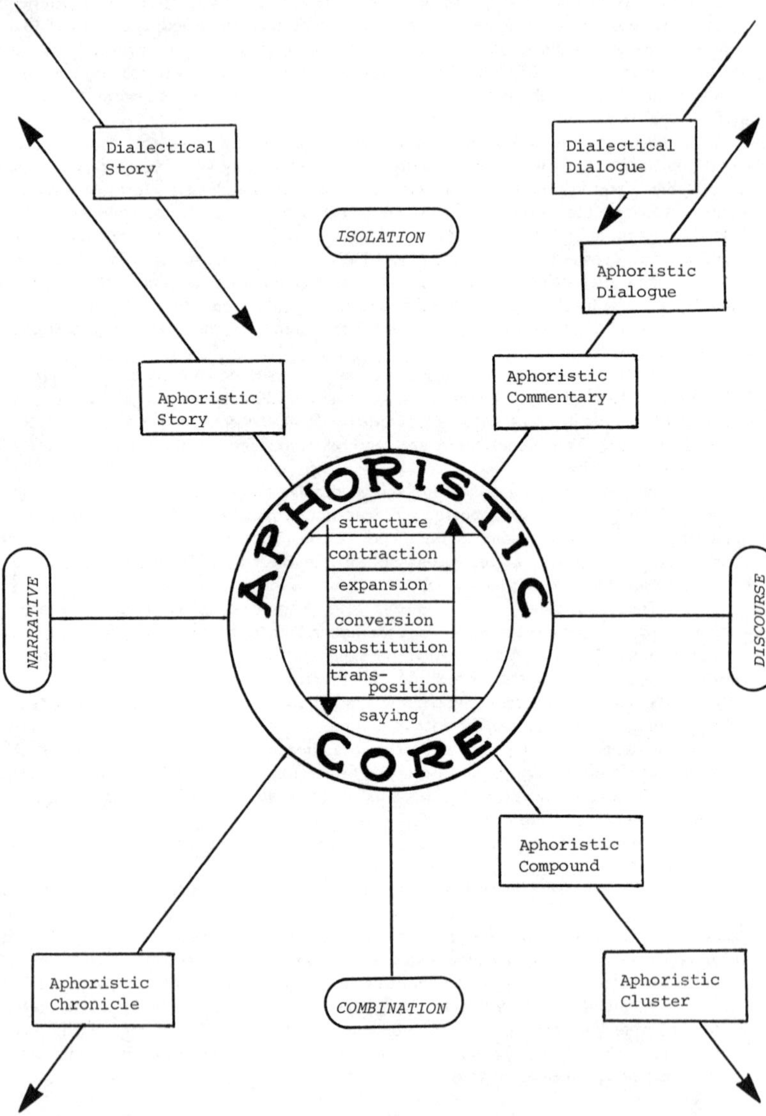

Works Consulted

Anonymous
    1912   *Papyri Greci e Latini. Vol. I: Nos. 1-112.* Pubblicazioni della Società
                Italiana per la ricerca die Papiri greci e latini in Egitto. Florence:
                Ariani.

Aune, David E.
    1978   "Septem Sapientium Convivium (Moralia 146B-164D)." Pp. 51-105 in
                Plutarch's Ethical Writings and Early Christian Literature. (Ed.)
                H. D. Betz. Studia ad Corpus Hellenisticum Novi Testamenti 4.
                Leiden: Brill.

Babbitt, Frank C., et alii (Trans.)
    1927-   *Plutarch's Moralia.* 16 vols. LCL. Cambridge, MA: Harvard Univer-
                sity Press.

Bacon, Francis
    1963   *The Works of Francis Bacon.* (Trans.) James Spedding, Robert Leslie
                Ellis, & Douglas Denon Heath. 14 vols. London: Longman, 1857-
                1874. Facsimile reproduction from Stuttgart/Bad Cannstatt:
                Frommann-Holzboog, 1963.

Baker, Aelred
    1964   "Pseudo-Macarius and the Gospel of Thomas." *VC* 18:215-25.

Bell, H. Idriss, & T. C. Skeat
    1935a   *Fragments of an Unknown Gospel and Other Early Christian Papyri.*
                London: Oxford University Press (See pp. 1-41).

    1935b   *The New Gospel Fragments.* London: Oxford University Press.

Brown, Norman O.
    1966   *Love's Body.* New York: Random House.

Brown, Raymond E.
    1966,   *The Gospel according to John I-XII & XIII-XXI.* AB 29 & 29A. Garden
    1970   City, NY: Doubleday.

Bultmann, Rudolph
    1963   *The History of the Synoptic Tradition.* (Trans.) John Marsh. New
                York: Harper & Row.

Butler, Harold Edgeworth (Trans.)
    1920-22   *The Institutio Oratoria of Quintilian.* 4 vols. LCL 124-127.
                Cambridge, MA: Harvard University Press.

Colson, F. H.
    1921   "Quintilian 1:9 and the 'Chria' in Ancient Education." *The Classical
                Review* 35:150-54.

Dodd, Charles Harold
    1963   *Historical Tradition in the Fourth Gospel.* New York: Cambridge
                University Press.

Gärtner, Bertil
    1961   *The Theology of the Gospel according to Thomas.*   (Trans.)
                E. J. Sharpe. New York: Harper & Bros.

Georgi, Dieter
    1972   "The Records of Jesus in the Light of Ancient Accounts of Revered
                Men."   Pp. 527-42 in *SBL 1972 Proceedings.*   2 vols. (Ed.)
                L. C. McGaughy. SBL.

Guillaumont, A., et alii (Trans.)
    1959   *The Gospel according to Thomas.* Leiden: Brill/New York: Harper &
                Row.

Hennecke, E., & W. Schneemelcher (Trans.: R. McL. Wilson)
    1973   *New Testament Apocrypha.* 2 vols. London: SCM.

Hicks, R. D. (Trans.)
    1925   *Diogenes Laertius: Lives of Eminent Philosophers.* 2 vols. LCL 184-
                185. Cambridge, MA: Harvard University Press.

Hultgren, Arland John
    1971   *Jesus and His Adversaries: A Study of the Form and Function of the
                Conflict Stories in the Synoptic Tradition.*   Union Theological
                Seminary, New York. Th.D. dissertation. Ann Arbor, MI: University
                Microfilms International.

    1979   *Jesus and His Adversaries: The Form and Function of the Conflict
                Stories in the Synoptic Tradition.* Minneapolis, MN: Augsburg.

Jeremias, Joachim
    1971   *New Testament Theology.* New York: Scribner's.

Kahn, Charles H.
    1979   *The Art and Thought of Heraclitus.* New York: Cambridge University
                Press.

Kee, Howard C.
    1963   "'Becoming a Child' in the Gospel of Thomas," *JBL* 82: 307-14.

Kelber, Werner H.
    1974   *The Kingdom in Mark.* Philadelphia: Fortress.

Koester, Helmut
    1979   "Dialog und Spruchüberlieferung in den gnostischen Texten von Nag
                Hammadi." *EvT* 39:532-56.

    1980a   "Apocryphal and Canonical Gospels." *HTR* 73: 105-30.

    1980b   "Gnostic Writings as Witnesses for the Development of the Sayings
                Tradition."   Pp. 238-56 (with discussion on pp. 256-61) in *The
                Rediscovery of Gnosticism.* Proceedings of the International
                conference on Gnosticism at Yale, New Haven, CT, March 28-31,
                1978. *Vol. 1: The School of Valentinus.* Studies in the History of
                Religions: Supplements to *Numen* 41/1. Leiden: Brill.

Lambdin, Thomas O. (Trans.)
1977   "The Gospel of Thomas." Pp. 118-30 in *The Nag Hammadi Library.* (Ed.) James M. Robinson. San Francisco: Harper & Row.

Lindars, Barnabas
1980-81   "John and the Synoptic Gospels: A Test Case." *NTS* 27:287-94.

Margolius, Hans
1963-64   "On the Uses of Aphorisms in Ethics." *Educational Forum* 28:79-85.

Mautner, F. H.
1976   "Der Aphorismus als literarische Gattung." Pp. 19-74 in *Der Aphorismus: zur Geschichte, zu den Formen und Möglichkeiten einer literarischen Gattung.* Wege der Forschung 356. (Ed.) Gerhard Neumann. Darmstadt: Wissenschaftliche Buchgesellschaft (Originally published in 1933).

Mayeda, Goro
1946   *Das Leben-Jesu-Fragment Papyrus Egerton 2 und seine Stellung in der urchristlichen Literaturgeschichte.* Bern: Haupt.

Migne, J.-P.
1903   *Patrologiae Cursus Completus: Series Graeca 34.* Paris: Garnier.

Nadeau, Ray
1952   "The Progymnasmata of Aphthonius in Translation." *Speech Monographs* 19:264-85.

Neirynck, Frans
1972   *Duality in Mark: Contributions to the Study of the Markan Redaction.* BETL 31. Leuven: Leuven University Press.

Pagels, Elaine & Helmut Koester
1978   "Report on the *Dialogue of the Savior.*" Pp. 66-74 in *Nag Hammadi and Gnosis.* Papers read at the First International Congress on Coptology, Cairo, December 1976. (Ed.) R. McL. Wilson. NHS 14. Leiden: Brill.

Perrin, Bernadette (Trans.)
1914-26   *Plutarch's Lives.* 11 vols. LCL. Cambridge, MA: Harvard University Press.

Perrin, Norman
1974   *The New Testament: An Introduction.* New York: Harcourt Brace Jovanovich.

Petersen, Norman R.
1980   "The Composition of Mark 4:1-8:26." *HTR* 73:185-217.

Pryke, E. J.
1978   *Redactional Style in the Marcan Gospel. A Study of Syntax and Vocabulary as Guides to Redaction in Mark.* SNTSMS 33. New York: Cambridge University Press.

Quispel, G.
    1964   "The Syrian Thomas and the Syrian Macarius." *VC* 18:226-35.

Robbins, Vernon K.
    1981a   "Summons and Outline in Mark: The Three-Step Progression." *NovT*
                    23:97-114.

    1981b   "Classifying Pronouncement Stories in Plutarch's *Parallel Lives.*"
                    Semeia 20:29-52.

Robinson, James M.
    1962   "The Formal Structure of Jesus' Message." Pp. 91-110 in *Current
                    Issues in New Testament Interpretation.* Essays in Honor of Otto A.
                    Piper. (Eds.) W. Klassen & G. F. Snyder. New York: Harper & Bros.

    1977   (Gen. Ed.) *The Nag Hammadi Library.* New York: Harper & Row.

Robinson, James M., & Helmut Koester
    1971   *Trajectories through Early Christianity.* Philadelphia: Fortress.

Schilling, F. A.
    1965   "What Means the Saying about Receiving the Kingdom of God as a
                    Little Child?" *ExpTim* 77:56-58.

Smith, D. M.
    1979-80   "John and the Synoptics: Some Dimensions of the Problem." *NTS*
                    26:425-44.

Spencer, Richard Albert
    1976   *A Study of the Form and Function of the Biographical Apophthegms in
                    the Synoptic Tradition in the Light of their Hellenistic Background.*
                    Emory University. Ph.D. Dissertation. Ann Arbor, MI: University
                    Microfilms International.

Spengel, Leonhard von
    1853-56   *Rhetores Graeci.* 3 vols. Leipzig: Teubner, 1953-56. Reprinted by
                    Frankfurt: Minerva, 1966.

Tannehill, Robert C.
    1981   "Introduction: The Pronouncement Story and Its Types" & "Varieties
                    of Synoptic Pronouncement Stories." *Semeia* 20:1-13 & 101-19.

Taylor, R. O. P.
    1946   *The Groundwork of the Gospels.* Oxford: Blackwell.

Wilson, R. McL. (Trans.)
    1973   "The Gospel of Thomas." Pp. 511-22 in *New Testament Apocrypha.*
                    (Eds.) E. Hennecke & W. Schneemelcher. Vol. 1. London: SCM.

THE NARRATOR IN THE FOURTH GOSPEL
INTRATEXTUAL RELATIONSHIPS

R. Alan Culpepper
Southern Baptist Theological Seminary

"Stories must be in the past, and the more in the past they are, one might say, the better it is for them, in their capacity as stories, and for the narrator, the whispering wizard of the imperfect tense."

Thomas Mann[1]

The narrator is a rhetorical device, the voice that tells the story and speaks to the reader. Since there is scarcely any literature on the subject of this paper,[2] our present task is "naming the whispering wizard" of the Fourth Gospel, which will mean defining the location and function of the narrator's comments, his point of view, and his relationships to the characters and the author.[3] The first two topics are dealt with in abbreviated fashion; the third will be the focus of this paper.

I. Expositional Mode

Narrators vary with respect to how much they know, as well as how much they tell, and when they tell the reader what must be known in order to understand the narrative world and its characters. Meir Sternberg calls this necessary, introductory or orienting information "exposition."[4] Sternberg observes that the exposition given by a narrator may either be concentrated in one place or distributed throughout a narrative. It may be preliminary (i.e., given before the beginning of the story itself) or delayed until it will have its desired effect at a later point in the narrative. It may either be given to the reader in chronological order or in some other order so that the reader must work out the chronological sequence. Exposition which is chronological, preliminary, and concentrated is "the basic norm of straightforward communication."[5] This "expositional mode" allows the reader's first impressions to be confirmed as the story progresses. Sternberg subsequently analyzes deviations from this expositional mode which have the effect of qualifying, modifying, or demolishing the reader's first impressions of a character or situation in the narrative world. In summary, he shows that an author's handling of the expositional material has a powerful effect upon the reader.

John's strategy conforms closely to the norm of chronological, preliminary, concentrated exposition. The narrator gives the reader a concentrated, more or less

---

[1]This paper is an abbreviated part of a longer work, *Anatomy of the Fourth Gospel*, to be published by Fortress Press. The epigraph is from Thomas Mann, *Der Zauberberg*, p. 5, and is quoted by Wolfgang Iser, *The Implied Reader* (Baltimore: Johns Hopkins University Press, 1974), p. 235.

[2]The comments and asides in the gospel have been studied by M. C. Tenney, "The Footnotes of John's Gospel," *BSac* 117 (1960) 350-64; and John J. O'Rourke, "Asides in the Gospel of John," *NovT* 21 (1979) 210-29. See also David W. Wead, *The Literary Devices in John's Gospel* (Theologischen Dissertationen, Bd. IV; Basel: Friedrich Reinhart Kommissionsverlag, 1970) 1-11. The most sophisticated analysis to date is in Wilhelm Wuellner's unpublished SNTS seminar paper, "Narrative Criticism and the Lazarus Story," esp. section 3, "Narration/Discourse/the Signifier: Narrating Elements."

[3]The Johannine narrator is not identified as male or female. We will refer to the narrator with masculine pronouns, however, for the sake of convenience and simplicity.

[4]Meir Sternberg, *Expositional Modes and Temporal Ordering in Fiction* (Baltimore: Johns Hopkins University Press, 1978) 1.

[5]Ibid., pp. 98-99.

chronologically arranged, block of exposition in the prologue, which proves to be reliable as the work progresses. Comments by the narrator are also distributed throughout the narrative and generally serve as introductions or conclusions to scenes, or whole sections, of the gospel, or as transitional or explanatory notes. Because his presence is overt rather than concealed and he makes comments to the reader which interrupt the flow of the narrative, the Johannine narrator is "intrusive."[6]

Not only *when* the exposition is given but *how much* exposition is given has a determinative effect upon the kind of response a narrative evokes from its readers. A narrator may tell the reader all the vital information, or the reader may be required to figure things out as the story progresses. The narrator may have only limited insight into the story or may supply privileged information which no ordinary observer would have, in which case the narrator is to a greater or lesser degree "omniscient." "Omnicommunicative" narrators tell what they know; others deliberately suppress vital information. Each narrator has a different effect upon the reader. An "unreliable" narrator may mislead and thereby alienate the reader by giving false or misleading information or by suppressing vital information. On the other hand, the narrator may win the reader's trust by giving reliable exposition early in the narrative.

The Johannine narrator is neither unreliable nor deliberately suppressive, but rather begins the narrative with an overview of the identity of the central figure and the course of the action to follow (John 1:1-18). From the beginning, the narrator shares his omniscient vantage point with the reader, so the reader is immediately given all that is needed to understand the story. Later, distributed comments reinforce the initial exposition. Like the narrator, therefore, the reader knows more than any of the characters who interact with Jesus and is never in danger of mistaking "the Syracusan for the Ephesian." Trollope's philosophy echoes that reflected in John: "Our doctrine is that the author and the reader should move along together in full confidence with each other."[7]

II. Point of View

Both Gérard Genette and Boris Uspensky have proposed distinctions which help to clarify and define the related matters of narrator and point of view.[8] Genette has distinguished between the two by showing that point of view, or "focalization," the term he prefers, is determined by whether the story is told from within by the main character or an omniscient author or from outside by a minor character or an author who has taken the role as an observer. The identity of the narrator is determined by whether the narrator is the voice of the author (as it is in John) or a character within the story.[9]

Uspensky has contributed significant conceptual refinements to the discussion of point of view by identifying five "planes" in which point of view may be expressed: the ideological (evaluative norms), the phraseological (speech patterns), the spatial (location of the narrator), the temporal (the time of the telling), and the psychological (internal or external to the characters).[10] We have already observed that the Johannine narrator is

---

[6]M. H. Abrams, *A Glossary of Literary Terms* (3rd ed.; New York: Holt, Reinhart and Winston, 1971) 134: "Within this mode [omniscient] the *intrusive narrator* is one who not only reports but freely comments on his characters, evaluating their actions and motives and expressing his views about human life in general; ordinarily, all the omniscient narrator's reports and judgments are to be taken as authoritative."

[7]Anthony Trollope, *Barchester Towers*, chapter 15; quoted by Sternberg, *Expositional Modes*, p. 259.

[8]Gérard Genette, *Narrative Discourse: An Essay in Method* (trans. Jane E. Lewin; Ithaca: Cornell University Press, 1979); Boris Uspensky, *A Poetics of Composition* (trans. V. Zavarin and S. Wittig; Berkeley: University of California Press, 1973).

[9]Genette, ibid., esp. pp. 185-94.

[10]Uspensky, *A Poetics of Composition*, p. 6 and passim. See also Norman R. Petersen, " 'Point of View' in Mark's Narrative," *Semeia* 12 (1978) 97-121.

undramatized, intrusive, and omnicommunicative. It is also readily apparent that the narrator in John usually speaks in the third person, as one outside the action, thereby providing the effect of the voice of a witness or observer.[11] This pattern is not maintained uniformly, however, since the first person plural, "we," is used in John 1:14, 16; and 21:24 (cf. 3:11).

    Psychological point of view: omniscient. A narrator's psychological point of view is determined by whether or not he or she is able to provide inside views of what a character is thinking, feeling, or intending. Omniscience in narrators is not a monolithic quality, however. There are various degrees of omniscience, since the source and extent of a narrator's knowledge may vary. Omniscient narration may be linked, for example, with a temporally retrospective point of view so that the narrator looks back on events which happened at some time in the narrator's past. In this case, it is as if the narrator "narrates experiences which took place some time ago, and has since had time to puzzle things out *post factum,* and can reconstruct the internal state of the people, imagining what they must have experienced."[12] We may now ask what the narrator in John knows, and how he knows what he tells us.

    The Johannine narrator knows that in the beginning the Word was with God and knows what is going to happen in the story before it happens. The narrator informs the reader that Jesus knew all things (2:24) and tells us at various points what Jesus was thinking and what he meant by what he said.[13] How deeply does the narrator take us into Jesus, and what is the "axis of his plunge"?[14] As numerous as the references are, the plunge is not deep. We are told that Jesus knew his betrayer, the time of his death, and various things about other people. What the narrator says Jesus knew about others gives us a reliable inside view of them as well. Yet, while the narrator exercises a privilege which is clearly artificial by providing us with an inside view of Jesus' mind, a measure of verisimilitude is preserved by the limited depth of the plunge and by coupling omniscience with retrospection, an aspect of the narrator's point of view we will discuss shortly.

    The question to be asked now is whether the narrator takes us inside other characters also, and if so how these "plunges" compare with the inside view of Jesus. We may work outwards from Jesus, considering first the disciples, then neutral characters, then his opponents. There are fairly numerous excursions inside the disciples as a group,[15] but they are rather shallow also. The kind of knowledge about the disciples that is revealed by the narrator is closely tied to his retrospective point of view and may be credibly accounted for as insight gained after the fact.

    Surprisingly, there are very few inside views of individual disciples. We never know what Peter, Andrew, or Thomas are thinking unless they tell us themselves. Judas is the only disciple of whom we get a significant inside view, and even then it is shallow and sketchy (12:4, 6; 18:2; cf. 13:2).

    Not only Jesus and the disciples but some of the minor characters as well are open to the narrator: the official, 4:53; the man at the pool, 5:13; Jesus' brothers, 7:5; the parents of the blind man, 9:22; Pilate, 19:8; Joseph, 19:38; and Mary Magdalene,

---

[11]Frank Kermode, *The Genesis of Secrecy: On the Interpretation of Narrative* (Cambridge, MA: Harvard University Press, 1979) 117: "The advantage of third-person narration is that it is the mode which best produces the illusion of pure reference. But it *is* an illusion, the effect of a rhetorical device."

[12]Uspensky, *A Poetics of Composition,* p. 96.

[13]For inside views of Jesus' mind, see: John 1:43; 4:1; 5:6; 6:6, 15, 61, 64; 11:5, 33, 38; 13:1, 11, 21; 16:19; 18:4; 19:28.

[14]Wayne C. Booth, "Distance and Point of View: An Essay in Classification," *Essays in Criticism* 11 (1961) 77.

[15]John 2:11, 17, 22; 4:27; 12:16; 13:28, 29; 20:9; 21:4.

20:14-15. As these verses show, the narrator does not make profound or prolonged plunges into any of these characters. Most of the comments are aesthetically or rhetorically motivated; they involve disclosures which enable the narrative to move more smoothly.

In reference to the last group of characters, "the Jews" and "the crowd," one finds that the narrator uses shallow inside views to characterize them, explain their actions, and draw attention to the division that develops as some believe while others plot Jesus' death.[16]

Spatial point of view: omnipresent. Distinguishable from omniscience but related to it is what is often called the omnipresence of the narrator. Chatman defines omnipresence as "the narrator's capacity to report from vantage-points not accessible to characters, or to jump from one to another, or to be in two places at once."[17] The Johannine narrator is not confined to a particular locale or group of characters but is free to move about from place to place to provide an unhampered view of the action. For example, the narrator is at the well when only Jesus and the woman are present, in the Samaritan village when she announces Jesus, and simultaneously (4:31) at the well to report Jesus' conversation with the disciples. While this freedom diminishes the narrative's verisimilitude, any threat which it poses is offset by the added authority it gives the narrator, and by implication the narrative.

Temporal point of view: retrospective. We have already noted that the narrator speaks retrospectively. This temporal point of view may be illustrated by such statements as "for the Spirit was not yet given because Jesus had not yet been glorified" (7:39). More specifically, the Johannine narrator tells the story from the temporal perspective of a group, "we," which advocates belief in Jesus after his resurrection. The narrator therefore speaks from some point in the future within the narrative world and interprets Jesus as no contemporary observer would have been able to.[18] The references to what the disciples did not know at the time but discovered after Jesus' resurrection (2:22; 12:16; 13:7; 20:9) suggest that the perspective of the believing community--should we say the Johannine community--is presented as absolutely necessary if one is to have an adequate understanding of Jesus.

John 12:16 provides an important clue to part of the process which conditioned the retrospective point of view which the author adopted for his narrator: "His disciples did not understand this at first; but when Jesus was glorified, then they remembered that this had been written of him and had been done to him." The reference emphasizes the role of memory and the study of scripture. The disciples are presented by the narrator as perceiving that passages being applied to the expected Messiah had been fulfilled by Jesus, or, more likely, that they noticed what could be taken as veiled allusions to what they remembered Jesus had done. Their perspective is therefore characterized as one informed by memory of an earlier time and the interpretation of scripture which they formulated subsequently. In John 12:16, and in fact throughout most of the narrative, memory and scripture are blended and reinterpreted. Memory provokes interpretation of scripture, and the latter overlays memory and gives it a new focus so that the story the narrator tells is set in a perspective no "on the scene" reporter would have. The narrator reflects on what occurred both before and after the events he narrates.

This perspective calls for a broadening of the concept of point of view along the lines proposed by Robert Weimann: texts derive from and act upon historical contexts,

---

[16]See John 5:16, 18; 7:15; 8:27, 30; 11:45; 12:9, 10, 11, 18, 42, 43.

[17]Seymour Chatman, *Story and Discourse: Narrative Structure in Fiction and Film* (Ithaca: Cornell University Press, 1978) 103; cf. p. 212.

[18]See Wead, *The Literary Devices in John's Gospel,* pp. 1-11; and Uspensky, *A Poetics of Composition,* p. 67.

and it is the author's relationship to society which is "the basis on which representation and evaluation are integrated through point of view."[19] In this broad sense, the Johannine narrator, who presumably expresses the perspective of the author, tells the story from a point of view which in its retrospection is informed by memory, interpretation of scripture, the coalescing of traditions with the post-Easter experience of the early church, consciousness of the presence of the Spirit, a reading of the glory of the risen Christ back into the days of his ministry, and an acute sensitivity to the struggles of the Johannine community.[20] But with this observation we have moved to the narrator's ideological or evaluative point of view.

Ideological point of view: reliable and stereoscopic.[21] No narrator can be absolutely impartial; inevitably a narrator, especially an omniscient, omnipresent, omnicommunicative, and intrusive one, will prejudice the reader toward or away from certain characters, claims, or events and their implications.[22] Nor is there any evidence that the Johannine narrator attempts to maintain neutrality toward his story: his function is to facilitate communication of the author's ideological or evaluative system to the reader.

For this reason, the narrator is established not only as omniscient and omnicommunicative but also as entirely reliable. All limits on our sense of his reliability are lifted by so structuring the narrative that the reader is elevated to the narrator's Olympian perspective on the characters and events, given this information at the outset and as necessary throughout the narrative, and then shown how the narrator's perspective is in fact confirmed by the action and character development that follows. We soon trust him implicitly and completely. The Johannine narrator is also entirely reliable in that "he speaks in accordance with the norms of the work (which is to say, the implied author's norms), ..."[23] The reliability of the narrator (as defined by Booth and used as a technical term) must be kept distinct from both the historical accuracy of the narrator's account and the "truth" of his ideological point of view.

All of the topics which are usually treated in discussions of the theology of the Gospel of John are, in fact, aspects of the implied author's ideological point of view as it is conveyed through Jesus and the narrator. One aspect of the narrator's ideological point of view merits special attention, however. For want of a better term, the narrator's point of view may be called "stereoscopic." The dictionary defines a stereoscope as an optical device with two eyeglasses which creates the illusion of solidity and depth by "assisting the observer to combine the images of two pictures taken from points of view a little way apart."[24] The term is appropriate, for the narrator views Jesus and his ministry from the twin perspectives of his "whence" and his "whither," his origin as the pre-existent *logos* and his destiny as the exalted Son of God. Only when these perspectives are combined can Jesus be understood. This stereoscopic perspective conditions not only what the narrator says but the gospel's entire characterization of Jesus. The narrator, who shares Jesus' knowledge of himself, knows that Jesus is the divine, pre-existent *logos* who was responsible for creation. The gospel narrative therefore portrays Jesus as the one who continues the creative work of the *logos* by creating eyes for a man born blind, restoring the dead to life, and breathing spirit into spiritless disciples. The narrator also knows that Jesus will be exalted to the Father, so he

---

[19]Robert Weimann, *Structure and Society in Literary History* (Charlottesville: University Press of Virginia, 1976) 237.

[20]Cf. Amos N. Wilder, *Early Christian Rhetoric: The Language of the Gospel* (Cambridge, MA: Harvard University Press, 1971) 69-70.

[21]Uspensky, *A Poetics of Composition*, p. 8.

[22]Wayne C. Booth, *A Rhetoric of Fiction* (Chicago: University of Chicago Press, 1961) 78.

[23]Booth, "Distance and Point of View," p. 72.

[24] *Webster's New Collegiate Dictionary*, 6th ed., s.v. "stereoscope."

prepares the reader to understand Jesus' death as exaltation rather than humiliation. these entrance and exit points, which are subjects of concern repeatedly in the gospel, condition the Johannine narrator's stereoscopic view of the ministry of Jesus.

IV. Relationships Within the Text

Up to this point we have been considering the identity of the narrator primarily as it is defined by his point of view, but the narrator may also be identified in terms of the way he relates to other figures in the narrative context, especially Jesus and the implied author. The narrator may be more or less identified with, sympathetic with, or distant from each of these figures, and the cumulative effect of these relationships defines in large measure the nature of the narrator's role.[25]

The narrator and Jesus. A great deal has already been said about the narrator's relationship to Jesus. The narrator knows who Jesus is and what he knows. They both know "all things." The narrator, however, shares as an authoritative interpreter of Jesus' words.

In John 11:11, Jesus tells the disciples that Lazarus has fallen asleep. The disciples miss Jesus' metaphor and therefore misunderstand. The narrator clarifies Jesus' statement for the reader: "Now Jesus had spoken of his death, but they thought that he meant taking rest in sleep. Then Jesus told them plainly, 'Lazarus is dead.' " Here, in a calculated way, the author presents the narrator as the one who understands Jesus' words even when the disciples do not. The importance of the narrator's role as interpreter becomes obvious when one skips the narration and reads only the dialogue. Without the narration the dialogue in this passage loses most of its significance. John 11:11-14 is not an isolated case; the narrator serves as the authoritative interpreter of Jesus' words in the following verses:

2:21   But he spoke of the temple of his body. Cf. 2:22.

6:6   This he said to test him, for he himself knew what he would do.

6:71   He spoke of Judas the son of Simon Iscariot, for he, one of the twelve, was to betray him.

7:39   Now this he said about the Spirit, which those who believed in him were to receive; for as yet the Spirit had not been given, because Jesus was not yet glorified. Cf. 19:30; 20:22.

8:27   They did not understand that he spoke to them of the Father.

12:33   He said this to show by what death he was to die.

13:11   For he knew who was to betray him; that was why he said, 'You are not all clean.'

18:32   This was to fulfill the word which Jesus had spoke to show by what death he was to die.

21:19   This he said to show by what death he was to glorify God.

21:23   The saying spread abroad among the brethren that this disciple was not to die; yet Jesus did not say to him that he was not to die, but, "If it is my will that he remain until I come, what is that to you?

Even when the interpretation does not occur in the immediate context of the saying, it is clear that the narrator is the authoritative interpreter of Jesus' words. For example, in John 5:44 Jesus asks the Jews, "How can you believe, who receive glory from one another and do not seek the glory that comes from the only God?" The narrator's words about the Jewish authorities at the end of chapter twelve return to his statement: "For they loved the glory of men more than the glory of God" (12:43). The implication is that the narrator understands Jesus' words and knows how they are to be interpreted. In addition

---

[25]See Booth, *The Rhetoric of Fiction,* pp. 155-59; Sternberg, *Expositional Modes,* pp. 259-60.

to Jesus' words, the narrator also interprets the words of the parents of the blind man (9:22), Caiaphas (11:51-53), Judas (12:6), and Isaiah (12:41). Then, in John 21:23, the narrator corrects the misunderstanding that was current among "the brothers" regarding the coming of the risen Lord before the death of the Beloved Disciple. By this point it has long been clear to the reader that the narrator is the authoritative interpreter of Jesus' words and therefore his interpretation has authority over any other interpretations. Actually, of course, the narrator interprets only a few statements. But what Jesus says, and the gospel as a whole, represents a massive, daring re-interpretation of Jesus. The narrator is only part of the larger whole in respect to this interpretation. Yet, the aura of reliability which is infused around the narrator goes a long way toward disposing the reader to accept the gospel's interpretation of Jesus.

In order to define further the relationship between the narrator and Jesus it is necessary to compare aspects of their points of view. In the farewell discourse, as elsewhere, Jesus has a distinctive point of view from which he interprets his mission, his departure and return, and the disciples' relationship to him. Since the narrator intrudes in a significant way only once during the farewell discourse (16:17, 19; see also 13:31; 17:1, and possibly 17:3), a comparative analysis of Jesus' point of view in the farewell discourse with the narrator's should provide a classic test for determining the relationship between the two and consistency of point of view throughout the gospel. The question may be put this way: Does the farewell discourse reflect the same point of view as the narrator's voice elsewhere in the gospel, or do these two—narration and discourse--offer different perspectives on Jesus?

The following paragraphs will show that Jesus' point of view as it may be inferred from the farewell discourse corresponds remarkably to that of the narrator. The two are omniscient, retrospective, and ideologically and phraseologically indistinguishable.

Jesus' omniscience may be inferred from what he says. Jesus knows when the disciples do not want to ask him the meaning of what he said (16:19). He knows that Peter will deny him three times that night (13:38). He explains to the disciples that his Father's house has many resting places and that he is going to prepare a place for them (14:2). He is entirely aware of his unique relationship to the Father (14:7, 9, 10, 11, 24; 15:1; 16:15; 17:11). He knows that the hour is coming when they will all abandon him (16:32), and that the ruler of this world is coming (14:30). Beyond that, the little while will pass (16:16, 20, 22), and they will see him again. In short, the farewell discourse shows that Jesus knows the spiritual orientation of the disciples (15:19; 17:16) and the world, the hearts and minds of the disciples, his own origin, mission, destiny, and relationship to the Father, and significant future events. Finally, just before the prayer in chapter 17, the author drives home the fact and significance of Jesus' omniscience by having the disciples say: "Now we know that you know all things, and need none to question you; by this we believe that you came from God" (16:30; cf. 2:24-25).

The temporal perspectives of the farewell discourse are notoriously difficult to sort out. In chapter 17 especially one finds retrospective statements:

17:4   I glorified thee on earth, having accomplished the work which thou gavest me to do, ...

17:6   I have manifested thy name to the men whom thou gavest me out of the world, ...

17:11   And now I am no more in the world, ...

With such pronouncements Jesus speaks from the position of the risen and exalted Lord: they characterize the significance of Jesus' life.

Although there are a few similar statements in the farewell discourse proper (e.g. 14:9), their prominence in chapter 17 is distinctive. In the earlier chapters the author presents Jesus as speaking proleptically about the events which were yet to occur: "And now I have told you before it takes place, so that when it does take place, you may believe" (14:29; cf. 13:7; 16:4). Among the things he discusses beforehand one may list: his departure, the coming of the Paraclete, their joy when they see him again (16:22-23), the greater works the disciples will do (14:12), the persecution they will experience (15:21), their expulsion from the synagogue (16:2-4), and Peter's death--though the reference in 13:36 is veiled. It is commonly thought that the author was in the midst of these events when he wrote. Therefore, while the narrator views Jesus retrospectively in the rest of the gospel, in the farewell discourse Jesus speaks proleptically of the life situation of the fictional narrator, which probably corresponds to that of the author himself. The link between Jesus and the later time is thereby maintained in the farewell discourse by Jesus' proleptic speech. It is the counterpart of the narrator's retrospective point of view, and it was the only narrative device open to the author for maintaining this linkage once he chose to place the material in the form of discourse from the mouth of Jesus.

The temporal point of view of the farewell discourse is, therefore, correlative to that of the narrator. By means of this linkage in perspective the author presents the significance of Jesus for the author's own time. The author's objective is transparent when Jesus says, "But I have said these things to you, that when their hour comes you may remember that I told you of them" (16:4).

An even clearer comparison between the point of view of the narrator and the farewell discourse can be drawn from Jesus' repeated references to his origin and his destiny. The parade example of this emphasis is John 16:28--"I came from the Father and have come into the world; again, I am leaving the world and going to the Father." The disciples respond acclaiming Jesus' omniscience and professing that it is sufficient basis for believing that he has come from God (16:29-30). The importance of Jesus' eternal whence and whither in the farewell discourse is clearly illustrated by its recurrence in the following statements:

14:12   . . . I go to the Father.
14:28   You heard me say to you, 'I go away, and I will come to you.' If you loved me, you would have rejoiced because I go to the Father; . . . .
16:5   But now I am going to him who sent me; yet none of you asks me, 'Where are you going?'
16:10   . . . because I go to the Father, and you will see me no more; . . . .
17:11   . . . , and I am coming to thee; . . . .
17:13   But now I am coming to thee; . . . .
17:18   As thou didst send me into the world, so I have sent them into the world.
17:24   Father, I desire that they also, whom thou hast given me, may be with me where I am, to behold my glory which thou hast given me in thy love for me before the foundation of the world.

Other examples could be added, but are unnecessary.

Before leaving the point, it is instructive to note that the one instance where the narrator intrudes significantly in the farewell discourse (with the possible exception of 17:3) follows Jesus' statement about the "little while," which concludes "because I go to the Father" (16:17). Immediately, the narrator tells us that the disciples spoke to one another and Jesus knew they wanted to question him (16:17, 19). Overcoming the disciples', and by inference the reader's, ignorance of Jesus' origin from above and return to the Father was consequential enough to justify this break in the flow of the discourse. The intervention of the narrator further confirms the emphasis given to Jesus' whence and whither in the discourse and fits the pattern established by the prologue and the stereoscopic perspective of the narrator elsewhere in the gospel.

The striking congruence in the points of view of the narrator and the farewell discourse, especially since the narrator remains silent through virtually all of these four chapters, is significant for establishing the perspective from which the reader is to view Jesus' life and death. Both Jesus and the narrator are omniscient and speak in retrospect--or prospect as discussed above--from the life situation of the Johannine community, while viewing Jesus' life in the context of his origin and destiny in glory. This consistency with respect to point of view in disparate elements of the gospel demonstrates the remarkable unity of perspective throughout John. The implication is that unless the readers see Jesus in the light of the narrator's temporal and ideological point of view, they cannot understand who Jesus was.

Commentators have identified numerous parallels to the discourse material among the pronouncements of Jesus elsewhere in the gospel, but it is more difficult to assess the relationship between the narrator's speech and the discourse material he reports. Nevertheless, it is worth asking whether there is a difference in idiom or speech patterns (i.e., Uspensky's phraseological plane) between Jesus and the narrator. The author controls both. Nevertheless, if there is any convergence between the idioms of these two distinct and disparate narrative elements, it is significant for the interpretation of the gospel. In addition to the verses cited above in which the narrator interprets the words of Jesus or another character, there are interpretative statements which are not related to a specific saying:

7:30   So they sought to arrest him; but no one laid hands on him, because his hour had not yet come.

8:20   . . . but no one arrested him, because his hour had not yet come.

12:16   His disciples did not understand this at first, but when Jesus was glorified, then they remembered that this had been written of him and had been done to him.

The correlation of the narrator's explanatory comments with the themes of the farewell discourse is surprising. The comments deal with Judas (6:71; 12:6; 13:11), Jesus' hour (7:30; 8:20), his glorification (7:39; 12:16), the giving of the Spirit (7:39), exclusion from the synagogue (9:22; 12:42), the Father (8:27), the significance of Jesus' death (11:51-53), and the manner of his death (12:33; 18:32). Missing are statements related to Jesus' going away and the unity and mutual love of the disciples. With these exceptions, the narrator's explanatory or interpretative comments deal with virtually all of the main themes of the farewell discourse, and with only one or two exceptions (11:13 and perhaps 12:41) every point at which the narrator intervenes to interpret a statement is related to concerns dealt with by the farewell discourse. Many of the themes of the farewell discourse, therefore, are foreshadowed by the narrator.

The interpretative comments also function as vehicles of plot development. Their effect is to focus the reader's attention on the betrayal, death, and glorification of Jesus and thereby build dramatic interest in how these events will occur. In this area the author is particularly skillful: he never shows his hand all at once, but he never leaves the impression that he is holding back on the reader.

In tracing the narrator's foreshadowing of the events related to Jesus' death, one sees that Jesus and the narrator share the same vocabulary and use terms with the same veiled or double meaning. The development cannot be traced here, but John 7:39 illustrates the pattern. In this verse, the verb $doxaz\bar{o}$, which is John's most important term for Jesus' death and resurrection, appears for the first time in the gospel. It will subsequently occur nine times in the farewell discourse and is always on the lips of Jesus except in 12:16 and 21:19, where the narrator speaks.[26] The narrator explains that the Spirit had not yet been given because Jesus had not yet been glorified. This linking of the coming of the Spirit to the death of Jesus receives substantial development later in the gospel, and in the farewell discourse in particular. In 7:30 and 8:20 the narrator explains the failure of the officials to arrest Jesus by saying, "his hour had not yet come." The mysterious significance of his hour was introduced by Jesus in 2:4. The narrator, who of course understands its importance, refers to it now in the context of the attempts by the Jews to arrest Jesus. The reader therefore begins to grasp its meaning. In 12:23 (and 17:1) Jesus ties the "hour" to his glorification. The narrator then introduces chapter 13 by saying that Jesus knew that the hour had now come. In similar fashion, the

---

[26]C. H. Dodd, *The Interpretation of the Fourth Gospel* (Cambridge: Cambridge University Press, 1953) 396.

narrator refers five times to the one who will betray Jesus (6:64, 71; 12:4; 13:2, 11) before Jesus himself finally alludes to his betrayer in 13:21. The reader is given a piece at a time, and slowly the pieces fit together, unveiling the course and meaning of coming events.

These examples show that the narrator uses or introduces most of the significant terms related to Jesus' death which figure prominently in the farewell discourse:

	Narrator	Farewell Discourse
hōra (hour)	7:30; 8:20; 13:1	16:32; 17:1; cf. 16:2
doxazō (glorify)	12:16	13:31, 32; 14:13; 15:8; 16:14; 17:1, 4, 5, 10
pneuma (spirit)	7:39; cf. 11:33; 13:21	14:17, 26; 15:26; 16:13
aposynagōgos (out of the synagogue)	9:22; 12:42	16:2

This sample of the evidence shows how the author has tied the farewell discourse to the gospel narrative by using the narrator to introduce some of its key terms earlier in the narrative. Moreover, the narrator and Jesus deal with the same themes and use the same key terms in the same ways. The death of Jesus is of such enormous significance that it is carefully foreshadowed and interpreted by both the narrator and the discourse material.

In the farewell discourse, and indeed in John generally, there is a remarkable uniformity in the idiom of the narrator and Jesus. There is certainly the theoretical possibility that the author has adapted the speech of his narrator to Jesus' idiom, but it is more likely that Jesus' speech is "contaminated" by authorial speech patterns. In John the "phraseological points of view," or speech characteristics, of the narrator and Jesus are so close that the narrator's phraseological point of view seems to be imposed on Jesus.[27] The difference between the idiom of the Johannine Jesus and the synoptic Jesus, on the one hand, and the similarity between this idiom and the language of the Johannine epistles, on the other hand, confirms that when Jesus, the literary character, speaks, he speaks the language of the author and his narrator.[28]

The ideological and phraseological planes of the narrator's point of view, which correspond to Jesus' point of view, subtly influence the presentation of Jesus and the other characters throughout the narrative. This influence can be seen most clearly when dialogue is created by, grows out of, illustrates, or is influenced by narration. For example, a new word is introduced in John 6:41 when the narrator explains that the Jews were "murmuring" (*egoggyzon,* a vividly onomatopoetic word) about Jesus. The word is carefully chosen because it evokes the murmuring of the Israelites against Moses (Exod 16:7-9, 12; 17:3; Num 11:1; 14:27, 29; 16:41; 17:5; Pss 59:5; 106:25). By describing the Jews' response to Jesus with this word, the narrator has led the reader to view the action in the light of the Exodus events. This context has already been established by the dialogue in 6:31-32. Jesus immediately picks up the narrator's description of what was taking place: in 6:43 Jesus says, "Do nor murmur (*goggyzete*) among yourselves." Later, the narrator tells us that Jesus' perception of what was happening even among the disciples corresponds to his own: "But Jesus, knowing in himself that his disciples murmured (*goggyzousin*) at it, . . ." (6:61). Since the narrator's description corresponds exactly to Jesus', the reader is all the more inclined to accept the narrator as a reliable guide to the meaning of Jesus' life. Other passages fit this pattern also. In John 1:32,

---

[27] Uspensky (*A Poetics of Composition,* p. 52) makes the following relevant observations: "The less differentiation there is between the phraseology of the described (the character) and the describing (author or narrator), the closer are their phraseological points of view. The two opposite poles are: the faithful representation of the specifica of the character's speech (the case of maximum differentiation), and the narrated monologue (the case of minimal differentiation)."

[28] On the substitution of points of view, see ibid., p. 119.

the narrator uses a characteristically Johannine word, "and John bore witness, ..." John's own words echo this description immediately: "And I have seen and have borne witness that this is the Son of God" (1:34). Here again, the narrator's interpretation of the meaning of an event is carried over into the dialogue.

Because of the similarity in Jesus' and the narrator's speech patterns, and because of the narrator's influence on dialogue, it is impossible to tell when Jesus or John the Baptist stops speaking in chapter three and when or if the narrator speaks. The identity of the speaker in 3:13 (or 16)-21 and 3:31-36 is a well-known problem.[29] The author often allows characters to fade from the narrative without notice, but does not normally change speakers without telling the reader. It is certainly not clear that a change of speakers is intended in these passages. The temporal perspective, terminology, and content of 3:13 (or 16)-21, 31-36 vary in appropriateness for Jesus (or John) and the narrator. It appears to be a classic instance of the blending of the narrator with Jesus' voice. There are numerous parallels between these verses and the prologue and the farewell discourse. There is also a change of temporal point of view in verses 13 and 14. The imposition of one time on another, one voice on another, requires the reader to hear Jesus speaking to the reader's time through the narrator and hence through the gospel. Chatman observes that when it is not possible to decide whether the words are a character's or the narrator's it may well be intended:

> The implication is "It doesn't matter who says or thinks this; it is appropriate to both character and narrator." The ambiguity may strengthen the bond between the two, make us trust still more the narrator's authority. Perhaps we should speak of "neutralization" or "unification," rather than ambiguity.
> . . . .
> Such statements imply that character and narrator are so close, in such sympathy, that it does not matter to whom we assign the statement. . . . A feeling is established that the narrator possesses not only access to but an unusual affinity or "vibration" with the character's mind. There is the suggestion of a kind of "in"-group psychology: . . . .[30]

This analysis fits suggestively with the gospel's portrayal of the Beloved Disciple, a matter we will consider shortly.

The overall effect of the similarity between the narrator's and Jesus' points of view, the relationship between narration and the farewell discourse, the narrator's influence on dialogue, and the blending of voices in chapter three points to a complex relationship between Jesus and the narrator. Both narrator and character, of course, can be vehicles for the implied author's ideology. In the gospel it appears that the narrator is adopting Jesus' point of view ideologically and phraseologically, but this is just the impression the reader gets of the situation. Actually, the author, who was probably informed by tradition handed down within the Johannine community, fashioned the character, Jesus, as he wrote and interpreted Jesus through both Jesus' dialogue and the narrator's interpretive comments. It is therefore not a matter of the narrator's speech being conformed to Jesus', but of both reflecting the author's speech patterns and expressing his ideological (or theological) point of view. The consonance between Jesus and the narrator is a result of the author's expression of his point of view through both

---

[29]See D. Moody Smith, *The Composition and Order of the Fourth Gospel: Bultmann's Literary Theory* (New Haven: Yale University Press, 1965) 126; Raymond E. Brown, *The Gospel According to John* (AB 29; Garden City, NY: Doubleday and Co., 1966) 1. 159-60; Dodd, *The Interpretation of the Fourth Gospel*, p. 308; Rudolf Schnackenburg, *The Gospel According to St. John* (trans. K. Smyth; New York: Herder and Herder, 1968) 1. 360-93.
[30]Chatman, *Story and Discourse*, pp. 206-07.

his central character and the narrator. The character is not as objective or removed from the narrator as the unsuspecting reader may think. As a result, the narrator is an absolutely reliable guide to what Jesus meant to the author, a view, or better, a belief which the author sought to convey to the reader.

The narrator and the implied author. Another of the narrator's significant relationships is to the author, or implied author. The distinction between the two may help to highlight the aesthetic and rhetorical choices which the "real" author made in writing the gospel, but there is no reason to suspect any difference in the ideological, spatial, temporal, or phraseological points of view of the narrator, the implied author, and the author. Because of the peculiar character of the gospel, the relationships among these entities are best approached by looking further at the three figures which have interpretive roles in the gospel: the narrator, the Paraclete, and the Beloved Disciple. Implicitly or explicitly the authority of each is emphasized. The omniscient narrator tells about Jesus retrospectively with the effect that the reader is led to trust his account. Jesus speaks of the future role of the Paraclete, the Spirit of Truth, who will teach the disciples all things, remind them of what Jesus said (14:26), and bear witness concerning him (15:26). The Beloved Disciple has borne witness (19:35; 21:24-25), and the narrator confirms that his witness is true. A strong, complementary relationship among these three Johannine interpreters of the Jesus tradition is therefore evident.

In *The Johannine School,* I argued that the similarity in the functions of the Paraclete and the Beloved Disciple within the Johannine community suggests that the community formed its understanding of the Spirit as Paraclete in the light of reflection on what the Beloved Disciple had done in their midst.[31] I shall not pursue that relationship further here. The key references for discussion of the relationship between the Beloved Disciple, the narrator, the implied author, and the author are John 19:35 and 21:24-25. Discussion of these verses has generally been concerned with their place within the gospel's composition history: Was 19:35 written by the evangelist or the redactor? Perhaps new insights can be gained by starting from the observation that it is the narrator who makes these comments.

Such a reading of John 19:35 reveals that it fits appropriately into the narration of the gospel. The narrator, who speaks about Jesus retrospectively, here relates something which happened subsequent to the crucifixion: namely, "the one who saw these things," presumably the Beloved Disciple, bore witness to them. Then, the narrator, who like the Paraclete knows all about Jesus, affirms that the Beloved Disciple's witness is true. The narrator, therefore, is not the Beloved Disciple but speaks as one who knows what is true, knows the mind of the Beloved Disciple, and knows that what the Beloved Disciple said is true. It is difficult to go further on the basis of this verse alone. The Beloved Disciple may be just another character through whom the author's point of view is communicated, or he may be an idealized representation of the author (hence a dramatic approximation of the implied author), or an accurate characterization of the author himself.

Before turning to the crucial, concluding verses of the gospel it will be helpful to review what the Beloved Disciple knows and what he tells in the course of the narrative. It may well be that the unidentified companion of Andrew in 1:35-40 is the Beloved Disciple. If so, as one of the first two disciples, he was with Jesus from the beginning of his ministry, the beginning of the story. There is some cogency in identifying both this disciple and Peter's unnamed companion in 18:15 with the Beloved Disciple. The explicit reference to the Beloved Disciple as "the other disciple" in 20:4 adds to the likelihood of this identification, but the narrative stops short of making it certain. The Beloved Disciple is introduced for the first time at the last supper. There, he is the one closest to Jesus. Jesus reveals to him the identity of the betrayer (13:25-

---

[31]R. Alan Culpepper, *The Johannine School* (SBLDS 26; Missoula: Scholars Press, 1975) 266-70.

26) through the dipping of the morsel. If the Beloved Disciple understands what Jesus means, he does not reveal Jesus' secret to Peter or any of the others before its time.[32] At the empty tomb the Beloved Disciple sees the grave clothes and believes (20:8), but does not tell Peter or any of the others what he understood. News of the resurrection reaches them through Mary Magdalene (20:18). The Beloved Disciple's silence about the empty tomb fits the pattern of the last supper scene and his seeing the water and the blood at the cross. He understands but does not bear witness until later. Luke would have said he "kept all these things, pondering them in his heart."

Virtually every part of John 21:24 is open to multiple interpretations except "this disciple," who must be the Beloved Disciple (cf. 21:20-23).[33] What are "these things" to which he has borne witness, John 21:23 and its immediate context (as Dodd argued), John 21, or the gospel as a whole?[34] Does ho grapsas mean "who wrote (these things)" or "who caused (these things) to be written"?[35] Who is denoted by "we," and what was their relationship to the Beloved Disciple?

Without needlessly multiplying entities, John 21:24-25 is open to interpretations involving one, two, or three persons. The one-person theory claims that the Beloved Disciple, the author, identifies himself here after implying that the community should not expect him to live until the parousia. This view founders upon four considerations: (1) John 21 seems to be an appendix added after the gospel reached its penultimate form, (2) it is more likely that 21:23 implies that the Beloved Disciple has died, (3) the writer identifies himself with the "we" over against "this disciple," and (4) it is unlikely that anyone would refer to himself as "the Beloved Disciple." One version in the two-person theory would say that 21:24-25 was written by the evangelist (the author of the rest of the gospel) and that the evangelist attributed his work to the Beloved Disciple, who may have been his mentor and the source of his material. Assuming this version of the two-person theory, the author at the end writes as a member of the group that has received the gospel written by the Beloved Disciple and attests to its truth. If this is the case, the Gospel of John is a pseudonymous writing in which the author subverts any suspicion that he has written it by attributing the gospel to the Beloved Disciple. A more common version of the two-person theory maintains that these verses are the work of an editor who identified the gospel's real author, the Beloved Disciple. This view is usually coupled with the assumption that the gospel's depiction of the Beloved Disciple is historically accurate. The three-person theory distinguishes the Beloved Disciple, the evangelist, and the editor as three separate persons. John 21:24-25 comes from an editor who attributed the gospel to the Beloved Disciple, the community's founding father, when in reality the Beloved Disciple was merely the source of the evangelist's material. If, as seems probable, John 19:35 comes from the evangelist, he too acknowledged the gospel's dependence on the Beloved Disciple.[36] Regardless of whether the Beloved Disciple was

---

[32]Cf. Marinus de Jonge, *Jesus: Stranger from Heaven and Son of God* (SBLSBS 11; ed. and trans. John E. Steely; Missoula: Scholars Press, 1977) 211-13.

[33]For a brief discussion of the problems involved in interpreting John 21:24-25 see: Stephen S. Smalley, *John: Evangelist and Interpreter* (Exeter: Paternoster Press, 1978) 80-81.

[34]C. H. Dodd, "Note on John 21, 24," *JTS* 4 (1953) 212-13. Dodd's view of this verse has not been widely accepted. Cf. Rudolf Bultmann, *The Gospel of John* (trans. G. R. Beasley-Murray; Philadelphia: Westminster Press, 1971) 717 n. 4; Brown, *John*, 2. 1123-24; C. K. Barrett, *The Gospel According to St. John* (2nd ed.; Philadelphia: Westminster Press, 1978) 588.

[35]Brown (*John*, 2. 1123) follows G. Schrenk, "*Graphō*," *TDNT* (Grand Rapids: Wm. B. Eerdmans, 1964) 1. 743, in adopting the weakened, causative, meaning. On the other hand, Barrett, *John*, p. 587; Barnabas Lindars, *The Gospel of John* (NCB; Grand Rapids: Wm. B. Eerdmans, 1981), p. 641; and de Jonge, *Jesus*, p. 221 n. 28, favor the more direct sense, "who wrote."

[36]Smith, *The Composition and Order of the Fourth Gospel*, p. 233; Brown, *John*, 2. 1127.

the evangelist, or wrote parts of the gospel or its source material, or just inspired its writing, the narrator's retrospective point of view may derive from his influence on the gospel. The debate over these alternatives, however, has not given much attention to the role of the narrator in the gospel. What difference does it make if these verses are taken as an integral part of the narration, i.e., as the words of the narrator?

First, the appearance of the narrator speaking in the first person at the end of the narrative should be seen as a common literary convention, not as something extraordinary or problematic. Uspensky has explored the function of framing in pictorial art and literature. Both present a strange new world which the viewer or reader must enter to comprehend it and then leave to re-enter the "real" world. In literature there are various devices which facilitate this transition from an external to an internal point of view at the beginning and from an internal to an external point of view at the conclusion. Among these are references to the narrator in the first person and the reader in the second person. John fits the pattern perfectly. The only clear references to "we" (omitting, for example, 3:11; 4:22) are at the beginning (1:14, 16) and at the end (21:24), and the reader is referred to directly with the second person plural in what is generally taken to be the original conclusion of the gospel (20:30-31). Uspensky did not have John in mind, but might well have, when he wrote:

> We have presented examples from folklore, but the same principle is evident in literature. Thus, for example, it is typical for some narratives that a first-person narrator who did not appear earlier in the story suddenly appears at the end. In other cases, this first-person narrator appears once at the beginning of the story, and then disappears . . . . his function, . . . is only to provide a frame for the story.
>
> Exactly the same function may be attributed to the unexpected address to a second person which occurs at the end in some narrative forms--that is an address to the reader, whose presence had been completely ignored until that moment.[37]

Uspensky also notes that the death of "the dominant representative of the authorial point of view in the story" is a device which effects a shift to the external point of view and produces what Frank Kermode called "the sense of an ending."[38] The death of the Beloved Disciple is implied by John 21:23. In all these respects, the conclusion of the gospel fits well-established patterns for framing a narrative.

The relationship between the narrator and the Beloved Disciple can be clarified further if one takes the view that the Beloved Disciple is an idealized characterization of an historical figure. Insofar as there is a consensus among Johannine scholars it is that there was a real person, who may have been an eyewitness to events in Jesus' ministry, and who was later the authoritative source of tradition for the Johannine community. The witness of the Beloved Disciple was probably also understood to be an expression of the work of the Paraclete. Because of his significance for the community, the Beloved Disciple was idealized by the author and given a role at the last supper, the crucifixion, the discovery of the empty tomb, and the appearance in Galilee. There is no corroborative evidence for his role, however, and he does not bear witness until after the resurrection and therefore does not affect events in the story.

On such a reading, the narrator finally identifies, or better, characterizes the implied author as the Beloved Disciple: "This is the disciple who is bearing witness to these things, and who has written these things" (21:24). Wayne Booth's definition of the implied author as the literary image of the artist should be recalled: "This implied author is always distinct from the 'real man'--whatever we may take him to be--who

---

[37]Uspensky, *A Poetics of Composition,* p. 147.

[38]Ibid., p. 148; Frank Kermode, *The Sense of an Ending: Studies in the Theory of Fiction* (New York: Oxford University Press, 1967).

creates a superior version of himself, a 'second self,' as he creates his work."[39] Not only does the evangelist create a superior version of himself as he writes, but the editor identifies this superior self ("who has written these things") as the Beloved Disciple. When the narrator dramatically pulls the curtain on the implied author in the closing verses of the gospel, the reader recognizes that the Beloved Disciple fits the image the gospel projects of its implied author as one who knows Jesus intimately, shares his theological perspective, and can interpret reliably, i.e., "his witness is true." The reader is thus given yet another reason for believing the gospel: its implied author is the Beloved Disciple. The narrator is presented as a member of the group ("we") which knows that the testimony of the Beloved Disciple is true. In the last verse the narrator adds that there are many other things which are not written here and comments that there is no end to the books that could be written.

In John 21:24, therefore, the editor characterizes the implied author (the superior self of the evangelist reflected in John 1-20, i.e., "he who has written these things") as the Beloved Disciple (the gospel's idealized portrayal of the evangelist's mentor). This conclusion not only assumes a three-person theory but relates it to the role of the narrator throughout the gospel. As a variation of the three-person theory it must also assume that the editor: (1) did not know the evangelist, or (2) was guided in his identification primarily by the internal evidence of John 1-20 rather than personal or community knowledge, or (3) used *ho grapsas* in its weakened, causative sense, or (4) deliberately sought to increase the authority of the gospel and honor the memory of the Beloved Disciple by this identification. These alternatives, which are not mutually exclusive, are listed in order of ascending probability. The last fits the evidence of John 21:24, the careful buttressing of the gospel's authority, and the idealization of the Beloved Disciple in John. The separation of the narrator from the implied author, which is without a parallel in ancient literature, probably came about, therefore, as a result of the idealizing of the Beloved Disciple and the comment of an editor rather than as a sophisticated ploy by an individual author.

Since the gospel is so daring in its perspective, its authority is established on the witness of the Beloved Disciple (an eyewitness), the reliability of the narrator, and the words of Jesus about the Paraclete. The narrator is not only omniscient but omnicommunicative and gives ample preliminary exposition in the prologue, which is confirmed by the story itself. All of these narrative devices incline the reader toward accepting the author's understanding of Jesus. In fact, the gospel makes use of virtually all of the devices available for heightening the credibility and authority of a narrative: appeal to tradition, a reliable narrator, inspiration (the Paraclete), eyewitness testimony, the authority of an esteemed figure (the Beloved Disciple), and the approval of a community.[40] Internally, the provision of historical, geographical, and descriptive detail which is either demonstrably true or verisimilar serves to confirm the claims the

---

[39]Booth, *The Rhetoric of Fiction,* p. 151.

[40]Scholes and Kellogg (*The Nature of Narrative,* pp. 246-47) describe the use of authority establishing techniques in antiquity: "By the end of Roman times virtually all the possibilities for establishing the authority of a narrative had been employed in one way or another. A writer dealing with the past could adopt any of a number of postures: he could be a historian (Tacitus), the inspired bard (Vergil, Ovid) or something in between (Lucan). A writer dealing with more recent times could present a personal eye-witness account in his own name (Augustine), a fictional account in a character's name (Petronius), or something in between (Apuleius). A writer more concerned with fictional than traditional, historical, or mimetic representation could offer a story with no justification (Xenophon of Ephesus' *Ephesian Tale*), one which carried its own esthetic and didactic justification (Longus' *Daphnis and Chloe*), or one which leaned toward eyewitness testimony (Achilles Tatius' *Leucippe and Cleitophon*)." See also pp. 242-43, 265-66.

narrative makes for itself.[41] There is no chance that the reader will miss the seriousness of the gospel's claim that it has the potential for a life or death effect on its readers. Such deliberate construction of credibility suggests a context of controversy in which John's distinctive stereoscopic Christology, the claim that Jesus was the pre-existent *logos* and exalted Son of God, was the divisive issue. It suggests further that one of the major purposes of the Fourth Gospel was to present a corrective view of Jesus. The disciples did not understand Jesus or his words during his ministry (12:16; 13:7). Only later did they understand. So, any account, whether written or oral, from an apostle or a prophet, which was not informed by the retrospective ideological point of view of this gospel could not present Jesus or his words in their true light.

Although the wizard has refused to give his name, we have heard his whisper. Our study of the role of the narrator, his point of view, and his relationship to Jesus and the implied author has at least established the contours of his identity.[42]

---

[41]Kermode, *The Genesis of Secrecy*, pp. 109, 118.

[42]While it is not my purpose to attempt to clarify further the gospel's composition history, this chapter may have certain implications for that task. The narrator's intrusive and interpretative comments cannot easily be attributed to an editor unless the editor is given a significant formative role in the gospel's composition or is virtually indistinguishable from the evangelist in his perspective. There is no evidence that they are later (or scribal) glosses, for they express a consistent point of view. Moreover, the correspondence in point of view between the narrator and the farewell discourse may be a significant indicator of a common origin for the farewell discourse and narrative material in the gospel. At least it renders problematic any theory which attributes either type of material to a source drawn from outside the Johannine community. In its present form, if not in its origin, the gospel must be approached as a unity, a literary whole.

POINT OF VIEW AND THE DISCIPLES IN MARK

Joanna Dewey

Graduate Seminary, Phillips University, Enid, OK

In this paper for the Group on Literary Aspects of the Gospels, I wish to address the question of point of view toward the disciples in the gospel of Mark. In their work presented at the meeting last year, Norman Petersen[1] and Robert Fowler[2] agreed that, in Mark, the point of view of Jesus is essentially the same as that of the omniscient narrator or implied author.[3] Therefore, whatever an actual reader may do, the implied reader accepts the point of view of the author, and thus identifies with Jesus. The question I wish to address is: does this identification of the implied reader with Jesus necessitate that s/he reject the disciples, or is it possible that the implied reader would also identify in some way with the disciples? Is the matter of Jesus and the disciples a matter of either/or, or is it a case of both/and--both a particular sort of identification with Jesus and another with the disciples?

In this paper I shall argue that it is theoretically possible and in fact the case that the implied reader would identify in some ways with Jesus and in others with the disciples. In doing so, I shall present evidence concerning point of view in regard to the disciples according to the categories of mood and voice developed by Gérard Genette in *Narrative Discourse: An Essay in Method.*[4] First, I shall describe the problem the narrative portrayal of the disciples presents for the implied reader. Second, I shall summarize Genette's narrative categories. Third, I shall apply his categories to Mark's portrait of the disciples. Finally, I shall conclude with a brief theoretical postscript on the usefulness and appropriateness of Genette's theory for understanding the markan narrative.

I

The portrait of the disciples is ambiguous in Mark. On the whole, the narrator of Mark has indicated clearly to the narratee which characters are approved and which scorned in the narrative world. Among the human characters, Jesus and some of the people Jesus heals are clearly good. The scribes, the Pharisees, the Herodians and the chief priests are equally clearly the villains of the piece. The information the narrator gives in regard to the disciples permits no such clear-cut decision. In some respects the disciples are presented quite favorably: they leave all to follow Jesus (Mk 1:16-20; 2:14), they successfully preach and cast out demons (6:12-13), they do--eventually--understand the necessity of suffering (10:35-40; 14:26-31), and they persevere in following Jesus almost (but not quite) to the end (14:50). On the other hand, they frequently fail to understand Jesus' parables (4:10-13; 7:17-18), his power over the sea (4:37-41; 6:48-52), and his ability to feed thousands (6:35-44; 8:1-9); they are very slow to grasp the need for suffering (8:32-9:1; 9:32-37; 10:35-46); and eventually, one disciple betrays Jesus, all flee at his arrest, and another denies him three times (14:10-11, 43-50, 66-72). Yet the

---

[1] " 'Point of View' in Mark's Narrative," *Semeia* 12 (1978) 97-121.

[2] "The Point of View of the Narrator of Mark (From the Point of View of the Narratee)," Paper circulated for the Literary Aspects of the Gospels Group, 1981. See also idem, *Loaves and Fishes* (SBLDS 54; Chico: Scholars Press, 1981) 149-83.

[3] In some narratives it is necessary to distinguish between the implied author and implied reader on one hand, and the narrator and narratee on the other. Since Mark employs an omniscient and fully reliable narrator, it would seem that the implied author and the narrator are one and the same, and also the implied reader and the narratee. Therefore, I use the terms interchangeably.

[4] (Tr. Jane E. Lewin; Ithaca: Cornell, 1980).

narrative of Mark 13 suggests to the implied reader that the disciples will be restored to Jesus and will play their part in the days between the empty tomb and the end.[5] Further, Jesus' saying in the Gethsemane scene, "the spirit indeed is willing, but the flesh is weak" (14:38), suggests a basis within the narrative for excusing the disciples' behavior at the time of the arrest.[6] How then is the narratee to evaluate the disciples?

Not surprisingly, scholars do not agree. The most negative evaluation of the disciples in Mark is probably still that made by T. J. Weden in 1971.[7] He views the disciples in the narrative as representatives of Mark's historical opponents, who are presented in the narrative as permanently deposed and discredited when they flee at the arrest. Transposing Weeden's historical thesis into a literary one, one could say that the implied author orchestrates their complete rejection by the implied reader.

Robert Tannehill may perhaps be said to represent the other extreme, the identification of the reader with the disciples:

> . . . a reader will identify most easily and immediately with characters who seem to share the reader's situation . . . [The author] composed his story so as to make use of this initial tendency to identify with the disciples in order to speak indirectly to the reader through the disciples' story. In doing so, he first reinforces the positive view of the disciples which he anticipates from his readers, thus strengthening the tendency to identify with them. Then he reveals the inadequacy of the disciples . . . [which] requires the reader to distance himself from them and their behavior. But something of the initial identification remains, for there are similarities between the problems which the first readers faced. This tension between identification and repulsion can lead the sensitive reader beyond a naively positive view of himself to self-criticism and repentance. The composition of Mark strongly suggests that the author, by the way in which he tells the disciples' story, intended to awaken his readers to their failures as disciples and call them to repentance.[8]

Tannehill posits the actual reader's identification with the disciples on the basis of similarity of situation and problems facing them both. While the description of the actual first readers goes beyond the available data, the similarity of situation would seem to apply to the implied reader. The implied author addresses the implied reader with demands just as within the narrative Jesus addresses the disciples with demands.

In a response to Tannehill's work given at the 1978 Seminar on Mark, Mary Ann Tolbert argued that, on the contrary, the implied reader would identify with Jesus:

> The ideal reader identifies with Jesus . . . . The ideal reader evaluates people and situations from the standpoint of the hero, Jesus. When Jesus favors the disciples, so does the reader; when Jesus despairs over the disciples, so does the reader. Not only is Jesus betrayed by the disciples, but the ideal reader is also betrayed by them.[9]

---

[5]Thus I accept Petersen's argument in regard to the implied reader's expectation of fulfillment of prophecy (*Literary Criticism for New Testament Critics* [Philadelphia: Fortress, 1978] 49-80). However, even if one does not accept the restoration of the disciples, most of my argument remains valid for the implied reader cannot make that decision until the end of the narrative.

[6]See Anitra Bingham Kolenkow, "Beyond Miracles, Suffering and Eschatology," *1973 Seminar Papers* (SBLASP 109; Society of Biblical Literature, 1973) 2. 160-70.

[7] *Mark--Traditions in Conflict* (Philadelphia: Fortress, 1971).

[8]"The Disciples in Mark: The Function of a Narrative Role," *JR* 57 (1977) 392-93. See also idem, "The Gospel of Mark as Narrative Christology," *Semeia* 16 (1979) 57-95.

[9]"1978 Markan Seminar: Response to Robert Tannehill," Paper circulated to the Seminar on Mark, 1978, p. 12.

Work on point of view in Mark suggests that Tolbert is indeed correct, at least in part. Using Boris Uspensky's planes of composition[10] Petersen has shown the alignment and implicit identification of the omniscient narrator with the principal character, Jesus:

> Mark's ideological standpoint is identical with that of his central character, Jesus
> . . . . all (characters) are evaluated by one point of view, the one shared by the
> narrator and the character, Jesus. . . .[11]

Tolbert, Petersen (and Fowler) have shown that there is an identification of the implied reader with the values of Jesus. But Tannehill still has a point: the situation of the implied reader is similar to that of the disciples, not to that of Jesus. And this similarity also suggests identification. What is needed is a theory to understand two different types of identification.

II

With the hope that Genette's subdivision of the overall category of point of view into mood and voice would help me to understand how the implied reader might identify with the disciples as well as with Jesus, I turned to the study of Genette.[12] In view of the multiplicity of Genette's technical vocabulary, I shall briefly summarize his work as it relates to my study.[13] At times I shall expand his descriptions with material from Susan Sniader Lanser's *The Narrative Act: Point of View in Prose Fiction.*[14]

Genette's categories of mood and voice, drawn from grammar, deal directly with issues related to point of view. Mood is a metaphorical extension of the grammatical concept of mood (subjunctive, indicative, etc.) to apply to different degrees of indicative or of affirmation. Distance and perspective are the two means of regulating narrative information that make up mood.[15] By distance, Genette refers to the distinction between pure narration or telling and pure mimesis or showing. Pure telling plus the obvious presence of a narrator provides the greatest distance; showing combined with the relative absence of the narrator increases closeness to the narrative. Showing is heightened by the sheer quanity of the information, the inclusion of unnecessary concrete details, and by direct speech of the characters.[16] Lanser adds that subjective or inside information also heightens mimetic effect.[17]

The second aspect of mood is perspective. Genette argues that most understandings of point of view confuse two issues, the question of *who sees* and the question of *who speaks*. A narrator speaks but may restrict his/her vision or perspective to that of a character in the narrative. Genette calls such a character who sees but does not speak a focalizer. The narrator may also be the focalizer, but s/he need not be. Perspective addresses the question of who sees and is divided into three types of focalization: (1) nonfocalized narrative presented by an omniscient narrator; (2) internal

---

[10] *A Poetics of Composition* (tr. Valentina Zavarin and Susan Wittig; Berkeley: University of California, 1973).

[11] "Point of View," p. 107.

[12] Genette prefers to restrict the term 'point of view' to perspective. I am continuing to use it as a general umbrella for all aspects of 'point of view.'

[13] See also Fowler's summary, "Point of View," pp. 11-12.

[14] (Princeton: Princeton University, 1981). In the following discussion I continue to use Genette's terminology rather than Lanser's.

[15] Genette, pp. 161-62.

[16] Ibid., pp. 162-85.

[17] Lanser, pp. 205-7.

focalization which may be fixed through one character or alternate among various characters and (3) external focalization in which there is no inside view of any character.[18] Lanser points out that focalization increases mimetic effect:

> The focalizer, usually a 'fleshed-out' character, can carry considerable *mimetic authority*--authority that attaches to the acting persona. In other words, the authority of intellection attaches most fully to the public voice (in Mark, the omniscient narrator), while that authority of lived (fictional) experience is more fully embodied in the focalizing character.[19]

Voice deals with who speaks, with the act of narrating as it appears in the text. Its three elements are person, narrative level and time of narrating.[20] Under person Genette deals with issues generally considered under the heading of first- or third-person narrative.[21] Narrative level is a means of describing the phenomenon of stories within stories (within stories).[22] The initial or first-level narrator is outside of the narrative (extradiegetic) and narrates the first-level narrative. A character within the first-level narrative relates a second-level narrative; a character in the second-level narrative narrates the third level, and so forth, as needed. As one changes level, the narratee changes along with the narrator. The first-level narrator addresses the primary narratee--in the case of Mark, the implied reader. The second-level narrator, him/herself a character in the first-level narrative, addresses the second-level narratee, also a character in the first-level narrative. Thus, the second-level narratee (the internal audience) is to the second-level narrator (internal character) as the implied reader is to the implied author. This notion of different narratees at different levels suggests a structural or situational similarity of the implied reader with the disciples-- both are narratees.

The higher the level of the narrative, that is, the greater the degree of embedding, the greater is the distance of the implied reader from the narrative. The implied reader has access to higher-level narratives only indirectly through the higher-level, internal narratees. Genette states, however, that the greater distance of the implied reader may not be perceived:

> And if the existence of an intradiegetic [higher-level] narratee has the effect of keeping us at a distance, since he is always interposed between the narrator and us ... it is true that the more transparent the receiving instance and the more silent its evocation in the narrative, so undoubtedly the easier, or rather the more irresistible, each real reader's identification with or substitution for that implied instance will be.[23]

Lanser develops her theory of narrative level considerably beyond Genette's work. Like Genette, she views narrative (diegesis) and mimesis as opposite poles on a continuum. Genette views the continuum as indicative of distance, part of mood. For Lanser, the two poles represent two different sorts of textual authority--narrative or conceptual authority on the one hand and mimetic or experiential authority on the other. Furthermore, Lanser attaches this continuum to narrative level. The lower the level (the closer one is to the implied author), the greater is the diegetic authority; the higher the level (the farther removed from the implied author), the greater is the

---

[18]Genette, pp. 185-94.
[19]Lanser, p. 142.
[20]Genette, pp. 214-15.
[21]Ibid., pp. 243-48.
[22]Ibid., pp. 227-31, 259-62.
[23]Ibid., p. 260.

mimetic authority.[24] Thus, for Lanser there are two kinds of authority in a narrative which function in inverse relationship to each other. Lanser's theory of two authorities may provide a clue to help understand the identification of the implied reader with both Jesus and the disciples.

Genette's time of narrating compares that time to the time of the story narrated. The time of narrating is prior for predictive narrative or prophecy, subsequent for the usual past-tense narrative, or simultaneous. Simultaneous narrating, when the emphasis is on the story being narrated, serves to make the narrative transparent to the story and thus heightens the mimetic effect.[25]

III

In this section I shall describe the employment of mood and voice in the markan narrative as far as it concerns the portrayal of the disciples, in order to see if Genette's (and Lanser's) theory can aid us in understanding the relationship of the implied reader to the disciples.

Mood: distance. The disciples are portrayed with a considerable degree of mimetic illusion, thus closeness. The disciples are often presented in direct speech: 4:38, 41; 5:31; 6:35-36, 37, 38; 8:4, 5, 16, 19, 20, 28, 29; 9:5, 11, 28, 38; 10:26, 28, 35, 37, 39; 11:21; 13:1, 4; 14:12, 19, 29, 31, 68, 71. Frequent inside views of the disciples' thoughts and emotions are given: 4:40, 41; 5:42; 6:48, 49, 50, 51-52; 8:16, 17-18, 21, 33; 9:6, 32, 34; 10:24, 26, 38, 41; 11:21; 14:10, 18, 19, 27, 30, 40, 72.[26] A variety of unnecessary concrete details that create a mimetic effect are included in narratives concerning the disciples: the implied reader is told not only that Simon, Andrew, James and John are fishermen, but that at the moment of being called, Simon and Andrew were casting out a net and James and John were mending theirs (1:16, 19). In the storm at sea, Jesus is not just asleep, but asleep on a cushion (presumably wet) at the boat's stern (4:37-38), etc. Yet the disciples do not appear to be portrayed with a greater degree of mimesis or closeness than other characters in the narrative. All the characters tend to use direct speech. There are inside views of Jesus, opponents, and people being healed as well. And there is probably a greater concentration of unnecessary detail in the healing narratives than elsewhere.

Mood: perspective. The markan narrative is almost entirely non-focalized-- presented directly by an omniscient and omnipresent narrator. The transfiguration scene, however, is visualized or focalized through the disciples. The narrator tells the story, constantly noting the disciples. Jesus takes Peter, James, and John and takes *them* up the mountain *alone by themselves;* Jesus was transfigured before *them;* Elijah and Moses appeared to *them;* Peter speaks; *they* were afraid; a cloud overshadows *them* and finally *they* no longer see anyone but Jesus (9:2-8). The implied reader sees what the disciples see, hears what they hear, and is conscious of their inner state, and thus is

---

[24]Lanser, pp. 140-45. Lanser views the focalizer as the highest narrative level. She does not explicitly discuss the placing of mimetic authority when there is no focalizer, which she says is often the case. However, her overall stress on the presence of different levels and her understanding of diegetic vs. mimetic authority as a continuum suggests that she would view all narratives as presenting a mimetic authority distinct from its diegetic authority.

[25]Genette, pp. 215-22.

[26]I have developed this list from Fowler's list of all inside views (*Loaves,* p. 166).

brought into close alignment with them.[27] In addition, the scene of the stilling of the storm is focalized through the disciples (4:36-41).

Focalization through other characters also occurs occasionally in the narrative. Focalization through Jesus occurs in 1:9-11, 16-20; 11:12-14, 15-17; 12:41-44 and 14:33-42. In addition 5:2-13 is focalized through the Gerasene demoniac, 5:25-29 through the woman with a flow of blood, 15:16-24 through the soldiers, and finally 16:1-5 through the women at the empty tomb. All the rest of the narrative is unfocalized.

Focalization, then, in the markan narrative does not appear to be a means of stressing any particular character since it occurs only rarely and scattered among various major and minor characters. (Considering that Jesus is the major character in virtually the entire narrative, the larger number of scenes focalized through him does not appear significant.) Genette's distinction of 'who sees' from 'who speaks' does not help to explain a dual identification of the implied reader in Mark.

Voice: Person. There is an omniscient narrator who is not a character in the narrative--in Genette's terms an extra-diegetic-heterodiegetic narrator.[28]

Voice: Narrative Level. The majority of the markan narrative--the story about Jesus—is presented directly by the first-level narrator, the omniscient narrator. A considerable portion of the gospel, however, is direct teaching by Jesus, a character in the first-level narrative. And some of this teaching seems clearly to be second-level narrative. The parable discourse obviously consists of stories within the first-level story (4:3-32). Also the apocalyptic discourse would seem to be second-level narrative, complete with second-level characters who speak in their own right, saying, "I am he!" or "Look, here is the Christ!" (13:6, 21). The following shorter passages spoken by Jesus might also be considered second-level narrative: 3:23-29; 7:6-23; 8:34-9:1; 9:39-50 and 12:1-11. Mark 3:23-29 and 8:34-9:1, alternatively, may be considered simply dialogue of first-level characters. In practice the dividing line is not always clear cut. There appears to be no second-level narrative in Mark with a narrator other than Jesus and no third-level narrative at all.

Second-level narrative of course has its own narratee. Jesus does not directly address the implied reader but rather other characters within the narrative world. The narratee for the parable discourse is at first the crowd, then at 4:10 it shifts to the twelve and those with them, and somewhere after that reverts back to the crowd. The narratee for the apocalyptic discourse is the inner group of disciples, Peter, James, John and Andrew (13:3). For the shorter second-level passages the narratees are as follows: 3:23-29, scribes; 7:6-23, scribes, crowd, disciples; 8:34-9:1, disciples and crowd; 9:39-50, disciples; 12:1-11, opponents and crowd. Even in those passages in which the disciples are not explicitly present, they may be assumed to be there since the disciples accompany Jesus continuously from 1:16 to 14:50 except for 6:12-29. Thus the disciples (or some of them) may be considered part of all the second-level narratees. The very construct of multi-level narration highlights the fact that there is a structural relationship between first- and second-level narrators and between first- and second-level narratees. Thus, there is built into the structure of Mark's narrative itself a relationship between the implied reader and the disciples (and other second-level narratees). Structurally, the implied reader is more akin to the disciples than to Jesus.

The structural relationship, however, may be developed in a number of different ways. As noted earlier, the existence of a second-level narratee may be used to increase

---

[27] A comparison of Luke's version of the transfiguration (Lk 9:28-36) helps to show the focalization in Mark by contrast. The lukan narrator views the scene from above, first showing Elijah, Moses, and Jesus in glory talking, and then showing the disciples struggling to stay awake.

[28] Genette, p. 248.

the distance of the implied reader from the second-level narrative by stressing the interposition of the internal narratee between the reader and the narrative. Or the second-level narratee may fade into the background, leaving the implied reader as the effectual direct addressee of the second-level narrative.

The latter seems to be the case in Mark. The close relationship between the omniscient narrator and the second-level narrator, Jesus, suggests the possibility of a close relationship between the two narratees. Both narrators are reliable and they are aligned, even identified, on the ideological plane--that is, they share the same values. On the first-level, the implied reader accepts the values of the omniscient narrator; on the second level, the disciples are the group in the narrative which most strongly attempts to follow Jesus (whether or not they succeed). Also the implied reader hears the private teaching to the disciples, thus aligning him/her more closely to the disciples than to other second-level narratees. Therefore, the implied reader and the disciples are aligned not only by structure but also by acceptance of the ideological stance of the omniscient narrator and Jesus.

The second-level narratees are presented in Mark 4 and 13, the two longest second-level narratives, so as to reinforce the implied reader's impression that s/he is part of Jesus' audience. In Mark 4, the second-level narratee fades into the background. For much of the narrative it is not even clear who that narratee is--crowd or inner circle. The implied reader is free to perceive him/herself as the narratee.

In Mark 13, on the other hand, the narrator is intrusive into the narrative. In fact both narrators, first- and second-level, intrude. In theory, the obvious presence of the narrators increases the reader's awareness of the narrating situation and thus increases the distance of the implied reader from the second-level narrative. However, the content of the narrative intrusions spell out that Jesus' speech is addressed directly to the implied reader as well as to the disciples. The first intrusion, "Let the reader understand" (13:14) is a violation of level.[29] The omniscient narrator intrudes into the speech of the second-level narrator in order to address the actual reader directly. The effect of the violation of level is not the merging of the first- and second-level narratees, but rather the placing of them side by side listening to Jesus. One would have to say either that the implied reader has become a character internal to the narrative world or the narrative world has been extended to include reality external to it.

The second intrusion, "And what I say to you I say to all: Watch" (13:37), is commentary by the second-level narrator, Jesus, extending his discourse to others besides the second-level narratee. Strictly speaking, this extension which is internal to the narrative applies to characters within it--other disciples, crowd, etc. But the implied reader has already been brought into the narrative at 13:14 and commanded to understand. The implied reader is likely to perceive him/herself as part of that 'all,' indeed as specifically addressed by it.[30] The warnings and promises of Mark 13 have become directly applicable to the implied reader.

The exploration of second-level narrative in Mark has suggested that the implied reader would identify in some way with the disciples. This identification is structural, or to use Tannehill's term, situational. The placing of the implied reader side by side with the disciples suggests that s/he should compare him/herself to the disciples. But it is not a question of the implied reader emulating the disciples' behavior; rather both the disciples and the implied reader are to live according to the behavior demanded by Jesus. So while the situation of the implied reader is that of the disciples, the criteria by which s/he is to be judged derive from Jesus (and the omniscient narrator). The relationships might perhaps be diagrammed as follows:

---

[29]Genette (pp. 234-36) calls this phenomenon a metalepsis.

[30]This is the common exegetical interpretation. See, for example, William L. Lane, *Commentary on the Gospel of Mark* (NICNT; Grand Rapids: Eerdmans, 1974) 483-84; Vincent Taylor, *The Gospel According to St. Mark* (2nd ed.; London: Macmillan, 1964) 524.

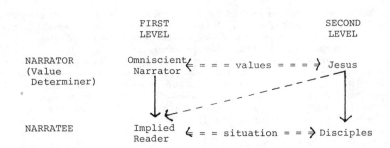

Thus, a consideration of narrative level suggests how the implied reader might identify both with Jesus and with the disciples: his/her values are those of Jesus, but his/her situation is that of the disciples.

   Voice: Time of Narrating. The time of narrating is more complex in the markan narrative (and the other gospels) than in many narratives. The bulk of the time of narrating is subsequent--that is, the omniscient narrator is relating events viewed as having already occurred in the past of the narrative world. In this case, the events would also be understood as past by the implied reader. The frequent use of the historic present, however, serves to make the time of narrating appear simultaneous with the story being narrated, thus bringing the past into the implied reader's present.

   Further, some of the events described by the second-level narrator, Jesus, are narrated prior to their occurrence: e.g. the passion predictions (8:31; 9:31; 10:33-34) and the apocalyptic discourse (13:5-37). Although the passion predictions refer to the future of Jesus and the disciples (the second level), these events are of course past for the omniscient narrator and the implied reader (the first level). However, the content of the apocalyptic discourse remains predominantly future for the omniscient narrator and the implied reader as well: the time the gospel is preached to all nations is the implied reader's present but the end of the age is future.

   On the temporal plane, the implied reader is more closely aligned with the events of the apocalyptic discourse than is the immediate narratee, the disciples. Indeed, the extension of prophecy up to and including the end of the age functions to incorporate the implied reader into the narrative world. Thus the effect of the shifts of time of narrating in Mark reinforces the inclusion of the implied reader into the narrative already noted in the analysis of narrative level of Mark 13.

   The time of narrating reverts in Mark 14-16 to subsequent narration--the events are viewed as in the narrator's and implied reader's past. And in these chapters, the disciples fail thoroughly to heed the warnings of Mark 13. The implied reader who identifies ideologically with Jesus (and the omniscient narrator) must condemn the disciples' behavior. Yet the situational identification with the disciples leads the implied reader to evaluate his/her own behavior in comparison with the disciples' behavior by the standards of Jesus.[31] Such narrative dynamics certainly invite the implied reader to critical self-evaluation and repentance. Thus, I agree with Tannehill's interpretation of the role of the disciples as a means of calling the (implied) reader to a new self-understanding. And if, indeed, the markan narrative points to the future restoration of

----

   [31]Actually the misunderstandings of the disciples throughout the markan narrative encourage the implied reader to see if s/he understands Jesus any better than they. The same dual identification is present: Jesus is the one to be understood but the disciples are the ones in the situation of trying to understand.

the disciples, then the reader is also given hope that however much s/he may have failed, restoration is possible.

The manipulation of time of narrating, then, functions both to strengthen the identification of the implied reader with the disciples and to force that reader into a critical comparison of his/her own behavior with that of the disciples, according to the values presented by Jesus.

Diegetic (narrative) vs. mimetic authority. Lanser's theory of two opposing textual authorities, the diegetic and the mimetic, appears to be a helpful concept for understanding the dual perspective of the implied reader in regard to the disciples--both identification and criticism. Or more precisely, it helps to explain the dual identification of the implied reader, on the one hand with Jesus, and on the other, with the disciples. She describes the diegetic authority as the "authority of intellection."[32] It appears similar to Uspensky's alignment of the ideological plane. This authority is greatest with the first-level narrator and declines as one reaches higher-level narrative or deeper embedding into the narrative world. And this is what is found in the markan narrative. The omniscient narrator carries the greatest diegetic authority, followed by the second-level narrator, Jesus. Indeed the very close alignment of the two makes their diegetic authority nearly identical. Both express the values according to which the implied reader is to judge (and be judged). Thus the implied reader guided by the diegetic authority in the text identifies with the ideology or values of Jesus.

But Lanser also stresses the presence of mimetic authority in a text, the authority of "lived ([albeit] fictional) experience."[33] As noted earlier, the higher the level the greater the mimetic authority.[34] I would argue that this mimetic authority is carried primarily by the disciples.[34] They are well embedded in the narrative, frequently functioning as the second-level narratee and never functioning as narrators. It is the disciples who show the implied reader what it is like to try to follow Jesus; it is they who illustrate vividly the difficulties of following him. The disciples are the model for the implied reader, not for instructions on how to follow Jesus but for the lived process of attempting to follow him. Since the implied reader is guided by the authority found in the narrative, s/he identifies on the diegetic level with Jesus and on the mimetic level with the disciples.

IV

Finally, I wish to discuss some theoretical questions raised by my investigation. First, how helpful was Genette's (and Lanser's) literary theory for the understanding of the markan narative in regard to the disciples? When I began this project I had hoped that Genette's division of the larger category of point of view into mood (who sees?) and voice (who speaks?) would help me to explain what I sensed as the double identification of the implied reader with Jesus and the disciples. This did not turn out to be the case. Although there is a slight tendency toward focalization from the perspective of the disciples, generally the 'person' who sees is the same one who speaks--the omniscient narrator. On the whole, Genette's basic division between mood and voice is irrelevant to the study of Mark's narrative.

This irrelevance may be due to some flaw in Genette's theory or to the nature of the markan narrative.[35] Genette is primarily interested in 'modern' texts, what Roland

---

[32]See above. Lanser, p. 142.

[33]Ibid.

[34]Other characters also periodically carry mimetic authority, especially the women at the empty tomb (16:1-8).

[35]The division between mood and voice may not be entirely valid. Mieke Bal ("Narration et focalisation: Pour une théorie des instances du récit," *Poétique* 29 [1977] 107-27) argues that focalization is an aspect of level and thus of voice. Lanser follows Bal in this (pp. 141, 201-15).

Barthes has called 'writerly' texts,[36] and his theory may be more useful when applied to such texts. And while the markan narrative is indeed a 'modern' text in some respects-- its open-endedness, its ambiguity and presentation of secrets, its order and use of repetition,[37] it is not modern in regard to point of view, the subject of this paper. The point of view in Mark is that of the omniscient narrator who both sees and speaks--a statement that can be made of virtually all narrative (epic and romance) until the rise of the novel in the eighteenth century, and indeed for much narrative since then.

Genette's poetics, then, as a comprehensive system for understanding point of view did not in the end assist my investigation. However, aspects of his theory, expecially distance, narrative level and time of narrating, proved very suggestive for me. Lanser's concept of diegetic vs. mimetic authority, which she builds upon Genette's concept of narrative level, provided a model for understanding the dual identification of the implied reader. Genette wrote, "The 'grid' which is so disparaged is not an instrument of incarceration, of bringing to heel, or of pruning that in fact castrates: it is a procedure of discovery, and a way of describing."[38] I have not adopted his grid, but he did lead me to a way of describing.

A second question I wish to consider is: was the literary theory necessary in order to understand the dual identification of the implied reader? Clearly the answer must be no. A careful reading of Tannehill's and Petersen's articles shows that Tannehill is stressing identification in regard to situation and Petersen in terms of valuation or ideology. A pragmatic analysis of the text of Mark could have led to much the same conclusions as the use of the theory did.

This does not mean, however, that the exercise in literary theory was superfluous. At last year's meeting, Fowler stressed the need for much greater precision in what we mean by point of view. And the literary theory of Genette and Lanser (and Uspensky) has led this writer at least to a much clearer understanding of the various concepts involved in point of view. In particular, I find useful the distinction of focalizer from the narrative voice, the notion of narrative level, and the distinction between diegetic and mimetic authority. Finally, Lanser's theory of diegetic vs. mimetic authority functioning in relation to narrative level informs me that the dual identification of the implied reader in Mark is probably not an unusual idiosyncracy of the gospel of Mark but a common feature of many narratives, there to be found once it is suspected. Thus, my employment of literary theory has not only helped me to understand an aspect of Mark which puzzled me, it also has given me useful tools for understanding other narratives.

Finally, an observation on the limitation of the literary theories used in this paper needs to be made. Reading is a *linear* process. Yet all three of these theorists, Genette, Lanser, and Uspensky, are essentially structuralists in their approach, interested in patterns and structures and not in the diachronic unfolding of the narrative.[39] Yet the actual identification of the implied reader with Jesus and/or the disciples occurs as a developing, changing process as the narrative unrolls. Thus my argument that the implied reader identifies with the disciples as well as Jesus, and my description of the nature of the identifications, needs to be tested by a diachronic scene-by-scene literary analysis of the markan narrative.[40] I believe such an analysis would confirm the dual identification of the implied reader. I suspect it would also confirm, in a more rigorous literary analysis, Tannehill's understanding of how the failure of the disciples functions to lead the (implied) reader to self-evaluation and repentance. But that is another paper.

---

[36]Genette, pp. 265-66.
[37]See Frank Kermode, *The Genesis of Secrecy: On the Interpretation of Narrative* (Cambridge: Harvard, 1979).
[38]Genette, p. 265.
[39]Petersen ("Point of View," p. 108) notes this as a limitation in Uspensky's work.
[40]Tannehill ("Disciples," "Christology") has begun this analysis.

PARTIES AND POLITICS IN PRE-HASMONEAN JERUSALEM:
A CLOSER LOOK AT 2 MACC 3:11

Robert Doran
Amherst College

The mention of Hyrcanus, son of Tobias, at 2 Macc 3:11 has given rise to much discussion on the parties and politics in Jerusalem prior to the accession of Antiochus IV. The reference is made in a speech attributed to Onias III, the high-priest. Combined with data from Josephus, the following connections and conclusions are often drawn from this verse:

1. This Hyrcanus of 2 Macc 3:11 is be identified with the Hyrcanus of Josephus, *Ant.* 12.186-222, 229-236. Either one must emend the text,[1] or say with E. Meyer, "ὁ Τωβίου ist hier wie sonst Geschlechtsname, nicht Vatersname."[2]

2. Following this identification, one infers that the mention by Onias III of this Hyrcanus means that the high-priest has reversed the opinion of his father Simon who had helped expel Hyrcanus from Jerusalem (*Ant.* 12.229). Since Onias describes Hyrcanus as "a man of very high position," Tcherikover goes on to state that Onias was his friend and that Onias was opposed to Hyrcanus' brothers, the Tobiads.[3] Finally, "it may well be therefore that (Hyrcanus) was in the habit of coming to Jerusalem personally and of meeting his friends there; and it may be believed that these meetings also possessed a political significance, since Hyrcanus, who was a supporter of Egypt, certainly would not have regarded the Syrian sovereign with favor and would have dreamed of the restoration of Palestine to the Ptolemies."[4] Tcherikover even makes Simon, son of Balgea, instigate the trouble by mentioning to the governor of Coele-Syria that Hyrcanus' deposits were in the temple.[5] Plöger also speaks of new political groupings and raises the possibility that Hyrcanus could have been destined by Egypt to head a neutral buffer-state between the Ptolemies and the Seleucids.[6] Mazar sees the expelled Hyrcanus as aiming to restore Ptolemaic rule apparently with the support of Onias III.[7] For Hengel, Onias III "was unable to cope with the party struggles and the influence of rich families, and put himself in the wrong by a pro-Ptolemaic policy and the acceptance of a bribe from the Tobiad Hyrcanus in Transjordan so that he was denounced by his opponents and finally summoned to answer for his conduct to king Seleucus IV Philopater in Antioch, where he was detained.[8] He modifies this opinion slightly later on when he still holds: "Onias seems to have been in close business relationship with the Tobiad Hyrcanus in Transjordan, who had been such a vigorous supporter of the Ptolemies before the

---

[1]V. Tcherikover (*Hellenistic Civilisation and the Jews* [New York: Atheneum, 1970] 461, n. 49) thinks those scholars may be right who suggested emending the text *Hyrkanou tou kai Tobiou.* However, A. Momigliano ("I Tobiadi nella preistoria del moto maccabaico," *Atti della reale Accademia della scienze di Torino* 67 [1931/32] 1971) had already accused this of capriciousness.

[2]E. Meyer, *Ursprung und Anfänge des Christentums* (Stuttgart: J. G. Cotta, 1925) 2. 134, n. 1.

[3]Tcherikover, *Hellenistic Civilisation,* 138-39.

[4]Tcherikover, *Hellenistic Civilisation,* 139.

[5]Tcherikover, *Hellenistic Civilisation,* 156. S. K. Eddy, (*The King is Dead. Studies in the Near Eastern Resistance to Hellenism 334-31 BC* [Lincoln: University of Nebraska Press, 1961] 205) implies the same thing.

[6]O. Plöger, *Theocracy and Eschatology* (Richmond: John Knox, 1968) 5.

[7]B. Mazar, "The Tobiads," *IEJ* 7 (1957) 138-39.

[8]M. Hengel, *Judaism and Hellenism. Studies in their Encounter in Palestine during the Early Hellenistic Period* (Philadelphia: Fortress, 1974) 1. 133-34.

conquest of Palestine by Antiochus III, and presumably reverted to this position after Magnesia."[9]

3. The continuation of pro-Ptolemaic and pro-Seleucid parties in Jerusalem is posited, and is made the basis for political analysis. "The defeat of Antiochus III by the Romans at Magnesia and the weakening of the Seleucid kingdom by the oppressive peace of Seleucus IV Philopater (187-175 BC) allowed the Ptolemaic party to become strong again, and the high-priest himself probably adopted a different political course. There was probably the hope of a re-conquest by the Ptolemies."[10] The idea of pro-Ptolemaic and pro-Seleucid forces in Jerusalem is reinforced by reference to two other texts in particular:

a) Josephus, *J.W.* 1.31-33:

> At the time when Antiochus, surnamed Epiphanes, was disputing with Ptolemy VI the suzerainty of Syria, dissension arose among the Jewish nobles. There were rival claims to supreme power, as no individual of rank could tolerate subjection to his peers. Onias, one of the chief priests, gaining the upper hand, expelled the sons of Tobias from the city. The latter took refuge with Antiochus and besought him to use their services as guides for an invasion of Judea. The king, having long cherished this design, consented, and setting out at the head of a huge army took the city by assault, slew a large number of Ptolemy's followers, gave his soldiers unrestricted licence to pillage, and himself plundered the temple and interrupted, for a period of three years and six months, the regular course of the daily sacrifices. The high priest Onias made his escape to Ptolemy and, obtaining from him a site in the nome of Heliopolis, built a small town on the model of Jerusalem and a temple resembling ours.

b) Porphyry, *Against the Christians,* as reported in Jerome, *In Danielem* 11:21-24 (FGH 260 F 49a):

> His brother Antiochus Epiphanes will stand in the place of Seleucus, to whom at first kingly honor was not given by those who favored Ptolemy, but later he obtained the kingdom of Syria by pretence of *clementia*.

What I would first like to do is to set the reference to Hyrcanus in context. Simon, of the tribe of Balgea,[11] out of pique reported to the governor of Coele-Syria that the temple is full of money not necessary for sacrifices and worship but which could be confiscated by the king (2 Macc 3:4-6). Seleucus sent his minister Heliodorus to get the money (3:7-8).

"After Heliodorus had reached Jerusalem and been courteously received by the high-priest, he told the high-priest the charges made against him and made plain why he had come. He asked if the accusations were true. The high-priest answered that there were deposits of widows and orphans, and a deposit of Hyrcanus son of Tobias, a man of high standing. It was not at all as the wicked Simon had slandered,[12] but the whole came to 400 talents of silver and 200 of gold. It was unthinkable that those who had trusted in the sanctity of the place and the sacredness of the temple respected throughout the whole world and in its

---

[9]Hengel, *Judaism and Hellenism,* 1. 272.

[10]Hengel, *Judaism and Hellenism,* 1. 272.

[11]See Tcherikover, *Hellenistic Civilisation,* 403-4.

[12]I agree with Habicht that this phrase does not modify Hyrcanus, but the whole affair of deposits.

inviolability should suffer loss. But Heliodorus, because of the royal command, roundly declared that these could be confiscated for the king's treasury." (3:9-13)

The story ends happily with Heliodorus scampering back to Seleucus empty-handed. As written, the story is full of rhetorical flourishes and pathos.[13]
   The mention of Hyrcanus appears precisely when the high-priest is pleading the case why the deposits should not be confiscated. As the story is told, Heliodorus simply rejects out of hand the plea, because Seleucus had ordered him to take the money (3:7). The implication is that Heliodorus saw the force of the argument, but blindly followed orders rather than listen to the truth and change his mind. In this situation, I cannot understand why one would think that Onias would deliberately throw in the face of the Seleucid minister that he had in the temple deposits from a Ptolemaic outlaw. Would Onias choose this moment to announce his alleged pro-Ptolemaic sympathies? It seems hardly likely. As for the suggestion that Hyrcanus was making trips to Jerusalem, this seems to go against what Josephus explicitly says about Hyrcanus after he was thrown out of Jerusalem: "he determined to go no more to Jerusalem, but settled in Trans-jordan" (Ant. 12.229). In sum, the context of the reference in 2 Macc 3:11 makes it unlikely that the author of 2 Maccabees was referring to a pro-Ptolemaic party. In fact, Onias, by his courteous reception of Heliodorus, seems to be on good terms with the Seleucids. One should not lay too much emphasis on this aspect, for the author is using this as a literary foil to highlight the dastardly behavior of the Seleucids.
   If one leaves aside the context, does the text still refer to Hyrcanus, son of Joseph, the anti-hero of Josephus? First, we do not know the names of the Tobiad family, even if we start with Tobias, father of Joseph the tax-collector (Ant. 12.160). We do not know how many brothers Joseph had--Josephus casually mentions another brother Solymius (12.186), and there may well have been others. Joseph has seven other sons besides Hyrcanus and their names are unknown (12.186). The Tobiad family goes back at least to the time of Ezra and Nehemiah (Ezra 2:60; Neh 2:19; 6:17-19), if not further.[14] Hyrcanus, a name of noble Persians,[15] seems to be widespread enough among Jews.[16] To identify the Hyrcanus of 2 Macc 3:11 with that of Josephus, Ant. 12.229, is to jump to conclusions based on the slimmest prosopographical evidence and on the desire to synthesize what little evidence we have.
   There is also no reason to accept Meyer's assertion that this is a *Geschlechtsname, nicht Vatersname.* The article placed before Tobiou is regularly found when the name of the son is in the genitive, cf. 2 Macc 4:21: *Apollōniou tou Menestheōs,* Apollonius, the son of Menestheus; 1 Macc 8:21: *Eupolemon huion Ioannou tou Hakkōs,* Eupolemus, the son of John, the son of Hakkoz. What one has in 2 Macc 3:11 is the regular form of son-father relationship. In the OT when *ben* is to describe tribal relationship, only once is the singular used as normally one finds the plural, e.g. *běnê ʿēber* (See BDB *ben* 1j). That singular usage is at Neh 10:39 (=LXX 2 Ezra 20:39): *hakkōhēn ben ʾahărōn, ho hiereus huios Aarōn.* No personal name of any individual is involved here, but it is a titular designation. At 2 Macc 3:11, the text speaks of Hyrcanus, son of Tobias. If one wants to read 'grandson' or 'Tobiad,' one has to emend the text.
   Caution should also be used with the other two texts referred to above, *J.W.* 1.31-33 and Porphyry. Tcherikover tries vainly to bestow some credibility on the Josephus

---

[13]For a fuller description, see R. Doran, *Temple Propaganda* (CBQMS 12; Washington: Catholic Biblical Association of America, 1981) 48-49.
   [14]See B. Mazar, "The Tobiads."
   [15]F. W. König, "Altpersische Adelsgeschlechter," *Wiener Zeitschrift für Kunde des Morganlandes* 33 (1926) 23-56.
   [16]John Hyrcanus I; Hyrcanus, son of Alexander Jannaeus; Hyrcanus, son of Herod the king of Chalcis; Hyrcanus, son of Josephus.

passage by replacing Onias by Jason, but even he is forced to admit that the number of errors makes the passage virtually useless: "it contains nothing that can enrich our knowledge to any considerable degree."[17] This, however, is the only passage in Josephus which speaks of pro-Ptolemaic and pro-Seleucid parties at work in Jerusalem! There is no mention of such forces at work when Josephus speaks of the expulsion of Menelaus and the Tobiads from Jerusalem by Jason in *Ant.* 12.237-241. Surely it is better to admit that if Josephus in *J.W.* 1.31-33 is wrong in holding that Antiochus was disputing with Ptolemy over the suzerainty of Syria and needed the Tobiads as guides to attack and capture Jerusalem from the Ptolemies, then he is also wrong in his description of the factions as pro-Ptolemaic and pro-Seleucid.

As for the report of what Porphyry said, one has to remember when reading it that:

1. Porphyry thought that the book of Daniel was composed by someone living at the time of Antiochus Epiphanes and that "whatever he wrote up till the time of Aniochus contained genuine history (*veram historiam*)." (Jerome, *In Danielem*, prologue.)

2. Porphyry thought that Coele-Syria legitimately belonged to the Ptolemies, having been given as dowry by Antiochus the Great when his daughter married Ptolemy. (*In Danielem* 11:17a.)

When therefore Porphyry reads in Dan 11:21 that "he will not be given kingly glory," Porphyry takes this as reliable information and, in the light of the Ptolemaic-Seleucid conflict over Coele-Syria which dominates Daniel 11, understands the text to mean that Antiochus was not regarded as king by those who supported Ptolemy. I find it difficult to believe that this extremely general description, "by those in Syria who supported Ptolemy," is based on precise historical information that Porphyry has obtained from his sources. Even if it were, however, it does not at all show that there were pro-Seleucid and pro-Ptolemaic parties *in Jerusalem*.

Finally, I would like to address the designation, so often found in current scholarship, of Hyrcanus as a loyal supporter of the Ptolemies. One has to remember exactly what we are dealing with. The Tobiads were tax-collectors, and whatever the difficulties one has with the Tobiad romance[18] Hyrcanus is portrayed as a successful wheeler-dealer who perhaps wanted some of the pie his father had obtained. The heart of the Hyrcanus narrative is how he ingratiated himself to Ptolemy. Ptolemy admired the spirit of the youth (*Ant.* 12.207), his clever replies (12.214, 219), and as reward showed him the highest honor, gave him splendid presents, and wrote commending him to his fathers and brothers and to all his governors and administrators (12.220) In all this, Hyrcanus has played the role of the young man who succeeds by his wit and cleverness.[19] I do not want to sound too cynical, but I do not think that Hyrcanus' behavior shows he had much loyalty for anyone except himself--certainly he has little for his father, and his treatment of his father's steward in Alexandria shows how little scrupulous he was. What Hyrcanus did in Transjordan remains a mystery--did he levy tribute on the barbarians (*Ant.* 12.222), or war continually on the Arabs, killing many and taking many captive (*Ant.* 12.229)? He seems to be acting independently, almost as a robber bandit, and not as tax-collector for the Ptolemies.[20] After the Seleucid takeover

[17]Tcherikover, *Hellenistic Civilisation*, 395. Tcherikover discusses this text on pages 392-95.
[18]See Tcherikover, *Hellenistic Civilisation*, 127-30; Hengel, *Judaism and Hellenism*, I. 269.
[19]See the excellent analysis by S. Niditch, "Father-Son Folktale Patterns and Tyrant Typologies in Josephus' *Ant* 12:160-222," *JJS* 32 (1981) 47-55.
[20]Tcherikover (*Hellenistic Civilisation*, 136-37) holds this notion as a consequence of his thesis that Hyrcanus purchased the post of tax-collector from Ptolemy. Tcherikover here seems to overlook the narrative motifs noticed by Niditch (see footnote 20). Hengel (*Judaism and Hellenism*, I. 269) thinks that Hyrcanus was probably

of Syria, in fact, he would have had a rather circuitous route to send the taxes to Ptolemy. Would such a character remain fanatically loyal to the Ptolemies, and stand by them even though their fortune had clearly waned? I very much doubt it. In fact, did tax-collectors normallly stick through thick and thin to their masters? Wouldn't they have changed allegiances as easily as clothes and adapted to political shifts with little hesitation? I suspect the latter.[21]

There seems to be no basis for the posited pro-Ptolemaic and pro-Seleucid parties in Jerusalem--2 Macc 3:11 offers no support for it, and Hyrcanus as head of a pro-Ptolemaic faction seems unlikely. The reasoning so far has been largely negative, so I should perhaps like to end on a positive note. If one wants to salvage anything from *J.W.* 1.31-33, it would be Josephus' use of the term *philotimia* to describe conditions in Jerusalem at this time. Ambition among the rich leaders of towns in the Greco-Roman world was a constant factor.[22] For Jerusalem at this time, we now have the Oniads, the Tobiads, and those of the tribe of Balgea, Simon and Menelaus (2 Macc 3:4; 4:23). Rather than appealing to pro-Ptolemaic or pro-Seleucid parties, one should, I think, be content to see at play the ambitions of the rich families of a small town.

---

given "supreme command over the cleruchy in Transjordania to protect the border against the Arabs."

[21]O. Plöger ("Hyrkan im Ostjordanland," *ZDPV* 71 [1955] 78) sees no problem in having Joseph and his other sons switch allegiance easily. He gives no reason why Hyrcanus would also not have so acted.

[22]The role of *philotimia*, the love of status, as a motivating factor in the Greco-Roman world was mentioned in passing by R. Mac Mullen, *Roman Social Relations. 50 BC to AD 284* (New Haven: Yale, 1974) 125. For an analysis of its role in Antonine society, see P. Brown, *The Making of Late Antiquity* (Cambridge: Harvard, 1978) 31-53.

JOSEPHUS' VERSION OF THE BINDING OF ISAAC

Louis H. Feldman
Yeshiva University

In a well-known essay comparing the narrative technique of Homer with that of the Bible, Erich Auerbach[1] concludes that in the Bible there is "exernalization of only so much of the phenomena as is necessary for the purpose of the narrative, all else [being] left in obscurity; the decisive points of the narrative alone are emphasized, what lies between is non-existent . . . ; thoughts and feelings remain unexpressed, are only suggested by the silence and the fragmentary speeches." On the other hand, "the Homeric poems conceal nothing, they contain no teaching and no secret second meaning."[2] Auerbach chooses to illustrate this contrast by comparing the Bible's account of the Aqedah, the binding of Isaac in preparation for sacrifice by his father Abraham, with Homer's account in Book 19 of the *Odyssey* of the recognition of Odysseus by the old nurse Eurycleia through the scar on his thigh. In the Biblical narrative, says Auerbach,[3] we are told "only what we need to know about him [Isaac] as a personage in the action here and now," and there is overwhelming suspense present. In contrast, the reader of Homer, because there are constant reminders of the earlier history of the personages, will find, even when the greatest catastrophes are occurring that there is no such suspense.

If, indeed, this contrast has validity, we may here suggest that Josephus, in his version of the Aqedah (*Ant* 1.222-236), which is surely the greatest of Abraham's actions, as Philo (*De Abrahamo* 32.167) has stated, has Hellenized the Biblical narrative so that it acquires precisely those qualities that are missing in the Bible--clarity, depth, and lack of suspense. Moreover, as a historian who is writing apologetically, Josephus is trying to answer the charge that Abraham did not do anything unique or remarkable--a charge that Philo (*De Abrahamo* 33.178) reports and also attempts to refute. And finally, Josephus, as an historian and apologist for Judaism, has detheologized the narrative.

Writing for an audience that would seek to know the background of the episode and would not be impressed with the Bible's stark and deliberate attempt to leave almost everything unexpressed, Josephus carefully sets the scene. To be sure, the rabbis[4] also elaborately set the stage for the Aqedah, but they stress the theological aspect of G-d's test of Abraham, relating how G-d asked Abraham to sacrifice his son in order to prove to Satan that Abraham was truly a man of faith and how Isaac sought to prove his superiority in faith to his brother Ishmael. For Josephus, however, the background material has a literary purpose, namely to provide proper motivation for what follows. Unlike the Biblical narrative, there is no suspense, since we are told at the very beginning (1.223) that Abraham obtained his goal of happiness by the will of G-d and that this was merely a trial of his piety. By eliminating, moreover, the direct command of G-d to Abraham, as well as Abraham's laconic response "Here I am," and by putting the whole scene in indirect discourse, Josephus diminishes the pathos, removes the suspense, and indicates that Abraham took all this in his stride.

---

[1] Erich Auerbach, *Mimesis, The Representation of Reality in Western Literature* (trans. from the German by Willard R. Trask; Princeton, 1953) 11.

[2] Auerbach, (above, note 1) 13.

[3] Auerbach (above, note 1) 10-11.

[4] *Yashar Vayera* 43b, *Bereshit Rabbah* 55.4, *Sanhedrin* 89b. See, in general, Louis Ginzberg, *The Legends of the Jews* (Philadelphia, 1909, 1925) 1.272-74; and 5.248-49, notes 226-229. The rabbis note, in particular, the vagueness of the opening phrase "after these things" (Gen 22:1) and attempt to fill in the details with a scene between G-d and Satan.

At the beginning of the pericope we are told (1.222), in an extra-Biblical remark, that Abraham passionately loved (ὑπερηγάπα , "loved exceedingly")[5] Isaac, whereas Gen 22:2 merely says "whom thou lovest." It is interesting that whereas the Septuagint renders *yeḥidekha* ("your only one," (Gen 22:2) by ἀγαπητόν ("beloved"), presumably because the translators were troubled by the fact that Isaac was not Abraham's only son, Josephus, who generally follows the Septuagint in his paraphrase of Scripture, especially for the Pentateuch, has μονογενῆ ("only born") to emphasize that Isaac was, for practical purposes, in terms of carrying on the family tradition, Abraham's only son.

To be sure, the rabbinic accounts[6] of the Aqedah likewise have extensive introductions and thus reduce the suspense of the narrative, but they are more concerned with explaining the problem of theodicy, that is, why G-d should have tested Abraham and Isaac[7] when He was omniscient and certainly knew the merits of Abraham and Isaac. Josephus, on the other hand, is concerned merely to have the event, as an historical narrative, possess the proper motivation and, as a story, flow smoothly. If, indeed, Josephus had developed the idea that G-d tested Isaac, this might have had considerable theological consequences, namely for the concept of Israel as the chosen people and for the justification of martyrdom, as we see, for example in 4 Macc 13:12.[8]

Though, to be sure, the rabbis (e.g. *Sifre Deuteronomy* 313) remark on Abraham's overwhelming love for Isaac, Josephus carefully explains that Abraham's great love for his son was due to the fact that Isaac was born (1.222) on the threshold of old age (ἐπὶ γήρως οὐδῷ), using a phrase very familiar to any reader of Homer or of Hesiod, who, together, constituted, in effect, the Bible of the Greeks. In Homer the phrase is particularly associated with the aged Priam, that most pathetic of all characters, who addresses his son Hector before the latter goes off to the battle with Achilles that will bring about his death while Priam is "in the path of old age" (ἐπὶ γήραος οὐδῷ, *Iliad* 22.60), his sons having perished before him. Again, Homer (*Iliad* 24.487) uses the same phrase when Priam addresses Achilles, begging him to return his son Hector's body, reminding him that Achilles' father was as old as Priam "on the deadly path of old age" (ὀλοῷ ἐπὶ γήραος οὐδῷ). The parallel of Abraham with Priam, both of whom are aged fathers, and of Isaac with Hector, both of whom are promising sons who are about to die in the flower of youth, would be especially clear to Josephus' readers, inasmuch as the the phrase ἐπὶ γήραος οὐδῷ had become almost a stock expression for the pathetic in life. Similarly, Odysseus, speaking as a stranger to Eumaeus the faithful swineherd, asks about his father Laertes, whom he had left behind on the threshold of old age (*Odyssey* 15.348). The parallel scenes in Homer may well have been in Josephus' mind, inasmuch as elsewhere (*Against Apion* 1.12) he shows his knowledge of Homer by mentioning him as an oral poet, noting his numerous inconsistencies and even realizing (*Against Apion* 2.155) that he nowhere employs the word νόμος. In addition, he quotes (*Ant* 19.92) Homer's *Iliad* (14.90-91) when discussing the conspiracy to assassinate Caligula. Finally, his portrait of Saul, especially in his last combat, as I have tried to show elsewhere,[9] is reminiscent of Homer's Achilles, who (*Iliad* 9.410-416) knew that if he remained to fight against the Trojans he would gain glory but would lose his life, and

---

[5]The same word (ὑπερηγάπησε) is used by Josephus in his description (*Ant* 12.195) of Joseph the Tobiad's love for his son Hyrcanus "as if he were his only (μόνου) son," a phrase similar to that used of Isaac (μονογενῆ, "only-born," *Ant* 1.222).

[6]Ginzberg (above, note 4).

[7]Targum Pseudo-Jonathan on Genesis 22:1 and Judith 8:26. See Ginzberg (above, note 4) 1.273-74 and 5.249, n. 229. The rabbis interpret *nissah* (Gen 22:1), "tested," as "proved," in the sense that G-d proved Abraham's virtue of faith to his accuser Satan, whereas Josephus translates the word literally.

[8]See Geza Vermes, *Scripture and Tradition in Judaism: Haggadic Studies* (2nd ed.; Leiden, 1973) 198.

[9]"Josephus' Portrait of Saul," to appear in *HUCA*.

yet chose this premature death deliberately. Again, the analogy with the aged father and the son who dies prematurely in his youth is implied. Hesiod, on the other hand, speaks of the son who abuses his aged father at the evil threshold of old age (κακῷ ἐπὶ γήραος οὐδῷ *Works and Days* 331), with whom Zeus is angry, and who in the end will pay for his wrongdoing. The comparison with Isaac, who honors his father, is again striking.[10] Finally, one thinks also of those most pathetic lines in Virgil's *Aeneid*, which had come to be regarded as a classic almost immediately after it had been written half a century before Josephus' birth, where, when Aeneas arrives in Carthage, he sees Priam in a painting of the Trojan War and remarks on the tragedy of life and on the mortality of things:

En primus! Sunt hic etiam sua praemia laudi;
Sunt lacrimae rerum, et mentem mortalia tangunt. (1.461-462)[11]

---

[10]The proverbial nature of the expression "upon the threshold of old age," as the height of the pathetic in life, is seen in Herodotus 3.14, where he tells how Psammenitus, king of Egypt, did not weep when he saw his daughter degraded and his son going to his death but broke into tears when he saw one of his boon companions who had lost his possessions and was begging "on the threshold of old age" (ἐπὶ γήραος οὐδῷ). The familiarity of the expression is also seen in the way in which Socrates, speaking to the old man Cephalus, says, "I would gladly learn of you what you think of this thing, now that your time has come to it, the thing the poets call "the threshold of old age" (ἐπὶ γήραος οὐδῷ). That this is a stock description of a helpless person is clear from the fourth-century B.C.E. Lycurgus, *Against Leocrates* 40, who speaks of "hurrying about helplessly on the threshold of old age" (ἐπὶ γήρως οὐδῷ). Moreover, that thesaurus of wise popular sayings, Menander (fragment 671, Kock), who lived at the end of the fourth and at the beginning of the third century, states that "it is most pitiable when on the threshold of old age (ἐπὶ γήρως ὁδῷ) just character has received the shock of an unjust fortune." Finally, Dionysius of Halicarnassus (*Roman Antiquities,* 8.35.3) to whom Josephus owes so much (see my forthcoming book *Josephus and Modern Scholarship* and my "Josephus' Portrait of Saul" [above, note 10], in describing the evils of war, mentions that parents upon the threshold of old age (ἐπὶ γήρως ὁδῷ) become slaves instead of free men. Abraham Schalit, in the notes to his Hebrew translation of Josephus' *Antiquitates Judaicae*, vol. 2 (Jerusalem, 1945) 39, note 250, declares that the expression was certainly due to Josephus' Greek assistants; but, as I, in my review of Henry St. John Thackeray's *Josephus the Man and the Historian*, in *JAOS* 90 (1970) 545-46, have noted, Josephus' statement (*Against Apion* 1.50) that he had fellow-workers for the sake of the Greek occurs in his discussion of the composition of the *Jewish War*. The very fact that the phrase is found in Dionysius of Halicarnassus would indicate that it is characteristic of first-century Greek rather than that it is the work of a special assistant.

[11]Inasmuch as Josephus prides himself (*Ant* 20.263-64) on the acquisition of his knowledge of Greek and thus must have possessed considerable linguistic aptitude, and inasmuch as the *Antiquities* was issued by Josephus after he had lived in Rome for over two decades, one would expect that he should have acquired a knowledge of Latin as well. Some of his sources for the period closest to his time were probably in Latin, especially the long account at the beginning of Book 19 of the *Antiquities* describing the assassination of Caligula and the accession of Claudius; see my "The Sources of Josephus' *Antiquities,* Book 19," *Latomus* 21 (1962) 320-33. Henry St. John Thackeray, *Josephus the Man and the Historian* (New York, 1929) 71-72 and 118-19, has remarked that occasionally the underlying Latin shines through and cites examples. David Daube, "Three Legal Notes on Josephus after His Surrender," *Law Quarterly Review* 93 (1977) 191-94, has also noted a Latinism in the *Life* (414) in the use of κελεύσαντος in the sense of *iubeo*, "to authorize."

Whereas the Bible proceeds directly to the Divine command to Abraham to sacrifice his child, Josephus builds up the poignancy of Abraham's decision to obey by shifting the center of gravity to Isaac through amplifying the virtues of the latter—his practice of every virtue (ἀρετήν), his devoted filial obedience (θεραπείας), and his zeal (ἐσπουδακώς) for the worship (θρησκείαν) of G-d. All of this calls forth still more the affection of his parents and indicates how great Abraham's faith is in that he is willing to sacrifice such a child. Philo (*De Abrahamo* 32.168) also, as Sandmel[12] has noted, describes Isaac in terms intelligible to his Greek readers, noting that he showed a perfection of virtues (ἀρετάς) beyond his years; but he adds that Isaac also possessed great bodily beauty and that Abraham cherished for him a strong tenderness (φιλο-στοργία, "family affection"). The rabbis also,[13] to be sure, note his virtues, particularly his piety and obedience; but Josephus presents a picture that omits Philo's stress on tenderness and the rabbis' on piety and that would appeal particularly to his Hellenized readers, for he states, in an extra-Biblical addition (1.223), that Abraham, because of Isaac's virtues, rested all his own happiness (εὐδαιμονίαν) in the hope that he would leave his son unscathed (ἀπαθῆ) when he died. The irony of the fact that Abraham the father seeks happiness only through his son matches a similar irony found in Euripides' *Iphigenia in Aulis,* with its similar situation of a father called upon to sacrifice his child, and where the chorus, catching sight of Queen Clytemnestra and of her daughter as they approach in a chariot, start their ode ironically, " ἰώ, ἰώ. μεγάλαι μεγάλων εὐδαιμονίαι, "Oh! oh! great happiness of the great!"[14]

Moreover, the term ἀπαθής ("unscathed") and the corresponding noun ἀπά-θεια (freedom from emotional disturbance) are particularly common Stoic terms with reference to freedom from emotion.[15] Indeed, for the Stoics to make love subservient to friendship was part of the pursuit of ἀπάθεια;[16] and, indeed, the whole Aqedah, with

---

[12]Samuel Sandmel, *Philo's Place in Judaism: A Study of Conceptions of Abraham in Jewish Literature* (Cincinnati, 1956) 72, note 322.

[13]Salomo Rappaport, *Agada und Exegese bei Flavius Josephus* (Wien, 1930) 19-20, no. 84; and Ginzberg (above, note 4) 5.249, note 230. Arthur Marmorstein, *The Doctrine of Merits in Old Rabbinical Literature* (London, 1920) 75-76 and 149, remarks, however, that the merits of Isaac are very seldom alluded to in the Aggadah.

[14]That Josephus was aware of Euripides in this part of his work seems indicated by the fact that just before he comes to the Aqedah he describes (*Ant* 1.218) the fleeing Hagar, who lays her child Ishmael at his last gasp under a tree and wanders away so that he may not die in her presence (θεῖσα τὸ παιδίον ψυχορραγοῦν, ὡς μὴ παρούσης τὴν ψυχὴν ἀφῇ, προῇει). Here, as Thackeray (above, note 11) 117-18, remarks, Josephus imitates Euripides' *Hercules Furens* 323-324, a play, which, according to Thackeray, ed. and trans., *Josephus,* (LCL; Cambridge, MA, 1930) 4.108, note *a,* seems to have been a favorite of Josephus or, if we accept Thackeray's theory, of his assistant, and where Amphitryon asks that he and his wife be killed so that they may not see their children at last gasp calling upon their mother (ὡς μὴ τέκν' εἰσίδωμεν ψυχορραγοῦντα καὶ καλοῦντα μητέρα). Moreover, elsewhere, as Thackeray (above, note 11) 118, notes, we even have in Josephus (*Ant* 14.96) an allusion to a lost play of Euripides, the *Ino.* Finally, Martin Braun, *History and Romance in Graeco-Oriental Literature* (Oxford, 1938) 44-93, has indicated how much Josephus is indebted to Euripides' *Hippolytus* in his great expansion of the incident of Joseph and Potiphar's wife (*Ant* 2.41-59).

[15]Cf., e.g., Dionysius of Heraclea the Stoic (third century B.C.E.) 3.34; Arrian, *Epicteti Dissertationes* 4.6.34; Antipater of Tarsus the Stoic 3. 109; Philodemus, *Concerning the Stoics* (*Herculanensia Volumina* 339.7). Robert J. Daly, "The Soteriological Significance of the Sacrifice of Isaac," *CBQ* 39 (1977) 58, is hardly warranted in his comment that "worthy of note [in Josephus' account] is the absence of the Stoic Flavor so prominent in Philo and especially 4 Maccabees."

[16]John Ferguson, *Moral Values in the Ancient World* (New York, 1959) 68.

its emphasis on freedom from emotion, is a prime example for Josephus of how Jewish values coincide with those of the Stoics. Josephus himself (*Ant* 1.46), in a a passage which has no parallel in the Bible, has the same juxtaposition of happiness and being unscathed in G-d's statement to Adam and Eve that he had decreed for them a life of happiness (εὐδαίμονα), unmolested (ἀπαθῆ) by all ill. In this Utopia,[17] all things that contribute to enjoyment and pleasure spring up spontaneously through G-d's providence (πρόνοιαν , a standard Stoic term), men have long lives, and old age does not soon overtake them. Isaac himself, in Josephus (1.276), using the two words "happiness" and "being unmolested," prays that G-d will protect his son Jacob and preserve him from every touch of ill (ἀπαθῆ κακοῦ) and grant him a blissful (εὐδαί-μονα) life. Josephus is thus presenting Abraham as seeking the Stoic goal of happiness as identified with ἀπάθεια. As I have noted elsewhere,[18] Josephus, in his portrait of Solomon, for example, consciously colors his narrative with Stoic phraseology to make it more intelligible and attractive to his readers. This identification of the goal of the forefathers with the goal of providence is reminiscent of the Stoic goal of ἀπάθεια as seen in Seneca (*Epistle* 90.37), Pseudo-Seneca (*Octavius* 404-405), and the unknown author of the *Aetna* ascribed to Virgil.[19] Indeed, since much of Josephus' projected audience was sympathetic to Stoicism,[20] it is not surprising that there are a number of Stoic touches in his paraphrase of the Bible in the *Antiquities*,[21] and his view of εἱμαρμένη, as Martin[22] has shown, is indebted to popular, non-technical Stoicism.

---

[17]Cf. my "Hellenizations in Josephus' Portrayal of Man's Decline," in Jacob Neusner, ed., *Religions in Antiquity: Essays in Memory of Erwin Ramsdell Goodenough* (*Studies in the History of Religions*, 14; Leiden, 1968) 341.

[18]"Josephus as an Apologist to the Greco-Roman World: His Portrait of Solomon," in Elisabeth Schüssler Fiorenza, ed., *Aspects of Religious Propaganda in Judaism and Early Christianity* (Notre Dame, 1976) 71.

[19]Cf. my article (above, note 17) 344.

[20]Cf. William Tarn and G. T. Griffith, *Hellenistic Civilisation* (3rd ed.; London, 1952) 325: "The philosophy of the Hellenistic world was the Stoa; all else was secondary."

[21]Cf. my article, "Abraham the Greek Philosopher in Josephus," *Transactions of the American Philological Association* 99 (1968) 146-49, where I note Josephus' use of Stoic terminology in connection with his proof for the existence of G-d (*Ant* 1.156). That it is the Stoics whom Josephus is there combatting is hinted at by the reference to the Chaldeans in the section (1.157) immediately after the one containing Abraham's proof, since, as Harry A. Wolfson, *Philo* (Cambridge, MA, 1947) 1. 176-177, and 2.78, comments, the Chaldeans, whom Josephus describes as opposed to Abraham's views, are in Philo (*De Migratione Abrahami* 32.179) prototypes of the Stoics. Moreover, Eduard Norden, *Agnostos Theos. Untersuchungen zur Formengeschichte religiöser Rede* (Leipzig, 1923) 19 n. 2, has remarked for example, that the phrase used by Josephus in Solomon's dedicatory prayer for the Temple, that G-d was now present and not far removed (*Ant* 8.108), shows Stoic influence. Again, the phrase that G-d sees all things and hears all things (πάντ' ἐφορᾶν καὶ πάντ' ἀκούειν, *Ant* 8.108) is reminiscent of the verse in Homer (*Iliad* 3.277), ἥλιος θ', ὃς πάντ' ἐφορᾷς καὶ πάντ' ἐπακούεις, which is cited and explained by the Stoic Heraclitus (*Questiones Homericae* 23). Again, as I (above, note 18) 90-91, have remarked, we have Stoic elements in the attribute ἀπροσδεές assigned to G-d, (*Ant* 8.111) and in the non-Biblical addition in Solomon's prayer that there is no more fitting way to appease G-d than through the voice "which we have from the air and know to ascend again through this element" (*Ant* 8.111-112; cf. H. van Arnim, ed., *Stoicorum Veterum Fragmenta* [Leipzig, 1903] 1. 21 and 243). Again, in dedicating the sanctuary at Bethel, King Jeroboam uses Stoic terminology in stating that every place has G-d in it, that there is no place set apart for Him, and that He hears and watches over His worshippers everywhere (*Ant* 8.227).

[22]Luther H. Martin, "Josephus' Use of *Heimarmene* in the *Jewish Antiquities* XIII, 171-3," *Numen* 28 (1981) 127-37.

The idea, moreover, that leaving one's son unscathed is a sine qua non for the achievement of happiness reminds one of the passage in Herodotus (1.30), where Solon tells Croesus that Tellus of Athens was happiest of all men, as indicated by the facts that his city was prosperous, that he had fine sons, that he lived to see children born to each of them, and that all his children survived him. The explicit comparison, which we have noted above, of Abraham with Priam is thus carried further in that the pathetic Priam saw all his sons die during his own lifetime and in that Abraham's hope (1.230) to see Isaac as the stay of his old age is about to be frustrated by G-d's command that he sacrifice his son.

We may also comment that Josephus' use of the word θεραπεία (1.222) in emphasizing Isaac's filial obedience may well have brought to mind for his readers who so admired Plato, who, as Hadas[23] has contended, was probably the most important single intellectual factor in the process of Hellenization in the East during the Hellenistic period, a passage in the *Laws* (886 C 6-9), where Plato is critical of the traditional theogony of the Greeks on the ground that it depicts the Greeks as not showing proper attendance (θεραπείας) toward and respect (τιμάς) for parents. Similarly, the Stoics emphasized this quality, as we see in Epictetus' remark (*Enchiridion* 30): "Is a certain man your father? In this are implied taking care of him, submitting to him in all things, receiving his reproaches." We must here emphasize that while the rabbis also stress the importance of filial obedience, Josephus' terminology would be recognized by his Greek readers as more closely reminiscent of Plato and of the Stoics.

It is true that the rabbis also assigned to Isaac a more active role in the story than does the Biblical narrative. In the oldest Targumic account,[24] Isaac gives his consent and, indeed, asks to be bound so that the sacrifice may be perfect; but, as Blidstein[25] has correctly noted, this new stress is announced more than it is explored. With Josephus, as with Euripides in the latter's *Iphigenia in Aulis*, it is the child that becomes a protagonist.

What follows is, in effect, a drama, commencing with a prologue, in which G-d appears to Abraham; the play proper, so to speak, containing a dialogue between Abraham and Isaac; and an epilogue in which G-d commends Abraham and predicts the glorious future of his descendants.

At the very beginning of the test, whereas the Bible (Gen 22:2) has G-d merely give an order to Abraham, Josephus, well aware that his readers would wonder at the seeming arbitrariness of such a command, has G-d build up to the order by first (1.224) enumerating three major benefits that He had bestowed upon Abraham, namely victory over his enemies in war, happiness (presumably in material matters), and the birth of a son. Thus the sacrifice may be seen here, as in Pseudo-Philo's *Biblical Antiquities* (32.2), as a logical repayment to G-d for His threefold benevolence. Rabbinic literature (*Tanḥuma Lekh Lekha* 13), on the other hand, saw no need to have G-d apologize, and so it is Abraham who justifies the sacrifice in his own mind as a repayment for G-d's great gifts to himself. This view of sacrifice would have been readily intelligible to a pagan Greek audience, as we may see in the comment of the old man Cephalus, representing traditional morality and religion, in Plato's *Republic* (1.331 A-B) that the great value of wealth is that it keeps one from having to leave life in the fear of owing debts to men or sacrifices to the gods.

---

[23] Moses Hadas, "Plato in Hellenistic Fusion," *Journal of the History of Ideas* 19 (1958) 3-13; idem, *Hellenistic Culture: Fusion and Diffusion* (New York, 1959) 72-82.

[24] Cf. Vermes (above, note 8) 194, who cites the Fragmentary Targum and the Targum Neofiti on Genesis 22:10. Cf. also George F. Moore, *Judaism in the First Centuries of the Christian Era: The Age of the Tannaim,* (Cambridge, MA, 1927) 1.539, who cites *Sifre Deuteronomy* 32, which goes so far as to state that Isaac bound himself.

[25] Gerald Blidstein, *Honor Thy Father and Mother: Filial Responsibility in Jewish Law and Ethics* (New York, 1975) 194, note 9.

That Josephus intended the account to be more than the story of Abraham's faithfulness to G-d and of Isaac's obedience to G-d and to his father is clear from the fact that Josephus (1.224) specifies that G-d told Abraham to take his child up to the Morian Mount, whereas the Bible (Gen 22:2) is vague in having G-d tell Abraham to offer his sacrifice "upon one of the mountains of which I shall tell you." The Septuagint (Gen 22:2), which is the text that Josephus follows for the most part, has "to the lofty land" (εἰς τὴν γῆν τὴν ὑψηλήν), with no mention of Moriah (perhaps, we may suggest, because μωρία means "folly"; and Josephus may well have been aware of the possible sneer, because of the similarity of the words μώριον and μωρία,[26] that might have been directed toward him and toward the Jews that Abraham had taken his son to a mountain of "folly." The fact that Josephus goes out of his way to mention Mount Moriah and to state (1.226) that it was there that King David later built the Temple seems thus to be deliberate. As a priest who had undoubtedly ministered in the Temple, Josephus, quite understandably, chose to emphasize that it was upon the site of their supreme indication of faith that the Temple was constructed, which was to be the central focus of the Jewish religion until its destruction in 70. Of course, it may be inferred from the Hebrew text that Isaac was bound on Mount Moriah but Josephus stresses this by repeating it (1.226) further in his account, as well as at a later point in his history (7.333), when he states that David purchased a site for the Temple in the very place where Abraham had brought his son Isaac to sacrifice him as a burnt-offering and where he refers the reader to his earlier account. Quite clearly, Josephus intends to have the reader associate the readiness of Abraham to sacrifice his son with the sacrifices that were, in effect, surrogate offerings at the site of the Temple itself, though Josephus, in his eagerness to avoid theological issues, omits the direct statement connecting the Aqedah with these sacrifices.[27] Even in his statement that the Temple was built on the site of the Aqedah, Josephus, seeking to maintain his posture as an historian rather than as a theologian, avoids stating that David (actually Solomon) built the Temple on Mount Moriah *because* Abraham had bound his son there. It is a case of *post hoc*, and not *ergo propter hoc*. Indeed, Josephus (*Ant* 7.333) says that it happened (συνέβη) that the Temple was built on the place where the Aqedah had occurred. The rabbis, of course, stress the causal relationship of the two events.[28]

One would have expected, as Kierkegaard does in his *Fear and Trembling,* that Abraham would have had some doubts about the sacrifice. And, indeed, this is precisely what we find in rabbinic sources (*Tanḥuma, Shelaḥ,* ed. Buber, 27), where we have a comparison of Abraham's struggle against temptation with that of Job. But theodicy is far removed from the mind of Josephus the historian, who is furthermore trying to build up the character of Abraham; and so we are told bluntly (1.225) that Abraham deemed that nothing would justify disobedience to G-d.

In seeking to present an apology for Abraham's extraordinary action, Josephus resorted to terminology reminiscent again of the Stoics. Thus he says (1.225) that in obeying the Divine command, Abraham reasoned that "all that befell His favored ones (οἷς ἂν εὐμενὴς ᾖ) was ordained by His providence (προνοίας). Whereas the

---

[26]For an example of this type of anti-Semitic attack note Lysimachus' attempt (*ap.* Josephus, *Against Apion* 2.21-27) to connect the word "Sabbath" with the disease of the groin in Egypt called *sabbo*.

[27]Daly (above, note 15) 58 finds it strange that Josephus makes no association with the Temple sacrifices, not even the Passover; but, we may remark, Josephus' purpose here is to present an historical narrative. To connect the sacrifice of Isaac with Passover, as do the rabbis (*Mekhilta of Rabbi Ishmael* on Exodus 12:13) and the Book of Jubilees (17.15-16; 18.3; 49.1), would have involved a theological discussion, which Josephus generally avoids.

[28]See *Bereshith Rabbah* 55.9 and other citations in Ginzberg (above, note 4) 5.253, notes 249 and 253.

rabbis[29] present a story of Satan's challenge to G-d to prove Abraham's faithlessness, an account which involves great problems of theodicy, Josephus, seeking to avoid theological entanglements, proceeds immediately to Abraham's obedience to G-d's command. The same confidence in G-d's providence is seen in Josephus' account of Amram's decision (Ant 2.219) to expose the infant Moses on the Nile rather than to continue to rear him in secret. Similarly, Moses, in his speech to the angry Israelites, exhorts them (Ant 3.19) not to despair of G-d's providence (πρόνοιαν). The same juxtaposition of G-d's graciousness (εὐμενῇ) and His Providence (προνοίας) that occurs in connection with Abraham is, moreover, found in Moses' last address to his people, where he renders thanks to G-d for bestowing these upon him. Indeed, as Attridge[30] has shown, the motif of G-d's πρόνοια is frequently found in Josephus' extra-Biblical additions in connection with many of his Biblical characters. We may add that Josephus may well, in this stress on πρόνοια, be answering the Epicureans, so abhorred by the rabbis ("Know what to answer the Epicurean," Avoth 2.14); and we may remark that, significantly, in the conclusion of his paraphrase of the book of Daniel, Josephus (Ant 10.278) states that the fulfillment of Daniel's prophecy proves "how mistaken are the Epicureans, who exclude Providence (πρόνοιαν) from human life and refuse to believe that G-d governs its affairs." Josephus' identification with the Stoics may be further seen in the fact that when Josephus (Life 12) declares that after going through the various sects he decided to join the Pharisees, he remarks that the Pharisees are a sect closely resembling (παραπλήσιος) "that which the Greeks call the Stoics" (τῇ παρ᾽ Ἕλλησι Στωικῇ λεγομένη).

One of the charges of the anti-Semites that Josephus attempts to answer in his treatise Against Apion (2.135) is that the Jews had failed to produce any geniuses. Hence, Josephus insists (Against Apion 2.136) that "our own famous men are deserving of winning no less praise" than the great heroes produced by the Greeks. Indeed, the Antiquities is full of extra-Biblical details to build up its major characters. In particular, Josephus' Abraham is a great general and no less, as I have tried to indicate elsewhere,[31] a rhetorician, scientist, and philosopher who presents a new proof for the existence of G-d from the irregularities of the movements of the heavenly bodies (Ant 1.156). Apparently, to judge from Philo's comment (De Abrahamo 33.178), there were "quarrelsome critics" who did not think Abraham's action in connection with the Aqedah to be great or wonderful; and Josephus is, therefore, particularly concerned to stress Abraham's faith. Thus he adds (1.255) that Abraham told no one in his household, not even his wife Sarah, about his resolve to sacrifice Isaac, lest they should attempt to hinder him from attending to G-d's service. To be sure, Philo (De Abrahamo 32.170) also adds that Abraham told no one of the Divine command; but Josephus is unique in giving the reason for this and thus in stressing Abraham's virtue. The rabbis, on the other hand, declare either that Abraham told Sarah nothing or that Abraham told Sarah that he was taking Isaac to study with Shem and Eber.[32] Josephus, however, had a difficult enough time in

---

[29]Ginzberg (above, note 4) 1.272-73, and 5.248-49, notes 227-228. Although we may argue that to submit to G-d's will is hardly an idea restricted to the Stoics, since it is found in the Mishnah (Avoth 2.4) also, the reason which Josephus gives for doing so, namely that all that befell His favored ones was ordained by Divine providence, has no rabbinic parallel as such.

[30]Harold W. Attridge, The Interpretation of Biblical History in the Antiquitates Judaicae of Flavius Josephus (Missoula, Montana, 1976) 71-76. See also, A. Lewinsky, Beiträge zur Kenntnis der religionsphilosophischen Anshauungen des Flavius Josephus (Breslau, 1887) 36-46; and George F. Moore, "Fate and Free Will in the Jewish Philosophies according to Josephus," HTR 22 (1929) 371-89.

[31]Above (note 21).

[32]Rappaport (above, note 13) 108, note 105; Ginzberg (above, note 4) 1.278 and 5.233; and Sandmel (above, note 12) 73, note 330.

trying to justify the deceit which Abraham practiced on Pharaoh and on Abimelech in connection with Sarah's relationship to himself, and he thus, as would be expected, sought to avoid further deceit of Sarah such as the rabbis ascribe to him. Moreover, Josephus may well have sought to avoid the inevitable equation in this respect of Abraham and Agamemnon, who, according to Euripides (*Iphigenia in Aulis* 98), attempted to deceive his wife Clytemnestra by writing a letter to her asking her to send their daughter Iphigenia to be married to Achilles, whereas his real intention was to sacrifice her. Similarly, Josephus avoids the embarrassment of Abraham's statement (Gen 22:5) that he and Isaac will return to the young men who had accompanied them, whereas the later statement (Gen 22:19) declares that Abraham did so and omits Isaac.[33]

A significant contrast between the style of the Bible and that of Josephus may be seen in the description of Abraham and Isaac proceeding to the sacrifice. On the one hand, we are kept in the dark as to which place Abraham saw (Gen 22:4), yet we are given the gruesome external details (Gen 22:6) that "Abraham took the wood of the burnt offering and laid it on Isaac his son; and he took in his hand the fire and knife." But we are told nothing of the inner thoughts of the pair, other than Isaac's question as to where the lamb for the offering is and Abraham's vague answer that G-d would provide one. Josephus (1.226), however, clearly identifies the place as the mountain which he has previously mentioned, but (1.227) on the other hand, omits the external details, as well as the phrase "and they walked together," a phrase which contributes to the suspense of the account in Genesis; and he creates a dramatic dialogue between father and son of the sort that Kierkegaard in his *Fear and Trembling* would have appreciated. He is not interested in presenting the details of the Aqedah as a proto-sacrifice, since these are theological; he is concerned, rather, with the two personalities who are involved. In particular, though generally averse to theologizing, Josephus presents (1.227) a defense of G-d's role in the event to readers who would undoubtedly raise questions about it, that G-d had "power alike to give men abundance of what they had not and to deprive of what they had those who felt assured of their possessions."[34] Attridge[35] has noted the neatly balanced gnomic form of this expression, which, we may suggest, sounds as if it came from a rhetorical or philosophical handbook.

One major addition to the Bible is Josephus' statement that Isaac was twenty-five years old at the time of the Aqedah.[36] Though his age is variously given (37, 36, 27, 26)

---

[33]The Midrash (cf. Ginzberg [above, note 4] 1.279 and 5.250, note 239) explains Abraham's statement as unconscious prophecy.

[34]Philo (*De Abrahamo* 32.175) similarly states on this passage, "To G-d all things are possible, including those that are impossible or insuperable to men."

[35]Attridge (above, note 30) 93.

[36]P. R. Davies and B. D. Chilton, "The Aqedah: A Revised Tradition History," *CBQ* 40 (1978) 521-22, suggest that the age of twenty-five is to be interpreted as the minimum for active military service, as is implied in the Dead Sea War Scroll (1QM 7.1-3), and that Josephus is thus depicting Isaac as a voluntary martyr, facing death with joy as an adult warrior. Again, as Philip R. Davies, *1QM, the War Scroll from Qumran: Its Structure and History*(Rome, 1977) 41-42, notes, in the Bible (Num 8:24) twenty-five is the lower limit for service in the tent of meeting by a Levite. Furthermore, the lower age limit for officers at Qumran (see the Zaddokite Document, 10.6) is twenty-five. But, we may remark, even if Isaac is not portrayed as holding the fanatical views of the Sicarii, such an implication would be out of character for Josephus in view of his strong opposition to such an attitude, though, we must admit, Josephus does have the Romans express admiration for such voluntary martydom at Masada (*War* 7.405). Davies and Chilton suggest that Isaac is the prototype of those who were active in the war against the Romans; but, as we have noted, Josephus' opposition to the war was so fundamental that this equation is hard to accept in view of Josephus' obvious admiration for Isaac. When, however, they conclude that Josephus cannot vouch for any pre-Christian Jewish

in rabbinic literature[37] and in Jubilees (17.15, where his age is 23), the important point is that Josephus has chosen to give his age, presumably because he considered it important to establish that Isaac was not a mere lad but a grown young man, and hence was able to make a deliberate choice as to whether he would consent to his being sacrificed. This is particularly important to Josephus in view of the fact that Iphigenia, with whom Isaac would certainly be compared by his Greek readers, did, in Euripides' play, heroically consent to be sacrificed. Josephus thus deliberately departs from the Biblical narrative, which refers to Isaac as a lad (*na^{c}ar,* Gen 22:5).[38] This further heightens the contrast between Isaac and Iphigenia, who is depicted as a young girl of scarcely marriageable age, considerably younger, apparently, than twenty-five. It also diminishes the horror that such a story would arouse in Josephus' readers, to judge from Lucretius' comments[39] in his retelling of the parallel story of Iphigenia. On the other hand, we may note that in his own parallel account of Jephthah's sacrifice of his daughter (*Ant* 5.264-266), Josephus does not give the age of Jephthah's daughter because he does not seek to diminish the horror of the act but instead castigates Jephthah for his rashness in making the vow to sacrifice the first creature to greet him after his victory in war.

The most important word, to judge from the way that the rabbis later refer to it, in the entire account is the word ^{c}*aqad,* "bound" (Gen 22:9), a *hapax legomenon* in the Bible. Franxman[40] remarks that we shall doubtless never know what gave rise to the tradition which Josephus has either invented or followed that has Abraham deliver a homily to Isaac rather than tie him up. We may, however, suggest that the actual binding of Isaac would probably have been too much for a Greek audience and would have been incriminating toward Abraham. Philo, too, as Sandmel[41] has noted, similarly omits mention of the actual binding, but he at least does portray Abraham as placing Isaac on

---

doctrine, since his work is contemporary with or even sometimes posterior to the New Testament, we may remark that there are so many places where Josephus agrees with Midrashic traditions, which almost certainly predate the New Testament, that this conclusion seems unconvincing. More likely, we may suggest, the age of twenty-five is to be seen as the minimum age, according to the Zaddokite Document (10.6) for judges in the community. My student, Larry Moscovitz, in an unpublished paper, has ingeniously suggested another solution to the mystery of Josephus' source for Isaac's age. He notes that according to the Adler manuscript of *Bereshith Rabbah* 56.8, as well as according to Rabbi Elijah Gaon of Vilna's emendation of *Seder Olam* 1, Isaac was twenty-six at the time of the Aqedah. This tradition is based upon the fact that Abraham spent twenty-six years among the Philistines and that Isaac was born after the first year there. However, inasmuch as Gen 22:1 says that the Aqedah occurred "after these things," if we presuppose that "these things" refers to the time immediately after Abraham left the Philistines, Isaac was twenty-five at that time.

[37] Cf. *Seder Olam* 1; *Bereshith Rabbah* 55.5.

[38] Philo (*De Abrahamo* 32.176), we may note, refers to Isaac as a child (παιδός), using a word related to its diminutive παιδάριον in the Septuagint (Gen 22:12).

[39] Lucretius, *De Rerum Natura* 1.101: "Tantum religio potuit suadere malorum."

[40] Thomas W. Franxman, *Genesis and the "Jewish Antiquities" of Flavius Josephus* (Rome, 1979) 161. See my forthcoming "Josephus' Commentary on Genesis" in *JQR,* in which I note that while we must be grateful to Franxman for his stylistic analysis of Josephus and for his attempt to compare the *Antiquities* with its Biblical source as well as with Philo, the Targumim, the Pseudepigrapha, and the Midrashim, at the same time we must express disappointment because he has missed numerous changes made by Josephus and has not answered the gnawing questions as to why Josephus claims not to have modified the Biblical account when he has manifestly done so, why he exhibits such a variety in his treatment of the Bible, and why he so often chooses to deviate from known exegetical traditions.

[41] Sandmel (above, note 12) 73, note 337.

the altar, whereas this detail is omitted by Josephus. We may further suggest that Josephus is thus deliberately heightening the heroism of Isaac in rushing (ὥρμησεν, 1.232) upon the altar. Thus Josephus, on the one hand, avoided the implication that Isaac had to be tied because, as the rabbis (*Pirke de-Rabbi Eliezer* 31) say, he might have shuddered at the sight of the knife and shrunk from the sacrifice, thus dishonoring his father, or because he might have struggled and thus have rendered the sacrifice ritually unsuitable (*Bereshith Rabbah* 56.8). Unlike the rabbis, who thus indicate that even the patriarchs were human enough to be tempted to disobey, Josephus, here as elsewhere,[42] paints his heroes larger than life and, in this case, as being above temptation. Moreover, as we have already noted, in his eagerness to avoid theological implications of the Aqedah, Josephus did not seek to depict the Aqedah as a sacrifice which presaged the sacrifices in the Temple.

Again, whereas in the Bible, Abraham begins to perform the sacrifice in mysterious and suspenseful silence (Gen 22:1), Josephus, in line with Homer's style, removes the veil of secrecy; and his description of Abraham's piety reaches its climax in Abraham's speech to Isaac (1.228-231), which he has invented and which, far from being an emotional or irrational outburst, *explains* his action rationally[43] and logically (in a fashion without rabbinic parallel), namely that since he was born out of the course of nature, it is fitting that he die not by sickness or war or any of the usual calamities by which men perish, but in this most unusual fashion as a sacrifice (1.230-231), as a result of which G-d, to whom he is giving this sacrifice, will, instead of his son, be his protector.[44] He asks (1.229) his son to bear this consecration (καθιέρωσιν) as befits one of noble birth (γενναίως). This nobility of birth is emphasized in the repetition of the same word (γενναῖον, 1.232), which Josephus uses to describe the nobility of spirit with which Isaac received his father's words. The fact that Josephus stresses Abraham's address to Isaac and does not have any appeal to G-d is contrasted with the rabbinic emphasis on Abraham's address to G-d in which he notes that though he could have argued against the Divine decree he did not do so; and he pleads, therefore, according to the rabbis, that G-d will defend Isaac's descendants when they come upon trouble.[45] The fact that Josephus omits such an appeal, fraught, as it is, with the

---

[42]See my forthcoming study of "Josephus' Portrait of Saul," to appear in *HUCA*. We may note that whereas the rabbis (Targum Pseudo-Jonathan on Genesis 22:1) indicate that G-d also tested Isaac, Josephus avoids this, since, presumably, it might lead to theological speculation about the fruits of this test, notably the rationale of martyrdom.

[43]Cf. James R. Lord, *Abraham: A Study in Ancient Jewish and Christian Interpretation* (Diss., Ph.D., Duke University, Durham, NC, 1968) 166. As Roland G. Bomstad, *Governing Ideas of the Jewish War of Flavius Josephus* (Diss., Ph.D., Yale University, New Haven, 1979) 2, has noted, the set speech, such as Abraham, we may suggest, here delivers in Josephus, in antiquity, "is a literary device used to further the aims of the historian, to present to the reader the author's interpretation of events, and to attempt to persuade him of the truth of that interpretation." As Lucian in his *Quomodo Historia Conscribenda Sit*-an essay whose ideals for the writing of history Josephus closely follows, as Gert Avenarius, *Lukians Schrift zur Geschichtsschreibung* (Meisenheim/Glan, 1956) has shown--declares, speeches afforded the historian "the counsel's right of showing your eloquence." Hence the speeches in a history are the natural starting point for any attempt to perceive the author's own views. On the liberties taken by Josephus in the speeches of Books 1 and 2 of the *Antiquities* see Martin Dibelius, "The Speeches in Acts and Ancient Historiography," in *Studies in the Acts of the Apostles* (trans. from the German by Mary Ling; New York, 1956) 138-91.

[44]Franxman (above, note 40) 159-60, says that Abraham breaks the news of the impending sacrifice so delicately to Isaac that "considering the rather unusual and unexpected charcter of what was intended, it is surprising tht Isaac got the point of what his father was saying." But we may object that Abraham clearly states that Isaac is now to die through the rite of sacrifice.

[45]Cf. Jerusalem *Taʿanith* 65D, *Bereshith Rabbah* 56.15, and other passages cited by Marmorstein (above, note 13) 76.

problem of theodicy, is again in line with his effort to avoid theological problems, which, apparently (*Ant* 1.25, 4.198, 20.268), he intended to deal with in a separate work. Abraham's calm, reasoned approach is in contrast with Agamemnon's pitiful apologetic in Euripides (*Iphigenia in Aulis* 1255-1275) in which he bewails his dilemma, claiming that if he does not do the will of the goddess Artemis and sacrifice his daughter his army in anger will slaughter him and his entire family. The speech of Agamemnon apparently, to judge from Seneca the Elder (*Suasoriae*, 3), where we have a sample of such an address, as well as Abraham's speech in Josephus, are examples of a progymnasmatic (preparatory) exercise called *ethopoeia*.[46] Again, the fact that Abraham makes no appeal to Isaac to sacrifice himself altruistically for the sake of his descendants or for the sanctification of G-d's name, as we find in rabbinic literature, removes the theological dimension and concentrates on the character of Isaac himself.

---

[46]See Leonardus Spengel, ed., *Rhetores Graeci*, vol 2 (Leipzig, 1854). Of the four rhetoricians whom Spengel cites--Theon, Pseudo-Hermogenes, Aphthonius, and Nicolaus--Theon, the oldest, is probably Aelius Theon, who would have been a younger contemporary of Josephus. Theon (*ap*. Spengel, 2.60-130) describes fifteen exercises designed to prepare a student not only for declamations but also specifically for writing history and poetry. One of the progymnasmatic exercises, moreover, of Aphthonius (*ap*. Spengel, 2.21-56, no. 11) presents the words that Niobe might have uttered after her children had been slain. In such a situation, we are told, a parent's remarks (as are, indeed, Abraham's in 228-231) should be concerned with the present, past, and future. One of the earliest progymnasmatic exercises taught by the grammarians involved the retelling of a single episode from myth, poetry, or history, with particular attention to the Isocratean virtues of the narrative art--clarity, brevity, and plausibility--and the six elements of agent, action, time, place, manner, and cause--qualities particularly discussed in Lucian's *Quomodo Historia Conscribenda Sit* and especially aimed at by Josephus in his retelling of the Aqedah episode. Though, to be sure, narratives based on poetical excerpts were more common, we do have exercises on papyri which are based on historical episodes. On progymnasmatic exercises see H. I. Marrou, *A History of Education in Antiquity* (trans. from the French by George Lamb; New York, 1956) 194-205; Helen F. North, "Rhetoric and Historiography," *Quarterly Journal of Speech* 42 (1956) 234-42; and Donald L. Clark, *Rhetoric in Greco-Roman Education* (New York, 1957) 177-212. While it is true that the address of a father to a son is not a distinctive type in classical rhetoric, the portrayal of the character of a father and of a son are features of *ethopoeia*, and progymnasmatic exercises occasionally created situations in which a father could address a child, as, for example, in Seneca the Elder. The fact that, as David L. Balch, "*Let Wives Be Submissive . . .*" *The Origin, Form and Apologetic Function of the Household Duty Code (Haustafel) in I Peter* (Diss., Ph.D., Yale University, New Haven, 1974) and "Josephus, Against Apion II. 145-296. A Preliminary Report," in George MacRae, ed., *Society of Biblical Literature 1975 Seminar Papers*, vol. 1 (Missoula, Montana, 1975) 187-92, has noted, Josephus, in his defense of the Jewish constitution (*Against Apion* 2.145-295), followed the standard rhetorical pattern for such encomia as described most fully in the later handbook by the third-century Menander of Laodicea (Περὶ ἐπιδεικτικῶν, in Leonardus Spengel, ed., *Rhetores Graeci* vol. 3 [Leipzig, 1856] 331-446) further supports the view that Josephus was, indeed influenced by the rhetoricians. Theon, in his preface, notes the utility of rhetorical exercises for the writing of history; and we may recall Cicero's famous remark (*De Legibus* 1.5) that history is an *opus . . . unum . . . oratorium maxime*. On this phrase see my discussion in *Cicero's Conception of Historiography* (Diss., Ph.D., Harvard University, Cambridge, MA, 1951) 149-69. (I am indebted to Prof. George A. Kennedy of the University of North Carolina for several suggestions in connection with Josephus' possible indebtedness to rhetorical theory.)

The degree of Abraham's faithfulness to G-d is all the greater because of his readiness to give up the son who was to be the protector (κηδεμόνα) and stay of his old age (γηροκόμον). One is reminded of Priam's speech (*Iliad* 22.38-76) begging his son Hector not to leave him bereft of the care of his children but to protect him in old age from ravening dogs. Similarly, Hesiod (*Theogony* 605) speaks of the curse of not having anyone to tend (γηροκόμοιο) one in one's baleful old age (ὀλοόν . . . γῆραϙ). Again, Medea says to her sons (Euripides, *Medea* 1032) that she had hopes that they would look after her in her old age. Indeed, as Josephus has elsewhere stated (*Ant* 4.261), in an extra-Biblical addition, the whole purpose of marriage is to produce children who will tend the old age (γηροκομήσουσιν) of one's parents.[47] The fact that Josephus in this brief pericope (1.222-236) on five occasions uses a form of the word for happiness[48] stresses how much happiness meant to Abraham; and yet his readiness to forego this shows how great was his faithfulness to G-d. The rabbinic accounts,[49] as well as Jubilees (18.6), are likewise full of embellishments at this point, but they stress the role of Satan, whereas Josephus omits this supernatural feature and focuses attention on Abraham himself.

Then, in a manifest addition, Isaac, who in the Bible is such a passive, secondary, and even shadowy figure, like Iphigenia, comes to the fore with a magnificently brave response. Just as Iphigenia (Euripides, *Iphigenia in Aulis* 1396) proclaims, "Shall I, who am a mortal, stand in the way of the goddess?", so Isaac exclaims (1.232) that he deserved never to have been born at all were he to reject the decision of G-d.[50] Isaac's statement (1.232) in Josephus that if the command to be sacrificed were the resolution of his father alone it would have been impious to disobey has no rabbinic parallel and, indeed, violates the rule that where a parent commands a child to do something in violation of the Torah (as this would be if it did not have G-d's direct sanction) the child should not obey.[51]

One would have expected that the climax of the narrative, where Abraham actually is about to slaughter his son, would be dramatized by Josephus even beyond the Biblical account, just as one finds in his treatment of Esther,[52] for example. Josephus,

---

[47]Cf. Josephus (*Ant* 5.336), where the son born to Boaz and Ruth is nursed by Naomi, "who on the counsel of the women called him Obed, because he was brought up to be the stay of her old age" (ἐπὶ γηροκομίᾳ) . Cf. also *Antiquities* 7.183, where the woman, one of whose sons has killed the other, asks David to spare the life of her remaining son so as not to deprive her of her last hope of support in old age (γηροκομίας).

[48]εὐδαιμονίαν (1.223), εὐδαιμονίαν (1.224), εὐδαιμονήσειν (1.228), εὐδαιμόνως (1.234), εὐδαιμόνως (1.236).

[49]*Yashar Vayera* 43b; *Sanhedrin* 89b.

[50]Pseudo-Philo (*Liber Antiquitatum Biblicarum* 32.3), as I (Prolegomenon to reprint of M. R. James, *The Biblical Antiquities of Philo* [New York, 1971] cxvii) have noted, has a parallel in language when Isaac asks: "What if I had not been born in the world to be offered a sacrifice unto Him that made me?" Thus both Josephus and Pseudo-Philo look upon the sacrifice as payment due to G-d; but there is also a difference in that Pseudo-Philo omits the concept that for Isaac not to allow himself to be sacrificed would be to disobey his father. For Pseudo-Philo the sacrifice is the fulfillment of a divine mission alone; for Josephus it is, in the first instance, the fulfillment of a human, that is a paternal, mission, and not only a divine mission. In short, Pseudo-Philo, like the rabbis (*Vayikra Rabbah* 2.11), emphasizes the theological consequences of Isaac's sacrifice, which, he says (32.3), will bring blessedness to all men; and all later generation will be instructed by his example. On Pseudo-Philo's view of the Aqedah see further Vermes (above, note 8) 199-202; Daly (above, note 15) 59ff.; and Davies and Chilton (above, note 36) 522ff.

[51]See *Yevamoth* 5b and *Sifra, Kedoshim* 1.10.87a; and Blidstein (above, note 25) 80-94.

[52]See my "Hellenizations in Josephus' Version of Esther," *Transactions of the American Philological Association* 101 (1970) 143-70.

however, well aware of the fact that the scene raised a major problem of theodicy, presents it in a matter-of-fact fashion: "The deed would have been accomplished had not G-d stood in the way" (ἐμποδών 1.233). Daly[53] has noted Josephus' disagreement with the Targumic idea that Isaac was actually sacrificed and with the Philonic view (*De Abrahamo* 33.177) that the sacrifice was considered as it if had been actually carried out; but he does not explain the reason, namely that Josephus is an apologist who seeks implicitly to contrast the Aqedah with the sacrifice of Iphigenia, which was actually consummated.

Next comes a remarkable addition in which G-d Himself presents an apology, that it was "from no craving for human blood" (ἐπιθυμήσας αἵματος ἀνθρωπίνου) that he had given the order to Abraham. This would seem to be in direct contrast to Artemis, who, according to the chorus in Euripides' *Iphigenia in Aulis* (1524-1525) "rejoices in human sacrifices" (θύμασιν βροτησίοις χαρεῖσα). Apparently, to judge from writers such as Lucretius (1.101), there were pagans also who could not accept the idea that the gods delighted in blood.

It is significant, moreover, that in the Bible it is an angel that appears to Abraham, whereas in Josephus, as in Philo (*De Abrahamo* 32.176), it is G-d Himself who addresses him, presumably because the subject was too important to be left to G-d's deputies.[54] Furthermore, the Bible does not explain why G-d had given the order and what should be learned from it. Finally, the Bible (Gen 22:13) implies that the appearance of the ram was by chance, whereas Josephus explicitly (1.236) declares that G-d Himself brought the ram into view. But Josephus does not explicitly tell us, as does the Bible (Gen 22:13), that Abraham offered the ram in place of his son, perhaps again because he sought to avoid the theological implication that the ram was a surrogate for the sins of man. Presumably, Josephus is attempting to answer those who might have difficulty in understanding such a command in the first place, especially since, as Pearson[55] has indicated, the practice of human sacrifice was rare in classical, let alone, Hellenistic, times. Somehow, as Franxman[56] remarks, Josephus is protesting too much and, indeed, seems to have found the manner of G-d's test of Abraham to be a bit embarrassing. We may suggest that inasmuch as G-d expressly forbids Abraham to slay his son and says that He has no craving for human blood, Josephus is expressing disagreement with the tradition that Isaac actually was slain or at least wounded.[57] One is reminded of Plutarch's comment (*Pelopidas* 21.4), on the vision that came to Pelopidas

---

[53]Daly (above, note 15) 58. Daly concludes that the theology of the Aqedah had, through the treatments of Philo, Pseudo-Philo, and Josephus become accessible to Christian writers by the beginning of the second century. We may, however, comment that it was not until the third century that extant Church Fathers refer to the Aqedah passage in Josephus, that they never refer to the passage in Pseudo-Philo, and that most likely they derive their theology of the Aqedah from a direct reading of the Biblical passage itself.

[54]Josephus' source for the fact that G-d Himself was present at the sacrifice may be, as Franxman (above, note 40) 119, note 12, has remarked, the ambiguity in the verses that G-d would provide (*yire'eh*) the lamb for a burnt offering (Gen 22:8) and that Abraham called the name of the place "The L-rd will provide" (*yire'eh*) (Gen 22:14).

[55]A. C. Pearson, "Human Sacrifice (Greek)," in James Hastings, ed., *Encyclopaedia of Religion and Ethics,* vol. 6 (Edinburgh, 1913) 847-49.

[56]Franxman (above, note 40) 161.

[57] *Pirke de-Rabbi Eliezer* 31, *Midrash Ha-Gadol* on Genesis 22:19, and other citations in Ginzberg (above, note 4) 5.251, note 243. See also Shalom Spiegel, *The Last Trial: On the Legends and Lord of the Command to Abraham to Offer Isaac as a Sacrifice: the Akedah* (trans. by Judah Goldin; Philadelphia, 1967) 3-8 and passim; and Vermes (above, note 8) 204-6.

instructing him to sacrifice a virgin with auburn hair, that some said that to believe in the existence of divine beings who take delight (χαίροντας) in the slaughter and blood (αἵματι καὶ φόνῳ) of men was perhaps a folly, and that even if such supernatural beings existed, they should not be obeyed, since they had no power, "for only weakness and depravity of soul could produce or harbor such unnatural and cruel desires" (ἐπιθυμίας).

Josephus is here stressing the difference between the motives of sacrifice of children in pagan mythology and that in the case of Isaac. In every instance[58] of the former, the sacrifice was for the sake of the country, whether to alleviate a famine, as in the case of Leos' sacrifice of his three daughters (Pausanias 1.5.2), or a plague, as in the case of Aristodemus' sacrifice of his daughter (Pausanias 4.9.4-5), or a drought, as in the case of the sacrifice of Phrixus, in whose place, as with Isaac, the god sent a ram (Apollodorus 1.9.1-2; Herodotus 7.197; Plutarch, De Superstitione 5).[59] Similarly, in Heliodorus (Aethiopica 10.16) King Hydaspes resolves to sacrifice his daughter Chariclea for the sake of his country. Likewise, in the case of Rome, where we hear of self-sacrifice in the instance of the devotio of Marcus Curtius (Livy 7.6.4) and in the cases of Decius Mus (Livy 8.9) and his son (Livy 10.28), it was to bring victory to the nation by plunging into the midst of the enemy. Philo (De Abrahamo 35.197), indeed, and, we may add, by implication, Josephus compare Abraham with other fathers, noting two major points of difference: first, that the latter gave their children to be sacrificed for the safety of their country or armies, and secondly, that they could not bear the sight and left to others the grisly task of killing their children.

The ending is, as Schalit[60] has remarked, a "happily-ever-after" finale, so typical of the Hellenistic novels. Moreover, Josephus develops further than does the Bible the Divine prediction of the blessings that will be showered upon Abraham and his descendants, presumably to build up Abraham still more. Yet, as Amaru[61] has noted, Josephus has deleted the theology of covenanted land, presumably because he did not want the land to be the focal point, with the implications that it had for the revolutionary theology of the Fourth Philosophy.

In summary, Josephus' treatment of the Aqedah is much more concerned with building up the character of Abraham and Isaac, just as he is elsewhere, as I have tried to show,[62] concerned with aggrandizing his other Biblical heroes, and deliberately plays down the aspects of theology and theodicy.[63] This emphasis on the biographical and on

---

[58]Euripides, in particular, seems to have been preoccupied with the concept of human sacrifice and treats it in no fewer than seven plays so far as we know: in Iphigenia in Aulis, retrospectively in Iphigenia in Tauris, in the sacrifice of Polyxena in the first half of Hecuba and in the first half of The Trojan Women, in the sacrifice of Macaria in the first half of the Heracleidae, in the sacrifice of Menoeceus in the Phoenissae, and in the sacrifice of Otionia in the fragmentary Erechtheus. The sacrifice of Iphigenia is also, we might add, alluded to by Clytemnestra in the Electra (1024-1025). A similar theme likewise appears in the Alcestis, where, after King Admetus' parents refused to die in his stead, his wife Alcestis heroically does so.

[59]Cf. Spiegel (above, note 57) 9-12.

[60]Schalit (above, note 10) 2.40, note 265. Schalit cites similar happy endings in Xenophon, Ephesiaca 5.15, and Apollonius of Tyre, Erotica 43.

[61]Betsy H. Amaru, "Land Theology in Josephus' Jewish Antiquities," JQR 71 (1980-81) 208 and 229.

[62]See my articles on Abraham (above, note 21), on Saul (above, note 42), on Solomon (above, note 18), and on Esther (above, note 52).

[63]It is striking that Josephus in the War, which has, especially as seen in the speeches, as noted by Bornstad (above, note 43) a clear theological lesson, has no indication in its proem that this is what the reader should derive from the work. On the other hand, the Antiquities, where, as we have noted, the theological element is played down, has in its proem (Ant 1.14) the statement that "the main lesson to be learnt from this

the study of character for its own sake, as I have tried to indicate elsewhere,[64] shows his
indebtedness to one of the great Greek schools of historiography, the Aristotelian, just as
his concern with the epic, rhetorical, and the tragic, which we see in the Aqedah
pericope, shows his debt to the other great Greek historiographical school, the Isocratean. In the case of Abraham, Josephus has presented us with a portrait of a philosopher
and scientist, an open-minded missionary, a resourceful general, and, as seen in the
climactic episode of the Aqedah, a knight of faith. Isaac, in turn, is the great exponent
of *pietas*.

As an apologist for the Jewish people, Josephus is particularly concerned with
showing the superiority of Judaism vis-à-vis pagan mythology, notably the parallel
sacrifice of Iphigenia. We may ask whether in making these changes Josephus was
following rabbinic tradition or that of Hellenistic-Jewish writers, such as Philo, or
inventing his own interpretations. To judge from the comparison with Philo, Pseudo-
Philo's *Biblical Antiquities*, and Midrashic traditions, we may conclude that while there
are many parallels, there is sufficient inner consistency in the uniquely Josephan characteristics and sufficient consistency with Josephan additions and changes elsewhere in
the *Antiquities* to make it likely that Josephus, whether for stylistic or apologetic
reasons or both, introduced a number of elements of his own. Cohen[65] has contended
that the Josephan enterprise shows sloppiness, inconsistency, and capriciousness. When,
however, one considers that Josephus spent at least a dozen years writing the *Antiquities*
(79/81-93/94), living on an imperial pension and without any additional duties, writing an
average of about ten lines of Greek a day,[66] we have a right to expect a careful and
consistent work, especially from so gifted a historian, and particularly in a pericope so
important to Jews as the Aqedah.[67] We agree with Franxman[68] in concluding that
"beneath the surface of Josephus' style we have found a more careful author . . . whose
alterations may represent exegetical traditions much better thought out than has been
heretofore supposed."

---

history by any who care to peruse it is that men who conform to the will of G-d . . .
prosper in all things beyond belief," as well as the admonition (1.15) that readers should
"fix their thoughts on G-d." We may perhaps explain that Josephus in the *Antiquities* is
presenting an apologetic for the Bible and consequently for G-d's deeds, but he does not
do so as a theologian but as a historian, noting the consequences of given actions by his
main characters.

[64]Above, note 42.

[65]Shaye J. D. Cohen, *Josephus in Galilee and Rome: His Vita and Development as
a Historian* (Leiden, 1979) 38-39.

[66]There are 7375 sections in Niese's edition of the Greek text of the twenty books
of the *Antiquities*. Each has an average of about six lines, making a total of 44,250 lines
of Greek. Twelve years contain 4380 days, hence the average of about ten lines a day.

[67]The Aqedah was already part of the *Zikhronoth* prayer in the Musaf service of
Rosh Hashanah in the first century, as Israel Lévi, "Le sacrifice d'Isaac et le mort de
Jésus," *REJ* 64 (1912), has indicated.

[68]Franxman (above, note 40) 289.

THE TEMPLE OF DENDUR

James M. Fennelly
Adelphi University

The Temple of Dendur stands extant within a large, separate glass enclosed wing at New York's Metropolitan Museum. In 1978 it was opened to the public, who discovered a diminutive, obscure, late Egyptian style temple from the debased Roman period, standing overwhelmed within the massive expanse of the new Sackler wing. Its opening did not receive enthusiastic reviews, eclipsed by the attention lavished on the King Tut Exhibition. In this paper, I would like to redress this injustice.

The Temple is a small building 13m (42.6 feet) long, 6.25m (20.5 feet) wide and 4.3m (14 feet) high). It has an entrance pylon standing east on the main axis creating a courtyard 9.2m (30.1 feet) long in front of the shrine. The Temple was originally located on the west bank of the Nile, facing east. It was 1033km (642 miles) south of Cairo, and 88.5km beyond the first cataract which is 3.5km (2.1 miles) south of the Tropic of Cancer. It was built early in the reign of Augustus Caesar, probably during the Praefecture of Petronius, following the defeat of the Nubian, Queen of Meroe. It appears to predate the Roman construction at Philae of ca. 15 B.C.E. (around the time when Augustus accepted the title of Pontifex Maximus). Dendur was constructed rapidly in front of a small Ptolemaic rock-chamber tomb. It was in Nubia on the outer edge of the Roman Empire. The last frontier post was 113km (70 miles) farther up the Nile at Primus (Qasr Ibrim), with the last permanent settlement under Roman domination just half that distance away. Dendur is one of perhaps six temples built in Egypt during the reign of Augustus, the most famous ones being Temple J at Philae (40 miles) down river and the foundations for the Horus Birth House at Dendera (half-way back to Cairo) with its Zodiac hemisphere, not to be completed until A.D. 35 by Tiberius. Augustus and the Romans were not concerned with Egyptian theology but they were particularly interested in the efficient economic operation and control of Egyptian temples. Temples were a means to the exploitation of Egypt's wealth which was necessary to bring stability to the entire empire. Rome's annual Egyptian income of about 60 million sesterces, plus the massive proceeds from Egyptian land sales, was a prime source of the capital which made possible Augustus's distribution to the plebs and the purchase of land for the settlement of his veterans. Augustus sold off old hieratic lands and transformed the Ptolemaic tax structure into the new and more efficient system known as Roman capitalism. Dendur is too small to play a role in this master economic plan. It is not like the important Nilometer at Philae which set the tax rate, nor is it a manifestation of Roman grandeur. Dendur is a toy, and that enhances its importance!

Classical Egyptologists have observed that the temple is not truly Egyptian. The dimensions and location of the rooms were conceived upon a foreign set of artistic assumptions. Previous generations of scholars accepted the facile premise (now universally rejected) that Roman Egypt was but a more efficient continuation of a Ptolemaic pattern of organization. In the same manner the Ptolemaic facade of Dendur disguises the essential nature of its Roman plan. Dendur was built according to conventions set down by Marcus Vitruvius Pollio, who advises that the length of the temple be two times its width. He also prescribed the ratio and pattern for the pronaos, antechamber, sanctuary, and the proportions and spacing of the columns. The external decoration abounds with scenes of the ubiquitous Augustus, in the costume of a Ptolemaic Pharaoh, performing liturgies to an assortment of upper Egyptian deities. The rounded corners of the stone blocks show that the building was constructed from previously cut stone and inscribed only in those places which can be seen from the outside. It was dedicated to two local brothers who reportedly drowned in the river. Their assonance of name, Petesi and Pihor, suggest that they are twins. Perhaps they were sons of a Nubian prince or princess. During Ptolemaic times they were identified with the Dioscuri who were popular with grecophiles throughout the length of the country. The Pharos at Alexandria had been dedicated to the Dioscuri/Gemini twin brothers, and papyrii and stelae abound with references to the cult of the twins at Philadelphia, Soknopaiou Nesos, Tebytunis, and Memphis. Much evidence for the cult of the twins has been found at Antinoopolis. At Karanis, during the reign of Vespasian, the Dioscuri were known by the assonate names of Pnepheros and Petesuchus. They appear to have an independent shrine within the sacred compound dedicated to the god, Serapis. With the arrival of Augustus and the Romans, the old Ptolemaic social structure was quickly transformed to accommodate Roman policy. On the lower register of the exterior of the south wall Augustus as Autokrator offers a bag of eye paint to Petesi, and adoration to his unnamed consort: the universal goddess in her Egyptian costume! Like the Greeks before them the Romans identified, as best as they could, the local deities with the universal qualities of the gods of their own pantheon: Isis with Vesta; Osiris and Janus; Horus and Apollo; Mandoulis and Mercury. The Romans were scandalized by the Egyptian proclivity toward animal representations of the gods. Dio Cassius reports that Augustus, being invited to visit the Apis bull remarked that he was accustomed to show reverence to the gods, not to cattle! (Dio 51:16) The discovery, on the frontier of the empire, of an obscure little tomb dedicated to two deified brothers who drowned in the Nile provided the Romans with the opportunity to construct a unique temple, one rich in mythology, history, mechanics, and the symbolism of the age. Dendur was conceived as an act of genius. It is not a commonplace building. It is as tiny as a toy and yet a paradigm of importance.

Petesi and Pihor had become local symbols for the Dioscuri commemorated in a tomb 3.5 km (2.1 miles) south of the modern marking for the Tropic of Cancer (well within the margin of acceptable accuracy for observations made across rough terrain by the naked eye--and 50 times more accurate than Syene-Aswan identification of Strabo). At the same time when Augustus himself was rebuilding and adorning the porch of the Temple of Castor and Pollux in the Roman Forum, his Prefect constructed Dendur at the outer edge of the empire, and the only point astride the Tropic of Cancer.

John Helgeland writes that religion produces assumptions for drawing the boundaries of the world. The center and edges are most critical because it is at these points that the imperial world is most vulnerable.

It was a time when the world had been overawed by the new mathematical science of astrology, which had absorbed into itself Greek mythology, pythagorean philosophy, and Roman polity.

The integrating power of Sol Invictus engulfed Helios both as Zeus Hypsistos and Amon-Re. Roman power was built on duty, valor, and efficient technology. On June 21 the sun shines overhead at Dendur. Its midday rays cast no shadow! The hemispheres of the sky are said to shift. The reign of the heavenly twin gives way to that of the earthly twin. It is the carnal one, the Autokrator, who gathers the harvest and rules over the earth.

The two brothers at Dendur are excellent representatives of the Dioscuri legend. The lower north panel on the exterior of the pylon is the temple dedicatory panel. It is June 21 when control of the world is temporarily given over to the human twin in the form of the Autokrator Augustus Caesar. On December 21 (which is also the birthday of Harpocrates) the divine twin takes command of the creative process and re-instills life into a decaying world. At death Augustus will seek apotheosis (similar to that granted to Horus) by the merit of loyalty he has shown in his life to the forces of the divine order. Petesi, whose name means "He whom Isis has given" (He is blue in color) bears the important cognomen "Agathodaemon," a term frequently used to designate the consort of Isis. A. M. Blackman was able to report in 1911 that some of the original colors were still recognizable in the upper registers of the pronaos offering scenes.

Pihor, called the prince or sheikh, appears ten times and was colored green, the same as the Osiris of vegetation. His name means "He who belongs to Horus"; the very earthly reflection of the divine Osiris. On the exterior of the north wall Augustus

"Autokrator" offers ointment to Pihor, and presents lotus flowers from the defeat of the powers of the Abyss to an enthroned Petesi. The heavenly twin is established above the carnal one on the north side of the building. The earthly Pihor does not appear on the south side of the building. The divine Petesi is the subject of two independent offering scenes on that most important side.

Inside the sanctuary on the west wall the most complete identification of the Dioscuri with Isis and Osiris is preserved. With the hieroglyph of heaven above him, Pihor stands adoring an enthroned Isis. His inscription reads, "Pihor, son of KKR, greatly praised in the underworld." Isis is described as, "Isis giver of life, mistress of Abaton, lady mistress of Philae, mistress of the southern foreign lands."

Beneath Pihor, in a manner consistent with certain panels of the east-west axis is the symbolic hieroglyph for *EARTH,* and beneath it the hieroglyph for *HEAVEN.* (Egyptian eschatology posits paradise beneath the earth and below the Nile, in a manner most congenial with Roman astrological theory.) Here, in the paradise below, Petesi adores the divine, enthroned Osiris. Above Petesi is the formula, "the Osiris, greatly praised in the underworld, Petesi son of *KWR."* The description of Osiris is badly damaged. This much may be read, "Osiris . . . (lacuna) . . . Onnophris, great god, Lord of Abaton." The reversal of priority manifest in the sanctuary stele marks the shift of the hemispheres at the moment of the summer solstice. The pattern is a gentle modification of the classical *dokna,* symbol of the Dioscuri. It is an archaeological verification of Franz Cumont's "Cercle de Petosiris" associated with Roman funerary customs.

Early imperial interest in judicial astrology has been well attested. The foremost horoscope of all time was associated with Augustus. He was reportedly born on 21 September (the autumnal equinox) and took for himself (as was the common practice) the sign of Capricorn, to mark the day of his conception, coordinate with the birth of Horus, (21 December--the winter solstice). This provided a standard pre-Julian 280 day gestation period of 10 lunar months. Contemporary speculation suggested that his soul, swathed in solar fluid, would lodge itself in a lunar integument within his mother on June 21 (the summer solstice). At death, that same soul would surrender its carnal body to rise to paradise as a star, being castorized (made like Castor) a visible god, a solar phoenix, at that moment when the sun came closest to earth. In classical Egypt while "western funerary temples . . . served the king when he was dead, they began to function while he was yet alive." (Nelson 149) But Roman genius becomes manifest only when we go beyond astrology, theology, and pythagorean philosophy.

The coefficients known to the Alexandrian mathematician Eratosthenes in 200 B.C.E. allowed him to measure the angle of the shadow cast by a gnomon in Alexandria at midday on June 21 and to multiply it by the distance to Syene (Aswan), thereby theorizing the earth's circumference at 28,725 miles. This event is reported to us in rather general terms by Cleomedes in the second century of this era. Cleomedes probably knew nothing beyond Aswan and certainly not of Dendur. But the clever Eratosthenes probably knew enough to add an additional 55 miles to make his circumference estimate more precise. During the early empire, Roman precision was able to ascertain from direct observation that the sun cast a shadow at Syene but not at Dendur. Vitruvius, whose work assisted us in identifying a Roman planned temple, contains a description of a remarkable water clock calibrated to harmonize with the new Julian solar calendar being implemented throughout the empire. After introducing the subject of the clock he describes its construction in detail. Vitruvius' clock was apparently designed for use at Dendur. June 21 introduces Cancer at the top, on the west wall for the apotheosis of the soul on the shadowless day. The south side of the shrine, with its special door, features Augustus with Petesi in the sign of Aries and leadership. Capricorn at the bottom of the clock dial faces into the sunrise, greeting the arrival of new life (Harpocrates' birth and Augustus' conception). This leaves Libra, the autumnal equinox, on the north with a depiction of Harpocrates standing behind Isis wearing his milk amulet and holding a pewit.

Upon further examination one finds a large water storage chamber cut into the southwest corner of the building abutting the west sanctuary wall carving. This space has been point dressed to hold a plaster facing creating a cistern for about 370 gallons of water. Replenishment would be easily drawn from the Nile. This cistern has an aperture through which a pipe might pass to connect a clock of the type just described. Six carefully drilled holes exist in the west wall to fasten the water clock firmly in place. Thus Dendur held a horological instrument, of the most advanced design, which was accurately set by the observation on June 21 of a shadowless column. It was a masterpiece of technology, actualizing Augustus' horoscope in a correctly located laboratory which demonstrated the new Julian solar calendar, so recently introduced, and harmonizing it with Egyptian and Greek mythology.

Roman suzerainty at Dendur lasted for little more than two centuries. The mechanical technology of the hydrolic clock created obvious maintenance problems at the edge of a remote frontier. By the end of the Julio-Claudians, the "toy" would be of little or no interest to the governed or the government. Although Dendur was designed according to Roman presuppositions, with slight modifications, it could become an acceptable Egyptian temple at last. The mythology of Dendur is essentially the Edfu creation epic.

A north doorway which could be opened and closed would provide an acceptable approximation to fulfill ritual requirements. Local priests viewing the temple from a native sense of pragmatism, cut just such a doorway in the north wall at the far edge of the Pronaos. In the process it became necessary to cut the right arm of Isis which held a *was* scepter (a prosperity stick). A bit of plaster covered the cut and a new upraised arm was carved to go above the doorway by an unskilled craftsman. The quality of the workmanship distinguishes it from the rest of the art on the exterior of the north wall. With this simple act Dendur became, at last, an acceptable Egyptian shrine. It was during this period that the Demotic inscription was cut before the face of Pihor, only a few feet from the new north door by Pakhom, son of Petusiri the Leshoni. He appears to have renounced certain claims to wealth for a personal freedom which allowed him to abandon his tax asylum at Philae. Being written in Demotic it should not be associated with the twentieth year of Augustus but rather the twentieth year of the Egyptian restoration of authority at Philae, when Suni was strategus and steward of Isis. Several Roman terms have remained in use following a native renaissance. That Pakhom, son of Petusiri, chose to cut his inscription before the face of Pihor reminds us that the earthly Dioscuri was a guardian of contracts. The fragments of the possible cult status of "Kupar" casually sighted in the village by H. R. Hall in 1910, which had the appearance of an Ethiopian king, may well have been part of this late Egyptian phase of development.

Dendur's third phase, following its use as a Roman Temple and as an Egyptian shrine is easily identified and dated by a coptic inscription cut in the thickness of the east jamb of the south door. It states that Abraham the priest, receiving the cross from Theodorus, bishop of Philae, had transformed the building into a coptic Christian Church on the twenty-seventh of Tobe, which is the feast day of S. Abifam, January 21, 577 A.D. Philae had remained a cult center for Isis and a stubborn holdout against Christianity until the time of Emperor Justinian (527-565). Following its conversion came the transformation of Dendur. Priest Abraham performed only a few alterations on the structure. The east-west axis of the building made it acceptable for an Orthodox church. The old sanctuary became the *bima* of the altar, and its wall the iconostasis. He closed off the unnecessary north door (which would have led most inauspiciously to the cemetery) and plastered over the hieroglyphs with their Augustan offering scenes. This act inadvertently protected the colors of the wall paints for an additional 1400 years! On the white plaster walls he painted icons of Egyptian Christian saints. The modern coptic liturgical calendar states that 27 Tobe is the day of the translation of the relics of St. Phoebammon, known as St. Abifam, a most popular local copt figure. Abifam was known for his healing powers. He appears in icons in the dress of a Roman nobel. What a fitting choice for Dendur. I, myself, would have preferred the work to have been speeded up by a fortnight so that the dedication might have fallen on the combined feast days of those noteworthy Coptic saints, Pihour, Pisoura and Asra, martyrs of the Diocletian persecution.

A. M. Blackman noted in 1911 that a portion of a Greek-Coptic inscription, painted in red, could still be seen above the inside of the sanctuary door. No trace of it remains due to the sixty years of intermittent flooding. What he saw suggests a slogan something like, "Jesus Savior; Christ Victor: Amen!"

One can only assume, from the decoration of similar shrines, that the favorite "horsemen saints" of the Castor/Pollux tradition might have apeared somewhere or other painted on the walls of the church.

There is, though, specific evidence that Abraham, or one of his priestly successors, constructed an additional room along the outside of the south wall to provide himself with a sacristy which had direct access to the church via the south door. While there is no suggestion whatsoever that the twins were remembered at Christian Dendur, the Coptic manuscripts found in December 1945 near Nag Hammadi stimulate the imagination with thoughts of Thomas Didymus, earthly twin of the heavenly Jesus. Reconstructed transformations of Egyptian mythology reach deeply into the origins of Christianity in Egypt. One can call to mind the old story of Si-Osiris, who was reborn to overcome an Ethiopian sorcerer, and who incidently takes his adopted father down through the seven halls of the underworld to show him the true nature of righteous judgment. This well known demotic tale was recorded in Greek on the back of a Claudian business document from 46/47 A.D. and again in a carefully edited Christian form as Gilmore (NTS 10.3, 1946) has demonstrated in the Gospel of Luke 16:19-31: the story of the Rich Man and Lazarus. Lazarus is "the one whom God helps." He rests beside cool water in a very Egyptian, Osirian paradise.

Islam does not come to dominate upper Egypt until the end of its own second century (mid ninth century A.D.). Although the first Aswan dam caused Dendur to be inundated part of each year, earlier visitors (such as Beato in 1870) suggest that a small semi-circle of stones stood at the entrance to the temple. A simple coat of whitewash over the Christian saints and the hint of a *mirab* could have made Dendur into a Mosque. By facing out, toward the river and about 12° south one is directed to Mecca and provided with a simple, functional cover from the brightness of the midday sun.

The current phase of Dendur, (who dares to say "final" to this hearty survivor of such vicissitudes) establishes it as an object of art in the Metropolitan Museum. Here too it faces east, looking out through its pylon, across a small pool which decorates its newly built landing pier. The pool sparkles with coins tossed in by modern "well-wishers" who seek to communicate with the unknown forces of "good luck." Here on fashionable Fifth Avenue it inspires the observer with the "numinous." Dendur remains a temple in its twentieth century American setting, visited by tourists (pilgrims), served by a curatorial staff (priests) and always under the protective eyes of museum guards. Its inner chambers remain sacro-sanct. The votive coins in the pool command silent petitions: Good luck (Agathodaemon) in business, love, marriage, or children: Dendur survives. It has been used as a temple, a shrine, a church, a mosque, and now the focal point for a wishing-well!

Bibliography

Aldred, C. The Temple of Dendur. New York: *The Metropolitan Museum Bulletin* XXXVI:I, 1978.

Baedeker, K. *Egypt and the Sudan.* 8th Edition. Leipzig: Baedeker, 1929.

Blackman, A. M.   The Sequence of Episodes in the Egyptian Daily Temple Liturgy. *Journal of Manchester Egyptian and Oriental Society* 26-53, 1918-19.

_____.   *Temple of Dendur.*   Cairo: Service des Antiquites de l'Egypte Temples immerges de la Nubie, 1911.

_____.   *L'Egypt des astrologues.*   Bruxelles: Edite par la Foundation Egyptologique Reine Elisabeth, 1937.

_____.   *La theologie solaire du paganisme Romain.* Paris, 1909.

_____.   *Recherches sur le symbolisme funeraire des Romans.* Paris, 1942.

Deonna, W.   The Crab and the Butterfly.   *The Journal of the Warburg and Courtauld Institutes* XVII.50 (1954) 47-86.

Evans, J. A. S.   A Social and Economic History of an Egyptian Temple in the Greco-Roman Period.   *Yale Classical Studies* 17, 143-283.

Fennelly, J. M.   Roman Involvement in the Affairs of the Egyptian Shrine.   *BJRL* 50 (1968) 317-335.

Harris, R.   *The Cult of the Heavenly Twins.* (Cambridge: University Press, 1906).

_____.   *The Dioscuri in the Christian Legends.*   London: C. J. Clay and Sons, 1903).

Helgeland, J.   "Time and Space: Christian and Roman."   *Aufstieg und Niedergang der romischen Welt.*   Ed. H. Temporini and W. Haase. Berlin: de Gruyter, 1979. II 23.2, 1285-1305.

Johnson, A. C.   Roman Egypt.   *An Economic Survey of Ancient Rome.*   Ed. Tenney Frank. New York: Octagon Books II, 1975.

Kenyon, F. G.   *Greek Papyri in the British Museum.* London: British Museum Manuscript Department, Greek Papyri I, 1893.

Meinardus, O. F. A.,   *Christian Egypt.* Cairo: Cahiers d'histoire Egyptienne, 1965.

Morgan, M. H.   *Vitruvius: The Ten Books on Architecture.* New York: Dover, (1960), 1914.

Otto, W.   *Priester und Temple im Hellenistischer Agypten.* Leipzig (Reprinted New York: Arno, 1975) 1905-08.

Woodcroft, B.   *The Pneumatics of Hero of Alexandria.* Ed. M. B. Hall (Re-published London: MacDonald, 1971) 1851.

MODELS FOR THE ORIGIN OF IRON AGE MONARCHY:
A MODERN CASE STUDY[1]

James W. Flanagan
University of Montana

Introduction

Recent studies on the transitional period linking the Late Bronze Age to Iron Age IC have called attention to the peculiar sequence of stages in the socio-political development of ancient Syro-Palestine. Where cultural evolutionists might expect egalitarian tribal social organization to develop toward stratified peasant and urban society, Syro-Palestine witnessed a reversed process. The stratified, centralized city states of the Canaanites began to disintegrate under pressure from new coalitions fired by an egalitarian ideal Retribalization followed, and a new confederation of tribal units began to dominate and control the resources of the region. Although their control was not complete in Iron IA, the egalitarian Yahwists were strong enough to evoke intense competition from alien, exogenous peoples associated with the Iron IB cultures. Over time, under pressures from outside military force and from internal expansion, the Yahwists evolved centralized leadership and organization that stabilized social order by unifying disparate, warring tribal, territorial, and political groups. In the minds of some of the more conservative egalitarian Yahwists, however, pacification was achieved at the expense of religious authenticity, because the new unity was accompanied by a return to the LB monarchical ideology and its oppressive institutions. But in spite of disagreements, a symbiosis of Yahwistic groups and authoritarian monopoly of force survived for a generation or two before it collapsed in the Great Schism at the end of Iron IC.

---

[1]The *SBL Seminar Papers* are dubbed "prepublished." In the jargon of the publisher's trade, that means they are statements of ideas, not yet final, but firm enough for the author to put them to the test. The only appropriate test is the criticism of one's peers.

I call attention to the tentative nature of this forum for several reasons. First, because what follows is not a final statement on any aspect of the sociology of monarchy. It is a partial report, in some ways personal, of my interest in a man and culture that I believe can be important for our work on ancient monarchical systems. It seems important to call attention to the man's fascinating life in order that others may also decide whether to proceed further with this sort of investigation.

Second, I should like to be clear that I respect the feelings and views of those who helped me gain access to the world described below. They include businessmen, scholars, and public officials who welcomed my interest in comparative studies and in the ancient world, but who also face the complex issues present in the Middle East. I state my views in this seminar for response and criticism pertaining to the development of monarchy in Iron Age I and do not do so in order to raise modern political questions. My interest is in the ancient world, a time before the boundaries that now divide the region existed. My plan is to review two cases as they unfolded "on the ground" in order to see what we can learn of one by studying the other. The *Seminar Papers* is an appropriate place to present preliminary results and to test initial reactions.

Research for this paper was supported in part by a Fellowship from the National Endowment for the Humanities, Centers Division, and the American Center of Oriental Research in Amman. I am grateful for the support of these institutions during the spring semester 1981. I am also grateful to Dr. Don Carlos Benjamin for agreeing to exercise his namesake's tribal claim on Iron Age leadership by serving as respondent and leader of the discussion of this paper.

My part in the discussions of this period has been focused upon the pivotal figure of David, commonly thought to be the first or second of the United Monarchs. I suggested, first, that the return to centralized monopoly of force was aided by the relocation of the capital under David (Flanagan, 1979). The move to heterogenetic Jerusalem from orthogenetic Yahwistic Hebron freed the leader from some of the political restraints imposed by conservative groups native to a traditional religious center.

More recently, I have suggested that the pattern of cultural evolution in Israel, a secondary society during Iron IA and IC, was the same as is typically found among pristine societies (Flanagan, 1981). The usual three stage development in archaic societies outlined by Elman Service (1975) applies equally to ancient Israel. Egalitarian social organization was followed by a period of chiefly leadership before evolving into kingship and statehood.

Although I has hardly the first to suggest chiefdom in Israel (Pedersen), and was deeply indebted to members of the Social World Group (Frick), these studies represented the beginnings of personal social scientific attempts to unravel the complicated, contradictory religious and political processes in Iron IC. What were the factors--the prime movers--that contributed to centralization, and how did the decentralizing religious beliefs contribute to developments that seem opposed to the religion's survival? Furthermore, what role did literature play in this process? Are the books of Samuel, where the story is told, history, religion, or political propaganda?

Further investigations have convinced me that the jury on these and related questions is still out. But they have not swayed me from my claim for chiefdom nor my belief that the literary record in Samuel is quite early. The period seems even more complicated than we have thought because it is extremely difficult to separate the underlying, indigenous religious attitudes in a secondary society from the overlay of political interpretation that forms a veneer in the surviving records (Flanagan, 1982a).

Method

Progress toward clarifying the early "monarchical" era can be made by continuing to appeal to a variety of disciplines and by approaching our problems with several methodologies. No doubt each method is fraught with problems that will elicit attacks and denials from members of opposing "schools." Methodology is particularly puzzling for scholars who reach across disciplinary boundary lines (Hammel; Talmon; Orme: 21-28). They face a dilemma: whether to march in where others fear to tread, or to stay in their own discipline and forego the venture altogether. The former is naive; the latter paralyzing.

Gottwald handled the problem by attacking it head on. He stated openly that the social scientific portions of his book combined structural-functional methods with those of cultural materialism (Gottwald, 1978: xxii). By admitting his appeal to several methodologies, Gottwald risked accusations of eclecticism from those who find such combinations "impure." However, the success of *The Tribes of Yahweh* has proven again that the most productive approach is to employ the best available techniques to answer one's questions and to solve one's problems (Harris: 290; Goody, 1969: 10).

In the discussion that follows, I tolerate methodological versatility. In the usual course of academic events, the claims I made about chiefs in Israel based on a comparison of the Bible and the work of Elman Service (1962; 1975) led me to look for a single parallel case that combined elements contained in David's experience. It is one thing to have a theoretical construct derived from generalizations made about many societies as Service has provided; it is another to have a single ethnological analogue that embraces personalities and forces parallel to those in the case under review (Goody, 1969: 7; see Verdon, 1980a; 1980b). The analogy will be strengthened if the parallel is drawn between societies that share a common environment and fall within the same broad cultural continuum. One cannot ignore analogues from other continents and civilizations, but, all things being equal, Middle Eastern cultures compared with others from the same region make stronger cases than, say, North American, African, or East Asian. Surely, the diversity and the political and religious fragmentation in the Middle East, especially where centuries separate the cases compared, are factors that may weaken the analogy, but it is important to look before rejecting. After all, we are not concerned with proving historical links nor with making political claims such as those that haunt the region today. Rather, we wish to cast light on the obscure by appealing to the less obscure. We move forward with a hypothesis of chiefdom, informed by evidence from anthropology, archaeology, and ancient literature, to find a test case in modern society that will enable us to bring more of the early records into focus.

Modern Parallel: Sources

As the Nile is to the history of Egypt, so Abdul Aziz bin Adbul Rahman bin Feisal al Saud is to the history of modern Saudi Arabia. It is impossible to speak of one half of each pair without the other; in each case the former is the stream of life flowing through the latter making its history possible.

Ibn Saud's life has been amply chronicled in biographies and histories, many written in English. His confidant, the indomitable and irascible Briton, Harry St. John Bridger Philby, was the first to supply an insider's view of the man Abdul Aziz and of the workings of his kingdom (Philby, 1952; 1955). A less intimate but more balanced biography was written by British author, David Howarth, in 1965. The prologue to this work draws explicit attention to the biblical air of the king's personality and deeds (8). A host of other books and monographs by British, American, and Dutch authors contain portraits of this powerful person (Van der Meulen; Lipsky; Rihani: 1928a, 1928b; Armstrong; Twitchell; Kheirallah; Bell).

Since 1980 three major works have appeared that situate Ibn Saud in his historical context and depict in detail the factors that contributed to his rise (Almana, 1980; Holden and Johns; Lacey; see also Quandt). Like the earlier studies, these depend on a combination of sources including hearsay evidence, government documents, camp stories, correspondence, diaries, and memos of early visitors, conversations with the king's associates and family, and journalists' accounts of daily affairs. Only Almana's is written by a Saudi citizen and a member of the king's court during the critical years of his rise. His work constitutes a primary source for my study.[2]

Sheikh Mohammed Almana is now an elderly man living in Al Khobar in the eastern province where he is Chairman of the Board of the Almana Hospital, the first Saudi-owned private hospital in the country. Born in Zubair on the trade route between Iraq and the Nejd, the central region of Arabia, Almana was taken to Bombay at the age of ten. He spent the next twelve years in India with his father where he was educated in Jesuit schools in Bombay and Punjab. The young man became fluent in English and Urdu as well as his native Arabic and was seemingly destined for the medical profession, a career encouraged by his father and by the Arab community in Bombay whom he often assisted in securing medical attention.

But Mohammed wanted to return to Arabia, for he had become fascinated by stories about Abdul Aziz and was determined to enter his service and that of his country. Almana went first to Basra in Iraq where he worked briefly as a clerk and writer for the English language *Basra Times*. Losing his job because of an office squabble

---

[2]Biographical information regarding the Ibn Saud presented here is based principally on the studies by Philby, Holden and Johns, Lacey, and especially Almana's book and interviews with him in Al Khobar. Biographical material pertaining to Almana is drawn from autobiographical sections of his book and from conversations with him, his family, his staff, and associates.

and being nearly destitute, Almana learned that a man from Zubair was visiting his rooming house and was accompanied by two members of Ibn Saud's staff. He convinced the *Times* editor to accept several interviews regarding the Arab Sheikh. He promised to forward them shortly and set off to interrogate his new acquaintances. Besides the interview, he secured from them a promise for help in acquiring a position in the court. On May 26, 1926, he began his service to Ibn Saud, eventually becoming the chief interpreter and translator for English and Urdu, a position he held until 1935 when he left Saudi Arabia to return to his father in Bombay. After a few years in India, he came again to his native country, this time to the eastern province where he worked as a translator for Caltex, now Aramco. Eventually, he left the oil company to form a construction firm and subsequently to build the hospital which he claimed satisfied his early ambition to be associated with the medical profession. Almana achieved a number of firsts in his long life: the first Moslem Arabian to speak English fluently; the first Saudi to own his own construction firm; the first to build a real hotel; the first to own a private hospital; the first to bring ice to Saudi Arabia. We might add, the first citizen in the court to write a biography of the king.

The years Almana served in the court were the years of nation building. The Hejaz had just been conquered and, with no further frontiers to challenge him, Ibn Saud had to devise means for settling the volatile tribesmen and for assuring their allegiance. This period, and the years of the king's rise beginning in 1902, form the major part of Almana's book. They were also central to our conversations when I visited the Sheikh in Al Khobar during June 1981. Our conversations were cordial and informal, and they ranged over topics having to do with the king, Almana's father's horse business, racing, Middle Eastern politics, bedouin life, and changes in the American image. The variety offered an opportunity to get to know the man and to determine how he might interpret information as he transmitted it. He spoke freely and with enthusiasm for his book. He is obviously a person of considerable stature who has few regrets about his life or his people. He placed no restrictions upon me, introducing me to his family and staff and encouraging me to visit with them as well. I was hosted in a most generous fashion as is typical in that part of the world. He appreciated my interest in him, his book, and his hero, and he seemed anxious to help enlighten the "formation of empire in the early Iron Age," as we referred to my project.

Ibn Saud's Roots

The story of Ibn Saud can be traced to Saud Ibn Mohammed Ibn Mugrin Ibn Markhan Ibn Ibrahim Ibn Musa Ibn Rabia Ibn Mana Ibn Assad Ibn Rabia Ibn Nizar Ibn Maad Ibn Adnan, his ancestor who was from a section of the Aneyza tribe and was invited in 1446 C.E. to settle in the region of Dariya (Almana, 1980: 257). The proximate history begins much later, however, with the time of Mohammed Ibn Saud (1726-65) and can be conveniently divided into three major periods. They are 1745-1818 when Mohammed Ibn Saud joined with the religious revival of Mohammed Ibn Abd al-Wahhab and agreed to be the movement's political arm in a combined effort to purify Arabia and to extend its influence throughout the Ottoman Empire; 1818-1902, a period first of relative independence for the House of Saud and then of submission to the rival Al-Rashid house in Ha'il (1865-1902); and 1902 until the present, that is, from Ibn Saud's capture of Riyadh which began the rise that led to the formation of modern Saudi Arabia (Almana, 1980: 257; Winder: 6-8). For our purposes, the last period is the most important, although we must recall that the roots of Ibn Saud's success reached back to the origins of the Wahhabi religious movement and that the Saud family for years had headed an elaborate tribal organization upon which centralized monarchy could be readily built.

Wahhabism, as it is called by outsiders,--Unitarianism to its adherents--represents a revival of the transcendental movement within Islam and stands as an alternative to the immanent wings such as the Sufi brotherhoods. Derived from the legal school of Ahmad Ibn Hanbal, it shares Hanbalism's insistence upon the absolute incomparability of

God. Puritanical in their application of this doctrine, the Wahhabis reject as polytheism all structures, persons, and beliefs that obscure the oneness of Allah. Saints are banned, ornate graves are shunned, sacred stones discarded, domes on mosques removed, and even formal observances of the Prophet's birthday are forbidden. Tobacco, music, silk, precious stones, ornate minarets, and prayer beads all fall under this stricture.

Obedience to the pristine law as it is found in the Koran, the Sunna, and the first three centuries of the *ijmā* is fundamental for the Wahhabis. They profess a strict egalitarianism that admits of no exception. The *jihad* is invoked as a means of expanding the community, but for them it is not limited to the "holy war." The ruler, the *imam*, may declare a *jihad* in order to justify his policies or strengthen his position, especially against those whom the Wahhabis consider polytheists (Winder: 8-15).

The political potential for leaders who embrace the movement is clear. The Ottomans were the first to feel its heat pressing against their cities' gates and fanning the emotions of the desert bedouin. The House of Saud aligned with the Wahhabi leaders, and, as we shall see, used its iconoclastic fervor to overcome tribal and regional differences by harnessing its religious passion for equality and purity to the aspirations of strong, central leadership.

By the time Abdul Aziz Ibn Saud was born, probably in November 1880, the Sauds had lost power and were living in abject poverty under the dominance of the Rashids. Dariya had been reduced to the ruins that it still is today. Two hundred years of struggle between the Rashids and Sauds for control of central Arabia had given the former ascendance, and Riyadh which the Sauds held was continually threatened. For our purposes it is neither necessary nor possible to recite a detailed chronology of Ibn Saud's life. This is readily available elsewhere, although even there, precise dates and numbers are seldom agreed upon by authors. A general outline will suit our needs, which we will follow with a closer look at the specific episodes that match those reported in the Iron Age.

Ibn Saud's Rise

The Saud family fled from Riyadh in 1890 first to Bahrain, then Qatar, and then Kuwait where they lived a restless life under the protection of the coastal shiekhs. The local rulers were originally from the Aneyza, the same tribe as the Sauds. During their stay, occasional raids were made against the Rashids, but none met with success. By the time the young Abdul Aziz reached his twentieth year, the boredom of his life, the longing for the excitement of battle, and pride spurred him to urge Sheikh Mubarak of Kuwait to equip him for the long trek toward his family's city. He recognized that he had no power base while under other's protection, and besides a recent loss in battle against the Rashids had cost Mubarak greatly, and the Saud welcome was running low.

Ibn Saud was given forty of the less desirable camels, a few men, and sent on his way. He hoped to win supplies, warriors, and the allegiance of tribes by raiding, but his efforts were not completely successful. He gained followers, perhaps 200, but not enough to satisfy him (Philby, 1952: 11). Here, biographers' reports begin to vary, probably because the tale of his adventure was recounted frequently by Ibn Saud, each time with elaboration typical of Arabian folk-lore (Howarth: 17; Lacey: 46-47). The young leader realized that this success depended on daring action, a heroic deed that would win the admiration and allegiance of large numbers instantly. He determined to capture Riyadh.

The journey took him from Kuwait, traveling by night and camping by day because of safety and Ramadan fast. After ten days he reached the vicinity of Riyadh, and only then did he announce his plans to his men. So hopeless did it seem that only a handful of men chose to accompany him into the city--some say six, others ten. The rest were told to stay in camp, but if the leader did not return by the break of dawn, to flee for their lives.

Ibn Saud scaled the city wall, landing on the terrace of a man he knew to have been a former servant of the Saud family. The man's wife had wet-nursed Saud when he was a baby, and so the intruder was quickly at home and learned all that the couple knew about the movements of Ajlan, the Rashid Amir of the city.

The governor routinely slept in the fortress under guard, but left the fort after morning prayer to go to a house across the street where he kept one of his wives. Abdul Aziz and his men advanced to the house to await dawn and their victim. As it happened, Ajlan's wife had also been wet-nursed by the same woman as Ibn Saud, thus bonding the two in a quasi brother-sister relationship and apparently preventing her from forewarning her husband (Almana, 1980: 36).

Ajlan emerged on schedule. Abdul Aziz, beside himself with excitement, sprang into the street, perhaps too soon for Ajlan managed to retreat through the fortress gate, and according to Almana, into the sanctuary of the mosque. Saud's cousin, Abdullah Ibn Jelawi, pursued him and cut him down with a sword. The surprise attack and the news of Amir's killing threw the garrison into turmoil. Rumors spread at once that a huge force had taken the city. Ibn Saud marched to the center of the courtyard, proclaimed himself victor, and the garrison surrendered.

All biographers record two consequences of the capture. First, the tactic was successful in winning the alliance of large numbers of followers. The Rashids had been oppressive, and no doubt the Sauds were a welcomed relief, but the sudden shift in loyalties must also be seen as evidence of the fragile and volatile relationships binding tribesmen. They deem impressions of power nearly as important as power itself. The economics of such shifts must also be stressed. The bedouin follow a strong leader, because it pays to do so. Bounty from raids moves among tribes with almost the same effects as currency flows through our economy. Therefore, the capture of Riyadh was important for Ibn Saud's rise because it launched him on an upward economic spiral that enabled him to satisfy the needs and whims of his followers. By expanding his tribal network through raiding he was able to attract still more support. As we shall see, within a few years this system forced severe problems when there were no more tribes to conquer. This is one case where success threatens success because the economy depends on continual expansion.

A second consequence of the capture was that the House of Saud was returned to the city. The young leader did not claim the sheikhdom for himself. Instead, he turned leadership over to his father, even kissing his feet and offering his back for his father's dismounting from his camel. Such deference is cited as a valuable quality in the man, one that he retained throughout his life. The father accepted the son's humility and abdicated at once, appointing the conqueror effective head of State and commander of the forces (Philby, 1955: 240).

Ibn Saud's Personal Qualities

From the capture in January 1902, the progress of Ibn Saud was steady, but not without setbacks. Over the next quarter of a century he built a coalition of tribes that expanded his influence throughout the entire Arabian peninsula except for the regions south of the Empty Quarter and the coastal sheikhdoms in the east that today form separate countries. Every commentator on Ibn Saud's success cites the same factors. Foremost were his personal qualities and his intimate knowledge of inter- and inner-tribal politics. Both equipped him exceedingly well for the personal legitimacy that every successful Arab leader must possess (Hudson: 18-20).

Descriptions of the leader have a decidedly biblical ring. The similarity to reports of David are so striking that several bear repeating. When listing Ibn Saud's advantages, David Howarth writes (Howarth: 27):

Next, he had his own physical distinction, and that was worth more. Most of the Bedouin were small, but he was six feet three and lean and muscular, and he could out-run or out-ride or out-shoot almost anyone else in the desert. He towered above his companions; nobody could ever neglect his persence. He was not merely handsome, his dark stern eyes and strongly-jutting nose, and his black hair and sparse beard and full lips with their suggestion, contradicting the eyes of amorous sensuality, made him the very type of Arab masculinity; and he was certainly aware of this quality and used it.

Elsewhere Howarth and Holden and Johns are content to repeat the description Gertrude Bell forwarded to the Arab Bureau after her first meeting with the man (Holden and Johns: 64):

Ibn Saud is now barely forty, though he looks some years older. He is a man of splendid physique, standing well over six feet, and carrying himself with the air of one accustomed to command. Though he is more massively built than the typical nomad sheik, he has the characteristics of the well-bred Arab, the strongly marked aquiline profile, full-fleshed nostrils, prominent lips and long, narrow chin, accentuated by a pointed beard. His hands are fine, with slender fingers, a trait almost universal among the tribes of pure Arab blood, and, in spite of his great height and breadth of shoulder, he conveys the impression, common enough in the desert, of an indefinable lassitude, not individual but racial, the secular weariness of ancient and self-contained people, which has made heavy drafts on its vital forces, and borrowed little from beyond its own forbidding frontiers. His deliberate movements, his slow, sweet smile, and the contemplative glance of his heavy-lidded eyes, though they add to his dignity and charm, do not accord with the western conception of a vigorous personality. Nevertheless, report credits him with powers of physical endurance rare even in hard-bitten Arabia. Among men bred in the camel saddle, he is said to have few rivals as a tireless rider. As a leader of irregular forces he is proved daring, and he combines with his qualities as a soldier that grasp of statecraft which is yet more highly prized by the tribesmen.

Almana, still fiercely loyal, adds a religious note by claiming that Ibn Saud grew to manhood " . . . gifted by God not only with all the talents and bravery of his ancestors, but also with a uniquely inspired hand of leadership capable of forging a permanent kingdom in the desert where others had failed" (1980: 26). His full portrait of the man is even more explicit (1980: 30):

By the time Prince Abdul Aziz Ibn Saud had reached his twentieth year it was already plain that God had marked him out for great things. In sheer physical size he towered above his companions, being fully six feet two inches tall, a most unusual and impressive height for a desert Arab. Everything else about his appearance was on the grand scale, from his strong, jutting nose to his full lips and fine beard. He had a natural kingly bearing and was dignified and graceful in his movements; as a horseman and warrior, he was beyond compare. From an early age he had about him a charm and magnetism which those who experienced it found impossible to describe in mere words. In short, he was a born leader, and had already built for himself in Kuwait a substantial personal following.

Although a skeptic might dismiss a portion of these descriptions as hero-worship or hyperbole, it is hard to deny impressions so consistent and widespread. Philby was awestruck by the man. British officer and Arabist William Shakespear claimed to have formed a warm friendship on his first meeting, and he never abandoned his affection and support for the leader (Holden and Johns: 41). He was so respectful that he accompanied Ibn Saud into battle against the Rashid forces and stayed to die when others fled ahead of the enemy sword. Even Franklin Roosevelt, himself two months away from death, was so impressed with the man that he remarked that he had learned more about Palestine in five minutes with Ibn Saud than from all the memoranda he had read on the subject (Holden and Johns [quoting Colonel Eddy] : 137).

Ibn Saud's Resources

When Ibn Saud turned his attention toward conquering, pacifying, unifying, and settling the warring tribes, he did not rely upon charm alone. His familiarity with tribal intrigues served him well. A villager by birth and residence, he learned the bedouin ways during his frequent wanderings, especially during his sojourn among the Al Murrah in the Rub al-Khali. An expert rider and swordsman, Ibn Saud is reported to have been so adept at following tracks as he had been taught by the Murrah that he could tell the sex, color, origin, and destination of a camel with only its footprint as evidence. He admired a similar ability of the Murrah whom he claimed with only a woman's footprint could determine the female's virginity (Lacey: 26)! Such stories probably tell us more about the society that passes them on than about the individual to whom they are attributed, but they also indicate that Ibn Saud was respected as a man who knew his way around the bedouin world.

Less suspicious are the reports of his prowess in the marital bed. Because the leader observed Arab norms requiring scrupulous privacy about his family life, no exact count of his wives, concubines, and slaves has been made. Estimates of wives range from twenty to three hundred. Many believe there were forty-five sons born of wives. No tally on daughters seems to have been kept, but this does not suggest that the role of women can be overlooked.

Marriage was of paramount importance for building the kingdom. Though he adhered scrupulously to the Islamic limit of four wives at one time, and he did have his favorites who forestalled divorce for decades, Ibn Saud used marriage as a political and military tool. He frequently divorced a wife (an easy matter in Islam) before embarking on a campaign in order to be able to add another legally if circumstances dictated. A hostile tribe could be easily subdued by the honor of the sheikh choosing one of their number as wife. The same ploy might gain passage through territory of a potential enemy or might make him privy to information he needed to decide the most advantageous course of action in a difficult situation.

Ibn Saud's military campaigns can be divided into three groups. First was the tedious series of raids and battles that won him allegiance of the sundry tribes in the central and eastern provinces. Almana insists that many campaigns there were *ghazzu*, raids designed for sport with little blood being shed and whose primary objective was to outmaneuver and outsmart the opponent. Circuitous routes and cat and mouse tactics characterized such endeavors. Still, the stakes were high, because his victories finally won Ibn Saud control of much of the Arabian peninsula and eventually the title of Sultan of Nejd.

The second phalanx was against the Hashemite Sherifs in the Hejaz. There the Turks and British played a prominent role that has been glamorized by T. E. Lawrence. The events were complex, but eventually the presence of the Hashemites became intolerable for the Saudis, and the Sherif was overthrown. The Hejaz now under Saudi control, Ibn Saud's domain stretched from coast to coast and gave him control over the lucrative pilgrimage routes and businesses that accompanied the Hajj to sacred Mecca. When the Sherifs were expelled, Almana states, the bureaucracy was kept intact except for the highest eschelons. In 1926, Ibn Saud accepted the title of King of the Hejaz and, in biblical fashion, bore it while he was still Sultan of the Nejd (Almana, 1980: 75).

With the peninsula now under his control, the King-Sultan had no new territories to raid. The expanded bureaucracy and his usual custom of giving generous gifts at his daily *majlis* created a serious strain on economic resources. Assistance from foreign governments was becoming available as part of their policies aimed more against other European powers than at helping the struggling leader. To establish a strong, stable, central government, Ibn Saud developed a plan for settlement that would turn the fickle loyalties of bedouin nomads into peaceful support from productive agriculturalists. The plan included establishing settlements around tribal wells and appointing religious *ulemas* who would instruct the settlers in the truths of their faith. For this, Ibn Saud restored Wahhabism to prominence and created the Ikhwan, the Brotherhood, to carry out his mission. Almana insists that establishing the settlements was one of the most important events in Saudi Arabian history, but that it is often overlooked by Westerners (Almana, 1980: 81).

The Ikhwan were to create political stability, but also they served economic and military purposes. The new agriculture production was to fuel the consumptive generosity of the leader, while the settled conditions were expected to provide a resource of men whose whereabouts would be known and whose loyalties could be trusted in times of war.

The transition was not easy nor was it complete. The bedouin have a saying, "the pleasure went out of the bedouin life when Faisal Ad-Dawish (Chief of the Mutair) first built a mud hut" (Almana, 1980: 81). Boundary lines and absence of raids made the settlers bored and restless. This coupled with religious intolerance made them eager to wage war whenever called by their Imam, Ibn Saud.

The Ikhwan became increasingly troublesome for their leader. Uncalled and unwarranted ruthless raids into neutral and Iraqi territory threatened the stability of the shakey alliance and hastened the intervention of the British. Matters became complex as they evolved beyond the point of toleration and led Ibn Saud into his third type of campaign, one directed against his own followers. Ikhwan leader Faisal Ad-Dawish, once subdued and pardoned because he was on the verge of death, recovered to plague Saud's peace again. This time there could be no further chance. Ibn Saud marched on the Ikhwan and suppressed them in a blood bath at Sibillah in 1929. The religious zealots who contributed so much to the Sultan's rise had overstepped their limits and had to be subdued. Ibn Saud remained faithful to his religious beliefs until his death, but he, unlike the Ikhwan, was able to adjust those beliefs to make room for modern life. Automobiles, radios, airplanes, and sophisticated technology all made their way into his land as did infidels from Europe, Britain, India, and America. But these were largely confined to the diplomatic center in Jeddah and the bedroom communities of Aramco in Dahran and the eastern province.

For our comparison, 1932 is an important year. Then, after peace had been restored, the Kingdom of Saudi Arabia was formed and His Majesty King of the Hejaz and Sultan of the Nejd became King of Saudi Arabia. Almana's claims about the change are interesting (Almana, 1981). He stated that when unification was being discussed, he proposed to name the nation "Arabia." However, Philby had gotten the king's ear and the decision had been made before his own proposal could be discussed. Almana believes his suggestion was the more suitable because it allowed for further expansion and for the formation of a united Arab kingdom. I asked whether the king shared his "vision," to which he replied, "I don't think he knew what I was talking about." No doubt, Almana's estimation is colored by his feelings for Philby, which are largely unfavorable.

Almana also insisted that the title of "king" was resisted by the king on religious grounds. "Only Allah is King," I was told. My host claimed that the title was first adopted after conquering the Hejaz because the office was already there. Ibn Saud simply replaced the Sherif and accepted the title, but refused to use it himself. Similarly the title "king" was not used in Riyadh even after formation of the kingdom, and Almana testified that the king preferred that it not be used in his presence. The man may have achieved regal splendor and power, but he always saw and spoke of himself in terms appropriate to a tribal sheikh.

The conquest and formation of a kingdom completed, Ibn Saud's fortunes were not immediately assured. The country still lived in a world full of aggressive powers who understood little of the Saudi ways and values. Britain and the United States were forced to find new reserves to fuel their transition to petroleum-based industry. Oil strikes in neighboring Bahrain tempted prospectors to search the Arabian lands for similar geological features.

The oil concessions transformed the history of Saudi Arabia and the world. But the change was slower than our recent memories tempt us to believe. Ibn Saud knew little about oil and cared more about water. In fact, Almana asserts that no one in the court was sophisticated enough to grasp fully what the concession seekers were talking about. But concessions were granted and new monies began to flow into the country bringing with them a host of problems for the conservative Wahhabis, but also the resources to stabilize the new kingdom. Tribes that benefited more from peace and international relations than they did from sporting raids were apt to choose the former and forego the latter. History was to show that the new resource, oil, would make the kingdom a stable entity by reinforcing a Saudi dynasty that has now continued through the succession of four of Abdul Aziz's sons.

Monarcy and its trappings did not obscure the chiefly traits of the founder-king. Comments made by those who knew or write about him confirm the charcteristics that Elman Service cites as distinctive features of chiefdom. Principal among them was Ibn Saud's use of the *majlis* as a means of keeping in touch with his people and for redistributing goods that he owned or were given to him. Late in his reign when he heard that members of his staff were shielding him from individuals seeking advice and assistance, he issued a mandate that had to be proclaimed by every sheikh and amir. He insisted that every citizen have access to him and that he would personally attend to their problems. The economy of chiefs was at work here as it had been throughout his entire life. Abdul Aziz Zanil Jawasir (1981), Almana's cousin who was attached to the political committee and eventually translator for Prince Faisal in the Hejaz, volunteered to me that the king never had money. "What he got, he would redistribute immediately." But the largess did not flow only one way. Visitors to the *majlis* brought all kinds of gifts depending on their rank and wealth (Almana, 1980: 178). Prestige, generosity, and wealth, all highly prized virtues in bedouin life, were communicated and were more valuable than the price of the gifts themselves.

Almana personally characterized life in the court as "semi-bedouin" and contrasted it with the cultural riches of Bombay where opera, concerts, and intellectual people abounded (Almana, 1981). The king was a shrewd and wise man, but, according to Almana, he was unable to read except for the Koran. This claim does not agree with the impression given by others, but I recall no one who makes an explicit statement contradicting Almana's.

The talents of an ancient sage dictated Ibn Saud's actions. As a result, his conduct, especially his treatment of enemies, appears contradictory or paradoxical. "Battles were usually of a small scale, where honor could be satisfied but few people actually hurt. One could almost liken desert warfare to a game of chess, in which the most skilled, alert general eventually 'checkmated' his opponent" (Almana, 1980: 25). But because "the bedouin were impossible material from which to build an empire" (Almana, 1980: 25), the leader had to keep fighting and winning. Any lull in the conflict would disappoint or bore the bedouin. Success could also turn them away if they thought they had received enough booty for awhile. Almana insists that winning Arabia was easier than keeping it. It took the wisdom of Ibn Saud to do both.

Against the background of such warfare, the paradox mentioned above falls into perspective. An example was the challenge to duel that Al Rashid presented Ibn Saud. The opponent sent a letter citing the futility of bloodshed and perpetual hostility suggesting a winner-take-all contest between just the two of them. Ibn Saud's size, agility, and experience seemed to dictate acceptance, but with his usual tact he declined. In his reply, he commended Al Rashid for his courage but went on to note that many times the man had indicated his willingness to die. Ibn Saud stated that he preferred to live and that "a man who wanted to live left the path of wisdom if he fought a man who wanted to die" (Almana, 1980: 45). Besides, such matters were Allah's business, and he would decide the final outcome.

When Ibn Saud's men did finally kill Al Rashid, it was by stealth. They entered the enemy's camp, took him by surprise, and hurried back to their leader bearing the victim's signet ring as proof of their success. Ibn Saud refused to believe until he saw the head of the deceased. The soldiers returned to the camp and fetched the gruesome trophy (Almana, 1980: 48).

Displaying the head of a victim was not uncommon in Ibn Saud's repertory of displays of strength. Such manifestations could offer irrefutable proof of victory that impressed the ordinary citizen in ways that assured him of their allegiance. No doubt the feelings were a blend of fear, hatred, respect, and pleasure, the dosage of each depending upon the occasion and the person.

But this manner seems to have been the exception rather than the rule for Ibn Saud. He was widely known as a person who was magnanimous in victory and courageous in defeat. His treatment of the Rashidi princes following the death of Al Rashid is an example. Many of them including the troublesome Mohammed Ibn Talal were taken not as prisoners but as honored guests into Riyadh where "in time, many of them were to become Ibn Saud's loyal and devoted subjects" (Almana, 1980: 59).

The dual purpose of such hospitality is clearly evident in Ibn Talal's case. Although he was a guest, he was kept under guard. On one occasion he tried to escape dressed in woman's clothing, an act that brought him embarrassment the rest of his days. Following that episode he was kept under still tighter guard, but allowed to accompany the king into battle, although still under close surveillance (Almana, 1980: 59).

The practice of co-opting one's enemy through forgiveness and generosity is not peculiar to Saudi Arabia. The practice assures the victor that the vanquished group will not rise again. Deprived of their leadership, the opposing group either is left aimless or is integrated into the loyal service of their former opponent. If the latter, the members have in a sense achieved their goal through defeat because they have gained access to the limited resources for which they formerly fought. The conqueror in turn has secured the talents of an individual who has already proven his ability to organize and mobilize a large following. In fact, there is a saying in some countries that the quickest way to high office is to plot a coup and fail! For the monarch, to have survived one or more attempts on his life strengthens his hand because he is perceived as an indomitable and durable leader. Besides, today's victor may be tomorrow's vanquished in the politics of the desert, and it makes good sense to forgive one's enemies.

Ibn Saud: His Significance for His Biographer

Detail could be added to detail in our description of the fascinating founder-king of Saudi Arabia, but none would change substantially the portrait drawn here. This is not to say that future research cannot shed additional light on this rich and largely unrecorded career. But the information we have in hand is sufficient to understand the processes and measures employed to turn a country of fickle, warring tribes into one of the richest nations in the world *within a single generation*.

We may examine the elements in our case study along two planes: first, on the plane of events themselves, and second, on the plane of the tradition and literature that brings knowledge of the events to our attention. I will look at the latter first.

Almana's position cast him in a role that was the functional equivalent of that of the ancient court scribes. In conversations about court life, he recounted events and depicted personalities as an insider would. This is a quality which reviewers note about his book (Little; Mostyn; Legg). He has warmth, knowledge, affection, and liveliness that other biographers, even Philby, lack. The author apparently shares my view, because when asked about Philby whom Almana did not like, he responded, "I knew him better than anyone else--without ever seeing him. I read everything he sent out of the office. He gave it to me (perhaps he was unsure of himself) even though he was not required to" (Almana, 1981). Referring to the court, he said,

> We were the king's brains, his arms, his legs, everything. We knew everything that was going on. We traveled with him and had access to his *majlis* anywhere. He got his information from us and we carried out his wishes. We would hear about where he had gone and what he had said even when we were not present. The court talked among themselves (1981).

He went on to describe how the court traveled with the king because it was his "personality." "Without us he would not be who he was." Almana, his brother, who also worked as a translator in the court, and his cousin from Bahrain (the translator in the Hejaz) agreed with the Sheikh's assessment.

In Almana's view, the relationship between the events and the book is very close. Speaking about his desire to write, he recalled that he was Jesuit trained ("They were very liberal. They did not harm my religion.") and had thought about writing a book like Yeats, Shelley, or Austen. Then he realized that he should be in Arabia and should write about Saud. He had been fascinated by the man from his early years, and in 1915 had begun to collect stories about him, with writing in mind. In three different contexts, I asked the same question, approaching it each time from a different perspective. Hoping to gain insight into the workings of the scribal mind, I asked on what basis he had selected the episodes finally included in the book. From all the available stories, memories, anecdotes, documents, and records, how did he choose the ones to be used? Always, I got the same reply: a denial that he had made a selection. Almana insisted that the book is a portrait, as the subtitle states, not a selection of materials. It is the king! I was given the impression that my question implied a lack of sensitivity for the integrity of the personality of Ibn Saud and for the biography that made him known. When asked for whom Almana wrote, the reply was, "the world." He insisted the book is for outsiders because "the Nejdi [Arabs in Central Arabia] already know these stories better than I." Regardless of whether friends and staff directly influenced the writing of the text, as has been hinted (Ohliger, 1981), it is clear that Almana considers the book his own and feels that it contains his portrait of Ibn Saud.

Attitudes such as Almana's assist us in comprehending the mind of a loyalist Iron Age scribe writing about David. We know that there was more than one way to tell the story (in fact the Bible contains several) and that the events controlled only a portion of the arrangement of the narrative. The general chronology was established by events, but the specific arrangement of stories within the general framework was left for the scribes to determine. Since many of us are convinced that a major portion of the Davidic material in the books of Samuel is the product of eye witnesses and court officers, why should we suspect that the narratives were contrived and mechanically constructed rather than enthusiastically compiled by someone close to its prominent figures? To those who do not share our views on the proximity of author to subject, we can now pose the question: Why should the telling of David's story have been postponed for generations or centuries? It is true that Sheikh Almana waited forty years until he had the leisure of semi-retirement and the nostalgia of age to help him. But in spite of the lapses of memory (which he admits) caused by delay, he did not surrender his task to his successors who might have done it more efficiently but surely not as effectively. He has lived to see the temptations of wealth, the deficiencies of sons who have not ruled as effectively as their father, and the passage of time which offers the advantage of hindsight. Still

Almana chose to tell the story of the man as he remembered him without great concern for the way history has or will judge the king. For Almana, Ibn Saud is *the* King, the founder, the man who remembered his origins. Others may write of his successors, but Sheikh Almana cares most about his friend and monarch.

If the authors of modern and Iron Age accounts can be compared, what about the heroes they describe? Here, in order to move to the level of event, we must pass over the structure of the two pieces of literature, although I believe a comparison of the arrangement of both would be fruitful. We must also note that neither account may be completely accurate in a technically historical sense. Both are interpretations of witnesses and authors whose recollection and use of details are at variance with those of other writers. This doesn't hamper our use of them in the study of Ibn Saud or David, but it cautions against an excessively literal comparison of their records.

The parallels between the maneuvers of David and Ibn Saud are striking even though it is sometimes difficult to determine which are relevant. Some may be accidents of history that tell us little about the process of state formation other than that two instances occurred in the same pattern. For example, consider the fact that Ibn Saud established a tribal confederation which he headed as a paramount chief before he turned to conquer the Hejazi kingdom which had already been formed by creating centralized rule among tribal groups. The way David used his chieftancy over Judah as a power base from which to secure the crown of the North appears similar. It is true that Ibn Saud was not an exiled member of the Hejazi court as David was of Saul's, but both did have at least one expulsion to his credit, the Al Saud from Riyadh and David from Gibeah and Jerusalem. But how much is useful for analogy, and how much is simply coincidence?

Posing the question in this manner is not methodologically sound because it leads one to pass judgment on evidence before the evidence has been fully presented. The advantage of using oral history, ethnography, ethnology, ethnohistory, ethnoarchaeology, and other descriptive methods is that they record what is "on the ground" rather than trying to determine a priori which evidence is relevant or what motives influence the actors as their lives unfold. Lévi-Strauss (18) seems on the right course toward relating the historical and anthropological disciplines when he asserts that "History organizes its data in relation to conscious expressions of social life, while anthropology proceeds by examining its unconscious foundations."

Efforts to link historical information with anthropology are the subject of many methodological debates, as was suggested in the introduction to this paper. Scholars such as Pitt-Rivers (128-131) and Goody (1976: 1-3) insist that the origins and histories of customs must be considered in any serious attempt to understand and critique society. French historian Duby, arguing on another front, relates medieval marriage laws to the entire social milieu of Western Europe, while Dorward and Johnson have challenged anthropologists to use ancient documents, missionaries' diaries, and traveler's notes as reliable supplements for the ethnographer's notebook.

Edmund Leach has launched the most sustained attack on historical anthropology (1961; 1969). While our attempt is to relate the present to the past, rather than vice versa as Pitt-Rivers, Dorward, and Johnson discuss, Leach cautions traffic on both sides of the chronological street. Although not totally pessimistic about relating anthropology to ancient societies, he warns archaeologists not to expect to open the "black box" of darkness that separates material substance from archaeological remains. He doubts that archaeologists can uncover the human institutions and procedures that transformed ancient substance into material artifacts (Leach, 1977: 175-76). Leach asserts that comparative ethnologies tell us little about the contents in the darkened zones of history, in part because societies differ so widely. His statements to biblical specialists interested in historical questions have been equally cautious (1980). Pressed on the subject he admits that we may be able to recover the general frameworks of biblical history, but denies that there is much hope of determining the details.

In spite of such monitions and similar cautions from others (Kovacs: 12), many of us are convinced that analogous parallels can be enlightening, at least when they compare a series of steps that form a cultural process. To repeat myself, the comparisons that cultural evolutionists have made in determining patterns of social development have been too successful to discard. We must be careful to compare items that serve similar functions in their own cultures, but many disciplines proceed to do this without the excessive paranoia that bothers some anthropologists and biblicists. The proof of the pudding is in the eating--if a comparison is cautiously drawn and is found to fit, use it.

Ibn Saud: Analogies

The number of analogies connecting Ibn Saud and Iron Age leadership have been implied in the outline of Saud's life supplied above. These need only be emphasized and several others added before drawing our conclusions.

The descriptions of Ibn Saud's and David's physical and personal characteristics are strikingly similar. It should be noted that remarks about height, bearing, dexterity, and leadership qualities are common in biographies of leaders, ancient and modern. For example, Saul also was reportedly a man of exceptional size and beauty, but he failed where others succeeded (1 Sam 10:23-24). Almana credits Ibn Saud's qualities to his divine vocation. The role the future king played as Imam, a role the head of State in Saudi Arabia still enjoys as a result of agreements with the Wahhabis, qualifies the chief's theocratic needs. His and David's ability to issue calls to arms, to pass judgments on legal and moral matters, and to claim exemptions from certain religious restraints testify to similar religio-ideological bases. Neither had a completely free religious hand, however, and the fact that they had to withdraw or postpone plans they otherwise would have implemented indicates that in some matters the *ulema's* and Yahweh's other spokesmen had the final word. David's temple and tax plans reveal this of him; Ibn Saud's avoidance of regal titles and his cautious attitude toward modernization are examples from his world. But still, the personal charism of both has been thought to be a product of divine intervention. Each enjoyed religious legitimacy.

Both men used the same tactics and techniques to achieve paramountcy and to transform their chieftancy into a kingdom. Here the parallels are particularly close and are strikingly similar to the factors cited by Service in his description of cultural evolution.

Intimate knowledge of tribal affairs allowed each leader to exploit alliances and tensions. Almana cited this as the most important advantage Abdul Aziz had over his opponents. In contrast, he claims that the Hashemite Sherifs had lost touch with the tribes and did not know what was going on (1981). The Hashemites had been educated abroad, and the Sherif had spent long years in Istanbul where he learned to think and speak like the Turks, a damaging habit he never overcame. On the other hand, Ibn Saud fought beside, camped with, prayed with, and played with the tribesmen of all ilks. His daily *majlis* was open to all whether in Riyadh or in the desert and villages throughout Arabia. He traveled purposely in order that the distant tribesmen could have access to him. The entire court moved to the Hejaz for several months a year, and he appointed family members and close friends to offices in order to be sure he was kept in touch with daily affairs.

We know less about David's contact with individual tribes, but he seems to have had a broad appeal. He is depicted as an individual who was popular with the people and one capable of amassing large followings (1 Sam 18:7). He identified with the outcasts and downtrodden (1 Sam 22:1-2). He appointed family members to positions of authority, no doubt for purposes of control, but also as a way of keeping in touch (2 Sam 8:15-18). He shared Ibn Saud's wisdom to forgive opponents (1 Sam 23 and 26) and he used the hospitality of house arrest to secure the allegiance of enemies and to decrease the chances of further unrest (2 Sam 9). Nevertheless, like Ibn Saud, he was not afraid to use violent slaughter in order to demonstrate his determination (2 Sam 24:1-14).

A footnote on the checks and balances of tribal politics will be helpful. It is the manner in which modern Middle Eastern monarchies set military forces against each other. In several countries a separate force comprised of bedouins serve the king directly but is not part of the regular military (Hudson: 179-180; Hoagland: 24). These special forces, the royal or national guard, have representatives of each of the tribes whose sheikhs enjoy a special relationship to the monarch whom they consider sheikh of the sheikhs (*sayyid*) rather than king of a nation--the   *primus inter pars* concept in another form. Therefore, it probably is not a coincidence that His Majesty King Fahd chose as his Crown Prince Abd Allah, Commander of the National Guard, and designated Sultan, Minister of Defense and Aviation, to replace Abd Allah as second in line of succession behind the Crown Prince during the recent succession in Saudi Arabia. Stability as well as continuity was thereby guaranteed. Sultan is a full brother of the new king, one of the Sudari Seven we shall mention below, while Abd Allah is a half brother who has no full brothers.

Marriage was a major factor in the successful rise of both Ibn Saud and David. Ibn Saud's use of matrimony has already been stressed, and here we need only mention that his wives enjoyed their own ranking system. Abdul Aziz's sister, Nura, was one of his closest advisors, but so were certain of his wives. In a family with 3,000 princes, the position of favorite wife is a coveted and powerful one because heirs and successors are often ranked according to a mother's position. For example, Hassah from the Sudari family has produced seven sons who have a particularly close relationship to each other and who hold especially prominent positions. Fahd is now King; Sultan, Minister of Defense and Aviation and second in line for succession; Abd Al-Rahman, a leading businessman; Nayif, Minister of Interior; Turki, former Deputy Minister of Defense; Salman, Governor of Riyadh Region; and Ahmad, Deputy Minister of Interior.

David's progeny was less plentiful, perhaps, but from existing records we can detect a similar vying for position based on one's rank in the genealogy and the importance of his mother. Marriages to Maacah, daughter of Talmai, the King of Geshur; to Abigail, wife of Nabal of Carmel; to Ahinoam of Jezreel; and to others strategically located could not have been accidents of love. In the military and political affairs surrounding his rise, each conjugal bond played a significant role by giving David control of or access to holding from which he would otherwise have been excluded. Jezreel and Geshur are two indications of this.

It was the favorite wife, Bathsheba, who was most successful in positioning her son. The Jerusalem genealogies credit four offspring to her and are explicit about her role in securing the crown for Solomon. There can be no doubt that wives played a major role in the politics of David's reign.

Both of our societies, as with other tribal groups, used genealogies to regulate and record the relative positions of family members. The Iron Age analogies have been discussed at length elsewhere, and have been proven to function the same as in other cultures (Flanagan, 1981; 1982).

In the case of Saudi Arabia, genealogies are a private matter. It is known that they are kept and that individuals in the power structure control them, making adjustments as actual relationships change with the normal rise and fall of fates. When asked about the repository or keeper of the genealogy, the response is usually similar to Alamana's. "No one keeps them. I don't know. They know who their family is." Modern corporations take a more aggressive attitude toward their importance. Several major genealogies of the royal family have been published and are used widely in order to determine advantageous commercial ventures (Lees). For outsiders working or doing business in Saudi Arabia, the labyrinthian administrative charts of corporations consti-tute an important parallel to the royal family tree. The successful businessman studies both for clues about the inner workings and changes in his partner's world.

The role of religion in the rise of our two subjects is one of the most striking parallels. Certainly it is not peculiar for religion to be exploited as a political tool, but its use in Arabia throws helpful light on several aspects of Iron Age empire building. In both it provided the ideological legitimacy needed for the leaders to rule (cf. Hudson: 20-23).

We have already noted the Wahhabi symbiosis with the House of Saud, the creation of the Ikhwan for military, agricultural, and religious purposes, the revolt of the Ikhwan, and the subsequent struggle to suppress them. The pattern corresponds closely to David's use of Yahwism. He began early to establish links with various tribes and villages through marriage and redistribution. Saul's house was included, along with those already mentioned above. He must have had support from the house of Nahash also (see Zeruiah) and have had good rapport with the Moabite leaders as well. The Philistines he ingratiated by his loyal service.

Our first clue regarding David's use of Yahwism is the abbreviated account of his decision to move to Hebron (2 Sam 2:1-3). Surely more could have been said than Yahweh approved the move. In any case, relocating from Ziklag to Hebron afforded him a link with Yahwist traditions and helped fulfill his own ambitions. The story from that point on is familiar—the move to Jerusalem, his expulsion from the city by conservative Yahwists, his need to suppress revolts led by his son Absalom and the Benjaminite Sheba. I have argued that pressure from the conservatives troubled David throughout his reign and came to expression around the figures of Saul and the ark (Flanagan, 1982b). I believe that David's "modernization" we have been calling "politization" or even "paganization" evoked resistance that forced him to proceed cautiously and at times restrained his progress completely. His response to such problems dictated many of his policies. For instance, the Levites and levitical cities, I believe, were part of his attempt to stabilize and pacify outlying areas by teaching the citizens loyalty to the central administration (Aharoni: 305). It all has a familiar ring when compared to Ibn Saud's relationship to the Ikhwan. What this means for our understanding of the Iron Age empire is that Yahwism was exploited for its political, unifying, pacifying potential. By providing David, chief of Judah, King of Israel, and King of All Israel, with a central core upon which to build further alliances, Yahwism served as his base.

But two additional factors must be noted. First, Yahwism did not make substantial inroads outside the early tribal Yahwist territory. Therefore, the basis of solidarity with and in those regions was other than religious, although the religious core he had in other regions gave David the political power to establish and maintain expanded territorial claims. In other words, the political power for the Yahwistic groups gave David strength sufficient for him to establish an empire, partly Yahwistic, partly non-Yahwistic.

Second, we should note that Israel and Judah, longstanding opponents, were never integrated politically. Thus, David exploited this separation by maintaining a check and balance between the two Yahwist groups as he did between the Yahwists and the non-Yahwists. We have cited other mechanisms dedicated to this balancing act, but we should not forget the one the biblical writers stress beyond all others, namely, his personal charm and magnetism. Elman Service has argued convincingly that leadership begets followers, rather than vice-versa. The entire story of Ibn Saud is in some sense a story of people seeking leadership because they recognize its advantage. The same must be admitted as an explanation for David's success. His personal appeal allowed him to use and abuse Yahwism in way others could not.

Redistribution is also central to the success of a rising chief. There is no need to repeat evidence I have presented elsewhere when I called attention to David's use of booty from raids as gifts to actual and potential followers (Flanagan, 1981). The economy of his early years was that of a redistributor.

Ibn Saud's largess and his redistribution of booty and wealth also require no repeating. Thus, the trait that Service considers central to the tactics of chiefs competing for paramountcy is shared by both leaders.

The two founder-kings also shared a similar advantage in trade, in attempts to exploit new agricultural potential, and in efforts to establish economically rewarding relationships with outside nations. Turkey, Britain, the United States, and India were the first to recognize the potential of Arabia. Everyone had his own plan, but all seemed to realize that the unification of Arabia would make two important contributions to trade and development. It would afford travelers and merchants passage across the entire peninsula from east to west for the first time, and it would pacify the region, making pilgrimage travel from the North possible again. By making Arabia an inviting place for foreign investment and for pilgrims, the economy would flourish. In fact, the pilgrim's trade in the Hejaz did rise sharply under Ibn Saud. The oil story in the Hasa, although slow to develop, brought untold wealth to the land. Ibn Saud's attempt at agriculture was less successful, but even that is reaping dividends today.

In the Iron Age, David's empire embraced the entire commercial region of the eastern Mediterranean. At its zenith, the empire encompassed all major land trade routes through the region and had access to the Mediterranean and Red Sea ports. Through treaty with the Phoenicians, he could reach the crafts and skills needed for seafaring as well as those needed for construction projects in Jerusalem. A similar treaty stretched his routes through Syria to the Euphrates. Agricultural production increased sharply in the newly pacified region as well. Each parallels in some fashion the developments in Arabia.

A final comparison needs to be drawn. Rapidly growing centralized administrations are often strapped for resources. They need large, new funds to support their expanding bureaucracy and programs. If the lower class will not be exploited excessively, as it usually is, additional sources of revenue need to be found or the accompanying exploitation will cause unrest usually leading to a peasant revolt. The Syro-Palestine and Arabian territories have long histories of this problem.

Ibn Saud's attempts to achieve stability through new resources were in part planned and in part coincidental. Settlement of bedouin in agricultural communities was one effort, conquering the lucrative pilgrim trade in the Hejaz another. Eventually, he realized the advantage of Western allies, such as Britain, who would pay him to resist the Turks and their agents, the Al Rashid. Relationships with foreign powers brought some revenues, enough to tide him over in time of crisis by enabling him to continue the rewards his followers expected from their chief. The Depression, of course, was an exceptionally difficult time.

Shortly after the Depression oil was discovered. Earlier Ibn Saud had received some revenues from the small, troublesome concessions he had granted, but with the discovery of the black gold, his immediate problems were solved. The new wealth brought its own agonies, those of lavish, corruptive excess, but from the beginning oil meant stability, peace, and continuity. Mechanisms for redistributing the new abundance were slow in coming, mostly because the royal family continued the tribal attitude of claiming the resources for the chief. The problem was not acute at first, however, and the revenues guaranteed, or at least assisted, the continuity of Ibn Saud's reign. Eventually the mechanisms for redistribution had to be established thereby creating what Hudson calls structural legitimacy (22-24).

The ancient parallel is less clear than we might hope, because only within recent years have archaeologists developed an interest in regions that would allow us to test our hypothesis. My claims must be muted for that reason, but it is not too early to make an informed guess. David's stability and his plan for expansion were related to the mineral resources within his empire. The true beginning of the Iron Age corresponded with his reign. Iron had been in use for some time, but the date when iron became the dominant utilitarian substance for manufacturing tools and weapons was the tenth century B.C.E. (Waldbaum; Wertime and Muhly). Recent studies have also demonstrated that, contrary to the opinion common among biblical scholars, the Philistines did not enjoy superior iron technology nor a greater number of iron implements (Stech-Wheeler, et al.). This suggests that there may be a parallel between the stabilizing effect of petroleum in modern Arabia and iron technology in ancient Syro-Palestine.

Conclusions

The parallels cited above pertain to two societies that evolved from uncentralized, shifting tribal affiliations to highly centralized nation-states within a single generation. We have compared individual traits of the leaders, mechanisms they used to achieve and maintain peaceful alliances, and resources they found at their disposal to enjoy and exploit. What I had asserted earlier about chieftancy and cultural development based on a comparison of the biblical record and a hypothesis of cultural evolutionists has been strengthened by comparing the Iron Age with a modern emerging nation.

My earlier claim was that Saul and David were more chiefs than kings, although monarchy had probably evolved by the end of the latter's reign. I remain convinced of my description, but on the basis of the comparisons in this paper would add a refinement.

Ibn Saud was certainly a king by the end of his life. Yet, he clung to the ways of a sheikh, even rejecting royal titles. He was, in a sense, a chief in king's robes. His subjects recognized the healthy paradox and loved him for it. He had gained the powers of a monarch without losing the heart of a sheikh, something his immediate successors could not claim, and something the present royalty has learned again. Leadership of this type lives in the betwixt and between, enjoying great power, but not exploiting it in a harmful, oppressive manner. Because such power is largely personal, it is difficult to hand on even where structures have been established and legitimated by the charismatic leader's use of them.

In such situations, several perceptions are at work simultaneously. The leader may see himself one way; the people may see him another. Or the people may be divided on how they perceive him and what his exact role is. For instance, Almana claimed that royal titles were not used in Riyadh because of religious resistance. Such titles were used in the Hejaz and were applied to Abdul Aziz from the day of his accession. In Jordan, a similar distinction can be made on the basis of the titles applied to the chief occupant of the palace by the townspeople and those used by the bedouin. The former speak freely about their king, but the latter shun the title in favor of the more chiefly *sayyid*, the sheikh of sheikhs mentioned above. The two perceptions co-exist, and government functions in spite, if not because, of them. They provide a way to have change and simultaneously not to have it.

In David's case, the tradition is confused about his exact role and title. *Nāgîd* and *melek* are both used, and scholars have devised explanations that discriminate between them on theological or chronological grounds. I suspect that even if such explanations are not inaccurate, they fall short of describing fully the complicated, conflicting impressions that David and his role made upon his people. When contrasted with Solomon, as Ibn Saud can be contrasted with his immediate successor-son, David appears sensitive, clever, and strong in ways his son does not. David was a king who did not forget the reasons for his rise. Therefore, our difficulty in separating Iron Age chiefs from kings owes in part to the confusion that existed in their titles, functions, and manners during the tenth century B.C.E.

Many other details that we would like to know are simply not available to us today. They lie buried beneath the hills and deserts of Syro-Palestine or locked in the minds and hearts of those who knew Abdul Aziz. Research on both fronts has just begun, so we must be satisfied with general comparisons until we can be more specific. But judgment and limitations of space have forced additional brevity here. A fuller treatment of the topic situating it in a broader context will expand arguments made here and will offer a fuller explanation for the emergence of empire in the early Iron Age.

Works Consulted

Abdul Aziz Zanil Jawasir
       1981   Conversations, Al Khobar, Saudi Arabia, June 1981.

Aharoni, Yohanan
       1979   *The Land of the Bible.* Revised ed. Philadelphia:
                               Westminster.

Almana, Mohammed
       1980   *Arabia Unified. A Portrait of Ibn Saud.* London: Hutchinson
                               Benham.

       1981   Interviews, Al Khobar, Saudi Arabia, June 1981.

Armstrong, Harold C.
       1938   *Lord of Arabia: Ibn Saud, an Intimate Study of a King.*
                               London: Penguin. Published London: Arthur Baker, 1934.

Bell, Lady Gertrude (ed.)
       1927   *Gertrude Bell, Letters.* 2 vols. London: Ernest Benn/ New
                               York: Boni and Liverlight.

Dorward, D. C.
       1974   "Ethnography and Administration: a Study of Anglo-Tiv
                               'Working Misunderstanding.' " *Journal of African History* 15:
                               457-477.

Duby, George
       1978   *Medieval Marriage.* Trans. Elborg Forster. Baltimore: Johns
                               Hopkins University Press.

Flanagan, James W.
       1979   "The Relocation of the Davidic Capital." *JAAR* 47: 223-244.

       1981   "Chiefs in Israel." *JSOT* 20: 47-73.

       1982a   "Genealogy and Dynasty in the Early Monarchy of Israel and
                               Judah." Pp. 23-28 in the *Proceedings of the Eighth World
                               Congress of Jewish Studies.* Jerusalem.

       1982b   "Social Transformation and Office." *The Word of the Lord Shall
                               Go Forth.* Ed. Carol M. Meyers and Michael Patrick
                               O'Connor. Cambridge, MA: American Schools of Oriental
                               Research. In press.

Frick, Frank S.
       1979   "Religion and Sociopolitical Structure in Early Israel: an
                               Ethno-Archaeological Approach." *Society of Biblical
                               Literature 1979 Seminar Papers.* Ed. Paul J. Achtemeier.
                               Missoula, MT: Scholars Press.

Goody, Jack
  1969   *Comparative Studies in Kinship*. Stanford: Stanford University
                         Press.

  1976   *Production and Reproduction*. Cambridge: Cambridge Univer-
                         sity Press.

Gottwald, Norman K.
  1979   *The Tribes of Yahweh*. Maryknoll, NY: Orbis.

Hammel, E. A.
  1980   "The Comparative Method in Anthropological Perspective."
                         Comparative Study of Society and History 22: 145-155.

Harris, Marvin
  1979   *Cultural Materialism*. New York: Random House.

Hoagland, Jim
  1982   "How Strong Are the Saudis?" *The New York Review of Books*
                         29, No. 5, April 1: 23-26.

Holden, David and Richard Johns
  1981   *The House of Saud*. London: Sidgwick and Jackson.

Howarth, David
  1980   *The Desert King. The Life of Ibn Saud*. London: Quartet
                         Books. Published London: William Collins, 1965.

Hudson, Michael C.
  1977   *Arab Politics*. New Haven: Yale University Press.

Johnson, Douglas H.
  1981   "The Fighting Nuer: Primary Sources and the Origins of a
                         Stereotype." *Africa* 51: 508-527.

Kheirallah, George
  1952   *Arabia Reborn*. Albuquerque, NM: University of New Mexico
                         Press.

Kovacs, Brian
  1980   "Contributions from Contemporary Social Theory to an
                         Understanding of the Rise of the Israelite Monarchy." Lecture
                         delivered before the Society of Biblical Literature. Dallas,
                         TX. Unpublished manuscript.

Lacey, Robert
  1981   *The Kingdom*. London: Hutchinson.

Leach, Edmund R.
1961   *Rethinking Anthropology*. London: Athlone.

1969   *Genesis as Myth*. London: Jonathan Cape.

1980   "Anthropological Approaches to the Study of the Bible During the Twentieth Century." Lecture delivered before the Society of Biblical Literature, Dallas, TX. Unpublished manuscript.

Lees, Brian A.
1980   *A Handbook of the Al Sa'ud Ruling Family of Sa'udi Arabia*. London: Royal Genealogies.

Legg, Paul
1980   "Arabic Topical Programs." British Broadcasting Network. July 19. Transcript.

Lévi-Strauss, Claude
1963   "Introduction: History and Anthropology." Pp. 1-27 In *Structural Anthropology*. Ed. Claire Jacobson and Brooke Grundfest Schoepf. New York: Basic Books.

Lipsky, George A.
1959   *Saudi Arabia*. New Haven: Human Relations Area Files.

Little Robert
1980   "New Book Defines Ibn Saud's Role Through Court Interpreter's Eyes." *Arab News*. July 6.

Mostyn, Trevor
1980   "Books." *Middle East*. July 18: 49.

Ohliger, Floyd W.
1981   Conversation by telephone, Princeton, NJ, March 1981.

Orme, Bryony
1981   *Anthropology for Archaeologists*. London: Duckworth.

Pedersen, Johannes
1940   *Israel, Its Life and Culture, III-IV*. London: Geoffrey Camberlege.

Philby, Harry St. John
1952   *Arabian Jubilee*. London: Robert Hale.

1955   *Sa'udi Arabia*. London: Ernest Benn.

Pitt-Rivers, Julian
1977   *The Fate of Shechem or the Politics of Sex*. Cambridge: Cambridge University Press.

Quandt, William B.
1981   *Saudi Arabia in the 1980s: Foreign Policy, Security, and Oil*. Washington: Brookings Institution.

Rihani, Ameen
    1928a   *Ibn Sa'oud of Arabia.* London: Constable.

    1928b   *Maker of Modern Arabia.* New York: Houghton Mifflin.

Service, Elman R.
    1962   *Primitive Social Organization.* 2nd ed. New York: Randon
                     House.

    1975   *Origins of the State and Civilization.* New York: Norton.

Stech-Wheeler, T., J. D. Muhly, D. R. Maxwell-Hyslop, R. Maddin
    1981   "Iron at Taanach and Early Iron Metallurgy in the Eastern
                     Mediterranean." *American Journal of Archaeology* 85: 245-
                     268.

Talmon, Shemaryahu
    1978   "The 'Comparative Method' in Biblical Interpretations--
                     Principals and Problems." *Supplements to Vetus Testamen-
                     tum* 29: 320-56.

Twitchell, K. S.
    1958   *Saudi Arabia.* 3rd ed. New York: Greenwood Press.

Van der Meulen, Daniël
    1957   *The Wells of Ibn Saud.* London: John Murray/New York:
                     Praeger.

Verdon, Michel
    1980a   "Shaking Off the Domestic Yoke, or the Sociological
                     Significance of Residence." *Comparative Studies in Society
                     and History* 22: 109-32.

    1980b   "From the Social to the Symbolic Equation: the Process of
                     Idealism in Contemporary Anthropological Representations of
                     Kinship, Marriage, and the Family." *Canadian Review of
                     Sociology and Anthropology* 17: 315-329.

Waldbaum, Jane C.
    1978   *From Bronze to Iron.* Göteborg: Paul Åströms.

Wertime, Theodore A. and James D. Muhly (eds.)
    1980   *The Coming of the Age of Iron.* New Haven: Yale University
                     Press.

Winder, R. Bayly
    1980   *Saudi Arabia in the Nineteenth Century.* New York:
                     Octagon. Published New York: St. Martins, 1965.

THE PROBLEM OF APOCALYPTIC GENRE AND THE APOCALYPSE OF JOHN *

David Hellholm
Linköping University, Sweden

For Geo Widengren
on his 75th birthday

1. *Models and Reality*[∅]

1.1. "Texts are abbreviations; they abridge, they simplify what is to be designated--and they do so by omitting."[1] This statement by Wolfgang Raible with reference to Edmund Husserl regarding such complex signs as texts can be illustrated by using a simple sign like "chair." The word or to be more exact: the concept "chair" contains only a small number of semantically distinctive characteristics (linguistically stated: *semes*) in comparison to what is common for existing chairs. Thus the concept "chair" is more abstract than the original! This is true as can be seen when we with Kurt Baldinger list the characteristics of the concept (linguistically speaking: *sememe*) "chair": (1) with solid material; (2) raised above the ground; (3) with a back; (4) for one person; (5) to sit on.[2] This is to say that we usually work with models and not with reality. A number of characteristics of an original chair are left out when in language we use the concept "chair": whether it is small or large, blue or red, of metal or wood is of no concern to the concept "chair." If specified, we, in fact, introduce a concept on a lower level of abstraction. This becomes immediately evident, if we add two further characteristics of "chair" to those pointed out earlier: (6) with arms and (7) with upholstery, thus producing the concept of "armchair." This is of great importance for the problem of genres, not least that of genres and subgenres, as I will try to show later.[3] The use of concepts is the very reason why language can function at all, that is, why we can communicate with one another and with generations past.

1.2. As I just tried to show models or signs can be more or less abstract and consequently we erect a hierarchy of models. If the concept "chair" is constituted of the five mentioned characteristics, we find that by selecting three of these let us say #1 (with solid material),[4] #2 (raised above the ground), and #5 (to sit on) we arrive at the even more

---

*Public lecture delivered on February 18, 1982 at the Divinity School, The University of Chicago.

[∅]Regarding concepts defined by extension I am--as far as textlinguistic analyses are concerned--in total agreement with Kurt Baldinger 1980, 269 (and cf. ibid., 25-61), when he writes that these "have no ontological implications concerning, for instance, the distinction between 'real' and 'fictitious' referents," see David Hellholm 1980, 34 and 88; Klaus Heger 1976, 35.

[1]Wolfgang Raible 1979a, 2, who refers to Edmund Husserl 1970, 354f.; cf. also Elisabeth Gülich/Wolfgang Raible 1977, 14ff.

[2]Baldinger 1980, 62ff., esp. 67 with table 4.

[3]See below §2.2.3.2., §2.2.3.3., and §3.3.4.

[4]Baldinger, ibid., includes only *semes* #2 and #5 in the *archisememe* "seat" (see below note 5) which thus are said to be the intersection of the *sememes* "armchair," "chair," "stool," and "sofa." This is a fallacy in Baldinger's theory, since it is hardly conceivable to have a *seme* of form and a *seme* of function without a *seme* of content. The reasons for this fallacy are firstly Baldinger's neglect of grouping the *semes*, and secondly his neglect of a hierarchical ranking of the *semes* themselves in spite of his statement that "a *seme* can be very specific or very general" (p. 81). *Seme* #1 (with solid material) can mean different things depending on the abstraction level; it can mean

abstract concept "seat." In linguistic terminology the concept at this abstraction level would be called an *"archisememe* ." We could easily generalize even further and say that "seats" themselves can be classified under still more comprehensive *"archisememes"* such as "furniture," thus constituting a *"superarchisememe"* and so on.[5]

Thus with regard to single signs it is possible to establish the hierarchy: "armchair," "chair," "seat," "furniture"; a hierarchy which is characterized by the rule: the larger the *intension,* the smaller the *extension* and vice versa.[6] In the words of Wolfgang Raible: "Signs with few characteristics have the character of "supreme-concepts," they can designate a number of things in an unspecified manner, while signs with many characteristics are typical sub-concepts, i.e. specified designations."[7]

1.3. If, instead of subordinating the *subsememe* "armchair" under the *sememe* "chair" and thus erecting a hierarchy of concepts, we take these two concepts as a true *"sememe -opposition,"* we encounter another problem, viz. that of mixed concepts, which is also highly significant for genre analysis. Klaus Heger has pointed to this problem in connection with the above mentioned *semes* #6 (with arms) and #7 (with upholstery). He writes: "As long as the person using the two *signemes,*[8] "chair" and "armchair," from among the seating furniture for the use of one person, encounters only furniture without upholstery and without arms or only furniture with upholstery and with arms, the multifarious definition in these alternatives makes no difference to him. However, as soon as there appears in his perspective corresponding seating furniture without upholstery but with arms and/or with upholstery but without arms, he is no better off than the analytical linguist and he finds himself encountering an insoluble task, that is, having to decide in favor of one or other of the alternative *seme*-pairs."[9]

Heger continues by giving two possible solutions: (a) by postulating a double polysemy or (b) by stressing a primary conceptual point (*begriffliche Schwerpunktsetzung*).[10] Another possibility, which in my opinion is preferable, is the above suggested conceptual hierarchization, in which an "armchair" is reckoned as a *subsememe* of the *sememe* "chair," and the acknowledgement of "empty positions," i.e., concepts without lexicalization, for the two "mixed *sememes.*" This solution is of theoretical significance for the question of mixed literary genres in two ways: (a) with regard to conceptual hierarchization and (b) with regard to historical development of genres and subgenres; both of

---

"solid" in opposition to "liquid" or "gas" but it can also mean "solid" in opposition to the less abstract concept "soft" and this is in fact the meaning presupposed by Baldinger, since he excludes the *sememe* "pouffe" when establishing the *semes* of the intersection. See further below note 14, and §3.3.4.

   [5]Baldinger 1980 distinguishes between *sememe* and *archisememe* and still further concepts of abstraction without, however, introducing proper terminology, thus either using an "empty position" (see ibid., 104ff.) or using the same lexeme on different conceptual levels. In order to avoid confusion I introduce the term *"superarchisememe"* for the next higher rank of conceptual abstraction.

   [6]Albert Menne 1973, 25, 75; Jens Allwood et alii 1977, 125ff.; Dieter Wunderlich 1979, 205ff.; Heger 1976, 59; Raible 1979a, 22.

   [7]Raible 1979a, 23.

   [8]See below note 17 (italics mine). The term *sign* in this paper is used for the most part in the sense of *signeme.*

   [9]Heger 1979a, 34 (italics mine). See also Baldinger's reference to a "border zone or zone of transition" (1980, 27).

   [10]Heger 1979a, 34f.

these having to do with the relationship between synchrony and diachrony in genre analysis.[11]

1.4 Before turning to the next section, I need to make two more--as I see it--important observations with regard to the distinctive characteristics of a concept.

1.4.1. First, then, it is easy to see that the five characteristics constituting the concept "chair" are to be found in other concepts as well, e.g., #1 (with solid material) is also a constitutive element of, e.g., a "car" and a "house"; #2 (raised above the ground) is also characteristic of a "table" or a "desk"; #3 (with a back) is a characteristic of a "sofa" and a "book" as well; #4 (for one person): taken in itself this characteristic is also a constitutive element of a "watch," a "ring," "glasses," etc.; #5 (to sit on) is certainly characteristic also of a "sofa," a "seat," a "bench," a "pew," and so forth. This observation makes it clear that it is by no means enough just to list a *number of characteristics* in order to arrive at a concept, but that we rather have to ask for the type, the sequence, and above all the interdependence and relationship of these *semes* to each other in constituting a *sememe* or on one abstraction level higher the grouping of the intersection of several *sememes* in constituting an *archisememe* and so on.[12] The concept then can be defined as an "abstraction from many realities which are related to each other."[13]

1.4.2. The second observation is perhaps not so evident but none the less of equal importance. When making use of Baldinger's characteristics of the concept "chair," I rearranged the sequential order of them to arrive at a grouping to which he has paid no attention. By doing so, I am able to show that these characteristics can be divided into three groups.
(a)   the first group is constituted by *seme* #1 (with solid material) and refers to *content*;
(b)   the second group is made up of *semes* #2 (raised above the ground) and #3 (with a back) and refers to *form*;
(c)   the third group is made up by *semes* #4 (for one person) and #5 (to sit on) and refers to *function* in a twofold way: (aa) for whom it functions and (bb) in what way or how it functions.
The importance of this threefold grouping becomes apparent, when we consider the *archisememe* "seat": Also on this level of abstraction we find the same grouping as on the lower abstraction level, viz., content, form, and function. This means that the grouping itself is not accidental or variable but rather constitutive and invariable: (a) the first group: *content* is constituted by *seme* #1 (with solid material); (b) the second group: *form* is in this case made up by only one *seme* on this level, viz., #2 (raised above the ground); here *seme* #3 is left out; (c) the third group: *function* is made up partly by a more general *seme* #4 (for persons) and *seme* #5 (to sit on).[14]

That the *grouping* of the *semes*, not the *semes* themselves, is indeed invariable becomes evident when we move to yet a higher level of abstraction, the *superarchisememe* as I called it:

---

[11]See below §3.3.4. with note 59.
[12]Cf. above note 4 and below note 14.
[13]Baldinger 1980, 62; see also below §3.3.2. # (b).
[14]This is precisely the intersection of the *sememes* "chair," "armchair," "stool," "sofa," and "pouffe." The last can be included or excluded depending upon the abstraction level of *seme* #1 (with solid material; see further above note 4 and below §3.3.4.). Unfortunately Baldinger has paid no attention to the necessity of abstract ranking of the *semes* as can be seen ibid., and in table 4 on page 67.

(a)   the first group is also here made up of the same *seme* #1 (with solid material);[15]
(b)   the second is also made up of the same *seme* as on the previous level, viz., #2 (raised above the ground);
(c)   the third group, however, is in this case constituted by a seemingly[16] new and more general *seme*, viz., to furnish. Here we also observe how on this abstraction level the concept has obtained its lexeme from its function.

This observation points to the obvious fact that the constituents of a *sememe* (i.e. concept), and *archiseme* or even a *superarchisememe* are made up of *semes* belonging to the three groups: content, form and function and that none of these groups are variable but indeed constitutive and will all have to be taken into account, when establishing or analyzing concepts. This circumstance is of far-reaching consequences, in particular, when we leave the single concept and move up to more complex signs or models such as texts and even genres.

2. Genres and Reality

2.1.   As the initial quotation from Raible/Husserl indicated the simplification of reality is not restricted to simple signs but applies also to more complex signs as sentences and texts. This has been elaborated in great detail by Klaus Heger in his work *Monem, Wort, Satz und Text* published in the 2nd edition in 1976. Time and space does not permit a development from the single sign *"monem"* all the way up to the complex sign *"text"* (= *signeme* [17]) on this occasion. Let me only briefly indicate how I see the relationship between the groupings established earlier with regard to the single concept "chair" and the more complex sign of a "sentence":[18]
(a)   the *propositional* aspect corresponds to content;
(b)   the *utterance* aspect--oral or written--corresponds to form;
(c)   the *illocutionary/perlocutionary* aspect corresponds to the function aspect as I have called it.

---

[15]See above notes 4 and 14.

[16]Here the need for a ranking of *semes* in abstraction levels becomes particularly apparent; see further above notes 4 and 14 and below §3.3.4.

[17]In his system Heger has replaced "*moneme*" with "*signeme*," since "it is obvious that the model should be usable not only for the analysis of minimal meaningful 'nits (*monemes*) but also for the analysis of meaningful units of higher hierarchical ranks" (Heger 1976, 40 with note 47; cf. also Baldinger 1980, 262). This in fact means as Heger states that the extended trapezium model referring to the level of *langue* "allows for being used there for *paradigmatic* as well as for *syntagmatic* analyses of *signemes*" (Heger 1976, 59; Baldinger 1980, 271; italics mine). For the sake of clarification I give the present form of the trapezium as found in Heger 1976, 58 and Baldinger 1980, 260:

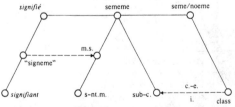

Abbreviations: m. = monosemization;   m.s. = monosemized   signeme;   s-nt. m. = *signifiant* of the monosemized signeme; c.-e. = relation of class to elements; i. = inclusion; sub-c. = subclass.

[18]Cf. Hellholm 1980, 52ff., esp. 56 with fig. 8. In addition to literature referred to there see now also Götz Beck 1980 and Werner Sökeland 1980.

Thus, even with regard to "*sentences*" the grouping remains intact and enables communication and understanding, since also here all three groups function in an interrelationship with one another.[19]

2.2. The even more complex sign "*text*" can have three different meanings that, from a methodological point of view, have to be kept apart:[20]

2.2.1. First, in ordinary language "text" usually refers to the realization of a certain entity *hic et nunc* or with regard to ancient texts *illic et tunc*. Used in this way text is understood as an individual work by itself, e.g., *The Red Room* by August Strindberg or *Anna Karenina* by Leo Tolstoy or, linguistically stated, as a manifestation on the level of *parole*; and yet we must not forget that such texts in comparison with reality itself are abbreviated models, since, as has been pointed out so neatly by Prof. Raible, "total information is almost equivalent to no information at all; only by means of reduction of the complexity, only by erecting simplified models will sense and coherence along with structures be recognizable."[21]

2.2.2. Second, in ordinary language text can be used as referring to a *group* or *class* of texts being held together by *one* specific invariant.[22] This is the case when we, e.g., ask the question in which way a certain text is similar to other texts. The possibility of grouping is abundant: we can talk about biblical texts or on a lower level of abstraction about New Testament texts or on a still lower level of abstraction about Pauline or Johannine texts. In doing so, however, we do not really enter the question of generic structures, since in all these instances we are concerned with only one specific invariant or isolated similarity in each case, viz., that it is a part of the Bible, or the New Testament, or the Pauline, or the Johannine corpus. I will illustrate this by going back to where I began, viz., with simple signs. If we take into account only one or if we expand it to even two *semes* #1 (of solid material) and #2 (raised above the ground), we could come up with such a bundle of things as "house," "table," "rock," "chair," "car," etc. These two *semes* were taken, one from the group of contents, the other from the group of forms. If we, however, add one *seme* more from the group of function #4 (for one person) we reduce the possibilities considerably and by adding #5 (to sit on) we arrive at the concept "chair."

From these examples we can draw three conclusions:
(a)   this type of taxonomical grouping or classification has little or no bearing at all on the question of generic structures;
(b)   there is a need to go beyond taxonomic-classifying procedures in order to arrive at a process of relating elements or characteristics to each other by investigating their interrelationship and function;
(c)   there is a necessity for all three groups of characteristics to be represented; the question of function cannot be left out!

2.2.3. Third, by "text" we can refer to a whole *hierarchy* of *concepts of generic nature*. In this connection we have to ask the question in which ways certain texts are structurally similar to each other and characteristically different from others. In dealing

---

[19]See Hellholm 1980, 57f. with references.
[20]Heger 1976, 26-28; Raible 1979b, 63.
[21]Raible 1979a, 4.
[22]Klaus Hempfer 1973, 27f., 106f., 224; Raible 1979a, 20; Heger 1976, 24-30, 60; the relevance of this type of groupings (Σ --Parole) for genre analysis is furthermore distinctly limited due to the fact that frequency classes cannot stand in syntagmatic contexts as pointed out by Heger, ibid., 29f., 60; cf. below §4.

with simple signs such as predicates, I tried to show the importance of establishing a
hierarchy of abstraction levels such as "armchair," "chair," "seat," "furniture." In dealing
with such complex signs as "genres," we have to proceed analogously, if genre-analysis is
to be successful at all. To my satisfaction there seems to be an increasing agreement
among linguists, literary critics, and even form-critics that such a hierarchization is an
absolute necessity. This is true, even if the terminology may differ and the theoretical
reflection may have reached various levels of awareness.

2.2.3.1. In *linguistics,* ever since de Saussure, one distinguishes between *parole* as the
level of actualization in speech and writing; *langue* as the level of a single-language
structure and *langage* as the level of language competence in general, i.e., language as
system.[23]

2.2.3.2. In *literary criticism* a similar although more detailed abstraction hierarchy is
being used in comparing the following generic concepts:[24]
(a) The "*communication situation*"; i.e., the factors characterizing the relationship
     between a sender and a receiver in which a speech-act is carried out;
(b) The "*mode of writing*" and "*type of writing,*" i.e., *ahistoric* generic invariants such
     as the narrative, the epic, the dramatic, or the satiric modes of writing.[25] That
     the generic concept on this abstraction level is of an *ahistoric* nature and none the
     less fully legitimate becomes obvious, when we turn to such a sign-model as "mam-
     mal." Nobody using the concept "mammal" is actually looking for the incarnation
     or the pure form of the mammal,--at least I hope so!
(c) The "*genre*" is the *historic* and concrete realization of the potential generic
     invariant structures of the "modes" and/or "types of writing" on the *ahistoric* level
     of abstraction. *Historic* realizations of the *ahistoric* concept narrative for instance
     are a novel, a biography, a tale, etc., just as historic realizations of the *ahistoric*
     concept "mammal" can be a "dog" or a "human being."
(d) The "*subgenres*": on an even lower abstraction level we find such realizations of
     the genre "novel" as "love-story," "detective-story," and so on. With regard to the
     concept "human being" it can be subdivided into the obvious subconcepts "female"
     and "male" by adding one *seme* more.

2.2.3.3. In *form-criticism* we also encounter a similar hierarchy of abstraction levels, a
fact which I can only briefly hint at on this occasion:
(a) "*Sitz im Leben*" is by and large the equivalence in biblical scholarship to the
     "communication situation" in linguistics and literary criticism although with
     considerably more attention paid to the situation of the sender than that of the
     receiver, to the origin rather than to the use.
(b) "*Mode of writing*" as a "name" for *ahistoric* generic structures is to my knowledge
     in biblical scholarship left with an "*empty position,*" i.e., a concept without
     lexicalization, in spite of the fact that the concept itself is there; after all we do
     talk about "Narrative Texts" or "Argumentative Texts" in connection with *genres*
     and about "Narrative Forms," "Sayings of Jesus," and "Middle Forms" in connection
     with *forms.*[26]

---

[23]Cf. Baldinger 1980, 150f.
[24]For the following cf. esp. Hempfer 1973, 26-29; Hellholm 1980, 62-64; Raible
1979a, 28.
[25]Concerning the question for a theoretical necessity of introducing the "type of
writing" as a level between "mode of writing" and "genre" see Hempfer 1973, 233f., note
102. Cf. in connection with the problem of the genre "Apocalypse" below §3.3.4.
[26]Concerning the differentiation *between* "form" and "genre (= *Gattung*)," see my
reference to Rudolf Bultmann's programmatic statement in RGG[2]II (1928) 418 and the
discussion in Hellholm 1980, 68. The distinction *between* "form" and "Gattung" on the
one hand and "genre" on the other by E. P. Sanders 1982, §2.1. and §5.1. is not very

(c)   *"Genre"* as a designation for historic generic structures has been employed since the formation of the form-critical school (*"Gattung"/"Form"*) and has like "Sitz im Leben" become to such a degree a part of biblical scholarship that even those scholars opposing new linguistic methods or theories today make use of them as an inherent part of their vocabulary and their conceptual understanding. We analyze the genre of "Gospels," "Letters" (although problematic[27]), and "Apocalypses" in connection with *genres,* and "Miracle stories," "Similitudes," or "Prophetic and Apocalyptic Sayings" in connection with *forms.*[28]

(d)   This also applies to *"subgenres"* as can easily be demonstrated by pointing to the concept "Synoptic Gospels."

2.3.   The hierarchic structures of the complex models of "single texts, subgenres, genres, modes of writing and communication situations" adhere to the same rule as the hierarchy of simple signs, viz. that the larger the *intension* the smaller the *extension* and vice versa. In variation of my quotation from Raible above we can say that generic structures with few characteristics have the character of "supreme-concepts," while generic structures with many characteristics are typical "sub-concepts." Applied to my topic today this means that there are fewer common characteristics of a "Narrative" than of an "Apocalypse," thus allowing more texts to be classified as "Narratives" than as "Apocalypses."

3. Genres and Paradigms

3.1.   So far I have deliberated on the hierarchical structures to be applied in genre analysis.

When I now turn to the problem of genres and paradigms, I will inevitably have to restrict myself to one generic concept, viz., that of an "Apocalypse." When entering upon a specific generic concept like "Apocalypse" we must not forget that genre designations function as *names* for texts.[29] This means first of all that genre designations are simple signs for more complex signs, that are themselves complex signs for a far more complex reality. However, this also means that, when analyzing texts as generic concepts, we have constantly to be conscious of the level on which we are posing our analyses. This does not *per se* favor any particular level of investigation; on the contrary it should explicitly be stated that text-linguistic and form-critical studies can legitimately be carried out on any of the levels, "subgenre," "genre," "mode of writing," etc., but that we can only move from one to any other, if we are aware of what we are doing.

3.2.   What are the characteristics, the *semes/noemes,*[30] of the macro-sign "Apocalypse"? That the answer to this question is by no means an easy one ought to be self-evident from our discussion so far and is indeed confirmed by the various suggestions

---

illuminating in view of the quotation from Gunkel (below note 43) and the fact that form-critics like Hans Conzelmann and Günther Bornkamm make a distinction precisely between *"Gattung* (= genre)" and *"Form"*; see Hellholm ibid.

[27] Cf. now, e.g., Karl Ermert 1979.

[28] See above note 26.

[29] See Raible 1972, 204ff.; idem, 1979a, 21ff.; Heger 1979, 49f.

[30] While *"seme* is defined as the minimal distinctive unit (of the content substance) with reference to the *sememe,* which is *bound to the structure of a given language,"* noeme is "a concept intensionally defined, which *does not depend on the structure of a given language,"* Heger 1976, 338f. (italics mine); see also Baldinger 1980, 267. In order not to predetermine at this point the status of the genre concept "Apocalypse," I give *seme/noeme* alternatively.

put forward by such scholars as Philipp Vielhauer, Klaus Koch, and in this country, John Collins and the SBL-group working with him.[31]   In order to avoid doing too much injustice to any one of these scholars I will list the following *semes/noemes* which include most characteristics mentioned in connection with attempts at defining the literary group "Apocalypse."

A.   *Content—Propositions and Themes (text-semantic aspect)*

s1   Eschatology as history in future form
s2   Cosmic history divided into periods ("Weltalterlehre")
s3   Description of the other-world
s4   Combat between dualistic macro-cosmic powers
s5   Combat between dualistic micro-cosmic powers and/or groups
s6   Other worldly mediators or revealers
s7   This-worldly recipients
s8   Addressees of recipient's revelation
s9   Paraeneses
s10   Command to recipient to reveal and/or to write by other-worldly mediator
s11   Systematization of numbers, etc.

B.   *Form—Style (text-syntactic aspect)*

s12   Narrative framework
s13   Epistolary prescript and/or postscript
s14   Removal to a this-worldly place of revelation
s15   Heavenly journey to an other-worldly place of revelation
s16   Account of vision(s)
s17   Account of audition(s)
s18   Interpretation of vision(s)
s19   Interpretation of audition(s)
s20   Discourse of mediators
s21   Dialogues between mediator(s) and receiver
s22   Heavenly writings (letters and/or books from Heaven)
s23   Quotations of the Supreme Divinity
s24   Communication embedment
s25   Pictorial language
s26   Pseudonymity
s27   Combination of smaller forms

C.   *Function—Communicative function (text-pragmatic aspect)*

s28   Intended for a group in crisis
s29   Exhortation to steadfastness and/or repentance
s30   Promise of vindication and redemption or more generally stated: consolation
s31   Authorization of message

---

[31]Philipp Vielhauer 1965, 583-94; idem, 1975, 487-92; Klaus Koch 1972, 24-33; John J. Collins 1979b, 28.

3.3. Is this listing of a substantial number of characteristics of Apocalypses pointed out by biblical scholars sufficiently to enable us to arrive at the concept "Apocalypse" in a *semasiological* approach[32] or are they all contained in the concept "Apocalypse" in an onomasiological approach?[33]

3.3.1. The *first observation* to be made is that practically no *semes/noemes* can be tied exclusively to the concept of Apocalypse.[34] Time and space do not allow for a scrutiny of all 31 *semes/noemes* but let me only point to a few constituents that normally are regarded as typical apocalyptic characteristics:
(a) *Eschatology*: not even this *seme/noeme* can be claimed to be an exclusive characteristic of an Apocalypse as its appearance in Pauline letters or in the Gospels demonstrates;
(b) *Visions*: neither are these nor are heavenly journeys reserved for Apocalypses as their appearance in Pauline, Hermetic, and Gnostic literature indicates;
(c) *Consolation* and *authorization*: even these two functional *semes/noemes* are typical not only for apocalypses, e.g., authorization can be achieved by pseudepigraphal letters also.

3.3.2. The *second observation* tells us that all these 31 *semes/noemes* in fact are not present in any single writing designated as an Apocalypse.[35] Where does this take us? What conclusions need to be drawn from this obvious state of affairs? In my opinion *two* to begin with:
(a) First, we must recall that the designation "Apocalypse" is a model abridging the model "text" which means that *per definitionem* we cannot expect all characteristics pertaining to single texts on the *parole* level to be included in a generic concept on various levels of abstraction;[36]

This takes us one step further: depending on where we locate the generic concept "Apocalypse," we can expect fewer or more characteristics to make up the concept; as a *supreme-concept* on the *ahistoric* level of "mode of writing" the determinative characteristics, the *semes/noemes* will inevitably have to be fewer; as a *sub-concept* on the historic levels of genre or subgenre the specific characteristics, the *semes/noemes* will have to be many more. And as stated twice already: the more *semes/noemes* the fewer Apocalypses, the fewer *semes/noemes* the more Apocalypses![37]

---

[32]I.e., starting from the sign (*signeme*) "Apocalypse" in order to arrive at a monosemized concept (*sememe*); see Baldinger 1980, 110-57; Heger 1979, 59, 60f. For the distinction between semasiology and onomasiology see further below §3.3.5.

[33]I.e., starting from the concept (*sememe*) "Apocalypse" in order to arrive at a proper lexicalization (*signeme*); see Baldinger, ibid.; Heger, ibid.; and cf. above note 32.

[34]As is the case with *semes/noemes* of simple concepts; cf. above §1.4.1. Cf., e.g., Paul D. Hanson 1963, 33; Jean Carmignac 1979, 17; idem, 1982, §1.; Michael Stone 1976, 440; Sanders 1982, §2.

[35]See above note 34.

[36]As Heger 1979, 52 and 60 points out only the determinative characteristics on the levels of *langue* or *langage* constitute *semes/noemes*, not, however, the specific characteristics of single texts. Cf. with regard to simple signs above §1.1.

[37]These deliberations show how essential it is to approach the question of genre not by utilizing merely inductive but rather by combining inductive and deductive methods; see further Hellholm 1980, 64-67 with notes and literature referred to there. Cf. also Gülich/Raible 1977, 18ff. and now Ermert 1979, 29f.; further above §1.4.2.; below §3.3.3. and §4.2.1.3.4. #(b).

(b)   Second, in my opinion this state of affairs leads to the same conclusion I drew
      earlier with regard to the simple predicate "chair":[38] it is by no means enough just
      to list a number of 31 characteristic *semes* or *noemes* in order to arrive at the
      generic concept "Apocalypse," but rather we have to ask for the type, the sequen-
      tial order and the interrelationship of these characteristics to each other in consti-
      tuting a possible genre "Apocalypse"; or on one abstraction level higher the
      grouping of the intersection of several types of texts on the same level in
      constituting a narrative.[39]

3.3.3. The *third observation* I have already revealed by grouping the above listed 31
elements in order to avoid repetition.[40] The problem of such groupings becomes
apparent as soon as one discovers that not a small number of characteristics could show
up in one or even two more groups as well depending on the perspective, e.g., from one
point of view the account of a vision is a stylistic or formal characteristic while from
another perspective it certainly belongs to the group of contents. This was particularly
striking in the classification of the *seme/noeme* 15, "Heavenly writing": from a literary
or *text-syntactical* point of view it is a specific form of revelation; from a *text-semantic*
point of view it is filled with content and from the perspective of *text-pragmatics* it has
a specific function in the macro-structure of the apocalyptic writing as such and, what is
much more important for our argument, of the generic structure of Apocalypses.[41]

From a semiotically and linguistically defined "communication-specific model of defini-
tion" this circumstance is in no way surprising, since pragmatics includes semantics and
syntactics, and semantics includes syntactics as well:[42]
Pragmatics: Relation between Signs, Designata, and Users = R(S,D,U);
Semantics: Relation between Signs and Designata = R(S,D);
Syntactics: Relation between Signs and other Signs = R(S,S').

When grouping the *semes* of the *sememe* "chair," I came to the conclusion that *semes* had
to be derived from all of the three groups, content, form, and function in order to

---

[38]See above §1.4.1.
[39]See esp. Hempfer 1973, 138ff., 190; Hellholm 1980, 67; Lars Hartman
1982, §3.2.2.
[40]Cf. the similar grouping in Hartman 1982, §3.
[41]The same is true also of s9 Paraenesis; an indication of this particular problem
in the grouping of the *semes* is the fact that Collins and the SBL-group include paraenesis
neither in the "Manner of Revelation" nor in the "Content: Temporal or Spatial Axis" but
set it apart as an entity by itself. The question of grouping of the *semes/noemes* as well
as the whole question of definition becomes exceptionally problematic, when Hartmut
Stegemann 1982, §5 #(8) note 107 writes: "In any event one can speak of a literary
'genre' if one does not understand this concept in the sense of a '*Gattung*' but orientates
oneself exclusively to the criteria of content (so. e.g., J. J. Collins 1979)." The reference
to Collins here is in my opinion misleading (cf. below, note 44) since Collins' "master-
paradigm" contains both criteria of form and of content. Furthermore, Stegemann
himself has convincingly pointed to the *seme* "authorization," a criterion of function, as a
determinative characteristic of the genre "Apocalypse" (cf. below note 141 and further
Raible 1979a, 27).
[42]For further details and references to relevant literature see Hellholm 1980,
22ff. For the importance of distinguishing between pragmatics (function of symptom and
function of signal) and semantics (function of symbol) with regard to synonymy, see now
Baldinger 1980, 212-53, esp. 230-40 and for functions of symbol, symptom, and signal in
the trapezium, ibid., 254-59. Cf. also Heger 1976, 45f. and already Karl Bühler 1934,
28ff.

establish the concept "chair." In apocalyptic research, up until the project of the SBL-group directed by Collins, that has been the starting point also in analyzing such complex models as generic concepts.[43] Now, Collins and the SBL-group give the following definition of the genre "Apocalypse":

> 'Apocalypse' is a genre of revelatory literature with a narrative framework, in which a revelation is mediated by an otherworldly being to a human recipient, disclosing a transcendent reality which is both temporal, insofar as it envisages eschatological salvation and spatial insofar as it involves another, supernatural world.[44]

This definition, operating on a fairly high abstraction level, brings to one's mind the question: why were Apocalypses ever written? From what Collins has noted elsewhere I believe he would answer something like this: each Apocalypse has its specific function but one cannot arrive at an invariant function.[45] This, however, does not resolve the problem at stake, since such an answer would only transfer the question from the level of *langue*, on which generic investigations operate, to the level of *parole*, dealing with single texts. I believe that one reason for the reluctance toward functional aspects as generic *semes/noemes* must be seen in connection with the lack of hierarchization of *semes/noemes* in the discussion of function, a problem I will return to in the next section. Another reason probably is the concentration on the "Sitz im Leben" aspect for genre definitions among form-critics instead of the integration of the three dimensions.[46] Personally I am inclined to think that such characteristics as s28 (intended for a group in crisis); s29 (exhortation to steadfastness or repentance); s30 (promise of vindication and redemption); or s31 (authorization of the message) are general enough to serve on the level of *langue* or even *langage*. This implies the conviction that these are

---

[43]That all three dimensions have to be taken into account was stressed by Hermann Gunkel 1924, 182f. (engl. translation in John Hayes 1980, 127f.) and idem, 1925 (ed. Hans Rollmann 1981, 283f.), when in a letter to Adolf Jülicher he writes: "Particularly displeasing to me is the word 'form*geschichtlich*' or even '*stil*kritisch'; I rather talk of '*Literaturgeschichte*' that organizes the material according to 'genres.' Genres I establish a) according to the common store of thoughts and moods, b) according to the similar Sitz im Leben, c) according to the constant forms of expression" (see also Rollmann's reference to similar statements by Gunkel in other works, p. 283 note 16; cf. also Sanders 1982, §1.3, who quotes from Gunkel's letter to Jülicher). The acknowledgment of the necessity of an interrelationship of all three dimensions in establishing genres is explicitly stressed in Gunkel 1924, 183: "Only where we have all three criteria preserved together . . . have we the right to speak of a genre." What Gunkel, however, does not discuss is the nature of the interrelationship or the possibility of a hierarchization of the criteria.

[44]Collins 1979a, 9. In this definition the groups "form" and "content" are represented.

[45]Collins 1982, 94: "Rather than assuming that there is a common setting and function . . . we need to examine the individual texts bearing in mind the differentiation of levels demanded by Knierim (1973)." Cf., however, above note 36 and Hellholm 1980, 13, 61, 64 with references.

[46]As Gunkel was right in rejecting genre definitions using only *formal* criteria (see above note 43), so are Collins and the SBL-group right in rejecting *function* as *the* decisive criterion. There is no equality between form, content, and function: " . . . as with all linguistic signs form has to be distinguished from function" (Raible 1979b, 68; Hempfer 1973, 113). This, however, does not justify the exclusion of the functional dimension, but rather its integration with the two other dimensions (so also Raible 1979a, 27 with note 45 and see Gunkel's statement [1924, 183] quoted above note 43).

indeed appropriate *semes/noemes* derived from the texts themselves. Thus, the grouping and hierarchization are derived *deductively* from the methodology applied, while the specific *semes/noemes* within the group are derived *inductively* from the texts themselves.[47]

For a paradigmatically established definition of the genre "Apocalypse" I would be willing to accept the definition quoted above, provided the following addition on the same level of abstraction: *"intended for a group in crisis with the purpose of exhortation and/or consolation by means of divine authority."*[48]

3.3.4. The *fourth observation* has to do with the hierarchization of the *semes/noemes* themselves. In John Collins' *master-paradigm* in *Semeia* 14 (1979) 6-8 he has paid due attention to this very important methodological approach. I can only emphasize my agreement at this point. When one turns, however, to the chart on p. 28 it becomes obvious that he has not carried his methodological insight over into practical use so that the characteristics listed there vary in abstraction, a feature which also returns in all the other contributions to that *Semeia* volume.[49] Now, we should be grateful to Collins for the hierarchization of the *semes/noemes* in his master-paradigm, especially since I have found no attempts at such a ranking in any other paradigm of apocalyptic *semes/noemes* available;[50] and yet I have to point to the fact that there remain serious problems with that master-paradigm as one striking inaccuracy demonstrates. In dividing existent Apocalypses into types Collins states that "the most obvious and fundamental distinction is between apocalypses which do not have an otherworldly journey (Type I) and those that do (Type II)."[51]

If we take a closer look at the paradigm, however, this "fundamental distinction" is not accounted for in the paradigm itself, since the *seme/noeme* #1.3. "other-worldly journey" has no equivalence in, e.g., a *seme/noeme* #1.2. "other-worldly revelation in this world" on the same level. On the contrary *semes/noemes* #1.1. "visual revelation" and #1.2. "auditory revelation" are said to be the corresponding *semes/noemes* to #1.3. "other-worldly journey," which obviously is incorrect, since both Apocalypses with or without other-worldly journeys have visual and auditory revelations. In the case of the Revelation of John we have both types represented in one and the same Apocalypse. Thus the

---

[47]Cf. below §4.2.1.3.4. #(b).

[48]Here I am in agreement with such scholars as Hartman 1982, §3.3. and §4.3. Sanders 1982, §7 and §8 and Tord Olsson 1982, §1.6.2. See, however, already Gunkel 1928, 62: "Who is speaking? Who are the listeners? What is the *mise en scène* at the time? What effect is aimed at?" (The German original is quoted in Hellholm 1980, 14). Cf. also the *elementa narrationis* (See Heinrich Lausberg 1973, 182f.): *quis, quid, ubi, quibus auxiliis, cur, quomodo, quando* (or in the words of the English rhetorician Thomas Wilson [16th century]: "Who, what, and where, by what help, and by whose: Why, how, and when, do many things disclose" [quoted from Heinrich Plett 1975, 12]). Cf. now also Collins 1982, 110.

[49]Adela Yarbro Collins 1979, 104f.; Francis T. Fallon 1979, 148; Harold W. Attridge 1979, 161-74.

[50]Theoretically, however, demands for such rankings have been advocated by others, e.g., Rolf Knierim 1973, 465; Hellholm 1980, 43f., 52, 70f.; Hempfer 1977, 14-21; Plett 1977a, 142f.: "In order to realize these (sc. rhetorical situations), a cultural typology of the rhetorical situations is needed" (ibid., note 38). Raible 1979a, 29: "In the range of the communication situation an establishment of types pertaining to the intentions of authors is important." Cf. further Hartman 1982, §3.4. and now also Collins 1982, 92-94.

[51]Collins 1979a, 13.

hierarchical arrangement, which is so commendable, must still be judged as imperfect and in need of improvement.

The need for a hierarchization of *semes/noemes* constituting generic concepts has to do with the hierarchic levels of abstraction made manifest in a *super-archisememe* like "mode of writing," and *archisememe* like "type of text,"[52] a *sememe* like "genre," a *subsememe* like "sub-genre" or the text itself like "The Apocalypse of John." This means: the more abstract the generic structure the more abstract, and the fewer, the *semes.*[53]

The simplified diagram below may serve as an example of such a heirarchy of generic concepts (*sememes*) for which a hierarchy of *semes/noemes* is required:[54]

One advantageous result of such a generic stemma of hierarchically arranged abstraction levels is the obvious fact that it provides the theoretical possibility for an author to generate and for recipients to recognize new and/or mixed genres and subgenres.[57] This is a possibility in those cases when *semes/noemes* from various *superarchi-* or *archisememes* in the process of ahistoric transformations are combined in historic *sememes* or *subsememes* or when *semes/noemes* from various *sememes* by means of historic transformation are combined in *subsememes* of various kinds.[58] Thus, the historic

---

[52]"Type" is here understood as an ahistoric constancy and not as a subgrouping of a genre; cf. the discussion in Hempfer 1973, 23f.

[53]Cf. above notes 4 and 14 and the discussion above §3.3.3.

[54]In the diagram below the following abbreviations are being used: Discourses = Discourses between the Risen Lord and His disciples; o.w. = other-worldly; Icar. = Icaromenippus.

[55]Concerning this genre see Vielhauer 1975, 680-92, esp. 690ff.; Helmut Koester 1971, 201ff.

[56]If in inductive investigations more texts of the mixed type appear, these would form another subgenre: "Apocalypses with *and* without other-worldly journey."

[57]Cf. above §1.3.

[58]See esp. Hempfer 1973, 27, 139-50 and cf. the discussion below §3.3.5.

development of new and/or mixed genres/subgenres can be accounted for and instead of a merely synchronic-static analysis we can also allow a diachronic-dynamic investigation of genres.[59]

3.3.5. The *fifth observation* has to do with "language in its fundamental function, in its *communicative function*" between sender and receiver.[60] This observation may simultaneously serve as a transition to the next section dealing with "Genres and Structures."

When designing the diagram above, I did not indicate by means of arrows in which direction it should be read. The reason for this is that it ought to function both ways as the following deliberations will try to show. The bipolarity between sender and receiver "correspond(s) exactly to the opposition between *semasiology* and *onomasiology*.[61] The hearer receives from his interlocutor forms, the meaning of which he must determine in order to understand them. Thus, the hearer's task is semasiological. The speaker, on the other hand, has to communicate mental objects (concepts). He must select designations[62] from the vocabulary placed at his disposal by his memory; he must link concepts to acoustic images, so converting them into *signifiants*; that is, his task is onomasiological."[63]

Now this differentiation between semasiology and onomasiology with regard to simple signs or concepts applies also to more complex signs and concepts, e.g., genres.

3.3.5.1. When writing an Apocalypse the author has at his disposal the structure of such a genre, i.e., the *sememe* or concept Apocalypse, and has to find the appropriate way of expressing his conceptual structure of this particular genre. This process of encoding, at least partly internalized,[64] occurs as transformation from various levels of abstractions or, in different terminology, from various deep structure levels[65] all the way to the single Apocalypse, or in other words, to the surface structure of an Apocalypse. This theory of transformation[66] provides a concept of structure, which is dynamic in so far as it allows diachrony in the development of generic structures[67] as well as superimposition of more than one generic structure at one level of abstraction upon a lower level in the hierarchy of conceptual abstraction as stated above.[68] This is the *onomasiological* approach, since it poses the problem from the viewpoint of the sender and his encoding of a given concept.

---

[59]See Hempfer 1973, 122ff., 131f., 140, 192-220; Eugenio Coseriu 1980, 134, 137f., 143; Raible 1979a, 8f., 23; Baldinger 1980, 277-309; Hellholm 1980, 64.

[60]Baldinger 1980, 132; cf. Hellholm 1980, 14-22; Hartman 1982, §3.3.

[61]Italics mine. Cf. above notes 32 and 33.

[62]"Signification proceeds from a *signifiant* (form) to a concept (mental object), and designation proceeds from a concept towards a *signifiant*" (Baldinger 1980, 110).

[63]Baldinger 1980, 132; cf. ibid., 110, 157-59, 211 and 306-8.

[64]Hempfer 1973, 126.

[65]Cf. Hempfer 1973, 141: "relative or absolute constancy of deep structures"; Ernst Ulrich Grosse 1979, 595: "On closer examination text as a totality almost always displays *several macro-structural dimensions* superimposing upon each other . . ."; Gülich/Raible 1977, 56ff.

[66]Cf. Jean Piaget 1970; Noam Chomsky 1965, 136: "Notice that in this view one major function of the transformational rules is to convert an abstract deep structure that expresses the content of a sentence into a fairly concrete surface structure that indicates the form."

[67]See above note 59.

[68]See above §3.3.4. and Hempfer 1973, 140-42.

3.3.5.2. When reading or listening to a text the receiver, who perceives forms already selected by the author, has to determine the structure of that text, in our case, not primarily of that particular text but rather its generic structure.[69] As will be shown in the next section a paradigmatic approach is hereby not sufficient; instead, a syntagmatic approach or a combination of both is necessary.

This process of decoding occurs as observations of the text as it stands, i.e. the generic surface structure, which is determined by a macro-structure of functional textsequences of various ranks.[70] This macro-structure must be recognizable on the surface level, since the receiver "obtains from the author neither a macro-structure nor a text deep structure but a text *tel quel*. Consequently there must exist signals--called delimitation markers--by means of which the reader or listener can arrive at such a macro-structure."[71] This is the *semasiological* approach, since it poses the problem from the viewpoint of the receiver and his decoding of a given macro-sign.

3.3.5.3. When analyzing or interpreting a text the scholar has to do justice to both aspects, the *onomasiological* as well as the *semasiological*. The role of the scholarly interpreter is thus different from that of the ordinary receiver.[72]

As indicated above "macro-structures always display an abstraction of the concrete text-form and are in all generative models established in the deep structure."[73] This is how a text is being analyzed from the point of view of the sender and the message he wants to communicate. "Notwithstanding, the existence of macro-structures must be recognizable on the text surface level" as we indicated above.[74] This is how a text is being analyzed from the point of view of the receiver in order for him to disclose the message communicated by the sender. Recognizing the appropriateness of these two approaches on the part of the interpreter, we must, however, not forget that in his analytical work the scholar is at first always put in the same position as the receiver: he has to work with the form that was given the text by the sender; he does not have immediate access to the deep structure of either a single text or a text representing a generic structure.

Therefore, the central phenomenon in recognizing the macro-structure is the delimitation of texts into *functional text-sequences* of different ranks.[75] The

---

[69]This is the reason, why we here must talk of *determining* the structure of texts.

[70]See below note 75; Gülich/Raible 1977, 56f.

[71]Gülich/Raible 1977a, 163; 1977, 54; William O. Hendricks 1973, 175: "Present day analysts . . . have not advanced beyond the work of Propp in that they continue to bypass what may be termed the 'textual surface' of narratives, i.e., the constituant sentences of the narratives as it is presented to the reader (hearer)." Teun A. van Dijk 1977, 149ff. and 1979, 519.

[72]See Hempfer's critique of E. D. Hirsch 1967 in Hempfer 1973, 251 note 387.

[73]Werner Kallmeyer/Reinhard Meyer-Hermann 1980, 254.

[74]Ibid.

[75]"Functional textsequences" denotes (a) *text delimitation* into textsequences of different ranks (syntactical macro-structure); (b) *semantic macro-structures* disclosing thematic text-sequences; (c) *pragmatic macro-structures,* i.e., *macro-speech acts* accomplishing a certain sequence of speech acts; cf. Hellholm 1980, 36, 60f., 76. See now also van Dijk 1979, 518ff.: "Semantic and pragmatic macro-structures are also systematically related. The semantic structure is the propositional content of the macro-speech act and, conversely, the macro-speech act is the pragmatic function of the theme or the topic of the text." Cf. also above note 42 and the quotation from Ermert 1979 below note 142.

delimitation is pursued by means of hierarchically ranked delimitation markers on the surface level.[76]

3.3.5.4. In conclusion it should be stated that there is a close connection between textual macro-structure and text-delimitation.[77] This connection reflects the two aspects of semasiology and onomasiology as described above: "Text-delimitation as a phenomenon on the surface level is on the one hand an *important way* to recognize macro-structures in the *process of reception and analysis*; on the other it is a *necessary result in realizing macro-structures* as well as in using principles of textuality *in the process of production*."[78] In this statement the three aspects or approaches of functional communication dealt with above have been taken into due consideration and it must be the starting point for an adequate approach to the whole question of genres and structures.

4. *Genres and Structures*

4.1. So far I have mainly discussed the problem of generic concepts from a paradigmatic point of view. In this lecture I have concentrated on paradigms,[79] since in genre analysis up until now this has been the prevailing method. It was my intent to present the paradigmatic approach, which works so well on simple models, to complex models in order to help us recognize its advantages but at the same time reveal its weaknesses. Its obvious strength is its simplicity, even if developed so as to try to take the relationship between the characteristic features and the grouping of these features and even the hierarchization of these characteristic *semes/noemes* into account. Its disadvantages are equally obvious: a paradigm has the tendency to remain taxonomic and static in spite of hierarchization, grouping into dimensions, and establishment of relationships between elements. In other words it has a tendency to be static instead of dynamic. I do not believe that we can do without paradigmatic analyses in genre investigations, but I also believe that a text-linguistic approach in its true meaning, i.e., as a syntagmatic approach on the level of macro-structures, is, if not an alternative, at least a necessary complement.

---

[76]See below §4.2.1.3.

[77]See below §4.2.

[78]Kallmeyer/Meyer-Hermann 1980, 251 (italics mine).

[79]So far this paper is a complement to my doctoral dissertation, in which I concentrated on syntagmatic aspects. When Collins 1981, 96 note 11 maintains that the approach in Hellholm 1980 "suffers from his failure to analyze the pattern of contents," he has not observed (a) that my approach was essentially syntagmatic and not paradigmatic, and (b) that in the analysis of the text of Hermas on pp. 140-89 the designation of content is in fact dealt with quite extensively and also utilized in the chart on pp. 136-39. The "content *pattern*" can, of course, only be dealt with after other Apocalypses have been analyzed syntagmatically too. This is the goal set for the first part of my second volume. My reasons for concentrating on a syntagmatic analysis was not--as Collins seems to believe--due to a dismissal of "any genre analysis which does not employ an explicit linguistic model" but to the very fact (a) that no syntagmatic analyses existed at the time (cf. now, however, even if only for a section of Daniel: Klaus Koch 1982, for 4 Ezra: Wolfgang Harnisch 1982, and for sections of Apc John: Lars Hartman 1980), and (b) that such analyses are *necessary* complements to the predominantly paradigmatic approaches in the field of scholarly research. The linguistic justification for syntagmatic analyses of various ranks is given above note 17.

4.1.1. When switching from the paradigmatic to the syntagmatic analysis, I will begin by listing six dimensions, noted by Raible and further developed by me, from which genre designations ought to derive their characteristics:[80]

(1)   *The communication situation between sender and receiver (text-pragmatic aspect)*

Here we have to distinguish between two levels of communication:[81]
(a)   *first,* the text*external* level between sender and receiver, between author and readers.
           Within this level of communication we encounter
    (aa)   the purpose of the author in writing his work, e.g., to persuade, to inform, to admonish, etc.;[82]
    (bb)   the description of the sender and his situation;
    (cc)   the description of the intended audience and its situation;
(b)   *second,* the text*internal* level between *dramatis personae* within the text itself.
           Within this level of communication we encounter
    (aa)   further textinternal levels of communication and their internal functions;
    (bb)   all levels of which have as their purpose to serve the course of the author in his communication with the readers on the external level.[83]

(2)   *The scope of objects (text-semantic aspect)*

Under this dimension we can subsume[84]
(a)   subject matters such as propositions, themes, motifs, etc.;
(b)   persons: individuals as well as types, e.g., this-worldly and other-worldly;
(c)   temporal and local constituents.

(3)   *The relationship to reality,* i.e., various possible worlds *(text-semantic aspect)*

Distinctions have to be made[85]
(a)   between this world and a fictive world of a novel for instance, and
(b)   between this-world and the other-world in religious literature
           (aa) with regard to the present as well as
           (bb) with regard to the future situation;[86]
(c)   between various this-worldly relations as under (b) above.

---

[80]Raible 1979a, 23-28. For a syntagmatic approach to the investigation of apocalyptic texts see Hellholm 1980, Hartman 1980, Lambrecht 1980, Harnisch 1982, and Koch 1982; cf. also above note 79.

[81]See Hellholm 1980, 43f., 77f., 83f. and the literature quoted there. Cf. now also Ermert 1979, 25, 27f., 32-41.

[82]See Hellholm 1980, 52-61, where the impact of modern speech-act theories upon genre analyses is discussed; Raible 1979a, 24. Cf. also above note 75.

[83]Hellholm 1980, 191.

[84]See, e.g., David Lewis 1972 and also Hellholm 1980, 88 note 67 for further references.

[85]See, e.g., van Dijk 1977, 29f.; cf. also Hellholm 1980, 87-91 with further references.

[86]Cf. Collins' temporal and spatial axis (1979a, 6ff.).

(4)   *Macro-syntagmatic structures of order (text-grammatical aspect* encompassing text- pragmatics, -semantics, and -syntactics)

Together with #1, #5 and #6 this is the eminently text-linguistic dimension,[87] since it encompasses

(a)   the macro-structures of the text, usually in combination with characteristics from other dimensions;

(b)   the relationship between macro-structures and micro-structures;[88]

(c)   the combination and/or overlapping of structures from other abstraction levels in the process of transformation.[89]

(5)   *The medium (text-grammatical aspect* encompassing text-pragmatics, -semantics, -syntactics)

Here we can distinguish between

(a)   the medium language in *combination with other media,* e.g., music, meter, rhythm, etc.;

(b)   the *carrier media* allowing the direct act of communication to be transferred into an indirect act, e.g., heavenly letters![90]

(c)   the *form media* allowing an act of communication to be transmitted in "forms," e.g., dialogues!

(6)   *The literary modes of presentation (text-grammatical aspect* encompassing text-pragmatics, -semantics, -syntactics)

In this dimension we have to distinguish between

(a)   various literary modes of representation such as narrative, dramatic, descriptive, instructive, and argumentative modes of presentation;[91]

(b)   the opposition between long and short ways of presentation, e.g., between "Gattung" and "Form."[92]

4.1.2. The advantage of this paradigm of syntagmatic dimensions, in spite of its more complex differentiation, is that it takes into account (1) the three major *paradigmatic* groups I mentioned earlier,[93] viz., content, form, and function and (2) the *syntagmatic* aspects, in forms of micro- as well as macro-syntagmatic structures.

Literally *textus/textura* means web and as such is two-dimensional. The first dimension of the web is made up by the warp; the second dimension is constituted by the woof.[94]

---

[87]It should explicitly be noted that textlinguistics has been defined as a *"transphrastic approach"* on the one hand and as a *"communication orientated approach"* on the other (so Kallmeyer/Meyer-Hermann 1973, 221ff.), thus taking *syntagmatic* and *functional* aspects into account; see further Hellholm 1980, 46ff.; Hartman 1980, 132, and now Coseriu 1981, 51ff. and 154ff.

[88]Cf. Raible 1979b, 69, 72. For my understanding of macro-structures see Hellholm 1980, 60f., 76 and above §3.3.5.; cf. also Gülich/Raible 1977, 53f.; van Dijk 1979, 519f. and below §4.1.2.

[89]See above §3.3.4. with note 58 and esp. §3.3.5.

[90]For the hierarchical levels of communication embedment see above note 81.

[91]See Raible 1979a, 27; Hempfer 1973, 128-36; Hellholm 1980, 64-66.

[92]Cf. above note 26.

[93]See above §3.3.3.

[94]See Roland Harweg 1979, 21, 148; idem, 1973, 69f.; Gülich/Raible 1977, 51-55; cf. also Hellholm 1980, 75f.

Transferred into *textus/textura* in the meaning of text, this also provides us at first with a two-dimensional aspect of texts:

(a)   the *first* dimension, the warp, constitutes the "chain-work" or liguistically stated, the *micro-syntagmatic* structure by means of syntagmatic substitution.[95] As in the weft this dimension is a necessary although not a sufficient condition for establishing texts;

(b)   the *second* dimension, the woof, is a necessary and in combination with the former, a sufficient condition for establishing texts.   This second dimension in its two different aspects allows specific patterns to stand out.   This is the *macro-syntagmatic* structure of texts and genres, operating not on the level of sentences but on the level of texts and textsequences.

The two aspects of the second dimension are:[96]

(1)   hierarchically arranged communication levels;
(2)   hierarchically arranged textsequences of different ranks.

Thus, we arrive in fact at a three-dimensional analysis of texts. These three dimensions will have to be used in a *macro-syntagmatic* approach to the analysis of generic structures:

The *first* step in the text analysis will be to divide the text into various functional communication levels, a possibility which is restricted to certain generic structures, primarily, but not exclusively, to narrative texts.

The *second* step will be to delimit the text into hierarchical and functional textsequences constituting--together with step one--the generic structures.[97]   Underlying these two *macro-structural* syntagmatic dimensions is the *micro-structural* syntagmatic dimension in form of syntagmatic substitution.[98]

As emphasized above more than once regarding paradigmatic analyses, now, regarding syntagmatic analysis, we likewise have to emphasize the importance of determining "interdependences and relationships between constituents of different dimensions" as the ones discussed above in paragraph 3.3.5.[99]   This becomes particularly important, when we enter the field of *macro-syntagmatic* analyses, since neither sentences nor textsequences of various degrees "have *per se* any function but only obtain their function from a superior totality, e.g., (with regard to tones) within a melody or, as far as texts are concerned, within a superior unity of meaning."[100]

---

[95]Harweg 1979, 21, 148; idem, 1978; Hellholm 1980, 30 with note 68.

[96]See esp. the analyses in Gülich/Raible 1975 and 1977a. Cf. also Hellholm 1980, 77f. and 78-189, and below §4.2.1.1., §4.2.1.2. regarding Hermas and §4.2.2.1., §4.2.2.2. regarding Apc John.

[97]See Gülich/Raible 1977, 53 and cf. Hellholm 1980, 75f. with further references. See also above note 75.

[98]Cf. Hempfer's distinction between *micro-structures* on the sentence level and *macro-structures* on the textlevel (1973, 144 and 179f.); so also Gülich/Raible 1977, 126f.; van Dijk 1977, 143; Franz von Kutschera 1975, 140; Hellholm 1980, 60f., 84f.; Grosse 1979, 609.

[99]Raible 1979a, 27.

[100]Raible 1979b, 69. Cf. Wilhelm von Humboldt 1836, 205: "Neither in concepts

4.2. The syntagmatic analysis of the functional macro-structures of genres[101] has to be
carried out by means of text-delimitations of generic texts as they are available to the
scholarly interpreter.[102] Thus, as indicated above, the analyst has to take the surface
structure of the text as his starting point in pursuing syntagmatic analyses in order to
arrive at the deep structure as conceived by the author.[103]

4.2.1. In my work on the Shepherd of Hermas I have utilized the syntagmatic method *in
extenso,* with special attention paid to the surface structure.

4.2.1.1. With regard to *communication levels* I arrived at a hierarchy of six levels of
communication:[104]

(1)	Level *one:* between author and addressees;
(2)	level *two:* between other-worldly mediators and the author as the human recipient;
(2a)	level *two-a:* between other-worldly mediators and the addressees;
(3)	level *three:* between a "Heavenly book" quoted in the text itself and the author;
(3a)	level *three-a:* between the "Heavenly book" and the addressees;
(4)	level *four:* between a quotation of an oath of the Supreme Divinity within the "Heavenly book" and the addressees.

This deep text-*pragmatic* embedment of the message from the other-world to this-world
recipients is the first most striking set of syntagmatic *semes/noemes* of the generic
concept "Apocalypse." All (sets of) syntagmatic *semes/noemes* constituting an Apocalypse are ranked in an abstraction hierarchy.

4.2.1.2. Regarding the *macro-structure* of the text as it emerges from the *text-
pragmatic-semantic-syntactic* delimitation of textsequences of different ranks, two
methodologically important observations are appropriate:

(a) the ranking of textsequences *per definitionem* leads not only to a sequential order
but also, and more importantly to the establishment of hierarchically and
functionally well-defined interrelationship between various textsequences, that is
to say, how textsequences on higher levels function within the next lower level in
rank all the way down to level $\emptyset$;[105]

(b) there is a necessity for establishing hierarchically defined delimitation markers of a
pragmatic, semantic, and syntactic nature, since in order to arrive at a delimitation
of texts into hierarchical textsequences there is a need for hierarchically defined
delimitation markers.[106] This task was undertaken in linguistics by Elizabeth

---

nor in language is anything isolated" (Quoted from Baldinger 1980, XVII); see further
Grosse 1976, 26; Gülich/Raible 1977, 53; Raible 1979a, 12f. note 17; Hempfer 1973, 140;
von Kutschera 1975, 130; Kallmeyer/Meyer-Hermann 1980, 242ff. With regard to
Apocalypses see esp. Stegemann 1982, §2.2.

[101]See above note 75.

[102]See above §3.3.5.2.; Gülich/Raible 1977, 54: "one can furthermore assume that
these textsequences which designate the macro-structure of a text, must be recognizable
directly on the surface of the text."

[103]See above §3.3.5.3.

[104]Hellholm 1980, 98.

[105]See above note 75.

[106]Cf. Gülich/Raible 1977, 54.

Gülich and Wolfgang Raible[107] as to descending analyses, by Klaus Heger[108] as to ascending analyses, and their efforts have been adapted and further developed by myself in my book on the Shepherd of Hermas for narrative texts, and in my essay on Romans 6 for argumentative texts.[109]

4.2.1.3. Here I can only give a brief summary of the most essential markers applying to narrative texts.[110]

4.2.1.3.1. *Delimitation markers on meta-level (pragmatic-semantic types).*

(1) *Meta-communicative clauses.*
These clauses function as signals for the beginning and ending of an act of communication, i.e., they make the linguistic communication situation the subject of a theme. These markers can be divided into two main groups one with an encoding (to say, to write), the other with a decoding (to hear, to read) function. Each of these can thematicize either oral or written acts of communication. The importance of these meta-communicative clauses lies mainly in the fact that they serve as signals for changes between various levels of communication and consequently among other things also signal out different dialogue phases and dialogue structures.

(2) *Substitution on meta level.*
Contrary to the syntagmatic substitutions on the *text-level* which link sentences on the micro-syntagmatic field together, the syntagmatic substitutions on the *meta-level* are manifestations (a) of various generic concepts such as "Narrative" (on the abstraction-level of "mode of writing"), "Revelatory writing" ("type of text"), "Apocalypse" ("genre"), "Apocalypse with other-worldly journey" ("subgenre") etc.,[111] and (b) of various textsequences of different ranks such as "vision," "letter," "scroll," etc.[112]

The substitution on meta-level functions in a two-fold but yet related way:

(a)   Precisely this type of substitution, through which a text or a textsequence is replaced by a meta-communicative part of a sentence, noun or verb, often plays a significant role on the surface level in delimiting the text into hierarchically arranged textsequences.[113]

(b)   In connection with the first function this type of substitution also "informs the receiver of the function of the text."[114] This function is particularly important, when the substitution is a manifestation of a generic concept such as "Gospel" or "Apocalypse," since a genre designation "rules the--nevertheless very many--possibilities of interpretation and curtails them: one laughs . . . at the death of an innocent man in a burlesque but one grieves therefore in a tragedy."[115] From a form-critical perspective the same function of literary genre designations has been acknowledged, e.g., by Hans Conzelmann and Andreas Lindemann: "If one reads a

---

[107]Gülich/Raible 1975; 1977a.

[108]Heger 1976; 1977.

[109]Hellholm 1980; 1983; cf. also above note 71.

[110]For further details see Hellholm 1980, 80-95.

[111]See above §3.3.4.

[112]The importance of redundance in the usage of "*substitution on meta-level*" is stressed by Grosse 1976, 143 note 4.

[113]Cf. esp. Gülich/Raible 1977, 44.

[114]Grosse 1976, 21; Hellholm 1980, 60, 86. This is the reason, why I talk about functional text-sequences, see above note 75; van Dijk 1977, 245; J. A. Austin 1975, 75.

[115]Raible 1979a, 15f. with reference to Wolf-Dieter Stempel 1971, 568.

miracle-story as a statement of facts, one inevitably fails to recognize its own intention, since such a miracle-story certainly is not drawn up as a statement of facts but constitute a literary product *sui generis.*[116] "This is the reason," says Wolfgang Raible, "why the genre as information about the essential gestalt characteristics of a text is eminently important for its interpretation."[117]

(3) Substitution on abstraction-level.
A middle position between substitutions on *text-level* and on *meta-level* is the substitution on *abstraction-level.* This type of *substituens* has a wider range of reference than the *substituendum* and frequently occurs in combination with verbs and prepositions indicating the end of a passage. The substitution on abstraction-level is often found in narrative writings as reductions of texts, textsequences, or even sentences in form of "abstract nouns," "pronouns and pronominal forms," certain "adverbs and conjunctions," and "verbs on abstraction-level."[118]   This type of substitution also serves the delimitation of texts into textsequences of different ranks although on a lower rank than the previous markers on the meta-level.

4.2.1.3.2. Delimitation-markers with direct textexternal analogon outside the meta-level (pragmatic-semantic types).

(1) Change in set of worlds.
As C. J. Fillmore has pointed out, "the discourse grammarians most important task is that of characterizing, on the basis of the linguistic material contained in the discourse under examination, the set of worlds in which the discourse could play a role, together with the set of possible worlds compatible with the message content of the discourse."[119]   Adhering to the principal of ontological neutrality[120] one can, by means of reduction, arrive at the following typologization in the classification of possible worlds:

Hellholm[121]		van Dijk[122]		Collins[123]	
(1)	this-world	(1)	[this world] ;	(1)	this-world of human recipients
	(a) actual world;		(a) "our actual world";		
	(b) fictive world;		(b) "a situation where the facts are different from the real or actual facts, but compatible with the postulates (laws, principles, etc.) of the actual world";		
(2)	other-world	´2)	"worlds with partly or fully different laws of nature, i.e., worlds which are increasingly *dissimilar* to our 'own' world."	(2)	other-world of a transcendant reality and super-natural mediators.

[116]Hans Conzelmann/Andreas Lindemann 1980, 5; cf. Bultmann 1963, 57.
[117]Raible 1979a, 15.
[118]See esp. Raible 1972, 150f., 194-203; further Hellholm 1980, 86f. with examples.
[119]Fillmore 1976, 88; cf. also Lewis 1972, 175, 213ff.
[120]See above note Ø.
[121]Hellholm 1980, 89.
[122]van Dijk 1977, 29f.
[123]Collins 1979a, 6ff.

Among the delimitation-markers of a primarily--although not exclusively[124]--semantic nature the "change in set of worlds" is the most important one, as can be seen from the important role it plays not only in text linguistic but also in form-critical apocalyptic research as the definition by Collins and the SBL-group reveals. The main difference, however, between this *seme/noeme* as used by Collins et alii on the one hand and the same *seme/noeme* used by Hellholm, Heger, and van Dijk on the other is that the former only used it paradigmatically while the latter used it *syntagmatically* as well, which according to our deliberations above is a distinct advantage.

(2) *Episode-markers etc.*
These demarcations are signals introducing (a) time and change of time and (b) localization and relocalization. Both of these can be divided into (aa) *absolute* episode-markers delimiting textsequences already established by preceding markers and (bb) *relative* episode markers delimiting textsequences already established by the absolute episode-markers.

(3) *Changes in the grouping of agents.*
This marker introduces changes in the main actors regardless of whether they are active (*agens*) or passive (*patiens*) agents. More important than changes of individual actors is the switch in groups of actors, which is in line with the above mentioned "change in set of possible worlds." Thus, the change in groups is a primary while the change in individuals is a secondary delimitating signal.

4.2.1.3.3.   *Delimitation-markers without direct textexternal analogon (semantic-syntactic types).*

(1) *Renominalization.*
This marker reintroduces an agent, who has been referred to by a pronoun, with a noun or his proper name. There seems to be a direct relationship between the change in the arrangement of actors and the renominalization, which is the reason why this marker often goes together with the previous one. This marker has only an *indirect* textexternal analogon as the "theory of mediated reference" discloses,[125] and is consequently of a semantic-syntactic character.

(2) *Sentence- and text-connectors: adverbs and conjunctions.*
These markers with no *analoga* in the textexternal field function *per se* only on higher grades, thus delimiting sentences and textsequences on the *micro-syntagmatic* level.[126] However, together with markers on lower levels these signals strengthen the delimiting function of the former.

4.2.1.3.4.   From the deliberations above on delimitation-markers three general conclusions can be drawn:
(a)   There is a direct proportionate correspondence between the inclusiveness[127] of the markers and their delimiting function: the more inclusive (pragmatic-semantic) markers distinguish *communication levels* and delimit *macro-syntagmatic* structures, while the less inclusive (syntactic) markers primarily delimit the *micro-syntagmatic* structures.[128]

---

[124]Cf. Siegfried J. Schmidt 1973, 238; Helmut Schnelle 1973, 237.
[125]Cf. already Bühler 1934, 385ff. esp. 390; in particular, however, Kallmeyer et alii 1977, 213-29; Hellholm 1980, 41, 94.
[126]Cf. Dressler 1973, 71.
[127]Cf. above §3.3.3. and §4.2.1.2. #(b).
[128]Cf. above §4.1.2.

(b)   As was the case with the grouping and hierarchizations of the paradigmatic
      semes/noemes,[129] so it is also with the syntagmatic delimitation markers: the
      grouping and hierarchization into pragmatic, semantic, and syntactic groups are
      derived *deductively* from the meta-theory applied,[130] while the specific markers
      (syntagmatic *semes/noemes*) within the groups are derived *inductively* from the
      texts themselves, thus providing a mediation between deductive and inductive
      methods.[131]

(c)   In order to delimit not only texts but also text-sequences in a hierarchical way,
      these markers are to be applied recursively on the various communication levels.

4.2.1.4. The delimitation of the Book of Visions in the Shepherd of Hermas on the macro-
structural level resulted in the following textsequential structure:[132]

(1)   The *first grade* of textsequences consists of two text parts: (a) the brief romance
      story followed by (b) the main visionary part;

(2)   The visionary part on the *second grade* of text-sequences is delimited into four
      visionary reports;

(3)   On the *third grade* each visionary report begins by a removal to a this-worldly place
      of revelation and is followed by the visionary account itself;

(4)   The visionary account on the *fourth grade* consists of a preparation to the vision in
      form of a prayer followed by the vision itself;

(5)   On the *fifth grade* each vision begins with an introduction followed by a dialogue
      between the other-worldly revealer or messenger and the human recipient *or* by
      listening to *or* copying a "Heavenly book/letter."

This hierarchical ranking of different textsequences in order arrive at the macro-
structure as conceived by the author is the second striking set of syntagmatic
semes/noemes[133] of the generic *sememe* (concept) "Apocalypse." I break off here since
my aim was only to show how the hierarchization of textsequences on the level of macro-
structures works when applied to a text belonging to the genre "Apocalypse."

4.2.2. Let me finally turn to the *Apocalypse of John* and see how the embedment in
communication levels and the hierarchical ranking of textsequences can be established
also in this text.

4.2.2.1. I will begin by discussing the syntagmatic *seme/noeme* that, alongside with the
change in worlds (from this-worldly to other-worldly), is the most striking macro-
syntagmatic feature of the generic concept "Apocalypse," viz., the *pragmatic embedment of communication levels.* According to the hierarchy of delimitation markers this
characteristic syntagmatic feature must be elaborated upon first. It is also appropriate
to begin our analysis with this *seme/noeme,* since it has to do in particular with the
problem of function and the relationship between function and content, i.e., between
pragmatics and semantics.

---

[129]See above §3.3.3.

[130]Cf. Hellholm 1980, 78f.

[131]See Hellholm 1980, 66 and 96. The deficit in Koch's (1982) otherwise very
helpful use of delimitation-markers on the surface level is precisely the lack of hierarchical grouping of these markers due to his insistence on primarily inductive investigations.

[132]See Hellholm 1980, 136-39, 190-96.

[133]For the first set of syntagmatic *semes/noemes* see above §4.2.1.1.

4.2.2.1.1. In analyzing the whole of the Apc of John, I have discovered many more and even much more complex levels of communication than I was able to establish for Hermas.

On this occasion I will merely list the most important ones and only those levels that serve as *meta-levels* for others.

(a) level *one*: between the author and the general christian audience (1:1-3 and 22:18-19);[134]

(b) level *two*: between the author and the more specified group of seven churches (1:4);

(c) level *three*: between other-worldly mediators and the author (Jesus himself in chaps. 1-3; angelic revealers/or Jesus Christ in the rest of the book);

(d) level *four*: between the "Heavenly scroll" and the author (6:1-22:5)

(e) level *five*: between the other-worldly mediators and the author within the "Heavenly scroll";

(f) level *six*: between God himself on the throne and the author within the "Heavenly scroll" with the command to the author to write down the words of the Supreme Divinity (21:5-8); (cf. in 1:19 Jesus' command to John: γράψον οὖν ἃ εἶδες καὶ ἃ εἰσὶν καὶ ἃ μέλλει γενέσθαι μετὰ ταῦτα and on the same level of communication Hermas 6:3: ἀλλὰ γνώρισον ταῦτα τὰ ῥήματα κτλ.).

4.2.2.1.2. Let us now take a closer look at the most embedded text, viz., the one in 21:5-8:

And he who sat upon the throne said: 'Behold, I make all things new.' Also he said: 'Write this, for these words are trustworthy and true.' And he said to me: 'It is done! I am the Alpha and the Omega, the beginning and the end. To the thirsty I will give water without price from the fountain of the water of life. He who conquers shall have this heritage and I will be his God and he shall be my son. But as for the cowardly, the faithless, the polluted, as for murderers, fornicators, sorcerers, idolaters, and all liars, their lot shall be in the lake that burns with fire and brimstone, which is the second death.[135]

From the point of view of pragmatics this is the text in Apc John with the most profound embedment:

(a) the words quoted in writing are God's own words;
(b) this statement of God is written down by the human recipient at the command of the Supreme Divinity himself;
(c) this textsequence is a part of the larger sequence called the "heavenly scroll";
(d) this scroll could only be opened by the lamb, Jesus Christ;
(e) the scroll and the breaking of its seals were shown to the author in a vision;
(f) the vision took place after a heavenly journey: vision within a journey;[136]
(g) this is written down in a text of a particular generic structure: an "Apocalypse";
(h) the concrete text is to be read to the congregation.

---

[134]See William Bousset 1906, 183 and 459.
[135]Translation from Yarbro Collins 1979a, 144.
[136]This phenomenon is to be compared to a "vision within a vision"; cf. James Brashler 1977, *passim,* esp. 135.

Even this *simplified* description of the embedment hierarchy is in my opinion very striking and from it *three* conclusions can be drawn:

(1)   the *first* conclusion has to do with *virtuality*. The parallel phenomenon in the *Shepherd of Hermas* and in the *Apc of John* other so called Apocalypses indicate that we have to do with a characteristic feature, which is not accidental and variant but on the contrary is constitutive and invariant; it is a *soeme/noeme*. This, however, does not mean that we should expect equally deep embedments of all texts of the generic concept "Apocalypse,"[137] but it does mean that some kind of hierarchic communication levels must be present;

(2)   the *second* conclusion has to do with *function*. In my book on Hermas I stated that there can be no doubt regarding the reason for the hierarchic embedment: it has to do with *authorization* of the message.[138] I am prepared to make the same claim now with regard to Apc John. This claim can furthermore be substantiated by three other circumstances:

   (a)   The self-definition of the Supreme Divinity on the throne: ἐγώ εἰμι τὸ ἄλφα καὶ τὸ ὦ, ἡ ἀρχὴ καὶ τὸ τέλος at the end of the heavenly scroll, functioning as an introduction to the quotation of his divine words (21:6).
   These words correspond to a similar self-designation at the beginning of Apc. John, viz., at the end of the epistolary prescript: ἐγώ εἰμι τὸ ἄλφα καὶ τὸ ὦ, λέγει κύριος ὁ θεός, ὁ ὢν καὶ ὁ ἦν καὶ ὁ ἐρχόμενος, ὁ παντοκράτωρ (1:8);

   (b)   the assurance by God himself that his words, which John is commanded to write down are πιστοὶ καὶ ἀληθινοί (21:5);

   (c)   the direct and programmatic statement of a hierarchic revelation embedment in the title 1:1-3: From *God*, to *Jesus Christ*, to an *angelic mediator*, to *John*, to the *readers*.[139]

   (d)   the letter-form as utilized by the author in 1:4 and 22:21.[140]

Here I am in agreement with Prof. Stegemann, when he claims that the *authorization* is the characteristic functional feature of Apocalypses.[141]

(3)   The *third* conclusion: there is a direct correspondence between the communication embedment on the *pragmatic* level and the content on the *semantic* level.

   (a)   In *Hermas the message is on the one hand* the promise (illocution) of the possibility of a second repentance for those who repent (proposition), and *on the other* a threat (illocution) of exclusion for those who abide in their sins (proposition). This is in fact the summary of the lengthy book by Hermas and it is a summary by God himself in an oath of his quoted in the "Heavenly writing."

---

[137]Cf. above §3.2.2. #(a) with note 36.

[138]Hellholm 1980, 191 with note 5.

[139]Cf. already Bousset 1906, 181: "The prophetic character of the book is emphasized with great energy (observe the *gradation of authorities*: God, Christ, the Angel, John) and it is commanded to the (ecclesiastical) lectors and to the audience" (italics mine). This passage has been analyzed along similar lines as I have pursued in this paper in Hartman 1980. See also Apc. 22:18-19 and for this passage cf. Bousset, ibid., 459f.; Hartman, ibid., 148.

[140]See Heinrich Kraft 1974, 28; Vielhauer 1975, 500.

[141]Stegemann 1982, §3.1.1.4.

(b)   In the *Apocalypse of John* the message is *on the one hand* the promise
        (illocution) to those who conquer that they shall live in unity with God in the
        new world of his (proposition), and *on the other hand* the threat (illocution)
        that the lot of the cowardly and unfaithful is ultimate separation from God
        described by the singular concept of a "second death" (proposition). This
        constitutes the summary of the Apocalypse of John from the lips of the
        Supreme Divinity on the throne.

        Thus, if *one function* in connection with summaries of the Supreme Divinity
        is *authorization* of the message, the *other function* can be defined as the
        promise of vindiction and redemption for the faithful and the *threat* of
        exclusion and death to the unfaithful.[142] Both functions are furthermore in
        each instance directly related to a positive and a negative proposition. We
        have to keep in mind, however, that these functions as well as propositions
        work on the level of *langue* or even *langage* and consequently must be fairly
        general and abstract, while the concrete exhortations and descriptions are
        given *in extenso* in the separate Apocalypses as single texts on the level of
        parole. This conclusion is in total harmony with my observation at the
        beginning of this lecture that texts are abbreviations of the reality and
        further more that summaries like the ones in Hermas 6 and Revelation 21
        certainly constitute further abbreviations omitting unnecessary details.

        Thus, *pragmatics* (i.e., communication embedment and illocutions) and
        semantics (i.e., positive and negative propositions) meet in both writings at
        the very center of the communication hierarchy.[143] This is obviously a
        virtual and invariant syntagmatic *seme/noeme* which together with other
        syntagmatic *semes/noemes* has to be taken seriously when syntagmatically
        defining the generic concept of Apocalypses and when interpreting single
        texts belonging to that genre.

4.2.2.2. I will conclude by outling in a preliminary way[144] the second set of syntagmatic
semes/noemes of the generic concept "Apocalypse," viz., the delimitation of its macro-
structure into hierarchically ranked textsequences.

4.2.2.2.1. When delimiting the text of Apc John the markers described above in §4.2.1.3.
will be utilized. The following abbreviations are being used in the analysis:

$1-n_{TS}$ = textsequences of different grades
$1-n_{TS}1-n$ = several textsequences of different grades;
MS = meta communicative sentences;
SM = substitution on meta-level;
SM(sur) = substitution on meta-level: surrogate;

---

[142]On the relationship between content and function, semantics and pragmatics
cf. Ermert 1979, 121 note 22: "The theme of a text must not be confused with its
function or with the intention of its producer, although there are connections between
the two. The latter designates the intended impact on account of the producer, the
former the subject matter of the text." Further see Kallmeyer et alii 1977, 99:
"Referential text-analysis--*text-semantic*--must not be confused with *text-interpretation*
. . . (which) also among other things implies a *pragmatic* analysis." Cf. also van Dijk
1979, 578ff. quoted above note 75.

[143]Taking the systematical relationship between semantic and pragmatic macro-
structures as described above note 75 into account, this is only what was to be expected.

[144]For a more definite textlinguistic analysis of Apc John and other apocalyptic
texts see the second volume of my studies in the Shepherd of Hermas, which is in
preparation.

SA = substitution on abstraction level;
CSW = change in set of worlds;
EM (a/r) loc./temp. = episodemarker (absolute/relative) local and temporal;
DP = dramatis personae: changes in (grouping of) agents;
RN = renominalization.

4.2.2.2.2. Text-delimitation of Apc John.

$^{\phi\phi}$TS   [ΑΠΟΚΑΛΥΨΙΣ ΙΩΑΝΝΟΥ]

$^{\phi}$TS   Prologue in form of a title: Apocalypse (1:1-3)

$\quad$ $^{\phi}$TS^1 Titulus proprius (1:1-2)

$\quad$ $^{\phi}$TS^2 Macarism (1:3)
^{1}TS^1 *Epistolary prescript* (1:4-8) [Form: epistolary address; DP: John-Seven
$\quad$ Churches]
$\quad$ ^{2}TS^{11} Address (1:4-5b)
$\quad$ ^{2}TS^{12} Doxology (1:5c-6)
$\quad$ ^{2}TS^{13} Motto in form of a prophetic saying (1:7)
$\quad$ ^{2}TS^{14} God's self-predication (1:8)
^{1}TS^2 *Visionary part:* "inner story" (1:9-22:5) [CSW: this-worldly → other-
$\quad$ worldly;   SM(sur): ἐγενόμην ἐν πνεύματι . . . ἤκουσα
$\quad$ . . . εἶδον;   EM(a) loc.: ἐν τῇ νήσῳ . . . Πάτμῳ;
$\quad$ temp.: ἐν τῇ κυριακῇ ἡμέρᾳ;RN: ἐγὼ ᾽Ιωάννης]

$\quad$ ^{2}TS^{21} *Revelation without other-worldly journey* (1:9-3:22)
$\qquad$ ^{3}TS^{211} Pneumatic enrapture at the place of revelation (1:9-10a)
$\qquad$ ^{4}TS^{2111} Situation report (1:9) [*DP*: John alone]
$\qquad\qquad$ ^{5}TS^{21111} Self-presentation (1:9a)
$\qquad\qquad$ ^{5}TS^{21112} Report regarding place of revelation (1:9b)
$\qquad$ ^{4}TS^{2112} Report on Pneumatic enrapture (1:10a) [*DP*: John-Pneuma]
$\qquad$ ^{3}TS^{212} Revelation of the message to the Seven Churches in Asia Minor
$\qquad$ (1:10b-3:20) [SM(sur): ἤκουσα . . . εἶδον; EM(a)temp.:
$\qquad$ ἐν τῇ κυριακῇ ἡμέρᾳ; DP: John-other-worldly revealers]
$\qquad$ ^{4}TS^{2121} Commissioning revelation of "one like a Son of Man" as an
$\qquad$ *introduction* to the copying of the seven-fold messages
$\qquad$ (1:10b-20) [DP: John-Son of Man]
$\qquad\qquad$ ^{5}TS^{21211} Auditory revelation (1:10b-11)
$\qquad\qquad$ ^{5}TS^{21212} Visionary revelation (1:12-20)
$\qquad$ ^{4}TS^{2122} The messages to the Seven Churches (2:1-3:22) [DP:
$\qquad$ Christ-John-Angels of the Churches-the Churches them-
$\qquad$ selves]
$\qquad\qquad$ ^{5}TS^{21221} To Ephesus (2:1-7)
$\qquad\qquad$ ^{5}TS^{21222} To Smyrna (2:8-11)
$\qquad\qquad$ ^{5}TS^{21223} To Pergamon (2:12-17)
$\qquad\qquad$ ^{5}TS^{21224} To Thyatira (2:18-29)
$\qquad\qquad$ ^{5}TS^{21225} To Sardis (3:1-6)
$\qquad\qquad$ ^{5}TS^{21226} To Philadelphia (3:7-13)
$\qquad\qquad$ ^{5}TS^{21227} To Laodicea (3:14-22)
$\quad$ ^{2}TS^{22} *Revelation with other-worldly journey* (4:1-22:5)   [SM(sur):
$\quad$ ἐγενόμην ἐν πνεύματι . . . εἶδον . . . ἰδού . . .
$\quad$ ἤκουσα; SA: μετὰ ταῦτα; EM(r) temp.: μετὰ ταῦτα; RN: ἡ
$\quad$ φωνὴ ἡ πρώτη ἣν ἤκουσα ὡς σάλπιγγος λαλούσης μετ᾽
$\quad$ ἐμοῦ;]

^{3}TS^{221} Pneumatic enrapture to a place of revelation (4:1-2a)

   ^{4}TS^{2211} Situation report in form of a vision with the purpose of producing change of revelatory location (4:1) [DP: John-ἡ φωνὴ ἡ πρώτη]

      ^{5}TS^{22111} Vision of the open door in heaven (4:1a)

      ^{5}TS^{22112} Audition of the command to a heavenly journey (4:1b)

   ^{4}TS^{2212} Report on Pneumatic enrapture (4:21) [DP: John-Pneuma]

^{3}TS^{222} Revelation of "that which is to come" (4:2b-22:5) [SM(sur): ἰδού . . . εἶδον; EM(r) loc.: ἐν τῷ οὐρανῷ; DP: John-Christ]

   ^{4}TS^{2221} Throne-room revelation as an *introduction* to the revelation of the "Heavenly Scroll" (4:2b-5:14) [DP: John-Christ]

      ^{5}TS^{22211} Vision of Supreme Divinity (4:2b-11)

      ^{5}TS^{22212} Vision of "Heavenly Scroll": written within and on the back, and sealed (5:1)

      ^{5}TS^{22213} Vision of angel in search of someone worthy of opening the scroll (5:2-5)

      ^{5}TS^{22214} Vision of the Lamb as the one worthy of opening the scroll (5:6-14)

   ^{4}TS^{2222} The revelation of the "Heavenly Scroll" (6:1-22:5) [DP: John-"Heavenly Scroll"]

      ^{5}TS^{22221} The summary revelation as the *scriptura exterior* (ἔξωθεν: 5:1) (6:1-7:17) [SM: numbering of the successive seals; SM(sur): καὶ εἶδον; EM(r) temp.: ὅτε; DP: Christ-revealer; RN: τὸ ἀρνίον]

         ^{6}TS^{222211} Vision of the first six seals pertaining to the macro-cosmic events (6:1-17)

            ^{7}TS^{2222111} First seal (6:1-2)

            ^{7}TS^{2222112} Second seal (6:3-4)

            ^{7}TS^{2222113} Third seal (6:5-6)

            ^{7}TS^{2222114} Fourth seal (6:7-8)

            ^{7}TS^{2222115} Fifth seal (6:9-11)

            ^{7}TS^{2222116} Sixth seal (6:12-17)

         ^{6}TS^{222212} Supplementary vision in form of an *intercalation* pertaining to the micro-cosmic situation of the church (7:1-14) [SA: μετὰ ταῦτα; EM(r) loc.: μετὰ ταῦτα; DP: τέσσαρες ἄγγελοι]

            ^{7}TS^{2222121} Sealing of the saints on earth (7:1-8)

            ^{7}TS^{2222122} Multitude worshipping God in heaven (7:9-14)

      ^{5}TS^{22222} The revelation as the *scriptura interior* (ἔσωθεν: 5:1) (8:1-22:5) [SM: numbering of the last seal; EM(r) loc. + temp.: ἐγένετο σιγὴ ἐν τῷ οὐρανῷ ὡς ἡμιώριον; DP: John--ἑπτὰ ἄγγελοι . . . n.b. not the Lamb!]

         ^{6}TS^{222221} Vision of the first six trumpets (8:1-11:14)

            ^{7}TS^{2222211} Introduction (8:1-5)

               ^{8}TS^{22222111} Opening of seventh seal (8:1) [DP: John-the Lamb]

               ^{8}TS^{22222112} Seven angels with seven trumpets (8:2) [DP: John - ἄλλος ἄγγελος]

8_{TS}22222113   Preparation in throne room for trumpet sounding (8:3-5) [DP: John - ἄλλος ἄγγελος]

7_{TS}2222212   Sounding of first six trumpets with first woe pertaining to macro-cosmic events (8:6-9:21) [EM (r) temp.: ἡτοίμασεν; DP: see RN; RN: οἱ ἑπτὰ ἄγγελοι . . .]

8_{TS}22222121   Preparation to sounding the trumpets (8:6)
8_{TS}22222122   First trumpet (8:7)
8_{TS}22222123   Second trumpet (8:8)
8_{TS}22222124   Third trumpet (8:10)
8_{TS}22222125   Fourth trumpet (8:12)
8_{TS}22222126   *Eagle's woe-cry* (8:13)
8_{TS}22222127   Fifth trumpet (9:1-11)
8_{TS}22222128   Passing of *first woe* (9:12)
8_{TS}22222129   Sixth trumpet (9:13-21)

6_{TS}222222   Supplementary vision in form of an intercalation: the "Little Scroll" pertaining to the micro-cosmic situation (10:1-11:14) [SM(sur): καὶ εἶδον;   DP: ἄλλος ἄγγελος ἰσχυρός]

7_{TS}2222221   Introductory preparation for the revelation of the "Little Scroll" (10:1-11)
7_{TS}2222222   Content of the "Little Scroll" pertaining to the micro-cosmic situation (11:1-13) [MS: δεῖ σε πάλιν προφητεῦσαι . . .   (10:11)]
7_{TS}2222223   The passing of the *second woe* and the prediction of *third woe* (11:16)

6_{TS}222223   Vision of the seven bowls: first part: (11:15-22:6) [SM; numbering of last trumpet; DP: φωναὶ μεγάλαι ἐν τῷ οὐρανῷ; ἄγγελοι ἑπτα ἔχοντες πληγὰς ἑπτὰ τὰς ἐσχάτας]

7_{TS}2222231   Introduction: first part (11:15-19)
8_{TS}22222311   Sounding of seventh trumpet (11:15a) [DP: John-seventh angel]
8_{TS}22222312   Preparation in the throne room for the emptying of the seven bowls (11:15b-19)   [DP: John - φωναὶ μεγάλαι]

6_{TS}222224   Supplementary vision in form of an *intercalation pertaining to the micro-cosmic situation of the church (12:1-14:20)* [SM: σημεῖον μέγα; EM(r) loc.: ἐν τῷ οὐρανῷ; DP: John - γυνή]
7_{TS}2222241   Vision of the woman and the Dragon (12:1-18)[DP: John - δράκων]

$7_{TS}2222242$ Vision of the beasts from the sea and from
the earth (13:1-18) [DP: John - θηρία]

$7_{TS}2222243$ Vision of the Lamb on Mount Zion (14:1-
5) [DP: John - τὸ ἀρνίον]

$7_{TS}2222244$ Vision of the three angels (14:6-13) [DP:
John-three angels]

$7_{TS}2222245$ Vision of the one like a Son of Man seated
on a cloud (14:14-20) [DP: John-Son of
Man]

$6_{TS}222225$ Vision of the seven bowls: second part
pertaining to macro-cosmic events (15:1-
16:21) [SM: εἶδον ἄλλο σημεῖον; EM(r)
loc.: ἐν τῷ οὐρανῷ; DP: John - ἄγγελοι
ἑπτὰ ἔχοντες πληγὰς ἑπτὰ τὰς ἐσχα-
τας . . .]

$7_{TS}2222251$ Introduction: second part (15:-1-15)

$7_{TS}2222252$ Emptying of the seven bowls of wrath
(16:1-16) [DP: John - φωνὴ μεγάλη
ἐκ τοῦ ναοῦ - ἑπτὰ ἄγγελοι]

$8_{TS}22222521$ Command to pour out the bowls on
the earth (16:1)

$8_{TS}22222522$ First bowl (16:2)

$8_{TS}22222523$ Second bowl (16:3)

$8_{TS}22222524$ Third bowl (16:4-7)

$8_{TS}22222525$ Fourth bowl (16:8-9)

$8_{TS}22222526$ Fifth bowl (16:10-11)

$8_{TS}22222527$ Sixth bowl (16:12-16)

$8_{TS}22222528$ Seventh bowl (16:17-21)

$6_{TS}222226$ Supplementary visions in form of *addendum*
pertaining both to micro-cosmic situation and
to macro-cosmic events (17:1-22:6) [SM:
δείξω σοι . . . καὶ εἶδον . . . ;
Em(r) loc. + temp.: καὶ ἦλθεν . . . ; DP:
εἷς ἐκ τῶν ἑπτὰ ἀγγέλων . . .]

$7_{TS}2222261$ Visions pertaining to the *micro-cosmic*
situation of the church (17:1-19:10) [DP:
John-this-worldly churches]

$8_{TS}22222611$ The judgment over Babylon by an
angelus interpres (17:1-18)

$9_{TS}222226111$ The vision (17:1-6)

$9_{TS}222226112$ The interpretation (17:7-18)

$8_{TS}22222612$ The Fall of Babylon (18:1-24)

$8_{TS}22222613$ Celebration in Heaven (19:1-10)

$7_{TS}2222262$ Visions pertaining to the *macro-cosmic*
events (19:11-22:5) [DP: John-godly +
anti-godly powers]

$8_{TS}22222621$ The final judgment (19:11-20:15)
[DP: John-Christ-Satan]

$9_{TS}222226211$ The victory of the equestrian
on the white horse (19:11-21)

$9_{TS}222226212$ The final victory over the
Dragon-Satan (20:1-10)

^{9}TS222226213   The Book of Life and the final
                      judgment (20:11-15)

^{8}TS22222622   The new creation (21:1-22:5) [DP:
                      John-New Heaven and Earth]

^{9}TS222226221   New Heaven and New Earth
                      (21:1-8)

^{9}TS222226222   New Jerusalem revealed by an
                      angeles interpres (21:9-22:5)

^{1}TS^{3} Epilogue in form of a visionary authentication (22:6-20) [SA: οὗτοι οἱ
         λόγοι . . . οἱ λόγοι τῆς προφητείας τοῦ βιβλίου τούτου
         etc. throughout the epilogue;   EM(r) temp.: καὶ ὅτε ἤκουσα καὶ
         ἔβλεψα; DP: John - Christ]

^{2}TS^{31} Attestation of the book and its motto on Christ's part (22:6)

^{2}TS^{32} Verification of the seer in an epiphany (22:8-9)   [RN:
         κἀγὼ 'Ιωάννης]

^{2}TS^{33} Paraenesis with citation of the motto on Christ's part (22:10-15)
         [DP: Christ]

^{2}TS^{34} Christ's statement of the revelatory transmission (22:16) [RN: ἐγὼ
         'Ιησοῦς]

^{2}TS^{35} Prophetic pneumatic saying with reference to the audience (22:17)
         [DP: τὸ πνεῦμα καὶ ἡ νύμφη etc.]

^{2}TS^{36} Canonization formula on Christ's part (22:18-19) [DP: Christ-the
         audience]

^{2}TS^{37} Christ's final citation of the motto with a prophetic cultic response
         (22:20) [DP: Christ - Church]

^{1}TS^{4} Epistolary postscript (22:21) [DP: John-The Churches]

4.2.2.2.3. This attempt at a delimitation of Apc John on the macro-structural level
resulted in the following textsequential structure:

(1)   The textsequence on the *nil grade* consists of the prologue functioning as a title[145]
      and is consequently meta-narrative in character.[146]
(2)   The *first grade* of textsequences consists of four text parts: (a) the epistolary
      prescript;[147] (b) the main revelatory part;[148] (c) the epilogue in form of a visionary
      authentication by Christ;[149] (d) the brief epistolary postscript.[150]
(3)   The visionary part is on the *second grade* divided into two major revelatory
      events:[151] (a) the revelation without an other-worldly journey and (b) with an
      other-worldly journey.[152]
(4)   On the *third grade* each visionary report (a) begins by a pneumatic enrapture on or
      to the place of revelation and (b) is followed by the visionary account itself.

---

^{145}See above §4.2.1.3.1. #(2) (b).

^{146}Cf. Hartman 1980, 132-34.

^{147}See above note 140.

^{148}So also Hartman 1980, 140f.; Ferdinand Hahn 1979, 147f.; Lambrecht 1980, 78.

^{149}With regard to 22:6 see Bousset 1906, 455; Günther Bornkamm 1959, 220; Ernst
Lohmeyer 1953, 177; August Strobel 1978, 179; otherwise Kraft 1974, 277; Hartman 1980,
145; Prigent 1981, 351. With regard to 22:18f. see Strobel 1978, 179; Moe 1965, ad loc.;
Hartman 1980, 148; otherwise Bousset 1906, 459; Lohmeyer 1953, 181; Kraft 1974, 281;
Prigent 1981, 360.

^{150}Cf. esp. Kraft 1974, 282.

^{151}Cf. Hahn 1979, 148f.; Lambrecht 1980, 79f.

^{152}Only at the beginning of each major section do we find the SM(sur): "I was in
the Spirit," which is a clear indication of the two-fold structure of the visionary part.

(5)   The visionary accounts on the *fourth grade* consist of (a) introductory revelation reports[153] ("Commissionary revelation" and "Throne-room revelation") followed by (b) the messages in written form (command to write to the seven churches; the visions contained in the Heavenly Scroll[154]).

(6)   On the *sixth grade* we encounter (a) the separate messages to the seven churches on the one hand and (b) the summary revelation as the *scriptura exterior* and the main revelation as the *scriptura interior* on the other.[155]

(7)   The most striking feature on *grade six* is the appearance of "Supplementary visions" in form of either *intercalations* within or an *addendum* to the seven-visions of seals, trumpets and bowls.[156] This leads to the openendedness of the first two seven-rows.[157] This compositional feature becomes all the more interesting when one recognizes that while the seven-visions are pertaining to macro-cosmic events the supplementary visions being *intercalations* pertain to the micro-cosmic situation of primarily the Church and the supplementary vision being an *addendum* combines macro-cosmic events with micro-cosmic situations.[158] The micro-cosmic situation is evidently the major concern of the author and the verification of these supplementary visions lies in the macro-cosmic events.   The interrelationship between macro-cosmic and micro-cosmic events is, furthermore, typical of apocalypticism in general and goes as far back as to the main features of Iranian apocalypticism.[159]

4.2.2.2.4. The preliminary analysis of the Apc John given above allows us to draw three conclusions:

(1)   The *first conclusion* has again to do with *virtuality*.   The macro-syntagmatic structure of Apc John is indeed very similar to the macro-structure of Hermas, which leads me to believe that we have to do with a characteristic feature, which is invariant and thus possessing the status of a *seme/noeme*. This, of course, does not mean that the macro-structure needs to be identical in all texts belonging to the generic concept (*sememe*) "Apocalypse," but it means that the macro-structure of "Apocalypses" has to be similar in all texts defined as "Apocalypses."[160]

(2)   The *second conclusion* has to do with the *interrelationship* of textsequences on different levels:
   (a)   When delimiting texts into textsequences one is looking for markers that separate one section or unit from another which is a necessary and legitimate task;
   (b)   By delimiting texts into textsequences of different ranks, however, the various text-units do not stand apart from and are not unrelated to each other, but are in fact linked to each other and only so is it possible to discover their interrelationship and to recognize their syntagmatic function in the overall structure of the text being analyzed;

(3)   The *third conclusion* has to do with *coherence* and in particular with the relationship between syntactic, semantic, and pragmatic types of coherence.[161] A text

---

[153]Cf. Vielhauer 1975, 497f.

[154]See esp. Bornkamm 1959; cf. now also Strobel 1978, 178.

[155]See above note 154 and further with regard to the scroll Yigael Yadin 1971, 222-34; Elisabeth Koffmahn 1968, esp. 10-30.

[156]See esp. Lambrecht 1980, 95-99.

[157]Lambrecht 1980, 87.

[158]See Vielhauer 1975, 505; Lambrecht 1980, 99.

[159]See Geo Widengren 1982, *passim*, esp. the conclusion in §8.

[160]See above §3.2.2. #(a) with note 36.

[161]See Hellholm 1980, 29-31, 37-42, 46-52.

lacking syntactic and even semantic coherence can from a pragmatic perspective possess a high density of coherence. The syntactic and semantic coherence of Apc John seems in many cases to be lacking and can probably only be fully explained by means of *diachronic* analyses and yet one has to admit that precisely where the semantic coherence seems to be missing, i.e., where we encounter the intercalations within and the addition to different rows of seven visions, there is a high degree of pragmatic coherence.[162]
This phenomenon is also typical of the Shepherd of Hermas, which indicates that we are dealing with an invariant and virtual syntagmatic *seme/noeme*, which together with other *semes/noemes* ought to be subject to serious investigations when trying to define the generic concept of an "Apocalypse" syntagmatically as well as when interpreting single texts belonging to that genre.

Bibliography

Allwood et alii (Allwood, J./ Andersson, L. G./ Dahl, Ö.)
    1977   *Logic in Linguistics* (Cambridge Textbooks in Linguistics) Cambridge 1977.

Althaus et alii (Althaus, H. P./Henne, H./Wiegand, H. E., eds.)
    1973   *Lexikon der Germanistischen Linguistik,* Tübingen 1973.

Althaus et alii (Althaus, H. P./Henne, H./Wiegand, H. E., eds.)
    1980   *Lexikon der Germanistischen Linguistik,* 2nd rev. and enlarged ed., Tübingen 1980.

Attridge, H. W.
    1979   "Greek and Latin Apocalypses," in Collins (ed.) 1979, 159-86.

Austin, J. L.
    1975   *How to do Things with Words,* 2nd ed., edited by Urmson, J. O. and Sbisà, M., Cambridge, MA 1975.

Baldinger, K.
    1980   *Semantic Theory.* Towards a Modern Semantics, Oxford/New York 1980.

Beck, G.
    1980   *Sprechakte und Sprachfunktionen.* Untersuchungen zur Handlungsstruktur der Sprache und ihren Grenzen (Reihe Germanistische Linguistik 27) Tübingen 1980.

Bornkamm, G.
    1959   "Die Komposition der apokalyptischen Visionen in der Offenbarung Johannis," in: idem, *Studien zu Antike und Urchristentum.* Gesammelte Aufsätze, Vol. 2 (BEvT 28) Munich 1959, 204-22.

Bousset, W.
    1906   *Die Offenbarung des Johannis* (MeyerK 16) Göttingen 1906 (Reprint 1966).

---

[162]See above §4.2.2.2.3. #(7).

Brashler, J.
1977   *The Coptic Apocalypse of Peter: A Genre Analysis and Interpretation*, Ph.D. Diss., Claremont 1977.

Bühler, K.
1934   *Sprachtheorie*. Die Darstellungfunktion der Sprache (Ullstein 3392) Frankfurt am Main etc., 1978 (Reprint of the 2nd unaltered edition 1965 = 1st edition 1934).

Bultmann, R.
1928   "Evangelien, gattungsgeschichtlich (formgeschichtlich)," *RGG*[2] Vol. 2, Tübingen 1928, 418-22.

Bultmann, R.
1963   *The History of the Synoptic Tradition*. Oxford/New York 1963.

Carmignac, J.
1979   "Qu'est-ce que l'Apocalyptique? Son emploi à Qumrân," *RevQ* 10 (1979) 3-33.

Carmignac, J.
1982   "Description du phénomène de l'Apocalyptique dans l'Ancien Testament," in Hellholm (ed.) 1982.

Chomski, N.
1965   *Aspects of the Theory of Syntax*. Cambridge, MA 1965.

Collins, J. J. (ed.)
1979   *Apocalypse: The Morphology of a Genre*. (*Semeia* 14), Missoula, MT 1979.

Collins, J. J.
1979a   "Introduction: Towards a Morphology of a Genre," in: idem (ed.) 1979, 1-20.

Collins, J. J.
1979b   "The Jewish Apocalypses," in idem (ed.) 1979, 21-59.

Collins, J. J.
1981   "Apocalyptic Genre and Mythic Allusions in Daniel," *JSOT* 21 (1981) 83-100.

Collins, J. J.
1982   "The Apocalyptic Technique: Setting and Function in the Book of Watchers," *CBQ* 4 (1982) 91-111.

Conzelmann, H./Lindemann, A.
1980   *Arbeitsbuch zum Neuen Testament* (Uni-Taschenbücher 52), 5th rev. ed., Tübingen 1980.

Coseriu, E.
1980   "Vom Primat der Geschichte," *Sprachwissenschaft* 5 (1980) 125-45.

Coseriu, E.
1981   *Textlinguistik.* Eine Einführung   (Tübinger Beiträge zur
               Linguistik 109) Tübingen 1981.

Davidson, D./Harman, G. (eds.)
1972   *Semantics of Natural Language.* (Synthese Library 40)
               Dordrecht/Boston 1972.

van Dijk, T. A./Petöfi, J. S. (eds.)
1977   *Grammars and Descriptions* (Research in Text Theory/
               Untersuchungen in Texttheorie 1), Berlin/New York 1977.

van Dijk, T. A.
1977   *Text and Context.* Explorations in the Semantics and
               Pragmatics of Discourse (Longman Linguistics Library 21)
               London/New York 1977.

van Dijk, T. A.
1979   "New Developments and Problems in Textlinguistics," in:
               Petöfi (ed.) 1979b, 509-23.

Dressler,W.
1973   *Einführung in die Textlinguistik* (Konzepte der Sprach- und
               Literaturwissenschaft 13) 2nd ed. Tübingen 1973.

Dressler, W. (ed.)
1978   *Current Trends in Textlinguistics* (Research in Text Theory/
               Untersuchungen in Texttheorie 2) Berlin/New York 1978.

Ermert, K.
1979   *Briefsorten.* Untersuchungen zu Theorie und Empirie der
               Textklassifikation (Reihe Germanistische Linguistik 20)
               Tübingen 1979.

Fallon, F. T.
1979   "The Gnostic Apocalypses," in: Collins (ed.) 1979, 123-54.

Fillmore, Ch. J.
1976   "Pragmatics and the Description of Discourse," in: Schmidt
               (ed.) 1976, 83-104.

Grosse, E. U.
1976   *Text und Kommunikation.* Eine linguistische Einführung in die
               Funktionen der Texte, Stuttgart 1976.

Grosse, E. U.
1979   "Von der Satzgrammatik zum Erzähltextmodell. Linguistische
               Grundlagen und Differenzen bei Greimas und Bremond," in:
               Petöfi (ed.) 1979b, 595-617.

Gülich, E./Raible, W.
1975   "Textsorten-Probleme," in: Moser (ed.) 1975, 144-97.

Gülich, E./Raible, W.
1977   *Linguistische Textmodelle.* Grundlagen und Möglichkeiten (Uni-
                       Taschenbücher 130) Munich 1977.

Gülich, E./Raible, W.
1977a   "Ueberlegungen zu einer makrostrukturellen Textanalyse:
                       J. Thurber, The Lover and His Lass," in: van Dijk/Petöfi (eds.)
                       1977, 132-75.

Gunkel, H.
1924   "Jesaia 33, eine prophetische Liturgie. Ein Vortrag," in: *ZAW*
                       42 (1924) 177-208.

Gunkel, H.
1925   "Letter from Hermann Gunkel to Adolf Jülicher from
                       8 September 1925," in: Rollmann 1981, 281-86.

Gunkel, H.
1928   "Fundamental Problems of Hebrew Literary History," in: idem,
                       What Remains of the Old Testament and Other Essays,
                       London/New York 1928, 57-78.

Hahn, F.
1979   "Zum Aufbau der Johannesoffenbarung," in: *Kirche und Bibel.
                       Festgabe für Bischof Eduard Schick,* Paderborn 1979, 145-54.

Hanson, P. D.
1963   "Jewish Apocalyptic Against its Near Eastern Environment," in
                       RB 78 (1963) 31-58.

Harnisch, W.
1982   "Der Prophet als Widerpart und Zeuge der Offenbarung.
                       Erwägungen zur Interdependenz von Form und Sache im IV.
                       Buch Esra," in: Hellholm (ed.) 1982.

Hartman, L.
1980   "Form and Message. A Preliminary Discussion of 'Partial
                       Texts' in Rev 1-3 and 22, 6ff.," in: Lambrecht (ed.) 1980, 129-
                       49.

Hartman, L.
1982   "Survey of the Problem of Apocalyptic Genre," in: Hellholm
                       1982.

Hayes, J. H.
1980   *An Introduction to Old Testament Study,* 2nd. ed., Nashville
                       1980.

Harweg, R.
1973   "Text Grammar and Literary Texts: Remarks on a Gram-
                       matical Science of Literature," in: *Poetics* 9 (1973) 65-91.

Harweg, R.
    1978   "Substitutional Textlinguistics," in: Dressler (ed.) 1978, 247-
                    60.

Harweg, R.
    1979   *Pronomina und Textkonstitution* (Beihefte zu Poetica 2) 2nd
                    rev. and enlarged ed., Munich 1979.

Heger, K.
    1976   *Monem, Wort, Satz und Text* (Konzepte der Sprache- und
                    Literaturwissenschaft 8), 2nd enlarged ed., Tübingen 1976.

Heger, K.
    1977   "Sigmenränge und Textanalyse," in: van Dijk/Petöfi (eds.)
                    1977, 260-313.

Heger, K.
    1979   "Text und Textlinguistik," in: Petöfi (ed.) 1979a, 49-62.

Heger, K.
    1979a   "Ungenauigkeiten in der angeblichen Ungenauigkeit
                    sprachlicher Zeichen," in: *Festschrift Kurt Baldinger zum 60.
                    Geburtstag 17. Nov. 1979,* edited by Höfler, M./Vernay,
                    H./Wolf, L., Vol. I, Tübingen 1979, 22-37.

Hellholm, D.
    1980   *Das Visionen buch des Hermas als Apokalypse.* Form-
                    geschichtliche und texttheoretische Studien zu einer literar-
                    ischen Gattung. Vol. I: Methodologische Vorüberlegungen und
                    makrostrukturelle Textanalyse (*ConNT* 13:1) Lund 1980.

Hellholm, D. (ed.)
    1982   *Apocalypticism in the Mediterranean World and the Near
                    East.* Proceedings of the International Colloquium on
                    Apocalypticism, Uppsala August 12-17, 1979, Tübingen 1982.

Hellholm, D.
    1983   "Paul's Argumentation in Romans 6." An essay to be published
                    in 1983. In expanded form this essay will be included in my
                    book: *Paul's Argumentation in Romans 5-8,* which is in
                    preparation.

Hempfer, K.
    1973   *Gattungstheorie.* Information und Synthese (Uni-Taschenbücher
                    133) Munich 1973.

Hempfer, K.
    1977   "Zur pragmatischen Fundierung der Texttypologie," in: Hinck
                    (ed.) 1977, 1-26.

Hendricks, W. O.
    1973   "Methodology of Narrative Structural Analysis," in: idem,
                    Essays on Semiolinguistics and Verbal Art (Approaches to
                    Semiotics 37) The Hague/Paris 1973, 175-95.

Hinck, W. (ed.)
1977   *Textsortenlehre-Gattungsgeschichte* (medium literatur 4)
                   Heidelberg 1977.

Hirsch, E. D.
1967   *Validity in Interpretation,* New Haven 1967.

von Humboldt, W.
1836   *Ueber die Verschiedenheit des menschlichen Sprachbaues und
                   ihren Einfluss auf die geistige Entwicklung des Menschen-
                   geschlechts,* Berlin 1836.

Husserl, E.
1970   "Zur Logik der Zeichen (Semiotik)," in: idem, *Philosophie der
                   Arithmetik.* Logische und psychologische Untersuchungen. Mit
                   ergänzenden Texten (1890-1901) (Gesammelte Werke, Vol. 12)
                   edited by Lothar Eley, The Hague 1970, 340-73.

Kallmeyer et al. (Kallmeyer, W./Klein, W./Meyer-Hermann, R./Netzer, K./Siebert, H. J.)
1977   *Lektürekolleg zur Textlinguistik.* Band 1: Einführung (Fischer
                   Athenäum Taschenbücher 2050) 2nd ed., Kronberg 1977.

Kallmeyer, W./Meyer-Hermann, R.
1973   "Textlinguistik," in: Althaus et alii (eds.) 1973, 221-31.

Kallmeyer, W./Meyer-Hermann, R.
1980   "Textlinguistik," in: Althaus et alii (eds.) 1980, 242-58.

Knierim, R.
1973   "Old Testament Form Criticism Reconsidered," in: *Int* 27
                   (1973) 435-67.

Koester, H.
1971   "One Jesus and Four Primitive Gospels," in: Robinson, J. M./
                   Koester, H.: *Trajectories Through Early Christianity,* Phila-
                   delphia 1971, 158-204.

Koch, K.
1972   *The Rediscovery of Apocalyptic* (SBT 22) London 1972.

Koch, K.
1982   "Vom profetischen zum apokalyptischen Visionsbericht," in:
                   Hellholm (ed.) 1982.

Koffmahn, E.
1968   *Die Doppelurkunde aus der Wüste Juda* (STDJ 5) Leiden 1968.

Kraft, H.
1974   *Die Offenbarung Johannes* (HNT 16a) Tübingen 1974.

von Kutschera, F.
1975   *Philosophy of Language* (Synthese Library 71) Dordrecht/
                   Boston 1975.

Lambrecht, J. (ed.)
        1980   *L'Apocalypse johannique et l'Apocalyptique dans le Nouveau
                                Testament* (BETL 53) Gembloux/Louvain 1980.

Lambrecht, J.
        1980   "A Structuration of Revelation 4,1-22,5," in: idem, (ed.) 1980,
                                77-104.

Lausberg, H.
        1973   *Handbuch der literarischen Rhetorik*. Eine Grundlegung der
                                Literaturwissenschaft, 2nd enlarged ed., Munich 1973.

Lewis, D.
        1972   "General Semantics," in: Davidson/Harman (eds.) 1972, 169-
                                218.

Lohmeyer, E.
        1953   *Die Offenbarung des Johannes* (HNT 16) 2nd enlarged ed.,
                                Tübingen 1953.

Menne, A.
        1973   *Einführung in die Logik* (Uni-Taschenbücher 34) 2nd ed.,
                                Munich 1973.

Moe, O.
        1963   *Johannes Uppenbarelse*. Bibelns sista bok (Tolkning av Nya
                                Testamentet 11) Stockholm 1963.

Moser, H. (ed.)
        1975   *Linguistische Probleme der Textanalyse* (Jahrbuch des Instituts
                                für deutsche Sprache 35) Düsseldorf 1975.

Olsson, T.
        1982   "The Apocalyptic Activity. The Case of Jāmāsp Nāmag," in:
                                Hellholm (ed.) 1982.

Petöfi, J. S. (ed.)
        1979a   *Text vs Sentence*. Basic Questions of Textlinguistics. First
                                part (Papiere zur Textlinguistik/Papers in Textlinguistics 20,1)
                                Hamburg 1979.

Petöfi, J. S. (ed.)
        1979b   *Text vs Sentence*. Basic Questions of Textlinguistics. Second
                                part (Papiere zur Textlinguistik/Papers in Textlinguistics 20,2)
                                Hamburg 1979.

Piaget, J.
        1970   *Structuralism*, New York 1970.

Plett, H.
        1975   *Einführung in die rhetorische Textanalyse*, 2nd ed., Hamburg
                                1975.

Plett, H. (ed.)
1977   *Rhetorik*.   Kritische   Positionen zum Stand der Forschung
                 (Kritische Information 50) Munich 1977.

Plett, H.
1977a   "Die Rhetorik der Figuren.   Zur Systematik, Pragmatik und
                 Ästhetik der 'Elocutio,' " in: idem, (ed.) 1977, 125-65.

Prigent, P.
1981   *L'Apocalypse de Saint Jean* (CNT 14) Neuchâtel 1981.

Raible, W.
1972   *Satz und Text*. Untersuchungen zu vier romanischen Sprachen
                 (Beihefte zur Zeitschrift für die romanische Philologie 132)
                 Tübingen 1972.

Raible, W.
1979a   "Gattungen als Textsorten." Unpublished paper from 1979 (pp.
                 1-30), of which the author kindly provided the present writer
                 with a copy.   For this favor I hereby express my sincere
                 gratitude.

Raible, W.
1979b   "Zum Textbegriff und zur Textlinguistik," in: Petöfi (ed.)
                 1979a, 63-76.

Rollman, H.
1981   "Zwei Briefe Hermann Gunkels an Adolf Jühlicher zur
                 religionsgeschichtlichen und formgeschichtlichen Methode,"
                 in: *ZTK* 78 (1981) 276-88.

Sanders, E. P.
1982   "The Genre of Palestinian Jewish Apocalypses," in: Hellholm
                 (ed.) 1982.

Schmidt, S. J.
1973   "Texttheorie/Pragmalinguistik," in: Althaus et alii (eds.) 1973,
                 233-44.

Schmidt, S. J. (ed.)
1976   *Pragmatik/Pragmatics 2*.   Zur Grundlegung einer expliziten
                 Pragmatik (Kritische Information 25) Munich 1976.

Schnelle, H.
1973   *Sprachphilosophie und Linguistik*. Prinzipien der Sprachanalyse
                 a priori und a posteriori (rororo studium 30) Reinbek/Hamburg
                 1973.

Sökeland, W.
1980   *Indirektheit   von   Sprechhandlungen*.   Eine   linguistische
                 Untersuchungen (Reihe Germanistische Linguistik 26) Tübingen
                 1980.

Stegemann, H.
1982   "Die Bedeutung der Qumranfunde für die Erforschung der
               Apokalyptik," in: Hellholm (ed.) 1982.

Stone, M.
1976   "Lists of Revealed Things in the Apocalyptic Literature," in:
               Magnalia Dei. The Mighty Acts of God. Essays on the Bible
               and Archaeology in Memory of G. Ernest Wright. Edited by
               Cross, F. M./Lemke, W. E./Miller, Jr., P. D., Garden City, NY,
               1976, 414-52.

Stempel, W.-D.
1971   "Pour une description des genres littéraires," in: *Actele celui
               de-al XII-lea congres international de lingvistică si filologie
               romanică,* Vol. II, Bucharest 1971, 565-70.

Strobel, A.
1978   "Apokalypse des Johannes," in: *Theologische Realenzyklopädie
               (TRE),* Vol. III, Berlin/New York 1978, 174-89.

Vielhauer, P.
1965   "Apocalypses and Related Subjects: Introduction," in:
               Hennecke, E./Schneemelcher, W./McL. Wilson, R. (eds.), *New
               Testament Apocrypha,* Vol. II, Philadelphia 1965, 581-607.

Vielhauer, P.
1975   *Geschichte der urchristlichen Literatur.* Einleitung in das
               Neue Testament, die Apokryphen und die Apostolischen Väter
               (de Gruyter Lehrbuch) Berlin/New York 1975.

Widengren, G.
1982   "Leitende Ideen und Quellen der iranischen Apokalyptik," in:
               Hellholm (ed.) 1982.

Wunderlich, D.
1979   *Foundations of Linguistics* (Cambridge Studies in Linguistics
               22) Cambridge 1979.

Yadin, Y.
1971   *Bar-Kokhba.* The Rediscovery of the Legendary Hero of the
               Last Jewish Revolt Against Imperial Rome, London 1971.

Yarbro Collins, A.
1979   "The Early Christian Apocalypses," in: Collins (ed.) 1979, 61-
               121.

Yarbro Collins, A.
1979a   *The Apocalypse* (New Testament Message 22) Wilmington, DE
               1979.

1 THESS 4:1-12 AND THE HOLINESS TRADITION (HT)

Robert Hodgson, Jr.

I. *Summary*

This paper presents a study in the tradition history of 1 Thess 4:1-12. It argues that the text belongs to a tradition of ethical exposition of the Holiness Code in Leviticus 17-26, a tradition known in Hellenistic and Palestinian Judaism prior to its appearance in the New Testament. Hellenistic Judaism witnesses to the HT in the LXX text of Leviticus 17-26 and in the hortatory poem of Pseudo-Phocylides, while within Palestinian Judaism the Damascus Document (CD) includes this pattern of ethical exposition. Naturally, other points along this trajectory could be identified, too (the Sifra on Leviticus for example), but for the purpose of this paper it is sufficient to describe the tradition in terms of two end points (the MT of Leviticus 17-26 and the NT witnesses) and the intermediate stations in the LXX, Pseudo-Phocylides, and CD.

Two discussion questions will be raised at the end. The first asks: In what form, literary or otherwise, was this tradition available to Paul? The second asks: Does the placement of 1 Thess 4:1-12 in a distinctly OT and Jewish tradition suggest anything about the sociology of the Thessalonian church? To the first question it will be replied that the testimony hypothesis[1] may explain how Paul had access to the HT, while to the second, the possibility is raised that Paul's use of an OT and Jewish tradition betokens the presence of believers attuned to that tradition, namely Jewish Christians.

II. *Methodology*

The paper begins by looking at some external evidence for the view that 1 Thess 4:1-12 is a traditional pattern of ethical exposition. A comparison with 1 Pet 1:1-2:3, 11-12, already largely drawn by E. G. Selwyn,[2] supplies such evidence. Next the paper takes up the matter of internal evidence for the same view, pointing out features within 1 Thess 4:1-12 that may qualify as evidence of traditional material. The actual tradition is worked out by first isolating the *topoi* in the MT of Leviticus 17-26 which correspond with the putative tradition behind 1 Thess 4:1-12 and 1 Pet 1:13-2:3, 11-12, then by setting forth a like arrangement of *topoi* in the Hellensitic (LXX, Pseudo-Phocylides) and Palestinian Jewish (CD) witnesses to the HT.

For the sake of the argument, the HT is determined to have three formal or structural parts: foundational statements, concrete demands, and motivations. Each witness to the tradition will be examined, first, in terms of its foundational statements, next in terms of its concrete demands, and finally in terms of its motivations. The foundational statements are assumptions or assertions about God and his people, and generally take the form "God is holy," "God's people are holy," "God's abode is holy," and so forth. These foundational statements serve to establish the condition for the possibility of fulfilling the concrete demand. The only witness to the HT not having such foundational statements is Pseudo-Phocylides, an omission that will be discussed below. The chief metaphor for depicting the behavior of this holy God and his holy people is "walking with his people" or "walking in the precepts." The concrete demands comprise the prescriptions and proscriptions regulating sexual, business, and social affairs. And, while strict philological parallels exist only now and then among the witnesses to the HT, the substance of the demands, and, from time to time, the grammatical form, overlap to a considerable degree within the broad categories of sexual, business, and social affairs. With

---

[1]Cf. R. Hodgson, "The Testimony Hypothesis," *JBL* 98 (1979) 361-78.

[2]E. G. Selwyn, *The First Epistle of St. Peter* (London: Macmillan, 1946) 370.

respect to the grammatical form of some of the demands, the paper calls attention to the use of the infinitive in Hebrew law codes generally, and the use of imperative infinitives in Pseudo-Phocylides CD, and 1 Thess 4:1-12 as possible indicators of the HT. The motivations include *topoi* such as God's vengeance or justice, concern for the outsider, and polemic against the heathen, and offer a rationale and goal for the concrete demands.

This paper is thus an attempt to compliment earlier studies of 1 Thessalonians which E. Krenz, A. Malherbe, and H. Koester[3] have prepared in their effort to work out the influence of the Graeco-Roman hortatory tradition upon 1 Thessalonians. It is, at bottom, a proposal that the inquiry into the tradition history of the letter continue to include OT and Jewish ethical material, a proposal already offered by Dibelius,[4] Dinkler,[5] Pax,[6] and others as well.[7]

III. *The HT in 1 Thess 4:1-12*

A. *External Evidence: 1 Thess 4:1-12 and 1 Pet 1:13-2:3, 11-12.* The comparison of 1 Thessalonians with 1 Peter offered by E. G. Selwyn[8] shows a common pattern of ethical exposition in 1 Thess 4:1-12 and 1 Pet 1:13-2:3, 11-12 which Selwyn attributed to a pre-Pauline catechetical tradition.[9] Though it is by no means clear that the agreements between 1 Thess 4:1-12 and 1 Pet 1:13-2:3, 11-12 confirm the existence of a pre-Pauline catechism, they do make a case for a pre-Pauline HT. The chart on the following page summarizes seven points of contact.

The pattern of exhortation in 1 Thess 4:1-12 breaks down in the following way:
1. Vv. 1-2 introduce the foundational statement in v. 3a that God's will is the sanctification (*hagiasmos*) of the church.
2. Vv. 3b-6a reproduce three concrete demands from the world of sexual and business affairs:
    a. on fornication (*porneia*)
    b. on taking a wife (*skeuos ktasthai*)
    c. and on transgressing and defrauding one's brother in business (*pragma*).[10]

---

[3]E. Krenz, "1 Thessalonians: A Document of Roman Hellenism," presented to the Seminar in 1979; A. Malherbe, "Exhortation in First Thessalonians," presented to the Seminar in 1981; H. Koester, "1 Thessalonians--Experiment in Christian Writing," in *Continuity and Discontinuity in Church History* (Leiden: Brill, 1979) 33-44.

[4]M. Dibelius, *An die Thessalonicher* (HNT 11; Tübingen: Mohr, 1937) 19-20.

[5]E. Dinkler, "Zum Problem der Ethik bei Paulus," *Signum Crucis* (Tübingen: Mohr, 1967) 233.

[6]E. Pax, "Konvertitenprobleme im ersten Thessalonicherbrief," *Bib Leb* 13 (1972) 24-37.

[7]In general cf. V. P. Furnish, *Theology and Ethics in Paul* (Nashville: Abingdon, 1968) 9-35; R. Asting, *Die Heiligkeit im Urchristentum* (Göttingen: Vandenhoeck und Ruprecht, 1930).

[8]Selwyn, 370-71.

[9]Cf. Ph. Carrington, *The Primitive Christian Catechism* (Cambridge: University Press, 1940); A. M. Hunter, *Paul and His Predecessors* (Philadelphia: Westminster, 1961). F. W. Beare (*The First Epistle of Peter* [Oxford: Blackwell, 1970] 216-20) surveys recent literature on traditional material in 1 Peter. For the sake of the argument I am assuming that 1 Peter is not literarily dependent upon 1 Thessalonians, but that whatever material they share derives from common pre-Pauline traditions. 1 Peter is pseudonymous, and was probably written in Rome during the latter years of Domitian or early in the principate of Trajan.

	1 Thessalonians	1 Peter
Foundational Statements	*hagiasmos* (4:3, 4, 7)	*hagios* (1:15, 16)
Material Demands: sexual life	*porneia* (4:3)	*epithymia* (1:14; 2:11)
Material Demands: business life	*pragma*	[lacking]
Material Demands: social life	*philadelphia* (4:9a) *agapan* (4:9b)	*philadelphia* (1:22a) *agapan* (1:22b)
Motivations	*ethnē* (4:5) *ekdikos kyrios* (4:6)	(*cf. 1:18*) *patēr krinōn* (1:17)
	hoi exō (4:12a)	(cf. 2:12a)

3.   Vv. 5 and 6b motivate these three counsels by reminding the church that unbridled lust belongs to the life of the heathen, and that God avenges all transgressions.

4.   V. 6c underlines again the consistency of Paul's earlier preaching with what he now writes.[11]

5.   V. 7[12] repeats the foundational statement, while v. 8 concludes that disobedience to this program of ethical behavior amounts to a denial of God.[13]

6.   Vv. 9-10a begin a second round of exhortation dealing with social affairs by disclaiming the need to address the theme of *philadelphia* since the church's *agapan* is well documented.

7.   Vv. 10b-11 urge more progress[14] and an aspiring to three things:
   a.   living quietly[15]
   b.   minding one's own business
   c.   and working.

8.   V. 12 motivates this final set of counsels by recalling the need to walk in such a way that wins the respect of outsiders[16] and promotes self-reliance.

---

[10]RSV: "that no man transgress and wrong his brother in this matter." If 1 Thess 4:1-12 does stem from the Holiness Tradition, then a proscription of unfair business practices is possibly meant.

[11]Does *diamartyresthai* refer to Paul's use of a testimony tradition? Cf. Acts 2:40; 28:23; LXX: Exod 18:20; 19:10, 21; 1 Sam 8:9.

[12]V. 7 forms an inclusion with v. 3a. Cf. Malherbe, "Exhortation," 13.

[13]Paul is possibly playing on a logion of Jesus (Lk 10:16) from Q. Cf. note 88.

[14]*Perisseuein* builds an inclusion with v. 1.

[15]Malherbe's observation (*Social Aspects of Early Christianity* [Baton Rouge: Louisiana State University, 1977] 25-26) that Paul is encouraging an Epicurean-like quietism in 1 Thess 4:11 suggests that Paul is redacting the Holiness Tradition at this point by supplementing it with Graeco-Roman hortatory motifs. Cf. below *Tradition and Redaction in 1 Thess 4:1-12.*

[16]*Peripatein* forms another inclusion with v. 1.

A similar pattern of ethical exhortation appears in 1 Pet 1:13-2:2, 11-12, although it is diffused throughout this section of the alleged baptismal homily constituting 1 Peter.[17]   The most striking features of the pattern in 1 Peter are its material and functional parallels with 1 Thess 4:1-12 as well as the common sequence of topoi. After the salutation in 1:1-2[18] and the panegyric on regeneration in 1:3-12[19] the pattern begins to emerge, and insofar as it preserves the sequence of 1 Thess 4:1-12 it runs:

1.   1:15-16 provide a foundational statement to the effect that, just as the God who called the believers is holy, so, too, they must be holy, an assertion for which Lev 19:2 LXX is the proof text.

2.   2:11 (cf. 1:14) regulates sexual affairs (*sarkikai epithymiai*).

3.   2:12 motivates the entire exhortation with a call for right behavior among gentiles and for a conscience so clear that it will not only disprove gentile calumny but lead to their praising of God as well.

Within this broad framework 1 Peter includes additional demands and motivations that recall the pattern of 1 Thess 4:1-12. Some of the most apparent are:[20]

1.   the exhortation in 1:14 to resist the passions (*epithymia*) of their former life in ignorance (*agnoia*: cf. 1 Thess 4:5);

2.   the exhortation in 1:22 to move beyond *philadelphia* to *agapan* (cf. 1 Thess 4:9);

3.   the motivating circumstance that God is both father and judge (*krinōn*; cf. 1 Thess 4:6c);

4.   the polemic against the gentile in 1:14, 18 (cf. 1 Thess 4:5).

B.   *Internal Evidence.*   Certain features of 1 Thess 4:1-12 betray the presence of traditional material insofar as they either correspond to how Paul edits tradition elsewhere or, by their awkwardness and opaqueness, suggest that the present context may not be the original one.

1.   In its present position 1 Thess 4:1-12 stands out in its narrower context. The first three chapters applaud fully the Thessalonian faith and life, and whatever concerns Paul in 1 Thessalonians 1-3 originates in local harassment of the community (2:14) and possibly in charges raised against him (2:3). In 4:1, however, Paul shifts to exhortation whose directness in view of chapters 1-3 catches the reader by surprise. The assumption

---

[17]Cf. Beare, *Peter*, 220-26.

[18]Note already the appearance of *hagiasmos* here. Apart from 8 occurrences in the traditional Corpus Paulinum (Rom 6:19; 1 Cor 1:30; 1 Thess 4:3, 4, 7; 2 Thess 2:13; 1 Tim 2:15; Hebr 12:14) it only appears at 1 Pet 1:2.

[19]1 Pet 2:4-10 may be left out of the discussion, since it is a tradition in its own right and does not directly derive from the ethical exposition of Leviticus 17-26. Cf. J. H. Elliot, *The Elect and the Holy* (Leiden: Brill, 1966); K. R. Snodgrass, "1 Peter 2:1-10: Its Formation and Literary Affinities," *NTS* 24 (1977/78) 97-106. Against Beare, 78, I would maintain that the *Haustafel* does not begin until 2:13.

[20]In the larger context of 1 Peter 2-3 cf. 1 Thess 4:3 with 1 Pet 2:15 (will of God); 1 Thess 4:4 with 1 Pet 3:7 (wife).

of actual moral lapses raises more questions than it answers, and one is on firmer ground to treat the text as conventional and prophylactic instruction.[21] With 4:13, however, the exhortation turns to what is clearly an actual problem, namely the untimely demise of certain Thessalonians and Paul's assurance that they, too, will be raised.[22] In sum, the exhortations in 1 Thess 4:1-12 cut across the grain of chapters 1-3 and, assuming the conventionality of 1 Thess 4:1-12, the text fits awkwardly into the parenesis that follows in 4:13-5:22 with its clear application to the Thessalonian situation.

2. 1 Thess 4:1 opens with the particle *loipon* which elsewhere signals Paul's transition to inherited material: Phil 3:1 (*to loipon*); 4:8 (*to loipon*).[23] Despite the ragged syntax, v. 1 provides a coherent heading for the exhortations that follow, exhortations which collectively describe the correct *peripatein* and *areskein theou*.[24] In writing that the Thessalonians have already received (*paralambanein*) these instructions, Paul uses a word that has the restrictive sense of receiving traditional material.[25] Paul says this again in v. 2 and a third time in v. 6, although the emphasis of v. 1 upon Paul's reception of the material is replaced by the assurance that the Thessalonians are acquainted with this body of instruction.[26]

3. 1 Thess 4:3-6 has the distinction of pressing more infinitives into service as imperatives than all other NT texts combined.[27] There are five such infinitives (matched by five in vv. 10-11!), the first three anarthrous, the last two with article and negation. While it may be simply a coincidence, it is nonetheless a curious one that the

---

[21] So B. Rigaux, *Les épîtres aux Thessaloniciens* (Paris: LeCoffre, 1956) 493; E. Best, *A Commentary on the First and Second Epistles to the Thessalonians* (London: Harper and Row, 1972) 178-79; and M. Dibelius, *An die Thessalonicher* (HNT 11; Tübingen: Mohr, 1937) 19-20 are typical. H. Baltensweiler ("Erwägungen zu 1 Thess. 4:3-8," *TZ* 19 [1963] 1) and C. H. Giblin (Analecta Biblica 31; *The Threat to Faith. An Exegetical and Theological Re-examination of 2 Thessalonians 2* [Rome: Pontifical Biblical Institute, 1967] 140) infer actual moral lapses among the Thessalonians.

[22] Cf. C. Roetzel, *The Letters of Paul* (Atlanta: Knox, 1975) 28 for the overall literary structure of 1 Thessalonians. If, however, one follows W. Meeks (*Writings of St. Paul* [New york: Norton, 1972] 3), who provides for a thanksgiving running through 3:13, then the position of 1 Thess 4:1-12, immediately after the thanksgiving, is unusual. Prof. Wm. Baird first called my attention to this issue. If, as Koester ("I Thessalonians") says, 1 Thessalonians is an experiment in letter writing, then it did not prove definitive, as the rather different organization of exhortation in Romans and Galatians shows. W. Schmithals's ("Die Thessalonicherbriefe als Briefkomposition," *Zeit und Geschichte* [Tübingen: Mohr, 1964] 295-315) discovery of seams and gaps in our text, leading to his notion of a compositie letter, is imaginative, instructive, and unconvincing.

[23] Cf. Best, *Commentary*, 154 and W. Klassen, "Foundations for Pauline Sexual Ethics," *SBL Seminar Papers* (Missoula: Scholars Press, 1978) 160.

[24] The HC summarizes its exhortations in materially the same way.

[25] 1 Cor 11:23 and 15:1, 3 are the two most familiar instances of this narrower meaning. Gal 1:9, 12; Phil 4:9 and 1 Thess 2:13 probably belong here, too. Cf. G. Delling, "*Paralambanō*," *TDNT* 4 (1967) 13-14.

[26] Cf. B. Rigaux, "Vocabulaire chrétien antérieur à la première épître aux Thessaloniciens," *Sacra Pagina* (2 vols.; Paris: LeCoffre) 2. 380-89.

[27] F. Blass-A. Debrunner-F. Rehkopf, (*Grammatik des neutestamentlichen Griechisch* [14th ed.; Göttingen: Vandenhoeck und Ruprecht, 1974] 315) restrict imperative infinitives in the NT to Rom 12:15 and Phil 3:16. C. F. D. Moule (*An Idiom Book of NT Greek* [Cambridge: University Press, 1953] 126-27) includes Luke 9:3; Acts 23:23; Tit 2:2.

great law codes of the Hebrew OT have a fondness for infinitive constructions that is really without parallel in the rest of the OT.[28] In two instances, Exod 20:8 and Deut 5:12, the infinitive serves as an imperative.[29] If this observation is of any relevance it would be that the extraordinary number of infinitives in 1 Thess 4:3-6 (and 10-11) may betray a semitism.[30]

Five more infinitives appear in 1 Thess 4:10b-11, although in this case they depend syntactically upon *parakalein*. The formal symmetry with vv. 3-6 is striking, and the possibility of a semitism may be raised here, too, especially if Paul or the putative tradition has consciously preserved the number ten.[31]

4. Because the material demands of vv. 3-6 are not only surprising but obscure as well, they may have originally had a different context. The assumption of a HT behind 1 Thess 4:1-12 has the advantage of offering a single tradition on the strength of which the sense of vessel (*skeuos*), fornication (*porneia*), to know (*eidenai*), and defraud (*pleonektein*) can be at least partially determined.[32]

C. *Summary.* The comparison with 1 Peter and the pointing out of four features within 1 Thess 4:1-12 as possible signs of a supporting tradition lead to the following question: Is there an identifiable tradition combining foundational statements about the holiness of God and his call to holiness with concrete exhortations in the areas of sexual, business, and social ethics, which motivates such behavior with references to God's vengeance, a concern for outsiders, and a polemic against the heathen? In the following section the thesis is developed that the ethical exposition of the Holiness Code of Leviticus 17-26 which appears in various forms in Hellenistic (LXX to Leviticus 17-26; Pseudo-Phocylides) and Palestinian Judaism (CD) provides such a tradition.

IV. *The Holiness Code (HC) of Leviticus 17-26* [33]

The relevant features of the HC may be summarized under the headings of its foundational statements or assertions about God, its concrete injunctions, and the motivations.

A. *Foundational Statements*

1. The most characteristic feature of the HC is its repeated assertion that God is holy; indeed "holy" and its derivatives appear nowhere in the OT more consistently as an

---

[28]C. H. Miller, "The Infinitive Construct in the Lawbooks of the OT," *CBQ* 32 (1970) 222-26.

[29]Cf. Hosea 4:2; Jer 7:9MT.

[30]This is a precarious point and I do not wish to press it. On the other hand, the imperative use of the infinitive gradually diminishes in Attic Greek (and in Hellenistic, too?) so that there is some justification in suspecting a semitism here. Cf. Blass-Debrunner-Rehkopf, 315-16.

[31]Again, one does not want to press a coincidence, but on sequences of ten and twelve commandments in the OT cf. M. Noth, *Exodus* (OTL; Philadelphia: Westminster) 160.

[32]Cf. the relevant entries in *TDNT*, the commentaries of Dibelius and Best, and W. Klassen, "Foundations," 165-68 for the alternatives.

[33]I have somewhat arbitrarily identified Leviticus 17-26 as the *terminus a quo* of the HT. There is some evidence that Ezekiel ought to be so designated. On the relationship between Ezekiel and Leviticus 17-26 cf. W. Zimmerli, *Ezekiel* (BKAT 13:1; Neukirchen-Vluyn: Neukirchener, 1969) 1.70-72.

attribute of God than in the HC. Typical is the refrain "Do this or that--because I the Lord your God am holy,"[34] while references to God's sanctuary,[35] God's holy name,[36] and to God's sanctification of people and objects[37] abound. Conversely, the HC warns against the danger of profaning God's holiness and holy things (Lev 20:3; 21:6; 12 passim).[38]

2. A corollary of God's holiness is that God has called his people to holiness, so that at least five times in the course of the HC one reads something like "you shall be holy; for I the Lord your God am holy."[39] In one instance (Lev 19:2) the call to holiness introduces a levitical decalog, in another (Lev 20:7) it rounds out preceding legislation (Lev 20:1-6), while in a third (Lev 20:26) the call concludes a series of injunctions (cf. Lev 20:10-25). It should be noted that Lev 20:7 and 20:26 serve as foundational statements for proscriptions of sexual offenses, so that already here the pattern observed in 1 Thessalonians and 1 Peter begins to emerge. A further refinement of this assertion contributes an entire chapter to the HC, namely Leviticus 23, the catalog of feasts of the Lord. These are those days on the festal calendar when God calls his people together as a holy convocation[40] an expression (cf. LXX klērē hagiai) which, materially and philologically, stands close to 1 Thess 4:7 and 1 Pet 1:15a.

In the sermonic conclusion to the HC, Leviticus 26, the figure of walking in the precepts of the Lord describes the anticipated response to God's call,[41] and this metaphor, though not peculiar to the HC, does provide another parallel for investigation. The same may be said about the assertion, found in the sacrificial legislation of Leviticus 19 and 22, that certain forms of sacrifice are not pleasing to god.[42]

B. The relevant injunctions of the HC fall into three groups: exhortations dealing with sexual behavior, business affairs and social obligations. Naturally, the HC embraces far more material than can be conveniently included here, so that only a representative selection will be offered. The selection is representative, too, insofar as different witnesses to the HT will draw upon different concrete injunctions from the code.

1. The sexual delicts against which Leviticus 18 and 20 militate may, broadly speaking, be summarized under the rubric of incest, that is, in the view of the HC certain degrees of blood and marriage kinship preclude sexual intercourse. The list of forbidden unions in Lev 18:6-18 reads like a litany, repeating again and again its proscription of uncovering the nakedness of one's father, mother, mother-in-law, and so forth,[43] concluding that such a practice is a wickedness. Vv. 19-23 continue, however, with injunctions against intercourse with a woman in menstruation, the worship of Molech, adultery,

[34]Cf. Lev. 19:2; 20:7, 26; 21:6, 8. Cf. W. Zimmerli, "Heiligkeit nach dem sogenannten Heiligkeitsgesetz," VT 33 (1980) 495, who points to the schema of the indicative-imperative as one feature of the HC. The Hebrew root is qdš.
[35]Cf. 19:30; 21:12; 26:2.
[36]Cf. 22:2, 32.
[37]Cf. 21:8, 15, 23; 22:9.
[38]Cf. 19:8, 12; 20:3.
[39]19:2. Cf. note 34.
[40]Cf. 23:2, 3, 4, 7 passim.
[41]Cf. 26:3, 21, 23, 27; also 20:23.
[42]Cf. 19:7; 22:20, 25; positively 22:27.
[43]Cf. K. Ellinger, "Das Gesetz Leviticus," ZNW 67 (1955) 1-26. Apart from chapters 18 and 20 the HC treats sexual issues also at Lev 19:20, 29; 21:7-9. The last passage is an especially interesting one since it regulates the type of wife the Aaronic priest might choose.

homosexuality, and sodomy, summing them up in vv. 22-23 as abominations and perversions.

Leviticus 20 recapitulates the legislation of Leviticus 18 and supplements it with provisions against wizardry, cursing parents, and the insertion of the call to holiness at vv. 7 and 26. V. 5 brands the worship of Molech as whoring; v. 13 calls homosexuality an abomination; and v. 21 sets incest off as impurity.

2. Under the heading of fair and unfair business practices one may subsume the legislation of the HC regulating the buying and selling of slaves and property during the jubilee year (Lev 25:13-17, 39-49), the timely distribution of wages (Lev 19:13), and the fairness of weights and measures (Lev 19:35). Lev 25:36 also forbids taking interest or increase from an impoverished brother.

3. The interest of the HC in social conduct is well known and may be treated summarily. Lev 19:17-18 contains the familiar injunctions against hating one's brother and taking vengeance as well as the positive counsels for reasoning with and loving one's brother. Legislation regulating the indenturing of slaves (Lev 25:43), stealing and lying (Lev 19:11), impartiality in justice (Lev 19:15), and so forth all belong here.

C. The HC motivates its legislation with warnings about God's vengeance, comparisons to the wickedness of the heathen, and a concern for the well-being of the sojourner. The sermonic conclusion to the HC warns of the consequences should the people not walk in the precepts given them. Lev 26:14-22 lists with an apocalyptic fervor the terrors, consumptions, fevers, plagues, and famines that God holds ready, a catalog of destruction that v. 24 summarizes as God's punitive walking with his people.[44] Although Leviticus 26 only obliquely refers to the wickedness of the nations by threatening to consign the people over to them (26:33, 38), the theme is most apparent in Leviticus 18 and 20, the sections of the HC dealing with sexual matters.[45] There the comparison is drawn between the ways in which God's people walk and the ways of the nations with a view to motivating right conduct. And, finally, a concern for the sojourner is evident in much of the legislation of the HC to the extent that the code strives to attract outsiders by including them in as many provisions as practicable.[46] This attention of the HC to the sojourner corresponds materially to 1 Thess 4:12a and 1 Pet 2:12.[47]

D. *Summary*. This survey of the HC indicates that at a number of important points the legislation of Leviticus 17-26 converges with what is presumed to be a traditional pattern of ethical exhortation behind 1 Thess 4:1-12 and 1 Pet 1:13-2:3, 11-12. With the HC as a *terminus a quo* the mediating stations along the way to the NT in Hellenistic and Palestinian Judaism may now be examined.

---

[44]Cf. Lev 26:11-12, a text which along with Lev 19:19 has affinities with the so-called Interpolated paragraph of 2 Cor 6:14-7:1. Cf. J. Fitzmyer, "Qumran and the Interpolated Paragraph in 2 Cor 6:14-7:1," *CBQ* 23 (1961) 271-80.

[45]Lev. 18:24-30; 20:22-26.

[46]Cf. Lev 17:13, 15; 19:10, 33-34; 23:22; 24:22.

[47]In general cf. W. C. van Unnik, "Die Rücksicht auf die Reaktion der Nicht-Christen als Motiv in der altchristliche Paränese," *Judentum, Urchristentum, Kirche* (Berlin: Akademie, 1964) 221-33 for a fuller discussion of a *topos* which is of course not limited to the HC.

V. *Hellenistic Judaism: LXX*[48]

A. *Foundational Statements.* The Greek translation of Leviticus in the LXX provides an early, if not the earliest witness to the HT. Its importance reposes in a special way in providing, for a body of Hebrew legislation, semantic equivalents in Greek which help guide the Hellenistic Jewish exposition of the HC. As in the case of the Hebrew text, relevant foundational statements, demands, and motivations will be highlighted, although in summary fashion to avoid repetition.

1. The foundational statement that God is holy translates in the LXX as "I am holy, the Lord, your God."[49] Similarly, God abides in a sanctuary,[50] his name is holy;[51] and God sanctifies his priests.[52] The call of the people at large to holiness is then "be holy" or a variation of this formula,[53] while the legislation providing for the feasts of the Lord calls the assemblies of the people "holy convocations," an expression which presupposes a God who calls to holiness and suggests a tradition out of which the two NT witnesses may have emerged.[54] Opposed to God's holiness and his holy things is, for example, the eating of a carcass or torn animal,[55] for that renders one *akathartos* "unclean" (Lev 17:15); intercourse with a woman in menstruation, for she has an *akatharsia* "uncleanliness" (Lev 18:19); and uncovering the nakedness of a brother's wife (Lev 20:21), for that, too, is *akatharsia*. Lev 22:3 provides that any priest who enters the sanctuary with an *akatharsia* will be cut off from his people.

2. The metaphor "to walk in the precepts" or simply "to walk"[56] describes the anticipated response to God's call, and is the material equivalent to the *anastrophē* and *peripatein* of 1 Pet 1:15; 2:12 and 1 Thess 4:1, 12.

B. The relevant injunctions in the LXX are those regulating sexual, business, and social ethics.

1. Incestuous unions are by definition those in which an "uncovering of nakedness" occurs among certain blood and marriage kin (cf. Lev 18:6-18; 20:11-21), and these alliances are branded as "wickedness," (Lev 18:17) and "uncleanliness" (Lev 20:21). The

---

[48]For the purpose of the paper the complicated textual history of the LXX is bracketed, and it is determined to be a late second or early third century Alexandrian translation of the MT. Cf. F. Cross, *The Ancient Library of Qumran and Modern Biblical Studies* (Garden City: Doubleday, 1958) 128-40.

[49]Cf. Lev 19:2 and note 34. The root word is *hagios*.

[50]Cf. Lev 19:30 and note 35.

[51]Cf. Lev 22:2, 32.

[52]Cf. Lev 21:8 and note 37.

[53]Cf. Lev 20:7.

[54]Cf. Lev 23:4 and note 40. The *hagiasmos* of 1 Thess 4:3, 4, 7 does not appear in the LXX text of Leviticus 17-26, although *hagiasma* "the holy place" does occur at Lev 25:5. It is otherwise rare in the LXX.

[55]On the relationship of the so-called apostolic decree of Acts 15 to this legislation cf. E. Haenchen, *The Acts of the Apostles* (Philadelphia: Westminster, 1971) 469. That the decree of Acts 15, like 2 Cor 6:14-7:1, is related to the HT is probable but beyond the scope of this paper.

[56]Cf. Lev 26:3, 21 and note 41: (*poreuesthai tois prostagmasin*). Paul's use of *peripatein* derives from the popular philosophical tradition. Cf. K. O. Brink, "Peripatos," *PW* Supplementary Volume 8 (1940) 899-949. In the LXX *peripatein* appears some forty times in either a literal or metaphorical sense, though not in Leviticus 17-26.

injunctions against adultery, homosexuality and sodomy (Lev 18:19-23) define these actions as "abominations," while the worship of Molech is "whoring" (cf. Lev 20:6).

2. The legislation in Leviticus which aims at business practices regulates the fair buying (ktasthai) and selling (apodidosthai) of property (25:13-17) and slaves (25:39-46), stipulates a timely payment of wages (19:13), and orders correct weights and measurements (19:35). The injunction against interest and profit-taking (pleonasmos) in Lev 25:37 is of special interest in light of 1 Thess 4:6a (pleonektein).

C. The Greek expression given to the motivations for holy behavior correspond both materially and, to some extent, philologically to the motivations of the HT assumed for 1 Thess 4:1-12 and 1 Pet 1:13-2:3, 11-12. God blesses his people when they walk in his precepts, but when they treat his judgments with contempt and reject his covenant, he will walk against them in anger.[57] The blessings and curses of Leviticus 26 motivate right conduct with threats of punishment and promise of reward in a manner similar to 1 Pet 1:17 and 1 Thess 4:6b with their references to God as judge and avenger respectively. The negative example of the nations reinforces continually the concrete injunctions of the HC, especially those regulating sexual behavior in Leviticus 18 and 20. Rounding out the proscription of incest, sodomy, worship of Molech, and so forth, Lev 18:24 warns against polluting one's self in this manner, because this is the way of the nations.[58] Concern to include the proselyte in the legislation is evident throughout the Greek text, appearing at least once as an expansion of the Hebrew text.[59] This deference may be the equivalent of what appears as a concern to generate good will among outsiders in 1 Pet 2:12a and 1 Thess 4:12a.

D. *Summary.* The exposition of the HC in the LXX includes foundational statements, concrete exhortation, and motivations various combinations of which constitute the HT in Hellenistic Judaism. It is not so, however, that every *topos* is represented in the subsequent witnesses; indeed, as the hortatory poem of Pseudo-Phocylides shows, it is possible to cull ethical demands from the HC without even referring to the concept of holiness, or to advance texts from the HC not included in the summaries above.

VI. *Hellenistic Judaism: Pseudo-Phocylides*[60]

A. Pseudo-Phocylides is a poem of some 230 lines of dactylic hexameter allegedly written by the sixth-century B.C. Ionic sage Phocylides. Its literary genre combines features of the wisdom poem and sentence collection or anthology. The poem's actual date is uncertain, but estimates range from 150 B.C. to A.D. 40. Its provenance is generally given as Alexandria, although the demonstration is a fragile one, resting on a single injunction against dissection of a human body, a custom associated with the practice of medicine in Alexandria. The poem is a manual for correct living, the bulk of whose injunctions stems from the LXX and Greek wisdom literature. Because it is written in a

---

[57] Cf. note 41.

[58] Lev. 18:24; cf. 18:1-3; 20:23.

[59] Lev 17:3; cf. note 46 for relevant texts of proselyte law.

[60] The treatment of Pseudo-Phocylides is indebted to P. W. van der Horst, *The Sentences of Pseudo-Phocylides* (Leiden: Brill, 1978) and M. Küchler, *Frühjüdische Weisheitstraditionen* (Göttingen: Vandenhoeck und Ruprecht, 1979) 261-302. References are to lines of the poem in van der Horst.

deliberately archaic Ionic style, its exposition of the HC is reflected more in material parallels than in philological ones, although the latter are not completely lacking. The Pentateuch, especially the great law codes, is mined extensively, so that van der Horst detects around thirty-five references and allusions to the HC alone.[61] If the author is a Hellenistic Jew, he is writing for a pagan audience with a view to winning it to a life that, at least ethically conforms to Judaism.[62] His chief interests are justice, honesty, moderation, faithfulness, concern for the poor, for the well-being of the household, and for moderation in sexual affairs. The principle of the collection is given at the end (228) when the author concludes his anthology with "Purifications are for the purity of the soul, not of the body," a sentiment which amounts to saying that his *dicta*, originally cultic, are now spiritualized and universalized.

B. The HT is diffused throughout Pseudo-Phocylides in such a way that any reconstruction necessarily pulls together texts that vary widely in position and function in the poem. Nonetheless, a recognizable pattern emerges, if one uses the threefold schema of foundational statements, material demands, and motivations. Especially prominent is the exposition of Leviticus 19--that part of the HC containing legislation regulating business and social obligations.[63]

C. Foundational statements deriving unambiguously from the HC do not appear in Pseudo-Phocylides because the poem as a whole scrupulously avoids mention of peculiarly Jewish cultic practices and concepts. Thus, references to Sabbath, circumcision, temple sacrifice, covenant, holiness, and so forth are conspicuously missing.[64] What foundational statements there are turn out to be, broadly speaking, sapiential: God is one, wise, and mighty (54); God rules over souls (111); God is the source of all prosperity (29). The writer of Pseudo-Phocylides has, in fact, gone to such lengths to excise or camouflage specifically Jewish foundational statements that on at least four occasions (75, 98, 104, 163) he makes assertions about the gods!

D. If foundational statements derived from the HC are wanting in Pseudo-Phocylides, material demands regulating business, social, and sexual life do appear. The four clearest instances of an ethical exposition of the HC are lines 10 (Lev 19:15), 14 (Lev 19:35), 19-24 (Lev 19:13), and 179-185 (Lev 18:8, 9, 16). In lines 9-21 Pseudo-Phocylides has gathered sentences dealing with the themes of social justice and fair business practices, so that in line 10 one reads "Cast the poor not down unjustly, judge not partially" as an abridgement and exposition of "Do not deal unjustly in judgment; do not show partiality to the poor; do not defer to the great." The most obvious modification of the LXX is the elimination of the great or powerful as one special focus of the injunction and the concentration on the plight of the poor. This refinement my reflect theological, social or economic forces in Alexandrian Judaism, although this cannot be discussed in detail here. In the same section (line 14) the poem calls for fair business practices with "Give a just measure, good is an extra full measure of all things," an injunction which appears to be an exposition of the LXX "Do not deal unjustly in (business) judgments: in length, weight or quantity." That Pseudo-Phocylides has the

---

[61]Küchler, 280-81 reduces this to four, so that the actual number will be somewhere in between. The following discussion will include only the more certain references to the HC.

[62]Whatever pertains to Jewish cultic life is carefully omitted from this poem: sacrifice, Sabbath, circumcision, and so forth.

[63]Cf. van der Horst, 66.

[64]Van der Horst's use of holy to translate *hosios* and derivatives at 1, 5, 37, 132, 219 is a *faux ami* and of no relevance to this study, unless one wanted to argue that Ps.-P. has translated the more OT and Jewish sounding *hagios* into the more Hellenistic *hosios*.

LXX text of the HC in mind seems clear, since line 15 plays on the so-called Kil'ayim law of Lev 19:19 (*heterozugos*).[65] Again, in line 19, the theme is fair business practices, and Pseudo-Phocylides has taken the levitical injunction against withholding a laborer's wages "Do not keep the wages of your worker overnight" and versified it with "To the laborer give his pay!" One of the striking features of line 19 is that it concludes a series of injunctions dealing with perjury, stealing, and payment of wages, a series that corresponds almost exactly to the sequence in Lev 19:11-13.

Toward the end of the poem (lines 179-85), in a section of counsels on marriage, chastity, and family life, Lev 18:8, 9, 16 are reworked into appropriate maxims, although there is no interest at all in the levitical notion that incest is forbidden because it involves an uncovering of the nakedness of a kinswoman. Line 179 runs "Touch not your stepmother, your father's second wife," and in so doing transposes the semitic idiom of the LXX to Lev 18:8 into proper Ionic Greek. Likewise, line 182 forbids intercourse with a sister, as does Lev 18:9. And, finally, the injunction in line 183 forbids intercourse with a sister-in-law, as does Lev 18:16. It should be noted, too, that the sequence of mother-in-law, sister, and sister-in-law is also the sequence in Leviticus, although the latter has included other degrees of kinship in the series as well.

While the four cases treated above represent the clearest cases of Pseudo-Phocylides's exposition of the HC, there are many other verses in which the poem may be reworking and versifying injunctions of the HC. Some of the more conspicuous are the injunctions against eating blood and food sacrificed to idols (31),[66] against compelling a wife to earn a living as a prostitute (177),[67] and against eating meat torn by animals (147-48).[68]

Before passing on to the motivations that Pseudo-Phocylides may have drawn from the HC, a word about the infinitive form of many of the poem's injunctions is called for. Above, it was noted that the ten infinitives that bulk so large in 1 Thess 4:1-12 may represent a semitism, going back to the use of the Hebrew infinitive construct in the law codes of the OT. Küchler has made a similar observation about Pseudo-Phocylides, although he has not linked it with the poem's redaction of the HC.[69] By his count Pseudo-Phocylides uses sixty imperative infinitives, but his explanation is that this feature of the text is part of the deliberate archaic style. That may be, but his second observation, that half of the infinitives occur in the first twenty lines, leads to another observation: lines 1-20 are to a large extent exposition of Leviticus 19, and thus one has again the, possibly fortuitous but nonetheless intriguing, occurrence of imperative infinitives in an ethical exposition of the HC. Küchler is correct in calling the imperative infinitives archaic but too quick to assume that they are Ionicisms. They may well be an expression of the poem's carefully shrouded yet real interest in reworking Jewish legal traditions for his day.

E. The motivations which Pseudo-Phocylides may owe to the HC are only two, for the poem has scrupulously avoided motivating right conduct with specifically Jewish topoi, just as it avoided grounding right conduct in such Jewish concepts as covenant and holiness. Thus, there is no polemic against the nations. What one does find is the concern to incorporate the outsider into its legislation and reference to God's judgment. In the first place, the poem concludes its section on mercy (lines 22-41) with the statement that "Strangers should be held in equal honor with citizens." Van der Horst suggests

[65]Van der Horst, 122; for the influence of the Kil'ayim law of Lev 19:19 on the interpolated paragraph of 2 Cor 6:14-7:1 (cf. Fitzmyer, "Qumran").

[66]Cf. Lev 19:26a (MT only). The LXX reads differently. Van der Horst considers line 31 a Christian interpolation from Acts 15:29.

[67]Cf. Lev 19:29.

[68]Cf. Lev 17:15.

[69]Küchler, 266-70.

that the poem has reworked a text such as Lev 19:34 with the intention of extending Jewish law to proselytes in Alexandria or, as appears more likely to him, with a view to moving the civic authorities in Alexandria to protect (Jewish?) peasants who have migrated to the city.[70] In the second place, Pseudo-Phocylides warns that "If you judge evilly, God will judge you thereafter" (line 11).[71]

F. *Summary.* Pseudo-Phocylides comprises, among other material, a series of injunctions that originates in ethical exposition of the HC. As such, the poem constitutes another link between the earliest formulation of the code in the Hebrew text of Leviticus 17-26 and the NT witnesses. The final stage of the tradition with which this paper is concerned comes from the literature of Palestinian Judaism, the Damascus Document.

VII. *The Damascus Document (CD)*[72]

The CD is a manual of theological exhortation and practical ordinances designed to animate, organize, and guide the life of the Essene community at Qumran. Originally discovered by Schechter in 1896-97 in a Cairo synagogue's geniza, later supplemented by finds from caves IV and VI at Qumran, the reconstructed document runs to eight pages of exhortation and eight of ordinances. The exhortation centers on the themes of obedience to the laws of the community, the holiness of the sect, the wickedness of outsiders, and the nearness of judgment, while the ordinances provide Essene halakah of the mosaic law. Not unexpectedly, exposition of the HC plays a role in the ordinances at key points, not to mention its influence in the exhortation itself. Dupont-Sommer dates the final redaction of CD to 63-48 B.C. principally because of the allusion to Pompei's capture of Jerusalem in 63 B.C. in CD VIII, 1-13.

A. Direct foundational statements of the sort "I the Lord your God am holy" do not appear in CD, but since there are in fact only four direct quotations from Leviticus in the whole document to begin with, such a finding is not surprising. If one, however, collects the assertions that are made about holiness in the document, then the presence of the HT in the form of a basic assumption about God, his people, and the things set apart for them is evident. Statements about holiness occur both in the exhortation and in the ordinances, although predominately in the former. CD's opening reviews the circumstances which called the Essene community into being: God turned away from Israel and from his holy place,[73] leaving only a remnant from among those whom he delivered over to the sword (i.e. Nebuchadnezzar). From this remnant some 390 years later a "root of planting" (i.e. the Essenes) sprang forth when God revealed to them his holy Sabbaths and glorious feasts, his testimony of righteousness, his ways of truth, and the desires of his will (cf. 1 Thess 4:3a). All this is done so that each man might perform the commandments and live through them,[74] an expression which Lev 18:5 has possibly inspired. To this remnant falls the duty of setting apart "holy things"[75] and of distinguishing between

---

[70]Van der Horst, 139-40.

[71]Cf. lines 16-17 on God who hates the perjurer.

[72]For the following section on CD I am indebted to A. Dupont-Sommer, *The Essene Writings from Qumran* (Cleveland: World, 1967) 114-63 and C. Rabin, *The Zadokite Documents* (Oxford: Clarendon, 1958). Text: E. Lohse, *Die Texte aus Qumran* (Darmstadt: Wissenschaftliche Buchgesellschaft, 1971) 63-107. References are to column and line numbers in Lohse.

[73]Cf. CD I.3-7. On the importance of the holy place (presumably the temple) cf. IV. 1 (= Ezek 44:15), 18; V. 6; VI. 12.16. Hebrew root is *qdš*.

[74]CD III. 14-16.

[75]CD VI. 20.

the holy and the profane.[76]   The sect's earliest members are designated men of holiness,[77] while the present members have each a holy spirit.[78]   Appropriately, the members walk in God's precepts in holy perfection.[79]

B. Both in the exhortations and the ordinances CD raises material demands that derive from ethical exposition of the HC. Following the outline of the earlier sections, injunctions regulating sexual, business, and social affairs are collected and briefly discussed. Describing the present distress and affliction of the sect, CD determines that the grounds for God's chastisement include, among other things, past sexual sin. Specifically, CD charges the defilement of the holy place to nonobservance of the law proscribing intercourse with a woman in menstruation, an application of Lev 18:19. The text continues with the observation that violation of the law of nakedness, that is, incest, also accounts for the holy place's defilement. While the HC does not specifically include women in its provisions against incest, CD does here: "This law is for men and for women."[80] The two specific cases which CD addresses are intercourse with the sister of one's mother (Lev 18:13) and with the brother of one's father (Lev 18:14). The ordinances also provide that sexual relations of any sort are forbidden within the city of the holy place, i.e. Jerusalem, an injunction which may be an application of Lev 15:18 to the life of the sectarians.[81]

Ordinances that apply strictly to business affairs include provisions against work on the Sabbath, none of which are directly derivable from the HC (cf. X. 14-XI. 18), although interestingly enough this whole section ends with a word play on Lev 23:38.[82] The selling of clean birds and animals, slaves and grain to gentiles is forbidden by CD XII. 8-11, a series of ordinances which is introduced by a warning against doing violence to a gentile in business affairs. That, by and large, CD comprises relatively little legislation pertaining to business may be due to the monastic and self-sufficient character of the community.

The ordinances regulating social affairs include one direct quotation from the HC (CD IX. 2), a text which is the beginning of the entire ordinance section as well as the beginning of a sub-section on community discipline. Quoting from Lev 19:18, it reads: "You shall not take vengeance or bear a grudge against the sons of your own people," going on then to apply this verse to the case of a brother reproving another brother without the benefit of witnesses. The same section (CD IX. 7-8) quotes Lev 19:17b-c: "but you shall reason with your neighbor, lest you bear sin because of him," interpreting it to mean that failure to rebuke a brother amounts to sin itself.

In the exhortation section of CD, Lev 19 has provided injunctions for the list of obligations incumbent upon the sect's membership (VI. 11-VII. 6). This is a section already observed to share the emphasis of the HC on walking in the holy precepts. Dupont-Sommer translates:[83]

> to separate themselves from the sons of the Pit, and to keep themselves from the unclean riches of iniquity. . . . to distinguish between the unclean and the clean (Lev 20:25 passim), to make known (the distinction) between sacred and profane, and to observe the Sabbath. . . . to set holy things apart. . . . to love

---

[76]CD VI. 17-18.

[77]CD IV. 6. The text has a lacuna here. Presumably a list of names preceded this honorific title. Cf. Dupont-Sommer, 127 n. 3.

[78]CD VII. 4; Cf. V. 11.

[79]CD VII. 4-5; Cf. II. 15-16; VI. 10; XII. 20-21.

[80]Cf. CD V. 6-11.

[81]Cf. Dupont-Sommer, 154 n. 4.

[82]Dupont-Sommer, 153 n. 6.

[83]132. Translation of French by G. Vermes.

each man his brother (Lev 19:18), and to support the hand of the needy, the poor, and the stranger, and to seek each man the well-being of his brother, and not to betray. . . . to keep from lust. . . . to reprove each man his brother according to the commandment (Lev 19:17). . . . and to bear no malice (Lev 19:18. . . . and to be separated from all uncleanliness. . . . For all who walk in these (precepts) in holy perfection. . . . the Covenant of God is assurance that they will live (Lev 18:5). . . .

Apart from material points of contact with the HC and the NT witnesses, another feature of this text stands out. The demands are almost all infinitives with the preposition "to," so that once again the fortuitous (?) combination of infinitives as imperatives with ethical exposition of the HC is noted.

C. The ways in which CD motivates right behavior may be summarized briefly under the usual headings of the vengeance and justice of God, concern for the outsider, and polemic against the heathen. CD opens with a reminder of divine judgment, so that in one sense this motivation overshadows the whole document: "Therefore hear now, all you who know justice, and comprehend the words of God! For He tries all flesh and will judge all those who scorn Him" (CD I. 1).[84] Concern for winning the support of the outsider may be present in the passage quoted at length above insofar as the community is called not only to support the needy and the poor but the stranger as well. Similarly, the ordinances proscribe the sending forth of strangers to do a job on the Sabbath (CD XI. 2) and exhort the protection of gentiles in business transactions (CD XII. 6). Polemic is reserved in CD not for the gentiles (i.e. Romans), to whom a certain deference is shown (cf. CD IX. 1), but for fallen-away sectarians and the sect's enemies in Jerusalem, presumably members of the Sadducean and Pharisaic parties.[85]

The charges raised against the sect's enemies are conventional and do not require elaboration here. Anticipating the discussion question about the sociology of the Thessalonian church, it may be said already here that the polemic that the HC levels against the heathen is transferred in CD to the internecine warfare conducted among parties in post-biblical Judaism. Charges of uncleanliness, whoring, riches, lack of wisdom, and so forth are thus by themselves ambiguous and can presuppose either gentile or Jewish audiences. This is also true of the charge of idol worship, which does not occur in CD but does appear in intertestamental literature of Jewish polemic against other Jews.

D. *Summary and Conclusions.* Ethical exposition of the HC appears at various points in the CD. Among its foundational statements are the references to the holiness of the sectarians and of the Sabbath and temple. The concrete demands include proscriptions of incest, of unlawful gain, and the positive counsels to brotherly love and to concern for the poor. CD motivates its demands with reminders of God's justice, with deference toward outsiders, and with a seasoned polemic directed toward enemies of the sect.

VIII. *Tradition and Redaction in 1 Thess 4:1-12*

The tradition of ethical exposition which has been traced from the MT of Leviticus 17-26, through its witnesses in Hellenistic and Palestinian Judaism, to the NT may help determine what exactly Paul is counseling in 1 Thess 4:1-12, especially in vv 3-6. The injunction to avoid *porneia* might be read in light of the proscription of incest found in the HT. That Paul knew of such a word association is clear from 1 Cor 5:1. The much

---

[84]Cf. CD II. 20; VII. 9-10; VIII. 18.
[85]Cf. CD I. 13-II. 1; II. 5-8; IV. 13-19; VII. 9-14; passim.

debated sense of *skeuos* might move toward rewsolution, too, if a semitism is involved in the usage of "wife" rather than a graecism "body," "person," "servant," and if one may presuppose the HT's combination of holiness with buying and selling. The concern of the HT to regulate business practices in general, but also its legislation against usury (Lev 19:36: *pleonasmos*) may pertain to 1 Thess 4:6 (*pleonektein*), while the exposition of the love command in Lev 19:18 ought to be taken into consideration in any exegesis of 1 Thess 4:9.

How has Paul edited the HT in order that it cohere with his own vision of theology and ethics, and in order that it speak to the Thessalonian situation? Two points may be raised in this connection. First, he has added foundational statements of his own in vv. 1 and 2 which then transform a basically Jewish code into a Jewish-Christian one: Paul speaks "in the Lord Jesus" and "through the Lord Jesus." Interestingly enough, these Pauline foundational statements bear specifically only on the authority or ground of Paul's ethical discourse. They account for why he can say what he says but not what he says. The actual tradition which Paul passes on does not refer to Jesus, only "God" and "Lord." Second, Paul has edited the HT in v. 11 by adding what Malherbe has correctly seen to be a call to quietism. Pax has identified isolation and anxiety as two problems endemic to conversion in general and possibly relevant to the church which 1 Thessalonians addresses. Does Paul's tradition and redaction in 1 Thess 4:1-12 aim at assuaging both problems with a program of ethical behavior that defines the call to holiness as a series of obligations which, on the one hand, promotes a sense of identity and self-sufficiency as a holy community, and, on the other hand, reduces the level of tension between the church and ousiders by encouraging the Thessalonians to maintain a low profile?

IX. *Discussion Questions*

A. With respect to the form of the HT that Paul might have known, one can point to the widespread practice in classical antiquity of preparing florilegia or anthologies for classroom and pulpit use.[86] Sentence collections, gnomologies, and testimony books all refer to the same basic genre, although florilegia generally contain some exposition while testimony collections do not. With examples of Graeco-Roman and patristic anthologies as precedents, J. Rendel Harris[87] proposed many years ago that NT writers collected OT excerpts especially in their polemic against the Jews. Not until the Dead Sea Scroll finds turned up a testimony collection (4Q Test), a florilegium (4Q Flor) as well as collections of legal texts with commentary (4Q Ord) did Harris's hypothesis attract the attention of contemporary scholarship. There would appear to be presently a widespread confidence in the validity of the hypothesis, at least to the extent that collections of OT texts in Qumran as well as collections represented by Pseudo-Phocylides, the Wisdom of Solomon, and the like establish a precedent for the use of similar collections in earliest Christianity. Possibly, one form in which the HT was transmitted was just such a collection of texts from the HC and elsewhere from which individual writers drew at their discretion. If such a collection existed, then it would explain, on the one hand, the recurrence of certain foundational statements, concrete demands, and motivations in many witnesses, and on the other hand, the clear dissimilarities among the witnesses.

J. M. Robinson[88] has argued convincingly that collections of sayings of the sages, originating with Jewish wisdom literature, survive well into late classical antiquity. Although Robinson's specific interest lies in placing Q and the Gospel of Thomas on this

---

[86] Cf. H. Chadwick, "Florilegium" *RAC* 7 (1969) 1131-59.

[87] J. R. Harris, *Testimonies* (Cambridge: Cambridge University, 1916-1920).

[88] J. M. Robinson, "LOGOI SOPHON: On the Gattung of Q," *The Future of Our Religious Past* (New York: Harper and Row, 1971) 84-130.

trajectory, his essay bears on Paul insofar as the literary genre of the sayings of the sages is really a sub-genre within the broad category of anthology literature. To the extent that Robinson has succeeded in showing that Q represents an excerpt tradition of dominical sayings, to that same extent one may infer the existence of other types of collections. In fact, there is probably some justification in claiming that Pseudo-Phocylides with its combination of OT legislation, sayings of the wise, *Haustafel*, and catalogs of *Peristasen*, vices, and virtues may represent a type of anthology familiar to Paul and earliest Christianity. Possibly, one could demonstrate, too, that collections of OT testimonies such as 4Q Flor and 4Q Test are the specific type of anthology which not only provided Paul with the HT but also encouraged the drawing up of the testimonies of Jesus, i.e. Q.[89]

B. If 1 Thess 4:1-12 reflects a tradition of ethical exposition of Leviticus 17-26, are there implications for the sociology of the Thessalonian church? Yes, if Paul intended 1 Thess 4:1-12 to be read and understood as OT-Jewish exhortation, which seems likely in view of the accent Paul places on holiness. This suggests that some of the Thessalonians at any rate may have been sufficiently steeped in OT and Jewish matters for such exhortation not to have been lost on them. Whether these people are Diaspora Jews, God-fearers or proselytes cannot be determined but Paul's readers are likely not to have been exclusively gentile Christians. Two points may be raised in this connection. First, while there is no literary evidence apart from the NT report of Acts for the presence of Jews in Thessalonica, there is some slight epigraphic and archaeological evidence which points in this direction, at least from the end of the second century A.D. onwards. E. Best reports a grave inscription, dated provisionally to the end of the second century and the remains of a fourth century samaritan syna-gogue.[90] Second, there is the much debated text of Acts 17:1-10 that presupposes a Jewish congregation and Jewish Christians in Thessalonica.

The defense of an exclusively gentile Christian congregation hinges especially on the meaning one gives to 1 Thess 1:9-10, verses into which Paul has worked up traditional material.[91] The drift of the argument is that the expression "turning from idols to serve the living and real God" presupposes gentile converts. Strictly speaking that is, of course, true: Jews already worship the living and real God and ought not to require such an exhortation. In practice, however, one finds charges of idol worship on the lips of Jewish reformers since the time of Nehemiah and Ezra (cf. Ezra 9 and the foreign wives; Nehemiah 9 and the recollection of the golden calf), and during the Maccabean period such charges were common (1 Macc 1:43, 47), while the wisdom literature, which cannot be said to address only gentiles, raises the charge of idol worship, too (Eccl 30:19; Epis.-Jer 1:72, Wisd Sol 14:11, 12, 27, 29, 30; 15:15). The Essene polemic against enemies of the sect includes a liberal application of the charge of idol worship in the form of tutelage to Belial (1QS I. 24; 1Qm I. 5 passim), charges directed against the other wings of Judaism. In short, Paul at 1 Thess 1:9, writes in a vein which may have both Jew and gentile converts in mind, or at least is using a tradition with such a group in mind.

[89]I have in mind a paper entitled "On the Gattung of Q: a Dialogue with J. M. Robinson" which will take up this discussion.

[90]Best, 59.

[91]Cf. I. Havener, "The Pre-Pauline Christological Credal Formulae of 1 Thes-salonias," presented to the Seminar in 1981.

THE TITLE *PAIS* IN LUKE-ACTS

Donald L. Jones
University of South Carolina, Columbia

Did Jesus understand his mission and death in terms of the Suffering Servant of Isaiah 53? Did a primitive Servant christology exist in the earliest Christian community? Among those who have answered these questions in the affirmative are Adolf Harnack,[1] Joachim Jeremias,[2] and Oscar Cullmann.[3] On the other hand, some have insisted that Jesus did not pattern his ministry on the Servant figure, and that other OT texts influenced him as much, if not more, than the Servant Songs of Isaiah 40-55. Further, there was no separate Servant christology with which to identify, and all interpretations of Jesus as the Suffering Servant, including that of vicarious suffering and atonement, were introduced later in the early church to explain his death. Advocates here include Henry J. Cadbury,[4] Morna D. Hooker,[5] and J. C. O'Neill.[6]

In the NT the title "Servant of God" (*pais tou theou*) is expressly given to Jesus five times: Matt 12:18 and Acts 3:13, 26; 4:27, 30. Likewise, in five passages quotations from the Servant Songs are applied to Jesus' mission: Matt 8:17; Matt 12:18-21; Luke 22:37; John 12:38; and Acts 8:32-36. Six of the nine texts cited are from Luke-Acts, including two of the three NT passages which directly connect Jesus' passion with the Suffering Servant: Luke 22:37; Acts 8:32-36; and 1 Pet 2:21-25. These observations suggest that any conclusions reached regarding Servant influence in Luke-Acts will be crucial for understanding that influence in the NT generally. Such is the purpose of this paper. Is there a primitive Servant christology in Luke-Acts?

Any quest for Luke's christology must confront the speeches in Acts. Research on the various titles applied to Jesus in these addresses contributes to the determination of Lucan christology by enabling one to observe the manner and extent to which Luke has taken over traditional designations and integrated them with his own conceptions.[7] Such a procedure is particularly helpful in dealing with the question which inevitably arises: Is the christology exhibited in Luke-Acts that which was current in the primitive Christian community shortly after Jesus' death, i.e., the middle of the first century A.D., or is the description of Christ's person and work that of Luke's own day, i.e., late first century

---

[1]"Die Bezeichnung Jesu als 'Knecht Gottes' und ihre Geschichte in der alten Kirche," *Sitzungsberichte der Preussischen Akademie der Wissenschaften: Philosophisch-Historische Klasse* 28 (1926) 212-38.

[2]"*Pais Theou* in the NT," *TDNT* 5 (1967) 700-717.

[3] *The Christology of the NT* (NT Library; rev. ed.; Philadelphia: Westminster, 1963) 51-82.

[4]"The Titles of Jesus in Acts," *The Beginnings of Christianity. Part I. The Acts of the Apostles* (ed. F. J. Foakes-Jackson and K. Lake; 5 vols.; London: Macmillan, 1920-33) 5. 364-70.

[5] *Jesus and the Servant: The Influence of the Servant Concept of Deutero-Isaiah in the NT* (London: SPCK, 1959).

[6] *The Theology of Acts in Its Historical Setting* (London: SPCK, 1961) 133-39.

[7]This view is shared by Stephen S. Smalley, "The Christology of Acts Again," *Christ and Spirit in the NT: In Honour of C. F. D. Moule* (ed. B. Lindars and S. S. Smalley; Cambridge: University Press, 1973) 81, who sees in the titles a "vital framework" for Lucan christology. For others, including Charles H. Talbert, "An Anti-Gnostic Tendency in Lucan Christology," *NTS* 14 (1967-68) 259-71, any who would find Luke's christology must begin not with titles, but with "the overall structure of his portrait of Christ." There is merit in each approach.

A.D.--indeed, of Luke himself? Elsewhere, based on considerations of the titles *christos* and *kyrios* in Luke-Acts, I have maintained the latter.[8]

A judgment on the nature of the Acts speeches is necessary. In another place[9] I have argued that, occasional traces of older kerygmatic or liturgical material notwithstanding, the evidence strongly supports the view that the speeches are of Lucan composition. For the purposes of this paper, then, we will assume that the addresses as we have them, rather than being accurate reports of speeches actually delivered, are products of Luke's dramatic imagination of what would have been appropriate for both the speakers and the occasions. Directed more to the reader than to the imagined audiences, the discourses possess far greater literary than historical significance. They are employed by Luke to interpret the narrative and illuminate the meaning of pivotal situations. This practice had its genesis and development among Greek and Roman historians, Thucydides in particular.

I. The Title *Pais* in Pre-Christian Judaism

Before examining the NT evidence, the Servant theme in pre-Christian Judaism, both Palestinian and Hellenistic, deserves brief notice. Since good discussions are available elsewhere,[10] we will not contribute to the protracted debate on the original identity of the Deutero-Isaianic Servant, except to say that in the OT the term "Servant of the Lord" (*ᶜebed Yahweh*) is a common expression frequently applied to the righteous in general who are loyal to the service of Yahweh and endure suffering and humiliation for his sake. A partial list of Israelites who are so called includes Moses (Exod 14:31; Num 12:7; Deut 34:5), David (2 Sam 7:5; 1 Kings 11:34), Isaiah (Isa 20:3), and Job (Job 1:8).[11] Nor will we search the Apocrypha, Pseudepigrapha, and other Jewish writings for Servant imagery, accepting instead Hooker's conclusion that there was no pre-Christian doctrine of a suffering Messiah based on Isaiah 40-55.[12] The absence of the Servant theme from Jewish literature suggests that neither this figure nor the idea of vicarious suffering was prominent at the time of Jesus.[13] We are not convinced by Eduard Lohse's argument that the concept of vicarious atonement was widespread in first-century Judaism, but Isaiah 53 was not adduced in support of it.[14] W. H. Brownlee[15] has suggested that the Qumran sect identified the Teacher of Righteousness with the Deutero-Isaianic Servant, but even if he is right, and the evidence is by no means conclusive, nowhere are the alleged sufferings said to have atoning value.

The importance which we attach to the Servant passages depends largely on our answer to the question of how the NT writers used the Old. According to C. H. Dodd,[16] the quotation of a few OT verses in the New serves as a pointer to the whole context of

---

[8] Donald L. Jones, "The Title *Christos* in Luke-Acts," *CBQ* 32 (1970) 69-76; "The Title *Kyrios* in Luke-Acts," *SBL 1974 Seminar Papers* (ed. G. MacRae) Vol. 2. 85-101.

[9] Donald L. Jones, "The Christology of the Missionary Speeches in the Acts of the Apostles," (unpublished Ph.D. dissertation, Duke University, 1966) 33-59.

[10] E.g., F. Hahn, *The Titles of Jesus in Christology: Their History in Early Christianity* (London: Lutterworth, 1969) 356-57.

[11] See J. E. Ménard, "*PAIS THEOU* as Messianic Title in the Book of Acts," *CBQ* 19 (1957) 91, and Cadbury, "Titles of Jesus in Acts," 365-67.

[12] *Jesus and the Servant*, 56-61.

[13] Rudolf Bultmann, *Theology of the NT* (2 vols.; New York: Scribner's, 1951) 1.31.

[14] *Martyrer und Gottesknecht* (FRLANT NF 46; Göttingen: Vandenhoeck und Ruprecht, 1955) 66-78; see R. H. Fuller, *The Foundations of NT Christology* (New York: Scribner's, 1965) 45.

[15] "Messianic Motifs of Qumran and the NT," *NTS* 3 (1956) 12-30, esp. 17-20; Fuller, ibid., 51-53.

[16] *The Old Testament in the New* (Philadelphia: Fortress, 1963) 12ff.

the quoted passage. We maintain with Cadbury,[17] however, that the NT writers utilized the Old in an atomistic way. When parts of Isaiah 53 are quoted, for example, we cannot assume that the whole chapter is in the quoter's mind; rather, he is calling attention to the actual verses quoted. This means that unless we can find in the NT specific references to vicarious suffering, we cannot assume that influence from Isaiah 53. By the same token, when we find the title *pais* or other allusions to the Servant Songs, we must avoid reading vicarious atonement into those contexts.[18]

The most common rendering of ᶜ*ebed* in the Septuagint is *pais,* possibly to avoid the menial word *doulos* in contexts which speak intimately of the Servant. The further Hellenistic Jewish writers moved from the Hebrew, the stronger became the tendency to interpret *pais* as "child" or "son" rather than as "servant." Thus, *pais theou* began to merge with the Hellenistic *huios theou,* but still no trace of the vicarious atonement theme can be seen.[19]

II. The Title *Pais* in the Synoptic Gospels

On turning to the NT evidence, we note immediately that *pais tou theou* is not closely associated with the Suffering Servant passages. The nearest to a direct connection is found in the quotation of Isa 42:1-4 (MT) in Matt 12:18-21 beginning "Here is my servant, whom I have chosen" (NEB). The context is the healing on the Sabbath of a man with a withered arm and the ensuing dispute with the Pharisees. Jesus, aware of their plot, withdraws, continues to cure all who are ill, and admonishes them "not to make him known." This is seen by Matthew as fulfillment of prophecy: Jesus is one who "will not strive" nor "shout" with the Pharisees. The quotation is related, then, to Jesus' healing miracles and his desire to avoid publicity. The atomistic exegesis of the OT prevalent in Matthew's day precludes reading into the few verses cited the concept of vicarious suffering expressed elsewhere in the Servant Songs. Even if Isaiah 40-55 were highly regarded in the Palestinian church, this one use of *pais* is not sufficient to establish that it was the key word to that material. If it were, we would expect to find far greater utilization of Servant imagery in the NT than is actually the case.[20]

Also in Matthew at 8:17, Isa 53:4a,b ("He took away our illnesses and lifted our diseases from us") is quoted and applied to Jesus' healing miracles rather than any expiatory suffering—a theme readily available elsewhere in Isaiah 53. Once more, atomistic interpretation prevents reading atonement into this context. That an express identification of Jesus with the Suffering Servant was not made here suggests that it was never made, either by Jesus or his early followers. Matthew's purpose in these two passages was to demonstrate that Jesus' work was foreshadowed in the OT, not to construct a doctrine on the meaning of that work.[21]

The words from heaven at Jesus' baptism (Mark 1:11 par.) "Thou art my Son, my Beloved; on thee my favour rests," widely held to be a combination of Ps 2:7 and Isa 42:1, are understood by Jeremias,[22] Cullmann,[23] and others[24] to have been more influenced by the latter than the former. They assume the descent of the Spirit (Mark 1:10) de-

---

[17]"Titles of Jesus in Acts," 369-70.

[18]Cf. Hooker, *Jesus and the Servant,* 21-23, and Fuller, *Foundations,* 46.

[19]O'Neill, *Theology of Acts,* 137, and Fuller, ibid., 66.

[20]See Hooker, *Jesus and the Servant,* 84, and O'Neill, ibid., 133-34.

[21]Wilhelm Bousset, *Kyrios Christos: A History of the Belief in Christ from the Beginning of Christianity to Irenaeus* (Nashville: Abingdon, 1970) 111; cf. Eduard Schweizer, *Lordship and Discipleship* (SBT 28; Naperville, IL: Allenson, 1960) 50, and Hooker, ibid., 83.

[22]"*Pais Theou* in the NT," 701.

[23]*Christology of the NT,* 66.

[24]E.g. Bousset, *Kyrios Christos,* 97 and Fuller, *Foundations,* 169-70.

pended on Isa 42:1b, and that behind Mark's clarification "my Son" (*huios*) there stood an original "my servant" (*pais*). We have no evidence, however, that Mark reinterpreted *pais* in this way--indeed, the term's use in Acts 3 and 4 militates against it since we would expect a similar change in the Lucan writings.[25] Even if this theory is accepted, and the evidence is far from conclusive, it does not warrant Cullmann's conclusion[26] that Jesus at his baptism consciously took on himself the Servant role, thereby initiating a primitive Servant christology in earliest Christianity. One should rather say that if the Servant element ever existed separately, it was so weak it was soon transformed into a Son christology.[27] The baptism tradition as we have it is a product of the early church; it is not derived from Jesus' personal reminiscences of the event. Atomistic exegesis will not permit the general similarity in thought between Mark 1:11 and Isa 42:1 to be construed as proof that Jesus understood himself to be the Suffering Servant of Isaiah 53.

Jeremias has collected several examples from the synoptic gospels which he believes show that Jesus thought about his suffering and death in the light of Isa 53.[28] We will look briefly at the most important of these passages, beginning with two texts from the Marcan passion predictions: Mark 9:12 and Mark 10:45 par.

In *The Mission and Achievement of Jesus*, R. H. Fuller[29] described Mark 9:12b ("Yet how is it that the scriptures say of the Son of Man that he is to endure great sufferings and to be treated with contempt?") as an original stratum in which Jesus speaks of his suffering in terms of Isaiah 53. Since then H. E. Tödt[30] has shown that *gegraptai* and *exoudenēthē* refer not to Isaiah 53 but to Ps 118:22. The Jews' rejection of Jesus has been reversed by the resurrection. This, Tödt maintains, is the earliest interpretation of Jesus' passion and death in the post-Easter community. Rather than reflecting Jesus' own self-understanding, the passion predictions can be used only as evidence for the kerygma of the early Palestinian church.

Tödt[31] has also argued that *diakonēthēnai* in Mark 10:45a ("Even the Son of Man did not come to be served but to serve") refers not to Isaiah 53, but to the original version of Jesus' service at table in Luke 22:27b: "Yet here am I among you like a servant." The Son of Man title in 10:45a has replaced an original "I" form and is therefore later. Only at 10:45b ("to give us his life as a ransom for many") does Tödt find, in agreement with Hahn[32] and Fuller,[33] an allusion to Isa 53:11 (MT). We support, however, Hooker[34] and C. K. Barrett[35] who see here no immediate connection with Isaiah 53. The phrase can hardly be regarded as an original expression of Jesus because the idea of atonement is omitted from the Lucan parallel.

Jeremias also regards the words over the cup: "This is my blood, the blood of the covenant, shed for many" in Mark 14:24 as a clear allusion to Isa 53:11 (MT) suggesting that Jesus' shedding of blood will be for many. But this saying over the cup is completely absent from the older and briefer text of Luke 22:17. Mark reports the words over bread (14:22) in brief: "This is my body" without any suggestion of the redemptive significance

---

[25]Hooker, *Jesus and the Servant*, 70.

[26] *Christology of the NT*, 66-68, 73; see Fuller, *Foundations*, 115-16.

[27]O'Neill, *Theology of Acts*, 134, 137.

[28]" *Pais Theou* in the NT," 712-13.

[29]Subtitle: *An Examination of the Presuppositions of NT Theology* (SBT 12; London: SCM, 1954) 55-64.

[30] *The Son of Man in the Synoptic Tradition* (NT Library; London: SCM, 1965) 163-70; cf. Fuller, *Foundations*, 118.

[31]Ibid., 200-11; see Fuller, ibid., 150.

[32] *Titles of Jesus*, 57.

[33] *Foundations*, 118.

[34] *Jesus and the Servant*, 74-79.

[35]"The Background of Mark 10:45," *NT Essays: Studies in Memory of T. W. Manson* (ed. A. J. B. Higgins; Manchester: University Press, 1959) 1-18.

of Jesus' death. In Luke 22:19a we also have simply: "This is my body" to which a later hand has added from 1 Cor 11:24-25 the words "which is given for you" and "poured out for you." Thus, the explanation of Jesus' death as having atoning, redemptive significance like that of the Suffering Servant is once again absent from Luke's account.[36]

The last of Jeremias' passages which we will discuss is Luke 22:37: "For Scripture says 'And he was counted among the outlaws.' " Here for the first and only time in the synoptics we have a clear reference to Isa 53:12. There is, however, no allusion to the essential function of the Servant--the vicarious bearing of sin.[37] This must have been part of the church's theological reflection on Jesus' passion. Such reflection, however, did not concentrate on any particular OT passage--in fact, the Passion Psalms (esp. 22 and 69) were much more prominent than Isaiah ever became. In such Psalms the passion of Jesus was found depicted in advance and in accordance with God's will. Passages like Luke 24:26, 44 express the divine necessity (*dei*) of this passion as foretold in Scripture. We conclude, then, with Tödt[38] and O'Neill,[39] that Jesus never explicitly referred to Deutero-Isaiah and that the Servant Songs only became popular as a proof text rather late in the church's history. Jeremias' supposed allusions to Isaiah 53 are in fact derived from other sources.

III. The Title *Pais* in Acts

The best example of a Deutero-Isaianic passage used to illustrate humiliation and exaltation in Acts is 8:32-36 where Isaiah 53, quoted by the Ethiopian eunuch, is applied by Philip to Jesus. For the first time in Acts we have a passage from the Servant Songs connected unmistakably with Jesus' passion. The fact that Philip begins with this text in conveying the good news of Jesus to the eunuch suggests only that Isaiah 53 served as a good introduction to Jesus' life and death, not necessarily that it was a passage of indispensable importance. The words quoted comprise the last three lines of Isa 53:7 (LXX) and the first three of v. 8 where the main themes are the Servant's humiliation and his submission to suffering. Reference, however, to suffering for the sins of others, so eloquently expressed both immediately preceding and following the quoted verses, is conspicuous by its absence. Luke amazingly has passed over all the vicarious passages with which Isaiah 53 abounds.[40] The chapter was significant for the author of Acts not because it connected suffering with sin, but because it appropriately illustrated the humiliation theme. It served as a proof text for the necessity of Jesus' passion, not as a treatise on its meaning.[41]

The humiliation theme illustrated by Deutero-Isaianic texts is applied in Acts to Paul as well as Jesus thereby casting doubt on the possibility of a specific Servant christology behind it.[42] As described in Acts 26:18, Paul's mission to open the eyes of Gentiles and "turn them from darkness to light" echoes Isa 42:7. Here Servant imagery is applied to Paul only a few verses before Isa 42:6 is referred to Jesus (Acts 26:23). The "light for the Gentiles" verse (Isa 49:6) is applied by Paul in Acts 13:47 to himself and

---

[36]Johannes Weiss, *Earliest Christianity: A History of the Period A.D. 30-150* (2 vols.; New York: Harper, 1959) 1.115.

[37]Cadbury, "Titles of Jesus in Acts," 366; and *The Making of Luke-Acts* (London: SPCK, 1958) 280n.; cf. also Hooker, *Jesus and the Servant*, 86.

[38]*Son of Man*, 200-211.

[39]*Theology of Acts*, 138.

[40]Cadbury, *Making of Luke-Acts*, 280n.

[41]Schweizer, *Lordship*, 50; see Hooker, *Jesus and the Servant*, 113-14.

[42]C. F. D. Moule, "The Christology of Acts," *Studies in Luke-Acts: Essays in Honor of P. Schubert* (ed. L. E. Keck and J. L. Martyn; Nashville: Abingdon, 1966) 170 n.37; cf. O'Neill, *Theology of Acts*, 134-35.

Barnabas. And at Acts 9:15 there is a possible application of Isa 48:6, 7 in the Lord's instructions to Ananias concerning the necessity of Paul's suffering. Because of this double application of Servant passages in Acts, it is extremely unlikely that Luke intended an exclusive identification of Jesus with that figure.

Further explication of the "humiliation-exaltation" theme in Acts is seen in Peter's speech in chap. 3. The association of the word *pais* in v. 13 with reminiscences (especially *edoxasen*) of Isa 52:13 (LXX) where the persecuted Servant is exalted may have suggested it to Luke as a particularly appropriate Messianic title. However, the leading feature of the fourth Servant Song—the atoning value of vicarious suffering—is missing. Since *edoxasen* is the natural word to use in this context, reference to Deutero-Isaiah is too weak to base on this one verse, as Cullmann[43] does, the existence of a distinct *pais* christology in the earliest church. We agree with Ernst Haenchen[44] that the glorification which Luke has in mind in 3:13 is not that of the resurrection but Jesus' earthly ministry.

Claiming Acts 3:12-26 as primary evidence, Fuller,[45] Hahn,[46] and Richard F. Zehnle[47] have interpreted Jesus' mission in terms of the Mosaic prophet-servant. The titles "Holy One" and "Righteous One" in v. 14 are viewed as examples of prophetic-servant vocabulary. When the adjective "holy" is applied to Jesus as it is here and at 4:27, 30 where it modifies "servant" we have struck a primitive tradition, and the title *ho dikaios* is elsewhere applied to Jesus in the Stephen speech (7:52) which they find impregnated with Mosaic prophet-servant christology. Moses was the "righteous one" *par excellence*. Their interpretation is supposedly clinched by the quotation in 3:22f. of Deut 18:15, 18f. regarding the raising up of the prophet Moses. This prophecy is fulfilled in Jesus. "God raised up his Servant" (v. 26). J. A. T. Robinson[48] is right that only here in Acts is *anastēsas* used of Jesus' historic ministry rather than his resurrection. The word is taken directly from Deut 18:15. However, I agree with Moule,[49] and have furnished the argument elsewhere,[50] that Robinson has not established his case for two distinctly different, primitive christologies side by side in Acts 2 and 3. We conclude, then, that the use of *pais* in Acts 3 does nothing to weaken the evidence for the rest of Luke-Acts, as we shall demonstrate, that Luke, rather than tapping a primitive christology, used the *pais* title interchangeably with "Son of God" and "Christ."

The most significant use of *pais* occurs in Acts 4 where Luke is in touch with traditional liturgical material. The prayer of the church in vv. 24-30 exhibits many marks which argue against its pre-Lucan origin and for its being a later Lucan construction. Like the Nunc Dimittis (Luke 2:29-32) it opens with the rare liturgical address *despota*. The peculiarly Lucan expression "to speak thy word with all boldness" (v. 29) reappears subsequently in narrative (v. 31). Herod is associated with Pilate in Jesus' death and only elsewhere at Luke 23:6-12. And the people of Israel are combined with the "peoples" of the Gentiles—again a feature unique to Luke (Luke 2:31f.; Acts 26:17, 23).[51] We support Haenchen[52] that with the prayer of Isaiah 37 as a model, Luke has

---

[43] *Christology of the NT*, 73; see O'Neill, ibid., 135.

[44] *The Acts of the Apostles: A Commentary* (Philadelphia: Westminster, 1971) 205.

[45] *Foundations*, 167-69.

[46] *Titles of Jesus*, 374-77.

[47] *Peter's Pentecost Discourse: Tradition and Lukan Reinterpretation in Peter's Speeches of Acts 2 and 3* (SBLMS 15; Nashville: Abingdon, 1971) passim.

[48] "The Most Primitive Christology of All?" *JTS* ns 7 (1956) 177ff.

[49] "Christology of Acts," 167-69.

[50] "*Christos* in Luke-Acts," 69-76, esp. 71ff.

[51] Ibid., 74 n.32.

[52] *Acts*, 228.

recast in prayer form an early Christian exegesis of Ps 2:1f (LXX) and has introduced *pais* out of dependence on 3:13.

In Acts 4:25ff. both David and Jesus are called the Lord's *pais,* suggesting that Luke intended no particular identification with the Servant. Further support for this is found in Luke 1:54 and 69 where *pais* is used of Israel and David respectively. The combination of both David and Jesus as Yahweh's Servant also occurs in the eucharistic prayer in the Didache 9:2f. Jesus is called God's *pais* in the prayer of the Roman congregation in 1 Clement 59:2-4; the Martyrdom of Polycarp 14:1, 3 and 20:2, a doxology; the Didache 10:2f.; the Epistle of Barnabas 6:1 and 9:2; and the Epistle to Diognetus 8:9, 11 and 9:1. Since all these writings are independent of one another, it is probably correct to assume dependence on a common liturgical tradition.[53]

It is striking that neither Acts 4 nor the Didache refers to Deutero-Isaiah. In Didache 9:2 the vine David speaks about is probably an allusion to Ps 80:8ff. In Acts 4:25ff. the OT quotation comes from Ps 2:1f., and the one reference in v. 27 to Isaiah (61:1) is not to a Servant passage.[54] Again, the use of Isaiah 61 here suggests to some[55] the appointment to prophetic office in the sense of the eschatological prophet like Moses. They see a further Mosaic association in v. 30: "Stretch out thy hand to heal and cause signs and wonders." We agree with Cadbury,[56] however, that the *iasis* together with *kai sēmeia kai terata* is a characteristic Lucan generalization of the sign of healing which had been central in the preceding chapters, especially 4:22.

In all likelihood, Luke understood *pais theou* as simply another designation for "Messiah."[57] This is in accordance with certain old Jewish prayers wherein David is called God's *ᶜebed* or *doulos.* In 1 Macc 4:30 and 4 Ezra 3:23 it is recalled that David slew Goliath and founded Jerusalem. "Servant" is here probably nothing more than a general title of honor. In Palestinian examples[58] "servant" occurs in parallelism with or close proximity to "the anointed one" and probably means nothing more than "chosen by God." In this context "servant" meant "Messiah" and had no special connection with Deutero-Isaiah.

Several have found evidence for belief in Jesus as the Deutero-Isaianic Servant in the use of *pais* in Acts 3 and 4. That it is found only here in what seems to be an early source confirms for them the primitive character of the title. In 1926 Harnack argued that the appearance of *pais* in the Acts speeches is evidence enough that the christology is embryonic and that Luke received and passed on early material.[59] Jeremias has claimed that the application of *pais* to Jesus here "belongs to a very ancient stratum of the tradition."[60] And describing the *pais* designation as the oldest answer to the christological question "Who is Jesus?", Cullmann says: "*The Acts of the Apostles* offers us the strongest proof of the fact that in the most ancient period of early Christianity there existed an explanation of the person and work of Jesus which we could characterize somewhat inaccurately as an *ᶜebed Yahweh* Christology--or more exactly as a 'Paidology.'"[61] Luke, according to Cullmann, preserves the memory that it was Peter who first interpreted Jesus' mission as that of the Deutero-Isaianic Servant of God and who designated Jesus as such. It is no accident that of the four passages in Acts which call Jesus *pais,* two appear in speeches ascribed to Peter and two in a prayer spoken when

---

[53]O'Neill, *Theology of Acts,* 135-36.

[54]Ibid., 136.

[55]E.g., Hahn, *Titles of Jesus,* 381, and Fuller, *Foundations,* 170.

[56]"Titles of Jesus in Acts," 368.

[57]Note the close proximity: "Servant," Acts 3:13, 26; 4:27, 30; "Christ," 3:18, 20; 4:26.

[58]See O'Neill, *Theology of Acts,* 136-37.

[59]"Bezeichnung 'Knecht Gottes.'"

[60]"*Pais Theou* in the NT," 702.

[61]*Christology of the NT,* 73.

Peter is present.[62] Finally, Moule[63] sees a clear distinction between the use of *pais* in chapters 3 and 4. Whereas the context in chap. 4 is liturgical, in chap. 3 apologetic claims are made for a crucified criminal by identifying him with another who received a criminal's treatment.

We claim, on the other hand, that Luke utilized *pais* compatibly throughout his two volumes. Aware of the long and diverse history of the term, he appropriately confined it in Acts to the early chapters in an attempt to give that material an ancient ring. The title "Servant of God" was in use rather late in the early church as seen from the Epistle of Barnabas where *pais* is inserted into two OT quotations to provide an explicit reference to Christ (Bar 6:1, Isa 50:8, 9 and Bar 9:2, Exod 15:26). The use of the adjectives "beloved" (*agapētos*) and "only begotten" (*monogenēs*) with *pais* in the Apostolic Fathers reflects influence of the words from heaven in the baptism and transfiguration traditions--further evidence that *pais,* while it can mean "servant," was understood primarily to mean "son."[64] Luke treats *pais,* concludes Haenchen,[65] as a formal expression for "Son of God."

IV. Luke's Interchangeable Use of *Pais, Christos,* and *Huios Theou*

We have seen that Luke uses *pais* synonymously for both "Christ" and "Son of God." But does "Son of God" mean "Christ" in the Lucan writings? In Luke 4:41 when the demons recognize Jesus as the Son of God he rebukes them and will not allow them to speak because "they knew that he was the Messiah." Here is perhaps the clearest illustration that for Luke "Christ" and "Son of God" are synonymous.[66] Of additional significance is the fact that the titles are lacking in the parallels.[67]

The trial of Jesus before the Council (Luke 22:66b-71) also reveals Luke's interest in *huios theou.* Jesus is asked (v. 67) "Tell us, are you the Messiah?" He answered: "If I tell you, you will not believe me." Three verses later to the question: "You are the Son of God, then?", he responds: "It is you who say that I am." Again, "Christ" and "Son of God" are used in parallelism.

In Acts Jesus is twice designated "Son of God"--at 9:20 and 13:33. In the former, following his conversion Paul proclaims him such in the Damascus synagogues. Two verses further it is clear that the title was not specially chosen because there again "Messiah" is used synonymously with "Son of God." Jesus is also called God's Son in 13:33 where Ps 2:7 is quoted. It is surprising, however, given Luke's usual "subordinationist" christology in which Jesus was "Son of God" from birth, that Luke should here seemingly apply this text to the resurrection, thereby giving some cause for an "adoptionist" interpretation. Our only comment is that even if Luke has cited the Psalm from an earlier tradition, he is careful not to insist on an "adoptionist" concept of which he does not approve. We conclude, then, since *pais* is used interchangeably for "Christ" and "Son of God" and since "Son of God" in Luke-Acts is just another way to express "Christ," that "Servant of God," "Son of God," and "Christ" are for Luke all synonymous. If such be the case, he could hardly be dependent upon a separate Servant christology even if one existed.

---

[62]Ibid., 74.

[63]"Christology of Acts," 169-70.

[64]E.g., 1 Clem 59: 2, 3; Mar Polyc 14:1, 3; 20:2; Diog 8:9, 11; cf. O'Neill, *Theology of Acts,* 139, 141.

[65] *Acts,* 205.

[66]Cadbury, "Titles of Jesus in Acts," 363, and O'Neill, *Theology of Acts,* 139.

[67]Matt 8:14-17 and Mark 1:29-34; see also Luke 8:28 and 9:35.

V. The Title *Pais* Elsewhere in the NT

The relevant material elsewhere in the NT can be presented briefly. While Paul himself may not have employed the *pais* concept, it has been argued that the language of the Servant Songs had become so much a part of the church's vocabulary that certain words used by Paul reflected an earlier identification of Jesus with the Servant. An oft-quoted example in this regard is Rom 4:25: "For he was given up to death for our misdeeds and raised to life to justify us." However, since *paradidōmi* appears to be the natural word to use in this context, one cannot link it definitely with any particular OT passage, including Isa 53:12c (LXX). Likewise, since *dikaioō* is used frequently in the Septuagint, there is no evidence either that it derived from Isaiah 53 or was an early Christian word taken over by Paul which reflected the Servant concept.[68]

1 Cor 15:3-5 also has been offered as evidence for a pre-Pauline tradition that Jesus was identified with the Servant of Deutero-Isaiah.[69] Supposedly, reference to the Servant Songs has been found in the phrase "in accordance with the Scriptures." But the phrase in itself is of a quite general nature and is not meant to denote any particular OT passage. It may bear more connection with Ps 118:22 than Isaiah 53. It has been further claimed that the words "for our sins" refer exclusively to Isaiah 53. However, it is as doubtful that Paul received a tradition of Christ's death for sin being foretold in the scriptures as it is that Jesus' disciples could have believed his death procured their forgiveness or that it was necessitated by their sins. It seems more probable that the association between death and the forgiveness of sins was due to the particular significance which Paul himself attached to the passion.[70] In sum, Paul makes no use of the Servant figure. If he had thought of Jesus as *pais theou,* surely he would have elaborated the argument!

There can be no doubt that 1 Pet 2:21-25 interprets Christ's passion in the light of Isaiah 53. The fourth Servant Song is used to emphasize Jesus' submission to humiliation, to connect his suffering with the sins of others, and as a proof text for the necessity of his death. The humiliation of Christ is the great example which slaves facing unjust punishment should emulate.[71]

Jeremias has suggested that indirect evidence for the antiquity of the *pais* title is furnished by the use of *ho amnos tou theou* in John 1:29, 36.[72] The description of the Messiah as a lamb was unknown in late Judaism and since the Aramaic *talya* means both "lamb" and "servant," possibly behind "the lamb of God" lies the Aramaic *talya dālaha* in the sense of *ᶜebed Yahweh.* This theory, however, rests on supposition and lacks evidence. While it is improbable that the primary reference of *pais* was to Isa 53:7,[73] it is likely that the Fourth Evangelist saw a secondary allusion to that chapter since the motif of a (slain) lamb and the achievement of atonement for all are among its characteristics. In John 12:38 a quotation from the Septuagint of Isa 53:1 is applied to the Jews' failure to believe the signs which Jesus performed. It is significant that the passage is not referred to Christ's death and resurrection. It has been argued that the title *arnion*, "lamb," used of the exalted Christ in Rev 5:6, 12 and 13:8 but never elsewhere is also derived from Isaiah 53. Jeremias regards *arnion* here as the equivalent of *amnos* in John 1:29, 36 and traces them both to Isaiah 53:7 and the double meaning in Aramaic of *talya.* However, the complete absence of the title from other early Christian

[68]Hooker, *Jesus and the Servant*, 122.

[69]Jeremias, "*Pais Theou* in the NT," 706.

[70]See Weiss, *Earliest Christianity*, 117-18, and Bultmann, *NT Theology*, 1.31.

[71]Bousset, *Kyrios Christos*, 111; cf. Hooker, *Jesus and the Servant*, 125 and Cadbury, "Titles of Jesus in Acts," 369.

[72]"*Pais Theou* in the NT," 708.

[73]See C. K. Barrett, "The Lamb of God," *NTS* (1955) 210-18.

literature shows that it was not a designation taken over from tradition, and other evidence of the influence of Isaiah 53 is lacking.[74]

Finally, the words "to bear the burden of men's sins" in Heb 9:28 seems to echo a similar phrase in Isa 53:12 (LXX). Christ is depicted not only as our great High Priest for the Day of Atonement ritual, but as the victim offered for sin as well. This idea may be derived from Isaiah 53 which also speaks of one who "bore the sin of many" not as a priest but in his own death. Thus, while no direct identification of Jesus with the Suffering Servant is made here, the imagery of Isaiah 53 lies behind this passage.[75]

VI. Conclusion

What can we conclude from the foregoing? First, the alleged references to Isaiah 53 both in the NT generally and in Luke-Acts in particular are, for the most part, ambiguous and inconclusive. Luke, especially in his gospel, seems deliberately to avoid the atonement theme. We found no evidence that Jesus connected his death with the forgiveness of sin or thought of his suffering as vicarious in nature. Jesus did not regard himself as fulfilling the mission of the Suffering Servant. As O'Neill puts it: "Those OT passages which we now distinguish as 'servant' passages became available for the illustration of the theme of Jesus' humiliation and glorification after *pais* had been established as a Christological title; they did not form the starting point for a so-called Servant Christology."[76]

Secondly, the christology of Luke-Acts is the "developed" christology of Luke and the Christian church at the close of the first century A.D. The Acts speeches represent the reading back of later christological thinking into earlier times. The crucial question regarding the use of *pais* in Acts is whether it implied an identification of Jesus with the Suffering Servant or whether it was ascribed to Jesus in the general sense of the OT concept of ᶜebed Yahweh, i.e., as a title of honor with no particular reference to Deutero-Isaiah. We have concluded the latter.[77] Luke applies *pais* to Jesus freely and adapts it to serve his own theological purpose. His use of the title first of David then of Jesus suggests that no particular reference is intended, and, most significantly, "Servant" is used interchangeably by Luke with two other titles--"Christ" and "Son of God."

Luke's utilization of *pais*, then, reveals a rather late development in Christian thought in that it is dominated by his own theological emphases and presupposes a certain amount of reflection upon Jesus' messianic mission. In short, the Lucan contexts in which Servant imagery appears reflect the christology of Luke's own day--indeed, of Luke himself; they do not preserve from the earliest Christian community a separate and primitive Servant christology--nor could they, since in our judgment, such a christology did not exist.

---

[74]Hooker, *Jesus and the Servant,* 126.

[75]Ibid., 123-24, and Bultmann, *NT Theology,* 1.31.

[76]*Theology of Acts,* 139.

[77]In agreement with this judgment is Emmeram Kränkl, *Heilgeschichtliche Stellung Jesu in den Reden der Apostelgeschichte* (BU 8; Regensburg: Pustet, 1972) 125-29, 211; see my review of Kränkl's work in *JBL* 93 (1974) 470-71.

CHRISTOLOGY AND ECCLESIOLOGY:
TITLES OF CHRIST AND MODELS OF COMMUNITY

Howard Clark Kee
Boston University

In his *Kyrios Christos,* written seventy years ago, Wilhelm Bousset set a basic pattern for the critical study of christology that has prevailed ever since.[1] One of the most widely-used studies in the field, Reginald H. Fuller's, *The Foundation of New Testament Christology,*[2] follows the conceptual and contextual categories of Bousset, in that the analysis concentrates on christological titles and classifies the background of the titles by using sharply defined categories into which the titles are then fitted. Bousset, it will be recalled, began with Jesus, but quickly moved to the so-called primitive Palestinian community, then to the hellenistic community before Paul, and finally to Paul and John. Proceeding beyond the New Testament, he depicted christology among the Gnostics, the apologists, and finally, Irenaeus. James Robinson and Helmut Koester, in their *Trajectories through Early Christianity,*[3] have declared in favor of other categories and historical methods than those of Bousset, but in practice dominant features of the Bousset approach to christology remain, as we shall see.

No one could quarrel with an analytical pattern, such as that advanced by Bousset, so long as its basic validity were to be confirmed by relevant evidence and by the interpretive results. Unfortunately, the discoveries of new documents from the period of early Christianity--especially the Dead Sea Scrolls and the Coptic Gnostic Library--do not confirm either Bousset's cultural categories or his historical judgments. More important, though less obvious, there are basic value judgments implicit in his work which are still operative and little recognized. Once discerned, these critical biases call into question both the approach of Bousset and the results of his undertaking. As we shall observe Bousset commends what happened in the development of christology from Jesus to Paul on the grounds that the apocalyptic mythology of the gospel tradition provided effective public relations for the young movement, and implies that Paul is to be admired in his reworking of the christological tradition, since he was at heart a proto-Protestant liberal.

Our procedure will be to examine briefly, but in some detail, Bousset's strategy, which became paradigmatic for critical theological conclusions. Then we shall scrutinize the avowedly alternative proposals of Robinson and Koester, before turning to our own methodological proposals.

I

Bousset was understandably reluctant to offer a detailed statement of Jesus' own christological views, although he ventured some opinions in passing as he described the view of the primitive Palestinian community. For the gospel tradition in its simple

---

[1]Bultmann commended Bousset's achievement in his foreword to the Fifth edition of *Kyrios Christos,* noting only that the shift from Son of Man to *Kyrios Christos* had become more readily understandable through research and discoveries subsequent to the appearance of Bousset's study, W. Bousset, *Kyrios Christos: A History of the Belief in Christ from the Beginnings of Christianity to Irenaeus* (tr. John E. Steely; Nashville: Abingdon, 1970) 7-9.

[2]London and New York: Scribner, 1965. Extremely useful as a detailed, well-documented survey of christology, is Dennis C. Duling's *Jesus Christ Through History* (New York: Harcourt-Brace-Jovanovich, 1979).

[3]Philadelphia: Fortress Press, 1971.

narrative dimensions, only the name of Jesus appears, but never the titles.[4] By contrast, "in the Son of Man sayings we have before us the deposit of theology of the primitive community,"[5] which provides the interpreter "the assured point of departure." "As soon as the symbol of Son of Man from Daniel was interpreted messianically, the Messiah had to become a supra-terrestrial figure."[6] The only new feature was the conception of the exaltation of the earthly Jesus to the dignity of the Son of Man, "which the Jewish Son of Man dogma naturally could not prefigure."[7] With Jesus' death, the hope of an earthly Son of David was shattered, but "we may suspect that the Messiah-Son of Man idea was approximately as ancient in the primitive community as the belief in Christ itself."[8] What gave rise to this faith was the series of visions of the Risen Jesus, which is to say "that in the souls of the disciples the rock-like conviction arose that in spite of death and apparent defeat, indeed precisely through all that, Jesus had become the supra-terrestrial Messiah in glory who would return to judge the world, and that this certainty made possible for them faith in the substance of the gospel which Jesus represented." The three factors which converged to create this faith were (1) the incomparable, powerful and indestructible impression which Jesus' personality left on the souls of his disciples, (2) the psychological law that shattered hopes swing to the opposite extreme of confidence, and (3) the fact that the ready-made image of the apocalyptic Messiah was at hand as a catalyst to produce this resultant faith.[9] This confession of Jesus as Son of Man was the "Shibboleth which separated the circle of Jesus' disciples from the Jewish synagogue," but it was central to the new faith of the primitive Christian community.[10]

The same theological view appears in the Fourth Gospel as well, and is transformed by the Ebionites and the author of the Pseudo-Clementines along gnosticizing lines in the concept of Jesus as the Primal Man.[11] At the hands of the writers of the first three gospels, everything is bent to support the claim that the crucified Jesus is the Messiah, king of the Jews, with the result that the "messianic thrust of the community tradition has rewritten history."[12] Bousset notes in passing that the so-called Johannine logion, Matt 11:27=Luke 10:22, betrays hellenistic kinship, and raises the question whether the Logia as a whole do not show "traces of a hellenistic spirit."[13] The title, Son of God, has too mythical a ring and would have been abhorrent to Jewish monotheistic piety, although Mark used it in his own addition to the tradition: the messianic secret.[14]

The faith of the community surrounded the picture of Jesus with "the nimbus of the miraculous," although "we are still able to see clearly how the earliest tradition of Jesus' life was relatively free from the miraculous."[15] From among the miracles, which Bousset saw as deriving from a variety of sources—folk, literary, Jewish and pagan—"the narrative of Jesus' transfiguration appears, in terms of total style, as a foreign element in the gospel narrative."[16] Although Bousset was obviously unhappy that the primitive community had fictionalized and surrounded the picture of Jesus "with the glitter of the

[4]Bousset, *Kyrios*, 33. The only exceptions, according to Bousset (Note 5) are Matthew's use of Christ in 11:2; 16:21; 1:1, 18.
   [5]Bousset, *Kyrios*, 39.
   [6]Ibid., p. 46.
   [7]Idem.
   [8]Ibid., 49.
   [9]Ibid., 50.
   [10]Ibid., 51.
   [11]Ibid., 54-56.
   [12]Ibid., 72.
   [13]Ibid., 83-89.
   [14]Ibid., 93-95.
   [15]Ibid., 98-106.
   [16]Ibid., 100-103.

miraculous," what seems to have troubled him most about the transfiguration was that, in his opinion, it fitted better with the hellenistic portrait of the divine savior figure than it did with the apocalyptic Son of Man. In fact, however, the transfiguration can best be understood as a feature of an apocalyptic world-view, as we shall note below.

Now, turning to the hellenistic community, Bousset asserts that Gentile Christianity was thriving in Antioch, Tarsus and Damascus at the time Paul was converted. Its distinctive designation for Jesus was *kyrios,* which was common as a mode of address, but relatively rare as a title.[17] In Syria and Egypt, especially, *kyrios* was used in connection with deities, both Greek (Zeus, Athena) and local (Serapis, Isis).[18] For the Christians, Jesus as *kyrios* held sway over the community, in particular as it gathered in worship. Their adaptation of this title for Jesus took place "in the unconscious, in the uncontrollable depths of the group psyche of a community," though it could have done so "only in an environment in which Old Testament monotheism no longer ruled unconditionally and with absolute security," i.e., outside of Palestine.[19] Once the transfer had been made, the Old Testament, with its use (in the Septuagint) of *kyrios* for Yahweh, was read christologically. As in the case of the identification in Palestine of Jesus with the apocalyptic power figure and the tricking out of his image with miracle stories, so in the hellenistic environment, "This change *had* to occur if Christianity was to compete effectively with the ruler cult and the other *kyrios* cults."[20] Although elements of the future orientation of the Jesus tradition survived, the center of gravity shifted to the present, with the result that in the *kyrios* cult, worship and sacrament "became the most dangerous and most significant opponents of the primitive eschatological outlook."[21] The danger lay in the urge to accommodate the picture of Jesus more closely to the gnostic myth and cult.

Paul embraced the *kyrios* cult, but added to it the dimension of intense personal feeling and the spiritual relationship with the exalted Lord. Paul is not interested in the ethical-religious personal image of Jesus of Nazareth, but in the "pre-existent, supra-terrestrial Christ," who was willing to give up the form of God for the form of a servant. It was not the Jesus who appeared to Paul on the road to Damascus who ignited the fire of his piety, but the powerful reality of the *kyrios* as experienced in the hellenistic communities: "Here the body of Christ was actually present; here the individual ceased to be, merged into the whole, and felt himself to be only a member of a body; here the new and blessed life-force overflowed from the head through all the members and bound them together with unbreakable bonds."[22] Paul's modification of this was "to transform it into individual mysticism, to ethicize it and transpose it out of the cult into the total personal life . . . ." He transforms the gloom and mysterious mood of the cultic experience of baptism (Romans 6), "and reorients it to the personal, interprets it spiritually-ethically, and enlarges it." Using the language of hellenistic piety, Paul converts communal and sacramental mysticism into personal mysticism."[23] His understanding of Christ is as the Last Adam, the New Man, but as one devoid of human characteristics; Paul has stripped the Messiah-Son of Man of his Jewish-Aramaic clothing and has accommodated this figure to the hellenistic myth of the Primal Man. "An actual community of nature between Adam and Christ is utterly alien to the apostle."[24] Similarly, Paul's doctrine of the Spirit has its closest affinity with the Hermetica and Gnosticism.[25] Though profoundly influenced by hellenistic thought world, Paul's view of

---

[17]Ibid., 119-30.
[18]Ibid., 140-45.
[19]Ibid., 146-49.
[20]Ibid., 151.
[21]Ibid., 152.
[22]Ibid., 155-56.
[23]Ibid., 156-57.
[24]Ibid., 178-79.
[25]Ibid., 186-87.

faith is "deepened and spiritualized . . . into a continuing vital relationship with God, into the center of all religious life."[26]

The fact that Bousset structured his analysis of christology in terms of titles—Son of Man and *kyrios*—seems to have foreclosed his even considering evidence that would have called into question the stark simplicity of his scheme. Since he finds the title, Son of Man, only in Dan 7:13—with some oblique references to 4 Ezra and the Similitudes of Enoch—he is free to ignore the rest of the book of Daniel, to say nothing of the whole body of Jewish apocalyptic literature. Elsewhere in Daniel, for example, one reads of the suffering of the faithful under the oppression of the authories; of the miracles by which God intervenes to preserve the obedient remnant; of Daniel's reassuring vision of a divine being, which his companions do not understand, but which results in the transformation of his appearance and his being reassured in his time of testing and humiliation (Dan 10:2-14); the promise of the resurrection of the faithful after an experience of unprecedented tribulation. The analogies between Daniel and the gospel tradition—especially Mark[27]—are obvious, and they obviate attributing these traditional themes of the gospels to Gentile savior cults. The fact that the chief motif in the gospel miracle stories is that of exorcisms, which are directly linked in the tradition with the defeat of the evil powers and the establishment of God's rule, shows that these, too, have their roots in apocalypticism, and are not merely transferred to Jesus from stories of Gentile wonder-workers.

The experience of Daniel in the divine encounter mentioned above is a fine example of Merkabah mysticism; the basic ingredients of that vision are likewise present in the vision Paul recounts in 2 Corinthians 12, which Gershon Sholem cites as a paradigm of the Merkabah experience. Personal reassurance in the midst of suffering, with the promise of eschatological vindication, is the essence of the throne mysticism of Judaism. One does not have to imagine Paul's mysticism as deriving from pagan paradigms. Indeed the pervasive significance of eschatological vindication in the letters of Paul has no counterpart in the hellenistic *kyrios*-cults. The basically apocalyptic outlook of Paul, especially evident in 1 Corinthians, 1 Thessalonians, Romans 8, Philippians 8, Bousset simply ignores.

Closely linked with wisdom—in one of its major strands—is apocalyptic. For Paul to set forth his understanding of Christ in terms of wisdom, therefore, is not to assume that the apostle is here merely transferring proto-gnostic notions of Jesus. Indeed, in 1 Cor 15:20-50, the Man from Heaven is pictured in purely apocalyptic terms. Similarly, the "secret and hidden wisdom" of 1 Cor 2:6-7 is apocalyptic wisdom, not of this age, hidden from the present world rulers, to be disclosed in the future for those who love God. For determining the connotations of wisdom for Paul, Bousset turns to selected passages from the Wisdom of Solomon, ignoring the fact that both there and in other basic wisdom writings, such as Sirach and Proverbs, there are importantly different understandings of the role of wisdom than the proto-gnostic theme which is used by Bousset as the exclusive foundation for his hypothesis about Paul's christology. Indeed it is precisely those aspects of wisdom which Bousset ignores that are most clearly akin to Paul's view of Jesus as God's agent. Wisdom's role as companion and co-worker with God in the act of creation (Prov 8:22-31) has its counterpart in Paul's claim that "what can be known about God" has been revealed by him since the creation, but that human beings have rejected this divine wisdom, choosing instead the darkness and futility of their senseless minds (Rom 1:19-21). The wisdom theme of the rejection of God's self-disclosure by the majority and the openness to wisdom of the faithful minority is common to Prov 1:24-33 and to the poignant passage in Romans 10:14-21 where Paul laments the refusal of Israel to hear God's message, and warns of judgment that will come as a result

---

[26]Ibid., 205.

[27]See my *Community of the New Age* (Philadelphia: Westminster, 1977) 43-49.

of the rejection. Conversely, the word of assurance to those who give heed to wisdom (Prov 1:33) has its analogue in Paul's commendation of those who, rejecting human wisdom, believe the gospel (1 Cor 1:21), and thereby not only partake of the wisdom of mature humanity--from which this age's wise and powerful are excluded (1 Cor 2:5-8)-- but also share in the common life with Jesus, "whom God has made to be our wisdom . . ." (1 Cor 1:30). Later in 1 Corinthians, when Paul discloses one of these divine mysteries (1 Cor 15:51), it is an eschatological promise, or more accurately, an apocalyptic secret, concerned with the end of the present age, the defeat of the God-opposing powers, and the renewal of the creation.

It is in this context--not that of a putative gnostic redeemer--that Paul speaks of Christ Jesus as "the man from heaven" and "the Last Adam" (1 Cor 15:45-49). Bousset cannot, of course, be faulted for not having known that in the apocalyptically-oriented Dead Sea community--in Palestine!--there would be documentation of exorcisms (Genesis Apocryphon) and of transforming mystical experience (Angelic Liturgy), both of which this scholar dismissed as impossible for Palestinian Judaism. But had he not read the Jewish texts so selectively and prejudicially, he would have seen that there is far more to the role of wisdom than he allows for by concentrating on the single strand that was later seized upon by the Gnostics. If he had searched more broadly, his portrayal of the christology of Paul and of the hellenistic community would not have been so simplistic.

Paradoxically, Bousset's christological investigation is both historicist and anti-historical. In historicist fashion, he reconstructs what the historical Jesus was like, behind the embellished portraits of him preserved in the gospels. Not surprisingly, Jesus appears as a model Protestant liberal: Bousset obviously admires "the stark heroism of his ethical demands, the picture of the great battler for truth, simplicity, plainness in religion, his critique of traditional piety, his trust in God, his regally careless way with respect to the values of this world, his call to obedience and his hope of God's rule."[28] Only in the final phrase is there an allusion to any of the culturally conditioned features of the Jesus tradition that pervade the gospels: the conflict with demons, the exorcisms, the expectation of the consummation of the age, the coming of the Son of Man. But if one interprets "the rule of God" in spiritualized terms, as preferred by Bousset's Paul, then Jesus appears in this portrait as an intellectually respectable religionist, genteel in his criticism of established religion and common values. Yet Bousset has not finished: he shifts into the realm of timeless truths with the observation that Jesus' preaching displays, not new insights, but "the eternal and universally valid . . . the wholeness and integrity with which this Eternal shines forth anew and comes to consciousness."[29] It is not surprising that Rudolf Bultmann should have written so affirmatively of Bousset's work, since he himself engaged in a similar reductionist enterprise when, in his *Jesus and the Word,* he dismissed the narrative tradition about Jesus' career, set aside the miracles, and transmuted eschatology into the perennial existential decisions about the future, which--responded to obediently--lead to the renewal of life.[30] Such interpretive enterprises are affirmations of theological prejudices in the guise of historical investigation.

II

In the joint work of James Robinson and Helmut Koester there are some method-ological analyses and proposals which offer important new possibilities for New

---

[28]Bousset, *Kyrios,* 116.

[29]Bousset, *Kyrios,* 117.

[30]Rudolf Bultmann, *Jesus and the Word* (tr. L. P. Smith and E. H. Lantero, from *Jesus*). New York, 1934. This process of "moderning tradition" is effectively explored and exposed by Peter L. Berger, in *The Heretical Imperative: Contemporary Possibilities of Religious Affirmation.* Garden City: Doubleday (Anchor Books), 1980, 87-113. Bultmann's reductionism is treated on pp. 93-104.

Testament interpretation, especially in relation to christology. Robinson expresses
regret that the "historicizing of theology was not carried through consistently, and the
divine continued to be shrouded in changelessness, perhaps as the outline of a dialectic
movement through history, or the progressive evolution of ethical ideals and institutions,
or the predetermined will of the Lord of history acted out in *Heilsgeschichte,* or a
constant understanding of existence beneath the flux of mythological and other
extraneous language patterns."[31] After the author's string of rejections of the major
interpretive options, including the existentialist mode of demythologizing associated with
Bultmann, the reader is led to expect an important new theological alternative. That
impression is strengthened when Robinson criticizes the history-of-religions approach to
the New Testament, which purported to be exploring the background of the communal
setting out of which a text arose, but which in fact merely "moved from fixed point to
fixed point, while the background tended to remain a static backdrop or stage setting."[32] Each of the so-called backgrounds was presented as a single, fixed position--
whether in rabbinic Judaism, Gnosticism, or a pagan cult or mystery religion. Instead,
Robinson wants to treat these historical factors as dynamic forces so that each limited
factor is seen to move "along as a variant or eddy within a broader religious or cultural
current." Even the same document can function in different ways at different times.
All this seems most promising methodologically, as a mode of treating evidence in its
own right and within the context where it arose and flourished.[33]

The work concentrates on two themes, both of which it seeks to revise drastically: the kerygmatic Christ and the historical Jesus. Both are regarded as constructs
of scholarship, ambiguous and ambivalent. What should properly be treated as kerygma
in the New Testament is the history of the transmission of the tradition. Since the
kerygma was always expressed in historically-conditioned language, there is an inevitable
alteration of meaning as the historical setting--and hence the linguistic expression--
change: "from Jew to Gentile, from Palestine to the Diaspora, from an apocalyptic to a
gnostic environment, from the social and political role of a Jewish sect to that of a world
religion--all these contextual alterations necessitated a rapid series of translations of the
kerygma."[34] The basic thesis is then set forth "that only the most penetrating analysis
of the specific historical situation in which the source was written is able to make
possible a penetration *within* the conceptualizations and traditions used *into* the point
being scored, which is really what should be referred to as the theology of the text."[35]
That set of agenda and these formulations of methodological approach to the task of New
Testament interpretation seem to be to be admirable, on the whole.[36]

In the analysis of the New Testament material, however--both that from the gospels and from Paul--historiographical problems arise which are analogous to those we
have found in Bousset's work. Both in method and in substance, Koester and Robinson in
their joint work are still locked into the Boussetian difficulties. We shall consider only
two of these problems: (1) the place of miracle in the gospel tradition; (2) the
christological implications of the wisdom tradition attributed to Jesus.

---

[31] James M. Robinson and Helmut Koester, *Trajectories,* 10.

[32] Ibid., 12.

[33] Ibid., 14-16.

[34] Ibid., 22-27.

[35] Ibid., 70.

[36] My chief misgiving about the methodological statement is the assertion that
"Man's being is not logically prior to his language but is constituted in terms of his
linguistic world," (26). If the meaning intended by this statement is that we have access
the experience of others only through verbal reports, whether oral or written, then the
statement is unexceptional. But if, as seems to be implied, the experience itself is
viewed as purely linguistic, then we are dealing with a reductionist ontology which is as
abstract as the essentialism that Robinson--in my view, correctly--is combatting.

In treating both the gospel and the Pauline material, the authors have recourse to the hypothesis of the "divine man." In the case of Mark, his collection of miracle stories "presents Jesus sufficiently in the role of a glorious divine man that it can culminate in what would otherwise be comprehensible as a resurrection story, but which here is simply the culmination of the cycle of miracle stories: the transfiguration. Mark has bound that cycle to the passion narrative in a rather jarring manner . . . ."[37] Robinson then shifts to the cycle of miracles in John where "there is direct, unambiguous, nonparadoxical, causal relation between the miracles that demonstrate Jesus to be a divine man, and the resultant faith . . . in him as just such a miracle worker." John, however, is said to be critical of this point of view; hence it must have been a continuing point of controversy in the early church. The author notes that "the evangelist is backing away from a kind of primitive Christian faith, embedded in traditions about Jesus as a miracle worker, on behalf of a more profound and spiritual Christianity."[38] Paul is similarly liberated from this primitive outlook concerning miracles, and hence opposes miracle workers, whom Dieter Georgi has identified as Paul's opponents in 2 Corinthians.[39] The absence of references in Paul's letters to the gospel tradition's portrait of Jesus is seen by Robinson as a kind of conspiracy of silence against the chief interests of the miracle workers. The apostle turns instead to the link between Jesus and wisdom, which is on the trajectory leading to Gnosticism.[40]

Koester seeks to make similar points, in his "One Jesus and Four Primitive Gospels." He regards the death and resurrection of Jesus as "the norm and pattern of the canonical gospel literature," a pattern which derives from Paul's definition of gospel.[41] The Gospel of Thomas is related to a version of Q from which the apocalyptic Son of Man is absent, and the radicalized eschatology of Jesus and the revelation of wisdom in his own words were dominant motifs. This version, however, Koester does not regard as a secondary variant, but as "very primitive." The apocalyptic expectations were added to the gospel tradition by Matthew and Luke in order "to check the gnosticizing tendencies."[42] The effort to represent Jesus as a divine man by means of his miracles is criticized by Mark by means of the crucified Jesus, as well as by Paul in 2 Corinthians, though it is blatantly present in the apocryphal gospels and acts.[43] The collections in which these miracles were reported, and used by Mark only to refute the claim that he was a divine man, were known as aretalogies. The church considered such a picture of Jesus to be heretical, and accepted as authoritative only those gospels in which the crucifixion and resurrection of Jesus countered the portrayal of him as a miracle worker. Only this latter sense of the gospel genre made the basic point that "faith remains bound to the criterion of the earthly Jesus."[44] Thus Koester takes his stand with Martin Kähler, who thought that the only important part of the gospels was the passion story, and who wanted to make a complete differentiation between the historical life of Jesus as reported in the gospel narratives and the crucified and risen Christ of faith.

III.

How appropriate are these interpretive specifics to the announced aim of Robinson to analyze the specific historical situation in which the sources were written? In my opinion we do well to leave aside the historicist questions as to authenticity of

---

[37] *Trajectories*, 48-49.
[38] Ibid., 52-58.
[39] Ibid., 59-66.   Dieter Georgi, *Die Gegner des Paulus im 2. Korintherbrief: Studien zur religiösen Propaganda in der Spätantike*, 1964.
[40] *Trajectories*, 113.
[41] Ibid., 163-64.
[42] Ibid., 186-87.
[43] Ibid., 189-91.
[44] Ibid., 204.

words of Jesus and historicity of narrative reports, concentrating instead on the writings
of the authors and the points of view represented therein. With that limit to the agenda
established, how useful are the interpretive lines laid down by Koester and Robinson for
handling the New Testament material? In spite of the promising proposals of Robinson,
has their detailed work moved the discussion of christology beyond the place in which it
has operated, by and large, since Bousset? In all candor, the results of the work done
under the new ground rules look very much like the outcomes under the guidelines laid
down at the turn of this century.

It is difficult to understand why, as authors who claim to analyze "the specific
historical situation" and who complain about those who appeal to history-of-religions
evidence but treat it as fixed phenomena in a static background,[45] Robinson and Koester
treat miracle as an unchanging entity, with an unaltered function. Worse still, they
classify all miracle workers as divine men, even though the term, *theios aner,* did not
have an unchanging meaning, and did not take on the connotations they attribute to it
until two centuries after the time of Jesus and more than a century after the latest of
the canonical gospels was written.[46] It is only in Philostratus (A.D. 170-244) that
Apollonius of Tyana (first century A.D.) is pictured as an itinerant wonder-worker,
philosopher and propagandist. The true aretalogies--which exist as extant texts, not as a
literary hypothesis--antedate the gospels, but they are concerned solely with the benefactions of deities, such as Isis and Asklepios. And while the wonders that accompany
the sage's peregrinations are recounted by Philostratus, there is no succinct literary
pattern in which his *aretai* are recited, as in the true aretalogies. Rather, Philostratus
has adopted the genre of the hellenistic romance in its later form.

If Koester and Robinson were faithful to their own avowed aim of dealing with
phenomena in terms of growth, adaptation and change, rather than as fixed entities, they
could have avoided the anachronism of importing third century *theios aner* into the
analysis of mid-first century documents. What would have been requisite is an analysis
of the phenomenon of miracle over the centuries before and after the rise of Christianity, drawing on both literary and inscriptional evidence, both Christian and pagan.[47]
The easy transfer from miracle in Mark to Johannine signs, referred to above is
vulnerable on at least two counts. In Mark, the miracles of Jesus are in fact central to
the tradition's portrayal of Jesus as the one in process of triumphing over Satan. The
disciples' problem with miracle is not that they regard highly Jesus' capacity to perform
them, but that they draw from that factor the wrong conclusions: that power alone will
bring in the Rule of God. What they fail to perceive on the far side of the cross is that
suffering and death are a necessary element in the accomplishment of God's purpose for
his people. Far from denigrating the performance of miracles, Jesus (according to Mark
9:39) rebukes the disciples for discouraging their being accomplished in his name. The
healings, and especially the exorcisms, are central to Mark's portrayal of Jesus, not as a
foil to be rejected, but as a basic to perceiving his messianic role.[48]

---

[45]Ibid., 11-12.

[46]Basic analysis of *theios aner* has already been done by David L Tiede, in *The
Charismatic Figure as Miracle Worker.* Missoula: Scholars Press, 1972, and by Carl
Holladay, *Theos Aner in Hellenistic Judaism.* Missoula: Scholars Press, 1978. Both have
shown that the "divine man" is not a fixed concept in the Greco-Roman world, but that it
shifts from the figure of a wise man (as in Philo of Alexandria) to the miracle worker, as
in Philostratus' *Life of Apollonius of Tyana.*

[47]The changing phenomenon of miracle during the late hellenistic and Roman
periods is discussed in my forthcoming study, *Miracle in the Roman World.* In this work,
the range of socio-cultural settings is portrayed, with the resultant shifts in both literary
genre for reporting the miracles and in the function which miracle is seen by the various
writers to fulfill.

[48]See my *Community of the New Age,* 119-144.

In John, although the miracles of Jesus are fundamental to the gospel as a whole, and to its christology, as 20:30-31 make obvious, they function for John in a manner that is significantly different from the more direct, straight-forward narrative style of Mark. Quite apart from the difficulty of separating out from John the alleged sign source,[49] the Johannine miracles are told in a style which is only superficially narrative, but which is in fact interested in the symbolic significance of the events. Here the closest analogy is not with an aretalogy, but with Plutarch's treatise on Isis, where he is not concerned with what visibly occurred but with its symbolic significance. The early second century shift in the import of miracles in the Isis cult resembles what was taking place in the Asklepios cult as well, as is apparent when one compares the testimonies to the *aretai* of the God from Epidauros and elsewhere in the hellenistic period with the role of Asklepios' benefactions in the heart and mind of Aelius Aristides, as reported in his Sacred Discourses. There he tells how he lived for years with regular access to the shrine of the god in Pergamum, enjoying bad health, treasuring the inner meaning and sense of purpose that the god provided him, part of the idle rich set--the second century equivalent of those gathered at Baden-Baden or Warm Springs, Georgia.[50] But it is the roles of Isis which best serve as a paradigm for the Johannine christology.[51] The Isis tradition by the second century of our era represented her in three related roles: (1) as the symbol of wisdom, through whom the world was created and sustained in its cosmic order; (2) as the personal benefactress of those in need, especially the ill or imperilled; (3) as the revelatory figure who addressed her devotees in the first person, enumerating her capacities: "I am Isis, the one who . . ." There can be no mistaking that this pattern of piety, expressing itself in this configuration of literary forms is mirrored in the Gospel of John. The Johannine portrait of Jesus is not the result of an agglutination of disparate elements, but the representation of a savior figure in modes and perspectives that were alive and appealing to an early second century readership. What is fundamentally different between Isis and the Jesus of John, of course, is that John is representing Jesus as an historical person: "The Word was made flesh, and dwelt among us" (John 1:14). There is no need to imagine sources or to conjecture theological debates lying behind the text of the Fourth Gospel. It has an integrity of its own, whatever its components may have been, which is illuminated by the extant Isis literature.

What must be taken into account in the analysis of christology in the New Testament is what Robinson calls for, but what he fails to employ: the changing patterns of social, cultural, linguistic, and literary usage in the various times and circumstances in which the Christian tradition was heard and responded to. The cosmic Christ of Colossians and the other literature of the later Pauline school must likewise be assessed against the dynamic background of changing understandings of redemptive figures, as evident in Aelius Aristides and Lucius Apuleius, in their respective portraits of Asklepios and Isis.

---

[49] An attempt to reconstruct the signs source, in Robert T. Fortna, *The Gospel of Signs: A Reconstruction of the Narrative Source Underlying the Fourth Gospel* (SNTSMS 11; Cambridge: Cambridge University Press, 1970). The major challenge to source theories about John is D. Moody Smith's *The Composition and Order of the Fourth Gospel* (New Haven: Yale University Press, 1965) in which he shows that though there were probably sources on which John drew, they can no longer be reconstructed, nor can their limits be determined.

[50] For details on the growth of and changes in the Asklepios cult, see my study in the forthcoming volume of essays presented at the McMaster University symposium, to be published by Fortress Press in the series edited by E. P. Sanders, *Jewish and Christian Self-Definition*, Vol. III, 1983.

[51] Documentation for this thesis is provided in my essay, "Isis, Wisdom, and the Fourth Gospel," in *Myth, Symbol and Reality*, ed. Alan Olson, in the Boston University Institute for Theology and Philosophy Series. Notre Dame: University of Notre Dame Press, 1980.

What must be avoided, however, is reading later developments back into the earlier period. There are useful analogies to be made between the glorification of Apollonius of Tyana as preacher-teacher-wonder-worker by Philostratus and early Christian writings. But the kinship is with the third and fourth century apocryphal gospels and especially the apocryphal acts, where sheer delight in the marvelous is a paramount feature. For example, there is seemingly little theological benefit to be gained from the story of the cooperative bedbugs, who in the Acts of John, leave the mattress so that the apostle can have a good night's sleep, but its charm matches some of those told about Apollonius' journey to Babylon and India. Above all, the miracles confirm the divine authority of the apostolic figures or effect judgment on those who reject the apostles or their message. The phenomenon of magic figures importantly in these narratives of the later second and third century, in both the pagan and Christian contests, so that one can easily discern the common cultural influences under which both the Christian propagandists and their secular--or, at least, non-Christian--counterparts are operating. In the New Testament apocryphal literature, the christological issue is minor or nonexistent. What has superseded it, is the authority of the church, conformity to which is now sought by these stories of divine confirmation of the authority of the apostles. This fundamental shift in the importance attached to miracles in the third and subsequent centuries should serve as a reminder to historians that they must not be misled by superficial similarities in phenomena such as miracles, but must ask rather how the phenomenon functions in an altered situation.

As Robinson reveals--probably inadvertently--in his discussion of the miracle in John, he finds miracles distasteful, or as he phrases it, "primitive," and he hence tries to make a case for a miracle-free version, "a more profound and spiritual Christianity," which he attributes to John.[52] But that is a statement of personal theological preference; it has no basis in historical evidence, nor is it a demonstrably accurate description of the theological outlook of the Fourth Evangelist. Similarly, Koester implies his low estimate of miracle in the Jesus tradition by crediting Mark with the effort to demolish the picture of Jesus as a "divine man" by emphasizing the gospel of the cross and resurrection.[53] Koester is free to express a theological preference for Paul's portrait of Jesus, without the miracles, but that provides no warrant for dismissing as a polemical ploy all the space Mark devotes to his portrait of Jesus as exorcist and healer. Or again, one may be uncomfortable with the apocalyptic expectation that pervades the Q material as we have it in the gospels, and one may correctly observe that the Q material as incorporated into the Gospel of Thomas has been deeschatologized. But that provides no basis for the historical conclusion that Q was originally non-eschatological, and that the element was later introduced into the tradition by those combatting Gnosticism by apocalyptic counterclaims.[54] The discovery of the immensely important Nag Hammadi Gnostic library vastly increased knowledge of second and third century Gnosticism, but it sheds no clear light on the question as to whether there was a pre-Christian Gnosticism. Instead, it seems to confirm the theory that Gnosticism was a growth on second century Christianity. The Gospel of Thomas is a prime example of the adaptation of earlier Christian tradition to portray Jesus as a Gnostic revelatory figure,[55] just as the Q material is thoroughly eschatological, rather than manifesting a sprinkling with later apocalyptic condiments. It is against backgrounds which exist in tangible form, rather than in terms of conceptual anachronisms, that the christological images are to be perceived and analyzed.

[52]Robinson, *Trajectories*, 58.

[53]Koester, *Trajectories*, 189.

[54]Ibid., 186-89.

[55]See my essay, " 'Becoming as a Child' in the Gospel of Thomas," *JBL* 82 (1963) 307-14.

IV.

The most serious deficiency in the approach to christology represented by Bousset and his heirs down to the present day is the failure to take into account the self-conscious Christian communities in and by which Jesus' messiahship was affirmed. The clues should have been read out of the Old Testament texts: in Daniel 7, "one like a son of man" is pictured as an individual (vs. 13), but then the recipient of the kingdom is identified twice (vv. 18, 22) as "the saints of the Most High." Similarly, the servant of 2 Isaiah is at times pictured as an individual (42:1) and at times as the whole of Israel (44:1). The Son of God is both the king (Ps 2:6-7) and the nation Israel (Hos 1:1). The effort to explain away these features by appeal to a later redactor is useless, since it was the finished text which was authoritative in both Judaism and early Christianity. Regardless of the christological image that is used by the various New Testament writers, each has a correlative image of God's people. Bousset was oppossed to that notion, as we have seen, and commends Paul for having played down the corporate nature of the Christian community, stressing instead personal mysticism.[56] Subsequent scholarly discussion has spoken often of "the community," but has meant by that an abstraction or an ill-defined group. Thus when form-critics speak of *Sitz-im-Leben,* they rarely go beyond the vague designations of preaching or worship, with no attention given to the distinctive features of the various communities among whom these phenomena functioned. That there were sharp differences among them in matters of admissions requirements and ritual obligations is evident from Paul's Letter to the Galatians, and in the uneasy feelings he betrays concerning his prospective (final) visit to the Jerusalem community. The most likely way to account for the lengthy, careful letter of self introduction that is his Letter to the Romans is to assume that there was an established Christian group there with which he had certain potential differences. The letter opens with a christological confession (Rom 1:3-4) which has no exact equivalent in his surviving letters, and is widely thought to include a credal formula which he had learned was in use in the church at Rome. It may be useful to sketch briefly the ways in which the correlated images of Messiah and his people vary among the four gospels and Paul. Although we shall not trace out the details here, this way of understanding christology also bears directly on ethical norms within the community, the stance of the community toward other religious, social, and political structures, and the pattern of authority that prevails within the community itself. We have already observed the fallaciousness of concentrating on christological titles, but there are certain images of Christ which are dominant in the gospels and Paul, and which relate directly to the respective views of the Christian community. We shall briefly sketch the characteristic features of each of these writings.

In both Mark and the Q tradition, the dominant designation for Jesus is Son of Man, understood in its apocalyptic context. Not merely the phrase itself from Daniel 7:13, but the whole of that apocalyptic work has influenced the writing of Mark. In the Q material, the weight falls on the *parousia* of the Son of Man, and the power to vindicate or to judge that he will manifest at the End of the Age: Luke 11:30, a sign to this generation; 12:16, a word against the Son of Man will be forgiven, i.e., in the eschatological judgment; 17:24-30, the unexpected appearing of the Son of Man; 12:40, the warning to be ready for his coming. The other two Son of Man words in Q have to do with another motif in apocalyptic: the popular rejection of the final messenger of God (Luke 9:58), and his befriending of the outcasts (7:34). In Mark, the Son of Man words also treat of his future coming at the End of the Age (8:38; 9:9; 13:26; 14:62), but they attest as well to his present authority to define true piety (2:10, forgiveness of sin; 2:28, sabbath observance), and above all to his suffering as part of the divine plan (8:31; 9:12; 9:31; 10:33; 10:45; 14:21, 41). Thus for Mark the entire career of Jesus is set in a context of eschatological significance by the dominance of this title. Not only the apocalyptic

---

[56]Bousset, *Kyrios,* 157.

discourse of Mark 13,[57] but the book as a whole is permeated by perspectives deriving from Jewish apocalyptic, and from Daniel in particular.[58] Thus, the major role of Jesus is one who by his earthly power redefines the community of the faithful, launches a major campaign to overcome the powers of evil, declares that his impending death is necessary to the divine plan and benefits "the lost." He also announces the circumstances of the approaching End of the Age, and commissions his followers to carry on the work until the End. The most suitable title by which to epitomize that messianic role is Son of Man.

Equally important for Mark (and for the Q tradition), however, is the new definition of the community of the faithful. In Luke 9:58, Jesus is the model of rejection that God's messengers can expect, just as he is one who befriends religious and social outcasts, joining with them in table fellowship (Luke 7:34). The so-called present Son of Man words in Mark (2:10; 2:28) are both concerned with the question of acceptance before God, through forgiveness of sin and by interpretation of the law against work on the sabbath, which Jesus has seemingly violated in the performance of acts of mercy.

What is apparent here is the issue which Jacob Neusner has recognized as the central concern of what became Mishnaic Judaism, beginning before the turn of the eras and taking definitive shape in the rise to power of Pharisaism following the first Jewish Revolt in A.D. 70: namely, "What are the qualifications for membership in the covenant people?"[59] The importance of that issue is obvious at Qumran, where the mainstream of Judaism is denounced as apostate, and the community of the New Covenant has withdrawn from society in order to maintain the true and pure worship, the correct interpretation of scripture, as disclosed through the One who Teaches Rightly, awaiting vindication by God's direct intervention in behalf of his people. It is not extraneous to Mark's concerns, therefore, that as the announcement of Jesus' death becomes more explicit (from 8:31 on), the issues discussed include Jesus' authority to interpret the divine will, the obligation of God's people to civil authority, marital relationships within the community, the question as to which is the greatest commandment (which culminates significantly in love of neighbor, 12:31). Nor is it surprising that, just before the first announcement of the passion, nearly an entire chapter is devoted to the matter of ritual purity versus moral purity (Mark 7). The two extended discourse sections of the gospel-- Mark 4 on the parables, and Mark 13 on the End of the Age--are both presented as special information, vouchsafed only to the inner circle which is the nucleus of God's people. The central cultic act linked with the death of the Messiah-Son of Man focuses on the shared body and the common cup which is "the blood of the New Covenant" (14:22-24), the full communion in which will be experienced only in the New Age (14:25). The destiny of the Messiah and that of his people are pictured in the same imagery, drawing on the same tradition in Judaism: the apocalyptic hope of vindication of those who, like Daniel and his companions, are faithful to death (13:26-27).

---

[57] The case for Mark 13 as a kind of *pesher* on Daniel is made persuasively by Lars Hartmann in *Prophecy Interpreted: The Formation of Some Jewish Apocalyptic Texts and of the Eschatological Discourse Mark 13 par.* (ConB NT Series 1; Lund, 1966).

[58] For a detailed presentation of the evidence, see my *Community of the New Age*, 43-48.

[59] Jacob Neusner has set forth this historical position brilliantly in the opening essays of his *Method and Meaning in Ancient Judaism*, Series III, Brown University Judaic Studies. Chico, CA: Scholars Press, 1981. Although Neusner is severely critical of the work of E. P. Sanders on the links between Paul and Rabbinic Judaism (*Paul and Palestinian Judaism*. Philadelphia: Fortress Press, 1977), on the ground of the allegedly uncritical use of the rabbinic sources, Sanders and Neusner agree that requirements for membership in the people of God were the paramount issues in Judaism in the New Testament period.

The dominant image in Matthew's gospel for portraying Jesus is power, and specifically royal power. In the genealogy (1:1-17), in the infancy stories (2:6; 2:15), in the account of Jesus' baptism, in the Q version of the temptation (4:3, 6), he is identified as descended from David and Son of God, in the tradition of Ps 2:6-7. This motif reaches its climax in the familiar post-resurrection announcement of Jesus (28:18, "All authority in heaven and on earth has been given to me.") The combination of supreme power and identification as Son of God stand at the turning point in Matthew: the confession of Peter as "the Christ, the Son of the living God," and the attendant claims of the triumph of his church over all the opposing powers. The power of his teaching is both implicit in Matthew's portrayal of Jesus as the New Moses, teaching the New Law on the mountain in Galilee, and explicit in the declarations, "You have heard it said of old . . . but I say to you," and in the claim to be the fulfillment of the law and the prophets (5:17). Those who mock him on the cross refer to him not only as king of Israel (as Mark reports), but as Son of God (27:39, 43).

Of equal importance for Matthew are the corollaries of this description of Jesus as the center of divine authority: the apostles are delegated authority by him. This is the case not only in the commissioning of the twelve (10:1-42), which has a briefer counterpart in Mark 6:1-13, but also in the uniquely Matthean passages about the keys of the kingdom (16:18-19), about the power to settle disputes in the church (18:15-20), about the solemn responsibilities of stewardship of divinely bestowed authority in the Parables of the Wise and Foolish Maidens and of the Talents in Matthew 25. The commissioning of the disciples in 28:19-20 derives directly from the power which Jesus now possesses ("Go therefore"), and provides authority in making disciples, in credal terms, in instruction, and carries with it the promise of the presence of the authoritative Jesus until the End of the Age. The extended discourse material of Matthew (Sermon on the Mount, Matt 5-7; the Commissioning of the Twelve, Matt 10; Parables of the Kingdom, Matt 13; Community Instruction, Matt 18; Polemic against the Pharisees, Matt 23; the Apoc-alyptic Discourse, Matt 24-25) provides the concrete instructional base and the pattern of administering apostolic authority within the church. It is not in the least surprising that the early church placed this book at the head of its canon.

Another distinctive feature of Matthew is his use of portent to underscore the divine authority of Jesus, as confirmed by cosmic signs. This feature, together with the advance disclosure by means of dreams concerning someone's having been destined by the gods for leadership, is an important factor in Roman histories written during the New Testament period: Tacitus, Suetonius, Dio Cassius, and even Josephus, who imitates the style and conventions of his Roman contemporaries.[60] The portents and dreams are regularly depicted as occurring before the birth, during the childhood, at the moment of entrance of public life, and at the death of these power figures of Roman history. One need only recall the following peculiarly Matthean narrative features to see how this evangelist has shaped his account along the lines of contemporary historiography:

Dreams: Concerning the birth of Mary's child (1:20)
                Warning to flee to Egypt (2:13)
                Advice to return to Nazareth (2:19)

Portents: The guiding star (2:2-9)
                The public attestation of Jesus (3:16-17)
                The earthquake at his death (27:51-54)
                The earthquake at his resurrection (28:2-4)

---

[60]For a detailed discussion of this aspect of miracle in Matthew, and in the historians of his period, see my forthcoming, *Miracle in the Roman World*.

Literate Gentiles reading Matthew in the late first century could not miss this claim of the hand of God powerfully at work shaping the life of Jesus from birth to death and resurrection, just as the narrative as a whole would convey the commissioning with power of Jesus' apostles.

Although Luke has used at least two of the same sources as Matthew (that is, Mark and Q), both his representation of the figure of Jesus and the literary modes through which he conveys it are significantly different. Although Luke uses the various christological titles--Son of Man, Son of God, Son of David--he frequently has simply "the Christ of God," as in Peter's confession (Luke 9:20) or adds the adjective, "chosen," as in the transfiguration story (9:35). Elsewhere Jesus links himself with wisdom (7:35; 11:49). Perhaps the most nearly characteristic use of the titles to depict the role of Jesus as Luke perceives it is in 19:10, where we read, "The Son of Man has come to seek and to save the lost." Although there are still elements of the apocalyptic function of the Son of Man in Luke, the christological roles are more directly linked with the prophetic tradition of Israel, with the emphasis on the themes of inclusiveness. It is surely by design that the birth of Jesus takes place in a stable and that his first visitors are shepherds. The impression that the work of the Son of Man is that of a seeking shepherd is confirmed by the familiar string of Lukan parables, the seeking shepherd, the seeking housewife, and the seeking father (Luke 15).

The prophetic role is even more explicit, beginning before Jesus' birth with the divine preparation for the incredulous husbands to receive their divinely commissioned sons, John and Jesus (Luke 1), in passages which obviously build on the divine gift of Samuel to his aged parents in 1 Samuel 1-2. The ecstatic utterances of Elizabeth, of Mary, of Simeon, of Zechariah (Luke 1-2) sound the themes of God's compassion on the poor and the deprived, including "all peoples" (1:30-31). The direct quotes from Isaiah in Luke 3 at the baptism and in Luke 4, as the text for Jesus' inaugural sermon in Nazareth, highlight the inclusion of all people in God's saving acts, and specify that it is the poor, the blind, the oppressed who are to hear the message of liberation. The sermon's use of Elijah and Elisha as forerunners of the opening to the Gentiles of a share in God's blessings (4:16-21) strengthens this feature of Luke's portrayal of Jesus. In addition to Q material in Luke 7:18-34 and 11:29-32, where the ministry to outsiders is announced and documented from the work of the Old Testament prophets, Luke includes unique material which illustrates both the outreach of Jesus to those beyond the ethnic or ritual or moral bounds of Jewish piety, as well as the responsiveness of the outsiders to his words and work. Women, whose place in Judaism was peripheral, figure prominently in Luke as both supporters of, and those who benefit from, Jesus (7:11-17, 34, 37; 8:1-3; 23:28-32). The Parables of the Good Samaritan, of the Pharisee and the Tax Collector, of the Rich Man and Lazarus, and of the Great Banquet confirm this central theme of Jesus as the divinely endowed agent of compassion and reaching out. The symbolism of the numbers in the two stories of Jesus' sending his messengers to carry forward his work--twelve (9:1-5) and seventy (10:1-2)--seems to point to the dual mission to Israel and to the Gentiles.

The picture of Jesus includes expectation of hostility and death from the outset (2:34-35), but when death comes it is received with tranquility (23:46) and expectation of immediate access to the presence of God (23:41-43), an inference which is confirmed by Stephen's utterance at the moment of his own death (Acts 7:56). The power title, Son of God, is missing in Luke's crucifixion scene (22:35, 70). The community is expected to share in Jesus' sufferings, as well as his rule (22:28-30). But even now it already participates in the Kingdom of God, whose powers are at work in its midst. They are the "little flock" to whom God has chosen to give the kingdom (12:32). The exorcisms are evidence of the presence of the kingdom in their midst (11:20). There is no need to be concerned with apocalyptic signs, since the kingdom is already evident among them (17:20-21). They stand at the turn of the eras, when the Old Covenant epoch and its messengers are features of the past and the powers of the New Age are already at work (16:16).

The sustaining and guiding power of the community is the Spirit, whose coming lies still in the future (Acts 1:8), but whose work will be an extension of what Jesus has made possible and begun. The abiding presence of Christ among his people, during his bodily absence, is vividly represented by Luke in the post-resurrection experiences of the disciples, when their burning hearts attest to his having made himself known to them in the exposition of the scriptures (24:27, 32) and in the breaking of the bread (24:35). Similarly in Acts, Paul's farewell to the church at Ephesus urges its leaders to care for and feed the flock (20:28).

An approach to christology which concentrated on a title or titles would not be ready to grasp the rich detail of Luke. The links of his literary method with ancient historiography have been superbly shown in the classic study by H. J. Cadbury, *The Making of Luke-Acts*.[61] The formal proem (1:1-4), the frequent allusions to reigning figures, and especially the synchronism in 3:1-2, are characteristic features of history-writing of the period, as are the speeches of Jesus in the gospel and of the apostles and others in Acts. Less widely recognized, however, is the influence on Luke of the hellenistic romance, which often concerned itself with the travels, trials, and divine guidance of the devotees of a deity--a genre which had its origins in the classical epoch, but which achieved great popularity as a vehicle for religious or philosophical propaganda in the second and third centuries.[62] With respect to both literary modes, Luke was obviously in tune with the culture of his time, as he sought to exploit its literary interests in behalf of the Christian movement.

Earlier we noted briefly the influence on the Gospel of John of the Isis cult and its methods of propaganda. Rather than the feminine term, *sophia,* which Isis devotees linked with their object of adoration, John identifies Jesus with a masculine equivalent, *logos.* The functions of the Logos in creation and in bringing together those who have shared in the divine illumination, and hence are partners in the faithful community, are fully set forth in the prologue to the Fourth Gospel.

The narratives of John seem to be told not merely to report the activities of Jesus, but with symbolic purposes, to represent a deeper level of meaning of or participation in the "life which was the light of human beings. (1:4). Occasionally the stories drift off without a narrative conclusion, as in the dialogue between Jesus and Nicodemus in John 3. There is no mention of Jesus' baptism or of the elements of bread and wine at the last supper, yet the imagery of water and wine permeate the narrative material: water and wine in the first sign at Cana (John 2); birth by water and Spirit (John 3); living water (John 4); washing as a means of being healed (John 5 and 9); the bread of life (John 6); the washing of the disciples' feet (John 13). In every instance the salvific role of Jesus involves participation by the potential beneficiaries.

The same viewpoint is evident in the "I am" sayings of John: the bread of life must be eaten; to acknowledge Jesus as "I am" involves keeping his word (John 8:52); the light of the world must be followed; the door must be entered; the shepherd lays down his life for the sheep; he who is the resurrection and the life must be trusted; the way provides access to the Father; the vine enables its branches to bear fruit. It is impossible, or at least inappropriate, to separate the Christ image from the destiny and responsibilities of his people. Even a title such as Lamb of God (1:29) includes awareness that he takes away the sin of the world. Both the titles and the activities of Jesus demand active participation. To analyze the titles in the abstract is to violate the clear intent of the gospel writer. The models of community implicit in John are not structural or hierarchical, but in the fullest sense communal. This is evident in the command to wash one another's feet, and in the post-resurrection scenes of John 20 and 21. Love is not merely an emotion or attitude, but a way of acting in behalf of others (21:15-19). Even in the closing statement about the significance of Jesus' signs (20:30-31), what he

---

[61]First published in 1927. Reprinted, London: SPCK, 1961.

[62]Also discussed in detail in my *Miracle in the Roman World.*

has done is to be believed by the community, so that its members may share in the life which Christ, the Son of God brings.

+ + + + + + + + + + + + + + + +

The criticism of standard scholarly christological research, that it treats concepts and titles as fixed entities, is valid, even though it has not been avoided by those who voiced it. What is required is two-fold: (1) there must be a disciplined, unrelenting effort to allow the New Testament writers to speak on their own terms, so that we respond to what they say without prejudicing their meaning by theological biases, by features of their life-world (such as apocalypticism) which we may find intellectually embarrassing, or by unacknowledged preferences for one of the christological options offered by the New Testament. Luther's preference for Paul, for example, has operated as a value judgment in assessing New Testament evidence, especially in German scholarship. But (2) christological study must adopt an approach which is perhaps symbolized by a statement in Acts 2:6, in the narrative of Pentecost: "Each one heard them speaking in his own language." To add to this notion the phrase from Hebrews 1:1, "In these last days God . . . has spoken to us by his Son," we perceive that God's address to humanity in Jesus was, and continues to be, heard in a variety of languages. Language differences involve cultural differences, or, as the sociologists of knowledge would say, differences in life-world. The task of christological research is to seek to hear the Word and to translate it into our own language--as faithfully as possible--as it was heard by the writers of the New Testament. It requires the abandonment of glib generalizations, and avoidance of appealing to anachronistic evidence. It demands holistic study of New Testament texts, rather than surgical analysis of hypothetical components or sources. It can perhaps avoid the foolish stance that, while it is fine for "all flesh to see God's salvation," they ought to see it our way.

THE FALL OF THE TEMPLE AND THE COMING OF THE END:
THE SPECTRUM AND PROCESS OF APOCALYPTIC ARGUMENT
IN 2 BARUCH AND OTHER AUTHORS

Anitra Bingham Kolenkow
Berkeley, California

2 Baruch begins by asking and receiving answers to two basic questions—one on the destruction of the temple (how long), the other on the end of the world (will it go to oblivion). The end of the world is moot and the pseudepigraphic author must ask about it. What are the functions of pseudepigraphy and of the endtime in 2 Baruch's period and where do 2 Baruch and his fellow authors fit in the spectrum of apocalyptic beliefs.

I. The Horror of the Present

There has been a recent scholarly tendency to see apocalyptic forecasts as mere hypotheses—games played by the wise. It is quite correct that apocalyptic is the production of literarily skilled and learned men. Its heroes, as von Rad noted long age,[1] are scribes (Enoch, Baruch, Ezra) and its revelations are written. It is also a genre of hypothesis (one writer is arguing against another about the future—2 Baruch would seem to be reacting against the arguments of 4 Ezra).[2] However, the use of literary skills and hypothetical arguments does not mean that the concerns are not real and the issues not moot. This is an age of horror. In most apocalyptic writings, the present is (as in Dan 12:1) the worst of all possible times—to be followed by the best of all times. Reading 2 Baruch, the words describe a time when the wise have been brought down to or below the foolish:[3]

48:33   For there shall not be found many wise at that time and the intelligent shall be but few.
70:5   The wise shall be silent and the foolish shall speak.

The lowering of the wise is a part of the time of confusion and chaos where the mean rule over the honorable. Who would not fear when the temple is destroyed and communities are slaughtered. bMak 24 a, b portrays a situation plainly. The heathen are worshipping at ease, most Jews are weeping at the sight of the prospering heathen—or at the sight of a fox coming from the ruined temple. Akiba, knowing of the prophecies of the destruction of Jerusalem (Mic 3:12; Jer 26:18-21) and seeing them fulfilled, now believes that Zech 8:4 may also be fulfilled. There is a great need for ultimate answers in such a time which lets the wise appropriate the prophecy of the past—and transmute into literature those fears and beliefs which usually belong to the underprivileged or opponents of existing power.[4] It is, of course, the skill of the prophet or person within

---

[1]G. von Rad, *Old Testament Theology* (New York, 1965) 2.306.

[2]For arguments on these points, cf. A. B. Kolenkow, *An Introduction to II Baruch 53, 56-74: Structure and Substance* (Harvard thesis, 1972) 9-26.

[3]Both 4 Ezra and 2 Baruch may be defined as apocalyptic in that they understand the present as the worst of times and see a better time coming, resulting from divine action in the present (not in the future as in eschatology). Apocalyptic is a form of "almost realized" eschatology and therefore used with or an alternate for miracles (cf. John). Eschatology, as described by Socrates (Phaedo 114d), cheers a man of sense when he is about to die.

[4]In this regard, the prophets become as those philosophers described by B.-A. Scharfstein, *The Philosophers* (New York, 1980). Scharfstein describes those who have lost their parents or for some other reason have been placed in a state of deprivation—

society who (for whatever reason) is able to gain perspective beyond himself and set ordinary life in divine perspective. Liminal knowledge becomes public written prophecy, taking on the garb of myth or the past so that it can be used to define the present and the future.

II. Giving Perspective to the End--Pseudepigraphy and Prophetic Myth

In such an age, myths give the ability to speak to and separate oneself and one's audience from the present. Vernant, Lattimore and others have talked of the use of alternate versions of myth to carry on an argument in a society. Snell emphasized the use of myth to distance oneself from the present situation.[5] Ancient society also knew well the use of myth or story from the past to describe the present, or the use of a past figure to speak about present problems. Numenius understood Plato as using Socrates to express Plato's views so that Plato would not face prosecution for his ideas of the gods (Eusebius *Prep Ev* 650d-651a). Further, to speak from the past not only gave freedom from present entanglements, it gave the authority of perspective and the proof of reliability, since as Philo said, fulfillment of past prophecies gives confidence in ones made of the future (VM 2:288).

Apocalyptic, like Socrates' evaluation of the gods, was a danger to the state. Apocalypticists were dangerous; they told when the endtime would occur and what would cause it--thus giving others the possibility of bringing it about (as prophets also gave magicians the timing and definition of right means to kill the emperor in the Roman world). They defined present power as evil and to be overcome, while present weakness was not rightful punishment but a result of temporary chaos; the present weak would be made strong or resurrected. This was part of the apologetic function of prophecy.

As part of their giving perspective from the past and from heaven, apocalyptic authors needed to argue from a divine viewpoint and/or from the point of view of an ancient worthy who was qualified to talk to God. The ability to consider themselves able to do the first is what gives the authors of the two versions of the Testament of Abraham (TA), or the gospels, their amazing freedom with citation of divine sayings. The two versions of TA present very different versions of the divine will. Each version, however, has God act and speak using biblical arguments and terminology. Thus the freedom gained for an author to speak as God is gained by putting language upon God which God would speak in that situation (cf. Thucydides on the writing of speeches according to what the speakers ought to have said in the situation).[6] This limitation of biblical or appropriate language also fosters the separation-distancing (as Snell described) of oneself (as author) from the situation--enabling one to speak more effectively to oneself or others.

In addition, to counteract or address this god, the author needed a figure of sufficient authority to talk to God--to argue against God, receive visions and then be moved to the divine viewpoint (as Abraham and Job are in the Bible). In 4 Ezra, Ezra both protests to God or an angel and talks back to vision. In 4 Ezra, what undoubtedly is

---

who are then enabled to use their knowledge to answer the normal problems of society. These are problems which, in the way of educated life, they might not have appropriated to themselves. In a time of chaos, they are forced to do so.

[5]J.-P. Vernant and P. Vidal Naquet, *Myth and Tragedy in Ancient Greece* (Sussex, 1981). R. Lattimore, *Story Patterns in Greek Tragedy* (Ann Arbor, 1969) 3ff. B. Snell, *The Discovery of the Mind* (Cambridge, MA, 1953).

[6]A. B. Kolenkow, "The Genre Testament and the Testament of Abraham," in Nickelsburg, ed., *Studies on the Testament of Abraham* (Missoula, 1976) 143ff.

most convincing to readers is that the situation forces Ezra to reply to Lady Jerusalem using the arguments which the angel has used to him. Again, to present this opponent-prophet, the author has to create a world consistent with its biblical context--thus the very careful use of the characteristics of the figure or the transfer of language and characteristics from one who would be assumed to have similar characteristics (as Abraham to Moses) in the creation of a new story-world.[7]

In the presentations of 4 Ezra and 2 Baruch, the two possibilities (of alternate stories for argument and of cross-over characterization) have been joined. 4 Ezra and 2 Baruch use similar language and structures in portraying different people. At the same time they portray opposite opinions--enough so that it may be argued that one is building on the other to argue with the other. Thus, 2 Baruch and 4 Ezra perform the functions of the alternate versions of TA (although they do not tell the same story) in that they argue with each other while at the same time using the same basic structures.

4 Ezra begins with a history (comparable to CD 2-3) which is used to protest the injustice of God by emphasizing the "cor malignum" and the fact that others have done more wickedly than Israel. Ezra becomes intercessor, taking on the functions of the "friend of God" (as Abraham in Genesis 15 or the angel in 1 En 13:4).[8] Then 4 Ezra uses Job and Daniel as major resources for his portrayal of divine speech. Job also furnishes Ezra with the model whose hero protests the justice of God and where "retributive history" theory (in the mouth of Job's opponents) is overthrown.[9] (The use of Ezra as intercessor, à la Abraham, however, puts Ezra at one remove from a person defending himself; he is, in fact, accused of ranging himself with the ungodly 8:47--as Abraham.) Then, however, Ezra takes up the argument of the divine, not only (as has been noted) in his reply to Lady Jerusalem, but in a theology of Adam and the Jobian power of God. Daniel furnishes the author with an ascetic model and with language and visions to which the author can give new meaning (cf. 12:12--not as to Daniel).

2 Baruch is not presented as changing his mind in the same way as 4 Ezra. 2 Baruch, instead of protesting, proclaims the divine power and prerogatives of Jobian divinity. He laments the situation of Adam's guilt (even using the same words as 4 Ezra). He asks questions and receives answers on the same topics discussed in 4 Ezra. He makes the Danielic structures of 4 Ezra a part of a new prophetic-historical configuration (36-40, 53, 56-74) which modifies the arguments of 4 Ezra. As Jeremiah and Deuteronomy, Baruch's Lord speaks of placing life and death before men (19:1). He may use the teaching of Jer 46:28 that God will not make a full end of Israel. However, he is also willing to give new revelation (against Jer 27:22; 52:18f.; 2 Macc 2:4-8) and use an alternate rabbinic teaching about the fate of the temple vessels--in order to proclaim heavenly continuities. 4 Ezra and 2 Baruch, however, are no mere conglomerates of arguments. The narrative power of both 4 Ezra and 2 Baruch is shown by the fact that different critics will consider one or the other the prior work.

---

[7]It is the power of dream or vision (or novelist) to use the features of one person to portray another or to combine several structures into a new whole with new meaning.

[8]Ezra, of course, is the one known for his confession of Israel's sin (Ezra 9). Thus, Ezra is portrayed in the beginning as one with those characteristics which are opposed to those he is known for. This "alternate" or opposite portrayal of Ezra may be compared with that of the vengeful Abraham in TA, when Abraham is normally portrayed as intecessor. One should note the relevance of the Enochian picture of angels for the monastic community at Qumran and later monastic communities. The angel who should be intercessor loses his power if he goes and mingles with women, "you were formerly spiritual."

[9]The use of Jobian argument in 4:5-9, 5:36-37 is important for an understanding of 4 Ezra, as has often been argued by this author.

III. Divine Retribution and the Endtime

The questions of divine retribution and the end of the world--as possible or threatened for the present--are alive and important in the Hellenistic and Greco-Roman eras. Jewish belief in divine retribution--as well as in the coming of the end time--is well known. The Greeks and Romans likewise used this belief as part of their "Weltanshauung." Those in power who wanted to control people, and the analysts who desired to control those in power, saw the heuristic value of such belief. Critias' *Sisyphos* says that laws were made first and then thinkers invented the gods so that men would not commit crimes in secret (Nauck *Frag Trag*[2] p. 77). Diodorus Siculus sees the appearance of figures like Eunus as keeping men virtuous:

> It is to the interest of society that fear of the gods should be deeply embedded in the hearts of the people. For those who act honestly because they themselves are virtuous are but few, and the great mass of humanity abstain from evil doing only because of the penalties of the law and the retribution that comes from the gods (XXXIV-XXXV: 2: 47).[10]

On the mythic level, Ovid's Metamorphoses picture the divine concern for the actions of mankind (cf. Philemon and Baucis). Orphic belief in the end of the world is tied to this. The crowds continue to be like the crowds of Seneca's *Hercules Oetaeus*:

> The overthrow of Hercules bids us believe the Thracian bard. Soon, soon, when to the universe shall come the day that the law shall be overwhelmed . . . then from the lost sky the affrighted sun shall fall . . . and Hercules asks for this revenge: Let this day wherein I die perish for the world . . . Now were it fitting to restore blind chaos . . . Why dost Thou spare the stars; Thou art losing Hercules, father.

As evidenced by Seneca's play, the world of antiquity was very conscious of the relation between the destruction of divine beings or temples and the destruction of cities or the world. Aesop knows that the place which kills him will be punished. As. Mos. 9-10 knows that the death of Taxo will bring earthly chaos and the rising of the righteous to the stars. 1 Cor 2:7-8 speaks of this age having crucified the Lord of glory and doomed to pass away. Paul also knows that if anyone destroys God's temple, God will destroy him (3:17).

> Note the ready motion between destruction of divine being and temple (4 Ezra 10:1--son means town or temple; cf. John 2:21--"Temple of his body").

Forecast destruction is, of course, a powerful support to religion--perhaps fostering both the growth of Qumran, with the fall of Jerusalem to Pompey occuring ca. forty years after harm to the teacher of righteousness (CDb 2:14, cf. Com Ps 37:1-7) and the growth of the Jesus movement forty years after the death of Jesus. With the fall of the temple, the forecast of the end of the world made apocalyptic into apologetic which explained the fall of the temple not as retribution, but as that evil event which triggered the end time.[11] Where an apocalypse portrays the destruction of the world following an attack on Jerusalem and the death of the Messiah (as in Hippolytus Ref 9:25), it may show a redefinition of a present defeat by a forecast destruction of the world. Indeed, any kind

---

[10]Cf. Justin, I Apol 12, on a God who punishes. On Justin's views of the end, cf. L. W. Barnard, *Justin Martyr* (Cambridge, England, 1967) 165-67.

[11]Cf. A. B. Kolenkow, "To Found or to Destroy," *Center for Hermeneutical Studies* (CHS) # 25, 27; "Beyond Miracles, Suffering and Eschatology," *SBL Seminar Papers*, 1973, II, 172.

of destruction following a man-caused disaster may then be turned into apocalyptic. In fact, histories, both Deuteronomic and apocalyptic, may be apologetic in that they argue beyond one destructive event as a punishment to say that that event itself is being punished.[12]

IV. A Spectrum of Messiah-Temple and Endtime Belief

By the first chapters of his book, the author of 2 Baruch shows himself fundamentally concerned with questions of the meaning of the fall of the temple and the end of the world. He shows divine responsibility for the fall of the temple and has God affirm that the world will not be destroyed. Where does the argument of 2 Baruch stand in the spectrum of options about the relationship between the coming of the endtime and the fall of Jerusalem (and/or the Messiah).

Deuteronomic history argues for a succession of punishments--with the punisher not necessarily being virtuous, but merely an agent of God. The Assumption of Moses says the Gentiles think that because Israel is in a state of sin, she will not be revenged if attacked (1:13; 5:1; 11:16-18).[13] However, if Taxo and his sons (being righteous) allow themselves to be killed, they will bring vengeance for themselves, including the world-chaos of the endtime.

Hippolytus Ref 9:25 says the Jews believe: the Messiah gathers all Jews in Jerusalem where they keep their ancient customs. Then there will be a conflict with foreign princes where the Christ will fall by the sword. A termination and conflagration of the universe will follow (at which time the resurrection will be completed and a recompense occur). Here one may see the motifs of an endtime-related obedience of the laws by the Jews in Jerusalem, an attack on these righteous with the death of their Messiah being followed by the destruction of the world. One may argue that this latter point is related to motifs like that of the death of Taxo or Hercules.

4 Ezra, in arguing beyond the idea of destruction for sins (and versus the Deuteronomic view) comes to see the death of the Messiah and/or the fall of the temple (4 Ezra 10:1; 7:29ff.) not as something which will be punished or serves as punishment, but as a preliminary to the birth of the new and as the will of God. (Cf., of course, John 12:29.)[14]

2 Baruch returns to the Deuteronomic process of divine retribution (for a time) as related to the fall of the temple (angels come so that the Gentiles may not say that they have done it by themselves). However, 2 Baruch does not say that the Messiah dies (unlike both Hippolytus and 4 Ezra) but rather stresses the continuity of his rule over the time which is the end of one age and the beginning of the next. Further, there is no post-Messianic destruction, but rather a peaceable transfer time between one age and the next.

---

[12]As one sees in the world of the 2nd century and later, philosophic doctrines also complicate the picture, especially the Stoic doctrines of creation and destruction. As Justin, Lactantius and Plotinus show, the question of the end of the world is a moot one between apologist-apocalyptists and philosophers. Justin's II Apol 7 says that both Stoics and Christians believe in the end of the world by fire, but he says they have different reasons. Lactantius Inst 7:3 asks if the Stoics can give a reason why they mix god with the world and say he can be destroyed--although Lactantius will admit that every philosophy has some part of the truth (7:7). Plotinus mocks the Gnostics (and those like 4 Ezra and Revelation) when the end does not occur and is rationalized by being made dependent on a certain number of individual souls (II 9, 20).

[13]A. B. Kolenkow, "The Assumption of Moses as a Testament," *Studies on the Testament of Moses*, Nickelsburg, ed. (Missoula, 1973) 72.

[14]4 Ezra 13 shows how 4 Ezra specifically contrasts with Hippolytus since 4 Ezra has the nations come to fight the messiah and he overcomes them (13:28-39).

V. 2 Baruch and 4 Ezra:
The Similarities of Subjects, the Difference of Approach

2 Baruch and 4 Ezra have many themes, portrait motifs and even word usages in common. Yet the two works often give contradictory or alternative answers from the divine. Each book has a scribal author talking to angels or God. Each book talks about Daniel's four empire vision. Each book uses a word for word language about Adam and similar language and structures especially in regard to visions and interpretations. However, unlike the four gospels or the two versions of TA (each giving an alternative presentation of the same story), these two works tell different stories--a rebuilder talks about the end of the world-age, a person present at the destruction talks about the continuities between one age and the next. It is the similar subjects, the similarities of wording and structure that allow one to see the conversation taking place. It is the differences which show the places of the authors in a spectrum of apocalyptic writing and give each a "Sitz im Leben" in the Judaism of the period.

When 2 Baruch begins his book with the two topics-questions--the fall of the temple (a present situation) and "whether the world will go back to nothingness"--he shows what is important to him and enables one to contrast his views with those of 4 Ezra. Where Ezra has emphasized the death of the son-temple and the sudden trans-figuration of Jerusalem--and talks of the field where evil is sown as passing away (4:29) and world return to primaeval silence (7:30). 2 Baruch begins by stressing the temporary nature of the temple's destruction, the continuity of the heavenly temple, and finally of a clear answer that the world-age will not be given over the oblivion. Where 4 Ezra 7 says the Messiah will die, 2 Baruch later answers that the Messiah will rule in peace for the age (73:1) and that there is a peaceful transfer from that which is corruptible to that which is incorruptible (74).

Other similarities and differences appear as one reads further. 4 Ezra emphasizes that the end comes through God (6:6), but that it is dependent on the filling up of a certain number. These are the seed (4:36), who are like Ezra the righteous and chaste (6:32)--versus the unrighteous and incontinency on earth (5:11); cf. also the pure life (7:122), the abstinent (7:125). In fact, 4 Ezra effectively argues that the endtime if brought about by a gathering of a certain number (chaste and ascetic as Ezra) and seems to be urging that, since the times are at an end, people can act to bring about the end by their own lifestyle (thus filling up the number of the ascetic).

The possibility of an ascetic life in this land[15] is pointed out when Ezra is asked to keep the ascetic diet of no meat and wine, but only herbs of the field (cf. also Daniel and his friends who eat neither the king's food or his wine, but only vegetables and water and yet thrive (Dan 1:8-16). In 13:42, the ten tribes become an image to show one may go to a land where they have never dwelt--and keep the statutes there as they have never kept them in their own land--and then return.

2 Baruch's revelation likewise emphasizes that the end is near and that it is dependent on a number--but of all who are to be born before the end (23:4-7). This revelation makes the coming of the endtime dependent on God and not on the number of the righteous--which a man can change--cf. Baruch's emphasis on God's use of foreigners, angels destroying Jerusalem (7:1), God brings a sign of the end or chaos (25:1). What 2 Baruch does say is that the end is near and that the righteous will see change (44:7).

---

[15]The term "Ardat" (9:26) is the Aramaic equivalent of "this land" in contrast to Azareth (the other land), suggesting that the original language of the book was Aramaic (cf. unpublished talk of the author, 1969). Does 4 Ezra also imply that the times are so evil that one must even eat in Palestine what one would normally eat in a foreign country?

(Thus, 2 Baruch also is not saying with certain rabbis that only when all Israel obeys the law will the end come.) 2 Baruch sees the rich possibility. Where 4 Ezra emphasizes the few, 2 Baruch says there are "not a few righteous." (The few, however, for 4 Ezra are the seed which will make a great harvest in the next age.) Although 4 Ezra mentions plenteousness in the future age (8:52), 2 Baruch describes flesh and wine (two things Ezra is not to eat and the Pythagorean gave up).

Further import of what 2 Baruch is saying may be gained by seeing where he mentions the virtues which are applied to Ezra in 4 Ezra. Where Ezra and those like him are the righteous and chaste (pure) and can save only themselves, in 2 Baruch, Hezekiah is righteous and Josiah is pure--the only one in his time--and theirs are good periods. Although foreigners (with God) have destroyed Jerusalem, the very possibility of man's saving Jerusalem is emphasized by God's request that the righteous get out (those who had works and prayed in Jerusalem) so that the city may fall (2:1, 2). Baruch and Jeremiah, pure from sins in his heart, are not captured. Works and prayers are what make a good period, but prayer is important even in a bad period--not only might it have saved Jerusalem, but 2 Baruch shows that it did save Manasseh in an evil period, as it had saved Hezekiah in a good period (63-65). 2 Baruch promises that the people who have been justified in the law will be able to acquire the world which does not die (51:3). Those who have been saved by their works and to whom the law has been a hope will see wonders in their time (51:7). Now is the time for works of the law and diligent prayer (84:8-10), as in the times of old when men trusted in their works and prayed (85:12). Although there is no place for prayer in the judgment (85:2; 2 Baruch agrees with 4 Ezra), 2 Baruch would emphasize that there will be leaders (46:4; 77:15; cf. 2 Baruch's common emphasis on the power of good or bad leadership). Leadership, indeed, is the point--and leadership would seem to be the concept which reinforces 2 Baruch's tie between one age and the next (with no destruction in between). (Is the argument that if Jeremiah and others had righteousness and power would not the Messiah have power to maintain continuity?) In the messianic age there is no stopping of works or riddance of beasts--but the works advance of themselves and wild beasts minister to man (73:6; 74:1) in a time which is the passage between corruption and incorruption. What one sees in 4 Ezra and 2 Baruch may be called salvation in the private sphere (4 Ezra) or public sphere (2 Baruch). 4 Ezra emphasizes the possibility of ascetics saving themselves. 2 Baruch says there is the power of righteous kings; stay among their people, the righteous, and you will be saved.

VI. The Integration of Views of the End,
of the Messiah or the Temple and of the Personal Life

If one aligns the individual teachings of 4 Ezra and 2 Baruch, the teachings of each may be argued to compose consistent wholes. 4 Ezra has an ascetic apocalypticism which emphasizes destruction preceding new creation. The ascetic lifestyle with its fasting and chastity is an alternate picture of the destruction of the body (which is often called divinization). On a world scale, this corresponds to the destruction of the world or the transfiguration of Jerusalem after sadness (as well as the death of the Messiah before the new age).[16]

Kabisch and Box[17] relate 4 Ezra's asceticism to the Essenes. The doctrine does look Pythagorean-Orphic and Josephus compared the Essenes to the Pythagoreans

---

[16]4 Ezra, as noted above, also teaches the reaping and passing away of the field where the evil was sown in order that, or to precede the new harvest (4:29, cf. 6:25, the end of my world).

[17]R. Kabisch, *Das Vierte Buch Esra auf seine Quellen untersucht* (Göttingen, 1889) 79. G. H. Box, *The Ezra Apocalypse* (London, 1912) 81. Cf. Porphyry, on Abstinence from Animal Food, for a Pythagorean view.

(Ant 15:371). What is important is the ascetic lifestyle proposed as a possibility. It is a commonplace that the tendency toward asceticism-monasticism occurs when people believe the endtime is coming. One is conscious of evil in oneself and in others--and believes a change of lifestyle is necessary. (One should also note that the monastic situation also fosters the continuation of belief in apocalyptic, even if the end does not occur. As T. Schwartz has rightly remarked, the cause is not only "cognitive dissonance" but the delight in the life modes fostered by apocalyptic.)[18] This may account for the emphasis on both ethics and the endtime in works like 4 Ezra and the Testaments of XII Patriarchs.

The danger in this situation is that the person may see the situation as so hopeless that God must be at fault. 4 Ezra therefore emphasizes that destruction is a process through which God promises new creation to the ascetic Ezra and those like him.

If one places 2 Baruch in the spectrum of apocalyptic thought, he is one who believes in national government, in law-obedience as a valid possibility--and a promise to the righteous in the time of the end. He uses a carefully constructed apocalyptic historiography as a way to move between *those* like 4 Ezra who suggest complete destruction and the salvation of only a few *and those* who argue that one should join the Gentiles in their prosperity. 2 Baruch teaches that there will be no giving of the world-age over to oblivion and that there is an alternation of bad and good periods with the bad always followed by the good and with the Messiah ruling over the righteous in the transition between the final good and bad periods. The chaos of the present is a sign of the end. Because the Gentiles are on top does not mean that one should join them. 2 Baruch portrays delights of the Gentiles as also failing (83:10-21) in this time. The sin now, as in past periods, is "mingling" with the Gentiles (56:12; 58:1; 60:1; cf. 42:4, 5). For both writers, the present is a time of horror. For 4 Ezra, the ascetic separatist, the need is to withdraw even from his own nation and give special teaching to the wise. For 2 Baruch, the advocate of law and government, the danger is that one may unite with the Gentiles and not attain the end promised to the righteous.[19]

---

[18]*Cargo Cult: A Melanesian Type-Response to Culture Contact* (unpublished paper, read in brief form at the 9th International Congress of Anthropological and Ethnological Sciences, Tokyo, 1968), esp. 78 (on states of expressive feeling, status inversion). This is a work of important insights for apocalyptic, magic and psychocultural dynamics (although some may feel this is overemphasized). For example, evidence is adduced for magic as an alternative or support to apocalyptic-prophecy. Cf. note 3 above.

[19]2 Baruch may be compared with the political theories of divine retribution (as III above) although moved by the apocalyptic situation, a "sign" giving immediacy to threat.

A JOINT PAPER
BY THE MEMBERS OF THE
STRUCTURALISM AND EXEGESIS
SBL SEMINAR

Brian Watson Kovacs, Editor

0.   At the moment of its enunciation, any communication has a spontaneous tempo-rality. The temporality may be that of speaker(s), hearer(s) or, commonly, both. In that sense, it is diachronic; its meaning comes into being through time and within the duree of human consciousness.

0.01   Some communications hardly come into being before they are lost. Though they flirt with textuality, in order to have any meaning at all, they are overwhelmed by their diachronicity--spontaneous temporality--and evanesce. People will little note nor long remember what they say.

0.02   Other endure. Their durability means that their spontaneous temporality, their diachronicity, gives place to a permanence of meaning that transcends the moment of enunciation and gives the message repeatability: at other times, in other places, and under changed circumstances. The message has become text, though in whatever form.

0.1   Textuality depends on the synchronicity of every message. Every message means something because of certain grounding structures which are independent of the spon-taneities of the moment of enunciation. Beauty is not just in the eye of the beholder, neither so is meaning.

0.11   For a text to *mean*, it must communicate something new, something unique which has never been uttered before.

0.12   For a text to be understood, it must be conditioned upon something, structures, which are more durable than even the textuality of the text.

0.121   If the text be solely conditioned upon the interrogatories which particular text-users, individuals, or communities, bring to the text, then the text a fortiori could not say anything truly new to the user. At best it could be an iconic representation of the consciousness(es) of the text-user or -using community.

0.122   The novelty of the text requires its grounding in certain conditions or commonalities which stand outside of ordinary temporality. Potency for meaning must reside in the text qua text, wherever else it may reside.

0.123   If the text have not this permanency, if it be not grounded synchronically, then its ability to mean must continue to drift, and in drifting ultimately disappear.

0.124   The capacity to mean requires generality, not particularity. The uniqueness of enunciation is created through the extraordinary complexity of a purely general system being used to create new artifacts (speech) by old means (grammar / syntax). Without a durable generality, meaning disintegrates even as it is forming: "You cannot step into the same river once" (Cratylus).

0.13   To communicate, the text-producer and text-user must share some synchronicity that conditions and endures in the text as text. What they share is the "grammar"--or, structure--of textuality.

0.2   Structures, grammar, stand outside of time. They lack the diachronicity of [shared] consciousness. They lack all duree. They are givens, necessary to the act of communication. For that reason, they may be called 'apodictic.' A caveat, however: what is undeniably certain is not meaning or any meaning but the conditions that enable a text or communication to mean at all.

0.201   It is certain that people communicate; consciousnesses do convey meanings to one another, both contemporaneously and through time. Without synchronicity, without the apodictic structures of communication, each consciousness would be a windowless monad locked in a world of the expected of its own creation.

0.21   Grammar / structure is not meaning; and it certainly is not message. The structure provides the conditions upon which an expressed agglomeration of signifiers may convey meaning when they are used according to its syntax. Thereby, the message retains its novelty and has the potency to stand over against the receiver—and even over against the sender as the message becomes text. Grammar does not mean. It does not depend on any particular consciousness. It provides the basis for intelligible communication precisely by its synchronic generality. If it be in any sense an artifact (Heidegger), it is an artifact prior to any consciousness and prior to any communication.

0.211   Signifiers, too, are synchronic. Syntactically organized and enunciated by and/or for a consciousness, i.e., diachronized with a duree, signs mean. Signs must be diachronized to mean. Even to become text, a message must first be expressed, i.e., diachronized. To mean *again*, a text must be rediachronized. It must be restored within duree. Outside of any duree, text and sign alike are pure structure.

0.3   The synchronic synchronizes the diachronic.

0.31   Structure grounds and conditions meaningful duree.

1.   Structuralism is, therefore, both Wissenschaft in the broad sense and science in the strict sense.

1.01   Structuralism does not provide a linguistic natural history. While particular morphological forms of language may each have their particular histories, structuralism is not interested in collecting accounts of such peculiarities. Nor is it interested in conventions. Its theory of communication grounds the possibilities for meaning in apodictic structures prior to any meaning. Structuralism focusses on these conditions.

1.02   Structuralism is also not simple observation and description. It is not "practical" in the sense of reporting the praxis of language users. At its worst, such reportage fragments what it observes. At best, it provides the material for inductive generalization which can never approach the apodicticity of grounding conditions.

1.1   Structuralism is practical science in the sense that it pursues hard data. It presupposes the empirical verifiability of models through data from texts. The data are organized and by interpretive models applied by structuralist students and researchers. But, the data arise from conditions independent of the models. Thus, structuralism is not humanistic or existential (Güttgemanns) interpretation; it is scientific analysis. The existence of grounding conditions does *not* mean that the science itself, nor any of its models, are apodictic. They instead are practical and must be verified through recourse to analysis of the evidence.

1.11   Grounding structures through their apodicticity offer the hope of scientific convergence or approximation. While models may differ in their (re-)construction of prior grounding conditions, gradually, better models should replace the merely good. Each succeeding generation of approximations should take us further along the analytic road.

1.12   [There is] validity and value [to] the kind of structuralism which posits broadly or even universally applicable models for comprehending the perceived regularities in texts--the kind of proposal found, for example, in Chapter Two of Daniel and Aline Patte's STRUCTURAL EXEGESIS: FROM THEORY TO PRACTICE. [T] his work could [not] be otherwise done than in a broadly "scientific" way--model-building and testing. One kind of criticism of such work [seems] trivial, namely that it uses quasi-mathematical tools (diagrams, "algebra"). In this criticism, [there seems to be] nothing more than knee-jerk humanism and even the "I was never much good at math" rhetoric. Anything remotely describeable as structuralism is going to go on using such tools in appropriate places. Another line of criticism is more serious, that this sort of analysis necessarily makes the text fit the model. That much structuralist work falls into this "reductionism" is clear. But to regard it as necessary and intrinsic is to misunderstand structuralist (and, more generally, scientific) method. Good structural analysis should proceed by defining levels of generality, so that it is appropriate at the first levels to account only for gross textual data. But what is not comprehended at a given level of generality *must* become the object of analysis at another level, so that the methodological model *must* provide for dealing with all the data. (Jobling)

1.2   Structural exegesis is a critical method which deliberately uses contemporary (modern) models for the study of biblical texts.

1.21   These are semiotic models accounting for the phenomenon "signification in discourse."

1.22   These semiotic models are valid only insofar as they have been established by means of a hypothetico-deductive research; i.e., a research which through theoretical reflection posits a hypothetical model then verifies it by applying it to texts originating in various cultures. At first, the applications to specific texts show the inadequacy of certain aspects of the model (or of the entire model) which then needs to be refined through additional theoretical reflection, and so on and so forth until the point when a model can be said to be *operational* because its verifications are conclusive. Since they have been established following the approach characteristic of scientific research, semiotic models are *scientific* in nature. According to the quality of the verifications (and of the theoretical reflection), they are, of course, more or less rigorous scientific models.

1.23   Semiotic models propose a scientific description of the nature of various aspects of a *universal* (human) phenomenon: signification in (human) discourses. The semiotic models insofar as they are operational (and thus have been verified through their application to a sample of discourse originating in a broad range of cultures) can claim to be a legitimate scientific model for this universal phenomenon.

1.24   Claiming scientificness and universality for the semiotic models is not making an absolute claim. As Kuhn has pointed out, a scientific model is based upon a given paradigm which both allows the scientists to perceive the reality out there *and* blinds the scientists to other dimensions of this reality. In other words, semiotic models, as any other scientific model, are culturally bound (and not absolute).

1.25   Because of the culture in which we live [, because it] is a technological culture, scientists, (among whom the semioticians) are bound to perceive any reality in systemic and thus structural terms--in terms of relations in systems of various sorts--rather than in diachronic, historical terms / characteristics of the preceding terms, see D. Patte, WHAT IS STRUCTURALIST EXEGESIS? /. Thus Patte's answer to Bernard Scott at the 1981 SBL-AAR meeting: indeed the semiotic model Patte uses is technological in nature.

1.26   Structural exegesis can also be called "technological" in another sense. As the technician applies scientific models of universal laws for resolving a specific problem, in the same way the structural exegete makes use of a knowledge of semiotic models (concerning the universal phenomenon of the happening of meaning in discourses) to study the specificity of a given text.   Thus structural exegesis can be said to be the technological application of the results of scientific research.

1.27   Consequently, the results of a structural exegesis are a "technological" (not necessarily highly technical!) re-presentation of the biblical texts--i.e., in terms of systems and relations. (1.2- 1.27 Patte)

1.3   Science is a techne of modern Western culture. When structuralism becomes practical, through application to specific texts, then it incorporates that culture and that science, however modeled.

1.301   We who are text-interpreters cannot free ourselves from our bondage to culture when we develop theories and methods for dealing with texts.

1.302   The cultural relativity of science does not a fortiori relativize its results, though in certain theoretical and philosophical systems, it may.

1.303   The cultural relativity of science does not relativize the conditions for com- munication sine qua non that it models. Relativity of models is not equivalent to relativ- ity of what is modeled. The apodicity of the structures of communication is theoretical, not practical.

1.31   In the present Western culture, technological in nature, exegesis must neces- sarily include the use of structural methods so as to fulfill its vocation, to open up the possibility of a valid hermeneutic of the biblical texts. /Patte proposes this argument in WHAT IS STRUCTURALIST EXEGESIS? Chapter I, q.v. The promises made in this line of argument are pursued in Patte's forthcoming PAUL'S FAITH AND THE POWER OF THE GOSPEL; A STRUCTURAL INTRODUCTION TO PAUL./

1.32   [Structuralism does not impose a foreign model on the text.]

1.321   First, the models used, despite their culturally bound formulation, represent universal phenomena. This is simply presupposing that the biblical texts are texts which belong to the process of meaningful human communication.

1.322   Second, structural exegesis indeed uses models which transcend any text. This is what is constantly done in any comparative study which needs to start with a definition of a topic (e.g., eschatology) that transcends and encompasses the specific definitions of that topic (the specific view of eschatology) in the texts being compared. By presenting the biblical texts in terms of categories (models), which are also applied to contemporary situations, it becomes possible to "compare" the biblical texts with these contemporary situations: hermeneutic takes place.

1.33   If you use a "technological" structural method of exegesis, [you are not] capitulating and giving in to the technological paradigm (or myth).

1.331   [Certainly,] when the technological paradigm is perceived as an absolute, as it is more and more in our culture, it becomes a myth out of which we need to be liberated. Yet, this does not mean that the technological paradigm in and of itself is an evil. Let us not throw the baby out with the bath water (that is, for instance, medical techniques) with the technological "spirit of stupor" which would make us perceive as good any coherent and functional system whatever might be its *telos*. What needs to be challenged is the absolutization of the technological paradigm.

1.332   In semiotic terms, this means that the semiotic system, thanks to which the "technological-paradigm-as-absolute" is established, must be transformed. Since this semiotic system is what, more and more, gives meaning, identity, and coherence to the present Western culture, it is useless to challenge it from outside. The alternative paradigm we would present would simply appear to be meaningless and purposeless to the participants via that culture--they have ears but do not hear, eyes but do not see-- anything outside their semiotic system as meaningful.

1.333   There are then two possibilities to free our culture of this myth: either from outside (the destruction of that culture and its participants--in the fiery wrath of a nuclear holocaust toward which it leads) or from inside (by a "coherent deformation"-- Malraux, Merleau-Ponty--of this semiotic system). The latter is what structural exegesis (or, more specifically, its results) accomplishes or will hopefully accomplish.

1.334   By re-presenting the biblical texts in "technological" terms (thus in systemic, relational terms), the biblical texts can made sense for the participants in that technological culture. Yet what makes sense, what appears as coherent, meaningful and able to provide a valid identity, is a paradigm (a system of convictions) which is *not* technological in nature. Thus the absolute character of the technological culture would (ideally?) become impossible to maintain. The scriptural faiths become viable *alterna- tives,* even though they are perceived in technological terms. If it was not obvious, this is what is involved in becoming Jew with the Jews, Greek with the Greeks. And the time is short!

1.335   If our culture is not rapidly freed from its absolutization of the technological paradigm, it will destroy itself--and this may be any day. Thus, it is urgent to develop technologically based methods--sociological, psychological, anthropological (as long as they are based upon a scientific model, i.e., reached through a hypothetico-deductive approach) as well as structural methods. (1.31- 1.335 Patte)

1.4   As science, structuralism is producing practical models which compete with one another in making sense of the currently available evidence.

1.401   At the present stage of structuralism's evolution, no one model or theory is clearly ascendant. Several seem to make substantial contributions to the conversation while differing from one another in substantive respects.

1.41   Hayden White (TROPICS OF DISCOURSE) distinguishes "two wings of the Structuralist movement": the "positivist" (Saussure, Piaget, Marxists) which aims at integration ("a unified level of human consciousness shared by all (people) everywhere") and the "eschatological" (Lacan, Levi-Strauss, Barthes, Foucault) which affirms "the irreducible variety of human nature." Jobling is not sure that White has the terms right but has the same strong sense of the bifurcation of structuralism and tends to put specific individuals in the same camps. Jobling has recently used the terms "constructive" and "deconstructive" for the two kinds of structural analysis which he thinks must always necessarily go together but which seem in practice to have gone separate ways (with biblical structuralism overwhelmingly on the "constructive" side). The constructive approach looks at the text in terms of its *manifesting* a meaning-system; the deconstructive, in terms of its *subverting* a meaning-system (aspiring but not attaining to the 'closure' of meaning--various terminology is available). It is helpful to look at the matter in relation to the hermeneutics of affirmation and suspicion. Human productions manifest deeply accepted values--and also obscure deeply feared contradictions. The hermeneutics of suspicion is an inalienable part of the development of structuralism. The moment of *subversion* of structure must be methodologically built into all structural analytic models. (Jobling).

1.42   Both Levi-Strauss' "formula" for the structure of myth as the mediation of opposites $[f_x(a) : f_y(b) :: f_x(b) : f_{a-1}(y)]$ and Greimas' "square" [his constitutional model or elementary structure of signification based on the logical square] are intended to describe the foundational level of cultural products, e.g., texts. Yet in an important sense Levi-Strauss' "formula" and Greimas' "square" are not equivalent, not parallel. Thus it is inappropriate to superimpose Greimas' square on Levi-Strauss' formula as Greimas (in *Diacritics*) has suggested:

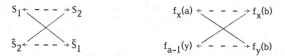

While Greimas' constitutional model may be represented by a square, Levi-Strauss' formula must be represented by a spiral (Maranda and Maranda). In reducing the structure of Levi-Strauss' formula to the structure of a logical square, Greimas appears to be attempting the feat that puzzled mathematicians from Hippocrates and Anaxagoras in the fifth century to Vieta in the sixteenth and Lindemann in the nineteenth--"squaring the circle" or in this case, squaring the spiral! Greimas' superimposition of the two models breaks down at the fourth element of Levi-Strauss' formula, but it is just this element that reflects the helicoidal structure of myth, its movement beyond its starting point to a new plane of experience, a new level of reality. In terms of mathematical models, while Greimas' square is isomorphic with a Klein group (Greimas and Rastier), Levi-Strauss' formula, because of its fourth element, not only is not isomorphic with a Klein group but does not meet the criteria of a "mathematical group" (Polzin) at all.] The essential conclusion to draw from this attempt is that Greimas and Levi-Strauss are raising different questions and offering different insights, and, although there are relationships and dialogue is healthy, ours is the loss if we move too swiftly or surely to accommodate one system of analysis to the other. (Malbon)

1.43   Structuralist models may differ by whether they postulate closed or open sign systems. A closed sign system, rather like a Gestalt, tends to close itself and the meaning system to which it is related. In a sense, as closure is approached, the sign system becomes predictable: the sequence of signs becomes self-generated, introducing the possibility of ellipticisms. The same closure may also apply to subsystems of signs. Given the presentation of certain signs in continuity with one another--having certain syntactic relations with one another--predictable sign sequences follow. Sometimes, though not by any means always, slight shifts in the predictable sequence are used to shift or undermine the predictable meaning system. Often, however, the conventions of the sign-using community prevent such manipulation of predicted sequences by attaching strong negative sanctions to their use. Open systems continually shift into new sign-syntax territory, along with their attendant meaning systems. Again, conventions of the sign-using community may even require that manipulation of established sign-syntax sequences not yield predictable outcomes: the system must not or should not close itself, but rather generates or should generate new agglomerations. In extreme cases, this exfoliation of signs may potentially continue without limit--its ellipticism comes at the point of recognition that the system cannot close.

1.44   Structuralist models may also differ in their corresponding theories of meaning. While structuralism per se is concerned with formal systemic relationships, the synchronicity of textuality, obviously structuralisms bear some relationship to the overall interpretive task, including hermeneutic and often exegesis. Thus, in analyzing a text, the appropriation of structuralist theories and methodologies presupposes some understanding of the nature of meaning. Early structuralist models tended to appropriate reference theories of meaning: the relation between sign and signified was assumed to be simple and often one-to-one. In addition, syntactic notions sometimes tended to locate signs serially, so that meaning arose from simple sequential composition. Signs produced meaning like connecting boxcars one after another produces a railroad train.

1.441   Increasingly, alternative theories of meaning and composition have appeared in structuralist models. One widely appropriated proposes that, at least in narrative, the relationship between structure and meaning is one of "polyvalent isomorphism." The structure of the text produces a pattern or morphos. This pattern bears some (unspecified) resemblance to diachronically experienced 'reality' and by that resemblance calls the experience (meaning) of that reality forth in the communication receiver. Because the relationship points only to the form or pattern and not to specific, exact elements of the 'reality,' typically various realities display some measure of correspondence with the proposed morphism. A monovalent isomorphism tends toward closure by systematically removing these ambiguities in some way. A polyvalent system tends toward openness, inviting the elaboration of more and more correspondences drawn from divergent areas of human experience. Monovalence and polyvalence should not be equated with openness and closure, since together these categories really define four possible structuralisms.

1.442   The question could be asked: "What value does linguistics, and, in particular, Transformational Grammar, have for the structural exegesis of the Bible?" There are some who would say, "None" or "Very little." There are others, however, who see great possibilities in such an application. Some scholars have already applied such studies to other works of literature. The book LINGUISTIC PERSPECTIVES ON LITERATURE contains a number of contributions in that field. Both poetry and prose are covered. Thomas Pavel, for one, deals with narrative prose. Pavel seeks to apply Transformational Grammar theory to narrative structure. He sees value in Chomsky's distinction between "competence" and "performance." Competence is the ability of a human, under ideal conditions, to produce an infinity of utterances. Performance is what is actually produced, which depends not only on competence but also on such factors as memory limitations and pertinence to the situation.

1.443   In applying the foregoing to narratives, Pavel sees the competence system containing a finite set of symbols and rules (including recursive rules) capable of producing an infinity of texts. "This infinity will never be realized completely, but nothing prevents the appearance of any of the potentially generatable stories of the grammar" (Ching, 192). There are also pragmatic rules which determine which of the generatable stories will be "acceptable." (Limitations of human memory are an example. THE THOUSAND AND ONE NIGHTS stretches memory toward those limits with its repeated embeddings.)

1.444   Although, in a psychologically real sense, transformational rules apparently do not take whole sentences and merge them, yet there is a sense in which something similar happens. We say that because a complex sentence represents meanings of two or more whole simple sentences. For the purposes of analyzing sentence meaning, then, it is helpful to look at the "kernel" sentences which make up the meaning of the complex sentences.

1.445   Something similar can be said of narratives and other forms of discourse. Robert Culley demonstrated with Genesis 2:4b-3:24 how various simple narrative sequences could be seen as put together to form the whole narrative by addition, embedding and paralleling (q.v.). He was apparently not trying to relate sentence structure to narrative structure, but the same kinds of changes occur in the former.

1.446   It should be noted that this is not a matter of "seriation." Chomsky, especially, saw "Markov processes" as inadequate to handle the complexity of language (q.v.). By transformational rules he attempted to get at the "depth" element of a correct representation of language. Phrase structure rules could not handle such a sentence as "The man who ate the cheese lying on the platter brought by the barmaid was a connoisseur." To decipher the structure of that sentence requires much more than seriation. Chomsky saw that.

1.447   Deep structure in Chomsky's original vision embodied simple structures, formed by phrase rules, easily related to meaning. Transformational rules changed those simple structures into more complex surface structures often not directly relating to meaning.

1.448   Thus, when we talk about applying Transformational Grammar theory to narrative or other discourse, we are *not* talking about simple seriation. Rather, we are talking about the ability of Transformational Grammar to handle some extremely complex structures that are capable of generating an infinity of sentences, or texts, as the case may be.

1.449   Nor does this mean that we see the composition of the meaning of sentences (or texts) as the mere addition of the meaning of the individual parts. Yet, as Jerrold Katz says: "An ideal speaker-hearer knows infinitely many distinct senses of infinitely many distinct sentences, and that could not be so unless these sentences obtained their senses compositionally" (p. 2). Somehow the meanings of the individual parts of the same sentence (and, to a lesser extent, other nearby sentences) in predictable ways to produce a composite meaning that is *not* a mere sum of the digits, so to speak. The particular configuration in which the words appear is part of what gives the meaning (e.g., "John hit the ball" vs. "The ball hit John"). Such facts probably have analogs in the capturing of meaning in narratives and other forms of discourse found in the Bible. (1.442- 1.449 Hutchinson)

1.45   Finally, structuralisms differ ontologically. While there is substantial concord that communication must be somehow grounded synchronically, theorists differ in the location and status of that grounding structure. Some locate it in human consciousness per se. Others locate it in human sociation. Some attribute structure to language or to the communication situation. Others still find some grounding in modes of being in the world. Thus, one finds structuralisms that use models drawn from psychology and psychoanalysis. Other models appropriate sociology, anthropology, or economics for their form. Yet others use folklore.

1.46   Based on the claims that structuralists make, one would expect the apodicticity of structure to lead not only to rapid approximations in practical scientific application but also to rapid convergence of theoretical models toward some similar solution. To some extent, this actually has occurred, e.g., in morphological theories of meaning and toward polyvalence. In other respects, however, structuralisms either do not converge or even seem to diverge.

2.   Structural exegesis and hermeneutic are not antithetical, but complementary methods for understanding biblical (symbolic) texts. Levi-Strauss and Heidegger, signification and meaning, are two sides of the same coin.

2.1   A comprehensive understanding of a biblical text requires three steps.

      a.   exegesis, which analyzes the definitions, denotations and connotations of symbols and their significance to a people;

      b. interpretation, which analyzes the actors (personae) and actions (ritual actions, mythemes) and oppositions to display their schematization, according to levels of signification (as in the STORY OF ASDIWAL) and/or syntagmatic paradigmatic permutations (as in "The Structural Study of Myth" re Oedipus legend); and

      c. hermeneutic, which articulates the symbolic text's meaning in resonance to the constitutive metaphors latent in the schematization of the myth or ritual and tacit in the whole and in the act of interpreting resonant to the ontogenesis of the human. Meaning is "for them" and "for us."

2.11   Troubetskoy's distinction between terms, relations, and structures is subsumed in the above steps.

2.12   Terms, relations, and structures do not alone constitute a system for systematic understanding. System also includes process of self-transformation (Piaget).

2.13   As including self-transformation, "system" includes metaphysical transformation, ontogenesis, the unfolding of the human phenomenon: human life, selfhood, personhood and individualness. Jung's "individuation" concept grounds Heidegger's hermeneutic and Levi-Strauss' structuralism.

2.14   A religious or other symbolic text is a manifestation, an unfolding of the phenomenon of the human, of human life, self, persona, and individuality.

2.15   Hermeneutic, as a philosophy of the essential, must articulate symbolic texts as latent metaphysics, ethics, psychology, and epistemology.

2.2   The synthesis of Heidegger and Levi-Strauss, hermeneutic and structuralism, is possible, if and only if, one grasps that constitutive metaphor is at the crux of a given symbolic text.

2.201   There are two types of constitutive metaphor, namely, "interpretive" and "onto-logical," and there are at least four kinds of interpretive metaphors.

2.202   Dialectical metaphor interweaves different significations of the same symbol on the same or different levels. (See Levi-Strauss' THE STORY OF ASDIWAL for analysis by levels.)

2.203   Rhetorical metaphor interweaves by "likeness" similar denotations / connotations on different levels (cf. Homeric simile).

2.204   Paradigmatic metaphor interweaves by "likeness" mythemes or symbols in a single vertical column / bundle of mythemes (see Levi-Strauss' OEDIPUS analysis by bundles).

2.205   Syntagmatic metaphor interweaves mythemes from different bundle columns.

2.206   Ontological metaphor articulates the significations of the schematisms by levels or by mythemes *as* the kerygma of human becoming, of the manifestation of Life.

2.21   Mythopoietic metaphors are not so much comparisons as differences between similarities.

2.22   The schematicism is the license for the poetic understanding of a mythopoietic text; it is one's 'poetic license.'

2.23   In a given interpretation, the number of interpretive metaphors is open-ended; this opens the way to a poetics of life.

2.25   Not "the symbol gives rise to thought" (Ricoeur), but the schematicism of symbols or complementary symbols give rise to thought, or rather to interpretation and hermeneutic. A religious symbol or symbolic act has no meaning except in dialectical relation to another. The friction of two symbols / symbolic acts sparks the act of understanding.

2.26   While religious symbolic texts are multileveled (so-called 'polyvalent'), they are not infinitely or indeterminately so; otherwise, understanding would be impossible. Exegetic ethnography is the basis for determining the limited and precise number of levels in a given symbolic text.

2.3   The most comprehensive and fruitful method of exegesis must be a "structural hermeneutic."

2.31   The full understanding of a myth or ritual is both metaphorical and thetic. The validity of an interpretation is tested by both its poetic beauty and its scientific precision.

2.32   If "language speaks," it is because symbols dialectically give rise to metaphor and thesis (ontological utterance).

2.33   Not the Levi-Straussian law of myth, but metaphor is the "depth structure," the life, of symbolic texts.

2.34   The law of myth is really the mathematical formalization and abstraction of permutations of the rhetoric / poetics of selfhood.

2.35   The Heideggerian model of hermeneutic (e.g., in DER WEG ZUR SPRACHE) is really not based on a primordial structure of ontogenesis or ontology, but on the primordial ethic of selfhood, where "self" is meant as in Kierkegaard, a relation that relates itself to its own self.

2.36   The Levi-Straussian law of myth should be more accurately called the "ideal structure" of myth, in contrast to its "depth structure," which is metaphorical. (2.- 2.36 Harrod)

2.4   Structuralism and hermeneutics are open to four analogous goals. Structuralists may aim toward: (1) philosophy (or ideology), (2) theory, (3) structural exegesis, or (4) narrative hermeneutics. A structuralist may choose any one of these four as her or his ultimate goal, though she or he may reach it via another goal (or goals) as penultimate. Thus, for example, in the MYTHOLOGIQUES, Levi-Strauss moves from an analysis of individual myths (structural exegesis) to a theory of myth to a philosophical (or ideological) understanding of what makes humanity human. In relation to philosophy (or ideology), both theory and analysis are forms of methodology. In relation to theory, both structural exegesis and narrative hermeneutics are forms of analysis. As theory is, in a sense, applied philosophy, so structural exegesis is theory applied to an "object" (a text) and narrative hermeneutics is structural exegesis applied to a "subject" (a reader) (Malbon, 318-21). Hermeneuts may aim toward: (1) philosophy (or theology), (2) theory, (3) biblical exegesis, or (4) existential understanding. This typology, however, is not to be viewed as static.   Bultmann, for example, shares much with the philosophical hermeneutics of Dilthey; yet Bultmann the pastor and New Testament scholar is concerned with biblical exegesis, and Bultmann the "demythologizer" and New Testament theologian aims at existential understanding of the biblical text. The sketching out of parallel typologies of structuralist and hermeneutical goals suggests that, in terms of their *aims,* certain structuralists may have more in common with certain hermeneuts than with other structuralists, and vice versa.

2.41   Presuppositions concerning language are intertwined with presuppositions concerning history for both structuralism and hermeneutics. Structuralism's insistence on the importance of synchronic study of language, including cultural "languages," correlates with its concern for history as the "historic." Hermeneutics' understanding of language as language-event correlates with its concern for history as the "historicity" of human existence in the world [on distinguishing "historical" / "historic" / "historicity" see Perrin, 27-28]. For structuralism, the historic is determined by syntagmatic and especially paradigmatic intra- and inter-relationships of cultural phenomena, and syntagmatic and paradigmatic are the two dimensions of language. For hermeneutics, the bridge between an historical text and the historicity of the reader is formed by language. Structuralism's approach to history as the historic predisposes structuralism to focus on the text in its literary or linguistic context, while hermeneutics' approach to history as the historicity of human existence in the world predisposes hermeneutics to focus on the reader in the context of his or her lived experience. Both structuralism and hermeneutics are approaches to meaning: while structuralism focuses on "meaning of," hermeneutics focuses on "meaning for." Structuralism might guide hermeneutics away from a premature application of the text to the reader. Hermeneutics might guide structuralism away from an immature abstraction of the text from the reader. Both structuralism and hermeneutics affirm that all textual meaning is contextual meaning. (2.4- 2.41 Malbon)

2.5   To what extent is the propositional content of statements in a narrative context determined by the discursive framework, i.e., by the concrete context of dialogical exchange either between the characters or between the author and reader? The very possibility of an entire text being ironic would seem to indicate that the propositional content of a text would be subordinate to the modal stance of the author toward his subject matter.

2.51   According to the linguist Robert Fowler, "propositions (facts) cannot be communicated without modality (interpretation)." He further explains, "As there is no sentence which does not imply a speaker taking a certain stance, so there is no text in which the content has not been filtered by an author who has selected and expressed the propositions and so set himself in a certain belief posture towards them" (p. 109).

2.6   If the governing semantic horizon of a narrative is established by the modal stance of the author toward his subject matter, can the meaning produced by this modal stance be reduced to a propositional content and analyzed on the basis of the logic of the semiotic square, or does this type of meaning operate according to another "logic"? When a writer chooses to compose a narrative rather than a philosophical essay, does this fundamentally affect the type of meaning produced by the narrative, or is this choice of style semantically neutral?

2.61   Oswald Ducrot argues that the starting point for understanding the semantics of a narrative is the enunciation rather than "la langue" because "the illocutory aspect of the activity of parole confers on it a necessary reference to itself and permits already the recognition of itself as the 'prime factor' indispensable to its structural study" (p. 114).

2.62   This would apply to the acts of speech, i.e., direct discourse, within narratives, and to the act of writing which produces the narrative as a whole. This viewpoint would thus attempt to understand the meaning of a narrative, ultimately, in terms of the type of meaning generated by adherence to or departure from the rules and functions of performative speech. The chief feature of this type of meaning is its primary reference to itself as an act of speech which causes this factor of self-reference to become fundamental to the significance of the statement. (2.5- 2.62 White)

2.7   The mode-lability of speech determines its model-ability.

2.701   In the process of in-form-ation, the text acquires as part of its morphos a remarkably durable mode-signification. We know how to take the text, i.e., we know what sort of text it is so that its structure communicates effectively with us when the text is re-hearsed and re-diachronized.

2.702   While there is no specific sign that codes for the text's modality, somehow that modality becomes clear from the relational-compositional morphos of the formulated text.

2.703   When the code is present, it is often possible for us to reconstruct a fragmentary or vague text from minute snippets of the whole. The text becomes like a hologram in which each fragment of the whole contains enough of the whole, of the entire communication / text, that the whole can be reconstructed from the fragment, though perhaps with some loss of precision or clarity. One has only to see portions of a scene from a grade-B 1950's U.S.-made "Western movie" and hear snatches of dialogue to make an impressively accurate reconstruction of the entire film. While "bad" or "camp" works are often humorously or irritatingly true-to-type/ -mode, so are very good exemplars of a genre.

2.71   Signification of modality might be intra, para- or extra-textual.

2.711   Particularly in dealing with ancient texts, some scholars have contended that the written text omits certain indications which are essential to produce a closed, coherent text (text with an intelligible and durable Gestalt). The text constitutes a *code*. Without an interpretive apparatus which was available only outside the text to certain text users could the system of signs be made to have sense. Such a system is highly fragile. If the extra-textual indicators become divorced from the text, it loses its ability to carry meaning. In effect, it becomes a pseudo-text since its morphological ability to control the exfoliation of meanings has been lost. Many structuralists would argue that the capacity of the text to mean implies its existence as a meaningful whole. The structure of textuality is grounded in the structures of personality and society. If so, then the extra-textual signs continue to reside in structures amenable to social or psychological (or anthropological or economic . . .) archaeology. We must dig up the signs again so that the text may mean once more.

2.712   Some modes seem to be indicated paratextually. Part of the text resides in elements necessarily presented with the text. The Editorial Page of a newspaper comes to mind. Its holographic quality lies in its format, texture, images, and lay-out. Even if no single word were legible (as is often the case in advertising and cartoons which present pseudo-editorial pages) we would know what we were "supposed to see." An editorial printed without a sign of designation on the wrong page can cause an uproar.

2.713   Most texts, perhaps all (?), sign "how to take" them intra-textually. Some of the claims of structuralists would seem to favor such a view. If that be so, then clearly matters of modality are not merely hermeneutic questions of ultimate interpretation but are structural questions that influence the selection and use of appropriate mode-ls.

2.8   How does meaning generated by performative speech relate in the narrative context to that produced by the semiotic square? What exactly is their place and mode of interaction at the semantic level? We might tentatively propose that the narrative as a dramatic form stems from the tension surrounding the semantic determination of the named characters, objects, and situations. The tension of the narrative would derive from the interplay between given meanings attached both to typical personages, objects, and situations and to those persons, objects and situations which are semantically undefined at the outset of the narrative. The movement and 'logical' development of the narrative thus would arise from the interaction on the modal level between the acting subjects and their language beginning with the writer and his subject matter.

2.81   The fundamental meaning of the narrative would thus stem ultimately from the extent to which closure is achieved. A secondary level of meaning may be extrapolated from the narrative having to do with the mediation of semantic systems which are structured logically.   While every narrative assumes such a logical system at the lexematic level, not every narrative is governed by a logical process at the discursive level. Those narratives which exhibit the most semantic closure at the discursive level would yield their most distinctive meanings to a strictly logical analysis, whereas those narratives which maintained a large degree of semantic openness would require analysis by means of a semantic system derived from the dynamics of the enunciation (2.8- 2.81 White)

2.9   Non-narrative texts present a particular challenge, especially to structuralist models derived from studies of folklore and myth.

2.91   Narrative "works" for models which treat correspondent meaning sequentially or serially. While a narrative may be framed, interrupted, or embedded, still its inherent transitivity facilitates its interpretation through step-by-step models. The narrative incorporates and must incorporate a dynamic, including the formulation of an agon and its resolution--a fact recognized since Aristotle.

2.911   Narrative may not be so simple as the railroad train metaphor would suggest. Meaning may be composed by inversion or by spiralling (cf. Patte and Patte). Still, narrative meaning and textuality clearly represent a special case, however important it may be.

2.92   Non-narrative texts do not automatically incorporate a dynamic, at least an obvious one. The morphos arises by composition. At the same time, it must operate through some 'logic' else there would be no motivation for the text-user to use the text as a whole. Even its compositional meaning must be one that drives the text-user through the text to its end in order for its meaning to emerge adequately. In that sense, even non-narrative texts must incorporate some transitivity and some agon-formation and -resolution at least in the relationship between enunciator and text and between text and text-user.

2.921   One way to formulate this transitivity is to place the non-narrative text in the context of the communication. This does not mean going back to the moment of enunciation as such, nor to the original performance. It does mean taking structuralism as a communication model, taking the emergent text as the signification of that communication, and seeing what "new" emerges as the text is used. In a sense, a non-narrative text becomes the sent object in the actantial model of communication. If this approach have validity, then the non-narrative text may not be so different from the narrative text as we might suppose.

2.10   If structuralism be a method for dealing with texts, then, unless it is to supplant all other interpretive methodologies (a claim which by-and-large is not being made), it must occupy some eventual location in the interpretive process. It may, by virtue of its presuppositions, not just be another criticism alongside many others, but it still must occupy some location within the overall sequence from coming into contact with a particular text to the point at which the informed text-user abandons the text with the one or the other suitably exhausted.

2.10.01   Some models of textual interpretation seem to treat exegesis as an assemblyline method. Exegesis consists of a series of workstations connected with one-after-another in an order that has a certain coherence in the assembly of the text's subsequent interpretation. Each step has its appropriate tools and procedures. Basically, each must be completed before the worker can proceed to the next step--or, as is often the case, turn it over to her or his colleague for manipulation in terms of that person's specialty. [In this sense, each scholar might become an expert in a particular criticism and stand at a particular workstation. One way to break into a job in the "plant" is to invent a new procedure and become its expert. Some of the criticism directed toward structuralism seems to emerge from such an image of exegesis and the exegetical profession.]   Later, down the line, the text may have to be subjected to some quality control, in which installed parts are tightened, checked, and calibrated. But, essentially, the text is a product, composed of interchangeable parts, interpreted on the assemblyline.

2.10.1   Aside from the Incompatibility and Sequential (Assemblyline) Models, at least four major possibilities (with their variants) emerge for relating structuralism to traditional exegesis. Each seems to have its advocates.

2.10.11   Antagonistic (Leninist) Model. Structuralism and traditional exegesis stand in fundamental conflict with one another. Each by itself distorts the text. While structuralism logically ought to have preference, historically it is subsequent to traditional interpretive methods and stands over against them all. The task of structuralism is to subvert traditional interpretation, unveil its distortions, and expose the uninterpreted sense of the text that has been heretofore hidden. Since structuralism also distorts, the ultimate exegesis must emerge from the radical conflict between these two approaches. Structuralism's role is to force interpretation toward a new level / dimension (through an Aufhebung) of exegesis not now available.

2.10.12   Dialectic (Hegelian) Model. Both structuralism and traditional exegesis are subsequent to the primordial communication event in which the then-enunciation acquired its textuality.   That primordial event cannot be recovered.   Its original diachronicity is irretrievably lost. But, in the rational analysis of the text, its textuality can ultimately give way for new text-users to a rediachronization of the communication. The text can speak again. Structuralism is one of two necessary approaches to the text which stand in tension--and conversation--with one another. Each proceeds simultaneously, though along different lines and different methods. Ultimately, the very process of interpretation forces them to consider one another and to relate their findings to one another. Out of that dialogue, sense emerges. Structuralism is the co-agonist of traditional exegesis.

2.10.13   Subordination Model. Structuralism deals with the apodictic. No other textual methods evoke the certain. Therefore, structuralism conditions and grounds all other approaches to the text. They are fundamentally distorted and invalid unless and until they are first given prior grounding through a thorough and completed structuralist analysis. Only then can any valid traditional study begin.

2.10.14   Synthetic Model. Ultimately, structuralism and traditional exegesis will have to make some peace with one another that leads each to incorporate the other into an entirely new approach to interpretation. Neither has primacy of place and neither can proceed without the other. Only fully integrated with one another can they together produce valid results. Each by itself is inadequate.

2.10.15   It is interesting to note that some scholars seem to be re-inventing exegetical procedures, under the rubric of structuralism, that parallel remarkably what traditional exegetes do.   That practical evidence will not decide the question of relationship to traditional methods but it is certainly interesting to observe.

3.   Structuralism must become structuralist exegesis.

3.01   [Some structuralists are] not interested in pursuing the above [philosophical and theoretical] kind of universalizing work, though [they are] very interested in testing the models proposed. Many members of the Seminar are interpreters of texts, and look to structuralism for an approach to exegesis. The application of deductive models [.] they find useful, but such application does not by itself amount to adequate exegesis. There are other things we need to do with texts, things indicated by historical-critical method, and "literary" or "aesthetic" things. Yet there is an important sense in which structuralism does not simply accept a division of labor; characteristically, it presses toward a *structural* account of the relationship among the diverse methods to be applied to texts. Such aspiration is intrinsic to structuralism (its "apodictic"), though [some scholars] do not see where strides have been made. One may offer a few thoughts about directions theory might take.

3.02   The relationships among diverse methods may be informed by Piagetian structural study of the development of human problem-solving. The text as manifesting a "mindset" (communal and / or authorial) requires data regarding sociological and psychological structures, and theory about how they relate to literary structures. For getting in touch with the historical-critical tradition we need to work on the *specific* structural elements of "historiographical" narrative (of which the Bible so largely consists--Hayden White's work is of some help here). In the absence of theory, one's exegesis remains necessarily eclectic; the trick, as Greimas says, is to work always at a *slightly* higher level of generality than the text demands. (3.01- 3.02 Jobling)

3.1   Not only structuralism, but a full structural hermeneutic should be applied to biblical texts.

3.101   A true biblical theology must be grounded in a structural hermeneutic of biblical texts.

3.11   Structural hermeneutic can and should be applied to the central texts of the Bible, namely the Hexateuchal tradition and the Gospel / Passion story.

3.12   The Hexateuchal and Gospel / Passion traditions are as available to a structural hermeneutic as any ancient myth or ritual.

3.121   The distinction between "myth" and "sacred history" (compare "cosmos" and "eschatology") is a matter of degree and not absolute or qualitative.

3.122   Old and New Testament materials are open to the same method as any other mythopoietic texts, similarly analyzable into levels of signification (e.g., political, economic, sociological, botanical, astronomical); schematisms, and constitutive metaphors.

3.123   The use of the technique of "typology" by New Testament creators is empowered by the "ideal structure" of the Old Testament mythologems.

3.13   The Exodus saga as a whole begs for a sytagmatic, paradigmatic and metaphorical understanding. It is ripe for structural hermeneutic. (3.1- 3.13 Harrod)
[Editor's Note: Prof. Harrod proceeds with a thorough, rich sketch of such an analysis of the Exodus saga which is too long to append here.]

3.14   [Similarly, a] n analysis of the text-linguistic function of New Testament miracle stories can greatly enhance our understanding of the structural dynamics of New Testament narrative. In a text-linguistic analysis, the relationship of the miracle story to the overarching narrative is perceived as analogous to the relationship of an individual word to a completed sentence.

3.141   Any word on its own has many communicative possibilities, the full spectrum of which is known as its semantic field. Only a word's specific function in a particular sentence determines which of these potential meanings is being drawn upon. One must therefore investigate both the semantic field of an individual term and its relationship to other terms in the sentence in order to discover its function within the sentence. Similarly, the total meaning of the sentence can be grasped only by an understanding of its constituent parts. Any inquiry into the meaning of a sentence must acknowledge this reciprocal relationship of the part to the whole--the part must be examined from the perspective of the whole, but at the same time the whole must be viewed with an eye to the particular qualities of each individual part.

3.142   By expanding this model from a sentence to a narrative, we are able to arrive at a method for text-linguistic analysis. The relationship of an individual term to the whole sentence is the same as the relationship of a small narrative unit, which we will call a macro-term, to the over-arching narrative in which it is contained. Like a word in a sentence, each macro-term has its own semantic field which receives a specific meaning from its use in the total narrative. The miracle story is the macro term with which this program is concerned.

3.143   The inquiry into the text-linguistic function of miracle stories in the New Testament narratives must follow a two-pronged approach. The first task is to locate and isolate the miracle stories within the narrative and then to identify their semantic field. In terms of narrative analysis, semantic field corresponds to the ideal narrative form and structure of the miracle story as an independent genre. The foundational studies of Propp and Greimas provide the basic methodological tools with which to work in delineating the genre of the miracle story. The work of both men is characterized by an attempt to understand the logical relationships underlying the surface manifestations in the narrative. Propp's analysis of Russian fairy tales was basically syntagmatic, his morphology composed of an inventory of functions--an action's relationship to the course of the story. Greimas, working from a similar functional foundation, modified Propp's morphological program to include both a paradigmatic and syntagmatic element. By referring to both Propp and Greimas, the syntagmatic and paradigmatic aspects can be classified in tandem, a necessity for any successful classification of genre.

3.144   This first task has close links with traditional form criticism, but also differs in important ways. One major difference is that the genre classification proposed here has a synchronic, not a diachronic, emphasis. It is concerned with the story in its present form, not as it might have been or as it developed through time. This marks a significant departure from traditional form criticism, whose aim, as Bultmann succinctly expresses it, is "to determine the original form of a piece of narrative, a dominical saying, or a parable" (p. 6).

3.145   The second task of text-linguistic analysis is to analyze the role which this independent miracle story genre (as determined by the first part of the program) plays when it loses its independent status and is incorporated into the overarching narrative: what aspects of the semantic field / form are highlighted, what happens to the "neutral" macro-term, etc. The emphasis is on a *relational* approach which emphasizes the dynamics of the literary interaction between miracle stories and the overarching narrative.

3.146   Just as the first part of the program is related to form criticism, this second part is related to redaction criticism. Both redaction criticism and text-linguistic analysis study the way independent units are incorporated into the overarching narrative and focus on the creative role in the choice and presentation of traditions. The major difference between the two lies in redaction criticism's traditional emphasis on the theological motivation in the author's use of traditions. The text is studied in order to clarify the author's theological perspective. Text-linguistics focuses on how the text as text functions, without singling out the theological motivation or historical development.

3.147   The most obvious application of this methodology is in the study of the function of miracle stories in the Synoptic Gospels. In addition, several other areas can be fruitfully investigated with this methodology:

(a) the question of "signs" and "miracles" is central to discussions of the Fourth Gospel. Text -linguistic analysis would provide a controlled methodology with which to approach this question.

(b) Text-linguistic analysis would provide an important control in the attempt to distinguish miracle story as genre from miracle story as action in the gospels and Acts.

(c) The application of the genre morphology to the birth narratives could yield important results in identifying the genre of these stories. One might be able to establish that some of the birth stories are indeed miracle stories. (3.14- 3.147 Preston)

4.   Some scholars, approaching structuralism out of the new criticism, propone criticisms of structuralist exegesis:

4.01   The analytic techniques of older American New Critics like Cleanth Brooks and W. K. Wimsatt provide exegetical tools which are better able to account for the unique content of scripture than prevailing narrative semiotic structuralist approaches. The structural analytic schemes of semioticians like Claude Bremond and A. J. Greimas entail that two different narratives with distinct characters and plots might have the same meaning provided they exhibit the same structures. On such grounds, scripture has no unique meaning. Likewise the uniqueness of biblical content and its distinctive features become less essential for exegesis. This subtle inattention to scripture's unique content can only be remedied by the use of more formal structural presuppositions, by the use of common interpretive questions posed to all narrative texts, which allow each text to provide its own distinct answers. American new critics have identified nine such formal structural patterns in light of which all texts shoud be interpreted. [They are commended] to structural exegetes: (1) What are the characters of the narrative in question like? (2) Are they real? (3) What is their motivation? (4) Are the characters consistent? (5) What do their actions say about the characters? (6) How is the narrative's plot organized? (7) How are its characters related? (8) What is the theme of the narrative? (9) How do the characters relate to the theme? Attention to these patterns leads the exegete to a concern with identity--description of biblical characters. As such structural exegesis might offer new patterns (horizons) for human existence in the contemporary world.

4.02   In order that the proper scriptural paradigms might be used on the proper biblical texts, more precise definitions of narrative literature, than to regard it as literature in which the author is a "sender," must be provided. A proposed definition borrowed from new criticism follows:

> Narratives are texts in which the chronological sequence of the events recounted is indispensable to the theme and meaning of the text. These events are realistically accounted, and so do not always follow in a smooth systematic pattern. Narratives often report everyday mundane events, which may be at cross-purposes. Such texts are characterized by an irreducible identification of character and action. In narrative literature one only knows the characters by what they do.

Thus the meaning of a narrative text can only be gained by understanding its literal content (Auerbach, pp. 18-20, 43; Frei, pp. 13-15). Since not all scripture exhibits these characteristics, structural techniques other than those applied to narratives must be discerned and used.

4.03   The meaning of a text and its appropriation are logically distinct. A narrative text's meaning is not a function of its impact (meaning-effect) on the interpreter. Narratives mean what they say. Their meaning can be determined by synchronic structural analysis, whose conclusions can be verified by community discourse. Insistence upon a role for the interpreter's reaction to a text in determining its meaning can lead to a relativizing or subjectivizing of scripture's meaning. In this connection attempts to relate a text's structural patterns to ontology may be of philosophical and apologetic interest. However, such endeavors are not relevant to the exegete's task. (4.01- 4.03 Ellingsen)

Contributors

[Editor's Note: The portions of the text contributed by each participating member of
the Seminar are indicated at the end of that section in the text. In some cases, minor
stylistic changes have been necessary. Material not otherwise attributed in the text
remains the responsibility of the Editor.]

Daniel Patte, Chairman
Mark Ellingsen
James B. Harrod
Arno Hutchinson,Jr.
David Jobling
Elizabeth Struthers Malbon
Gail O'Day Preston
Hugh C. White
Brian Watson Kovacs, Editor

Selected Bibliography

Auerbach, Erich.
    1953   MIMESIS. Princeton University Press.

Bultmann, Rudolf.
    1963   HISTORY OF THE SYNOPTIC TRADITION. New York: Harper & Row.

Ching, Marvin, Michael Haley and Ronald Lunsford, eds.
    1980   LINGUISTIC PERSPECTIVES ON LITERATURE.   London: Routledge &
              Kegan Paul.

Chomsky, Noam.
    1957   SYNTACTIC STRUCTURES. The Hague: Mouton.

Culley, Robert.
    1980   "Action Sequences in Genesis 2-3." SEMEIA 18: pp. 25-33.

Ducrot, Oswald.
    1978   "Structuralisme, enonciation et semantique." POETIQUE 33 (Feb.).

Fowler, Roger.
    1981   LITERATURE AS SOCIAL DISCOURSE. Bloomington: Indiana University
              Press.

Frei, Hans W.
    1974   THE ECLIPSE OF BIBLICAL NARRATIVE. New Haven: Yale University
              Press.

Greimas, A. J.
    1977   DIACRITICS 7.

_____. and F. Rastier.
    1968   "The Interactions of Semiotic Constraints." YALE FRENCH STUDIES 41.

_____.
    1966   SEMANTIQUE STRUCTURALE. Paris: n.p.

Katz, Jerrold.
    1977   PROPOSITIONAL STRUCTURE AND ILLOCUTORY FORCE. Cambridge:
    1980   University Press by arrangement with Thomas Y. Crowell.

Levi-Strauss, Claude.
    1966-   MYTHOLOGIQUES. (Various).
    1971

Malbon, Elizabeth Struthers.
    1980   "'No Need to have Anyone Write'?: A Structural Exegesis of I Thessa-
              lonians." SBL SEMINAR PAPERS: 301-36.

Patte, Daniel.
    1982   PAUL'S FAITH AND THE POWER OF THE GOSPEL: A STRUCTURAL
              INTRODUCTION TO PAUL. Philadelphia: Fortress. (Forthcoming.)

_____.
    1975   WHAT IS STRUCTURALIST EXEGESIS? Philadelphia: Fortress.

_____. and Aline Patte.
    1978   STRUCTURAL EXEGESIS: FROM THEORY TO PRACTICE. Phila-
              delphia: Fortress.

Perrin, Norman.
    1974   THE NEW TESTAMENT: AN INTRODUCTION. New York: Harcourt
              Brace Jovanovich.

Polzin, Robert M.
    c.1977   BIBLICAL STRUCTURALISM. Philadelphia: Fortress.

Propp, V.
    1979   MORPHOLOGY OF THE FOLKTALE. Austin: University of Texas Press.

Thompson, John B.
    1981   CRITICAL HERMENEUTICS: A STUDY IN THE THOUGHT OF PAUL
              RICOEUR AND JüRGEN HABERMAS. Cambridge University Press.

White, Hayden
    1978   TROPICS OF DISCOURSE. Baltimore: Johns Hopkins University Press.

THE LEGITIMIZING ROLE OF THE TEMPLE
IN THE ORIGIN OF THE STATE[+]

John M. Lundquist
Brigham Young University

Thus, if the ancient Mesopotamian historian is to give any meaningful account of his materials at all he must of a necessity relax the stringent claim of "what the evidence obliges us to believe" and substitute for it a modest "what the evidence makes it reasonable for us to believe," for it is only by taking account of evidence which is suggestive, when the suggestion is in itself reasonable, rather than restricting himself to wholly compelling evidence, that he will be able to integrate his data in a consistent and meaningful presentation. In replacing "what the evidence obliges us to believe," with "what the evidence makes it reasonable for us to believe" the historian--at the peril of his right to so call himself--leaves, of course, except for details of his work, the realm of knowledge to enter that of reasonable conjecture. This may not be altogether palatable to him, but since the nature of his materials allows him no other choice the best he can do is to accept it as gracefully as possible and with full awareness of its consequences in terms of limited finality of the results possible to him.[1]

I may be accused here of ideationalism, or something vile like that, but that is all right with me. My current research centers on religious systems expressed in art. In my estimation, there was strong ideological motivation in these early societies, particularly as embodied in religious systems, and this is something that materialist archaeologists tend to ignore. If some of these scholars found themselves transported to some of these societies they pretend to reconstruct, they would not recognize, I suspect, much around them.[2]

I

It is the thesis of this paper that the state, as we presently understand that term as applying to archaic societies (I will presently give a number of attempts to define this term) did not come into being, indeed could not have been perceived to have come into being in ancient Israel before and until the temple of Solomon was build and dedicated. Solomon's dedicatory prayer and the accompanying communal meal represent the final passage into Israel of the "divine charter" ideology that characterized state polities among Israel's ancient Near Eastern neighbors. (I will discuss shortly the implications of the Deuteronomic dating of 1 Kings 8 for the above claim.)[3] In the ancient Near East temple building/rebuilding/restoring is an all but quintessential element in state formation, and often represents the sealing of the covenant process that state formation in the ancient Near East presumes.[4] We find significant earlier vestiges of temple symbolism

---

[+]See end of paper for list of abbreviations.

[1]Thorkild Jacobsen, "Early Political Development in Mesopotamia," *Toward the Image of Tammuz and other Essays on Mesopotamian History and Culture*, (ed. William L. Moran; Cambridge: Harvard University Press, 1970) 133-34.

[2]Michael Coe, "Comments on Professor Sanders' Paper," *Reconstructing Complex Societies*, (ed. Charlotte B. Moore; Supp. to BASOR, 20; Cambridge: The American Schools of Oriental Research, 1974) 117.

[3]George E. Mendenhall, "The Monarchy," *Int* 34 (1975) 166-68. John Bright Fs.

[4]"The ideal of the covenant is then prevalent everywhere in the traditions of this occasion, and we may thus conclude that Solomon at the dedication festival actually renewed the covenant with Yahweh." Geo Widengren, "King and Covenant," *JSS* 2 (1957) 8.

(à la my Typology below) in earlier moments in Israelite history, at the mountain in the time of Moses, during the time of the Conquest, as recorded in Joshua 8 and 24, and in fact, according to Menahen Haran: "In general, any cultic activity to which the biblical text applies the formula 'before the Lord' can be considered an indication of a temple at the site, since this expression stems from the basic conception of the temple as a divine dwelling place and actually belongs to the temple's technical terminology."[5] However, only with the completion of the temple in Jerusalem is the process of imperial state formation completed, making Israel in the fullest sense "like the other nations."[6] The ideology of kingship in the archaic state is indelibly and incontrovertibly connected with temple building and with temple ideology.

It is important to note at this stage that I am not attempting to introduce the temple as the central feature in a "prime mover" hypothesis concerning the origin of the state. The process of early state formation is a very fluid one, a process that can go either forward or backward.[7] I am not introducing the temple as the primary cause of state formation, but rather as an integrative, legitimizing factor that symbolizes, and I believe in the ancient mind would have symbolized, the full implementation of what we today call the "state."[8]

---

[5]*Temples and Temple Service in Ancient Israel* (Oxford: Clarendon, 1978) 26.

[6]1 Sam 8:20. See also George E. Mendenhall, "The Monarchy," 157.

[7]See the views of Richard N. Adams, "The Early State: Theories and Hypotheses," *The Early State* (ed. Henri J. M. Claessen and Peter Skalnik; Studies in the Social Sciences, 32; The Hague: Mouton, 1978) 22; George E. Mendenhall, *The Tenth Generation* (Baltimore: Johns Hopkins University Press, 1973) 188-89; for summaries of the various prime mover theories of state origins, see J. Stephen Athens, "Theory Building and the Study of the Evolutionary Process in Complex Societies," *For Theory Building in Archaeology* (ed. Lewis R. Binford; Studies in Archaeology; New York: Academic Press, 1977) 353-57, with a valuable chart on p. 354.

[8]Relatively rare in scholarship is the attempt by scholars to define analogues to the term "state" from ancient sources. For Mesopotamia we have the description of "primitive democracy" for the Protoliterate period by Thorkild Jacobsen, for which he chooses "the relatively noncommittal term 'Kengir League' " in place of "state" or "nation." See "Early Political Development in Mesopotamia," 140. Also noteworthy is Jacobsen's contribution to *Before Philosophy, The Intellectual Adventure of Ancient Man*, An Oriental institute Essay; Baltimore: Penguin Books, 1972, 137-99, under the title "The Cosmos as a State." Here as elsewhere ("Foreword," in Robert McC. Adams, *Heartland of Cities, Surveys of Ancient Settlements and Land Use on the Central Floodplain of the Euphrates*, Chicago: University of Chicago Press, 1981, xiv) he recognizes the state primarily as the "monopoly of violence," or, quoting Max Weber, a community becomes a state when it "successfully displays the monopoly of a legitimate physical compulsion. See *Before Philosophy*, 156. For Jacobsen, in Mesopotamian myth Anu and Enlil "embody, on a cosmic level, the two powers which are the fundamental constituents of any state: authority and legitimate force." Ibid. Similarly Robert McC. Adams, writing from the evidence of the preliterate Uruk period remains of the central Euphrates floodplain of Iraq: "Among its features were: deities whose cults attracted pilgrimages and voluntary offerings; intervals of emergent, centralized, militarily based domination of subordinate centers that had been reduced to the status of clients, alternating with other intervals of fragile multicenter coalition or local self-reliance . . ." (*Heartland of Cities*, 81). "A better case can be made that the primary basis for organization was of a rather more traditional kind: religious allegiance to deities or cults identified with particular localities, political subordination resting ultimately on the possibility of military coercion, or a fluid mixture of both" (Ibid., 78). Dr. Mendenhall's characterization of the transition from the Federation to the State in ancient Israel states that "when a population emerges from a community to a political monopoly of

Recently I have been engaged in an attempt to identify commonalities in the temple practices/ideologies of the various ancient Near Eastern traditions. My main purpose in such an endeavor has been to construct a model or typology that will assist scholars in understanding "the social foundations of ancient polytheism,"[9] insofar as ancient temples can be seen to embody and to express central and crucial elements of such systems. The purpose of such a typology is to allow for "explanatory power in dealing with a set body of data." It will "point beyond the surface to the underlying patterns and processes; it will explain as well as identify."[10] It is true that I conclude that the main, if not all of the elements of the following typology were accepted by and taken into the religious system of ancient Israel--and this at a time far antedating the introduction of the monarchy. Folker Willeson wrote many years ago that "if the temple ideologies of the different nations are able to display certain traits, common throughout the whole ancient world, it may be a special branch of the Chaos-Cosmos ideology."[11] This is the ideology that I attempt to identify and describe in what follows. I introduce the typology here because it will play an interpretive role later in this paper.[12]

---

force, it almost inevitably imitates models best known and most accessible to it" ("The Monarchy," 159). He further writes: "The foundation of the community had nothing to do with a social agreement concerning divine legitimacy of social power structures--this entered from paganism with David and Solomon--but with common assent to a group of norms which stemmed from no social power" (*Tenth Generation*, 195). His definition of the state which Israel took over from its neighbors during the period of the united monarchy is then ". . . the maximization of human control. It is the divine power incarnate in the state or even the person of the king which guarantees the success of the daily economic activities of the subjects, just as it is the king who guarantees the military protection with the same divine delegated authority" (Ibid., 192). Perhaps the most suggestive formula for an ancient definition of the state comes from the Sumerian King List, which yields the formula "the state = a king (invested with kingship by the gods) + a (capital) city." This most important point can be deduced, I believe, from Giorgio Buccellati's "The Enthronement of the King and the Capital City in Texts from Ancient Mesopotamia and Syria," *Studies Presented to A. Leo Oppenheim* (Chicago: The Oriental Institute, 1964) 54-61. This introduces us to the controversial problem of the role of urbanism in the origin of the state, an issue to which I will return later. For the present, see Adams, *Heartland of Cities*, 52-129, and especially 75-81. Buccellati found that texts from Syria, including the OT, come closer to the Sumerian than to the Akkadian formulas of expressing what I call above a definition of state polities in the ancient Near East. Although I will introduce highly sophisticated evidence below for the proposition that Israel did not achieve state formation until the monarchy, and thus that the period of Judges cannot be considered a time of state formation in Israel, it is probable that the OT gives us this very picture in a manner highly reminiscent of the stylistic simplicity of the Sumerian King List. The very refrain of Judges, "in those days there was no king in Israel; everyone did what was right in his own eyes," tells us that this period cannot be considered the time of Israelite state formation, either according to ancient views, or our own, while the theme of 1 Samuel 8, "give us a king, that we may be like the other nations," alerts us to the fact that, in the ancients' views as well as the views of modern research, a state polity is being introduced.

[9] George E. Mendenhall, *The Tenth Generation*, 192.

[10] Lee Daniel Snyder, "Modeling and Civilization: Can There Be a Science of Civilization?" (*Abstract for International Society for the Comparative Study of Civilization*, Typescript, 1982, 1-2).

[11] "The Cultic Situation of Psalm LXXIV," *VT* 2 (1952) 290.

[12] Perhaps a more succinct definition of what I mean by "ideology" is the following: "The central value system is constituted by the values which are pursued and affirmed by the *élites* of the constituent sub-systems and of the organizations which are

II

The Typology

1.   The temple is the architectural embodiment of the cosmic mountain.

2.   The cosmic mountain represents the primordial hillock, the place which first emerged from the waters that covered the earth during the creative process. In Egypt, for example, all temples are seen as representing the primordial hillock.

3.   The temple is often associated with the waters of life which flow from a spring within the building itself--or rather the temple is viewed as incorporating within itself such a spring or as having been built upon the spring. The reason that such springs exist in temples is that they were perceived as the primeval waters of creation, *Nun* in Egypt, *Abzu* in Mesopotamia, *Těhôm* in Israel. The temple is thus founded upon and stands in contact with the waters of creation. These waters carry the dual symbolism of the chaotic waters that were organized during the creation, and of the life giving, saving nature of the waters of life.

4.   The temple is associated with the tree of life. (The above four taken to-gether constitute what I call a "primordial landscape," which we can expect to see reproduced architecturally and ritually in ancient Near Eastern temple traditions.)[13]

5.   The temple is built on separate, sacral, set apart space.

6.   The temple is oriented toward the four world regions or cardinal directions, and to various celestial bodies such as the polar star. Astronomical observation may have played a role in ancient temples, the main purpose of which was to regulate the ritual calendar. Since earthly temples were viewed as the counterparts of heavenly temples,[14] this view also would have contributed to the possible role of temples as observatories.

---

comprised in the sub-systems. By their very possession of authority, they attribute to themselves an essential affinity with the sacred elements of their society, of which they regard themselves as the custodians. By the same token, many members of their society attribute to them that same kind of affinity . . . . The *élites* of . . . the ecclesiastical system affirm and practice certain values which should govern intellectual and religious activities (including beliefs). On the whole, these values are the values embedded in current activity. The ideals which they affirm do not far transcend the reality which is ruled by those who espouse them. The values of the different *élites* are clustered into an approximately consensual pattern." (Edward Shils, "Centre and Periphery," *Selected Essays by Edward Shils*, Chicago: Center for Organization Studies, Department of Sociology, 1970, 3 [*sic*]).

[13]For the presence of such a "landscape" in the mythical texts from Ras Shamra, see Frank Moore Cross, "The Priestly Tabernacle in the Light of Recent Research," *Temples and High Places in Biblical Times*, Proceedings of the Colloquium in Honor of the Centennial of Hebrew Union College-Jewish Institute of Religion; Jerusalem: The Nelson Glueck School of Biblical Archaeology, 1981, 170-72.

[14]Bruno Meissner, *Babylonien und Assyrien*, Vol. 2, Kulturgeschichtliche Bibliothek, 4; Heidelberg: Carl Winter, 1925, 107-12, 409-10; for this imagery in the OT and in the texts from Ras Shamra, see David Noel Freedman, "Temple Without Hands," *Temples and High Places in Biblical Times*, 21, 28; and Frank Moore Cross, "The Priestly Tabernacle in the Light of Recent Research," Ibid., 170.

7.   Temples, in their architectonic orientation express the idea of a successive ascension toward heaven.[15] The Mesopotamian ziggurat or staged temple tower is the best example of this architectural principle. It was constructed of various levels or stages. Monumental staircases led to the upper levels, where smaller temples stood. The basic ritual pattern represented in these structures is that the worshippers ascended the staircase to the top, the deity was seen to descend from heaven, and worshippers and deity were then thought to meet in the small temple which stood at the top of the structure.

8.   The plan and measurements of the temple are revealed by God to the king or prophet, and the plan must be carefully carried out. The Babylonian king Nabopolassar stated that he took the measurements of Etemenanki, the temple tower in the main temple precinct at Babylon, under the guidance of the Babylonian gods Shamash, Adad, and Marduk, and that "he kept the measurements in his memory as a treasure."

9.   The temple is the central, organizing, unifying institution in ancient Near Eastern society.

A.   The temple is associated with abundance and prosperity, indeed is perceived as the giver of these.[16]

B.   The destruction or loss of the temple is seen as calamitous and fatal to the community in which the temple stood. The destruction is viewed as the result of social and moral decadence and disobedience to god's word.

10.   Inside the temple and in temple workshops images of deities as well as living kings, temple priests, and worshippers are washed, anointed, clothed, fed, enthroned, and symbolically initiated into the presence of deity, and thus into eternal life. Further, New Year rites are held at which time texts are read and dramatically portrayed which recite a pre-earthly war in heaven, the victory in the war by the forces of good, led by a chief

---

[15]"The Sumerians and their successors found a special significance in the height of the temples." (Eric Burrows, "Some Cosmological Patterns in Babylonian Religion," *The Labyrinth*, ed. S. H. Hooke, London: Society for Promoting Christian Knowledge, 1935, 60).

[16]These ideas are clearly expressed in Neo-Sumerian temple hymns, particularly in the Cylinder inscriptions of Gudea of Lagash and in the Keš Temple Hymn. For the latter see Gene B. Gragg, "The Keš Temple Hymn," in *The Collection of the Sumerian Temple Hymns* (ed. Ake W. Sjöberg and E. Bergmann; Texts from Cuneiform Sources, 3; Locust Valley: J. J. Augustin, 1969) 168 (lines 22-30) and 173 (lines 90-95). For Gudea see F. Thureau-Dangin, *Die Sumerischen und Akkadischen Königsinschriften* (Vorderasiatischen Bibliothek, 1; Leipzig: J. C. Hinrichs, 1907) 86-141. Many years ago Julius A. Bewer wrote an article in which he compared the religious and social role of the temple as it is depicted in the Cylinder inscriptions of Gudea with similar associations in the prophecies of Haggai. Gudea attributes wide reaching social, legal, and economic reform as well as agricultural abundance to the building of the temple (see point # 15, below). Bewer's article ("Ancient Babylonian Parallels to the Prophecies of Haggai," *American Journal of Semitic Languages and Literatures* 35 [1919] 128-33) retains considerable value. Of course, such claims of prosperity in temple hymns and building dedications may be fictional, as has been proved, for example, for the prices claimed by Shamshi-Adad I in his dedicatory inscription for the "Enlil" temple in Ashur. In this case, we are dealing not with genuine piety, but with political propaganda. See Albert Kirk Grayson, *Assyrian Royal Inscriptions*, I (Records of the Ancient Near East; ed. Hans Goedicke; Wiesbaden: Harrassowitz, 1972) 20-21.

deity, the creation and establishment of the cosmos, cities, temples, and the social order. The sacred marriage is carried out at this time.

11.   The temple is associated with the realm of the dead, the underworld, the afterlife, the grave.   The unifying feature here is the rites and worship of ancestors. Tombs can be and in Egypt and elsewhere are essentially temples (cf. the cosmic orientation, texts written on tomb walls which guide the deceased into the afterlife, etc.).   The unifying principle between temple and tomb can also be resurrection.   In Egyptian religion the sky goddess Nut is depicted on the coffin cover, symbolizing the cosmic orientation (cf. "Nut is the coffin.").

12.   Sacral, communal meals are carried out in connection with temple ritual, often at the conclusion of or during a covenant ceremony.

13.   The tablets of destiny (or tablets of the decrees) are consulted both in the cosmic sense by the gods, and yearly in a special temple chamber, ubšukinna in the Eninnu temple in the time of Gudea of Lagash.   It was by this means that the will of deity was communicated to the people through the king or prophet for a given year.

14.   God's word is revealed in the temple, usually in the holy of holies, to priests or prophets attached to the temple or to the religious system that it represents.

15.   There is a close interrelationship between the temple and law in the ancient Near East.   The building or restoration of a temple is perceived as the moving force behind a restating or "codifying" of basic legal principles, and of a "righting" and organizing of proper social order.

16.   The temple is a place of sacrifice.

17.   The temple and its ritual are unshrouded in secrecy.   This secrecy relates to the sacredness of the temple precinct and the strict division in ancient times between sacred and profane space.

18.   The temple and its cult are central to the economic structure of ancient Near Eastern society.[17]

It is evident that at least one major function of ancient temples is missing from this list.[18]   The most obvious feature that is missing is the political function of the temple in the ancient Near East (George E. Mendenhall, Private Communication).   In terms of the present paper, the temple plays a legitimizing political role, and serves as "the ritual functioning system that establishes the connection between deity and king." (George E. Mendenhall, Private Communication).   I will thus add to the typology an

---

[17]This list constitutes a revision of that which appears in John M. Lundquist, "What is a Temple? A Preliminary Typology," *The Quest for the Kingdom of God, Studies in Honor of George E. Mendenhall* (Winona Lake, IN: Eisenbrauns, 1982) and John M. Lundquist, "The Common Temple Ideology of the Ancient Near East," *The Temple in Antiquity* (Religious Studies Center Monograph Series; ed. Truman G. Madsen; Provo, UT: Brigham Young University, In Press).   In both these studies I provide extensive validations for the typology.
[18]Of course, there may be many such missing; but as Snyder writes: "A good model need not be perfect in every detail as long as it stimulates empirical testing and refinement, but until the model is relatively complete, effective testing is impossible." ("Modeling and Civilization: Can There Be a Science of Civilization?" Typescript, 1981.)

additional item: "The temple plays a legitimizing political role in the ancient Near East," or, as stated above: "The ideology of kingship in the archaic state is indelibly and incontrovertibly connected with temple building and with temple ideology." It is this latter permutation of this latest addition of my typology that I will now continue to develop in the present paper.

III

It is necessary now to discuss the issue of state formation as it relates to ancient Israel. Theories of state formation have been widely tested on ancient and ethnographic populations,[19] but have only recently begun to be applied to ancient Israel. I am not aware of any published archaeological field projects within Palestine that have gone into the field with an explicit research strategy in which hypotheses of state origins in the country were tested, in the way say, that Henry Wright has field tested and refined his ongoing hypotheses in Iraq and Iran,[20] or in the way that Robert McC. Adams has tested and refined theories of state origins over many years of surface survey in Iraq.[21]

A number of recent publications have succeeded in demonstrating that Israelite society during the period of the Judges should be classified as a chiefdom, taking the three-fold evolutionary schema of Service (tribe, chiefdom, archaic civilization) as a model.[22] Mendenhall, for example, characterizes Israel during this period as "an oath-bound unity of the village populations of ancient Palestine that was oriented first toward the realization of the ethical rule of Yahweh as the only Suzerain, and secondly toward the avoidance of the reimposition of the imperialism of the foreign-dominated regimes of the Palestinian power structures--the city-states.[23]

In one of the most interesting and challenging claims made in recent years for the ability of field archaeology to reconstruct the social structure of ancient societies, Colin Renfrew presented a list of twenty features characteristic of chiefdoms "not one of . . . which cannot be identified in favorable circumstances from the archaeological record."[24] This list includes:

1.   a ranked society.
2.   the redistribution of produce organized by the chief.
3.   greater population density.
4.   increase in total number of society.
5.   increase in the size of individual residence groups.

---

[19]Claessen and Skalnik, *The Early State*, 109-530; Henry T. Wright, "Toward an Explanation of the Origin of the State," *Origins of the State, The Anthropology of Political Evolution* (ed. Ronald Cohen and Elman R. Service; Philadelphia: Institute for the Study of Human Issues, 1978) 49-68.

[20]"Toward an Explanation of the Origin of the State," 57-66.

[21] *Heartland of Cities*, 27-51. Evidently the researches of Prof. Lawrence Stager on the distinctions between highland and lowland villages during Iron Age Palestine will go far to correct this deficit, once they are more fully published.

[22]Elman R. Service, *Origins of the State and Civilization* (New York: W. W. Norton, 1975) 303-8; James W. Flanagan, "Chiefs in Israel," *JSOT* 20 (1981) 47-73; Frank S. Frick, "Religion and Sociopolitical Structure in Early Israel: An Ethno-Archaeological Approach," *SBL 1979 Seminar Papers* (Vol. II; ed. Paul J. Achtemeier; Missoula: Society of Biblical Literature/Scholars Press, 1979) 233-53; George E. Mendenhall, "Social Organization in Early Israel," *Magnalia Dei, Essays on the Bible and Archaeology in Memory of G. Ernest Wright* (ed. Frank Moore Cross, et al.; Garden City: Doubleday, 1976) 132-51.

[23]"Social Organization in Early Israel," 136.

[24]"Beyond a Subsistence Economy: The Evolution of Social Organization in Prehistoric Europe," *Reconstructing Complex Societies*, 73.

6.   greater productivity.
7.   more clearly defined territorial boundaries or borders.
8.   a more integrated society with a greater number of socio-centric statuses.
9.   centers which coordinate social and religious as well as economic activity.
10. frequent ceremonies and rituals serving wide social purposes.
11. rise of priesthood.
12. relation to a total environment (and hence redistribution)--i.e., to some ecological diversity.
13. specialization, not only regional or ecological but also through the pooling of individual skills in large cooperative endeavors.
14. organization and deployment of public labor, sometimes for agricultural work (e.g., irrigation) and/or for building temples, temple mounds, or pyramids.
15. improvement in craft specialization.
16. potential for territorial expansion--associated with the 'rise and fall' of chiefdoms.
17. reduction of internal strife.
18. pervasive inequality of persons or groups in the society associated with permanent leadership, effective in fields other than the economic.
19. distinctive dress or ornament for those of high status.
20. no true government to back up decisions by legalized force.[25]

Flanagan concluded his recent study with the statement that "most of the elements of Renfrew's list of twenty characteristics of chiefdoms cited above can be documented in Israel. These indicate both the presence of chiefs and the absence of a strong centralized monopoly of force equipped with laws during the time of Saul and the early years of David."[26]

Numerous theories have been propounded to define the state and to account for its emergence. These theories can be roughly divided into two classes: the "prime mover" theories, according to which a single variable, such as irrigation works, population growth, religious influence, trade, or environmental factors, is posited as the primary

---

[25]Renfrew, 73.

[26]"Chiefs in Israel," 69. We must keep in mind the very vigorous opposition that was raised against Renfrew's claims for archaeology at the conference in Cambridge where he presented the above list of features. Ruth Tringham rejected outright the ability of archaeologists to recognize ten of the items on the list from the archaeological record, and granted the remaining items only with "very rigorous backup information on the environment, economy, and technology. . . ." (Ibid., 88). On a more general level, she accused Renfrew of "very simplistic use of ethnographic analogy which would make many an anthropologist shudder." (Ibid., 89). As such, Tringham was mirroring the stinging criticisms made against what he considered the overoptimistic and naive use of ethnographic data by archaeologists by Edmund Leach, in his now famous, "Black Box" summary lecture at the 1971 Sheffield seminar on the explanation of culture change. (The Explanation of Culture Change: Models in Pre-history (ed. Colin Renfrew; Pittsburgh: University of Pittsburgh Press, 1973) 761-71. Leach's criticisms were answered by D. H. Mellor at the same conference ("Do Cultures Exist?" Ibid., 59-72). The point is that biblical scholars and Syro-Palestinian archaeologists should exercise care and discrimination in the extent to which they adopt models from other disciplines for application to biblical problems. There is always the danger expressed by Michael Coe, who said that "archaeologists tend to be somewhat retrograde in the models which they adopt from other fields of study." (Reconstructing Complex Societies, 116).

moving force in the development of complex social organization;[27] the other main class of theories tend to be cybernetic or systemic in nature, "in which multiple possible sets of causes in the ecology, economy, society and intersocial environment may singly or in combination produce more permanent centralized hierarchies of political control.[28] Claessen and Skalnik offer the following *working definition* (emphasis theirs) of the state: "the early state is the organization for the regulation of social relations in a society that is divided into two emergent social classes, the rulers and the ruled." They then offer the following "main characteristics of the early state:

1.   There is a sufficient *number* of people to make possible social categorization, stratification and specialization.
2.   Citizenship is determined by residence or birth in the *territory*.
3.   The *government* is *centralized*, and has the necessary sovereign power for the maintenance of law and order, through the use of both authority and force, or at least the threat of force.
4.   It is *independent*, at least de facto, and the government possesses sufficient power to prevent separatism (fission), and the capacity to defend its integrity against external threats.
5.   The productivity (level of development of the productive forces) is developed to such a degree that there is a *regular surplus* which is used for the maintenance of the state organization.
6.   The population shows a degree of *social stratification* that emergent social classes (rulers and ruled) can be distinguished.
7.   A *common ideology* exists, on which the legitimacy of the ruling stratum (the rulers) is based.[29]

Gregory Johnson has defined the state as "a differentiated and internally specialized decision making organization which is structured in minimally three hierarchical levels."[30]   In his essay published in 1978 Henry Wright defined the state as "a society with specialized decision-making organizations that are receiving messages from many different sources, recoding these messages, supplementing them with previously stored data, making the actual decisions, storing both the message and the decision, and conveying decisions back to other organizations. Such organizations are thus internally as well as externally specialized."[31]   This definition, by the way, underlines the extraordinary role of record keeping in early states and points us toward a recognition of the complexity of the bureaucratic structure that we can expect to find. It also raises the question of the place of writing in the origin of the state. Certainly in the ancient Near East we have writing in each example of state formation. As Adams has written, writing and other forms of craftsmanship guaranteed that "a highly significant segment of the population must have been given or won its freedom from more than a token or symbolic involvement in the primary processes of food production."[32]   On the role of writing in

---

[27] J. Stephen Athens, "Theory Building and the Study of Evolutionary Process in Complex Societies," 353-57; Henry Wright, "Toward an Explanation of the Origin of the State," 49-52.

[28] Ronald Cohen, "State Origins: A Reappraisel," in *The Early State*, 70; see also Henry Wright, "Toward an Explanation of the Origin of the State."

[29] "The Early State: Theories and Hypotheses," 21, 639-40. Emphasis theirs.

[30] Quoted in Adams, *Heartland of Cities*, 76.

[31] "Toward an Explanation of the Origin of the State," 56.

[32] Adams, *Heartland of Cities*, 80: Mendenhall has emphasized the great dependence that the burgeoning monarchy of Israel would have had on an extensive scribal bureaucracy, the lack of which in traditional Israelite society would have necessitated David and Solomon turning to the well-established Jebusite bureaucracy to

general as a concomitant of state origins Lawrence Krader has written: "The relation between the formation of the state and the development of script, of writings, is not a chance correlation, but a coordination with interacting consequence in the service of the former."[33]   Finally, Ronald Cohen's recent definition of the state emphasizes it as "a centralized and hierarchically organized political system in which the central authority has control over the greatest amount of coercive force in the society. Sub-units are tied into the hierarchy through their relations to officials appointed by and responsible to a ruler or monarchical head of state. These officials maintain the administrative structure of the system and attempt to ensure its continuity by having among them a set of electors who choose and/or legitimate a new monarch."[34]

According to Service "there seems to be no way to discriminate the state from the chiefdom stage." He then quotes Sanders' and Marino's *New World Prehistory* (p. 9): "Differences between chiefdoms and states are as much quantitative as they are qualitative."[35]   Claessen and Skalnik distinguish the state from chiefdoms in the latter's lack of a "formal, legal apparatus of forceful repression," and also its incapacity to prevent fission.[36]   Cohen sees fission as the main feature that distinguishes chiefdoms in comparison with states: "The state is a system that overcomes such fissiparous tendencies. This capacity creates an entirely new kind of society. One that can expand and take in other ethnic groups, one that can become more populous and more powerful without necessarily having any upper limits to its size or strength."[37]

If we compare Renfrew's list of characteristics of chiefdoms, above, with the definitions of the state that have been cited, it would be possible to conclude that the only, or perhaps better the major, features that distinguish the two would be the presence of stratified society in the state, in the place of ranked society in the chiefdom,[38] and the inability of the chiefdom to enforce its will legally or by force; in other words, the chiefdom lacks the monopoly of force (Renfrew's point #20, but see below). Otherwise it would probably be fair to say, a la Sanders and Marino, that the state constitutes "more of the same." This comes out in a rather interesting way in Wright's successive working models of his field work in southwestern Iran. His Figure 5 (p. 60) emphasizes, for example, *"Increasing* population," *"Increasing* competition for land," while Figure 6 (p. 62) develops a model of *"Increasing* population," *"Increasing* demand for goods," *"Increasing* interregional exchange," *"Increasing* competition." His Figure 7 (p. 64), his working model for 1970, emphasizes *"More* specialization in herding," *"More* demands by nomads for goods and food," *"More* raiding," *"More* grain production in lowlands."[39]   Thus it seems that even though the variables that he tested changed as his successive field work established certain variables as untenable or irrelevant, the field

---

fill this need. See "The Monarchy," 159-62. See also Ronald Cohen, "State Origins: A Reappraisal," 36-37.

[33]"The Origin of the State Among the Nomads of Asia," *The Early State,* 104.

[34]"State Origins: A Reappraisal," 36.

[35]*Origins of the State and Civilization,* 304.

[36]"The Early State: Theories and Hypotheses," 22.

[37]"State Origins: A Reappraisal," 35; any more formal study of the development of the state in ancient Israel than the present one will have to deal with the issue of fission with regard to the break-up of the Israelite monarchy in the time of Jeroboam. What does this say for the nature of the Israelite state? Does it disqualify the monarchy of David and Solomon from the category of early state? Flanagan, by the way, sees David "on the boundary line between chiefdom and kingdom." ("Chiefs in Israel," 67).

[38]For this distinction, see Service, *Origins of the State and Civilization,* 44-46, quoting Fried.

[39]"Toward an Explanation of the Origin of the State." Of course, his working models are much more complicated and extensive than the excerpts given here. Emphasis added.

work also apparently demonstrated an evolutionary increase in these variables in the development from a chiefdom to the state.

One of the most interesting archaeologically based studies of the transition from chiefdom to statehood in recent years, and one that I feel has great potential for application to field work based tests of hypotheses of state formation in ancient Israel's homeland (evidently it will demand this type of field testing, following the example of Henry Wright, Adams and others, before major progress will be made in bringing ancient Israel into the orbit of primary state formations) is that of William T. Sanders and Joseph Michels and others on the Kaminaljuyu Project, at the site of Kaminaljuyu, in the Valley of Guatemala. Sanders gave a tentative summary of some of the results of the field work, especially as they relate to the problem of state formation, at the conference on Reconstructing Complex Societies.[40] I am going to summarize what appear to be the main points of Sanders' article, especially as they relate to his views of chiefdoms and the state. I will also make reference to comments made on Sanders' paper at the conference by Martin Diskin.[41]

The majority of Sanders' conclusions that will be quoted here refer to the following archaeological phases at Kaminaljuyu: Terminal Formative (Verbena-Arenal Phases--100 B.C.-300 A.D.); Early Classic (Aurora Phase--300-500 A.D.); Middle Classic (Amatle I--500-700 A.D.); Late Classic (Amatle II--700-1000 A.D.). (97). To begin with, Sanders introduces the problem of the relationship between civilization and the state. He defines civilization as "a large, internally complex society. By internally complex we mean that a civilization is a society composed of many sub-societies each with its own value systems and life styles, and that these distinctions are based primarily on differences in occupation, wealth, and political power. By large, we mean societies at least with populations in the tens of thousands. There is also a growing tendency among cultural anthropologists interested in complex societies to consider a state level of political organization as one of their fundamental characteristics."[42] Sanders defines the state "as a political system involving adjucative [sic] power and explicit manifestation of force." (98).

Sanders evidently sees the chiefdom stage of political development prevailing at Kaminaljuyu through the Terminal Formative period, at which time the transition to the state begins, with full state formation completed by Late Classic times. A number of features stand out as characterizing a chiefdom form of political development at Kaminaljuyu: Chiefs can often mobilize much greater expenditure of public resources for the building of temples and tombs than on personal residences for themselves. (109). It is toward the end of the Terminal Formative that larger expenditures of labor begin to be devoted to the building of "elite residential platforms." (109). In general though, it is the ability of the leader of a state to exercise "adjudicative rather than mediating functions," to "command the control of strategic resources (particularly agricultural land)," and to demand a greater "scale and sophistication of civic buildings" that distinguishes the state from a chiefdom. (109). Further, the chiefdom seems to place a much greater emphasis on the funerary cult, "with the implications that ancestral spirits or chiefs themselves were the main objects of worship rather than high gods." (110). This pattern would support the assumption that "the political system was still structured along

[40]"Chiefdom to State: Political Evolution at Kaminaljuyu, Guatemala," Reconstructing Complex Societies, 97-113, 118-19.
[41]"The Costs of Evolution," Reconstructing Complex Societies, 113-16.
[42]p. 97; Thus "civilization" implies "the state." Thus also Anatolii M. Khazanov, "Some Theoretical Problems of the Study of the Early State," The Early State, 89: "Civilization is a broader concept than the state. Aside from the latter it also embraces a written language . . . and the concept of towns. . . . The obvious fact is that the contemporary state, like any more or less developed state of the past, presupposes a civilization."

kinship lines." (110). Sanders argues that a series of ceremonial platforms of the Arenal Phase, although implying "the ability of a leader to amass labor for ceremonial construction," (and thus implying the state), nevertheless "strongly suggests that these were funerary temples dedicated to dead chiefs or lineage ancestors rather than to high gods," (thus implying a chiefdom) (103). As matters develop during the Terminal Formative, population increased considerably, a situation that leads to political instability in a chiefdom, because of its tendency "to be stable only on the lowest levels of political integration" (111). At this point we reach the stage of a "paramount chiefdom," involving a much greater population, when "unusually able and vigorous men with great charismatic power achieve a paramount position during their own lifetime, and sometimes this paramountcy survives through the reigns of a number of succeeding chiefs, but generally involves a period of less than 100 years in total length" (111).

One of the most interesting phenomena, appearing during Early/Middle Classic times and heralding the advent of the state, is the introduction of large, centralized monumental building projects, with the architecture modelled after a major adjacent culture. Sanders writes that the style of the architecture is a "slavish imitation of the architecture of the great site of Teotihuacan in central Mexico implying a very close, special relationship between the two sites" (106). Along with a deemphasis on the funerary cult, there seems to be the introduction of high gods, "particularly the imported god Tlaloc, from Teotihuacan," and a corresponding "reorganization of ceremonialism towards temple construction" (111). Sanders writes in general of a major ideological change during this time, apparently attributable to the infuence of cultural and religious influences coming from Teotihuacan. In response to a question posed during the discussion period at the conference "whether the similarity in architecture between Teotihuacan and Kaminaljuyu was the result of foreign invasion of people living there or a result of imitation by the local people," Sanders replied "that there was a drastic architectural reorganization. There was a sudden shift from the style of the buildings in the main civic center of a community which had a long tradition of elite culture with its own sculptural and architectural style. The centers were abandoned; and the new center, a massive acropolis, was built in foreign style. Simultaneously with this was the introduction of the Tlaloc religious cult from Teotihuacan. But whereas at Teotihuacan there were several avatars of Tlaloc, there was only one of these versions found in foreign areas; and it is the same one whether at Tikal or Kaminaljuyu. There seems to have been a highly organized religious system which came in and replaced the native religion, and many of the religious artifacts disappeared. . . ." (121).

More generally Sanders speaks of enormous increases in population from Middle Formative to Late Classic times, necessitating great structural changes "if the society were to hold together" (111). One such change was "the disappearance of the ranked lineage type pattern," (111) a situation expanded by Martin Diskin in his comments to Sanders' paper: "But the shift from rank society . . . to stratified society is best seen in the economic sphere where specialization and exchange mechanisms signal class or caste distinction and mobility is increasingly curtailed."[43]

During the Late Classic population in the Valley of Guatemala doubled, but at the same time "there is clear evidence of a retraction of population, in which many slope areas were abandoned and settlement was concentrated in a few prize agricultural portions of the valley, where soils were deep and fertile and where erosion was a minor problem" (107). Intensive agricultural practices are introduced at this time. It appears that the people of the Late Classic occupied perhaps 35% of the amount of land that had been farmed during the Terminal Formative. This led to a social setting in the Late Classic of "intense competition over land resources; on the intrasocial level this would produce unequal access to land, patron-client relationships and social stratification. On the intersocietal level competition would lead to intense warfare and increasing

---

[43]"The Costs of Evolution," 115.

centralization of political authority" (113). Martin Diskin elaborated these developments by positing "political control and monopoly of power . . . over the producers"; the "peasant group . . . subject to the superior power of a political elite," and "its alternatives severely restricted"; "with the growth of new social forms, the costs are borne by ever increasing levies in the forms of taxes, services, and what Wolf generally calls 'rent.' This condition, that of rent payer, becomes irreversible. Usually this is so not only because of the power of the state . . . but because local production patterns become 'adjusted' to state needs and less and less toward self-sufficiency."[44] In his response to the comments on his paper, Sanders elaborated the theory behind such developments further: ". . . one of the interesting things that archaeologists have indicated in many chronological sequences, or cultural historical sequences, is a general reduction in the quality of the average technology of individuals as one proceeds through time . . . as the political system gets more highly stratified, as the holdings of the peasants get smaller, and as they contribute more and more to the system, obviously their purchasing power declines, and one may get an overall decline in peasant technology." Sanders then generalized this principle into a distinguishing feature defining one of the differences between a chiefdom and a state. We would note the movement "from a chiefdom level, where the individual still has a fair amount of independent action and the farmer, in particular, an ability to produce surpluses to a highly evolved political state where there is a class of people who are really living on the bare subsistence level, getting very close to Wolf's caloric minima and replacement level" (118).

The implications for ancient Israel of some of the patterns of cultural evolution at Kaminaljuyu, as suggested by Sanders, seem very obvious to me, although it is not my purpose in this paper to attempt to draw out these implications. Especially important seem the problems of marshalling of strategic resources, particularly for public building, in the chiefdom and the state; the role of funerary cult in Palestine during chiefdom and state,[45] with the attendant implications for the worship of ancestors in a kin-based religious setting; massive architectural undertakings under foreign aegis in connection with major ideological re-adjustment as the society is transformed from a chiefdom into a state; population trends and changes in social structure, especially at the top; the introduction of charismatic leaders during the "paramount chiefdom" stage, at a time when population has increased considerably (of course, the issue of charismatic leadership during the period of the Judges in Israel has been extensively studied[46]); comparative agricultural usage in chiefdom and state, and patterns of land use intensification; the comparative role of peasants in chiefdom and state, including the resource flow between rulers and ruled and other evidence of class division; technology at the village peasant level in chiefdom and state.[47] Finally, the study of the political evolution has

[44]"The Costs of Evolution," 114.

[45]W. F. Albright, *Archaeology and the Religion of Israel*, 5th ed. Garden City: Doubleday Anchor, 1968, 102-4, with notes; W. Boyd Barrick, "The Funerary Character of 'High Places' in Ancient Palestine; A Reassessment," *VT* 25 (1975) 565-95, and Abraham Malamat, "King Lists of the Old Babylonian Period and Biblical Geneologies," *JAOS* 88 (1968) 173, n. 29.

[46]Abraham Malamat, "Charismatic Leadership in the Book of Judges," *Magnalia Dei, Essays on the Bible and Archaeology in Memory of G. Ernest Wright*, 152-68. Malamat writes, interestingly, of the process of the "routinization of charisma," (164) that results in the monarchy.

[47]Many of these issues are treated in some length by George E. Mendenhall, particularly in "The Monarchy," and in "Social Organization in Early Israel." Also valuable is Flanagan's "Chiefs in Israel," and Frick, "Religion and Sociopolitical Structure in Early Israel: An Ethno-Archaeological Approach," whose study is the first, as far as I am aware, to apply a theory of Israelite chiefdom to the archaeological evidence. Especially interesting in Frick's study is his discussion of Iron Age I agricultural practices, which

suggested that "the structure, functioning and evolution of early states of all times and places show marked similarities. These findings give us reason to believe that it may be possible to develop a generally acceptable definition of the early state and to infer some of its basic characteristics."[48]   While we must observe the cautions of Flanagan that "Human societies are not so easily typed, and thus the factors interrelating processual phenomena militate against facile generalizing,"[49] we can still welcome the extent to which ancient Israel's cultural history has been brought into the general pattern and discussion of tribe--chiefdom--state, and applaud continued attempts to refine our knowledge of this process.

IV

In introducing the temple as an institution of ancient Near Eastern society[50] and its role in state formation I want to emphasize a fundamental principle laid down by Barbara Price: "By definition the processes of state formation--pristine or secondary--involve major institutional transformations resulting in turn from significant bioenergetic change."[51]   Price relies primarily on two types of data, architecture and settlement patterns, to provide reliable measures of the extensive bioenergetic changes that state formation represents. "The greater the energy encapsulated in a piece of data, the more reliable will be its evidence, the greater the number of problems for which its application will be relevant and valid. . . . Stronger evidence of social, political, and economic [I would add, religious] processes can be derived from other kinds of material evidence, such as architecture, assuming that it is its scale or mass rather than its style that is emphasized."[52] And finally, " 'A building,' if appropriately analyzed, is thus theoretically capable of providing information on a fairly wide range of problems."[53]   Similarly for

---

appear to have been oriented toward subsistence, rather than toward the needs of a centralized bureaucracy, which fits the picture from Kaminaljuyu (244-46). Also of great interest is Normal K. Gottwald, "Early Israel and the 'Asiatic Mode of Production' in Canaan," *Society of Biblical Literature 1976 Seminar Papers*, ed. George MacRae, Missoula: Society of Biblical Literature/Scholars press, 1976, 145-54.   Gottwald's discussion can benefit by seeing the Asiatic Mode of Production within the wider theory of state origins, as is done, for example, by Claessen and Skalnik, "The Early State: Models and Reality," *The Early State*, 643, 647-49, and by being more specific in placing "Early Israel" at some defined point along the Chiefdom--State spectrum, as Flanagan, Frick, Mendenhall, and I have attempted to do. Also of interest here is the view of Barbara Price concerning the data from Kaminaljuyu, that Kaminaljuyu represents a secondary state, developing from a ranked society under pressure from the primary state, centered at Teotihuacan. Is it possible that the Israelite monarchy, is, technically, an example of a secondary state, developed from a ranked society under the pressure of the Philistine/Phoenician states that surrounded it? See Barbara Price, "Secondary State Formation: An Explanatory Model," *Origins of the State*, 170-79. Such a view could be read into Mendenhall, 'The Monarchy," 157-60. See also Claessen and Skalnik, "Limits: Beginning and End of the Early State," *The Early State*, 626: "State formation is *not* caused by war, but is greatly *promoted* by war, or by the threat of war and by social stress" (emphasis theirs), and Abraham Malamat, "Charismatic Leadership in the Book of Judges," 164. See also G. W. Ahlstrom, "Where Did the Israelites Live?" *JNES* 41 (1982) 133-38.

[48]Claessen and Skalnik, "The Early State: Theories and Hypotheses," 5.

[49]"Chiefs in Israel," 49.

[50]One of the "Great Organizations" described by A. Leo Oppenheim in *Ancient Mesopotamia, Portrait of a Dead Civilization*, Rev. ed. Comp. by Erica Reiner, Chicago: The University of Chicago Press, 1977, 95-101, 106-9.

[51]"Secondary State Formation: An Explanatory Model," 166.

[52]Ibid., 164-65.

Sanders, who relies heavily on the evidence of architecture, settlement patterns and craft specialization to measure the evolution of civilization, "civic architecture clearly relates to the institutional characteristics of any culture, so that the changing patterns of civic architecture of archaeological sites in a given area should provide important clues. . . ."[54]

The introduction of the concept of civic architecture as an important clue to some of the central distinguishing features of ancient civilization must also at the same time introduce us to the "tell" as the main target configuration of a given ancient civilization that the archaeologist will be interested in investigating.[55] Of course this does not mean that the archaeologist explores the tell to the exclusion of its hinterlands--its resource area. An effective approach to the understanding of complex society in its formative periods requires a balance between the investigation of the "central city or the urban complex," and "the relations of the urban center to its surroundings and the effects of the urban system on the entire region."[56] An archaeological study of the temple in the ancient society will however, in general, locate us on the mound itself, perhaps indeed on an acropolis within or on the mound itself, which acropolis will often, but not always be located at the rough geographical center of the mound.[57] What I am getting at here is that the temple stands at the "center" of ancient Near Eastern societies, not necessarily at the geographical center for, as Edward Shils writes: "The central zone is not, as such, a spatially located phenomenon. It almost always has a more or less definite location within the bounded territory in which the society lives. Its centrality has, however, nothing to do with geometry and little with geography."[58] The ideological or sociological center of ancient societies does not necessarily stand at the geographical center. "The centre, or the central zone, is a phenomenon of the realm of values and beliefs, which govern the society. It is the centre because it is the ultimate and irreducible; and it is felt to be such by many who cannot give explicit articulation to its irreducibility. The central zone partakes of the nature of the sacred."[59] It is in this sense that I believe that temples often stood at the "center" of ancient Near Eastern society, including Israelite Society in the time of the temple of Solomon.[60]

It should be noted however that none of my studies of the origins of the state referred to above had any role for the temple in the process of state formation. Although I want to reemphasize that I am not introducing the temple as a prime mover hypothesis for state origins, I do feel that its exclusion in state formation hypotheses is a mistake. In response to the opening quote of this paper, which originally appeared as a criticism by Michael Coe of William Sanders "materialist" ignoring of religious systems, Sanders replied that he ignored these factors "since this type of study does not lead to

---

[53]Ibid.

[54]"Chiefdom to State," 98.

[55]G. Ernest Wright, "The Tel: Basic Unit for Reconstructing Complex Societies of the Near East," Reconstructing Complex Societies, 123-30.

[56]Charles Redman, "Research Design for a Regional Approach to Complex Societies," Reconstructing Complex Societies, 133, 136.

[57]For sketch views of a variety of configurations which major mounds in Syria assume, especially noting the relationship of an acropolis to the remaining area encompassed within the fortification wall, see W. J. van Liere, "Capitals and Citadels of Bronze Age Syria in their Relationship to Land and Water," AAAS 13 (1963) Fig. 3A, B, C.

[58]"Centre and Periphery," 1. Emphasis his.

[59]Shils, Ibid.

[60]See also Jonathan Z. Smith, Map is Not Territory (SJLA; Leiden: E. J. Brill, 1978) 98-101, 107-19; 186-89.

scientific generalization."[61]   Combining the influence Sanders grants to civic architecture with the textual evidence that we have for the importance of the temple in
ancient Near Eastern society, we can indeed formulate testable hypotheses with regard
to the role of the temple and other religious/ideological values in ancient society.
Perhaps this is what Robert McC. Adams had in mind in faulting the reconstructions of
Wright and Johnson for omitting "in the face of overwhelming evidence not only of its
importance as a historic force elsewhere but of incontrovertible archaeological evidence
that it was the predominant preoccupation precisely in the Uruk period . . . any concession of a special role for religion and religious institutions."[62]

The central position of temple building/rebuilding/restoring in the royal inscriptions of the kings of ancient Western Asia is well known.[63] In general the pattern for
these kingdoms would seem to be similar, a pattern that would also fit the Israelite state
under Solomon: the state is not necessarily fully formed immediately upon the accession
to kingship of a given charismatic figure. As with Israel in the time of David, state
formation began in that time, but was not finalized until the reign of his successor.
Further, the process of temple building/rebuilding/dedication does not necessarily take
up the king's main attention in the first year or two of his reign. If we may take the
Babylonian Year Names as an example of this, in most cases the first few years were
taken up with building/rebuilding walls, defeating remaining enemies, in general solidi-
fying their control over their kingdom. Then, in the case of Sumuabum, the first king of
the First Dynasty of Babylon, for example, it is the fourth year that bears a name connected with temple building; in the case of his successor, Sumulael, it is the seventh; in
the case of his successor Sabium, the eighth; in the case of Hammurapi, it is the third.[64]

In most cases under discussion here we will be dealing, strictly speaking, with
secondary state formations, and not with pristine states. And, as I suggested above, this
is in all probability the correct designation also for Israel under David, Solomon, and
their successors. But, as Price maintains: "All by definition are equally states."[65] The
examples that I will refer to here for the role of the temple in state formation will come
from polities that in my opinion can bear either the pristine or secondary state
designation.

To begin with I would like to introduce an example that represents a conflation of
evidence for the importance of temples in the state from two different periods of the
history of southern Iraq during the third millennium B.C. I am referring to the Temple
Oval at the Early Dynastic I-II site of Khafaje in the Diyala Valley (an archaeological
example) and the Cylinder inscriptions of Gudea of Lagash (ca. 2143-2124 B.C.), which
describe the process of building a temple to the god Ningirsu.

Although separated in time, these two bodies of evidence both bear the same
witness to what Mallowan calls "the fantastically extravagant effort Early Dynastic man
was prepared to go" to please his god.[66] The site of Khafaje, of which Mound A was
excavated by an Oriental Institute team during the 1930's, lies just to the east of
Baghdad, on the Diyala River. The extra-ordinary development of this temple dominated

---

[61]"Chiefdom to State," 119.

[62]Heartland of Cities, 77.

[63]A. Leo Oppenheim, Ancient Mesopotamia, 108-9.

[64]A. Ungnad, "Datenlisten," RLA 2 (1938) 174-78; for the surviving year names of
the Sargonic Dynasty, which, along with the First Dynasty of Babylon can be considered a
secondary state, see Ibid., 133-34.

[65]"Pristine states achieve this level of integration through systemic operation of
essentially autochthonous processes; secondary states, as defined, reflect regular
processes of interaction/competition of expanding states vis-a-vis non-state organized
populations." ("Secondary State Formation: An Explanatory Model," 170).

[66]Max E. L. Mallowan, "The Early Dynastic Period in Mesopotamia," CAH I/2
(1971) 270.

city plan fits into the late Early Dynasty I and Early Dynasty II when so many changes took place that were to characterize the era of "primitive monarchy" of the earliest historical Sumerian states. The "implosive" (R. McC. Adams) process of urbanization, the building of the first city walls at Uruk, large scale palace architecture and monumental temple platforms further characterize the E.D. I and II periods in southern Mesopotamia. This was a period of major state development.[67] As far as Gudea is concerned, he was the second governor of the most important post-Akkad, pre-Ur III state in southern Mesopotamia. The building materials for the temple he built came from as far away as the Amanus Mountains, Ebla, and the Jebel Bishri.[68]

The Temple Oval at Khafaje dominated a city settlement that was surrounded by a 6 to 8 meter wide defense wall. A number of other important temples, chief among them the many levels of the Sin Temple, and sections of private houses were also excavated. The building process involved in the ancient construction of the Temple Oval was truly phenomenal. The Oval is surrounded by a double wall which enclosed an area of about 8,000 square meters. This area was prepared for the construction of the temple by being excavated to a depth of over 8 meters. Then clean, sandy soil was brought into the excavation site from elsewhere, and laid into the pit. The excavators estimated "a volume of not less than 64,000 cubic meters [of sandy soil], the equivalent of 6½ million basket loads as soil is carried nowadays."[69] The foundation walls of the oval were then raised on the sand base, the sand being limited to the area encompassed by these walls.[70] The original excavation for the foundations of the Temple Oval cut through earlier, apparently Early Dynastic levels of houses, but there was also evidence that parts of the foundations had been founded on a reclaimed swamp.[71] This "staggering amount of labor" was "entirely preliminary to the brickmaking and the erection of the massive structure itself."[72]

What was the meaning of such a procedure? Ellis writes that "I know of no ancient text that explains the reason for this."[73] I have attempted elsewhere[74] to connect such a practice with temple ideology attested in Egypt at a much later period. A. J. Spencer has written of the enormous expenditure of labor that went into fulfilling the "mythological requirements" of temples in the Late and Ptolemaic Periods.

---

[67]Edith Porada, "The Relative Chronology of Mesopotamia, I, *Chronologies in Old World Archaeology* (ed. Robert W. Ehrich; Chicago: The University of Chicago Press, 1965) 161-63; Robert McC. Adams, "Patterns of Urbanization in Early Southern Mesopotamia," *Man, Settlement and Urbanism* (ed. Peter J. Ucko et al.; Cambridge: Schenkman, 1972) 735-50; Wiliam W. Hallo and William Kelly Simpson, *The Ancient Near East: A History* (New York: Harcourt Brace Jovanovich, 1971) 42-46.

[68]Adam Falkenstein, Eva Strommenger, "Gudea," *RLA* 3 (1971) 676-78.

[69]Henri Frankfort, *Oriental Institute Discoveries in Iraq, 1933/34, Fourth Preliminary Report of the Iraq Expedition* (OIC, 19; Chicago: The University of Chicago Press, 1935) 32. (Unfortunately, I was unable to consult the final report for the temple Oval, *OIP* 53). See also Pinhas Delougaz, Harold D. Hill, and Seton Lloyd, *Private Houses and Graves in the Diyala Region* (OIP 88; Chicago: The University of Chicago Press, 1967) 24-25.

[70]Henri Frankfort, *Fourth Preliminary Report*, 32-33.

[71]Henri Frankfort, *Progress of the Work of the Oriental Institute in Iraq, 1934/35, Fifth Preliminary Report of the Iraq Expedition* (OIC 20; Chicago: The University of Chicago Press, 1936) 15-17.

[72]Ibid., 17.

[73]Richard S. Ellis, *Foundation Deposits in Ancient Mesopotamia* (Yale Near Eastern Researches, 2; New Haven: Yale University Press) 12, and 6-34 for descriptions of various building rites connected with temples.

[74]"What is a Temple? A Preliminary Typology."

The construction of the vast temple enclosure walls in undulating brickwork is an obvious example. Another effect, closely related to the substructure of the peripteral temples, is the development of a new style of foundation for large cult temples in the Late Period . . . . The entire area to be occupied by a Late-Period temple was dug out into an enormous rectangular pit, which was then lined with strong brick retaining walls and filled up to the top with sand. Over this sand bed were laid several courses of stone to create a platform on which to build the temple.[75]

Attested examples of this type of structure have been found in the Delta and in Upper Egypt. Fortunately, this building procedure is given a mythological foundation in an Edfu text which describes the building of the temple there: "He excavated its foundation down to the water, it being filled up with sand according to the rule, being constructed of sandstone as an excellent work of eternity."[76] Thus, "The temple had to rest on a bed of sand, as a representation of the primaeval mound, and it was desireable that this sand should extend down to the subsoil water, as the Mound (emphasis his) had stood in the Nun."[77] Thus in this case we have a textual attestation for the enormous amount of work that Egyptians in this period were prepared to undertake in order to fit the temple building to mythological presuppositions. As Spencer writes, "The effects of religious belief on architecture were not, as some have claimed a vague symbolism . . . ."[78]

The same hold true, I believe, for a case such as the Temple Oval, particularly when we consider the extent to which mythological traditions of ancient Mesopotamia viewed temples as being founded in and arising out of the sweet waters of the abyss, the home of the god of wisdom Enki. I have given considerable evidence for this connection elsewhere.[79] A fairly common Sumerian phrase states that the temple's *temen* (foundation) "is sunk into the *abzu*."[80] One Neo-Sumerian hymn exhibits a kind of inner or chiastic parallelism of the first two words of two successive lines which, as I have tried to show elsewhere,[81] very possibly approaches the primeval mound-temple ideology of Egypt. Line 4 of this hymn begins "Abzu, shrine," (*abzu èš*), while line 5 begins "House, holy mound," (*é du₆-kù*), where *èš* and *é* are synonymous and *abzu* and *du₆-kù* are synonymous.[82] The reclaimed swamp on which the Temple Oval was built could thus take on a greater significance in the light of the above.

The Gudea hymns "give a vivid picture of the ideology behind the temple building, and they are the best examples which an be found on Sumerian soil."[83] Many scholars

[75]A. J. Spencer, "The Brick Foundations of Late-Period Peripteral Temples and their Mythological Origin," *Glimpses of Ancient Egypt, Studies in Honor of H. W. Fairman* (ed. John Ruffle, G. A. Gaballa, and Kenneth A. Kitchen; Orbis Aegyptiorum Speculum; Warminster: Aris & Phillips, 1979) 133.

[76]Ibid.

[77]Ibid., and see point # 2 in my typology, above.

[78]Ibid.

[79]"The Common Temple Ideology of the Ancient Near East," drawing especially on the temple foundation hymns of Gudea, and on Neo-Sumerian temple hymns. The same picture is found in the *Enuma elish*.

[80]A. Falkenstein, "Sumerische Bauausdrücke," *Or* 35 (1966) 236.

[81]"The Common Temple Ideology of the Ancient Near East."

[82]Ake W. Sjöberg and E. Bergmann, *The Collection of the Sumerian Temple Hymns, Texts from Cuneiform Sources* 3 (Locust Valley: J. J. Augustin, 1969) 17, 50. For *du₆-kù*, "shining (holy) mound" see A. Deimel, *Šumerisches Lexikon*, II/3 (Rome: Verlag des Päpstl. Bibelinstitutes, 1934) 459.

[83]Arvid S. Kapelrud, "Temple Building, A Task for Gods and Kings," *Or* 32 (1963) 58.

have recognized the relevance of the Gudea inscriptions to the OT.[84] Kapelrud has pointed out the main parallels between traditions of temple building in which "the gods" are the main protagonists, as in the *Enuma elish*, and the Baal Cycle from Ras Shamra, and those in which kings are the center of attention, as with Gudea, Moses, and Solomon.[85] With the former the main elements are: "1. A victorious god after battle; 2. He wants to have his own temple; 3. Permission asked from the leading god; 4. Master builder set to work; 5. Cedars from Lebanon, buiding-stones, gold, silver, etc. procured for the task; 6. The temple finished according to plan; 7. Offerings and dedication, fixing of norms; 8. A great banquet for the gods." In those instances where kings are depicted as temple builders, Kapelrud found the following elements: "1. Some indication that a temple had to be built; 2. The king visits a temple overnight [incubation]; 3. A god tells him what to do, indicates plans; 4. The king announces his intention to build a temple; 5. Master builder is engaged, cedars from Lebanon, building-stones, gold, silver, etc. procured for the task; 6. The temple finished according to plan; 7. Offerings and dedication, fixing of norms; 8. Assembly of the people; 9. The god comes to his new house; 10. The king is blesed and promised everlasting domination."[86] (One would have to add to this list, also, a great banquet for all the people.)

The the purposes of this paper, the most important aspect of temple building, its legitimizing role in the establishment of a dynasty, is most clearly expressed in the Gudea Cylinder B. Once the temple had been completed, it was necessary that its god, Ningirsu, should be led inside and formally installed as "king." (B II 5, B V 1). Ningirsu, in his turn, had in the meantime been carried to the Temple of the Abyss of Enki in Eridu, the most ancient and honored temple in Sumer, to receive the legitimizing approval of Enki for the temple that Gudea was building in Lagash.[87] Ningirsu then returns from Eridu and is majestically ushered into his temple during the New Year festival.[88] During this festival, the sacred marriage rite is carried out between Ningirsu and Bau, the destinies are fixed, and a communal meal is shared by the inhabitants of the city.[89] The gate through which Ningirsu would have been led into the temple was at the same time one of the city gates. This was the *ká.ki.lugal.ku₄*, "the gate through which the king (Ningirsu) enters." Next to this gate stood a pillar (^{giš}ti), "a heavenly *nir* that extends to heaven."[90]

To return to Cylinder B, Gudea, depicted as a priest who leads the processions, prayers and sacrifices, receives his kingship in perpetuity from Ningirsu. One of the key passages is B VI 14-18, which reads, in Falkenstein's translation: ". . . dass (Ningirsus) Stadt, das Heiligtum Girsu, Gereinigt, der 'Thron der Schicksalsentscheidung' aufgestellt, dass Szepter langer Tage geführt werde, dass der Hirte Ningirsu für Gudea das Haupt

---

[84]In addition to Kapelrud, and Bewer, cited above, see Richard D. Barnett, "Bringing the God into the Temple," *Temples and High Places in Biblical Times*, 11, and Moshe Weinfeld, *Deuteronomy and the Deuteronomic School* (Oxford: Clarendon Press, 1972) 35, 248-50.

[85]"Moses is 'to a great extent depicted in royal categories'," Kapelrud, ibid., 61, quoting Ivan Engnell.

[86]Kapelrud, ibid., 62.

[87]A II 11, B III 9. And see E. Douglas van Buren, "Foundation Rites for a New Temple," *Or* 21 (1952) 293, 296-97, and Richard S. Ellis, *Foundation Deposits*, 7-8.

[88]A Falkenstein, *Die Inschriften Gudeas von Lagaš* (AnOr 30; Rome: Pontificium Institutum Biblicum, 1966) 120.

[89]Falkenstein, ibid.

[90]References to the Gudea Cylinders are taken from F. Thureau-Dangin, *Die Sumerischen und Akkadischen Königsinschriften*, abbreviated *SAK*. See also A. Falkenstein, *Die Inschriften Gudeas von Lagas*, 121, 137 and Gudea Cylinder A XXV 5-8). According to Deimel, ^{giš}ti is a "biegsame Stange; Rippe; Pfeil (*mit Bronze dazu verarbeitet*): *Šumerisches Lexikon*, II/1, 150, emphasis added.

(wie) eine schöne Krone zum Himmel erhebe . . . ."[91] Another passage, important for the
thesis presented here, is B VIII 13-19, where Ningirsu is presented as having returned
from Eridu (again, the introduction of Eridu as the main, legitimizing temple center in
the ideology which underlies the Gudea Cylinders), and "der Thron in der 'wohlgebauten'
Stadt gefestigt werde, dass für das Leben des guten Hirten Gudea die Hand (zum Gebet)
an den Mund geführt werde . . . ."[92] Here we have the ultimate "legitimizing"
connection, bringing together all the main factors that I believe were involved in the
establishment of the "divine charter" ideology in ancient Near Eastern state polities: the
god in his temple, which temple was built by divine instruction by the king of the city
after it was duly authorized and approved by Enki of the "Temple of the Abyss" in Eridu;
then the king, the "good shepherd" was handed a scepter of perpetual rule, guaranteeing
the authority and legitimacy of his throne; all of this carried out, of course, in the
temple itself (which of course, as mentioned above, underscores the priestly functions of
the king, at least in this tradition).[93]

Thus we have an ancient theory of state origins, centered around the building of a
temple to the main deity of the city, and the establishment of a dynastic system through
this means. The Gudea inscriptions give us perhaps the clearest view of this process (the
fact that they may give us a fanciful and idealized picture,[94] does not detract from their
value as a theoretical statement of an ideology, a "constitution" if you will, a statement
of how things should be, as viewed through the eyes of temple poets, the intellectuals of
that day). The site of Khafaje, as an example, begins to show us how this theory would
have been carried out architecturally, how the architecture of the temple would have
related to the city plan as a whole,[95] and what the implications of this arrangement
would be for the economic role of the temple in the city.[96]

Leaving the evidence introduced above, we should mention in passing that two of
the most famous religious epics of ancient Near Eastern literature, the *Enuma elish* and
the Baal Cycle from Ras Shamra, give us a similar temple centered view of state origins,
a view in which the legitimizing decisions of the cosmic deities are transferred to earth
and to the earthly monarch, the whole process symbolized by and centered in the building

---

[91] A Falkenstein and W. van Soden, *Sumerische und Akkadische Hymnen und
Gebete* (Bibliothek der alten Welt; Zurich: Artemis, 1953) 170.

[92] Ibid., 172.

[93] Of course, Gudea is not strictly a *lugal*, "king," but an *ensi*, "governor." For a
discussion of the evolution of these terms in ancient Sumerian texts, along with an
emphasis upon the priestly functions of the *en*, see Thorkild Jacobsen, *Toward the Image
of Tammuz*, 375.

[94] Samuel Noah Kramer, *The Sumerians, Their History, Culture and Character*
(Chicago: The University of Chicago Press, 1963) 137-40.

[95] It is interesting to note here that the best preserved city gate at Khafaje was
found situated just to the northwest of the Temple Oval, so that entry into the city gate
at this point would have given one a direct view of the gate of the Temple Oval itself.
See *OIP* 88, 24-25 and Plate I.

[96] This is a question that I am not discussing here, although it is well known that
temples served, among other things, as treasuries, and that they were often looted,
either by the local king in order to pursue warfare or other foreign policy ventures
(2 Kings 16:8), or by conquerors (1 Kings 14:25-26). The Eninnu, built by Gudea, had a
"treasury," which apparently served both as his own royal treasury and as temple
treasury. It is described as being filled with various precious and semi-precious stones
and metals. See A. Falkenstein, *Die Inschriften Gudeas von Lagaš*, 131. According to
Edmond Sollberger, the possibility exists that there was a "marked evolution from
simplicity to luxury" in the furnishings and treasures found in temples during the third
millennium B.C. See "The Temple in Babylonia," *Le Temple et le Culte* (CRRA 20;
Istanbul: Nederlands Historisch-Archeologisch Instituut, 1975) 34.

of a temple. Of great interest here is a point made by Jonathan Z. Smith in his critique of Mircea Eliade's views of "Center" symbolism: "Eliade has not, to my knowledge, dwelt on the significance of the fact that the Babylonian creation epic, *Enuma elish*, is not so much a cosmogony as it is a myth of the creation of a temple."[97] With regard to the Baal Cycle, we have the recent statement of Frank Moore Cross: "Ba'l founded his temple on Mount Ṣāpōn in order to make manifest his establishment of order, especially kingship among the gods. The earthly temple of Ba'l manifested not only Ba'l's creation of order, but at the same time established the rule of the earthly king. There is thus a tie between the temple as the abode of the king of the gods and the temple as a dynastic shrine of the earthly king, the adopted son of the god. The temple and kingship are thus part of the 'orders of creation,' properly the eternal kingship of the god of order, the eternal dynasty of his earthly counterpart."[98]

If we thus use the above statement of Cross as a summary description of the temple centered state polity, keeping in mind the evidence from Gudea, the evidence of the extraordinary, "fantastically extravagant" (Mallowan) building practices associated with temples as at Khafaje, referring at the same time to my typology, above, especially points 1-4 (the "primordial landscape"), then I think that we can begin to answer the question of how a building can play such an important role in legitimizing centralized, monarchical, dynastic authority in the ancient Near Eastern state.[99]

---

[97]*Map is Not Territory*, 99.

[98]"The Priestly Tabernacle in the Light of Recent Research," 174. I have devoted considerable space in my article "What is a Temple? A Preliminary Typology," to validations derived from *Enuma elish* and the Baal Cycle.

[99]Of course, the "fantastically extravagant" effort that went into the temple building means corvee labor, and extensive oppression of the masses by the ruling classes, which is what we expect in the early state, at least at certain levels of its evolution. See Claessen and Skalnik, "The Early State: Theories and Hypotheses," 20-21. But remember point # 7 in Claessen and Skalnik's "main characteristics of the early state," above: "A *common ideology* exists, on which the legitimacy of the ruling stratum (rulers) is based." Elsewhere (*The Early State*, 640) they elaborated this point, adding that the "basic concept [of the common ideology] is the principle of reciprocity between the ruler in the center and his subjects living for the greater part in agrarian communities . . . ." We would assume that the oppressive labor requirement imposed by the building of the Temple Oval would have transgressed this "principle of reciprocity," and of course, in the matter of the succession to the kingship of Israel, following Solomon's death, we know that this principle was broken, and we have a record of the acrimonious negotiations which accompanied its breaking, and the subsequent division of the kingdom (1 Kings 12). But we must also remember two important factors that relate to this point: 1. "By their very possession of authority, they [*the elites*] attribute to themselves an essential affinity with the sacred elements of their society, of which they regard themselves as the custodians. By the same token, *many members of their society attribute to them that same kind of affinity*." (Edward Shils, "Centre and Periphery," 3. Emphasis added.) And 2. "The common man, lastly, remains an unknown, the most important unknown element in Mesopotamian religion." (A. Leo Oppenheim, *Ancient Mesopotamia*, 181). Therefore we must assume the probability that temples played unifying, integrating, positive, genuinely pious roles in the ancient community, and that, to some extent, perhaps impossible to define, even corvee would not have been viewed as an entirely onerous duty in connection with temple building. For a view of the positive, pious aspects of Mesopotamian temple establishments, see J. N. Postgate, "The Role of the Temple in the Mesopotamian Secular Community," *Man, Settlement and Urbanism*, 813-18, 820-21. Postgate gives evidence for the general horror that would have been felt in the community at the sacking of the temple treasuries (815 and note 18).

Before leaving this section I would like to refer to two additional pieces of evidence that support the thesis of the paper. First is the stele of the Assyrian noble Bel-Harran-bel usur, who, sometime during the reign of Shalmaneser IV, founded his own, presumably independent city in the desert west of Ninevah. So great was the weakness of the central power at this time that Bel-Harran-bel-usur was able to claim total independance on his stele, calling in the first instance on the Babylonian gods Marduk and Nabu, ignoring Ashur and ignoring the Assyrian king. He himself claims to have established the freedom of the city, exempting it from certain taxes and establishing certain endowments. We can safely call this foundation a secondary state, I believe. In the stele itself, after he has named the gods who have authorized his new city, we read: "Bel-Harran-bel-usur . . . who fears the great gods, they have sent and,--the mighty lords, at their exalted word and by their sure grace, I founded a city in the desert, in a waste. From its foundation to its top I completed it. A temple I built and I placed a shrine for the great gods therein. Its foundation I made firm as the mountains are set down, I established its foundation (walls) for all eternity. Dur-Bel-Harran-bel-usur I called its name,--in the mouth of the people, and I opened up a road to it. I inscribed a stele, the images of the gods I fashioned on it, in the divine dwelling place I set it up."[100] This seems, to me at least, to point out the centrality of the temple building in state formation, even in so ephemeral a polity as Dur-Bel-Harran-bel-usur was.

The second piece of evidence that I would like to introduce here is the thesis of the very important recent article of Richard D. Barnett.[101] Barnett, starting off from Solomon's prayer of dedication for the Jerusalem temple (1 Kings 8), examines evidence from Hittite and neo-Hittite gateway reliefs which illustrate the process by which the gods of these cities were ritually and ceremoniously invited into the city and installed, whereby they took up their residence in the city's temples. The reliefs generally show a procession of nobles and soldiers, male and female worshippers, approaching the seated deity of the city where a feast is in process. In the case of Carchemish, the "worship at the gate" motif appears to have terminated at the chief temple itself, although the excavations were not able to demonstrate this conclusively. Especially interesting is the building inscription of Azitawadda which states at one point "Having built this city and having given it the name of Azitawaddiya, I have established Ba'l-Kmtryš in it. A sacrific(ial order) was established for all the molten images . . . May Ba'l-Kmtryš bless Azitawadda with life, peace, and mighty power over every king . . . ."[102] I have pointed out above the possibility that the temple gate at Lagash through which Ningirsu was introduced into the Temple was also one of the main city gates, and the fact that the Temple Oval was built directly adjacent to a main city gate. The process of memorializing the introduction of a city's gods into their temples, in some cases temples that were built just inside the city gate (as at Alaca Huyuk for example), by means of wall reliefs that depict a sacral procession with banquet (see my point # 12 of the typology, above, and "What is a Temple? A Preliminary Typology," for a description of the role of sacral meals in covenant ceremonies) further supports the thesis that temple building was central to the ancient state formation process.

V

Ancient Israel developed from a chiefdom to a (in all probability secondary) state during a period of about two generations, covering the span of the Iron Age IC period (about 1000-918 B.C.). As I suggested above, the process of evolution from chiefdom to state is graphically recounted in the OT, in terms that are familiar to the modern student

---

[100]AR 1, 295-96; A. T. Olmstead, *History of Assyria* (Chicago: The University of Chicago Press, 1951) 167-69, and 203-4 for Bel-Harran-bel-usur's decline under Tiglath-pileser III.
[101]"Bringing the God Into the Temple," 10-20.
[102]*ANET* 3rd ed., 654.

of such processes in ancient societies. From the refrain that ends the book of Judges,[103] to Samuel's admonitions concerning the institution of kingship in 1 Samuel 8,[104] to Nathan's (first) oracle to David in 2 Samuel 7 informing him that he should not build a house for Yahweh,[105] to the night vision/dream of Solomon during the incubation at the high place of Gibeon where he presumably received the instructions that he should build the temple,[106] to the actual building and dedication of the temple the OT gives us an extraordinary and apparently unmatched ancient narrative of the tensions, debates, political and theological argument that accompanied the advent of the dynastic state. Again, the state was not "caused" by the introduction of the temple and the accompanying divine charter ideology; the temple is a symbol of a "major institutional transformation," resulting "from significant bioenergetic change," (Barbara Price, above, note 51), and thus signals to us, as I believe it did to the Israelites of that period and to their neighbors that they had achieved a state, "like all the other nations."[107] We might as well take the ancient record at its own word.

But what of the Temple of Solomon? The "cosmic-universal rule"[108] implied by the Israelite monarchy demanded a temple that incorporated the same cosmic symbolism as did temples in the surrounding region. I believe that Albright's description and interpretation of the various cosmic features in the Temple of Solomon, such as the two pillars, Jachin and Boaz, the Sea, the twelve bulls, the altar of burnt offerings, and the platform, kîyôr, on which, according to the Chronicler Solomon stood while uttering the prayer of dedication (2 Chr 6:12-13), have not been effectively either superseded or refuted.[109] In spite of whether Jachin and Boaz served as structural columns within a bit Hilani porch,[110] or whether they were free standing pillars, which has been the

---

[103]Robert G. Boling, *Judges, Introduction, Translation, and Commentary* (AB 6A; Garden City: Doubleday, 1975) 256, 258, 273, 293; but see also Moshe Weinfeld, *Deuteronomy and the Deuteronomic School*, 169-70, with notes. The debate over the editorial strand to which these passages should be assigned and the view of the monarchy that they represent is irrelevant to my argument, which is simply that the passages reveal self-knowledge on the part of the Israelite editors of various stages of political evolution and the implications of these stages for the Israelite community.

[104]See Moshe Weinfeld, ibid., and William McKane, *I and II Samuel, Introduction and Commentary* (Torch Bible Commentaries; London: SCM Press, 1963) 66-69; see also P. Kyle McCarter, Jr., *I Samuel, A New Translation* (AB 8; Garden City: Doubleday, 1980) 156-62. I have suggested above, note 47, the possibility that Israel represents a secondary state that was formed under the pressure of the Philistine/Phoenician states surrounding her. McCarter (ibid., 160) writes that: ". . . it might be argued that a king is requested out of military necessity. Israel's pre-monarchical institutions have become inadequate to cope with new political realities, especially the Philistine threat." But he rejects this explanation.

[105]William McKane, *I and II Samuel*, 217-19, and Moshe Weinfeld, *Deuteronomy and the Deuteronomic School*, 194, for the presumed Deuteronomic editing of vs. 13a, and 247-48. See also Frank Moore Cross, *Canaanite Myth and Hebrew Epic, Essays in the History of the Religion of Israel* (Cambridge: Harvard University Press, 1973) 241-64.

[106]Arvid Kapelrud, "Temple Building, A Task for Gods and Kings," 59-60, and Moshe Weinfeld, *Deuteronomy and the Deuteronomic School*, 250-54.

[107]1 Sam 8:20. See P. Kyle McCarter, *I Samuel*, 160-62; Frank Moore Cross, *Canaanite Myth and Hebrew Epic*, 243, and George E. Mendenhall, "The Monarchy," 157.

[108]Frank Moore Cross, ibid., 265.

[109]William Foxwell Alright, *Archaeology and the Religion of Israel*, 138-50, with notes.

[110]Jean Ouellette, "The Basic Structure of Solomon's Temple and Archaeological Research," *The Temple of Solomon* (ed. Joseph Gutmann; American Academy of Religion, Society of Biblical Literature Religion and the Arts, 3; Missoula: Scholars Press, 1976) 8-11, with notes.

opinion of most scholars,[111] it is undeniable, in my opinion, that they had a major symbolic purpose in relationship to the sanctuary. Pillars built with such symbolic purpose would probably point us toward free standing structures, and we can generally agree with S. Yeivin that "a custom of erecting twin columns in front of the facades of temples (without any architectural relation to the building) was current in the western part of the Fertile Crescent (the area of Israel, Phoenicia, Syria) at least since the XIIIth century B.C.E. and till the IInd century C.E."[112]

The symbolic purposes played by such pillars could well have included those mentioned as possibilities by Albright, namely, "they may have been regarded as the reflection of the columns between which the sun rose each morning to pour its light through the portico of the Temple into its interior,"[113] or that, "Like the Egyptian, 'djed' symbol they may also have denoted 'endurance,' 'continuity,' in which case their dynastic role would become self-evident."[114] It is this latter that I think is especially important in the light of the thesis of this paper. I assume that the pillars played a major role in legitimizing the temple and the dynasty of David in the minds of the people. In other words the pillars, Jachin on the south, carrying the message that Yahweh had established the dynasty and the temple, and Boaz on the north, carrying the message that the power that emanates from the sanctuary is that of Yahweh.[115] An old suggestion by R. B. Y. Scott seems most interesting and relevant here. Scott drew upon an example from Cylinder A of Gudea of Lagash, as well as other Near Eastern evidence to demonstrate the hypothesis that the words "Jachin" and "Boaz" were parts of two inscriptions, "of which the opening words came to designate the pillars on which they appeared."[116] The relevant passage in Gudea is A XXII 24–XXIV 7, where Gudea has stones brought into the temple precinct and fashioned into six steles each of which bears a sentence name. These were set up on the temple terrace, apparently surrounding it, at various gates leading into the temple, and inside the temple itself. One of these, which was stationed at the *ká.sur.ra.* gate, was called, in Thureau-Dangin's translation: "der Herr des Sturmes Enlil, welcher nicht seinesgleichen hat, blickt mit günstigem Auge auf Gudea, den Grosspriester [*en*] Ningirsus."[117] The next stele mentioned, stationed toward the rising sun, bore the name: "der König der (brausenden) Wirbelwinde Enlil, der Herr, der nicht seinesgleichen hat, hat in seinem reinen Herzen erwählt Gudea, den Grosspriester Ningirsus."[118] The following stele, erected at *šu.ga.lam*, the main entrance to Eninnu,[119] bore the name "der König, durch den die Welt ruht, hat befestigt den Thron Gudeas, des Grosspriester Ningirsus."[120] Thus each of these steles bore an inscription that identified the ruling dynast with the chief god of the city, and, particularly in the case of the stele at the *šu.ga.lam* gate, specifically legitimized the throne of Gudea.

---

[111]Ibid., 7, with notes.

[112]"Jachin and Boaz," *PEQ* 91 (1959) 20. But note also the bronzed pillar that stood near the gate through which Ningirsu would have been led into the Eninnu temple in Lagash: see above, note 90. The phenomenon is not limited to the Levant.

[113]*Archaeology and the Religion of Israel*, 143, and notes. See also H. Van Dyke Paranuk, "Was Solomon's Temple Oriented Toward the Sun," *PEQ* 110 (1978) 28-33.

[114]Ibid.

[115]John Gray, *I and II Kings, A Commentary* (2nd ed.; The Old Testament Library; Philadelphia: Westminster, 1970) 187.

[116]"The Pillars Jachin and Boaz," *JBL* 58 (1939) 146.

[117]*SAK* 115.

[118]Ibid.

[119]A. Falkenstein, *Die Inschriften Gudeas von Lagaš*, 140-41.

[120]Ibid. I would also like to recall the "bronzed" pillar that stood outside the gate "through which Ningirsu enters" the temple. See note 90, above.

R. B. Y. Scott's suggested reconstruction for the inscription on Jachin was: "He (Yahweh) will establish the throne of David, and his kingdom to his seed forever." And for Boaz: "in the strength of Yahweh shall the king rejoice," or some such, drawing on language well known from the Psalms.[121] In Scott's more recent discussion of the same problem he wrote that "It seems probable that the names of the pillars in Solomon's royal temple, where he officiated as high priest, were derived from the initial words of dynastic inscriptions like that of Gudea."[122] This view seems to me by far the most reasonable and the most likely explanation of the pillar's significance, adding more evidence for the legitimizing political role of the temple and its appurtenances, and allowing us to see more clearly just how a building could have played such a role in ancient societies.

One additional role played by pillars in the ancient Near East, that of witnesses of covenant ceremonies, can be proposed. Widengren has pointed out the central role of the king in Israelite covenant making during the period of the monarchy. He found three main elements present in such ceremonies: 1) the king plays the central role, calling the assembly and reading from the book of the law; 2) the king himself appears "before the Lord," thus assuming the role of high priest; and 3) "The covenant is made in the temple."[123] I have argued elsewhere for the centrality of the role of the temple in ancient Near Eastern covenant rituals ("What is a Temple? A Preliminary Typology"). Covenants are sealed in temples or near pillars standing near temples, and thus derive their binding efficacy on the ancient society from the temple's authoritative, legitimizing position within the society. We have a classic example of the role of a pillar, presumably either Jachin or Boaz, in the covenant renewal ceremony of Josiah, as recorded in 1 Kings 23:2-3: "The king went up to the House of the Lord, with all the men of Judah and all the inhabitants of Jerusalem: priests, prophets, and all the people, small and great. And he read in their ears all the words of the book of the law which had been found in the House of the Lord. The king stood by the column and made a covenant before the Lord . . . ."[124] The pillar must play here the same legitimizing role that I have described for the state itself. The process of "state renewal" in Israel, which is after all what the covenant making process is during the period of the monarchy, and what we have also on other occasions where the pillars play a similar role (1 Kings 11), derives its power from the temple.[125]

The temple was finished in Solomon's eleventh year (ca. 959), in the eighth month (Bul), and dedicated the following year in the seventh month (Ethanim). The eleven month delay between completion and dedication could well be attributed to Solomon's

---

[121]"The Pillars Jachin and Boaz," 148-49.

[122]IDB 2. 781.

[123]"King and Covenant," 3.

[124]"King and Covenant," 5-7. See also George E. Mendenhall, "Covenant Forms in Israelite Tradition," BAR 3, 35: "Provision for deposit in the temple and periodic public reading," with the accompanying explanation: "Since the treaty itself was under the protection of the deity, it was deposited as a sacred thing in the sanctuary of the vassal state . . . ." See also John Gray, I and II Kings, 188, where he writes that "On the evidence of the association of the pillars with the covenant in the two passages in Kings, Jachin and Boaz might be survivals of the standing stones of witness to the covenant at the central sanctuary, cf. Josh. 24.26f. . . ." And see Widengren, "King and Covenant," 12-17.

[125]Of course, it was obvious that Jeroboam would have to found new temples that would legitimize his dynasty, also under the aegis of Yahweh, as he intended. His choice of shrine centers and of symbols represents an archaizing attempt to establish a temple cultus that would have all the appearance of legitimacy in the eyes of his subjects that the Jerusalem temple held. See Frank Moore Cross, Canaanite Myth and Hebrew Epic, 73-75.

wish to dedicate the temple at the New Year, during the Feast of Tabernacles.[126] We must distinguish here between Spring and Fall New Year's festivals. In Israel there was an older, Spring New Year, and a more recent Fall New Year, the latter, "falling on the New Year common to Canaan and Egypt, in Israel became the great feast of the era of kingship . . . ."[127] Generally speaking, the New Year in the Mesopotamian tradition began in the Spring, with the modification that there may have been a cultic year that began in the Fall. The Babylonian Akitu Festival, for example, took place mostly in Nisan, earlier in Adar.[128] Thus while it is technically correct that "sanctuaries are dedicated at the Near Year," according to De Moor, we must distinguish temple dedications/festivals that took place at the Spring New Year, such as the Gudea Eninnu Temple and the *Enuma elish*/Akitu in Babylon, and those that took place during the Fall New Year, such as the Baal Temple at Ras Shamra, and the Temple of Solomon.[129]

With regard to Solomon's prayer of dedication of the Jerusalem Temple itself, most authorities are agreed that large parts of the prayer in 1 Kings 8 are the work of the later Deuteronomic editor. Gray sees vss. 1-11 as preserving an authentic account of what actually happened on that occasion, and vss. 62-66 as reflecting "a genuine tradition of the significant assembly of the sacral community Israel at the dedication of the new central sanctuary, but this is the work of the Deuteronomistic compiler . . . ."[130] Montgomery sees "the original elements of the story" contained in vss. 1, 3, 5, and 6.[131] It is important here to note the importance of post-dedication post-New Year public feasts in all the traditions that have been discussed above: Gudea, Babylonian (*Enuma elish*), Ugaritic, etc.[132] Most authorities assume that vss. 62-66 have been worked over by the Deuteronomic editor, and that the numbers are too large.[133] Weinfeld see vss. 12-13 as a summary of the original prayer, which he compares with similar statements in the dedicatory prayers of Gudea and Esarhaddon.[134]

Two important Deuteronomic elements in the prayer of Solomon are the "name theology," as seen in vss. 17, 18, 19, 20, 44, 48, where the temple is seen as having been built to the "name" of Yahweh, rather than as his actual dwelling place. Contrast this

---

[126]"He was obeying a venerable Oriental tradition according to which sanctuaries had to be dedicated preferably on New Year." (Johannes C. De Moor, *New Year With Canaanites and Israelites, Part One: Description*, Kamper Cahiers; Kampen: J. H. Kok, 1972, 18). See also John Gray, *I and II Kings*, 206-8, and James A. Montgomery, *The Book of Kings, A Critical and Exegetical Commentary* (ed. Henry Snyder Gehman; ICC; New York: Scribner's, 1951) 186-88. Montgomery would excise *beḥāg* "as a backreference from v. 65." (187.

[127]Frank Moore Cross, *Canaanite Myth and Hebrew Epic*, 123, with notes and 238.

[128]Svend Aage Pallis, *The Babylonian Akîtu Festival* (Copenhagen: Bianco Lunos Bogtrykkeri, 1926) 27-30. And see H. Hunger, "Kalender," *RLA* 5 (1977) 297-303.

[129]For Ras Shamra, see further Johannes De Moor, *New Year With Canaanites and Israelites, Part Two: The Canaanite Sources*. See also H. W. Fairman, "Worship and Festivals in an Egyptian Temple," *BJRL* 37 (1954-55) 187: "The traditional time for the dedication of a temple was either on the eve of New Year's Day, or on New Year's Day ...the ceremonies on the temple roof on New Year's Day included the annual rededication of the temple and its gods: the union with the sun not only brought renewal of fertility and welfare to Egypt, it renewed for another year the life and powers of Edfu, Horus, and the gods who lived with him in the temple."

[130]*I and II Kings*, 203.

[131]*The Book of Kings*, 186.

[132]See "What is a Temple? A Preliminary Typology," and item number 12 of my typology, above.

[133]See 2 Chr 29:31-36 for a similar event with more manageable numbers and Montgomery, *The Book of Kings*, 199-200, for additional examples.

[134]*Deuteronomy and the Deuteronomic School*, 35-37.

with Pss 74:2 and 76:3, where the Temple on Mount Zion is seen as the dwelling place of Yahweh, "an earlier conception," more in line with Near Eastern views of temples.[135] The other Deuteronomic feature of the prayer that stands out strongly is the view that the temple is a house of prayer, rather than a cultic center, the actual dwelling of Yahweh. Vss. 41-43 are especially important here, where Yahweh will listen to the prayers of foreigners who come to the temple to honor his name.[136] The important point that I want to make, in the light of the Deuteronomic argument, is that the pre-Deuteronomic sources of the OT that make reference to the Temple of Solomon place that edifice in the pattern well known to us from other ancient Near Eastern temple traditions.[137] To put it another way, the Deuteronomic argument is largely irrelevant as far as the main thesis of this paper is concerned: the Israelite state (a pre-Deuteronomic polity), was capped by a legitimizing temple/cult system that was intimately related to other such systems in the Near East.[138]

+List of Abbreviations used in this paper that are not identified in the Society of Biblical Literature, "Instructions to Contributors," or otherwise identified in the paper:

AAAS Annales Archéologiques Arabes Syriennes. Damascus.

CRRA Compte Rendu de la . . . Rencontre Assyriologique Internationale.

OIC   Oriental Institute Communications. Chicago.

RLA   Reallexikon der Assyriologie. Berlin.

---

[135]Weinfeld, *Deuteronomy and the Deuteronomic School*, 194-98. See also Frank Moore Cross, *Canaanite Myth and Hebrew Epic*, 254.
[136]Weinfeld, ibid., 37, 195-99.
[137]Ibid., 250-55, and Arvid Kapelrud, "Temple Building, A Task for Gods and Kings."
[138]Only as the present paper was finished did I receive a copy of Norman K. Gottwald, *The Tribes of Yahweh, A Sociology of Liberated Israel* (Maryknoll: Orbis Books, 1979). See, for example, 371-74. Also of exceptional value is G. W. Ahlstrom, "Heaven on Earth—At Hazor and Arad," *Religious Syncretism in Antiquity, Essays in Conversation with Geo Widengren* (ed. Birger A. Pearson; American Academy of Religion and the Institute of Religious Studies, UCSB, Series on Formative Thinkers, I; Missoula: Scholars Press, 1975) 67-83, with many references.

UNDER THE SHADOW OF MOSES:
AUTHORSHIP AND AUTHORITY IN HELLENISTIC JUDAISM

Burton Mack
Claremont

INTRODUCTION

The topic for this paper is the notion of authorship in the literary traditions of Second Temple Judaism. Three theses will be proposed and discussed in general terms in the first part of the study. In the second part the theses will be tested by analyses of three authors in the tradition of Jewish Wisdom—Ben Sira, the author of the Wisdom of Solomon, and Philo of Alexandria.

The first thesis will be that the notion of authorship as it occurred during this period was strongly indebted to Greek literary practice and conceptuality, learned in the process of Hellenization. The second thesis will be that with the discovery of the significance of authorship the status of the written text was given a particular kind of authority. This authority was a function of the relationship which a text (*logos*) was understood to sustain with its author (*ethos*). Thus the increased authority of the five books of Moses during this period corresponded to the increase in the significance of Moses himself as a figure of authority. The linkage for this correspondence may be found in the notion of authorship itself. The third thesis will be that, as the authority of Moses and his books increased throughout the period, the acknowledgement of authorship of new literatures became increasingly problematic. The reason was that the reading of the books of Moses as authored and authoritative left less and less room for other original compositions which could be read in turn in their own right, i.e., on their own "authority," or compete with the literary authority which Moses came to have. In order to describe this phenomenon of authorial competition more clearly Harold Bloom's theory of the "anxiety of influence" will be used.

The set of theses does not intend to provide a sufficient account for the emergence of Moses' books as authoritative for Judaism. Complex relationships among a variety of cultural, historical factors were in play. Scholars working in the field of Second Temple Judaism are aware of some of these factors. Needs internal to Jewish self-definition determined ways in which the literary manifestations of its traditions were read and invested with varying degrees and kinds of authority as foundational scriptures. Encounter with other cultural traditions called for certain apologetic moves, one of which was the need to heighten the significance and function of the scriptures as national epic in competition with other epic traditions. And in the process of Hellenization, a process probably begun and carried largely at the level of recognizing Greek *paideia* as a literary phenomenon, a wide range of new significations of Jewish literature itself came to be explored. The notion of authorship was therefore but one factor among many in the emerging authority of the books of Moses during the period. But it may have been an important factor.

Nothing can be said about the relative importance of such a factor in the process of canonization, however, until the notion itself is clarified, documented across the range of literatures written during the period, and assessed in relation to other forces and factors at work in the process. The theses presented here are to be taken as a first attempt to describe the notion itself, and to suggest a way of understanding its significance as that notion which set in motion a variety of authorial postures on the part of those who continued to write in the tradition of Moses. The attempt to describe the Hellenistic notion of authorship is itself the more important move at this point. If there is value to it, and if it can be shown that Jewish authors of the period understood authorship in its terms, the entire spectrum of authorial postures in Jewish literature of the period presumably could be assessed and compared using our thesis as control. The literatures would range from anonymous cultic, poetic and visionary writings, through pseudonymous compositions to the varieties of midrashic texts, and on to signatured commentaries and histories. In this paper only a small probe can be made in the interest of arguing for the plausibility and value of this approach for a fresh reading of those literatures which may be placed easily in the "School of Moses."[1]

PART I: AUTHORSHIP AND THE ANXIETY OF INFLUENCE

A. *Authorship Among the Greeks*

We engage now a consideration for which there is very little precedent in scholarly discussion. The reasons for this are two-fold. The first is that the marks of authorship in Greek literature are so obvious that the phenomenon itself has simply been taken for granted by scholars in the field. The second is that the notion of authorship itself, at those times when it has come under critical investigation, as in the case of general literary theory, quickly has involved such a complex of philosophical, linguistic, and psychological issues as to appear problematic, unmanageable at least for scholars working with ancient texts. There are, however, certain observations which can be made about authorship as understood and practiced by the Greeks which do not at first require the articulation of a complex psychological theory. Only after making them will a recent theory of authorship be suggested which can help us with one important aspect of the notion and serve as a bridge to considerations we will want to make about the problem which the Greek notion of authorship created for Jewish writers of the Hellenistic period.

The observations to be made about the Hellenistic notion of authorship are based on commonplaces of classical scholarship about aspects of Hellenistic culture in general. They can only be presented here briefly and in an outline as indications of the phenomenon we seek to delineate. At this point they form a set of characteristics which merely mark out the cultural arenas within which a more precise description would have to be sought. But taken as a set they do present us with the contours of what may be a coherent conceptuality of a common literary experience. It is the suspicion of such coherence which allows us to speak of a notion of authorship at all and to seek its manifestations in Jewish literature of the period.

The set includes the following items: 1) *Literacy* as the fundamental requirement and manifestation of the Hellenistic *ideal* of human excellence and achievement (*aretē* via *paideia*); 2) *Signature* (and/or attribution) as the way in which authorship was acknowledged as a person's achievement; 3) the *competitive spirit* which motivated all forms of literary accomplishment; 4) *recognition* as the way in which reward for successful literary accomplishment was given; 5) *originality* as the way in which an individual could establish authorial recognition (i.e., compete) over against strong precursors in a literary tradition.

1. The Emergence of a Literary Culture: We may begin with the usual description of Hellenistic culture as "literary."[2] The archaic orientation to physical prowess and

---

[1]While the concept of "authority" has long been recognized as a matter for scholarly investigation in the formation of communities and their traditions in early Judaism and Christianity, discussions of authorship as a significant factor in the attribution of authority are curiously absent. A cursory glance at recent monographs on the subject will illustrate. See John H. Schütz, *Paul and the Anatomy of Apostolic Authority* (New York: Cambridge, 1975); Bengt Holmberg, *Paul and Power* (Lund: Gleerup, 1978); Walter Schmithals and Antonias Gunneweg, *Authority* (Nashville: Abingdon, 1982).

[2]That Hellenistic culture (*paideia*) was "literary" is a generalization commonly accepted by scholars. See such a classic statement as that of H. I. Marrou, *A History of Education in Antiquity* (translated from the third French edition by George Lamb; New York: Sheed and Ward, 1956). There are summary statements in his "Conclusion. Classical Humanism" at the end of Part Two.

valor, the *aretē* of the aristocratic warrior, came to an end in the sixth and fifth
centuries with the emergence of the *polis* and its needs for the sophistic or rhetorical
education of its citizens.[3] With the development of rhetorical skills and theory came
preference for prose composition and the emergence of a popular educational system
which would focus upon letters. Isocrates (436-338 B.C.E.)--rhetor, educator, author--
may be taken as a representative and founding figure for this new orientation.[4] In his
Evagoras, which Isocrates exhibits as the first prose encomium (of a ruler), the subject is
still the ideal warrior-king marked by brave deeds and exploits. But the notion of *aretē*
is already being recast, even and especially for the ruler, in the direction of the new
educational enterprise with its concerns for learning, ethics, and discourse. The ideal
ruler must now be wise, a move in re-characterization of the warrior-king which became
normative for the Hellenistic era and can be traced through the Kingship treatises to
Plutarch's lives.[5] But wisdom comes through learning. And learning comes through discourse. And so it happened that the characterization of the superior man changed dramatically from its archaic ideal to include now those skills which had to do with speech.
Alongside the image of the warrior-king that of the teacher and sage emerged to focus
the new civic ideals. And alongside the older *aretē* manifest in glorious deeds the considered speech of the man of excellence marked the new cultural values. With this shift
in the definition of virtue *paideia* itself became both the way (as education) and the goal
(as culture) for the achievement of human well-being. And *paideia* had to do with words
now--being well read and being capable of considered speech. The curriculum was now
oriented to literature.

2. The Rewards for Literary Achievement: Composed speech now became that
human activity by which the superior individual could exhibit excellence. The Greeks
were never clear on the relationship of (natural) endowment to human achievement, and
this is reflected in their many and continuous debates about the prerequisites for education and literary accomplishment. For poets the muses tended to be credited; for prose
writers mastery of the *technē*. But for both the age-old desire for superiority, measured
still by the image of the warrior's valor and victory in battle, continued to motivate
achievement. The writer will be tested in the arena of literary competition.

The competitive spirit is clearly in evidence throughout the entire history of
Greek literary accomplishment. Its manifestations vary from genre to genre, but in
those intended for public performance, including both poets and writers of prose, it was
not unusual for formal competition to be institutionalized and prizes given for the
winner. Pindar gloried in his victories in competition with other odists; the dramatic
poets vied for prizes; Demosthenes received the crown for his orations; Hellenistic
legend even created a scene of competition between Hesiod and Homer.[6] The reward
was recognition, fame, and glory.

---

[3]In addition to Marrou's study noted above, see W. Jaeger, *Paideia. The Ideals of
Greek Culture* I-III (translated from the second German edition by Gilbert Highet; New
York: Oxford, 1939-1945; second edition Oxford: Blackwells, 1954; subsequent reprints
in paperback).
    [4]See Marrou, *History of Education*, Part One, Chap. VII: "The Masters of the
Classical Tradition II: Isocrates."
    [5]The classical study on the "Kingship treatises" is still E. R. Goodenough, "The
Political Philosophy of Hellenistic Kingship," *Yale Classical Studies* 1 (1928) 55-102.
    [6]On the competition between Hesiod and Homer in Hellenistic biographic
traditions see Mary R. Lefkowitz, *The Lives of the Greek Poets* (Baltimore: Johns
Hopkins, 1981) 5, 8-9, 18-22.

Where competition was not formalized it surfaced in other ways. Isocrates was at pains to show the novelty of his accomplishment as a creator of the prose encomium by claiming a distinctive use of words not possible for poets and never attempted by philosophers.[7] Philosophers, for their part, informally institutionalized the competitive nature of their schools, marked by their demands for articulate discourse, polemic, and the aspiration for acknowledged literary accomplishment.[8] Teachers candidating for positions even in the country villages frequently had to compose and perform competitively. And student competition in composition and recital was the order of the day. A person was judged by his way with words.

Thus signature was called for as the expected correlate to literary achievement. The author's words were understood to be his own. If his description was graphic, his poetry moving, his maxims telling, his philosophical discourse convincing, his rhetoric persuasive--he could count on being lauded. Readership and audience were therefore always in view. It was the author's intention to be read (or heard), gaining recognition and approval from those he sought to persuade. If he succeeded his name would be known. And if his text was good enough to be read again and again, throughout the generations, why that was immortality. Excellence, then, was now to be manifest not only in daring deeds, but also in the crafting of speech. The arena of *aretē* had shifted, but the competitive spirit remained. Recognition and fame for superior and lasting achievement in composition marked the authorial consciousness and indicated the significance of signature.

But with whom did one compete? As odist with contemporary odists? As creator of new genre with writers of traditional genres? As author with one's subjects? Or as ephebe with strong precursors? The answer seems to be with all of them. All of these competitive relationships may indeed be discerned in the history of Hellenistic authorship and must be taken into account in any comprehensive discussion. In this article we can merely indicate the possibility of determining in general three such relationships important for our study. The first is that between an author and other contemporary authors in formalized competition, usually within a given genre. The second is more subtle, that between an author and the subject of his discourse with which or whom glory must be shared. The third is that between an author and his precursors whether working within the same literary genre or not. The case of formalized competition in Greek literary history is too well known to need further documentation here. But the other two competitive relationships need some discussion.

The second relationship in which an author shares glory with his subject can be illustrated in the composition of an encomium. The encomium was a discourse of praise for esteemed and valued persons, things, institutions and their achievements. But as Pindar knew, and as Isocrates reveals, the successful writing of encomia not only assured the person praised of glory, but the author who praised of fame and glory as well. The intricate balance of such shared glory is hardly an overt competition between author and subject. But it does present yet another consideration for the author in quest of literary achievement and its rewards. That consideration is that one write about a strong and significant subject. A strong subject will enhance the chances for being read. As

---

[7]Isocrates, *Evagoras* 8-11.

[8]One might read Diogenes Laertius' *Lives of Eminent Philosophers* with these questions in mind. The history is related as a series of "*successions*" following earlier biographical historians such as Sotion. The "successions" are lines of continuity *and discontinuity* in philosophical traditions from teachers to students who then become teachers themselves. The mark of the philosopher is articulate discourse as espousal. The points of discontinuity in the "successions" are marked by new and "original" teaching which differs from that of one's precursors, and is strong enough to establish a new series of successions in continuity. The mark of the founder of a school is invariably that he was the "first" to have articulated or espoused a certain teaching.

Isocrates says in the *Evagoras*, the encomium is a memorial in written form which may be published abroad and may continue to be read by the subject's descendants, thus extending his renown in a way not possible for the traditional funeral games and monuments.[9] What he does not say in so many words, but surely knew, is that that would assure his own fame as well. In the encomium he has compared Evagoras to other rulers and found him to be superior. He has also compared his own work to other authors, and the reader knows what Isocrates hopes for--that his readers will find his encomium worth the reading and remember him for his fine achievement.

The third competitive relationship, that between an author and his precursors, introduces yet another factor into the equation, that namely of the function of tradition itself. In order to see the several ways in which an author might respond to strong precursors we need to discuss the development and transmission of literary traditions in relation to authorial achievement.

3. The Development of Literary Traditions: The age of oral epic came to an end with the written texts of Homer and Hesiod, and the emergence of signatured authorship of lyric poetry, odes, dramatic poetry, and prose literatures during the sixth and fifth centuries.[10] The significance of the text being written, of course, is that the precursor continues to manifest presence as an author. And with the presence of precursors literary traditions may begin. Homer was given pride of first place for poetic style and his epic came to be understood as the beginning of Greek history, culture, and literature. It would not be a misuse of the term "canon" to designate the important role his works played throughout the history of classical and Hellenistic Greek culture and education. To use Harold Bloom's term we may call Homer's epic a "strong" text. Acquaintance with the (oral) epic tradition preceding Homer now had to be won by reading him. After him, and this is the mark of his achievement, another epic need not be written. Now there were rhapsodists, interpreters of the written text, whose mark of achievement was rather in memorization and performance than in composition.

For a time during the eighth and seventh centuries other authors did indeed compose epic poetry, though we know only of those who took as their subjects epic traditions other than "Homeric" (e.g., the Theseus and Heracles sagas).[11] But only one other writer from this period produced another "strong" text, and he did so not by competing expressly with Homer and the other epics of Aristocratic culture, but by turning to 1) mythic origins and 2) to non-aristocratic folk-themes for his subjects. With this move Hesiod created a new literature by carving out a space not already occupied by Homer and filling it with his own strong compositions. But if not overtly competitive for the same turf, to extend the metaphor, Hesiod's poetry was nevertheless a kind of supplement to that of Homer's, making the necessary "additions" to it, as it were, in order to make it "complete." Looked at in this way, then, Hesiod did stand in a competitive relationship to Homer, one which the Greeks themselves recognized early on and resolved by distinguishing their respective strengths. If Homer was the master of the style of epic verse, Hesiod was to be given pride of place for content--poetry which possessed abiding moral significance.

As for the emergence of other forms of poetry--lyric, elegy, encomiastic odes, drama--one suspects in general, and can detect here and there in specific instances, that the desire for individual accomplishment impelled originality in two directions: in the selection of new themes and in the development of new genres. We have already noted this phenomenon expressed in the case of Isocrates' *Evagoras*. Another more subtle but clear instance would be Aristophanes' re-casting of drama in the comic mode with its

---

[9]Isocrates, *Evagoras* 73-77.
[10]There is a fine discussion of the transition from oral to written epic in Albin Lesky, *Geschichte der griechischen Literatur* (2nd ed.; Munich: Francke, 1963) 29-58.
[11]See A. Lesky, *Geschichte* (note 10) 126-27.

overt parodies of his own precursors in the dramatic tradition! In *The Frogs* it is even
the case that the parody of Aeschylus and Euripedes is presented as a competition
between them for the place of honor as the best poet in Hades! A third example of the
way in which creativity and competition appear to be conjoined is given with Thucydides. He does not acknowledge Herodotus as precursor, though he does compare his own
work to Homer's epic. He is at pains, however, to argue that his war, the war between
Athens and Sparta which he will write, is the greatest war the Greeks have fought, far
greater than others about which others have written.[12] Could it be that the glory of the
classical period, that namely so many new literary genres and themes were created, was
the result of competition? Most of them do exhibit the spirit of competition with other
writers, both those of other genres and those writing in the author's own mode of
composition.

But soon this period of literary creativity appeared to come to the full. By the end
of the fifth century the major classifications of literature were acknowledged, distinguished, and compared: epic, lyric, elegy, ode, and drama as forms of poetry; speeches,
including encomia and apologies, tracts, philosophical writings, educational treatises, and
histories, including memorabilia, as forms of prose. Critique, praise, and blame were the
order of the day when reference was made to authors and writings whether by name or by
type. And the process of selecting and acknowledging strong texts and authors eventually produced the roster of giants who stood at the beginnings of the several literary
traditions and marked their courses.[13]

Once the strong texts were there the problem of original composition within a
genre became acute. It was exacerbated by the Hellenistic orientation to rhetoric as an
art and the concomitant requirement of learning to compose through education, i.e., with
and from a teacher. Now the student as ephebe had to learn how to write (and think) at
first by imitating teachers and strong precursors. But this meant that the aspiring
student now competed with those from whom he had learned, those whose writings he had
read and imitated, if he wished to establish himself independently. Relatively few were
able to do so, though the history of philosophy, with its plurification of schools by strong
and independent thinkers and writers may be read in this way, as may the history of
drama and rhetoric with their own twists and turns. For most though learning through
mimesis set the constraints for literary pursuits and inaugurated the age of scholarship
and criticism.

It was during this time that the phenomenon of pseudonymous authorship
appeared. Such writings as the Homeric Hymns and the Letters of Socrates reveal the
curious reticence of some creative authors to sign their own works, and the solution
which was found by attributing them to persons whose authority was already established. Pseudonymity is probably to be distinguished from anonymous authorship, at least
in the form of anonymous scribal activity of the kind which had long occurred in the context of established institutions with their needs for archives, chronicles, and composed
materials for institutional use (including poetries for liturgical use). Pseudonymity knows
about authorship as an individual and public activity, but avoids authorial competition by
trading in a firmly established literary tradition with its canons and authorities. Rewards
for literary accomplishment would therefore be highly problematic. We probably must
suppose a sub-cultural readership within which some form of recognition of the "real"
author would have been possible for such pseudonymous works. But as a response to the
weight of pervasive canonical literature and its cultivation pseudonymity was probably a
precarious solution at best with short-lived rewards at most. Better appears to have
been the discovery of style as that arena open for individual, creative performance in a

---

[12]Thucydides, Book I, Sections I-II.

[13]The process of "canonization" was completed by the literary critics, especially
in Alexandria, at the end of the Hellenistic period. With them the lists appear, i.e., the
nine lyric poets, the five dramatic poets, etc.

literary culture dominated by the mimetic ideals. But with this move we find ourselves at the end of the Greco-Roman age and at the beginning of the Second Sophistic.

4. The Disclosure of the Author in His Writing: There is one other aspect to the Greek view of authorship which needs to be observed. It surfaced early in the Hellenistic period and eventually determined a wide range of literary activities, both critical and compositional, which set the stage for the *imitatio Graecae* of the Romans and the Second Sophistic. It was the notion that the considered and composed speech of an author was an expression of his own character.

The rootage for such an idea lay deeply imbedded in the classical orientation to language and literature as the field of human endeavor within which the new *aretē* was to be cultivated. The theoretical foundation for such an idea was worked out expressly in the later technical handbooks of the rhetorical tradition. It proposed a close correspondence between an author's speech (*logos*) and his character (*ethos*), and was discussed primarily in terms of the speaker's need to establish credibility early on in the introductory section of the speech. Aristotle is explicit about this credibility having to do with the character of the speaker, and that it must be achieved by the way in which he uses words no matter how well known he may already have been to his audience.[14] Thus the convincing manifestation of a speaker's *ethos* by means of what and how he spoke was considered one of the three essential components of persuasive composition, the other two being the rhetorical power and logic of the speech itself (*logos*) and its forthright engagement of the listeners-readers at the point of their own investment in the issue, thesis, or theme under consideration (*pathos*).

As a literary device the construction of speeches for persons needing characterization (*prosōpopoiïa*) had already been used in historiography by Thucydides with telling force, and the dramatic poets put it to constant use. With it *logos* took its place beside *praxis* as a means by which a person's *ethos* and *aretē* could be disclosed. *Prosōpopoiïa* became a primary skill to be learned in the preliminary exercises of rhetorical training, and with it the creation of characters (*ethopoiïa*) became a possibility as well.[15] Thus the skilled author could, with words, create or disclose the character of his subjects by having them come to speech.

For the reader and critic, then, the sayings and speeches of persons encountered in literary tradition were understood to be significant disclosures of character. Plutarch explained that the character, motivations, and workings of a person's mind were better revealed in the words he spoke than in the deeds he performed.[16] This is no doubt an exaggeration on his part, but it does express an assumption about the importance of speech which clarifies to a great extent the rationale behind the way in which he composed his lives with their prominent usage of anecdotal material (*chreiai*) in combination with encomiastic description of great achievements. The teachers of rhetoric had long since taken note of the *chreiai* among the anecdotal material of which the earlier "biographies" (in the Aristotelian tradition) were composed. They saw in them just that combination of carefully composed *logos* with its speaker's *ethos* which defined the rhetorical situation itself.[17] For teachers of rhetoric, literary critics, and authors of literatures dealing in character-study and characterization, what a person said was understood to be telling.

---

[14]Aristotle, *Rhetoric* I, ii, 4.

[15]The earliest extant *progymnasmata* is of Theon of Alexandria, first century C.E. It contains a discussion of *prosōpopoiïa*. See Christianus Walz, *Rhetores Graeci* I (Stuttgart: Cottage, 1832) 235-39.

[16]Plutarch, *Sayings of Kings and Commanders, Moralia* 172 c.

[17]See Theon's statement about the *chreia* in the introduction to his *Progymnasmata* (C. Walz, *Rhetores Graeci* I, 148, 12-15). "Indeed the (rhetorical) exercise with the *chreia* not only produces a certain facility with words, but a worthy character as well, if we exercise with the apophthegms of the sages."

Behind and through all of this the notion of authorship itself was at work. A person's words were understood to be his own. They revealed what he had seen of the world, how he had looked upon it, what his judgments and contentions were, and how skilled he was in clarifying that in words. Speech was espousal, and the author was understood to "stand behind" what he said. What one said, then, disclosed the kind of person one was. It is not surprising therefore to learn that, in the course of time, the biographies of the great authors of the canons of literature themselves were made possible precisely by means of this principle. Mary Lefkowitz has shown that the Hellenistic and Greco-Roman biographies of Homer and Hesiod, the lyric and dramatic poets, as well as of later authors were all fictions based almost entirely on the authors' writings themselves.[18] From the written works, in addition to clues here and there for reconstructing names, dates, and places, it was the impression the author gave of himself through the kind of literature he wrote, and its tone, which enabled others to characterize him.

The close association which *logos* and *ethos* had for Hellenistic readers and authors is revealed in concerns which came to be expressed about care in selecting literature to be read in the first century C.E. Theon of Alexandria made a point of advising the selection only of "approved" authorities for exercises in rhetorical training.[19] Plutarch's treatise on how to study poetry marshalled all the known modes of literary criticism as means by which the teacher was to discredit the speeches of persons in Homer's epic who were considered unworthy of emulation. Seneca cautioned against reading any authors but those whose character was preeminently virtuous. He explained that "*conversatio*" with their words would have its effect in the formation of the reader's own character, though he did not know quite how this happens.[20] We see here already the ethical and mimetic concerns of the Second Sophistic. By now everything was or had to be authored. Even the anthologies of traditional gnomological material will have to be attributed to some appropriate canonical authority, as for instance, the *Monostichoi* of "Menander" attest. And all of the important figures in the canonical lists of sages and philosophers conversely must have written works attributed to their names, as Diogenes Laertius attests. Authorship and authority now belong together and each will be judged in terms of ethical considerations. Those who win approval as models worthy of emulation will now be imitated without shame.[21] In the Second Sophistic the new author's glory will be manifest more in the style of his praise and *imitatio* of the canons, than in new and original compositional creations.

B. *A Theory of Authorship and Anxiety*

Biblical scholars (and indeed classicists as I read them) have found it difficult to approach their ancient texts with questions about authorship and authority in mind. The reason may be that the notion of canon appears to be a given even as we make our first approaches. With it comes the long tradition of reading and scholarship in just these texts which determines for us the stance of a scribal interpreter. But if we want to understand our texts as literary compositions, as indeed we do, and see them as enactments of vital human engagements with social experience and cultural history, we need to inquire about the act of authorship.

We may consider now a theory of authorship which Harold Bloom has proposed recently, especially in his *Anxiety of Influence* (1973), and *A Map of Misreading*

---

[18]See references to Lefkowitz in note 6.

[19]Theon in Walz, *Rhetores Graeci* I, 212, 15.

[20]Seneca, *Epistle* 11, 8; 94, 40.

[21]See Seneca on the imitation of Socrates in Klaus Döring, *Exemplum Socratis* (Wiesbaden: Steiner, 1979) 18-42.

(1975).[22] Bloom is a literary critic with particular expertise in the traditions of Romantic poetry. The significance of his theory for us lies in the fact that it addresses the question of authorship as a question about literary tradition itself. He is concerned not only to describe the process of creative composition, but to understand the intricate and integral relationship of the poet's precursors to that process. With Bloom the notion of canonical tradition as authority is essential to an understanding of authorship. We will find it helpful as a moment of transition from our discussion of the Greek notion of authorship to considerations of Jewish authorship during the Hellenistic period. Here only the barest outline of the main ideas in Bloom's theory can be given.

1. The Ephebe and His Precursor: We may begin with Bloom's observation that one learns to write by reading. Before the ephebe has written a poem, or even aspired to write a poem, he has read a poem. In the reading he has learned what a poem is, and if the reading awakens the poem within, the desire to write his own poem, the poem read becomes his precursor. Precursors are strong poems, written by strong poets, those who attract strong readers. They mark the fine and exemplary achievements of a literary tradition as read and recognized by subsequent readers. In the reading of one's precursors one sees what it is to have written a strong and lasting poem. Unfortunately one discovers in the process as well, that the poem is already there, has already been written.

Having learned about poetry in just this way, Bloom says, the ephebe experiences a sense of "belatedness." One has come on the scene too late, for the poem which can engender poesis has already been written. If one aspires now to write a poem, one must struggle with the problem of influence, of writing merely in imitation of the strong precursor. This creates anxiety precisely because the relationship to the precursor is now ambivalent and tensive. Caught in this bind the would-be poet seeks to deny his precursor's influence upon him, and to write an "original" poem all his own. In so doing the poet reveals his deepest desire, the unacknowledged source of his pretentions and refusal to acknowledge the influence of his precursor. It is the desire to be "the first," the first in time to see and say what the poem sees and says, the first in rank to achieve what a poem is. Ultimately, as Bloom reads the romantic poets, one desires to have been the first poet, the first human being, self-engendered and without precursors at all. And should the ephebe contend successfully, why then, the new poem will appear in its own strength of superior achievement. And the precursor's poem? Why it will now appear to have been written under the influence of the ephebe's successful poem, even though that poem was written later!

2. The Ratios of Misprision: There is a series of clever moves on the part of the late poet which make it possible to achieve this illusion. Bloom calls the "revisionary ratios," relationships which the poet establishes with his precursor's text. We cannot discuss them here adequately, for the theoretical foundations root deeply in a complex psychology of authorship, and the argumentation draws heavily upon the full range of current discourse in literary criticism. But we may dare the attempt to simplify and translate these ratios in the interest of a description of a process which we can use to compare and contrast Greek and Jewish authorial postures.

All of them are moves made by the poet in the course of re-"reading" his precursor in such a way as to "make room" for his own poem as an "original" composition. The moves themselves are probably to be understood as psycholinguistic, i.e., they occur in the author's own mind and heart in the process of reading and writing as a complex and elongated act. They may or may not be evident separately in the text of the poem as completed, except in the sense in which all belong to a single posturing, the result of

[22]Harold Bloom, *The Anxiety of Influence* (New York: Oxford, 1973); *A Map of Misreading* (New York: Oxford, 1975).

which determines the way in which the poem dares to be presented. They chart, instead, the author's experience, caught in the bind of the anxiety of influence. All are ways in which the author "misreads" his precursor, as well as ways in which he takes courage to write his own poem.

1) *Clinamen* or "swerve" refers to that point at which a modicum of novelty is introduced in the "reading" of the precursor's poem which makes it possible to depart from it, to need to write it over again, to "correct" it by means of writing the new poem.

2) *Tessera* or "completion" refers to the way in which the new poem is understood "merely" to "complete" the meaning which the old poem intended, but did not express. That the new poem does this antithetically or dialectically, however, means that the old poem is really being read as inadequate.

3) *Kenosis* or "emptying" refers to the way in which a poem feigns humility with respect to its precursors, but in such a way that even the precedent poetry is humiliated, brought to the level, that is, of "mere" human speech.

4) *Daemonization* or "inspiration" refers to the poet's daring entertainment of the thought that he is in touch with the spirit or power of poesis. This spirit was encountered at first in the precursor's poem, but now is believed to be transcendent to it and available to the belated poet as well.

5) *Askesis* refers to the poet's willingness to deny aspects of his own imaginative endowment in order to attain his own private control of his capacities in a state of solitude. But the capabilities relinquished are the very ones most manifest in the precursor's poem, and the move thus serves to truncate the authority of the precursor himself.

6) *Apophrades* or the "return of the dead" refers to the willingness at last to have the new poem read in the light of the old. But the "uncanny effect" (Bloom's words) is that the precursor now appears to have imitated the later poet!

According to Bloom these ratios give an account of the battle which the belated poet must engage with his precursor(s). We need not discuss them in detail at the level of psychological theory. The important thing is that Bloom has noticed the relationship of the act of writing to that of reading and related both to the phenomena of history, tradition, and canonization of literary authorities. That such a theory could be developed for the tradition of romantic poetry is impressive in its own right, and suggests its potential significance for the study of other literary cultures. If some form of "anxiety of influence" is endemic to authorship which needs or aspires to be "original," Bloom's theory may be doubly helpful. This is because he has given an account of the reasons why the belated author fails to acknowledge his indebtedness to his precursors. We have wondered about this silence in the case of Hellenistic authors, and we will see that an author's position on the question of precursor-acknowledgment is a significant criterion for distinguishing types of Jewish literature written during the period. Bloom's ratios, then, can alert us to the possibility of authorial competition behind certain maneuvers which a text may manifest in relation to its precursor(s).

Interlude: Milton, Homer, and Moses

Harold Bloom works out his theory of poetry and criticism with the romantic poets in view. They all stand, he claims, under the imposing authority and shadow of Milton as their strong precursor par excellence. With him and the intervening history of other strong poets the modern poet must do battle in a heightened consciousness of belatedness which makes this tradition different from earlier forms of tradition (MM 35). One might ask, then, whether and how his theory of criticism can be used to investigate readership and authorship in earlier literary traditions. Bloom is, after all, working from within a living tradition or poetry and its criticism, which includes express notions of authorship, influence and creativity. And it is a tradition wherein recognized competition already is limited to genre-specific activity.

We must exercise caution, indeed, in the attempt to interpret ancient literary traditions with Bloom's theory in mind. The reason is that, as Bloom indicates in so many words, his theory discloses the melancholy of a cultural age as well as the sense of authorship and its ruses which identify the poets of that age. But if we know that the task of literary criticism, even and especially when focused on the chains of readership-authorship of a specific literary tradition, implies a cultural criticism as well, we may take heart.

We have seen that the Greek notion of authorship, worked out in terms of evidences contained within its own literary texts, and correlated with observations about Greek cultural aspirations in general, does manifest a set of features similar to Bloom's description of the romantic poet. The Greek may not have suffered as consciously a sense of belatedness. Nor were they as appalled by literary and cultural "continuities," a mark of modern Romanticism according to Bloom (MM 36). But we have noted the desire to be "first" as definitive. And we have noted the ratios of competition at work. If the arena of competition was not as circumscribed as that for the romantic poet, both by genre and by traditional canons of authorities, it does not mean that the swerves were less devious. We have suggested that the creation of new genres was itself a way to compete with strong precursors, and that the self-conscious desire for fame was a fundamental factor in literary achievement. It may well be that a psychology of originality (desire for absolute independence) is not yet consciously present in Greek literary culture, but late Hellenistic reflections on *mimesis* show that the phenomenon of influence (i.e., the effect of the reading of an author by a later would-be author) had been discovered and named.[23] If the melancholy of the belated poet needed to wait for modern times, then, it is probably because the challenge of authorship in the meantime could be managed by moves less subjective. These seem to have been given largely with the mastery of rhetoric, and especially its skills in matters of style and delivery, which carried the day for a thousand years. But if this is so, the basic equation of the inter-relationship between precursor and author may work to help us unravel the "hidden roads that go from poem to poem" (AI 96) in the classical traditions too. Taking note of the dissimilarities in cultural setting, we dare nevertheless to seek now evidence for the Greek notion of authorship among Jewish authors of the Hellenistic period, then to trace out several instances of the "hidden roads."

C. Jewish Authorship During the Hellenistic Period

We turn now to the Jewish literature written during the Hellenistic period. To test our thesis on all of the literature of the period as a whole is not possible. But we can make some observations about the nature of the literary activity in general which may indicate the significance of our set of questions and prepare us for a closer look at the three authors we have in mind.

1. The Marks of Authorial Consciousness: Literature written before the period of Hellenistic influence appears not to bear the marks of desire for individual recognition, i.e, authorship of original composition. One may marvel at the lasting literary accomplishments which thus remained anonymous--several re-writings of the epic history, the creative composition of the book of Job, the careful formation of the book of Proverbs-- to say nothing of psalms, songs, cultic codes, and reflective poetry which found their places somewhere in the process of collecting and arranging written materials. One may speak perhaps of a scribal and institutional mentality which found its rewards for written

---

[23]See, for instance, Quintilian, *Inst. or.* II, vii, 2-4; that by means of imitative composition students "will form an intimate acquaintance with the best writings, will carry their models with them, and unconsciously reproduce the style of speech which has been impressed upon the memory."

accomplishments in ways other than public acknowledgment of an individual's originality. Even in the case of the prophets, for whom original speech and public expression were definitive, authorship, though acknowledged by signature, is qualified by the usual disclaimer. This seems to be something more severe than the Greek poet's reference to the Muses. It rejects any claim to human achievement in the transmission of oracular materials.

With the first person accounts of Nehemiah, however, the signature of Ben Sira to his work, and the strong sense of authorial presence of Qohelet, the period of Hellenistic influence begins. For the next three to four hundred years there was an explosion of literary activity in spite of some strong and pervasive conservative cautions against writing things down at all. New genres were borrowed, adapted, and created in the process, and the literary energies unleashed were exceptionally vigorous. It is significant, though, the extent to which much of this literature remained anonymous and/or pseudonymous. This is especially true of visionary and apocalyptic literature. But as one moves to more reflective poetries, such as Hodayot or the Wisdom of Solomon, wisdom collections (Ps. Phocylides), and on to some histories (Jubilees, Maccabees), the targumim, and sectarian instructions, the phenomenon continues to be in evidence. Signatured works, of which there are quite a few, tend to be recastings of the epic history of Moses in the form of exegetical histories (Demetrius, Artapanus, Eupolemos, Josephus), epic poetry (Philo the Poet), dramatizations (Ezekiel the Tragedian), or commentaries (Aristobulus, Philo). The curiosity, then, is that signature appears to have been acceptable as long as the works were clearly dependent upon Moses as precursor. Where there is not the case, where works are marked by "originality" (as in the case of apocalyptic visions and reflective poetry), anonymity and pseudonymity are the rule. Is it possible that this curiosity may be clarified by recourse to Bloom's theory?

2. In the Shadow of Moses: It is at least obvious to all that the period under consideration is precisely that during which the books of Moses achieved that authority which we call canon. The process was slow. The literary reference intended by the term Torah is still fluid in Sirach at the beginning of the second century B.C.E. But shortly thereafter, and certainly by the middle of the first century B.C.E., the five books of Moses had been recognized as a literary unit of singular significance, at least by some groups, and were being read and interpreted with exceptional care.

It also happens that the importance of Moses as a figure of authority increased markedly during just this time. He was assigned a growing list of roles as the encomia, biographies, and myths about him developed. But at the center of the cluster of characterizations attributed to him appears to be those roles which cast him as the author of very significant literature. He is everywhere the legislator, but also the philosopher and sage, the one who discovered writing and wrote the epic history of the creation of the world. Inspired as prophet, and the very incarnation of virtue itself, Moses comes to be the leader the king of his people. Is there a link between the authority of Torah and the authority of Moses for Judaism in this period? The answer seems to be yes. And the connection appears to include the relationship of an author to his literary accomplishments. We may even dare now to suggest that Moses' rise to authority may have been a direct result of the increasing significance of the five books, and that it was the Hellenistic notion of authorship which made it possible to elaborate his character and roles in keeping with the genre and function of his scriptures. It may even have been the case that legends which reified Moses' being in the presence of God were impelled by the need to attribute appropriate authorship to scriptures for which very heightened claims were wont to be made.

If this is plausible Bloom's theory of the "anxiety of influence," adjusted for any specifically Jewish casting, may indeed help us investigate the relationship of authorship and authority during this period. If the books of Moses as Torah were indeed in the process of becoming singularly important as the community's epic, legislation, and book of ethical instruction, and if their author was fast becoming reified as quasi-divine source and model for the community's wisdom and ethical guidance, the combined authority of the two would mark out an arena of literary achievement confronted with which even the strongest of would-be authors would yield. To the extent that the Greek notion of authorship was known, accepted, and at work among Jewish writers of the period, the "ratios of misprision" would function as well. All of the literary forms, including the apocalypse, may indeed be "midrashic," i.e., under the shadow of Moses' Torah, devising ways to (mis)interpret it. But given that common restraint, the range of options open to would-be authors appears to have been quite broad. The trick would have been first to clear a space for one's own composition, and second to keep from competing overtly with Moses. We will look at the achievements of three authors now from this point of view.

PART II. THREE AUTHORS IN THE SCHOOL OF MOSES

Each of the authors to be considered stood within the tradition of wisdom, though the type of wisdom discourse varies. Each understood himself to be a teacher who offered instruction in his writings and thus came to speech with a sense of the teacher's authority. For each of them, too, the books of Moses appear to have been the strongest precursor literature, though with varying degrees of acknowledgment. Each had read Moses carefully, i.e., misread or interpreted him, and, each presents us with this reading in the form of an original literary accomplishment. Because they all share this relationship to Moses both as teachers and as authors, it should be possible to test our thesis with them. It is important to keep in mind the way in which these three authors span the period under investigation. Ben Sira wrote ca. 180 B.C.E.; "Solomon" ca. 50 B.C.E.; and Philo ca. 15-40 C.E. This will allow us to trace any indications of development which may surface as we compare the three modes of authorship.

A. Ben Sira

1. The Marks of His Authorship: That Ben Sira was conscious of being an author is one of the more noteworthy things about him. This has long been acknowledged by scholars who have seen in the fact of his signature that which distinguishes him from earlier Jewish writers and which demonstrates his Hellenistic learning. His book throughout projects a very strong sense of care in composition and pride in literary accomplishment. There are numerous passages which may be taken as self-referential, and some which should be read that way.[24] Almost all of them have to do with his work as a scholar, teacher, and author. We may take a closer look at one of these passages, the poem about the scribe in Sir 39:1-11.

The poem makes three statements about the scribe. The first is that the scribe will devote himself to the study of literature. The Torah is mentioned first, but is immediately joined by the "wisdom of all the ancients," prophecies, accounts of noble men, gnomologies, etc. Wide experience is also mentioned, a common *topos* in the depiction of the Hellenistic "renaissance man." Apparently the range of literatures to be mastered was to match the range of experience recommended, i.e., as far ranging and international as one could manage. This agrees with what we know about Ben Sira's library in general. We can determine that almost all of the Hebrew scriptural corpus was there, of course. But he also had read, apparently with critical approval, both Greek and Egyptian literatures exemplifying the genres of historiography, biography, the prose encomium, gnomology, aretalogy, and hymn.[25] According to the poem about the scribe,

---

[24]Sir 24:30-34; 33:16-18; 39:12-16, 32-35; 42:15; 44:1; 50:27.

[25]On Ben Sira's use of the Hebrew scriptures and Hellenistic gnomology, see Theophil Middendorp, *Die Stellung Jesu ben Siras zwischen Judentum und Hellenismus* (Leiden: Brill, 1973). On historiography and biography see Martin Hengel, *Judaism and*

he was to investigate this literature thoroughly, seeking to work through its subleties and enigmas, and come to an understanding of its wisdom. This is a remarkable disclosure of that scribe at work who will not continue merely to be a scribe. This scribe, pouring over his texts, is seeking to win through to an account of things which he calls wisdom. Each text will be investigated as to its wisdom. But that means that all of the texts are being read, misread, just from this point of view. Wisdom is the normative principle for the critical reading of all texts. We will see that this wisdom is eventually to be disclosed as Ben Sira's own endowment.

The second statement made about the scribe in the poem is that he will pray for the spirit of understanding. This is cast at first in terms of traditional pieties and prophetic conceptualities. But the importance of this move is clearly more than an acknowledgment of the scribe's religiosity. It is a not too subtle invocation of the Muses in Jewish dress. "If the Great Lord is willing, he will be filled . . . he will pour forth words of wisdom." The goal, then, is to come to speech for one's self. And the "spirit of understanding"? Why that is the Muse itself which has been courted in and through all of the texts the scribe has studied. If now it comes to him, too, his daemonization (to use Bloom's term) is accomplished, and his precursors may be left "behind." The question is whether his coming to speech means authorship, and whether that authorship can be tested against his reading of his precursors. If so, the old prophetic "word of the Lord" is now dealing self-consciously in literary tradition.

That the scribe's coming to speech means authorship of written material can be demonstrated. Following the poem a mysterious person comes to speech as one who is "filled like the moon at the full." The language used here is reminiscent of language used elsewhere in the book to describe wisdom itself.[26] Then a call goes forth to "sing a hymn of praise" to the Lord for all his works. The hymn of praise follows. Then Ben Sira confesses: "Therefore from the beginning I have been convinced, and have thought this out, and *left it in writing*: 'The works of the Lord are all good.' " (Sir 39:32)

This self-disclosure about Ben Sira's aspirations and achievements as an author, coming as it does at the end of reflections about the scribal scholar as author, indicates a mode of literary activity which can be tested by a study of Ben Sira's book of wisdom as a whole. Recent studies have begun to explore the way in which Ben Sira incorporated the literature he read into his book. We are still far from a comprehensive study and assessment. But it is already evident that he drew heavily upon a wide range of literature for words, themes, tropes, ideas, modes of arrangement and argumentation, as well as generic patterns. But he did so in a very creative way. Cross-cultural correlations of traditional materials were achieved;[27] double allusions to disparate traditions in a single saying can be found;[28] new literary patterns are formed;[29] and new mythology is coined.[30] All was achieved by literary skill--the (mis)reading the (re)writing of traditional literatures as original composition. No explicit references to precursors as authors are made in the course of "borrowings" (from citations, paraphrases, and allusions

---

Hellenism (Philadelphia: Fortress, 1974) 1.136. On indebtedness to the Hellenistic prose encomium see Thomas Lee, *Studies in the Form of Sirach 44-50* (Dissertation, University of California, Berkeley, 1979). On the aretalogy see Hans Conzelmann, "The Mother of Wisdom," in *The Future of Our Religious Past* (ed. James Robinson; New York: Harper and Row, 1971) 230-43.

[26]Sir 24:13-17, 25-27, 30-34.

[27]To take but one example, the study of friendship in Sir 6:5-17 would have sounded familiar to a Greek reader until vs. 16 where Yahweh piety is introduced.

[28]A remarkable observation by Middendorp, *Stellung*, 24-25 (see reference in note 25).

[29]The hymn in praise of the fathers, Sir 44-50, is a case in point.

[30]The poems which deal with wisdom's origin and quest may be Ben Sira's own, thus marking a significant mythological reflection.

through to working with themes, schemata and genres given with the precursors). But in the poem about the scribe, in several references to the Torah which *might* be taken as reference to scriptures, and in the reference to the "book of the covenant, the Torah Moses commanded" (24:23), Ben Sira reveals that he knows that his "sources" are literary, i.e., are authored, i.e., that he has precursors. This is a telling revelation. With the consciousness of authorship on Ben Sira's own part must have come the awareness that the texts before him too were authored. And with this awareness the very notion of literary tradition was possible for the first time. Before Ben Sira we have no indication that Jewish wisdom was transmitted as literary tradition. Can the awareness of authorship on Ben Sira's part be due to Greek influence?

The answer must be Yes for a very simple reason. At the end of the poem about the scribe it is said that, should he win through to wisdom and succeed in coming to speech: "Nations will declare his wisdom, and the congregation will proclaim his praise" (39:10). This of course, is the familiar Hellenistic theme of fame and glory for literary achievement. Glory itself is a theme to which Ben Sira returns again and again throughout the book in ways which show that he fully intends its ambivalence to evoke Jewish cultic (theological) traditions as well as Hellenistic public (anthropological) culture. Used as a term for reward for literary accomplishment it brings Ben Sira's view of authorship very close to that of the Greeks. Only the characteristic of overt competitiveness with peers seems to be lacking. But that theme too may be present elsewhere in the book, if we understand wisdom in general now to be a literary activity. Wisdom, Ben Sira says, "will exalt him above his neighbors, and open his mouth in the midst of the assembly. He will find gladness and a crown of rejoicing, and will acquire an everlasting name" (15:5-6).

Even the phenomenon of sharing glory with the subject of one's poem is present in Ben Sira's literary activity. In the case before us the creator's works are praised. And Ben Sira as author of the hymn of praise receives praise as well. In the case of the hymn in praise of the fathers, the heroes of Israel's history are praised and said to have been praised. And Ben Sira as author of the hymn knows that he will be praised as well. Without him the heroes must go without also.

And so the question now is raised: What about Moses? How has Ben Sira ranked Torah and Moses among his many precursors? How has he read him? And has he suffered under his shadow?

2. Ben Sira's Reading of Moses: Ben Sira reveals intense preoccupation with the books later to be called the five books of Moses. It is not clear whether he understood Moses to have authored them all as a unit (as Torah), but it is clear the Moses is associated with the material. It is also clear that Moses was given the law in order to teach it to Israel (45:5). Moses, then, was important for Ben Sira in ways appropriate to our concerns, and the literature associated with him appears to have been very important indeed for the theologically reflective poetry in Ben Sira's book. This in itself is quite a finding. It means that a wisdom scribe took up the epic history of Israel for reading and interpretation, i.e., began a kind of wisdom-midrash in a creative literary mode.

We are not able here to document Ben Sira's reading of the five books. It will have to suffice to note that much of the more reflective poetry about wisdom--her quest and destiny, as well as about Adam (or the reader)--and his quest for wisdom, works with images and themes given in Genesis and Exodus.[31] It should also be noted that the first seven figures in the roster of heroes (44:16-45:26) form a literary unit having to do with the establishment of the essential covenants basic to Ben Sira's view of Second Temple

---

[31]Cf. Sir 14:20-15:8 with its allusions to Exodus motifs; 16:26-17:14 with outright references to events from Genesis and Exodus; 24:1-29 as a mythological reading of Genesis and Exodus as epic history; 39:17-31 as a reflection upon the Exodus story; and 44:16-45:26 as a recital of the epic history of Genesis and Exodus.

Judaism. Only these seven are taken from the five books, which means that it has been read as primordial epic history on the model of Hellenistic historiography. It can therefore be shown that Moses is very, very important for Ben Sira's work as mythologist and theologian.

Nevertheless, no citations are acknowledged. The hymnic history, where dependence upon the precursor texts is most obvious, even and especially at the point of outright borrowing of descriptions and phraseology, is presented as an original composition which is able to stand on its own independently of other texts. It reads well from beginning to end as a majestic, encomiastic rehearsal of Israel's history right up and into Ben Sira's own time. It climaxes with a marvelous description of the people gathered at the temple and the glorious High Priest Simon coming out to pronounce the blessing and the name. All of that Moses could not have achieved in a poem, could not have known. Moses, then, is one of several "sources" for Ben Sira's work. He is probably the most important source for certain "foundational" issues and "epic" canons. But he stood to Ben Sira as Homer and Hesiod stood to Hellenistic historiographers and prose encomiasts, i.e., those who "competed" by creating other genres. Thus, Moses as author and authority is only in the making here. There was no need either to deny him his importance and influence, or to single him out for exceptional and superior performance. Ben Sira could manage composition and signature comfortably in Moses' presence as author, and on Moses' own literary turf. Whence then Ben Sira's need for daemonization?

3. Belated but Glorious: The appeal to the spirit of wisdom does function in a way analogous to the Greek invocation of the Muses and Bloom's ratio of misprision which he calls daemonization. It thus belongs to the phenomenon of authorship, and does function in Ben Sira's poem to establish the authority of the scribe as author. We have also found Ben Sira to acknowledge frankly the fame and glory with which the scribe may be rewarded, and even to glory in that glory without compunction. The reason seems to be that the notion of authorship reflected here is just now being explored, with gusto and delight one might add, and has not advanced to the point of establishing the authority of one's precursors on the basis of authorship in such a way as to inhibit outright rewriting. But the notion of authorship is certainly in the process of being extended to them and this will set the stage for subsequent developments of considerable significance for later writers.

Ben Sira himself appears to have sensed already something of his own belatedness however. He is, as he says, the "last on watch," "like one who gleans after the grape-gatherers." But: "By the blessing of the Lord I excelled, and like a grape-gatherer I filled by winepress" (33:16). Here we see that even Ben Sira, standing at the beginning of this literary period, has not been spared some sense of belatedness and a certain melancholy if not anxiety about influence. But it is only a touch. The precursors as authors are not yet clearly enough delineated to have to do them battle. And so for a brief, glorious moment in the history of Jewish authorship signature is dared openly and the rewards are accepted gleefully. The "Spirit of wisdom" here establishes continuities with precursors (the prophets?), as well as claim to superior achievements among peers. But it can work its will as daemon, too, easily and soon. When it does the distinction between author and precursor will have to be clarified if there is to be any new "originality."

B. *The Wisdom of Solomon*

The Wisdom of Solomon may appear at first glance to be an unlikely example of Jewish authorship under the shadow of Moses. It is, for one thing, pseudonymous, making it very difficult to assess the sense of authorial consciousness. It also lacks explicit reference to Moses as author as well as to the five books either as law or as epic history. But its pseudonymity is curious. And its (mis)reading or re-writing of the epic history and exodus credo betrays a long, studied, and passionate encounter with its unacknowledged precursor. Certainly by the last half of the first century B.C.E. Moses had risen to ethereal prominence as founder figure for Judaism, and his Torah was firmly in place as the single most important scripture, whether as cultic code, epic history, or ethical instruction. We need only to suppose the connection between authority and authorship, a connection we have theorized would develop, and one which can be demonstrated shortly for Philo, in order to pursue our inquiry. As it appears the author of the Wisdom of Solomon places high on the scale of the anxiety of influence.

      1. The Marks of His Authorship: This is poetry written anonymously. In the case of the two fine prayer-report cycles in Wisdom 7-9, however, it could appear as a pseudonym. This is because a *prosōpopoiïa* has been invented, clearly intended for King Solomon, and based upon the well-known story about his pious and noble request for wisdom. It is apparently on the basis of this rhetorical characteristic that the entire document came to be regarded as a pseudonym. It does show the degree to which the author was able to efface self-reference throughout the work. But it should also be noted that Solomon is nowhere mentioned in the text. Indeed, all of the figures treated in the book are unnamed. It is, then, primarily and at first an anonymous poetry.

      In spite of its anonymity, however, the poetry is strong and its address to readers is direct. The author clearly has something to say and is quite capable of saying it. He is skilled both in rhetoric and poetics, moves comfortably and creatively between Jewish and Hellenistic sensibilities, and is capable of dialectic thought. His book is certainly an original composition about which he must have been pleased, and of which, let us say, he must have been proud. Why then is it anonymous?

      The traditional answers to this question range from considerations of the inappropriateness of the author to project himself into the audience-setting which he imagines, to archaizing as a way to trade on the authority of traditional figures, to evocation of apocalyptic models (which combine pseudonymous authorship, visionary experience, and predictions of the future from a point in the past). But the book as a whole really does not work as an Apocalypse of Solomon, nor would his (anonymous!) authority really have been all that helpful, it seems, in lending weight to the appeal in Wisdom 1-5 to the "rulers of the earth" as audience. Nevertheless there is something about the problem of matching the authority of the author with the audience addressed which may help us in our investigation. Even if the audience is merely imagined to be the "rulers of the earth," thus engaging in a serious fiction, the author may not have hoped to be able to pose as standing plausibly in their presence, and thus will have found signature inappropriate. But there is more. The seriousness of the issue is such that, though the author passionately desires his ethic and message to be heard by those who have not yet heard it, he knows that, even if they were to hear it, it would not be accepted, understood. This frustration determines the move to very strong claims to authoritative speech and triggers, in fact, a modulation in the *ethos* of the author toward that of the "prophet and friend of God" (7:27) who can speak for (and in the persona of?) wisdom herself: "To you then, O Monarchs, my words are directed . . . set your desire on my words; long for them, and you will be instructed . . . I will tell you what wisdom is. . . ." (6:9, 11, 22).

      With this the author does take his place with the king-elect in Wisdom 7-9 who knew, too, (or came to know) all about wisdom and all about wisdom's world in the midst of mortals whose "reasoning is worthless" (9:14). Such a staggering claim to wisdom may indeed appear to be reason enough to inhibit signature. There are touches of humility, to be sure, in the confessions of the king-elect about his need to quest and pray for wisdom. But the humility is really a ruse. For by means of feigned humility the author's claim to knowledge is now made absolute. He has his wisdom from God himself (7:17; 9:9-10, 17)!

      Thus the question of authorship and authority becomes quite complex. Anonymity is no longer merely a matter of using an appropriate literary device. The author has chosen to assume the persona of the faceless, nameless king-elect who received the knowledge of all that there is from God himself. Why?

2. The Misprision of Moses: We may begin again by noting that, though Ben Sira also could assume the persona of wisdom herself, he knew that her spirit was essentially exegetical, that his approach to her was through the study of texts. In the Wisdom of Solomon there is no longer any acknowledgment of the books, or of the study of the books, or of the literary activity of the "king" of wisdom. Everything rides on prayer, spirit, and *praxis*, power, and achievement. Even the few references to the law, places where one might expect a sidelong glance at the literary sources of the author's wisdom, refer to it in non-literary terms. The law belongs to the new cosmic wisdom: "Love of her is the keeping of *her* laws, and giving heed to her laws is assurance of immortality" (6:18). In Wis 18:4 it is the "*light* of the law" which is to be given to the world; in Wis 16:11 the scriptures, if indeed the scriptures are meant, are referred to as oracles and thus taken up into the discourse about God's speech as that which makes events to happen. So there is no reference to written law, no references to other textual traditions, no precursors in sight.

This does not mean, however, that the author has not read Moses! The lovely poem about those whom wisdom rescued in chap. 10 is clearly a "reading" of Genesis and Exodus from a certain point of view. Seven figures are rescued and it is not too difficult to name them, though the author does not do so. The first is Adam and the last is Moses. The series as a whole forms a hymn in praise of wisdom's activity "from the first." One might compare Ben Sira's encomiastic hymn in praise of the fathers where the primordial period of covenant establishment is succeeded by a review of the history of Israel in the land up until the author's own time. In Wisdom 10 the primordial epic (Genesis-Exodus) has been read as the story of wisdom's saving activity which, once seen, is paradigmatic for all time. No subsequent history need be related.

It is also clear that Wisdom 11-19 is a very creative (mis)reading of the Exodus story. The re-casting is achieved by re-writing in a powerful poetry which deals in symbolism, irony, dialectic, and cosmic mythologization. The result is to make of Moses' account a mythic moment in history which articulates and makes available to the imagination the pattern of the "help" which comes from God for his people "at all times and in all places" (19:22). It is this poetic misprision of the Exodus story to which the entire composition has been leading as its climax. With it the author has laid claim to the credo-significance of the Moses-story tradition in the interest of his wisdom view of the world and his concern to address the "rulers of the world."

Only now it is clear that the audience is really not those kings out there, but fellow Jews who share with the author his concerns about times of trouble and testing. They will easily have noted the midrashic and revisionary aspects of the poem and offered praise (or blame). So the author will be in competition with Moses as his precursor after all! The exaggerated degree of daemonization corresponds exactly with the radicality of the misreading of Moses' text. It appears to be a severe case of the anxiety of influence, and a precarious solution to the author's relationship to his precursor. With Philo another tack will be taken.

C. *Philo of Alexandria*

1. That Moses has written well: With Philo the superior status and authority of Moses and his Five Books are finally expressly acknowledged. What we have suspicioned to be the case for earlier authors is now articulated clearly. Moses is quite a writer! It is not just that he alone entered into the presence of God, that he alone received the law, that he alone fully incorporated in his own life the law he legislated. No. He wrote the books which document all of that--and much more besides. His Five Books are the founding document for the Jewish nation. They include all one needs to know, from a full account of the creation of the world, through the epic history of the beginnings of the

people Israel, to the legislation of the law which serves as constitution for Israel's institutions and ethical code for its life together as a religious society. And he wrote it well! This theme becomes a commonplace in Philo and serves over and over again as a point of departure by which Philo moves away from Moses' text and gains entre into his own task of interpretation. According to Philo, Moses was not only a master of rhetoric and prose composition. He was extremely skilled in subtleties, nuances, double entendre, and allegory. Every letter and turn of phrase in his (even Greek!) text was carefully crafted, intentionally significant, and worth poring over. His literary skills were such that all he wrote had the mark of the oracle about them, and all other Jewish authors after him were merely to be understood as "in his school."

2. That Philo will merely interpret: Philo too, of course, understood himself to be merely a student of Moses, "in his school." He acknowledged forthrightly, of course, that he (Philo) was the author of his commentaries (and treatises). He even describes on occasion his work at the desk as a scholar-author, and it is clear that he found it all rewarding. So what we have now are two texts. Moses' text, the precursor, is cited literally and fully both as lemma for comment and as reference or citation in the course of the development of theses and argumentations. Philo's text, the student's, is presented merely as a commentary upon Moses. Questions about the text are raised, observations are made, and significations are worked out.

Throughout the entire set of commentaries the reader is repeatedly told that Philo merely intends to lead the quest for the meaning which Moses intended. Thus Moses' wisdom or *logos* or vision of things as a whole is established as the goal of the investigation. Only Moses really knew or followed the *logos* fully, according to Philo. But because Moses has written the books so well, and provided for us clues here and there, we should be able to read our way into his view of things as a whole. Philo will lead the way.

As one reads along however, and one does real along, one soon becomes enchanted (if that is the right word) with Philo's own clever way with words and argumentation. Time after time the meaning of Moses' text does unfold before the reader's eyes, but not so that the *logos* is fully seen, of course. So one reads on, curious about the next citations and the next moves which Philo, as the leader of the quest, will need to make. Eventually, of course, it begins to dawn on the reader that the *logos* under investigation is actually Philo's own view of things, and that his attribution of it to Moses is the master stroke of deception. But that does not happen until one has read a lot of Philo!

So Philo will be read. And he achieved it by feigning merely to "interpret" Moses' superior text. But interpretation (as misreading) is exactly the swerve which the ephebe must make in order to write his own poem. Philo's swerve is most disarming. He does not deny his precursor. Indeed, he exaggerates its superiority and originality, and says that no one will ever be able to do it better. Then he cites it outright, and offers merely to comment upon it. That is clever. Because no one would ever imagine that Moses' text meant what Philo says it meant--without Philo's text. So we have two texts, the strength of the first assuring that the second will be read, and the strength of the second assuring that its author will be known. Eventually, reading along, one hardly notices that Philo's periods become longer and longer, until finally there is a whole theme-treatise purporting to elucidate a single word of Moses' text. And if that were not suspicious enough, here comes the *vita*. The opening lines are as follows:

> I purpose to write the life of Moses, whom some describe as the legislator of the Jews, others as the interpreter of the Holy Laws. I hope to bring the story of this greatest and most perfect of men to the knowledge of such as deserve not to remain in ignorance of it; for, while the fame of the laws which he left behind him has travelled throughout the civilized world and reached the ends of the earth, the man himself as he really was is known to few. (Vita Mosis I 1-2).

For this task, Philo explains he will draw both upon the sacred books and upon the oral traditions of the elders (V. Mos. I.4). He will complement the fame of Moses' laws by writing a prose encomium of their author. Here commentary is no longer necessary; original composition may be allowed. Philo will take the writings of Moses and construct from them an encomium of Moses! With it Philo will assure Moses' fame as the man who stands behind his books. But if he succeeds in doing that, he will have taken his own place openly in the roster of authors for all time as well. And that, of course, is the old double-glory game all over again.

CONCLUSION

Our study can hardly be considered to have demonstrated the phenomenon under investigation. But it has mapped out an arena within which an investigation may be pursued. That investigation will have to do with the notion or notions of authorship as manifest in the literatures of the Hellenistic period both Greek and Jewish. We have made the attempt to outline certain characteristics of Greek authorship and to point to their presence in certain Jewish writings of the period. We have theorized that a strong moment of competition is involved in notions of authorship that aspire to individual originality. We have used Bloom's theory of the anxiety of influence to help us conceptualize this aspect of the act of writing, and to set it within the context of literary tradition with its canons and precursors. Two moments of authorship thus come into view as important considerations for tracing the "hidden roads" that go from text to text within a literary tradition. The one is the authorship of the precursor text as it is imagined or presupposed by the belated writer-to-be. The other is the authorship of the belated writer himself. The two stand in competition with one another, though this is seldom acknowledged due to the belated author's need to disavow being influenced.

We have theorized that the emergence of the authority of Moses for Jewish circles during the Hellenistic period may have been due to the increasing importance of those books associated with him. The thought that these books were authored was probably learned from the Greeks early on in the process of Hellenization by scribal scholars who discovered the rewards for accomplished composition. But once the notion of authorship of Moses had established his authority in keeping with the singular importance of his books, scribal scholars and other Jewish authors found it increasingly difficult to sign their works as original compositions. Three examples of authorship in the "school of Moses" were given which suggested three different authorial postures. In each case the mode of authorial self-reference could be shown to be related to a corresponding view taken by the author of Moses and his books and their authority.

Should it be possible to establish the thesis presented here for discussion—a thesis about authorship, authority, and anxiety—its importance for a range of related literary and cultural phenomena of interest to biblical scholars would be assured. Not only would the process of canonization look different than it now is understood to have occurred. Our notions of (literary) tradition and the ways in which we have understood relationships among texts would need to be revised. What Bloom has suggested as a theory of authorship is actually a thoery of the social-historical context and function of literature from the perspective of the act of authoring. What his thesis would mean for criticism (scholarship) then is quite revolutionary. The essentially rhetorical aspects of the cultural function of reading and writing literature call now to be worked out. And the act of appropriation (reading) as an act of violence (misprision) would need to be clarified in terms of some cultural-anthropological theory. Only at the end of such a theoretical investigation would we dare return to the question of where, within the battle of words which determines literary tradition and canonization, we may expect to find the enduring *logos*.

JESUS AND THE "WILDERNESS GENERATION":
THE DEATH OF THE PROPHET LIKE MOSES ACCORDING TO LUKE

David P. Moessner
Basel, Switzerland

It has become a maxim in the halls of NT scholarship that Luke affords the crucifixion no particular atoning significance in his account of the salvation history fulfilled in Jesus of Nazareth.[1] The most one can maintain is that the author of Luke-Acts has included a few traditional formulae which speak of vicarious sacrifice or redemptive blood (e.g. Luke 22:19b-20; Acts 20:28).[2] While it is conceded that *suffering*--both for Jesus (e.g., 9:22; 12:50; 13:33; 17:25; 18:31; 22:15, 19-20, 22, 37; 24:7, 25-27, 46; Acts 3:18, 24; 7:52; 8:32-35; 13:27; 26:22, 27) and his disciples (e.g., Luke 9:23-25; 12:11-12; 14:26-27; Acts 9:16; 14:22; 17:3; 20:23; 21:11-14)--plays an important role in the overall *plan* of God,[3] nevertheless the real emphasis within the divinely ordained journey of salvation from Galilee to Jesus' "taking up" in Jerusalem is upon that final stage of the resurrection or exaltation. "The exaltation of Jesus is the supreme saving event in Luke's eyes, since it is the act whereby God confirms the status of Jesus."[4]

Yet we may wonder whether ascribing such a prominent idea as suffering and death simply to the "will of God" does justice to the critical function Luke accords this reality in the *structuring* of his salvation narrative. The whole path of Jesus is portrayed as one of rejection and cross-bearing in which those who cannot share in this suffering are excluded from the "gaining of life" (Luke 9:23-24; 14:26-27; cf. 9:58; 13:31-33; etc.). Jesus is reported to be "totally controlled" by the death awaiting him (12:50),[5] and if, as seems probable, 22:43-44 are to be regarded as ancient, if not authentic,[6] this death is

---

[1] See the surveys by C. H. Talbert, "Shifting Sands: The Recent Study of the Gospel of Luke," *Int* 30 (1976) 389, 391; W. G. Kümmel, "Current Theological Accusations Against Luke," *ANQ* 16 (1975) 134, 138; idem, *Introduction to the New Testament* (rev. ed.; Nashville: Abingdon, 1975) 149; cf. I. H. Marshall, *Luke: Historian and Theologian* (Exeter: Paternoster, 1970) 169-75; H. Flender, *St. Luke: Theologian of Redemptive History* (London: SPCK, 1967) 157-62; contra, L. Morris, *The Cross in the New Testament* (Exeter: Paternoster, 1965) 63-143.

[2] E. g. Kümmel, "Accusations," 138: "While Luke by no means entirely removes the redemptive significance of the death of Jesus he does not stress it." For earlier estimates, see e.g. P. Vielhauer, "On the 'Paulinism' of Acts," *Studies in Luke-Acts* (Fs. P. Schubert; ed. L. E. Keck and J. L. Martyn; Nashville: Abingdon, 1966) 45 (first appearing in 1950/51); H. Conzelmann, *The Theology of St. Luke* (London: Faber and Faber, 1960) 201-2; U. Wilckens, *Die Missionsreden der Apostelgeschichte* (WMANT 5; Neukirchen: Neukirchener, 1961) 216: "Die Tod Jesu hat keine Heilsbedeutung, und damit fehlt der lukanischen Christologie überhaupt jede inhaltliche Soteriologie."

[3] Kümmel, "Accusations," 138: Luke's "chief interest lies in the fact that the death of Jesus corresponds to the will of God"; Flender, *Luke*, 158: Jesus' "suffering is not only a human crime permitted by God, but was planned by his living, active will"; Marshall, *Historian*, 172, commenting on the "Servant" christology of Deutero-Isaiah in Luke: "In the Servant in fact we see the supreme case of a person who goes to suffering by the will of God."

[4] Marshall, *Historian*, 169; cf. Flender, *Luke*, 159-62; Conzelmann, *Luke*, 199-206; Talbert, "Sands," 389.

[5] See e.g. on συνέχω, H. Köster, *TDNT* 7, 884-85.

[6] B. M. Metzger, *A Textual Commentary on the Greek New Testament* (London: United Bible Societies, 1971) 177 (ancient, but not original); I. H. Marshall, *The Gospel of Luke* (NIGTC; Exeter: Paternoster, 1978) 832: "the internal evidence inclines us to accept the verses as original."

indeed depicted as an agonizing ordeal of the greatest magnitude. Moreover, what protrudes out at every crucial turn of events in the Acts is the fate of the disciples-apostles to follow their Master in the way of *suffering*: First the apostles (4:3, 18, 21; 5:17-26, 33, 40-41), then Stephen (6:9-14; 7:54-8:3), then the whole congregation of disciples (8:1; 11:19) are persecuted for the "sake of the name" (e.g., 9:16); and it has been pointed out that Paul's conversion is actually a calling to *suffer* (9:16), with his final trip to Jerusalem patterned after the way to the cross (e.g., 20:22-23; 21:11-14, 30-36).[7] When we are told repeatedly by Luke that both Jesus' and his followers' suffering fulfills a divine "must" (δεῖ, 9:22; 13:33; 17:25; 22:37; 24:7, 26, 46; Acts 1:16; 9:16; 14:22; 17:3; 23:11), then we may legitimately question whether this necessity is to be construed simply as the path of the "righteous" or of the martyr(s) which leads to glory.[8] Does not Luke himself perhaps supply a more specific and pivotal content to his "will of God?"

The suggestion put forth in this paper is that in the final two-thirds of his Gospel, Luke presents the journey of Jesus on a New Exodus to Jerusalem whose death, like Moses' in Deuteronomy, *must* occur in order to effect deliverance for a still-necked, disobedient nation. As such, this death, like that of Moses, expresses God's judgment upon this monolith of rebellion, and therefore, *atones* for the sin of the people. But because Jesus is the eschatological Prophet like Moses (Deut 18:15-19) whom God raises and exalts from the dead, his death enables and ushers in the final consummated salvation of the Exodus deliverance, granting Israel a second opportunity to receive this life even as this life is extended to the nations (the Acts).

We cannot attempt any kind of comprehensive analysis of Luke's theology of "suffering" and "death," or of "resurrection"-"exaltation"-"glorification" and related themes. Our focus will be limited to Luke 9-24 and to Peter's speech in Acts 3:12-26 where the motifs of the Prophet like Moses are explicitly developed.[9] Our investigation will unfold in three stages: Part I will provide a quick overview of Moses' calling in Deuteronomy with special attention to the *role* that his *death* plays;[10] Part II will argue that Luke 9:1-50 presents a four-fold Deuteronomic Exodus typology[11] which governs the

---

[7]H. J. Cadbury, *The Making of Luke-Acts* (New York: Macmillan, 1927) 231-33; G. Bouman, *Das dritte Evangelium* (Düsseldorf: Patmos, 1968) 74; for survey and literature, see esp. A. J. Mattill, "The Jesus-Paul Parallels and the Purpose of Luke-Acts: H. H. Evans Reconsidered," *NovT* 17 (1975) 15-46, esp. 30-37.

[8]Cf. e.g. Talbert, "Sands," 389: "In Luke-Acts Jesus' death is viewed primarily as part of the divine plan and as a martyrdom of a righteous man, which serves as the dominical basis for Christian suffering"; cf. F. Schütz, *Der leidende Christus* (BWANT 89; Stuttgart: Kohlhammer, 1969) 97-112.

[9]Space does not permit inclusion of Acts 7:37, the other explicit citation of Deut 18:15-19 in the Acts. On the Exodus typology as its context, see esp. L. T. Johnson, *The Literary Function of Possessions in Luke-Acts* (SBLDS 39; Missoula: Scholars, 1977) 70--76.

[10]Our methodology in both Parts I and II will follow a literary analysis of the text as *story*, as defined by the Russian 'Formalists' (see e.g. *Readings in Russian Poetics* [ed. L. Matejka and K. Pomorska; Cambridge: MIT, 1971] 3-37; *Russian Formalism* [ed. S. Bann and J. E. Bowlt; Edinburgh: Scottish Academic, 1973] 6-19, 26-40, 48-72). For an application to the NT, see N. R. Petersen, *Literary Criticism for New Testament Critics* (Philadelphia: Fortress, 1978) 24-92, esp. 33-48.

[11]For our understanding of typology, see L. Goppelt, *Typos: Die typologische Deutung des Alten Testaments in Neuen* (BFCT 43; 2d ser.; Darmstadt: Wissenschaftliche, 1966).

Analysis of the "form-content" of the "journey section" in Luke (9:51-19:44) in current exegetical discussion has ossified into a static "journey" form into which Luke has "poured" the content of various sayings of Jesus. By using the 'Formalist' notion of

portrayal of Jesus in the remainder of the Gospel; and Part III will marshal evidence to contend that an *atoning* import is the only logical one for the death of Jesus within the argument of Acts 3:12-26.

Unfortunately limitations of space prevent the sort of systematic approach to the meaning of Jesus' death which is so needed in contemporary Lukan studies. Yet it is hoped that the imprint of the career and atoning death of the Prophet like Moses will emerge clearly as a pregnant picture of the Lukan "will of God."

I

Moses has led the pilgrim tribes of *all Israel*[12] to the borders of the Promised Land in the valley opposite Beth-peor (Deut 3:29; cf. 34:6). There, under the baneful shadows of the Nebo massif (32:49-50; 34:1; cf. 1:37; 3:27; 4:21-22), he takes the people through a renewal of the covenant at Mt Horeb by leading them back in memory to that momentous revelation at that *mountain* and their ensuing wilderness wanderings from *Kadesh-Barnea* (1:6-11:32).[13]   Before the recitation and expounding of the Law (12:1-26:19), it already becomes manifest that in these two seminal experiences Moses' lot to *suffer* and *die* was irrevocably cast.

When at the mountain out of the midst of the fiery cloud God began to *speak* to the gathered assembly of Israel (4:12-13, 33, 36; 5:4, 22, 24; 9:10; 10:4), the people were so terrified that they implored Moses to mediate the *voice* (φωνή) of Yahweh for them (5:4-5, 22-31).   This then becomes Moses' great calling to *utter the voice* of the Lord to the people[14] (e.g., 4:5, 14, 40; 5:27-28, 30-31; 10:5; 32:46-47; cf. 30:2, 8 etc.) by teaching them all His commandments that they might live in the land which they were to possess as an inheritance of the covenant to Abraham, Isaac, and Jacob (1:8; 6:10; 9:5, 27, 29; 29:13-15; 30:20; 34:4).   But though they had promised fidelity to Moses' God-given word (5:27), even while Moses is still on the mountain speaking "face to face" with God (cf. 34:10), the people at the base rebel by worshipping an image, the molten calf (9:8-21; cf. 4:15-19).   At once the Lord's anger is so overwhelming that only Moses' suffering submission in the intercession of 40 days and nights can appease His wrath sufficiently to save the people from total annihilation (9:18-20, 25-29; 10:10-11).

So the Lord continues His promise to them by *sending* Moses onward from Horeb at the head of the people to the land of promise (10:11; 1:7). But it would seem to no avail. Despite the searing discipline (4:36) of *seeing* the very *glory* of God on the *mountain* (5:24) and *hearing* His great *voice* from the *cloud of fire* (4:11) the people are intractable in defying Moses' authority. At Kadesh-Barnea, some eleven days journey (cf. 1:2), all Israel and especially her "men of war" (2:14-16) spurn the voice of the Lord through Moses and spite Moses' leadership altogether as first they "murmur" against the

---

"plot motivation" and "plot device" (cf. n. 10), we will be attempting to show that Luke has dynamically structured the "story-stuff" of the journey around a four-fold movement within a Deuteronomic Exodus typology.

[12] 1:1; 5:1; 11:6; 13:11; 18:6; 27:9, (14); 29:2, (10); 31:1, 7, 11 (2x); 32:45; 34:12.

[13] This portrait of his calling is indebted heavily to G. von Rad, *Old Testament Theology* (2 vols.; New York: Harper & Row, 1962-65) 1. 289-96; idem, *Deuteronomy* (OTL; London: SCM, 1966) passim. For questions of tradition and redaction, cf. e.g., E. W. Nicholson, *Deuteronomy and Tradition* (Oxford: B. Blackwell, 1967) esp. 18-36; M. Weinfeld, *Deuteronomy and the Deuteronomic School* (Oxford: Clarendon, 1972) esp. 179-89, 320-70; N. Lohfink, "Darstellungskunst und Theologie in Dtn 1,6-3,29," *Bib* 41 (1960) 105-34, esp. 107-10.

[14] Cf. von Rad, *Theology*, 1. 294: "The most impressive corroboration of this all-embracing mediating office of proclamation is of course the fact that the corpus of Deuteronomy is put into the form of words of Moses (and so not of Jahweh) spoken to Israel"; cf. Lohfink, "Darstellungskunst," 106 n. 4.

call to battle and then go up against the Lord's command (1:19-46). With that, two epoch-making judgments fall upon Moses and his egregious entourage: (i) Only the children (παιδίον, 1:39; cf. vv. 34-38; 11:2; 31:13) of the assembled people at Horeb will become the future possessors of the land; the entire older generation will be wiped out (1:35; 2:14-16); (ii) "On account of"[15] (1:37; 3:26) the people's intransigence Moses *must suffer* the anger of the Lord, the anguish of being choked off from the land of promise, and thus ultimately *die* without the promised deliverance--all *because of*[16] the sin of his people (1:37; 3:26; 4:21-22; cf. 9:18-20, 25-29; 10:10-11; 31:2, 14; 32:50-52; 34:4).

These two themes become the double-beat *leitmotiv* which like a dirge undertones the whole of Deuteronomy. The first is sounded as the relentless, interminable *stubbornness* of *all* Israel to heed God's voice through Moses, even from the moment they left Egypt (e.g. 9:6, 7, 13, 27; 10:16; 12:8; 29:19; 31:27). They have been "rebellious"[17] (1:26, 43; 9:7, 23, 24; cf. 21:18, 20; 31:27) as long as Moses has known them (9:24). They are "evil" or "presumptuous"[18] (9:4-5, 27; 17:13; 18:20, 22; 19:16; 25:2), "sinful"[19] (5:9; 9:18, 21; 15:9; 19:15; 21:22; 23:21-22; 24:15-16; 30:3), "proud"[20] (8:14; 17:20), *slow to believe* and "hearken"[21] (9:23; 32:20; cf. εἰσακούω, 1:43; 9:23; 21:18), refusing *discipline* and *training*[22] (4:10-14, 36; 5:5, 23-30; 8:2-5, 16-17; 9:6-29; 11:2-12) without "understanding"[23] (32:28; cf. 4:6; 11:2). They need new "eyes to see and ears to hear" (29:4); or as Moses himself sums up, they are *en masse* a "stiff-necked," "faithless," and "crooked generation" (32:5, 20; 1:35).

It is only against this refrain that the echo of Moses' *suffering* and *death,* (ii) can be heard as a clarion call to effect deliverance precisely through this means. For it is not the case that the younger generation, the "children" on the mountain who take possession of the land, are blameless while their "fathers," the "men of war," receive the punishment. Rather, it is striking how this generation at the "border" is lumped with their predecessors as one solidary mass of a disobedient, perfidious people, such that their sin is at once linked to that of their "fathers," on the one side, but also to the necessity of Moses' tragic fate, on the other. At three strategic junctures in the *story time*[24] the necessity of Moses' death is woven into the progression and ultimate completion of the *present generation's* deliverance. (a) Moses' suffering mediation and intercession for the people at *Horeb* is forged to Yahweh's sentence at *Kadesh-Barnea:* Moses' cry for relief from the "burden and strife" of a contrary people "at that time" (i.e., Horeb, 1:9) is granted--ironically, if not heartlessly--in the subsequent and *explicit* announcement of his death (1:9, 12 ⟶ 34-40; cf. 9:7-21 ⟶ 22-24). Though the present generation was only "children who this day have no knowledge of good and evil" (1:39), nonetheless they are made culpable for that grave disobedience: "The Lord was angry with me also on account of *you*" (1:37). "When the Lord sent *you* from Kadesh-Barnea . . . then *you* rebelled against . . . the Lord" (9:23). (b) As if to dispel any notion that

---

[15]1:37--בגללכם--δι' ὑμᾶς; 3:26--למענכם-- ἕνεκεν ὑμῶν.

[16]Cf. T. W. Mann, "Theological Reflections on the Denial of Moses," *JBL* 98 (1979) 486: "Nowhere in the deuteronomic explanations does Moses refer to his own responsibility; the blame falls squarely on the people."

[17]מרה (Hi.); סרר-- ἀπειθεῖν, -ής; cf. Mann ("Denial," 484) on *mrh*: "It seems to have been introduced into the vocabulary of the wilderness theme by the Deuteronomist."

[18]רשעה; זדרן; סרה; רשה; זוד (Hi.)--ἀσέβ-, -εια; -ημα; ἀσεβεῖν.

[19]עון; חטאת; חטא-- ἁμαρτία.

[20]רום-- ὑψωθῇς.

[21]שמע; שמה-- εἰσακούειν.

[22]E.g. 8:5-- יסר (Pi.)-- παιδεύειν.

[23]תבונה-- ἐπιστήμη.

[24]In contrast to "plotted time"; see nn. 10, 11.

Yahweh's anger was assuaged by the death of the older evil generation or that the Exodus continued to the borders of Canaan through the "uprightness" or innocence of Caleb or Joshua or the "children" of the mountain, the narrator has Moses repeat Yahweh's sentence to him *"at that time"* (3:23),[25] i.e., *when the possession of the Trans-Jordan area was completed.* Moses' plea to enter the land is met with "anger on *your* account" (3:26a). *Because of* the sin of the *audience* Moses is addressing, he must die (3:27). (c) The third announcement removes any vestige of the possibility that Moses' death is, after all, merely parallel to the main event of the deliverance or that his denial outside the land is simply an example "of the tragic dimension of human experience."[26] After reviewing the affairs at Beth-peor following the time of the second declaration of his demise (4:1-9), Moses harks back to the revelation of Yahweh at Horeb to warn against apostasy and uses that watershed event with its sequel at Kadesh-Barnea (4:10-19) to summarize and typify his audience's *present* state of affairs *"this day"* (4:20b). They stand freed from their bondage in Egypt, ready to pass over into the land, to be sure (4:20), but--again--Moses must die, precisely because "on account of you,"[27] Yahweh *"swore* that I should not cross the Jordan nor enter into the good land which the Lord your God is giving you as an inheritance. For *I* must die in this land, *I* must not cross the Jordan, but rather *you* shall cross over that you may take possession of that good land"[28] (4:21-22). In short, without Moses' death they would not receive the gracious act of deliverance that Yahweh is now bringing to pass[29] (cf. 31:2, 14; 32:48-50;[30] 34:4) even as they are forewarned not to continue their rebellious ways once they have entered the land, lest they meet the same fate as their fathers (4:23-28). Thus it is at each of the three critical turns of events in the developing story that *"Moses' death"* moves the action of Yahweh's deliverance forward to its climax at the boundaries of the land and enables the people to cross over to their promised inheritance.[31]

The pen-portrait is now distinct. Moses has emerged as a *suffering mediator, sent* from Horeb to lead the "faithless" and "crooked generation" of "children" to the promised salvation by *dying* outside the land. More precisely, we can distinguish a four-fold *dynamic* to his prophetic vocation:

(i) On the mountain Moses' calling to be the mediator of God's life-giving words (the Law) on the Exodus journey is revealed most formidably by the *voice* (φωνή) out of the fiery cloud to the gathered assembly of *all* Israel;

(ii) From the mountain the persistent *stubbornness* of the people to hearken to this voice is divulged through the twisting of this voice in the *image* of the molten calf; this defiance in turn illustrates the unwillingness of the people to "hear" this voice from the beginning;

---

[25]See 3:29-4:1.

[26]So Mann ("Denial," 486) referring to H. Barzel, "Moses: Tragedy and Sublimity," *Literary Interpretations of Biblical Narratives* (ed. K. R. R. Gros Louis et al.; Nashville: Abingdon, 1974) 129.

[27]For the three parallel synonymous expressions (1:37; 3:26; 4:21), see S. R. Driver, *Deuteronomy* (ICC; Edinburgh: Clark, 1902) 27.

[28]The emphatic "I" is twice sharply contrasted to the emphatic "you."

[29]Driver, *Deuteronomy*, 71.

[30]Usually ascribed to the P account; cf. e.g. von Rad, *Deuteronomy*, 201; Mann, "Denial," 483.

[31]We are not suggesting that a developed, *theoretical* explanation of Moses' death as atoning or redemptive is offered in Deuteronomy. Yet within the plotted dynamics of the story, Moses' death is indispensable to the enactment of the Exodus deliverance and occupation of the land, an event which *must* be accomplished as an execution of Yahweh's wrath/judgment and, consequently, an explanation of the raison d'être of Moses' denial. For interpretations of "vicarious" in a "substitutionary" and/or "representative" sense, see e.g., von Rad, *Theology*, 1. 294-95; G. E. Wright, "Exegesis of Deuteronomy," *IB* 2. 339-40.

(iii)   Accordingly, while Moses is still on the mountain and as he descends and is *sent* on the Exodus his calling is disclosed to be a *suffering journey to death*;

(iv)   As a result, his calling does not effect deliverance for all those who follow him to the Promised Land but only for the new people of the land, the *"children* of the mountain."

At the core of this dynamic is the double-stroke of Israel's stiff-necked opposition to the voice of the Lord through Moses and the consequent tragic fate of this prophet. As later generations of the Deuteronomist historians colored his career,[32] Moses' death outside the land was a *necessary* punishment for the sin of all Israel--even of the "children" who like their fathers proved themselves to be the "stubborn" and "crooked" "wilderness generation."

II

It has long been recognized that Luke's account of Jesus' mountain transfiguration (9:28-36) introduces his subsequent "journey" to Jerusalem (9:51-19:44).[33]   But from a literary standpoint the whole of 9:1-50 performs such a function through Luke's[34] carefully carved continuity in audience and scenery. In this way, before Jesus' journey to his "taking up" is signally announced (9:51), Luke sets forth a four-fold *Exodus typology* of the prophetic calling of Jesus which conforms closely to that of Moses in Deuteronomy as we have outlined it above. This typology in fact becomes the *organizing principle* for the rest of the story in the Gospel. As the scheme is set out it is important to bear in mind that the correspondence in "type" is not a function of a mechanical, rote-like parallelism in the sequence of events or description of details. It is *not* suggested that a one-to-one analogy in the chronology of episodes in Deuteronomy exists in Luke 9:1-50 or in the following journey and events in Jerusalem, or that every event or subject in the one has a mirror image in the other. Rather, what we discover is a *profound correspondence in the calling, execution, and fate of the calling* of the one who is the Prophet like Moses (Deut 18:15-19), effecting a New Exodus for a renewed people of God:

(i)   Only Luke of the three Synoptists speaks of Jesus' transfiguration taking place "while he was praying" (9:28b, 29a); like Moses Jesus is one who *speaks directly with God*.[35]   As his robes begin to "flash like lightning" (ἐξαστράπτω) and the "appearance"

---

[32]See nn. 13, 25.

[33]So e.g. Conzelmann, *Luke*, 57-59; J. H. Davies, "The Purpose of the Central Section of Luke's Gospel," *SE* II (=TU 87; Berlin: Akademie, 1964) 164-65; D. Gill, "Observations on the Lukan Travel Narrative and Some Related Passages," *HTR* 63 (1970) 218-21; C. C. McCown, "The Geography of Luke's Central Section," *JBL* 57 (1938) 64-66; P. Schubert, "The Structure and Significance of Luke 24," *Neutestamentliche Studien für Rudolf Bultmann* (BZNW 21; ed. W. Eltester; Berlin: A. Töpelmann, 1954) 181-82.

[34]Or perhaps his sources'. For 9:7-50 and esp. Herod's perplexity (9:9) as raising question of Jesus' identity and in 9:10-50 depicting Jesus' authoritative status in preparation for the "Teacher par excellence" of the journey section, see J. A. Fitzmyer, "The Composition of Luke, Chapter 9," *Perspectives on Luke-Acts* (ed. C. H. Talbert; Danville: Association of Baptist Professors of Religion, 1978) 149-52.

[35]It may be objected that since Luke alone presents Jesus at *prayer* in other instances (e.g. 3:21; 5:16; 6:12; 9:18), and that Exodus also portrays Moses speaking directly with God (e.g. 19:9-13), this detail does not say very much, if anything at all. But this feature takes on added weight within the *interlocking* picture of Jesus with the Moses of Deuteronomy (see below) in which the Mosaic portrait is clearly distinguished from the J and E accounts in Exodus (cf. e.g. von Rad, *Theology*, 1. 291-95). That Jesus is often at prayer merely shows the consistency of Luke 9:28-36 with the rest of the Lukan presentation.

(εἶδος)[36] of his face is altered, suddenly (ἰδού) Moses and Elijah "appear" "in glory" (ἐν δόξῃ, 9:29b-31a) with him.   Luke alone would have his readers behold *three* glowing personages who must have created quite a spectacle for the unwitting spectators. As with the Horeb theophany the mountain was "burning with fire" (cf. Deut 4:11-12, 15, 33, 36b; 5:23). Again it is only Luke who states that the three disciples saw Jesus' glory (τὴν δόξαν αὐτοῦ, v 32b--Deut 5:24!). Peter, dumbfounded and stumbling over every word, suggests that they make three tents (9:33b) when, just "as he was speaking," a *cloud*[37] comes and "overshadows" them (9:34).[38]   The disciples are "frightened" as the cloud engulfs them and a "voice from the cloud" (φωνή ... ἐκ τῆς νεφέλης) declares, "This is my Son, my Chosen One, *hearken to him*" (αὐτοῦ ἀκούετε, v 35). Now it is the heavenly *voice* (φωνή) of Horeb which, Moses reminds the people time and time again, is their *life* (Deut 4:11-13, 33, 36; 5:22, 23, 24, 25, 26; 8:20; 18:16; cf. for the future 4:30; 13:4, 18; 15:5; 26:14, 17; 27:10; 28:1, 2, 9, 13, 15, 45, 62; 30:2, 8, 10, 20). To *hearken* is to live, to disobey to die. And not only to this voice in Moses but also in the *"prophet like"* him who shall "arise" (ἀνίστημι) "among his brethren" after him are they to "*hearken to him*" (αὐτοῦ ἀκούσεσθε, 18:15b).[39] Here it is curious that of the three versions of this heavenly voice, only Luke in *both* diction and word order matches the LXX of 18:15b.[40] Thus, like *all* Israel, who on the mountain hundreds of years earlier *witnessed* the authoritative revelation of the *divine voice* through Moses, so now on the mountain the three disciples, representing the "Twelve" and hence the *twelve* tribes of *all* Israel, *witness* the definitive revelation of the *divine voice* through Jesus, God's Chosen Son. *Like Moses Jesus is called to mediate the voice of God.*

As Jesus determines to head for Jerusalem (9:51), Luke sketches a portrait of one whose authority can only adequately be described as the "voice of God." "On the way" (9:57, 58-10:20) Jesus issues orders and sends out ambassadors on a mission that brooks no rival. His command to *follow* him transcends any observance of the Law as it is currently perceived and enforced (9:59-60);[41] the *words* of his emissaries bear such a force that to heed (ἀκούω)[42] is to make effective the eschatological life of the rule of God (10:5-6, 9), while to reject them already unleashes the verdict of the final judgment (10:10-12, 13-15, 16, 17-20). When confronted by one of the leading authorities of the covenant Law, there is no doubt that as Jesus finishes his parable of the uncompassionate priest and Levite with, "Go and do likewise" (10:37b), he claims for himself the *authority* to declare where the life of the Law is present and where it is not (10:25-37). The conclusion is unavoidable that the "dead who are to bury their own" (9:60) are those who are missing the eschatological life of the life-giving Law in the Kingdom entourage of the "teacher" who utters directly the will of God (10:25, 28, 37; cf. v 38).

---

[36]Cf. (LXX) Exod 24:10, 17--only Luke has this verbal link with the Exodus account.

[37]Cf. (LXX) Exod 40:35; Pss 90 (91):4; 139 (140):7; Prov 18:11.

[38]Whether the disciples, or Jesus and Moses and Elijah are meant, is not decisive for our thesis; cf. Marshall, *Gospel,* 387.

[39]It must not be overlooked that the *authority* of the prophet like Moses is tied directly to Moses' authority *revealed at Horeb* (18:16-17).

[40]If any direct textual dependence is involved, this parallel would seem to indicate familiarity with the LXX account rather than any deliberate "change" or Matthew or Mark, esp. given the latters' divergent emphases (see n.58).

[41]See e.g. W. Grundmann, *Das Evangelium nach Lukas* (THKNT 3; 8th ed.; Berlin: Evangelische, 1978) 205.

[42]ποιέω (e.g. 10:25, 28, 37; 11:42 etc.) and φυλάσσω (11:28; 18:21) are the other key verbs.

Between the two Deuteronomic pillars[43] of the *Shema* (10:27a--Deut 6:5) and the Decalogue (18:20[44]--Deut 5:16-20) Luke fills in his portraiture of a prophet-teacher whose *own word* defines "what one must do to inherit eternal *life*" (10:25; 18:18). Mary, who "was hearkening to his *word*" "has chosen the better part" (10:39b, 42); Jesus' words to the *crowds* are wiser than Solomon's and greater than Jonah's as they (and *not* his miraculous deeds) evoke the eschatological blessing of God's rule for those "who hear the word of God" in him "and keep it" (11:28, 29-36; cf. vv 14-27); to the *Pharisee leaders* of the people comes the prophetic indictment that "you pass by justice and the love of God; these you ought to have *done* without neglecting the other things. . . . It shall be required of this generation" (11:42, 51b, 37-41, 43-50, 52); and to his *disciples* (cf. 12:1b) Jesus claims in his own presence to be an eschatological messenger who, according to their reception of *him*, will determine their fate in the court of God Himself (12:8-9; cf. vv 1-7, 10-12, 22-34). That is to say, he *speaks* for God: "Fool, this night your soul is required of you" (12:20), or "It is your Father's good pleasure to give you the Kingdom" (12:32b), or "Blessed is that servant whom his lord finds so *doing* when he comes" (12:43). It is no wonder that this "Lord" (13:23) who journeys on through the towns and villages toward Jerusalem, *teaching* in their streets (13:22), controls the door into the banquet hall of salvation: "You will weep . . . when you see Abraham . . . and all the prophets in the Kingdom of God but you yourselves thrust out" (13:28, 23-27, 29-30). Only those who follow by actually *hearkening* to his *word* will avail themselves of the covenant life fulfilled in their midst (14:35! cf. 14:1-34; 15:1-2, 3-32). To the proud, prestigious, and presumptuous[45] of Israel comes the categorical warning: "They have *Moses* and *the prophets*, let them hearken to them. He [Abraham] said to them, 'If they do not hearken to Moses and the prophets neither will they be convinced if someone should rise from the dead' " (16:29, 31, 1-13, 14-18, 19-30; 17:1-10, 11-19, 20-37; 18:1-8, 9-14, 15-17). What Luke presents, then, is *eschatological halakoth* from the mouth of one who not only stands in the line of Moses and the prophets, but will also consummate them through the raising up of this voice from the dead. Jesus speaks with nothing less than the authority of the author of the Law himself!--"Do this and you will *live*" . . . "and receive . . . in the coming age *eternal life*" (10:28b; 18:30).

As the journey episodes intensify as Jesus nears Jerusalem, the life he bears and speaks is manifest among those who submit to his authority: "Your faith has saved you" (18:42); "Today salvation has come to this house" (19:9); "If these were silent the very stones would cry out" (19:40). It is thus when he enters the Temple that he is ensconced there by the people (λαός)[46] as *the teacher* of Israel (19:47-48). He is the one who has the authoritative *word* to which the chief priests, scribes, and elders (cf. 9:22) can only protest, "By what authority (ἐξουσία) do you do these things? Who gave you this authority?" (20:2). "But they were not able in the presence of the people to catch him by what he said" (20:26a); "for they no longer dared to ask him any question" (20:40; cf. 20:1-8, 9-19, 20-26, 27-39, 41-44, 45-47). This prophet-teacher, then, who "stirs up the people, teaching throughout all Judea, from Galilee even to this place" (23:5) must die. Yet not even death can prevent this voice from declaring the decisive life-giving word from God as foretold by "Moses and all the prophets" (24:25-26, 44-47). For by virtue of the resurrection and glorification of this prophet the apostles will stand up in Solomon's Portico to announce that what Moses had prophesied in Deut 18:15-19 has at last been culminated (Acts 3:22-23). Now even Peter, of the trembling trio on the mountain, will boldly resound to "all the people" of Israel the thunderous voice from that mountain: "Hearken to him" (Deut 18:15b ⟶ Luke 9:35b ⟶ Acts 3:22b).

---

[43]M. D. Goulder's expression in, "The Chiastic Structure of the Lucan Journey," *SE* II (= TU 87) 196.

[44]Luke's order matches the LXX.

[45]Including the "disciples"; see below on (iii), in Part II.

[46]For Luke's use of λαός, see P. S. Minear, "Jesus' Audiences according to Luke," *NovT* 16 (1974) 81-109.

(ii) It is only Luke of the Evangelists who dares mention that while Jesus is transfigured "in glory" with Moses and Elijah the disciples *sleep*! (βεβαρημένοι ὕπνῳ, 9:32a).[47] Only *after* they have "awakened" (v 32b) do they "see" Jesus' glory and the two men. What is more, Luke does not spare Peter and his companions further embarrassment when Peter, astir with "greatness in the air," thinks that the group needs a "booth" for each of the "glorious" figures--"not knowing what he was saying" (9:33b). It is then, "*as he was speaking*" (9:34a), that a *cloud* comes and the "voice out of the cloud" commands the *terrified* disciples to obey the voice of God in Jesus, His Elect Son. Like the people of Israel on Horeb who in their stubborn resistance to obey the voice of God through Moses had to be *disciplined* by the *shock* of the *thundering voice* from the fiery cloud (Deut 4:36), so the disciples in their stuporous response to the voice of God through Jesus also have to be *overwhelmed* by the *traumatic voice* from out of the cloud. Luke continues (v 36) that "after the voice had *spoken* Jesus was found alone" and the disciples "were mute," "telling no one *in those days*[48] anything of what they had seen" (ἑώρα-καν). For it was true of them that they had "this day" (ἐν τῇ ἡμέρα ταύτῃ) "seen (εἴδομεν) God *speak* with man and man still live!" (Deut 5:24b).

It may be objected that this second analogy hardly holds together when it is recalled that in fear of their own lives the Israelites *eagerly* accepted Moses' mediation of the divine voice on the mountain, in contrast to the halting *ambivalence* of the disciples who do not even comprehend the "life and death" matters in their midst at all. But what we are presenting is a typological correspondence far more fundamental than a specific sequence or episode within a momentous revelation. To penetrate these deeper dimensions it will be necessary to see how Luke's casting of the disciples on the *mountain* is, like Deuteronomy, carefully engrafted into the behavior of the crowd below on the plain (9:1-27, 37-50).

In 9:1-6 Jesus "sends" out the Twelve with "power" (δύναμις) and "authority" (ἐξουσία) to continue the *same* activity in which he himself has been engaged, sc. healing and preaching the Kingdom of God (v 2; cf. 9:11). Herod's stance to both Jesus' and his emissaries' amazing feats is then dovetailed into this sending out (9:7-9): Herod has "heard of all the things that were being done"; folks are buzzing with speculation that "John the Baptist had been raised" (ἠγέρθη) or that "Elijah had appeared (ἐφάνη) or that "one of the prophets of bygone days had arisen"[49] (ἀνέστη; cf. ἀναστήσω, Deut 18:15, 18); as for Herod, he is at a loss just what to think--he must "see" (ἰδεῖν) this Jesus for himself! (9:9; cf. 23:6-12). The disciples' activity here is without doubt *identified* with Jesus' fame; to hear about their work is to force a decision about Jesus.[50] They appear to be *one* with their master in the *power* and *authority* granted them.

The Twelve return (9:10) and report but no response by Jesus is given except that he takes them "apart" to Bethsaida. The "crowds" (ὄχλοι, v 11), however, who have thronged Jesus for some time now,[51] learn where he is going and follow him. While it is not explicitly stated that these *crowds* represent the same folk who are voicing their opinions about Jesus (9:7-8), yet it is interesting that right at this point, after Jesus has *spoken* about the Kingdom of God, *healed*,[52] and with his disciples *fed* these crowds in a *desert* place (ἐν ἐρήμῳ τόπῳ, v 12b; cf. ἐν τῇ ἐρήμῳ, Deut 8:2), Jesus asks his disciples just what these *crowds* are thinking about him (9:18). And they report almost

---

[47]For linguistic issues, cf. Marshall, *Gospel*, 385.

[48]Luke 9:36b-- ἐν ἐκείναις ταῖς ἡμέραις.

[49]This phrase unique to Luke.

[50]A vivid illustration of the *shaliaḥ* concept, cf. Luke 9:10-- οἱ ἀπόστολοι. See C. K. Barrett, "*Shaliaḥ* and Apostle," *Donum Gentilicium: New Testament Studies in Honour of David Daube* (ed. E. Bammel and W. D. Davies; Oxford: Clarendon, 1978) 88-102.

[51]E.g. 6:17, 19; 7:9, 11, 12, 24; 8:4, 19, 40, 42, 45.

[52]These first two activities match those of the Twelve (9:2).

verbatim the same sentiments that are troubling Herod's ears (v 19). The popular feeling is that Jesus is a great prophet, comparable to the greatest of the OT figures. The reader is led to believe, then, that these opinions are emerging essentially from the *same crowds*. Peter, on the other hand, not content to be marked by such commonality, goes beyond this stance, acknowledging Jesus to be God's own "Anointed" (τὸν χριστὸν τοῦ θεοῦ, 9:20). But unlike the other Synoptists no praise or blessing by Jesus is accorded this insight; no period of private correction and teaching is awarded the disciples' confession.[53] Instead, Jesus, "charging" and "commanding" them to silence and in the same breath (εἰπών)[54] telling them that "the Son of Man must suffer many things . . . ," *continues on* by telling (cf. ἔλεγεν,[55] v 23) *all* that they too must suffer if they want to save their lives by following him (9:23-26). The sequence here is quite different than in Mark and Matthew. For Luke presents one continuous *scene* in which the *same crowds* remain close by as a theatrical backdrop for the disciples' performance. This lack of interaction of Jesus with his disciples might appear to "level" them with the masses, to join them with the popular currents of the crowds. *All* must follow Jesus and *all* alike must suffer. Yet however different this picture, without Mark and Matthew as foils and stylistic variances notwithstanding, Luke's account is straightforward and intrinsically logical. The disciples *are* distinguished from the crowds *confessionally* and *spatially* by a relative privacy where Jesus is praying "alone," in addition of course to their commissioning (9:1-6) and special assistance in feeding these multitudes.

But as we pursue the advancing lines of the plot this suspicion is borne out as the disciples' *solidarity* in power and authority with Jesus takes marked turns in the opposite direction. The divergences in audience and sequence with Mark and Matthew do indeed become signposts of a fundamentally different terrain which lies ahead. The great tableau of Jesus' *following* which extends from 9:10-27 climaxes with Jesus prophesying to all that some among them will not "taste death" before they "see" (ἴδωσιν, v 27) "the Kingdom of God." "Now about eight days *after these sayings*," Peter, James, and John--in spite of themselves--"see" (εἶδον, v 32) Jesus *glory* on the mountain. "The next day" when they have descended, Jesus is met by a "great crowd" (ὄχλος πολύς, 9:37b) only to learn from one of them (ἀπὸ τοῦ ὄχλου, v 38a) that his *disciples* "were unable" (οὐκ ἠδυνήθησαν, v 40) to heal this man's "only son" (cf. v 38b). Jesus' response: "You faithless and crooked generation!" ('Ω γενεὰ ἄπιστος καὶ διεστραμμένη, 9:41a). Here Jesus lumps his disciples together with one solid mass of a disbelieving, perverse people. Indeed just as earlier the people's faithless twisting of God's commandment in the molten calf at the base revealed their *stubborn perversity* as Moses descends the mountain, so now as Jesus descends the mountain the disciples' faithless twisting of their divinely bestowed power and authority with the man's only son at the base reveals the *stubborn perversity* of the whole generation. Moreover, Moses' charge to the people that they are a "stubborn and crooked generation" (γενεὰ σκολιὰ καὶ διεστραμμένη, 32:5), and "a perverse (ἐξεστραμμένη) generation, children in whom there is no faith" (οὐκ ἔστιν πίστις, 32:20) is matched here by Jesus: in both, the zealous anger of the Lord who confronts an obdurate generation "in the wilderness" comes to expression. And Moses' cry of desperation at Horeb, "How can I bear alone the weight and the burden of you and your strife?" (1:12), is echoed remarkably again by Jesus here at the base of the mountain: "How long am I to be with you and bear you?!" (Luke 9:41).[56] Jesus laments that he must endure this faithless mass

---

[53]Contrast Mark 8:31-32; Matt 16:17-19, 21, 24-28.

[54]Cf. e.g. W. Grundmann, "Fragen der Komposition des lukanischen Reiseberichts," *ZNW* 50 (1959) 255-56.

[55]Cf. Marshall, *Gospel*, 373: "He went on to say"; for this use of the imperf. cf. BDF (Chicago: University of Chicago, 1961) §329.

[56]The disciples are "at strife" in 9:46-48 (see below); see n. 58 for the different import of this lament in Matt 17:17 and Mark 9:19.

any longer; even the disciples, who hardly more than a week earlier had confessed his Messiahship, are pulled into and *identified* with this crooked lot. They in fact are the very provocators of this outburst. Their "impotence" at the base of the mountain becomes a striking demonstration of their *ambivalence* at the top. The *whole generation,* disciples and all, are like their Horeb counterparts--one disobedient, rebellious mass.

That this portrayal is not happy coincidence is startlingly confirmed as the scene unfolds. Luke moves at a quick pace. While the crowds "marvel" at the "majesty" (μεγαλειοτης, 9:43) "of God . . . and all that he was doing," Jesus tells his disciples again in sobering if not stern words, "Let these words sink into your ears (ὦτα) . . . ." (9:44). The disciples fare no better this time than with Jesus' first prediction of his passion as Luke stresses in four different phrases their *incapacity* to grasp these words: They (a) do not "understand" (b) that which has been "concealed" from them, (c) "in order that they should not perceive"; and (d) "they were *afraid* (cf. v 34b) to ask him about this saying" (9:45). They are like their frightened wilderness predecessors who remain *slow to believe* and *hearken* (Deut 9:23; 32:20), a people "without understanding" (32:28), even though they had witnessed the "majestic" (μεγαλεῖος, 11:2-7) deliverance of God. Despite the mighty signs in their midst and the glory on the mountain they re-embody that people to whom Moses so well observed: "You have seen all the things the Lord did . . . the signs and those great wonders. Yet the Lord has not given you a heart (καρδία) to know or eyes to see or ears (ὦτα) to hear, even to this very day" (29:2b-4).

But as with the Israelites, the disciples' and the whole generation's "crooked" perfidy is not simply summed up by uncomprehending unbelief. For immediately Luke continues on at the *same* time and in the *same* "crowded" arena with the disciples arguing which of them is the "greatest" (9:46-48). That they could squabble about their own importance in the midst of these crowds right when they had failed miserably at casting out a "demon" (δαιμόνιον, v 42) from one of their *children* seems almost as if Luke here has resorted to "burlesque." With the powerful perception of a prophet Jesus penetrates all the way to their "hearts" (εἰδὼς . . . τῆς καρδίας αὐτῶν, 9:47a) and places a "child" (παιδίον) by his *own side.* The point: Unless one can humble his puffed-up heart, and *"in my name"* associate with, i.e., "receive" (δέχομαι) a person as small (μικρότερος) and insignificant as a *child,* that one will be *unable* to "receive" Jesus and thus also the One who has "sent" Jesus (9:48). There is no point in being at Jesus' side unless one is humble enough to be at a "child's" side. The rebuke to the disciples could hardly be more scathing. They are failing to *obey* Jesus' *voice* through "proud and patronizing hearts."

That this is the pith of the problem in its Lukan context is illustrated by the next pericope which again continues on *uninterrupted* in setting. John "answers" that they (i.e., the disciples) "saw (εἴδομεν) someone casting out *demons* (δαιμόνια) in your *name*"; they forbade him, because he does not *follow with us*" (ἀκολουθεῖ μεθ᾽ ἡμῶν, cf. 9:11, 23). Not only are the disciples blind and deaf to the true authority of Jesus' voice, but their presumptuousness also makes them numb to Jesus' discipline. What they "see" in this Jesus who performs mighty works is foremostly that which makes themselves "mighty" as well. That is to say, they *cannot* recognize and fall in line with Jesus' authority structure but insist that "true following" (cf. 9:23-27) requires a "falling in line" with *them.* The resonance of ἐν τῷ ὀνόματί σου (9:49) with ἐπὶ τῷ ὀνόματί μου (9:48) is loud and clear. Jesus' retort is also equally unequivocal. He *forbids* them to "forbid" the person who is working "in Jesus' name"[57] since such a one is obviously not "against" the disciples but is "for them" (9:50). Jesus' pointing to the child in v 48 as an object lesson in submission to his authority has been of no account whatever. The disciples are too caught *up* in their own "prominence" to *stoop* to the side of the child. They are like their obstinate antetypes--*refusing discipline* and *training* (Deut 9:6-

---

[57] There is no indication by Jesus that his authority is being abused by the "unknown" exorcist.

29; cf. 4:36; 5:23-30; 8:2-5, 14-20; 11:2-7). Their glimpse of Jesus' divine glory on the mountain has revealed their own self-"glory" on the plain (Deut 5:24; Luke 9:32).[58]

We are now in a position to see how the incidents at the base of the mountain interpret the behavior on the summit and in fact all that precedes the ascent (9:1-27). The contrast of the disciples with the "unknown exorcist" could not be starker. He *has* the *power* and *authority* to exorcise *demons* because he works in Jesus' name, sc. *he has submitted to the divine voice in Jesus*. This incident (9:49-50), which at first seems to be attached arbitrarily by Luke, indeed renders Jesus' lament and charge in 9:42 fully comprehensible. The disciples are *unable* to exorcise the demon from the child because they have not submitted to this divine voice; and they *cannot* because their "hearts" are bloated beyond response to the "child" in their midst. They are at *base* no different from the rest of the "twisted, unbelieving generation" of the crowds. Thus what we have is the same fundamental *distortion of the divine voice* as at Horeb. In both, the command to hearken to the *authority* of the Lord through His mediator is completely contorted to the authority of their own "imagination." As the *image* of the molten calf divulges the rebellious refusal to obey the voice of God in Moses, so the *image* of self-importance of the disciples reveals their stubborn refusal to obey the voice of God in Jesus. The idol of the one is as real as the idol of the other. Thus in both Deuteronomy and Luke 9 the *reluctance and fear of listening to the voice of God on the mountain is truly a foreboding revelation of the "wilderness generation" on the plain*. And the incomprehension, strife, conceited hearts, imperviousness to discipline, etc., all become salient signs of "this generation's" crooked unbelief. We can schematize this basic *dynamic or response* in both Deuteronomy and Luke 9:1-50 as follows: Reluctance and Fear of Hearing the Voice on the Mountain ⟶ Stubborn Perversion of this Voice on the Plain ⟶ Incomprehension, Strife, Conceit, Rejection of Discipline, etc. by Whole Generation. What was true of the miraculous signs and feeding for the wilderness people of God becomes true again for the "wilderness generation" in Luke: "You have been rebellious against the Lord from the day that I knew you" (Deut 9:24; cf. 8:3, 15-20).

At several pivotal points in the developing contour of the "voice of God" to Jerusalem Luke again presents a Jesus who confronts the "wilderness generation" which like their fathers forms an obstinate monolith of resistance. In 11:14-54, although encountering five types of response, Jesus levels them all to *one mass* of an "evil generation" (vv 29, 50-51).[59] "Marvelling" amazement (v 14b), a charge of alignment with "Beelzebul" (v 15), "testy" skepticism (v 16), naive, uncommitted admiration (vv 27-28), and censorious "amazement" (v 38) all stand condemned at the final judgment for failing to *repent* at the "sign" of the preaching of the one "greater" "here" in their midst (vv 29-32). Smaller groups (vv 15-16), a nameless individual (vv 27-28), and Pharisees (vv 37-54; cf. v 37a--"while he was speaking") all emerge from the burgeoning *crowds* of "this generation" (ἡ γενεὰ αὕτη, v 29) to be spattered by the "blood of all the prophets shed from the foundation of the world . . . from the blood of Abel to the blood of Zechariah" (v 51a). It is precisely "this generation" which "consents to the deeds of *your fathers*" (v 48). Whereas in 9:1-50 it was the *disciples' inability* and lack of *authority* which spark Jesus' indictment of the crowds (9:41), it is now the resistance to Jesus' *ability* and *authority* from the individuals, groups, and leaders of the crowds themselves

---

[58] A comparison of the *disciples* in the corresponding Matthean and Markan passages discloses that only Luke reflects a developed complex of Exodus motifs which determines the whole *tenor* and *structure* of the story of Jesus: Mark 9:14-50--the disciples are *bound* to Jesus through their confessing, albeit naive and insufficient, faith and as such are set apart from the unbelieving and, in part, even hostile crowds; Matt 17:14-18:35-- even more than Mark the disciples are distinguished from the *unbelieving* and *perverted* crowds (17:17a) by their faith and responsibilities as *guardians* of that faith.

[59] Although only "others" (11:16a) are "seeking a sign," yet Jesus accuses the *whole generation* of this (v 29).

which provokes this same rebuff. "Yes, I tell you, it shall be required of *this generation* (v 51a).

As the crowds swell to the "thousands" (12:1) Jesus turns alternately to the disciples (12:1b, 22) and the masses (12:15, 54) to warn them to discern and heed the "sign" (cf. 11:16) in their midst that is already "on the way" to "accuse" them before the "judge" (12:58). The crowds of this generation have already become like their leaders, "hypocrites" (12:56 ⟶ 12:1 ⟶ 11:37-54). By refusing to repent they will bring upon the whole nation (cf. the fig tree)[60] the destruction "normally" associated with their "worst sinners" (13:1-5); a calamity experienced by *some* is a ready illustration of the calamity awaiting *all!* (vv 3, 5).

Farther along the way (cf. 17:11) Jesus is confronted again by a stubborn generation that seeks a "sign" (17:20-21 ⟶ 11:29). He does not mince his words when he tells "the Pharisees" that the Kingdom of salvation (cf. 17:19) they are searching for is already in their midst. The leaders of "this generation" remain like their "unknowing" followers (cf. 11:29-36, 43-46; 12:55-57),[61] calloused to the "effective presence" of the Kingdom already "here" in their presence (cf. ἰδοὺ ὧδε, 17:21 ⟶ 11:30b, 32b). So Jesus once again turns to his disciples to admonish them not to fall prey to a *generation* that, once they have inflicted his suffering and rejection (17:25), will continue as the generations of Noah and of Lot to "eat and drink," "buy and sell" etc., totally hardened to the redemptive warning of the past and oblivious to the future day of the Son of Man (17:24, 30). Such a day will *not* come when "men say to *you*, 'Look here (ὧδε) it is!' " (17:23 ⟶ 21 ⟶ 12:54-57 ⟶ 11:30b, 32b, 16).

With the sights of Jerusalem in full view Jesus weeps for a people that have remained blind to the "things that would lead to peace" (19:41-42). Jerusalem, symbol of God's covenant salvation and yet of a nation's stiff-necked rejection of God's messengers (13:33-35), proves itself again to be the "wilderness generation" that spurns the *Exodus visitation* of God (19:44b ⟶ 9:31 ⟶ LXX Exod 3:16; Gen 50:24-25). Therefore, as in 587 B.C.E. and already predicted by Moses (Deut 4:25-28; 28:45-68),[62] God will visit them for destruction (cf. Jer 6:15; 10:15; Isa 29:6). In the Temple Jesus proceeds to etch this nation's behavior into the "people's" minds; their leaders are like the impudent tenants of a vineyard who, repeatedly mistreating the owner's mesengers, force him to give the vineyard *to others*[63] (20:9-28, esp. v 16). It is no coincidence that Luke begins his Acts with Jesus' charge to the "wilderness generation" at the mountain--now echoed ironically by Peter--"Save yourselves from this 'crooked generation' " (Acts 2:40b ⟶ Luke 9:41 ⟶ Deut 32:5), and closes his story with the prophet's foreboding pronouncement of a "blind," "deaf," and "hard-hearted" people: "This people's heart has grown dull . . . therefore . . . this salvation of God has been sent to the Gentiles; they will hearken" (ἀκούσονται, Acts 28:27a, 28; Paul citing Isa 6:9-10).

(iii) It is only Luke of the Gospel writers who discloses that while the disciples slumber Moses and Elijah converse with Jesus about his "exodus" (ἔξοδος) "which he was to fulfill in *Jerusalem*" (9:31). We have already seen that Luke explicitly links Jesus' *words* about bearing a *cross* and *losing* one's *life* directly to the mountain glorification (9:23-27 ⟶ 28). These words are in turn an amplification of the Son of Man's *suffering rejection* and *death* at the hands of "elders, chief priests, and scribes" (9:22), that is by the Sanhedrin *in Jerusalem*. Moreover, in the context of 9:51 where "the days (pl.) of his "taking up" in Jerusalem are (lit.) "becoming completely full," that is, "had already

---

[60]E.g. Hos 9:10; Joel 1:7; Jer 8:13; 24:1-8; Mic 7:1.

[61]12:57 intimates an unwitting acceptance of someone *else's judgment*, most likely from their leaders, 12:1.

[62]For these Deuteronomic traditions, see O. H. Steck, *Israel und das gewaltsame Geschick der Propheten* (WMANT 23; Neukirchen: Neukirchener, 1967) 139-43.

[63]See F. W. Danker, *Jesus and the New Age* (St. Louis: Clayton, 1972) 201.

arrived,"[64] it is certain that the exodus Jesus fulfills *in* Jerusalem is also one that he fulfills on his way *to* Jerusalem, i.e., through a *journey* to that city. Hence his *exodus* is both a "going out" *to* as well as a "departure" *from* Jerusalem. *Like Moses, then, Jesus' calling to a journey of suffering and death is revealed to those on the mountain who would follow behind him to reach the "promised land" of salvation* (Deut 1:6-9; 10:11; Luke 9:22-25 ⟶ 32 ⟶ 51).

As Jesus descends and is met by the "wilderness generation" his cry of desperation like Moses' lament reveals the palpable *necessity* of his suffering. "How long must I be with you and put up with you" voices the sentiment not of a normal mortal but of one who is clearly reckoning with a *departure* from "this generation"[65] in the imminent future. This *necessity* is suddenly voiced again, this time in the most ironic of settings. As the chorus of the *crowds of men* marvel approval, Jesus tries to shake his disciples from the monolithic snare of sin by warning them of these *same men* into whose hands he is about to be "delivered" (παραδίδωμι, 9:44b;[66] cf. 9:23, 25, 18). It is not only the Sanhedrin that is going to force Jesus' death, but so is *this same twisted generation*! The base of the mountain again confirms what has already been divulged at the top. And it now becomes transparent that Herod's *beheading* of John the Baptist with his desire to "see" Jesus (9:9 ⟶ 23:8) is an *omen* of *ill* on par with the "crowds' " (9:11-19) or the "disciples' " (9:20, 27, 28-36, 37-50) ability to "see" Jesus. Consequently, together with Herod symbolizing the hardened nation, the disciples' desire to dismiss rather than feed the *laos* in the wilderness is, like the Exodus antetype (Deut 8:2-5, 14-17), a poignant demonstration of the whole generation's stubborn refusal to accept discipline and hence to heed the voice of the mountain revelation. The *grounding* for the death of Jesus is thus already the *same* as for Moses in Deuteronomy. *Because of* the intransigent sin of the people, a resistance so powerful that even gestures of redemption are twisted around to strife, jealousy, and conceit, Moses/Jesus must *suffer and die*.

As Jesus and his retinue continue onward from the mountain on the New Exodus, the various *dramatis personae* of the "wilderness generation" emerge along Jesus' path to merge eventually into one solid front of disobedience and even hostile opposition. As they cross over into Samaria, the *disciples* can only think of calling down more of that "glorious fire" or the mountain (9:29-34) to vindicate their *own* status as the *mighty men of war* for their Messiah-Deliverer (9:54--Deut 1:41; 2:16). But for Jesus' stiff rebuke the disciples would "gird on his weapons of war and go up and fight!" (Deut 1:41). Jesus must warn all who would wish to follow that his journey will be one long trek of rejection, not unlike that through the Samaritan village--"without any place to lay his head (9:57-58). His own ambassadors will be like "lambs in the midst of wolves" (10:3; cf. vv 6b, 10-12, 16b).

At table fellowship with the leaders of "this generation" the one *greater* than Solomon and Jonah who is "here" links them to the *persecution* and *murder* of all the prophets throughout Israel's history. Luke records that as he departed, "the scribes (οἱ γραμματεῖς) and the Pharisees began to oppose him fiercely . . . waiting to catch him in something he might say" (11:53-54). The ploy thickens instantly when Jesus goes directly to warn his disciples of the "leaven of the Pharisees which is hypocrisy" (12:1). This infectious infuence, which engages Jesus as a "teacher" while simultaneously undermining the "something greater," will be fully exposed (12:2). Those who endure will undergo persecution and trial (12:4-7, 11-12); but their allegiance will be rewarded by

---

[64]Cf. Acts 2:1 for the best analogy; cf. also J. H. Davies, "Purpose," and Schubert, "Structure," 184-85, for the linguistic relation of 9:51 to 9:31.

[65]See M. Dibelius, *Die Formgeschichte der Evangelien* (Tübingen: J. C. B. Mohr, 1971) 278.

[66]9:23-25 along with probable paranomasia on ὁ υἱὸς τοῦ ἀνθρώπου with χεῖρας ἀνθρώπων (cf. J. Jeremias, *TDNT* 5, 715) indicate a *generic* sense of "man," or the *generation* of Jesus' day; cf. 17:25.

acclaim before the throne of God (vv 8-9). They should therefore not be in fear of those who at most can *kill* the body (v 4). Rather, they are to fear God and submit to his chosen ambassador (vv 5, 8-10).

As the large audience scene unfolds, however, it becomes alarmingly apparent that the large band of disciples are succumbing more and more to this leaven. They are told not only that slovenliness in preparing for the coming judgment will result in disaster (12:35-48), but that this judgment is also *already* in their midst, straining relentlessly to its fulfillment (vv 49-53). For Jesus himself *has come* (vv 49, 51) to cast eschatological fire right through the center of the households of Israel (vv 52-53). As the "accuser" is "on the way" these households "from now on" will be torn asunder! (vv 58, 52a). Stiff-necked opposition to his sending is now welling up so ominously that Jesus is becoming engulfed by the "baptism" of death (v 50). That "immersion" in the obdurate "wilderness generation" at the mountain is fomenting inexorably to its eruption. The destiny of this judgment is inescapable; it is becoming all-consuming and explosively real. "How I wish it were already ignited!" (v 49a).[67]

Opposition to Jesus intensifies even as he intensifies his warning to disciples and crowds and puts his "hypocritical adversaries to shame" (13:15, 17). In 13:31-35 Jesus learns that Herod already has a "death warrant" out on his life. Undeterred, he tells these Pharisees in effect that indeed Herod will have his day (cf. 23:6-12), but not until he has journeyed on his divinely ordered sending as a *prophet* to the heart of a stubborn nation (vv 32-33). With this prophet's lament and cry of judgment in vv 34-35, it has become certain that the judgment required of "this generation" for all the murders of Israel's prophets and messengers is due to its killing of the prophet Jesus who forms the "omega point" of this entire history. Luke follows immediately with another instance of "this generation's" determination to trip up Jesus in his Exodus sending (14:1-6 ⟶ 13:31-35 ⟶ 11:53-54). The leaders and their "many" (14:16) are already on the brink of exclusion from the Kingdom banquet which Jesus' journey is inaugurating (esp. vv 15, 17, 21-24). When--at some point later on the journey (cf. 14:25)--the Pharisees scoff at Jesus' talk of crisis and ultimate obedience and the dangers of prestige and wealth, he retorts with a parable mirroring the "many" with its influential leaders who have become so immune to the signs and warnings of the present time that not even the raising up of a prophet from the *dead* can jolt them into repentance (16:14-31). Thus it happens that the solid front of lepers of the Jewish nation (17:11-19) becomes emblematic of what already has become abundantly evident: Jesus "must (δεῖ) *suffer* many things and be rejected by *this* generation" (17:25). Jesus must die.

At 18:31-34 Jesus informs the "Twelve" that the imminent journey "up to Jerusalem" will bring to fruition everything written about him by the prophets. But "this generation" remains obtuse (18:34; cf. 9:44b). With the monolithic house of "scorn" in place (19:7, πάντες;cf. vv 14, 20-27, 39-40, 44b), it is not long once Jesus has entered the Temple that forces of opposition are set in motion. Representatives of each of the three functionary groups of the Sanhedrin are actively *plotting* to kill Jesus (19:47). And with Luke's mention of the "scribes" (γραμματεῖς, v 47) we encounter once again the Pharisees-scribes whom Jesus had arraigned *at table* as leaders of the *laos* and whom he will again so indict (11:43-46 ⟶ 14:7-11 ⟶ 20:45-47; cf. 20:19-20, 39-40).[68] But just when these plotters again loom into the picture (22:2), the story takes what must surely be a most ironic twist. Judas, one of the *"Twelve"* (22:3), makes the decisive move to "deliver" Jesus over to the scribes and chief priests

---

[67]Cf. Marshall (*Gospel*, 547) in noting the relation between the coming fire of judgment upon the world and Jesus' "baptism" of death: "His baptism is the pre-condition for what is to follow."

[68]As in 20:47 it is the *Pharisees'* scribes of 11:47-52 who will receive the "greater condemnation" for their detrimental influence upon the people; *pace* J. A. Ziesler, "Luke and the Pharisees," *NTS* 25 (1978-79) 146-57.

(cf. 22:48). What Jesus had forecast to the "wilderness generation" at the base of the mountain (9:44) and disclosed privately to the Twelve (18:32) is now consummated by one from this innermost band of followers[69] (παραδίδωμι, 22:48 ⟶ 22:3 ⟶ 18:32 ⟶ 9:44). Instead of Jesus the accuser handing the crowds over to the judge (12:57-59), one of his own disciples will hand him over to the judges of the Sanhedrin!

And yet Luke has prepared his readers for this development. Already at the mountain the disciples had demonstrated their solidarity with the generation of "men" into whose hands Jesus is to be delivered over to death (9:44). And on the journey they had certainly fared no better! Now as Jesus prepares to eat the Passover meal as an anticipation of his *suffering* (22:15; cf. 17:25; 9:22), the *hands of this generation* are once again with him *at table* (22:22a ⟶ 14:1 ⟶ 11:53-54; cf. 9:44). *"Woe* to that man by whom he is delivered over" (22:22b ⟶ 11:42-52!). Even as Jesus again declares that his death must take place according to the will of God (22:22a ⟶ 9:44-45), so the disciples again begin to argue which of them is the greatest! (22:24-27 ⟶ 9:46-48). That they could quarrel over their own importance in the pall of Jesus' death can only serve here to seal their incorporation with the "wilderness generation" whose leaders are epitomized by their *striving for rank at table* (11:43; 14:7-11; 20:46). Not only this, but when Peter of the mountain triad is told that he is going to deny that he even "knows" his master, he protests that he is *ready* to go with Jesus to prison and death--again, "not knowing what he was saying" (22:33-34; cf. vv 54-62; 9:33b).

Again Luke moves at a quick pace. While *praying* on the mountain (Olivet) Jesus comes over to his disciples to discover that instead of "alert" and "ready" (22:33 ⟶ 12:37, 40), they are *sleeping!* (22:45-46 ⟶ 9:32). Suddenly the band of chief priests, Temple police, and elders of the people--led by one of the *Twelve*--descends upon Jesus to spirit him away to the house of the high priest. Only Peter follows at a distance, soon to deny his "Lord" *three times* (22:54-62). The assembly of the leaders of the people then condemn Jesus for claiming to be the *"Son* of God," thereby acknowledging negatively what the voice on the mountain had already declared (22:70-71 ⟶ 9:35), and lead him before Pilate where they accuse him of perverting the people and of threatening Caesar through his own royal aspirations (23:1-5). With that, Pilate sends Jesus to the nation's king who, now "seeing" Jesus (23:8 ⟶ 9:9), joins his soldiers in mocking this "Christ" (23:11; cf. 9:20). Jesus is then shuttled back to Pilate to stand one final time before the crowd, now called interestingly enough, "the people" (ὁ λαός), who in turn stand with their leaders and the chief priests (23:13). The whole nation is assembled! The people, their leaders, their priests, their king, their Gentile governor of the kings of the nations (22:25) all condemn Jesus to death. *Three times* Pilate tries to persuade release of Jesus; but each time it falls on the deaf ears of a nation that is unrelenting to the end: "For they all cried out together, away with this man. . . . Crucify him, crucify him. . . . And they were urgent . . . and their voices prevailed" (23:18, 21, 23). At last Pilate *delivers* him over (παραδίδωμι, 23:25 ⟶ 18:32 ⟶ 9:44) to their will. "This generation" has spoken; Jesus must die.

Luke then recites the drama of the "wilderness generation" at the mountain. One by one in a mounting suspense of stubborn resistance and twisted treachery the "hands of men" link to form the monolith of the Exodus people that forces the death of the prophet Jesus in Jerusalem. It is indeed a "faithless and crooked generation" (9:41). And while it has become obvious that the external circumstances, kind of cooperation, and immediate causes of Jesus' death are anything but parallel to Moses' death in Deuteronomy, nevertheless the *theological* explanation of the basis or cause of their deaths is the same:[70] *because of* the intransigent disobedience of the people to the voice of God in his

---

[69]On the disciples' involvement, see esp. P. S. Minear, "A Note of Luke xxii 36," *NovT* 7 (1964-65) 128-34.

[70]Curiously, even the *plotted* portrait of this calling is similar. As later generations of Deuteronomists impressed the passion of Moses as the signet for the whole

messenger-prophet, God has determined that Moses/Jesus *must die*. It is only in the light of this perspective that the curious juxtaposition in the Acts of the *accusations* against the entire nation with the *pronouncements* of the *necessity* of God's foreordained plan in the Scriptures can be clarified (2:23--23a, 31; 3:13b-15--18, 20-24; 4:10--11; 25b-27--25a, 28; 7:51-52a--52b; 10:39b--42-43; 13:28--27, 29; cf. 5:35-39). As Peter crisply states 2:23, "Men of Israel . . . this Jesus, delivered up according to the determined plan and foreknowledge of God, *you* crucified and killed through the hands of lawless men"; or e.g. "*you* killed the author of life whom God raised from the dead. . . . Moses said, 'The Lord your God will raise up for you a prophet like me from among your brethren" (3:15a--22a, quoting Deut 18:15a).

(iv) It is only Luke of the Synoptists who links the figure of a *child directly* to the *mountain revelation* (9:47-48). Only the *childlike* can heed the "voice" of the mountain and "receive" this Jesus who has been *sent* by God *from the mountain* (v 48). Already in 9:23-25 Jesus had set forth the indispensable conditions of this receiving, or of this following him on his exodus to Jerusalem. One must deny himself, take up his cross daily and follow him (v 23); for the one who wishes to "save" his life will in fact lose it (v 24a). Now what we find in 9:46-47 are the disciples trying desperately to "save" their lives, promoting instead of denying themselves. With the *child* at *his* side, Jesus says in essence that such behavior can only lead to destruction of life as it stifles the life-giving liberation of the Prophet's exodus to death and exaltation. That is precisely why the "anonymous exorcist" (vv 49-50) is *for* (ὑπέρ) the disciples since his *childlike* submission is a powerful promotion for the following Jesus demands.

It is the case with this fourth line of the typology as well that it functions as a constitutive principle for the rest of Luke's story in his Gospel. For side by side with the ever-growing monolith of resistance Luke counterposes a steadily increasing stream of "Wisdom's" (cf. 7:35) or "Abraham's" (cf. 13:16, 28; 16:22; 19:10) *children* who for a time, in submitting to Jesus' authority, do crack the monolith into the divided house of Israel (cf. 12:51-53). Already in contrast to the mission of the Twelve and especially to the behavior of the disciples on the mountain and with the Samaritan village, our author describes the return of the Seventy(-two) messengers in tones strikingly reminiscent of the "anonymous exorcist" (9:49-50). Like he, they evince the *authority* to cast out *demons* (δαιμόνια, 9:49--10:17) *in your* (Jesus') *name* (ἐν τῷ ὀνόματί σου 9:49-- 10:17) and thus are likened by Jesus to the *submission of the child* (παιδίον, 9:47-48; νήπιοι, 10:21). Immediately the story of the "*wise* and *learned*" lawyer follows as a foil to the *childlike* Samaritan who illustrates what submission to Jesus the teacher entails with respect to "the Lord your God" and "your neighbor" (10:25-37; esp. vv 25, 27).

As he presses onward (cf. 10:38; 13:22), women (10:39; 13:10-17), the crippled and infirm (13:10-17, 32; 14:1-6, 21), tax collectors and "sinners" (15:1-2; cf. vv 3-32; 16:19-31), and "foreigners" (17:11-19; cf. 13:29; 14:23) all display the childlike reception of Jesus which is tantamount to the flow of Abraham, Isaac, and Jacob and all the prophets into the Kingdom of god (13:22-30; esp. v 28). It is therefore in the midst of this current that Jesus' "woe" to the disciples against the "falling away" of "these little ones" (τῶν μικρῶν τούτων, 17:2b) in 17:1-3a is to be felt. With Luke's use of οὗτοι, these "little ones" are most probably pictured right in the midst of the disciples.[71] Either

---

(1:9, 12; 1:37; 3:25-28; 4:21-22), so Luke posits premonitions of the deadly resistance to come (2:34-35; 4:16-30; 5:35; 6:16). And in both, notices of Moses'/Jesus' suffering and death are concentrated before and after the giving of the Law/eschatological *halakoth* (Deut 1:37; 3:25-28; 4:21-22; 9:18-21, 25-29; 10:10; 31:2, 14, 23; 32:48-52; 34:4--Luke 9:22, 23-25, 31, 41, 43b-45, 51; 18:31-34; 19:47; 20:9-18, 19, 20, 26; but cf. 12:49-50; 13:31-33; 17:25). Consequently in Luke as in Deuteronomy, the *necessity* of Moses'/Jesus' suffering and death is first adumbrated and then announced in advance of the fuller mountain manifestation of the monolithic disobedience.

[71] Marshall, *Gospel*, 641.

literal children, or more probably the "poor" and "outcast," i.e., the "least" in society, are signified here, especially since Luke has thrust a constant parade of these "weak" and "powerless" before his readers' eyes from 14:1 (viz. 14:1-6, 21-24; 15:1-32; 16:19-31). Once again the symbol of the *child in their midst* (9:46-48) is a palpable warning of the response required to receive the life in their midst. As we have already seen, the disciples now are facing the gravest danger of succumbing to the hindering leaven of hypocrisy. They must "take heed to yourselves" lest their inflated image destroy the servant status to which Jesus has called them (17:7-10 —→ 9:46, 49-50; cf. 17:3b-4, 5-6; 12:41-48). "For the one who is *the least* (ὁ μικρότερος) *among you all*, he it is who is great" (9:48b).

With the two countermovements continuing to crescendo (cf. 17:11-19, 20-21, 22-18:8), Jesus points a parable to "some who were confident in themselves that they were righteous, while snubbing others" (18:9-14). Whereupon the *disciples* "look down" upon *children* coming to Jesus (18:15) in a manner frightfully familiar in the Pharisee's disdain for the "sinner" tax collector in vv 9-14, esp. v 11. As in 9:46-48 Jesus places the children (παιδία) by his side and chides the disciples for *hindering* them: "for of *such is* the Kingdom of God. Truly I say to you, whoever does not *receive* the Kingdom of God *like a child* (ὡς παιδίον) cannot enter into it" (18:16-17).

Jesus' approach to Israel's center is marked by a childlike following--of the *blind* who "sees" (18:35)[72] and of a "sinner" tax collector, "small of stature," who repents (19:3, 8)--against the backdrop of the "citizens" who "do not want this man to reign over us" (19:14).[73] Jesus exclaims that *salvation* has come to these children of Abraham *today* (19:10; 18:42b); but as for that mass of rebellion, when the journeying king returns, "Bring them here and slay them before me" (19:27b). Jesus is then heralded as *king* by the great company of disciples who were looking for the Kingdom of God to *appear* straightaway as Jesus strides "triumphantly" into Jerusalem (cf. 19:11, 34-40). The people are electric with expectation as he teaches in the Temple with an uncanny authority (19:48b; 20:19, 26, 40; 21:38; cf. 18:43b). Yet in spite of all this, Jesus strikes an entirely contrary pitch by warning of *doom* and *destruction*; the people are to "watch" and "pray" unceasingly, lest through "carousing and drunkenness" they fall into the eschatological crisis that will come upon them suddenly like a snare (21:8-36). "Truly I say to you, *this generation* will not pass away until all has taken place!" (v 32). At the Passover table Jesus again interjects a sombre note into an atmosphere charged with anticipation of great and glorious things! (22:15, 21-23, 24). Once again he must resort to the image of the *child* to fight the disciples' misguided vanity. And yet again his words fall on deaf ears. Not even his warning of "Satan's sifting" of Peter (and the others, ὑμᾶς, v 31) pierces the veil of a proud generation that is slow to believe and hearken, a people that will take its "teacher" to the cross.

The events that follow are now well known. The *laos* of the "wilderness generation" (9:13b) consolidate behind their leaders to execute a false prophet who was to have "redeemed" Israel (cf. 24:19-21). Thus even as the innocent children of Mt. Horeb were later to blend into the crooked generation of their fathers to necessitate the death of Moses at the end of the Exodus journey, so now even the "children" of Jesus' Exodus journey are incorporated into "this generation" of the people of Israel to compel Jesus' death at the end. Once the period of the Acts begins, Luke will no longer distinguish various groups like tax collectors and sinners, Pharisees, lawyers, etc. but speak rather of the "men of Israel" (e.g. 2:29) or "peoples of Israel" (4:27) or "this crooked generation" (2:40). And though he underscores the leaders' role in both volumes[74] and describes a

---

[72]The "blind" man *follows* in contrast to the "rich" man (18:18-30) who cannot.

[73]The *journeying* "nobleman" in 19:12-14 mirrors Jesus' journey "to receive a kingdom" (v. 12): 9:51 —→ 22:69.

[74]Luke 6:7, 11; 7:30; 9:22; 11:47-12:1; 16:14; 19:47; 20:19, 26, 40; 22:2, 4, 52; 23:6-12, 51; 24:20; Acts 4:10; cf. 4:27.

childlike submission by a "lawless one" even as Jesus hangs alongside him as one "reckoned with the lawless," (22:37; 23:42), yet the spectacle before Pilate and the accusations against the people in the Acts make it clear that in Luke's presentation the *whole generation* has coalesced into an obdurate folk that demands Jesus' death. Like Moses, Jesus must die.

But the story of this Prophet like Moses is not at an end. Just as through Moses' death the "children" of the first Exodus *do* enter the land of the promised deliverance, so now through Jesus' death the "children" of the New Exodus enter the life of the *fulfilled* deliverance of the covenant of Abraham (Acts 3:18, 24-25). Though the people like their forerunners hundreds of years earlier acted in "ignorance" (Acts 3:17--Deut 29:4; 32:28-29; cf. 4:6; 11:2), yet they now have the unprecedented opportunity to have their sins "blotted out" and to receive "times of respite" from the judgment of God which come from the "presence of the Lord" (3:17, 19b-20a). For now Peter dares to announce the fulfillment of Moses' words in Deut 18:15-19 and to assert unabashedly, "And it shall be that every one who does not *hearken* to that prophet will be destroyed from the people" (3:23). Once again only those who submit to this voice will receive the life which now flows through the powerful presence of the "name"[75] (3:16, 6). And now it is the command of this Prophet like Moses "to repent and turn around" (3:19a), that the people may at last be delivered from the monolith of *evil* (πονηρία, 3:26--Deut 4:25; 9:18; 28:20; 31:29) of a froward generation. *Those days*[76] proclaimed by "Moses" (3:22-23) and "all the prophets" (v 24) have--finally--come to their fulfillment.

In keeping with the Deuteronomic Exodus typology it is significant that Luke places Peter's speech in Acts 3 in the midst of the blessings of the covenant to the fathers now perceived to fulfill the description of life in the "land" à la Deut 30:1-10. Moses had predicted that this stubborn people would be punished and would later be restored to the land with even greater blessing[77] (e.g. 28:36-38, 63-68; 29:28). Now in Acts 2-5: (a) The *gathering* of the dispersed people of Israel from all the corners of the earth in Deut 30:1b, 3b-5 is beginning to be fulfilled at the Feast of First Fruits (Pentecost) in Jerusalem (2:5-12). It is primarily from this group that the first "believers" are drawn (2:14-41; cf. 3:11); (b) The "crooked" hearts (2:40) of the Horeb covenant people are "cleansed" through the baptism of the Holy Spirit as they turn and repent and thus fulfill (LXX) Deut 30:6a (1:5; 2:1-4, 37-41; cf. 3:19, 26); (c) Those whose hearts are purged hearken to the preaching of the apostles to bring about the obedience to the voice of the Lord as Moses envisions in Deut 30:2, 8, 10 (2:37, 41-42; 4:4; 5:25-26, 32; cf. 3:21-24); (d) The sins of this young community are "released" or "removed" (ἄφεσις) in the sense that their ill effects are "cured" or "counteracted" (ἰάομαι) according to the prediction of (LXX) Deut 30:3a (2:38; 5:31; cf. 3:19, 26); and (e) The "singleness" or "oneness" of "heart and soul" that characterizes the restored covenant community fulfills Moses' prophecy of the *oneness* or *wholeness* of heart devoted to the Lord in Deut 30:2, 6, 10 (4:32; cf. 2:42, 44). Now all of these points are fittingly summed up in the *eating* and *rejoicing* "before the Lord" by the young "First Fruits" community: "Day by day, attending the Temple together and breaking bread in their households, they partook of food, full of joy and with a singleness of heart, praising God and finding favor with the whole people" (2:46-47a). Here at last the crowning of the first Exodus in Deuteronomy in the eating and rejoicing at the central place "before the Lord" (Deut 26:1-11) finds its full fruition in the eschatological jubilation of the New Exodus life.

---

[75]Cf. the presence of the Lord in His "name" in Deuteronomy, e.g. 12:5, 11, 21; 14:23-24; 16:2, 6, 11; 18:5, 7, 19-20!; 21:5; 26:2.

[76]Cf. Luke 9:51-"the days of his taking up."

[77]Though not termed a "New Exodus," the return is both a restoration and a consummation of the first Exodus; and in 28:68 the people will *again* be enslaved in Egypt.

III

We shall now mention briefly several additional points in Peter's speech in Acts 3 which cohere with the Deuteronomic Exodus-New Exodus typology and thus enhance the portrait of Jesus' *death* that we have presented above:

(1) It is curious what little reference is made in 3:12-26 to the *resurrection*. Only in v 15b does Peter state that "God raised him [i.e. "the author of life"] from the dead," while v 13a speaks of Jesus' "glorification." In both verses the divine action *reverses* the *result* of the action of the people, viz. "delivering up," "denying," and "killing" God's "servant," "the Holy and Just one" (v 14), and "the author/pioneer of life." Because of this reversal the one who was dead is now alive again and therefore, as one vindicated by God, present to infuse life into the body of the lame man (vv 1-12). There is no indication whatever that this raising up from the dead itself releases the people from the guilt and consequent punishment for the death of this *innocent* man Jesus (cf."holy and just," v 14; Pilate wanted to release him, v 13b; a "murderer" instead was released, v 14b);

(2) The *people's* guilt, in fact, is stressed in vv 13, 14, 15, 17, and 19. In v 19 this guilt is explicitly acknowledged as still in *effect* by virtue of the call to "repent" and "turn around" "with the *result* that" (εἰς . . . ὅπως ἄν, vv 19, 20a). As is well known, the dominant idea in the Judaism of Jesus' day was that only when acknowledgment/confession of sin accompanied a sacrifice, or when a confession of guilt preceded the death of a criminal/Law breaker, did the sacrifice/death effect atonement.[78] By the conjunction of v 18--Jesus' *suffering* (i.e. death)--with v 19 (οὖν), it is now certain that the call to repentance is coupled to the guilt of the *death* of Jesus.[79] That is to say, without this repentance the "blotting out of sin" and "times of respite/reprieve" (vv 19-20) would not become effective in the lives of the hearers, as v 23 reiterates. The idea is all but explicitly uttered that 'by virtue of'/'by means of' Jesus' death this removal/forgiveness of sin (v 19) coupled with the *eschatological* fulfillment of salvation (v 20) is *now* a reality and available to the hearers;

(3) This understanding of Jesus' death is supported further by v 26 where the *purpose* of the first sending of Jesus, God's "servant," is to "bless you by turning each of you from your evil." The following progression in thought is summed up in this verse: (i) A potent power of *blessing* is now (cf. pres. εὐλογοῦντα) in force (v 26b; εὐλογέω here resonates with the *blessing* (εὐλογηθήσονται) that was to be fulfilled as the raison d'être of the "covenant" to "Abraham" and "your fathers"[80] (v 25); (ii) This promise of blessing has already been *fulfilled* in Jesus, God's servant (v 26), since: (a) "The God of Abraham and Isaac and Jacob . . . and of our fathers" has *already* "glorified"/"exalted" His servant (v 13a); (b) "*You* are the sons of the prophets and of the covenant" (v 25a), and this God has already sent His servant to "*you first*" with this blessing (v 26); (c) This sending was long ago foretold by "all of the prophets, from Samuel onward, who spoke and proclaimed *these* days" (v 24). "These days" are linked both forward to the "sons of the prophets" of v 25a (sc. sons of those prophets of v 24) and backward by the copula (καί) at the beginning of v 24 to the *first* prophet, viz. Moses, who predicted the "prophet like me" (vv 22-23). It is clear, therefore, that God's servant who has already been sent in v 26 is also the fulfillment of the *prophet like Moses*; (iii) Hence it follows that the *primary referent* of the "raising" (ἀναστήσας) in v 26 is to the ἀναστήσει of

---

[78]See e.g. E. Lohse, *Märtyrer und Gottesknecht* (FRLANT 46; Göttingen: Vandenhoeck & Ruprecht, 1955) 25-29.

[79]See e.g. G. Stählin, *Die Apostelgeschichte* (NTD 2; Göttingen: Vandenhoeck & Ruprecht, 1963) 66.

[80]Recall the importance of this expectation in Deuteronomy; see the beginning of Part I above.

v 22, sc. to the prophet's calling and life, and not to the "raising up from the dead."[81] This interpretation harmonizes perfectly with the usual sense of the aorist participle in tandem with the aorist verb as *preceding* in time/sequence. Consequently, Jesus' mission to Israel was to "turn away" the people from their (collective) *evil*, and this mission is still in effect in the blessing available to the hearers in the present; (iv) Since v 26 sums up the fulfillment of the covenant and the prophets, it is significant that the *only* event within the mission of Jesus foretold by these prophets which is *explicitly* said to be *fulfilled* (ἐπλήρωσεν) is the *suffering* (death) of God's Christ in v 18. As we have already seen that the reference to "ignorance" in v 17 does not remove their guilt and its consequences (v 19), this means that the only aspect of this mission which is singled out and tied, on the one side, to the cause for repentance (vv 18-19), and, on the other side, to the active power available to remove the cause of this guilt (i.e., "your evil"), is Jesus' *death*;

(4) In light of nos. (1)-(3) above the heavy concentration of accusation against the people in vv 13b-15, 17 followed immediately by the *offer* of forgiveness and eschatological rest from judgment in vv 19-20 takes on added importance. Between these two realities of guilt and release stands the *pivot* verse 18--the *death* of "the Christ." And this fulfillment is depicted in v 26 as an energetic power of blessing, not simply as an attitude or subjective mindset of God. In other words, God in His graciousness has *not* simply overlooked the "tragic" and "ignorant" mistake of the Jewish people;[82] the event of dying was integral to the breakup of the corporate evil (v 26). "You killed . . . that your sins may be blotted out . . . to bless you!";

(5) In contrast to Jesus' warnings and pronouncements of judgment upon the *whole* nation which we traced in the journey and the Temple teaching, there is no such blanket condemnation here. The "times of respite" are already available; the *power* to turn from the monolithic evil has already been unleashed. The *evil* and *crooked* generation of Luke 11:29 and Acts 2:40 has been broken apart by the repentance/faith of 3000 people of Israel from all over the world (2:5-12, 41; cf. 4:4; 5:14). Now the proclamation is that the unrepentant *individual* will be cut off *from* the *people* (3:23). And through most of the remainder of Acts the final judgment denotes the universal assize of the living and the dead (e.g., 10:42; 17:31; 24:15, 25; cf. 2:20). Only at the end in 28:25b-28 do the ominous tones of blanket denunciation revive the threat of a general destruction of Israel which Jesus had pronounced (but cf. Acts 7:51-53; 13:41). When this observation is joined to the intrinsic relation between Jesus' baptism of *death* and the *judgment* of the nation in Luke 12:49-53 that we delineated above,[83] then here is one more indication that the "divine must" of Jesus' *death* is central to the removal of the divine judgment hanging over the "stiff-necked" nation.[84]

To conclude, in the last two-thirds of his Gospel and at the beginning of the Acts Luke portrays a Jesus who, like Moses, *must die* to effect deliverance for his people. But

---

[81]As E. Haenchen (*The Acts of the Apostles* [Oxford: Blackwell, 1971] 210), F. F. Bruce (*The Book of the Acts* [NICNT; Grand Rapids: W. B. Eerdmans, 1954] 94), and Stählin (*Apostelgeschichte*, 69) also maintain; cf. also 13:33. It is very unlikely that the *aorist* "sent" (ἀπέστειλεν) of v 26 refers to the present sending of the risen Christ through the apostles since v 20 speaks of a *future* sending (ἀποστείλη) at the "consummation of all things" which *follows* (ἄχρι) the *present* "receiving" of "Christ Jesus" by or in "heaven" (v 21); *pace* G. Schneider, *Die Apostelgeschichte*, I. Teil (HTKNT 5; Freiburg: Herder, 1980) 330.

[82]E.G. Vielhauer, "Paulinism," 45.

[83]See (iii) in Part II.

[84]Note how Jesus' identity/solidarity with *sinners* reinforces this connection: e.g. Luke 3:15-17, 21-22; 5:27-39; 7:36-50; 13:10-17; 15:1-32; 19:1-10; 22:39-46; 23:39-43.

now this *divine must* is fulfilled in the eschatological *Prophet like Moses* whose death, consummating Moses and all the prophets, delivers the people at last from the stiff-necked monolith of the "wilderness generation."   "For this means life to you" (Deut 30:20b).

THE APOCALYPSE OF ABRAHAM
AND THE DESTRUCTION OF THE SECOND JEWISH TEMPLE

James R. Mueller
North Carolina State University

I

Calling to mind previous destructions, and subsequent renewals, of the Temple, the devastation visited upon the Second Temple in 70 C.E. changed forever the directions Judaism would take. Although one "direction" came to predominate in later years, especially after the failure of the Bar Kokhba revolt, the period immediately following the burning of the Jerusalem Temple witnessed a profusion of responses.[1] The authors of the age were confronted with the classic questions of theodicy and covenant.[2] How could God permit his people to suffer such a radical disconfirmation; how could he allow the wicked to dominate and enslave those people with whom he had covenanted?

The post-70 apocalypses tackle these related issues using a variety of styles, forms, questions, and answers.[3] While all the authors assume that salvation will ultimately derive from an intervention by God, or his agent, who will initiate a new era of justice, each seer also plots a course for the present and immediate future. This present is seen as a time of decision for the reader: "Both the temporal eschatology and the otherworldly revelation provide a framework which sets the present time and place of humanity in urgent relief. All the apocalypses are therefore hortatory in purpose, whether this purpose is expressed explicitly or not."[4] As such each apocalypse, even though it may share the eschatological outlook of its contemporaries, does not recommend the same course of action as every other apocalypse.[5] The reader must

---

[1]For a full discussion of the period, see E. Schürer, *The History of the Jewish People in the Age of Jesus Christ* (new English version rev. and ed. by G. Vermes and F. Millar; Edinburgh, 1973) see esp. pp. 484-557; and the other standard works too numerous to catalog here. For a combination historical and literary introduction to the period, cf. G. W. E. Nickelsburg, *Jewish Literature Between the Bible and the Mishnah* (Philadelphia, 1981) pp. 277-309.

[2]See in this regard the recent article by M. E. Stone, "Reactions to Destructions of the Second Temple," *JSJ* 12 (1982) 195-204. Stone concentrates on the two major apocalyptic responses to the destruction, 4 Ezra and 2 Baruch. Also see the recent work of J. Neusner, esp. his discussion of late first-century "apocalyptic response" to the destruction in "Judaism in a Time of Crisis: Four Responses to the Destruction of the Second Temple," *Judaism* (in press) pp. 313-27 (esp. pp. 315-17); and idem, "The Mishnah in Context: Ways Not Taken," *Judaism: The Evidence of the Mishnah* (Chicago, 1981) pp. 25-44 (esp. pp. 28-37).

[3]This variety is evident in the collected essays *Apocalypse: The Morphology of a Genre*, ed. J. J. Collins; *Semeia* 14 (1979). See especially, "Introduction: Towards the Morphology of a Genre," and "Jewish Apocalypses," both by J. J. Collins, pp. 1-59; as well as in J. H. Charlesworth, *The Pseudepigrapha and Modern Research with a Supplement* (SCS 7S; Chico, CA, 1981); and hopefully in the near future, in idem, ed. *The Old Testament Pseudepigrapha* (Garden City, NY, in press).

[4]Collins, *Semeia* 14 (1979) 26.

[5]I am indebted here to the work of B. McGinn, *Visions of the End: Apocalyptic Traditions in the Middle Ages* (Records of Civilization 96; New York, 1979); and idem, *Apocalyptic Spirituality* (The Classics of Western Spirituality; New York, 1979). McGinn, responding to the thesis of N. Cohn (somewhat muted in the revised version of his *The Pursuit of the Millennium* [New York, 1970]) that apocalyptic literature is basically "protorevolutionary," contends: "it is possible to specify broad ways in which the

make a decision for or against the hortatory demands of the individual author. Couched in the visions, dialogues, and exhortations each author signals those actions and commitments required of the reader which will enable that reader to be assured of a place in the glorious future.[6] Thus each author, while essentially negative in his world-view, maintains a somewhat more positive view of his audience's capability to assure their own place in the future redemption to be offered by God in the new age.[7] The purpose of this paper is to examine the Apocalypse of Abraham in terms of its demands on the audience, but first a few preliminary remarks on the work itself are in order.

II

Perhaps the least studied of the apocalypses dated to the time between the two Jewish Revolts against Rome,[8] the Apocalypse of Abraham is usually dealt with as two distincly different legendary accounts of the patriarch.[9] The first part (chapters 1-8) deals with Abraham's rejection of the idol-worship of his father and his search for and acceptance of the "true God" (7:11):

---

rhetoric of apocalypticism has been used in support of the political and social order. The two most fundamental approaches during our period might be described as the *a priori* and the *a posteriori*: the one making use of the already established apocalyptic scenario to interpret current events and thus to move men to decision and action, the other reacting to political and social change by expanding the scenario to include transcendentalized versions of recent events, thus giving final validation to the present by making a place for it at the End" (*Visions,* p. 33).

[6]For an example of this line of thinking see the works cited in the previous note, and my "A Prolegomenon to the Study of the Social Function of 4 Ezra," *SBL 1981 Seminar Papers* (ed. K. H. Richards; Chico, CA: Scholars Press, 1981) pp. 259-68; and H. C. Kee, " 'The Man' in Fourth Ezra: Growth of a Tradition," *SBL 1981 Seminar Papers,* pp. 199-208: "Rather than merely transmitting tradition, the apocalypticist characteristically adapts and transforms the tradition on which his life-world is built, in order to demonstrate its relevance to the time and circumstances of his own community" (Kee, p. 199).

[7]As such the paranesis found in the apocalyptic writings serves a "pastoral" function for the author's present. The author seeks to align himself with what he deigns to be the proper course of action required by the new situation (in our case the destruction of the Temple) in light of the envisioned future redemption. He also condemns those actions or actors that precipitated the crisis now facing the community. Cf. J. J. Collins, "The Apocalyptic Technique: Setting and Function in the Book of the Watchers," *CBQ* 44 (1982) 91-111.

[8]A quick glance at the bibliographical studies of the Pseudepigrapha by G. Delling, *Bibliographie zur jüdisch-hellenistischen und Intertestamentarischen Literatur 1900-1970* (TU 106[2]; Berlin, 1970[2]); and J. H. Charlesworth, *The Pseudepigrapha and Modern Research;* shows a ratio of 116:51:25 in the number of studies on 4 Ezra, 2 Baruch, and the Apocalypse of Abraham, respectively.

[9]R. Rubinkiewicz has proposed instead of the two-fold structure, a seven-fold schema. See his "La vision de l'histoire dans l'Apocalypse d'Abraham," *Aufstieg und Niedergang der römischen Welt* (eds. W. Haase and H. Temporini; Berlin/New York, 1979) II. 19. 1, pp. 137-51; and idem, *L'Apocalypse d'Abraham (en slave). Edition critique du texte, introduction, traduction et commentaire* (Diss. Pontifical Biblical Institute; Rome, 1977).

You are searching for the God of gods, the Creator, in the understanding of your heart. I am he. Go out from Terah, your father, and go out of the house, that you too may not be slain in the sins of your father's house. (8:3f.)[10]

The episode concludes with the utter destruction of the house of Terah. The second, more extensive section is an extended midrash on the sacrifice offered by Abraham in Genesis 15.[11]

Why has so little attention been given to this Apocalypse? Three reasons are immediately evident: (1) the document is preserved only in Slavonic, a language few experts of intertestamental literature are comfortable with;[12] (2) the Slavonic versions owe their preservation to the medieval dualist Bogomils, who adopted and adapted the pseudepigraphon;[13] and (3) the possibility that the document is not early and Jewish, and does not represent a late first-century reaction to the destruction of the Temple.[14] The first two reasons require little or no discussion, but will be taken into account in our discussion of the third reason given: the problem of the date of the pseudepigraphon. Can we with any degree of certainty date the Apocalypse of Abraham to the decades following the First Revolt, and thus use the document as a witness to the social and religious life in the aftermath of the destruction of the Temple?

III

Any discussion of date must move carefully along three lines: the external evidence, the internal evidence, and the evidence of a shared *Zeitgeist*. By "shared

---

[10]Translations from the Apocalypse of Abraham, unless otherwise specified, are taken from the translation of R. Rubinkiewicz, revised by H. G. Lunt, which will appear in the forthcoming *Old Testament Pseudepigrapha*.

[11]For a more complete summary of the contents of the Apocalypse, see Nickelsburg, *Jewish Literature*, pp. 294-99; L. Ginzberg, "Abraham, Apocalypse of," *JE*, vol. 1, pp. 91f.; or J. Licht, "Abraham, Apocalypse of," *EncJud* vol. 2, cols. 125-27.

[12]Because I have not been able to work with the Slavonic versions of the text, the work presented herein must be considered provisional. I have worked with the modern language translations currently available: G. H. Box-J. I. Landsman, *The Apocalypse of Abraham* (London, 1919); G. N. Bonwetsch, *Die Apokalypse Abrahams. Das Testament der vier-Märtyrer* (Studien zur Geschichte der Theologie und der Kirche 1; Leipzig, 1897); P. Riessler, *Altjüdisches Schrifttum ausserhalb der Bibel* (Augsburg, 1928); and Rubinkiewicz, rev. by H. G. Lunt, *The Old Testament Pseudepigrapha*. A French translation and commentary by M. Philonenko should be available in the near future. For a discussion of the Slavonic manuscripts, see the works cited above, plus E. Turdeanu, "L'*Apocalypse d'Abraham* en slave," *JSJ* 3 (1972) 153-80.

[13]"Succinctly put, it is abundantly clear that the Bogomils inherited some Jewish apocryphal documents and that they created new apocryphal writings; on the one hand, the Bogomils were created by some of the pseudepigrapha; on the other, they created new ones." J. H. Charlesworth, "Christian and Jewish Self-Definition in Light of the Christian Additions to the Apocryphal Writings," *Jewish and Christian Self-Definition* (ed. E. P. Sanders, with A. I. Baumgarten and A. Mendelson; Philadelphia, 1981) vol. 2, p. 29. While most commentators agree that 29:3-13 is a later, Christian interpolation (R. Meyer, "Abraham-Apokalypse," *RGG*[3] vol. 1, col. 72; J. B. Frey, "Abraham, (Apocalypse d')," *DBSup* vol. 1, col. 31; Ginzberg, *JE* vol. 1, p. 92; Licht, *EncJud* vol. 2, cols. 126f.; Rubinkiewicz, *ANRW* II. 19. 1, pp. 139-44; et al.), there is a general uncertainty about the presence of interpolations in other parts of the document. Rubinkiewicz (*ANRW* II. 19. 1, pp. 139-44) isolates several glosses, notably all of chapter 7, and sections of chapters 10, 18, and 23.

[14]Cf. the previous note.

Zeitgeist" I mean the witness, not necessarily of literary dependence, but of shared concerns. As such this line of evidence is probably the weakest link in the argument, but when coupled with the external and internal evidence, I hope to demonstrate that the Apocalypse of Abraham fits into the same time period as the Syriac Apocalypse of Baruch and 4 Ezra.

The external evidence for dating the Apocalypse is scant and elusive. The stichometry of Nicephorus (806-815) mentions a book of "Abraham," but the 300 lines attributed to it make it unlikely that the reference is to the Apocalypse.[15] An "Apocalypse of Abraham" is mentioned by Epiphanius (*Haer.* 39.15) which is ascribed to the Sethians, but little is known of its contents except that Epiphanius declares it to be "full of all wickedness."[16] Origen quotes from an "Apocalypse of Abraham" (*In Lucam,* homily 35), but this is surely not from our Apocalypse.[17] Lastly, two passages in the Pseudo-Clementines relate traditions about the patriarch: (1) Abraham as an astrologer (*Recognitiones,* Book 1, 32:3f.), and (2) Abraham as the recipient of visions of the divine, of the beginning, and of the end of the world (*Recognitiones,* Book 1, 33:1f.). The second tradition reads as follows:

> Therefore Abraham, when he was desirous to learn the causes of things, and was intently pondering on what had been told him, the true Prophet appeared to him, who alone knows the hearts and purpose of men, and disclosed to him all things which he desired. He taught him the knowledge of the Divinity; intimated the origin of the world, and likewise its end; showed him the immortality of the soul, and the manner of life which was pleasing to God; declared also the resurrection of the dead, the future judgment, the reward of the good, the punishment of the evil,-- all to be regulated by righteous judgment: and having given him all this information plainly and sufficiently, He departed again to the invisible abodes.[18]

This passage relates revelations given to Abraham which are highly reminiscent of the Apocalypse, and yet the imprecise language does not permit a strict identification of the source used by the author.[19] The external evidence, therefore, is not conclusive with

---

[15]Nicephorus (PG 100, col. 1059). Ginzberg has suggested that if the first eight chapters (the legend of Abraham's conversion from idolatry) and the unspecified gnostic and Christian interpolations were removed "only about three hundred lines would remain" (*JE* vol. 1, p. 92), but the thematic unity (the problem of idolatry) and cross references between the two sections (the reference to Iaoel having ordered Terah's house burned in 10:11, the comparison of the idol of jealousy to "a carpenter's figure such as my father used to make" in 25:1, and the question put by God to Abraham regarding Terah's failure to abandon his idol-worship in 26:3) indicate that the two major sections of the document form a cohesive whole. This structure would correspond roughly to the combination of legend and apocalypse found in the canonical book of Daniel, cf. J. J. Collins, "The Court-Tales in Daniel and the Development of Apocalyptic," *JBL* 94 (1975) 218-34; and idem, *The Apocalyptic Vision of the Book of Daniel* (HSM 16; Missoula, MT, 1977).

[16]Box-Landsman, *The Apocalypse of Abraham,* p. xvii. Rubinkiewicz is convinced that the work mentioned by Epiphanius is identical to a document used by the Audiens, whose content we know from Theodore bar Konai, and is not the same as our Apocalypse (*The Old Testament Pseudepigrapha;* for a more detailed analysis, see his Rome dissertation).

[17]PG 13, col. 1889. Cf. Ginzberg, *JE* vol. 1, p. 92.

[18]The translation is from T. Smith, "Recognitions of Clement," *Ante-Nicene Fathers* (ed. A. Roberts and J. Donaldson; Grand Rapids, MI, rev. American ed. 1951) vol. 8, p. 86.

[19]For most of the preceding references to witnesses to the Apocalypse of Abraham, especially the Clementine material, I am indebted to the work of Rubinkiewicz (*The Old Testament Pseudepigrapha*).

regard to a late first-century date for the Apocalypse, but it does indicate an interest during the first few centuries C.E. in the figure of Abraham as the recipient of divine revelations about the future, a role noticeably present in Genesis 15, the chapter upon which the latter part of the Apocalypse is based.

The internal evidence points more strongly to a date near the end of the first century. First, the strong possibility exists that the Slavonic versions of the Apocalypse are translations from a Semitic original, probably through a Greek intermediary.[20] Rubinkiewicz and Lunt propose the following as evidence for a Hebrew or Aramaic *Grundschrift*: (1) "the use of parts of the body instead of a simple pronoun" (1:4; 17:23; 22:2; 27:6); (2) the use of the "positive instead of a comparative" (1:5; 6:9); (3) "the prepositions are sometimes utilized according to Hebrew rather than Slavonic syntax" (8:4; 12:10; 27:11); and (4) "the syntax of the temporal phrases," especially the introduction of a phrase by the verb *hyh* (1:4, 7; 2:5; 5:4, 10, 11; 8:5).[21] One may add to this list the following from the work of Box and Landsman: (5) the characteristic use of the Abrahamic reply, "Here am I"; and (6) the use of proper names which reflect a knowledge and understanding of Semitic languages, i.e., (Merumath (= *ʾeben Mĕrūmā*, "stone of deceit") and Barisat (= *bar ʾishtā*, "son of the fire").[22]

Second, the author of the Apocalypse makes explicit reference to the destruction of the Temple:

> And I looked and I saw, and behold the picture swayed. And from its left side a crowd of heathens ran out and they captured the men, women, and children who were on its right side. And some they slaughtered and others they kept with them. Behold, I saw (them) running to them by way of four ascents and they burned the temple with fire, and they plundered the holy things that were in it. And I said, "Eternal One, the people you received from me are being robbed by the hordes of the heathen. They are killing some and holding others as aliens, and they burned the temple with fire and they are stealing and destroying the beautiful things which are in it." (27:1-5)

This description, coupled with the high likelihood of a Semitic original, while not conclusive, is the best evidence for a date near the end of the first century.[23]

---

[20]A. Rubinstein, "Hebraisms in the Slavonic 'Apocalypse of Abraham,' " *JJS* 4 (1953) 108-15; and idem, "Hebraisms in the 'Apocalypse of Abraham,' " *JJS* 5 (1954) 132-35. Rubinkiewicz has proposed that "it may be that this pseudepigraphon was translated directly from Hebrew into Slavonic," a suggestion that is not adopted by H. G. Lunt: "There can be no question that this text, like the whole Slavonic culture of Bulgaria of the time, was translated from Greek" (*The Old Testament Pseudepigrapha*).

[21]Rubinkiewicz and Lunt, *The Old Testament Pseudepigrapha*. Lunt also cites examples to show that a Greek intermediary was highly likely: "The translation contains Greek words well known from Old Church Slavonic (*adŭ*: *ʾhaidēs*, Hades'; *aerŭ*: *ʾaēr*, air'; *stuxija*: *ʾstoicheion*, element'), along with the conventional bizarre rendering of Gehenna as 'fiery race' (by a confusion of *géena* with *geneá* or some other derivative of the root *gen-*) and numerous literalistic phrases that make better sense in Greek than in Slavonic.

[22]Box-Landsman, *Apocalypse of Abraham*, p. xv.

[23]Rubinkiewicz has proposed a more precise dating of the Apocalypse to 79-81 C.E. based on an interpretation of the ten plagues which are to befall the heathens before the End. He speculates that five of the plagues (1, 3, 5, 7, 9) relate to the First Jewish Revolt, and the remaining five refer to the eruption of Vesuvius in 79 C.E. (*The Old Testament Pseudepigrapha* in a note supplied by J. H. Charlesworth). Cf. also Rubinkiewicz's Rome dissertation *L'Apocalypse d'Abraham*, pp. 201f.; and idem, *ANRW* II. 19. 1, p. 137, n. 1.

Even more convincing in this regard are the ways in which the destruction described above left its mark on the author of the Apocalypse.[24] He shares with the authors of 4 Ezra and 2 Baruch the abiding concerns of the post-70 mentality: the problem of evil and the problem of the uncertain destiny of the chosen people. Although not as persistent as the protagonist in 4 Ezra, the figure of Abraham pushes for an answer to the apparent contradiction between God's goodness and omniscience, and the exisence of evil in the creation:

> Eternal, Mighty One! Why did it please you to bring it about that evil should be desired in the heart of man, because you are angered at what was chosen by you[25] . . .him who does useless things in your light(?). (23:14)[26]

The author also searches for the reason that God has allowed his Temple to be destroyed and his chosen people to be conquered and exiled. After receiving a vision of the Temple and the abominations being carried out within it ("boys being slaughtered" on the altar "in the face of the idol," 24:2), Abraham asks God about the scene. God responds:

> This temple which you have seen, the altar and the works of art, this is my idea of the priesthood of the name of my glory, where every petition of man will enter and dwell; the ascent of kings and prophets and whatever sacrifice I decree to be made for me among my coming people, even of your tribe. And the body you saw is my anger, because the people who will come to me out of you will make me angry. And the man you saw slaughtering is he who angers me, and the sacrifice is a killing of those who are for me a testimony of the judgment of the completion at the beginning of creation. (25:4-6)

In what follows this passage Abraham witnesses the destruction of the Temple and God explains that "all that you have seen will happen on account of your seed who will (continually) provoke me because of the body which you saw and the murder in what was depicted in the temple of jealousy . . . ." (27:7)[27]

The authors of 4 Ezra, 2 Baruch, and the Apocalypse of Abraham share in the turmoil, the *ethos,* which pervaded Palestinian culture following the devastation of the Temple. Though not giving the same answers, they deal with the same questions. They each reflect on the questions of theodicy and covenant, not in abstraction at a date far removed from the events they reflect on, but from the heart in the aftermath of the

---

[24]The emphasis on the destruction of the Temple in the Apocalypse of Abraham may also point to a Palestinian origin for the work: "In a very real sense, therefore, for the Christian Jews, who were indifferent to the Temple cult, for the Jews at Qumran, who rejected the Temple, for the Jews of Leontopolis, in Egypt, who had their own Temple, but especially for the masses of diasporan Jews who never saw the Temple to begin with, but served God through synagogue worship alone, the year 70 cannot be said to have marked an important change. . . . It was significant primarily for the religious life of various Palestinian Jewish groups, not to mention the ordinary folk who had made pilgrimages to Jerusalem and could do so no more." Neusner, *Judaism* (in press) p. 314.

[25]Box-Landsman translate here "willed by you" (*Apocalypse of Abraham,* p. 71).

[26]For a discussion of this question and the answer(?) to it in chapter 24, cf. A. Rubenstein, "A Problematic Passage in the Apocalypse of Abraham," *JJS* 8 (1957) 45-50.

[27]Cf. also the utter destruction of the idolatrous Terah in chapter 8. As Nickelsburg rightly states: "The emphasis on cult is missing in *4 Ezra* and for the part in *2 Baruch*" (*Jewish Literature,* p. 299). This emphasis may also indicate an early date for our Apocalypse, a date prior to the devastating Second Jewish Revolt and the emergence of the Mishnah as the code of normative Judaism.

destruction of the Temple. These common concerns, along with the scant external evidence and the more solid internal evidence, make a date in the last decades of the first century C.E. likely.[28]

IV

Having located the concerns of the Apocalypse of Abraham in the late first century C.E., we now turn our attention to the responses our author makes to the problems he encountered. As can be seen from the quotation of 25:4-6 above, heavy emphasis is placed on the cult. Improper cultic practices have brought about the destruction of the Temple; future redemption will bring about a renewal of proper cultic practices (29:18).[29] Noticeably absent is any mention of the Torah as a key element in the redemptive process.[30] Only in one passage is the keeping of the commandments related to salvation:

> For the makers will see in them justice, (the makers) who have chosen my desire and manifestly kept my commandments, and they will rejoice with merrymaking over the downfall of the men who remain and who followed after the idols and their murders. (31:4)

But here the ones who keep the commandments are contrasted with those who follow after idols. Perhaps in this passage the author understands the commandments to represent non-idolatrous worship and not the keeping of the Law. Later in the same chapter the idolatry theme is reiterated: "And they glorified an alien (god). And they joined one to whom they had not been allotted, and they abandoned the Lord who gave them strength" (31:7f.).

Is there then no moral exhortation, no demand on the reader as to the proper course of action to be taken? Although not prominent, and not connected to the vision of redemption in the later chapters, the author does make a few general recommendations in the form of condemnation for fornicators, thieves, and the like. But the actions described are very general and the avoidance of such behavioral pitfalls does not guarantee salvation.[31]

---

[28]As always caution is indicated in any attempt to date documents based on inferences. In this particular case, no one line of evidence is sufficiently strong to bear the weight of the final conclusion, but the cumulative effect, or better the convergence of probabilities, tends to support the date indicated. Hopefully more certainty will be possible as the Slavonic pseudepigrapha come under closer scrutiny.

[29]Contrast 2 Baruch 10:9-12. The importance of proper sacrificial practices for our author is evident also in his portrayal of Abraham's sacrifice in chapters 11-15. Throughout these chapters the angel instructs Abraham regarding the sacrifice and Abraham does all that the angel commands. Thus the sacrifice is completed according to the divine will. The author portrays the perversion of proper practices as coming as a result of the disappearance of the instructing angel after the time of Abraham: "And I will go with you visible until the sacrifice, but after the sacrifice invisible forever" (11:5). Also relevant here is Abraham's recital of the heavenly song: "Accept my prayer and delight in it, and (accept) also the sacrifice which you yourself made to yourself through me as I searched for you" (17:20).

[30]Nickelsburg, *Jewish Literature*, p. 299.

[31]Box-Landsman postulate that the list may be a reflection on the Decalogue, commandments 7, 8, and 10 (*Apocalypse of Abraham*, p. 72), but this suggestion does not help to explain the condemnation of the naked men standing with their foreheads together.

What does the author recommend? In the last days, God will judge the heathen nations who have mistreated Abraham's descendants. This period will witness the ten plagues enumerated in chapter 30. In chapter 29 God promises Abraham that following the ten plagues:

> . . . from your seed will be left the righteous men in their number, protected by me, who strive in the glory of my name toward the place prepared beforehand for them, which you saw deserted in the picture.[32] And they will live, being affirmed by the sacrifices and the gifts of justice and truth in the age of justice. And they will rejoice forever in me, and they will destroy those who have destroyed them, they will rebuke those who have rebuked them through their mockery, and they will spit in their faces. (29:17-19)

All of the action described will be carried out by God, in consort with those who truly return to him, "before the age of justice starts to grow" (29:14). In a similar vein in chapter 31 God tells Abraham:

> And then I will sound the trumpet out of the air, and I will send my chosen one, having in him one measure of all my power, and he will summon my people, humiliated by the heathen. And I will burn with fire those who mocked them and ruled over them in this age and I will deliver those who have covered me with mockery over to the scorn of the coming age. (31:1f.)

Here again the downfall of the wicked is contrasted with the rejoicing of the righteous nation gathered from their dispersion. The implication, much stronger in the first passage quoted above, is that the people presently being oppressed will rise up to destroy the gentile overlords. Following the ten plagues, which will devastate the heathen, the reconstituted seed of Abraham will be given free reign to destroy the unrighteous and re-establish the cultus. In chapter 31 there is added to the scenario the figure of "the chosen one," who will gather the dispersed righteous and help initiate the destruction of the unrighteous. In both descriptions the oppressed are urged to take an active role, to help supplant the rule of the idolaters.

V

The most striking feature of the Apocalypse of Abraham lies in its recommendation to its audience to take action. When the ten plagues are completed, God and his people will bring down the oppressors from their high places. As such the Apocalypse stands in contrast to the relative pacifism recommended in 4 Ezra. In 4 Ezra God and the ones sent from God bring about redemption of the righteous and destruction of the wicked (see the final vision, "the man from the sea"). Our Apocalypse represents a mind-set that saw the possibility of renewal only through the re-establishment of the cult and of proper sacrificial practices. As such salvation and renewal were available only to those who returned to God from idolatry and who would strive with God, or his "chosen one," toward

---

[32]Box-Landsman translate the final clause: "which thou sawest devastated in the picture"; and identify the place, correctly I think, as Jerusalem.

the place which had been destroyed, i.e., Jerusalem. Thus the Apocalypse of Abraham stands as an example of a response to the destruction of the Second Temple which may have contributed to the atmosphere which precipitated the revolt of Bar Kokhba.[33]

---

[33] I have intentionally left my conclusion as a suggestion rather than an outright claim for two reasons, both of which have been mentioned previously, but bear repeating: (1) the provisional nature of any thesis based on modern language translations; and (2) the uncertain extent to which the original document has been adapted by those who transmitted it, especially applicable in this case because of the presence of the Bogomils.

I wish to express my thanks to Prof. J. H. Charlesworth for making available to me the work of Rubinkiewicz and Lunt from the new edition of *The Old Testament Pseudepigrapha*.

THE SUICIDE ACCOUNTS IN JOSEPHUS:
A FORM CRITICAL STUDY

Raymond R. Newell
Mount Union College

We often find among Jewish revolutionaries in the first century A.D. a strong willingness to commit suicide[1] rather than fall into the hands of their Roman conquerors. Yigael Yadin has brought this attitude to the attention of the modern world by his archaeological work at Masada--the final stronghold of the Jewish Revolt of A.D. 66 where, according to Josephus, nearly a thousand people killed themselves to avoid Roman capture.[2] Josephus, a Jewish commander who had surrendered to the Romans and who wrote the history of the revolt, records the Masada incident as well as many other suicides. This present study seeks to examine places in the writings of Josephus describing suicides. Although discussions of reasons for suicide among the various revolutionary groups of the first century exist, none really take into account the form Josephus used when describing suicides.[3] There is, in fact, little form-critical work on Josephus[4] though this method has proven quite helpful in illuminating the content and setting of various materials in biblical studies. Consequently, the following investigation constitutes a form-critical study of suicide accounts in the works of Josephus. Hopefully such a study will help reveal the import of Josephus' description of self-inflicted deaths during the turn of the eras.

The investigation proceeds along the following lines: (1) examination of various suicide stories in Josephus, determining if these various stories share basic identifiable structures; (2) search for parallels to these structures in contemporary Greek, Roman, and Jewish writings, asking whether Josephus drew upon suicide narrative genres to depict suicides of first century revolutionaries; and (3) investigation of the history of these genres to determine their function at various stages of their development in both literary and social settings. Under this final category we will suggest how first century revolutionaries and Josephus understood suicide.

---

[1] H. Fedden, *Suicide: A Social and Historical Study* (London: Peter Davies, 1938) 29, points out the word "suicide" is itself of fairly recent origin, appearing about the middle of the seventeenth century. In ancient times expressions such as "self-murder," "to fall by his own hand," and so on were used.

[2] Y. Yadin, *Masada: Herod's Fortress and the Zealot's Last Stand* (New York: Random House, 1966). Masada has brought forth much debate among Jewish scholars, especially about the Jewishness of the mass suicide there. See especially the survey article, L. H. Feldman, "Masada: A Critique of Recent Scholarship," *Christianity, Judaism and other Greco-Roman Cults: Studies for Morton Smith at Sixty. Part Three. Judaism Before 70* (ed. J. Neusner; Leiden: Brill, 1975) 218-48.

[3] W. Farmer, *Maccabees, Zealots and Josephus* (New York: Columbia University, 1956) 69-70, and M. Hengel, *Die Zeloten* (Leiden: Brill, 1961) 272-77. On suicides specifically reported by Josephus see D. Daube, "Josephus on Suicide and Liability of Depositee," *Juridical Review* 9 (1964) 212-24, and the series by L. D. Hankoff, "The Theme of Suicide in the Works of Flavius Josephus," *Clio Medica* 11 (1976) 15-24; "Flavius Josephus. First-century A.D. View of Suicide," *New York State Journal of Medicine* 77 (1977) 1986-1992; "Flavius Josephus. Suicide and Transition," *NYSJM* 79 (1979) 937-42.

[4] Cf. Listings in L. Feldman, *Scholarship on Philo and Josephus, 1937-1962* (New York: Yeshiva University, 1963) and H. Schreckenberg, *Bibliographie zu Flavius Josephus* (Leiden: Brill, 1968), and *Bibliographie zu Flavius Josephus. Supplementband mit Gesamtregister* (Leiden: Brill, 1979).

I. Forms of Suicide Narratives in Josephus

Suicide stories in Josephus do not share uniform length. They may extend anywhere from a few lines to several pages. In fact, in a majority of cases suicide receives only short notice by Josephus. Such brief notification of suicide is found in Josephus' description of the fall of Jotapata (*J.W.* III. 329-331):[5]

> The Romans, remembering what they had borne during the siege, showed no quarter or pity for any, but thrust the people down the steep slope from the citadel in a general massacre. Even those still able to fight here found themselves deprived of the means of defence by the difficulties of the ground: crushed in the narrow alleys and slipping down the declivity, they were engulfed in the wave of carnage that streamed from the citadel. The situation even drove many of Josephus' picked men to suicide; seeing themselves powerless to kill a single Roman, they could at least forestall death at Roman hands, and retiring in a body to the outskirts of the town, they there put an end to themselves.

Other examples of short suicide episodes are found in *J.W.* I. 150; II. 49-50; III. 424-25; IV. 78-79; 433-436; *Ant.* XIII. 362-363; XVII. 261-263. Despite their brevity, all share some common characteristics. Normally Josephus appends the suicide episode to the end of battle scenes where the situation has become quite hopeless. A person or group facing a hopeless plight makes the decision for suicide, and states the reason for that decision. Then appears a simple concluding statement about the person or group's death. So the suicide episode itself consists of two major elements: (1) the reason for the suicide and (2) the act of suicide; but a description of a hopeless situation generally precedes the episode. In one instance, the death of Abimelek (*Ant.* V. 252), Josephus describes the hopeless situation just as briefly as the reason for the suicide and the act itself. In a couple of instances, the description of the hopeless situation also doubles as the reason for the suicide. For example, one Eleazar, follower of Simon bar Giora, entered Herodion to ask for its surrender:

> The guards, ignorant of the object of his visit, promptly admitted him, but at the first mention of the word "surrender" drew their swords and pursued him, until, finding escape impossible, he flung himself from the ramparts into the valley below and was killed on the spot (*J.W.* IV. 519).

This type of suicide episode is also found in *Ant.* XII. 236; XV. 358-359; XX. 80.

A few exceptions to this form of suicide episode exist. In two cases, Josephus does not include a description of a hopeless situation. Interestingly, both examples deal with Roman suicides. *J.W.* IV. 547-548 tells of Otho's suicide after his defeat at Bedriacum in Gaul. Both reason for the act and the act itself are cited, but the presence of a hopeless situation is not self evident. Perhaps it can be implied from Otho's defeat, but the text contains no description of immanent capture or death. The other case found in *Ant.* XIX. 273 concerns the suicide of one of Caligula's assassins:

> As for Sabinus, he was not only released by Claudius from the charge but allowed to retain the office which he held. Nevertheless, deeming it wrong to fail in loyalty to his fellow conspirators, he slew himself, falling upon his sword till the hilt actually reached the wound.

---

[5]Throughout this paper, quotations from Josephus will be taken from the *Loeb Classical Library* version of his works, translated variously by H. St. J. Thackeray, R. Marcus, and L. H. Feldman. All citations from classical sources will also come from the *Loeb* series.

Here only reason and act are described. Absence of the hopeless situation receives emphasis because Sabinus had been allowed to go free. Another exception to the usual form is found in *Ant.* XIV. 70. There the order is rearranged: (1) description of the hopeless situation, (2) the act of suicide, and (3) reason for the suicide. In this passage's parallel in *J.W.* I. 150, however, we find the normal order of situation, reason and act. Perhaps, *Ant.* XIV. 70 merely rearranges for stylistic reasons the earlier account in the *Jewish War*.[6]

In form the short suicide episode in Josephus contains two elements: (1) reason for the suicide and (2) the act of suicide. Normally, a third element, a description of some hopeless predicament, is included as an introduction to the suicide episode. This latter component, however, is not mandatory. When we move from these short suicide episodes to longer narratives about suicide, we find these same basic elements also present.

The first place where suicide acts as the subject of a narrative is in *J.W.* I. 312-313. This pericope is placed within the context of Herod's destruction of the Galilean bandits:

> It was then that one old man, the father of seven children, being asked by them and their mother permission to leave under Herod's pledge, killed them in the following manner. Ordering them to come forward one by one, he stood at the entrance and slew each son as he advanced. Herod, watching this spectacle from a conspicuous spot, was profoundly affected and, extending his hand to the old man, implored him to spare his children; but he, unmoved by any word of Herod, and even upbraiding him as a low-born upstart, followed up the slaughter of his sons by that of his wife, and, having flung their corpses down the precipice, finally threw himself over after them.

Several elements in this story merit comment: (1) the story centers on the act of one person caught in a dangerous situation; (2) the whole family is killed; (3) a speech was reportedly given by the story's protagonist, here recorded indirectly; and (4) the story climaxes with self-murder by the central figure.[7] No reason for familiacide and suicide is given within the story, although Josephus introduces it by saying many of the bandits "preferred death to captivity." This story represents one example of such a choice on the part of one bandit. We would say, consequently, that no description of a totally hopeless situation exists; rather, the central subject is given a choice. He may surrender and save himself and his family, or he may die at the hand of Herod's attacking soldiers (cf. *J.W.* I. 311). Rather than accept either a life of captivity or death at enemy hands, the old man chooses suicide for his family and himself. The parallel to this story in *Ant.* XIV. 429-430 shows the same basic components, rearranged. Again, this reordering probably occurred for stylistic reasons. In the *Antiquities'* version, reason for the suicide is given after the act rather than as an introduction to the story. The speech and offer of immunity are also found after the description of the deaths.

After describing the slaughter of resident Jews by the Scythopolitans, Josephus relates the story of Simon, son of Saul (*J.W.* II. 469-476). This is one of the most self-contained, dramatic suicide narratives.[8] Saul, one of the resident Jews who fought with

---

[6]H. St. J. Thackeray, *Josephus: The Man and the Historian* (New York: Jewish Institute of Religion, 1929) 106-7, notes that with *Ant.* XIV, Josephus started going over ground he had covered in his *Jewish War*: "Now while it was customary for ancient historians to make free and unacknowledged use of published works of their predecessors, without any sense of what we should call 'plagiarism,' it was almost a point of honour with them to vary the phraseology." This rule was especially important for an author who had already written on the same area.

[7]Cf. F. Loftus, "The Martyrdom of the Galilean Troglodytes (B. J. i 312-13; A. xiv 429-30)," *JQR* 66 (1975/76) 212-23, for a tradition historical analysis of this story.

[8]Hankoff, "Flavius Josephus. Suicide and Transition," 940.

the Scythopolitans against attacking Jewish revolutionaries, found his faithfulness to his city over that to his people rewarded by treachery from the Scythopolitans. Fearful of the Jews in their midst, they call them to a grove and there attack them. Witnessing this assault, Simon draws his sword; but rather than charge his assailants, he delivers an extended speech which describes his situation as just punishment for having fought against his kinsmen, concluding with the statement: "This, God grant, shall be at once the fit retribution for my foul crime and the testimony to my courage, that none of my foes shall be able to boast of having slain me or glory over my prostrate body" (*J.W.* II. 473-474). He then proceeds to kill his father, his wife, and children, and finally--with all eyes upon him--he plunges his sword into his own throat. Here we find elements similar to those in the story of the death of the old bandit: (1) emphasis centers on the action of one person caught in a hopeless situation; (2) a speech is given containing the reason for the act; (3) the protagonist kills his family; and (4) the central character kills himself. Simon prefers that he and his family die by his own hand rather than by the enemy's.

Turning to the other suicide narratives, we find the element of familiacide no longer present, although the other components remain: (1) one person in a hopeless situation, (2) the reason for the act, usually given in a speech, and (3) the act of suicide. Herod's brother Phasael, captured and marked for execution and believing it shameful to suffer at the hands of his enemy, dashes his head against a rock (*Ant.* XIV. 367). Ahithophel, counselor of David who sided with rebellious Absalom, finding his advice spurned and realizing the revolt is a failure, delivers a speech--reported indirectly--"it is better for him to remove himself from the world in a free and noble spirit than surrender himself to David," then hangs himself (*Ant.* VII. 228-229). This latter story proves particularly interesting for the present investigation because for once Josephus' source, the Bible, is available for evaluating how he dealt with information in forming his own narrative.[9] 2 Sam 17:23 contains the original Ahithophel story: "When Ahithophel saw that his counsel was not carried out, he saddled his donkey, and he went to his house, to his city. Then he set order to his house and he hanged himself; and he died and he was buried in the grave of his father." Here we find no description of a hopeless situation or reason for the act; only the course of action receives description. This suggests Josephus' responsibility for adding the other two elements to his narrative. In recounting two other biblical suicides, Samson (*Ant.* V. 314-317) and Saul (*Ant.* VI. 370-372), Josephus follows his source more closely than in the case of Ahithophel. The three elements of hopeless situation, reason for act, and the suicide also appear in these two stories. However, it must be noted that the biblical versions (cf. Judg 16:23-31; 1 Sam 31:3-6) also contain these three components to some extent.

Josephus even uses this basic three component outline in narrating a fake suicide (*J.W.* V. 317-324). A group of ten Jews led by a certain Castor are caught in a tower under attack by one of Titus' battering rams. Castor pretends to implore mercy from Titus, and the latter stops the battering before the tower falls. Titus invites Castor's company to surrender. Five of the Jews pretend to go along with Castor, but five "cried out that they would never be slaves of the Romans so long as they might die free men." This latter group then raises their swords to public view, strike their breast plates, and fall down as if dead. This impresses the Romans until they discover it is all a ruse to get them to stop their attack on the tower. The outline appears again in the narrative on the death of Longus, one of the Roman soldiers trapped when Jews burn the western portico of the Temple (*J.W.* VI. 186-187). In this pericope, the speech containing the reason for

---

[9] On Josephus' use of his sources, see, B. Niese, "Josephus," *Hastings Encyclopedia of Religion and Ethics* 7 (1914) 569-79; A. Peletier, *Flavius Josèphe adaptateur de la Lettre d'Aristée. Une réaction atticisante contre la Koine* (Paris: Klincksieck, 1962); S. J. D. Cohen, *Josephus in Galilee and Rome. His Vita and Development as a Historian* (Leiden: Brill, 1979), and T. W. Franxman, *Genesis and the "Jewish Antiquities" of Flavius Josephus* (Rome: Biblical Institute, 1979).

suicide is not delivered by the victim but by his brother, who implores Longus "not to disgrace his own reputation or the Roman arms."

Thus, in the suicide narratives the same basic outline apparently surfaces. The story as a whole normally centers on the action of one individual faced with a hopeless situation, either death at the hand of the enemy or--equally bad--surrender into the enemy's hand. We must remember that in the days of Josephus, captivity meant slavery; the slave no longer had control over his own life. The hopeless situation is briefly described at the beginning of the narrative. Whereas this depiction of the hopeless plight was not mandatory for the brief suicide episode, it becomes so for the longer suicide narrative. Next appears the reason for the suicide in the face of such an unacceptable predicament, usually a speech reported either directly or indirectly. Finally, the act of suicide itself is briefly described.

Emphasis of the suicide narrative apparently focuses on the second component, the speech in which the reason for suicide is stated. These narratives normally devote their greatest space to this element. A description of the situation sets the stage for the speech while the final act validates ideas presented in the speech. Sometimes another element, familiacide by the central character, is added to the narrative; but this functions much as does the suicide--it further verifies convictions expressed in the speech. The act follows the reason and is totally dependent on it. Even in Josephus' more extended suicide narratives, these basic components are maintained and emphasized.

No doubt the most famous of Josephus' suicide narratives describes the mass suicide by revolutionary defenders trapped on Masada (J.W. VII. 320-401). With their fortress facing capture on the morrow, the leader of the revolutionaries, Eleazar, delivers first one speech and then immediately another exhorting his followers to kill themselves, their wives, and their children rather than be captured by the Romans. The men personally kill their wives and children, and in turn are killed by ten men selected by lot. One from this group then kills the other nine executioners and, finally, himself. Josephus reports a total of 960 people died in this manner on Masada; only two old women and five children, hidden during the slaughter, escaped. In this extended account we again find the basic elements of suicide narrative. Although this story tells of a large group action, in many ways it still focuses on one person, Eleazar, the leader of the Sicarii.

The great bulk of this narrative is reserved for the two successive speeches supposedly delivered by Eleazar. The importance of the speeches found here and in other suicide narratives should not be underrated. As has already been pointed out, the speeches comprise the central element in these narratives. To this can be added the general importance of speeches in ancient historiography. Speeches, either direct or indirect, were used by ancient historians both to show their own oratorical skills and to express their own points of view on the subject at hand.[10]

These two Eleazar speeches have received a great deal of scholarly analysis.[11] Both speeches contain their own unity and form. The first (J.W. VII. 323-336)

---

[10]For a fine analysis of Eleazar's speeches see D. R. Runnalls, "Hebrew and Greek Sources in the Speeches of Josephus' Jewish War," Ph.D. Dissertation, University of Toronto (1971) 232-74. Runnalls argues that the speeches in Josephus are more than propaganda; they reveal the central purpose of the author, 346. Cf. R. G. Bomstad, "Governing Ideas of the 'Jewish War' of Flavius Josephus," Ph.D. Dissertation, Yale (1979) 1-3.

[11]W. Morel, "Eine Rede bei Josephus (Bell. Iud. VII 341 sqq)," Rheinisches Museum für Philologie 75 (1926) 106-14; O. Bauernfeind and O. Michel, "Die beiden Eleazarreden in Jos. bell 7, 323-336; 7, 341-388," ZNW 58 (1967) 267-72; H. Linder, Die Geschichtsauffassung des Flavius Josephus in Bellum Judaicum (Leiden: Brill, 1972) 33-40; Runnalls, "Hebrew and Greek Sources," 232-74; D. J. Ladouceur, "Studies in the Language and Historiography of Flavius Josephus," Ph.D. Dissertation, Brown (1977) 99-100; Bomstad, "Governing Ideas," 90-135.

concentrates on the need for suicide in this situation because of the principle first enunciated by Judas the Galilean that the Jew must not subject himself to any man, only God (cf. *J.W.* II. 118); it portrays Eleazar as acknowledging God's historical judgment on the Jewish people in the failure of the revolt; and it concludes with a call to suicide in order to pay the death penalty imposed by God directly to him and not to the Romans.[12] Here Josephus comes closest to depicting faithfully the theological tradition of the Sicarii on Masada, although this speech bears the marks of his own thesis that the struggle for freedom is wrong.[13] The theme of the second Eleazar speech (*J.W.* VII. 341-388) appears to pick up a popular Hellenistic belief that death is freedom for the soul (cf. *J.W.* VII. 344). Consequently, O. Bauernfeind and O. Michel label the entire second speech a Hellenistic *Seelenrede*--a speech on the immortality of the soul.[14] Helgo Lindar, however, indicates this theme only goes through 17 of the 48 sections of the speech. The second oration also contains a reiteration of the theme presented in the first speech that suicide is demanded by the historical hour, and it concludes with a lament over the misery of the revolt's survivors.[15] The section on the idea of the soul's immortality which emerges from popular Hellenistic thought constitutes, then, just one element in the second speech serving the overall purpose of justifying suicide.[16] The second speech serves to intensify the message of the first speech.[17]

One other extended suicide narrative appears in *J.W.* III. 346-391. This relates Josephus' account of his own participation in a suicide pact at Jotapata. Josephus faces the choice of surrender to the Romans or death by their hands. When he decides to surrender, his companions speak to him about committing suicide instead. Then Josephus delivers a long speech about why suicide is unnatural and irreligious. His comrades find his arguments unconvincing, so Josephus agrees to commit suicide with them. They draw lots, and "by fortune or by the providence of God"[18] Josephus is left alone with one other man whom he convinces to surrender with him. Although in the end, Josephus does not kill himself, this story can still be considered an extended suicide narrative. The various elements are present: the account centers mainly on the actions of one person, Josephus, in the face of death or surrender, even though others are involved; the situation is described; a speech containing characteristics of a philosophical diatribe[19]--only here it opposes suicide; and finally, the act is described. The unusual aspect is that Josephus uses the suicide narrative form to *attack* the suicide idea. In other words, Josephus uses the form, but alters its function.

In conclusion, Josephus uses two basic forms in narrating examples of suicide. The short suicide episode consists of (1) a reason for the suicide and (2) a description of the act. Normally these episodes are appended to battle scenes where one side's position is depicted as hopeless, offering only death or captivity; but such a dire situation is not necessary for use of a suicide episode. Suicide narratives are longer, including at least several lines. These suicide narratives generally focus on one individual's action and consist of three basic elements: (1) description of a hopeless situation, (2) reasons for

---

[12] Linder, *Geschichtsauffassung*, 33-34; Runnalls, "Hebrew and Greek Sources," 240-41.

[13] Linder, *Geschichtsauffassung*, 34.

[14] "Eleazarreden," 267-68; cf. Hengel, *Zeloten*, 269-70.

[15] Linder, *Geschichtsauffassung*, 35-36.

[16] Ibid., p. 39; Runnalls concurs, arguing that the speech reflects more Jewish ideas than Greek, "Hebrew and Greek Sources," 258-74.

[17] Linder, *Geschichtsauffassung*, 35; Bauernfeind and Michel, "Eleazarreden," 267-68.

[18] D. Daube, "Typology in Josephus," *JJS* 31 (1980) 30, points out this famous line does not have the best textual basis.

[19] M. Braun, *Griechischer Roman und hellenistische Geschichtsschreibung* (Frankfurt am Main: Vittorio Klostermann, 1934) 85-86 note.

suicide in the face of such a plight (given in the form of direct or indirect speech), and (3) a report on how the act ensued. These suicide narratives are subject to extensive expansion, primarily by increasing the length and/or number of speeches promoting (or attacking) suicide. The narratives focus on these speeches. Sometimes the familiacide element is added to the suicide depiction, emphasizing the extent to which the person is willing to carry out his beliefs cited in the suicide oration.

The question naturally arising from the presence of such forms for suicide reports in Josephus is: Did he create these forms himself or borrow them from elsewhere? In order to answer this question, it is necessary to examine how suicides were viewed in the cultural setting of Josephus' life. Since Josephus was a Jew, we would normally begin the search for suicide forms within Jewish literature. We must remember, however, that Josephus (whose native language was Aramaic) wrote the *Jewish War* and the *Antiquities* in a respectable Atticized Greek for a Hellenistic audience. While it was once fashionable to claim that all Hellenistic coloring in Josephus' writings depended on the work of assistants,[20] research over the last couple of decades has disproved this.[21] Most recent scholarly work argues that Josephus is largely responsible for the construction and writing of his own historical works and places his writings firmly within the Greco-Roman historiographic tradition.[22] Combined with Josephus' probable use of Hellenistic sources, it seems most reasonable to assume that if Josephus borrowed the forms of suicide episode and suicide narrative from elsewhere, it was from the Hellenistic milieu rather than purely Jewish culture. Consequently, investigation of forms in which suicide was reported in the Greco-Roman world appears necessary.

II. *Suicide Forms in Greco-Roman Literature*[23]

The oldest mentions of suicide in Greek literature lie in Homer's *Odyssey* which mentions the suicides of Oedipus' mother (*Od.* XI. 271ff.) and Aias (*Od.* XI. 548ff.), though not in any special form which brings situation, reason, and act together. A particular form for reporting suicide does not appear until the famous histories of the fifth century B.C. In Herodotus' *The Persian Wars*, the majority of suicides are reported without any form (cf. I. 24; II. 100, 131); but in two cases the suicide episode form seems to be used. One Othryadas, "prevented by a sense of shame from returning to Sparta after all his comrades had fallen, laid violent hands upon himself in Thyrea" (I. 82). Here we find in a brief sentence both reason for the suicide and the act of suicide. The same form is employed in telling about the death of Pantites, a survivor of Thermopolae (VII. 232). Neither example is preceded by a description of a hopeless situation. Thucydides tells of two group suicides in his *History of the Peloponnesian War*. The first relates the self-murders of a group of Messenians captured by Corcyraeans in the form of a suicide episode (III. 18. 3) introduced by description of a hopeless situation. The other example, again involving Corcyraeans, describes the suicide without the use of any specific form (IV. 48. 1-4).

---

[20]Thackeray, *Josephus*, 100-118.

[21]Cf. the critiques found in G. C. Richards, "The Composition of Josephus' *Antiquities*," *CQ* 33 (1939) 36-40; R. J. H. Shutt, *Studies in Josephus* (London: S.P.C.K., 1961) 59-78; and especially Ladouceur, "Studies," 25-42.

[22]H. W. Attridge, *The Interpretation of Biblical History in the Antiquitates Judaicae of Flavius Josephus* (Missoula: Scholars Press, 1976) 29-70.

[23]For a survey of this material see K. A. Geiger, *Der Selbstmord in klassischen Altertum. Historisch-kritische Abhandlung* (Augsburg: Huttler, 1888); A. W. Mair, "Suicide (Greek and Roman)," *Encyclopedia of Religion and Ethics* 12 (1925) 26-33; A. J. Droge, "MORI LUCRUM: Paul and Ancient Theories of Suicide," unpublished paper presented at the SBL Annual Meeting, Dec. 21, 1981, 1-9.

In Rome, suicide became relatively common, particularly during the civil wars and under the Empire. Cicero (106-43 B.C.) mentions suicides several times. He uses the suicide episode form when speaking of the father of Marcus Crassus: "that he might not live to see his enemy victorious, ended his life with the same hand with which he had often dealt death unto his foes" (*Pro Sestio* 48). Cicero speaks of suicide at other times, though not in any set form (cf. *OBScaurus* III. 1; 4). In the *Gallic Wars* of Julius Caesar (ca. 102-44 B.C.), we find both the suicide episode and the suicide narrative. The mass suicide by survivors of Sabinus' command is succinctly reported in a suicide episode: "In the night, despairing of safety, they killed one another to a man" (V. 37). Another example of this form is found in VI. 31. The suicide narrative form is used in the story about centurion Marcus Petronius who, overwhelmed by the enemy, shouts to his men the reason for his suicidal act, and dies (VII. 50).

Interestingly, the greatest Hellenistic use of the suicide narrative form occurs in the period from about A.D. 40-120, the time of Josephus' own life and writings. Seneca (ca. 2 B.C.-A.D. 65) employs this form in speaking about the death of Cato (*On Providence* II. 9-12). The speech placed in Cato's mouth is reported in a very eloquent direct speech.[24] In his long poem, *The Civil War*, Lucan (A.D. 39-65) employs an extended suicide narrative when describing the death of Vulteius and his men, followers of Caesar (IV. 465-581). A company of 600 men, trapped on a raft, are attacked by several thousand. They are able to fight off their attackers through the day, but during the night Vulteius delivers a speech exhorting his soldiers to show their true freedom and devotion to Caesar by committing suicide rather than be captured. The next day, at the height of the battle, Vulteius called his men to turn their swords from their enemies and kill each other. Lucan concludes his story with the statement: "cowardly nations will not understand how simple a feat it is to escape slavery by suicide; . . . the purpose of the sword is to save men from slavery."

Tacitus (ca. A.D. 56-sometime after 117) reports several suicides ordered by Nero; he portrays Seneca's death using the suicide narrative form (*Annals* XV. 12-14). Seneca reportedly delivers two speeches, one to his friends and one to his wife. Tacitus' narrative presents an unusually detailed account of the act itself. In his depiction of the similar death of Lucan (*Annals* XV. 70), Tacitus mentions a speech given--recitation of one of Lucan's poems describing a soldier's suicide--but he does not include it. Ironically, then, two men known to employ the suicide narrative form to describe suicides of others later had their own deaths told in that same form. Tacitus, however, does not use this form when depicting the final moments of Vestinus (*Annals* XV. 69). In *The Histories*, Tacitus uses the suicide narrative form to relate the death of Emperor Otho (II. 47-49). Here again, two speeches are found, one to a group and one to his nephew. Both contain reasons why, under the circumstances, he should kill himself. The greatest use of suicide narratives in Greco-Roman literature, excluding Josephus, occurs in *The Lives* by Plutarch (before A.D. 50-after 120). The death of Brutus is described in an extended suicide narrative which contains two speeches, one reported directly and one reported indirectly (*Brutus* LII. 1-5). Plutarch's version of Cato's death continues through several chapters with many of his speeches recorded both directly and indirectly (*Cato the Younger* LXVI-LXX). Antony's suicide, too, is told in an extended suicide narrative (*Antony* LXXVI. 2 - LXXVII. 4). Slow death brought on by his wound allows a unique feature in the Antony suicide--portrayal of him giving a speech after he performs the suicidal act, yet before he dies. Another minor variation on Plutarch's use of the suicide form lies in his account of Themistocles' death (*Themistocles* XXXI. 3-5). Rather than reporting a speech, Plutarch describes Themistocles' train of thought which eventuates in

---

[24]In Epistle LXXI. 15-16, Seneca again cites Cato's death speech, but not in the context of a suicide narrative. This speech contains a line suspiciously reminiscent of Josephus: "The whole race of man, both that which is and that which is to be, is condemned to die" (cf. *J.W.* VII. 343).

his suicide. The ideas present are, nonetheless, the same as those normally appearing in suicide speeches. Only once does Plutarch not use the suicide narrative to describe a self-inflicted death, that of Otho (*Otho* XVII. 1-3).

It is not necessary to proceed further in study of Greco-Roman suicide forms to draw some conclusions about their relationship to the forms found in Josephus. That form in Josephus we designated suicide episode is found as early as the Greek historical writings of the fifth century B.C. The form entitled suicide narrative, on the other hand, does not seem to appear until the first century B.C. Rome. The evidence of the *Gallic Wars* might suggest that the succinct suicide narrative form found its original setting in official Roman military commentaries. The extended suicide narrative usually appears in historical writings, occasionally in rhetorical speeches. Apparently, these types of narratives enjoyed great popularity in literary historical circles during the same time period Josephus wrote the *Jewish War* and the *Antiquities*. At least two distinct genres for reporting suicides in historical writings appear to have existed in the Greco-Roman world during the late first and early second centuries A.D. Thus we cannot credit Josephus with creating these forms. Before we can firmly conclude that Josephus borrowed these forms solely from the Hellenistic world, however, we must investigate forms used by Jewish writers to report suicides. Although standing withing the Greco-Roman historiographic tradition, Josephus still received his primary education within Palestinian Jewish circles. It would be hard to believe that his Jewish background had no effect on his writings.[25] Some aspects in Josephus' use of suicide narratives differ from normal Greco-Roman usage of the genre. For example, great differences often exist in the content of speeches giving reasons for the suicide as presented by Josephus and Greco-Roman authors. Perhaps an investigation of the way Josephus' Jewish tradition reported suicides will help explain various peculiarities in his use of apparent Greco-Roman literary genres.

III. Suicide Forms in Jewish Literature

The Old Testament reports only five suicides: Abimelech (Judg 9:54), Samson (Judg 16:30), Saul and his armor bearer (1 Sam 31:4-5; 1 Chr 10:4), Ahithophel (2 Sam 17:23), and Zimri (1 Kings 16:18). Ahithophel's death, as already noted, only describes the act. Samson, serving in captivity, seeks vengeance on his enemies. His death wish receives no explanation and emphasis centers on the number he killed rather than on the suicide act itself. Zimri's death is described in the sparest of terms with no discernible form. The stories of Abimelech and Saul, however, reveal similarities to the suicide narrative. Abimelech, mortally wounded, asks to be killed to escape dishonorable death and is slain by his armor bearer. Saul's death follows the same outline, although he is responsible for his own death (but compare the Amalekite's story in 2 Sam 1:6-10). These two stories possibly reveal a primitive Jewish form of the suicide narrative. The major argument against such a contention is that the deaths of Abimelech and Saul constitute parts of continuous narratives and cannot really be separated form-critically from their context. They may contain some elements of suicide narratives, but not in one self-contained unit as is the case with most Greco-Roman and Josephan uses of this genre (cf. the stories of Marcus Petronius, Cato, Vulteius, Lucan, Seneca, Simon, the old bandit, Phasael, and Longus). Only in the biographical writings of Plutarch do we find the suicide narrative as part of a longer, continuous account. These biographies, however, are themselves a type of genre which definitely differs from Old Testament narratives of sacred history. Therefore, although initially the deaths of Abimelech and Saul impress us as suicide

---

[25]In the past it was very popular to question Josephus' Jewishness; cf. N. Bentwich, *Josephus* (Philadelphia: Jewish Publication Society, 1914) 56-57; but recently it has become more popular to accept seriously Josephus' Jewishness; cf. D. Daube, "Typology," 33-36.

360   SBL 1982 Seminar Papers

narratives, they are not. We should add, though, that superficial similarity between the Greco-Roman suicide narrative and death accounts of Abimelech and Saul helped enable Jews to assimilate this form when they came in contact with, and found need for it.

Jewish tradition cites several suicides during the Maccabean revolt, with its struggle against the Hellenizing pressures of the Jewish leadership. 2 Maccabees, an epitome in Greek of the now lost five volume history of Jason of Cyrene (ca. 100 B.C.) records the very dramatic suicide of one Razis (2 Macc 14:37-46). About to be captured by Nicanor's soldiers, Razis tries to kill himself, but with little immediate success. His sword blow is not true; he tries to jump into the crowd but this too fails; finally, he throws his own entrails at the crowd before he dies. Though a self-contained unit, this story does not follow the suicide narrative form. It seems almost like an expanded version of the suicide episode. It is preceded by an introduction depicting a typically hopeless situation. The reason for the suicide is stated: to avoid falling "into the hands of sinners and suffer outrages unworthy of his noble birth." Description of the act, however, causes problems. Normally, a suicide episode contains only a brief description of the act; in the Razis story, however, attempts at death are depicted in detail and brought to a climax with the final successful act. Perhaps this story of Razis shows how the suicide episode was eventually expanded in Greek historical writings, but it is definitely not related to the normal Hellenistic suicide narrative form.

4 Maccabees (ca. A.D. 30), a book devoted to graphic description of the martyrdom of a Jewish family, contains one suicide narrative (4 Macc 12:1-19). The youngest boy, having witnessed the death of his brothers, is offered life if he obeys the king's command to eat unclean meat or death if he does not. The lad asks to be freed from his fetters, runs to a brazier, delivers a speech attacking the king and proclaiming his own faithfulness to God's commandments, and throws himself into the fire. This work also contains an example of a suicide episode in the account of the mother's death (4 Macc 17:1). Here then are two examples of Jewish use of these suicide forms. 4 Maccabees is a Hellenistic Jewish work, written originally in Greek and reveals a strong dependence on Hellenistic rhetoric and philosophy.[26] Therefore, its use of the suicide episode and narrative can probably be credited to borrowing from the Greco-Roman world rather than any specifically Jewish background.

The manner in which the books about the Maccabean revolt portray martyrdom needs also to be viewed. 1 Macc 2:29-38 tells of the death of a thousand people in a cave because they refused to defend themselves on the Sabbath. There is some similarity to the end of this story and the suicide episode, but it is doubtful this story can be so classified. The martyrdoms portrayed in 2 Macc 6:18-7:42, apparently the basis of the story told in 4 Maccabees, has no discernible relation to the suicide forms; although the death speeches are a typically Hellenistic element. The martyrdoms of the first six sons in 4 Macc 8:1-12:1 almost appear to follow an extended suicide narrative form. The hopeless situation of these young men necessitates choosing between death in obedience to God's will or life in obedience to the king's will. Each one delivers an extensive speech about his willingness to die for the Law, then dies. Although there is no act of suicide here, the demand to be killed rather than live in disobedience to God might be considered a type of passive suicide, similar to asking servant or friend to slay you (cf. Abimelech, Saul, Vulteius, Brutus, Antony, and Eleazar). This brief review suggests that as the Jews struggled to find a form by which the experience of martyrdom could be described, they turned at least in part to the suicide forms of the very Hellenistic culture which was the major cause of such martyrdoms.

When one turns to the rabbinic literature, he finds only two stories about suicide which are at all near in form to the suicide narrative. In b. Giṭ 57b appears a story of 400 boys and girls who commit suicide to avoid being used by their captors for immoral

[26]M. Hadas, The Third and Fourth Books of Maccabees (New York: 1953) 100-103, 115-18.

purposes. The situation is briefly described, speeches are given, and the commission of the act is stated. The unusual part of this report is that the speech is a citation of a biblical verse with a brief interpretation. The form of this story definitely follows the Greco-Roman suicide narrative genre. It has been altered to fit rabbinical needs by making the basis of the suicidal act an appropriately interpreted biblical verse rather than a rhetorical speech. That such alterations of a basically Hellenistic form took place is shown by the narrative which immediately follows the tale of the 400 boys and girls in b. Giṭ 57b. For here is found the rabbinic version of the story of the martyrdom of the mother and her seven sons. Rather than speeches on their loyalty to God even to death found in the Jewish Hellenistic versions (2 Macc 7:1-42 and 4 Maccabees), each son recites a verse from the Torah which disallows his worship of an idol. Here is perhaps an example of a form which may once have been tied to Hellenistic suicide genres, but which has developed into a new form more appropriately called a temptation story (cf. Matt 4:1-17; Luke 4:1-13). In the rabbinic tradition, then, the Hellenistic suicide narrative did not maintain its form, but was adapted to other purposes--primarily to witness to the absoluteness of God's commandments.

This conclusion draws partial confirmation when one looks at the primary way suicides are described in rabbinic literature. B. Ketub. 103b reports that on the death of Rabbi Judah, the compiler of the Mishnah, a bath kol announced that all those present at his death would enjoy the life of the world to come. Upon hearing this, a fuller who had not called on the Rabbi that day killed himself. Then a bath kol announced that he too would live in the coming world. This form is also found in the story about the suicide of Jakum of Ṣẹrorot (Midr. Pss 11:7 and Gen. Rab. 65:22). Jakum, stung by the word of Jose ben Joezer who was on the way to his own martyrdom, committed a very ingenious suicide. He drove a beam into the ground, built a row of sticks with a wall of stones on them, and placed a sword pointing upward in the center of a pile of fuel under the beam. The account continues: "After lighting a fire under the sticks of wood beneath the stones he hanged himself from the beam and thus strangled himself. The rope broke, and he fell into the fire, the sword met him, and the wall of stones tumbled upon him" (Midr. Pss 11:7). Jakum did this to impose upon himself the four death penalties: stoning, burning, beheading, and strangulation. After all this, the story depicts Jose ben Joezer as seeing Jakum precede him into the Garden of Eden. A similar story concerns the martyrdom of Rabbi Hanina b. Teradion and the suicide of his executioner (ʿAbod. Zar. 18a). This rabbi was wrapped in a Torah scroll and set on fire; but to make sure he suffered, water-soaked tufts of wool were placed over his heart. His disciples advise him to open his mouth and breathe in the fire so that he will die more quickly. R. Hanina b. Teradion, however, refuses to do so: "Let Him who gave [my soul] take it away, but no one should injure himself." The executioner asks if he helps the rabbi die sooner, will he enter the life to come. When answered "Yes," the executioner removes the tufts of wool. The rabbi dies, and the executioner throws himself into the fire. A bath kol announces both have been assigned to the world to come.

Some scholars have used parts of these rabbinic stories--especially the words of Hanina b. Teradion--to prove that the rabbis were against suicide.[27] These narratives cannot really be used for such conclusions because something else is going on in them which tells of death/martyrdom and suicide. Their purpose is not specifically to attack or defend suicide. Rather, the intent of these stories is to demonstrate, as the story of Hanina b. Teradion concludes, "One may acquire eternal life in a single hour, another after many years" (ʿAbod. Zar. 18a). Suicide functions in these narratives as a way of

---

[27] Cf. J. Hamburger, "Selbstmord, Selbstmörder," Real-Encyclopädie für Bibel und Talmud 2, 1 (1883) 1111; G. Margoliouth, "Suicide (Jewish)," Encyclopedia of Religion and Ethics 12 (1925) 37; A. Cohen, Everyman's Talmud (London: J. M. Dent, 1949) 75; C. W. Reines, "The Jewish Attitude Toward Suicide," Judaism 10 (1961) 165; and S. Goldstein, "Suicide in Rabbinic Literature," Ph.D. Dissertation, Yeshiva University (1978) 55.

showing the earnestness of the person's sorrow over his past evil. They act as a self-inflicted death penalty (*Midr. Pss* 11:7; *Gen. Rab.* 65:22) which cancels the suicide's past sins and makes it possible for him to enter into eternal life. Also present may be the idea that it is a person's relationship with God the moment he dies which decides his path after death. From this interpretation it appears that these rabbinic stories of death/ martyrdom and suicide are not some type of suicide narrative. Rather, they should be designated righteous-unrighteous salvations stories.[28]

Suicide appears elsewhere in rabbinic materials in interpretations of the Bible for legal purposes. Although suicide is generally seen in negative terms in these inter-pretations, it is not absolutely forbidden. The verse in Genesis 9:5, "And surely the blood of your lives I will require," is explained as referring to one who strangles himself; but exceptions to this interpretation are also pointed out (*Gen. Rab.* 34:13; cf. *B. Qam.* 91b). Haim Cohn comments that eventually, "the law was settled to the effect that where one is required to commit idolatry, adultery, or murder, he must kill himself or let himself be killed rather than commit any of those crimes (*Sanh.* 74a; Sh. Ar. YD 157)."[29]

These views reaffirm the thesis that Josephus' use of suicide episode and narrative depends almost totally on Greco-Roman models. His extensive use of religious reasons in narratives about Jewish suicides, however, probably derives from Jewish modes of han-dling this form. Examination of Jewish suicide stories has shown that, in Josephus' day, it would not have been unnatural for a Hellenized Jew to resort to the Greco-Roman suicide episode and narrative to describe suicides--and perhaps even martyrdoms--among his own people. The natural question arising from such a conclusion is: Why would this have been the case? To formulate an answer, we must move beyond a description of suicide forms and their history to a discussion of their setting in life. It is not enough to demonstrate that these genres existed; one also has to attempt explanation of why they were formulated and why they developed as they did. Consequently, it is essential to examine the function of suicide episodes and narratives in their setting in Greco-Roman culture, Judaism, and the writings of Josephus.

IV. *Settings of Suicide Accounts*

Officially, ancient Greek religion, as A. W. Mair has pointed out, always regarded suicide "as a crime, a violation of the social order."[30] Yet most of the suicides recorded in Greek literature are viewed favorably. For example, the oldest reported suicide--that of Jocasta--is depicted by Homer as a perfectly natural and dignified way out of an un-bearable situation.[31] Other suicides found in Greek writings are seen as having only the highest motives.[32] Because of this, A. Alvarez has commented, "So far as the records go, the ancient Greeks took their lives only for the best possible reasons: grief, high patriotic principle, or to avoid dishonor."[33] Suicide to preserve one's honor became especially important in the Greek military sphere. Henry Fedden notes that the idea grew among the Greeks, "that is was not consonant with one's dignity and the way a man should die, to fall alive into the hands of one's enemies."[34] He cites the deaths of the

---

[28]Cf. the story of Jesus and the penitent thief on the cross (Luke 23:39-43). Perhaps the suicide of Judas also should be seen in light of this type of story (Matt 27:3-5). If an executioner of a righteous man could enter eternal life by suicide (ᶜ*Abod. Zar.* 18a), perhaps so could one who had betrayed a righteous man. Obviously, however, the later Christian tradition did not understand Judas' act in this manner.

[29]"Suicide," *Encyclopedia Judaica* 15 (1971) 491.

[30]"Suicide," 30.

[31]Cf. Fedden, *Suicide,* 55; A. Alvarez, *The Savage God: A Study of Suicide* (New York: Bantam, 1973) 56.

[32]Cf. Mair, "Suicide," 27-28 and Alvarez, *Savage God,* 56-57 for examples.

[33]*Savage God,* 57.

[34]*Suicide,* 56.

oligarchs of Corcyra, Isocrates, and Demosthenes as examples of this type of suicide.[35] The Spartan law that no soldier might turn his back on the enemy might almost be considered an institutionalization of this belief.[36]

In this setting, where officially suicide was a crime but where under certain circumstances it was not only right but expected, one can explain the formation of the suicide episode. Merely to report the action of suicide was not enough; one also had to report the reason, citing one of the socially acceptable motives for suicide. To record a justifiable suicide, one had to preface it with its justification. This genre developed most probably in military histories of wars where suicides to preserve personal honor would most necessarily be reported.

This Greek idea of the suicide to avoid dishonor was either passed on to or shared with other peoples who came under Hellenic influence. In fact, this concept even had a monument built to it. In 228 B.C. one Attalos, a ruler over Pergamum, defeated the Gauls in battle. He built several monuments commemorating this deed. One statue on one of these monuments became popular in Roman times, several copies being extant. It portrays a single Gaul with his wife, killing himself. Christine Havelock describes the action taking place in this statue:

> Rather than yield to the enemy, whom he seems to sight over his right shoulder, he first kills his wife and then plunges the dagger into his own breast. It is a grim and tragic scene indeed. The wife sinks slowly to the ground away from the supporting hand of her husband--the only significant point of contact between them, which death will soon nullify. Mouth, head, arms, and drapery--everything about her droops. Though blood gushes from his wound, he, on the contrary, is passionately active.[37]

She goes on to point out that the reason for such depiction of a defeated enemy was to emphasize the magnitude of Attalos' triumph. The enemy is presented as so noble and courageous that the ruler's defeat of him "takes on epic proportions."[38] A brave and noble soldier was expected to destroy himself rather than allow himself to be captured.

The Romans also shared this understanding. Most of the suicide stories deal with the deaths of soldiers or officers facing imminent capture. This is interesting since officially suicide was a crime for Roman soldiers. As Karl Geiger points out, it was considered an unauthorized departure from the army, i.e., desertion, and a violation of the soldier's oath of service.[39] This understanding, that suicide was a crime, apparently was applied only to instances when a soldier tried to kill himself to avoid difficult service.[40] Evidently, it was also a crime for a Roman soldier to be captured by an enemy. We know that any legion that lost its eagle in a battle was disbanded.[41] Josephus records one incident where a Roman soldier who had been captured by the Jews and had subsequently escaped was dismissed from his legion, judged unfit to be a Roman soldier (*J.W.* VI. 362). Caesar reports a mass suicide of some troops who had been defeated and were facing capture as a natural and expected act (*Gallic War* V. 37). The strength of the Roman belief that a brave and noble soldier will kill himself to avoid capture is

---

[35]Ibid., 56.

[36]Ibid., 26.

[37]*Hellenistic Art* (Greenwich, CT: New York Graphic Society, 1968) 146.

[38]Ibid., 146.

[39]*Selbstmord*, 75; Cf. E. Durkheim, *Suicide* (New York: The Free Press, 1951) 331. On the Roman military oath see G. Watson, *The Roman Soldier* (New York: Cornell University, 1969) 49-50.

[40]Geiger, *Selbstmord*, 75.

[41]Watson, *Soldier*, 128.

summarized at the end of Lucan's account of the suicide of Vulteius' men: "the purpose of the sword is to save every man from slavery" (*Civil War* IV. 581). If there was no specific written law that a Roman soldier would commit suicide to avoid capture, it was apparently such a strong element in the soldier's code that it acted as a legal precept. Emile Durkheim has explained that in this type of situation a person kills himself "not because he assumes the right to do so, on the contrary, *because it is his duty*. If he fails in this obligation, he is dishonored and also punished. . . ."[42] Suicide, then, to the Roman mind, was demanded in any situation where a person faced capture. If suicide was not performed, the man was held in disrepute.

In this setting, it is understandable how the suicide narrative was formulated. The situation had to be described which warranted suicide as well as the reason given. Essentially, there appear to be some legal reasons behind the situation; the reason for the suicide had to be reported to keep the person from suffering legal repercussions. According to the law, the property of a soldier committing an illegal suicide went to the state. If there were extenuating circumstances, however, the man's family received his estate.[43] The suicide narrative, therefore, probably originated in the official commentaries of a military campaign. It both cleared the suicide's legal record and, since under certain situations suicide was a highly honorable act, extolled his personal bravery. The suicide narrative was probably the ancient Roman equivalent to citation for valorous action under fire found in modern military battle reports.

The original setting was altered, however, when the commentaries were polished up and published for public reading.[44] Probably, at this point, reasons for the suicide were given the form of a speech placed in the mouth of the person about to kill himself. We must remember that generals, like Caesar, who published their commentaries were basically civilian politicians who had been trained in the rhetorical schools and who learned there the skills of speech making. Interestingly, subjects for speeches in schools of rhetoric often deal with suicides. One of the first exercises in learning rhetoric in Rome was impersonation which, as Donald Clark states, "required the pupil to compose an imaginary monolog which might appropriately be spoken or written by a historical, legendary, or fictitious person under a given circumstance."[45] Cato before his suicide seems to have been an especially popular subject for such subjects.[46] More advanced rhetoric students learned declamation, one kind being the *suasoria*--an attempt to persuade a person or group to do or not do something. The *suasoria* usually contained historical or quasi-historical material.[47] Some examples of *suasoria* topics dealing with taking one's life are: Cicero's decision whether to plead for mercy from Antony, escape to Brutus, or die nobly; "The soldiers cut off by the Carthaginians deliberate what to do;" and "The wounded in Sicily implore the Athenians who are retreating to put them to death with their own hands."[48] These rhetorical exercises prepared the future politician-generals to place in the mouth of a soldier about to take his life a speech describing the glorious reasons for his act. Perhaps at first these speeches were reported indirectly, described from the viewpoint of the general. Such indirect speeches may have approximated what was actually said on the occasion.[49]

The suicide narrative quickly moved from a literary setting in the commentaries to one in historical writings. This transition was made possible by the historians' use of

[42]*Suicide*, 219; Cf. Fedden, *Suicide*, 17.

[43]Geiger, *Selbstmord*, 75.

[44]Ladouceur, "Studies," 67, 69, 93ff., for important comments on these commentaries.

[45]*Rhetoric in Greco-Roman Education* (New York: Columbia University, 1957) 199.

[46]Ibid., 220.

[47]Ibid., 213.

[48]Ibid., 220-21.

[49]Thackeray, *Josephus*, 42.

military commentaries as sources.[50]   Probably with this change in literary setting, speeches detailing the reason for suicide came to be reported directly. As has already been noted, ancient historians used such speeches to display their rhetorical skills as well as to express their personal views. The speech of the suicide victim became an exercise in impersonation. Speeches became longer and more developed, greatly expanding the suicide narrative. So succinct reports of suicide to avoid capture found in the commentaries developed into expanded suicide narratives containing long rhetorical speeches. Such change in function brought expansion in length. Where the original suicide narrative cited a valorous deed and cleared the dead soldier from legal repercussions, now the expanded form became the historian's means of expressing his opinion of such an act. With the expression of the writer's views, however, the suicide narrative developed into a voice for the popular upper-class philosophy of the day.

Greek philosophy had primarily stood against suicide; but during the Hellenistic period a philosophy developed which was very favorable to suicide: Stoicism.[51] For the Stoic, life and death are indifferent.[52]   One lives by reason in accord with nature.[53] Suicide enters when circumstances arise which interfere with this manner of life. Robert Hicks explains that for the Stoic:

> When a life in accordance with nature is no longer possible, when we have no means to life, when we can only live by loss of personal honour or through dereliction of duty, then we must obey the call and go. Under such circumstances to remain in life is an act of cowardice as heinous as if we should shrink from death for country or friend; nay, more, it would render all our surviving life useless.[54]

To die rationally and nobly became as important as to live rationally and nobly.

Stoicism became especially popular among the upper class in the first century A.D. under the Empire.[55] Fedden explains that with the harsh aftermath of the civil wars and the despotic type of rule exhibited by someone like Nero, the upper stratum could feel no security: "Unless it were possible to develop an indifference to death, life for these people would have been an intolerable nightmare of fears, tremors, and tortured expectations. To live at all it was necessary to be brave."[56] Stoicism was indeed, as Alvarez has characterized it, a "philosophy of despair";[57] but its advocacy of suicide under certain circumstances made it possible--strange as it is to say--for the upper class to survive. As Fedden notes, "Thanks to the proximity of death, man stood invincible on earth: his spirit need never be subdued, his body need never be tamed."[58] This, then, was the dominating philosophy among those who wrote histories and biographies at the end of the first century A.D. In this context, it is understandable why the suicide narrative became so popular. Seneca could use it in a philosophical treatise (*On Providence* II. 9-12); Lucan could adapt it into a poetical form (*The Civil War* IV. 465-581); Tacitus could use it in historical works (*Annals* XV. 12-14; 69; 70; *Histories* II. 47-49); and Plutarch could use it in biographies (*Cato the Younger* LXVI-LXXII; *Brutus* LII. 1-5; *Otho* XVII. 1-3; etc.). The speeches in the suicide narratives became ways for their authors to express their own personal attitudes toward suicide.

---

[50]Cf. ibid., 38-40.

[51]Cf. Mair, "Suicide," 30; Alvarez, *Savage God*, 58.

[52]Mair, "Suicide," 30.

[53]Ibid., 30.

[54]*Stoic and Epicurean* (New York: Russel & Russel, 1962) 100. Cf. Mair, "Suicide," 30; Alvarez, *Savage God*, 58; Droge, "MORI LUCRUM," 4-8.

[55]Mair, "Suicide," 57; Droge, "MORI LUCRUM," 1, calls it a "suicide cult."

[56]*Suicide*, 84-85.

[57]*Savage God*, 64.

[58]*Suicide*, 78.

The suicide narrative became such a popular literary genre that it in turn influenced how a person committed suicide. The speech, which entered the suicide narrative as a literary method of the historian, apparently became a requirement for one wishing to commit suicide. Mair comments concerning the suicides under Nero, "It appears that in those times every suicide was more or less a *poseur*, who was expected to make his suicide remarkable by some notable word or act."[59] Tacitus' narrative of Seneca's death contains speeches as required by the form; but it also records that Seneca dictated to his secretary a long discourse before his death which was published (*Annals* XV. 13). Tacitus also notes that Lucan recited one of his poems before he died, but he does not record the words (*Annals* XV. 70). These examples suggest that the literary genre entitled suicide narrative came to influence the way a person committed suicide. In effect, it was expected! To do the deed correctly, one had to deliver some kind of oration before death. This is understandable when we remember that the individual's main contact with suicide before he attempted it was probably through narratives about suicides of great men in the past. The literary form for reporting suicides became the form for proper suicides.

So the Roman setting in which Josephus wrote was one which believed that an honorable man--especially a soldier--would kill himself rather than be captured. The Stoic philosophy had strengthened this belief extensively, so that suicide became almost a duty for one caught in an impossible situation. Suicide forms had been adapted to serve almost as mini-treatises on the Stoic attitude toward suicide. The original forms still existed in commentaries and in historical writings, but most popular was the expanded suicide narrative concerning the death of some famous individual which gave free play to an author's rhetorical skills and beliefs on the subject.

Judaism, as has been suggested, had no native suicide genres but adopted Hellenistic suicide forms. With this adoption, however, there was also an adaptation. While the Hellenistic suicide episodes and narratives give reasons of personal or national honor for the act, Jewish examples of these genres present religious reasons. William Farmer has explained that during the Hellenistic period Jewish nationalism was characterized by "zeal for the Torah": "Behind this zeal for the Law lay the more fundamental and original zeal for the covenant God of Israel known to Elijah--a God who had chosen a particular people and was, in his love for his people, exceedingly jealous of all other gods."[60] A Jew was not faithful to some personal sense of honor, and he did not seek to live in accord with nature; rather, he was first and foremost faithful to the God of Israel and he lived in accord with God's laws. It was this absolute devotion to God and his commandments which opened Judaism to the experience of suicide and martyrdom. Razis, for example, must kill himself to avoid capture by the heathen (2 Macc 14:37-46). Martin Hengel explains that such action was necessary because captivity made further observance of the Torah impossible.[61] The thousand who were destroyed in the cave passively accepted death rather than fight on the Sabbath and break God's law (1 Macc 2:29-38). 4 Maccabees tells of the martyrdoms and suicide in one Jewish family because of their refusal to eat unclean meat (cf. 2 Macc 7:1-42; *b. Giṭ.* 57b). The situation did not really change with the coming of the Romans. Josephus reports that when Pompey captured the Temple, priests were struck down in the midst of their rituals because they put "the worship of the Deity above their own preservation" (*J.W.* I. 150). On this same occasion others are reported to have committed suicide.

Another element which supported this willingness to die for God was a growing belief in an afterlife. Razis at the moment of his death calls upon the Lord of life and spirit to give him back the entrails which he has just hurled at his enemies (2 Macc 14:46). The four hundred boys and girls who kill themselves are said to have done so in

---

[59]"Suicide," 32.
[60]*Maccabees,* 49.
[61]*Zeloten,* 276.

the belief that they would be resurrected (*b. Giṭ.* 57b). The righteous-unrighteous salvation stories all have such a belief as their primary basis (*ᶜAbod. Zar.* 18a; *b. Ketub.* 103b; *Gen. Rab.* 65:22; *Midr. Pss* 11:7). Farmer states, "It is this belief in the resurrection of the body which largely accounts for the astounding phenomenon of mass martyrdom as well as mass military heroism on the part of the Jews in the Greco-Roman Period."[62] This is probably an overstatement. The Sadducees, who did not believe in an afterlife (*J.W.* I. 165), were apparently willing to die for their God (cf. *J.W.* I. 150). The concept of a future life of bliss, however, undoubtedly made it easier for the devoted Jew to commit suicide or accept martyrdom for faithfulness to God.[63]

The greatest number of Jewish suicides evidently occurred among various revolutionary groups of the first century A.D. Josephus pictures these revolutionaries as sharing a common understanding that God alone was their lord (*J.W.* II. 118; *Ant.* XVIII. 23). With this belief, many zealous Jews could not tolerate the Roman claim to rulership over the Holy Land. Therefore, they resorted to armed violence in attempting to overthrow Roman rule.[64] This ultimately ended in failure; but up through the final defeat at Masada, Josephus records many incidents where Jewish rebels freely committed suicide to avoid falling into Roman hands. They refused to accept a life of captivity where they would have a human master and where they could no longer follow God's commandments. Hengel explains there were other considerations for the revolutionaries concerning their families. If captured, the women would be delivered up to shame and the children were in danger of themselves growing up as heathens, worshipping idols.[65] These fighters for Israel's freedom also probably shared an idea of an afterlife into which they would enter because of their zeal for the Law (cf. *J.W.* VII. 343-350).[66]

The various revolutionary groups, then, shared with other Jews a strong belief in following the laws of God. As they were more willing than others to actively pursue the sole rulership of God over Israel, so were they more willing to actively take their own lives when they were faced with a hopeless situation which would not allow them to live by God's commandments. Normally, the propensity to commit suicide on the part of various revolutionaries is considered as another form of martyrdom.[67] The present study would suggest that the opposite is the case: martyrdom is another form of suicide. The idea of suicide under certain circumstances seems to have entered Judaism most strongly during the Hellenistic period. Hellenistic suicide ideas and forms were adapted by Judaism. If this is the case, it implies that suicide preceded martyrdom among Jews faced by Hellenistic oppression. Perhaps the story of the thousand in the cave (1 Macc 2:29-38) shows the point of departure from active suicide to passive martyrdom. If one could not lift the sword to defend oneself on the Sabbath, could one lift it to kill oneself? Although this is a very hypothetical suggestion, it does explain how martyrdom

[62] *Maccabees,* 190; cf. Hengel, *Zeloten,* 275-76.

[63] An example of this is found in *J.W.* I. 653. The men who tore down Herod's eagle from the Temple are asked by the king, "And why so exultant, when you will shortly be put to death?" They answer, "Because, after our death, we shall enjoy greater felicity."

[64] Cf. Hengel, *Zeloten,* 267; within the last decade the unity of the revolutionaries has been seriously questioned; cf. M. Smith, "Zealots and Sicarii, their Origins and Relation," *HTR* 64 (1971) 1-19; D. M. Rhoads, *Israel in Revolution: 6-74 C.E. A Political History Based on the Writings of Josephus* (Philadelphia: Fortress, 1976); and R. A. Horsley, "Ancient Jewish Banditry and the Revolt against Rome, A.D. 66-70," *CBQ* 43 (1981) 409-32; "Josephus and the Bandits," *JSJ* 10 (1979) 37-63; "The Sicarii: Ancient Jewish Terrorists," *JR* 59 (1979) 435-58.

[65] *Zeloten,* 276.

[66] Cf. Hengel, Zeloten, 275-76. Note the relationship of the fourth philosophy with the Pharisees (*Ant.* XVIII. 23), a group which believed in an afterlife (*J.W.* II. 163; *Ant.* XVIII. 14).

[67] Hengel, *Zeloten,* 268.

might have developed within certain circles. Martyrdom might then be considered one of the ways Hellenistic ideas about suicide were adapted by Judaism. Certain revolutionaries, however, retained the more Hellenistic idea of active suicide when faced with a hopeless situation. Hengel has stated that the heroic contempt for death exhibited in suicides by Jewish revolutionaries was a unique attitude for the classical world and must have appeared as madness to the Romans.[68] The present investigation, however, has shown that exactly the contrary was true. An indifference to death exhibited by suicide was a common attitude in the Hellenistic world of the first century. Rather than non-understandable madness to the Romans, the revolutionaries' propensity to commit suicide was probably one place the Romans could understand and sympathize to some extent with their strange enemy.[69] Ironically, with their suicides to keep from being captured by the Romans, the revolutionaries--especially the Sicarii of Masada--were possibly most captive to the alien influences they were fighting against.

In conclusion, the setting in which Josephus' use of the suicide episode and narrative has to be placed is one in which both Jews and Romans considered suicide a very honorable and, indeed, at certain times an obligatory act. The Roman attitude was shaped by concepts of personal honor and living in accord with nature while the Jewish attitude was fashioned by concepts of God's rulership and absolute obedience to his will; but both peoples agreed that suicide was a viable way for the individual to avoid change in his life situation repugnant to him Josephus took over the Greco-Roman suicide episode and narrative to portray such deaths. Some of these were probably borrowed directly from his sources. The story of the old bandit (J.W. I.312-313), for example, probably comes from Nicholas of Damascus' history of Herod's reign.[70] The succinct narrative about the death of Longus (J.W. VI. 186-187), on the other hand, probably derives from official Roman commentaries on the Jewish War.[71] Josephus, however, would have been the one who placed a story like that of Ahithophel into the proper suicide narrative form (Ant. VII. 228-229). He is also undoubtedly responsible for the extended suicide narrative form of the story of the fall of Masada (J.W. VII. 320-401). For the most part, then, Josephus' uses of the suicide genres fit directly into the typical settings in life common for such stories in both Greco-Roman and Jewish circles.

Because of his own personal setting in life, however, Josephus could not wholeheartedly advocate the type of action described in the suicide genres. After all, he was a defeated general who had refused to commit suicide, freely surrendering to his conqueror. Because of this personal situation, the function of at least one suicide narrative is apologetic. Josephus must defend his own avoidance of an action deemed honorable by many of his own people and his Roman patrons. He performs this task by using the rhetorical speech of the expanded suicide narrative to express anti-suicide arguments (J.W. III. 346-391).[72] Here he carries on a discussion not so much with his revolutionary subordinates as with his Hellenistic readers. The arguments for suicide he cites in order to disprove (J.W. III. 363-368) may have been held by the soldiers under his command;[73] they were probably held by many of Josephus' readers. Josephus draws on Hellenistic philosophical ideas which ran counter to suicide as well as ideas we meet in later rabbinic materials to explain his surrender. First, he justifies his act by claiming

---

[68]Ibid., 266.

[69]On Roman attitudes toward people in the empire cf. J. P. V. D. Balsdon, Romans & Aliens (Chapel Hill: University of North Carolina, 1979), especially on suicide, 249-52.

[70]Nicholas probably included this account of the suicides of the bandits to glorify Herod, just as Attalos erected monuments to the suicidal Gauls he defeated.

[71]Cf. T. Rajak, "Flavius Josephus: Jewish History in the Greek World," Ph. D. Dissertation, Oxford (1974) 169.

[72]Cf. Ladouceur, "Studies," 93-94, where he notes how Josephus inverts the Duel of Champions form also.

[73]Cf. Hengel, Zeloten, 268-69.

that he had a message from God which had to be delivered to Vespasian (*J.W.* III. 353-354). He then argues against the piety of suicide. He writes in words reminiscent of Hanina b. Teradion: "For it is from Him [God] that we received our being, and it is to Him that we should leave the decision to take it away" (*J.W.* III. 371). He adds a statement that the suicide is punished by God in the afterlife, not honored (*J.W.* III. 375). He refers to an unknown Hebrew rule about dishonorable treatment of the suicide's body as well as such laws in other nations (*J.W.* III. 376-378). Finally, he concludes by attempting to convince his opponents that surrendering to a conqueror is not dishonorable.

Josephus has often been excoriated as a traitor to his religion and people because of his surrender to the Romans. To the contrary, by his surrender, Josephus might have been most faithful to the beliefs of the Pharisaic party in which he claimed membership. In the later rabbinic materials, as we have seen, suicide was allowed as a means of cleansing great apostasy against God. While Josephus was convinced the revolutionaries stood guilty before God and therefore should commit suicide (*J.W.* VII. 332-333), we see no evidence that he saw himself in such a state. The rabbis also would accept suicide to avoid the great sins of idolatry, adultery, and murder. Surrender to the Romans involved none of these dangers for Josephus (*J.W.* III. 346-349). Consequently, if Josephus was a Pharisee, he could not kill himself in the situation in which he found himself at Jotapata and still remain faithful to his party's beliefs concerning when suicide was justifiable. Like Johanan b. Zakkai, Josephus too bent before the will of God as he perceived it and surrendered to the Romans. Also like Johanan b. Zakkai, Josephus never abandoned his religion and his people. He spent the rest of his life defending them before the Roman world. It must have taken the bravery of a prophet to defend the Jews in the very court of the Flavian family which had destroyed Jerusalem and the Temple.

ENTERING THE KINGDOM LIKE CHILDREN:
A STRUCTURAL EXEGESIS

Daniel Patte
Vanderbilt University

The six texts selected by J. Dominic Crossan--Matthew 18:1-5 (or 9?); Matthew 19:13-15; Mark 10:13-16; Luke 18:15-17; John 3:1-6; Gospel of Thomas 22--form a corpus admirably suited for structural exegesis. They can be compared to the variants of a myth studied by Lévi-Strauss. Studying their structural relations should allow us to specify the features of their common theme as well as to elucidate the specific connotations which this theme takes in each of these texts.

As a starting point for our study we need to identify, at the level of the textual manifestation, the common theme of these six texts. Reflecting upon the nature of this theme we shall then select an approach suited for our comparative study.

1. IDENTIFICATION OF THE TEXTUAL MANIFESTATIONS OF THE COMMON THEME

1.0   These six texts have in common a clearly recognizable theme--which can also be called a tradition or a mytheme. Yet the textual constants found in these six texts are very few. All of them can be expressed in a single statement: *a pronouncement by Jesus relating "entering the Kingdom" with "childhood" addressed to a character with an overall positive relation to Jesus.* (This applies to all the texts except Matt 19:13-15, which is a weak variant and does not include the verb "entering." The true variant is in Matt 18:1-5.)

1.1   In each case Jesus utters the pronouncement. It is addressed to a collective or individual character--the disciples, except in John 3 where it is Nicodemus. This character has an overall positive relation to Jesus--this is clear in the case of the disciples, and Nicodemus comes to Jesus with a positive evaluation of his ministry (John 3:2). Yet the pronouncement is contrasted to a misapprehension by the character of a situation or of a statement by Jesus (except in Matt 18:1-5). But this situation or statement is in itself a variable in our corpus, despite the parallelism between the synoptic texts.

1.2   In our formulation of the constants in the pronouncement, relating "entering the Kingdom" with "childhood," the term "childhood" should be read in a very broad sense. In Mark 10 the term "children" is not qualified. In Matthew 18 the children are apparently old enough to stand. In Luke 18:15 they are "babies" (although they are called "children" in 18:16-17). In Thomas 22 they are "children being suckled." Finally, it is the "new born" which is the concern of John 3.

2. THE APPROACH NEEDED FOR THE STUDY OF SUCH A COMMON THEME

2.0   Our main task will be to compare the different meanings that this common theme has in the six texts. This involves comparing the various forms this common theme takes when it is set in the midst of the specific networks of relations which characterize each of our texts.

In order to undertake this task we must first note that the common theme is itself characterized by two sets of relations: (a) the relations between Jesus and his addressees; and (b) in the pronouncement itself, the relation of "entering the Kingdom" to "childhood." The nature of these relations defines the ways in which the theme can be set into a wider relational network and in so doing can acquire various connotations. For indeed, relations have very specific natures and cannot be grafted upon relations of a totally different species.

2.10   The first relation is a reported enunciation: Jesus speaking to his disciples or Nicodemus. According to Greimas' theory, this is a relation of the discoursive syntax. In other words, it is a relation in the discourse (the text) which manifests, together with other relations of the same type, the relation between the enunciator and the enunciatee of the text. It has the effect of constructing a reader, indeed a receptive ideal "reader," as well as a credible and persuasive "author." More specifically, this relation is part of the process of characterization. Each of the texts poses Jesus as the character who displays the true understanding of a situation or statement. As such Jesus is like the enunciator who has a true understanding of the story he/she tells.

Jesus' addressees have a twofold qualification. (1) Either by their name (disciples defined earlier in the texts and in various ways as characters in a positive relation with Jesus) or by their own statement (Nicodemus stating "we know that you are a teacher come from God" John 3:2) they are posited as characters who acknowledge Jesus' authority and thus are receptive to his teaching. As such they are like the enunciatee, the ideal "reader," who is receiving this true teaching. (2) But Jesus' addressees are also cast in a somewhat negative light (except in Matt 18:1-4; in the other texts the negative connotation is more or less marked). They misinterpret either a situation or a statement from Jesus or at least they do not know something (as in Matt 18:1-5). Yet they are not rejected but rather corrected. They do lack true understanding, they need teaching or instruction, but are given what they lack. As such they are like the ideal reader constructed by the text who needs the true understanding provided by the enunciator.

2.11   Thus this first set of relations of the common theme belongs to the *discoursive syntax*. We can expect that it will be set in the various discoursive structures of the six texts. The relations of the common theme as constants can be viewed as a constraint which limits the range of the possible discoursive strategies--i.e., the range of the possible investments of the discoursive structures. Yet, because it establishes only a few syntactical relations, it leaves open the possibility of many variations at the discoursive level.

Our comparison of these six texts needs therefore to involve a study of the discoursive structures of these six texts. Yet because of the nature of our corpus--made of short passages of much longer texts (Gospels)--we can expect only partial results. Discoursive structures are manifested most clearly throughout an entire discourse. Yet because of the common theme as constant, our comparative study should allow us to reach significant results at the level of the discoursive syntax.

2.20   The pronouncement itself is characterized by the relation between the "entering the Kingdom" and "childhood." This is the relation between a "function" or better a transformation--"entering the Kingdom"--which belongs to narrative syntax and a "state," or semantic category--"childhood"--which belongs to narrative semantics.

2.21   The first set of relations discussed above (2.10 and 2.11) can be said to be simple in the sense that it interrelates terms belonging to the same structural level--discoursive syntax. As such it functions as a fairly strong constraint which drastically limits the number of possible variations. This set of relations establishes a definite pattern which must be respected in the entire discoursive syntax. By contrast, in the case of this second set of relations--between "entering the Kingdom" and "childhood"--we are dealing with a complex relation in the sense that it interrelates terms belonging to different structural levels--narrative syntax and narrative semantics.

The complexity of this relation appears when one realizes that in a discourse (or text) the relation between narrative syntax and narrative semantics is a relation between two systems: a narrative syntactical system and a narrative semantic system. The correspondence--or, more technically, the isotopic (by contrast to isomorphic) relation-ship--of these two systems is a correspondence of *relations* involving each time several terms. The syntactical system establishes a series of transformations in relations of cause and effect (a first transformation allowing the performance of another), in rela-tions of complementarity (several transformations contributing together to the perfor-mance of another) and in polemical relations (transformations opposing the performance of others). The syntactical relations indirectly correspond (that is, not in a one-to-one correspondence, yet nevertheless according to specific laws; see Patte and Patte, 1978, ch. II and Patte, 1981) to semantic relations. The (narrative) semantic system establishes a series of semantic terms in relations of implication (or correlation), of contradiction or of contrariety. This is true in the case of a simple semantic system--including a single semantic field, or isotopy--as well as in the case of a complex semantic system--includ-ing several isotopies. In this later case the terms set in relations can belong to different isotopies and be interrelated through what is called a metaphorical relationship which is nothing other than either a relation of correlation (the most comon case), or of contra-diction or again of contrariety.

Now, in the common theme the relation between narrative syntax and narrative semantics is limited to the relation between a single term from each of the two systems. This means that *each term remains essentially undefined.* For indeed, a transformation--such as "entering the Kingdom"--is defined through its relations with other transformations in a given syntactical system. Similarly a semantic term--such as "childhood"--is defined through its relations with other semantic terms in a given semantic system. This means the relation between "entering the Kingdom" and "childhood" posited by the common theme is a very weak constraint. This relation can be conceived in a great number of ways since each of its terms is undefined and thus can be variously defined by being inserted in widely different either syntactical or semantic systems.

2.22   Our comparative study of the six texts needs therefore to involve (a) a study of the narrative syntactical system of each text so as to determine how, in each instance, the transformation "entering the Kingdom" is defined; (b) a study of the "narrative" semantic system of each text so as to determine how, in each instance, the semantic term "childhood" is defined. Even though we are dealing with very short texts--and thus with very partial syntactic and semantic systems--we should be able to reach significant results because both of these systems are characterized by patterns of relationship which are manifested in each of their parts. Thus we can expect to find a great diversity in meaning given to the relation between "entering the Kingdom" and "childhood," but we should be able to elucidate in such case at least some of the characteristics of this relation.

2.3   Finally, we have to take into consideration the correlation in the common theme of the two sets of relations. Discursive syntax--such as that of the relations between Jesus and his addressees--and narrative syntax and semantics are necessarily interrelated in a given discourse. Thus the correlation between the two sets of relations of the common theme is certainly another constraint contributing to the limitation of the field of possible variants.

Unfortunately semiotic research has not yet been able to define in any detailed fashion the nature of the relations between semio-narrative structures (including narra-tive syntax and semantics) and discursive structures. We will therefore have to proceed with caution on the basis of our knowledge of these various structures taken separately. Yet it remains clear that through their correlation the two sets of relations of the common theme define each other somewhat.

3.   COMPARISON OF THE SIX TEXTS IN TERMS OF THEIR DISCOURSIVE SYNTAX:
     THE RELATION BETWEEN JESUS AND HIS ADDRESSEES

3.0   Our goal in this first part of our structural exegesis is to determine how the
relation between Jesus and his addressees is specifically defined in each text. For this
purpose we need to study the discoursive syntax of each of these texts. In the "generative trajectory" (the overall structural model for a discourse proposed by Greimas), the
discoursive syntax involves three processes: characterization, temporalization, and spatialization. It is the stage of the generative trajectory in which characters are constructed in such a way that they might be recognizable and (at least to a certain extent),
believable ("realistic") for the intended reader. A character is constructed on the one
hand through its relations with other characters and on the other hand through the establishment of its competence as subject with a wanting (will, *vouloir*), a knowing (know-how
or knowledge, *savoir*), and a being able to (power, ability, having the necessary tools,
pouvoir). Similarly a time frame and space frame are constructed in such a way that the
narrative might be located in a time and space framework which might make sense for
the intended reader.

This discoursivization process, with its concern to establish a link between enunciator and enunciatee, is, of course, building upon the narrative syntax and semantics (of
the enunciator). And therefore there is necessarily some overlap between the discoursive
syntax and the narrative syntax. Yet by focussing our attention on the three processes of
discoursivization briefly described above, it is possible to isolate the discoursive syntactical system which characterizes a text. Following this procedure will allow us to elucidate the specific view of the relation between Jesus and his addressees in each text.

3.1   *The Relation between Jesus and the Disciples in Mark 10:13-16*
Since most of the discoursive syntax of Mark 10:13-16 is devoted to characterization, let us begin by the two other aspects of the discoursivization process.

3.11   *Temporalization.* The only time markers in this text are those found in the
past tenses of the verbs (primarily aorists). The absence of any other time marker leaves
the time framework largely undefined. Of course, as reader of what precedes in the
Gospel of Mark, the enunciatee is also under the constraints of the time markers elsewhere in the Gospel which we cannot study here. Yet if we consider the pronouncement
story in and of itself, the enunciatee is left with a large freedom to set this story in a
time framework of his/her choice. In other words, the presence of rather weak time
markers gives to the pronouncement story a timeless quality. The reader is in the same
time frame: before the time for entering the Kingdom (an undefined future weakly
marked by an aorist subjunctive with a double negative).

3.12   *Spatialization.* There is no space marker denoting a specific concrete
location. Yet a threefold space is nevertheless constructed:
     (a)   There is space *near* Jesus, indeed very near Jesus, in his arms (10:16a) being
touched by him (10:13b, 16c). It is a euphoric space in which one is blessed by Jesus
(10:16b) as the children are.
     (b)   The *Kingdom* is also a space in which one enters (10:15c). It is a space which
is clearly euphoric since it is presupposed that the addressees (the disciples) wish to enter
it. The juxtaposition of these two euphoric spaces--the one in the narrative form, the
other in the pronouncement--has the effect of correlating them. Being near Jesus (in the
arms of Jesus) is like being in the Kingdom. Since the space "near Jesus" is very narrow
(limited to direct contact with Jesus), the space *Kingdom* is itself very narrow.
     (c)   A third space, *away from Jesus,* is occupied by the children and those who
being them to Jesus (10:13). By comparison with the two other spaces it is dysphoric:
the children should not stay in that space (10:14).

The disciples are in an ambiguous position. They form the border between the two spaces: neither near Jesus ("in his arms") as the children (10:16), nor away from Jesus. In fact, they are rebuked for attempting to establish a clear borderline between the spaces "away from Jesus" and "near Jesus." One of the goals of the story is to make clear that the passage from the dysphoric space "away from Jesus" to the euphoric space "near Jesus" should remain open.

3.13   *Characterization.* Except for the people who bring the children to Jesus, who are merely characterized by their will to do so, the only other active subjects are the disciples and Jesus.

Through the term used to designate them, the "disciples" are posited as being in an overall positive relation with Jesus. Yet in our text they are primarily characterized by their opposition to the people bringing the children and thus indirectly to the children and by the fact that they are the addressees of Jesus' pronouncement which objects to their attitude. A closer look at the text will allow us to specify the nature of the Jesus-disciples relationship.

First, let us take note that Jesus' words are presented as being the result of his "seeing" and of an emotional reaction, "(he) was indignant" (10:14). Verbs of perception and those expressing emotion often introduce the interpretation/evaluation of a situation by a character. This is certainly the case here since we find not one but two interpretation markers. Jesus interprets a twofold situation. On the one hand, a positive value is attributed to the bringing of children to him. On the other hand, a negative value is attributed to the disciples' negative attitude toward this first situation. This means that the disciples' attitude is itself interpretative in nature despite the fact that there is only a weaker interpretation marker in 10:13c (yet note that *epitimaō* is derived from *timaō*).

Thus, the conflict between Jesus and the disciples is first of all the conflict of two interpretations of a concrete situation, "people bringing children to Jesus." More precisely, it is a conflict of evaluations, that is of an interpretation of the positive (euphoric) or negative (dysphoric) value of the concrete situation.

In addition, it is a conflict regarding the concrete attitude (doing) one should have vis-à-vis this concrete situation: allowing the children to come to Jesus or hindering them to do so. In Greimas' terminology this is a conflict of "deontic modalities," that is, concerning what one *has to do* in such a situation. This observation is furthermore confirmed by the fact that after the interpretative pronouncement the text comes back to the concrete situation by showing Jesus taking in his arms the children who have thus been allowed to come to him. The performance of the proper action--the action that one has to do in a specific situation--is thus underscored.

Thus it becomes clear that what is at stake is the establishment of the will (wanting) of the disciples as subjects rather than the establishment of one of the other competencies (knowing and being able to) of the subject. Jesus through his pronouncement does not impart to his disciples a knowledge (a teaching) which they need in order to carry out an action that they already want to carry out, but rather the *very will* to carry it out. Using another vocabulary, that of the covenant, we could say that Jesus by his pronouncement imparts to the disciples a vocation, that is a perception of their identity and purpose as elect, rather than the means to carry out their vocation (the Law).

This observation is confirmed by an examination of discursive features of the pronouncement. To begin with Jesus is alone to speak. In contrast with most of the other texts we shall study, the disciples do not ask a question. They do not have any questions. They know what should be done! They are deliberately carrying out a program of action on their own. But what they want to do, their will, is wrong. They have a wrong perception of what they should do. The two imperatives (*aphete, mē kōluete,* 10:14) aim at transforming their will, by showing them what they should do, what is the proper will they should have. Note that this is not imposed as a "must" (*devoir*) by the mere authority of the speaker (as a dictator imposes his will upon his subjects). Rather it is through a proper interpretation of the situation that the disciples' proper will is to be established. They should allow children to come to Jesus *because* the Kingdom of God belongs to those such as the children. In other words, the true reality of the situation "people bringing children to Jesus" can be perceived by the disciples only if they interpret it in terms of the Kingdom of God. When one does this it appears that the situation has to be interpreted positively (as a euphoric situation and not as a dysphoric one). The Kingdom is for those such as the children. Consequently it is proper to let them come to Jesus. Of course, such a conclusion demands viewing Jesus as directly related to the Kingdom. Thus, in summary, the disciples are not the passive receptors of a new will. They have to participate in the establishment of their new will in joining Jesus in his interpretation of the situation in terms of the Kingdom.

The discoursive features of Mark 10:15 make it clear, once again, that the goal of the pronouncement is the one suggested above. I want to refer to the negative form of the injunction "whoever does *not* receive the Kingdom like a child shall *not* enter it." This negative form is purely a feature of discoursive syntax, since, as we shall see below, it does not play any role in the narrative syntax of Mark 10:13-16. A positive formulation in an imperative form--receive the Kingdom like a child and you shall enter it-- would leave the addressees in a relatively passive role of receptor of a new will. By contrast the negative formulation with the indefinite relative clause demands the involvement of the addressees who, at the very least, have to prolong this statement by thinking: "but I want to enter the Kingdom and thus I need to receive it like a child." Thus it is the addressees who formulate what is the proper will and not the addresser.

3.14   Finally, the text describes Jesus interacting with the children. For the disciples this new situation should be interpreted in terms of the pronouncement and the pronouncement in terms of the new situation. But the fact that this interpretation by the disciples is not given makes it clear that this description is for the readers. The readers are thus those who are expected to carry out this twofold interpretation (as we shall do below) and thus find themselves in the position of the disciples. Thus, beyond their interpretation of what it means to receive the Kingdom like a child, they are also invited to establish their own will and course of action on the basis of their interpretations of various situations in terms of the Kingdom. These include situations belonging to any time period (see above 3.11) and in any space where they can identify a space "near Jesus," a space of "the Kingdom," and a space "away from Jesus" (see above 3.12).

3.2   *The Relation between Jesus and the Disciples in Matt 18:1-5*
Despite the parallelism with Mark 9:33-37, regarding the question "who is the greatest in the Kingdom," we shall compare Matt 18:1-5 to Mark 10:13-16 because it is in this context that Matthew chose to set the pronouncement to the disciples about entering the Kingdom like a child.

3.21   *Temporalization.* In addition to the past tenses of the verbs, we find another time marker, *en ekeinē tē hōra* (18:1a), which has the effect of locating in a general way the pronouncement story in the past time of Jesus' ministry. Thus at the outset it is made clear that the meaning of the story can be properly understood only in the context of "that time," the time of Jesus' ministry. This weakens the effect of the undefined future of the Kingdom.

3.22   *Spatialization.* There is no space marker denoting a specific concrete (geographical) location. As in Mark 10 a space is nevertheless constructed. Yet it has a quite different character.

(a)   There is the space *near Jesus.* Yet it is conceived in a broader sense. It is no longer a space where one touches and is touched by Jesus. It is now a circle which includes Jesus and the disciples (who come to Jesus, 18:16) and in the midst of which a child can be put. The fact that this is indeed a euphoric space is only marked indirectly by the presence of Jesus, which is positively marked since the beginning of the Gospel, and in opposition to 18:6.

(b)   The *Kingdom* is also a space in which one is (18:1c) and one can enter (18:3d). This euphoric space (for the same reason as in Mark 10 and, in addition, as the space of "life," 18:8) is once again juxtaposed to the space near Jesus. They are thus correlated. Since the space "near Jesus" is now wider, a circle rather than a point (of contact), the Kingdom is itself a wider space. Despite other connotations of the phrase "of heaven," heaven is also perceived as a location as is clear from its opposition to the Gehenna.

The following verses (6-9) include three dysphoric spaces:

(a)   The deep of the sea as the space for those who make stumble (*skandalizō* the little ones (18:6).

(b)   The *world* as the space where *skandalon* occurs (18:7). This is a space outside of the circle near Jesus in which the disciples are exhorted to reject whatever is a cause of stumbling (a hand, a foot, an eye).

(c)   A space of *eternal fire* (18:8), the Gehenna of fire (18:9), which is the dysphoric counterpart of the Kingdom.

Thus, as compared with what we found in Mark, the spaces have become more "spacious" and the separation of the euphoric from the dysphoric spaces is strongly marked (by contrast with the pronouncement story in Mark which aimed at breaking the separation between these spaces).

3.23   *Characterization.* We shall focus our remarks on the characterization of the disciples and Jesus.

The disciples are not only posited as being in an overall positive relation to Jesus (through the term "disciples" used to designate them), but are also characterized in the pronouncement story as being in a positive relationship with Jesus. They come to Jesus (18:1b), and their question (18:1c) is answered by Jesus (18:4) rather than being rejected as illegitimate.

By contrast with Mark 10:13-16, none of the characters is presented as interpreting a concrete situation previously described in the text (note the absence of interpretative markers) and acting accordingly. Rather the disciples address a question to Jesus. As such they are characterized as lacking knowledge (information) concerning a specific topic--an aspect of the existence in the Kingdom. As the one who answers the question, Jesus is characterized as one who knows, who has information that others do not have. Thus the relation Jesus-disciples is a relation teacher-pupils.

More specifically, through their questions the disciples show that they are confident that they belong to the Kingdom. The only question is who is the greatest in it. There is no hint that the establishment of the will of the disciples is at stake. The use of the logion found in Mark 10:15 would then be problematic since its negative form is aimed at involving the addressees in the establishment of their own will. And thus it is not surprising to find a quite different function of the saying. Instead of having a function at the level of discursive syntax, the negative verbs function now at the level of the narrative syntax, thanks to their juxtaposition with a statement using a series of positive verbs. The addressees do not have any longer to construct the positive statement; Jesus utters it. Thus the only involvement of the disciples is to acknowledge and to express that they lack knowledge. Jesus is providing all the knowledge they need.

3.24   Even though this is anticipating our study of the relation between Kingdom and childhood, we can note that this discursive characterization of the relations between the disciples and Jesus is closely related to the attitude of humility described in 18:4. By their question and their attitude as pupils of the teacher Jesus, the disciples demonstrate that they belong to the Kingdom. Thus the readers are invited to identify with the disciples and enter in the same relationship with Jesus, asking the disciples' question as well as listening with them to Jesus' answer. As such the readers are called to identify with the time of the disciples--"that time" (see above 3:21)--so as to listen to Jesus' words and consequently, so to speak, to "withdraw" from their present time. In the same time they need to withdraw from the world where *skandalon* occurs so as to be in the space "near Jesus," listening to him because they are aware of their lack of knowledge, and as such belonging to the Kingdom rather than to the world and the Gehenna (see above 3.22).

3.3   The Relation between Jesus and the Disciples in Matt 19: 13-15

3.31   *Temporalization.* The addition of the time marker *tote* to the past tense of the verbs has the same effect as *en ekeinē tē hōra* has in Matt 18:1-5. It inscribes the pronouncement story in the time of Jesus' ministry whether it is interpreted "in that time" or "then." See above 3:21.

3.32   *Spatialization.* A threefold space is constructed similar to that in Mark 10:13-16 (see above 3.12). It is enough to note the differences:
(a)   The space *near Jesus* is not as intimate as in Mark. Jesus does *not* take the children into his arms. It is not even sure that he touches them. The phrase *epitheis tas cheiras autois* may be understood as a liturgical gesture which might not involve actual physical contact. At any rate, physical contact is not as emphasized. Thus the space "near Jesus" is not as narrow as in Mark (and thus more like the one in Matt 18:1-5, see above 3.22a). Furthermore, "laying his hand on the children" is presented as something Jesus does as he goes away from them. Laying his hand on the children is expressed in a subordinate clause of th principle verb *eporeuthē*. This has the effect of minimizing the positive value of the space "in direct contact with Jesus."
(b)   The space *Kingdom* is mentioned, but also de-emphasized as space (there is no mention of "entering the Kingdom").
(c)   The space "away from Jesus" is presented as being dysphoric as in Mark 10:13-16 (see 3.12c). But the physical separation from Jesus is not necessarily dysphoric since his departure after laying his hand on the children is euphoric.

3.33   *Characterization.* The comparison with Mark 10:13-16 is instructive. The two clear interpretative markers (*idōn* and *ēganaktēsen*) as well as the second part (heavily interpretative in form) of the pronouncement have disappeared. Thus the interpretative dimension of *epitemēsan* which remains is de-emphasized if not completely bracketed out. Thus, even though the first part of the pronouncement remains approximately the same, it becomes a teaching expressing how to conduct oneself as disciples in such a situation. This teaching provides the disciples with the knowledge necessary to carry out in a special circumstance the program in which they are already established as willing subjects. This program is nothing other than their vocation as disciples. In other words, what is at stake is not their will to be disciples nor their status as disciples (by contrast to Mark 10 according to which by behaving as they did the disciples showed they did not belong to the Kingdom), but indeed the performance of their vocation in a specific circumstance. Thus Jesus, while correcting them, does not address a fundamental reproof to them. He is not "indignant." Thus the relation of Jesus to the disciples remains one of teacher to willing pupils as in Matt 18:1-5 (see 3.24).

3.4   The Relation between Jesus and the Disciples in Luke 18:15-17

3.41   *Temporalization.* Exactly as in Mark 10:13-16 (see above 3.11).

3.42   *Spatialization.* A threefold space is constructed as in Mark 10:13-16 (see above (3:12). The only difference is that it is no longer expressed that Jesus touched the children (babies) after the interruption of the program by the disciples. Thus the space "near Jesus" is not as intimate as in Mark, and more like in Matt 18:1-5 (see 3.22). Yet here it is a "verbal" space delimited by Jesus' call.

3.43   *Characterization.* At the outset the characterization in Luke 18:15-17 appears as being different from that of either Mark or Matthew. To begin with it is not clear that the pronouncement is addressed to the disciples. Nestle (following the best witnesses) can be translation: "But Jesus called them (the babes) to him, saying. . . ." "Saying" is a subordinate clause of "called the babies to him." Thus the addressees are those who are associated with the babies, that is, those who brought them and possibly other people with them, as well as the disciples who rebuked them. (The variant found in other good witnesses--which can be translated "But Jesus calling them to him, said"--de-emphasizes somewhat the association of the addressees with the babies. Thus they could be the disciples alone. Yet one would expect *autois* which remains absent. This is another reason to prefer Nestle's text.)

Thus the disciples--despite their name which relates them to Jesus--are not the privileged addressees of Jesus. They are among other addresses of Jesus. Furthermore, Jesus "bypasses" them to directly call the babies to him.

The disciples in and of themselves are characterized as interpreting (evaluating) a situation and acting accordingly, as is expressed by the interpretative marker *idontes* (18:15c) and the weaker interpretative marker *epetimon.* Thus the establishment of their will as subject of the program is what characterizes them. Consequently, as in Mark 10:13-16, the pronouncement aims at the correct establishment of their will by the addressees.

The interpretative marker *idon* is not repeated concerning Jesus. But the adversative *de* which sets Jesus in opposition to the disciples expresses that Jesus is himself interpreting the situation. Yet the absence of strong interpretative markers has the effect of de-emphasizing the interpretative relation between the situation and Jesus' pronouncement. The relation is less direct. This is furthermore manifested by the fact that Jesus relates to the children as if the disciples--who are part of the situation that Jesus interprets--were not present. The only reference to the disciples' attitude is in the *mē koluete auta* of the pronouncement. Yet, because of the absence of reference to the disciples in the description of Jesus' action, this negative injunction acquires a much more generalized value. Thus the relation of Jesus to the disciples and their concrete attitude is minimized.

The same is true of Jesus' relation to the children. He is characterized as *calling* to himself the babies. This is his only relation to the children: Mark 10:16 is totally missing. What happens after the call is not mentioned.

This characterization of Jesus has several effects. First, it is consistent with his role of enticing his addressees to participate actively in the establishment of their own will: a call demands a response. Second, the disciples are no longer under a fundamental reproof. Their misinterpretation and mishandling of the situation does not jeopardize their status as disciples belonging to the Kingdom (as was the case in Mark). Third, the pronouncement is less directly related to the concrete situation of "people bringing babies to Jesus." In fact, its second part, 18:17, becomes a quite general statement concerning the way in which the Kingdom should be received (like a child), which does not need to be interpreted any longer in terms of Jesus' concrete involvement with children.

3.44   Consequently in Luke the addressees are indeed called upon to participate in the establishment of their will to be persons who belong to the Kingdom by interpreting correctly their relation to the Kingdom. But by contrast with Mark where the concrete situation is central--one is in the right relationship to the Kingdom if one relates the concrete situation in which one is to the Kingdom by means of the interpretation--in Luke the concrete situation is secondary.

Being in the right relationship to the Kingdom is to a certain extent removed from the concrete situation in which one finds oneself. It seems that we can conclude that the concrete situation and one's relation to the Kingdom belong to two discrete realms. And thus the interpretation of the concrete situation remains important but only as an allegorical interpretation, that is, only as it gives the possibility of understanding aspects of the other realm. Yet the two realms are not completely separated. Those in the realm of the concrete situation--the children--can be brought into the realm of the Kingdom through Jesus' call. Thus the two realms are related in two ways: (a) the concrete situation by being interpreted allegorically gives the possibility of understanding aspects of the relations within the realm of the Kingdom; and (b) this interpretation gives the possibility of identifying those who should be called to enter the realm of the Kingdom. These tentative conclusions on the basis of our study of the characterization are consistent with the timeless quality of the pronouncement (see 3.41 and 3.11) and the "verbal" nature of the space "near Jesus" (see 3.42). Yet they need to be verified by our analysis of the narrative syntax and semantics since they involve the perception of the Kingdom.

3.5   The Relation between Jesus and Nicodemus in John 3:1-6

3.51   *Temporalization.* Besides the past tenses of the verbs there is only one time marker, *nuktos* (3:2), which would need to be interpreted together with all the time markers of the Fourth Gospel. Yet it is clear that this is a secondary time marker which specifies a time span within a broader time frame that remains largely undefined (as in Mark and Luke), so much so that the reader still belongs to it. In fact, in John 3:1-6 there is no future which closes the time of the pronouncement (in 3:12 the future is the time when people will believe when they will be taught heavenly things, a time which apparently is still future for the reader).

3.52   *Spatialization.* As in the previous cases no concrete space is mentioned, but a fourfold space is nevertheless constructed.
(a)   A space "near Jesus" where verbal exchanges take place. It is thus a verbal space not in the sense that it is created verbally (by a call as in Luke). This is a euphoric space since Jesus is described as "performing signs" and having God "with him."
(b)   A space "away from Jesus," the space where Nicodemus was among the Pharisees. By its juxtaposition with the preceding it is dysphoric at least to a certain extent.
(c)   A space "with God," the space from which Jesus comes (3:2) identified as "heaven" in 3:13.
(d)   A space "Kingdom" that no one can see (3:3) and "enter" (3:5), which is related to "water and the spirit."
(e)   The "mother's womb" (3:4) is another dysphoric space. This is a part of a space of the "flesh," (3:6) opposed to the space of the spirit (the Kingdom).
Thus the concrete spaces (away from Jesus with the Pharisees, the "mother's womb" and the flesh) are dysphoric. The euphoric spaces are verbal, in relation with the divine, and spiritual.

3.53   *Characterization.* Nicodemus is characterized as "ruler of the Jews," but also by the fact that his proper name is given. As such he is presented as having a personal identity in a specific program. As a full-blown subject he is presumed to have all the competencies (will, knowledge, ability) needed to carry out this program. He addresses Jesus as one who has knowledge (3:2): he makes a statement (rather than raising a question). The use of the respectful "Rabbi" to address Jesus posits their relation as that of two knowledgeable persons. Furthermore since his statement is not contradicted by Jesus, this knowledge is posited as valid. This knowledge is the result of an interpretation of Jesus' activity as the performance of signs that one cannot perform without God. This interpretation is thus performed thanks to a "knowing how to interpret what is from God" that Nicodemus shares with the other Pharisees (*oidamen*). It is based upon an evaluation of the power (ability) displayed in somebody's concrete activity (*dunatai*). Similarly his evaluation of Jesus' statements both in 3:4 and 9 is in terms of power (note the repetition of *dunatai*): what a human being is able to do in 3:4; what God is able to do in 3:9 (taking the impersonal form as an indirect reference to God).

The fact that in 3:4 and 9 Nicodemus asks questions shows that his relationship with Jesus has changed. He acknowledges a lack of knowledge and posits Jesus as having that knowledge.

Jesus is characterized as performing signs (in Nicodemus' statement) and as one who has knowledge and can impart it. This knowledge that he has and that Nicodemus lacks also concerns power (ability). But it now concerns being able to see the Kingdom (3:3) and to enter it (3:5), that it, an ability which pertains to the "spiritual" realm, rather than an ability which pertains to the performance of action in the "physical" ("fleshly") realm (3:6, 10-13). The Pharisee Nicodemus is thus characterized as having knowledge (knowing how to interpret the manifestations of power) concerning the physical realm. Thus he can identify God's power in the physical activity of Jesus. Note that this is very similar to the ability to interpret concrete situations in terms of the Kingdom which, according to Mark, is sufficient. By contrast, here, while this ability to interpret physical situations is posited as valid, it is presented as insufficient. One also needs to be able (*dunatai*) to interpret or identify (*idein*, 3:3) spiritual realities, and thus gain knowledge about that realm.

Jesus' pronouncement aims therefore at establishing this competence--this "ability" or "knowing how to identify (interpret) spiritual realities"--of the subject rather than the subject's will. This presupposes that the Pharisee Nicodemus has already the correct will: that of identifying manifestations of God (as he did in 3:2b) and of acting accordingly (as he did by coming to Jesus in 3:2a).

The negative form of the pronouncements once again invites the participation of the addressee and calls him to establish himself as willing subject, but here, of a secondary program aimed at acquiring this ability. He has to be willing to be born again. But, in fact, Nicodemus refuses to be the addressee or does not have the ability to do so. He does not know how to interpret (understand) Jesus' pronouncement (3:10-13). Or, in other words, he does not believe (3:12).

3.54   Believing is thus defined as agreeing to be Jesus' addressee. But, in the text, Jesus' pronouncement is left without addressee. The readers have to fill up that role and to become believers. They can do so since they belong to the time frame of the text (see 3.51) and the space frames can be theirs (since the space of the Pharisees is redefined in broader terms as a "fleshly," physical space, see 3.52).

3.6   *The Relation between Jesus and the Disciples in Thomas 22*

3.61   *Temporalization.* The time of the exchange between Jesus and disciples is set in an undefined past since there is no other time marker than the verb tenses (see Thomas 85:20, 23, 24. I follow Guillaumont's notations for Log. 22 as lines 20-35 or Pl. 85). The pronouncements are then in the present (21-22) and primarily in the future (23, 25-35) marked by the repeated time marker *hotan*, when (25, 31), and *tote*, then, and the future (35). This future of the pronouncement story remains future for the readers (they have not yet entered the Kingdom). Thus the time of the pronouncement story encompasses that of the readers.

3.62   *Spatializations.* There is no concrete space described and no verb of movement in the story frame. It includes therefore only one space, the dialogic space which includes Jesus, the disciples, and children.

By contrast, in the pronouncements spatialization plays a large role. There is the space of the Kingdom (that people shall enter, mentioned three times, 22, 24, 35). And the condition for entering the Kingdom is expressed in 26-28 in terms of a unified space (or is it a space which is the negation of space division): "when you make the inner as the outer and the outer as the inner and the above as the below. . . ."

When we bring together these two observations, it appears that the space of Jesus (of his ministry) is already fulfilling the conditions for entering the Kingdom: it is unified.

3.63   *Characterization.* Unlike Mark 10:13-16 and Matt 18:1-5 and 19, but like John 3 and to a certain extent similarly to Luke 18:15-17, the personages are exclusively characterized by their verbal performances.

Jesus is first characterized as interpreting (he "saw") a situation "children who were being suckled." Neither Jesus nor the disciples directly intervene in this concrete situation. This situation is related to them only through their interpretation (Jesus' interpretation accepted by the disciples) as being similar (*homoioi eisin* proposes R. Kasser) to another situation: the situation of those who enter the Kingdom, that is, that of Jesus and the disciples as the rest of the dialogue shows. Thus, as in Luke 18:15-17, we find two discrete realms related by what can be termed an allegorical interpretation (but here, unlike in Luke, this interpretation is not the occasion of a call of the children which introduces another relation between the two realms). Thus, coming back to our observation concerning spatialization, the two discrete spaces, that of the "children being suckled" and that of "Jesus and the disciples," are united into a single space through Jesus' interpretation. Is this what is expressed toward the end of Jesus' second pronouncement: the concrete situation--the concrete "image," *eikon*--is perceived as ("made into") the image of another situation (34)?

The disciples address a question to Jesus (23-24). This is acknowledging that they lack knowledge that Jesus has, as in Matt 18:1-5. Yet here it is not a knowledge concerning an aspect of the existence in the Kingdom. It is rather a knowledge concerning their status in relation to the Kingdom, the issue raised by the discoursive syntax of Mark 10:13-16 and Luke 18:15-17. In these texts the addressees are enticed to adopt this status by (having the will of) becoming in different ways correct interpreters of a situation in terms of the Kingdom (see 3:44). By contrast here the disciples acknowledge that they do not know how to interpret their status in relation to the Kingdom in terms of Jesus' first pronouncement. They see themselves as children (23) but do not know whether they will enter the Kingdom or not (or at least are not sure of it). They question their ability to interpret their status and Jesus' first pronouncement. But they are also in quest for this ability that they trust Jesus can give them.

3.64   Jesus is thus characterized as one who has this ability to interpret correctly on the one hand the relation between a concrete situation and the Kingdom, and on the other hand the relation of the disciples to the Kingdom. As is expressed in the second pronouncement, this is an ability of "making one" these three situations, and this two by two. The disciples shall enter the Kingdom when they shall do the same.

The relation Jesus-disciples is a relation teacher-willing pupils (comparable to that of Matt 18:1-5, since the disciples ask a question of Jesus, see 3.24). But here the teaching that is transmitted is no longer a knowledge (a piece of information about greatness in the Kingdom exemplified by the children who in their concrete situation do belong to the Kingdom), but an ability to interpret, that is, to relate allegorically two discrete realms. The transmission of knowledge (information) in and of itself (the first pronouncement in Thomas 22) is not enough. One needs also, and indeed primarily, to know-how-to-interpret, the ability to interpret, as Jesus does. Thus the relation Jesus-disciples is here more like master-apprentices.

By comparison with John 3, we find here also two levels of interpretation: the interpretation of a concrete "physical" situation and that of a "spiritual" situation characterized by a "spiritual" ability. In John 3 these two levels of interpretation are distinguished and even opposed. The ability to interpret the spiritual reality has nothing to do with the ability to interpret the physical reality and to perceive God at work in it. In Thomas 22, by contrast, the two levels of interpretation are brought together. Interpreting a concrete situation is deriving from it a knowledge concerning the realm of the Kingdom, in the same way that interpreting a situation in the realm of the Kingdom (the disciples as children) provides knowledge concerning the realm of the Kingdom. These two levels of interpretation in Thomas 22 might, in fact, correspond to the second level of interpretation in John 3 (note that John 3:12, "telling heavenly things," suggests a third level; the first level of John 3, that of the Pharisaic interpretation being left out of consideration in Thomas 22). But this can only be established by a study of the entire Gospels of John and Thomas.

3.7   The preceding remark points out the tentative nature of our conclusions regarding the characteristics of the discursive syntax of the six passages we have studied. They merely suggest what seem to be the implications of our observations about the discursive syntax of very short passages of much longer texts (the Gospels). Without any doubt they would have to be refined and possibly corrected in light of a study of the discursive syntax of the entire Gospels. The discursive syntax is a system that encompasses an entire discourse. Yet this system is characterized by patterns which are repeated in various ways through the entire system. And thus our conclusions based upon the study of short passages are preliminary assessments of what characterize the discursive syntax of the entire Gospels. But in this tentative way I believe our analysis shows how the constant relation "Jesus-people in an overall positive relation with Jesus" has been defined in various ways by being inserted in different systems of discursive syntax.

4.   COMPARISON OF THE SIX TEXTS IN TERMS OF THEIR NARRATIVE SYNTAX AND SEMANTICS: THE RELATION BETWEEN "ENTERING THE KINGDOM" AND "CHILDHOOD"

4.0   In this second part of our structural exegesis our goal is (a) to determine how "entering the Kingdom" and "childhood" are defined in each text by being inserted in, respectively, a specific narrative syntactical system and a specific semantic system; and (b) to show how they are interrelated. For this purpose we need in each case to establish the syntactical system that I term "system of pertinent transformations" (see Patte and Patte, 1978, Ch. II), that is, the system established by the text by opppsing two by two (narrative) transformation manifested by the verbs of the category "doing" (to which "entering the Kingdom" belongs). This will allow us to deduce from it, in a second stage of our analysis, the narrative semantic system which is made up of interrelated oppositions of semantic terms (among which "childhood") manifested by the states--the subjects and their qualifications--associated with the pertinent transformations.

4.1   *The Relations between "Entering the Kingdom" and "Childhood" in Mark 10:13-16*

4.11   *"Entering the Kingdom" as defined in the syntactical system.*

4.111   In this text there are only three clear oppositions of transformations that we can list as follows (the verses are broken down in subsections by attributing a subsection to each verb. For instance, "14b" means second verb in verse 14).
14b, having an indignation vis-a-vis the disciples vs 13c, having a negative evaluation of the people who bring the children (this awkward rendering of the verbs

ēganaktēsen and *epitimēsan* attempts to account for the reflexive character of these verbs of emotion without denying their other dimensions).

14d, giving permission to the children (to come to Jesus) vs 14f, hindering them.

16c, laying his hand on (touching) the children vs 13b, Jesus not touching them (since this intended transformation is interrupted by the disciples).

The last two oppositions (14d vs 14f and 16c vs 13b) belongs to the primary level of the text. On the positive side, giving permission, 14d, leads to Jesus' touching the children, 16c. On the negative side, hindering the children, 14f, leads to Jesus' not touching them, 13b. Both these sequences of action presuppose that an interpretation (evaluation) of the euphoric or dysphoric value of "Jesus touching the children" and consequently of "giving them the permission to approach Jesus" took place. The contradictory evaluations are expressed by the opposition 14b vs 13c.

4.112   15c, "Not entering the Kingdom," does not belong to the system of pertinent transformations of this text (it is a negative transformation that does not have a positive counterpart; in this form it it therefore an element of the discoursive syntax which we have discussed above). Yet it is defined through its relations to the transformations of the system of pertinent transformations.

"Not entering the Kingdom" is closely associated with "not receiving the Kingdom as a child," 15b, which cannot be equated with hindering (which is doing something to the children, who are receivers of the object hindrance) but indeed can be correlated with "having a negative evaluation of the children," 13c. In each case it is a reflexive action, "not attributing an object (an evaluation of the children, or the Kingdom) to oneself." Consequently, "not entering the Kingdom" belongs to the interpretative level of the text. It is what happens to the interpreting subject in a syntactic unfolding other than the unfolding of the primary story, and as a consequence of the interpretation.

4.113   Thus, in the positive side of the syntactical system, a correct interpretation of the relation between Jesus and the children ("receiving the children") brings about two syntactic developments: on the primary level, giving permission to the children to approach Jesus so that Jesus might *bless* them by taking them in his arms and laying his hand on them (note that "blessing," *kateulogei,* is the principal verb in 10:16); and, on the interpretative level, the interpreter's entrance into the Kingdom.

Thus, in the narrative syntactical system of Mark 10:13-16, "entering the Kingdom" is correlated (is like) "being blessed by Jesus as one who is in his arms and upon whom he lays his hand." Entering the Kingdom of God is not so much something one does, but rather something which happens to someone: it is being blessed.

4.12   *"Childhood" as defined in the semantic system.*

4.120   Following the methodology established and applied in Patte and Patte, 1978, Ch. II and III, from the system of pertinent transformations one can deduce the organization of the narrative semantic system (which I also called "symbolic system" and which is nothing else than the "system of convictions," of self-evident truths, held by the enunciator). For this it is enough to organize the system of pertinent transformations in such a way as to have a narrative progression along either the principal or the polemical axis (according to the way in which the story unfolds) with the interpretative levels branching out of the primary level at the point of interpretation. Since to an opposition of the semantic terms (manifested by the subjects of the transformations and their qualifications), it is enough to replace the transformations by their subjects and simultaneously to slide the negative axis upward to obtain the shape of the semantic system (for the theoretical justification of this apparently mechanical move see Patte and Patte, 1978, Ch. II, and Patte, 1981).

4.121   In the case of Mark 10 all this operation is quite simple since we are dealing with only three sets of pertinent transformations. Furthermore, since the interpretative level is based upon the interpretation of whether or not the children should approach
Jesus and be touched by him (which happens to be the second and last set of pertinent
transformations), the two levels can be represented as a continuous system. The progression along the two axes is identical.   Thus its organization does not present any
difficulty.   The first opposition of transformation is 14d vs 14f (giving permission to the
children vs hindering them), followed by 16c vs 13b (Jesus laying his hand on the children
vs not touching them).   Then the interpretative opposition of transformations follows,
14b vs 13c (Jesus' indignation vs the disciples' negative evaluation).   Furthermore, from
the above discussion of the syntax, we know that the next opposition would have been
"entering the Kingdom" vs "not entering the Kingdom." (Even though this opposition is
not expressed, this observation shall be useful below.)

Following the process described above, we can thus establish the shape of the
semantic system as follows. We replace the transformations by their subjects as a short-
hand marker for the subjects *and* their qualifications. By convention the above representation must be read from bottom to top (movement toward the more important semantic
categories). The verse numbers are kept to mark the relation of the semantic terms with
the transformations. We thus obtain one complete semiotic squares and two half
squares. The top half square can then be completed: on the positive axis it is the
semantic terms corresponding to "entering the Kingdom" which are nothing else than
those (the true disciples) who interpret the situation of the children in terms of their
relation to the Kingdom. As is the case in most stories, the main semantic category is
not related to a pertinent transformation so that its semantic character might be more
directly manifested.

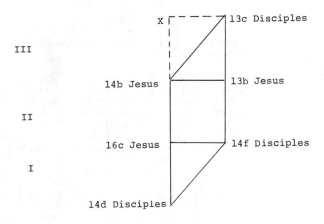

Each of these subjects has very few qualifications (there is no descriptive statement about any of them). Therefore we can expect that their primary qualifications are
their respective competence as defined by the narrative unfolding.

4.122   Let us first consider square no. I, a half square involving the relations of
contradictions 14d Disciples vs 14f Disciples, of contrariety 16c Jesus vs. 14f Disciples,

and of implication 14d Disciples 16c Jesus. All these subjects are merely defined by the action they perform. Furthermore two of them (14d and 14f) are merely expressed in an imperative form. Thus their subjects are only qualified by a "will" (and not "knowledge" and "being able to" which would be present if the actions had been described as performed). This means that in this square the respective "will" of these two subjects is related to the "will" of the subject of 16c.

Hindering (14f) involves "wanting to separate the children from Jesus" as qualification of the subject "disciples." Giving permission (14d) involves "wanting to let approach the children to Jesus" as qualificant of the subject "disciples." Laying his hand on them (16c) after taking them in his arms involves "wanting to invite the children with oneself (Jesus) in an intimate fashion." If we now remove the elements common to these three semantic terms, we are left with the contradictory opposition /non-separation/ vs /separation/, the contrary opposition /union/ vs /separation/ and the implication /union/ /non-separation/.

This can be summarized as follows:

```
16c will to unite child-  ──────────────┐   14f will to separate
ren with Jesus                          │   children from Jesus
/UNION/                                 │   /SEPARATION/


14d will to let approach
(= not to separate)
children from Jesus
/NON-SEPARATION/
```

Thus /separation/ is posited as having a negative value, while /union/ and consequently /non-separation/ are posited as a positive value.

4.123   In square no. II the contrary opposition /union/ vs /separation/ becomes a subcontrary opposition and is defined further by its insertion in a new set of values.

Let us first consider the contradictory opposition of 16c (Jesus reunited with the children and blessing them) with 13b (Jesus separated from the children by the action of the disciples). Let us underscore that in 16c Jesus' action involves "blessing" and "laying his hand" on the children. He is thus defined as having the power to give a blessing, and thus as "holy" or "sacred." Thus Jesus as "holy" is in /union/ with the children, who are defined here as those who need to receive a blessing and thus are themselves "not holy" or "profane." Thus the value manifested in 16c can be approximately formulated as "holy" as in union with the profane (in order to bless it).

In 13b the subject is Jesus as he should be from the disciples' perspective: separated from the children (not touching the children). In view of the fact that the disciples are followers of Jesus (who have recognized in him a religious authority), the definition of Jesus involved here is certainly of a religious order. The contradictory opposition defines this negative religious definition of Jesus: since he is "holy" he should be separated from what is not holy, from the profane. The people who bring the children and wish that they be touched by Jesus, and the children who passively accept this, should not be allowed near him. Thus the value manifested in 13b can be approximately formulated as "holy as separated from the profane which would passively accept union with it."

From these observations it appears that the disciples who hinder the children (14f) do this because they are characterized by their "commitment to the separation of the

holy from the profane," which they view as their role as disciples. Then Jesus'
indignation (14b), as contradictory with 14f, is a "(righteous) wrath against the separation
of the holy from the profane."

For brevity's sake we will not push the analysis further by considering the other
relations of the square. It is clear that they could be established by refining the
categories further: each contains an attitude (passive acceptance, commitment, wrath)
and a relation between holy and profane. But his would not help us toward our goal of
defining the value ascribed to the children. Let us summarize our brief discussion in the
following schema:

```
14b                              13b
/(righteous) wrath              /holy as separated from
against separation               the profane which would
of holy from                     passively accept union
profane/                         with it/
```

```
16c                              14f
/holy as in union               /commitment to separation
with the profane                 of holy from profane/
which passively
accepts union with
it/
```

From this study of this part of the semantic system we can draw conclusions
regarding connotations attached to Jesus, the disciples, and the children in our text.
Jesus is presented as a manifestation of the divine (holy) which breaks away with and
fundamentally rejects a view of the divine separated from profane human affairs. Indeed
the divine manifestation needs to be intimately related to human affairs so as to bring its
blessing. The disciples are presented as fundamentally misunderstanding their role and
vocation. Indeed, they are the followers of a wrong Jesus. They are not truly disciples.
By their attitude they demonstrate that they hold a view of divine manifestation which is
totally incompatible with Jesus' ministry. Finally, the children are defined as those who
are in need of blessing, and thus are profane in need of the holy, and are furthermore
open to a union with the holy (initiated by somebody else, the people bringing them and
wanting them to be touched by Jesus). By contrast to the active commitment of the
(false) disciples, the children are characterized by a passive acceptance, a mere
openness, of an intimate relation with the divine.

4.124   In square III (a half square that we shall complete), at first we find only one
new opposition: the contradictory opposition 14b (Jesus' indignation) vs 13c (the disciples' rebuke). This is the relation of two evaluations. In 13c the disciples have a negative evaluation of the people bringing the children to Jesus so that he might touch them,
or more abstractly in light of the values discussed above, "a negative evaluation of other
people's desire to unite holy and profane, in terms of a view of the separation of the holy
and the profane." In 14b Jesus' indignation is a "negative evaluation of the negative
evaluation . . . in terms of a view of the union of the holy with the profane."

In 13b (contrary to 16c and in relation of implication to 13c), Jesus as viewed by the disciples would not touch the children because of his "evaluation of his own status in terms of a view of the separation of the holy and the profane."

7c
(true disciples)

13c
/negative evaluation/of
other people's desire to
unite holy and profane/
in terms of a view of the
separation of holy and
profane/

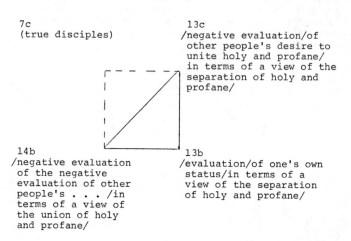

14b
/negative evaluation
of the negative
evaluation of other
people's . . . /in
terms of a view of
the union of holy
and profane/

13b
/evaluation/of one's own
status/in terms of a
view of the separation
of holy and profane/

Consequently, the fourth term of the square has to be an /evaluation/ of one's own status / in terms of a view of the union of holy and profane/. This is the comple: qualification that the true disciples should have.

4.125   As the second part of 10:14 makes clear, in order to choose the proper course of action (the proper will which defines their indentity as true disciples), they should evaluate (something) /in terms of the Kingdom/. The phrases /in terms of the Kingdom/ and /in terms of a view of the union of holy and profane/ are equivalent. Consequently, the Kingdom of God is defined in Mark 10:13-16 as the union of the holy and the profane. More precisely, since by the term "profane" we designate the children and the people who bring them, the Kingdom involves the union of the divine with normal human beings (by contrast with holy people).

As 10:15 makes clear, the disciples are not merely called to evaluate the concrete situation but primarily their own status vis-a-vis the Kingdom: will they enter the Kingdom or not? Now the Kingdom is for those such as the children (10:14), that is (see above 4.123), for those who passively accept an intimate relation with the divine. Since the children are only defined by an attitude (although a passive one) toward the relations between holy and profane, the phrase *hos paidion* must be interpreted "as a child receives the Kingdom" (and not, the Kingdom is "like a child" as could also be read). In other words, the Kingdom is for those who receive the Kingdom passively, without effort and without even conceiving that the union of the holy and the profane could be questioned, because they totally conceive of themselves in terms of a view of reality in which the holy and the profane can be united as it will be in the Kingdom.

4.2   *The Relations between "Entering the Kingdom" and "Childhood" in Matt 18:1-5*

4.21   *"Entering the Kingdom" as defined in the syntactical system.*

4.211   In this passage Jesus and the disciples are not in a polemical relationship. Thus the only oppositions of transformation are to be found in the pronouncement, that is, in a discourse. This is to say that the (narrative) transformations are no longer cast in the framework of a narrative development. It is as if they were extracted from it in order to be case in the framework of an argument. For the sake of the argument, transformations which would have belonged to different narrative developments can be brought together and opposed, in a kind of telescoping of various stories.

This is what happens in the discourse beginning in Matt 18:3. It begins with a negative statement, 18:3, followed by a positive statement which can be deduced from it, 18:4-5 (note the "*oun*," in 18:4a, whose effect is carried to the next verse by the "*kai*" of 18:5a), followed by another negative statement, 18:6ff. In this way the discourse sets the following oppositions of transformations:

4a (humbling oneself like a child) vs 3d (not becoming like children).

Furthermore, "not entering the Kingdom," which can be understood as not attributing the Kingdom as object to oneself as receiver, is opposed to "receiving Jesus," that is, attributing Jesus as object to oneself as receiver. Thus we find a second opposition of transformations:

5b (receiving Jesus) vs 3e (not entering the Kingdom).

Finally, "receiving a child," 5a, is clearly opposed by the discourse to "scandalizing a little one," 6a. This involves a very specific understanding of "receiving a child" as giving a good "reception" as object to a child as receiver (by contrast to the strictly narrative understanding of it as attributing a child as object to oneself as receiver).

5a (receiving a child) vs 6a (scandalizing a little one).

4.212   In the syntactical system, "entering the Kingdom" is thus defined as equivalent to "receiving Jesus." Furthermore, it is equivalent to "receiving a child" (since when one receives a child, one receives Jesus), which is to be contrasted with "scandalizing a little one." "Entering the Kingdom" is the result of "becoming like a child," which is "humbling oneself." When one truly does so, one is then the greatest in the Kingdom.

4.22   *"Childhood" as defined in the semantic system.*

4.221   Since, as we saw above, "receiving a child" and "receiving Jesus" are posited as equivalent, there is no progression from the opposition 5a vs 6a to 5b vs 3e. Consequently, the system of pertinent transformation has only two stages. First the oposition 4a (humbling oneself) vs 3d (not becoming like a child), and then the double opposition 5a and 5b vs 61 and 3e.

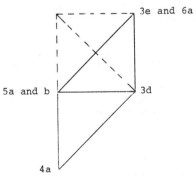

The shape of the semantic system of this short passage is thus as on the preceding page (all the subjects are indefinite and thus we do not write them).

We have only two half squares. Furthermore, since all the subjects are indefinite, their semantic value is limited to their competence. The best defined is that of the subject in 3d: the negative competence of the subject (not becoming like a child) involves "not having turned." And thus the competence of the subject of 4a (humbling oneself) involves "having turned."

"Not having turned" is in itself largely non-defined (it can take many different connotations). Yet through its relationship of implication with 6a (and 3e), it is defined. For indeed, those who scandalize the little ones are themselves defines by 18:7-9. Without studying these verses in detail we can say that they are those who do not remove what scandalizes them (even if it is a hand, a foot or an eye). In other words, those who scandalize the little ones (6a) are sinners, and "not turning" is not turning away from sin, that is, not removing what is sinful in oneself.

Consequently, the subjects who "humble themselves as a child" (4a) are those who have competence to have turned away from their sin, i.e., converted from the scandalous way of the world (7). And those who have humbled themselves and thus can receive Jesus or a child (5a and b) are those who remove from themselves what is sinful, and thus admit to lacking something (as someone maimed or lame or with only one eye, 8 and 9).

The semantic system corresponds exactly therefore to the discoursive syntactical system: being like a child, being humble is accepting, acknowledging that one lacks something important (a hand, a foot, an eye are important parts of the body that one would not like to miss), for instance, the right knowledge that Jesus imparts. (This equivalence of the two levels means that, at least at this point in the Gospel, it is presupposed that the enunciatee shares the system of deep values—the system of convictions—of the enunciator: this is a discourse from Matthew's church to Matthew's church.) This means that being like a child is also being able to "receive a child." If one perceives oneself as lacking something, one can welcome those who likewise perceive themselves as lacking something important.

4.3   *The Relations between the "Kingdom" and "Childhood" in Matt 19:13-15*

4.31   *The Syntactical System*. The system of pertinent transformation is somewhat similar to that of Mark 10:13-16 with one important difference. The opposition of transformation between Jesus' (14a) and the disciples' (13d) actions is an opposition of two performances with other people as receivers and no longer directly an opposition of interpretation (note again the absence of interpretative markers, see 3.33). As we shall see, there remains an interpretative *semantic* dimension, but it is not a narrative syntactical feature. This opposition can be represented as follows:

14a (giving a mandate to others) vs 13d (rebuking, giving the opposite mandate, to others).

14b (giving permission to the children) vs 14c (hindering them).

15a (laying his hand on the children) vs 13b (not doing it).

The system of pertinent transformations is thus different. First, note that here "rebuking (the children)" (13d) and "hindering them" (14c) is the same transformation since 13d is no longer presented as interpretative. Thus the oppositions of 14a vs 13d and 14b vs 14c are a single step of the system of transformations. Jesus' pronouncement (14a) is equivalent to giving the permission to the children to come to him. Thus the system of pertinent transformations is reduced to two oppositions:

15a   vs   13b
14a, 14b   vs   14d, 14c

Since "entering the Kingdom" is not to be found as a transformation, we do not need to discuss further the syntactical system.

4.32   *"Childhood" as defines in the semantic system.*

4.321   From the preceding system of pertinent transformations we can deduce the shape of the semantic system. It includes two half squares.

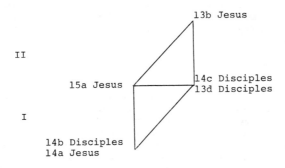

4.322   Let us consider square no. I, a half square and first the relation of contradiction between 14a, 14b vs 13d, 14c. The fact that Jesus as speaking is now one of the subjects of the term 14a, 14b makes it clear that in addition to the will to let the children come to Jesus, the "knowledge of what to do vis-a-vis the children" is involved (declaring something involves having the knowledge of what is declared). It is a knowledge which involves relating the children to the Kingdom: it is knowing how to relate the Kingdom to a specific situation. This is an interpretative competence, which shows that in Matthew the entire episode is set on an interpretative level (by contrast with Mark, which distinguishes the interpretative level from a primary narrative level). This implies that the disciples' rebuke is in fact the rejection of people (those who bring the children and the children) who had the proper interpretative knowledge. This rebuke is thus based upon a wrong interpretative knowledge.

Thus in a first approximation the contradictory opposition 14a, 14b vs 13d, 14c can be formulated as follows: "will to relate Jesus to children based on knowledge of the children's relation to the Kingdom" vs "will not to relate Jesus to the children (or to separate them) based on wrong knowledge of the children's relation to Jesus and an absence of knowledge of the children's relation to the Kingdom."

In the contradictory opposition 15a vs 13b of half square no. II, Jesus' action of "laying his hand on the children" is correlated with "praying" (13c) and "going away" (15b). Once more we would need to complement the study of this text with the rest of the Gospel, especially to know exactly how to interpret "praying." Yet in the partial semantic system we are dealing with, the "relation" dimension of his action is certainly important. Praying involves indeed "establishing a relation between something (the children) and the divine." Thus Jesus through his actions manifests "the competence (including the will and ability) to relate the children to God" in 15a and the opposite (contradictory) in 13b. Furthermore, the immediate going away of Jesus expresses that Jesus' relation to the children is secondary: it is simply the means by which the children are related to God. After laying his hand on and praying for the children he can immediately depart.

In view of the limitation of space, we shall not propose a more detailed and complete study of the semantic system (which would demand analyzing a longer passage so as to have at least one full square). The above remarks are enough to show that, in this text, the statement "the Kingdom of heaven is for those such as the children" means that the children and those who are like them are such--have the necessary qualifications--that they can be established in relationship with God. Thus they are not yet in this relationship with God--not yet participant in the Kingdom of heaven--but are proper candidates for it. They should be allowed, therefore, to approach Jesus whose role is to establish such people in this relationship with God. What are the qualifications which make someone "like a child" is not expressed here, but it was done in 18:1-6. Such are the conclusions we can reach on the basis of this short text, but they have to be understood as quite tentative. A study of the rest of the Gospel would allow us to verify and to refine them.

4.4   *The Relations between "Entering the Kingdom" and "Childhood" in Luke 18:15-17*

4.41   *"Entering the Kingdom" as defined in the syntactical system.*
There are only two oppositions of pertinent transformations. The disciples and Jesus are opposed as interpreting a situation in opposite ways (note again the interpretative markers) and as consequence either calling the children to himself or rebuking them.
16a (calling the children to oneself) vs 15d (hindering them).
The other opposition is the one concerning "giving permission" and "hindering."
16c (giving permission to the children to come to Jesus) vs 16e (hindering them).
The latter opposition belongs to the primary narrative level (which does not unfold beyond this point). The former belongs to the interpretative level. Therefore, the system of pertinent transformations needs to be organized as follows:
        16a   vs   15d
        16c   vs   16e
"Entering the Kingdom" (17c) belongs to the interpretative level (which encompasses all the text except 15a and b, and 16c, d and e) together with "receiving the Kingdom like a child" (17b), Jesus' pronouncement to undetermined addressees (16b, and 17a), and Jesus' call of the children to himself (16a). Receiving the Kingdom like a child (17b) is thus correlated to Jesus' calling to himself the children (16a, a pertinent transformation). The question is then to know how to interpret *hōs paidion*. The correlation of 17b with 16a has to be taken in account. "Calling to himself" can be understood as equivalent to "receiving." This correlation displaces the relation with the end of the first part of the pronouncement. Thus is appears that Luke interprets 17b as "receiving the Kingdom as one receives a child" (the Kingdom is like a child). This would fit the description of the children as "babies," who, as infants, are not in a position to perform acts such as "receiving the Kingdom," but are indeed received (as in Matt 18:5).

4.42   *"Childhood" as defined in the semantic system.*

4.421   The shape of the semantic system can be derived from the above system of pertinent transformations.

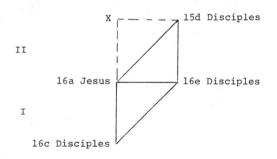

As in the case of Matt 19:13-15, we have only two half squares. It is therefore difficult to reach very clear results. Yet in this case the discussion of the syntactical system suggests that the following opposition would be receiving the Kingdom vs not receiving it (17b). Therefore the contrary of 15d Disciples would the hypothetical subject of "receiving the Kingdom."

The half square no. I is quite similar to that found in Mark 10:13-16. It could be written in the same way except that in Luke 18:15-17 the /union/ of the children with Jesus is no longer emphasized (by Jesus' taking the children in his arms). It is simply their relation which is manifested by his call. Thus we can represent this half square as follows:

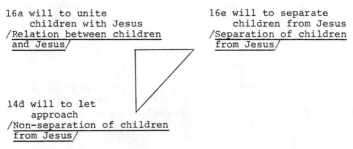

```
16a will to unite              16e will to separate
    children with Jesus            children from Jesus
/Relation between children     /Separation of children
 and Jesus/                     from Jesus/




14d will to let
    approach
/Non-separation of children
 from Jesus/
```

In half square no. II, the disciples (15d) are qualified as having a cognition (*idontes*) of the babies. But they ignore what will be pointed out by Jesus, namely, the relation of the children with the Kingdom. In fact, by rebuking the babies the competence that they have for performing this action involves a conviction, the /knowledge that there is *no relation* between the children and the Kingdom/.

As we noted above (see 3.43), Jesus ignores the disciples. He acts as if they did not exist. And thus he is qualified as having a /lack of knowledge that there is *no relation* between the children and the Kingdom/.

By contrast, at the interpretative level the disciples who hinder the children (16e) /*lack* knowledge of the relation between the children and the Kingdom/ (a relation expressed in the next phrase of the text).

The fourth term of the square has therefore to be a /knowledge of the relation between the children and the Kingdom/. This is indeed a qualification that we can expect for those (including Jesus) who receive the Kingdom in the right way so that they will enter it.

We obtain the following square:

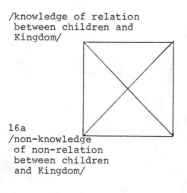

```
                               15d
/knowledge of relation         /knowledge of non-relation
 between children and           between children and
 Kingdom/                       Kingdom/



16a                            16e
/non-knowledge                 /non-knowledge
 of non-relation                of relation
 between children               between children
 and Kingdom/                   and Kingdom/
```

The nature of this "relation" is not defined by the semantic system of the short passage under study. But as we suggested above, it is defined at the level of the syntactic system (which is also the level of the theological affirmations). The Kingdom is like a child (a baby) and thus the Kingdom should be received as a child is received. At the discoursive level this cognitive nature of the relation opens the possibility of a kind of allegorical interpretation of the situation of the children to gain knowledge concerning one's relationship to the Kingdom (see 3.44).

4.5   The Relations between "Entering the Kingdom" and "Childhood" in John 3:1-6

4.51   "Entering the Kingdom" and "childhood" as defined by the syntactic system.
An opposition of pertinent transformations at the primary narrative level is found in 3:2.

2f (performing signs) vs 2e (not performing signs).

The other oppositions belong to the interpretative level. A first one opposes Nicodemus' question to Jesus' sayings.

5a, b (3a, b, c) (Jesus' response) vs 4a (Nicodemus' question).

There is only one other opposition of pertinent transformations (and a weak one at that since it is expressed in the passive form, yet in 4e the subject of the passive form, strangely enough, has a competence . . . being able to, *dunataî*).

3d, 5c (being born again) vs 4e (being born from the womb).

Thus the system of transformations can be written:

3d, 5c	vs	4e
5a, b (3a, b, c)	vs	4a
2f	vs	2e

As is clear, "entering the Kingdom" is related to "being born from above" (*anōthen*), from water and spirit" and not "from the flesh" (5, 6). Thus in John 3:1-6 the two terms of the common theme, "entering the Kingdom" and "childhood," are both expressed in a syntactic form. In other words, what is emphasized is no longer the state "being like a child or infant," but the process "becoming (like) an infant" as a necessary transformation for "entering the Kingdom." This transformation is itself the result of cognitive transformation (as is made clear in 3:10-12 and by the opposition to the cognitive activity of Nicodemus). The passive form of the verb shows that this transformation of somebody as an infant is something which happens to somebody as birth happens to an infant. Yet it is linked with believing as an active cognitive performance of the subject (12).

4.52   The semantic system.

4.521   The shape of the semantic system can be represented as follows:

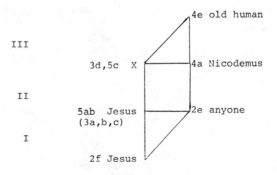

There is no point in spending much time on the analysis of the semantic system. Despite the qualification "old human being" in 4e, "childhood" is not a pertinent semantic feature. The semantic system, thanks to the many repetitions, is quite apparent on the surface of the text. On the negative axis we find semantic features concerning "human ability" (not from God nor with God) in 2e, "human knowledge and ability to interpret" in 4a, and "human nature, flesh" in 4e. By contrast, on the positive axis we find semantic features concerning "ability originating in the divine and resulting from conjunction with the divine" in 2f, "knowledge originating in the divine and from the Spirit" in 5a, b and other passages, and "the believers' nature as from above, water and the spirit" in 3d and 5c. This is the opposition of the "spiritual realm" to the "physical, fleshy realm," which also plays an important role at the discursive level. As in Matthew 18, the semantic system and discursive system coincide, and thus it is presupposed that the views (the system of convictions) of the enunciator and the enunciatee are the same. The discourse is from (a member of) the Johannine community to the Johannine community. "Being born from above (and again)" is thus entering this system of convictions. Consequently, entering the Kingdom is nothing more than entering the Johannine community of faith (as is further suggested by the allusion to baptism, 5).

4.6   *The Syntactic and Semantic Systems of Thomas 22*

There is no opposition of narrative transformations in this passage. The positive transformations (and they are many) are only defined in terms of the discoursive syntax (see above 3.6). They remain totally undefined at the level of the semio-narrative syntax. In other words, the enunciator does not impose any syntactic system as normative. The enunciatees are free to include the positive transformations in whatever narrative system (and thus life situation) that they choose.

The same is true, consequently, of the semantic system. In other words, no definite system of convictions, no definite view of reality is imposed by the enunciator. The enunciatees are free to cast the positive values expressed in this text in whatever semantic system they choose. This is fitting with our conclusions regarding the discoursive system. The discourse aims at teaching how to interpret, and indeed gives all freedom to the enunciatees to do so. Thus the enunciatees are those who should determine for themselves what the relation is between "entering the Kingdom" and "childhood."

5. It remains to draw conclusions which would involve a discussion of the interpretations of these passages by other New Testament scholars. Space does not permit it, and hopefully this will take place in the seminar as this structural exegesis is discussed together with the papers by J. Dominic Crossan and Vernon Robbins.

Bibliography

Greimas, A. J. and J. Courtès, *Semiotics and Language: An Encyclopedic Dictionary.* Bloomington: Indiana University Press, 1982.

Guillaumont, A., H. Ch. Puech, G. Quispel, W. Till and Yassah 'Abd Al Masih, *The Gospel According to Thomas: Coptic Text Established and Translated.* Leiden: Brill and New York: Harper & Brothers, 1959.

Kasser, Rodolphe, *L'Evangile selon Thomas.* Neuchatel (Switzerland): Delachaux & Niestlé, 1961.

Patte, D., *Carré sémiotique et syntaxe narrative, Documents de Recherche* III, 23.
    1981. Paris: Groupe de Recherches semio-linguistiques.

Patte, D. and A. Patte, *Structural Exegesis From Theory to Practice*. Philadelphia:
    Fortress, 1978.

RETHINKING THE RELIGIOUS CRISIS OF THE ROMAN REPUBLIC

Charles Robert Phillips, III
Lehigh University

Communis opinio usually holds that considerable religious disenchantment plagued the first century Roman Republic.[1] Beginning with the Social Wars at the start of the century, continuing through factionalism and triumvirates and culminating with the horrors of Civil War, the social fabric weakened. In consequence, the Romans, denied the possibility of consolation by a religion of "cult acts, devoid of belief" sank into a deep gloom. Finally Augustus conveniently appeared as the restorer of the Old and Good, shaping a new Roman order from chaos. This paper concentrates on three problems of that characterization. First, while not denying the importance of first century unrest, it argues that the extant literary sources' emphases on a crisis have produced misplaced scholarly emphases. Second, the crisis, such as it was, did not arise *ex nihilo* but had a long history as reflected in tensions among the orders. Third, and consequently, scholarship on Roman religion has usually not given sufficient attention to crucial socio-economic factors of first century history.

Classical scholarship, traditionally a perquisite of elites, has regularly emphasized the primacy of literary evidence for posing questions and framing answers to those questions. But full literacy in classical antiquity always belonged to an extremely small group: the situation resembles nothing so much as one elite talking across the centuries to another.[2] As for the first century crisis, citations from Cicero and Varro, buttressed by gloomy allusions in Augustan authors, have commonly provided the evidence.[3] Varro, always a notorious fan of the excerpt, survives largely in quotations often made for many different reasons.[4] Cicero's philosophical statements of skepticism must be balanced against the considerable religious concern his other writings reveal. Both have been taken as models: against their skeptical utterances the events of the first century assume near manic dimensions. This position will not do. Ciceronian and Varronian assumptions can at best represent the sometime utterances of litterateurs: they cannot, unqualified, form the basis for generalization even to other members of the elite, let alone all of Roman society. Put differently, the concern in false oracles, the manipulation of omens and profanations of mysteries may just as easily provide evidence for a system's strengths which the believers manipulate on that basis.[5]

---

[1]I wish to thank Professor Morton Smith for valuable criticism of this paper. The notes are allusive, not all-inclusive; fuller treatment on many topics appears in my *Rethinking Augustan Poetry* (Brussels, forthcoming) and "Sociology of Religion in the Roman Empire to A.D. 284," *ANRW* 2.16.3 (forthcoming).

[2]Sobering: A. Mócsy, "Die Unerkenntnis des Lebensaltens im römischen Reich," *AAntHung* 14 (1966) 387-421. Economic factors need more consideration, i.e., *IG* I^2 374. 279-81 (price of papyrus equals a laborer's daily wage, ibid. 404-7). But cf. the wildly fluctuating book prices later: Gel. 3.17, Mart. 1.117.15-17. Forgeries: Gal. 15.505K. False ageing to increase price: Arist. *Categ. Sch.* in Arist. 28a13ff.

[3]Varro 2a Ag(=August. *C.D.* 6.12); Cic. *N.D.* 2.9-10, 3.87, *Div.* 1.29, 90, 105, *Leg.* 2.33; Sal. *Cat.* 36, 53; Liv. *Praef* 9, 3.20.5, 6.41.8; Hor. *Carm.* 1.2, 1.12.59, *Epod.* 7, 16.9; Prop. 3.13.58-66; Verg. *Ecl* 4, 6; P. Jal, *La guerre civile à Rome* (Paris, 1963).

[4]Varro: B. Cardauns, *ANRW* 2.16.1.94. Anecdotes: Richard Saller, "Anecdotes as Historical Evidence for the Principate," *G. & R.* 2nd Ser. 27 (1980) 68-83; E. Gabba, "True History and False History in Classical Antiquity," *JRS* 71 (1981) 50-62.

[5]False oracle to restore Ptolemy XII: Cic. *Fam* 1.1.1-2, 1.4.2, *Q. fr.* 2.2.3. Misuse of omens: Cic. *Att.* 4.3.4, *Phil* 1.31,2.82-4; D.C. 39.32.1; Plut. *Cat. Mi.* 42, *Pomp.* 52; cf. Cic. *Sest* 129. Profanations: Cic. *Pis.* 11, *Har.* 8-9, *Dom.* In general: L. R. Taylor, *Party Politics in the Age of Caesar* (Berkeley, 1968) 76-79; H. D. Jocelyn, "The Roman Nobility

Of course, the first century saw many upheavals. Proscriptions, devastation of land and famine affected all in varying degrees.[6] Factors such as the mob and religious cynicism at Rome itself, while perhaps more limited in geographical impact, certainly affected the city's residents.[7] But, given conditions of full literacy in the ancient world, skeptical utterances in literary sources cannot provide a sound basis for generalization to all of society. Those sources, the products of rhetorical, philosophical, and poetical sophistication, were written by those most able, and most concerned, to find profound philosophical and religious implications in the events. How much philosophical gloom would a provincial family of four, extracting a livelihood from a seven *iugerum* plot, feel even if it could read *Laomedonteae . . . periuria Troiae* (Verg. *G.* 1. 502) or *scelusque fraternae necis* (Hor. *Epod* 7. 18)? How many could savor the political, historical and religious legitimations of Aeneas/Augustus in the *Aeneid,* since the whole Aeneas tradition had long been the plaything of the learned, lettered antiquarians?[8] The farmers of Vergil's first and ninth *Eclogues* speak with a primarily literary voice. Of course, that family of four could appreciate certain things: indeed, it had probably suffered far more acutely than Vergil's bucolic swains. Julius Caesar's coins could carry the germs of messages to those not privy to the in-house *gens* histories: at the same time, the circulation of coins is, at best, willy-nilly.[9] The Ara Pacis could make a strong visual impact on lettered and unlettered alike, but how many farmers, given the stern nature of Italian agriculture, could come to Rome and scan it? Likewise, Augustus' inscriptional testament, the *Res Gestae,* probably had a far smaller audience than is regularly assumed for it.[10] Thus, while an already restricted group read the statement on temple rebuilding (20.4), a far smaller group would be able to compare it with Appian's account (5. 87, 97) of the temples Octavian and Friends had pillaged to raise money for their wars.[11] For the moment, then, many conclusions must be negative. All the "crisis" statements in the literary sources must be considered in context of the sociology of Roman literacy and must not be made to speak for all of Roman society. Of course, popular religious discontent existed: the curbing of astrology and Sibyllines implies specific need to control religious outlets more open to the lower orders than were the traditional state cults.[12] Nevertheless, the late first century religious "crisis" as regularly described seems the plaything of Roman authors. The further enshrinement of those authors as canonical in classical education has ensured that their emphases would become those of later scholarship. This will not do: the religious "crisis" was nothing new.

and the Religion of the Republican State," *Journal of Religious History* 4 (1966/67) 89-104; Olivia Dix, *History and Prodigy in the Late Republic* (Diss. Univ. East Anglia, 1978).

[6]Proscriptions: Peter Brunt, *Italian Manpower* (Oxford, 1971) 326-31. Devastations: App. *B.C.* 3.49; Cic. *Fam.* 10.33.4, *Phil.* 3.31; D.C. 46.54.3; Labeo ap. *Dig.* 19.2.15.2; Jal 478-88. Famine: App. 5.18, 22, 25, 67, 77, 92, 99.

[7]Mob rule: Cic. *Att.* 1.3.13, 2.1.8, *Sest.* 6, 28, 34, 38, *Pis.* 1-11; liberated thugs: D.H. 4.24.5; P. Brunt, "The Roman Mob," *Past and Present* 35 (1966) 3-27 and previous note 551-3.

[8]T. J. Cornell, "Aeneas' Arrival in Italy," *LCM* 2 (1977) 77-83, opposing implicitly G. K. Galinsky, *Aeneas, Sicily and Rome* (Princeton, 1969).

[9]Coins: S. Weinstock, *Divus Julius* (Oxford, 1971). Lucius Julius Caesar on his *gens*: S. *Aen.* 1.287. Cf. coins of Sex. Julius Caesar (c. 130-25 B.C.): Sydenham 56, *RE* 10.475 # 150.

[10]Jocelyn 96.

[11]Suet. Aug. 30, Liv. 4.20.7. *Vetustate conlapsum* almost a codeword: *CIL* 3.1790, 3342, 13.7281, *ILS* 3741, *AE* 1974. 574: it did not mean worship ceased: Paus. 8.42.11-13. G. Bodei Giglioni, "Pecunia fanatica: L'incidenze economica dei templi laziali," *Riv. Stor. Ital.* 89 (1977) 33-76.

[12]Suet. *Aug.* 31.2, D.C. 56.25.5.

Max Weber observed that there exist in society certain groups privileged enough to recognize the potential benefits of a higher socio-economic status but yet unable to attain that status. This aptly describes the subgroup of plebeians who extracted significant concessions from the patricians early in the fifth century. Ogilvie has argued that the concessions reflect plebeian strength rather than weakness, but that strength would primarily lie in the leverage of the subgroup whose economic interests brought it close enough to the patrician order to desire some of its perquisites.[13] This is the same group for whom the Lex Canuleia (445 B.C.) and the Lex Ogulneia (300 B.C.) mattered: the less propertied would be in no position, financial, social or psychological, to marry a patrician or attempt duties of state religion. But despite this crossing of economic and social interests, the control of state religion always lay in patrician hands. Thus the institution of two plebeian religious cults (Mercury, 495 B.C.; Ceres/Liber/Libera, 496 (493) B.C.) at the same time as the extraction of the other concessions evidences religious discontent throughout the plebeians. Again, the institution of the equestrian cult of the Dioscuri after the battle of Lake Regillus (499 (496) B.C.) demonstrates patrician self-awareness of the need to offer concessions to a significant group.[14] Nevertheless, those concessions did not significantly change patrician domination, a fact which Polybius noted approvingly (6.56.6-12). *Auspicia ad patres redeunt* makes the point well: the other orders had varying amounts of leverage as a function of particular historical circumstances.[15] Patrician control of legitimating mechanisms such as the Sibyllines offered a kind of switch, which could be turned on and off. And it quite conveniently gave the patricians relief whenever theological ennui struck them.[16] Patricians, then, dominated both causes and cures of religious malaise across the centuries.

Put simply, the lower orders of the fifth and fourth century suffered relative deprivation. They had their private devotions and agrarian cults, but those cults could not mitigate exclusion from state cults. The continuing success of the elite-dominated military expeditions of those centuries only furthered the frustration as a stream of Roman victories confirmed the apparent "rightness" of the established order.[17] But that very military machine not only furthered the disenchantment but, in time, provided relief. Continuing Roman military involvements required ever larger levies of soldiers enrolled under increasingly difficult conditions of service. Small farms were abandoned, soon to be engulfed by latifundia: as the dispossessed migrated to urban centers, the sense of deprivation vis à vis the state cults grew. Tensions arose, but as long as Rome expanded through Italic regions the various religious alternatives would be limited to patrician sponsored imports. The Pyrrhic, Punic and Macedonian wars changed things. Each not only brought armies into contact with significantly different cultures but also, as the pacification of the defeated proceeded, ensured a stream of new influence into Italy. The willingness of the lower orders to "grab" at the state cult of Jupiter, however, shows that the imports had not entirely eliminated discontent.[18]

Surely it is significant that the third century saw the importation of several powerful foreign cults: Aesculapius (293 B.C.), Magna Mater (204 B.C.). Each, in various ways, was open to lower orders. Each also demonstrates that the religious boundaries were becoming more fluid. Thus the Ogulneius who as tribune had sponsored the religious laws of 300 B.C. was, as aedile, joined by his brother, also an aedile, in the importation of Aesculapius.[19] Their interests most obviously looked both to their order and to the upper order. Again, third century numismatic evidence suggests the patrician interests in the

---

[13]Robert Ogilvie, *A Commentary on Livy Books 1-5* (Oxford, 1965) 294.

[14]A. Momigliano, "Procum Patricium," *JRS* 56 (1966) 21-22; cf. Ogilvie, 347.

[15]A. Magdelain, "Auspicia ad patres redeunt," *Collection Latomus* 70 (1964) 427-73.

[16]A. Gagè, *Apollon romain* (Paris, 1955) 421-44.

[17]Keith Hopkins, *Conquerors and Slaves* (Cambridge, 1978) 25-37.

[18]J. R. Fears, *ANRW* 2.17.1.50-1.

[19]Liv. 10.6.3-4, 47.6; V. Max. 1.8.2.

Magna Mater.[20] Not even the legendary past was exempt: in the second century the
patricians destroyed the recently-discovered priestly books attributed to Numa (V. Max.
1. 1. 12).[21] Two conclusions follow. First, cults can only take hold if a constituency
exists for them. Second, while the brothers Ogulneius appear as intermediaries, the ultimate control remained vested in the patricians.

Thus the centuries before the first century had plenty of religious discontent on all
levels. While discontent on the part of the lower orders bulked large, it existed in the
upper orders as well: the elite, after some initial hesitancy, seems readily to have
adopted Greek philosophical systems. Nevertheless, it is one thing for a senator amidst
his ancestral imagines to con a Stoic tract and perhaps shun his family's traditional
priesthoods, and quite another for a freedman not to have that luxury. Thus the long
first century vacancy for the position of Flamen Dialis has probably received too much
emphasis. Roman pacification of the Mediterranean region had meant continued contact
with other religious systems, making it increasingly easy for those who wished to "drop
out" of traditional systems to do so. The evidence for that at the elite levels requires
careful handling: Cicero's religious allusions in his orations may not readily be dismissed
as mere rhetoric. Indeed, the various "crisis" statements seem more a function of
changing socio-political circumstances: "What is really disguised behind this moralizing
language is a transformation of the relationship between religion and society."[22] One
should take a balanced view of the Augustan religious innovations in this connexion: the
Augustales did offer some religious expression to the hitherto marginal group of freedmen, but the financial perquisites excluded all but the very wealthiest.[23] Nevertheless,
the various literary expressions of optimism were just as genuine as the previous gloom:
the problem arises when scholarship does not recognize that this was a group talking
largely to itself.

The military elite of the Roman Republic practiced nearly continuous war, partly
through cultural conventions for gaining glory, partly through patriotism, partly through
greed. This spirit of martial aggrandizement, although initially blind to the spiritual
needs of others, through its very tenacity at last produced remedies, culminating with
Augustus. At the same time, Augustus put that elite out of significant existence. Those
who lamented the problems of the late Republic wanted a restored Republic, but on their
own terms of political gamesmanship. The Principate was not what they had in mind.

Literary expressions have value provided they be not taken as normative for social
history. Unfortunately, many of the models for late Republican history were formed
from literature before significant use was made of other evidence. When that evidence
began to proliferate, it was assimilated to the model based on literature. This imbalance
still needs redress. A crisis, even if perceived by a small group, does not suddenly burst
forth like a conceptual Athena from the head of Zeus. Attention to antecedents must
cast the critical net widely to integrate views via attention to all manner of data from
all the social strata. Who was saying what to whom?

---

[20]G. A. Grueber, *Coins of the Roman Republic in the British Museum* (London,
1910) 1, 126-27.

[21]A. S. Pease, "Notes on Book Burning," in *Munera Studiosa* (ed. M. H. Shepherd and
S. E. Johnson; Cambridge, MA, 1940) 150-54.

[22]John North, "Religious Toleration in Republican Rome," *PCPS* 205 (1979) 96.

[23]John D'Arms, *Commerce and Social Standing in Ancient Rome* (Cambridge, MA,
1981) 126ff.

EXEGETICAL RESTRAINT IN GREGORY OF NYSSA'S
DE VITA MOYSIS

Gregory A. Robbins
Wichita State University

What sort of work is Gregory of Nyssa's *De vita Moysis?* In the section devoted to Gregory's writings in the third volume of his *Patrology,* Johannes Quasten places it among Gregory's exegetical works, but characterizes it as "a mystical treatise" in which Moses is "the symbol of the mystic migration and ascension of the soul to God."[1] That description reflects what has been the dominant interpretation of much of Gregory's corpus. Overwhelming attention has been focused on the so-called "mystical" elements in several of Gregory's works and in *De vita Moysis* in particular and to the question of whether Gregory was the founder of Christian mysticism, as Daniélou believes,[2] or whether he inherited the idea from Alexandrian Christianity, an opinion to which Völker ascribes.[3]

During the last decade or so some have begun to challenge the very presuppositions of this trend of research. Ekkehard Mühlenberg, for example, has noticed that *In canticum canticorum,* considered by many to be one of Gregory's most profound mystical treatises, has no concept at all of mystical union. Mühlenberg accuses scholars of transplanting the "unio mystica" concept from Western medieval theology into the patristic period to interpret the Greek fathers' notion of the ascent of the soul.[4] In their excellent introduction to a long-needed English translation of *De vita Moysis,* Abraham Malherbe and Everett Ferguson wisely avoid using the imprecise and slippery term "mysticism" and prefer to speak of Gregory's distinctive "spirituality."[5]

More recently, an attempt has been made to locate Gregory's writings on the virtuous life within the broader context of polemical theology.[6] In an important monograph on *De vita Moysis,* Ronald E. Heine contends that Gregory's debate with Origenism (especially Origen's speculation on the finitude of God and the satiety of souls) and Eunomianism (on the comprehensibility of God and Eunomius' opposition to the Cappadocians' brand of ascetic spirituality) provides the background against which one ought to read the treatise.[7]

Heine recognizes that his proposal marks a radical departure from earlier interpretations of *De vita Moysis* and he anticipates two possible objections. First, would Gregory still have been wrestling with these controversial issues near the end of his life when he was no longer active as an ecclesiastical statesman? This line of questioning, Heine replies, assumes a late date for the work--after 390.[8] Despite Gregory's own

---

[1]J. Quasten, *Patrology, Vol. III: The Golden Age of Greek Patristic Literature from the Council of Nicea to the Council of Chalcedon,* (Utrecht/Antwerp, 1960), p. 265.

[2]J. Daniélou, *Platonisme et Theologie Mystique,* (Theologie 2, Paris, 1944). Daniélou, *Gregoire de Nysse, La Vie de Moïse,* (SC 1, Paris, 1955). Daniélou and H. Musurillo, *From Glory to Glory: Texts from Gregory of Nyssa's Mystical Writings,* (London, 1961).

[3]W. Völker, *Gregor von Nyssa als Mystiker,* (Wiesbaden, 1955).

[4]E. Mühlenberg, *Die Unendlichkeit Gottes bei Gregor von Nyssa. Gregors Kritik am Gottesbegriff der klassischen Metaphysik,* (Göttingen, 1966).

[5]A. Malherbe and E. Ferguson, *Gregory of Nyssa, The Life of Moses* (New York, 1978) pp. 1-23, especially 9-14.

[6]R. Heine, *Perfection in the Virtuous Life,* (Patristic Monograph Series, No. 2, Philadelphia, 1975).

[7]Ibid., pp. 1-26.

[8]The date assigned to the treatise by Daniélou, *Gregoire de Nysse, La Vie de Moïse* (n. 2, above), p. ix, and by W. Jaeger, *Two Rediscovered Works of Ancient Christian*

references to his "old age" in *De vita Moysis*,[9] Heine suggests that the mid-380's would not be an improbable date for the composition of the work.[10] Second, how does one reconcile the general nature of the treatise (a response to a young man's request for counsel concerning the perfect life, I.2) with the thesis that its central themes are really rooted in polemical theology? Heine counters that toward the end of the treatise (II.316) Gregory comes very close to revealing that the person for whom he has written the work --a person who remains unidentified throughout[11]--is a priest. Heine maintains that if Gregory's young friend were a priest and Gregory wrote the treatise with the priesthood specifically in view, it is not impossible to imagine why these themes from Gregory's polemical theology are woven into a guide to the virtuous life. Virtue, for a man who led and taught in the church, had to be carefully regulated by the rule of orthodoxy. Both his belief and his life had to be correct by this standard. Certain aspects of Origenism deviated from orthodox doctrine. Eunomianism was heretical and could lead to moral laxity. It would be strange indeed, says Heine, for a bishop who was a major figure in the defense of orthodoxy to write a treatise for the edification of the priesthood in a period of theological controversy and not offer a defense against those positions he believed threatened the church.

As compelling as these recent suggestions are, they have not, in my estimation, sufficiently taken into account the exegetical character of *De vita Moysis* and the shape of the work as a whole. Gregory of Nyssa wrote several treatises dealing with the virtuous life--*In psalmorum inscriptiones, In canticum canticorum, Vita Macrinae, De virginitate, Quid nomen professione Christianorum sibi velit, De perfectione, De instituto Christiano,* and *De castigatione*--in addition to *De vita Moysis.*[12] Some of these works are entirely exegetical, while others are conspicuous because of their lack of scriptural reference. Is that significant? Although Gregory often turned to Moses as a model of virtue,[13] he could appeal to other biblical worthies as well.[14] In the opening pages of *De vita Moysis* Gregory notes that Abraham and Sarah might have served equally well as guides to the virtuous life (I.12). Gregory could appeal to non-biblical models, too. "Indeed," argues Gregory in chapter 24 of *De virginitate*, "examples of holy lives for them to follow are not wanting in the living generation. Now, if ever before, saintliness abounds and penetrates our world."[15] If other models of virtue were available to Gregory, why did he choose Moses (again)? If we want to say, as Heine does, that a theological polemic and historical circumstances have a direct bearing on the content of the work, and if the work is an exegetical one, as *De vita Moysis* certainly is, it seems logical to ask how these factors shape the exegesis in the sense that they determine the

---

Literature: Gregory of Nyssa and Macarius (Leiden, 1954) pp. 119, 130. See also: G. May, "Die Chronologie des Lebens und der Werke des Gregor von Nyssa," in M. Harl, ed. *Ecriture et Culture Philosophique dans la Pensee de Gregoire de Nysse,* (Leiden, 1971), pp. 63ff.

[9]I.2. References to passages in *De vita Moysis* reflect the section numbers in Malherbe's and Ferguson's English translation (n. 5, above), as well as those in Daniélou's Sources Chrétiennes edition (n. 2, above).

[10]Especially significant are the references to his advanced age in his works against Eunomius written in the early 380's. See Quasten, op. cit., pp. 257-58, and Malherbe and Ferguson, op. cit., p. 149, n. 6.

[11]I.2; II.319. Cf., Malherbe and Ferguson, op. cit., pp. 2, 149, n. 4.

[12]Quasten, op. cit., pp. 263-69.

[13]Malherbe and Ferguson, op. cit., pp. 9, 20-22.

[14]Ibid., pp. 20-22.

[15]Translated by W. Moore and H. Wilson in *The Nicene and Post-Nicene Fathers, Vol. V,* (Grand Rapids, 1976) p. 369.

questions posed and the results obtained.[16] We ought to ask how theology and historical circumstances play a role in the formulation of exegetical methods. Within the context of a discussion of the virtuous life, does Gregory's debate with Origenism and Eunomianism, as outlined by Heine, do justice to the exegetical character of the work and the methodology employed?

These remarks are not intended to imply that Heine is unconcerned with such issues. In a rather brief section, he attempts to account for the structure of the work by noting that Gregory's theological predisposition made the life of Moses particularly attractive to him. Moses' career is appealing to Gregory because certain climactic events are tailor-made for Gregory's purposes: to underline his anti-satiety position, to argue for the incomprehensibility of God. Heine draws our attention especially to the dynamic character of Gregory's vocabulary throughout the work.[17] There can be no doubt, however, that Heine focuses most of his attention on the theophany[18] sections and the sort of theological language found there. He makes no attempt to explain in detail the fact that, in this work, Gregory not only tells the *whole* story of Moses' life, but does so *twice*. Nor does he devote much comment to the content of the exegesis in the individual sections, the citations and allusions[19] to other biblical texts within them, or the transitions in the *theoria* sections.[20]

Heine has not been the only one to suggest that Gregory's *De vita Moysis* might have a polemical thrust. Werner Jaeger, in his extremely provocative little book, *Early Christianity and Greek Paideia,* remarks in passing that he thinks *De vita Moysis* was written chiefly as an answer to accusations made by certain Christians against Gregory's work, complaining that he was interpolating foreign philosophy into the Bible.[21] Near the end of his life, Gregory had to counter rather severe criticism about his exegetical method in the wake of an attack within the church against the excesses of Origen.[22] Jaeger notes elsewhere that the staunch champions of this new anti-Origenistic traditionalism were Methodius of Olympus and Epiphanius of Salamis.[23] In his anti-heretical work, *Panarion,* Epiphanius included a long chapter about Origen (chapter 64) in which he criticized not only individual details but the entire mentality and principles by which

---

[16]For a systematic attempt to do just that see R. A. Greer, *The Captain of Our Salvation,* (Tübingen, 1973).

[17]Heine, op. cit., pp. 97-114.

[18]E.g., the narrative about the burning bush (II.22-26), the revelation of the Law at Sinai (II.162-166), and the request to see God (II.221-222, 231-239, 249-255).

[19]Malherbe and Ferguson, op. cit., p. 18, have noted correctly that: "It is characteristic of Gregory's later writings that he gives a Scriptural grounding to his spiritual doctrine. Not only is the whole *Life of Moses* based on Scriptural narrative, but also the spiritual interpretations are given a Scriptural basis wherever possible. The frequent Scriptural citations will bear this out. In the Introduction he says: 'It seems good to me to make use of Scripture as a counselor in this matter' (I.11). The prophets and apostles are the instruments of the Spirit, trumpeting forth the divine message (II.159). The treatise is replete with such affirmations of the divine nature of Scripture. The Spirit who has inspired Scripture must guide its interpretation (II.173)." The question I wish to pursue is: Why is it necessary for Gregory to make these statements?

[20]On Gregory's preference for the term *theoria* when urging the reader to go beyond the literal sense of the biblical text, see: Malherbe and Ferguson, op. cit., p. 7, especially their suggestion that Gregory's choice may reflect an accommodation to the Antiochian attack on *allegoria.*

[21]W. Jaeger, *Early Christianity and Greek Paideia,* (London, 1977) p. 81.

[22]Quasten, op. cit., p. 266, notes that in the preface to *In canticum canticorum* Gregory defends against several ecclesiastical authors the necessity for, and the right to, a spiritual interpretation of Scripture. The section concludes with high praise of Origen.

[23]Jaeger, *Two Rediscovered Works* (n. 8, above), p. 120, n. 2.

Origen attempted to reconcile Christian revelation with philosophical truth on the basis of rational thought. Epiphanius described Origen as "blinded by Greek *paideia*." After the *Panarion* was published in the 370's, the criticism spread and a reaction of enormous proportions against "Origenism" was to follow it, coming to a crest in the early 390's.

That Gregory was affected by this movement seems clear from the obvious tendency toward conservatism in exegesis that characterizes his later exegetical works.[24] On occasion he found it necessary to clarify his own position. Consider the opening lines of *De instituto Christiano*, the last of Gregory's works on the virtuous life which represents, according to Jaeger, a concentrated synthesis of everything Gregory had written prior to it:

> So I write you these seeds of instruction, selecting them from the fruits the Spirit has given me, but often using as well the words of Scripture as proof of what I say and to clarify my interpretation of their meaning, lest I seem to abandon the divine gifts sent from above and to substitute for them the poor products of my own mind, or to shape an ideal of piety in accordance with the doctrines of exotic philosophy and, inflated by vain pride, to interpolate them in my ignorance into the Scriptures.[25]

Jaeger locates this document in the mid-390's, not long after the date usually assigned to *De vita Moysis*--maybe 3 to 5 years.

There are still other factors I think we must keep in mind if we are to fully appreciate the exegetical reserve we encounter in Gregory's *De vita Moysis*. While Moses had long held a prominent place in the thinking of Jews and Christians,[26] he also had his detractors.[27] When considering the 4th century, Julian the Apostate comes immediately to mind. As John Gager has noted,[28] Julian was not only the last significant political and religious representative of Greek and Roman pagan culture in the ancient world, he was also the last pagan writer to deal extensively with Moses. In his invective, *Against the Galileans*, Julian depicts Moses as a rather deficient lawgiver who compares unfavorably with the likes of Plato, Socrates, Thales and others (184B).[29] Moreover, Julian asserts that the Hebrews never originated any science or philosophical study (178A). By comparing Moses' creation story (49A-D, 57B-66A) with Plato's, by analyzing Moses' cosmology (96C-E), and by considering his account of the confusion of tongues (134E), Julian attempts to prove that Moses is also a deficient theologian whose God is god over a very small portion indeed (148B). Since these criticisms are imbedded in a vituperous assault on Christianity, the implications for Christians, who appeal to Moses and who, in Julian's opinion, constantly *mis*-interpret Moses by reading Jesus into such passages as Deut 18:18 and countless others (253C), are quite serious. Julian anticipates Origen's critics when he scoffs at Christians who "nibble at the learning of the Hellenes" and yet persist in maintaining the supremacy of their scriptures (229C). Again, the conclusions he draws are most telling:

---

[24]M. Canevet, "Exegese et theologie dans les Traites Spirituels de Gregoire de Nysse," in Harl, op. cit., pp. 148-68. In her conclusion she states: "Ce qu'il (Gregory) perd en richesse par rapport à Origène, il le gagne en pureté de ligne."

[25]Jaeger, *Two Rediscovered Works*, pp. 115ff.

[26]Malherbe and Ferguson, op. cit., pp. 5-7, 144, n. 24.

[27]J. Gager, *Moses in Greco-Roman Paganism*, (SBLMS 16; Nashville, 1972).

[28]Gager, op. cit., pp. 101ff. Cf., R. MacMullen, *Paganism in the Roman Empire* (New Haven, 1982), pp. 132-35.

[29]All references are to W. C. Wright's translation, *The Works of the Emperor Julian, Vol. III* (London: Loeb Classical Library, 1913-24).

> But you yourselves know, it seems to me, the very different effect on the intelligence of your writings as compared with ours; and that from studying yours no man could attain to excellence or even to ordinary goodness, whereas from studying ours every man would become better than before, even though he were altogether without natural fitness (229D).

Similar remarks are to be found in Julian's famous "Rescript on Christian Teachers" written in June of 362 from Antioch.[30]

Such considerations tend to bring our earlier questions into sharper focus. In the face of more tradition-oriented, anti-Origenist critics within the church and recent pagan criticism from without, Gregory's penchant for allegorical exegesis had to be held in check. His method of interpretation of scripture could not stray too far from the literal meaning of the text; if it did, it had to be justified. Similarly, in appealing to Moses as a model for the virtuous life of the Christian, Gregory not only had to demonstrate that such a biblical personage could be a credible model to emulate, but in fact had to reclaim him for the church from the hands of its cultured despisers. Such concerns, I am convinced, have dictated the shape of *De vita Moysis* and the sort of exegesis we find there.

That Gregory of Nyssa knew the works of Philo of Alexandria and incorporated parts of Philo's work into his own has long been recognized.[31] With respect to Gregory's *De vita Moysis*, the influence of Philo's own depiction of Moses is clear.[32] While a detailed comparison of Gregory's *De vita Moysis* and Philo's is not possible here, I would like to suggest that not only did the two-part format of Philo's *Vita Moysis* appeal to Gregory, by which the literal and speculative readings of the narrative are bound together (for the reasons outlined above), but also the apologetic intention of Philo's work, being concerned to present Moses as a virtuous person well-suited to assume the responsibilities of legislator, priest, and prophet—but especially those of the priest.

> I intend to write the life of Moses, whom some call the lawgiver of the Jews. . . . For while the fame of his laws has spread throughout the world and reached the ends of the earth, not many know him as he really was. Greek authors have not wanted to record him as worthy of memory, in part out of envy and also because in many cases the ordinances of local lawgivers are opposed to his (I.1f.).[33]

> The chief and most essential quality required by a priest is piety, and this he (Moses) practised in a very high degree, and at the same time made use of his great natural gifts. In these, philosophy found a good soil, which she improved still further by the admirable truths which she brought before his eyes, nor did she cease until the fruits of virtue shown in word and deed were brought to perfection. Thus he came to love God and to be loved by Him as have been few others (II.13.66ff.).

If Heine is correct in assuming that Gregory wrote his *De vita Moysis* for a young priest, and if I am right in suggesting that Gregory has unmentioned exegetical dialogue part-

---

[30]Ibid., p. 117.

[31]Jaeger, *Two Rediscovered Works*, p. 78, cites evidence that medieval scribes recognized Philo's influence on Gregory. Daniélou, *Gregoire de Nysse, La Vie de Moïse*, pp. xiv-xv, lists specific parallels. Malherbe and Ferguson, op. cit., pp. 6, 141-94 passim.

[32]J. Daniélou, "Orientations Actuelles de la Recherche sur Gregoire de Nysse," in Harl, op. cit., pp. 9-12. Daniélou also points to the influence of Philo's *The Posterity of Cain* upon Gregory's *De vita Moysis*. Cf., Malherbe and Ferguson, op. cit., p. 6.

[33]The quotes from the *Vita Moysis* are from F. H. Colson's *The Works of Philo*, (London: Loeb Classical Library).

ners, then the overall shape of the work is not unimportant. Gregory's decision to imitate Philo's *Vita Moysis* was not simply a matter of convenience. Gregory and Philo had similar concerns.

But to a certain extent, Gregory is even more cautious than Philo in accomplishing his aims. For example, in offering an interpretation of Exod 12:35-36, where the Hebrews despoil the Egyptians, Philo had no difficulty in coming to terms with the implication that Moses condoned the action, arguing that the Hebrews were receiving but a bare wage for all their time in servitude and were retaliating not on an equal but on a *lesser* scale (I.25.140f.). Gregory, however, feels compelled to seek a "loftier meaning" (II.112-116). He worries over the implications of such an act at Moses' command. There is an attempt here to clear Moses from any sense of impropriety that might make him unworthy as a model of virtue. There is, then, a plea to the reader to go beyond the obvious sense of the text. Given the scorn a literal reading of the text might attract, the allegorical interpretation is more fitting than the obvious one. There are countless passages throughout Gregory's *De vita Moysis* where such appeals are made by Gregory in defense of the exegesis he proffers.

Such appeals are not an invitation to a flight of exegetical fancy. In this instance, the allegorical interpretation is no less problematic than the literal. By suggesting that the spoils from Egypt ought to be understood as the wealth of pagan learning, Gregory must expound on the relationship of rational, secular pursuits to the life of virtue. In essence, Gregory admits the truth of Julian's charge noted above. Moral and natural philosophy, geometry, astronomy, dialectic, etc., do, in fact, lie beyond the purview of the church, even outside the church. But when used properly (and this is Gregory's real concern), within the context of the virtuous life, these disciplines "adorn the divine temple of the mystery," i.e., they build up the faithful.

Who is best qualified to take on this task, which involves, as I have suggested, a number of risks? Clearly not everyone.

> The multitude was not capable of hearing the voice from above but relied on Moses to learn by himself the secrets and to teach the people whatever doctrine he might learn through instruction from above. This is also true of the arrangement of the church: Not all thrust themselves toward the apprehension of the mysteries, but, choosing from among themselves someone who is able to hear things divine, they give ear gratefully to him, considering trustworthy whatever they might hear from someone initiated into the divine mysteries. It is said, "Not all are apostles, nor all prophets," but this is not now heeded in many of the churches. For many, still in need of being purified from the way they have lived, unwashed and full of spots in their life's garment and protecting themselves only with their irrational senses, make an assault on the divine mountain. So it happens that they are stoned by their own reasonings, for heretical opinions are in effect stones which crush the inventor of evil doctrines (II.160-161).

Heine claims that Gregory has in mind the virtuous priest who knows how to dodge the crushing stones of Origenism and Eunomianism. I have attempted to augment his proposal by pointing to currents in the late 4th century that call for an individual who can avoid literalism while practicing imaginative exegetical restraint.

PRONOUNCEMENT STORIES AND JESUS' BLESSING OF CHILDREN:
A RHETORICAL APPROACH[+]

Vernon K. Robbins
University of Illinois at Urbana-Champaign

This paper contains analysis of the literary units in the NT Gospels and the Gospel of Thomas that feature poignant speech and action concerning children. Each of the synoptic Gospels contains two different stories about Jesus and children: (1) Matt 19:13-15; Mark 10:13-16; Luke 18:15-17; (2) Matt 18:1-5; Mark 9:33-37; Luke 9:46-48. In addition, John 3:1-8 has a discussion about being born again to see the kingdom of God, and Gospel of Thomas 22 has a discussion about suckling infants entering the Kingdom.

The commonly accepted approach to gospel traditions that contain poignant sayings is either to ignore the actions of Jesus in the story or to consider the actions to be secondary to the sayings.[1] In other words, it is presupposed that the transmission of speech attributed to Jesus holds the key to the history of the gospel traditions in which Jesus is the main character. The accompanying result of this approach to gospel traditions is to suggest that most settings are contrived artificially to provide a situation for sayings to occur, and in many instances the settings have been created out of the idea in the major saying in the story.

The analysis in this paper challenges the traditional approach on the basis of evidence in the history of chreia traditions in Graeco-Roman literature.[2] First, evidence in chreia traditions suggests that actions often are as important as sayings, and in some instances actions are prior in the tradition. In other words, in some stories a poignant action within a particular setting has been the occasion for the production of one or more sayings. The sayings have been produced to explain the action, to supplement the thought in the action, or to relate the thought in the action to some other thought or action. Secondly, specific sayings are often prior in the tradition to generalized sayings, i.e., maxims. This paper suggests, therefore, that the history of the traditions in the gospels needs to be re-assessed to identify sayings that have developed out of settings characterized by poignant action and generalized sayings that have arisen to supplement or replace specific sayings in specific settings.

[+]This paper was written during Spring, 1982, while the author was a Visiting Scholar at the Institute for Antiquity and Christianity under the sponsorship of the SBL-Claremont Fellowship. I am deeply grateful to the participants at the Institute and to the Fellowship program for a most pleasant and stimulating environment for this research.

[1]Only very meagre use of chreia traditions to understand gospel stories has occurred in previous scholarship. See Martin Dibelius, *From Tradition to Gospel* (New York: Charles Scribner's Sons, 1935) 152-64; R. O. P. Taylor, *The Groundwork of the Gospels* (Oxford: Basil Blackwell, 1946) 75-89; William R. Farmer, "Notes on a Literary and Form-Critical Analysis of Some of the Synoptic Material Peculiar to Luke," *NTS* 8 (1962) 301-15; Arland J. Hultgren, *Jesus and His Adversaries: The Form and Function of the Conflict Stories in the Synoptic Tradition* (Minneapolis: Augsburg, 1979) 33-36.

[2]The author is indebted to members of the Chreia Project at the Institute for Antiquity and Christianity, Claremont, for their translations and analyses of portions of the *Progymnasmata* concerning the chreia. Edward N. O'Neil, Burton L. Mack, and Ronald F. Hock are leaders of the Chreia Project, with James R. Butts as the Research Associate. For an account of the origins, goals, and scope of the Chreia Project, see Edward N. O'Neil, "The Chreia in Greco-Roman Literature and Education," *The Institute for Antiquity and Christianity Report: 1972-80* (ed. Marvin W. Meyer; Claremont: Institute for Antiquity and Christianity, 1981) 19-22.

The conclusions in this paper are attained by means of analysis informed by ancient rhetorical treatises.[3] While rhetoric means many things to many people, in this paper it refers to techniques of persuasion and argumentation as they are embodied in literature. Rhetorical analysis, therefore, is undertaken in the form of analysis of techniques of persuasion and argumentation in the literary units in which children are the object of Jesus' speech and demonstrative action.[4] Rhetorical analysis of the units about children seems especially appropriate, because the units contain all three components of a rhetorical situation: (1) speaker; (2) speech and/or demonstrative action; and (3) audience. The presence of these three components means that the units create the rhetorical setting of a mini-speech. Through these three components in the mini-speech situation, persuasion and argumentation operate through three modes: (1) character (ethos); (2) thought (logos); (3) response (pathos). The speaker embodies character (ethos), the speech and demonstrative action contain thought (logos), and the audience responds (pathos) to the character and the thought.[5] Accordingly, in the units concerning children, Jesus embodies authoritative character (ethos), Jesus' speech and demonstrative action contain thought (logos), and the disciples and the reader respond (pathos) to the actions and speech in the setting.

Since the limitations of space make it impossible to present a complete rhetorical analysis of the stories concerning children, this paper presents only a revised history of the tradition and an initial consideration of the function of the stories in each of the gospels as construed on the basis of evidence both in rhetorical treatises and in literature contemporary with the gospels. The steps in the analysis are based especially on data in the *Progymnasmata* of Aelius Theon of Alexandria, written during the latter part of the first or early part of the second century C.E.,[6] and in the writings of Plutarch, written 90-120 C.E.[7] The data from Theon shows that people who learned to compose in Greek began their training with exercises performed on short literary units like the units in the synoptic gospels. The exercises in Theon's *Progymnasmata* represent widespread educa-

---

[3]The major rhetorical treatises written prior to or during the first century C.E., available in English (e.g., in Loeb Classical Library), include Aristotle, *Ars Rhetorica*; the *Rhetorica ad Alexandrum*; Cicero, *De Inventione, De Oratore*; the *Rhetorica ad Herennium*; Quintilian, *Institutio Oratoria*. For an excellent introduction to rhetoric in antiquity, see Donald L. Clark, *Rhetoric in Greco-Roman Education* (New York: Columbia University Press, 1957); for more detailed accounts, see George A. Kennedy, *The Art of Persuasion in Greece* (Princeton: Princeton University Press, 1963); idem, *The Art of Rhetoric in the Roman World* (Princeton: Princeton University Press, 1972).

[4]By demonstrative action, I mean the kind of action that demonstrates a thought. One of the most well told stories containing a demonstrative action is found in Plutarch, *Alexander* 65.6-7 [3-4] where Calanus first walks around on the edge of a shrivelled hide with parts of the hide continually rising up, then stands in the middle of the hide holding it all down, to explain the difficulties of maintain control of a government while travelling in expeditions designed to expand the outer boundaries of the regime.

[5]For a discussion of ethos, logos and pathos in ancient rhetorical treatises, see Aristotle, *Ars Rhetorica* 1-2 (esp. 1.2.3-6,); Cicero, *De Oratore* 2.27.114-115. For a secondary discussion, see Clark, *Rhetoric*, pp. 52-58, 74-75, 80.

[6]For the text of Aelius Theon's *Progymnasmata*, see T. Christian Walz, *Rhetores Graeci* (Stuttgart and Tübingen: J. G. Cotta, 1832) I, pp. 137ff.; Leonhard von Spengel, *Rhetores Graeci* (Leipzig: Teubner, 1854) II, pp. 59ff. For the date and importance of Aelius Theon, see W. von Christ and W. Schmid, *Geschichte der griechische Literatur, Nachklassische Periode* (6th ed.; Munich: Beck, 1919) II. 1, pp. 460-61.

[7]For the importance of Plutarch's writing in relation to early Christian literature, see H. Dieter Betz (ed.) *Plutarch's Theological Writings and Early Christian Literature* (SACHNT 3; Leiden: Brill, 1975); idem, *Plutarch's Ethical Writings and Early Christian Literature* (SACHNT 4; Leiden: Brill, 1978).

tional practice going back to the beginning of the first century B.C.E.,[8] and they show that variations in data and phrasing in brief literary units was understood as a rhetorical exercise that prepared the student for the incorporation of traditional stories and sayings into full-length speeches.[9] In other words, writing brief literary units in varying ways was a preparatory exercise for adapting a unit to the argumentative setting in which it would occur. In turn, the data from Plutarch show how an author employed the insights gained from his training in composition, adapting and rewriting brief stories and apophthegms as he incorporated them into an extended literary document.

The analysis and interpretation in this paper unfold in four steps. First, we will exhibit Theon's definition of a chreia, list the exercises Theon says were used in the educational setting, and illustrate an exercise that is especially important for under-standing the relation of the chreia to the stories about Jesus and the children. Analysis of the exercises performed with the chreia during the preliminary stage of rhetorical training suggests that the synoptic stories about Jesus and the children should be understood as moderately expanded chreiai. In other words, instead of rejecting the importance of the chreia for understanding stories with pointed sayings and actions, as did both M. Dibelius and A. Hultgren,[10] this study uses the exercises with the chreia as a springboard for analysis and interpretation. Secondly, moving out from chreiai in Theon's *Progymnasmata* to chreiai as they were composed in the setting of literature contemporary with the gospels, the analysis of the six synoptic stories about Jesus and the children suggests that two chreiai existed in early Christian tradition: (1) a chreia in which Jesus responds with a saying when the disciples attempt to hinder people from bringing children to him; and (2) a chreia in which Jesus responds with a demonstrative action when they are concerned to know who is the greatest. This analysis breaks with the tradition that "the interest of the apophthegms is entirely confined to sayings of Jesus"[11] to argue that the history of the tradition concerning Jesus' blessing of the children can be accurately unravelled only if the analysis is as sensitive to settings and actions as to sayings. Thirdly, the analysis of moderately expanded chreiai in the synoptic gospels and in literature contemporary with them shows a tendency either to transform sayings with a specific reference to sayings with more general reference, or to add general maxims to specific sayings. These changes allow the story to contribute more directly to argumentation in the document in which it is being incorporated. This generalizing activity appears to produce general sayings and maxims that, within time, may become separated from the chreia. Fourthly, the production of general sayings within chreia traditions is juxtaposed with the attraction of general maxims to a chreia tradition. This investigation provides the basis for analysis of the settings of dialogue and discourse in the Fourth Gospel and the Gospel of Thomas about being born again and about being a suckling infant in order to enter the kingdom.

Therefore, working through the units about Jesus and the children, we will suggest that early traditions in the form of chreiai portrayed a specific image of Jesus' character (ethos) by means of pointed speech and action (logos) designed to evoke a positive response (pathos) toward a particular system of thought and action perpetuated by early Christians. As the traditions were transmitted through succeeding generations of

---

[8]For a discussion of the formation of a standard set of preliminary exercises by the first century B.C.E. and the importance of the *Progymnasmata* of Aelius Theon of Alexandria for understanding the development in Greek and Roman circles, see Stanley F. Bonner, *Education in Ancient Rome* (Berkeley and Los Angeles: University of California Press, 1977) 250-59.

[9]See Bonner, *Education*, pp. 254-55.

[10]See Dibelius, *Tradition*, pp. 152-64; Hultgren, *Jesus*, pp. 33-36.

[11]Rudolf Bultmann, *The History of the Synoptic Tradition* (trans. J. Marsh; New York and Evanston, 1963) 62. Accordingly, Dibelius, *Tradition*, p. 48 says: "The action of the narrative has no independent value for the preacher."

believers, the character of Jesus was molded in terms of more spiritualistic, esoteric wisdom. In this setting the emphasis fell more and more on the portrayal of a "logic" for entering and seeing the kingdom. This logic was explored by means of a setting of dialogue and extended discourse that subordinated poignant action to poignant speech.

In particular, the conclusion will be drawn that the synoptic writers had been trained to perceive stories about personages in terms of discrete literary units that were fair game for expansion and modification. The conclusion is near to hand that the authors of the synoptic gospels had learned to compose Greek in a setting that had incorporated preliminary exercises of rhetorical education as they are discussed and illustrated in Theon's *Progymnasmata*. Both as they wrote their gospels and as they read other people's collections or complete narratives they saw the material in terms of the discrete units they had been taught to see and write in the educational setting where they had learned to compose in Greek. Also, in accord with their level of rhetorical training, they expanded or condensed these literary units—incorporating, excluding and rewriting—by means of procedures they understood to be persuasive rhetorically.

Rhetorical Composition in the Chreia

From the point of view of a rhetorician like Theon, the six literary units about children in the synoptic gospels are chreai that have been expanded in various ways by different authors. For Theon, a chreia is:

σύντομος ἀπόφασις ἢ πρᾶξις μετ' εὐστοχίας ἀναφερομένη
εἴς τι ὡρισμένον πρόσωπον ἢ ἀναλογοῦν προσώπῳ,

a brief statement or action with pointedness attributed to some specific person or something analogous to a person.[12]

The essential attributes of a chreia, therefore, are the presence of a personage (πρόσωπον) by means of attribution of the statement or action, and the presence of a statement or action that is "well-aimed" (ἀπόφασις ἢ πρᾶξις μετ' εὐστοχίας), i.e., that directs the reader's thought in a striking manner. Through convention, the statement or action in the chreia was written by means of one or more participial clauses in the first part followed by a finite verb that introduced the statement or action. One of the chreiai Theon gives as an example is as follows:

Ἐπαμεινώδας, ἄτεκνος ἀποθνήσκων, ἔλεγε τοῖς φίλοις,
δύο θυγατέρας ἀπέλιπον, τήν τε περὶ Λεῦκτραν νίκην,
καὶ τὴν περὶ Μαντίνειαν·

Epameinondas, as he was dying childless, said to his friends: "I have left two daughters—the victory at Leuctra and the one at Mantineia"[13]

---

[12]Theon, *Progymnasmata* 201, 16-18 (Walz). The understanding of this definition often has been confused by the later textual tradition that placed μετ' εὐστοχίας after ἀναφερομένη under the influence of the definitions in Hermogenes and Aphthonius. The later *Progymnasmata* used the term ἀπομνημόνευμα (reminiscence) in the definition and shifted the emphasis further toward the attribution, thus losing touch with the emphasis on the "well-aimed" quality of the chreia as it existed during the first centuries B.C.E. and C.E. The reference to "something analogous to a person" refers to a written document attributed to a certain person.

[13]Theon, *Progymnasmata* 213, 14-17 (Walz). See Bonner, *Education*, p. 258.

A chreia like this one would be used with the student during his preliminary rhetorical training in order to teach him how to compose in a clear and persuasive style. Theon says that the student would write and rewrite the chreia according to the following exercises:

(1) Write the chreia clearly either in the same words or in different words (recitation; ἀπαγγελία);

(2) Rewrite the chreia by changing the person, number and cases so that the chreia would be written in first, second, third and dual persons, and in the five cases (inflection; κλίσις);

(3) Write comments on what was said or done in the chreia (ἐπιφώνησις);

(4) Write objections to the chreia from the opposite points of view (ἀντιλογία);

(5) Expand the chreia (ἐπεκτείνειν);

(6) Condense the chreia (συστέλλειν);

(7) Refute the chreia (ἀνασκευάζειν);

(8) Confirm the chreia (κατασκευάζειν);[14]

These exercises prepared the student for using the chreia rhetorically within extended prose composition where any person and number may be required in the verbs, various cases would be needed to express the circumstances surrounding the statement or action, and various lengths would be desired for the inclusion of greater or less detail. Also, these exercises influenced the oral skills of the student, since the student was asked to express the exercises orally as well as to write them.[15]

While it is not necessary to recount what Theon says about each of the exercises with the chreia, his illustration of the expansion of a chreia is pertinent to our analysis. To illustrate the expansion exercise, Theon expands the chreia cited above into the following form:

> Ἐπαμεινώνδας, ὁ τῶν Θηβαίων στρατηγός, ἦν μὲν ἄρα καὶ
> παρὰ τὴν εἰρήνην ἀνὴρ ἀγαθός, συστάντος δὲ τῇ πατρίδι
> πολέμου πρὸς Λακεδαιμονίους, πολλὰ καὶ λαμπρὰ ἔργα τῆς
> μεγαλοψυχίας ἐπεδείξατο· βοιωταρχῶν μὲν περὶ Λεῦκτρα
> ἐνίκα τοὺς πολεμίους, στρατευόμενος δὲ ὑπὲρ τῆς πατρίδος
> καὶ ἀγωνιζόμενος ἀπέθανεν ἐν Μαντινείᾳ. ἐπεὶ δὲ
> τρωθεὶς ἐτελεύτα τὸν βίον, ὀλοφυρομένων τῶν φίλων τά
> τε ἄλλα, καὶ διότι ἄτεκνος ἀποθνήσκοι, μειδιάσας,
> παύσασθε, ἔφη, ὦ φίλοι, κλαίοντες, ἐγὼ γὰρ ὑμῖν
> ἀθανάτους δύο καταλέλοιπα θυγατέρας, δύο νίκας τῆς
> πατρίδος κατὰ Λακεδαιμονίων, τὴν μὲν ἐν Λεύκτροις,
> τὴν πρεσβυτέραν, νεωτέραν δὲ τὴν ἄρτι μοι γενομένην
> ἐν Μαντινείᾳ.

---

[14]Theon, *Progymnasmata* 210, 3-6 (Walz).
[15]See Bonner, *Education*, pp. 254-55.

Epameinondas, the Theban general, was of course a good man even in time of
peace, but when war broke out between his country and the Lacedaemonians,
he performed many brilliant deeds of courage. As a Boeotarch at Leuctra,
he triumphed over the enemy, but while campaigning and fighting for his
country, he died at Mantineia. While he was dying of his wounds and his
friends were particularly grief-stricken that he was dying childless, he
smiled and said: "Stop grieving, friends, for I have left you two immortal
daughters: two victories of our country over the Lacedaemonians, the one at
Leuctra, who is the older, and the younger, who has just been born to me at
Mantineia.[16]

Immediately the reader will notice how the expansion has produced a sequence of
sentences containing participial clauses and finite verbs. The unity of the story is
maintained through the use of conjunctions. The saying has been expanded through direct
address, command and greater detail. The author has shifted from ἔλεγε to introduce
the saying in the condensed form to ἔφη in the expanded form. Also, a participle
(μειδιάσας; laughing) is included to introduce a circumstantial gesture and attitude in
the setting of the finite verb that introduced the speaking.

The procedures for expanding the chreia bridge the gap between the chreiai and the
stories with pointed sayings and actions in the gospels called "pronouncement stories" in
recent research, and previously called paradigms or apophthegms.[17] The rejection of a
relationship between the gospel stories and chreiai has arisen, partially, because of a lack
of periodic composition in the gospel stories. But periodic composition was not emphasized during the stage of learning to expand and condense the chreia, and Theon, as we
see, did not compose his example of the expanded chreia in one periodic construction.
The problem in scholarship, we therefore suggest, has arisen both from a failure to
analyze the procedures for expanding and condensing the chreia in the *Progymnasmata*
and from a failure to analyze the actual instances of chreia traditions in extended
literary settings comparable to the gospels.

Rhetorical Composition in the Chreia
About Children Belonging in the Kingdom

One of the chreiai that existed in early Christian tradition recited a scene in which
the disciples were preventing little children from coming to Jesus, to which Jesus
responded, "Let the children come to me, and do not hinder them, for to such belongs the
kingdom of God (Heaven)."[18] This chreia underlines the little stories in Matt 19:13-15;
Mark 10:13-16 and Luke 18:15-17. The basic structure of the chreia is:

(a)   people were bringing children to Jesus, that he might touch them;

(b)   the disciples rebuked the people;

(c)   Jesus said, "Let the children come to me, and do not prevent them, for to
       such belongs the kingdom of God."

---

[16]Theon, *Progymnasmata* 213,17-214,4 (Walz).

[17]For recent analysis of units previously called apophthegms and paradigms, see
Robert C. Tannehill (ed.), *Pronouncement Stories, Semeia* 20 (1981).

[18]Cf. Dibelius, *Tradition*, p. 43, where Mark 10:13ff. is listed among the "pure"
paradigms; and Bultmann, *History*, p. 32, where Mark 10:13-16 is considered a "complete
apophthegm."

This sequence is rhetorically complete, and it contains the natural ingredients for a chreia that ends with a poignant saying. The challenge for composition of the chreia in a condensed form (as a periodic construction) would be to express the people's bringing of the children and the disciples' rebuking of the people as an introduction to Jesus' response to the disciples' action. If a person were to write a condensed form of the story in a manner similar to Theon's composition of the Epameinondas chreia, it might look something like this:

'Ιησοῦς, ἰδὼν τοὺς μαθητὰς ἐπιτιμῶντάς τινας τοὺς προσφέροντας παιδία αὐτῷ ἵνα αὐτῶν ἅψηται, εἶπεν αὐτοῖς, ἄφετε τὰ παιδία ἔρχεσθαι πρός με καὶ μὴ κωλύετε αὐτά· τῶν γὰρ τοιούτων ἐστὶν ἡ βασιλεία τοῦ θεοῦ.

Jesus, when he saw his disciples rebuking certain ones who were bringing children to him in order that he might touch them, said to them, "Let the children come to me and do not hinder them; for to such belongs the kingdom of God."

The story in this condensed form would exhibit the ethos of Jesus through a statement that countered the disciples' decision not to let people bring the little children to him. Jesus' response contains the assertion (logos) that little children belong to the kingdom of God, and this thought embodies the ethos of Jesus that brings forth a positive response (pathos). By his willingness to give individual attention to little children, who cannot confer expensive gifts or positions of authority in return for favors, Jesus manifests good moral character and good will.[19]

Interpretation of the earliest form of the tradition would be facilitated greatly if we knew the motivation and occasion, as perceived in the story, for bringing the children to Jesus. What social context makes this action appropriate? The only clue lies in the comment that the goal was for Jesus to touch the children, i.e., to lay his hands on them. The best possibility, on the basis of the evidence recently presented by J. Sauer, appears to be a tradition of healing children by taking them into one's arms.[20] Whether the presupposition is healing or some other form of blessing, the interest in Jesus' touching of the children is essential for understanding the development of the story in the tradition.

Instead of writing the chreia in a condensed form, all of the authors of the gospels compose a moderately expanded chreia by means of a paratactic sequence. The form of the gospel units is therefore like Theon's expanded chreia rather than like the form of a condensed chreia with a periodic construction. In other words, the chreia in the gospels takes the form of a pronouncement story with a length that stands half-way between the condensed chreia and the expanded chreia produced as an example by Theon.

In this paper, the stories in the synoptic gospels are discussed individually to delineate the rhetorical features peculiar to each unit in its fully constituted form. No preconceived notion of literary dependence is imposed, since such a procedure easily leads to a lack of perception of the rhetorical nature of the presently constituted form. When the analysis has implications for conclusions about literary dependence, the implications are introduced. Otherwise, the order in which the stories are discussed arises from the inner logic of the paper itself rather than from a decision about one author's dependence on another.

---

[19]Cf. Aristotle, *Ars Rhetorica* 2.1.5; Clark, *Rhetoric,* pp. 74-75.

[20]Jürgen Sauer, "Der ursprüngliche 'Sitz im Leben' von Mk 10:13-16," *ZNW* 72 (1981) 40-49.

Matthew 19:13-15

Matthew composes an expanded form of the chreia by introducing the laying on of hands at the beginning and the end. He uses only one participle, ἐπιθείς, in the midst of independent clauses connected by conjunctions to construct the story:

> Τότε προσηνέχθησαν αὐτῷ παιδία, ἵνα τὰς χεῖρας ἐπιθῇ
> αὐτοῖς καὶ προσεύξηται· οἱ δὲ μαθηταὶ ἐπετίμησαν
> αὐτοῖς. ὁ δὲ Ἰησοῦς εἶπεν, Ἄφετε τὰ παιδία καὶ
> μὴ κωλύετε αὐτὰ ἐλθεῖν πρός με, τῶν γὰρ τοιούτων
> ἐστὶν ἡ βασιλεία τῶν οὐρανῶν. καὶ ἐπιθεὶς τὰς χεῖρας
> αὐτοῖς ἐπορεύθη ἐκεῖθεν.

Then children were brought to him that he might lay his hands on them and pray, but the disciples rebuked them. Then Jesus said, "Let the children come to me, and do not hinder them, for to such belongs the kingdom of heaven." And when he had laid his hands on them, he went away.

In the form in which Matthew composes the story, Jesus responds to the disciples' action both with a saying and with an action (laying his hands on the children). The portrayal of action as well as speech creates a form the ancient rhetoricians called a mixed chreia (μικτὴ χρεία).[21] If a chreia makes its point through speech alone, it is called a sayings chreia (λογικὴ χρεία); if it makes its point through action alone, it is called an action chreia (πρακτικὴ χρεία); but if it makes its point through both speech and action, it is called a mixed chreia (μικτὴ χρεία). The presence of both speech and action allows the character (ethos) of Jesus to emerge in the story not only through the thought (logos) expressed in the speech but through the thought (logos) expressed by the action. The action of laying his hands on the children manifests good character in Jesus that produces a strong favorable response (pathos). Matthew has emphasized the action of Jesus by repeating τὰς χεῖρας ἐπιθῇ αὐτοῖς (Matt 19:13) in the form of ἐπιθεὶς τὰς χεῖρας αὐτοῖς in the last line (Matt 19:15). The rhetorical significance of this emphasis lies in the attempt of the narrator of the story to control the response (pathos) of the reader. The action which frames the saying transmits an image of Jesus as a personage with morally reputable character traits.

The action frames a saying in which Jesus rebukes the disciples. The intensity of the rebuke of Jesus is emphasized by means of the verb of rebuke, ἐπετίμησαν, and the commands to let the children come and not to hinder them. The presence of the γάρ clause makes the saying rhetorically complete. The γάρ clause supplies the reason, the basis, for the command. As the *Rhetorica ad Herennium* explains:

> The reason, by means of a brief explanation subjoined, sets forth the causal basis, establishing the truth of what we are urging (2.18.28).

Supplying a statement of the reason is important rhetorically whenever an assertion, even if not unreasonable, is obscure. As Aristotle explains:

> In all cases where the statements made, although not paradoxical, are obscure, the reasons should be added as concisely as possible (*Ars Rhetorica* 2.21.8).

As an example, Aristotle recites the following:

---

[21] See Theon, *Progymnasmata* 202,18-20; 206,1-8 (Walz).

Stesichorus said to the Locrians that they ought not to be insolent, lest their cicadas should be forced to chirp from the ground (*Ars Rhetorica* 2.21.8).

In parallel to the saying of Jesus in Matt 19:14, Stesichorus provides a basis for his command not to be insolent by explaining that their insolence would produce devastation of their land so that no trees or plants would exist upon which the cicadas could sit and chirp. In Matt 19:14, Jesus explains to the disciples that, since children such as these belong to the kingdom of heaven, they should not prevent the children from coming to him.[22]

The statement that supplies the reason for accepting the children may or may not appear to be sufficient for a modern reader. Perhaps it would have been sufficient to an ancient reader if it was presupposed that little children were not punished by God (or the gods). In any case, Matthew adds Jesus' laying of his hands on the children, with the additional comment that people were bringing the children so that he might pray for them (Matt 19:13), with the result that the story becomes persuasive through the ethos of Jesus manifested in action as well as in speech.

It appears that Matthew includes both the laying on of hands and the praying to contribute to the effectiveness of the story in its present setting where marriage and divorce have arisen as a debated issue. As a result of Jesus' discussion of divorce with Pharisees in Matt 19:3-9, the disciples conclude that Jesus' views on divorce should be taken as a directive not to marry at all (Matt 19:10). Matthew uses the little story about the disciples' prevention of children from coming to him to argue that Jesus' teaching about divorce (and about eunuchs: Matt 19:11-12) is not to be understood as an injunction against marriage which belittles the place of little children in this age and the coming age. Jesus' ethos in the story emerges both in the action of laying his hands on the little children and insisting that the disciples let the children come to him. The manifestation of Jesus' ethos is also present in the personalized form of the saying in the story, which emphasizes the necessity to let the children come "to me." Thus a positive response (pathos) to the inclusion of little children in the kingdom of heaven is evoked through the ethos of Jesus in the story as it manifests itself in the thought (logos) both in Jesus' speech and in his action.[23]

Mark 10:13-16

Mark also composes the story in such a manner that it accentuates both the speech and the action of Jesus:

> Καὶ προσέφερον αὐτῷ παιδία ἵνα αὐτῶν ἅψηται· οἱ δὲ
> μαθηταὶ ἐπετίμησαν αὐτοῖς. ἰδὼν δὲ ὁ Ἰησοῦς
> ἠγανάκτησεν καὶ εἶπεν αὐτοῖς, "Αφετε τὰ παιδία ἔρχεσθαι
> πρός με, μὴ κωλύετε αὐτά, τῶν γὰρ τοιούτων ἐστὶν ἡ
> βασιλεία τοῦ θεοῦ. ἀμὴν λέγω ὑμῖν, ὃς ἂν μὴ δέξηται
> τὴν βασιλείαν τοῦ θεοῦ ὡς παιδίον, οὐ μὴ εἰσέλθῃ εἰς
> αὐτήν. καὶ ἐναγκαλισάμενος αὐτὰ κατευλόγει τιθεὶς
> τὰς χεῖρας ἐπ᾽ αὐτά.

---

[22]Theon gives an example of this phenomenon in the chreia, *Progymnasmata* 204,7-205,1 (Walz).

[23]It is important for the ethos of the personage to be manifest within the story itself rather than for it to be imported from outside the story. See Aristotle, *Ars Rhetorica* 1.2.4: "This confidence must be due to the speech itself, not to any preconceived idea of the speaker's character."

For Mark, the story builds in a three-part sequence.[24] The first part sets the stage for the speech and action of Jesus:

> And they were bringing children in order that he might touch them, but the disciples rebuked them.

The second part includes two statements in the speech of Jesus and introduces an attendant emotion (pathos) of Jesus as he speaks:

> And when Jesus saw it he was indignant and said to them, "Let the children come to me, do not hinder them, for to such belongs the kingdom of God. Truly I say to you, whoever does not receive the kingdom of God like a child shall never enter it."

The third part accentuates the action of Jesus in a threefold statement:

   (a) and taking them in his arms
   (b) he blessed them,
   (c) putting his hands on them.

It is impossible to know, given the knowledge of the expanding and condensing of the chreia in an educational setting, if Matthew has seen and condensed Mark's form of the story or Mark has seen and expanded Matthew's form of the story. What we can see is Mark's interest in accentuating both the speech and the action of Jesus in a three-part episode that climaxes in Jesus' taking, blessing, and touching of the children.

First, we should notice the expansion of the speech of Jesus in the story, since the expansion introduces a new feature--a maxim. The saying in Mark 10:14 (par. Matt 19:14; Luke 18:16) is specific, so that the saying would not be intelligible apart from the setting. Such a saying, responding to a specific situation, creates a "unitary" story.[25] The saying and the setting stand in an integral unity. In addition to the specific saying, the Markan story contains a second general saying:

> Truly I say to you, whoever does not receive the kingdom of God like a child shall never enter it.

This general saying, in contrast to the specific saying, is a maxim. A maxim (γνώμη), according to Aristotle's definition, is:

> ἀπόφανσις, οὐ μέντοι περὶ τῶν καθ' ἕκαστον, οἶον ποῖός τις 'Ιφικράτης, ἀλλὰ καθόλου· καὶ οὐ περὶ πάντων καθόλου, οἶον ὅτι τὸ εὐθὺ τῷ καμπύλῳ ἐναντίον, ἀλλὰ περὶ ὅσων αἱ πράξεις εἰσί, καὶ αἱρετὰ ἢ φευκτά ἐστι πρὸς τὸ πράττειν.

> a statement, not however concerning particulars, as, for instance, what sort of a man Iphicrates was, but general; it does not even deal with all general things, as for instance that the straight is the opposite of the crooked, but with the objects of human actions, and with what should be chosen or avoided with reference to them. (*Ars Rhetorica* 2.21.2)

---

[24]For the nature of the three-part sequences in Mark, see the author's "Summons and Outline in Mark: The Three-Step Progression," *NovT* 23 (1981) 97-114.

[25]For a discussion of unitary stories, see Hultgren, *Jesus,* pp. 20-21, 67; cf. Bultmann, *History,* p. 47.

Maxims therefore have two basic characteristics: (1) they are general rather than specific; and (2) they concern themselves with human actions. A sayings-chreia usually ends in a specific saying, with the result that both the setting and the saying are essential to the story. The saying alone, or the setting alone, would be incomplete.

It is not unusual, however, for a saying in a chreia to be generalized or to be supplemented by a general maxim when the story is used in an extended literary setting. One of the reasons for this tendency is that maxims as well as good actions make speeches ἠθικός, i.e., they establish the reliable character of the speaker. As Aristotle says:

> He who employs them in a general manner declares his moral preferences; if then the maxims are good, they show the speaker also to be a man of good character. (Aristotle, *Ars Rhetorica* 2.21.16)

Thus, when an author incorporates a chreia into an extended literary setting depicting the speech and action of an important personage, there is a natural rhetorical basis for generalizing the statement.

The tendency for a saying in a chreia to be transformed or expanded into a maxim-like statement is well illustrated by a chreia about Alexander in the writings of Plutarch. In Plutarch's *Alexander,* a tradition about the famous king is written in the form of a condensed chreia:

> ἀλλὰ καὶ τῶν περὶ αὐτὸν ἀποπειρωμένων εἰ
> βούλοιτ' ἂν 'Ολυμπίασιν ἀγωνίσασθαι στάδιον,
> ἦν γὰρ ποδώκης, "Εἴ γε," ἔφη, "βασιλεῖς
> ἔμελλον ἔξειν ἀνταγωνιστάς."

> . . . nay, when those around him inquired whether he would be willing to compete in the foot-race at the Olympic games, since he was swift of foot, "Yes," he said, "if I were to have kings as competitors." (*Alexander* 4.10)

In this setting, Plutarch composed the chreia by means of a genitive absolute and a γάρ clause, ending the unit with a saying that has particular reference to the setting. In Plutarch's *De Alexandri Magni Fortuna Aut Virtute,* however, the story has the following form:

> ποδωκέστατος γὰρ τῶν ἐφ' ἡλικίας νέων γενόμενος καὶ
> τῶν ἑταίρων αὐτὸν ἐπ' 'Ολύμπια παρορμώντων, ἠρώ-
> τησεν, εἰ βασιλεῖς ἀγωνίζονται· τῶν δ' οὐ φαμένων,
> ἄδικον εἶπεν εἶναι τὴν ἅμιλλαν, ἐν ᾗ νικήσει μὲν
> ἰδιώτας, νικηθήσεται δὲ βασιλεύς.

> Since he was the swiftest of foot of all the young men of his age, and his comrades urged him to enter the Olympic games, he asked if kings were competing. When they replied no, he said that the contest was unfair, for in a victory he would be victorious over commoners but a defeat would be the defeat of a king.

In this setting, Plutarch has composed the chreia by means of two sentences connected with the conjunction δέ, a phenomenon observable in Mark 10:13-14. By this means the chreia has been expanded into a little story in which Alexander asks a question in the first sentence and gives his response (using the verb εἶπεν) in the second sentence.

In the expanded form in *De Alexandri Fortuna* the reponse on the lips of Alexander is much more nearly a general maxim about kings and commoners:

The contest would be unfair, for in victory I would be victorious over commoners, but a defeat would be the defeat of a king.

This transformation of the saying gives the story a generalized rhetorical quality about the philosophic spirit within Alexander's kingship. A king with philosophical insight is not so eager to attain glory that he can be lured into a type of competition in which nothing significant can be achieved but something significant can be lost. Only a slight further adjustment could make the statement a free-floating maxim:

> A contest between kings and commoners is unfair, since the king's victory would be a victory over commoners, but a defeat would be the defeat of a king.

The expansion of the chreia is therefore a significant form of rhetorical composition. Plutarch, by transforming the specific response in the condensed form of the chreia into a more generalized statement in the expanded form, has composed a story that advances his argument in the treatise that Alexander's success was as fully attributable to his philosophic spirit as to the hand of Fortune (*Moralia* 326D-E).

The presence of the maxim in Mark 10:15 points in a similar manner to rhetorical composition in the Gospel of Mark. The difficulty in understanding the origin of the maxim, however, lies in a step in the tradition of which no literary example is extant. It is widely recognized that the specific saying in Mark 10:14 and the maxim in Mark 10:15 contain two different dimensions that make it unlikely that one has emerged from the other.[26]

(1)   Mark 10:14 refers to "belonging" to the kingdom while Mark 10:15 refers to "receiving and entering" the kingdom;

(2)   Mark 10:14 refers in the plural to τὰ παιδία while Mark 10:15 contains the singular ὡς παιδίον.

From this, however, the improper conclusion has been drawn that the maxim in Mark 10:15 is "an originally independent dominical saying, inserted into the situation of vv. 13-16."[27] It is most likely that the maxim arose directly in relation to the chreia tradition. The key for understanding the emergence of the saying lies in Jesus' action of receiving the little children into his arms. As one can see from Luke 2:28, the verbal equivalent of ἐναγκαλισάμενος αὐτά (Mark 10:16) is ἐδέξατο αὐτὰ εἰς τὰς ἀγκάλας. The δέξηται in the maxim has arisen from Jesus' action of receiving the children into his arms.

On the basis of the tendency to develop general sayings out of specific sayings within chreia traditions, it is likely that the maxim in Mark 10:15 first existed as a comment after the statement that Jesus received the children into his arms. The general maxim evolved from the specific statements in Mark 10:14 in a manner generally analogous to the relationship between the specific and the general sayings in Plutarch, *Alexander* 4.10 and *De Alexandri Fortuna* 331B. First, once the statement has been made that Jesus "received" the children into his arms, it would be natural to refer to "receiving" the kingdom rather than "belonging" to it. Second, in a general saying beginning with the singular ὃς ἄν, it would be natural to couch the statement about children in the singular ὡς παιδίον. Third, the statement about "entering into" (εἰσέλθῃ εἰς) the kingdom in the second part of Mark 10:15 is the natural terminology to use in relation to the "coming to" (ἔρχεσθαι πρός) in Mark 10:14.

---

[26]Cf. Sauer, "Mk 10:13-16," p. 35.
[27]Bultmann, *History*, p. 32.

Once the importance of "receiving the children" is seen for understanding the origin of the maxim in Mark 10:15, it is clear that the maxim originally referred to "receiving the kingdom as one receives a child," as suggested by W. K. L. Clarke and F. A. Schelling.[28] The ellipsis in the saying presupposed that παιδίον was an accusative parallel to τὴν βασιλείαν τοῦ θεοῦ:

Verily I say to you, whoever does not receive the kingdom of God as [he should] receive a child, shall certainly never enter it.

The maxim drew from the chreia tradition the obvious conclusion that Jesus' receiving of the children presented an analogy for receiving the kingdom. Just as it should be a natural response to accept a child into one's arms rather than to refuse it, so it should be a natural response to accept the kingdom of God with all the benefits and responsibilities that accompany it.

The origin of the maxim in Mark 10:15 has been confused both because of its position prior to the statement that Jesus received the children into his arms and because of the maxim about "becoming like a child" in Matthew 18:3. Probably the position of the maxim results from Mark's rhetorical composition. The placement of the maxim exhibits the same rhetorical strategy present with Mark 2:10. In both instances a maxim that has arisen out of a setting characterized by specific sayings and actions has been placed within the story itself, and the maxim exhibits a lack of completely satisfactory integration into the story. Matt 18:3, in turn, is an adaptation of Mark 10:15 to another chreia tradition.[29]

The maxim in Mark 10:15 contributes to Mark's interest in intertwining the speech and action of Jesus throughout his gospel. The unity of Jesus' speech and action is announced at the beginning of the narrative in Mark 1:22-28.[30] Mark 8:27-10:45, the general section in which the story of Jesus and the children occurs, contains extensive teaching of Jesus, yet the teaching is systematically placed within the setting of actions of Jesus. In the particular sub-section in which this story occurs, Mark 9:30-10:21, the author has applied the teaching about the arrested, killed and rising Son of man (9:30-32) to discipleship by means of a discussion about greatness (9:33-34) that has led into teaching by means of both demonstrative action and speech concerning a child (9:35-37).[31] After this three-part introduction of the section, Mark alternates scenes that mention children (9:42-50; 10:13-16, 23-31) with scenes that do not mention children (9:38-41; 10:1-12, 17-22). Through this procedure, the author also alternates maxims about entering the kingdom (9:47; 10:15, 24-25) with general teaching concerning discipleship and community life (9:40-41; 10:11-12, 21). The presence of the maxim in Mark 10:15, therefore, links this specific story with the argumentation about children, kingdom and discipleship that the author is developing in Mark 9:30-10:31. In the same manner in which a person accepts a child, so he should accept the kingdom of God, which means "following" in discipleship (Mark 10:21, 28).[32] Without the maxim, Mark 10:13-16

---

[28]W. K. L. Clarke, *New Testament Problems* (London: SPCK, 1929) 36-38; F. A. Schelling, "What Means the Saying about Receiving the Kingdom of God as a Little Child?" *ExpT* 77 (1965-66) 56-58.

[29]Contra Barnabas Lindars, "John and the Synoptic Gospels: A Test Case," *NTS* 27 (1981) 287-94. Lindars makes the case well for a relationship between Matthew 18:3 and John 3:3, but he has not made the case for the emergence of Mark 10:15 from a saying about "becoming like a child."

[30]See, e.g., Joachim Gnilka, *Das Evangelium nach Markus* (EKK II.1; Zürich and Neukirchen-Vluyn: Benziger and Neukirchener, 1978) 76-82.

[31]For the three-part structure of this unit, see Robbins, "Summons," pp. 103-4.

[32]The integral relation between the kingdom and following is established at the beginning of the gospel in Mark 1:14-20: see the author's "Mark 1:14-20: An Inter-

would contain a statement about children belonging to the kingdom, but it would contribute in a less direct way to the discussion about entering the kingdom in this section. The presence of the maxim enables the story to contribute directly to the argument in the section in which it occurs.

Luke 18:15-17

In contrast to Matthew and Mark, Luke composes the story in the form of a sayings-chreia without pointed action:

Προσέφερον δὲ αὐτῷ καὶ τὰ βρέφη ἵνα αὐτῶν ἅπτηται·
ἰδόντες δὲ οἱ μαθηταὶ ἐπετίμων αὐτοῖς. ὁ δὲ Ἰησοῦς
προσεκαλέσατο αὐτὰ λέγων, "Ἄφετε τὰ παιδία ἔρχεσθαι
πρός με καὶ μὴ κωλύετε αὐτά, τῶν γὰρ τοιούτων ἐστὶν
ἡ βασιλεία τοῦ θεοῦ. ἀμὴν λέγω ὑμῖν, ὃς ἂν μὴ δέξηται
τὴν βασιλείαν τοῦ θεοῦ ὡς παιδίον, οὐ μὴ εἰσέλθῃ
εἰς αὐτήν.

Now they were bringing even infants to him in order that he might touch them, but when the disciples saw it they began to rebuke them. Then Jesus called to them, saying, "Let the children come to me and do not hinder them; for to such belongs the kingdom of God. Truly, I say to you, whoever does not receive the kingdom of God like a child shall never enter it."

Instead of exhibiting the ethos of Jesus through both action and speech, the Lukan story contains speech that includes the maxim along with the specific saying, without adding any comment about Jesus' action after the saying.

Since only the Markan and Lukan forms of the story contain the general maxim, the interpreter must conclude that some relationship stands between the two. There is a greater likelihood that Luke has condensed the Markan form of the story than that Mark has expanded the Lukan form, since the saying with particular reference and the maxim rest uneasily side by side apart from Jesus' action of receiving little children into his arms. The Lukan form results from removing the action to emphasize the speech of Jesus.

When the action is removed from the end of the story, a specific saying followed by a general maxim concludes the unit. This phenomenon emphasizes the speech of Jesus in such a manner that the unit contributes well to the argumentation about the kingdom of God that has been introduced in Luke 17:20 with the question about the time when the kingdom would come. By allowing the sayings to stand at the end of the story, Luke has created a sequence of three stories that end with a maxim. These maxims, with their supporting statements, represent a sequence of argumentation that describes the means by which a person may enter the kingdom:

(1)   The publican rather than the Pharisee went down to his house justified, for every one who exalts himself will be humbled, but he who humbles himself will be exalted (Luke 18:14);

(2)   Since children belong to the kingdom of God, whoever does not receive the kingdom of God like a child shall not enter it (Luke 18:16-17);

(3)   but there is no one who has left house or wife or brothers or parents or children for the sake of the kingdom of God, who will not receive manifold more in this time, and in the age to come eternal life. (Luke 18:29-30)

---

pretation at the Intersection of Jewish and Graeco-Roman Traditions," *NTS* 28 (1982) 220-36.

It would appear that Luke is interested in creating a sequence of argumentation by means of general conclusions that stand in the form of maxims at the end of these stories.

With the Lukan form of the story about Jesus and the children, the maxim loses its relationship to Jesus' receiving of children and becomes a general conclusion to a specific story. The conclusion now means that "as children belong to the kingdom," so "anyone who does not humble himself to become like a child before God (as the publican did: Luke 18:14) shall not enter the kingdom of God." There is a special form of humbling oneself, however, that must be considered. Anyone who has left home and loved ones, "for the sake of the kingdom of God" shall receive great rewards now and eternal life in the future (Luke 18:29-30). In other words, the maxim receives its meaning from the sequence of argumentation in the narrative.

Conclusion

While the direction of the rhetorical interest in the story varies from author to author in the synoptic gospels, each story builds on the statement that the disciples should let the children "come to him" because "to such belongs the kingdom of God (Heaven)." It is often overlooked that the presence of this saying introduces two rather than one crucial emphases: (1) me; and (2) kingdom of God. As Jesus comes to speech in the story, he presents himself as accepting the kingdom of God by accepting children. The presence of Jesus in the story is underscored by Jesus' reference to himself in relation to the children.

The image of Jesus in the story is essential for understanding the meaning of children in the story. Jesus embodies a model for proper action as he counters the action of his disciples. Most of all, Jesus is depicted as accepting whatever belongs to the kingdom of God. Because of the depiction of Jesus' acceptance of children, the story may be used in rhetorical settings where it is implied that people who are "like children" will enter the kingdom. It is doubtful that this rhetorical interest is present in the Markan use of the story. Rather, the goal is an explanation of following that requires an acceptance of concepts and actions that appear unacceptable. In contrast, Matthew and Luke use the story in a setting that suggests the necessity for humbling oneself and becoming like a child.

Rhetorical Composition in the Chreia about Greatness

Another chreia that existed in early Christian tradition presented an issue among the disciples concerning who was the greatest, to which Jesus responded by setting a child either in their midst or by his side. This chreia lies behind the little stories in Luke 9:46-48; Mark 9:34-37 and Matt 18:1-5. The basis structure of the chreia was:

(a)   The disciples were discussing who was the greatest;
(b)   Jesus put a child either in their midst or beside himself.

The challenge for composition of the chreia was to highlight the issue about greatness sufficiently to make the action a pointed response to the issue. If one were to construct the unit in the form of a condensed chreia, it could become:

προσελθόντων τῶν μαθητῶν τῷ 'Ιησοῦ καὶ λεγόντων τίς μείζων, λαβὼν παιδίον ἔστησεν αὐτὸ ἐν μέσῳ αὐτῶν [παρ' ἑαυτῷ].

When the disciples came to Jesus and said, "Who is the greatest?," taking a
little child, he set it in their midst[by his side].

This unit has resisted interpretation as a unitary tradition, because the decisive point is
the action of Jesus of putting a child either in their midst or beside himself instead of
making a statement that directly addresses the issue of greatness.[33] Jesus' selection of
the child functions similarly to the action of Pythagoras in the following chreia:

Πυθαγόρας ὁ φιλόσοφος, ἐρωτηθείς, πόσος ἐστὶν ὁ τῶν
ἀνθρώπων βίος; ἀναβὰς ἐπὶ τὸ δωμάτιον, παρέκυψεν ὀλίγον,
δηλῶν διὰ τοῦτο τὴν βραχύτητα.

Pythagoras the philosopher, on being asked how long the life of man is, went
up to his bedroom and looked back out for a short time, showing thereby its
brevity.[34]

This is an action chreia (πρακτικὴ χρεία) in which the issue raised in the first part is
answered through a demonstrative action.

A concern about greatness and the action of putting a child in their midst (or by his
side) is common to all three gospel stories reciting this tradition. Thus it is quite evident, once an interpreter has worked through Theon's *Progymnasmata*, that the essential
unit ends with Jesus' action. Yet all the stories add one or more sayings to the action of
Jesus. Does this not suggest that a different history of the tradition must be pursued?

Analysis of action-chreiai in literature contemporary with the gospels shows that
there was a natural tendency to add some kind of statement after a demonstrative action
as the story was told in an extended literary setting. An excellent example merges in a
tradition about a Laconian:

Λάκων, ἐρομένου τινὸς αὐτόν, ποῦ τοὺς ὅρους   τῆς
γῆς ἔχουσι Λακεδαιμόνιοι; ἔδειξε τὸ δόρυ.

A Laconian, when someone asked him where the Lacedaemonians had the
boundaries of their country, showed his spear. (Theon, 206,6-8; Walz)

Once the Laconian has shown his spear, the question has been answered. Nevertheless, it
was natural for authors to add a saying of some sort that explained the action. Thus, in a
version of this in which it is attributed to Agesilaus the Great, Plutarch writes the chreia
as follows:

᾿Ερωτηθεὶς δέ ποτε ἄχρι τίνος εἰσὶν οἱ τῆς
Λακωνικῆς ὅροι, τὸ δόρυ κραδάνας εἶπεν
"ἄχρις οὗ τοῦτο φθάνοι."

Being asked once how far the boundaries of Laconia extended, he said, with a
flourish of his spear, "As far as this can reach." (*Moralia* 210E,28; cf.
218F,2; 267C)

The saying is expanded further, however, in the version in Plutarch's *Lysander*:

---

[33]Cf. Bultmann, *History*, pp. 142-43, who discusses Mark 9:37 in relation to Mark
9:41 without considering the possibility that Mark 9:33-34, 36 was an early unitary
tradition.
[34]Theon, *Progymnasmata* 206,3-6 (Walz).

Ἀργείοις μὲν γὰρ ἀμφιλογουμένοις περὶ γῆς ὅρων καὶ
δικαιότερα τῶν Λακεδαιμονίων οἰομένοις λέγειν δείξας
τὴν μάχαιραν, "Ὁ ταύτης," ἔφη, "κρατῶν βέλτιστα περὶ
γῆς ὅρων διαλέγεται."

For, when the Argives were disputing about boundaries, and thought they
made a juster plea than the Lacedaimonians, he showed his sword and said to
them: "He who is master of this discourses best about boundaries."
(*Lysander* 22.1; cf. *Moralia* 190E,3; 229C,6)

In this version a saying that is nearly a general maxim accompanies the action of pointing
to the sword. The saying explains the meaning of the action in a form that could, with
slight adaptation, be separated from the chreia ("He who is master of the sword discourses best about boundaries").

The tendency to add one or more sayings to an action chreia is observable in the
gospel accounts where Jesus puts a child in front of the disciples in response to their
discussion of greatness. In fact, by the time the tradition reaches the gospel writers, it
ended with a saying that included at least the following words:

Whoever receives one such (or "this") child in my name receives me (Matt
18:5; Mark 9:37a; Luke 9:48a).

The problem is that the setting in the action-chreia is not a natural introduction for the
saying.[35] Matthew attempts a transition through two other sayings (Matt 18:3-4), and
Luke unifies the story by framing the saying with the issue of greatness (Luke 9:46, 48).
It appears that the saying emerged from the action-chreia by a process similar to the
emergence of the maxim about "not receiving" in the other chreia (Matt 19:13-15; Mark
10:13-16; Luke 18:15-17). The clue again stands in the addition of ἐναγκαλισάμενος
αὐτό (Mark 9:36). As soon as Jesus is depicted as "receiving" the child into his arms,
the story is ready for the development of sayings about "receiving." When the portrayal
of the ethos of Jesus in the selection of a child as "one who is greatest" includes the
action of "receiving" him into his arms, the story is a natural springboard for the saying:

Whoever receives one such child in my name receives me.

In other words, the saying depicts Jesus as putting his ability to command respect on the
line. If they will not accept this child as "great," then they are not receiving the action
and thought which he himself embodies. Again, however, it is virtually impossible to
decide if Matthew's version is a partial condensing and partial expanding of Mark or
Mark's version is a partial condensing and partial expanding of Matthew, although the
presence of ἐναγκαλισάμενος αὐτό, the natural bridge for the saying about
receiving, suggests that the Markan version preserves a crucial feature for the
development of the tradition that has been lost in Matthew's version. On the other hand,
the presence of the longer saying in Luke suggests that the Lukan version is a rewriting
of the Markan form of the story.

Luke 9:46-48

Again it will be instructive to approach the stories individually. Luke composes the
story with admirable efficiency, creating a rhetorically apposite literary unit in the
setting in which Jesus' suffering and death as the Son of man has been introduced for the

---

[35]For this reason only the history of the sayings has been discussed; see Bultmann,
History, pp. 142-43; Gnilka, *Markus*, II.2, pp. 54-58.

first time in the narrative (Luke 9:18-45). He constructed the story by means of two participles in the midst of independent clauses connected by conjunctions:

Εἰσῆλθεν δὲ διαλογισμὸς ἐν αὐτοῖς, τὸ τίς ἂν εἴη
μείζων αὐτῶν. ὁ δὲ Ἰησοῦς εἰδὼς τὸν διαλογισμὸν
τῆς καρδίας αὐτῶν ἐπιλαβόμενος παιδίον ἔστησεν αὐτὸ
παρ' ἑαυτῷ καὶ εἶπεν αὐτοῖς, "Ὃς ἐὰν δέξηται τοῦτο
τὸ παιδίον ἐπὶ τῷ ὀνόματί μου ἐμὲ δέχεται, καὶ ὃς ἂν
ἐμὲ δέξηται δέχεται τὸν ἀποστείλαντά με· ὁ γὰρ μικρότερος ἐν πᾶσιν ὑμῖν ὑπάρχων οὗτός ἐστιν μέγας.

And an argument arose among them as to which of them was the greatest. But when Jesus perceived the argument in their hearts, he took a child and put him by his side, and said to them, "Whoever receives this child in my name receives me; and whoever receives me receives him who sent me; for he who is least among you all is the one who is great."

Luke's skillful composition begins and ends the story with the issue of greatness. His use of the two participles εἰδώς (ν) and ἐπιλαβόμενος, the two finite verbs ἔστησεν and εἶπεν, and the γὰρ clause at the end[36] integrate the unit syntactically. Moreover, the διαλογισμός among the disciples provides the rhetorical link between the first sentence and the second sentence.[37] Through this careful composition, Luke adds one more step to the argument about greatness which is introduced in Luke 1:15 and developed throughout the narrative in Luke 1:32, 46, 49, 58; 7:16, 28; 9:43, (46, 48); 22:24, 26, 27; and Acts 2:11; 5:13; 8:9, 10; 10:17; 19:17, 27-28; 26:22.

Once again the story is constructed so that it ends with a maxim that contains a supporting statement:

Whoever receives this child in my name receives me, and whoever receives me receives him who sent me, for he who is the least among you is the one who is great. (Luke 9:48)

It is instructive, further, to notice that the next unit in Luke also ends with a saying that contains a supporting statement:

Do not forbid him, for he who is not against you is for you.

This manner of composing a unit, at least in the settings concerning Jesus and children, appears to be a Lukan characteristic.

In Luke 9:46-48, in contrast to Luke 18:15-17, the ethos of Jesus manifests itself through both action and speech. As Jesus takes the little child and sets him alongside himself over against the disciples, his own quality of greatness is demonstrated in his willingness to side with a little child rather than the powers and abilities which bring greatness to most people. Luke emphasizes the speech of Jesus, however, in the final part of the story. As Jesus comes to speech, the thought already exhibited in Jesus' action of receiving the child as great is explained in terms of the disciples' willingness or unwillingness to accept the child, and along with the child, Jesus himself. Their response (pathos) to Jesus' acceptance of the child as great establishes the condition on which they

---

[36]A γὰρ clause is a common phenomenon at the end of a chreia, as discussed above in the section on Matthew 19:13-15.

[37]Cf., e.g., the repetition of πατρίς in the first two sentences of Theon's expanded chreia on Epameinondas, cited above in the section on rhetorical composition in the chreia.

do or do not receive God (the one who sent Jesus) on their side. Therefore, the final statement about greatness, "He who is least among you all is the one who is great," receives its persuasive power through the ethos, logos, and pathos of the story.

Matthew 18:1-5

Matthew composes a little story out of the chreia with a somewhat different rhetorical interest. Matthew also writes the story with respectable efficiency, using the two participles λέγοντες and προσκαλεσάμενος in three sentences that link the issue of greatness with entrance into the kingdom of Heaven. Through his composition, Matthew creates a story that begins a specific argument about entrance into the kingdom that is developed in Matt 18:6-14. He links the discussion with the theme of "humbling oneself," which had been introduced in Matt 11:29 and further developed in Matt 23:12, and he continues the discussion of the kingdom of Heaven that pervades the narrative virtually from beginning to end. The story is composed as follows:

Ἐν ἐκείνῃ τῇ ὥρᾳ προσῆλθον οἱ μαθηταὶ τῷ Ἰησοῦ
λέγοντες, Τίς ἄρα μείζων ἐστὶν ἐν τῇ βασιλείᾳ τῶν
οὐρανῶν; καὶ προσκαλεσάμενος παιδίον ἔστησεν αὐτὸ
ἐν μέσῳ αὐτῶν καὶ εἶπεν, Ἀμὴν λέγω ὑμῖν, ἐὰν μὴ
στραφῆτε καὶ γένησθε ὡς τὰ παιδία, οὐ μὴ εἰσέλθητε εἰς
τὴν βασιλείαν τῶν οὐρανῶν. ὅστις οὖν ταπεινώσει
ἑαυτὸν ὡς τὸ παιδίον τοῦτο, οὗτός ἐστιν ὁ μείζων ἐν τῇ
βασιλείᾳ τῶν οὐρανῶν. καὶ ὃς ἐὰν δέξηται ἓν παιδίον
τοιοῦτο ἐπὶ τῷ ὀνόματί μου, ἐμὲ δέχεται.

At that time the disciples came to Jesus, saying, "Who is the greatest in the kingdom of heaven?" And calling to him a child, he put him in the midst of them and said, "Truly, I say to you, unless you turn and become like children, you will never enter the kingdom of heven. Therefore, whoever humbles himself like this child, he is the greatest in the kingdom of heaven, and whoever receives one such child in my name receives me."

Matthew's composition, through a procedure similar to Luke's, begins and ends the story with the issue of greatness in the kingdom of heaven. Matthew's rhetorical interest in the kingdom in the story, however, manifests itself in the composition of two sayings prior to the saying about receiving one such child in my name. The sayings are:

(1)   Truly, I say to you, unless you turn and become like children, you will never enter the kingdom of heaven;
(2)   Whoever humbles himself like this child, he is the greatest in the kingdom of heaven.

Matthew has created the first saying by adapting the maxim that had developed out of the sayings-chreia tradition (Mark 10:15; Luke 18:17).[38] The second saying in the story was created by adapting the saying about greatness both to entrance into the kingdom of heaven and to humbling oneself, which evidently existed in a free-floating maxim in Mediterranean culture.[39]

---

[38]Bultmann, *History*, p. 32, is right about this, versus Lindars, "John and the Synoptic Gospels," pp. 288-89. Lindars has addressed the history of the sayings of Jesus at one step further removed from the unitary traditions than Bultmann's analysis. Instead of taking further steps away from the unitary traditions, it is necessary to give them much more serious attention.

[39]Only when a saying has a widespread presence in a cultural setting, as this one

426   SBL 1982 Seminar Papers

Mark 9:33-37

Mark approaches the story with a slightly different rhetorical interest than either Luke or Matthew. His composition of maxim-like material in the story, however, reminds one of Matthew's approach. Mark composes the story using four participles (γενόμενος, καθίσας, λαβων, ἐναγκαλισάμενος) and six finite verbs. If the composition is not sophisticated, it is nevertheless appropriate and effective. The story is composed as follows:

Καὶ ἦλθον εἰς Καφαρναούμ. καὶ ἐν τῇ οἰκίᾳ γενόμενος ἐπηρώτα αὐτούς, Τί ἐν τῇ ὁδῷ διελογίζεσθε; οἱ
δὲ ἐσιώπων, πρὸς ἀλλήλους γὰρ διελέχθησαν ἐν τῇ ὁδῷ
τίς μείζων. καὶ καθίσας ἐφώνησεν τοὺς δώδεκα καὶ
λέγει αὐτοῖς, Εἴ τις θέλει πρῶτος εἶναι ἔσται πάντων
ἔσχατος καὶ πάντων διάκονος. καὶ λαβὼν παιδίον
ἔστησεν αὐτὸ ἐν μέσῳ αὐτῶν καὶ ἐναγκαλισάμενος αὐτὸ
εἶπεν αὐτοῖς, Ὃς ἂν ἓν τῶν τοιούτων παιδίων δέξηται
ἐπὶ τῷ ὀνόματί μου, ἐμὲ δέχεται· καὶ ὃς ἂν ἐμὲ δέχηται,
οὐκ ἐμὲ δέχεται ἀλλὰ τὸν ἀποστείλαντά με.

And they came to Capernaum; and when he was in the house he asked them, "What were you discussing on the way?" But they were silent, for on the way they had discussed with one another who was greatest. And sitting down, he called the twelve and said to them, "If anyone would be first, he must be last of all and servant of all." And taking a child, he put him in the midst of them; and on taking him in his arms he said to them, "Whoever receives one such child in my name receives me; and whoever receives me, receives not me but him who sent me."

Mark is interested, with this story, in developing the theme of the rejection, death, and rising of the Son of man that had first been introduced in Mark 8:31. After this theme has been reintroduced in Mark 9:31, Mark uses the chreia about greatness as a setting to introduce a maxim that recalls the teaching in Mark 8:34:

If someone wants to follow after me, let him deny himself and take up his cross and follow me.

In Mark 9:35, this theme is restated in the following maxim:

If someone wants to be first he must be last of all and servant of all.

This maxim is a restatement that is repeated at the end of the immediate section of which it is a part (Mark 9:30-10:31). Therefore Mark 9:35 provides a frame around the section with Mark 10:31:

But many who are first will be last, and the last, first.

All of this is moving toward the last verses in the overall section (8:27-10:45) that sum up the argument and ground it in the ethos and logos of Jesus:

___

has, should the interpreter readily suggest its presence as a free-floating maxim. Otherwise, the possibility for the emergence of a general saying from a chreia tradition should be given prior consideration.

Whoever is great among you shall be servant of all, and whoever wants to be first among you, shall be slave of all, for even the Son of man came not to be served but to serve and to give his life as a ransom for many. (Mark 10:43-45).

Mark's composition of the story in Mark 9:33-37 is therefore an exercise in rhetorical composition. The story contributes to the argument in the overall section by expanding the setting in which the issue of greatness arises (Mark 9:33-34) and by introducing a maxim (Mark 9:35) that links the story with the teaching in Mark 8:34-9:1. The maxim in Mark 9:35 prepares for the maxim at the end of the immediate section (Mark 10:31), and it moves the discussion toward the conclusion of the entire section in Mark 10:43-45. Then, with the ending of the story (Mark 9:36-37) Mark creates an excellent transition to the story about the man casting out a demon "in my name."

Each author, therefore, has composed the story by using rhetorical techniques that he understands to be natural procedures with a chreia tradition. Each author observes and preserves the essential elements of the chreia--the issue about greatness and the action with the child. Also, each author expands, condenses, and rewrites the story so that it furthers the argumentation he is pursuing in his extended literary composition.

Conclusion

The chreia about greatness, in contrast to the chreia where the disciples were hindering the children, appears to have ended originally with an action of Jesus rather than a saying. Before the story reached the writers of the synoptic gospels, however, the chreia about hindering the children had influenced the chreia about greatness. The first step appears to have been the addition of a comment that Jesus took the child into his arms (Mark 9:36). This comment, accordingly, created the link for adding sayings about "receiving." Interestingly enough, the sayings concern "receiving Jesus":

Whoever receives one such child in my name receives me.

This saying then created the setting for the addition of other sayings (Mark 9:37; Luke 9:48).

The importance of the statement about "receiving Jesus" becomes evident when the interpreter observes an absence of any reference to the kingdom in the early forms of the story. This means that the common tradition shared by the two chreiai is not a reference to the kingdom but a reference to "me." In other words, the building blocks of both traditions are the ethos of Jesus as constituted by his action and speech. It should be no surprise that Matthew rewrites the chreia to include sayings about the kingdom (Matthew 18:3-4). But the earliest form of the tradition suggests that the ethos of Jesus as constituted by his action and speech is primary to the theme of the kingdom. Thus, once again, Jesus' act of receiving children lies at the heart of the tradition, and upon this manifestation of Jesus' character the authors of the synoptic gospels built expanded chreiai that supported the argumentation in which they engaged in their literary documents.

Rhetorical Composition
in the Fourth Gospel and the Gospel of Thomas

Once two chreia traditions had been generalized by appending, inserting, or transforming specific sayings into maxims, both the maxims and the settings were ready to be used in literary units that were more artistically constructed. The further development of the traditions about Jesus and the children is evident in John 3:1-21 and Thomas 22. These two literary units have the characteristics of a dialogue that has developed by generalizing both the settings and the sayings that existed in previous chreia traditions.[40] Such a procedure was not unique to Christian tradition, however. During the fourth century B.C.E., Xenophon created settings for dialogue in a manner that parallels the compositional procedure in the Fourth Gospel, and the Gospel of Thomas. In *Memorabilia* 3.9.14-15, two sayings-chreiai featuring inquiries are used to pursue a topic in the fashion of a dialogue:

> Ἐρομένου δέ τινος αὐτόν, τί δοκοίη αὐτῷ κράτιστον
> ἀνδρὶ ἐπιτήδευμα εἶναι, ἀπεκρίνατο Εὐπραξία. ἐρομένου
> δὲ πάλιν, εἰ καὶ τὴν εὐτυχίαν ἐπιτήδευμα νομίζοι εἶναι,
> Πᾶν μὲν οὖν τοὐναντίον ἔγωγ', ἔφη, τύχην καὶ πρᾶξιν
> ἡγοῦμαι· τὸ μὲν γὰρ μὴ ζητοῦντα ἐπιτυχεῖν τινι τῶν
> δεόντων εὐτυχίαν οἶμαι εἶναι, τὸ δὲ μαθόντα τε καὶ
> μελετήσαντά τι εὖ ποιεῖν εὐπραξίαν νομίζω, καὶ οἱ
> τοῦτο ἐπιτηδεύοντες δοκοῦσί μοι εὖ πράττειν. καὶ
> ἀρίστους δὲ καὶ θεοφιλεστάτους ἔφη εἶναι ἐν μὲν
> γεωργίᾳ τοὺς τὰ γεωργικὰ εὖ πράττοντας, ἐν δ'
> ἰατρείᾳ τοὺς τὰ ἰατρικά, ἐν δὲ πολιτείᾳ τοὺς τὰ
> πολιτικά· τὸν δὲ μηδὲν εὖ πράττοντα οὔτε χρήσιμον
> οὐδὲν ἔφη εἶναι οὔτε θεοφιλῆ.

> When someone asked him what seemed to him the best pursuit for a man, he answered: "Doing well." Then when questioned further, whether also he thought good luck a pursuit, he said: "On the contrary, I think luck and doing are opposite poles. For to hit on something right by luck without search I call good luck, to do something well after study and practice I call doing well; and those who pursue this seem to me to do well. And the best man and dearest to the gods," he said, "are those who do their work well; if it is farming, as good farmers; if medicine, as good doctors; if politics, as good politicians. But he who does nothing well is neither useful in any way," he said, "nor dear to the gods."

The first question and answer is a sayings-chreia in and of itself featuring a participle in the first part followed by the finite verb ἀπεκρίνατο to introduce the response. Immediately, however, another question is introduced which takes the discussion of the topic a step further. This time, after a participial clause that introduces the question, the response is introduced by the finite verb ἔφη. As the response extends into a series of statements, the author twice more introduces ἔφη as a means of maintaining the presence of the speaker in the statements. We may further notice the post-positive γάρ in the second statement after the inquiry, signalling that the remaining statements provide the reasons for holding the view that "luck and doing are opposites." Finally, we should notice that the last saying is a general maxim: "He who does nothing well is neither useful in any way nor dear to the gods."

This unit, like the previous units, takes the reader from a specific issue to a generalized statement. In this instance, two chreiai have been placed in a series to compose one unit, and the response in the final chreia has been expanded to provide a series of statements. With the generalized statement at the end of the unit, Xenophon has

---

[40]For recent discussions of the nature of dialogue traditions in the apocryphal gospels, see Helmut Koester, "Gnostic Writings as Witnesses for the Development of the Sayings Tradition," *The Rediscovery of Gnosticism* (*SupNumen* 41.1; Leiden: Brill, 1978) 238-56 and the discussion, pp. 256-61; idem, "Dialog und Spruchüberlieferung in den gnostischen Texten von Nag Hammadi," *EvT* 39 (1979) 532-56; idem, "Apocryphal and Canonical Gospels," *HTR* 73 (1980) 105-30.

presented a point of view that contributes to his argument in the *Memorabilia* that Socrates himself engaged in doing things useful throughout his life.

The scene in Thomas 22 has been constructed in a manner similar to the scene in Xenophon's *Memorabilia*. The major difference is that the first unit begins with a chreia in which Jesus observes suckling children rather than one which features an inquiry:

> Jesus saw children that were being suckled. He said to his disciples: "These children being suckled are like those who enter the kingdom."

After this unit, however, the scene continues with an inquiry from the disciples, followed by Jesus' response:

> They said to him: "If we are children, shall we enter the Kingdom?" Jesus said to them: "When you make the two one, and make the inside like the outside, and the outside like the inside, and the upper side like the under side, and when you make the male and the female into a single one, so that the male will not be male and the female will not be female; when you make eyes in place of an eye, and a hand in place of a hand, and a foot in place of a foot, an image in place of an image, then you shall enter."

In contrast, John 3:1-21 builds out of a sequence of three statements by Nicodemus. Instead of the concern with attribution of the responses in a chreia, the scene begins with careful attribution of the recipient of the teaching: "a man named Nicodemus, a man of the Pharisees, a ruler of the Jews." In this dialogue tradition, therefore, the ethos of the speaker is so well established that the ethos of the recipient of the teaching receives the major attention. The first statement Nicodemus makes is an encomium (a statement of praise) to Jesus:

> Rabbi, we know that you are a teacher come from God, for no one is able to do these signs which you do unless God is with him.

The second and third statements, then, are simply questions that respond in amazement to Jesus' statements:

(a) "How is anyone able to be born when he is old? Can he enter a second time into his mother's womb and be born?" (John 3:4).
(b) "How can this be?" (John 3:9).

These statements are simply the remarks of a person who is providing the setting, in the context of a dialogue, for the sage to continue his teaching.

In both traditions, the sayings and the settings of the earlier chreia traditions about Jesus and children have been generalized. In Thomas 22, Luke's suggestion that βρέφη (new-born infants) were being brought to Jesus (Luke 18:15) has been used as a beginning point. Then, the statement to the disciples in Matt 18:3 that "unless they turn and become like children, they will never enter the kingdom of heaven" serves as a beginning point for the disciples' response:

> If we are children shall we enter the kingdom?

In the Gospel of John, on the other hand, the presence of children in the situation has been lost. Following the interest in the newborn infant, a maxim is developed in which Jesus tells Nicodemus:

> Truly, truly, I say to you, unless one is born anew, he cannot see the kingdom of God (John 3:3).

This maxim has changed the issue from "entering" the kingdom of God to "seeing" it, since the dialogue is engaged in the process of bringing light to the meaning of the kingdom of God so that he who believes may see. The next maxim attributed to Jesus, however, is couched in terms of "entering":

> Truly, truly, I say to you, unless one is born of water and spirit, he cannot enter the kingdom of God. That which is born of the flesh is flesh, and that which is born of the spirit. . . . (John 3:5-6).

In this context, the general imagery of the settings of Jesus and the children, and the sayings about the children and others belonging to the kingdom or entering the kingdom have been used to create a dialogue setting that extends into a discourse on believing in heavenly things, coming to the light and seeing the works of God (John 3:10-21).

Summary and Conclusions

Rhetorical analysis based on insights from chreia traditions raises serious questions about the conventional conclusions about the gospel traditions where maxims occur in stories containing poignant actions and sayings. Our study of the two chreia traditions concerning Jesus and the children suggests that specific sayings and actions in specific settings stand at the beginning of the tradition. In some instances, as in the chreia where Jesus rebukes the disciples for not allowing children to come to him, the stories produce a general maxim that interprets the speech and action in the setting. In other instances, as in the chreia where Jesus sets a child before the disciples as an answer to their question about greatness, maxims that were either produced in relation to other chreiai or had been free-floating traditions were inserted into the story to give it a new rhetorical direction.

The analysis suggests, therefore, a revised agenda for investigation of the traditions about Jesus in the gospels. First, for every occurrence of a story an interpreter should probe the interrelation between the rhetoricity within the story itself and the rhetorical function of the story within its literary setting. Second, in the absence of uniform sayings in a story, the possibility must be entertained that a poignant action rather than a poignant saying ended the earliest form of the tradition. Third, it is necessary to distinguish between free-floating maxims and maxims that have arisen through a rhetorical process in which a general statement has been created as commentary on a chreia tradition. Fourth, interaction among different chreia traditions must be analyzed to distinguish between components integral to the earliest form of a tradition and components that have arisen through influence from another chreia tradition. Fifth, dialogue situations characterized by a sequence of maxims must be distinguished from chreia traditions to which maxims have been added.

The scenes concerning Jesus and children in the Fourth Gospel and the Gospel of Thomas constitute dialogue situations rather than chreia traditions. In this literary setting, both settings and sayings from chreia traditions are generalized to create a dialogue that presents a theme through a particular kind of logic expressed within generalized sayings. In this format, the specific settings and responses characteristic of chreia traditions have been replaced by generalized settings and sayings. The artistic and rhetorical goal of developing a theme in the manner of a dialogue introduces a generalization of scenes and sayings taken from earlier traditions.

MARS IN THE INSCRIPTIONS

Vincent J. Rosivach
Fairfield University

The most common religious artifact surviving from Roman antiquity is the inscription. Literally thousands survive, constituting our broadest source of information on religion in the Roman empire during the early centuries of the first millennium. Most of the inscriptions are quite brief and typically formulaic in character, but despite this they are still valuable, for through them we come in contact with a world of religion removed both geographically and socially from the world represented in our other written sources, literary and apologetic. This paper studies inscriptions dealing with Mars and related gods to see what they can tell us about these deities and their worshipers in roughly the first three centuries A.D.

The paper is based on the relevant inscriptions contained in Dessau's *Inscriptiones Latinae Selectae* (3rd ed.) which is assumed to be a representative sample of the contents of the larger *Corpus Inscriptionum Latinarum*. Some 350 inscriptions were studied, approximately 125 dealing specifically with Mars, the remainder dealing with related gods or used for purposes of comparison. A detailed consideration of all these inscriptions would be impossible within the present paper; instead general categories and representative examples are discussed, as the best way of suggesting the kinds of information which can be derived from the inscriptions. More complex inscriptions have been translated into English while shorter ones have been left in Latin; errors in Latin transcriptions reflect errors in the original texts.

One group of inscriptions consists of religious records of various sorts. This group would include, e.g., the *Acts of the Arval Brethren*, the various *fasti* (calendars) listing religious festivals and holy days, and *ferialia* (ritual calendars) prescribing the rites to be performed at a particular site on specific days. An example of this last would be the *feriale* found at Cumae (*ILS* 108) which prescribes rites in honor of the emperor Augustus, including bloodless sacrifices to Moles Martis (probably "the Might of Mars") on the anniversary of the dedication of the temple of Mars the Avenger, and to Mars the Avenger on the anniversary of the birthday of Julius Caesar whose death Augustus avenged at Philippi. All the inscriptions in this group arise from "official" (as opposed to personal) religion. They are valuable for what they tell us of the external forms of that religion, particularly in Rome and nearby Italy, as well as for the fossilized evidence they preserve of the earlier stages of Roman religion (e.g., the *carmen Arvale* preserved in *ILS* 5039). These inscriptions are thus a necessary part of the total picture, but they are also limited in that they tell us only what was done, and perhaps why the community as a whole did it (for the emperor's health, etc.), but they are too general to tell us much about the personal religious experience of those participating in the rituals they describe.

We come closer to this personal element--and also broaden our scope beyond Rome and its environs--through dedicatory inscriptions. There are inscriptions to Mars from throughout the Latin-speaking empire, announcing the dedications of temples, statues, and the like. More often than not, however, the inscriptions are on simple stone plaques, and what is dedicated is the plaque itself, erected in some public place to announce the dedicator's devotion and/or the god's power. Some of these plaques are elaborately decorated, but others are small and plain, and were obviously not very expensive to produce. Romans who achieved any distinction in life usually liked to make note of it in their inscriptions, e.g., "to Mars Augustus for the health of the *imperator* Caesar M. Antonius Gordianus . . . M. Antonius Valentinus, Roman knight, city councilman of the municipality of Apulum, priest of the altar of the *numen* of the emperor, *coronatus* of the three Dacias, gave as a gift" (*ILS* 7129). And so when no mention is made of office or rank, as is often the case in the simpler inscriptions (e.g., Marti Albiorigi Sex. Cornelius

Sacratus v. s. l. m.," *ILS* 4542), it is probably because there was in fact nothing to distinguish the dedicator from the broad social mass.

The typical dedicatory inscription has three parts:

1. the name of the god or gods to whom the dedication is made expressed in the dative case;
2. the name of the dedicator in the nominative case, with any information about himself he wishes to include (e.g., civil or military office);
3. the reason for the dedication usually expressed by some conventional abbreviation.

The most common reason for a dedication is the fulfillment of a vow (*v(otum) s(olvit) l(ibens) m(erito)*, etc.). In a vow one promised to do something for a god if the god will do something for the person making the vow. If the god does what was asked for, the person making the vow reciprocates by fulfilling his promise. The dedication thus serves both to declare the dedicator's gratitude to the god, and to manifest the god's power by announcing what he has done for the dedicator, presumably in the hope that he will continue to show his favor in the future. Other inscriptions announce gifts to the gods (*d(onum) d(edit)*), sometimes specifying favors sought in return, and a few are responses to a god's command. All are, at least in form, public manifestations of a personal religious experience, the belief of an individual that a god has or can intervene in his life, and the need which he feels to act as a consequence of that belief.

In Roman paganism one acknowledged the existence of all the gods, but one chose only a few, or perhaps only one, to whom to address prayers and vows. The gods in the dedicatory inscriptions were rarely specialized by function. Rather, whichever of the traditional gods one chose, one tended to pray to them all in much the same way and for much the same things. Apart from iconography there is little in the inscriptions to distinguish the gods from each other. There is also little to explain why one god was chosen in preference to another, though local influences are one obvious factor. In the case of Mars it is widely recognized that the Celts frequently identified their local tribal gods with Mars, as can easily be seen from such inscriptions as "Leherenno deo Mandatus Mansueti f(ilius) v. s. l. m." (*ILS* 4533) and "Leherenno Marti Titullus Amoeni fil. v. s. l. m." (*ILS* 4533b), both from Ardiege in southwest France, or "Petiganus Placidus Toutati . . . votum solvet anniversarium" (*ILS* 4691), from an army camp in Rome, and "Marti Toutati Ti. Claudius Primus Atii liber(tus) v. s. l. m." (*ILS* 4540), from Britain. Mars was always identified as the special patron and protector of the Romans, and this may well be why the Celts so frequently chose him to represent their own tutelary deities. In all events, it seems quite likely that in Celtic contexts the name of Mars, even when not specified by an epithet such as Leherennus or Toutas, was still likely to evoke, not the Mars of Roman mythology, but a somewhat more universalized version of the old Celtic tribal deity, standing in the same relation to his worshipers as did the old tribal god, but no longer identified with a specific geographical area or group of people. Outside the Celtic areas inscriptions to Mars are usually put up by soldiers, many of whom have Celtic backgrounds. But whether the inscriptions were put up by soldiers or civilians, the image which they present is not significantly different from that of Mars in the Celtic area inscriptions.

This Mars of the inscriptions has little if anything to do with classical mythology. For example, in classical mythology Mars was paired with Venus, but this pairing appears in none of the inscriptions studied for this paper, which is perhaps surprising inasmuch as other similar mythological pairs do occur (e.g. Mercury/Maia, *ILS* 3206-9, 6389-90; cf. Aesculapius/Salus = Hygeia, 3841, 9258). Rather Mars is paired occasionally with a female tribal deity (e.g. "Marti et Nemetonae Silvini Iustus et Dubitatus v. s. l. l. p.," *ILS* 4586). More frequently, however, he is paired with Victoria who is herself a Romanized version of this same female tribal deity, as can be seen, e.g., from the pair of inscriptions "deae Brigantiae sacrum Congenniccus v. s. l. m." and "d(eae) Vict(oriae) Brig(antiae) . . . T. Aurelianus d(onum) d(edit) . . ." (*ILS* 4717, 4719, both from Britain).

Clearly this is how we should understand Mars and Victoria in inscriptions such as *ILS* 7309a ("in h. d. d. deo Marti et Victoriae contubernium Marti cultorum posuerunt, v. s. l. l. m.") where there is no suggestion of a military function for either deity. But even in a "military" inscription such as *ILS* 2485, set up in 198 by a detachment of Pannonian cavalty temporarily stationed in North Africa ("I(ovi) o(optimo) m(aximo) Iun(oni) reg(inae) Min(ervae) Marti Vict. Auggg. pro salute impp. . . vexill. leg. III Aug. . . v. s."), Jupiter, Juno, and Minerva are the standard Roman Capitoline triad, and Mars and Victoria almost certainly represent the native deities of the cavalrymen who set up the inscription (cf. *ILS* 4833, from an altar set up by a group of cavalry veterans on their discharge in 141, where the same list is extended to include, among others, the typically Celtic grouping "Herculi . . . Mercurio . . . Silvano . . . Eponae Matribus Sulevis . . ."). The Celtic pairing of Mars and Victoria appears even in inscriptions, including non-military ones, from non-Celtic areas, e.g. *ILS* 3159 from Dacia cited below; this is important, for it suggests that the Celtic Mars could also be present in many of the inscriptions from non-Celtic areas dedicated to Mars alone. (Although further discussion of Victoria is beyond the scope of this paper, we should note that Victoria by herself often appears to be something of a symbol for imperial power, and not simply the tribal goddess when she is coupled with Mars.)

We normally think of Mars as a warrior god, and this is the way he is usually represented when his portrait appears with inscriptions (e.g. *ILS* 4633 where Camulus = Mars Camulus, cf. 235, 4550). We also find inscriptions, all of them set up by soldiers, to "Marti militari" (*ILS* 3155), to "deo Marti arm." (*ILS* 3156), to "deo Marti militiae potenti" (*ILS* 2296), and to "Marti campestri" ("of the camp," *ILS* 2416). But despite such dedications, which are but a small fraction of the whole, and despite his iconography, there is something decidedly unwarlike about Mars in most of these inscriptions. There are inscriptions from soldiers, as we would expect, but there are also inscriptions from civilians, both male and--at first glance surprisingly--female (e.g. "Curtilia Prepusa Marti Loucetio v. s. l. l. m.," *ILS* 4572a). Further, none of the inscriptions under study gives Mars a gift, or fulfills a vow made in the hope of military success. In fact, more often than not the reason for the inscription is not even specified beyond the standard v. s. l. m. or d. d., but when the reason is given it is almost always for someone's good health ("pro salute") or simply on their behalf ("pro . . ."), both of which probably come down to the same things. (Allied to this is the notion of Mars as protector, e.g. "Marti patr. conservatori et bonae Victoriae L. Ael. Rufinus pro se et suos v. l. p.," *ILS* 3159, cf. 3160 cited below.) A concern with health is not unique to inscriptions to Mars, but is found in inscriptions to many different gods, and is an interesting index of how precarious one's physical well-being was at the time. Sometimes it is a question of health restored after illness, as in *ILS* 4569, a bilingual inscription from Coblenz thanking Mars in Greek and Latin hexameters: "Corporis adque animi diros sufferre labores / dum nequeo mortis prope limina saepe vagando, / servatus Tychicus divino Martis amore / hoc munus parvom pro magna dedico cura." (Mars is *Ares Lenos* in the Greek.) At other times, however, the *salus* is question may simply be the maintenance of good health rather than a cure. One's vow may be for oneself (e.g. "deo Marti Corotiaco Simplicia pro se . . .," *ILS* 4558), for one's family (e.g. "ex voto Marti Lelhunno ob sanitatem suam et suorum Tib. Claudius Faustinus v. s. l. m.," *ILS* 4534) or for others (e.g. the drill sargeant's concern for the troops under his command in *ILS* 2453: "Marti Aug. sac(rum) C. Cusp. Secundus exercitator leg(ionis) II Adi(utricis) pro salute militum et sua, quod evocatus vovit, centurio solvit l. m.").

One's prayer may also be for the health of the emperor, e.g. *ILS* 2485 and 7129 cited above. Self-announcement and a visible display of loyalty to the ruler may play a greater role than religion in both these inscriptions, but the references to the emperor are also part of a much larger pattern which the inscriptions to Mars share with inscriptions to other gods. Indeed, to one unfamiliar with this body of inscriptions it is extraordinary how many of them do refer in one way or another to the emperor.

Sometimes the reference is to a specific emperor (as in *ILS* 2485 and 7129; cf. also 5074 cited below), but far more often the reference is generic, with the adjective "Augustus" used as a synonym for "imperial" in inscriptions directed to the *numen* or the *genius* of the emperor (e.g. "Num. Aug. et Marti Mogentio Gracchus Aregnutis fil. v. s. l. m.," *ILS* 4577; cf. the "genio sing. Aug." listed in 2181). Sometimes the adjective "Augustus" modifies the god's name (e.g. "Latobio Aug. sac. pro salute Nam. Sabinae et Iuliae Bassillae Vindonis Ver mat. v. s. l. m.," *ILS* 4567; cf. 2453, 5074 cited above), sometimes the inscription itself is "Augusto sacrum" on an analogy with inscriptions "Marti sacrum," "Iovi sacrum," etc. (e.g. "Aug. sacr. Marti Boluinno et Dunati C. Domiti Virilis decurio pro salut. sua et Iul. Thalli Virilliani fili et Avitillae Aviti fil. uxoris, v. s. l. m.," *ILS* 4547). And sometimes the inscription is prefaced with the abbreviation *in h(onorem) d(omus) d(ivinae)*, the "domus divina" being the imperial government, not the Olympian household (e.g. "in h. d. d. deo Marti Cicollui Pudens Pudentiani fil.," *ILS* 4544; cf. "in honorem domus divinae et pagi Sextanmandui Marti Mulloni . . . ," 7053a). Of special interest are those inscriptions which incidentally include references to the emperor in prayers and vows which are clearly concerned with personal rather than political matters (e.g. the dedicator's prayers on behalf of his children in *ILS* 4586b: "i. h. d. d. Marti Leucet. et Victoriae . . . Severinus pro suis filis Sperato et Pupo . . ."; cf. 4547 and 4567 cited above), for they give us some idea of how much the emperor was part of the ordinary forms and formulae of the religion of the time.

Of particular interest is a group of inscriptions which their dedicators tell us were set up *ex iussu*, at the command of the god (e.g. "Marti Beladoni T. Fl. Iustus ex iussu," *ILS* 4546; "Marti Rigisami Ti. Iul. Eunus ex vissu," 4581; "ex vissu" may be either metaphasis for "ex iussu" or a misspelling of "ex visu," "as a consequence of a vision"). Here the inscriptions speak of an experience of the god which is more intimate and direct. In the case of inscriptions fulfilling vows, for example, the dedicator believes that the god has heeded his prayer and intervened on his behalf, manifesting himself through his acts. In these *ex iussu* inscriptions, however, the dedicator believes that the god himself has in some way made his will known to him, as the dedicator of *ILS* 3160 insists: "Marti Aug. conservatori corporis sui, Mercurialis Aug(usti) n(ostri) vil(icus) *ex iussu numinis ipsius* sigillum marmoreum posuit."

It is a particular kind of closeness when the god speaks, or perhaps even appears, to an individual, as the dedicators of the *ex iussu* inscriptions believe Mars has done to them. Different inscriptions speak of another kind of closeness between god and man, friendship ("Marti amico et consentienti sacrum. Hermias dedicavit idemq. vovit," *ILS* 3161) and something perhaps even closer ("Flavia Cuba firmani filia Cosono *deo Marti suo* [her own god Mars] hoc signum donavit Augusto," *ILS* 4559). And finally, from another point of view there is the closeness of the "contubernium Marti cultorum" who set up *ILS* 7309a cited above, a group of worshipers who, for whatever reason, felt a need to do something extra for Mars, to join together in a corporate body to honor their god.

In almost all these inscriptions the religious experience is expressed through some conventional formula ("ex iussu," "votum solvit," etc.), but this is no reason for believing that the religious expression is any less sincere or the experience less real. Indeed it is unlikely that Roman society of the first centuries A.D. would have developed these conventional formulae if the religious experiences which they represent were not a common feature of that society. From another point of view, it is also in the nature of these inscriptions that they announce this religious experience to the community at large, and on occasion one senses that the primary intent of an inscription is less religion and more the self-advertising of the dedicator (e.g. *ILS* 5074, from North Africa and dated 239: "To Mars Augustus, protector of our lord *imperator* Caesar Marcus Antonius Gordianus . . . Quintus Calvius Rufus aedile, at his own expense . . . in honor of his aedileship, instead of the customary gifts to the people, made (this statue) . . . and, at his own expense, presented a boxing and gymnastic show . . ."). But if it is clear that some inscriptions owe less to religious experience and more to a desire to display oneself before the community, we should not be too ready in every instance to emphasize this element of public display so as to deny the genuine religious experience which must underlie many of these inscriptions. And even in those inscriptions where the primary intent is self-advertisement, the fact that that self-advertisement takes the form of a religious dedication again suggests something about the place of religion in the society which produced these inscriptions. In sum, the evidence of the inscriptions suggests that old pagan religion, as exemplified by the worship of Mars, had not atrophied, as we are often told, but continued to develop so as to provide meaningful personal religious experiences for a large number of people in the first centuries A.D.

VARIETIES OF RABBINIC RESPONSE TO THE
DESTRUCTION OF THE TEMPLE

Anthony J. Saldarini
Boston College

The course that Rabbinic Judaism took after 70 C.E. was greatly influenced by the lack of a Temple as a cultic and symbolic center. Yet no Rabbinic work thematically treats the loss of the Temple and its effects on Judaism. This topic along with many others of great interest to modern scholars receives only isolated mention in scattered exegetical comments and in the course of Talmudic arguments. The halakic literature treats problems occasioned by the loss of the Temple as they occur, but does not ordinarily enter into an extended discussion of the destruction itself or a systematic account of adaptations made. Nevertheless, were all explicit and implicit references to the Temple and its loss collected and studied in context, we would have an extensive and unworkable mass of material. This literature does not contain a response to the loss of the Temple, but many responses both complementary and contradictory to one another. What the literature says about the loss of the Temple varies with the nature of the literary context, the limits of the Scriptural verse being interpreted, the social situation spurring the author to teach and the attitudes presumed by his generation. We often cannot date texts, nor locate them in communities; when we can, we are often limited in our knowledge of the social situation. This paper will discuss four related collections of material on the destruction of the Temple to discern the authors' different and often contrasting views and varied interests. Attention will be focused on the final forms of the texts, their literary structure and peculiarities and their setting within a larger context. The historicity of the events and the development of the traditions will receive brief treatment at the end.

A sketch of some of the Rabbinic materials available for study in connection with the destruction of the Temple will help keep the limited sources studied here in perspective. Two obvious and major responses to the loss of the Temple are the Mishna and the Bar Kosiba War. The Bar Kosiba War shows that resistance to Rome did not cease with the defeat in 70 C.E. and that the people and attitudes which prompted the fighting remained an important part of Judaism, though poorly represented in Rabbinic literature. The Mishna is the first and most important body of literature to emerge in the post-Temple period. One must deduce its response to the loss of the Temple from its structure and content, from what it says, what it leaves implicit and what it leaves out. Jacob Neusner has argued that Mishna creates orderly world to replace the world lost when the Temple was destroyed and Israel subjugated. The Mishna gives Israel identity and emphasizes the role of human intention in the sanctification of life.[1] In addition, the rise of Rabbis themselves as leaders and of their schools and of other institutions as places of influence within Judaism is a response to the loss of the Temple (though a reliable history is very difficult to reconstruct from the anecdotes in Rabbinic literature).

Certain sections of the midrash deal extensively with the destruction of the Temple. Lamentations, written in response to the destruction of the first Temple, becomes a vehicle for further reaction to the loss of the second Temple as well as other disasters in Jewish history. Two sections from this collection will be studied below. Pesikta de Rab Kahana, Piskas 13-22 and Pesikta Rabbati, Piskas 26-37 contain homilies on the loss of the Temple in connection with Tisha b'Av, the day of mourning for the loss

---

[1] J. Neusner, *Judaism: The Evidence of the Mishnah* (Chicago: University, 1981) ch. 3, "Divisions, Tractates, Principal Ideas between the Wars," pp. 77-121; also pp. 271 and 283. See also *Method and Meaning in Ancient Judaism: Second Series* (Chico: Scholars, 1981) 212-13.

of the Temple.[2] Further materials on mourning customs and motives surrounding Tisha
b'av can be found in m. Taanit 4:6-8, t. Taan. 4:9-14 and b. Taan. 28b-31a. M. Sotah 9:9-
15 gives a list of things which have gone wrong since the Temple was destroyed. (See
also t. Sotah 15:10-15; b. Sotah 47a-49b.) B. Shabbat 119b gives a list of seven reasons
why Jerusalem was destroyed. The "mourners for Zion," a group who engaged in
ascetical practices because of the loss of the Temple, are engaged in debate and brought
into line with moderate Rabbinic teaching in t. Sotah 15:11-12 and b. Baba Bathra 60b.

Numerous stories about people and events connected with the destruction of the
Temple are scattered through the literature. Johanan ben Zakkai is a central figure,
some of whose material will be studied. The *taqqanot* (decrees) said to have been issued
by Johanan are another subject for discussion. They give an idea of what later
generations thought had to be done after the Temple was gone. Other stories concern
Rabbi Sadok who fasted forty years that the Temple not be destroyed, Martha bat
Boethius who came to a tragic end in the siege, the Jewish girl picking barley grains out
of the excrement of a horse after the destruction (numerous variants of this story exist)
and the priests throwing the keys to the Temple back to God in heaven. Each of these
literary units as well as numerous others not listed requires extensive literary analysis in
context and in comparison with other versions of the same material, followed by
historical and sociological analyses of the traditions in a larger context.

Here we shall analyze and compare four groups of material which have common
elements but also individually distinctive shapes and purpose. They contain the story of
Johanan ben Zakkai's escape from Jerusalem and descriptions of the siege and
destruction of Jerusalem as well as some stories about how the war came about and its
consequences. The texts are found in the Fathers According to Rabbi Nathan, Version A,
ch. 4 and Version B, chs. 5-9, b. Gittin 55b-59a and two places in Lamentations Rabba.[3]
Except for Lamentations Rabba they are coherent literary units which can be studied as
a whole in a specific context. They are well known and often taken for granted, yet their
exact message and limits have not been explored. For example, numerous treatments of
the beginning of Rabbinic Judaism cite Johanan ben Zakkai's interpretation of Hos 6:6, "I
desire loving kindness and not sacrifice, the knowledge of God rather than burnt
offerings," as the charter of Judaism after the destruction. Yet this verse with its
interpretation, that study and good deeds replace Temple sacrifices, is found only in the
two versions of the Fathers According to Rabbi Nathan. It is a fundamental tenet of
post-destruction Judaism only within certain circles, according to the specific meaning it
has in its literary context and as part of a coherent and complex group of ideas and
themes.

The Fathers According to Rabbi Nathan

An extended discussion of the destruction of the Temple and its consequences
dominates the interpretation of the saying of Simeon the Righteous as found in both
versions of the Fathers According to Rabbi Nathan. This hermeneutical decision reveals
something of the attitudes of the commentators. Simeon the Righteous was most
probably the high priest Simeon II who flourished about 200 B.C.E. and who is
immortalized by an elaborate description in Ben Sira, ch. 50.[4] Simeon is said to be

---

[2]In 1981 at the SBL meeting Lewis Barth delivered a paper on Pesikta de Rab
Kahana 13-22 entitled, "The Three of Retribution and Seven of Consolation in Pesikta
deRab Kahanah: The Problem of Historical Context." Abstract S 94.

[3]The Fathers According to Rabbi Nathan (*'Ābôt dĕ Rabbî Nātān*) will be
abbreviated ARN. Version A will be ARNA and Version B ARNB. Lamentations Rabba
will be Lam. Rab.

[4]See Josephus, *Antiquities,* 12.4.10 and George F. Moore, "Simon the Righteous," in
Jewish Studies in Memory of Israel Abrahams (New York, 1927), pp. 348-64.

"among the last of the Great Assembly" (Abot 1:2). The Great Assembly is pictured in Rabbinic literature as a body of leaders/elders/scholars who fill the gap between the last of the prophets and the first of the pairs of Rabbinic leaders who are dated to the second century, B.C.E. All these leaders, including Simeon, are part of the chain of tradition found in Mishna Tractate Abot and they serve as the guarantors of accurate, coherent and authoritative teaching within the tradition from the Biblical to the Rabbinic period.[5] Simeon's saying concisely summarizes the old order in Judaism before the destruction of the Temple; the commentary on it in ARN adapts the old order to the new situation of Judaism after the destruction. Simeon's saying reads: "On three things the world stands--on the Torah, on the Temple service and on acts of loving kindness." Judah Goldin has argued that in a pre-destruction context this saying has a natural meaning different from the interpretation given to it in ARN.[6] The saying originally meant: "On three things the Age stands--on the Torah (meaning books of Torah), on the Temple service and on acts of piety." The word *ʿôlām* means "world" in Mishnaic Hebrew, but its earlier Biblical meaning is temporal, "age." Torah in Rabbinic writings means both the Bible and later traditions (the oral Torah) and it often refers specifically to *study* of Torah. *Gĕmîlût ḥăsādîm*, acts of loving kindness, probably included both cultic and social acts which were fulfillment of the commandments.[7] In Rabbinic literature this term tends to refer to a more restricted range of acts of charity. The pre-destruction meaning of Simeon's saying, then, encompasses Scripture, the Temple and the believer's actions in response to both. The foundations of life while the Temple existed were revelation from God found in the Bible, the cultic center which plays such a central role in the Bible and the activities of Jews in response to Biblical commandments and to the demands of worship in the Temple. The core of Judaism, its foundations and boundaries, are summarized concisely in Simeon's saying. The challenge for the post-destruction commentators was to make sense out of the elements of this saying, to reestablish the foundations of Judaism while providing for continuity in the tradition.

The Fathers According to Rabbi Nathan, Version B

The Fathers According to Rabbi Nathan exists in two versions which have extensive similarities and differences. The relationships between the versions are complex and show a long process of development. Though some have dated these works to the seventh century or later, an argument can be made that the core of the traditions took shape in the second and/or third centuries.[8] This study will accept the traditions in their final form and make historical comments only when possible and appropriate. The commentators in both versions of ARN have included their views on the destruction of Jerusalem and the Temple within the chain of tradition, the longest and most organized section of

---

[5] A. Saldarini, *Scholastic Rabbinism* (Chico: Scholars, 1982) chs. 2 and 5.

[6] J. Goldin, "The Three Pillars of Simeon the Righteous," *PAAJR* 27 (1958) 43-58. Goldin argues that the saying derives historically from Simeon himself. Since the chain of tradition in Abot probably dates from either the first or second century, C.E., the historicity of the attribution to Simeon is doubtful. However, Goldin's analysis of the terms in the saying transcends the historical point. See A. Saldarini, "The End of the Rabbinic Chain of Tradition," *JBL* 93 (1974) 97-106 and *Scholastic Rabbinism*, 22-23.

[7] Goldin, "Three Pillars," 44-47.

[8] Saldarini, *Scholastic Rabbinism*, chs. 9 and 10. The text of ARN is found in S. Schechter, *Aboth de Rabbi Nathan* (Vienna, 1887). Version A is translated by Judah Goldin, *The Fathers According to Rabbi Nathan* (New Haven: Yale, 1955) and Version B by Anthony J. Saldarini, *The Fathers According to Rabbi Nathan, Version B: A Translation and Commentary* (SJLA 11; Leiden: Brill, 1975).

both versions.[9] The chain of tradition serves to establish the Rabbinic school of thought, master-disciple relationships, the central symbol of Torah and the most important activity, study of Torah. Torah study leads to good deeds, especially those which support the relationships among and activities of the members of the school. Torah serves as symbol for God revealed, as an authoritative basis for the school and its activities, and as a central reference point for all other aspects of life, Judaism and Jewish history. The Rabbis are presented as both teachers and models, in the Hellenistic mode. They are analogous to Simeon the Righteous, a symbol for the glory of the Temple and the great leaders of old. Within this symbolically intense context the commentators treat the destruction of Jerusalem and the Temple.

A quick review of ARNB, chs. 5-9 reveals that under the phrase "Torah" the commentator briefly gives the reason for the destruction of Jerusalem and the exile. Under the phrase "Temple service" he treats the agricultural fertility promised by Scripture when the Temple worship was faithfully carried out. The mention of Temple brings with it a long digression on the destruction of the Temple (chs. 6-7). The final phrase "deeds of loving kindness" initiates a discussion of how both Torah and deeds of loving kindness have become replacements for the sacrifices lost when the Temple was destroyed. The discussion of loving kindness then leads to a long digression on marriage and the nature of women. This final digression is a return to the subject of life after the loss and death connected with the destruction.

The first term, "Torah," is followed by four parallel cases of things affected adversely by the sin of *neglect* of Torah. That Israel, the tribes of Judah and Benjamin and the land (which was left desolate) went into exile and Jerusalem was destroyed because of the sin of neglect of Torah is proved by appropriate Scriptural verses which say that the people rejected, forsook or would not listen to Yahweh's Torah or words. Both the destruction and the diaspora, in the sixth century and in the first, are attributed to neglect of Torah which seems to mean disobedience to God's commands as well as inattention to his words. However, the phrase "neglect of Torah" (*biṭṭûl Tôrâ*) in Rabbinic literature has the connotation of the neglect of *the study* of Torah (cf. b. Shabbat 32b, for example). In context in ARNB with its emphasis on both study of and obedience to Torah this potent phrase probably has both connotations. In any case, neglect of the central symbol and central teaching of Judaism has resulted in the destruction of Biblical Judaism as it existed both geographically and cultically. The examples and the topic being pondered concern the first and second exile and destruction, not Torah which is presumed rather than discussed.

The phrase "Temple service" is in Hebrew ʿabôdāh, the service. The importance of that worship for life and world is succinctly stated by the commentator: "And so you find that while the Temple service existed, the world was blessed, low prices were prevalent and grain and wine were plentiful; people ate until satisfied and domestic animals ate until satisfied. . . . But once the Temple was destroyed, blessing left the world. . . ." This thematic comment is followed by the exegesis of a series of verses (Deut 11:15-17; Hag 1:11; 2:16; 1:6; 3:17) which detail the evils to come because of cessation of the Temple service. Using classical Biblical ideas the commentator associates the Temple with agricultural fertility, the availability of food for human life and general prosperity. The Temple is established as crucially necessary for human life, not something long lost and now irrelevant. Its absence explains the troubles of the present and demands some adaptation. The reality of the Temple's loss will be emphasized in chs. 6-7 and the adaptation necessary in ch. 8. Before developing the rest of this theme, the commentator at the end of ch. 5 pictures briefly what life will be like when the Temple is rebuilt using verses from Jeremiah and Habakkuk (3:18-19).

The comments made on the first two phrases of Simeon's saying, Torah and Temple service, assume the loss of the Temple and respond to it, first by giving the reason for

---

[9]See Saldarini, *Scholastic Rabbinism*, chs. 3 and 4.

the destruction and then by describing the value of the Temple and effects of its loss. A more detailed account of the destruction of Jerusalem and the Temple logically follow. Both ch. 6, which describes Johanan ben Zakkai's escape from Jerusalem, and ch. 7, which describes the siege, the destruction and the fate of Titus, begin the same way: "When Vespasian came and besieged Jerusalem. . . ." Each chapter stands independently and ch. 7 describes the central topic, the actual destruction. However, ch. 6 which climaxes with the founding of Johanan ben Zakkai's school at Jamnia offers hope before the destruction and sets the scene for the replacement of the Temple in ch. 8.

Johanan ben Zakkai's Escape from Jerusalem

The story of Vespasian's fruitless negotiations with the besieged in Jerusalem, Johanan ben Zakkai's subsequent escape from Jerusalem, and his meeting with Vespasian during which he predicts that Vespasian will become Emperor and Vespasian grants him permission for a school in Jamnia is well known. The meeting has often been treated as simply historical, though it exists in four versions with significant differences and presents numerous chronological and sociological problems. Actually, Johanan's escape from Jerusalem is a preliminary part of the dramatic action which climaxes with Johanan's meeting with Vespasian and especially with the granting of permission for a school. The story functions on its own primarily as a foundation legend for the Rabbinic school which traced its origins from Johanan and Jamnia.[10] The story is filled with ironies and reversals. Johanan and Vespasian agree that Jerusalem is lost and the Jerusalemites who resist the siege are presented as foolish. Johanan proclaims Vespasian Emperor and Vespasian encourages the foundation of Rabbinic Judaism. Actually, Johanan ensured that Vespasian's conquest of Jerusalem became also a victory for Judaism, which survived through the Rabbinic school founded at Jamnia.[11] The story presents the Rabbinic view of what was at stake in the conflict over Jerusalem, the survival of Judaism, not the defeat of Rome; and also what the solution to the conflict must be, Torah not military action.

The story of Vespasian and Johanan is divided into three scenes, each introduced by a temporal marker, "When." The three scenes are:

1. "When (kĕše-) Vespasian came and besieged Jerusalem" followed by negotiations.

2. "When (kêwān še-) Rabban Johanan ben Zakkai saw that the people were not willing to listen to him" followed by his escape.

3. "When (kêwān še-) Rabban Johanan ben Zakkai got outside the gate of Jerusalem followed by the meeting with Vespasian.

---

[10]A. Saldarini, "Johanan ben Zakkai's Escape from Jerusalem: Origin and Development of a Rabbinic Story," *JSJ* 6 (1975) 189-204; Peter Schäfer, "Die Flucht Johanan b. Zakkais aus Jerusalem und die Gründung des 'Lehrhauses' in Jabne," in *Aufstieg und Niedergang der Römischen Welt. II Principat. 19:2 Religion. Judentum* (ed. H. Temporini et al.; Berlin/New York: de Gruyter, 1979), pp. 43-101. See especially p. 93. Schäfer reviews all previous literature with special attention to the historicity problem and shows the many difficulties associated with parts of the story.

[11]Jacob Neusner, *Judaism: The Evidence of the Mishnah* (Chicago: University, 1981) pp. 307-28 in an analysis of this story in Version A demonstrates an underlying pattern of clash between Rabbi and general which is found elsewhere, which has Biblical parallels in Jeremiah and which stresses the superiority of one who knows Scripture. Some of his observations pertain to this story.

The first scene takes place inside Jerusalem, the second is the transition from inside to outside, the third takes place in the Roman camp outside Jerusalem. The first scene, the negotiations, has a negative result. The third scene, the interchange between Johanan and Vespasian, has a positive result in that Johanan gets his school and Vespasian his crown. The danger caused by Vespasian's siege of Jerusalem in scene one is resolved in a complex and ironic way. The danger to Johanan ben Zakkai is resolved in scene two when he escapes from Jerusalem. The danger to Judaism caused by the threat to the Temple and city is resolved by the founding of the Rabbinic school at Jamnia. Ironically, the danger to Jerusalem and the Temple is simply dropped after the first scene; the danger remains, but its outcome, the destruction, is not mentioned.

The fate of Jerusalem is resolved in an understated and indirect way through contrasting predictions of Vespasian's fate. In the first scene, Johanan warns the Jerusalemites that they face destruction. They reply: "As we sallied forth against the previous commanders and slaughtered them, so will we sally forth against this one and kill him." This prediction, unsupported by anything but imprudent bravado, is false. In the third scene, Johanan predicts that Vespasian will become Emperor because Scripture says "that this Temple will be destroyed only by a king, as it says: 'And Lebanon shall fall by a mighty one.' (Is. 10:34)." This prediction, based on Scripture and given by the expert interpreter of Scripture, comes true. The loss of Jerusalem is presumed and the focus of the story is shifted to those actors who remain on stage after its loss, Rome and the Rabbis. Those left in real control of history are the Rabbis who know accurately what is planned by God, the unstated power who controls history. The human cause of the destruction in this story is not Vespasian, who is an actor controlled by God, but the Jerusalemites who refuse to listen to Johanan in scene one, in contrast to Vespasian who does listen to him in scene three. Johanan, who stands as a symbol for the Judaism which survived the destruction, evades the danger of death in Jerusalem by leaving Jerusalem (ironically) disguised as a corpse. He arises from the coffin in which he was carried out and begins a new way of life in Jamnia. Thus the loss of Jerusalem and the Temple is here a story of death leading to life.

The Horror of Destruction

The next chapter of ARNB, ch. 7, begins the same way ch. 6 began, "When Vespasian came and besieged Jerusalem . . . ," but it approaches the destruction from the side of loss and sorrow. Thus the author of ARNB has provided contrasting and balancing chapters on the destruction, first understating its horror to show hope and survival, then describing the horror with full force. The action centers on the successful siege and then on the arrogant and blasphemous actions of the evil destroyer of the Temple, Titus. It is divided into ten incidents arranged chiastically.

  1. Siege. The Jews fight vigorously despite famine.
  2. The wall is destroyed until finally a pig's head lands on the altar, making it unclean.
  3. Titus profanes the Temple. Scriptural warrants given.
  4. Titus challenges God to come and face him. Scriptural warrants given.
  5. The booty is packed for the triumph in Rome.
  6. A gale threatens the ship.
  7. Titus challenges God by saying he has power only over the sea.
  8. God condemns Titus to death by a mosquito.
  9. Titus enjoys his triumph.
 10. The mosquito enters Titus' nose and eats his way into Titus' head. (The size of the mosquito receives elaboration.)

The first five items detail the destruction of Jerusalem and the second five the reversal, Titus' destruction by God. Jerusalem remains destroyed and drops out of the narrative after the first five items. Actually, the core of the narrative is a contest between two kings, God and Titus. Titus besieged Jerusalem in #1 and God "besieges" Titus with a mosquito in #10. The Jews lack food in #1 and a mosquito eats Titus in #10. Titus challenges God in #4 and seems to be unanswered. In #7 he challenges him again and is decisively answered. The wall of Jerusalem is destroyed and the altar profaned in #2 and in #9 by contrast Titus enjoys his triumph in Rome. However, ironically Titus' triumph is immediately reversed. Titus' profanation of the Temple in #3 parallels his condemnation to death in #8. Many of the details and elements concerning Titus are often repeated in Rabbinic collections. Here they have been arranged into a sophisticated whole which describes and admits the defeat associated with the destruction of Jerusalem and the Temple, but which affirms at the same time God's power and continuing control over human events as well as his sovereignty over all people, even the man who appears to have bested him in battle. Though no reason is given for the destruction, God's justice prevails in the punishment of Titus. In the second half of the series of incidents, the loss of the Temple recedes into the background and God comes forth to replace personally and directly the loss of his special city and house.

Having provided for the future of Judaism in ch. 6 and for the demise of the destroyer of the Temple in the first part of ch. 7, the author finally turns to a direct and sorrowful reaction to the loss of the Temple. Johanan ben Zakkai, waiting to hear of the fate of Jerusalem, is compared to Eli waiting to hear of the fate of the ark (1 Sam 4).[12] Unlike Eli, who marks the end of an era, Johanan does not die from shock, but mourns with his disciples. In ch. 8 he will reappear again with a positive response to the loss of the Temple. On the basis of Zechariah 11:2 a series of Biblical figures (the patriarchs, Zedekiah, the princes of Judah and Benjamin and the people of Jerusalem) are said to have mourned with Johanan. Thus Johanan's reaction to the loss of the Temple symbolizes the mourning of all Israelites, just as his leadership after the loss symbolizes the "rebirth" of Judaism. The author of ARNB then provides one more backward look at Jerusalem and the Temple. First, the coming destruction was known ahead of time through Scripture. Zech 11:1 says "Open your doors, O Lebanon . . . ," and forty years before the destruction the people used to find the gates of the Temple open of their own accord in the morning. Second, as the Temple was burning, the priests went up on the roof and threw the keys to the gates and Temple back to God in heaven, confessing, "We were not faithful custodians, (worthy) to eat from the stores of the king." God ultimately controls his house, both its administration and destruction. Humans can only accede faithfully to the divine will. Though the priests admit guilt, the reasons for the destruction of the Temple are not emphasized; its destruction is left in the same realm as the mystery of God's presence--something uncontrollable, beyond understanding and demanding human attention to God's will in whatever way it manifests itself.

The response to the loss of the Temple and Jerusalem is centered around Hos 6:6, "For I desire loving kindness ($hesed$) and not sacrifice, the knowledge of God, rather than burnt offerings." Loving kindness is associated with deeds of loving kindness, the creation of humans and male-female relations and holds together a group of disparate comments which describe human life in its most basic reality along with life after the destruction of the Temple. Hos 6:6 is taken to mean that words of Torah replace burnt offerings and acts of loving kindness ($gĕmîlû ḥăsādîm$) replace sacrifices. Rabbi Simeon makes the centrality of Torah even more explicit by saying that *study of* the words of Torah is more precious to God than burnt offerings and sacrifices. Loving kindness is further described by four Scriptural verses which show that acts of loving kindness fill the earth, extend from earth to sky, reach higher than the sky and extend from one end of the earth to the other; in the interpretation of the verses God's loving kindness is equated with human acts of loving kindness and is shown to be constitutive of the universe.

---

[12]Neusner, *Judaism*, 322 shows how Johanan in the escape story is parallel to Jeremiah.

Hos 6:6 is used again as the key to the story of Rabbi Joshua's complaint to Johanan ben Zakkai that the Temple's atonement for sins is lost to Judaism. Johanan says that Jews have another atonement and quotes the first half of Hos 6:6 that God desires loving kindness (that is, acts of loving kindness) and not sacrifice. Simeon the Righteous' saying that the world stands on acts of loving kindness exerts an influence on Johanan ben Zakkai's solution to the loss of atoning sacrifices from the ritual of Judaism and ties together the interpretation of Simeon's saying and its association with the destruction.

The story of Johanan's answer to Joshua is followed by a dispute, which occurs in various other contexts, about whether a scholar who is studying should leave his studies to take part in a wedding procession (or funeral cortege). The recognized answer is that they should only if there are insufficient other people in the procession. However, this rule is followed by a teaching of Rabbi Judah that he and his disciples enthusiastically take part in a wedding procession in imitation of God who himself prepared the bride for Adam. Behind these materials is the ongoing dispute over the relative value and place of study in relation to acts of loving kindness; however, here the dispute serves to enhance the importance of both and then leads into a long development on the nature of humans and male-female relations. Ps 139:5, "You have formed me behind and in front, and you lay your hand upon me," initiates the discussion of Adam, creation and finally the creation of Eve. In ch. 9 Gen 2:23, "Bone of my bones," initiates a long series of contrasts between males and females. Themes in these digressions are sexuality, love, procreation and implicitly the very nature of humans, life and the universe. Thus, even though the Temple and Jerusalem, that is, the visible center of Judaism, are gone and the cult which governed contact with God is in disarray, humans still find themselves in a natural relationship with God in a universe founded on loving kindness.

In summary, the author of ARNB does not lament at length the loss of the Temple and Jerusalem nor does he offer elaborate and sophisticated reasons for this disaster. Mourning is restrained, conventional reasons for the disaster such as sin or neglect of Torah are adduced without emphasis and even the enemy Rome is fairly evaluated. The author's concern is known by his context in Simeon's saying on the foundations of the world. Torah, Temple and good deeds explain both Judaism and creation. The loss of the Temple requires a shift of emphasis to both Torah and good deeds. The author stands in the Rabbinic tradition and attributes the survival of Judaism to his tradition and specifically to the leadership of one man, Johanan ben Zakkai. He is indifferent to Johanan's politics, to Vespasian's role in destroying Jerusalem (he reacts to Titus' challenge to God rather than to the bare fact of his destruction of Jerusalem and the Temple) and for the most part to the lamentable effect of the destruction to the people inside and outside Jerusalem. He wishes to demonstrate on the basis of both Scripture and creation that life goes on, that God remains present and active, that Judaism retains a coherent center in Torah and in acts of loving kindness and that all this has a basis both in God and in the nature of the universe. His demonstration of these realities takes place in his development of the chain of tradition as an authoritative basis for the Rabbinic school of Judaism as both a mode of interpreting and a way of living Judaism. This way of life demands both study of Torah and the living of Torah. This section has a slightly greater emphasis on living Torah, that is, on acts of loving kindness.

The Fathers According to Rabbi Nathan, Version A

The two versions of ARN share both structure and materials, but differ in many particulars and in some important features. Version A will be treated more briefly than Version B with attention to its main features and its significant differences from Version B. ARNA, ch. 4 comments on each of the phrases of Simeon the Righteous' saying (Torah, Temple, acts of loving kindness) in order and then adds as an appendix the story of Johanan ben Zakkai's escape from Jerusalem and a more brief account of the siege, destruction and mourning which followed. It lacks the long digression on creation, Adam and Eve and the differences between men and women found in ARNB, chs. 8-9.

ARNA begins its commentary on "Torah" by quoting Hos 6:6 to show that "the study of Torah is more beloved by God than burnt offerings." From this the conclusion is drawn that "when a sage sits and expounds to the congregation, Scripture accounts it to him as though he had offered up fat and blood on the altar." Three points should be noted. ARNA begins immediately with the replacing of the Temple sacrifices, even before it recounts the loss of the Temple. It does not even pause to account for the loss of the Temple, in contrast to ARNB. Second, ARNA stresses that Torah and study of Torah replace sacrifices and it immediately uses Hos 6:6 for this purpose. Later, under the phrase "acts of loving kindness" ARNA will use Hos 6:6 again and stress ḥesed and acts of loving kindness, as did ARNB. However, ARNA here as often stresses Torah and study of Torah slightly more than ARNB (though these themes are important to both versions).[13] Third, ARNA mentions sages teaching and scholars studying and so explicitly compares the activities of the Rabbinic school to the sacrifices offered and activities carried on in the Temple. Whatever is said about the Temple and its loss and in favor of acts of loving kindness, study of Torah occupies pride of place and colors our reading of the rest of the chapter. ARNA brings up the controversy over whether scholars should join wedding and burial processions and Rabbi Judah's strong emphasis on weddings in imitation of God's attention to Adam and Eve. However, the citation of Gen 2:23, "Bone of my bone," does not lead into a long digression on male and female nor is there a heavy stress on human love and procreation, as in ARNB. ARNA subordinates all firmly to Torah. Goldin's translation suggests that the material on God's care for Eve, the bride, belongs under the phrase "acts of loving kindness."[14] Though this is the arrangement in ARNB, the material on the bride seems to go with the controversy over study versus taking part in wedding processions and belongs with the discussion of Torah here. In addition ARNA combines under the phrase Torah the three themes (or three options) which govern human relations with God: sacrifices, Torah and natural life and love. With the loss of the Temple, sacrifices are gone and must be replaced with Torah. Yet, despite the emphasis on Torah, life itself, created and fostered by God, must also be nurtured.

The theme of fertility and life is continued in the discussion of the Temple service. As in ARNB, the Biblical idea that agricultural fertility and so life itself depend on the Temple is presented using the same passages from Deuteronomy and Haggai. The poignancy of the loss of the Temple is indirectly conveyed by the last sentence of the section: "Thus you learn that there is no service more beloved of the Holy One, blessed be He, than the Temple service."

The importance of "acts of loving kindness" is established through reference to Hos 6:6 again, but this time "loving kindness" is interpreted as the basic constituent of creation on the basis of Ps 89:3, which is understood as "The world is built with loving kindness." Secondly, Hos 6:6 is used again in the story of Johanan ben Zakkai teaching Joshua that acts of loving kindness replace the atonement which took place at the Temple. Finally and significantly, Daniel is cited as an example who replaces the sacrifices lost in the first destruction with acts of loving kindness performed in the diaspora. The acts of loving kindness? "He used to outfit the bride and make her rejoice, accompany the dead, give a perutah to the poor, and pray three times a day--and his prayer was received with favor." Prayer, alms giving and attention to weddings and funerals all are familiar pious practices essential to the integrity of the community. They govern fundamental relationships among humans and with God and they foster concern for all members of the community and promote love (ḥesed) among them. This emphasis stands in stark contrast to the death and destruction which follow in the account of the loss of Jerusalem.

---

[13] J. Goldin, "The Two Versions of *Abot De Rabbi Nathan,*" *HUCA* 19 (1946) 97-120, develops this thesis with numerous examples.

[14] p. 182, n. 14.

Johanan ben Zakkai's Escape from Jerusalem

The version of Johanan's escape in ARNA is similar to ARNB and reflects a common tradition, different from the versions of the story found in b. Gittin 56a and Lamentations Rabba 1:5 (#31).[15] However, the two ARN versions of the story have each been written to make different points. The structure of the two stories and the relationships of the characters differ as does the climax of the story. At the beginning of the story Vespasian and Johanan appeal to the Jerusalemites in the same words and receive exactly the same rejection from them. The parallel between the two and lack of conflict between them are more pronounced here than in ARNB. The two identical dialogues with the Jerusalemites emphasize the Jerusalemites' stubbornness and over-confidence in themselves (in implicit opposition to God whose intentions Johanan correctly interprets).

When Johanan leaves Jerusalem in a coffin, the guards do not try to stop the disciples or threaten to pierce the "corpse." Rather, Johanan's exit is allowed on the basis of halaka, that a corpse is not allowed to remain in Jerusalem overnight. This reference to halaka is consistent with ARNA's emphasis on Torah and on the decrease in conflict in ARNA's version of the escape compared to ARNB. When Johanan ben Zakkai meets Vespasian, he first makes his request for Jamnia, and only afterwards predicts that Vespasian will become Emperor. This order is justified because Vespasian has heard from spies that Johanan ben Zakkai is friendly to him and so is motivated to grant his request. More important to the author, the school at Jamnia is not a gift in response to the prediction that Vespasian will be Emperor, but rather something which Johanan achieved on his own recognizance. Johanan is master of the school both as teacher and as founder.

Johanan ben Zakkai then brings up the subject of Vespasian's approaching sovereignty. His motive is not given, but the prediction is based on Scripture and so Johanan's warrant for predicting Vespasian's accession to the throne is the truth from God found in Scripture.[16] That Vespasian is an enemy of Judaism is secondary to the reign of God over events, a reign known from Scripture. Note that in contrast to ARNB Johanan's prediction does not cause Vespasian to charge Johanan with treason; harmony prevails in their relationship. The prediction that Vespasian will be Emperor because Jerusalem must be conquered by a king leads to two events: Vespasian hears that he has been proclaimed Emperor and then Jerusalem is destroyed. The author of ARNA has melded the end of the story of Johanan's meeting with Vespasian into the brief account of Jerusalem's destruction. All hangs on God's will as known from Scripture and the two events are recounted briefly and dispassionately.

The final act of siege in the capture of Jerusalem is that "a swine's head was brought and set into the catapult, and this he (Vespasian? Titus?) hurled toward the (sacrificial) limbs which were on the altar.[17] It was then that Jerusalem was captured." Again in ARNA halaka is the key. When the sacrificial cult is defiled, the Temple and Jerusalem are no more. Fighting, flames, and Titus are not mentioned because they are irrelevant. As in the escape story, so in the account of the siege God prevails though his presence is left unstated.

Reactions to the loss of Jerusalem are twofold: Johanan waits for news of Jerusalem as did Eli. Johanan the rabbi replaces Eli the high priest. Johanan lives while Eli died. Johanan mourns with his disciples. The reader knows that they then adapted Judaism to live without the Temple. A midrash on Zech 11:1-3 shows the priests throwing the keys of the Temple back to heaven and various Biblical figures mourning. ARNA,

[15]Saldarini, "Escape," esp. 190-91 and 202-3.
[16]Neusner, *Judaism*, 307-28 develops the theme of Johanan as interpreter of Scripture dominating the future Emperor.
[17]Titus' blasphemous actions in the Temple are recounted earlier in ch. 1.

ch. 4 ends, oddly enough, with an account of the three things by which God distinguished humans from one another: voice, taste ($n\check{e}^c\bar{\imath}m\bar{a}h$) and appearance. This triad matches the triad found in Simeon's saying at the beginning of the chapter.[18] It also turns the focus on humans after the destruction, much as ARNB, chs. 8-9 described humanity at great length.

In summary, ARNA stresses Torah and fulfillment of Johanan's scriptural prediction. It has more emphasis on harmony and less on confrontation, danger and war than ARNB. At a couple of crucial points halaka provides the key to the action. Though several themes form the core of the chapter, Torah dominates as both the key to understanding the loss of the Temple and the basis for Judaism after that loss.

Babylonian Talmud, Tractate Gittin

B. Gittin 55b-59a comments on m. Gittin 5:6 which explains a rule called *sicaricon*. A sicaricon is a Gentile who acquires a Jew's land in Palestine through duress. Since the land belongs to Jews by divine mandate it is inalienable and real ownership resides with the original owner. A person who buys the land from a Gentile does not acquire real title. Since the Mishna also wishes to encourage Jews to repurchase land from Gentile conquerers, it provides some protection for new owners and rules for compensating the original owner. (See also t. Gittin 3:10.) The complex of problems surrounding this rule need not detain us because the rule for us is important as the context for stories concerning the destruction of Jerusalem. The first sentence of the Mishna says: "There was no (law of) sicaricon in Judea in the case of those slain in war; from (the time of) those slain in war and since, there is (the law of) sicaricon there."[19] The war referred to in this mishna is not clear. The Talmud interprets the sentence to mean that the law of sicaricon did not exist during the war ($bah\check{a}r\hat{u}g\hat{e}~hammilh\bar{a}m\hat{a}$) but came into existence after the war ($m\bar{e}h\check{a}r\hat{u}g\hat{e}~hammilh\bar{a}m\hat{a}$) and asks how the rule could be instituted after the war when threats against Jews would presumably be less. Two answers are given. Rabbi Judah says that the rule was in existence during the war but was simply not applied. Rabbi Assi says that after the war the government issued three successive decrees ranging from more to less severe. The threat to Jews from the first two decrees prompted the law of sicaricon. The decrees form a neat triad. First, not to kill a Jew was a capital offense; then to kill a Jew was punishable by a small fine of four zuz; finally to kill a Jew was a capital offense. In the first two periods a Jew could be coerced into silence by threat of death; in the third period a Jew says "Let him take it today; tomorrow I will sue him for it."[20] Since the time being discussed and the law itself relates to war and its effects, the Talmud digresses (55b-58a) with comments on three conflicts which led to destruction: the destruction of Jerusalem, Ṭur Malkaʾ and Bethar. After the digression the Talmud returns to a discussion of how the Rule works.

Two of the three wars referred to are easily identified: the destruction of Jerusalem took place during the Great War with Rome in 66-70 and the destruction of Bethar during the Bar Kosiba War in 132-135. Ṭur Malkaʾ, Aramaic for the King's Mountain, may refer to Samaria.[21] When this destruction occurred is not clear from the text and not

---

[18]See Goldin's translation, n. 39.

[19]Later in this mishna *sicaricon* refers to the person who has seized the property. The term is best translated as (the law of) usurping occupant.

[20]The general description of the decrees leads commentators to identify them with the decrees of Hadrian after the Bar Kosiba War. But the decrees form a neat literary structure that helps answer the Talmudic question; they are not accurate historical description and could fit any time Jews have been persecuted. The first decree, that to leave a Jew alive was a capital offense, is a concise way of expressing savage repression and persecution, not the record of an imperial decree.

[21]See the references ad loc. in the Soncino translation, p. 254, n. 4.

important for this study. It and the other two conflicts are developed in similar ways and under same rubric as a triad. The three wars are introduced by a Scriptural verse and by enigmatic statements about the cause of each war.

> Rabbi Johanan said: What is the meaning of the verse, "Blessed is the man who fears the Lord always; but he who hardens his heart will fall into calamity." (Prov 28:14) Through a Qamsaᵓ and a Bar Qamsaᵓ Jerusalem was destroyed; through a cock and a hen Tur Malka' was destroyed;through the shaft of a litter Bethar was destroyed.[22]

The relationship between the verse and the three examples is not immediately clear. The Soncino translation (p. 254, n. 2) suggests that these materials illustrate "the endless misery and mischief caused by hardness of heart." The development of each of these incidents illustrates many things besides hardness of heart and the term hardness of heart is not specifically referred to nor used to hold the section together. There are some incidents where insensitivity and misunderstanding cause the destructions, but the link is not strong or dominant. That these three destructions illustrate in some way the meaning of the verse brings out very clearly that we are not dealing with history and that the "Talmudic Sages were hardly interested in history per se."[23]

First, the similarities among the three incidents will be examined and then the materials associated with the destruction of Jerusalem will be presented in greater detail. The incident which is said to have begun the war that resulted in each of the destructions is trivial. Bar Qamsa' is invited to a supper instead of Qamsa'. When he is expelled, he makes the Romans suspicious of the Jews and conspires to worsen relations between them and cause the war of 66-70. The war in which Tur Malka' is destroyed comes about when Roman soldiers take a cock and hen from a wedding procession and a fight ensues which is interpreted as rebellion. The Bar Kosiba war is caused by the servants of the Emperor's daughter who cut down a tree to replace a shaft of her litter. The tree had been planted to make the canopy of a girl when she married. Again a fight ensues and it is interpreted as rebellion. The last two incidents are very similar; the first is more complex in its plot. The last two are concerned with a wedding, one in progress and one in the future. The first is concerned with another kind of celebration, a formal supper. In all three stories the Romans misunderstand a Jewish custom, conflict ensues because of that and the conflict is then misinterpreted again by the Romans as general rebellion. Two further peculiarities might be mentioned. In the first two wars, the Emperor receives a sign that he is to conquer. In the last two the enormous amount of blood spilled in the slaughter is graphically described. These three groups of material are held together by parallels and similarities, but they are not tightly organized. The materials concerning Jerusalem have several peculiarities which must be examined.

The treatment of the destruction of Jerusalem begins with the story of Bar Qamsa' as the cause of Jerusalem's destruction. At the end of the section on Jerusalem, another reference is made to this story to form an inclusion. Between, three people are said to have been sent to destroy Jerusalem: Nero, Vespasian and Titus, with each treated in turn. Nero refuses to attack and becomes a convert; Vespasian leaves before the siege is completed and grants Johanan ben Zakkai Jamnia; finally, Titus destroys Jerusalem. Only Titus is treated as evil and shown being punished in the next world.

---

[22]The introductory formula for the verse, *mᵓy dktib*, is typically Babylonian. In Aramaic the cock and the hen are *tarněgôlāᵓ* and *tarněgûltāᵓ*, similar in sound the way *Qamsa'* and *Bar Qamsa'* are.

[23]Naomi G. Cohen, "The Theological Stratum of the Martha b. Boethus Tradition: An Explication of the Text in *Gittin* 56a," *HTR* 69 (1976) 187.

The story of Qamsa' and Bar Qamsa' is a comic story with a tragic ending which embodies both the serious and the trivial.[24] A man giving a formal dinner sends his servant to invite his friend Qamsa'. By mistake the servant invites his enemy, Bar Qamsa'. The host throws his enemy out despite the enemy's attempt to negotiate, so the enemy goes to the Gentile authorities with charges that the Jews are rebelling. He puts a blemish on a sacrifice sent by the Emperor to test the Jews' loyalty so that his charges will be substantiated by the Jews' refusal to sacrifice the blemished animal. The story seems to contain two strands which have been joined; it rests upon some well-known themes and some subtleties to make a complex point which does not provide a single satisfying cause for the war with Rome but does show its nature and consequences within an intricate set of social relationships.

The setting and plot, a mistaken invitation to a dinner, is a standard topos in comedy and this sets a tone for the story contrary to the tragic atmosphere one would expect. The mixed-up invitations are a trivial mistake, but the mistake leads to world shaking consequences for Judaism, the destruction of the Temple. The similar names cause the mistake; a person's friend and enemy have almost the same name and are hard to distinguish. On a larger scale, the Emperor has difficulty distinguishing whether the Jews are "friends" or enemies in revolt. Likewise, the Rabbis dispute over the treatment to be accorded Bar Qamsa', who is a threat to Judaism. The names themselves are humorous in two ways. First, the obvious repetition and confusion of two names and second the Aramaic meaning for *qamṣā$^{\circ}$* which is "locust." The host has invited a locust to dinner; locusts destroy.[25]

The host of the dinner sees Bar Qamsa' and challenges his presence because he is his *ba'al děbābā$^{\circ}$*, that is, his opponent. This idiom means literally a master of evil speech, of whispering. The Soncino translation interprets it as "You tell tales about me," a meaning appropriate to the relationship between the two men. In addition, the term is used for informers who provide information and accusations to the Roman government and thus the host's characterization of Bar Qamsa' foreshadows his actions later in the story. For the moment a humorous negotiation between the two men ensues. Bar Qamsa', wishing to avoid ejection, offers first to pay for what he eats and drinks, then for half of the supper and finally for the whole supper. The host rejects his overtures and ejects him. The presuppositions of their negotiation are left silent: the guest's desire to preserve his honor and avoid shame and the host's obligation to show honor through hospitality to his guests.[26] Though the situation is complex, the socially harmonious mode of handling this embarrassing situation would have to include a way for the mistakenly invited guest to save face. Instead, the host treats him with unmitigated hostility and defeats him socially by ejecting him in such a way that he loses his honor and suffers shame. Thus a "war" begins.

The very next line of the story widens the conflict from a conflict between Bar Qamsa' and his host to a conflict between Judaism at large and Bar Qamsa': "Since the Rabbis were seated there and did not stop him, this shows that they agreed with him."

---

[24]Y. Baer, "Jerusalem in the Times of the Great Revolt," *Zion* 36 (1971) 170 (Hebrew). J. Derenbourg, *Essai sur L'Histoire et la Géographie de la Palestine* (Paris: Imprimerie Imperiale, 1867) 267, judges this story a striking example of the way that "deux siècles à peine après la destruction du temple, l'imagination bizarre des docteurs dénaturait les événements, en les transformant en un conte amusant." He advances no rationale for this transformation.

[25]Derenbourg, *Essai*, 267 suggests that the name may be an historical reminiscence of a pro-Roman citizen of Tiberias mentioned in Josephus, *Life*, ch. 9 (#33): *kompsòs ho toû kompsoû*. Baer, "Jerusalem," 169-70 agrees.

[26]For a useful analysis of honor and shame applied to New Testament studies, see Bruce J. Malina, *The New Testament World: Insights from Cultural Anthropology* (Atlanta: Knox, 1981), ch. 2.

Bar Qamsa' enlists an ally against Judaism, the Roman government. Bar Qamsa' tells the Emperor that the Jews are rebelling; in so doing, he suggests a parallel between his own rejection and the rejection of Rome. The Aramaic idiom for informing is relevant to the story. *ăkal qûrṣā*ʾ (or qarṣāʾ) means literally to "eat destruction" or "to eat something cutting." Because he was refused food at the meal, Bar Qamsa' goes and "eats destruction," that is, informs and conspires with the Romans in such a way as to bring about the destruction of the Temple. Bar Qamsa' convinces the Emperor to send a sacrifice to the Temple to see if the authorities will offer it (a sign of loyalty) or whether they will reject it (a sign of rebellion). Now the two protagonists are the sages, that is, the Jewish authorities, and the Roman Emperor; Bar Qamsa' and his host take secondary positions. A domestic conflict has been transmuted into a total social conflict; a contest over individual honor has been transformed into a contest over the honor of the Empire versus the honor of the Temple.

As Bar Qamsa' is bringing the offering to the Temple, he inflicts a physical blemish on it which makes it unsuitable for sacrifice according to Jewish law, but leaves it still suitable under Roman law. Thus Bar Qamsa' creates a cultural misunderstanding very similar to the misunderstandings which are said to have prompted the wars which caused the destruction of Tur Malka and Bethar. The dilemma consequent on the presentation of the blemished animal has two solutions: first, the Rabbis are inclined to offer the blemished animal "in order not to offend the government" (miššûm šĕlôm malkût). Rabbi Zechariah ben Abqulas stands up for the honor of the Temple and Jewish law by pointing out that people will say blemished animals are offered at the Temple. The Rabbis implicitly agree with his argument that the honor and integrity of the Temple must be preserved at the expense of the honor of the Emperor. They then propose to kill Bar Qamsa' so that he will not inform the government about their rejection of the sacrifice. This is thinkable because informers are traitors and enemies of society. Bar Qamsa' is now to Judaism what he was originally to the host of the supper: someone to be totally rejected as an enemy. However, Zechariah ben Abqulas turns the Rabbis to another dilemma. Bar Qamsa' has not yet informed on their action; all he has done is blemish a consecrated animal, not a capital offense. With this dilemma the story ends. It is assumed but not stated that the Jewish authorities did not kill Bar Qamsa', that he did inform and that the war and destruction of the Temple resulted.

Different interpretations of this story have been suggested, two of them in the Talmud itself. The comment of Rabbi Johanan immediately following the story will be treated momentarily; first let us examine the comment which comes at the end of the whole section dealing with the destruction of Jerusalem: "Note how serious a thing it is to put a man to shame, for God espoused the cause of Bar Qamsa' and destroyed his house and burnt his Temple" (b. Git. 57a). Implicit in this line is the judgment that Bar Qamsa' was treated wrongly both by the host at the supper and the Rabbis in attendance there. This interpretation introduces a new actor into drama, God. In the plot of the story, Bar Qamsa' enlists the aid of Rome as a powerful ally. The Talmudic interpreter sees behind Bar Qamsa'ʾs actions the hand of God righting the injustice done to Bar Qamsa'. The human causes of the destruction of the Temple are transcended and God's zeal to protect justice is seen as the ultimate value which is even more important than the preservation of the Temple. Thus, that which was lacking in the story, respect for another's honor and dignity, caused the loss of the Temple. Respect for another's honor is implicitly encouraged as essential for just relations within the Jewish community and with God. Survival of Judaism without the Temple depends on actions which do not shame others. The meal among friends, the sacrifices at the Temple (meal between God and his people), the relationships between Jewish authorities and people and finally the relations between Judaism and the Roman government are intimately linked in this story and in the interpretation of the world given by the Talmudic author.

The second interpretation of the Bar Qamsa' story is appended immediately to the story. "Rabbi Johanan said: Through the humility of Rabbi Zechariah ben Abqulas our

house has been destroyed, our Temple burned and we ourselves exiled from our land."
The Soncino translation renders the key word, ʿinwĕtānûtô, as scrupulousness and Neusner
translates the related Tosefta text (Shab. 16:7) as fastidiousness. Rashi interprets the
meaning as "patience" (sablānût). The exact connotation of the word is not immediately
clear, nor is its relationship to Zechariah's opinions voiced in the Rabbinic debate clear.
Further light can legitimately be thrown on this enigmatic saying from the parallel in t.
Shab. 16 (17):6 (Zuckermandel, 135; Lieberman, 77). There the problem is what to do
with bones and shells on the table during Sabbath. The House of Hillel says one takes
them from the table; the House of Shammai says the entire table is removed and shaken
out (outside). Zechariah did not accept either opinion, but threw them under the couch.
Rabbi Jose comments: "The humility of Rabbi Zechariah ben Abqulas burned the
Temple." In the Tosefta Jose is clearly criticizing Zechariah's indecisiveness and irre-
sponsibility; a sage should make halakic decisions in unclear cases.[27] Jose says that this
kind of unwillingness to decide is what caused the destruction of the Temple.[28] Jose
does not make clear the basis for his statement; it is possible and even somewhat
probable that the Talmudic story is an attempt to illustrate what Rabbi Jose means in
the Tosefta and that the Talmud makes the further move of saying that Zechariah
actually caused the destruction of the Temple by being unwilling to make hard decisions
in dealing with Bar Qamsa'. Instead of striving to interpret the law so as to protect the
Temple, he advised following usual procedure and caused further misunderstanding and
destruction.[29]

    The Bar Qamsa' story in b. Gittin shifts focus half way through from a dispute over
how to treat a guest to an halakic dispute over relations with the Roman Empire. The
final comment by Rabbi Johanan lays upon the sages the ultimate responsibility for
making difficult decisions in all areas and thus keeping order in society. The Rabbis at
the banquet did not intervene to maintain proper relations between the host and Bar
Qamsa' and to smooth over a socially awkward situation. From that conflict resulted an
awkward situation with the Roman Empire and again the Rabbis do nothing to solve the
complex issues surrounding the blemished sacrifice but follow the advice of Zechariah
ben Abqulas.   The story implies that the sages are responsible for keeping order by
settling difficult cases of law and by preserving harmony within the community.   In
addition, the Jewish community and its leaders should stress accommodation rather than
conflict. Had the "negotiations" between Bar Qamsa' and his host been successful (with
the help of the Rabbis present), then Bar Qamsa' would not have gone to the Roman
government and the war would not have begun. Had the sages fulfilled their larger
responsibilities by creating some way out of the dilemma of the blemished sacrifice
brought from the Emperor, that is, had they worked out an accommodation and halakic
solution to the problem of relations with the Roman government, the community would
have preserved its integrity and its Temple. Thus without explicitly saying so the
humorous story of Bar Qamsa' criticizes the actions of the Rabbis (who are assumed to
have been in control before the Temple was destroyed) and encourages more adequate
leadership from later generations of sages.

_____

[27]See Baer, "Jerusalem," 170 and reference to Lieberman in n. 152.
    [28]Baer, "Jerusalem," 170 associates the name Abqulas with the Greek eukolos
which means "easily satisfied, good natured, content," and is used of Socrates by
Aristophanes in the Clouds. Baer notes another suggestion which originated with Jost
(1821). Josephus, War, 4:225 mentions a zealot named Zechariah ben Amphikallos. The
Greek text of his name is not certain. If there is an historical reminiscence here, it does
not function in the story.
    [29]Historically one of the acts leading to war with Rome was the refusal of the
Jewish authorities at the Temple to offer sacrifice for the welfare of the Emperor.
However, this act was intentionally done as an act of independence (Josephus, War,
2:411-418). In the Talmudic story the basis for decision is halaka, not politics.

The sequence of events leading to the destruction of Jerusalem continues with a brief section on Nero and longer sections on Vespasian and Titus. Nero shoots arrows in all four directions and they all fall in Jerusalem. Nero then decides (on the basis of Ezek 25:14) that God wants to destroy the Temple and blame Nero for it. So Nero runs away, becomes a proselyte and has a descendent Rabbi Meir. This brief account of Nero's career is no less striking and confusing than the Bar Qamsa' story which preceded it. Naomi Cohen has shown that Meir's name is Anatolian and that he was probably associated with Nero because Nero was said in Roman legend to have escaped to Asia Minor and hidden there. The story may also be a polemic against the later Christian legend of Nero redivivus who will return at the end from the East.[30] In context the Nero story serves several functions. First, it shows that God willed the destruction of the Temple. Nero learned by shooting the arrows and interpreting the Scriptural verse that he had been chosen as God's instrument; he also discerned that like the instruments of God's anger in the Bible, he would in turn be rejected. Note that the first line of the story reads: "He sent against them Nero the Caesar." Similarly the section on Vespasian begins "He sent against them Vespasian the Caesar." There is no antecedent for "he" in the text. The Soncino translation interprets the text to mean the Emperor sent Nero. (That a general should be called a Caesar is an understandable confusion.) But the ambiguous pronoun may also refer to God, who retains control over events even when they seem as destructive to Judaism as the loss of the Temple. One final point. That Nero, a notorious figure in Roman history, finally becomes a Jew and even produces a great authority like Meir furthers the theme of God's sovereignty. Despite the loss of Jerusalem Judaism ultimately triumphs over its enemies, in this case by winning Nero over.

Vespasian and Johanan

The interaction between Vespasian and Johanan ben Zakkai still does not result in the destruction of Jerusalem. This is reserved for the third figure in this sequence, Titus. Rather, Vespasian prospers by becoming Emperor in accordance with Scripture and God's will: because he is to destroy Jerusalem, he must be a king (Isa 10:34). Thus the theme of God's dominance over events continues. Vespasian also helps the survival of Judaism by giving Johanan a school in Jamnia. Because we have studied this story as it occurs in ARNB, here we shall note some salient differences in the treatment of the story and their effect on this section of b. Gittin.

Vespasian does not encourage the Jerusalemites to surrender nor does he know of Johanan ben Zakkai through spies before he meets him. Johanan does not suggest to the Jerusalemites that they surrender; the Rabbis do that. Thus at the beginning of the narrative the focus is moved from Vespasian and Johanan to Jerusalem and its inhabitants. The situation in the city is more fully described than in ARN through a contrast between the three rich men, Nakdimon ben Gorion, Ben Kalba Shabua' and Ben Zizith Hakeseth, who could have kept the city supplied for 21 years, and the Biryoni, the zealots, who destroyed the supplies and would not negotiate. The gravity of the situation is communicated by the tragic and curious story of the rich woman Martha bat Boethius who died strangely.[31] Johanan ben Zakkai enters the story when he asks his nephew, Abba Siqra,[32] who is head of the Biryoni, to get him out. Even Abba Siqra acknowledges

---

[30] Naomi G. Cohen, "Rabbi Meir, a Descendant of Anatolian Proselytes," *JJS* 23 (1972) 51-59.

[31] Naomi G. Cohen, "The Theological Stratum of the Martha b. Boethus Tradition: An Explication of the Text in Gittin 56a," *HTR* 69 (1976) 187-95 traces various historical reminiscences in the text and suggests a polemic against misuse of wealth by certain Jewish leaders.

[32] Abba Siqra' probably connotes "father" or leader of the *sîqārîn*, the *sicarii* and is a title.

that the Biryoni are irrational. The danger and confusion are enhanced by two double challenges faced by Johanan. The guards at the gate twice wish to harm his "corpse" and Vespasian rejects his royal greeting with the dilemma that Johanan has either treasonously and falsely declared him Emperor or, if he is Emperor, Johanan has treasonously not paid him homage until now. Johanan escapes the dilemma by pointing out that the Biryoni coerced him. In all these scenes the Biryoni are the evil force and the Rabbis, Johanan, Johanan's nephew and even Vespasian are forces for order and so part of God's plan for Judaism.

In the dialogue with Vespasian Johanan is twice judged to have lost an opportunity to save Jerusalem according to b. Gittin. When Johanan says that the Biryoni are in control in Jerusalem, Vespasian presents him with a conundrum: "If there is a jar of honey around which a serpent is wound, would they not break the jar (to get rid of) the serpent?" Johanan has no answer to refute Vespasian. Either Rabbi Jose or Rabbi Akiba applied to Johanan Isa 44:25, "(God) turns back wise men and makes their knowledge foolish." Johanan should have said that we grab the snake with tongs and leave the jar intact. The same verse from Isaiah is used of Johanan's reply to Vespasian when Vespasian grants him a request. Johanan asks for Jamnia, its sages, the family chain of Rabban Gamaliel and physicians to heal Rabbi Zadok. He should have asked Vespasian to let the Jews off this time. The answer given to this criticism is the same as the reason given for Johanan's desire to leave Jerusalem at the beginning of the story: he wanted to save a little (*pôrtā'*). The little, in contrast to Jerusalem and the Temple, is the Rabbinic school and leadership. Implicit in this comparison and criticism is the fact that God did preserve Judaism through what Johanan requested and despite the destruction of Jerusalem.

Johanan's authority and power are shown in his command of Scripture, something treated above in the comments on ARN. Johanan correctly predicts that Vespasian will be Emperor. In addition, when Vespasian hears that he is Emperor, one of his feet swells and he cannot put on his boot. Johanan explains what happened on the basis of Prov 15:30, "Good news makes the bone fat." He cures the condition by having Vespasian see someone he dislikes on the basis of Prov 17:22, "A downcast spirit dries up the bones."

The end of Johanan's meeting with Vespasian shows clearly that Jerusalem is lost and prepares the way for Titus. Vespasian says, "I am now going and will send someone to take my place." Vespasian then grants Johanan the request noted above. The request for Jamnia guarantees that Johanan and the sages are safely out of the way before Titus comes to destroy Jerusalem. In addition Johanan asks for physicians to cure Rabbi Zadok. Zadok had fasted for forty years so that Jerusalem might not be destroyed (as recounted in the course of the Martha bat Boethius story previously) and his cure means the end of his fast. Jerusalem is lost.

The final figure of the three is the wicked Titus who begins with a challenge to God: "Where is their God, the rock in which they took refuge?" (Deut 32:37). Titus' blasphemous actions (illustrated by Biblical verses to show that even the desecration of the Temple is within the ambit of God's will), his challenge to God during the storm at sea and his death by a gnat which enters his head are recounted. After Titus' painful death is described, the story is told of Titus' nephew consulting the dead Titus to find out who is of most repute in the next world. Israel, Titus replies, and so even he gives testimony in favor of Israel. The Temple and Jerusalem cease; Israel lives.

In summary, the stories associated with the destruction of Jerusalem in b. Gittin stress God's control over events, the lesser importance of human actions, the Rabbis' authority and responsibility for the survival of Judaism and Israel's ultimate victory over her enemies even though the Temple and Jerusalem have been lost.

Lamentations Rabba

Lamentations Rabba (or Rabbati) is a commentary on Lamentations the bulk of which is usually dated to the fifth-sixth centuries. It and Genesis Rabba are the earliest midrashim in the Rabba collection. Like the Biblical Lamentations the commentary speaks mostly of the destruction of the Temple and Jerusalem, melding together the first and second destructions and bringing in other wars and disasters from Jewish history as well. The commentary begins with a large number of proems, has extensive comments on chs. 1 and 2 and briefer remarks on chs. 3-5. There is no critical edition; I use the usual printed edition. There is also an edition by Buber and a number of Geniza fragments. We cannot study discrete chapters, as we did in ARN and b. Gittin, since the whole book is on the destruction.[33] We shall look at Lam. Rab.'s treatment of two stories, the Bar Qamsa' story and Johanan's escape from Jerusalem. Each manifests some striking changes which reveal attitudes toward the loss of Jerusalem and the Temple.

The Bar Qamsa' story is found in the comments on Lam 4:2 (#4): "The precious sons of Zion, worth their weight in fine gold." As is the case all through Lam. Rab. the commentator seeks to illustrate the verses with incidents and events. Here he wishes to show how the Jerusalemites are "precious," that is, how they spend money on one another and especially the customs surrounding their formal suppers and invitations to them. "Precious" refers to the expense, to the honor and to the care expended on and shown to one another. Thus the bar Qamsa' story becomes an example of failure in this regard. The plot of the story and comments by the author are recast (in comparison with the version in b. Gittin) in such a way that the shame brought upon Bar Qamsa' is the key, and the responsibility for its rests totally on Zechariah ben Abqulas.

As an example of the honor with which Jerusalemites treated one another and their care in these matters the commentator says: "None of them would attend a banquet unless he was invited twice." The mix-up in the invitation of Bar Qamsa' illustrates the importance of this rule. The story itself stresses Bar Qamsaʾ's desire to avoid shame. When the host tells him to leave he explicitly asks him not to put him to shame and he offers first to pay for what he consumes, then to consume nothing and finally to pay for the whole meal. Instead of *the Rabbis* being present as in b. Gittin, Rabbi Zechariah ben Abqulas is present and the commentator says explicitly that he could have prevented this behavior but did not. Thus the humility of Rabbi Zechariah is first his meekness and lack of assertiveness in the face of the host's misbehavior toward Bar Qamsa'. Rabbi Zechariah, who only enters the story in the second half in b. Gittin, here is integral to the whole story. The author of Lam. Rab. has integrated the elements of the story and made it more coherent.

The author introduces more verisimilitude and graphic detail into the rest of the story in comparison with b. Gittin. Bar Qamsa' voices explicit resentment that he has been expelled while they sit in comfort at the supper. He goes to the governor (šilṭôn), not the Emperor. He charges that the Jews substitute inferior animals for the prime animals sent by the government for sacrifice, not that they are in rebellion. The governor is unwilling to accept the charges and Bar Qamsa' must return to convince him. Bar Qamsa' is not simply given an animal to bring to the Temple for sacrifice; an officer comes with him and while the officer sleeps, Bar Qamsa' blemishes the animals. When the priest at the Temple will not offer the animals, the messenger tells the king that the charge is true and he comes to destroy the Temple.

In Lam. Rab. the story becomes more human and easy to understand. The halaka concerned with blemishes is not noted, as it is in the Talmud. The discussion among the Rabbis about whether to offer the blemished animals or not, and whether to kill Bar Qamsa' or not as well as Rabbi Zechariah's ribid opinions on these subjects are omitted. The problem is simply the shame visited upon a guest and the reluctance of a leader, Rabbi Zechariah, to take a stand in a social situation. The Jews are not accused of rebellion, but simply of insulting the ruler, again a matter of honor and shame. At the end of the story the commentator offers two possible interpretations. First, "Hence the

---

[33]For a survey of the major themes and attitudes in Lam. Rab., see Shaye J. D. Cohen, "The Destruction: From Scripture to Midrash," *Prooftexts* 2 (1982) 18-39.

popular saying: "Because of the difference between (the names) Qamsa' and Bar Qamsa' was the Temple destroyed." Second, the line from Tosefta Shabbat 16:6, "The humility of Rabbi Zechariah ben Abqulas burnt the Temple."[34] In both cases the Temple's destruction is caused by ordinary human failing, the mix-up of two names or a social failing. No stress is laid on the actions or responsibility of the Gentile government. The officials act reasonably; it is a fellow Jew, Bar Qamsa', who provokes the trouble.

Johanan ben Zakkai's Escape

Lam 1:5 (#31), "Her foes have become the head," is illustrated by the story of Johanan ben Zakkai's escape from Jerusalem and meeting with Vespasian in which he predicts that Vespasian will be Emperor because only a king can destroy Jerusalem. As with the Bar Qamsa' story, this story is recast to fit the views of the author and it also has some details which fill in gaps and give it verisimilitude. Most strikingly Johanan ben Zakkai is presented as a wise man, who contests both the zealots and Vespasian's advisors. Vespasian is not a sympathetic figure, does not grant Johanan a school in Jamnia and himself presides over the destruction of Jerusalem.[35]

Lam. Rab. says that Vespasian besieged Jerusalem for three and a half years, a number familiar from Daniel. Vespasian has four generals outside the city and in Jerusalem there are four councillors, namely the three rich men named in b. Gittin with Nakdimon ben Gorion's name divided into two to make a parallel group of four. Each of the four was capable of providing supplies to the city for ten years, a total of *forty* years. The general of Arabia, Pangar, has a major role near the end of the story.[36] A final character is Ben Battiah, the nephew of Johanan, who was in charge of all the supplies and burned them, threatened to execute Johanan when he seemed to disagree and finally helped him escape contrary to the policy of his fellow zealots. His name, from the root *bṭḥ*, trust, security, etc., is ironic because he burns the stores rather than preserving them, he fights for a city which will not remain secure and he deceives his fellow zealots to effect Johanan's escape.

Johanan's character is different here compared to the other versions, especially b. Gittin. When Ben Battiah burns the stores, Johanan laments saying woe (*wwy*). When threatened by Ben Battiah because of this, he claims to have spoken a similar exclamation of approval (*wh*). The commentator remarks, "Through the difference between 'woe' and 'wah' Rabbi Johanan ben Zakkai escaped death; and the verse was applied to him, "And the advantage of knowledge is that wisdom preserves the life of him who has it' (Qoh 7:12)." Johanan manifests his wisdom to Vespasian when he predicts that he will be proclaimed Emperor on the basis of Scripture and it comes true and also (in an incident unique to Lam. Rab.) when he is able to tell the time of day and night though locked in a lightless chamber. Johanan's knowledge of Torah allows him to recite it and his familiarity with recitation means he knows how long it takes him to recite. Johanan passes two further "tests" which he failed in b. Gittin and for which he was criticized

---

[34]Cohen, "The Destruction," 27-28 notes that Lam. Rab. has the tendency to blame various leaders within Judaism for the disaster. He is incorrect in saying that the regular printed edition of Lam. Rab. speaks of Rabbi Zechariah ben Abqulas' insistence on halakic minutiae. B. Gittin brings this up.

[35]Some of the added details of this version of the story stem from Josephus or a source common to Josephus and the midrash. See Schäfer, "Die Flucht," 93-97 who cites other literature and moderates some of the extravagant claims of literary dependence found in Baer, "Jerusalem," 171-84.

[36]Schäfer, "Die Flucht," 97 is probably correct in seeing an anti-Islamic polemic in the introduction of Pangar, general of *Arabia;* this is contrary to Baer's hypothesis of an anti-Christian polemic on the basis on the identification of Pangar with Abgar (pp. 171-75).

there. The author of Lam. Rab. seems to be directly refuting the criticism of Johanan in the Talmud and presenting him instead as an ideal wise leader of Judaism, a model for later Rabbinic leaders. When Vespasian presents the conundrum of the snake nested in a jar (wound around the jar in b. Gittin), Johanan enters into a contest with Pangar as his adversary. Johanan suggests getting a charmer to charm the snake out and leave the jar intact. Pangar says to kill the snake and break the jar. The same problem is presented again as a snake in a tower and equivalent answers are given. Johanan then challenges Pangar, saying that recommending destruction for Jerusalem may bring destruction also to him in Arabia, a neighboring country. Pangar replies that he is only trying to help Israel. Johanan says that Pangar's intentions, good or evil, will be discerned later.

Johanan shows his wisdom further by explaining to Vespasian why his foot swelled up and how to get it down, as was seen also in b. Gittin. Finally, when Vespasian grants Johanan a favor, Johanan first asks that Jerusalem be spared. This, according to b. Gittin, is what he should have requested and did not. The author of Lam. Rab. revises the story to remove blame from Johanan. Johanan then asks that the Western Wall be spared, a request which is formulated to match what historically happened. Finally, he requests that all who leave before the fourth hour be spared, that is, he is pictured as trying to save some of the people along with one of the walls.

Several other things at the end of this story require comment. First, Johanan does not ask for Jamnia and a school there. The author of Lam. Rab. does not want to attribute something as central to Judaism as the Rabbinic school to the largesse of an enemy of Israel.[37] Second, Vespasian does not know Johanan ben Zakkai and though he grants him some favors, he is much more the enemy of Israel. He remains at Jerusalem until the end and Titus is not mentioned nor does he play any role in the destruction. Third, attention is focused on the physical remains of Jerusalem, the Western Wall. Pangar, Johanan's adversary, is assigned to destroy that wall. (The other three generals are assigned to the other walls.) He says he did not destroy it for the glory of Vespasian, but when he jumps off the wall as a test of his good intention, he dies. This is to fulfill what Johanan predicted about his intentions earlier when he said he wanted to help Israel. His death shows that he lied. Fourth, the study of Torah is brought in not through the founding of the school at Jamnia, but through the cure of Rabbi Sadok. Vespasian asks Johanan if there is anyone he wants to save and Johanan names Rabbi Sadok who had been fasting (unsuccessfully) to save Jerusalem. Johanan notes that he eats one fig and teaches 100 sessions in the academy. Jews need no help from Vespasian to preserve Torah.

In summary, Johanan prevails over the zealots in Jerusalem, Pangar outside Jerusalem, and even Vespasian by his wisdom. He saves what he can of Judaism and is linked to what remains: the Western Wall.

Historical Problems

This study has elucidated the responses to the loss of the Temple contained in four groups of materials. The collections of stories, sayings and comments have been taken as a whole in context with only occasional reference to the development of traditions and the relationships among the sources. A few further comments on the relationships among the sources and their historicity are in order. Baer attacks those who have taken the Rabbinic stories as historical and argues that they are late, based on a fifth century source which itself depends on Josephus and other sources. He also says that the two versions of the Fathers According to Rabbi Nathan are dependent upon b. Gittin and Lam. Rab. and are a summary of them.[38] Baer's position stands on hypothetical sources and improbable literary relationships. He uses medieval sources as evidence for writings

[37]S. Cohen, "The Destruction," 32.
[38]Baer, "Jerusalem," 169 and passim for historical sources.

in the fifth century, misreads some texts and fails to show a clear relationship among the four Rabbinic texts.[39] Baer is very probably correct in many particulars, especially that Josephus has influenced the Rabbinic traditions. E. E. Halevy reviews the four sources with especial attention to Hellenistic parallels. He concludes that the two versions of ARN are first, Lam. Rab. derived from them and then b. Gittin derived from the previous three.[40] He also tries to unite all accounts around a central question about who was responsible for the destruction of the Temple. His analysis is too broad and general and it fails to account for numerous parts of the narrative and peculiarities in each version. Schäfer has most judiciously evaluated the parallels to Josephus suggested by Baer and the historical probability of the various parts of the narrative of Johanan's escape from Jerusalem and some of the materials associated with it. He concludes that it is likely that Johanan did flee Jerusalem, but the course of events and his motives cannot be recovered from the literature. The prediction to Vespasian that he would be Emperor and the gift of Jamnia to Johanan are not historical. Vespasian might have known about Johanan through spies and Johanan probably planned some accommodation with the Romans.[41] Schäfer takes the sources out of context and compares them with careful attention to their historical probability in comparison with other historical sources. This study gives more attention to the context of each source and the redactional purpose of each incident and is less confident of our ability to reach a firm historical evaluation of the events.

The story of Johanan ben Zakkai's escape from Jerusalem comes to us in two traditions, each tradition containing two versions. The differences between the two versions in the ARN tradition are explained by their differing purposes, as developed above. B. Gittin and Lam. Rab. have much in common and form another tradition. Lam. Rab. defends Johanan ben Zakkai against accusations made in b. Gittin and also changes the request Johanan made of Vespasian by omitting Jamnia. Thus, Lam. Rab. has a clear literary dependence on b. Gittin.[42] We really do not know when or how Johanan ben Zakkai left Jerusalem or what his relations with the Romans were. The story of his escape and request for Jamnia functions as a foundation story for the Rabbinic school. Johanan meets and deals as an equal or superior with the Roman general. He is a hero and founder, not an historical figure, in these stories. Schäfer suggests reasonably that Johanan's application of Isa 10:34 to Vespasian may originally have been a messianic prophecy which was later combined with the story of Josephus' meeting with Vespasian and prediction of his ascendency.[43] The story of Pangar, the general of Arabia, and Vespasian's swollen foot are later and separate incidents, the former a polemic, as noted above, and the latter a story illustrating the meaning of a verse and showing Johanan's Scripture-based wisdom.

The accounts of Titus' blasphemy in entering the Temple, his challenge to God and God's conquest of him using a gnat occur in many places in Rabbinic literature and are an independent group of materials used differently by each source. They express horror at the loss of the Temple, and imaginative reconstruction of the desecration of the Temple and a vindication of God's power and justice in the horrible death of Titus. They are omitted in Lam. Rab. and placed elsewhere in ARNA. The Bar Qamsa' story, as analyzed above, is a sophisticated comic story which responds to a tragic event. It is hardly

---

[39]See Saldarini, "Johanan ben Zakkai's Escape," 196-97 and Schäfer, "Die Flucht," passim.

[40]E. E. Halevy, Šaᶜărê Haᵓăggādâ (Tel Aviv: Armoni, 1963) 209-28. His work is marred by lack of method and his parallels are undisciplined. On p. 216 he compares only ch. 7 of ARNB and omits ch. 6.

[41]Schäfer, "Die Flucht," 98 summarizes his conclusions.

[42]See this argument in more detail in Saldarini, "Johanan ben Zakkai's Escape."

[43]Schäfer, "Die Flucht," 87-88. See also Saldarini, "Johanan ben Zakkai's Escape," 198-99.

history. The story of Joshua lamenting the loss of the Temple's atoning powers and Johanan's answer using Hos 6:6 solves a theological problem on the basis of exegesis. Johanan's historical role and attitudes in the crisis remain obscure. He serves the theological and social purposes of some Jews associated with the Rabbinic school by founding the school and articulating the solution to some post-destruction theological and social problems. This is especially true in ARN where Torah and good deeds replace the Temple's sacrifices and atonement.

Summary

Johanan ben Zakkai is one of the central figures in all the sources. In ARN he is the founder of the Rabbinic school which replaces the Temple as institutional center in the way of life created by the Rabbis. He also works out solutions to the loss of sacrifice at the Temple. In b. Gittin he is blamed for not having saved the Temple and the people of Jerusalem and he is less central to the narrative than in ARN. In Lam. Rab. he is defended against the charges brought in b. Gittin and he is more sharply presented as an example to Judaism, especially as a wise leader. This emphasis on Johanan's wisdom in Lam. Rab. is complementary to a lack of interest in the loss of the Temple ritual and the Temple itself.[44] None of the sources assigns any value to fighting the Romans, nationalism, patriotism or martyrdom. a silence remarkable in comparison with other literature from the second century, B.C.E. on. Rather, God is sovereign and victorious over his enemies and the Rabbi is God's faithful follower through wisdom based on Scripture. Thus, b. Gittin criticizes the Rabbis for not protecting Judaism from internal and external conflict when it presents the tragedy of the Bar Qamsa' story and the faults in Johanan's dealings with Vespasian.

The settings in each of the sources and the elements of humanity and its universe brought into play differ. In ARN fertility, human nature, the central symbols of Judaism (Torah and Temple) and human good deeds are related to one another in such a way as to adjust for the loss of the Temple. These values and aspects of life are set within the historical and social setting of the Rabbinic school which engages in study as a faithful adherence to God and revelation. Halaka is the most important statement of God's will and good order. B. Gittin recounts a variety of stories to bring out the comedy and tragedy characteristic of a complex of social relationships among Jews and parallel political relationships with the Empire. Lam. Rab. reduces these complexities to personal relationships among the actors, e.g., Johanan's relationship to his nephew, Ben Battiah, and Rabbi Zechariah's reticence at the supper where Bar Qamsa' was insulted.

Though none of the four sources studied here theorize about the loss of the Temple or systematically develop its consequences, they do reveal attitudes and reaction to the crisis by their choice and arrangement of materials and by their unique ways of telling stories associated with the destruction of Jerusalem. Some of the literary methods and theological perspectives are subtle and sophisticated; none of their reactions is simple. The loss of the Temple was too traumatic for a simple discursive statement. To understand the range of reaction to the loss of the Temple we must "by indirection find directions out."

---

[44]S. Cohen, "The Destruction," 24. Lam. Rab. concentrates on God's enduring love for and presence among Israel.

THE USE OF PRONOUNCEMENT STORIES
IN SUETONIUS' *LIVES OF THE TWELVE CAESARS*

Richard P. Saller
Swarthmore College

Pronouncement stories in Suetonius' biographies invite our attention for several reasons. They were an important aspect of his method of composition, as demonstrated by numbers alone: about 199 instances can be found in a text of some 250 pages. This high frequency can be compared to the handful found in the extant works of Suetonius' predecessors in the Latin biographical tradition, Cornelius Nepos and Quintus Curtius. Suetonius organized his biographies not in continuous chronological narratives, but as catalogues of deeds, virtues, and vices.[1] Self-contained pronouncement stories and anecdotes formed units easy to organize in these categories.

Aside from the intrinsic interest in pronouncement stories for understanding Suetonius' composition, they may be of some value for comparison with other authors' use of them. It seems to me (without having conducted a full study of other authors) that Suetonius' use is likely to be unusual in several respects. First, the subjects of Suetonius' biographies (in contrast to Plutarch's, for example) were not chosen for their virtue or wisdom or talent; rather, Suetonius wrote about them because they reached the imperial throne, many by accident of birth and in spite of their vices. Consequently, most of the biographies are very negative, as are the pronouncement stories in them. In many of these negative stories it seems quite possible that Suetonius was playing off the expectations of his audience, who had been trained by memorizing *exempla* of the virtuous and *chreiai* of the wise.[2] In a second respect Suetonius was unusual, in that as secretary *ab epistulis* he had access to and quoted from imperial archives and other documentary evidence in some of his *Lives.*[3] Some of his pronouncement stories were taken from documentary or archival material: in these cases we have pronouncements that are not the result of literary or oral tradition.

In this paper I wish to begin with a discussion of the distribution of the pronouncement stories in two classification schemes, together with comments about dificulties arising from classification. Then I will analyze briefly how Suetonius uses such stories to characterize the emperors: how some classes of stories appear to be suited to particular character types and how Suetonius manipulates the expectations of his readers.

Classification

Various classification systems have been suggested for pronouncement stories. In this section Suetonius' stories will be divided in accordance with two of them, that delineated in antiquity by the rhetorician Theon for *chreiai* and the one recently suggested by Vernon Robbins.[4]

Theon's system included three categories: voluntary, situational, and responsive. Voluntary pronouncement stories, in which the pronouncement is unprovoked by the situation or another person, are the least common in Suetonius: only 21 out of 199. In

---

[1] G. B. Townend, "Suetonius and His Influence," in *Latin Biography* (ed. T. A. Dorey; London: Routledge & K. Paul, 1967) 83-84. On the historical veracity of these stories, see my "Anecdotes as Historical Evidence for the Principate," *Greece and Rome* n.s. 27 (1980) 69-83.

[2] Harold C. Gotoff, "Cicero's Style of Relating Memorable Sayings," *Illinois Classical Studies* 6.2 (1981) 311.

[3] Townend, "Suetonius," p. 87.

[4] Theon, *Progymnasmata* III; Vernon K. Robbins, "Classifying Pronouncement Stories in Plutarch's *Parallel Lives*," *Semeia* 20 (1981) 29-52.

some cases these appear as voluntary because they have been taken out of context by the author, and in fact, many are simple pronouncements rather than pronouncement stories. For example, to support his statement that Augustus thought that "nothing suited a general less than haste and rashness," Suetonius cites four sayings of Augustus, including "a safe commander is better than a bold one" (in Greek) and "whatever is done well enough is done quickly enough" (*Aug. 25.4*). Altogether, only 4 of 21 of the pronouncements appear in a narrative context.

The situational pronouncement stories are by far the most numerous class (113) in Suetonius' biographies. The line between voluntary and situational is not always clear to me, because I am not certain how immediate the situation provoking the saying must be. As evidence that Nero was at least an accomplice to Claudius' murder, Suetonius points out that Nero "was accustomed, in accordance with a Greek proverb, to praise mushrooms (in which food Claudius received the poison) as the food of the gods" (*Nero 33.1*). The saying, one of Nero's most memorable, fits into the general context of Claudius' murder, but, as told by Suetonius, is not prompted directly by the situation. Therefore, I have classified it as voluntary. Under the notable sayings (*dicta notabilia*) issuing from Domitian's lips, Suetonius includes the following: "of a certain man's head whose hair color was a mixture of reddish and grey, he said that it was snow sprinkled with mead" (*Dom. 20*). Again with this pronouncement, the context is left rather vague by the author. I have classified it as situational, assuming that behind the compression the reader is to understand something like "when Domitian saw a man . . . , he said . . . ." This pronouncement may be worth considering in another respect. The sayings in pronouncement stories are supposed to be "pointed" or "well-aimed." The fact that Suetonius quoted this as one of two examples of Domitian's *dicta notabilia* suggests that we may have tastes very different from Suetonius as to what is "pointed" and what is worth remembering. Consequently, I have been inclined to use Suetonius' inclusion of sayings in the biographies as *prima facie* evidence that they are notable and in some sense "well-aimed," rather than trusting my own judgment.

Whatever the uncertainty of classification in the preceding cases, the situation in most stories is clear. For instance, in reporting the events preceding Nero's death, Suetonius wrote: "Indeed, it had been observed that [Nero] had sung in public as his last piece "Oedipus the exile" and had ended with this verse: 'Wife, mother, father, command me to die' " (*Nero 46.3*). To return to the issue of "pointedness," it should be noted that in this story, as in some others, the "point" was not intended by the speaker, but was perceived from the viewpoint of the audience and reader, who suspected that Nero had killed his mother, father, and wife.

Responsive pronouncement stories are usually easy to identify and in terms of frequency are intermediate between situational and voluntary pronouncement stories (64 of 199). A classic response, exhibiting more wit than usual in emperors, is found in the biography of Tiberius (52.2): after the death of Tiberius' son "when delegates from Troy came consoling the emperor somewhat too late, as if the memory of his grief had already faded, he laughed at them and answered that he grieved for their sake, because they had lost their exellent citizen Hector."

The identity of the party to whom the emperor is responding is sometimes left rather vague by Suetonius. Another story about Tiberius and his reluctance to take the throne offers an extreme case of this. "The reason for his hesitation was fear of danger threatening from every side, so that he often used to say that he was holding a wolf by the ears" (*Tib. 25.1*). The party drawing the response is so vague here that I was at first inclined to classify this story as something other than responsive.

Emperors spent much of their time replying in writing to questions from their administrators and petitions from their subjects.[5] It is not surprising, then, that some of

---

[5]Fergus Millar, *The Emperor in the Roman World* (Ithaca, NY: Cornell University Press, 1977) 203-72.

the pronouncements in Suetonius' *Lives* were in the form of written responses. The biography of Tiberius contains a story of this kind: "to his governors who were urging that the provinces be burdened with tribute, he wrote back that it was the job of a good shepherd to shear his flock, not to flay it" (*Tib.* 32.2). Suetonius could have had documentary evidence for such pronouncements in the senate (recorded in the *acta senatus*). A statement quoted in *oratio recta* and so perhaps taken from the *acta senatus* forms the basis for another story about Tiberius: "Once when the senate was demanding that attention be given to charges of this type [insults to the emperor] and those guilty of them, he said, 'We do not have so much spare time that we should involve ourselves in more business; if you open this window, you will allow nothing else to be done; the hatreds of all men will be brought to you on this pretext' " (*Tib.* 28).

The above classification scheme seems to me to be so general as not to be very useful in analyzing the pronouncement stories beyond the obvious: by and large emperors did not make pronouncements unprompted, but were usually depicted as reacting to situations and, less often, to remarks or actions directed at them.[6] Robbins' more elaborate scheme enables us to proceed with a more interesting analysis.

In Robbins' tripartite division of pronouncement stories (aphoristic, adversative, affirmative), the aphoristic category is further subdivided into description and inquiry. Some one-sixth (34) of the stories in Suetonius fall into this general class, and nearly all of those into the subclass of descriptive (32). Some of the most famous imperial sayings are descriptive aphorisms. Vespasian displayed his customary wit to the end. As death approached, Suetonius tells us, Vespasian exclaimed, "Oh, I think I am becoming a god" (*Vesp.* 23.4). Domitian's most famous saying is reported without much context: "He used to say that the condition of the emperors was most wretched, because their claim to have discovered a conspiracy was not believed unless they were killed" (*Dom.* 21).

Suetonius includes only two aphoristic inquiry stories in his biographies. To illustrate Vespasian's wit and affability, the following story is presented. "Having been overcome by a certain woman who claimed that she was dying of love for him, after he took her to bed he gave her 400,000 HS. When his steward asked how he wanted this amount entered in the accounts, he said, 'for Vespasian in love.' " (*Vesp.* 22). For the most part, these imperial aphorisms were remembered not for their wisdom, but for their cleverness. The fact that they are a relatively common class suggests that the latter quality was valued in emperors.

Nearly half of the stories (113) can be classified as adversative pronouncements, with 86 falling into the correction subclass and 27 in the dissent subclass. Robbins has further subdivided the correction stories into self-, direct, and indirect correction. Self-correction was not a popular pastime among emperors, to judge from the small number (7) of such pronouncements. Two of the seven are attributed to Titus. "Once after supper having remembered that he had given nothing to anyone all day, he uttered that memorable and justly praised saying: 'Friends, I have lost a day' " (*Titus* 8.1). Similar pronouncements are attributed to earlier rulers, including Alexander the Great.[7] Unfortunately, there is no way of knowing whether Titus had heard the story told of others and decided to use the saying himself, or, on the other hand, the story came to be told of him because it fit his character. (It may be noted that several other sayings were attributed to more than one emperor--e.g., variations on "let them hate as long as they fear" in *Tib.* 59.2 and *Gaius* 30.1).

Emperors were far more inclined to correct others in their presence than themselves, if the number of direct correction stories can be used as a guide (44, making it the largest subclass). In some cases the correction was spoken in jest. Vespasian, "after

---

[6]This corresponds to Millar's image of an essentially passive emperor in the above cited work.

[7]For similar stories about other rulers, see Otto Luschnat, "*Diem Perdidi*," *Philologus* 109 (1965) 297-99.

he had put off one of his closest assistants who was seeking an office for someone he claimed was his brother, summoned the candidate himself into his presence; he granted the office without delay after exacting the money that the candidate had promised to his supporter; when the assistant pressed the matter presently, Vespasian said to him, 'Look for another brother for yourself; you think this one is yours, but he turns out to be mine' " (*Vesp.* 23.2). Other corrections were deadly serious. "Because a jester loudly ordered the corpse in a passing funeral procession to tell the dead Augustus that his legacies left to the plebs were not yet paid out, Tiberius ordered the jester, who had been dragged before him, to receive what was owed and to be led away to execution, bidding him to tell the truth to his father [Augustus]" (*Tib.* 57.2). In both of these stories the emperor produces a short saying whose "pointedness" depends on the emperor's ability to turn the situation on his interlocutor. Many of the other direct correction pronouncements are much less pointed, as we shall see.

It is not always easy to distinguish between direct and indirect correction stories, because Suetonius on occasion fails to indicate clearly whether the corrected party was present. For example, when Gaius "was about to murder his brother whom he suspected of having taken precautions with antidotes on account of a fear of poisons, he said, 'What! an antidote against Caesar?' " Whether this remark was heard by the doomed Tiberius Gemellus or not, Suetonius leaves unclear. There are two or three other stories of this kind. The class of clearly indirect corrections is large, comprising 32 stories. Some leave no doubt that the criticism is indirect, because the criticized party was dead at the time of the pronouncement, as in the famous line of Julius Caesar that "Sulla did not know his ABCs when he laid down his dictatorship" (*Iul.* 77). As indicated above, correction stories, direct and indirect, form by far the largest subclass (interestingly enough, 43% of the total—precisely the proportion discovered by Robbins in his study of Plutarch).[8] Why should this kind of story have been so popular? Perhaps it was because the emperor's subjects were particularly interested in how he used his authority—i.e., how he criticized and corrected his subjects. Certainly the fact of imperial power was an indispensable part of the background for the "point" of many stories.

The second subclass of adversative stories is dissent, which in turn is subdivided into objection (the main character responding to dissent by a second party) and rebuff (the main character being rebuffed in a final saying of a secondary character). There are only 7 dissent-objection stories in Suetonius' *Lives*, despite the expectation that the dramatic tension inherent in such stories might make them popular. Indeed, Suetonius tells one of the seven in a way to diminish the dramatic impact. When Vespasian "was fearful because he had been banished from Nero's court, and was asking what he should do and where he should go, one of the servants controlling admission to the court threw him out and ordered him to go to Morbovia [i.e., go to hell] . When this servant later pleaded for pardon, Vespasian did not flare up at him except in words—in fact, about as many and of the same kind" (*Vesp.* 14). The last line of this story could obviously have been told with more rhetorical "point."

It might be suggested that dissent-objection stories are rare because dissent from an absolute ruler is not a particularly salutary pursuit. But then it would be difficult to explain the much higher frequency of dissent-rebuff stories (20). Suetonius relates a sort of double rebuff story about Tiberius in the context of his long hesitation over accepting the throne after Augustus' death. "He kept the senate in suspense with a clever delay so that some lost patience and one shouted out in the uproar: 'Either let him do it or withdraw!' Another remarked critically in his presence that others accomplished tardily what they had promised, but *he* promised tardily what he had accomplished" (*Tib.* 24.1). In this, as in many of the dissent-rebuff stories, the emperor's critics are not given a specific identity.

---

[8]Robbins, "Classifying," p. 38.

The third class consists of affirmative stories, including both commendations (praise from the main character) and laudations (praise of the main character from a second party). The frequency of this class is comparable to that of aphoristic stories (39). Commendations can be further broken down into self-, direct, and indirect commendations. If emperors were far more likely to criticize others rather than themselves in pronouncement stories, they were far more likely to commend themselves (20). The self-praise is sometimes straightforward, as in Caesar's "veni, vidi, vici" pronouncement. In other instances the self-praise is also self-exhortation. As a part of Augustus' attempt to revive old Republican values as exemplified by the great leaders of the past, Augustus "dedicated statues of all in triumphal dress in the two porticoes of his forum, even proclaiming in an edict that he had devised this so that both he himself, as long as he lived, and rulers of later ages would be required by citizens to live up to the standard of those men" (*Aug*. 31.5). In still other cases, the self-commendation is two-edged. Nero's exclamation just before his death--"How great an artist perishes in me!"--is both genuine self-praise from Nero's point of view and from the readers' point of view the culmination of a pattern of ridiculous and undignified behavior unworthy of an emperor (*Nero* 49.1).

I have separated from self-commendation another closely related subclass, self-defense, of which there are eight examples in the *Lives of the Twelve Caesars*. One pronouncement attributed to Caesar by Suetonius illustrates how close the two subclasses are: "Caesar, having been disturbed by these [threatening actions of Marcellus] and believing, as they say he often was heard to remark, that it would be more difficult to push him, the leading man of the state, down from the first rank to the second rank than from the second to the lowest, he resisted with all his power, partly through the veto of tribunes and partly through the other consul Servius Sulpicius" (*Iul*. 29.1). Here Suetonius has subordinated a well-known saying of Caesar in the narrative rather than using it as the climax of a self-contained story. Caesar was both praising and defending himself. In other stories the self-praise is less prominent, making them less easy to include in the category of self-commendation.

Suetonius reports only 5 direct commendation pronouncements, of which 3 emanated from Claudius. One of the others comes at the end of the story of Nero's death, which includes several pronouncements. "Now he encouraged Sporus to begin to lament and beat his breasts; now he begged that someone help him by example to seize death; meanwhile he complained about his own slowness in these words: 'I am living disgracefully and basely [in Latin] --it does not become Nero, it does not--it is necessary to be resolute in such affairs--come, rouse yourself [in Greek].' And now horsemen were approaching with orders to bring him back alive. As he perceived their approach, he said in fear: 'The thunder of swift-footed horses is beating against my ears' [*Iliad* 10.535] and drove a dagger into his throat with the help of his secretary Epaphroditus, a *libellis*. And to a centurion who broke in at this point and, placing a cloak on his wound, pretended that he had come to help, Nero replied no more than: 'Too late' and 'This is loyalty' " (*Nero* 49.3-4). Nero's first pronouncement is self-correction; the second is one of many sayings quoting a line of Homer or another poet. The final saying is a direct commendation, but ironic from the viewpoint of the reader. Suetonius' imperial biographies contain no indirect commendations, leaving a total of only 5 commendations of others.

There is one other pronouncement that I have classified as a direct defense. Augustus "gave legal judgments not only with the greatest diligence, but also with leniency, as shown by the fact that, to keep a defendant clearly guilty of parricide from being sewn up in the sack,[9] because only those who confessed suffered this punishment, he is said to have asked: 'Surely you did not kill your father?' " (*Aug*. 33.1).

---

[9]The traditional punishment for parricides was to be sewn up in a sack along with a cock, a dog, a snake, and a monkey, and then be thrown into a river or the sea.

The final subclass is the laudation, in which I have included predictions of future greatness. Of the 5 laudations, 3 are predictions of this kind. Included in the biography of Galba is a prediction of Augustus. "It is established that when Galba came as a boy to pay his respects to Augustus, Augustus pinched his cheek and said, 'Child, you also will have a nibble at this power of mine' " (*Galba* 4.1). This and the other two predictions do not actually praise the main character, but since they are affirmative pronouncements by a second party about the main character, I have classified them with laudations, to which they are related.

So far I have accounted for 186 of 199 pronouncements in this classification scheme. The remaining 13 are hybrids, i.e., pronouncements which could be put into more than one category. For example, Suetonius claims that among his other mad pursuits Gaius "even considered destroying the poems of Homer, asking why this should not be permitted to him when it was permitted to Plato who had thrown Homer out of the state which he established" (*Gaius* 34.2). This saying seems to me to be a combination of indirect correction of Homer and self-commendation insofar as Gaius placed himself in a class with Plato.

Suetonius' Use and Manipulation of Story Types

Having classified the pronouncement stories, we can now move on to examine how certain types of stories correspond to character types and how Suetonius manipulates stories to produce negative characterizations. In addressing the first question, I began by looking at which emperors appear most prominently in which class of story.

Titus was known as a benevolent and generous emperor whose rule did not last long enough for negative traits to emerge. Titus was sufficiently conscious of his own behavior that he was able to criticize himself, and so 2 of the 7 self-correction pronouncements were from Titus (including the "I have lost a day" story related above). In both cases what is self-correction from the perspective of Titus turns out to be a commendation in the eyes of the reader because both sayings require the assumption that Titus was usually generous. Titus is also well-represented in the group of self-commendation stories, along with the arrogant Gaius, but Titus' pronouncements in this class are really self-exhortations, unlike Gaius'. The harmony enjoyed under Titus is reflected in the complete lack of direct or indirect correction stories attributed to him--the only emperor who is not credited with a direct correction. There is one possible exception. When two patricians were said to be conspiring against Titus, he ostentatiously pardoned them. "It is even said that, after checking their horoscope, Titus confirmed that danger threatened both, but at some other time and from someone else, as turned out to be the case" (*Titus* 9.2). It is not clear whether this pronouncement is direct or indirect, and though the pronouncement is adverse, the fact that the harm does not come from Titus (contrary to expectation) serves to highlight his benevolence.

In sharp contrast to Titus, Tiberius, Gaius, Nero and even Augustus early in his rule were known for their cruelty, and all are well represented in direct and indirect correction stories (48 of the 79 stories in these two subclasses concern these four emperors). Tiberius was harsh, but at least a man of strong character and courage--qualities reflected in the fact that most of his correction pronouncements are direct (11 of 14). Gaius, on the other hand, was maniacally cruel with no strength of character, and so did not usually confront the party of whom he was critical (7 of his 9 correction pronouncements are indirect). Another facet of Gaius' unbalanced character was his megalomania, depicted in the large number of self-commendation stories attributed to him (6--twice as many as attributed to any other emperor). The strange tone of some of these contributes to the picture of mental imbalance. "And indeed at night he constantly used to invite into his embrace and bed the full and gleaming moon, and by day indeed he used to talk secretly with Capitoline Jupiter, now whispering and offering his ear in turn, now speaking more clearly and not without threats. For this saying was heard from him in a threatening tone: 'Either lift me or I will lift you.' " (*Gaius* 22.4). This line was taken from Homer's wrestling match between Ajax and Odysseus (*Iliad* 23.724).

The dissent-objection stories in Suetonius do not display the wisdom of the emperors, but their wit or self-restraint. Most of this kind of story were told about Vespasian (4 of 7), who was noted for both of these qualities. "When he met Demetrius the Cynic on a journey after having condemned him to exile and Demetrius deigned neither to rise for nor to greet the emperor, even barking out some insult, Vespasian thought it sufficient to call him 'cur' " (*Vesp.* 13). This story gains "point" in the context of the emperor's absolute power: the fact that Vespasian issued a saying (and that of only one word) rather than an order for execution makes the story noteworthy for the restraint exhibited. The content of the saying is secondary. (This was also true of the Morbovia story cited above in which Suetonius does not bother to quote Vespasian's words.)

Nearly half of the dissent-rebuff stories (9 of 20) were told of two rulers, Julius Caesar and Claudius, but they are prominent in this group for different reasons. Most of Julius Caesar's life was passed during the Republic, when outrageous abuse of political opponents was taken for granted. Suetonius reports two Ciceronian pronouncements abusing Caesar, "and lest anyone have any doubt at all that Caesar suffered a reputation for vice and adultery, the elder Curio in a speech calls him 'a man for all women and a woman for all men' " (*Iul.* 52.3). It is perhaps not to Suetonius' credit that he takes such pronouncements so seriously and does not understand them as a part of the routine rhetoric of late Republic politics.[10]

Political invective was generally suppressed under the emperors, but Claudius' reputation as a buffoon nevertheless invited dissent-rebuff stories. We are told that Claudius' mother Antonia used to refer to dull-witted people as "more stupid than her son Claudius" (*Claud.* 3.2). Later in life Claudius "allowed his freedmen to acquire and seize so much wealth that, when he was once complaining about the poverty of the imperial treasury, it was said with good reason that it would overflow with money if he should be taken into partnership by his two freedmen" (*Claud.* 28). Here, in contrast to the rebuffs of Caesar, the criticism of the emperor is anonymous—the safest kind.

Claudius is also prominent in the small group of direct commendation stories, being the main character in 3 of the 5. In all 3 Claudius is represented as either incompetent or the kindly old fool (*Claud.* 40.2, 43; *Otho* 1.3). The fact that there are so few direct commendations and that most of those were intended as negative comment on the speaker suggests that generosity in the praise of others was not a highly valued imperial quality or, alternatively, that such pronouncements did not make for rhetorically interesting stories.

Having been brought up on *exempla* and *chreia*, the educated Roman reader must have expected pronouncement stories to end with sayings notable for their wisdom or cleverness. When pronouncement stories violated that expectation, Suetonius surely anticipated his readers would take note and form their ideas of the emperor's character accordingly. We noted above that Vespasian was known for his quick wit and hence is well represented in direct correction and dissent-objection stories of the traditional kind. In contrast, Claudius, known for his dullness, fails in these exchanges. "When he was about to drain the Fucine lake, he first held a naval battle show. But when the combatants shouted, 'Hail emperor, those who are going to die salute you,' and Claudius replied, 'Or not,' no one would fight after this remark on the ground that a pardon had been granted. After hesitating over whether to destroy all of them by fire and sword, he finally jumped up from his seat and, running around the lake shore with some unseemly tottering, he forced them into battle partly by threat and partly by encouragement" (*Claud.* 21.6). Claudius' bungling is displayed, as what begins as a direct correction story drags out because not even humble combatants are impressed by the authority of Claudius.

---

[10]Ronald Syme, *The Roman Revolution* (Oxford: Clarendon, 1939) 149-61.

It seems to me that Claudius' reply in the above story is really not so bad, but in other stories his pronouncements are flat or ridiculous. "When a debate concerning butchers and wine-sellers was going on in the Senate, Claudius cried out: 'I ask you, who can live without a snack?' And then he described the abundance of the old taverns where even he was once accustomed to seek wine" (*Claud.* 40.1). Suetonius reports this pronouncement, which displays neither the dignity nor the wit expected of an emperor, to illustrate Claudius' carelessness in speaking. In a group of stories about Claudius' hearing of legal cases, Suetonius writes: "In a certain case it is believed that Claudius read out from a tablet written ahead of time his judgment that he decided in favor of those who had told the truth" (*Claud.* 15.3). These and other inane pronouncements must have made a stronger impression on a Roman reader, educated to appreciate clever use of language, than on a reader today.

If Claudius' sayings make a point because they are flat or silly, many of Gaius' are "well-aimed" because they show him to be mad and/or vicious. Several pronouncements are put in the mouth of Gaius during his strange expedition to Gaul. When his army had been drawn up at the seashore and "no one knew or had any idea as to what he was about to undertake, he ordered the troops to gather seashells and to fill their helmets and the folds of their clothing, calling the shells 'spoils of Ocean owed to the Capitoline and Palatine' " (*Gaius* 46). Gaius' actions are mad and his pronouncement, though cast in imaginative language, shows that his imagination is working outside the bounds of normal human reason. At the end of the expedition Gaius "announced a donative for each soldier of 100 denarii, and, as if exceeding every standard of liberality, he said: 'Go away happy, go away rich' " (*Gaius* 46). The language of the pronouncement was intended to have a poetic touch, but in fact serves to show the reader that Gaius had lost touch with reality (donatives many times greater had been paid by previous rulers).

Other pronouncements of Gaius with nice rhetorical "pointing" show that this is the cleverness of a cruel tyrant. "When an ex-praetor from his retirement in Anticyra where he had gone for his health asked too often for an extension of his leave, Gaius ordered that he be killed and added that the letting of blood was necessary for a man whom hellebore did not help for so long" (*Gaius* 29.2). The pronouncement is a wicked perversion of an aphoristic description. In one of his most famous sayings Gaius, "angry at the mob for showing favor to a side against his own preference, shouted out: 'Would that the Roman people had one neck' " (*Gaius* 30.2). Again, the use of language here is clever, but rather than exhibiting wisdom, reveals a megalomaniacal cruelty.

Gaius and Claudius are not the only emperors of whom Suetonius tells unconventional pronouncement stories, but their pronouncements regularly shock or violate the audience's expectation of sayings that are clever or wise.

My aims in this paper have been modest: to show the pervasiveness of pronouncements in Suetonius' biographies, to offer an indication of the kinds of stories recounted and a brief glimpse at the literary use made of them. Much more remains to be done. A rhetorical analysis of the sayings could be profitably undertaken, as well as a more thorough consideration of Suetonius' place in the history of the use of pronouncement stories in the Greco-Roman tradition. Is it merely coincidence that Suetonius' biographies, the first extant in Latin to incorporate pronouncement stories on a large scale, were written in the early second century after Christ, a generation after Quintilian's and Theon's discussions of *chreiai* in education? Finally, more attention needs to be given to the relation between pronouncement stories and the old Roman tradition of inculcating *exempla* of famous men in their children.

THE SALVATION OF THE JEWS IN LUKE-ACTS

Jack T. Sanders
University of Oregon

What is the theological position of the author of Luke-Acts regarding the salvation of the Jews? Can Jews be saved or not? The question is of course most acute regarding the author's opinion of the possibilities that exist at the conclusion of the Book of Acts. Can Jews be saved after Paul's quotation of the Isaiah passage to his Roman Jewish hearers and his interpretation of that passage, as described in Acts 28:23-28? But the question must also be posed for the period covered by Luke-Acts. To what degree does the author intend to describe a "mission to Israel" in his two volumes? The standard view of scholarship on the subject is that (in the theology of the author of Luke-Acts), after the end of Acts, Jews no longer have the opportunity to accept the gospel, because they have so completely rejected it during the period covered by Luke-Acts. Thus Jacob Jervell refers to "the common opinion that Luke describes the Jews as a whole as rejecting the gospel."[1] In support of Jervell's assessment, one may refer to the two most important commentaries on Acts, those of Loisy and of Haenchen, as well as to the important monograph study by Conzelmann, *Die Mitte der Zeit;* although the views of these authors on the subject, as we shall see, are not entirely uniform.

In his study of the theology of Luke-Acts, Conzelmann explained, regarding the "hope of Israel" (Acts 1:6; 28:20), that "the emphatic passage, 28:28 . . . , shows who now shares in this hope: salvation is passing to the Gentiles." Thus one "can see quite clearly how Luke thinks of the Christians, according to plan, taking over the privileges of the Jews as one epoch is succeeded by the next."[2] It is the change of epochs that is significant; the Jews have had their *last* chance; the gospel now goes *from* the Jews *to* the Gentiles. Conzelmann distinguished, however, between "the Jews" and the individual Jew. Thus, while "the Jews" oppose Christianity, "for the individual the way of salvation is open, now as always. The polemic is at the same time a call to repentance."[3] Loisy, of course, had already noted the shift of the gospel from the Jews to the Gentiles at the end of Acts, and he explained that Christianity was, for the author (that is to say, for the "redactor" in Loisy's understanding) of Acts, "if one dare say it, the true Jewish religion. It is only that the Jews, by an inconceivable blindness,[fully attested elsewhere in Acts], have repulsed God's gift." But the gospel had *first* to be offered to them: It is a part of the function of the concluding part of Acts for the "redactor" to "render the position believable that the proposal of the gospel had not been made to the pagans before having been made to the Jews."[4] Haenchen, then, takes essentially the same position as Conzelmann. Thus he refers to "the transfer of the saving proclamation from the Jews to the Gentiles,"[5] and he tenders the explanation of the conclusion of Acts that

---

[1]J. Jervell, *Luke and the People of God* (Minneapolis: Augsburg, 1972) 44.

[2]H. Conzelmann, *The Theology of St. Luke* (New York: Harpers, 1960) 163; cf. also pp. 145, 160, 212, and also Conzelmann's statement in his commentary on Acts that, after the conclusion of Acts, "Luke no longer considers that there is any success of the Christian mission among 'the Jews' " (Conzelmann, *Die Apostelgeschichte* [HNT 7; Tübingen: Mohr (Siebeck), 1963] 149). A somewhat similar interpretation is given by J. Gnilka, *Die Verstockung Israels. Isaias 6,9-10 in der Theologie der Synoptiker* (SANT 3; Munich: Kösel, 1961) 132, who views Jesus' earthly ministry in Luke as a "last grace period" for the Jews.

[3]Conzelmann, *Theology,* 145; also Gnilka, *Verstockung,* 146.

[4]A. Loisy, *Les Acts des Apôtres* (Paris: Nourry, 1920) 939.

[5]E. Haenchen, *Die Apostelgeschichte* (MeyerK 3; 7th ed.; Göttingen: Vandenhoeck & Ruprecht, 1977) 691-92. Cf. also Haenchen, "The Book of Acts as Source Material for the History of Early Christianity," *Studies in Luke-Acts* (ed. L. E. Keck and J. L. Martyn; Philadelphia: Fortress, 1980) 259-65.

the author was bringing two purposes together, one to show that the gospel was convincing (thus some of the Jewish audience were "persuaded" or "convinced" but not converted, just as the Pharisees in Acts 23:7-10 spoke on Paul's behalf but did not become Christians) and the other to show that the period of Jewish salvation was past and that salvation henceforth would be offered only to Gentiles (thus Paul's citation and interpretation of the Isaiah passage).[6] Loisy and Haenchen do not, however, think of the continued possibility of the salvation of individual Jews.[7]

If Jervell could cite the views thus far sketched, however, as a "common opinion," it was his own persuasion that such common opinion was in large part mistaken and that, in fact, "Luke does not describe a Jewish people who, as a whole, reject the early Christian message, and in which the believing Jews are exceptions." Acts contains, indeed, "numerous references to mass conversions of Jews."[8] On the other side of the coin, Gentiles do not begin to be saved only after a Jewish rejection of the gospel; rather, "from the beginning of the mission it is certain that according to Scripture and in agreement with the missionary command, the Gentiles have a share in salvation."[9] It is thus clear that Jervell rejects the notion that, in the development of the early church, salvation is offered first to the Jews and then to the Gentiles. There exists no first period during which the gospel is offered to the Jews alone, which is then followed by a second period of turning to the Gentiles; rather, from first until last, some Jews accept the gospel and others reject it. Thus, in the early part of Acts, the Sadducees reject the gospel, and in the period of the Gentile mission, some diaspora Jews convert while others do not, just as in the closing scene of Acts.[10] Rather than seeing a division in Acts between Jew and Gentile, therefore, Jervell finds a division between "obdurate" Israel and "repentant (i.e., Christian)" Israel.[11] This renewed Israel is then composed of both Jews and Gentiles--that is, those who accept the gospel. "The addition of Gentiles is part of the restoration of Israel."[12] This understanding of Acts leads Jervell to conclude that the author of Luke-Acts gives a theological explanation for the fact that the church of his own day is Gentile while a non-Christian Judaism still exists. That theological solution is that the Apostles have already offered the gospel to all the Jews who would

---

[6]Haenchen, *Apostelgeschichte*, 697.

[7]Cf. Haenchen, "Source Material," 278: "Luke has written the Jews off."

[8]Jervell, *People of God*, 42.

[9]Ibid., 43.

[10]Ibid., 48.

[11]Ibid., 49. This position is not so different from that of Conzelmann, who refers to "penitent" and "impenitent." This division among the Jews allows Luke a "sharpness of polemic" against them "but at the same time avoids a summary Christian anti-Semitism" (Conzelmann, *Theology*, 146). This division could be seen as early as the distinguishing of "two distinct groups" in the response to John's baptism (ibid., 21); cf. also p. 190: "the true or the false Israel." The position was also shared by A. Harnack, *The Acts of the Apostles* (New Testament Studies 3; New York: Putnam's, 1909) 286-87 and G. W. H. Lampe, *St. Luke and the Church of Jerusalem* (Univ. of London: Athlone, 1969) 9-10, both of whom saw the later Apologists as taking the position which Jervell now describes as the "common" one, and both of whom saw Luke as half way between Paul and that position. Thus Lampe, ibid., 9, refers to "two 'successions' in Israel." Gnilka, *Verstockung*, 143, also sees the Jewish rejection of the gospel as an opting out of Israel. On p. 151 he endorses Conzelmann's position and sees Luke as attempting to distinguish Church from Israel without hurting the Jews: It is the leaders and those who follow them who are at fault. With Conzelmann, however, he also emphasizes the epochal plan of Luke-Acts and thus sees the final position of Luke-Acts as being that the Jews have rejected their own proper salvation; cf. ibid., 153.

[12]Jervell, *People of God*, 60. F. Menezes, "The Mission of Jesus according to Lk 4:16-30," *Bible Bhashyam* 6 (1980) 258, comes to the same conclusion.

accept. "How can the church," he asks, attempting to state Luke's problem, "justify its neglect of the Jewish mission while it preaches the Messiah of Israel?" Luke's answer, according to Jervell, is that the Apostles "have gathered the repentant Israel and have given to Gentiles a share in the salvation that comes from the repentant people of God."[13] It is this theological position, according to Jervell, which explains the role of the Jews in Luke-Acts, and not the epochal scheme proposed by Loisy, Conzelmann, and others.[14] *After the conclusion of Acts,* however, there is no need for any further attempt to convert Jews, since "there can be no talk about a renewed mission to Jews without . . . calling into question the right of Gentiles to the promises."[15]

A second recent work, Eric Franklin's *Christ the Lord,*[16] has also sought to show the incorrectness of the epochal explanation of Jewish salvation and rejection in Luke-Acts and to support the explanation that salvation of Jews continues throughout, with only those Jews who reject the gospel being rejected. While Franklin is more willing than Jervell to agree that the Jews as a whole reject the gospel,[17] nevertheless he goes beyond Jervell in proposing that, even after the conclusion of Acts, Jews may still be saved. "The final episode at Rome," he argues, "is to be understood as a justification of Christianity in spite of its refusal by the Jews rather than as a turning aside from them"; and he adds, "Paul's work among the Jews at Rome is not a total failure ([Acts] 28:24)."[18] On the issue of whether the author of Luke-Acts intends to describe an epoch of the offering of the gospel to the Jews, after which they no longer have an opportunity to accept it, Franklin is quite clear. "Christianity" at the end of Acts "is still put forward as the 'hope of Israel' (28:20)"; and he understands Paul's statement in 28:28 that the gospel will henceforth go to the Gentiles as "less a programme for the future than a justification of what has happened" in the course of the Gentile mission described in Acts.[19]

It is thus clear that an answer to the question regarding the salvation of the Jews in Luke-Acts hangs on the interpretation of the closing verses of Acts and also on the acceptance or rejection of Loisy's and Conzelmann's epochal understanding of the work.

---

[13]Jervell, *People of God,* 68. A similar position is maintained by C. Burchard, *Der dreizehnte Zeuge. Traditions- und kompositionsgeschichtliche Untersuchungen zu Lukas' Darstellung der Frühzeit des Paulus* (FRLANT 103; Göttingen: Vandenhoeck & Ruprecht, 1970) 113-77; on p. 176 he holds that, "in Luke's sense [the Gentile church] is an ecumenical church without Jews."

[14]Cf. also F. Mussner, "Wohnung Gottes und Menschensohn nach der Stephanusperikope (Apg 6,8-8,2)," *Jesus und der Menschensohn. Für Anton Vögtle* (ed. R. Pesch, et al.; Freiburg, et al.: Herder, 1975) 291-92. Jervell's position is supported by D. L. Tiede, *Prophecy and History in Luke-Acts* (Philadelphia: Fortress, 1980) 10: "It is the 'unpersuaded' or 'unbelieving' Jews (14:4; 28:24) . . . who generate a division among the 'Jews' which is displayed before the Gentiles (cf. 14:4; 23:7)." Tiede goes even farther than Jervell in seeking to counteract the notion that the author of Luke-Acts himself harbored some kind of hostility toward Jews by proposing that the author was himself, in fact, some kind of Jew ("at home in the synagogue," ibid., 8), although Tiede leaves open the possibility that the author may have been in some manner a Gentile adherent of Judaism (ibid., 10).

[15]Jervell, *People of God,* 69.

[16]E. Franklin, *Christ the Lord. A Study in the Purpose and Theology of Luke-Acts* (Philadelphia: Westminster, 1975).

[17]Ibid., 99-108.

[18]Ibid., 114. S. Sandmel, *Anti-Semitism in the New Testament?* (Philadelphia: Fortress, 1978) 73, also refers to "a residual concern in Luke to win Jews to Christianity"; but he bases this judgment on Luke's "pity" for the Jews, which turns out to be rather short-lived; cf. further below.

[19]Franklin, *Christ the Lord,* 115.

Can any further clarity on these points be achieved? We begin with the former issue, the concluding scene of the Book of Acts.

What is the point of Paul's citation of Isa 6:9-10 LXX to his Roman Jewish hearers in Acts 28:26-27 and of his interpretation thereof in v. 28: "This salvation of God has been sent to the Gentiles; they will listen"? In order to understand this concluding statement of Paul's in Acts, it is necessary first of all to recall that it is not an isolated statement, but that it is the third in a chain of similar statements. In Acts 13:46, after a mixed reaction to his preaching of the gospel to the Jews in Antioch of Pisidia, Paul announces to them, "Since you thrust it from you and judge yourselves unworthy of eternal life, behold, we turn to the Gentiles"; and, in Acts 18:6, after opposition to the gospel develops in the synagogue in Corinth, Paul declares, "From now on I will go to the Gentiles," and he moves next door. In all these cases Paul has been "persuading" Jews,[20] but it is not entirely clear of what; and it is not certain that he has been converting them. If the "standard" position regarding Luke's attitude toward the salvation of the Jews is correct, then the "persuasion" of these three accounts does not necessarily refer to conversion, but, even if this "persuasion" does refer to conversion, we have in any case a reiteration or an ascending emphasis on Jewish rejection of the gospel and on the exclusion of the Jews from salvation. If Jervell and Franklin are correct, however, then the persuasion certainly does refer to conversion, and the three occurrences of the announcement of turning to the Gentiles do not refer to the exclusion of the Jews but rather show that, in spite of the perceived general opposition of Jews to the gospel, still, where it is preached, some Jews convert.

Haenchen remarks regarding Acts 28:28, "The transfer of the saving proclamation from the Jews to the Gentiles is thereby established here (as in 13:48; 18:6)."[21] Jervell, however, finds that Acts shows throughout how the preaching of the gospel divides the Jews into two groups, those who believe and those who reject, and this is how he understands the closing scene in Acts. "Once more we find the familiar picture of some believing, others unbelieving";[22] and he supports his observation with this reasoning: "If it is really Luke's intention to describe the complete rejection of the gospel on the part of the Jews, then it is very strange that he seems to emphasize clearly the division among the Jews and appears to speak about the unbelief of only a portion of the Roman Jewish community."[23] Franklin's position is less a direct opposition to the "standard" opinion about Jewish rejection in Acts than is Jervell's--he does, as noted above, agree that the Jewish rejection of the gospel in Acts is total--nevertheless he affirms that "Paul's work among the Jews at Rome is not a total failure (28:24). . . . Christianity is still put forward as the 'hope of Israel' (28:20), a designation that suggests that even now the Jews are unlikely to be abandoned. . . . Paul's final statement is not a rejection of

---

[20]Acts 13:43: [Παῦλος καὶ Βαρναβᾶς] ἔπειθον [τοὺς Ἰουδαίους] προσμένειν τῇ χάριτι τοῦ θεοῦ; Acts 18:4: [Παῦλος] ἔπειθεν τε Ἰουδαίους καὶ Ἕλληνας; Acts 28:24: οἱ μὲν [τῶν Ἰουδαίων] ἐπείθοντο τοῖς λεγομένοις [ὑπὸ Παύλου].

[21]Haenchen, *Apostelgeschichte*, 691-92. R. B. Rackham, *The Acts of the Apostles. An Exposition* (London: Methuen, 1901) 220, emphasizes that the Apostles turn to the Gentiles only when the Jews push them to it. L. Cerfaux and J. Dupont, *Les Actes des Apôtres* (La Sainte Bible; Paris: Editions du Cerf, 1964) 128, refer in this regard to "*un fil conducteur.*" Similarly also Harnack, *Acts*, 128-29. Cf. further Conzelmann, *Apostelgeschichte*, 149 and E. Preuschen, *Die Apostelgeschichte* (HNT 4/1; Tübingen: Mohr [Siebeck], 1912) 86.

[22]Jervell, *People of God*, 63; cf. his entire chapter, "The Divided People of God," ibid., 41-74. A. George, "Israël dans l'oeuvre de Luc," *RB* 75 (1968) 514-15, also considers the instances of persuasion to be accounts of conversion.

[23]Jervell, *People of God*, 63.

the Jews."[24]   Obviously it cannot be both ways.   We turn therefore to a further examination of the "persuasion" of the Jews.

Of the numerous places in Acts where the word πείθω occurs,[25] only in the three accounts of Paul's turning to the Gentiles (13:43; 18:4; and 28:23-24) and in 17:4 and 19:26 may this "persuasion" be understood to refer to conversion to Christianity.   The occurrence in 17:4 sheds little light on the precise meaning of the three accounts that include announcements of turning to the Gentiles, since the usage in 17:4 is exactly the same as in the three other passages: It is Jews who are persuaded, but this persuasion is followed immediately by a Jewish attack on Paul.   The instance that most likely involves the meaning "conversion" for "persuasion" is 19:26, where Demetrius charges that Paul has "persuaded and turned away a considerable company of people," so that they are no longer willing to consider idols gods.   Even here, however, the meaning of "conversion" for "persuasion" is not crystal clear, since the author of Luke-Acts may mean only to have Demetrius say that Paul has persuaded people not to believe in idols, not that he has converted them to Christianity.

Luke's normal word for conversion is "belief," often connected with an account or mention of baptism.[26]   Thus the first conversions in Acts, after Peter's first sermon, are characterized by baptism (2:41), after which it is said that "all who believed were together"; or Acts 14:1 refers to Jews and Greeks at Iconium who "believed"; and the reference to Jewish Christians in 21:20 (to which we must return below) is to "those who have believed."   It is thus striking and surely not accidental that just following both 13:46 and 18:6 we find accounts of such belief/conversion.   In 13:48 we read that "as many [of the Gentiles] as were ordained to eternal life believed," and 18:8 relates how "Crispus . . . believed in the Lord . . . ; and many of the Corinthians . . . believed and were baptized."   In Acts 13:44-49, therefore, and in 18:4-8 we have the pattern: *persuasion* of Jewish hearers, opposition on the part of Jews to the gospel, announcement of turning to Gentiles, belief (Gentile and, in chapter 18, Jewish) and baptism.[27]   The fact that, in both cases, belief/conversion is mentioned later, after the announcement of turning to the Gentiles, supports the contention that the earlier "persuasion" is not conversion. Acts 28:23-28 then begins the pattern and follows it through exactly up to the point at which the turning to the Gentiles is announced.   This announcement is more elaborate here than in the two previous occurrences of the pattern, but the pattern breaks off at this point.   The final turning has been announced; no belief is mentioned.   When one adds to these observations Dibelius' notice that the three announcements of the turning to the

---

[24]Franklin, *Christ the Lord*, 114-15.

[25]On πείθω and πιστεύω in Luke-Acts, cf. H. J. Hauser, *Strukturen der Abschlusserzählung der Apostelgeschichte (Apg 28,16-31)* (AnBib 86; Rome: Pontificio Instituto Biblico, 1979) 62-66.

[26]Cf. the similar explanation given by U. Wilckens, *Die Missionsreden der Apostelgeschichte* (WMANT 5; 2d ed.; Neukirchen-Vluyn: Neukirchener Verlag des Erziehungsvereins, 1963) 182-83.   Cf. also Conzelmann, *Theology*, 229 and S. Brown, *Apostasy and Perseverance in the Theology of Luke* (AnBib 36; Rome: Pontifical Biblical Institute, 1969) 46-47.

[27]Loisy, *Actes*, 937, and Haenchen, *Apostelgeschichte*, 691, have seen this point correctly.   Even E. Jacquier, *Les Actes des Apôtres* (EBibl 2d ed.; Paris: Gabalda, 1926), whose commentary was intended to present a properly Catholic interpretation of Acts after that of the heretic Loisy, admits (p. 758) that "it does not seem that their conviction was sufficient to lead them to faith."   It is thus mistaken for Wilson, Conzelmann, and others to think that Acts 28:24 refers to conversion of some of the Jews; cf. the discussion in S. G. Wilson, *The Gentiles and the Gentile Mission in Luke-Acts* (SNTSMS 23; Cambridge: University Press, 1973) 226 n. 1.   Cf. further Loisy, *Actes*, 523.   F. Stagg, *The Book of Acts.   The Early Struggle for an Unhindered Gospel* (Nashville: Broadman, 1955) 265, also thinks that the persuasion of these accounts is conversion.

Gentiles occur, respectively, in Asia Minor, on the Greek mainland, and in Rome[28]--thus in all the major geographical areas of Paul's missionary activity--then one should see that the author of Luke-Acts has not set up a pattern that implies continued missionary activity among the Jews after the conclusion of Acts; rather, he has emphasized the thoroughness of the mission to the Jews and the thoroughness of their rejection of the gospel. J. Gnilka correctly observes that "Luke . . . gains the possibility, by this presentational means, of keeping the Jewish obduracy all the more impressively before the eyes of the reader; and thus the consequences that follow therefrom become weightier."[29] Acts 28:25-28 is Luke's final judgement on the Jews, after which it would be foolish, in Luke's opinion, to waste any further missionary effort on them.[30] The correctness of this assessment will be borne out further in the following observations.

It is usually not noticed that, aside from the questionable references to Jewish "persuasion" under Paul's preaching, there is precious little Jewish conversion to Christianity in the diaspora, according to Acts. In 14:1 "a great crowd of Jews and also of Greeks[at Iconium] believed"; in 17:11-12 the Jews at Beroea "received the word with all eagerness. . . . Many of them therefore believed"; and, as mentioned previously, Crispus and his household believed in Corinth (18:8). There are no other clear references to Jewish conversion to Christianity in the context of the Gentile mission in Acts! Even if one were to add the four cases of persuasion, still these seven accounts of Jewish conversion would be meagre. Surely the author of Acts intends to show that the conversion of Jews to Christianity as a result of Paul's mission was an oddity, and that the normal response was one of open hostility.[31] This very disappointing result of the Gentile mission in gaining Jewish converts to Christianity, as sketched by the author of Luke-Acts, would certainly justify Paul's final speech, the meaning of which is that *it is inherent in being Jewish to be incapable of understanding* (especially the gospel), and that God therefore sends his missionaries to the Gentiles, who *are* capable of understanding.[32]

Franklin recognizes this Lucan theme, even though Jervell does not, and therefore gives over a considerable amount of space to the discussion of it, especially in terms of Stephen's speech at his martyrdom.[33] Franklin sees that "the main point of the speech is to show that the hostility of the Jews to the Christian proclamation is of one piece with

---

[28]M. Dibelius, *Aufsätze zur Apostelgeschichte* (FRLANT N. F. 42; 4th ed., ed. H. Greeven; Göttingen: Vandenhoeck & Ruprecht, 1961) 129. Cf. also Haenchen, *Apostelgeschichte*, 691-92; Gnilka, *Verstockung*, 146; Wilson, *Gentiles*, 226.

[29]Gnilka, *Verstockung*, 147.

[30]That this is Luke's intention has also been correctly seen by Overbeck (W. M. L. DeWette, *Kurze Erklärung der Apostelgeschichte* [4th ed. revised by R. Overbeck; Leipzig: Hirzel, 1870]) 480-81 and by Loisy, *Actes*, 938-39. Cf. further R. P. C. Hanson, *The Acts in the Revised Standard Version with Introduction and Commentary* (Oxford: Clarendon Press, 1967) 255: Acts 28:28 is "a fine summary, in a sentence, of the main message of Acts."

[31]So also Sandmel, *Anti-Semitism*, 98-99; J. Weiss, *Earliest Christianity* (New York: Harper, 1937) 665. The statement of Tiede, *Prophecy and History*, 10, that "Luke was eager to document the success of Christian preaching among the Jews in the face of great opposition" is true only of Acts 1-6, not of the successive phase(s) of the Christian mission.

[32]Cf. also Weiss, *Earliest Christianity*, 666. It is not that--as Hauser, *Apostelgeschichte*, 69, thinks--it is the nature of Jews to disagree, but that it is their nature to oppose the gospel. It is Hauser's lack of clarity regarding the use of πείθω in Acts (cf. above, n. 24) that clouds his vision here.

[33]Franklin, *Christ the Lord*, 99-108. Jervell does not discuss Stephen's speech except to characterize it as marking the end of the missionary effort of the twelve in Jerusalem (*People of God*, 77).

the hostility to the purposes of God which is characteristic of their history."[34] The climax of this long harangue--which the author, of course, places on the lips of Stephen[35]--is reached in 7:51: "You always resist the Holy Spirit. As your fathers did, so do you." It is inherent, endemic in the Jewish people to behave so, and it was therefore no surprise that they killed the "Righteous One," since they had always persecuted and killed all the prophets (v. 52--hardly a historically accurate description of the fate of prophets in ancient Israel).[36]

This hostility of the Jewish people to the purposes of God, so vehemently denounced here and portrayed ad nauseam throughout the rest of Acts right up to the concluding scene, can occasionally be called ignorance. Peter, in his second sermon, tells his hearers that he knows that they acted "according to ignorance" in killing Christ, wherefore they now have the opportunity to repent (Acts 3:17, 19);[37] and Paul, in his first missionary sermon, explains that the Jerusalemites "were ignorant of [Christ] and of the voices of the prophets which are read every Sabbath" (Acts 13:27). There can be little doubt that the author of Luke-Acts intended these formulations to be similar.[38] Both mention both the people generally (in Peter's speech "you," in Paul's "those dwelling in Jeruslam") and also archontes, and these are the only places in Acts where ignorance is mentioned, except for Paul's sermon at Athens, where he first (Acts 17:23) picks up on the dedication Agnōstō Theō and then (v. 30) explains that God had "overlooked the time of ignorance" in offering salvation on the occasion of Paul's visit to the city. It appears, therefore, that, according to the author of Luke-Acts, God is willing to overlook ignorance regarding himself and his plan of salvation, even when that ignorance leads to the

---

[34]Franklin, Christ the Lord, 103. So also N. A. Dahl, "The Story of Abraham in Luke-Acts," Studies in Luke-Acts (see n. 5) 148: "Stephen's own history is the continuation of that history which began by God's revelation to Abraham; it leads to the preaching in Samaria and beyond." Thus Dahl correctly sees the Stephen episode as the main turning point in Acts.

[35]The literature on the speeches in Acts and on the Stephen episode is enormous and cannot all be surveyed here. One should note particularly Wilckens, Missionsreden (who does not, however, discuss the Stephen speech); Haenchen, Apostelgeschichte, 265-81; J. Bihler, "Der Stephanusbericht (Apg 6,8-15 und 7,54-8,2)," BZ N. F. 3 (1959) 252-70; J. Zmijewski, Die Eschatologiereden des Lukas-Evangeliums (BBB 40; Bonn: Hanstein, 1972); C. H. Talbert, Literary Patterns, Theological Themes, and the Genre of Luke-Acts (SBLMS 20; Missoula: SBL, 1974) 96-97; and esp. R. Pesch, Die Vision des Stephanus. Apg 7,55-56 im Rahmen der Apostelgeschichte (SBS 12; Stuttgart: Katholisches Bibelwerk, s.d.) 32, 38-39.

[36]The theme is so pronounced that nearly all commentators have seen it; cf. esp. Overbeck (DeWette), Apostelgeschichte, 110, and Loisy, Actes, 345-47. E. Kränkl, Jesus der Knecht Gottes (Regensburg: Pustet, 1972) 112, refers to Jewish guilt as a "roter Faden" running through the speech. Cf. Bihler, "Stephanusbericht," 266, 270; Overbeck (DeWette), Apostelgeschichte, 94. Gnilka, Verstockung, 144-45, also sees that it is here the Jews' own fault that salvation goes over from them to the Gentiles. Haenchen, "Judentum und Christentum in der Apostelgeschichte," ZNW 54 (1963) 168, notes that there "the Jews had not ever even been the people of God."

[37]Wilckens, Missionsreden, 98, observes that the early speeches in Acts must combine the "Jesus Kerygma," dealing with Jesus' death, with "the call to repentance"; but he is also keenly aware of the anti-Jewish polemic in Acts: "Whereas the passion tradition simply established . . . human dealing with the Son of man, the statements of the sermons [in Acts] have throughout a sharply accusatory note" (ibid., 119, emphasis his). Gnilka, Verstockung, 141, observes that Jewish ignorance excuses the Jews but does not acquit them.

[38]Cf. further Wilckens, Missionsreden, 134.

murder of Christ himself, *until the gospel is preached*.[39] The preaching of the gospel should remove all ignorance, and ignorance cannot be an excuse for rejecting God's will after the preaching of the gospel. Thus Peter's sermon excuses the former ignorance of the Jews, just as Paul's sermon at Athens excuses the former ignorance of the Gentiles (who show their intellectual honesty, one may note, by recognizing their ignorance and by erecting a statue to it); but Paul's sermon at Antioch does not mention Jewish ignorance as an excuse, it rather *accuses* the Jews of ignorance![40] The Jerusalemites could not even understand the Bible, although they heard it read every Saturday. They could find Jesus guilty of no crime deserving capital punishment (Acts 13:28), but they still urged his death.[41] As Stephen charged at the conclusion of the mission to Jerusalem, and as Paul also charged at the conclusion of the Gentile mission, the Jews "always resist the Holy Spirit"; they "hear but never understand." We may, of course, inquire whether the preaching of the gospel in the face of Athenian ignorance was more successful than the preaching of the gospel in Pisidian Antioch or in Jerusalem, but the author of Luke-Acts never entertained such a question. For him, the details of the narrative he lays before us should not obscure the overriding truth that Jews reject the gospel whereas Gentiless accept it. "They will hear" (Acts 28:28). Theology does not like to be confused by facts.

Jervell, however, views the facts themselves differently. "Mass conversions of Jews," he writes, "are again and again reported"; and he cites "2:41 (47); 4:4; 5:14; 6:1, 7; 9:42; 12:24; 13:43; 14:1; 17:10ff.; (19:20); 21:20."[42] Franklin gives a somewhat different set of passages in Acts (4:4; 5:12-16; 9:26-28; 11:2, 29-30; 12:25; 15:22; 21:20), and his position regarding them is again rather more cautious than that of Jervell: It is not that conversions are "reported" in these passages; rather, one sees in them that "Luke points out that many in Jerusalem did accept the Christian proclamation."[43] Only those references to Jewish conversion that follow Acts 9 are of concern to us here, since such conversion in the first nine chapters of Acts is not at issue.[44]

Whether Acts 12:24, "The word of God grew and multiplied," refers to new conversions is not entirely clear. While it is possible that the note--entirely disconnected, as it is, from its context--refers to new conversions, it is markedly different from the previous summary statements that explicitly mention conversions. Even if we were to allow that conversions were implied, it would still not be clear who has been converted, since

---

[39]Conzelmann, *Theology*, 90, observes that "after the Resurrection . . . unbelief becomes inexcusable"; cf. also ibid., 93. While that is not incorrect, it is also clear that it is not the resurrection itself, but the preaching about it that provides the κρίσις Conzelmann also, ibid., 92, thinks that the accusation against the Jews and the excuse of ignorance stem from the interplay between Luke and his source and (ibid., 145) that "for the individual the way of salvation is open, now as always"; but the themes are rather related to Luke's epochs. Cf. further ibid., 162 n. 1. Gnilka, *Verstockung*, 141, has seen the point exactly; cf. also Kränkl, *Knecht*, 106.

[40]This point is widely recognized. Cf. Loisy, *Actes*, 233; Haenchen, *Apostelgeschichte*, 206, n. 3, 210; Conzelmann, *Apostelgeschichte*, 76; Hanson, *Acts*, 143; A. Wikenhauser, *Die Apostelgeschichte* (RNT; 3d ed.; Regensburg: Pustet, 1956) 155; Kränkl, *Knecht*, 103. Even Jacquier, *Actes*, 400, sees that 13:27 is an accusation. It is this difference that Sandmel, *Anti-Semitism*, 73, has overlooked in finding "a residual concern in Luke to win Jews to Christianity"; cf. above, n. 18. Sandmel correctly, however (ibid., 98), observes that "the theme of Jewish guilt for the death of Jesus is ascribed not to whatever Jews were present but to all the Jews in Jerusalem."

[41]Wilckens, *Missionsreden*, 134.

[42]Jervell,   44. A critique of Jervell's position on this point is also given by Wilson, *Gentiles*, 222-24.

[43]Franklin, *Christ the Lord*, 103.

[44]I do not intend by this statement to take a position regarding the much debated issue as to whether the Samaritans are Jews or Gentiles.

the gospel has already expanded into Samaritan and Gentile regions. Verse 25, of course, does not refer to conversions. Acts 19:20, however, similarly to 12:24, reports that "the word of the Lord grew and prevailed mightily." Not only can this note not be used to show that there were Jewish conversions, since it falls within the Gentile mission, but its context weighs heavily on the side of considering neither it nor the similar 12:24 as summaries of conversions, since its reference is to the gospel's destruction of magic in Ephesus! The point is just what the note maintains: The *power* of the gospel increased. This "power" is not limited to the winning of converts to Christianity, and references to such power should not necessarily be so taken. Three of the references in Acts mentioned by Jervell--13:43; 14:1; and 17:10-12--have already been discussed (Jervell has overlooked Acts 18:8). Acts 15:22 does not refer to any new conversions.

We are brought, therefore, to Acts 21:20, "You see, . . . how many thousands there are among the Jews who have believed." Does this attestation mean, as Jervell takes it, that the number of Jewish converts in Jerusalem has increased since the events narrated in chap. 10?[45] It does not. In the first place, the statement is not a "report" of a "mass conversion of Jews," since it is not a "report" in the sense of a narrative at all. It is a summary of what has already happened. If Acts 21:20, however, is a summary, then it summarizes earlier conversions of Jews in Jerusalem, either reported or not reported. Jervell has to assume that the summary of Acts 21:20 refers to unreported conversions of Jerusalem Jews which have taken place since chap. 10. This assumption is not necessary, however, since the 3000 of Acts 2:41, the unspecified additional number of 2:47, the 5000 men (plus additional women?) of 4:4, the multitude of 5:14, the multiplying disciples of 6:1, and the greatly multiplying disicples of 6:7 will surely produce the "so many myriads" of 21:20. We are therefore able to arrive at the sum given in 21:20 without the assumption of a single Jewish convert in Jerusalem after 6:7.[46] It is therefore not proper to assume, as Jervell does, that Acts 21:20 refers to such additional converts *when that is the very point that needs to be proved.*

But if Acts shows us "many myriads" of Jews who are converted before chap. 10 and only a few who are converted in the context of the Gentile mission, it is also true that the myriads of Jewish conversions in the first part of the book are not matched by myriads of Gentile conversions in the latter part, so that, while there are rather more Gentile conversions than Jewish conversions in the Gentile mission, the latter part of Acts is hardly an account of mass Gentile conversion to Christianity. The author of Luke-Acts seems more concerned to show, in Acts 12-28, the universal and pervasive hostility of the Jews to the gospel and how this hostility of the Jews repeatedly forces the preaching of the gospel to Gentiles.[47] Thus it is the purpose of the characterization

---

[45] While Franklin is more cautious at this point, I take his implication to be at least similar to Jervell's opinion about Acts 21:20. There is a variety of opinions among commentators on this issue. G. Stählin, *Die Apostelgeschichte* (NTD 5; Göttingen: Vandenhoeck & Ruprecht, 1962) 277, agrees that the reference is to new converts; but Overbeck (DeWette), *Apostelgeschichte,* 381, and Loisy, *Actes,* 794, think of all Jewish Christians, including those in the diaspora. Haenchen, *Apostelgeschichte,* 582, sees a hyperbole, and Jacquier, *Actes,* 632, votes both for all Jewish Christians and for a hyperbole. H. J. Holtzmann, *Die Apostelgeschichte* (HKNT 1/2; 3d ed.; Tübingen and Leipzig: Mohr [Siebeck], 1901) 131, thinks that the myriads are in Jerusalem.

[46] G. Lohfink, *Die Sammlung Israels. Eine Untersuchung zur lukanischen Ekklesiologie* (SANT 39; Munich: Kösel, 1975) 51-55, also describes massive Jewish conversions in the first section of Acts but resistance in the rest of the book. The "reversal . . . in 6:8-8:1 occurs abruptly and suddenly" (p. 54). The "true Israel" responds to the gospel immediately; the Israel that rejected the gospel in that first period of opportunity is incorrigible and "became Judaism" (p. 55).

[47] Jervell, *People of God,* 44, also notes the small quantity of Gentile conversions in Acts but reaches, as may be imagined, a conclusion different from the one presented

of the Gentile mission in Acts 12-28 to show, not that myriads of Gentiles were converted, but that consistent and pervasive Jewish hostility to the gospel drove the Christian preachers from this place to that, saturating the several regions of the Gentile world with their preaching, finally even Rome itself.[48] It was this contrast that led Johannes Weiss to note, "The victory of Gentile Christianity and the repression of Jewish Christianity have their literary reflection in the Book of Acts."[49]

One more aspect of the pervasive Jewish hostility toward the purposes of God, especially toward the gospel (as it is represented in Acts), deserves to be mentioned, and that is that the hostility of the Jews to the gospel is part of God's plan, it being his will to offer salvation to the Gentiles and to accomplish that by the means of Jewish rejection of the gospel.[50] This theme is seen most clearly in Acts 13:42-49, the account of the conclusion of Paul's first missionary activity, at Pisidian Antioch. Here Paul "urges" (ἔπειθον, i.e., "persuades") the Jews to continue in grace (v. 43), then they turn on him (v. 45), in response to which Paul pronounces the divine necessity and, by implication, foreknowledge of the chain of events: "It was necessary (ἀναγκαῖον) that the word of God should be spoken first to you. Since you thrust it from you, . . . we turn to the Gentiles" (v. 46). While Paul does not here give a reason for the necessity of preaching first to the Jews, that reason will have been obvious to the author of Luke-Acts: to the Jews were given the prophecies in the first place.[51] But the Jewish rejection of the gospel must be just as much a necessity as the preaching to them in the first place--that is, God must have known in advance of their rejection, since the rejection is followed by the prophecy of the Gentile mission, Isa 49:6 (Acts 13:47). Thus the pattern: proclamation to the Jews, rejection by them, proclamation to the Gentiles--is the divine plan. Had the Jews accepted the gospel, and had they thereby not forced the

---

here. Wilson, *Gentiles*, 227-33, presents a refutation of Jervell on this point but does not emphasize the role of Jewish rejection of the gospel portrayed by Luke for the Gentile mission. M. Tolbert, "Leading Ideas of the Gospel of Luke," *RevExp* 64 (1967) 445-46, sees that it is the Jews, not the gospel, who are to blame for their not being saved. Thus E. Trocmé, *Le "Livre des Actes" et l'histoire* (Etudes d'histoire et de philosophie religieuses 45; Paris: Presses Universitaires de France, 1957) 118, considers Acts 13-28 "the trial of Israel, particularly of its *diaspora*." Cf. further Haenchen, "Judentum und Christentum," 175-76, who observes that "the entire *course of the Christian missionary Paul's life* is determined by the argument with the Jews."

[48]Since the Gentile mission, the hostility of the Jews, and salvation of the Gentiles are not the topic of this paper, they will not be discussed further here; but it seemed necessary to refer, at least briefly, to the major themes of the latter part of Acts in order better to clarify the issue of Jewish salvation in Acts 12-28. For the conflicting viewpoints, cf., on the one hand, Loisy, *Actes*, 541, and Conzelmann, *Apostelgeschichte*, 77-78, and *Theology*, 212, and, on the other hand, Jervell, *People of God*, 64-67, and Franklin, *Christ the Lord*, 119-24 and 139-44, Haenchen, *Apostelgeschichte*, 398, takes a middle position.

[49]Weiss, *Earliest Christianity*, 672. Wilckens, *Missionsreden*, 119, observes that the mission to the Jews "is, as a whole, determined by this polemical tendency."

[50]Conzelmann, *Apostelgeschichte*, 77, refers to the "*heilsgeschichtliche Prinzip*"; Loisy, *Actes*, 541, to the "*disposition providentielle*." Cf. also E. Lohse, "Lukas als Theologe der Heilsgeschichte," *Das Lukas-Evangelium. Die redaktions- und kompositionsgeschichtliche Forschung* (Wege der Forschung 280; ed. G. Braumann; Darmstadt: Wissenschaftliche Buchgesellschaft, 1974) 79-80. Hauser, *Apostelgeschichte*, 76-79, confirms the temporal distinction (a time of salvation for the Jews is followed by a time of salvation for the Gentiles) and the element of divine economy but denies that Jewish rejection propels the gospel toward the Gentiles. He has, I believe, overlooked the nuances observed above, pp. 475-76.

[51]Also Wilckens, *Missionsreden*, 134.

Gentile mission, they would have thwarted the purposes of God!   This theological construction then also underlies the exchange between Paul and the Roman Jews in the concluding scene of Acts, and it lies equally behind Acts 7:51-53.   Especially in the conclusion of Stephen's speech we see that this divine necessity provides no more excuse for the Jews than does their ignorance. They still fall under the accusation of rejection; and, for the author of Luke-Acts, there is no longer, after the time of Acts 28:28, any salvation of any Jews.[52]   They have consistently, in keeping both with God's plan and with their natural disposition, rejected the gospel and have thereby judged themselves "unworthy of eternal life" (Acts 13:46). If this, however, is the position of the author of Luke-Acts found in Acts after chap. 10, then how can it be explained that myriads of Jews are converted to Christianity before chap. 10? The answer lies in the recognition of Luke's periodization of history.

The contrast between the earlier and later periods in Acts is so marked--and so obviously schematized--that it is impossible to overlook it. In the opening chapters, when the Christian preaching is confined to Jerusalem, myriads of Jews convert to Christianity, as has just been noted, and the former opposition of the Jews to God's plan is excused as ignorance, as was explained above.[53]   In chaps. 6-7, then, comes the martyrdom of Stephen, in whose final words the Jews are denounced as incorrigible and whose death leads to the expansion of the gospel outside Jerusalem.[54]   The author of Luke-Acts has a little difficulty making the transition from the Jewish mission to the Gentile mission,[55] but it is begun by Peter in chap. 10 and gets underway in chap. 11 or in chap. 13. From chap. 13 on the Jews take the place in Acts that has already been described.

For Conzelmann, who has discussed the successive periods in Luke-Acts in great detail, all of Acts, of course, belongs to Luke's "epoch of the church," but "the initial period comes to be thought of as a unique kind of period; . . . it stands apart as the unique period of the witnesses," and is characterized both by the persecution of the church and by peace in the church.[56]   Loisy also notes that "from this point [sc. the

---

[52]This is also, in general, the view of J. C. O'Neill, *The Theology of Acts in Its Historical Setting* (2d ed.; London: SPCK, 1970) 87-95. O'Neill does, however, hold out the possibility of an eventual "conversion of Israel" (ibid., 87 n. 1). Similarly Rackham, *Acts*, 505. "So through the fall of the Jews came the salvation of the Gentiles"; yet he adds that those who believe were not rejected. Gnilka, *Verstockung*, 149, states that "a new Israel has come into existence, but the old Israel . . . in its entirety is not included therein"; cf. further ibid., 150.

[53]With keen insight, Wilckens, *Missionsreden*, 182, has seen that the mission to the Jews in "the first Jewish Christian phase of church history" is, in Acts, a reformulation of "the general pattern of Hellenistic Christian conversion." This "*ordo salutis* for the guilty Jews" then appears as a "generally inclusive and normative image of conversion."

[54]Cf. Bihler, "Stephanusbericht," 266: "*Das Judentum kann nicht mehr Gottesvolk sein*"; cf. further ibid., 270. Haenchen, "Source Material," 262, observes that, in the first part of Acts, the author "has constantly steered the plot toward a climax. . . . This conflict reaches its climax in the stoning of Stephen and the flight of the entire congregation (8:1)."

[55]Haenchen, *Apostelgeschichte*, 113, 289-90, q.v., offers an explanation of chaps. 8-11 that may suffice for now. It seems superfluous to discuss further here the transition from chap. 7 to chap. 12, since it is clear that Luke gets us, in the intervening chapters, from the Jewish to the Gentile mission. Cf. also Dibelius, *Apostelgeschichte*, 146; Gnilka, *Verstockung*, 150 n. 105.

[56]Conzelmann, *Theology*, 210. Cf. also Conzelmann, *Apostelgeschichte*, 50: The martyrdom of Stephen "prepares theoretically the transition to the Gentile mission"; further Conzelmann, *History of Primitive Christianity* (Nashville and New York: Abingdon, 1973) 35. The pronounced parallelism between the martyrdoms of Jesus and of

martyrdom of Stephen] this conclusion [pronounced by Paul in Acts 28:25-28] is prepared by showing that Israel was never worthy of the promises made to it";[57] and Haenchen observes that "the expulsion of the primitive congregation by this unbelieving Israel brought about and justified the Gentile mission."[58] Even Jervell is forced to recognize the transition, and observes that "Stephen's sermon, which marks the conclusion of missionary activity in Jerusalem, signifies the end of the apostles' direct missionary activity to Israel."[59]

This "initial" and "unique" (Conzelmann) period of the church described in Acts 1-6, during which time myriads of Jews convert, is partially to be explained by the viewpoint of the author of Luke-Acts elucidated by Haenchen in his discussion of the conclusion of Acts. There, he observed, Luke was attempting to bring together two viewpoints: one, that the gospel was "in essential agreement with Judaism" and, two, that the Jewish rejection of the gospel brought about the Gentile mission.[60] To this "essential agreement" of the gospel with Judaism one will want to add Luke's conviction that the gospel

---

Stephen (cf. below n. 62) convince me of the superiority of Conzelmann's analysis to later attempts to improve on his position. In the theology of the author of Luke-Acts, an early and never-to-be-repeated phase of the time of the church, which was inaugurated by the martyrdom of Jesus, was brought to a close by the martyrdom of Stephen, which in turn inaugurated the time of the Gentile mission, that continues (theoretically) down to this day. Different dividing points for the history of the church have been proposed by Talbert, *Patterns*, 106, and by H. C. Kee, *Jesus in History* (New York: Harcourt Brace Jovanovich, 1977) 189-90.

[57] Loisy, *Actes*, 320. Dahl, "Abraham," 151, also sees that the salvation of the Jews is of no concern to Luke after the Stephen episode.

[58] Haenchen, *Apostelgeschichte*, 289.

[59] Jervell, *People of God*, 77. Hauser, *Apostelgeschichte*, 238, argues that the offering of salvation to the Jews is not over until the end of Acts. While we must keep clear the distinction between *offering* of salvation and *acceptance* of it, we need to note that Hauser has given an adequate and satisfactory explanation of the continued preaching of the gospel to the Jews in Acts right up until the end: Rome symbolizes "the end of the earth" for Jews as well as for Gentiles; when the Jews have finally rejected the gospel in Rome, they have rejected it in all the world. Hauser, himself, then confuses the issue when he adopts the view of Jervell, Conzelmann, and others that individual Jews still have the opportunity to be saved. One cannot have it both ways. Either the Jews have rejected the gospel everywhere, since Stephen's death, or they have not. Conzelmann's epochal explanation is also supported by Wilckens, *Missionsreden*, 96-100, esp. p. 97. He also notes (p. 97) that it is in keeping with this epochal understanding that Jesus' ministry was among the Jews, concluding in Jerusalem. G. Bornkamm, "The Missionary Stance of Paul in I Corinthians 9 and in Acts," *Studies in Luke-Acts* (see n. 5) 201, clarifies the Lucan perspective by a contrast with Paul: "While Paul views the Jewish and Gentile missions as simultaneous enterprises, Luke sees them as forming a *succession*." Cf. also M. Hengel, *Acts and the History of Earliest Christianity* (Philadelphia: Fortress, 1979) 87, who refers to "Luke's pattern of a mission to the Jews, rejection by the Jews, mission to the Gentiles, which runs like a scarlet thread right through his work." Cf. further Hanson, *Acts*, 102, who states that Stephen's "speech does not so much prepare us for the movement of the Church's mission towards the Gentiles as for its movement away from the Jews"; and E. Richard, "The Polemical Character of the Joseph Episode in Acts 7," *JBL* 98 (1979) 265: "The Stephen speech . . . is . . . a farewell speech to Judaism."

[60] Haenchen, *Apostelgeschichte*, 697. The need to bring together these two conflicting views is also noted by J. A. Fitzmyer, "Jewish Christianity in Acts in Light of the Qumran Scrolls," *Studies in Luke-Acts* (see n. 5) 235, who observes that "during all this growth the Christian group is marked off from the Jewish people as such"; cf. further ibid., 234-39.

was always "persuasive" or "powerful"[61] as well as the geographical plan laid down in Acts 1:8, and one will have Luke's rationale for the salvation of the Jews in Acts 1-6. Luke makes this theology effective with the theme of excusable ignorance. The preaching of the gospel offers a second chance to the Jews after their initial rejection; but, after appropriate success, the gospel is rejected in the same way in which Jesus was rejected. This second rejection (which incudes, N.B.! a rejection by diaspora Jews as well, Acts 6:9) is shown to be a sequel to the first rejection by the parallelism between the martyrdom of Jesus and that of Stephen. The Stephen episode, therefore, is properly viewed as containing, in microcosm, Luke's entire theology about the Jews.[62]

We noted at the outset that the positions of Jervell and of Franklin stood or fell on the answer to two questions, whether Acts 28:25-28 represents a final rejection of the Jews and whether the epochal understanding of Acts put forward by Loisy, Conzelmann, and others was correct. The analysis here presented has shown the incorrectness of Jervell's and Franklin's positions. The theology of the author of Luke-Acts regarding the salvation of the Jews, if we may now summarize it briefly, is that the Jews are by nature stubborn and both unable and unwilling to recognize the will of God, even though God had for centuries attempted to explain his will to them alone. This racial characteristic-- which then also happens to coincide with the divine plan--led them to kill the prophets, to kill the Messiah; and, when God was even willing to excuse those earlier murders on the basis of ignorance and to offer them still one other chance at salvation in the preaching of the gospel, *the truth of which is attested by the conversion of myriads of them*, still they rejected God's salvation and murdered Stephen just as they had murdered Christ, thus forcing the gospel to go to the Gentiles (which movement was, after all, God's plan). In the context of the Gentile mission, then, the Christian preachers still attempted to convert Jews, but the success of the early days of the church was no longer there, and the Jewish response to the gospel was primarily one of hostility. The Gentile mission therefore served to attest the truth displayed in the martyrdom of Stephen, which Paul finally and for the last time announces at the end of Acts. A final solution of the Jewish problem has been indicated.[63]

---

[61]Cf. again the discussion above, pp. 471, 475.

[62]Again, an analysis of the Stephen episode would take us beyond the scope of this paper. The parallelism between Jesus' martyrdom and Stephen's is well explained by Talbert, *Luke and the Gnostics. An Examination of the Lucan Purpose* (Nashville and New York: Abingdon, 1966) 76; Talbert, *Patterns*, 97; and W. Radl, *Paulus und Jesus im lukanischen Doppelwerk* (Europäische Hochschulschriften 23/49; Bern: Herbert Lang; Frankfurt: Peter Lang, 1975) 237; and one may also note that his speech is the longest of all the speeches in Acts (cf. Dibelius, *Apostelgeschichte*, 143-46).

[63]On the position sketched here, cf. also in general K. Löning, "Lukas--Theologe der von Gott geführten Heilsgeschichte (Lk, Apg)," *Gestalt und Anspruch des Neuen Testaments* (ed. J. Schreiner; Würzburg: Echter-Verlag, 1969) 222. Haenchen, "Source Material," 278, says the "Luke has written the Jews off." In light of this understanding, it is shocking to read a statement like that of Hengel, *Acts and History*, 64: "There is not a trace in his work of the ancient antisemitism which was similarly not unknown to him." Hengel's reference, ibid., to Luke's awareness of Gentile antisemitism, as is found in Acts 16:20-21, does not reduce Luke's own consignment of the Jews to ruin. The argument of G. Braumann, "Das Mittel der Zeit. Erwägungen zur Theologie des Lukasevangeliums," *ZNW* 54 (1963) 135-40, that Luke presents no opposition between Judaism and church, and that Judaism and paganism are both secular political entities that stand over against the church as both mission field and opponent, so that the only opposition in Luke-Acts is that between saved and unsaved, is so obviously contrary to our evidence that it will have to be assigned the label, "tour de force." Braumann seems not to have read Acts 28:28.

This once-only chance for salvation given to the Jews by the author of Luke-Acts is expressed not only in the Acts, but in the Gospel of Luke as well. As a matter of fact, when Luke and Acts are viewed together, then one is able to see that their central theme is the two-sided Jewish rejection (the Jews' rejection of the gospel and God's rejection of them) and the carrying of the gospel to the Gentiles.[64]

Following the two preliminary chapters of Luke, the author presents the ministry of the Baptist, Jesus' baptism, and the temptation. All that is preliminary to the activity of Jesus, which is the subject of the Gospel; and *that activity begins with Jesus' denunciation of the Jews and his announcement that salvation is sent to the Gentiles.*[65] It is widely recognized, of course, that Luke has pulled the scene of Jesus' preaching in Nazareth forward from its earlier setting in his sources to make it the opening scene of the public ministry (Luke 4:16-30). What is thereby accomplished? The answer to that question can be found by looking at the differences between Luke, on the one hand, and Matthew and Mark, on the other. Only Luke includes here a prophecy of the mockery thrown at Jesus in Luke 23:35 and parallels, "Physician, heal yourself"; only Luke includes the examples of the Gentiles in Elijah's and Elisha's time--the Sidonian widow and Naaman the Syrian--and throws it into the teeth of the Jewish hearers that there were Israelite widows and lepers in those days; and only Luke tells of the attempt by the Jewish hearers to stone Jesus. Thus the statement of Jesus to his Jewish audience that God favors Gentiles over Jews--and what other inference could be drawn from his examples?[66]--leads to Jewish hostility, just as in Acts the proclamation of the gospel

---

[64]Thus W. C. Robinson, Jr., *Der Weg des Herrn. Studien zur Geschichte und Eschatologie im Lukas-Evangelium* (TF 36; Hamburg-Bergstedt: H. Reich/Evangelischer Verlag, 1964) 39, 43, 67, understands the Lord's "way" in Luke-Acts to be a way to the Gentiles. This is also the view of Zmijewski, *Eschatologiereden,* maintained at length in an analysis of Luke 20:5-36. Cf. esp. p. 316: "The radical hardening of Judaism leads to its radical rejection. . . . At the same time, however, this hardening provides the means with the help of which God can realize his universal plan of salvation. Salvation goes finally over to the Gentiles by the rejection of Israel." Cf. in general ibid., 43-325. So also R. Morgenthaler, *Die lukanische Geschichtsschreibung als Zeugnis* (Zurich: Zwingli, 1949) 1. 188: "If anything is clear, then it is this [overall conception]; it says that salvation is going over from the Jews to the Gentiles. . . . This and only this is the key to the riddle of the construction of the Lucan work."

[65]C. G. Montefiore, *The Synoptic Gospels* (2d ed.; London: Macmillan, 1927) 2. 395, has seen the role of this pericope exactly, as has also Loisy, *Les Evangiles synoptiques* (Ceffonds, près Montier-en-Der (Haute-Marne): published by the author, 1907-8) 1. 839. Cf. also W. Grundmann, *Das Evangelium nach Lukas* (THKNT 3; 7th ed.; Berlin: Evangelische Verlagsanstalt, 1974) 119; E. Klostermann, *Das Lukasevangelium* (HNT 5; 2d ed.; Tübingen: Mohr [Siebeck], 1929) 62; F. Hauck, *Das Evangelium des Lukas* (THKNT 3; Leipzig: Deichert, 1934) 63. W. J. Harrington, *The Gospel According to St. Luke* (New York, et al.: Newman, 1967) 87, calls the pericope a "synopsis" of Luke-Acts. Cf. J. Wellhausen, *Das Evangelium Lucae* (Berlin: Reimer, 1904) 10; Holtzmann, *Apostelgeschichte,* 20; J. A. Fitzmyer, *The Gospel According to Luke (I-IX)* (AB 28; Garden City, NY: Doubleday, 1981) 529; I. H. Marshall, *The Gospel of Luke. A Commentary on the Greek Text* (The New International Greek Testament Commentary; Grand Rapids, MI: Eerdmans, 1978) 178. So also Sandmel, *Anti-Semitism,* 76-77. Tolbert, "Leading Ideas," 442-43, has correctly emphasized the importance of Jewish rejection in the framework of the narrative of Luke-Acts, namely Luke 4:16-30 and the closing scene of Acts. Radl, *Paulus und Jesus,* compares Luke 4:16-30 with Acts 13:14-52, seeing both as *"Eröffnungsperikopen"* (p. 97) and as presenting "the opposition of Jews and Gentiles" (p. 98).

[66]H. Schürmann, *Das Lukasevangelium,* erster Teil: *Kommentar zu Kap. 1,1-9,50* (HTKNT 3; Freiburg, et al.: Herder, 1969) 236-39, makes this meaning abundantly

leads to hostility; and the Jews take Jesus out of the city to stone him, just as in Acts the Jews take Stephen out of the city to stone him.[67] Naturally, Jesus escapes, since this is only the beginning of the public ministry, and he cannot be killed by the Jews until the end; but the author of Luke-Acts has here set the course of the entire two-volume work straight toward the conclusion in Acts 28:25-28.[68] Another way of emphasizing that point is to observe that, just as Luke's entire theology about the Jews may be seen in the Stephen episode, so Luke's theology about the plan of God's salvation is contained in microcosm in the first scene of the public ministry:[69] God's salvation is coming to the Gentiles and not to the Jews; the Jews react to that "gospel" message in a hostile manner; their final rejection at the end of Acts is therefore a foregone conclusion at the outset of Jesus' public ministry. The salvation of the Jews was never at any time of any concern to the author of Luke-Acts. For him, theirs is the role of those who seek to thwart the purposes of God.

We have seen that the theme of two-sided Jewish rejection is dominant in the Acts and is also prepared in the Gospel of Luke. Is there, however, some difference between the two works in this regard? Is the Gospel of Luke less strongly disposed to reject the possibility of Jewish salvation than is the Acts? Is the Gospel "more subtly" antisemitic than the Acts?[70] Once one begins to look for the standard theme of Jewish rejection, it soon becomes clear that it is hardly less prominent in the Gospel than in the Acts.

We may begin again with the opening scene of the public ministry, the preaching and rejection in Nazareth. After his miraculous escape from stoning, Jesus does a few

---

clear. "πατρίς," (v. 24), he notes, "becomes ambiguous in the context," meaning both "father city" and, from v. 25 on, "fatherland" (ibid., 237-38). Cf. also Haenchen, "Historie und Verkündigung bei Markus und Lukas," *Das Lukas-Evangelium* (see n. 50) 300; Kee, *Jesus in History*, 195; E. E. Ellis, *The Gospel of Luke* (The Century Bible, New Edition; Greenwood, SC: Attic Press, 1966) 96, 98; Harrington, *St. Luke*, 88-89; E. J. Tinsley, *The Gospel According to Luke* (The Cambridge Bible Commentary, NEB; Cambridge: University Press, 1965) 53-54; Löning, "Theologe," 218-20. The way in which a few modern commentators endorse Luke's antisemitism is disheartening. The worst that I have encountered is A. Plummer, *A Critical and Exegetical Commentary on the Gospel According to S. Luke* (ICC; 4th ed.; Edinburgh: Clark, 1910) 128-29: "To this day the position remains the same; and Gentiles enjoy the Divine privileges of which the Jews have deprived themselves." J. M. Creed, *The Gospel According to St. Luke* (London et al.: Macmillan, 1969) 66, takes the references to Elijah and Elishah to be justifications of the absence of miracles in Nazareth. This is to overlook the references to Israel in vv. 25, 27.

[67]Similarly H. Gollwitzer, *Die Freude Gottes. Einführung in das Lukasevangelium* (5th ed.; Berlin-Dahlem; Gelnhausen/Hessen: Burckhardthaus, s.d.) 54.

[68]Conzelmann's understanding of this important pericope (*Theology*, 33, 38) is inadequate; cf. Tolbert, "Leading Ideas," 442-43, and Radl, *Paulus und Jesus*, 97-98.

[69]So also Schürmann, *Lukasevangelium*, 1. 225; Menezes, "Lk 4:16-30," 250; further, Marshall, *Gospel of Luke*, 178: "Many of the main themes of Lk.-Acts *in nuce*." Fitzmyer, *Luke*, 529, has come close to seeing this when he states that the story is an "encapsulation" of "the entire ministry of Jesus and the reaction to it." Cf. J. W. Packer, *Acts of the Apostles* (The Cambridge Bible Commentary; Cambridge: University Press, 1966) 222 (on Acts 28:28): "Since the Jews refused to listen, *this salvation of God has been sent to the Gentiles*, who will. This is the whole burden of Luke's great work. The mission to the Gentiles has been foretold by Simeon (Luke 2:32). The gospel narrative led up to Israel's rejection of the Messiah, as Stephen reminded his hearers (7:52). Therefore, it is now the Gentiles' turn and they will accept the message."

[70]This is the opinion of Sandmel, *Anti-Semitism*, 73, who finds "in Luke a frequent subtle, genteel anti-Semitism," whereas in Acts the subtlety "recedes and the anti-Semitism becomes overt and direct."

deeds and says a few sayings, and then (9:51) he starts the journey toward Jerusalem. Immediately he gets underway and he is rejected by some Samaritans (9:51-56), but this rejection is different in two ways from the standard Jewish rejection. On the one hand, a reason is given for the Samaritans' rejecting Jesus (he is journeying toward Jerusalem), and, on the other hand, when the opportunity is given to destroy the Samaritans (v. 54), Jesus rejects such a possibility.[71]   The scene at the outset of the Travel Narrative provides an interesting contrast and comparison with the rejection scene (in parable) at the conclusion of the Travel Narrative.[72]   Here (19:11-27), Jesus tells of a throne pretender who journeys to another country in order the receive authority over his realm, who is followed by some of his subjects who oppose his rule, and who then slays his opponents after having received his kingdom and having returned to it--all a thinly veiled allegory of Jesus, who departs to heaven to come again in power, whose rule is opposed by the Jews, and who will destroy them when he returns. This framework for the Travel Narrative--excusable and excused Samaritan rejection vs. unforgiveable Jewish rejection; rejection of destruction vs. promise of destruction--determines its tone throughout and allows the careful reader to observe the standard pattern of Jewish rejection, already indicated at the beginning of the public ministry, throughout the Travel Narrative.[73] Thus we can recognize the parable of the Good Samaritan (10:29-37) as being directed against the (religious) Jews and as showing the Samaritans to be superior in their response to the will of God; and the parable of the Great Supper (14:15-24), with its two invitations to the uninvited, as again rejecting the (religious) Jews while seeking out either Jewish religious outcasts or Samaritans, and Gentiles.[74]

When we once recognize the pervasive character of the theme of Jewish rejection in the Gospel, then we are not surprised when the Jews carry out the most infamous act of rejection possible by themselves murdering Jesus, an act which Luke accomplishes, as is well known, by omitting the scene in which the Roman soldiers mock Jesus (Mark 15:16-20a and parallels) and moving directly from "he delivered Jesus to their will" (Luke 23:25; cf. Mark 15:15) to "and as they led him away" (Luke 23:26; cf. Mark 15:20b).[75] Finally, the Lucan version of the "Great Commission" (24:44-49) simply takes as given the theme of Jewish rejection and of the consequent sending of salvation to the Gentiles. The "forgiveness of sins" is to go to "πάντα τὰ ἔθνη," and it is to begin "from Jerusalem."[76]   The apostles, however, are to remain in Jerusalem (only) until they

---

[71]So also K. L. Schmidt, *Der Rahmen der Geschichte Jesu* (Berlin, 1919) 267. Schmidt notes (p. 268) that one may learn from the following verses "that Jesus is not rejected by the Samaritans everywhere." He sees this characterization as part of Luke's "*Missionspolitik*," since "many Samaritans became Christians" (ibid.). Conzelmann, *Theology*, 65, sees the two rejections as parallel, inaugurating the main stages of Jesus' public ministry.

[72]For a fuller discussion of this point, cf. my article, "The Parable of the Pounds and Lucan Anti-Semitism," *TS* 42 (1981) 660-68. Lohse, "Lukas als Theologe," 79, connects the three rejections in Luke 4:30; 9:51-56; and 19:37 to three periods in Jesus' ministry but does not note the theologically loaded differences among the three episodes.

[73]Cf. M. D. Goulder, *Type and History in Acts* (London: SPCK, 1964) 59: "The theme of Luke 10-13 is the failure of Israel, its keyword is ὑποκριταί." Loisy, *Evangiles synoptiques*, 2. 102, also contrasts the attitude toward the Samaritans in Luke 9:51-56 to the attitude toward the Jews in 4:16-30. Fitzmyer, *Luke*, 827, thinks that Jesus' rejection of retribution is a rejection of identification with Elijah. What will he propose for 19:27?

[74]Sandmel, *Anti-Semitism*, 77-80, gives these and other instances of antisemitic constructions in the Gospel of Luke.

[75]See also Weiss, *Earliest Christianity*, 664; Creed, *St. Luke*, 283, 285, very mildly.

[76]So also Lohse, "Lukas als Theologe," 81. Weiss, *Earliest Christianity*, 661, takes this to mean that "the original destination of the Twelve to Israel [as in Matthew] is

receive the heavenly power. The Jewish mission of Acts 1-6 seems hardly to be envisioned here and is, indeed, inconsequential in view of the overall soteriological plan of Luke-Acts.[77]

---

completely forgotten"; and he contrasts the Lucan programme of Acts 1:8 ("to the ends of the earth") with the narrative of Acts, which confines the twelve to Jerusalem.

[77] The tone of these remarks on the opinion of the author of Luke-Acts about the salvation of the Jews has probably made my own attitude clear, but for the record, I should like to state that, as far as I am concerned, Jews--and all other people--are entirely free and welcome to convert to Christianity--and to any other religion--if they so wish.

2 BARUCH
A STORY OF GRIEF AND CONSOLATION

Gwen Sayler
University of Iowa

2 Baruch, or the Syriac Apocalypse of Baruch, is a Jewish document composed as a response to the crisis precipitated by the destruction of Jerusalem in 70 C.E. Probably because of its length and complexity, the book has not been the object of extensive scrutiny. With the exception of the annotated editions of R. H. Charles and P.-M. Bogaert,[1] the text has been analyzed almost exclusively in conjunction with an examination of 4 Ezra.[2] Moreover, even Bogaert and Charles assume that 4 Ezra is a model in some way for the structure and/or content of 2 Baruch. As a result, there has been almost no research on 2 Baruch as a piece of literature in its own right, apart from any perceived relationship to 4 Ezra. This paper is a step toward an analysis of 2 Baruch as a document which presents its own unique response to the events of 70 C.E.[3]

Although the assumed relationship between 4 Ezra and 2 Baruch has hindered research on 2 Baruch as a document in its own right, one discussion of 4 Ezra does, in fact, provide a key to the structure of 2 Baruch. This key is the pattern of movement from grief to consolation, identified in 4 Ezra by Earl Breech.[4] He summarizes his approach to 4 Ezra as follows:

> This paper (about the form and function of 4 Ezra) has been written with the conviction that the structure and meaning of 4 Ezra are mutually determinative. I would suggest that the formal principle which structures 4 Ezra as a literary composition is what may be called the pattern of consolation. The form of the work is constituted by the narrative of Ezra's movement from distress to consolation, from distress occasioned by the destruction of Jerusalem, to consolation by the Most High himself who reveals to the prophet, in dream visions, his end-time plans.[5]

In what follows, I will argue that the author of 2 Baruch responds to the events of 70 C.E. by composing a story--a story in which Baruch and then his community move from grief to consolation. The story is carried by sections of narrative prose, which are supplemented by units of other literary genres (laments, a discourse, prayers, conversations, and visions). By means of this story, the author develops the issues with which he is concerned. He does this by clustering and arranging the various units into seven major blocks of material, in which he raises and then resolves the issues of the book.[6] As the story unfolds, it becomes clear that these issues are as follows: the

---

[1] R. H. Charles, ed., *APOT* (Oxford: Clarendon, 1913), 2. 481-521; P.-M. Bogaert, *Apocalypse de Baruch* (SC 144-45; Paris: Le Cerf, 1969).

[2] The most detailed examinations of 2 Baruch in conjunction with 4 Ezra include: W. Harnisch, *Verhangnis und Verheissung der Geschichte* (FRLANT 97; Göttingen: Vandenhoeck & Ruprecht, 1969); A. L. Thompson, *Responsibility for Evil in the Theodicy of 4 Ezra* (SBLDS 29; Missoula: Scholars Press, 1977).

[3] This paper is a condensation of my University of Iowa Ph.D. dissertation on the structure and content of 2 Baruch. The dissertation is being completed at the time of this writing.

[4] Earl Breech, "These Fragments I Have Shored against My Ruins: The Form and Function of 4 Ezra," *JBL* 92 (1973) 267-74.

[5] Ibid., 269.

[6] Unlike Daniel or the Apocalypse of Abraham, the narrative and apocalyptic sections of 2 Baruch are not nearly separated from each other. Rather, they are

vindication of God's justice and power in reference to the destruction; and the survival of
the faithful Jewish community in the aftermath of the destruction.

In order to show how the story told in 2 Baruch develops, I will take the reader
through the text, block by block. The purpose of the analysis is not to argue that the
seven blocks begin and end at certain places. Rather, I will use the author's division into
blocks to trace the development of the primary issues from their introduction to their
resolution.

After I have discussed 2 Baruch, I will compare it with three contemporary Jewish
documents. The comparison will illustrate the similarities and differences in these responses to the destruction of Jerusalem.

ANALYSIS OF 2 BARUCH

Block 1 (Chapters 1-5)

*Block 1 consists of a narrative introduction (1:1), a conversation between God and
Baruch (1:2-5:4), and a narrative conclusion (5:5-7). This block establishes the setting of
the story, announces the action that is to follow, and identifies as the author's primary
concern the implications of the destruction for Israel and the nations.*

The narrative introduction (1:1) establishes the fictional setting of the story as the
days before the fall of Jerusalem to Babylon in 587 B.C.E. Conversation begins as God
tells Baruch that the city will be destroyed because of the people's sins. Baruch is to
lead those who are like him outside the city so that their works and prayers can no longer
protect it. From the opening chapters, it is apparent that *time* will be a major concern
throughout the book.[7] The destruction will be of *temporary duration*, as will the
dispersion of the people (1:2-2:2).

Baruch reacts to the revelation with a death-wish and a series of questions which
reduce to three: the survival of Israel; the future of the world; and the efficacy of God's
words to Moses about Israel (3:4-9). God responds to these questions by reemphasizing
the *temporary* nature of the destruction and of the chastening of the people. He also
contrasts the earthly city with its heavenly counterpart (4:1-6), thereby alluding to His
later comments about the eschatological resolution to the present crisis (see below,
Block 5).

Before Baruch obeys God's exhortation to go and do as He had commanded him
(4:7), he raises one more concern: his grief that the enemy will destroy God's city and
then return home to boast before their idols. God assures him that the enemy will not
overthrow the city (5:1-3).

The block concludes with another segment of narrative prose. Baruch leads the
honorable men outside the city to Kidron valley. The first day of the story ends as he
tells them what he has heard, and together they weep and fast until evening (5:4-7).

Block 2 (Chapters 6-20)

*Block 2 consists of a narrative introduction and description (6:1-10:4), a lament
(10:5-11:7), a discourse (chap. 12), and a conversation between God and Baruch (chaps.
13-20) This block probes the issue of theodicy from one perspective: the appropriateness
of God's choice to exercise His justice by destroying Jerusalem. God's defense of His
justice toward Israel and the nations evolves into a discussion about the righteous and*

---

integrated throughout the book. Narrative phrases (i.e., "I said," "I went") consistently
are used to introduce and/or conclude the non-narrative portions of the account.

[7]Because the dimension of *time* is an essential element in all facets of the story
told in 2 Baruch, I have italicized references to it throughout the paper. I do not intend
thereby to give the impression that the book is only about *time*; rather, I want to
emphasize how *time* is a factor in the development of each of the book's primary issues.

wicked within Israel. His explanation of His method of chastening the nations and Israel provides the basis for the discussion.

The narrative, dropped at the end of Block 1, continues on the second day of the story. Baruch departs from the righteous men in the Kidron valley and is lifted over the walls of Jerusalem. There he watches the angels bury the Temple vessels and set fire to the walls prior to the enemy's entrance into the city (6:1-8:2). Thus, he receives visual confirmation of God's earlier assurance that the enemy would not overthrow the city (cf. 5:1-3). After the destruction has occurred, Baruch and Jeremiah mourn and fast for a week. Then Baruch instructs Jeremiah to join the exiles in Babylon, while he remains in the Temple ruins to receive revelations about *the last days* (8:3-10:4).

As he sits in the Temple ruins, Baruch utters a lengthy lament (10:5-11:7). It is bracketed by death-wishes (10:6; 11:6-7), and contains exhortations to all life to cease functioning because of the desolation of Mother Zion. Near the end of the lament, Baruch interrupts his exhortations to tell Babylon that Jewish grief is infinite because she prospers while Zion is desolate (11:1-2). This interjection anticipates his subsequent discourse.

This discourse (chap. 12) emphasizes the dimension of *time*. Baruch warns Babylon that her prosperity will not endure *for all time; in its time,* divine anger, now restrained by *long-suffering,* will awake against her. After the discourse, Baruch fasts seven days before God once again converses with him (12:5).

God opens the conversation by explaining His method of chastening the nations and Israel (chap. 13). He tells Baruch that he will be preserved until the *consummation* as a witness:

> So that, if ever those prosperous cities say: "Why has the mighty God brought upon us this retribution?" You . . . can say . . . This (is the) evil and the retributions which are coming upon you and upon your people *in its time* so that the nations may be totally chastened. . . . And if they say *at that time*: "how long?," you will say to them: you who have drunk the strained wine, drink also the dregs, the judgment of the Lofty One who has no respect of persons. Therefore, He had before no mercy on His own sons, but afflicted them as His enemies, because they sinned. They were therefore chastened then that they might be pardoned.[8] (13:4-10)

Thus, God's anger toward the nations will not awake until the *consummation.* Then they will be punished fully for all their sins. In contrast, the present chastisement of Israel is *temporary* and will lead to her pardon.[9]

God's explanation of His method of chastening the nations and Israel is unacceptable to Baruch for two reasons: 1) too few Gentiles will be left at the consummation to experience the promised retribution (14:1-3); and 2) the destruction of Zion despite the righteousness of some of its inhabitants only demonstrates the futility of righteousness (14:4-7). Baruch reiterates his frustration by concluding that God's ways are incomprehensible (14:8-19). We will see later (Block 6) how his attitude eventually changes.

God defers Baruch's question about the delay in retribution against the nations until a later conversation. In response to Baruch's second assertion, He defends the justness of His present dealings with Israel. The basis of God's defense is the eschatological destinies of the wicked and righteous within Israel (15:1-8). Each Jew is responsible for

---

[8]Except for the few instances in which my translation differs from that of R. H. Charles, the quotations of the text are taken from his English edition of 2 Baruch (*APOT* 2. 481-521).

[9]For an excellent discussion of this perspective on God's method of chastening Israel and the nations, see K. Stendahl, "Hate, Retaliation, and Love in 1 QS x, 10-17 and Romans 12:19-21," *HTR* 55 (1962) 343-55.

his/her decision vis-a-vis the covenant relationship. Because violators of the Torah transgressed the covenant with conscious intent, they will suffer torment.[10] This world is a place of suffering for the righteous; however, the future world will be a crown of great glory for them.

God's defense does not satisfy Baruch. His complaint that *time* is *too short* to acquire the measureless (16:1) introduces a new part of the conversation. God uses the example of the life spans and legacies of Adam and Moses to argue that the shortened life span resulting from Adam's sin does not negate the individual's ability to choose his/her destiny (17:1-4). Baruch's reply gets to the heart of the problem as he perceives it:

> He that lit (Moses) has taken from the light, and *few* are those who have imitated him. But *many* of those whom he lit have taken from the darkness of Adam and have not taken delight in the light of the lamp. (18:1-2)

At this point, the question of responsibility has been re-phrased in terms of the *many* Jews who have not chosen the way of the Torah, in contrast to the *few* Jews who have.

The distinction between the *many* and the *few* within a discussion of theodicy is not unique to 2 Baruch. It is significant in Chapters 15-18 because it raises the question of the identification of the true Israel: who are those *few* Jews worthy to inherit the future world?

God responds (19:1-3) to Baruch's concern about the *many* and the *few* by paraphrasing Deut 30:15-20. The stipulations of the covenant are still in effect; the Torah rebukes those who transgress it.

God encourages Baruch to anticipate the *consummation*, instead of despairing over the *present* shameful treatment of the righteous (19:4-8). Then He brings the conversation to a conclusion by giving Baruch instructions and promising him that he will receive further revelations about the *methods of the times* (20:1-6).

Block 3 (Chapters 21-30)

Block 3 consists of a narrative introduction (21:1-3), a prayer (21:4-26), and a lengthy conversation between God and Baruch (chaps. 22-30). This Block probes the issue of theodicy from one specific perspective: the perceived delay in the manifestation of God's power to the nations. Baruch's impatience with the time remaining until the consummation provides the basis for the discussion.

The narrative continues as Baruch leaves the Temple area and goes alone to the Kidron valley. There he fulfills the first instruction given to him (cf. 20:5) by sanctifying himself and fasting seven days (21:1-2). After the week has passed, he carries out the second instruction (cf. 20:6) by returning to Mt. Zion (21:3), which is the setting for his first prayer.

Baruch's prayer (21:4-26) reveals his impatience with the *delay* in the manifestation of God's power caused by His *long-suffering*. The prayer begins with an acknowledgment of God's power over creation and of His knowledge of the *consummation of the times* (21:4-17). Then Baruch asks:

> *How long* will that which is corruptible remain, and *how long* will the time of mortals be prospered, and *until what time* will those who transgress in the world be polluted with much wickedness? (21:19)

---

[10]The identification of Jews as the object of God's judgment is evident in His statement: "Man would not have known My judgment unless he had accepted My Torah and I had instructed him in wisdom. But now, because he transgressed knowingly. . . ." (15:5-6).

His impatience culminates in the petition:

> Command therefore in mercy, and accomplish all that You said You would bring, that Your might may be made known to those who think Your *long-suffering* is weakness. And show to those who know not, and let them see that it has happened to us and to our city until now according to the *long-suffering* of Your power because on account of Your name, You have called us a beloved people. (21:20-21)

The references to God's long-suffering indicate that Baruch here is pleading that God implement *immediately* the judgment which Baruch announced in his discourse (chap. 12). By expressing concern that God's failure to exercise His power will be misperceived, Baruch also returns to a theme in his initial conversation with God--the relationship of God's power to the enemy's triumph over His city (5:1). Here, as there, Baruch is concerned with all Israel in contrast to the nations rather than with divisions within the Jewish community.

The prayer concludes as Baruch expresses his desire that God seal Sheol and let the treasuries of souls restore those persons preserved in them (21:23-24). A sense of immediacy is evident in his final words: "And now show Your glory *quickly*, and *do not delay* what You have promised" (21:25).

In the subsequent conversation (chaps. 22-30), Baruch's impatience over the *delay* in the manifestation of God's power is resolved by a glimpse of God's plan for mankind, which extends *throughout time*. As He indicated He would do (cf. 20:6), God again reveals Himself and speaks to Baruch (22:1). He uses Baruch's impatience as a foil to illustrate that consolation is possible only when a project is completed (22:2-8). Then He introduces the *temporal boundaries* of his plan for mankind:

> . . . when Adam sinned and death was decreed against those who should be born, then the multitude of those who should be born was numbered, and for that number a place was prepared where the living might dwell and the dead might be guarded. Unless therefore that number is fulfilled, the creature will not live again, for My spirit is the Creator of life, and Sheol will receive the dead . . . (23:3-5).

Thus, the final manifestation of God's power cannot occur until the completion of the process which began when Adam sinned. God assures Baruch that when all the steps in the plan have been fulfilled, the final judgment will occur. *At that time*, God's long-suffering to all generations will be seen by all mankind (24:1-2).

In response to Baruch's query regarding *how much time* is left (24:3-4), God describes in considerable detail the twelve parts of the *last times*, the Messianic era of peace and fecundity, and the resurrection (25:1-30:5).

Block 4 (Chapters 31-43)

Block 4 consists of a narrative introduction (31:1-2), Baruch's speech to the elders of his community (31:3-32:7), a conversation between Baruch and his people (32:8-34:1), a lament (chap. 35), a vision (chaps. 36-37), a prayer (chap. 38), and a conversation between God and Baruch (chaps. 39-43). This block continues the discussion of Block 2 by describing the eschatological judgment against Rome and by delineating further the identity and destiny of the many Jews who have chosen the darkness of Adam (cf. 18:1-2). In addition, Baruch's encounter with the elders of his community introduces the second cycle of the story, as the people begin to express their grief at the thought of life without Baruch's leadership.

The second cycle of the story begins as Baruch goes to his people and tells them to assemble the elders in the Kidron valley (31:1-2). His message to the elders (31:3-32:7) is succinct and reflects the revelation he just has received:

> . . . the days come when everything will become the prey of corruption . . . but if you prepare your hearts to sow in them the fruits of the Torah, it will protect you *in that time* when the Mighty One will shake creation. (31:5; 32:1)

When the people observe Baruch departing from them after his speech (32:8), they assume that he is leaving them permanently. They react with panic. Accusing Baruch of forsaking them like a father his orphan children, they lament that death would be preferable to life without him. They also accuse him of violating Jeremiah's commands to him to care for them (32:9-33:3). Baruch responds by assuring them that he is leaving them only temporarily to return to the Temple ruins and seek further enlightenment (34:1).

Thus, as Baruch begins to speak his first cautious words of *hope* about the *future,* his community begins to express their *grief* at the thought of a *future* without him. Baruch mourned the destruction of "mother Zion"; they mourn the departure of "father Baruch."

There are a number of indications that the reaction of Baruch's community to his temporary departure from them is modelled after Baruch's reaction to the announcement of the destruction (Block 1). Both texts begin with a narrative introduction followed by a message which announces a forthcoming disaster (1:2-4; 31:3-6). Baruch's reaction to God's words to him and the people's reactions to Baruch's departure from them both contain a death-wish—Baruch's, because he cannot endure the destruction of his "mother" (3:1-2); and his people's, because they can not envision life without the guidance of their "father" (32:7-33:3). In both texts, the conversation between the protagonists introduces questions regarding the appropriateness of what is happening (3:4-9; 5:1; 33:1-2). A temporal element is essential to the assurances given in each segment. God assures Baruch that the destruction and dispersion are temporary (4:1; 5:3), while Baruch assures his people that his departure from them is temporary (34:1).

Baruch's community temporarily recedes from the story, as Baruch goes alone to the Holy of Holies. There he laments his inability to mourn sufficiently over what has happened to the Temple (chap. 35). This lament is Baruch's final expression of distress over the destruction; from this point forward, his attention is directed to the ongoing life of the faithful community in this *present time* and to the final eschatological judgment.

After his lament, Baruch falls asleep and sees a vision (chaps. 36-37). A vine and fountain approach a great forest and gradually uproot it. Finally, only one cedar tree is left. The vine confronts the cedar and announces its demise. The tree disappears, and a field full of unfading flowers appears.

Baruch awakes (37:1) and responds to the vision with a prayer for its interpretation (chap. 38). As He did previously (chaps. 22-30), God replies to Baruch's prayer by initiating further conversation with him (chaps. 39-43). The first subject is the interpretation of the vision (chaps. 39-40). Baruch learns that it describes the defeat of Rome[11] and its last wicked leader (the forest and the cedar tree) by the Messiah (the vine and fountain). After the Messiah has convicted and killed the last Roman leader, he will inaugurate an era of peace and fecundity, which will last until *the times previously mentioned* are fulfilled. Thus, through the vision Baruch gets a glimpse of what will happen when God's anger awakes and His retribution falls on Rome (cf. chaps. 12-13).

Baruch responds to the interpretation by asking who will be worthy to live *at the last times* (41:1-6). The specific objects of his concern are two groups within Israel—apostates and proselytes:

---

[11] God does not state explicitly that the vision refers to "Rome." However, by describing the forest as the fourth kingdom which will follow Babylon (39:1-5), He clearly infers that this is the case.

To whom will these things be, and how many (will they be)? or who will be worthy to live *at that time?* . . . . For lo, I see many of Your people who have withdrawn from Your *covenant* and thrown off from themselves the yoke of the *Torah*. But others again I have seen who have forsaken their emptiness and fled for refuge. What therefore will be to them? Or how will the *last times* receive them? (41:1-5)

God's reply is brief and to the point:

As for those who before *submitted,* and afterwards withdrew and mingled them- selves with the seed of mingled peoples, the *time* of these was the former. . . . And as for those who before knew not but afterwards knew life, and mingled with the seed of the people which had separated itself, the *time* of these is the latter. . . . (42:4-5)[12]

The use of the terms "covenant," "Torah," and "submit" connect this conversation to the conversation between God and Baruch in Block 2 (chaps. 13-20). In the former discussion, God emphasized the torment awaiting the *many* Jews who had chosen to sin despite the fact that they had received the Torah and the covenant (15:1-19:3). In the present conversation, the "sin" of these *many* Jews is described further as assimilation to the ways of the nations.

As was the case in Block 2 (20:3-6), God concludes the conversation by giving Baruch instructions and promising him that he will receive further revelations (43:1-3).

Block 5 (Chapter 44-52)

Block 5 consists of a narrative introduction (44:1), Baruch's speech to his designated successors (44:2-45:2), a conversation between Baruch and his community (chaps. 46-47), a prayer (48:1-24), and a conversation between God and Baruch (48:25-52:7). This Block integrates motifs from the earlier discussions on God's justice (Blocks 1, 2, 4) and His power (Blocks 1, 2, 3) for two purposes: 1) to explicate the characteristics of the faithful community, here identified as "Israel," and to describe the basis of its existence in the present time; and 2) to describe the eschatological judgment, which will result in the exultation of the righteous and the torment of the wicked at the end of time. In addition, the second cycle of the story continues to evolve, as Baruch announces his impending death and initiates a transfer in leadership from himself to his designated successors. He also promises that leadership under the Torah never will be lacking for the faithful community.

The story continues (44:1) as Baruch fulfills the first instruction given to him (cf. 43:3) by returning to his people. He selects certain persons and delivers a testamentary speech in which he transfers the leadership of the community from himself to them.

Behold, I go unto my fathers according to the way of all the earth. But withdraw not from the way of the Torah, but guard and admonish the people who remain, so that they do not withdraw from the commandments of the Mighty One. (44:2-3)

Therefore, as much as you are able, instruct the people, for that work is ours. For if you teach them, you will make them alive. (45:1)[13]

---

[12]The text is corrupt. I have followed the logical emendation of R. H. Charles, *APOT* 2. 502.

[13]Previously, Baruch "instructed" Israel (31:3). Now he tells his designated successors to "instruct" the people (45:1).

Within the speech, Baruch also shares part of the revelations he has received.   He promised his hearers that endurance in the Torah will lead to the sight of the consolation of Zion, and to participation in the eschatological world and *time* (44:7-15).

Baruch's successors react with anger and panic to the announcement of his impending death.   Accusing God of humiliating them, they ask Baruch how the community can survive without his leadership (46:1-3).   Previously, Baruch reacted to the destruction of Jerusalem with anger and panic; here his successors respond in a similar way to the announcement of his forthcoming death.

> There are several indications that the reaction of Baruch's successors to the announcement of his impending death is modelled after Baruch's reaction to the sight of the destruction of Jerusalem (Block 2--chaps. 6-11). Both texts begin with a narrative introduction in which Baruch either returns to or leaves Jerusalem (6:1; 44:1). In the first text (6:3-8:5), the sight of the destruction was accompanied by visual confirmation for Baruch that angels from a transcendent realm had deprived the enemy of any real claim to victory. However, Baruch's reaction to the destruction in the form of his lament (10:6-11:7) indicated that the sight of the angelic intervention was not sufficient to console him. In the present text, the announcement of Baruch's impending death is accompanied by the assurance that there are resources for the faithful community to survive in this world and to participate in a future, transcendent realm (44:1-45:1). However, the angry reaction of Baruch's successors to his words (46:1-3) indicates that the promise of participation in the future world is not sufficient to console them.

Baruch promies his hearers that the faithful community will never lack leadership under the Torah, and he exhorts that community to submit to the Torah and its teachers.[14]

> The throne of the Mighty One I cannot resist; nevertheless, there shall not be wanting to Israel a wise man or a son of the Torah to the race of Jacob. But only prepare your hearts, that you may obey the Torah, and submit to those who in fear are wise and understanding, and prepare your souls not to withdraw from them. For if you do these things, good tidings will come to you. (46:4-6)

Thus, the community can be consoled about the loss of Baruch and can face the future confidently without him.

After dismissing his successors, Baruch fulfills the second instruction given to him (cf. 43:3) by returning to Mt. Zion and fasting for seven days (47:1-2). Then he utters his third prayer (48:1-24). In this prayer, Baruch intercedes for the faithful community whom he addressed just previously. After praising God's power over time and space (48:1-10), he petitions:

> Protect us in Your compassion, and in Your mercy help us. Behold the *few* who have submitted to You; and destroy not the hope of our people, and cut not short the *times* of our aid. (48:18-19)

Baruch's description of this community of the *few* (cf. 18:1-2) emphasizes that these people are "Israel,"[15] and that the Torah is the basis of their continued existence:

---

[14]The change in audience from Baruch's successors to the entire community is not explicit. However, the context indicates that this is the case.

[15]Based on the preceding conversation between God and Baruch (chaps. 41-43), this community includes faithful Jews and proselytes.   The precise meaning of the term "proselyte" is ambiguous throughout 2 Baruch.

For this is the nation which you have chosen, and these are the people to whom You find no equal. . . . In You do we trust, for lo, Your Torah is with us, and we know that we will not fail as long as we keep Your covenant. To *all time* we are blessed . . . because we have not mingled with Gentiles. For we are all one named people, who have received one Torah from One; and the Torah which is among us will aid us, and the surpassing wisdom which is in us will help us. (48:20-24)

Baruch's community is Israel; Baruch is confident that the Torah guarantees their survival *in this present time.*

The description of the community in this prayer must be read against the backdrop of the description of the *many* in Block 4 (chaps. 41-43): they have kept the covenant (48:22) rather than withdrawing from it (42:3); they base their trust on the presence of the Torah among them (48:22) rather than throwing off the yoke of the Torah (41:3); they, unlike the Jews mentioned in 42:4, have not mingled with the Gentiles.

In contrast to the prayer's emphasis on *this time,* the conversation which follows (48:26-52:7) integrates the themes of God's justice and power in order to describe the eschatological judgment at the *end of time.* As a result of the knowledge he gains about the future, Baruch is able to acknowledge God's justice and power even in the *present time.*

The initial part of the conversation (48:29-47) describes God's eschatological judgment against the nations.[16] A description of the tribulations which will occur *at that time* (48:31-37) is followed by God's indictment of the peoples of the earth:

. . . *in all those times* they polluted themselves, and they overreached. Each man walked in his own works, and did not remember the Torah of the Mighty One . . . each of the inhabitants of the earth knew when he was transgressing, but My Torah they did not know because of their pride. (48:38, 40)

The time of judgment is approaching: "the Judge is coming and will not delay" (48:39).

Baruch responds to what God has just said about the nations by acknowledging the justness of God's plan for mankind:

. . . You (God) commanded the dust to produce Adam, and You know the number of those who are born from him, and how much they have sinned . . . their end will convict them and Your Torah, which they have transgressed, will requite them *on Your day.* (48:46-47)

Baruch's previous impatience has been allayed because now he can view the present from the perspective of the final times.

This perspective dominates the words with which Baruch interrupts his conversation with God to address the righteous:[17]

. . . surely, as in a *short time* in this world which passes away you have endured much labor, so in that world to which there is no end you will receive great light. (48:56)

---

[16]The text does not refer explicitly to the nations. However, the terms used to describe the recipients of judgment are borrowed from earlier sections (chaps. 12-13) which deal with the nations.

[17]The technique of interjecting a direct address out of context was used earlier in Baruch's first lament (11:1-2). There, as here, the address anticipated the following discussion. Cf. 54:17-18.

Basically, Baruch here repeats *to the righteous* what God revealed *to him* in Block 2 (15:7-8).

The remainder of God's comments deal with the eschatological destinies of the righteous and the wicked. In response to Baruch's question about the shape of the resurrected bodies (49:2), He describes the details of the eschatological judgment. The Torah will be the criterion of final condemnation or exaltation.

> The terminology used by God to describe the burial and resurrection of the dead previously was used to describe the burial and ultimate restoration of the Temple vessels (50:2; 6:8-9). Similarly, the description of the exaltation of the righteous (51:7-14) contains motifs originally appearing in God's comments about the heavenly city (4:2-6; 51:7-11) and in Baruch's first lament (10:17; 51:10). Thus, there is a definite parallelism at work. The righteous dead and the Temple vessels will remain in the earth until the judgment. They then will be raised to the heavenly world and Temple.

The element of *time* remains essential in God's concluding remarks. The righteous have chosen *the time* which will not age them, and in which they will be delivered from the world of tribulation (51:8-14). Those persons who will perish have not chosen *this time;* they have selected *that time* whose limits are full of groans and lamentations. They have rejected the *time of glory* (51:16).

Baruch's response to God's words emphasizes further his realization that the *future time* offers the best perspective from which to approach the *present time.* He acknowledges that continued lamentations over the *present desolation* of Zion (cf. 10:5ff.; chap. 35) are inappropriate; lamentations should be reserved for the *future torment* (52:3). His second address to the righteous encourages them to make his perspective their own:

> . . . rejoice in the suffering which you now suffer: for why do you look to the aberration of those who hate you? Make ready your souls for that which is reserved for you, and prepare your souls for the reward which is laid up for you. (52:6-7)

Essentially, the major concerns of 2 Baruch have been resolved. Baruch has attained consolation regarding God's justice and power in relation to "mother Zion," and his community has been assured that they have the resources to move from grief over the loss of "father Baruch" to consolation.

Block 6 (Chapters 53-76)

Block 6 consists of a narrative introduction (53:1a), a vision (53:1b-11), a prayer (chap. 54), and a conversation between the angel Ramiel and Baruch (chaps. 55-76). This Block emphasizes in three ways the vindication of God as just and powerful: 1) through Baruch's praise of God's justice and power; 2) through the application of God's general plan for mankind to the details of Israel's history; and 3) through Baruch's doxology and rhetorical exhortation to his people.

The story continues as Baruch falls asleep and sees another vision (53:1-11). A cloud with the likeness of lightning at its top rains twelve sets of alternating dark and light waters on the earth. After a final shower of dark waters, the lightning seizes the cloud, hurls it to the earth, and takes dominion over the earth.

Baruch awakes (53:12) and prays that the vision be interpreted for him (chap. 54). The consolation available to the righteous is emphasized in his description of God's revelatory activity among His people:

> You reveal to those who fear You what is prepared for them, that they may be comforted. You show great acts to those who do not know; You break up the

enclosure of those who are ignorant; and light up what is dark, and reveal what is hidden to the pure, who in faith have submitted to You and Your Torah. (54:4-5)

After petitioning God to reveal the interpretation of the vision (54:6), Baruch reverses his earlier laments by uttering a lengthy doxology (54:7ff.). The same Baruch who once summoned life to cease because of the "desolation of this mother" (10:5-11:7) now affirms "blessed be my mother among those who bear . . ." (54:10). His praise of God culminates in his definitive vindication of God's justice and power:

And justly do they perish who have not loved Your Torah, and the torment of judgment will await those who have not submitted to Your power. For though Adam first sinned and brought untimely death to all, yet of those who were born of him, each one of them has prepared for his own soul torment to come, and again each one of them has chosen for himself glories to come. (54:11-15)

Baruch interrupts his prayer to address the wicked, admonishing them to turn to their deserved destruction (54:17-18). Then he concludes the prayer by reiterating his conviction that the righteous will be glorified and the wicked will experience God's vengeance at the *consummation* of the world (54:21-22).

After his prayer, Baruch contemplates the condemnation which awaits the wicked (55:1-2). Suddenly, the angel Ramiel appears, and initiates a conversation with him (chaps. 55-76). His interpretation of the vision (chaps. 56-74) applies God's general plan for mankind to the details of Israel's history. The cloud represents the duration of the world. The bright and dark waters which rained upon the earth reflect high and low points in Israel's history. The interpretation culminates in the advent of the Messiah (the lightning), who appears after the twelve sequences of waters and the final turbulent waters. He inaugurates an era of paradaisical peace and fecundity, in which the curses brought about by Adam's sin are reversed (chaps. 72-74).

Baruch's response to Ramiel's words is a doxology (75:1-8). His earlier frustration over God's incomprehensibility (cf. 14:8-19) dissolves into praise of God (75:1-6). However, the doxology is not Baruch's final word. He returns to the covenantal imagery of Blocks 2, 4, and 5 in order to deliver a rhetorical address to his community:

But if we who exist know from where we have come, and submit to Him who brought us out of Egypt, we shall come again and remember those things which have passed, and shall rejoice regarding that which has been. But if now we know not from where we have come, and recognize not the principate of Him who brought us out of Egypt, we shall come again and seek after those things which have been now, and be grieved with pain because of those things which have happened. (75:7-8)

Knowledge and submission will lead to rejoicing--knowledge of the revelations Baruch has received about the *future* and the *past* of his community; and submission to the God who continues to be in a covenant relationship with His faithful people in the *present time*.

The conversation concludes (chap. 76) as Ramiel announces that after forty days Baruch will be taken from the earth.[18] He instructs Baruch to use the interim period to instruct the people so that they might learn to live *at the last times.*

---

[18]The announcement that Baruch will be taken from the earth after forty days establishes a typology between Baruch and Moses, which is continued in the next block.

Block 7 (Chapter 77)[19]

    Block 7 consists of a narrative introduction (77:1). Baruch's speech to his community (77:2-10), a conversation between Baruch and his community (77:11-17), and a narrative conclusion (77:18-26). This Block forms an epilogue to 2 Baruch. Speaking with the authority of Moses, Baruch delivers his testament to the people. Then, as necessitated by the story, he leaves them permanently. He writes and sends letters to the diaspora, thereby indicating that his message is authoritative for all Jews everywhere.

    After he has assembled all his people (77:1), Baruch delivers his final message to them. His speech (77:2-10) emphasizes that the dispersions of the twelve tribes and the destruction of Jerusalem were due to the people's sins. However, Baruch promises the people that if they direct their ways properly, their dispersed brothers will return to them.

    The people respond by assuring Baruch that they will remember the good things of God as best they can. However, they request that Baruch write a letter to the brothers in Babylon to strengthen them before his death. The reason for this request is as follows:

> For the shepherds of Israel have perished, and the lamps which gave light are extinguished, and the fountains have withheld their stream from which we used to drink. And we are left in the darkness, and without the counsel of a shepherd,[20] and in the thirst of the desert. (77:13-14)

Baruch quickly reassures them:

> Shepherds and lamps and fountains come from the Torah, and though we depart, the Torah remains. If therefore you have respect to the Torah, and are intent upon wisdom, a lamp will not be wanting, and shepherd will not fail, and a fountain will not dry up. (77:15-16)

Thus, the survival of the community is guaranteed because the Torah, which spawns its own teachers, endures throughout time. Here Baruch expresses the definitive answer to his earlier question about the future of Israel and the efficacy of God's words to Moses about Israel (cf. 3:5, 9).

    The story in 2 Baruch concludes as Baruch leaves the people and writes two letters. He sends one letter to Babylon with three men. The other letter he sends by eagle to the nine and one/half tribes (77:18-26). In this way, his message is conveyed to all Jews everywhere.

        The type of leadership envisioned by the author of 2 Baruch poses an interesting puzzle. Although there is a clear transference of leadership to Baruch's designated successors, the exact identity and function of these successors is never given. Throughout the book, Baruch clearly functions as a prophet. Thus, it is quite possible that his people's panic is due to the fear that prophetic leadership will cease with his death. If this is so, then the "shepherds" whom Baruch promises will arise from the Torah easily could be prophetic leaders. This hypothesis supports the argument that not all Jews believed that prophecy had ceased in the time of Ezra.

---

    [19]This analysis of 2 Baruch assumes that chapters 1-77 comprise the entire book. I do not believe that the Epistle of Baruch (chapters 78-87) is an integral part of 2 Baruch. The decision to omit the Epistle is defended at length in my dissertation.

    [20]The phrase "without the counsel of a shepherd" is corrupt. I am following the emendation of F. Zimmerman, "Textual Observations on the Apocalypse of Baruch," *JTS* 40 (1939) 151-56.

Summary

This analysis has revealed that 2 Baruch indeed tells a story--a story in which Baruch and then his community move from grief to consolation. Baruch's laments give way to doxology because of the revelations he has received from God; and his community's fears are replaced by consolation as he shares these revelations with them.

The questions which Baruch raises in the wake of the destruction introduce the issue of God's justice and power relative to the destruction. As a result of his conversations with God, Baruch acknowledges that his questions have been answered. Because of the knowledge he gains about the *future times,* Baruch is able to affirm God's justice and power in the *present time.*

Throughout the book, Baruch shares the revelations he has received with his people. Their reactions to him develop the issue of the survival of the faithful community in the aftermath of the destruction. Because of the knowledge they gain about the *future times* and about the ongoing leadership under the Torah in the *present time,* Baruch's community is able to accept his death and to face *their own future* with confidence.

The contrast between the "private" and the "public" Baruch is noteworthy. In his private conversations with God, Baruch probes the theological ramifications of the destruction. It is in this context that the issue of God's justice and power is raised and resolved. In his public encounters with his people, Baruch applies what he has learned to the practical needs of his community. Here the issue of God's power and justice is secondary to the people's primary concern--the survival of the community after Baruch's death.

The dimension of *time* is an essential element in all facets of the story told in 2 Baruch. All of the evidence indicates that the *delay* in the *consummation* must have been problematic for the community for which 2 Baruch was composed. The resolution to this problem is summarized in Baruch's final doxology (chap. 75). Consolation is possible through knowledge of the *eschatological future* and of *Israel's past* within the context of God's plan for mankind. This knowledge, coupled with submission to the Torah and its teachers, makes *life in the present* worth living and guarantees entrance into the *future world and time.*

OTHER RESPONSES TO THE DESTRUCTION--A COMPARISON

In this part of the paper I will compare 2 Baruch with three contemporary documents--4 Ezra, Pseudo-Philo, and the Apocalypse of Abraham. The comparison will illustrate the similarities and differences in these responses to the destruction of Jerusalem.

2 Baruch and 4 Ezra

As I noted in the introduction to this paper, scholars have tended to assume that 2 Baruch and 4 Ezra are addressing the same questions.[21] However, the preceding analysis of 2 Baruch indicates that the books are controlled by substantially different responses to the events of 70 C.E. These differences are apparent in at least five ways.

(1)   Although both books use the destruction of 587 B.C.E. as a model for the destruction of 70 C.E., the relationship of the main character to that event differs significantly. Baruch witnesses the destruction and immediately reacts to it. He laments the desolation of Zion and raises questions about the concrete implications of the destruction for the future of Israel and of the nations. He does not speculate about the theoretical implications of the event.

In contrast, Ezra appears in Babylon thirty years after the destruction. The desolation of Zion and the prosperity of Babylon form the basis of his theoretical speculations

---

[21]See above, notes 1 and 2.

about the effects of the evil heart on Adam's descendants (3:1ff.). While Baruch laments the particular event, Ezra probes the universal implications of the human weakness which he believes was responsible for the event.

(2)   Because of their different relationships to the destruction, Baruch and Ezra raise substantially different questions in response to the events of 70 C.E. Baruch argues that God's method of administering justice in this particular situation is ineffective, and he is impatient with God's failure to exercise His power to the nations immediately. The individual's ability to fulfill the Torah is not an issue in Baruch's questions. In contrast, Ezra's basic premise is that the propensity to sin resulting from the evil heart makes it impossible for almost anyone to fulfill the Torah and thereby to obtain life. The sins which prompted God to deliver His city to the enemy are the last in a long string of examples of the effects of the evil heart (3:19-26; 7:116-120). Thus, Ezra's question is actually an accusation: God places demands on His people which they cannot fulfill, and then punishes them for their failure to do so. In addition, Ezra protests that God humiliates His people further by allowing nations more wicked than they to punish them (3:27-36).

(3)   Uriel's responses to Ezra's grief also are addressed to questions different from those discussed by God and Baruch. The distinction between the *many* and the *few* occurs in the conversations between God and Baruch and in Uriel's words. In 2 Baruch, the distinction is used to identify as Israel the *few* Jews who have remained loyal to the Mosaic heritage, in contrast to the *many* Jews who have chosen the darkness of Adam. The question of whether the human will is free is not a part of the discussion.[22]

In 4 Ezra, Uriel uses the distinction to defend God's decision to let the *many* sinners perish, while the *few* righteous persons obtain salvation (7:11-14, 20-25, 70-73, 127-8:3). The issue here is the difficulty of obtaining final salvation, not the present identification of Israel. Central to Uriel's argument is the assertion, contra Ezra, that the individual is completely free to make his/her decision vis-a-vis God.

(4)   Although Ezra and Baruch both move to consolation because of the revelations they receive about the future, the nature of those revelations differs significantly. Baruch converses with God, and gains knowledge which enables him to acknowledge that his questions have been answered. Moreover, repeatedly he shares the revelation he has received with his community.

In contrast, Ezra sees the heavenly city (9:38-10:58), and he receives two visions of the end-time, which are interpreted for him (11:1-12:34; 13:1-52). Although obviously he is consoled, Ezra never explicitly acknowledges that his accusations have been refuted. Moreover, much of the revelation he has received is for the exclusive use of the wise within his community (12:35-39; 14:44-48).

(5)   The relationship of Baruch and Ezra to their communities illustrates yet another difference between the two books. Baruch is a pastoral figure to all his people; he shares the revelations he has received with them, transfers the leadership from himself to others when his death approaches, and reassures them that their continued survival is guaranteed because of the Torah and the leaders it will spawn. Moreover, his community's response to him plays an important role in the unfolding of the story.

In contrast, Ezra has very little contact with his people, and he offers only superficial responses to their fears that he is abandoning them (4:16-19; 12:40-49). Moreover, his community's response to him plays an important role in the unfolding of the story.

In contrast, Ezra has very little contact with his people, and he offers only superficial responses to their fears that he is abandoning them (4:16-19; 12:40-49). Moreover, he is told to withhold certain esoteric knowledge from the general public and to transmit

---

[22]Similarly, Baruch is not addressing the question of whether the will is free in his later comments about the effects of Adam's sin on his descendants (48:42-47; 54:15, 19). Rather, he is expressing his consolation; because of the revelations he has received about the future, he can acknowledge God's justice and power in the present times.

it only to a wise elite within the community. The conclusions of the books emphasize these differences. Baruch sends letters to the diaspora so that all Jews everywhere might share the revelations he has received; Ezra writes the Torah for the general community, and books of esoteric knowledge for the wise within the community.

The contrasts between the encounters of Baruch and Ezra with their communities provide a particularly interesting point of comparison. Baruch's three encounters with his community are essential to the story which is being told. Ezra also meets with his people or their leader three times (4:16-19; 12:40-49; 14:27-36). In the first two meetings, the people or their leader express a feeling of abandonment similar to that expressed by Baruch's community. In the final encounter, Ezra delivers a speech to all the people which bears little, if any, relationship to the revelations he has received throughout the book. Interestingly, none of the three encounters are essential components in the development of the book; if they were omitted, their absence hardly would be noticed.[23]

2 Baruch and Pseudo-Philo

Pseudo-Philo shares 2 Baruch's concern about the survival of the Jewish community in the troubled years ca. 70 C.E. Both books emphasize that God remains loyal to His covenant commitment to His people, despite their oppression by the nations.[24] Both books also assert that submission to the Torah is essential to the community's survival, and both promise that God will continue to raise up leaders for His people.[25] The issue of ongoing leadership is the most striking similarity between the books. In both instances, a perceived threat to the community's survival is countered by the assurance that new leaders will appear to guide the community.

The primary difference between the books is apparent in the Biblical models used as the basis for both documents. The author of 2 Baruch uses the destruction of 587 B.C.E. as the basis from which to raise and to resolve questions originating in the wake of the destruction of 70 C.E. In contrast, the author of Pseudo-Philo resolves similar kinds of questions by applying the Biblical pattern of sin/punishment/repentance/deliverance directly to the situation of his community. On the basis of this pattern, he expresses the conviction that God will deliver His people in the present time as He did in the past. Although there are hints that the ultimate resolution of Israel's dilemmas will occur only on an eschatological level (i.e., 28:6-9), the eschatological resolution is not as central in Pseudo-Philo as it is in 2 Baruch.

Thus, Pseudo-Philo and 2 Baruch agree that God will continue to raise up leaders for the faithful community. However, the authors of the two books express this conviction from different perspectives. Because of the revelation they have received about the *future*, Baruch's community can be confident that their survival is guaranteed in the *present time*. Because of the example of God's activities in the *past*, Pseudo-Philo's community can be confident that God will act to deliver them in the *present time*.

---

[23]In fact, this is what scholars tend to do. The encounters between Ezra and his people are mentioned only rarely in analyses of 4 Ezra. Earl Breech ("These Fragments") tries to incorporate them into his analysis of 4 Ezra; however, his attempt is not particularly convincing.

[24]See Pseudo-Philo 9:3; 12:8; 18:5-11; 19:9; 30:2-4; 35:2-6; 7:4; 32:1; 53:8; 59:3; 21:4; 23:12-13; 28:4; 60:2.

[25]For an excellent survey of the major leaders and their functions in Pseudo-Philo, see G. W. E. Nickelsburg, "Good and Bad Leaders," in J. Collins and G. Nickelsburg, eds., *Ideal Figures in Ancient Judaism* (SCS 12; Chico: Scholars Press, 1980) 49-65.

2 Baruch and the Apocalypse of Abraham

   2 Baruch and the Apocalypse of Abraham both address the question of the oppression of Israel by the nations. In addition, they share a concern with God's justice toward the wicked and the righteous within Israel.[26] The emphasis on cultic defilement in the Apocalypse of Abraham is particularly interesting in this context. As part of his argument that the cult in Jerusalem was defiled prior to the destruction, the author describes the idolatrous activities of Manasseh in the Temple (chap. 25). In 2 Baruch, these activities are described within the cloud/waters vision (chaps. 64-65).[27]

   Despite the similarities, there are significant differences between the books. They have different settings and forms: 2 Baruch tells a story which is set in 587 B.C.E., while the Apocalypse of Abraham describes the mystical ascent of Abraham back at the beginning of Israel's history (chaps. 9ff.). Moreover, the issue of ongoing leadership under the Torah is completely lacking in the Apocalypse of Abraham. Perhaps the most striking difference is the personification of evil in the figure of Azazel in the Apocalypse of Abraham (chaps. 13-14, 23-24). Here the author of the Apocalypse is much close to the "evil heart" imagery of 4 Ezra than he is to 2 Baruch.

---

[26] See the Apocalypse of Abraham 13, 23-27, 29, 32.

[27] Although not discussed in this paper because of limitations in space, there is evidence in 2 Baruch to suggest that the author perceived that the Temple cult was defiled prior to the destruction.

DOES LUKE MAKE A SOTERIOLOGICAL STATEMENT IN ACTS 20:28?

Waldemar Schmeichel
Kalamazoo College

Scholars have intermittently observed that for Luke the death of Jesus does not function as a saving event, that Luke does not understand the cross as a soteriological datum. Such a claim relies on the near absence of *anti/peri pollōn* or *hyper hēmōn/ hymōn* language in conjunction with the cross or the death of Jesus and has frequently been systematized into the conclusion that Luke does not have a *theologia crucis*. Methodologically as diverse scholars as M. Dibelius, H. J. Cadbury, C. H. Dodd, and J. M. Creed[1] have expressed themselves in agreement with such a conclusion. More recently U. Wilckens could assert, "The death of Jesus has no redemptive significance, and hence the Lukan christology in general lacks any substantial soteriology."[2] H. Conzelmann agreed, "The decisive thing is that Luke says nothing about the redemptive significance of the cross and that he does not link forgiveness with the death of Jesus."[3] Finally, E. Haenchen can speak of a "soteriologisches Loch"[4] in Lukan theology.

However, one may object to the equation of a soteriology with a *theologia crucis,* the above statements reflect an unconscious *Tendenz* on the part of scholarship as a whole to approach the question of a Lukan soteriology from the vantage point of the redemptive significance of the death of Jesus. The reasons for this *Tendenz* are quickly apparent when one recalls the long shadow of Paul, Luke's traditionally held theological mentor, and the centrality of the *theologia crucis* there. As a result, to the extent Paul's theology remains suggestive for an inquiry into Lukan thought, Pauline ideas will nuance the questions we ask of Luke.

A second reason for such a *Tendenz* is more concrete and more problematic. Luke-Acts actually contains two passages in which unambiguous *theologia crucis* language is found: Luke 22:19b-20 and Acts 20:28. The former is the long text of the Lukan Lord's Supper, and if the towering influence of Westcott and Hort[5] is granted, as it is in the RSV and the NEB, we are dealing with an example of a Western non-interpolation. In such a case the Lukan Lord's Supper text does not contain language applying the cup and the bread/body to human salvation. If, however, Westcott and Hort are overruled and the long text is allowed, as is a growing consensus today,[6] we have the phrase "this cup which is poured out for you. . . ." But the fact that such language occurs in a liturgical context diminishes any conclusion one would want to draw from it other than that Luke accepted a hallowed phrase from traditional worship. Indeed, J. Jeremias has demonstrated the

---

[1]Martin Dibelius, *From Tradition to Gospel* (trans. by B. L. Woolf; New York: Ch. Scribner's Sons, 1934) 201; Henry J. Cadbury, *The Making of Luke-Acts* (New York: Macmillan, 1927) 280 and *The Beginnings of Christianity,* Part I, Vol. 5 (ed. by F. J. Foakes Jackson and Kirsopp Lake; London: Macmillan and Co., 1933) 366; Charles H. Dodd, *The Apostolic Preaching and Its Development* (New York: Harper and Bros., 1949) 25; John M. Creed, *The Gospel According to St. Luke* (London: Macmillan and Co., 1930) LXXII.
[2]Ulrich Wilckens, *Die Missionsreden der Apostelgeschichte* (WMANT 5; Neukirchen: Neukirchener Verlag, 1961) 216.
[3]Hans Conzelmann, *The Theology of St. Luke* (trans. by G. Buswell; New York: Harper and Row, 1960) 201.
[4]Ernst Haenchen, *Die Apostelgeschichte* (MeyerK 5; 13th ed.; Goettingen: Vandenhoeck & Ruprecht, 1961) 689.
[5]Brook F. Westcott and Fenton J. Hort, *The New Testament in the Original Greek* (Cambridge: Macmillan and Co., 1881-82) Vol. I, p. 177; Vol. II, Appendix, pp. 63-64.
[6]Joachim Jeremias, *The Eucharistic Words of Jesus* (trans. by N. Perrin; London: SCM Press, 1966) 152-56.

non-Lukan language in the Lord's Supper text and shown the traditional character of liturgical language in general.[7]

This leaves us with Acts 20:28 and its phrase "to feed the church of the Lord which he obtained with his own blood" (RSV). The fact that this is the only unambiguous language in all of Luke-Acts--26% of the whole New Testament!--in which the death of Jesus is described soteriologically, ought to have given pause to scholars long ago. On the contrary, scholars were strangely inhibited by this pericope toward three distinct conclusions.

1. Luke lived and thought in an environment of such pervasive *theologia crucis* understanding that he found it singularly unnecessary to belabor the point of his agreement with such theology. Thus Luke 22:19b-20, Acts 20:28 and the servant passages in the beginning of Acts are all clues for a *theologia crucis* in Luke-Acts which point to and take for granted this broader background, J. Jeremias, for example, argues.[8] Above all, the relative clause in Acts 20:28 "shatters" any contention that Luke does not understand the death of Jesus soteriologically. Proceding from the same evidence E. Lohmeyer had earlier maintained that such an argument therefore "kaum richtig sein duerfte."[9] More recently H. J. Michel agreed, "Dagegen beweist Apg. 20:28 zusammen mit Lukas 22:19, dass Lukas den Gedanken des Suehnetodes kennt, ihn akzeptiert und ihn so wenig mit seinen Ansichten im Widerspruch sieht, dass er ihn gelegentlich auch anfuehrt."[10]

2. A second position treats Acts 20:28 as a singular exception to an otherwise consistent absence of a soteriology of the cross. Thus E. Haenchen hears only here a "soteriological echo" in Acts:[11] K. Lake allows vs. 28b the status of an unsupported exception,[12] and V. Taylor judges it to stand out "boldly against the background of Acts."[13] However, none of these scholars pursued the matter beyond that point, but seemed content to allow the judgment of exception to be self-explanatory.

3. A third position, found in more recent studies, subsumes the death of Jesus under a conception of the salvific character of his whole life[14] or it is made to function in the context of *Heilsgeschichte* with a clear emphasis on the *Heil* in that *Geschichte*. Thus H. Flender insists, "Die Frage nach der Heilbedeutung des Kreuzes darf daher nicht isoliert gestellt werden. Das Kreuz ist innerhalb des ganzen Heilsgeschehen zu verstehen."[15] Similarly F. Schuetz, "In den lukanischen Schriften bildet die Passion jedoch

[7]Ibid., 155.

[8]Ibid., 158.

[9]Ernst Lohmeyer, "Vom Christlichen Abendmahl,"*ThRu* 9 (1937) 181.

[10]H. J. Michel, *Die Abschiedsrede des Paulus an die Kirche Apg. 20:17-38* (Munich: Koesel Verlag, 1973) 89. Cf. also Eduard Lohse, *Maertyrer und Gottesknecht. Untersuchungen zur urchristlichen Verkuendigung vom Suehnetod Jesu Christi* (FRLANT 46; Goettingen: Vandenhoeck & Ruprecht, 1955) 188-89 and W. G. Kuemmel, "Luc en accusation dans la theologie contemporaine,"*ETL* 46 (1970) 265-81, esp. 275.

[11]Ernst Haenchen, *The Acts of the Apostles* (trans. and ed. by R. McL. Wilson; Philadelphia: Westminster Press, 1971) 92, n. 6.

[12]Foakes Jackson and Lake, *Beginnings*, Vol. 5, 220.

[13]Vincent Taylor, *The Atonement in New Testament Teaching* (London: Epworth Press, 1940) 21. For further analogous judgments cf. Wilckens, *Missionsreden,* 184, n. 4; Conzelmann, *Theology,* 201, 230; Helmut Flender, *St. Luke Theologian of Redemptive History* (trans. by R. H. and I. Fuller; Philadelphia: Fortress Press, 1967) 157, n. 2; Ferdinand Hahn, *The Titles of Jesus in Christology* (trans. by H. Knight and G. Ogg; New York: World Publishing Co., 1969) 187; Guenther Voss, *Die Christologie der lukanischen Schriften in Grundzuegen* (Brueges: Desclee de Brouwer, 1965) 130.

[14]Richard Zehnle, "Jesus' Death in Lucan Soteriology," *TS* 30 (1969) 443, and Wilckens, *Missionsreden,* 185.

[15]Flender,*St. Luke,* 141.

einen festen Bestandteil der Geschichte als Geschichte Gottes mit der Welt, d. h. als Offenbarungsgeschichte."[16] Or the death of Jesus is subsumed under the resurrection. So A. George writes, "Sa nouveaute est d'insister sur le salut par la resurrection, et c'est bien des les origines un trait fondamental du message de l'Evangile."[17]

The paradigmatic function of the death of Jesus is stressed by G. Voss and G. Schneider. The former recognizes in the Lukan presentation "die Offenbarung seines Weges der vertrauenden Sohneshaltung als das Urbild menschlichen Selbstvollzugs."[18] The latter argues, "Der Maertyrer bekehrt solche, die sein Martyrium erleben, und er ruft diejenigen zur Nachahmung auf, die den Martyrerbericht lesen . . . Doch haengt das Zuruecktreten des Suehnegedankens bei dem dritten Evangelisten mit der Absicht zusammen, Jesu Sterben als Vorbild fuer den Christen zu zeichnen."[19]

These assessments in their individual ways agree that soteriological language is in fact used in Acts 20:28 to speak of the death of Jesus (cf. the reference to blood). The disagreements center on the theological significance of that language in the Lukan intent. Is it traditional? Is it stylistic? Is it emphatic? The answer is complicated by a significant textual problem which has accustomed Acts 20:28 to prominence, for the nineteenth century frequently tested its textual theories and judgments on it.[20]

Yet despite such long and concentrated attention--since J. J. Wettstein, E. Abbot documents[21]--no generally agreed upon results have accrued. The reason, in my judgment, lies in the peculiar interplay between the textual and soteriological problem areas and specifically in the fact that mainly the former was seen to be an issue while the text's soteriological assertion was throughout granted its full weight. In this inquiry I shall regard the textual and soteriological questions to be separately open for investigation by permitting the former the natural flow of its logic while the latter, though always a shadow, will first of all stay in penumbral background. Then I shall turn to the soteriological assertion itself and examine its force and validity against these broader questions: Given our present concern for the individual thought of the author, what did Luke have in mind when he used "God" or "Lord," "obtained," "church," "blood," and "his own" in the relative clause of a complex sentence? Given also a certain body of knowledge we have obtained from and about Luke, how does Acts 20:28 cohere with what we already know?

In the context of the speech to the elders of Ephesus Luke has Paul say *"Poimainein tēn ekklēsian tou . . . hēn periepoiēsato dia tou haimatos tou idiou."* (to feed the church of . . . which he obtained with his own blood). The ellipsis above can be filled either by *theou* from B etc. reading "the church of God" or by *kyriou* from p[74]AC∗D etc. reading "the church of the Lord."[22] Neither reading can establish itself by MS evidence alone, and ultimately arguments from internal probability will have to become decisive.

---

[16]Frieder Schuetz, *Der leidende Christus* (Stuttgart: Kohlhammer, 1969) 96.

[17]August George, "Le sense de la mort de Jesus pour Luc," *RB* 80 (1973) 217. For a broad overview of the issue cf. Anton Buechele, *Der Tod Jesu im Lukasevangelium. Eine redaktionsgeschichtliche Untersuchung zu Lk 23* (Frankfurt: Knecht, 1978); Charles Talbert, "Shifting Sands; The Recent Study of the Gospel of Luke," *Int* 30 (1976) 381-95, esp. p. 389, and Joseph A. Fitzmyer, *The Gospel According to Luke (I-IX)* (AB 28; Garden City, NY: Doubleday, 1981) 22-23, 219-27.

[18]Voss, *Christologie,* 130.

[19]Gerhard Schneider, *Verleugnung, Verspottung und Verhoer Jesu nach Lukas 22:54-71* (Munich: Koesel, 1969) 187, 188.

[20]For a review of the text critical issues and their significant literature cf. Charles F. DeVine, "The 'Blood of God' in Acts 20:28," *CBQ* 9 (1947) 381-408.

[21]Ezra Abbot, "On the Reading 'Church of God,' Acts 20:28," *BS* 33 (1876) 314.

[22]Bruce M. Metzger, *The Text of the New Testament* (New York: Oxford University Press, 1964) 234.

However, here for the first time it is imperative that the soteriological question in the form of the *haima* reference not be allowed to encroach on the textcritical issue.

The phrase "church of God" is a known New Testament expression occurring twelve times in the letters traditionally ascribed to Paul, while the phrase "church of the Lord" is not found in the New Testament, although *ekklēsia tou kyriou* is frequent in the LXX.[23] One could, of course, speculate that an author as septuagintally aware as Luke could appropriate the LXX phrase for a singular occasion. But as plausible as such a suggestion would seem to be, its speculative nature is all too evident.

When we turn to the *haima* reference, we focus on the central term of this passage which historically has overshadowed all other terms. A case in point is W. Bousset, "In 20:28 we are quite certainly to read *ekklēsia tou kyriou* (not . . . *theou* which is impossible because of the following *to haima to idion*."[24] A current example comes from H. J. Michel, "Der Sinn ist eindeutig: Das Blut Christi (=Kreuzestod) ist der Preis fuer den Loskauf der Gemeinde, die somit Gottes Eigentum wird.[25] Thus understood the term *haima* becomes a cipher not only for the person of Jesus, but for the passion story and specifically a soteriological appropriation of that story. As such it has come to determine what the other words in this sentence mean, indeed, can mean: The sentence as a whole is understood to come out of the conceptualization of the *theologia crucis*. All the details in it are now shaded to clarify this superficially so persuasive conclusion. The first casualty of this approach is the phrase "church of God" and the patripassian claim that it is God's blood which obtained the church. Beginning with the fifth century textual tradition we have repeated evidence of "Lord" being substituted for "God" with the implicit understanding that, of course, Jesus is meant by "Lord." Such substitution enhances the soteriological clarity of this sentence by having found conceptual room for the *sōtēr* himself.

If we, however, keep the soteriological issue at a distance, overwhelming evidence supports the reading "church of God." The MS evidence is stronger for such a reading, New Testament parallels can readily be found, a fact which is not true for its alternative, and the *lectio difficilior*, the rule of thumb which gives textual priority to grammatically and/or theologically more difficult readings, is most compelling for it as the suggestion for a patripassian meaning amply illustrates.

But a stronger argument can yet be made with a closer investigation of Luke's use of *haima*. It is widely used in the New Testament and frequently expresses the redemptive significance of the death of Jesus, especially in the Pauline literature and in the letter to the Hebrews.[26] It is also widely found in Luke-Acts, and it is imperative to determine whether Luke shares the general New Testament understanding at least in some instances or whether he employs the term in his own distinctive way.

The occurrences of *haima* in Luke-Acts can be classified into five categories: 1. as a simple physiological term (Luke 8:43-44; 13:1; 22:44; Acts 1:19; 22:20); 2. in conjunction with Jewish dietary laws (Acts 15:20, 29; 21:25); 3. in apocalyptic imagery (Acts 2:19-20); 4. in the Lord's Supper tradition in conjunction with the new covenant (Luke 22:20); and 5. as an oath formula (Luke 11:50-51; Acts 5:28; 18:6; 20:26). Of importance to us are only the last two categories of which the former, the longer text of the eucharistic statement, can be disregarded on the liturgical grounds I had argued above.

I am calling the expression "to be innocent/guilty of someone's blood" or to have "someone's blood required from someone" an oath formula on the basis of the Joshua 2:19 and Ezekiel 3:18, 20 injunctions. Both passages speak of high degrees of responsibility

---

[23]Ibid.

[24]Wilhelm Bousset, *Kyrios Christos* (trans. by J. E. Steely; Nashville: Abingdon, 1970) 289, n. 145.

[25]Michel, *Abschiedsrede,* 88.

[26]E.g., Rom 3:25; 5:9; Eph 1:7; Col 1:20; Heb 2:14; 9:12, 14, 18; 10:19, 29; 13:20.

for the lives of others. Should these be in jeopardy or forfeited as a result of my action or inaction, their blood shall be upon my hands in the same manner as if I had actually spilled it, i.e., killed them. It is in the context of this formula, I contend, that Luke comes as close as he does to use *haima* theologically. His intention is nowhere more apparent than in Acts 5:27-32 where the death of Jesus and the blood expression in our formula are interrelated in the same scene. The high priest in exasperation confronts the uncooperative apostles with the charge, "You intend to bring this man's (i.e., Jesus') blood upon us." This gives Luke the most propitious opening to have Peter pick up this reference to blood as a statement of judgment and reinterpret it as a saving statement. Instead, Peter responds, "God exalted him (Jesus) at his right hand as Leader and Savior, to give repentance to Israel and forgiveness of sins" (5:31). The blood statement in so close a sense relationship to the death of Jesus remains an oath formula while the death of Jesus leads to resurrection and exaltation for which then a soteriological force is claimed. As here so in the other references in this category (Luke 11:50-51; Acts 18:20, 26) the adjuring dimension prevails for *haima* and a soteriological nuance is nowhere suggested. Consequently, we have no Lukan encouragement to see in the *haima* of 20:28 a soteriological cipher. On the contrary, the evidence seems to point away from such a conclusion.

I now regard two issues as firmly established. Luke in fact wrote the "church of God" and he did not use *haima* as a cipher for the soteriological identity and function of Jesus. But the traditional soteriological language of Acts 20:28 beckons to find him there.

One immediate attempt is to see *theos* as a title for Jesus and this passage to affirm not only the soteriological function of his death but also the divinity of his being.[27] This patently is an imputed ascription made against the evident restraint the New Testament as a whole reserves for it and against the ambiguity attending to the few examples where Jesus and *theos* may refer to the same subject.[28] Further, the clearly subordinate position Jesus occupies toward the Father makes such an identification most implausible for Luke.

A second *Notloesung,* first proposed by Westcott and Hort, considers the possibility that *huios* (son) may have dropped out after *idios* (his own) "at some very early transcription affecting all existing documents."[29] Thus the difficult "blood of his own" would become the familiar "blood of his own son." E. Haenchen has also taken recourse to such a conjecture, but without an attempt to explain his choice.[30] More recently H. J. Michel justified such procedure on pragmatic grounds. "Diese Ergaenzung geschieht hier nicht ins Blaue hinein, sondern entspricht genau dem allseits unbestrittenen Verstaendnis der Stelle und ergibt als einziger Loesungsversuch einen sowohl grammatakalisch wie inhaltlich vernuenftigen Satz."[31] One could paraphrase Michel's argument in the following manner: "There is no ambiguity as to what Luke seems to mean here. We are only frustrated by his problematic choice of language and grammar." J. Dupont expresses the necessary objection: "Der Exeget hat den Text so zu erklaeren, wie er dasteht, und nicht, wie er ihn wuenscht."[32]

---

[27] DeVine, "The 'Blood of God,' " 394, 404, 408. Cf. the pointed criticism by Dupont, *Paulus,* 107-8.

[28] Vincent Taylor, "Does the New Testament Call Jesus God?" *ExpT* 73 (1961/62) 116-18. But cf. Oscar Cullmann, *The Christology of the New Testament,* (trans. by S. C. Guthrie and C. A. M. Hall; Philadelphia: Westminster, 1963) 306-14.

[29] Westcott and Hort, *New Testament,* Vol. II, 99-100.

[30] Haenchen, *Acts,* 589. Cf. the confidence of the American Bible Society which has the TEV translate, "Be shepherds of the church of God, which he made his own through the sacrificial death of his Son."

[31] Michel, *Abschiedsrede,* 25.

[32] Jacques Dupont, *Paulus an die Seelsorger. Das Vermaechtnis von Milet (Apg. 20:18-36)* (trans. from the French by F. J. Schierse; Duesseldorf: Patmos Verlag, 1966) 108.

A third proposal, equally speculative, assumes a change of subject in the relative clause, reading "the church of God which he, Jesus, of course, obtained with his own blood." This suggestion becomes somewhat more plausible with the assumption of traditional material Luke may have incorporated into this sentence. The word "church" required "God"; the word "blood" required "Jesus," and as the mind travelled over familiar territory, Luke's quill did not keep up. What was familiar to him, was also familiar to his readers who unconsciously made the necessary change of subject,[33] and only scholars who labor over their Greek take offence.

A further and more substantial way of introducing Jesus into Acts 20:28 is the translational ambiguity inherent in *tou haimatos tou idiou* which can be rendered adjectively as "his own blood" or substantively as "the blood of his Own," or more freely "the blood of one who was his Own." F. J. Hort observed, "This remarkable form seems to imply some peculiar force lying in the word *idiou*,"[34] which force would seem to require a substantive rendering. Such resolution is mitigated, however, by the absence of the singular *ho idios* as an independent substantive in New Testament literature, although the plural occurs, including four times in Luke-Acts (masculine: Acts 4:23; 24:23; neuter: Luke 18:28; Acts 21:6). The independent singular, however, is occasionally found in the papyri as a form of address implying near relationship.[35]

What is not warranted on the basis of such evidence is the use of the independent substantive as equivalent to and expressive of *ho idios huios*.[36] This caution is demanded by the near absence of christological contexts in which *idios* occurs. In over 125 instances where some form of *idios* is used in the New Testament, only once, Romans 8:32, is a christological phrase! Paul refers to God "who did not spare his own Son (*tou idiou huiou*)."

Thus Acts 20:28 presents *ho idios* twice in a unique form: Not only is this the sole New Testament example of the absolute use of the singular number of *idios*, it further--in traditional interpretation--is meant in a christological sense implying the word *huios*. Since the only instance of a christological usage of *ho idios* (Romans 8:32) readily supplies *huios*, the traditional soteriological understanding of Acts 20:28 builds its argument on a unique interpretation of a phrase which in turn stands on a unique formulation of that phrase. Even the analogical detour to *ho agapētos, ho monogenēs*, and *ho eklektos* "which are all Greek renderings of the Hebrew *yahid* ('only one,' 'solitary') and are often used with the added *huios*"[37] does not do more than point to the possibility that such usage was theoretically available. The fact that it is not used this way has to be a decisive consideration.

Further, the often noted analogy of *tou idiou huiou* of Romans 8:32 to *tou agapētou huiou* of Gen 22:16 (LXX) in the sense of the "only son" (Hebrew) has to be cautiously examined. Therefore O. Cullmann can certainly not be correct with his suggestion that "'his Own' was a title which early Christians gave to Jesus, comparable with 'the Beloved.'"[38] *Ho idios* apart from our problematic text is a non-existent phrase in the New Testament!

---

[33]I. Howard Marshall, *Luke: Historian and Theologian* (Grand Rapids: Zondervan, 1971) 173. Some have even gone so far as to recognize a prefiguration of trinitarian thought in this text. Dupont, *Paulus*, 112, writes, "Erst zum Schluss des Verses erscheint, gleichsam in sein Blut gehuelt, die Gestalt des Sohnes."

[34]Westcott and Hort, *New Testament*, 99.

[35]James H. Moulton, *A Grammar of New Testament Greek* (Edinburgh: Clark, 1908) 1. 60; and *The Expositor*, Ser. VI, Vol. 3 (1901) 277; James H. Moulton and George Milligan, *The Vocabulary of the Greek New Testament* (London: Hodder and Stoughton, 1930) 298.

[36]Foakes Jackson and Lake, *Beginnings*, 5. 372; Westcott and Hort, *New Testament*, 99.

[37]Foakes Jackson and Lake, *Beginnings*, 4. 262.

[38]Metzger, *Text*, 236; cf. Reginald H. Fuller, *The Foundations of New Testament Christology* (New York: Ch. Scribner's Sons, 1965) 201, n. 34.

Thus the continued scholarly effort to grasp *ho idios* on a larger scale than the author apparently intended has involved these efforts in a severe amount of supplementation. For the purposes of this study I shall regard *idios* in a neutral sense to mean simply "belonging to someone" or "own." Only the actual context can enrich that meaning.

Up to this point this study has had a negative and dismantling thrust. I pressed the soteriological claims and assumptions of each of the terms in the sentence under investigation and reviewed representative interpretations. None could sustain themselves once they were taken from under the umbrella of soteriological pre-understanding. On the other hand, the history of scholarship was hardly capricious in its treatment of Acts 20:28. By understanding it soteriologically, it was able to make sense out of a complicated sentence.

I now turn to the constructive part of interpreting the Lukan sentence "to feed the church of God which he obtained with the blood of his own one." Denied recourse to christological and soteriological categories, we need to ask the obvious question: Whose blood obtained the church? I would like to propose the thesis that it is Paul and his martyr blood which was shed in the service of establishing and obtaining the church of God. To substantiate this daring departure from traditional interpretation, I turn to the context of the speech and to the function it serves in the Book of Acts.

First of all, let us note a peculiarly Lukan stylistic habit. H. Conzelmann has pointed to the Lukan bracketing of the life of Jesus.[39] After the temptation story (Luke 4:13) Satan departs; before the Passion "Satan entered into Judas" (Luke 22:3). Between these two points "the middle of time" develops. N. Perrin sees this same feature with a different agent.[40] At the baptism (Luke 3:21-22) Jesus receives the Spirit, and on the cross he returns it to God (23:46). Between these two points Jesus is the exclusive bearer of the Spirit and functions by its guiding power.

Without the benefit of such clear verbal correspondence but with a pointed reference to Paul's beginning--"the ministry which I received from the Lord Jesus" (Acts 20:24)--we find an analogous trait in Paul's story. In Acts 9:15-16 God introduces Paul to Ananias as "a chosen instrument of mine" with the immediate qualification "how much he must suffer for my name." In Acts 20:28 Luke recaptures the sense of the phrase "God's instrument" by the term *idios* (his own) with the prior recognition that the blood which obtained churches was Paul's who fulfilled the condition of his call. I contend that the Lukan bent of mind which understood history in providential terms[41] and thus worked with a promise-fulfillment pattern, did not only see this pattern at work between an Old Testament promise and a New Testament fulfillment. Rather, the same pattern is at work within the much shorter span of Paul's life, for instance, when a beginning charged with a specific purpose is recognized at the end with the discharge of that purpose.

Important for this argument is the acknowledgment that this speech makes in fact an allusion to Paul's martyrdom (cf. vss. 22-27, 38) which for structural and theological reasons Luke cannot make more explicit than he does. His propensity to reach for the beginning when the end is irrevocably taking shape I adduce as first evidence for such a

---

[39]Conzelmann, *Theology*, 28 et passim. This period Conzelmann has called "satansfreie Zeit" for which he has been severely criticized but in substance unjustly so. The slogan is wrong, but apart from it two distinctly aggressive postures of Satan function in relationship to each other. For a critical evaluation cf. P. Schuyler Brown, *Apostasy and Perseverance* (Rome: Pontifical Biblical Institute, 1969). For a correctively positive judgment, cf. Schneider, *Verleugnung,* 1969, 181-82.

[40]Norman Perrin, *The New Testament: An Introduction* (New York: Harcourt Brace Jovanovich, 1974) 201, and *Christology and a Modern Pilgrimage. A Discussion with Norman Perrin* (ed. H. D. Betz; Claremont: The New Testament Colloquium, 1971) 56.

[41]Siegfried Schultz, "Gottes Vorsehung bei Lukas," *ZNW 54* (1963) 104-16.

conclusion. Further support I find in the following. Apart from the subsequent oracle of Agabus (21:10-14) this is the only Lukan reference to Paul's eventual fate.[42] From the presupposition of considerable Lukan compositional activity in Acts, some such reference is logically mandatory, for Luke recounts five hearings before various officials: before the Sanhedrin (22:30-23:10); Felix (24:1-23); Felix and Drusilla (24:24-25); Festus (25:6-12) and Festus and Agrippa II (26:1-32).[43] Luke owes the logic of his own compositional structure that he communicate some outcome of these hearings. This he cannot do at the conclusion of Acts, for his purpose is the glorious progression of the gospel which requires an upbeat ending for the "end" of Paul's story. For that same reason the drama of Paul's death cannot be directly told, for another Lukan purpose was to comfort a hard pressed church[44] by pointing to Roman tolerance and to missionary success. Since Paul in Acts 20 has reached his missionary plateau--Luke does not seem to know Romans 15!-- he presses here as it were the martyr's crown on his head.[45] The rest of Acts in the Lukan purpose could not sustain Paul's martyr story, and Luke is content to make some oblique yet unmistakable references to it. The Holy Spirit with uninterrupted frequency ("in every city," vs. 23) points to "imprisonment and afflictions."[46] Paul accepts the implications of such testifying and concludes for himself, "I do not account my life of any value nor as precious to myself" (vs. 24), and for his audience (readers!) that "all of you ... will see my face no more" (vs. 25). The elders unambiguously indicate that they understood the nature of his "departure" (vs. 29). In their only response to Paul's varied speech[47] "they sorrowed most of all because of the word . . . they should see his face no more" (vs. 38).

It is further often the characteristic of a farewell speech not to mention death specifically. Its euphemistic stand-in, however, does not mislead the audience which often responds specifically to that fact, as is the case in vs. 38.[48]

Since we are dealing with a speech of sufficient length (eighteen verses), we have a right to inquire into its internal structure, its movement of thought and compositional peculiarities. I will now approach this speech as its own entity with reciprocal internal elements by simply asking, "What does the speaker/author say and how has he organized his thoughts? (In all of this I will, of course, limit myself to the specific interest of this paper.)

Paul is speaking to church leaders from Ephesus who will carry on his work, and he commends continuation of that work in the manner in which he himself was accustomed to perform it. The beginning of the speech deals, therefore, with the past and is an overview of Paul's job performance. Its striking feature is the care and completeness with which Paul's church building efforts are surveyed. His integrity and the discharge of his calling are couched in language which abounds with practical absolutes. Paul is accounted for by an historical absolute ("all the time from the first day," vs. 18), a temporal absolute ("night and day," vss. 18, 31), spatially ("publically from house to house," vs. 20), emotionally ("all humility and tears," vs. 19), materially ("in all things I have shown you that by toiling . . . " vss. 33-35), by a universal absolute ("to Jews and to Greeks," vs. 21; "every one," vs. 31), by an absolute message ("anything profitable," vs. 20; "the whole counsel of God," vs. 27), by his exhaustive effort ("I did not cease to

---

[42] Heinz Schuermann, *Traditionsgeschichtliche Untersuchungen zu den synoptischen Evangelien* (Düsseldorf: Patmos Verlag, 1968) 326.

[43] Martin Dibelius, *Aufsaetze zur Apostelgeschichte* (ed. by H. Greeven; FRLANT 42; Goettingen: Vandenhoeck & Ruprecht, 1951) 178-79.

[44] Frieder Schuetz, *Der leidende Christus* (Stuttgart: Kohlhammer, 1969).

[45] Dibelius, *Aufsaetze*, 136. Translated by author.

[46] Perhaps by prophets, cf. Agabus (Acts 21:10-14).

[47] Haenchen, *Acts*, 595.

[48] Cf. Dupont, *Paulus*, 147 and the biblical examples cited on pp. 9-17, and Michel, *Abschiedsrede*, 35-72.

admonish," vs. 31; "I did not shrink from . . . " vss. 20, 27; "I am going to Jerusalem," vs. 22; cf. Luke 13:33) finally culminating in an absolute declaration of discharged responsibility ("I am innocent of the blood of all of you," vs. 26) that categorically divides the Pauline ministry from any possible post-Pauline aberrations.

It took all these absolutes to build the church--whether at Ephesus or elsewhere--Luke has Paul suggest. There were trials and plots from the start (vs. 19); there was the death of the builder at the end. It took all of this including the blood of one who wanted to "accomplish (his) course and the ministry which (he) received from the Lord Jesus" (vs. 24). When Paul was called to the missionary task, it was introduced to him to entail an emphasized amount of suffering (Acts 9:16). This task when Luke surveys it at the moment of its formal completion by its nature and the Pauline way of doing it pushed Paul to the practical limits of human devotion. The suffering foreseen from the start also became absolute. Therefore, belonging to the practical absolutes of Paul's missionary life is his absolute *martyrion.*

The question, of course, has to be asked, why is Luke safe-guarding the Pauline ministry in such careful ways? The answer has to do with a concrete issue in which Paul's church obtaining work was heretically undermined.[49] Indeed, W. Bauer[50] has made plausible a picture of widespread gnostic apostasy of the churches in Asia Minor reaching into the first century of the Common Era. Already John's Revelation--a roughly contemporary work with Acts looking at the same general region--can document gnostically sounding difficulties (Rev 2:2, 6, 14-15, 20-24; 22:15).[51] Luke desires to exonerate Paul from any suspicion--perhaps even charge[52]--that his founding work was deficient by putting a wedge between a pre-Pauline orthodoxy and post-Pauline heresy (vss. 29-30). We must recall that this is the only speech in Acts to an exclusively Christian audience[53] and, more specifically, to the "clergy" of that audience (vs. 17 "elders"). Since it is a literary creation[54]--the Ephesian elders "heard" it for the first time when they read it in the scroll of Acts!--the audience Luke envisioned was his universal readership and specifically the clergy among them. It is therefore a statement of professional accountability in the form of a testament Paul places into the hands of the orthodox clergy[55] while at the same time--the only time in Acts!--he warns them against inner-Christian heresy.

Here we find the fundamental reason for the speech and why Luke leaves no room to deduce other than an orthodox tradition from Paul's work. Secret and post-Miletian contacts with these churches are excluded since Paul worked openly (vs. 20) and was arrested at the end of his journey. Whatever tradition Paul had, is now in the trust of the elders, and the absolutes surrounding his missionary discharge do not allow for a variant appeal to his authority.

---

[49]For an overview of the "kirchliche Situation," cf. Schuermann, *Untersuchungen,* 312-22 and the literature noted there. Especially Walter Bauer, *Orthodoxy and Heresy in Earliest Christianity* (trans. and ed. by R. A. Kraft and G. Krodel; Philadelphia: Fortress, 1971) 77-94.

[50]Bauer, *Orthodoxy,* 77-94.

[51]Haenchen, *Acts,* 596.

[52]Guenther Klein, *Die Zwoelf Apostel. Ursprung und Gehalt einer Idee* (Goettingen: Vandenhoeck & Ruprecht, 1961) 183.

[53]Jaques Dupont, "Les discours missionnaires des Apôtres," *RB* 69 (1962) 50, n. 27 and *Paulus,* 130-31 has attempted to build an argument on that fact. Since in addition this is also the only instance in Acts where the death of Jesus has soteriological application, Dupont brings these two singular factors into causal relationship. The audience of faith is the proper *Sitz im Leben* for the *theologia crucis!* Since for the most part Acts envisions a missionary context, it is not at all surprising that the "positive account of the drama of Calvary" is absent in Acts.

[54]Dibelius, *Aufsaetze,* 157.

[55]Schuermann, *Untersuchungen,* 310-12; Klein, *Apostel,* 184.

More indirectly, Luke defends Paul by taking him out of the arena of human judgment. Paul received his ministry "from the Lord Jesus" (vs. 24) in an unmediated and
unmotivated divine commissioning. God chose him as his instrument without consultation, and at the end he still identifies with him as someone who is his own. Since Paul
is the issue of the speech, vs. 28 needs to be understood against the background of that
issue.[56]

Let me pull these observations together and bring them to bear on the movement of
thought principally in the first section of the speech, vss. 18-27, which is a summary
review of Paul's missionary activity. This section subdivides into three sense segments
which are linguistically interrelated with sufficient care to recognize composition and to
attach importance to the movement of that composition.[57]

The first segment (vss. 18-21) is an encompassing survey in absolutizing language of
Paul's way of doing his job. The second segment, vss. 22-25, using a prophetically
predictive cast virtually assures Paul's martyrdom. In constructing that segment Luke
had to be sufficiently transparent without being depressingly realistic and thus create a
cloud from under which the subsequent narrative of Paul's "witness in chains" could not
escape.[58] This pre-occupation with what Luke knew about Paul's fate and what his
narrative permitted him to tell found its linguistic release and particular form in Paul's
assertion of a clear conscience, "I am innocent of the blood of all of you," vss. 26-27, or
segment three.

Now that the term "blood" has been introduced in a derivative sense, Luke can use
it in the next sentence (vs. 28) where a shift takes place from the past to the future and
from Paul to the elders. Paul is handing over to the authority of elders a church which
he established with extreme labor (vss. 18-21) costing him his life (vss. 22-25) but leaving
him with a clear conscience (vss. 26-27). In his advice to these elders this church is
described as "established by the blood of one who was His Own" (vs. 28). Since just a
moment ago Paul had rather encompassingly narrated how he established that same
church--by absolute effort (vss. 18-21) and absolute sacrifice (vss. 22-25) confirmed by a
clear conscience (vss. 26-27)--we are under compulsion to heed the contextual argument
and understand "the blood of one who was His own" to be a summary reference to the
review of Paul's ministry just completed (vss. 18-27). Therefore, "blood" belongs to the
absolutes of Paul's church building life and clearly epitomizes them (vss. 18-21). It also
is the harsh reality behind the pious words of vss. 22-25, both the eventual outcome of
Paul's way of doing things and a historical fact, now an element of church tradition.

It is now necessary to explain the function of *idios* as a cipher for Paul. Its
presence in vs. 28b and my way of understanding it make Paul as the speaker refer to
himself impersonally as "His (God's) own one" or "der Eigene."[59] This is generally
dictated by Luke's veiled language about Paul's martyrdom and specifically by the
penetration of that veil with the term "blood." The realism of the latter, however, is
softened by the oath formula and rendered emotionally inoffensive as long as it does not
appear in sense proximity to the word "Paul." Therefore, in vss. 22-25 Paul's identity as
the sufferer of a (future) harsh fate is unambiguous, but that fate is not specified, i.e., no
blood reference. In vs. 28b a realistic blood reference describes how the church is
obtained, but the identity of Paul whose blood this is has to remain veiled. In other
words, *idios* in vs. 28b serves the same function that the form of a prophetic casting of

[56]Ernst Kaesemann, *Essays on New Testament Themes* (trans. by W. J. Montague;
SBT 41; London: SCM Press, 1964) 145.

[57]On the general structuring of the speech cf. Haenchen, *Acts,* 595-96; Klein,
Apostel, 179-80; Schuermann, *Untersuchungen,* 311; Dupont, *Paulus,* 17-20. For an
extension of structure into a possible use of sources cf. Thomas L. Budesheim, "Paul's
'Abschiedsrede' in the Acts of the Apostles," *HTR* 69 (1976) 9-30.

[58]Haenchen, *Acts,* 597.

[59]Conzelmann, *Die Apostelgeschichte* (HNT 7; Tuebingen: J. C. B. Mohr, 1963) 18.

Paul's martyrdom serves in vss. 22-25; to walk a careful linguistic line between concealment and revelation. When the identity of the sufferer is explicit, the extent of his suffering is vague (vss. 22-25). When its extent and nature are clear, the identity is vague (vs. 28b).

It is, however, not quite apparent why Luke chose *idios* rather than another term. Three possible reasons can be derived from the context. 1. Since the living Lord called Paul to be his "chosen instrument" (Acts 9:15), that same special sort of belonging[60] is recapitulated by *idios* within the dialectic requirements of the speech. 2. It is a euphemism for death, Paul having returned "unto the Lord." 3. Reaching into the controversy between the orthodox and the Gnostics for a right to Paul Luke affirms that in life and death he first of all belongs to God.

However, if the middle voice of *periepoiēsato* is appreciated, as in the NEB, we can recognize a certain extension of the middle force to reach and call for *idios*: "The church of God which He obtained *for Himself* by the blood of someone who is *his own*." The emphasis here is both theocentric and biographical. Just as Luke found it essential twice to explain Paul and his actions by reference to God's compelling call and authorization (22:4-16; 26:9-18), he in this case once again takes refuge in the divine necessity and identification with what Paul has done. In short, however problematic the Asian church situation may have appeared to Luke and his contemporaries, Luke's final explanation inseparably links God's and Paul's church building work: The churches in Asia are God's churches; God obtained them for himself; the agent of that obtaining God calls "his own."

Even if we now can decipher the meaning of Acts 20:28, the very fact that such a process is necessary alongside the argument that Luke self-consciously constructed this speech requires justification. The usual answer has been that Luke reworked a traditional statement which may have had its *Sitz im Leben* in the eucharistic tradition and toward which the language of Psalm 74:2 may have contributed greatly. Such an argument, however, has to assume that Luke had before him a traditional statement which may have spoken of a "shepherding by Christ" and made a specific soteriological point by reference to "his blood."[61] Luke's adaptation of such a statement would imply a critical judgment on the *theologia crucis,* for according to this assumption Luke took an assumption of what Jesus had done for the church and transformed it into what Paul has done for it.

Such an argument, however, takes its primary orientation from the soteriological traditions surrounding the death of Jesus and in subtle ways prejudges the conclusions. I think the proper context out of which to approach 20:28 is the missionary/martyriological setting of the whole speech and the tension that exists between the biographical facts of Paul and the gospel purpose of the Book of Acts.

Against this background and with the identity of God's church obtainer now disclosed, let us ask directly, "How did he perform his task?" The answer we have found to be: by self-giving and exhaustive work in a whole-counsel ministry! This surprisingly untheological conclusion is re-enforced by the preview Paul gives to the elders of heretical dissention they will have to expect. Rather than theological guidelines or ecclesiological strictures Luke provides a practical answer for the future consistent with Paul's work in the past. He counsels alertness and bases that counsel on Paul's own example of hard work, "For three years I did not cease night or day to admonish every one with tears" (vs. 31). Paul in effect is saying: "Through such exhaustive efforts I built the church. If you follow my example rather than any specific theology, you will keep it orthodox."

---

[60]Moulton, *Grammar,* 89.

[61]Gerhard Delling, *Der Kreuzestod Jesu in der urchristlichen Verkuendigung* (Goettingen: Vandenhoeck & Ruprecht, 1972) 94.

The strikingly untheological tenor of the speech[62] is an additional argument against a self-conscious soteriological assertion in 20:28b. Within the framework of the traditional understanding of the passage, the incidental nature of the soteriological phrase by itself requires support before it can be made a theological point of departure. If we couple incidental soteriological language to an untheological context and then recall the textual and translational uncertainties, any argument for a soteriological assertion in 20:28b begins with what appears to me to be insurmountable cumulative weaknesses.

The speech, however, does provide a soteriological hint that is consistent with Lukan thought, and if taken on its own terms, either releases vs. 28b from soteriological obligation or demands reconciliation with it. Vs. 21 in "extreme condensation"[63] offers a peculiar division of labor between God and Jesus: *metanoia* (repentance) has to do with God while *pistis* (faith) concerns Jesus.[64] If we assume that Luke in fact meant this distinction, as his subordinationism evident elsewhere surely requires that we must, we are confronted with a soteriological base oriented toward God (vs. 21) in juxtaposition to one relying on a specific fact in the life of Jesus (vs. 28). That these two positions should co-exist within the compass of one book would require interpretive dexterity. That with the maintenance of a soteriological assertion in vs. 28b they are part of one carefully composed speech makes the substantial modification of one or the other mandatory.

Although *metanoia* and its derivatives are prominent in Luke-Acts,[65] they are not connected with the death of Jesus.[66] Most often they are used absolutely and in a moral sense. Where a distinction is made, it is clearly God who authorizes and empowers repentance (e.g., Acts 11:18; 17:30; 20:21; 26:19). Where Jesus in mentioned, there is never a causal connection between his person/activity and repentance. Most clearly Acts 3:19 makes the "blotting out of sins" dependent on the decision to repent and on nothing else! Similarly the soteriological parable of the Prodigal Son (Luke 15:11-32) equates the act of repentance with the remembering of the father's house and the decision to return to it.[67]

---

[62]Haenchen, *Acts*, 597. A more encompassing judgment on Luke's nontheological orientation is given by C. K. Barrett, "It would perhaps be wrong to describe him (Luke) as either a theologus gloriae or a theologus crucis: he is not sufficiently interested in theology . . . to be called a theologus of any colour." "Theologia Crucis--in Acts?" in Carl Andersen and Guenther Klein, eds., *Theologia Crucis*. E. Dinkler Festschrift (Tuebingen: J. C. B. Mohr, 1979) 84. A more moderate statement comes from Paul S. Minear, "Dear Theo: The Kerygmatic Intention and Claim of the Book of Acts," *Int* 27 (1973) 148-49.

[63]The commentaries are strangely unimpressed by this verse noting mainly, as does Haenchen, *Acts*, 591, its condensed wording. Dupont, *Paulus*, 61, however, recognizes its division and accounts for it by appealing to the dual audience of Paul's preaching just mentioned, the Greeks and the Jews. To the Greeks would apply "repentance to God," i.e., a turning away from other, false, gods, and to the Jews who already are turned to the right God "faith in our Lord Jesus Christ." This, however, leads to a two-track soteriology as well as a quantitative notion of faith in Jesus to a faith in God already present.

[64]Acts always connects *pisteuein* and derivatives with *kyrios*. The only exception is 16:34 which is especially strange following vs. 31. Acts 27:25 does not use *pisteuein* in the sense of Christian faith. Cf. Bousset, *Kyrios Christos*, 288, n. 145.

[65]R. Michiels, "La conception lucaniene de la conversion," *ETL* 41 (1965) 43.

[66]Cadbury, *Making*, 288; Otto Betz, "The Kerygma of Luke," *Int* 22 (1968) 133.

[67]My purpose here is merely to suggest what I conclude to be an alternative area for a Lukan soteriological understanding and not pursue this question any further. For studies which have worked with an analogous assumption cf. Wilckens, *Missionsreden*, 178-86; Flender, *St. Luke*, 135-62; Conzelmann, *Theology*, 218-34. Cf. also Joseph Gewiess, *Die urapostolische Heilsverkuendigung nach der Apostelgeschichte* (Breslau: Verlag Mueller und Seiffert, 1939). On Acts 13:38 cf. Conzelmann, *Theology*, 230, n. 1.

It is in this context that the Lukan soteriology needs to be sought, a context that has a great deal in common with Old Testament prophetic preaching, particularly the assumption that the human act of turning to God requires no new enabling reality, e.g., the death of Jesus. In short, the soteriological touchstone consonant with Lukan thought is provided by vs. 21 while vs. 28 functions in a martyriological/apologetic context as a summary reference to the first two sections of the speech. At the moment Paul passes the church into the hands of elders, it is a necessary qualifier for what kind of church is being passed on by a man standing in what kind of relationship to it.

Let me summarize. I attempted to achieve a negative and positive result in this study. Negatively I wanted to show that pressed specifically our text has an ill-founded soteriological reputation. Positively I developed a possible variant understanding of what Luke intended to say and why he said it so obliquely. For the former purpose I allowed due weight to those arguments which were impressed by the Lukan emphases on a non-soteriological death of Jesus wondering if a lone verse in the book of Acts was sufficient to reverse the tide, as J. Jeremias, for one, so emphatically insists. When additionally that verse is textually compromised and interpretively ambiguous, the question has to be narrowed from, "Can Acts 20:28b rescue a soteriology of the cross for Luke?" to "What could Luke possibly have had in mind in this uncharacteristic statement?"

I examined *idios* and found it theologically neutral. I turned to *haima* and proved it soteriologically barren. Unless we are prepared to reduce Acts 20:28b to a stylistic embellishment to recall Pauline color,[68] we have to explore a more substantially positive Lukan intent.

I began with a sporadically current emphasis that the Miletian speech is in fact as close as Luke can come to narrate Paul's martyrdom and adduced the most relevant evidence. The opening section of the speech (vss. 18-21) is a display of practical absolutes of Paul's missionary habits that carries an apologetic impulse. The Pauline churches were threatened by and succumbing to gnostic influences. Whether to defend Paul from any concrete charges of responsibility (so G. Klein) or to prevent his heretical appropriation, Luke emphasizes the continuity of an open tradition and the orthodox office.[69]

Against this generally accepted background I tried to understand the positive function of vs. 28b. I noted the movement of thought from absolutes (vss. 18-21) to martyrdom (vss. 22-23) which received a personal conclusion in Paul's biblically phrased disclaimer of professional negligence (vss. 26-27). The mental pre-occupation with a martyrdom Luke knew had happened but which his narrative required as a forboding event of the future suggested the familiar "I am innocent of the blood of all of you."

With this declaration the review of Paul's life ends and attention shifts to the elders who now will inherit what Paul has obtained. In vs. 28 "the church" is mentioned the only time within the speech, and as Paul passes on this church to Spirit appointed elders, it is "the church of God," by all means, but it is also the church of Paul. Luke combines the empirical and final rights to the church by a closely dependent relationship between Paul and God: Paul is God's "own" and God obtained the church "for himself." Therefore, what God did through Paul he did for himself. The failure of the Asian churches in orthodox judgment can not be attributed to Paul but ultimately is a mystery of the divine purpose.

When that church is passed on, it is not a church without a history, rather the elders inherit a blood-obtained church by God's own man. In the review of Paul's life Luke had given content as to how the church was obtained. Now the relative clause in vs. 28b,

---

[68]Cf. Eric Franklin, *Christ the Lord* (Philadelphia: Westminster, 1975) 66: "This speech . . . is Luke's defence of Paul against those who have been belittling the apostle and as such is an accomodation to Paul's beliefs rather than an expression of his own theology."

[69]Schuermann, *Untersuchungen,* 322-40.

principally the terms "blood" and *idios,* are the ciphers for that review. For "blood" epitomizes the absolute efforts in vss. 18-21 and, now softened by the oath formula in vs. 26, is not too harsh a term for the envisioned martyrdom (vss. 22-25). *Idios* identified Paul without breaking the veil his martyrdom necessarily has to wear in the Lukan structure.

Rather than in vs. 28b, Luke alludes to his soteriology in vs. 21 where repentance as the human decision orients itself to God. Faith in Jesus complements this orientation but does not substantially alter it. Acts 20:28b is, therefore, not a soteriological reference but an apologetic one which uses Paul's martyrdom to epitomize his exhaustive effort on behalf of the church. To H. Shuermann's two orthodox defenses for a heretically threatened church, tradition and office,[70] I would add a third, hard and dedicated work by the office holder![71] Although he stands in the closest relationship to God, is God's own, he will spend his own blood to establish and obtain his church. Thus Luke writes in Acts 20:28, "Shepherd the church of God which he obtained for himself by the blood of the one who is his own."

---

[70]Ibid., 323.

[71]Perhaps in this connection it becomes more plausible why Luke ends the speech having Paul state his economic self-reliance culminating in the non-synoptic quotation from Jesus, "It is better to give than to receive."

IS THERE AN HERMETIC HERMENEUTIC?[+]

Ellen Shanahan
Temple University, Philadelphia

The Corpus Hermeticum is the body of literature composed in Greek in late antiquity and ascribed to Hermes Trismegistus. In its broader meaning, Hermetic literature includes earlier astronomical, medical, and magical works, the philosophical and religious tractates of the second and third centuries, C.E., and later alchemical writings. While they commanded wide popularity in antiquity as witnessed by testimonies in writings of the Christian Fathers and pagan philosophers and by early translations into Latin and Syriac,[1] the writings have suffered a troubled history of transmission and interpretation since that time. This paper discusses the Corpus Hermeticum which was available to scholars at the beginning of the twentieth century, the reasons those scholars considered the Corpus Hermeticum worthy of study, some of the presuppositions they brought to their work, and their conclusions. I suggest that in the main because of their initial interests, whether in the history of religions or in the relation of the Hermetica to early Christianity, these scholars overlooked the principle of interpretation employed by the authors of the Hermetic tractates themselves. The work of Richard Reitzenstein, G. R. S. Mead, Walter Scott, Hans Jonas, C. H. Dodd, Arthur Darby Nock, André-Jean Festurière, and Karl-Wolfgang Tröger is briefly reviewed.

The second part of the paper turns to the Corpus Hermeticum itself in order to investigate the coherence of the literature. Why is this collection of writings called a "body" at all? Does nothing more than the name *Hermes* give the Corpus Hermeticum its identity? I suggest that there is a specific principle of interpretation, or hermeneutic, at work in the texts, and seek to illustrate it with examples from three tractates. The first is the short tractate (C.H. III) which at first appears to be in the style of a midrash on the Genesis 1:1-2:4a creation account. The second uses language common to mystery cult rituals (C.H. VII), and the third deals with the popular topic of cosmological speculation (XI, 6-8, 19-22). In each case the Hermetic author points to the provisional nature of the salvific hope offered by the tradition presented and then shows the superiority of the Hermetic way to salvation or deification.

Richard Reitzenstein notes that "die Überlieferung ist ausserordentlich schlecht, aber einheitlich."[2] The manuscript tradition of which he spoke comes to us from a single copy of the Hermetic tractates dating from the eleventh century. When it came into the hands of Michael Psellus, it was in poor condition and had been mutilated: all that survives of the second tractate is its title, and the text breaks off abruptly after the eighteenth tractate. The surviving seventeen tractates comprise the bulk of the known religious Hermetica. These are supplemented by a long tractate preserved only in Latin from pseudo-Asclepius and a number of fragments collected by Johannes Stobaeus, some of which duplicate parts of the tractates, although twenty-seven are not preserved elsewhere. The discoveries at Chenoboskion allow us to add to the store of religious Hermetica a previously unknown "Discourse on the Eighth and Ninth" (NH VI, 6), as well as a prayer of thanksgiving (NH VI, 7) and a discourse of Hermes to Asclepius (NH VI, 8) which had been known from the Latin Asclepius.

Numerous difficulties attend the student of the Corpus Hermeticum. There had not been a reliable critical edition of the whole Corpus until the appearance of Nock's edition in 1938. Second, we possess only a small portion of a once extensive body of literature: to what degree the surviving materials are representative of the whole cannot be known. One must assume that what we have, replete with repetitions and contradictions as it is, is not substantially different from the lost texts.[3] The twentieth-century scholar is unlike the Hermetist of the third century in assigning various texts to the categories of

---

[+]The notes for this article are available from the author.

science, magic, philosophy, and religion. For the latter, all the materials were investigations into the nature and structure of reality, discussions of the role and expectations
a person might have in such a world, and instruction in the means to achieve one's goals.
The task of relating the religious Hermetica to the rest of the Hermetic literature needs
much attention. Festugière's work is the only substantial contribution to the task.

I

Given all these difficulties, it is a wonder that anyone has deemed the Corpus Hermeticum worthy of serious scholarship. Fortunately there have been a small number who
have been interested in the text and its place in the history of the religions of late
antiquity and have contributed to our knowledge and understanding of the field. It is
important to note the presuppositions, assessments, and interpretations of those who
have devoted their skills and talents to the study of the Corpus Hermeticum in order to
judge the value and limitations of their contributions. The following brief survey is not
complete: one will notice immediately the absence of mention of Bousset, Pietschmann
and Josef Kroll. The omission of the names of younger scholars--Tröger being the only
one considered--may not be apparent as immediately, but the work of William Grese and
Jean-Pierre Mahé is important and signals continued interest in the Corpus
Hermeticum.[4]

Richard Reitzenstein's first interest was in an historical and literary study of the
text. He was influenced by nineteenth-century evolutionary theory and the correlative
search for origins. He came to see the value of the Corpus Hermeticum as a record of an
important religious movement in late antiquity.[5] His critical edition of four tractates is
a masterpiece of careful, technical scholarship, the standard of which was not met again
until Nock and Festugière collaborated on their edition and translation. Originally,
Reitzenstein emphasized the Egyptian influences on the text, but after his move to
Göttingen afforded him the opportunity to study Mandaean and Manichaean texts, he
came to see their sources in the Hermetica as well. His reassessment appears in his
Hellenistic Mystery Religions where he notes "three writings that exhibit significant
Iranian influence," i.e., C.H. I, XI, and XIII.[6] According to Reitzenstein, the Hermetica
are "literary mystery" in which the "reader is to experience such a mystery in his
imagination. The miraculous power which is connected with the action of the mystery
can also be attached to the word, even the written word."[7] The edition by Reitzenstein
is replete with parallels between the Corpus Hermeticum and the records of various
oriental mystery religions, bolstering his argument that the major influences on the
Hermetica are oriental, and not Greek or philosophical.

In 1906, G. R. S. Mead published a three volume work, one volume of prolegomena,
two of translations.[8] Although he claimed to come to the text with the same philological
interests as he attributes to Reitzenstein, Mead had theosophical interests which make
themselves apparent throughout the work. Thus while he claims to be writing both
according to the "methods of scholarship and criticism," he also intends to provide a
means for the "initiatory process towards an understanding of the Archaic Gnosis."[9]
Mead hopes to make a "small contribution to the preparation of the way leading towards
a solution of the vast problems involved in the scientific study of the origins of the
Christian faith,"[10] but sees the source of the Corpus Hermeticum in Egyptian myths,
which reflect a *philosophia perennis*. Mead claims to base his translation on the best
available editions, but he does not reproduce the Greek text from which he worked. The
contribution which his work makes is to provide a readable English version of all the
tractates, excerpts, fragments, and testimonies. He frequently indicates cognates to
Greek words to give the reader a sense of the nuance of the original.

Walter Scott attempted a critical edition and English translation of the whole
corpus which was published between 1924 and 1936.[11] The profusion of square and
pointed brackets--both single and double--and the use of Coptic letters makes the Greek

text almost unreadable. But most scholars agree that Scott has so badly emended the texts that the effort is not worthwhile. Scott sees the Corpus Hermeticum arising from small religious, philosophical schools with neither cult nor sacraments.[12] Thus he emphasizes the Greek influence on the text, but because he fit the text to his own notions, neither the edition nor his ideas are taken very seriously.

Hans Jonas understood Gnosticism to be a religion, not just a movement or heresy, and he included Hermeticism within that religion. According to Jonas, "there was abroad in the Hellenistic world gnostic thought and speculation entirely free of Christian connections." The Hermetica "not only are purely pagan but even lack polemical reference to either Judaism or Christianity."[13] Though not all the Hermetica are gnostic, the Poimandres, C.H. I, is especially so and he finds "eine interessante antignostische Glosse, eingesprengt in einen spezisisch gnostischen Zusammenhang" in C.H. IV, 4.[14] Jonas does a long exegesis of C.H. XIII as a mystic-ecstatic transformation[15] and discusses the Urmensch in terms of C.H. I.[16] His section on "Gottesschau u. Vollendung" also emphasizes tractates I and XIII,[17] thus including Jonas with the many scholars who attend only or primarily to these two tractates. Jonas's most significant contribution to the study of Hermeticism is methodological: less important than the unveiling of the origin of concepts is the understanding of the new ways in which they were used.[18]

C. H. Dodd, primarily known for his Biblical studies, extended his scope to the Greek tradition in order to elucidate the milieu in which early Christianity spread. His estimation of the Corpus Hermeticum was high; he referred to it as a religion "of a singularly pure and spiritual kind."[19] In his work on the gospel of John, Dodd sets verses of the gospel in parallel with lines of C.H. XIII.[20] He can, however, only conclude that the examined tractates and all the Hermetica "represent a type of religious thought akin to one side of Johannine thought without any substantial borrowing on one side or the other."[21]

Arthur Darby Nock was essentially a classicist, but one of extremely wide interests. He sees an Egyptian framework for the tractates, but that they "contiennent extrêmement peu d'éléments égyptiens. Les idées sont celles de la pensée philosophique grecque populaire, sous une forme très éclectique, avec ce mélange de platonisme, d'aristotélisme et de stoïcisme qui était alors si répandu; çà et là paraissent des traces de judaïsme, et probablement aussi, d'une littérature religieuse dont la source ultime est l'Iran: par contre nulle marque évident ni de christianisme ni de néoplatonisme."[22] Although this summary is not particularly enlightening, Nock substantiates his claims with detailed introductions to each of the tractates, which give evidence of his acquaintance with all the relevant parallels. Nock's collaborator, André-Jean Festugière also emphasizes the Greek background of the Hermetica, though his magisterial Révélation d'Hermès Trismégiste demonstrates that the identification of Greek elements is not a simple matter.[23] A classicist of broad scope, Festugière contributed not only a felicitous translation but made available the astronomical and magical Hermetica in coherent synthesis.

Karl-Wolfgang Tröger has focused his interests on C.H. XIII[25] and the Hermetic texts in the Nag Hammadi corpus. He finds the tractate to be gnostic and related to the mysteries, although Grese does not find his arguments to be convincing.[26] His work on the Nag Hammadi materials places him in the group which emphasizes a gnostic and oriental background for the Hermetica. The inclusion of Hermetic materials in the Nag Hammadi corpus has given impetus to those who would include Hermeticism under the general category of gnosis, and those who would note the Egyptian elements in the materials, as does Labib.[27] An exception to this trend, however, is Pheme Perkins who in her recent work on gnostic dialogue fails to consider the hermetic dialogues in the Nag Hammadi material.[28] The analysis of the characteristics of this genre applied to the Hermetic dialogues would be a significant step in the recognition of the latter as interpretive and critical writings.

II

We turn now to a consideration of the texts themselves. We have noted that scholars have frequently proceded to analyze the Corpus Hermeticum by means of parallels to other ancient literature, whether that of the mystery religions, Greek philosophy, or emergent Christianity. This method helps to place the Hermetica in its social and intellectual milieu, but I find it inadequate to the critical genius the Hermetica displays. The tractates were written as means of salvation or deification by persons fully aware of the other salvation schemes available in late antiquity. The authors were convinced that these means were inferior to the salvific knowledge of one's own divine origin and nature[29] which is revealed in the Hermetic tractates. The tractates are mystagogic:[30] they assume that the reader is interested in the Hermetic path, but is also conversant with at least one other religious position, probably one still practiced. One cannot determine conclusively whether the tractates are records of actual instructions, models for use by Hermetic teachers along the lines of sermon outlines, or purely literary compositions, as Reitzenstein suggests. I think that most fall into the second category of model instruction although some tractates display more literary characteristics. The author of the tractate introduces a religious topic either by means of dialogue or exposition, usually being fair in the representation of the content, but then proceeds--sometimes subtly, sometimes more obviously--to show the incompleteness of that tradition or content. The culmination is an illustration of the Hermetic doctrine, often described in terms of its simplicity or self-evident nature. I offer three examples.

Tractate III opens with the statement that God is divine and the source of mind, nature, and matter. To show forth wisdom, God created all things. A paragraph closely following Genesis 1 continues: darkness and chaos are permeated by a "subtle, intelligent breath" which imparts the divine power so that all things are divided--light from darkness, the heavy from the light, dry land from water. Before the embellishment of creation is described, however, a paragraph on the articulation of the seven heavenly spheres and their gods is inserted. Each of these gods then produces that for which he is responsible: quadrupeds and creeping animals, fishes and birds, herbs, grasses and flowering plants. God is responsible for the generation of humankind, which in turn is ordained to increase and multiply, rule as master over nature, discover the sciences and arts, and contemplate the works of God and God by means of his works. While the description of the various astral gods bringing forth the lower creation is a common formulation probably of Stoic origin, the four ends of humanity are similar to rabbinic midrash on Genesis.[31] The logical conclusion, presented next, conflates Jewish and Stoic elements: it is the lot of humans to live and then to die; the names of those who did great deeds will live on, but for most there is oblivion.

But the Hermetist is dissatisfied with the sequence of generation and dissolution. If God is the source of mind, nature, and matter, and these in turn bring about the visible creation, then dissolution must be followed by regeneration. As long as the astral gods are maintained by God in their spheres, just so long will their creations continue to be renewed because "the divine is the entire cosmic composition renewed by nature: for it is in the divine that nature has her foundation" (C.H. III, 4). The Hermetic conclusion is that anything which originates with God must, like God, not be able to pass into oblivion. Because the divine nature is the foundation for all creation, creation is none other than what the divine nature is.

Tractate VII begins with a common hortatory injunction to wakefulness and sobriety in place of the drunkenness of ignorance.[32] A nautical motif is introduced in the first sentence, "You are being swept away." Ignorance is said to flood the land, to prevent coming to anchor in the safe harbor of salvation. This language is reminiscent of the mystery cults in some of which navigational events played more than a metaphoric role, as a cursory reading of the Ship of Isis section in Apuleius' *Metamorphoses,* Book XI, reminds us.[33] A second motif is that of ignorance as a garment--a fabric of ignorance, a prop of evil, a dark jail, a conscious corpse, and even a tomb which one carries about. Oftentimes, the disrobing and investiture with new garments is a ritual act of initiation in the mystery cults, but in this text there is no new garment to be donned. The Hermetist claims that the garment of evil and ignorance weighs one down and prevents one's looking up to see the true and the good which dwell above.

For the Hermetists, the body which needs safe harbor from the storm and needs to be clothed is not an adequate expression for the essential human nature. In each of the three paragraphs of the tractate are references to "look upward with the eyes of the heart" by means of which one can "hear what you must hear and see what you must see." The critique of the mystery cults offered here is that the mysteries deal with sensory experiences, which only further engorge the person with mere matter and further ensnare him with ignorance. Thus, the mysteries do not succeed in their aim of liberation. It is only when one sees with the mind and heart that one sees the good and the true--and knows that one is united with the divine in knowledge.

Tractate XI has two sections which deal with cosmology: paragraphs 6-8 and 19-22. In the first section, Nous invites Hermes to "look with mind's eye," that is, to contemplate with or by means of Nous, the cosmos, the hierarchy of the seven spheres, the sun, the moon, and the earth with its multitude of living beings. In the second section, Nous invites Hermes to "bid your soul to travel": by land, the oceans, through the heavens and the spheres of the planets, and even beyond the boundaries of the cosmos, if there be such a thing. The reason for this mental exercise is that this is the way in which God comprehends all within himself. Hermes is to conceive of God in precisely the way God conceives of the cosmos--by thought. Nous then instructs Hermes, "If you do not make yourself equal to God you cannot comprehend God, because like is known only by like." (XI, 20) How does one make oneself equal to God? Simply by doing what God does, that is, thinking as God does, reconciling opposites within oneself. "Think that for you nothing is impossible": grasp all the sciences, find your home in every place, make yourself higher than the heights, lower than the depths, containing at once heat and cold, the dry and the moist. Be everywhere at once, and every age at once: not yet begotten, in the womb, an infant, a child, adolescent, adult, old, dead, in the world beyond the grave.

This audacious instruction is not just permitted, it is demanded. The one who says, "I don't know anything. I can't do anything. I'm afraid" has nothing to do with God, cannot grasp the good or the beautiful, and hence is evil. The epitome of evil is not to know God. (XI, 21) The tractate concludes by insisting that such knowledge--of the cosmos, of God--not only is something the human person is capable of, but once begun is simple. To hope to know God is the path to that knowledge "for everywhere God will come to meet you" in all places and times, for there is nothing which is not God. God, the seeker, the path and the knowledge: all are God.

Cosmological speculation was a popular form of religious discourse in late antiquity, but the Hermetist transcends all other examples of the genre. He makes of the astral journey the very activity of God in comprehending the cosmos. He invites the listener to make him or herself equal to God and confirms the invitation by asserting that "there is nothing which is not God." The doctrine of correspondence ratifies the Hermetic claim: like is known only by like, so if one knows anything at all one knows God.

In conclusion, the Hermetic principle of interpretation operates by means of description, augmentation with Hermetic doctrine, and implicit critique of the original religious position. The Hermetic authors seem not to realize that this process is as much a method as the interpretive methods which they analyze and find lacking. The blind spot in the Hermetist's eye is precisely his inability to critique his own method. Simplicity and self-evidence are taken for truth. The Corpus Hermeticum is both self-contradictory and self-referential literature. The next step in substantiating my theory of an Hermetic hermeneutic would be to carry out an Hermetic interpretation of one tractate by means of another tractate.

THE PRONOUNCEMENT STORY IN THE HADITH LITERATURE
OF ISLAM

R. Marston Speight
National Council of Churches

The hadith literature of Islam consists of many collections of anecdotes, reports, statements and prescriptions on a variety of subjects, all containing words and deeds attributed to the Prophet Muhammad, to his Companions and to other Muslims of the early Islamic period.[1] It is to this material that Rudolf Bultmann made reference in his *The History of the Synoptic Tradition,* English translation, page 42, note 1: ". . . in the tradition of Islam there are also apophthegmatic items which would repay study." His authority for that reference is I. (not J.) Goldziher, *Muhammedanische Studien* II, 1890, one of the basic studies by non-Muslims of the hadith literature.

The Arabic word, "hadith," commonly means "event" or "report." Its plural is "ahadith," but this form is used only for small numbers of events or reports. The form, "hadith," is used both as a singular and as a collective noun, and, in its technical, religious sense, has found its way into *Webster's Third New International Dictionary* as follows:

hadith, pl. hadith or hadiths
1:   a narrative record of sayings or customs of Muhammad and his companions
2:   the collective body of traditions relating to Muhammad and his companions

So in this paper "hadith" will be used uniformly to cover the singular, plural and collective meanings, according to Webster's definition.

Hadith texts are a basic source of doctrine and practice in Islam. They were preserved and transmitted first of all for the purpose of providing the community of Muslims with authoritative information regarding the interpretation of the Qur'an and the ways of fulfilling the duties of private, social and cultic life. Beyond this primary function of the texts, historians have discerned a variety of secondary concerns which they reflect. Hadith take the form of short unconnected pieces, each of which is preceded by its chain of authorities. They were originally transmitted orally, and after they were recorded in writing they did not undergo literary recomposition. The material retains the distinctive characteristics of oral composition. As hadith were transmitted orally they underwent a certain amount of creative transformation, so that any given piece of material may exist in several different versions. The compilers of written collections were careful not to tamper with the texts as they were delivered to them by recognized specialists in hadith transmission. Although the variant readings are mostly of inconsequential difference from each other, sometimes a careful form critical study of the different versions of a text yields important results.

---

[1] The best general introduction in English to the hadith literature is the article, "hadith," in the *Encyclopedia of Islam,* New Edition. Other introductory books are: Ignaz Goldziher, *Muslim Studies,* Vol. II, trans. by C. R. Barber and S. M. Stern (Chicago: Aldine Publishing Co., 1971); Alfred Guillaume, *The Traditions of Islam* (reprint of 1924 edition; Beirut: Khayat's, 1966); Muhammad Zubair Siddiqi, *Hadith Literature* (Calcutta: Calcutta University, 1961).   A few of the collections of hadith have been translated into English, such as: Al-Bukhari, *Sahih al-Bakhari,* trans. by Muhammad Muhsin Khan (9 vols.; Chicago: Kazi Publications, 4th revised edition, 1979); Muslim ibn al-Hajjaj, *Sahih Muslim,* trans. by Abdul Hamid Siddiqi (Lahore: Sh. Muhammad Ashraf, 1971).

A number of oral literary forms are found in the hadith literature,[2] but for the purpose of this paper only pronouncements and pronouncement stories will be identified. I have examined about sixty-five texts with reference to the typology of pronouncement stories outlined by Robert C. Tannehill[3] and to the description of chreiai in Greek rhetoric, as given by Vernon K. Robbins.[4] These two frameworks for classification, the first emphasizing content and the second emphasizing form, are convenient vehicles for an initial presentation of pronouncements and pronouncement stories in the hadith literature.

Most of the examples chosen for presentation here are taken from the *Musnad* of Al-Tayalisi, a collection of 2,767 hadith dating from the latter part of the eighth century A.D. The compiler died about 819 A.D. His *Musnad* was published in Hyderabad, India in 1903. It is one of the earliest extant collections of hadith. The other authoritative compilations were completed in the course of the ninth and tenth centuries, as a result of intensive research by some of the most remarkable figures in the history of Islamic thought. Additional examples in this paper are taken from the ninth century collections of Al-Tirmidhi, Ibn Hanbal, Al-Bukhari and Muslim. The translation of the Arabic texts was done by myself.

Voluntary Pronouncements

Many hadith consist of simple statements, giving information or reporting an action, either in a prosaic fashion or in stylized formulas, such as comparison, promise, prophecy, epigram, metaphor, rhyme, numerical saying, antithesis, blessing, curse, prescription, judgment and prohibition. When the statement is pointed it corresponds to the definition of a voluntary chreia, that is, "a pointed statement or action delivered by an individual on his own free will."[5] Here are some examples of voluntary pronouncements.

Ibn Mas'ud reported: I saw the Prophet praying while wearing his sandals (Al-Tayalisi, No. 395).

The pointedness of this statement is not evident without the background of Islamic practice in prayer. The pronouncement is intended to correct the opinion that one had to remove the sandals to pray. This text is thus a correction pronouncement, according to Tannehill's typology, even though the opinion corrected is not explicitly expressed.

'Abd Allah b. Mas'ud reported: The Messenger of God traced a line for us and said, "This is the way of God." Then he traced lines on his right and on his left and said, "These are ways, and Satan invites men to go in each one of them." Then he recited the verse from the Qur'an, "This is my straight path" (Qur'an 6:153) (Al-Tayalisi, No. 224).

Here the pronouncement consists of both a symbolic action, the tracing of lines, and explanatory statements, reinforced by a citation from the Qur'an.

---

[2]Cf. R. Marston Speight, *The Musnad of Al-Tayalisi: A Study of Islamic Hadith as Oral Literature*. Unpublished doctoral dissertation, Hartford Seminary Foundation, 1970.
[3]Robert C. Tannehill, "Introduction: The Pronouncement Story and its Types," *Semeia* 20 (1981) 1-13.
[4]Vernon K. Robbins, "Identifying and Interpreting Pronouncement Stories in Mark: A Rhetorical Approach." A paper read at the Pacific Society of Biblical Literature meetings, Stanford University, March 26, 1982.
[5]Ibid., p. 3.

Jubayr b. Mut'im reported: The Prophet said, "Prayer in this, my mosque, is better than a thousand prayers (or he said, "a hundred") in another one, unless it be the Mosque of al-Haram" (Al-Tayalisi, No. 950).

The pronouncement is in the form of a comparison. The words in parentheses are those of the guarantor who thus acknowledges that in another version of the saying, the number was a hundred instead of a thousand.

Thawban reported: I heard the Messenger of God say, "There is no Muslim who prostrates himself in prayer but that by virtue of that prostration God will elevate him a degree and reduce his sin" (Al-Tayalisi, No. 986).

The pronouncement is in the form of a conditional promise, introduced by an exceptive formula.

Anas b. Malik reported: The Prophet said that God said, "If a man draws near to me by the space of a span I draw near to him by the space of a cubit; and if he draws near to me by the space of a cubit, I draw near to him by the space of a fathom" (Al-Tayalisi, No. 1967).

Here the conditional promise states that God will outdo man in overcoming the distance separating the two.

Ibn 'Umar reported: The Messenger of God said, "Whoever drinks wine in the world will not drink it in the hereafter unless he repents" (Al-Tayalisi, No. 1857).

This is an antithetical assertion according to a pattern often found in the literature. One of the joys of Paradise, according to Islam, will be the abundance of non-inebriating wine.

Situational Pronouncements

Often the hadith texts are in the form of a simple narrative in which a situation is briefly described which calls forth a response from the speaker or actor. When this response is a pointed statement or action, it may be identified as a pronouncement, and the whole text as a pronouncement story of the situational type.[6] Some examples of this type are as follows.

(Guarantor):   Abu Ma'mar reported:
(Situation):   A man got up and started praising a certain prince.
(Action pronouncement):
          Al-Miqdad b. al-Aswad threw dirt in his face
(Saying pronouncement):
          and said, "The Messenger of God directed us to throw dirt in the face of flatterers" (Al-Tirmidhi, zuhd, 43).

Robbins writes, "If there is action in the first part of the chreia, the action is not directed toward the person who makes the statement or performs the action at the end." The pronouncement occurs when "the person to whom the chreia is attributed . . . engages the situation with a pointed saying or action."[7] In the above story the man who praised the prince was not doing anything to Al-Miqdad, but the latter challenged what

---

[6]Ibid., p. 4.
[7]Ibid., p. 4.

he was doing with his own action and statement. This is a correction story, according to the typology of Tannehill.[8]

(Guarantor):	Ibn Mas'ud reported:
(Situation):	When we were praying behind the Messenger of God we said, "Peace be upon God, peace be upon Gabriel, peace be upon Michael.
(Saying pronouncement):	

> Then the Messenger of God turned to us and said, "Do not say, peace be upon God, for God is peace; but say, greetings, prayers and good things to God; peace be upon you, O Prophet, with God's mercy and blessings; peace be upon us and upon the righteous servants of God; I witness that there is no deity but God, and that Muhammad is His servant and His messenger" (Al-Tayalisi, No. 249).

Again, in this situational-correction story the Companions in prayer were not directing their action toward the Messenger of God, but he intervened upon hearing their faulty formulation.

(Guarantor):	'Ali reported:
(Situation):	The Prophet sent out a raiding party and put someone in charge of it, commanding the men to obey him. A fire broke out in the party and their leader ordered them to defy danger to put it out. Some did so, but others said, "We fled from the fire and refused to obey." Later they came to the Messenger of God and told him what had happened.
(Response as pronouncement):	

> The Messenger of God said, "Even if they had had to enter the fire, their obligation to obey orders would have held and it will hold until the day of resurrection. There shall be no obedience to man if it involves disobedience to God (may He be praised and exalted), but obedience is necessary in that which is good" (Al-Tayalisi, No. 109).

This is a situational-correction story in which the action of the situation takes place in the absence of the respondent, but is brought to his attention by his interlocutors, and thus elicits his pronouncement response.

Responsive Pronouncements

As defined by Greek rhetoric, a responsive pronouncement is one in which a saying or an action in the situation "invites or initiates the response."[9] The hadith literature contains a large number of responsive pronouncements. The most common pattern is that of question and answer. The question provides the situation and the answer is the responsive pronouncement. Some examples are as follows.

(Guarantor):	Ibn Mas'ud reported:
(Question as situation):	

> We said, "O Messenger of God, will what we did in the Jahiliyya[10] be held against us?"

---

[8]Tannehill, op. cit., pp. 6, 7.
[9]Robbins, op. cit., p. 5.
[10]The preislamic period of ignorance.

(Response):   The Messenger of God replied, "Whoever does good in Islam will
                   not be punished for what he did either in the Jahiliyya or in Islam;
                   but whoever does evil in Islam will be punished both for what he
                   did in the Jahiliyya and in Islam" (Al-Tayalisi, No. 260).

The above is an inquiry story, according to the typology of Tannehill,[11] even as are
the other question and answer texts.

(Guarantor):   Sa'id b. al-Harith reported:
(Question as situation):
                   Ibn 'Umar said, "Is it not forbidden to make vows?"
(Response):   The Prophet said, "A vow neither hastens nor delays anything, but
                   by means of a vow a miser can be separated from his wealth"[12]
                   (Al-Bukhari, nudhur, 26).

The next example is slightly more complex, containing two questions and two
responses.

(Guarantor):   Usama b. Sharik reported:
(Question as situation):
                   The Bedouins asked the Messenger of God, "Shall we not use
                   medicines?"
(Response as pronouncement, inviting a further question):
                   He said, "Yes, O People of God, use medicines. God provides
                   either healing or a remedy for each disease, that is, except for
                   one."
(Second question):
                   They said, "O Messenger of God, what is that one?"
(Second response as pronouncement):
                   "Old age" (Al-Tirmidhi, tibb, 2).

Sometimes the respondent himself asks a question, inviting his hearers to request
the information to which reference is made in the question. This pattern is seen in the
following example.

(Guarantor):   The father of 'Abd al-Rahman b. Abi Bakra reported:
(Question by respondent):
                   The Messenger of God said, "Shall I not tell you about the most
                   serious of the great sins?"
(Reiteration of question by hearers):
                   His listeners replied, "Yes, indeed, O Messenger of God."
(Response as pronouncement):
                   He said, "Making someone an associate with God in His sover-
                   eignty, then disobedience to parents,"--here he sat up from his re-
                   clining position--"then false testimony, or untrue words." And the
                   Messenger of God kept on talking about the great sins until we
                   wished he would stop (Al-Tirmidhi, birr, 4).

---

[11]Tannehill, op. cit., p. 10.
[12]Only by the incentive of a vow can a miser be persuaded to give up any of his
wealth.

Occasionally the situation is of such a nature as to suggest the quest story as described by Tannehill,[13] that is, the inquirer shows a concern for personal guidance which seems to go beyond the mere desire for information. For example,

(Guarantor): 'Abd Allah b. 'Amr reported:
(Complaint as situation):
> A man came to the Messenger of God and said, "O Messenger of God, I recite the Qur'an, but I find that my head does not understand it."

(Response as pronouncement):
> The Messenger of God replied, "Your heart lacks faith, for truly, faith is given to a believer first, then the Qur'an" (Ibn Hanbal, No. 6604).

Another kind of responsive pronouncement emerges out of a situation in the form of an act. The following example is also a commendation story, as described by Tannehill.[14]

(Guarantor):   Abu Mas'ud al-Badri reported:
(Act as situation):
> A man came to the Prophet bringing a bridled she-camel as alms.

(Response as pronouncement):
> The Messenger of God said to him, "By virtue of this alms you will have seven hundred she-camels on the day of resurrection" (Al-Tayalisi, No. 610).

In the next item, a description story,[15] the respondent himself provides the situation by his action, and then gives a pronouncement as his response to the situation.

(Guarantor):   Salim reported on the authority of his father
(Situation):   that 'Umar kissed the Black Stone
(Response as pronouncement):
> and then said, "By God, I know that you are a stone, and if I had not seen God's Messenger kissing you, I would not have kissed you" (Muslim, hajj, 484).

Often the situation is described in the tersest way, as in the following.

(Guarantor):   Jabir b. 'Abd Allah reported:
(Situation):   I heard the Messenger of God say, three days before his death,
(Response as pronouncement):
> "No one dies but that he has good thoughts toward God" (Al-Tayalisi, No. 1779).

There seem to be few objection stories[16] in the hadith, but the following illustrates that type. It shows another way in which the situation can invite or initiate the response. The first speaker objects to the behavior of the responder.

---

[13]Tannehill, op. cit., p. 9.
[14]Ibid., p. 7.
[15]Ibid., pp. 10, 11.
[16]Ibid., pp. 8, 9.

(Guarantor):   Anas b. Malik reported:
(Situation as objection):
                      A man of the Ansar said to the Prophet, "You put so-and-so in a
                      place of authority, but you did not do that for me."
(Response as pronouncement):
                      Then the Prophet said, "After me you will see selfishness, but
                      persevere until we meet together around the Pool (hawd)[17] (Al-
                      Tayalisi, No. 1969).

In the next example, a correction story, the situation consists first of an action by
the respondent, and then a question and answer exchange between the respondent and
another person. Finally the correction response is given as a rhetorical question, and it is
followed by a pointed statement which is the pronouncement. The story is more complex
than any seen heretofore in this presentation.

(Guarantor):   Abu Hurayra reported:
(Situation):   The Messenger of God passed by a pile of grain. He put his hand
                      into the midst of it, and his fingers encountered moisture. He
                      exclaimed, "O merchant, what is this?" The owner of the grain
                      said, "It has been damaged by the rain, O Messenger of God."
(Response):   Then he replied, "If that is the case, why not put the damaged
                      grain on top of the pile so that people can see it?" Then he con-
                      cluded, "Whoever practices fraud is not one of us" (Al-Tirmidhi,
                      buyu', 72).

The Combination of Types

Having identified examples of the three types of chreiai and shown how they are
developed into pronouncement stories in the case of the situational and the responsive
types, I shall now give examples of hadith in which two types are combined. First of all
there is a voluntary pronouncement leading to a responsive one. Both of the examples
are commendation stories.

(Guarantor):   Ibn Mas'ud reported:
(Voluntary pronouncement):
                      The Messenger of God said, "No one will go into hell who has even
                      a tiny grain of faith in his heart. And no one will go into paradise
                      who has even a tiny grain of pride in his heart."
(Situation arising out of the pronouncement):
                      A man asked him, "O Messenger of God, I like to keep my clothing
                      freshly washed, my head anointed, my sandal thongs in good con-
                      dition"--and he mentioned other things, ending with the strap of
                      his whip--"Is this a sign of pride, O Messenger of God?"
(Response as pronouncement):
                      He said, "No, that shows comeliness. Truly, God is beauty, and
                      He loves comeliness. By contrast pride is seen in one who acts in
                      stupid ignorance and who despises other people" (Ibn Hanbal, No.
                      3789).

(Guarantor):   Abu Sa'id al-Khudri reported:

---

[17]An eschatological reality.

(Voluntary pronouncement):

> The Messenger of God preached; saying, "God has given a choice to a person, either the world or what is with God. The person has chosen what is with God."

(Situation arising out of the pronouncement):

> Abu Bakr wept and we were astonished that he should weep because of what the Messenger of God had said. But Abu Bakr informed us that the Messenger of God was himself the one who had been offered the choice.

(Response as pronouncement):

> Then the Messenger of God said, "The one who has been most generous to me with his companionship and his possessions is Abu Bakr. If I should take a Friend (khalil) other than my Lord he would be Abu Bakr. We are united in brotherhood and the comradeship of Islam" (Al-Bukhari, Fada'il al-sahaba, 3).

Another combination seen is that of two responsive pronouncement stories, one emerging out of the other. In the following example the guarantor, Mujahid, tells the entire story. He is the respondent in the first story, and it is his exchange with Ibn 'Abbas that provides the first situation. Then the first responsive pronouncement by Mujahid elicits a reminiscence from Ibn 'Abbas which provides a new situation, calling forth a response from a new respondent, the Messenger of God.

(Guarantor):   Mujahid reported:

(First situation):

> I went in to see Ibn 'Abbas and said to him, "O Ibn 'Abbas when I was with Ibn 'Umar he recited a certain verse and wept." Ibn 'Abbas said, "Which verse was it?"

(First response as pronouncement):

> I replied, "Whether you publish what is in your heart or hide it, God will make reckoning with you for it" (Qur'an 2:284).

(Second situation):

> Ibn 'Abbas said, "When that verse was revealed the Companions of the Messenger of God were filled with great distress, that is to say, they were thoroughly troubled. They said, 'O Messenger of God, we are doomed if what we have said and done is to be held against us. Besides, we have no control over our hearts.'

(Second response as pronouncement):

> "The Messenger of God said to them, 'Say, we have heard and we have obeyed.' Then this verse takes the place of the other one, 'The Messenger believes in what was sent down to him from the Lord, and the believers . . . ' up to: 'God charges no soul save to its capacity; standing to its account is what it has earned, and against its account what it deserves' (Qur'an 2:285-86). So they were delivered from their worries and they accepted responsibility for their deeds" (Ibn Hanbal, No. 3071).

The large number and varying complexity of hadith texts suggests that other combinations of types might be found as an ongoing inventory of pronouncement stories is made. Other subjects for research suggest themselves. The rhetorical devices used in the pronouncements might be analyzed. There may be correlation to discover between content and type of pronouncement story, as well as between the personalities involved as primary guarantors and the types of expression or the content of the stories. If a pronouncement is found to exist in more than one type of story it might be useful to determine whether or not this fact reveals anything about the history of the tradition that the pronouncement represents. Finally, no study of pronouncement stories in the hadith can long ignore a consideration of the uses to which those texts were put by Muslims. Hadith were a formative influence in the science of Qur'an exegesis, in the development of doctrine and cult, in the teaching of ethics and in the nurture of devotion. This literature is one of the basic sources for the history of Islamic thought.

Works Consulted

Al-Bukhari, Muhammad b. Isma'il. *Sahih al-Bukhari*. Cairo: Dar wa-Matabi' al-Sha'b, n.d.

Bultmann, Rudolf. *The History of the Synoptic Tradition*. Translated by John Marsh. Revised edition. New York: Harper and Row, 1968.

Ibn Hangal, Ahmad. *Al-Musnad*. Edited by Ahmad Shakir. 14 vols. Cairo: Dar al-Ma'arif, 1949-55.

Al-Mubarakfuri, Muhammad 'Abd al-Rahman. *Tuhfat al-Ahwadhi bi Sharh Jami' al-Tirmidhi*. Edited by 'Abd al-Wahhab 'Abd al-Latif and 'Abd al-Rahman Muhammad 'Uthman. 10 vols. Al-Madina al-Munawwara: Al-Maktaba al-Salafiyya, 1963-67.

Muslim b. al-Hajjaj. *Sahih Muslim*. Edited by Muhammad Fu'ad 'Abd al-Baqi. 5 vols. Cairo: Al-Halabi, 1955.

Robbins, Vernon K. "Identifying and Interpreting Pronouncement Stories in Mark: A Rhetorical Approach." A paper read at the Pacific Society of Biblical Literature meetings, Stanford University, March 26, 1982.

Tannehill, Robert C. "Introduction: The Pronouncement Story and its Types." *Semeia*, 20 (1981) 1-13.

Al-Tayalisi, Sulayman b. Dawud. *Al-Musnad*. Edited by Abu al-Hasan al-Amruhi, et al. Hyderabad: Majlis Da'irat al-Ma'arif al-Nizamiyya, 1903.

EUSEBEIA IN AELIUS ARISTIDES

Stephen A. Stertz

Various attempts have been made to analyze the vocabulary of Aelius Aristides. Volume II of Wilhelm Schmid, *Der Atticismus* (Stuttgart, 1889) is a pioneer attempt, discussing unusual words on pp. 187-246 and particles on pp. 301-9. Attempts to examine specific aspects of Aristides' vocabulary from the viewpoint of investigating the authenticity of disputed orations include J. E. Harry, "On the Authorship of the Leptines Orations ascribed to Aristides," *AJP* 15 (1894) 66-73, and B. Keil, "Eine Kaiserrede (Or. XXXV)," *N. Ak. G.*, 1905, 381-428. More recently J. H. Oliver produced "Greek indices," compiled by hand, excluding particles (of stylometric importance) and subject to criticism, of two major orations, the oration *To Rome* (*The Ruling Power, Transactions of the American Philosophical Society* 43, 4, 1953), and the *Panathenaica* (*The Civilizing Power*, ibid., 58, 1, 1968).

An examination of Aristides' religious ideas or in fact ideas in general through stylometric analysis, with or without a computer, has never been systematically conducted. The suggestion that an analysis of the orations be made was put forth by Bette Forte, *Rome and The Romans as the Greeks Saw Them* (PAAR 28, 1972), 409ff, who, however, did not specifically mention stylometry.

The idea of such an investigation first occurred to me in 1978, when I attempted to disprove the authenticity of the *Eis Basilea* (Or. 35 Keil) in my article "Pseudo-Aristides ΕΙΣ ΒΑΣΙΛΕΑ," *Classical Quarterly* 29 (1979), 172-97. I obtained a grant-in-aid from the American Philosophical Society and, with the technical assistance of Professor Malcolm Brown of Brooklyn College, using the City University of New York computer center, searched the 200,000 word corpus of Aelius Aristides (excluding the so-called *Aristides Rhetoric*, considered by virtually all scholars to be spurious (cf. e.g., André Boulanger, *Aelius Aristide* (Paris 1923), 156 n. 1) for a number of words, including both particles (of stylometric significance for determining date and authenticity) and words illustrating Aristides' political and religious ideas.

One of the words in the latter category (a total of thirty-six words were searched, in all forms) is *eusebeia*, or rather all forms of the *euseb-* root. It was discovered that all forms appear under one hundred times in the entire corpus of Aristides (the exact figure is not given because the results so far are in preliminary form and may vary by a very small percentage, insignificant for statistical purposes; however the orations discussed in detail below have been carefully checked). A cursory inspection of the orations of Dio Chrysostom, who flourished a little earlier than Aristides, and of Libanius, a fourth-century admirer and to some extent imitator of Aristides, indicate that forms of *eusebia* appear far more frequently than in Aristides.

There are, for example, only about a half dozen occurrences in the very long oration (about 34,000 words, or about one-sixth of the total length of the corpus, again excluding the spurious so-called *Aristides Rhetoric*) 13 in Dindorf's edition, 1 in the Lenz-Behr edition, the *Panathenaica*. Although the oration is considered by some scholars, such as C. A. Behr (*Aelius Aristides and the Sacred Tales* [Amsterdam, 1968] p. 129, and Oliver, 1968, op. cit., p. 33) to date from the reign of Antoninus *Pius*, such punning seems to be alien to Aristides' style (the word appears five times in the much shorter *Eis Basilea*, oration 9 in Dindorf's edition, 35 in Keil's, but the latter oration is generally not considered to have been written by Aristides; see my article in *Classical Quarterly*, cited above, especially at p. 181; C. P. Jones, "Aelius Aristides ΕΙΣ ΒΑΣΙΛΕΑ," *JRS* 62 (1972) 134-52, argues otherwise). In the *Panathenaica*, as elsewhere, Aristides uses the concept of *eusebeia* in a highly conventional, rhetorical, sense, as part of commonly found *topoi* of the kind described later by Menander Rhetor. Here Athens is called "pious," as in 149. 25 Jebb. At 191. 3 *eusebeia* is coupled with intelligence, given in adjectival superlative form as *phronematos*, and gentleness, similarly given as *praotetos*, as attributes of the city. Elsewhere, at 180. 16, it is said that to call Athens a child of Zeus is an act of piety. At 182. 29 Aristides says that it is one's own, and elsewhere, at 139. 25, *eusebeia* is coupled with that old attribute of the good person or city, *philanthropia*. The word *eusebeia* appears again on the following line, a rare example of repetition in Aristides. There is relatively little of an explicitly religious nature in this long oration. Invocations to the gods are either decorative or excuses to recite patriotic myths. In few of these passages does any form of the word *eusebeia* appear.

No form of the word is found in the oration *To Rome*, oration 14 in Dindorf's edition, despite the generally accepted date in Pius' reign (cf. Boulanger, op. cit., p. 161). The oration is considered by many scholars to be earlier than the *Panathenaica*, but still date from the same reign. As I will point out, there seems to be no correlation between chronology and the use of this word. Rome is praised in other terms. As in the *Panathenaica*, there is very little of an explicitly religious nature in the oration, little more than the highly conventional invocation at the opening of the oration--which includes a joke--and at the end.

Examining a few of the shorter orations, a generally similar pattern is found. In the early hymns, numbered 1 to 5 by Dindorf, forms of *eusebeia* occur only twice in about ten thousand lines: in orations 3 Dindorf, 46 Keil, *To Poseidon*, and 5 Dindorf, 40 Keil, *To Heracles*. According to Behr, op. cit., p. 129, these orations come last, chronologically, in this group. Boulanger, loc. cit., dates some of the other three orations in this group as very early in the rhetor's career. In both cases usage is, as usual in Aristides, incidental and part of highly conventional rhetorical *topoi*. Thus in oration 3, at p. 25, line 29 Jebb, there is a passage which may be translated, "or truly it would not be possible to say this *piously*, while making a speech about the gods." The word is used adverbially, in passing. In oration 5, p. 33, line 26 Jebb, Theseus is called "the oldest of the Greeks and most *pious* toward the gods." The same phenomenon is again encountered.

The word *eusebeia* in any form is also totally absent from the *Lalia eis Asklepion*, about 1,160 words in length, perhaps too short for the absence of the word to be of purely statistical significance apart from the subject matter. However, we are not speaking of a particle. Aristides was devoted to the god Aesculapius, as he states repeatedly in his *Sacred Tales* and elsewhere. He had been licked by the sacred dogs and was one of the great hypochondriacs of antiquity. It might therefore be expected that, if the word *eusebeia* played an important part in Aristides' devotions, it would certainly be found in a hymn to Aesculapius, however short. In addition, Behr (op. cit., p. 130) gives a very late date, after Aristides' illness and visits to the shrine of the god, to this oration, which is number 6 in Dindorf's edition and 42 in Keil's.

In a number of other hymns addressed to Aesculapius, for example 38 Keil, 7 Dindorf, the *Asklepiadae*, about 1,510 words long, dated A.D. 147, relatively early in Aristides' career by Behr (op. cit., p. 128), the word is lacking, as it is in Aristides' funeral orations, such as 31 and 32 Keil, the funeral orations by Eteoneus and Alexander respectively, dated fairly late by Behr (loc. cit.), but earlier in Aristides' career by Boulanger (loc. cit.). It is interesting that the deceased is in neither case praised as "pious." Analysis of other orations, although less complete as of this writing, reveals similar tendencies.

To summarize, despite Aristides' strong feelings of devotion to Aesculapius and his interests in the cults of his native Asia Minor, he very seldom invokes, at least directly, the concept of peity, *eusebeia*, and when forms of the word do appear, they are used in very conventional, time-honored, formulae, as are such words as *eubolia, megalopsychia*, and *philanthropia*, usages going back to Plato and Demosthenes, strong influences on Aristides, as Oliver points out in *The Ruling Power*. The apparent lack of sincerity in Aristides' disquisitions on religious matters did not escape Boulanger as early as 1923 (op. cit., p. 209). Stylometric analysis of the use of the word *eusebeia* fully confirms his insight. Nevertheless, Aristides was certainly no skeptic like Lucian. He was a practicing rhetor and expressed himself according to the traditional canons of his expression. As is well known, he lived in an age which placed no high value on originality. An examination of the *Sacred Tales* should be sufficient to dispel any suspicion of religious skepticism on Aristides' part.

Although there are signs of an attempt to avoid excessive use of certain words and formulae (see for example Schmid, op. cit., passim, and the remarks in Keil's and my articles about Aristides' reluctance to pile up abstractions), both for euphonic reasons and in order to avoid too mechanical and amateurish an effect (a comparison between the orations of Aristides and, for example, the early orations of the emperor Julian would be instructive in this regard), it is not easy to determine whether purely stylistic factors explain the paucity of references to *eusebeia*, which seems to characterize all periods of Aristides' career (although additional research is needed regarding the chronology of his orations; nevertheless several can be dated from internal evidence) and to distinguish him from certain other orators. Additional study of religious references, particularly in Aristides' addresses to emperors, which have received relatively less attention from this viewpoint than the hymns or the *Sacred Tales*, is needed, and the use of stylometric evidence will be helpful in this direction.

MITHRAS AND PERSEUS

David Ulansey
Princeton University

As is well known, according to Franz Cumont--the founder of the field of Mithraic Studies--the Mithraic tauroctony or bull-slaying scene represents a moment in the Persian legend of the god Mithras, and the figures portrayed in the scene can be connected with elements of Persian mythology. However, in the past several years, a number of scholars have been working on a new, astronomical interpretation of the tauroctony, in which the tauroctony-figures represent not characters out of Persian myth, but rather represent certain stars and constellations. Such an interpretation was first suggested in 1865 by K. B. Stark, but was more or less dismissed by Cumont at the turn of the century.[1] Owing to Cumont's double authority as a leader in the study of both Mithraism and ancient astrology, subsequent generations of scholars followed his lead, and Stark's theory fell into complete neglect. However, following the general attack on Cumont which occurred at the First International Congress of Mithraic Studies in 1971, the meaning of the tauroctony again became an open question, and Stark's theory began to reemerge as a possible alternative to Cumont.

Thus, at the 1973 meeting of the American Philological Association, Roger Beck read a paper titled "On the Composition of the Mithraic Tauroctony" in which he re-examined and carried forward Stark's hypothesis. Beck's paper was not published, but in a subsequent article on the astronomical significance of Cautes and Cautopates--the torchbearers who almost always accompany Mithras in the tauroctony--in which he connects them with the stars Aldebaran and Antares, Beck summarizes the argument of his earlier paper as follows:

> Suppose that we watch this scene as Antares rises in the east and Aldebaran sets in the west. What do we observe? We see spread along the half of the ecliptic that separates these two stars a band of constellations which includes the counterparts of all five animals present in the bull-slaying scene: Taurus the bull, Canis Minor the dog, Hydra the snake, Corvus the raven, Scorpius the scorpion. To these we can add another important individual star, Spica the wheat-ear, the lucida of Virgo, whose counterpart in the tauroctony is the metamorphosed tail of the dying bull. Also visible in this same band of constellations are Leo and Crater, which recall the lion and the cup frequently present in reliefs from the Rhine-Danube frontier. . . . All that I need do here is emphasize the simple and indisputable fact that the same objects--arranged, moreover, in much the same order--figure both as constellations and as elements in the Mithraic tauroctony.[2]

Two years after Beck read his original paper, S. Insler, who did not know of Beck's work, independently proposed a similar interpretation of the tauroctony. Like Beck, Insler connects the bull with the constellation Taurus, and then goes on to say that "all of the other figures which play a major role in the iconography of the bull-slaying scene--scorpion, snake, raven, krater, lion, and dog--likewise correspond to the constellations Scorpio, Hydra, Corvus, Krater, Leo major, and Canis minor. . . ."[3] More recently,

---

[1] Franz Cumont, *Textes et monuments figurés relatifs aux mystères de Mithra*, Brussels, 1899, v. 1, p. 202.
[2] Roger Beck, "Cautes and Cautopates: Some Astronomical Considerations," *Journal of Mithraic Studies*, v. 2, #1, p. 10.
[3] S. Insler, "A New Interpretation of the Bull-Slaying Motif," in *Hommages à Maarten J. Vermaseren* (ed. M. B. de Boer; Leiden: Brill, 1978) 2. 525.

Alessandro Bausani of Rome and Michael Speidel of Hawaii have published interpretations of the tauroctony based on the astronomical correlations proposed by Beck and
Insler.[4]

If Beck and Insler are correct in their claim that the tauroctony-figures represent
constellations, then there arises an obvious question which, however, Beck and Insler
themselves strangely enough do not address. This question is the following: If, as Beck
and Insler claim, all of the figures surrounding Mithras in the tauroctony represent constellations, is it not likely that Mithras himself also represents a constellation?

Now, if we assume that the figure of Mithras does represent a constellation, an
obvious direction in which to begin looking to discover what constellation that might be
is to examine the region of the sky which corresponds to the position of Mithras in the
tauroctony: namely, the region of the sky directly above Taurus the Bull. And here we
are confronted with the following startling fact, which supports our assumption that
Mithras represents a constellation: directly above the constellation of the Bull--and thus
in a position in the sky exactly analogous to that of Mithras in the tauroctony--we find
not an eagle or a swan or a bear, but rather we find the constellation figure of a young
man with one leg extended and the other bent, carrying a knife, and wearing a Phrygian
cap! This constellation directly above the Bull, which bears such a striking resemblance
to the figure of Mithras, is the constellation which since at least the 6th century B.C. has
been seen as representing the hero Perseus.

As we mentioned above, the constellation-figure of Perseus resembles Mithras in
several ways, perhaps the most important being that Perseus is usually represented as
wearing a Phrygian cap. The cap which Perseus wears is known as the Cap of Darkness,
and was a divine gift which enabled him to become invisible. Just as the Phrygian cap is
the trademark of Mithras, so is the Cap of Darkness the trademark of Perseus. The fact
that Perseus' Cap of Darkness was usually portrayed as being a Phrygian cap probably has
to do with a fact which provides another important connection between Perseus and
Mithras: namely, the fact that Perseus was believed by the ancients to have had a strong
connection with Persia. Thus, for example, Herodotus says that Perseus, through his son
Perses, gave his name to Persia and the Persian people.[5]

There are numerous other examples of iconographical and mythological parallels
between the figures of Perseus and Mithras. These similarities, however, can provide no
more than circumstantial evidence for the connection between Mithras and Perseus
which we have hypothesized on the basis of the new astronomical interpretation of the
tauroctony. However, beyond such external similarities between the two figures, there
does exist another body of evidence which provides strong historical support for our
hypothesis of a connection between Mithras and Perseus. This evidence consists of the
fact that the historian Plutarch traces the origin of Mithraism to the region of Asia
Minor known as Cilicia, while archaeological evidence tells us that one of the most
important cults in Cilicia in Greco-Roman times consisted in the worship of none other
than the Greek hero Perseus![6]

The possibility of a connection between Mithraism and the cult of Perseus in Cilicia
has been suggested before, most notably in 1917 by A. L. Frothingham, the founder of the
American Journal of Archaeology. According to Frothingham, Tarsus, the capital city of
Cilicia, was the home of a complex syncretistic religion involving Anatolian, Greek, and
Persian elements. The local Anatolian hero-god was named Sandan, and according to
Frothingham:

---

[4]Alessandro Bausani, "Note sulla preistoria astronomica del mito di Mithra," in
Mysteria Mithrae (ed. Ugo Bianchi; Leiden: Brill, 1979) 503-11; Michael Speidel, *Mithras-
Orion* (Leiden: Brill, 1981).

[5]Herodotus, VII, 61, 3.

[6]Plutarch, *Vita Pompeii*, 24; on Perseus in Cilicia see Louis Robert, "Documents
d'Asie Mineure," *Bulletin de correspondance hellénique*, #10 (1977), p. 98ff.

The Greek element in Tarsus found the equivalent to Sandan in their own Heracles blended with Perseus. . . . What I particularly aim to prove in this paper is: (1) That the killing of Medusa by Perseus was considered by the Greeks of Tarsus and Asia Minor as the equivalent of the sacrifice of Sandan. (2) That the sacrifice of the Divine Bull by Mithra was regarded by the Persians of Tarsus and elsewhere as also corresponding to the sacrifice of Sandan. Both these scenes appear on the coins of Tarsus. (3) That the scene of the Lion slaying the Bull, which is the coat of arms of the city, is also and primarily the emblem of the sacrifice of Sandan. Whatever may have been the primitive naturalistic meaning of the lion slaying the bull, it was never a mere animal fight, but always symbolic and religious. . . . Perseus, the Destroyer, was called the winged lion, and Mithra as slayer was the lion, and merely takes the place of the lion on the back of the bull as an anthropomorphic substitute.[7]

Like K. B. Stark's astronomical interpretation of the tauroctony, owing to the authority exercised by Cumont, Frothingham's hypothesis has up till now been completely ignored. However, I believe that my discovery of the possibility of an astronomical connection between the figure of Mithras and the constellation Perseus provides strong and unexpected new support for Frothingham's general hypothesis (if not for all of its details) of a connection between the cult of Mithras, whose origins Plutarch traces to Cilicia, and the Cilician Perseus-cult.

Two particular points made by Frothingham deserve further discussion. First, Frothingham suggests that central importance be given to the lion-bull combat scene which was the coat of arms of Tarsus and in which, according to Frothingham, Mithras simply takes the place of the lion and thereby becomes the bull-slayer. In the context of the new astronomical interpretation of the tauroctony, this suggestion of Frothingham's gains additional support when we note Willy Hartner's recent demonstration that the lion-bull combat motif originated and continued to serve through most of its five thousand year history as a symbol whose essential significance was astronomical.[8]

Second, Frothingham claims that the figure of the Gorgon Medusa whom Perseus killed was an important element in the syncretistic process out of which Mithraism emerged. In this connection it is interesting to note the striking similarity between the figure of the Gorgon, with its animal-like head and winged, snake-entwined body, and the figure of the Mithraic lion-headed god, whose body also has wings and is entwined with snakes.

I would now like to return to the subject of Mithraic astronomy, and examine in greater detail the interpretation of the tauroctony offered by Beck and Insler. As Beck and Insler have pointed out, the figures that accompany Mithras in the tauroctony can be connected with particular constellations as follows: bull-Taurus, dog-Canis Minor, snake-Hydra, cup-Crater, raven-Corvus, scorpion-Scorpius, lion-Leo. The question that immediately arises in response to this list is: what is the connection between these particular constellations which would lead one to place them together in a group such as we find in the tauroctony? As Beck says,

As Antares rises in the east and Aldebaran sets in the west . . . we see spread along the half of the ecliptic that separates these two stars a band of constellations which includes the counterparts of all five animals present in the bull-slaying scene.

---

[7]A. L. Frothingham, "The Cosmopolitan Religion of Tarsus and the Origin of Mithra" (abstract only), *American Journal of Archaeology* 22 (1918) 63-64.

[8]Willy Hartner, *Oriens-Occidens* (Hildesheim, 1968) 227-59.

However, it is not enough merely to point out that these constellations are present in the same general area of the sky, for there are a number of other constellations in the same area which are not paralleled in the tauroctony, such as Gemini, Cancer, Libra, Centaurus, and Lupus, to mention only those which lie below or on the ecliptic. It thus remains to be explained why *only* those constellations listed by Beck and Insler are paralleled in the tauroctony.

The clue necessary to answer this question is given to us by Porphyry, who says in his *Cave of the Nymphs* that "Mithras is placed on the celestial equator."[9] Now the celestial equator, which consists of the projection of the earth's equator onto the celestial sphere, was, along with the ecliptic and the Milky Way, one of the three major circles which ancient astronomers and astrologers used to divide the sky. In addition, the places where the celestial equator crosses the ecliptic determine the spring and autumn equinoxes. The celestial equator, however, has a very slow movement, called "precession," which was first discovered by Hipparchus around 125 B.C., and thus the places where it crosses the ecliptic--the equinoxes--also move very slowly. Thus, in the first century B.C. the equinoxes were in Aries and Libra, but a few thousand years earlier they were in Taurus and Scorpius. It is here that Porphyry's statement provides the key to understanding the tauroctony. For if we place the spring equinox in Taurus, as it was around 3,000 B.C., then the celestial equator will pass through the following, and *only* the following, constellations below and on the ecliptic: Taurus, Canis Minor, Hydra, Crater, Corvus, and Scorpius! This list is exactly the same as that arrived at by Beck and Insler except that Leo is missing.[10] However, Leo fits perfectly into our solution, since when the spring equinox is in Taurus, the summer solstice will be in Leo. Further, if we follow the celestial equator above the ecliptic in this position, then just above Taurus it passes through a constellation which, as we have seen, plays a central role in the astronomy of the tauroctony--namely, the constellation Perseus.[11]

But why would anyone want to adopt as the central icon of their religion a symbolic picture of the celestial equator of 3,000 B.C.? By way of conclusion, I would like to present two possible answers to this question. First, the discovery of the precession of the equinoxes by Hipparchus in 125 B.C. amounted, for those who understood it, to the discovery that the entire cosmos possessed a previously unknown movement. It is not difficult to imagine philosophical and religious circles associated with the great University of Tarsus--which, as Strabo tells us, included many important Stoic philosophers--in which such a discovery would be seen as having deep religious significance.[12] In such circumstances, it is also easy to imagine that the divine being responsible for moving the cosmos in this new manner might--in typical Stoic fashion--become the object of allegorization and personification, and in Tarsian religious circles what better candidate could be found to personify this new cosmic force than the god of the city, the hero Perseus, whose cosmic significance was already manifest in his existence as a constellation? The hero slaying the bull would represent that divine power which, in remote antiquity, had destroyed the power of the bull by moving the entire sphere of the fixed stars in such a way that the spring equinox moved from the constellation of Taurus into Aries. Finally, knowledge of this secret movement and of the divine force responsible for it could come to be seen as a source of power and as a means of escape from the powers of fate and of

---

[9] *De Antro Nympharum*, 24.

[10] I would refer the wheat-ear on the bull's tail in the tauroctony not, as Beck and Insler do, to the star Spica, but rather to a common Mesopotamian symbol, consisting of a bull and an ear of wheat, which, according to Hartner (op. cit., p. 230), symbolized the constellation Taurus, with the wheat-ear representing its brightest star Aldebaran.

[11] In his recent book *Mithras-Orion*, Michael Speidel also concludes that the tauroctony represents the celestial equator, although he places it in a different position than I do, and claims that Mithras represents not Perseus but Orion.

[12] Strabo, *Geography*, 14, 5, 13-15.

the stars. Such knowledge would thus become both highly sacred and extremely valuable, and would therefore be jealously guarded and revealed only to those who proved themselves worthy.

A hint as to a second possible answer is given to us by Frothingham. As we said earlier, Frothingham claimed that the tauroctony originated out of the lion-bull combat scene which was the coat of arms of Tarsus; and, as we also mentioned earlier, this same lion-bull combat motif, which actually originated in Sumerian times, had, according to Hartner, an essentially astronomical significance. It is thus possible that ancient astronomical and astrological traditions surrounded the use of this symbol, and that among these there might have been a tradition in which it was recalled that the spring equinox was once in Taurus. As we said earlier, when the spring equinox is in Taurus, the celestial equator passes through the constellation Perseus, and thus if it was believed that the spring equinox had once been in Taurus in some remote past (i.e., in what Eliade would call "sacred time"), then the construction of a hypothetical celestial equator with equinox in Taurus would allow the worshippers of Perseus in Tarsus to attribute a new cosmic significance to their hero, who could now be called "the ruler of the celestial equator in sacred time."

REPENTANCE AND REDEMPTION IN HOSEA[+]

Jeremiah Unterman
Wichita State University

Definition of Terms

Repentance is equivalent to the prophetic use of the root שׁו"ב as a spiritual *return*, which, in its fullest sense, encapsulates three sequential steps, as in Jer 3:12-13: (1) acknowledgment of sin (at least inwardly, if not an outward confession), i.e., that Israel has willfully disobeyed God; (2) the cessation of sin; (3) the return of the people to the path of obedience and faithfulness (cp. vv 22-25). Whether complete repentance can lack step (3) is doubtful. Whatever is less than "return" cannot truly be called "return." it may then take another name, such as "confession" or, perhaps, "seeking" (דרשׁ), and the texts in which these other expressions appear must be investigated to see whether or not complete repentance is implied.

Redemption is the spiritual act of God reaccepting Israel, which is accompanied by the physical acts of God--returning Israel to the land, increase of agriculture and population, reinstitution of the Davidic monarchy, reunification of the people, etc. Similarly, repentance is the spiritual act of the people's will in reaccepting God accompanied by the acts of physical obedience.

Introduction

It is an axiom of Biblical thought that once Israel has sinned, and while it still dwells in a divinely-sanctioned Israelite state in the land of Israel, it must repent in order to avoid destruction and/or exile. But what if the hoped-for repentance is not realized and the threat of destruction and/or exile is carried out? How then can the positive relationship between God and Israel be renewed? Is repentance a condition of the redemptive process, or not? This study will investigatethe role of repentance, if at all, in those passages in Hosea which are concerned with redemption.

However, the clarification of the role of repentance in Hosea's prophecy is hardly a simple matter, for it depends upon the composition of the book--an issue of some controversy and complexity. Three representative scholarly approaches follow.

Three Critical Approaches

1. Y. Kaufmann, succeeded by H. L. Ginsberg, has maintained that the authorship of ch. 1-3 derives from a prophet other than the author of ch. 4-14, and that the former lived in the 9th cent. B.C.E.[1] Kaufmann claims that the two parts of the book differ in style, phraseology, use of symbols, objectivity and lyricism, ideology (and conception of the people's specific sin), and attitude toward Baalism.[2] Ginsberg[3] agrees with Kaufmann in the main,[4] but, among other comments, emphasizes the emotionality of Hosea II to the point of asserting that this prophet depicts God as restoring Israel unconditionally because of his "unmerited love," while Hosea I "does not speak at all of

---

[+]Dedicated to my parents and first teachers, Roslyn Eisen Unterman and Theodor Herzl Unterman, on the occasion of their 45th wedding anniversary.

[1]Y. Kaufmann, תולדות האמונה הישראלית, Vol. 3 (Jerusalem, 1967), p. 99.

[2]Ibid., pp. 93-97.

[3]H. L. Ginsberg, "Hosea," *EncJud* (Jerusalem, 1971), 8. 1012-16, 1018-19.

[4]Ginsberg, "Sudies in Hosea 1-3," *Yehezkel Kaufmann Jubilee Volume* (Jerusalem, 1960), p. 50, n. 1.

YHWH's love either with reference to the past, present, or to the future. . . ."[5] That Ginsberg holds this position despite verses such as 2:20-25 is quite surprising and rather untenable.

To discuss and attempt to refute the claims of these two scholars in a comprehensive fashion deserves the treatment of a separate article.[6] Suffice it to say here that the entire book of Hosea contains 197 verses, and yet according to the superscription of 1:1, Hosea prophesied from the reign of Jeroboam II through that of Hezekiah! Although the maximum number of years would surely be far too large (784-698 B.C.), most scholars posit a term of 25 years for Hosea's prophecies (750-725). Even if the extreme view of H. Tadmor is accepted[7] (that the terminus ante quem of the book is 738), Hosea is still left with a dozen years of activity. Certainly, if ch. 1-3 are from Hosea's early prophecies and the rest from later ones, enough time can elapse to explain certain differences of style, phraseology, symbolism, and even development of ideology. All too often the prophets are not perceived by modern scholars to have characteristics which should be attributed to every thinking, reflective individual--the traits of complexity and growth, and the very human feature of not being completely, or consistently, logical. This is one of the major reasons, if not the foremost one, why many scholars deny the authenticity of numerous prophetic passages. Indeed, in Hosea, particularly, there are many elements of relationship between ch. 1-3 and 4-14: cp. 2:10 with 14:9d; 2:15 with 13:6 (the root שכ"ח); 2:10 with 11:3 (the use of the root יד"ע); דגן ותירוש ותירוש in 2:10, 11, 24; 7:14; גפן and/or תאנה in 2:14; 9:10; 10:1; 14:8; etc. (Kaufmann names a few others).[8] These linguistic connections are strong witnesses against the division of the book.

2. As has just been noted, there are wide differences of opinion among scholars concerning the dates of Hosea's prophecies (although there is unanimous agreement that Hosea did not prophesy after the fall of Samaria). These divisions reflect the absence of clear indications of dates in the text. This reality, in turn, makes the sure reconstruction of an historical development of Hosea's ideology extremely difficult if not impossible. Nonetheless, G. Fohrer[9] attempts just such a reconstruction by rearranging the order of the prophecies as follows: 5:15-6:6; 14:2-9; 3:1-5; 2:16-25. Thus, he arrives at the convenient conclusion that after initially believing in repentance as a prelude to redemption, the prophet abandons that hope when his prophet experience makes him realize that Israel is incapable of repenting. Hosea then turns to a belief in redemption which is effected solely through God's grace. J. Bright accepts this reconstruction.[10]

3. Unlike Fohrer, H. W. Wolff accepts the order of the prophecies in the book, but sees the one in ch. 2 as being built upon Israel's repentance (by placing 2:9 after 2:15).[11] Later, he opines, Hosea understands God's love to be the only precondition to Israel's restoration. This stand forces him to view 14:2-4 as "an invitation to return (which)

---

[5]"Hosea," *Enc Jud* 8. 1022.

[6]On the matter of Baalism, see E. Halpern, *Hosea* (Jerusalem, 1976) pp. 11-13 (Hebrew).

[7]H. Tadmor, "הרקע ההיסטורי של נבואת הושע" *Y. Kaufmann Jubilee Vol., pp.* For a review of the controversy, see Halpern, pp. 9-12. Ginsberg, "Hosea," p. 1018, lowers the terminus ante quem to 734. The authenticity of 1:1 has also been debated (cp. Isa 1:1; Mic 1:1; and the works cited here).

[8]Ibid., p. 95, n. 2.

[9]G. Fohrer, "Umkehr und Erlosung beim Propheten Hosea," *Studien zur alttestamentlichen Prophetie*, BZAW 99, pp. 222-41.

[10]J. Bright, *Covenant and Promise* (London, 1977), pp. 92-93.

[11]H. W. Wolff, *Hosea, Hermeneia*, (trans. by Gary Stansell; Philadelphia, 1974), pp. xxvii-xxix.

already presupposes this love." Thus, through arbitrary and illegitimate methods Wolff and Fohrer arrive at the same (preconceived?) conclusions concerning the development of Hosea's ideology.

The above attempts at analysis having been found wanting, the relevant passages in Hosea shall now be examined.

Hosea

2:4-25 [12]

2:4-25 appears to be a continuous literary unit. Most commentators see 2:18-25 as a later addition (even if authentic to Hosea) by an editor.[13] However, the first words of v 18, וְהָיָה בַיּוֹם הַהוּא,assume some prelude! Furthermore, one would expect that a prophecy of redemption which succeeds a prohecy of punishment would contain references to, and a reversal of, that punishment, and this is exactly what occurs here: cp. v 19 with v 15; vv 18-19 with v 4; חית השדה in v 20 and v 14; יד"ע in v 22 and v 10; v 23 with v 5; v 24 with v 11; רח"ם in vv 21, 25, and v 6.

And now to the matter at hand:

Although the root שו"ב does not appear, v 4b contains an element of repentance: God calls for a cessation of sin, specifically idolatry, by Israel (ריבו באמכם to avert the impending (ריבו . . . ותסר זנוניה מפניה ונאפופיה מבין שדיה punishment of vv 5-15. Some scholars have sought to find the people's positive response in v 9b--.ואמרה אלכה ואשובה אל אישי הראשון כי טוב לי אז מעתה[14] However, if this was, indeed, repentance then the following verses, 10-15, are anomalous, and even paradoxical, for the punishment of vv 5-8 continues and worsens (cp.מעתה of v 9b with v 12--ועתה . . .). Furthermore, the שוב of v 11 seems to reflect in direct contrast the ואשובה of v 9, for the immediately preceding לכן in v 11, which introduces further punishment, is, by definition, consequential. Thus, it appears that the statement placed in the mouth of the faithless mother Israel in v 9b is only the expression of selfish concern--כי טוב לי אז מעתה.[15] The use of the comparative here

---

[12]2:1-3 appears out of context. Wolff, p. 26, J. M. Ward, *Hosea* (New York, 1966), p. 27, and others place these verses at the end of the chapter, and, indeed, they have no continuity with the surrounding verses. Ideationally, they discuss the effects of redemption. Once removed, 1:9 flows smoothly into 2:4 and creates a larger unit starting with 1:2: cp. ופקדתי in vv 4 and 2:15;והשבתי in vv 4 and 2:13;זנ"ה in vv 2 and 2:4, 6, 7; שב"ר in vv 5 and 2:20; vv 4, 6, 8 with 2:24-25. 1:7 has long been considered a Judahite interpolation (cf. the commentaries), but the succession מלחמה, חרב, קשת appears only here and 2:20 in the entire Bible! The verse itself predicts God's mercies and salvation to Judah.

[13]For example, see Wolff, p. 48, and J. L. Mays, *Hosea* (OTL; Philadelphia, 1969), pp. 36, 46.

[14]So many of the commentators, such as O. Procksch, *Die kleinen prophetischen Schriften vor dem Exil, Erläuterungen zum Alten Testament* 3 (Stuttgart, 1910); A. Weiser, *Das Buch der zwölf kleinen Propheten* (ATD 24; Göttingen, 1949); W. Rudolph, *Hosea, Kommentar zum Alten Testament* (Stuttgart, 1966). However, in order for them to hold this opinion they have been forced to place vv 8-9 after v 15. Kaufmann, p. 107, Wolff, and Ginsberg, "Hosea," p. 1011, too, see this as genuine repentance.

[15]T. K. Cheyne, *Hosea* (CBSC) (Cambridge, 1897) comments "it is not so much the expression of penitence, as of a longing to escape from the sense of misery." G. von Rad, *Old Testament Theology*, Vol. 2, trans. by D. M. G. Stalker (London, 1965), p. 142, adds, "Israel . . . failed to see that she had been brought into a *status confessionis* before Jahweh because of these gifts; rather, she fell victim to a mythic divinisation of husbandry and of its numinous, chthonic origins." Ward, p. 38, feels that because Israel

("for it was better for us/me x than y") is reminiscent of the type of amoral physical gratification sought by the generation of the desert, who also longed for the comforts of a fertile land rather than desert-like desolation (Exod 14:12--כי טוב לנו עבד את מצרים ממתינו במדבר similarly, Num 11:18; 14:3). At the best, then, the statement in v 9b is false repentance, a theme which reoccurs in the book (5:6; 6:1-4).

It is only after punishment, not repentance, that the process of redemption is initiated. Vv 16-17 depict the renewal of the "marriage" between God and Israel as reminiscent of the inception of the relationship as it occurred in the Sinai desert (l7b--וענתה שמה כימי נעוריה וכיום עלתה מארץ מצרים). However, it may not be necessary to assume that this redemptive process is preceded by exile from the land. The punishment in vv 5-15 explicitly indicates only drought and wild beasts (a sequence which also appears in Lev 26:19-22). The "desert" mentioned in v 16 is, in reality, part of the Promised Land--v 17a: ונתתי לה את כרמיה משם ואת עמק עכור לפתח תקוה. The site herein indicated is the Judean Desert since עמק עכור appears to be near Jericho (Josh 7:1-26; 15:7). The words והשכבתים לבטח in v 20 do not have to presuppose exile (cp. Job 11:18), but rather insecurity, and the same may be said for the expression וזרעתיה לי בארץ of v 25 where the reference may be to agricultural increase (in agreement with vv 23-24 and in reversal of the punishment of v 11; cf. v 10).

The reconstitution of a fertile agriculture is, thus, depicted in historical terms, since it was from the Valley of Achor that Joshua's armies are viewed rising to conquer the hill country. The renewed fertility will be magnified over that of pre-punishment days, for the Valley of Achor will become full of vineyards.[16]

Thus, vv 16-17a portray God wooing and giving a dowry to Israel, which results in a positive response (vv 17b-18). It is God, too, not the people, who ensures their loyalty (v 19). In other words, the people's acknowledgment of God's lordship is preceded by actual divine acts of redemption. These acts continue in a new covenant, which differs from the Sinaitic one by guaranteeing a completely peaceful existence of Israel, and harmony with wild animals (v 20, which hearkens back to Genesis 1-2; similarly, Isa 11:6-9). Additionally, the relationship between God and Israel will be eternal (v 21a), of mutual, correct behavior (v 21b), and Israel's obedience is secured (v 22). These sureties are accompanied by natural harmony and crop production.

Nowhere in the prophecy of redemption in vv 16-25 is there any indication of Israel's confession of sin, or promise of the cessation of sin, or decision to return to God. Acceptance of God (vv 18, 25b) and obedience (v22b) are results of God's redemptive acts. We must conclude, then, that Hosea 2:4-25 demands sincere repentance to avoid divine punishment (vv 4-5), but that once judgment has been executed, God will restore Israel, assuring the people's fealty, in a process in which repentance (or even confession) has no part.

3:4-5[17]

V 3 symbolizes the coming isolation of the people Israel predicted in v 4. Neither verse seems to imply exile, but rather a period when Israel will have neither government,

---

"has not changed her means or goals, she has not changed at all." U. Cassuto, "The Second Chapter of Hosea," *Biblical and Oriental Studies,* Vol. 1, trans. by Israel Abrahams (Jerusalem, 1973), p. 124, argues that "she designated the Lord 'my first Husband,' and thus showed that she did not yet realize who and what He was to her . . . the implication is that she thinks that others like Him exist."

[16]Similarly, the prophecy of restoration in Amos 9:13-14.

[17]Modern scholarship has concerned itself with the authenticity of 3:1-5 as well as its relationship to the previous chapters, and the dating of these verses (for treatments of the text, see Ward, pp. 47-52). For an unusual approach, see Halpern (pp. 80-90), who claims that vv 4-5 refer back to the period of the Judges as a symbolic lesson for Hosea's personal life.

nor ritual. This end to local political and religious institutions indicates, perhaps, oppressive rule by foreigners. The words אין מלך of v 4 appear to allude to the frequent אין מלך בישראל in Judges (17:6; 18:1; 21:25; cp. 19:1) in prophecy of a similar time of anarchy. On the other hand, the words כי ימים רבים ישבו seem to suggest the punishment of the generation of the desert (Deut 1:46; Josh 24:7). After this period of desolation Israel will return to God and will come "tremblingly" to the divine "bounty."[18] It is puzzling that this prophecy contains no description of divine acceptance of the people's repentance other than the oblique שובו. Nonetheless, it seems clear[19] that repentance succeeds punishment and precedes restoration, in contradistinction to chapter 2. Neither chapter, though, indicates exile.

5:4-7

In 5:4 the people's sins do not allow them to return to God.[20] As a result, they suffer an undetermined punishment in 5:5--וישראל ואפרים יכשלו בעונם כשל גם יהודה עמם. Apparently, though, the reference is to destruction of some type,[21] for in 4:5 כשל is paralleled to דמה, which indicates death (cp. 10:7, 15 and the contexts there). 5:6 then predicts the people's attempt to return to God, which is rejected--בצאנם ובבקרם ילכו לבקש את יהוה ולא ימצאו חלץ מהם.[22] That this repentance is insincere is indicated by the reference to the sacrificial animals. Elsewhere (6:6; 4:1-2; etc.) Hosea emphasizes the primacy of morality and fealty to God rather than cultic service. 5:7, despite its difficulties,[23] relates further punishment.

The implication of these verses is that true repentance would have brought about a cessation of punishment, and probably redemption.

5:14-6:4

5:14 views God as bringing destruction upon the people. Then, in v 15, God waits for the repentance which will result from the people's distress.[24] 6:1-3 reveals the desire of the people to return to God (לכו ונשובה אל יהוה--6:1) in obedience (ונדעה נרדפה לדעת את יהוה--6:3) in order to be saved, healed, and restored (כי הוא טרף וירפאנו יך ויחבשנו יחיינו מימים . . . ויבא כגשם לנו--6:1-3). It is noteworthy that there is no admission of sin contained in this exhortation, rather, only a concern for self-preservation. This, too, then, is not true repentance, but lip-service, and is so recognized by God in v 4.[25] True repentance implies steadfast loyalty (חסדכם כענן בקר וכטל משכים הלך--cp. 6:6; 2:21; 4:1; 10:12; 12:7), while Israel is concerned only with immediate gratification--יחיינו מימים ביום השלישי יקמנ־ה (v 2). Again, the implication is that sincere return would result in redemption. This seems to be the focus of the double לך מה אעשה לך "What shall I do for you" (cp. 2 Sam 21:3, 4; 2 Kings 4:2), i.e., God would restore Israel if it were deserved.

---

[18]Ginsberg's definition, "Hosea," p. 1013, cp. Jer 31:12, 14.

[19]Contra F. I. Anderson and D. N. Freedman, *Hosea,* Anchor Bible (New York, 1980), p. 307, who refer to v 5 as "cryptic remarks."

[20]Wolff, p. 99: "it is no longer humanly possible for Israel to 'return' from her idols to God."

[21]Cp. Abarbanel.

[22]Wolff, p. 100, thinks that there may be a reference here to Canaanite ritual.

[23]Particularly, the word חדש (cf. the commentaries).

[24]יאשמו as Jacob Milgrom, *Cult and Conscience* (Leiden, 1976), p. 5 has shown, means "they are punished." Similarly 10:2 and14:1 (see n. 16, loc. cit.).

[25]Contra Anderson and Freedman, p. 426.

6:11b-7:2[26]

6:11b should be taken together with 7:1-- עמי כרפאי [27] בשובי שבות
לישראל. In these verses, God's desire to redeem Israel is thwarted by their evil deeds,
deceitful acts, and their refusal to acknowledge their responsibility to God for their sin
(7:2--ובל יאמרו לבבכם כל רעתם זכרתי). Again, the inference is that genuine
repentance would have opened the door for redemption.

7:10, 13-16

7:10 reiterates Israel's refusal to return to God despite the punishment that has
already come to pass (v 9). This pattern is repeated in vv 13-16. V 13b can be
interpreted "and I, should I redeem them!?! and they have spoken lies against me!"[28] or,
"Yet, I would redeem them, but they have spoken lies against (or, about) me." The lies
may be in reference to false repentance (but, cp. 2 Kgs 17:9-11). V 14 repeats Israel's
obstinacy and reemphasizes their concern with material things, "grain and new wine."
Their "mourning" indicates that they have already experienced punishment. In v 16,
ישובו לא על[29] may, once more, reassert their rejection of God.

10:3

The first acknowledgment of guilt appears in 10:3 as a response to chaos, but no
positive statement is forthcoming from God.

10:12

10:12 is an unanswered call for repentance-- נירו לכם ניר ועת לדרוש את
יהוה.

11:1-11

Despite the obscurity of the text of ch. 11 certain significant observations are
possible. Israel has declined to repent--(v 5) כי מאנו לשוב. V 7 is, admittedly, a
crux. Nonetheless, it is exceedingly implausible that it infers the people's repentance.[30] V. 8 relates the beginning of God's redemptive decision in words which

---

[26]For an ingenious reconstruction of 6:11-7:1 see Tur-Sinai, פשוטו של מקרא,
Vol. 3B, who understands this passage as meaning that the sins will be erased when God's
redemption comes.

[27]שוב שבות does not have to be explained as return from captivity or exile, cp.
Job 42:10. Ginsberg, "Hosea," p. 1020, translates "Whenever I would make my people
whole again" (similarly, Wolff). The attachment of 6:11b to 7:1 was seen by A. B. Ehrlich,
מקרא כפשוטו, Vol. 3, and many others.

[28]Similarly, Wolff et al.

[29]The Septuagint translates for לא על, εἰς οὐδέν, i.e., לא יועיל cp. Jer
2:8, 11. Cp. Ps 78:57, the only other appearance in the Bible of קשת רמיה.

[30]Logically, repentance in v 7 would be incongruous after v 5. ואל על is
interpreted as a reference to Baal by Wolff and Ward. Others (Cheyne and Halpern)
follow rabbinic commentators: Rashi-- כשהנביאים מלמדים אותם לשוב אלי
תלואים הם אם לשוב אם לא לשוב בקושי ישובון אלי . . . ואל הדבר אשר
Ibn Ezra--עליו יקראוהו הנביאים יחד לא ירוממוהו עמי לא יאות לעשותו;
משובה לעולם לגנאי . . . ואל עליון יקראוהו . . . נביאי השם וכולם
(משובתי) כשלא . . . לא ירומו ראש Abarbanel (Metzudat David concurs)--
ירצה לשוב מחרון אפו . . . משובת האל יתברך היא כפי הדיו והמשפט הישר

underscore the fact that repentance is not a factor, but rather a spontaneous act of divine mercy-- נכמרו נחומי. The expression נהפך עלי לבי יחד נכמרו נחומי parallels נכמרו רחמים in Gen 43:30; 1 Kgs 3:26. The familial relationship hovering over all three verses (cp. vv 1, 3, 10) points to the instinctive flood of compassion and love.[31] God's promise not to eradicate Israel is delivered in v. 9.[32] Although the authenticity of vv 10-11 has been questioned,[33] the return from exile and the obedience to God follow logically. Whether אחרי יהוה ילכו of v 10 represents return after the fact of redemption, or a description of Israel's future loyalty, is a moot point. In either case repentance did not lead to redemption.

12:7-10

12:7-10 represent the typical prophetic pattern of call to repentance (v 7)[34] in order to avoid punishment, here viewed as exile (v 10b; cp. v 15). These verses, then, are outside our purview.

13:14

Apparently, 13:14a, מיד שאול אפדם ממות אגאלם, must be taken as a rhetorical, incredulous question (cp. 7:13b),[35] otherwise the following verses (14b-14:1) make no sense.

14:2-9

Much of the wording of 14:2-9 is uncertain. Nevertheless, certain essentials are clear. 14:2 is a plea to Israel to return to God, for it has already suffered punishment

---

[31] Ehrlich's view differs slightly-- ; . . . היו תולין תשובתם בתשובת האל יתברך קירומו של עמי תלוי בחזרתי שאחזור בי ואנחם על אשר נתתים לפני אויב ואשיב ואושיעם מידו, והם קוראים "אל על" "אל הערל אשר בצוארם, ואף על פי כן לא ארים את הערל מעל לחייהם כאשר עשיתי לפנים. Cp., also, Kaufmann, p. 145, n. 75. Contra Anderson and Freedman, p. 589.

[32] Although there is much wisdom and knowledge in the commentary on Hosea by Anderson and Freedman, one must take exception to their reading and translation of v 9, "I will certainly act out my burning anger. I will certainly come back to destroy Ephraim. For I am a god and not a human. I, the Holy One, will certainly come into the midst of your city" (pp. 574-75). Despite their acknowledgment of the "sentiment" of v 8 (p. 589), Anderson and Freedman maintain that for YHWH not to act with strict justice would be deceitful (pp. 589-90). How do they explain the (now) paradoxical depiction of restoration that appears immediately in vv 10-11? They do not. All they say is "There is an abrupt change at this point" (p. 591). Such sophism is hardly worthy of these two excellent scholars. The compassionate content of vv 8 and 10 necessitates the negative לא in v 9 and not the asseverative. Furthermore, they ignore the fact that v 9b is a parallelism--

כי אל אנכי ולא איש
בקרבך קדוש ולא אבוא בעיר.

Thus, if YHWH comes into the city, according to Anderson and Freedman, then He also claims that He is a man.

[33] For a review of scholarship, see Ward, p. 194.

[34] Ginsberg, "Hosea's Ephraim, More Fool than Knave," *JBL* 80 (1961) 342-43, feels that the first phrase of v 7 should be corrected to באהליך תשב. Rudolph maintains the text and understands it to mean that Israel shall return *with the help of* her God.

[35] So Ehrlich, Rudolph, Mays, Wolff, Halpern, etc. Contra Anderson and Freedman, p. 639.

(כִּי כָשַׁלְתָּ בַעֲוֹנֶךָ).[36] V 3a is a further exhortation to verbal repentance. Whatever the
meaning of 3b,[37] v 4 is a confession of the futility of disloyalty to God, a rejection of
idolatry, and recognition of divine mercy. These words, placed in the mouth of the
people by the prophet, contain none of the elements of false repentance previously
expressed by the people. There is no refusal to accept responsibility for sin, nor any
selfish preoccupation with material benefit. The earnest declaration elicits God's
assurance of restoration.[38] He will heal and love them, for his anger is turned away (v
5). The many metaphors of plant growth in vv 6-9 promise Israel's reinvigoration and
secure existence under God's care. The reference to the striking of roots in v 6 appears
to point to a return from exile. Certainly, the placement of this passage at the end of
the book denotes a redemption after all the predicted punishments have come to pass.
Equally certain, the positive response of the people to the summons to repentance is an
essential prelude to redemption.

Conclusions

The frequent obscurity of the text impedes understanding.[39] It is, therefore, with
some trepidation that the following concluding remarks are made.

1. A summons to repentance, which is *not* part of a prophecy of judgment or one
of redemption, appears only in 10:12.[40] Calls to repentance which are in reality parts of
prophecies of judgment, and, consequently, express the refusal of Israel to repent, are
found in 2:4 and 12:7 (with vv 8-10).[41] 14:2-3 is the one call to repentance found in a
prophecy of redemption.

2. False or insincere repentance appears in 2:10; 5:6; 6:1-3; 7:14 and 8:2.[42]

3. Refusal to repent is found in 7:2, 14, 16; 8:10; 11:5 and 12:9.

4. Whereas redemption in 14:5-9 is based on a call to repentance to which the
people respond positively, 3:5 predicts, not calls for, repentance as a stage between
punishment and (assumed) restoration.

5. 2:16-25 and 11:8-11 are prophecies which depict redemption despite the
people's lack of repentance.[43]

6. 5:4 and 7:2 hint at the inability of Israel to repent due to their habitual sins.

The similarity between passages found in diverse sections of the book, illustrated
above, point to the improbability of delineating an historical pattern. It would be facile
to claim that an editor arranged the materials improperly, and that a rearrangement

---

[36]See on 5:4-7, and Wolff, p. 234.
[37]Cp. the commentaries and R. Gordis, "The Text and Meaning of Hosea 14:3," *VT* 5
(1955) 88-90.
[38]Contra Wolff, p. 237.
[39]Is it to this reality that the unique statement in Hosea 14:10 was penned by an
editor (מִי חָכָם וְיָבֵן אֵלֶּה נָבוֹן וְיֵדָעֵם)?
[40]Even here Wolff, p. 186, has connected this verse to a prophecy of judgment, but
vv 12-13a have the effect "Do this (v 12) . . . for that is what has happened to you (v 13)."
[41]V 9 is the people's response to the call in v 7.
[42]10:3 has not been included here because it appears to contain words of mourning
which the prophet predicts the people will utter, rather than repentance.
[43]1:7 is incongruous. 2:1-3 appears out of context.

would, indeed, bring a pattern to life. However, it seems much more probable that the inconsistency of the message of redemption reflects the inner turmoil of the prophet. Hosea is caught on a tension wire between two poles. On the one hand is judgment: Israel has sinned, suffers, and must repent or suffer further destruction. On the other hand is mercy: Israel seems incapable of repentance, but how can God, who loves the people as a father/husband, annihilate them!?! So, Hosea vacillates between one pole and the other, sometimes prophesying redemption dependent upon repentance, sometimes not. Sometimes Hosea feels that Israel does not deserve the benefits of God's love unless it repents, and sometimes God's love overwhelms his senses. The prophet finds a rationale for the latter in the Exodus traditions (2:16-17; 11:1), [44] but the tension is never resolved.

Hosea, more so than Amos, is the first prophet to exist on the edge of national disaster, and, thus, the need to relate repentance and redemption is more critical with him than with Amos. Also, he has no prophetic models to follow, for he conceives of no innocent remnant, as does Amos.[45] Therefore, it is not surprising that he has more than one view of the redemptive process. But, it is of more than passing interest that Jeremiah, too, will in his lifetime have more than one view of redemption, and will go to Hosea for *his* models.

Methodological Observations

It is a highly problematic issue whether modern biblical scholarship can be categorized as scientific or artistic. Certainly, in attempting to uncover the truth of a biblical matter, the scholar must always be conscious of his inability both to completely dissipate the mists that obscure the past and to entirely loose the mental fetters placed upon him by his own life-experiences.

One of the purposes of the foregoing analysis has been to illuminate some of the pitfalls of tendentious scholarship, particularly the lack of appreciation for the complexity of a human being. Narrow-mindedness in scholarship can be defined as the consistent use of only some critical approaches while eschewing others. The true scholar must be holistic[46] in study--anything and everything that can serve as a tool to better understand the text must be used. Obviously, in any given case some methods will be more appropriate than others. In any one of the vast majority of research papers published today, various historical and literary methods are used, but far too often the received text is ignored. Difficulties and incongruencies are commonly explained as textual corruptions: copyist misspellings, misplacement of verses, illogical order of passages, faulty dates, incorrect attribution of scholarship, etc. Mistakes, of course, occur, but such mistakes should be considered only after every other available means of analysis has been applied and tested. Unfortunately, scholars resort very quickly to interpreting the text in a way which is totally at odds with its received state. Thus, as has been shown above, Kaufmann and Ginsberg have divided *Hosea* into texts originating in different centuries without considering all the evidence. Fohrer and Wolff have forced interpretations on the text by reordering it. All of these four scholars have been

---

[44] See U. Cassuto, "The Prophet Hosea and the Books of the Pentateuch," *Biblical and Oriental Studies*, Vol. 1, pp. 88-89.

[45] A necessary implication of Amos 9:8-10, which is perfectly consistent with 2:6-7, 12; 3:9; 4:1; 5:11-12.

[46] "Holistic" used in this context is adopted from Moshe Greenberg, for example, "The Vision of Jerusalem in Ezekiel 8-11, a Holistic Interpretation," *The Divine Helmsman* (ed. J. L. Crenshaw and S. Sandmel; New York, 1980), pp. 143-64. This method is also called "Total Interpretation"--see the masterpiece by Meir Weiss, *The Bible and Modern Literary Theory* (2d ed.; Jerusalem, 1967; Hebrew). An expansion and English translation will soon be published.

motivated by a desire to understand the thought of the prophet. That has been the desire of the present author, too, but the attempt here has been to understand Hosea *through* the received text, not by reshaping or slicing it. Therefore, the question asked was, "What does the text mean as it stands?" A plausible answer did present itself. Whether or not that answer is correct may never be known, but at least it was derived from an approach which attempted to take the received text, the basis for all such study, seriously.

THE IMAGE OF WOMAN IN PHILO

Judith Romney Wegner
Brown University

This study of the image of woman as portrayed in Philo's writings has two objectives. The first is simply to present a selection of passages that bear on the theme and to analyze the part it plays in Philo's thought. The second task is to see whether we can discern either specifically Greek or specifically Jewish influences on Philo's depiction of women. To this end, we shall briefly compare Philo's ideas with those found in some Greek sources which were certainly available to him. We shall likewise compare Philo's view of women with what is found in some Jewish talmudic or midrashic texts. These may reflect traditions already current in the Palestine of Philo's day, though it is not assumed or concluded that he knew them. The further goal of the study is to stimulate comparative exploration of the image of women in the two ancient cultures--Hellenistic and Judaic--which together have shaped attitudes to women in the predominantly Christian West.

I. *Woman in Philo as Allegory*

It is impossible to read far in Philo without noticing that he holds fixed views concerning the nature of women; for he airs these views at every turn. At the same time, it seems that he had no great interest in women as a topic for sustained discussion, or his scriptural exegesis would surely have included a book on this subject, for there is ample scriptural material on which to draw. Instead, Philo's strictures on women are scattered throughout his work, frequently appearing as incidental comments (sometimes gratuitous) in other contexts. We shall begin by looking at Philo's use of woman as an allegorical device

1. *Gender and human attributes*

A basic theme of Philo's cosmology, and certainly of his allegorical use of scripture, is the relationship between gender and certain characteristics of the human soul. Having first told us that mind or intellect (*nous*), the "sovereign element of the soul," is the image of God in which man was created (Op. Mund. 69 on Gen 1:26), Philo asserts as an axiom that mind is a masculine attribute, while feeling or sense-perception (*aisthēsis*) is a feminine attribute: "for in us, mind corresponds to man, the senses to woman" (Op. Mund. 165). Mind, moreover, is superior to sense-perception (Leg. All. 222).

Nous is for Philo the soul's rational quality, *aisthēsis* its irrational quality. The relationship between this polarity and the male-female polarity in Philo is well explained by Richard Baer as follows:

> That the male-female polarity is associated with the irrational part of the soul, not with the higher *nous*, finds further confirmation in Rer. Div. Her. 133ff, a description of the division of all things into equal parts and opposites through the agency of the *logos tomeus*. In Rer. Div. Her. 138-9, a text deserving close attention, Philo points out that just as God separated the living from the lifeless, so he further divided the living into rational and irrational species. The rational species he divided into mortal and immortal, "and *of the mortal* he made two portions, one of which he named men and the other women." Here it is clear that the male-female polarity originated from the sphere of the mortal, not from that part of man which was created after the image of God.[1]

---

[1] Richard A. Baer, Jr., *Philo's Use of the Categories Male and Female* (Leiden: Brill, 1970), p. 19.

Since *nous* is the immortal part of the soul, in the image of God, the woman, who is fashioned from the mortal aspect of man, has no part in *nous*, the soul's rational quality, but only in *aisthēsis*, the soul's irrational quality. Time and again, throughout his works, Philo makes this distinction—and not in a neutral way, but always so as to depreciate the female.

This distinction appears from the outset, in Philo's discussion of the biblical creation myths. At the commencement of his argument, Philo wants to discourse at length on the first part of Gen 1:27, "And God created man in the image of God," without considering the last part of the verse, "male and female created He them." For this purpose, he declares at Op. Mund. 76 that "male and female" are two species of the genus *anthrōpos*, which though mentioned here had not yet taken shape. This taxonomy of the sexes as two species of the genus may surprise the modern mind; but it enables Philo to discuss the relationship between man and God without addressing himself to the question of male and female.[2] This, however, tends to blur the distinction between "mankind" (*anthrōpos*, a masculine noun) and "man" as the human male. For the effect of dropping the female from the discussion, while continuing to speak of the supposedly sexless *anthrōpos* in masculine terms, is not evenhanded, as we see from the following passage at Op. Mund. 134:

> . . . there is a vast difference between the man thus formed [at Gen 2:7] and the man that came into existence earlier [at Gen 1:27] after the image of God; for the man so formed [*sc.*, at Gen 2:7] is an object of sense-perception (*aisthētos*) . . . , consisting of body and soul, man or woman, by nature immortal, while he [masc. pron. *ho*] that was after the (Divine) image was an idea or type or seal, an object of thought (only), incorporeal, neither male nor female. . . .[3]

Philo's definition of the *anthrōpos* created in God's image as "neither male nor female" is interesting for two reasons. First, it directly contradicts the language of the verse, which specifically states that God created *anthrōpos* "in the image of God . . . , male and female" (*kai eikona theou epoiēsen auton arsen kai thely*). Philo's exegesis thus gives an interpretation that is diametrically opposed to traditional Jewish exegesis on the verse, that both male and female were created in God's image and both partake of the divine spirit.[4] This divine spirit, which God breathed into the *man* at Gen 2:7 (LXX *pnoēn*) seems to correspond with the *pneuma*, which Philo asserts is the essence of the rational faculty. Thus, at Det. 83-84:

> To the faculty which we have in common with the irrational creatures, blood has been given as its essence; but to the faculty which streams forth from the fountain of reason breath (*pneuma*) has been assigned; not moving air, but, as it were, an impression stamped by the divine power, to which Moses gives the appropriate title of "image," thus indicating that God is the Archetype of rational existence, while man is a copy and likeness. By "man" I mean not the living creature with two natures, but the highest form in which the life shows itself; and this has received the title of "mind" and "reason." This is why he says that the blood is the life of the flesh [Gen 9:4] , being aware that the fleshly nature has received no share of mind,

---

[2]The connection between this postponement of the male-female question and the cosmology of Plato's *Timaeus* is discussed below.

[3]This and all citations of Philo are from the Loeb Classical Library translations.

[4]For the notion that the *ādām* of Gen 1:27 contained both male and female elements, see b. Ketub. 8a, b. Berak. 61a, b. Erub. 18a. Nahmanides, commenting on Gen 1:27, says that "the creation of man was, from the first, male and female, and His divine spirit (*nišmātō*) was included in them both." (*neśāmâ* is the word translated as *pnoēn* at Gen 2:7.)

. . . but man's life he names "breath," giving the title of "man" *(anthrōpos)* . . . *to that God-like creation with which we reason*. . . .

Secondly, Philo's definition of anthrōpos as "neither male nor female" is at odds with his discussion, which throughout speaks of man in his relationship to God in masculine terms. While this is in part dictated by the grammatical gender of *anthrōpos*, that gender itself (in a language like Greek, whick does possess a neuter gender) begs a very important question; at the very least, it obscures the equal relationship of male and female to *anthrōpos*, whether both are to be excluded or both included. Thus the mere employment of the term *anthrōpos*, with its masculine article and pronoun, coupled with the exclusion of consideration of the female in the discussion of man's reception of the rational faculty from God, creates an ineluctable nexus between rationality and masculinity which lends weight to this point in Philo's argument.

The exclusion of woman from Philo's discussion of the first creation myth at Op. Mund. 65-88 is repeated at several points (Conf. 169, Fug. 68-70 and Mut. 30ff). In all these passages, Philo argues that the plural form, "Let *us* make man in *our* image," (Gen 1:26) indicates that God was assisted in man's creation by other beings; this, he says, explains why man has both "good" qualities (which come from God) and "bad" qualities (which come from God's partners in man's creation). This Gnostic notion is here quite neutrally expressed. But later, we learn from Philo's discussion of the second creation myth that "good" qualities are those associated with the male and "bad" qualities those associated with the female. For when he finally considers the fleshly man of Genesis 2:7ff, Philo makes much of the distinction between the two sexes; man has the "male" attributes of mind and reason (*nous* and *logos*), while woman has the "female" attributes of body and sense-perception (*sōma* and *aisthēsis*). *Sōma* is a "bad" thing; for, as Philo tells us at Op. Mund. 152, the creation of woman "begat bodily pleasure, which is the beginning of wrongs and violation of law." Like *sōma*, *aisthēsis* is a female attribute, as we learn at Leg. All. 2:38:

> "He built it to be a woman" (Gen 2:22), proving that the most proper and exact name for sense-perception (*aisthēsis*) is "woman."[5] For just as the man shows himself in activity and the woman in passivity, so the province of the mind (*nous*) is activity and that of the perceptive sense (*aisthēsis*) passivity, as in woman.

Unfortunately, says Philo, mind becomes the slave of sense-perception when man succumbs to the desire for intercourse. Commenting on Gen 2:24, "Therefore shall a man cleave to his wife," Philo concludes at Leg. All. 2:50:

> For the sake of sense-perception the Mind, when it has become her slave, abandons both God the Father of the Universe, and God's excellence and wisdom, the Mother of all things, and cleaves to and becomes one with sense-perception and is resolved into sense-perception so that the two become one flesh and one experience. Observe that it is not the woman that cleaves to the man, but conversely the man to the woman, Mind to Sense-perception. For when that which is superior, namely Mind, becomes one with that which is inferior, namely Sense-perception, it resolves itself into the order of flesh which is inferior, into sense-perception. . . .

It is because of the power of sense-perception over mind, we learn at Op. Mund. 165, that the serpent spoke first to Eve rather than to Adam:

---

[5]This explanation, as we discuss below, bears a curious resemblance to traditional (talmudic) exegesis of Gen 1:22, which draws a similar conclusion from a folk-etymology connecting the verb "build" with the noun "intuitive understanding."

Pleasure [i.e., the serpent] does not venture to bring her wiles and deceptions to bear on the man, but on the woman, and by her means on him. This is a telling and well-made point: for in us mind corresponds to man, the senses to woman; and pleasure encounters and holds parley with the senses first, and through them cheats with her quackeries the sovereign mind itself. . . .

Another explanation, given in Quaest. Gen. 1:33, exploits the notion of woman's inferior intellect from another angle. The serpent:

. . . deceives by trickery and artfulness. And woman is more accustomed to be deceived than man. For his judgment, like his body, is masculine and is capable of dissolving or destroying the designs of deception; but the judgment of woman is more feminine, and because of softness she gives way and is taken in by plausible falsehoods which resemble the truth.[6]

The related question, "Why did the woman, rather than the man, pick the fruit from the tree?" (Gen 3:6) is answered at Quaest. Gen. 1:37 as follows:

It was fitting that the man should rule over immortality and everything good, and the woman over death and everything vile.

This somewhat obscure comment seems to suggest that, by picking the fruit of the Tree of Knowledge, the woman is responsible for God's subsequently barring man's access to the Tree of Life; hence the woman condemns mankind to mortality and death. For good measure, Philo adds a second explanation, which, as before, connects woman with sense-perception and man with mind. It had to be the woman who picked the fruit because:

In the allegorical sense . . . woman is a symbol of sense [-perception] , and man of mind. Now of necessity sense comes into contact with the sense-perceptible and by the participation of sense, things pass into the mind; for sense is moved by objects, while the mind is moved by sense.

Here it seems that the lofty male principle of mind is so far above noticing material things, that only the mediation of feminine sense-perception can bring him down to that level.
    A final question on this subject is asked and answered at Quaest. Gen. 1:43, interpreting Gen 3:8:

Why, when they hid themselves from the face of God, was not the woman, who first ate of the forbidden fruit, first mentioned, but the man; for (Scripture) says, "Adam and his wife hid themselves"?

The question is answered as follows:

It was the more imperfect and noble element, the female, that made a beginning of the transgression and lawlessness, while the male made the beginning of reverence and modesty and all good, since he was better and more perfect.

Hence, where the woman initiated the sin, it was the man who initiated the atonement.

---

[6]This explanation calls to mind the talmudic statement that "women are tender-hearted" (b. Meg. 14b), implying that they will subordinate reason to emotion, as well as the statement (at b. Qid. 80b) that "women are weak-minded," which leads to similar results.

The man's guilt is thus mitigated in two ways: first, he sinned only because the woman seduced him; second, he was the first to repent.

These examples make it clear enough that, in his discussion of masculine and feminine attributes, Philo has a pronounced male chauvinist bias. It would be unfair, though, to overlook the fact that, on rare occasions, he treats the sexes with relative impartiality. One such instance is at Quis Her. 164, where he acknowledges the indispensability of both sexes for the reproductive function:

> Equality too divided the human being into man and woman, two sections unequal indeed in strength, but quite equal as regards what was nature's urgent purpose, the reproduction of themselves in a third person.

Finally, one refreshingly positive reference to woman occurs at Cher. 59-60, where Philo actually sees some value in sense-perception:

> . . . the Mind was docked of all its powers of sense-perception, thus truly powerless. It was but half the perfect soul, lacking the power whereby it is the nature of bodies to be perceived, a mere unhappy section bereft of its mate without the support of the sense-perceiving organs, whereby it could have propped as with a staff its faltering steps. And thus all bodily objects were wrapped in profound darkness and none of them could come to the light. For sense, the means whereby they were to become the objects of knowledge, was not. God then, wishing to provide the mind with perception of material as well as immaterial things, thought to complete the soul by weaving into the part first made the other section, which he called by the general name of "woman" and the proper name of "Eve" thus symbolizing sense.

Philo's acknowledgment that, in the last analysis, man cannot function without woman suggests that his true attitude was one of ambivalence towards women rather than the prejudice against them that seems to inform most of his statements about them.[7] Nonetheless, complementarity does not imply equality; and it is quite clear that Philo perceives woman as categorically inferior to man.

2. Gratuitous depreciation of women

Philo's insistence on female inferiority accounts for two annoying tendencies in his writing. One is that he sometimes seems impelled to insult women quite gratuitously, when the context does not invite this; the other is that, when the context forces him to concede some good in a woman, he sometimes insists that the quality in question is a masculine rather than feminine trait. One such gratuitous insult occurs at Quaest. Gen. 4:148, where Philo expounds Gen 25:5-6, "And Abraham gave all that was his to Isaac his son, and to the sons of his concubines he gave gifts."

> So much superior was Isaac to (the sons) of the concubines as are possessions to gifts. Wherefore (Scripture) recently described Isaac as motherless, and it calls those born to the concubines fatherless. Accordingly, those who were harmonious in the father's family are of the male progeny, while (the sons) of the women and those of inferior descent are certainly to be called female and unvirile, for which reason they are little admired as great ones.

This remarkable piece of exegesis depends upon some rather strained interpretations of the biblical text. Philo's statement that scripture describes Isaac as motherless

---

[7] We discuss below a similar ambivalence toward women in traditional Jewish exegesis.

can only be based on Gen 24:67, "and Isaac was comforted for the death of his mother."
But to claim, as does Philo, that he never had a mother is very strange, especially since
the exegesis of Gen 25:5-6 does not call for anything of the kind. Similarly, Philo's
suggestion that the sons of the concubines were fatherless seems to be based on their
rejection by Abraham as his heirs. But Gen 25:6 makes it clear that the gifts were in lieu
of inheritance, for it continues, "Abraham let them go while he was yet alive." This is
far from saying that he rejected them as his sons.[8] The entire passage in Philo seems to
be a highly contrived excuse to depreciate the female.

The same can be said of Philo's explanation of the preference of Jacob, the younger
twin, over Esau, the elder at Quaest. Gen. 4:160, expounding Gen 25:25:

> But a distinction should be made between "first-born" and "first-begotten." For the
> one is (the offspring) of female and material matter, for the female gives birth; but
> the first-begotten is a male and (the offspring) of a more responsible power, for it
> is the property of the male to beget.

This piece of biological nonsense is equally devoid of any scriptural basis. Once more,
the passage seems highly contrived.

Another gratuitous insult to females appears at Quaest. Exod. 1:7, concerning the
prescription of a male animal for the paschal sacrifice:

> Q.   Why does (Moses) command (them) to take a "perfect male sheep of one
>   year?" (Exod 12:5)
>
> A.   (It is to be) perfect. . . . For an imperfect (sacrifice) is not worthy to be
>   brought to the altar of God. And it is to be male, first, because the male is
>   more perfect than the female. Wherefore it is said by the naturalists that the
>   female is nothing else than an imperfect male.[9]
>
> Q.   Why is a sheep chosen?
>
> A.   Symbolically, as I have said, it indicates perfect progress and at the same
>   time the male. For progress is indeed nothing else than the giving up of the
>   female gender by changing into the male, since the female gender is material,
>   passive, corporeal and sense-perceptible, while the male is active, rational,
>   incorporeal and more akin to mind and thought.

Here Philo has clearly amplified both answers beyond anything warranted by Exod 12:5.
We may suppose it more likely that the sacrifice of male animals originates in the purely
practical desire to preserve potentially productive females--if anything, a superior
evaluation of the female. In the particular case, of course, the paschal sacrifice was
linked to the death of the firstborn Egyptian males, making a male sacrifice more apposite. But Philo contrives to exact from the verse his pound of female flesh.

---

[8]The translator's footnote to this passage is misleading. The sons of concubines
were not "illegitimate" in Semitic law. Cf. the story of Jephtha in Jud 11:1ff, where
Jephtha's half-brothers drive him away to prevent his inheriting from their common
father as he otherwise would. The fact that he was the son of a concubine did not per se
disqualify him from inheritance. Ths sons of concubines could, however, remain slaves
unless the father freed them during his lifetime. The word way^e šalḥem in Gen 25:6
probably has the technical sense of emancipation, "he released them." Abraham was
favoring his concubines' sons, not rendering them "fatherless."

[9]The classification of the female as nothing but an imperfect male is found in
Greek sources. Cf. Aristotle, *De Generatione Animalium* 775a; Plato, *Timaeus* 90a ff.

Yet another insult occurs as the sting in the tail of Philo's explanation of the use of women's earrings to make the golden calf (Exod 32:2, explained at Post. 166):

> The calf, you observe, is not made out of all the things with which women deck themselves, but only their ear-rings (Exod 32:2), for the lawgiver is teaching us that no manufactured god is a God for sight and in reality, but for the ear to hear of, and vogue and custom to proclaim, and that too a woman's ear, not a man's, for to entertain such trash is the work of an effeminate and sinewless soul.

Clearly the exegesis here was adequate without the final comment; but that comment is in keeping with Philo's propensity to get as much mileage as possible out of the male-female dichotomy.

Perhaps the ultimate insult to woman appears in Mig. 205-6, where Philo is discussing the story of the daughters of Zelophehad (Num 27:1-11). Here, he offers the following ingenious explanation of why Zelophehad had produced only daughters and no sons:

> Do you not notice, that the five daughters of Zelophehad . . . are of the tribe of Manasseh [whose name means] "from forgetfulness" . . . "and he had no sons" (Num 27:3) but only daughters, for whereas the faculty of memory, being naturally wide awake, has male progeny, forgetfulness, wrapt in a slumber of reasoning power, has female offspring; . . .

Daughters, then, are begotten in a fit of absentmindedness in the first place![10]

3. The anomaly of virtuous women

Philo is faced from time to time with the need to account for the excellence of some of the women in scripture. One such case is the matriarch Sarah. She must receive praise as the founding mother of the Hebrew people. True, Sarah's main significance for Philo is allegorical; she personifies virtue (Abr. 206, Ebr. 59-61 and elsewhere). Nonetheless, in the assumed historical context of Genesis, she is a woman; and the appearance of such excellence in woman requires explanation. Philo's solution is to prove from scripture that Sarah is an exception to the rule of female inferiority. This he does, in Quaest. Gen. 4:15, by offering an extraordinary interpretation of Gen 18:11, "The way of women had ceased for Sarah." While conceding at the outset that the verse refers literally to menstruation, Philo proceeds to offer an allegory:

> What is the meaning of the words, "There ceased to be to Sarah the ways of women"?
>
> The literal meaning is clear. For (Scripture) by a euphemism calls the monthly purification of women "the ways of women." But as for the deeper meaning, it is to be allegorized as follows. The soul has, as it were, a dwelling, partly men's quarters, partly women's quarters. Now for the men there is a place where properly dwell the masculine thoughts (that are) wise, sound, just, prudent, pious, filled with freedom and boldness, and kin to wisdom. And the women's quarters are a place where womanly opinions go about and dwell, being followers of the female sex. And the female sex is irrational and akin to bestial passions, fear, sorrow, pleasure and desire, from which ensue incurable weaknesses and indescrib-

---

[10]Though he gives no indication here, it is possible that Philo knew that the Hebrew roots for "male" and "memory" are identical (zkr).

able diseases. He who is conquered by these is unhappy, while he who controls them is happy. And longing for and desiring this happiness, and seizing a certain time to be able to escape from terrible and unbearable sorrow, which is (what is meant by) "there ceased to be the ways of women"--this clearly belongs to minds full of Law, which resemble the male sex and overcome passions and rise above all sense-pleasure and desire.

At Ebr. 59-61, Philo removes Sarah completely from the world of women:

> For the customs of women still prevail among us, and we cannot as yet cleanse ourselves from them or flee to the dwelling-place where the men are quartered, as we are told that it was with the virtue-loving mind, named Sarah.[11] For the oracles represent her as having left all the things of women . . . (Gen 18:11).

To this, Philo adds the following extraordinary claim:

> She is declared, too, to be without a mother, and to have inherited her kinship only on the father's side and not on the mother's, and thus to have no part in female parentage. For we find it said, "Indeed she is my sister, the daughter of my father, but not of my mother" (Gen 20:12).

Here, Philo does not begin, as in Quaest. Gen. 4:15, by noting the literal meaning of the cited verse. This may simply be because he is not systematically expounding scripture here, while there he was following the traditional style of giving first the literal and then the figurative interpretations.[12] But it is also true that, while Gen 18:11 at least states that the way of women had ceased for Sarah (thus opening the way to allegorical interpretation), Gen 20:12 certainly does not declare Sarah to be without a mother, but merely points out that she was Abraham's half-sister born of a different mother.

Another biblical figure whose excellence Philo could not overlook was Miriam. With her, as with Sarah, he seems to have felt constrained to explain that she really was not a typical woman. Thus, to justify Miriam's leadership qualities described at Exod 15:20, Philo asserts that in her case, sense-perception was a virtue rather than a defect. Thus (at Agr. 80) Miriam personifies:

> . . . sense perception made pure and clean. For it is right with both mind and sense to render hymns and sing blessings to the Godhead without delay. . . .

Though Philo does not cite scripture here, his basis for declaring Miriam "pure and clean" is presumably the story of her healing from leprosy described at Num 12:14-15.

One interesting instance of Philo's praising a woman occurs in a historical rather than biblical context. In Leg. 319, Philo asserts that the following praise of Julia Augusta, great-grandmother of Gaius Caligula, was contained in a letter sent by Agrippa to the Emperor to persuade him to rescind a decree that his statue be placed in the Temple at Jerusalem:

> Under such an instructor in piety [sc., Augustus] , your great-grandmother Julia Augusta adorned the temple with golden vials and libation bowls and a multitude of

---

[11]Latin virtus, from vir, certainly has masculine etymological connotations. Whether the same is true for Greek aretē has recently come into question.

[12]As Marcus points out in his Introduction to Questions and Answers on Genesis and Exodus, "Philo's twofold method of interpretation is a forerunner of the fourfold method used by Rabbinic and Patristic commentators." Philo (Loeb ed.) Supp. I, p. ix.

other sumptuous offerings. What made her to do this, as there was no image there? For the judgments of women as a rule are weaker and do not apprehend any mental conception apart from what their senses perceive. But she excelled herself in this as in everything else, for the purity of the training she received supplementing nature and practice gave virility to her reasoning power, which gained such clearness of vision that it apprehended the things of mind better than the things of sense. . . .

On reading these words, one has a definite sense that, if the pen was the pen of Agrippa, the voice is the voice of Philo. For here, just as with the biblical heroines, Philo seems impelled to make a special point of the unfeminine character of Julia's excellence by stressing the "virility" (*arrenōtheisa*) of her reasoning power. This passage, incidentally, shows Philo able and willing, for political gain, to praise a woman without resort to scriptural proof texts where none was to be had.

So great is Philo's reluctance to leave any excellence whatever to the female, that he divests even the Sabbath of its traditional feminine aura. In Spec. Leg. 2:56, while conceding that some call her virgin,[13] Philo claims that the seventh day is motherless:

. . . begotten by the father of the universe alone, the ideal form of the male sex with nothing of the female.

In fact, this is at odds with Philo's own description of the seventh day as female and virgin at Mos. 2:210. But that passage is a rare deviation from Philo's monotonous insistence on relegating females to an inferior status.

This concludes our survey of passages that reveal Philo's stance on masculine and feminine attributes and his attitude toward woman in the abstract. We turn now to consider his view of women's social status as reflected in the laws.

II. Women in Philo: Social Status Under Law

As we have seen, Philo has much to say about woman in an allegorical way, as the personification of sense-perception. He has far less to say about women in real life. This is in keeping with his general preference for figurative exegesis over literal exposition of text; he tends to mention women only incidentally to other topics. Philo did not find women important enough to devote a book, or even a section of a book, to sustained discussion of the place of real women in his real world. The closest he comes to this is at Spec. Leg. 3:8-71, where he brings together under the general rubric of the seventh commandment all the Mosaic legislation on sexual morality. The section discusses consanguinity laws and other prohibited sexual conduct (Leviticus 18), laws of rape and seduction (Exod 22:16-17, Deut 22:23-29), the law of the suspected adulteress (Num 5:12-31) and the law governing accusations of unchastity against new brides (Deut 22:13-21). The discussion follows the biblical text closely, and is mainly concerned to endorse Mosaic morality as a model for Philo's own community, in contrast to the immoralities (notably homosexuality among Greeks and incest among Egyptians) practiced in gentile cultures of Philo's day.

Here, just as in Philo's allegories, the treatment of women is more incidental to the general discussion than as a topic in their own right. Thus, Philo simply takes for granted the double standard in adultery. This offense occurs only when a man has intercourse

---

[13]In the Hebrew Scriptures, the word *šabbāt* (sabbath) is, with few exceptions, treated as masculine. Yet the sabbath in traditional Jewish parlance has generally been feminine, being called "queen" and "bride." Philo's statement that some call her virgin may reflect such a perception among Alexandrian Jews of his day.

with another man's wife or betrothed wife (Deut 22:22ff), but not when a married man has intercourse with an unmarried woman, since the law forbade polyandry but permitted polygyny. He takes equally for granted that a young marriageable girl is virtually the property of her father, who may permit or deny her in marriage to her seducer, without consulting her wishes (Spec. Leg. 3:70). He even accepts the view, implicit in Deut 22:29, that the forced marriage of a rapist with his victim constitutes some "consolation" for the girl (Spec. Leg. 3:71).

The general flavor of this section of Philo's writings is uncompromisingly Judaic rather than Hellenistic. This is precisely to be expected; for it is historically true that family law, dealing as it does with the most basic of human activities, has always been closely bound up with religion in traditional cultures and continues to claim adherence even when members of minority groups become acculturated in all other respects to the laws and customs of a more progressive majority culture.[14] Hence it is no great surprise that Philo values the Hebrew sexual morality over the Greek, even while adopting the more sophisticated Greek culture in matters of science and philosophy.

Elsewhere in the *Special Laws*, Philo cites a few other pentateuchal laws pertaining to women. At Spec. Leg., 1:105-6, he finds it appropriate that the high priest is required to marry a virgin (Lev 21:13-14), for:

> [by] mating with souls entirely innocent and unperverted [high priests] may find it easy to mould the characters and dispositions of their wives, for the minds of virgins are easily influenced and attracted to virtue and very ready to be taught. But she who has had experience of another husband is naturally far less amenable to instruction.

Again, at Spec. Leg. 2:24, Philo voices his approval of the law (Num 30:4ff) whereby fathers and husbands can annul religious vows of daughters and wives:

> That is surely reasonable, for the former, owing to their youth, do not know the value of oaths, so that they need others to judge for them, and the latter often, through want of sense, swear what would not be to their husbands' advantage. . . .

There is one place, outside the *Special Laws*, where Philo presents a catalogue of the most important biblical laws as he sees them. This is in the *Hypothetica*, according to its subtitle an "apology for the Jews." The work is known to us only from the fact that it is cited in Eusebius.[15] The purpose of the work seems to have been an apology for Jewish law to the Hellenistic world. After a historical introduction, Philo offers a list of the principal pentateuchal laws. He commences, naturally enough, with those whose transgression invokes the death penalty (murder, adultery, etc.). For our present discussion, however, it is interesting to see which law Philo places at the head of the non-capital laws that immediately follow. It is this:

> 7.3. Other rules again there are of various kinds: wives must be in servitude to their husbands, a servitude not imposed by violent ill-treatment but promoting obedience in all things.

This rule is apparently based on Gen 3:16, "Thy desire shall be to thy husband, and he shall rule over thee." Its significance here consists in Philo's placing it at the head of the

---

[14]As witness the adherence of a surprising number of modern, well-educated Jews to archaic Jewish marriage and divorce laws. Likewise, in Israel and the more progressive Arab states, while all other laws are modeled on the civil and criminal codes of modern European countries, family law remains the province of religious authorities.
[15]*Praeparatio Evangelica* 8, 5:11-7:20.

list of non-capital laws.[16] This surely indicates the importance he attached to it and implies his view of the rightness of the subjection of wives.

The sociocultural perception of women that underpins their subordination in law is aptly reflected at Spec. Leg. 32-34, where Philo's view of women's status is expressed in his use of metaphors for intercourse and childbearing. He speaks there of "sowing wheat and barley" and calls the womb a "cornfield." Mating with a barren woman is described as "ploughing the hard and stony land." These metaphors, of course, are common to many cultures, including both Semitic and Hellenistic. Thus, Plato speaks of "the ploughland of the womb";[17] and the mishnaic law that began to take shape not long after Philo's time specifically compares the acquisition of a wife to the acquisition of a field.[18] The general sense of all these metaphors is that women were perceived more as chattel than as persons.

Thus far, we have considered Philo's use of woman as allegory and his perception of women as the object of laws. As for his personal feelings about women, some light may perhaps be shed on this by the following vitriolic diatribe, which appears in another fragment of the *Hypothetica* cited by Eusebius (Hyp. 11.14-17). While the context makes it not entirely clear whether the view expressed is Philo's own or one that he attributes to the Essenes, it seems quite consistent with much else that Philo has to say about women:[19]

> For no Essene takes a wife, because a wife is a selfish creature, excessively jealous and an adept at beguiling the morals of her husband and seducing him by her continued impostures. For by the fawning talk which she practises and the other ways in which she plays her part like an actress on the stage she first ensnares the sight and hearing, and when these subjects as it were have been duped she cajoles the sovereign mind. And if children come, filled with the spirit of arrogance and bold speaking, she gives utterance with more audacious hardihood to things which before she hinted at covertly and under disguise, and casting off all shame she compels him to commit actions which are all hostile to the life of fellowship. For he who is either fast bound in the love lures of his wife or under the stress of nature makes his children his first care ceases to be the same to others and unconsciously has become a different man and has passed from freedom into slavery.

This diatribe has the ring of personal conviction; it is hard to believe that its author did not speak from the heart. In Philo's defense, it must be said that a similarly hostile view of women appears in Jewish exegetical sources, which may well reflect views already current in other Jewish communities of Philo's day.[20] Such views may, indeed, have been universally prevalent in all cultures of the ancient Near East.

---

[16]Since the fragment is known only from Eusebius, who no doubt had some interest in promoting St. Paul's identical view of women's place, one must proceed here with some caution. It is assumed, in the absence of other evidence, that Eusebius gives Philo's list exactly as he found it.

[17]*Timaeus* 19d.

[18]M. Qid. 1:1 provides that a woman may be acquired "by money, by deed, or by intercourse." M. Qid. 1:5 provides that land may be acquired "by money, by deed, or by usucaption."

[19]F. H. Colson, the translator of the *Hypothetica*, takes a different view, namely, that the passage represents "not, I think, . . . Philo's definite opinion, but rather . . . what might be plausibly argued by the Essenes." *Philo* (Loeb ed.) vol. 9, p. 442.

[20]Thus, Gen. Rabbah 18:2 says of the creation of woman from man: "God said: 'I shall not create her from the head, lest she hold up her head too proudly; nor from the eye, lest she be a coquette; nor from the ear, lest she be an eavesdropper; nor from the mouth, lest she be too talkative; nor from the heart, lest she be too jealous; nor from the hand, lest she be too acquisitive; nor from the foot, lest she be a gadabout; but from a

III. Philo's View of Women: Possible Sources

Philo was heir to two cultures, Jewish and Greek. While the dominant influence on his work was certainly the Hellenistic world of which Alexandria was the epicenter, it is clear that he was also Philo Judaeus in fundamental ways: loyal to his ethnic community, the Jewish people, and devoted to his ancestral heritage, the Jewish scriptures. True, his exegesis often wears a Greek apologetic guise, particularly when he emphasizes the allegorical as opposed to the literal meaning of the Torah; but his Jewish identification is abundantly clear. It is therefore interesting to speculate on the combination of sources that may have shaped his attitudes to women and might form the basis of fruitful research.

Throughout this study, we noted a number of resemblances or differences between Philo's statements and views found in either Greek or Hebrew literature. We shall briefly review these here, as a general indication of possible directions for further research.

A crucial theme of Philo's cosmology and anthropology seems to be his distinction between masculine and feminine categories, in which the man personifies *nous*, intellect, and the woman *aisthēsis*, sense-perception. The notion that men are "thinkers" while women are "feelers" is common in many societies to this day. Perhaps it is universal; but in the West it is surely a heritage from one or both of the principal traditions that have shaped western thought: Greek philosophy and Jewish theology.

Thus, we noted that Philo's distinction between *nous* and *aisthēsis* appears also in "mainstream" Jewish tradition. It is found, for instance, in the Babylonian Talmud, where it is based on a folk-etymological play on the unusual verb used in Gen 2:22, "And the Lord God *built* the rib, which he had taken from the man, into a woman." The Hebrew verb, *bny*, "build" is an anagram of the root *byn*, meaning "to understand [intuitively rather than cerebrally] ." Hence, the sages claimed that the use of this verb showed that God gave more *bīnâ*, "intuitive understanding" to the woman (b. Nid. 45b). *Bīnâ* was contrasted with *ḥokmâ*, "cerebral wisdom," thought to be a masculine attribute; the Talmud ascribes to R. Eliezer of the second century the statement that "there is not wisdom (*ḥokmâ*) in women but with the distaff" (b. Yoma 66b).[21]

These talmudic statements may well reflect traditions that are far older than the sixth-century date of redaction. It seems quite likely that Jewish tradition in Philo's time perceived men as stronger in intellect and women as stronger in intuition. While intuition is not precisely the same as sense-perception, it seems to have been opposed to intellect in the same way. This tradition may have been known to Philo, though his exegesis of Gen 2:22 at Leg. All. 38 wrongly claims that the word "woman" (rather than the word "built") is connected with the notion of "sense-perception." (Indeed, the very fact that Philo offers the interpretation without a Greek etymology suggests that he may consciously be citing a Jewish tradition; his lack of Hebrew would account for the etymological mistake.)

On the other hand, Philo's insistence on *nous* as the higher part of man's nature and hence the respect in which man is made in God's image, while *aisthēsis* belongs to man's lower nature and appears only after the later division into sexes, seems to owe more to

---

part of the body which is hidden . . . so that she should be modest.' " But, as Gen. Rabbah 45:5 tells us, all was in vain; for woman is "greedy (like Eve), eavesdropping (like Sarah), lazy (like Sarah), jealous (like Rachel), irresponsible (again, Sarah!) and garrulous (like Miriam). She is thieving (like Rachel) and a gadabout (like Dinah)." Scriptural proof texts are adduced in support of all these strictures.

[21] R. Eliezer was playing with words. The noun *ḥokmâ* appears rarely in the Pentateuch, except in Exodus 28-36, where it refers exclusively to manual skill in the making of priestly accoutrements and decorations for the tabernacle. Eliezer, then, was saying that a woman lacked *ḥokmâ* in the intellectual sense required for scholarly study.

Greek than to Jewish cosmology. Philo's whole discussion of the relationship between God and man in the context of the Godlike attribute of *nous* depends on the Platonic view of the creation of sexual parts as postponed until after the rest of the body is complete.[22] At that point, women are created from imperfect men:

> Of those who were born as men, all that were cowardly and spent their life in wrongdoing were, according to the probable account, transformed at the second birth into women.[23]

This seems to be the source of Philo's reference at Quaest. Exod. 1:7 to the naturalists' assertion that the female is "nothing else than an imperfect male."

A related proposition in Philo's scheme is his notion that the archetypal *anthrōpos*, created in God's image, was neither male nor female. This, we saw, was diametrically opposed to the traditional Jewish view that mankind was created in God's image male *and* female. Hence we may conclude that Philo here draws exclusively on Greek rather than Jewish cosmology.

Philo's perception of the female as intellectually inferior to the male appears in Jewish tradition in such statements as "woman are weak-minded" (or "light-minded") at b. Qid. 80a and b. Shab. 33b. Since, however, this view appears also in a Roman law code of the second century, the *Institutes* of Gaius, it was very likely prevalent throughout the ancient Near East.[24]

Finally, we noted Philo's ambivalence toward women when, despite all his strictures about them, he admits at Cher. 59-60 that the masculine principle of *nous* is only half the soul and thus needs to be complemented by feminine *aesthēsis*. A similar ambivalence appears throughout traditional Jewish exegesis on women; for all their strictures, the sages maintained that "a man without a wife lives without joy, blessing and good" and hence a man should "love his wife as himself and respect her more than himself" (b. Yeb. 62b).

Conclusion

Based on the material presented here, the main conclusion to be drawn concerning the sources of Philo's views on women is that some of his statements seem to draw on Greek sources, others on Jewish sources. A basic Platonic influence seems clear, in the notion of the higher, masculine *nous* and the lower, feminine *aisthēsis*. This may or may not be related to the Jewish polarity of masculine wisdom and feminine intuition; Philo may perhaps have drawn on oral traditions preserved among the Jews of Alexandria on this point. Some of his ideas, again, were surely the intellectual property of the entire Near East of his day. Hostility to women, in particular, seems universal in patriarchal societies, all of which perceive man as the normal "self" and woman as the mysterious "other." Further research alone can provide a basis for more specific conclusions.

---

[22]F. M. Cornford, *Plato's Cosmology (The Timaeus)* (1937, 1966 ed.), p. 291.

[23]Ibid., p. 356, translation of *Timaeus* 90e-91a.

[24]Cf. Gaius I.44: ". . . the early lawyers held that women even of full age should be *in tutela* on account of their instability of judgment (*propter animi laevitatem*). The talmudic expression *nāšîm daʿatām kallāh* exhibits a semantic correspondence between *kallāh*, "light" and *laevitas* as well as between *daʿat*, "mind" and *animus*.